The **Rough Guide** to

Scotland

written and researched by

Rob Humphreys and Donald Reid

with additional contributions by

Colin Hutchison

ROUGH
GUIDES

NEW YORK • LONDON • DELHI

www.roughguides.com

Contents

Architecture insert
following p.168

Festivals insert
following p.360

The great outdoors
insert following p.600

◀◀ Eilean Donan Castle ◀ Gearrannan, Lewis

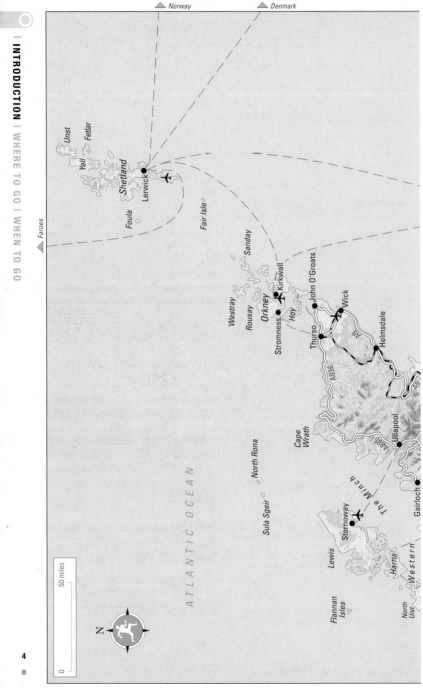

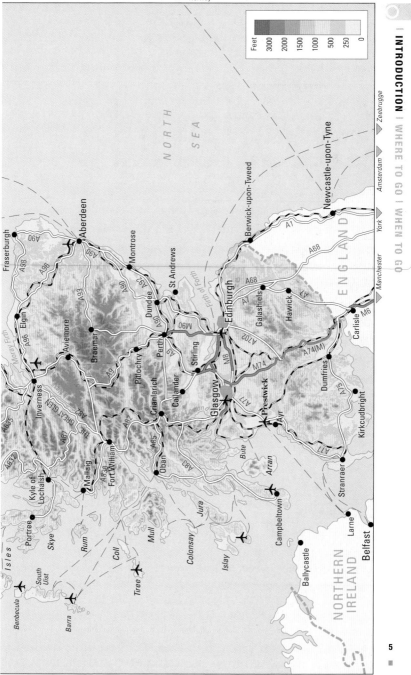

© Crown copyright

Introduction to
Scotland

Scotland not only defies description, it gets positively irritated by it. Clichéd images of the place abound – postcards of wee Highland terriers, tartan tins of shortbread, ranks of diamond-patterned golf jerseys ... and they drive many Scots to apoplexy. And yet Scotland has a habit of delivering on its classic images: ruined castles really do perch on just about every hilltop, in summer the glens inevitably turn purple with heather and, if you're lucky, you just might bump into a formation of bagpipers marching down the village street on gala day.

Scotland is a difficult country, where Celtic hedonism intertwines, somehow, with stern Calvinism, where the losers of battles (and football games) are more romanticized than the winners. It's often defined by its scenery – known to make poets weep, but half the time hidden under a pall of drizzly mist. The country's major contribution to medieval warfare was the chaotic, bloodcurdling charge of the half-naked Highlander, yet it's civilized enough to have given the world steam power, the television and penicillin. Chefs from Paris to Prague rhapsodize over Scottish wild salmon and Aberdeen Angus steaks, even while the locals are tucking happily into another deep-fried supper of haggis and chips.

Naturally, the tourist industry tends to play up the heritage and play down the contemporary, but beyond the tartan lies a modern, dynamic nation. Oil and microprocessors now matter more to the Scottish economy than Harris tweed. Edinburgh still has its genteel Royal Mile, but just as many folk are drawn by its clubs and cappuccino culture, while out in the Hebrides, the locals are more likely to be building websites than shearing sheep. The Highland huntin' shootin' fishin' set are these days outnumbered by mountain bikers and wide-eyed whale-watchers. Much as folk bands are knocking out old tunes on electronic fiddles, reinvention of tradition has become a Scottish art form.

Stuck in the far northwest corner of Europe, Scotland is remote, but it's not isolated. The inspiring emptiness of the wild northwest coast lies barely a couple of hours from Edinburgh and Glasgow, two of Britain's most dense and intriguing urban centres. Ancient ties to Ireland, Scandinavia, France and the Netherlands mean that — compared with the English at least — Scots are generally enthusiastic about the European Union, which has poured money into infrastructure and cultural projects, particularly in the Highlands and Islands. By contrast, Scotland's relationship with the "auld enemy", England, remains as problematic as ever. Despite the new Scottish parliament established in Edinburgh in 1999, with its new-found power to shape Scottish life, many Scots still tend to view matters south of the border with a mixture of exaggerated disdain and well-hidden envy. Ask for a "full English breakfast" and you'll quickly find yourself put right. Old prejudices die hard.

▲ Otter, Aviemore

Fact file

• Scotland covers an **area** of just over 30,000 square miles, has a 2300-mile-long coastline and contains over 31,460 **lochs**. Of its 790 **islands**, 130 are inhabited. The highest point is the summit of Ben Nevis (4406 ft), while the bottom of Loch Morar is 1017 feet below sea level.

• The **capital** is Edinburgh (population nearly 450,000), and the largest city is Glasgow (over 600,000). While the number of people worldwide who claim Scottish descent is estimated at over 25 million, the **population** of the country is just 5 million – 1.3 percent of whom (roughly 66,000 people) speak **Gaelic**.

• Scotland is a constituent territory of the **United Kingdom** of Great Britain and Northern Ireland. The head of state is Queen Elizabeth II. It is a **parliamentary democracy** whose sovereign parliament sits at Westminster in London, with elements of government business devolved to the separately elected Scottish Parliament which sits in Edinburgh.

• **Whisky** accounts for 13 percent of Scotland's exports and is worth over £2 billion annually, but Scotland also manufactures over 30 percent of Europe's personal computers and 65 percent of Europe's ATMs.

Where to go

Whisky

The Scots like a drink. Somehow, a Scot who doesn't like (or, worse, can't handle) a dram of "Scotch" – although whisky is rarely described as such in Scotland – isn't wholly credible. No Highland village or cobbled Edinburgh street would be complete without its cosy, convivial pub – and no pub complete without its array of amber-tinged bottles, the spirit within nurtured by a beguiling and well-marketed mix of soft Scottish rain, glistening Highland streams, rich peaty soil and tender Scots craftsmanship.

But not only is whisky the national drink, it's often regarded as the national pastime too, lubricating any social gathering from a Highland ceilidh to a Saturday night session. And the tradition that whisky be drunk neat says far more about Scottish society's machismo than its epicurean instincts: the truth is that a splash of water releases the whisky's flavours. It's no surprise, then, that the canny Scots also turn a healthy profit bottling the country's abundant spring water and selling it around the world.

Even if you're planning a short visit, it's still perfectly possible, and quite common, to combine a stay in either Edinburgh or Glasgow with a brief foray into the Highlands. With more time at your disposal, the opportunity to experience the variety of landscapes in Scotland increases, but there's no escaping the fact that travel in the more remote regions of Scotland takes time, and – in the case of the outer islands – money. If you're planning to spend most of your time in the countryside, it's most rewarding to concentrate on just one or two small areas.

The initial focus for many visitors to Scotland is the capital, **Edinburgh**, a dramatically handsome and engaging city famous for its magnificent castle and historic Old

▼ Live music, Taybank pub, Dunkeld

Town. Come here in August and you'll find the city transformed by the Edinburgh Festival, the largest arts festival in the world. An hour's travel to the west is the country's largest city, **Glasgow**, a place quite different in character from Edinburgh. Once a sprawling industrial metropolis, Glasgow has done much to improve its image by promoting its impressive architectural heritage and lively social and cultural life. Other urban centres are inevitably overshadowed by the big two, although the transformation from industrial grey to cultural colour is injecting life into **Dundee**, while there's a defiant separateness to **Aberdeen** with its silvery granite architecture and oil prosperity. **Stirling** is well worth visiting for its wonderful castle and historic importance, while **Perth**, **Dumfries** and **Inverness** are pleasant county towns serving a wide rural hinterland.

You don't have to travel far north of the Glasgow–Edinburgh axis to find the first hints of **Highland** landscape, a divide marked by the Highland Boundary Fault which cuts across central Scotland. The lochs, hills and wooded glens of the **Trossachs** and **Loch Lomond** are most easily reached, and as a consequence busier than other parts. Further north, **Perthshire** and the Grampian hills of **Angus** and **Deeside** show the Scottish countryside at its richest, with colourful woodlands and long glens rising up to distinctive mountain peaks. South of Inverness the mighty **Cairngorm** massif offers hints of the raw wilderness Scotland can still provide, an aspect of the country which is at its finest in the lonely north and western Highlands. To get to the far north you'll have to cross the **Great Glen**, an ancient geological fissure which cuts right across the country from Ben Nevis to **Loch Ness**, a moody stretch of water rather choked with tourists hoping for a glimpse of its monster. Scotland's most memorable scenery is to be found on the jagged

The Kirkcudbright conundrum

Gearraidh na h-Aibhne (A 858)
Uig (B 8011)
Bearnaraigh (B 8059)

Ionad Tursachan Chalanais
Callanish Stones Visitor Centre
Dun Charlabhaigh
Carloway Broch
Gearrannan
Garenin Blackhouse Village
Taigh Tughaidh Arnoil
Arnol Blackhouse Museum

At some point or other, most visitors will fall foul of the peculiarities of Scottish pronunciation. Hikers wishing to embark on the West Highland Way, for example, first have to negotiate the linguistic hurdle of the footpath's starting-point at Milngavie – pronounced "mill-guy". Seemingly innocuous place names, the unwary will discover, can be pronounced idiosyncratically: Avoch like "och"; Crovie as "crivie"; Culzean like "cullane"; Glamis most definitely as "glahms". Other common names to come a cropper on are Kirkcaldy ("kircoddy") and Kirkcudbright ("kircoobree"). Even the labels on some whiskies can be hard to swallow, particularly on Islay ("eye-la") in Argyll ("argyle"), where drinkers have to get their mouths around Bunnahabhainn ("bunna-have-an") and Caol Ila ("culleela"). Stress is important, too: the island of Benbecula must be pronounced with the stress on the second syllable; ditto the town and whisky of Bowmore. And when you think you've finally cracked Scots pronunciation, it's time to get really stuck into the nettlebed of Gaelic, in which the seemingly unpronounceable town of Gearraidh na h-Aibhne is anglicized to become Garynahine.

west coast, stretching from **Argyll** all the way north to **Wester Ross** and the looming hills of Assynt. Not all of central and northern Scotland is rugged Highlands, however, with the east coast in particular mixing fertile farmland with pretty stone-built fishing villages and golf courses, most notably at the prosperous university town of **St Andrews**, the spiritual home of the game. Elsewhere the whisky trail of **Speyside** and the castles and Pictish stones of the **northeast** provide plenty of scope for exploration off the beaten track, while in the southern part of the country, the rolling hills and ruined abbeys of the **Borders** offer a refreshingly unaffected vision of rural Scotland.

▲ Fruitmarket Gallery Café, Edinburgh

The grand splendour of the Highlands would be bare without the **islands** off the west and north coasts. Assorted in size, flavour and accessibility, the long chain of rocky Hebrides which necklace Scotland's Atlantic shoreline includes **Mull** and its nearby pilgrimage centre of **Iona**; **Islay** and **Jura**, famous for their wildlife and whisky; **Skye**, the most visited of the Hebrides, where the snow-tipped Cuillin peaks rise up from deep sea lochs; and the **Western Isles**, an elongated archipelago that is the last bastion of Gaelic language and culture. Off the north coast, **Orkney** and **Shetland**, both with a rich Norse heritage, differ not only from each other, but also quite distinctly from mainland Scotland in dialect and culture – far-flung islands buffeted by wind and sea that offer some of the country's wildest scenery, finest bird-watching and best archeological sites.

When to go

The **summer** months of June, July and August are regarded as high season, with local school holidays making July and early August the busiest period. While the locals celebrate a single day of bright sunshine as "glorious", the weather at this time is, at best, unpredictable; however, days are generally mild or warm and, most importantly, long, with daylight lingering until 9pm or later. August in Edinburgh is Festival time, which dominates everything in the city and means accommodation is hard to come by. Elsewhere, events such as Highland Games, folk festivals

Munro-bagging

Just as the Inuit have hundreds of words for snow, so in Scotland a hill is rarely just a hill. Depending on where you are in the country, what it's shaped like and how high it is, a hill might be a ben, a mount, a law, a pen, a brae or even a pap. Even more confusing if you're keen on doing a bit of hill walking are "Munros". These are the hills in Scotland over 3000 feet in height, defined by a list first drawn up by one Sir Hugh Munro in 1891. You "bag" a Munro by walking to the top of it, and once you've bagged all 284 you can call yourself a Munroist and let your chiropodist retire in peace. Of course, there's no need to do them all: at heart, Munro-bagging is simply about appreciating the great Scottish outdoors. It's advisable, however, not to get too obsessed by Sir Hugh's challenge: after the Munros you might hear the call of the "Corbetts" (hills between 2500 and 2999 feet) or even the "Donalds" (lowland hills above 2000 feet).

▼ Princes Square, Glasgow

or sporting events – most of which take place in the summer months – can tie up accommodation, though normally only in a fairly concentrated local area. If you're out and about in the Highlands throughout the summer, you won't be able to avoid the clouds of small biting insects called **midges**, which can be a real annoyance on still days, particularly around dusk.

Commonly, **May** and **September** throw up weather every bit as good as, if not better than, the months of high summer. You're less likely to encounter crowds or struggle to find somewhere to stay, and the mild temperatures combined with the changing colours of nature mean both are great for outdoor activities, particularly hiking. Note, however, that September is prime stalking season for deer, which can disrupt access over parts of the Highlands.

The **spring** and **autumn** months of April and October bracket the

The weather

"There's no such thing as bad weather, only inadequate clothing," the poet laureate Ted Hughes is alleged to have said when asked why he liked holidaying on Scotland's west coast, given that it always rains there. For those who don't share Hughes' cavalier attitude to the elements, the weather is probably the single biggest factor to put you off visiting Scotland. It's not so much that the weather's always bad, it's just that it is unpredictable: you could enjoy the most fabulous week of sunshine in early April and suffer a week of low-lying fog and drizzle in August. Out in the islands, they say you can get all four seasons in a day. The saving grace is that even if the weather's not necessarily good, it's generally interesting, exhilarating, dramatic and certainly photogenic. Then, the sun finally coming out is truly worth the wait. A week spent in a landscape swathed in thick mist can be transformed when the clouds lift to reveal a majestic mountain range or a hidden group of islands far offshore.

season for many parts of rural Scotland. A large number of attractions, tourist offices and guesthouses often open for business on Easter weekend and shut up shop after the school half-term in mid-October. If places do stay open through the winter it's normally with reduced opening hours; this is the best time to pick up special offers at hotels and guesthouses. Note too that in more remote spots public transport will often operate on a reduced winter timetable.

◄ Snow-dappled slopes of Buachaille Etive Mhor, Glen Coe

Winter days, from November through to March, occasionally crisp and bright, are more often cold, gloomy and all too brief, although Hogmanay and New Year has traditionally been a time to visit Scotland for partying and warm hospitality – something which improves as the weather worsens. While even tourist hotspots such as Edinburgh are notably quieter during winter, a fall of snow in the Highlands will prompt plenty of activity around the ski resorts.

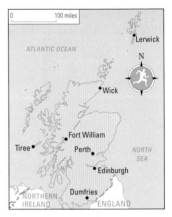

Scotland's climate

The table shows average daily maximum temperatures and monthly rainfall.

	Jan	Feb	Mar	Apr	May	Jun	Jul	Aug	Sep	Oct	Nov	Dec
Dumfries												
°C	6	6	8	11	14	17	18	18	16	13	9	7
mm	103	72	66	55	71	63	77	93	104	106	109	104
°F	42	43	47	52	58	63	65	65	61	55	47	44
inches	4	2.8	2.6	2.1	2.8	2.5	3	3.6	4	4.1	4.3	4.1
Edinburgh												
°C	6	6	9	11	14	17	18	18	16	13	9	7
mm	47	39	39	38	49	45	69	73	57	56	58	56
°F	43	44	47	52	58	63	65	65	61	56	48	45
inches	1.8	1.5	1.5	1.5	1.9	1.8	2.7	2.8	2.2	2.2	2.2	2.2
Fort William												
°C	6	7	9	11	15	17	17	17	15	13	9	7
mm	200	132	152	111	103	124	137	150	199	215	220	238
°F	43	44	47	52	58	62	63	63	60	55	48	45
inches	7.8	5.1	5.9	4.3	4	4.8	5.3	5.9	7.8	8.4	8.6	9.3
Lerwick												
°C	5	5	6	8	10	13	14	14	13	10	7	6
mm	127	93	93	72	64	64	67	78	113	119	140	147
°F	41	41	43	46	50	55	57	57	55	51	45	43
inches	5	3.6	3.6	2.8	2.5	2.5	2.6	3	4.4	4.6	5.5	5.7
Perth												
°C	6	6	8	12	15	18	19	19	16	13	9	7
mm	70	52	47	43	57	51	67	72	63	65	69	82
°F	42	43	47	53	59	64	66	65	61	55	47	44
inches	2.7	2	1.8	1.7	2.2	2	2.6	2.8	2.5	2.5	2.7	3.2
Tiree												
°C	7	7	8	10	13	15	16	16	15	13	10	8
mm	120	71	77	60	56	66	79	83	123	125	123	123
°F	45	45	47	51	55	59	60	61	58	55	49	47
inches	4.7	2.8	3	2.3	2.2	2.6	3.1	3.2	4.8	4.9	4.8	4.8
Wick												
°C	6	6	7	9	11	14	15	15	14	12	8	7
mm	81	58	55	45	47	49	61	74	68	73	90	7
°F	42	42	45	49	52	58	60	60	57	53	47	44
inches	3.2	2.3	2.1	1.8	1.8	1.9	2.4	2.9	2.7	2.8	3.5	3.2

40

things not to miss

It's not possible to see everything that Scotland has to offer in one trip – and we don't suggest you try. What follows is a selective taste of the country's highlights: great places to visit, remarkable buildings, breathtaking scenery and unforgettable journeys. They're arranged in five colour-coded categories, which you can browse through to find the very best things to see and experience. All entries have a page reference to take you straight into the guide, where you can find out more.

01 **Mousa, Shetland** Page **773** • The mother of all Iron Age brochs, on an island off the coast of Shetland.

02 Iona Page **368** • The home of Celtic Christian spirituality, an island of pilgrimage today as in antiquity.

04 Golf at St Andrews Page **443** • The most famous fairway in world golf, and you can play for next to nothing at the neighbouring Himalayas putting green.

06 Burrell Collection, Glasgow Page **308** • An unconventional but impressive museum at the heart of Glasgow's cultural renaissance.

03 Jarlshof, Shetland Page **774** • An exceptional archeological site taking in Bronze Age, Iron Age, Pictish, Viking and medieval remains.

05 Islay Page **391** • Hebridean island with no fewer than seven whisky distilleries, and wonderfully varied birdlife that includes thousands of wintering geese.

07 **Hill walking** Page **62** • The array of challenging but accessible hills makes walking one of the best ways to enjoy Scotland.

08 **Shetland folk festival** Page **770** • Shetland is the place to experience traditional folk music, and the annual folk festival is the best time to do it.

09 **Whale-watching, Mull** Page **361** • Close encounters with a very different type of Highland wildlife.

10 **Dunnottar Castle** Page **532** • Memorably dramatic ruined fortress, surrounded by giddy sea cliffs.

11 **Scottish Parliament** Page **108** • Enric Miralles' startling, contemporary design has transformed the old Holyrood area of Edinburgh.

12 Glasgow School of Art
Page **297** • Finest example of the unique style of Glasgow architect and designer Charles Rennie Mackintosh.

13 Eigg Page **690** • Perfect example of a tiny, friendly Hebridean island with a golden beach to lie on, a hill to climb and stunning views across the sea to its neighbour, Rùm.

14 Stirling Castle Page **410** • The grandest castle in Scotland, with a commanding outlook over Highlands and Lowlands.

15 Highland Games See the *Festivals* colour section • An entertaining blend of summer sports day and traditional clan gathering, held in locations across the Highlands.

16 **Kinloch Castle, Rùm** Page **688** • Stay in the servants' quarters of this Edwardian hideaway or in one of its few remaining four-poster beds.

17 **Staffa and the Treshnish Isles** Page **365** • View the basalt columns of Staffa's Fingal's Cave from the sea, and then picnic beside the puffins on the Isle of Lunga.

19 **Pubs** Page **50** • Forget the great outdoors and install yourself in one of Scotland's cosy and convivial hostelries.

18 **Museum of Scotland, Edinburgh** Page **113** • The ivory Lewis chessmen are part of the superb collection of artefacts.

20 **Arbroath "smokies"** Page 48 • An unsung delicacy – haddock smoked over traditional wood fires, best savoured in this unpretentious east-coast port town.

22 **The Falkirk Wheel** Page 419 • Less a wheel, more a mighty claw, this engineering and design marvel lifts boats between two stretches of canal.

21 **Calanais, Lewis** Page 705 • Prehistoric standing stones that occupy a serene setting in the Western Isles.

23 **St Magnus Cathedral, Kirkwall** Page 737 • A medieval cathedral in miniature, built by the Vikings using the local red and yellow sandstones.

24 **Caledonian forest** Page 594 • The few gnarled survivors of the great ancient Highland forests are majestic characters.

25 **Melrose Abbey** Page **190** Ruined Cistercian abbey situated in the most beguiling of Border towns.

26 **The Cairngorm mountains** Page **557** • Natural splendour and terrific outdoor activities.

27 **Flying above Orkney** Page **728** Take an exhilarating aerial tour of the archipelago in an eight-seater plane.

29 **DCA, Dundee** Page **498** • The Dundee Contemporary Arts centre, an inspiring focus for the town's up-and-coming cultural scene.

28 **Edinburgh Old Town** Page **90** • Lose yourself in the capital's medieval cobbled streets and closes.

30 **Edinburgh Festival** Page **147** •
The world's biggest festival of theatre and the arts transforms Edinburgh every August.

31 **Pictish stones** Page **508**
• Intriguing stone carvings by the ancient Picts are found up and down the east coast.

32 **Hogmanay** See the *Festivals* colour section • New Year celebrations, with whisky, dancing and fireworks staving off the midwinter chill.

33 **Glen Coe** Page **587** • Moody, poignant and spectacular glen within easy reach of Fort William.

34 **Gearrannan, Lewis** Page **704** • Stay in the thatched blackhouse hostel in this beautifully restored former crofting village.

35 **South Harris beaches** Page **708** • Take your pick of deserted golden beaches in South Harris, or further south in the Uists.

36 Maes Howe, Orkney
Page **732** • Europe's best-preserved Neolithic chambered cairn also contains fine examples of Viking runic inscriptions and drawings.

37 West Highland railway
Page **621** • One of the great railway journeys of the world.

39 Loch Fyne Oyster Bar
Page **342** • Pick up a picnic or enjoy fine dining at Scotland's top smokehouse and seafood outlet, located just outside Inveraray.

38 Tobermory
Page **360** • The main town on the beautiful island of Mull, and Scotland's most picturesque fishing port.

40 Skye Cuillin
Page **679** • The most spectacular mountain range on the west coast, for viewing or climbing.

Basics

Basics

Getting there

There are a few nonstop flights to Scotland from North America, but not from Australia or New Zealand; in any case, you'll get a much wider choice – and usually lower fares – if you fly via London. From continental Europe and parts of Britain, the cheapest and quickest way to reach Scotland is by plane. However, road and rail connections from around Britain are pretty straightforward, and there are direct ferries to Scotland from Ireland, Belgium and Scandinavia.

Scotland has three main **international airports:** Glasgow, Edinburgh and Aberdeen. Glasgow handles most nonstop scheduled flights from North America; all three have a reasonable spread of European flights. Glasgow Prestwick also has a few scheduled flights to and from Europe, and transatlantic flights via Dublin, but most of its custom comes from budget and charter airlines. Note that although Glasgow, Edinburgh and Aberdeen are well linked into the **domestic** network, there are no flights from Glasgow Prestwick to anywhere else in Scotland.

Airfares depend primarily on availability, but they also depend on the **season**, with the highest fares charged from mid-June to mid-September and around Christmas and New Year. Fares will ordinarily be cheaper during the rest of the year, which is considered low season, though some airlines also have a "shoulder" season – typically April to mid-June and mid-September to October.

Booking flights online

Loads of people book tickets online nowadays and good deals can often be found through discount or auction sites, as well as through the airlines' own websites.

ⓦ **www.cheapflights.com** (US); ⓦ **www .cheapflights.ca** (Canada); ⓦ **www.cheapflights .com.au** (Australia). All the sites offer flight deals, details of travel agents and links to other travel sites.

ⓦ **www.cheaptickets.com** Hawaii-based discount flight specialists (US only) whose search engine claims to dig up the lowest possible fares worldwide; the one drawback is its cumbersome log-in procedure.

ⓦ **www.etn.nl/discount.htm** A hub of consolidator and discount agent Web links, maintained by the non-profit European Travel Network.

ⓦ **www.expedia.com** (US); ⓦ **www.expedia .canada** (Canada) Discount airfares, all-airline search engine and daily deals.

ⓦ **www.gaytravel.com** US gay travel agent, offering accommodation, cruises, tours and more.

ⓦ **www.hotwire.com** Bookings from the US only. Last-minute savings of up to forty percent on regular published fares. Travellers must be at least 18 and there are no refunds, transfers or changes allowed. Log-in required. If you're looking for the cheapest possible scheduled flight, this is probably your best bet.

ⓦ **www.lastminute.com.au** (Australia only) Good last-minute holiday package and flight-only deals.

ⓦ **www.priceline.com** Name-your-own-price website that has deals at around forty percent off standard fares.

ⓦ **www.qixo.com** A comparison search that trawls through other ticket sites – including agencies and airlines – to find the best deals.

ⓦ **www.skyauction.com** Bookings from the US only. Auctions tickets and travel packages using a "second bid" scheme, just like eBay. You state the maximum you're willing to pay, and the system will bid only as much as it takes to outbid others, up to your stated limit.

ⓦ **www.travelocity.com** Destination guides, best deals for car hire, accommodation and lodging as well as fares. Provides access to the travel agent system SABRE, the most comprehensive central reservations system in the US.

ⓦ **www.travelshop.com.au** Australian website offering discounted flights, packages, insurance and online bookings.

ⓦ **travel.yahoo.com** Incorporates some Rough Guides material in its coverage of destination countries and cities across the world, with information about places to eat and sleep.

From North America

If you want to fly nonstop into Scotland **from North America**, there's a limited choice:

Continental from New York to Glasgow and Edinburgh or one of the Canadian budget airlines, Zoom or Transat. Most other airlines, and all flights to other Scottish airports, route through London, Manchester, Dublin or Paris.

Figure on six to seven hours' **flight time** nonstop from the east coast to Glasgow, or seven hours to London plus an extra hour and a quarter from London to Glasgow or Edinburgh (not including stopover time). Add three or four hours more for travel from the west coast. Most eastbound flights cross the Atlantic overnight, reaching Britain the next morning; flying back, departure times tend to be morning or afternoon, arriving in the afternoon or evening.

Return **fares** (including taxes) to Glasgow from New York are $400–500 low season, $600–800 high season; from Canada around C$750 low season, C$1000 high season.

Airlines in North America

Aer Lingus ℡1-800/IRISH-AIR, ⓦwww.aerlingus.com

Air Canada ℡1-888/247-2262, ⓦwww.aircanada.com

Air Transat ℡1-866/847-1112, ⓦwww.airtransat.ca

American Airlines ℡1-800/433-7300, ⓦwww.aa.com

bmi ℡1-800/788-0555, ⓦwww.flybmi.com

British Airways ℡1-800/AIRWAYS, ⓦwww.ba.com

Continental ℡1-800/231-0856, ⓦwww.continental.com

Delta ℡1-800/241-4141, ⓦwww.delta.com

United Airlines ℡1-800/538-2929, ⓦwww.united.com

Virgin Atlantic Airways ℡1-800/862-8621, ⓦwww.virgin-atlantic.com.

Zoom Airlines ℡1-866/359-9666, ⓦwww.flyzoom.com

Discount travel companies

Air Brokers International ℡1-800/883-3273, ⓦwww.airbrokers.com. Consolidator and specialist in round-the-world tickets.

Airtech ℡212/219-7000, ⓦwww.airtech.com. Standby seat broker; also deals in consolidator fares.

Educational Travel Centre ℡1-800/747-5551 or 608/256-5551, ⓦwww.edtrav.com. Low-cost fares

worldwide, student/youth discount offers, and Eurail passes, car rental and tours.

New Frontiers ℡1-800/677-0720, ⓦwww.newfrontiers.com. Discount firm, specializing in travel from the US to Europe.

STA Travel US ℡1-800/329-9537, Canada ℡1-888/427-5639, ⓦwww.statravel.com. Worldwide specialists in independent travel; also student IDs, travel insurance, car rental, rail passes and more.

Student Flights ℡1-800/255-8000 or 480/951-1177, ⓦwww.isecard.com/studentflights. Student/youth fares, plus student IDs and European rail and bus passes.

TFI Tours International ℡1-800/745-8000 or 212/736-1140, ⓦwww.lowestairprice.com. Well-established consolidator with a wide variety of global fares.

Travel CUTS US ℡1-800/592-CUTS, Canada ℡1-888/246-9762, ⓦwww.travelcuts.com. Popular, long-established student-travel organization, with worldwide offers.

Worldtek Travel ℡1-800/243-1723, ⓦwww.worldtek.com. Discount travel agency for worldwide travel.

Tour operators in North America

Abercrombie & Kent ℡1-800/554-7016, ⓦwww.abercrombiekent.com. Classy operator with a strong reputation, offering various packages including cruises and rail tours around Scotland.

Adventures Abroad ℡1-800/665-3998 or ℡604/303-1099, ⓦwww.adventures-abroad.com. Walking and sightseeing tours of Scotland.

Backroads ℡1-800/GO-ACTIVE, ⓦwww.backroads.com. Guided walking packages in the Scottish Highlands and Islands.

CIE Tours ℡1-800/CIE-TOUR, ⓦwww.cietours.com. Escorted coach tours and self-drive packages.

Golf International Inc ℡1-800/833-1389, ⓦwww.golfinternational.com. Scottish golf vacation specialist.

Home at First ℡1-800/523-5842, ⓦwww.homeatfirst.com. Flights, cottages, car rental and golf packages.

International Gay Travel Association ℡1-800/448-8550, ⓦwww.iglta.org. Trade group with lists of gay-owned or gay-friendly travel agents, accommodation options and other travel-related services.

Jerry Quinlan's Celtic Golf ℡1-800/535-6148 or 609/465-0600, ⓦwww.jqcelticgolf.com. Customized golf tours of Scotland.

Mountain Travel Sobek ℡1-888/MT-SOBEK, ⓦwww.mtsobek.com. Hiking holidays in the Highlands.

Prestige Tours ☎ 1-800/890-7375, ⓦ www
.prestige-tours.com. Fly-drive, all-inclusive coach
tours and city breaks.
Rail Europe ☎ 1-877/EUROVAC; ⓦ www
.raileurope.com. Rail, air, hotel and car reservations
in the UK.

From Australia and New Zealand

Flight time from **Australia** and **New Zealand** to Scotland is at least 22 hours, and can be more depending on routes and transfer times. There's a wide variety of routes, with those touching down in Southeast Asia the quickest and cheapest on average. To reach Scotland, you usually have to change planes either in London – the most popular choice – or in another European gateway such as Paris or Amsterdam. One exception to this is if you fly via Dubai, from which Emirates has daily flights direct to Glasgow. Given the length of the journey involved, you might be better off including a night's stopover in your itinerary, and indeed some airlines include one in the price of the flight.

The cheapest direct scheduled flights to London are usually to be found on one of the Asian airlines. Average return **fares** (including taxes) from eastern gateways to London are A$1500–2000 in low season, A$2000–2500 in high season. Fares from Perth or Darwin cost around A$200 less. Return fares from Auckland to London range between NZ$2000 and NZ$3000 depending on the season, route and carrier.

Airlines in Australia and New Zealand

Air New Zealand Australia ☎ 13 24 76, ⓦ www
.airnz.com.au; New Zealand ☎ 0800/737 000,
ⓦ www.airnz.co.nz
British Airways Australia ☎ 1300/767 177, New
Zealand ☎ 09/966 9777; ⓦ www.ba.com
Cathay Pacific Australia ☎ 02/9667 3816, New
Zealand ☎ 09/275 0847; ⓦ www.cathaypacific.com
Delta Australia ☎ 02/9251 3211, New Zealand
☎ 09/379 3370; ⓦ www.delta.com
Emirates Australia ☎ 1300/303 777 or 02/9290
9700, New Zealand ☎ 09/377 6004; ⓦ www
.emirates.com
Garuda Indonesia Australia ☎ 1300/365 330
or 02/9334 9944, New Zealand ☎ 09/366 1862;
ⓦ www.garuda-indonesia.com

KLM Australia ☎ 1300 303 747, New Zealand
☎ 09/302 1792; ⓦ www.klm.com
Malaysian Airlines Australia ☎ 13 26 27, New
Zealand ☎ 0800/777 747 or 649/379 3743;
ⓦ www.malaysiaairlines.com
Qantas Australia ☎ 13 1313, New Zealand ☎ 09/
357 8900 or 0800/808 767; ⓦ www.quantas.com
Singapore Airlines Australia ☎ 13 1011 or ☎ 02/
9350 0262, New Zealand ☎ 09/379 3209; ⓦ www
.singaporeair.com
Sri Lankan Airlines Australia ☎ 02/9244 2234,
New Zealand ☎ 09/308 3353; ⓦ www.srilankan
.aero
Thai Airways Australia ☎ 1300 651 960, New
Zealand ☎ 09/377 3886; ⓦ www.thaiair.com
Virgin Atlantic Airways Australia ☎ 02/9244
2747, ⓦ www.virgin-atlantic.com.

Flight agents

Flight Centre Australia ☎ 13 31 33 or 02/9235
3522, ⓦ www.flightcentre.com.au; New Zealand
☎ 0800 243 544 or 09/358 4310, ⓦ www
.flightcentre.co.nz
Holiday Shoppe New Zealand ☎ 0800/808 480,
ⓦ www.holidayshoppe.co.nz
Northern Gateway Australia ☎ 1800/174 800,
ⓦ www.northerngateway.com.au
STA Travel Australia ☎ 1300/733 035 or 02/9212
1255, ⓦ www.statravel.com.au; New Zealand
☎ 0508/782 872 or 09/309 9273, ⓦ www
.statravel.co.nz
Trailfinders Australia ☎ /9247 7666 or
☎ 1300/780 212, ⓦ www.trailfinders.com.au
ⓦ **www.travel.com.au** Australia ☎ 1300/130 482
or 02/9249 5444; New Zealand ⓦ www.travel
.co.nz, ☎ 0800/468 332

From England and Wales

Crossing the border from England into Scotland is straightforward, with **train** and **bus** services forming part of the British national network. If you add on the time spent getting to and from the airport and checking in, **flying** is no quicker than travelling by train or coach unless you're heading out to the Highlands and Islands. Budget airfares are only really competitive on popular routes such as London to Edinburgh and Glasgow, and, again, if you add on the cost of travel to and from the airport (and remember to include airport tax), the savings on the same journey overland are often minimal – and then, of course, there's the environmental impact to consider.

The most competitive **airfares** from England and Wales are with the no-frills budget airlines. The leaders in the field are Ryanair, who fly into Glasgow Prestwick, and easyJet, who fly into all the major Scottish airports from London and other regional airports. You can pay as little as £20 for a rock-bottom one-way ticket and £40 for a return (including tax). However, the cheaper tickets need to be booked well in advance and are either non-refundable or only partially refundable, and non-exchangeable. For more reasonable flight times and/or a more flexible, refundable fare from these same budget airlines, you're looking at more like £80 return, a price that British Airways – with a range of flights out of many English airports – can often compete with.

Airlines in Britain

Air Wales ℡0870/850 9850, ⊛www.airwales.com

British Airways ℡0870/850 9850, ⊛www.ba.com

bmi ℡0870/607 0555, ⊛www.flybmi.com

bmibaby ℡0870/264 2229, ⊛www.bmibaby.com

easyJet ℡0871/750 0100, ⊛www.easyjet.com

Eastern Airways ℡0870/366 9100, ⊛www.easternairways.com

Flybe ℡0870/889 0908, ⊛www.flybe.com

Jet2.com ℡0871/226 1737, ⊛www.jet2.com

KLM ℡0870/507 4074, ⊛www.klm.com

Ryanair ℡0871/246 0000, ⊛www.ryanair.com

ScotAirways ℡0870/606 0707, ⊛www.scotairways.com

Flight agents in Britain

North South Travel ℡01245/608 291, ⊛www.northsouthtravel.co.uk. Friendly, competitive travel agency, offering discounted fares worldwide. Profits are used to support projects in the developing world, especially the promotion of sustainable tourism.

STA Travel ℡0870/160 0599, ⊛www.statravel.co.uk. Worldwide specialists in low-cost flights, overlands and holiday deals. Good discounts for students and under-26s.

Trailfinders UK ℡020/7938 3939, ⊛www.trailfinders.com. One of the best-informed and most efficient agents for independent travellers.

By train from England and Wales

Glasgow and Edinburgh are both served by frequent direct **train** services from London,

and are easily reached from other main English towns and cities, though you may have to change trains en route. GNER trains depart from **London King's Cross** and run up the east coast via Peterborough, York and Newcastle to Edinburgh, with some going on to Glasgow, Aberdeen or Inverness, while Virgin trains run up the west coast from **London Euston** via Crewe, Preston and Carlisle to Glasgow. Virgin also runs several other long-distance direct services to Scotland that don't originate in London: from **Penzance**, **Plymouth** and **Bournemouth** to Edinburgh or Glasgow via Birmingham and then either the east or the west coast.

Journey times from London can be as little as 4hr 20min to Edinburgh and 4hr 45min to Glasgow; from Manchester or York, knock off about 2hr; from Bristol add about 2hr; from Penzance, it takes just over 10hr. Beyond Edinburgh or Glasgow, allow another 2hr 30min to reach Aberdeen, or 3hr 30min to Inverness.

Fare structures are fiendishly complex, but if you simply turn up at the station, the cheapest off-peak fare available will be around £85 return; if you book in advance you can get £10–20 off and occasional special offers can bring the price down even further. Return fares from Manchester to Glasgow are around £30 if you book in advance, but more like £50 on the day; from Bristol to Edinburgh, advance returns cost around £70, but over £100 on the day. Various discount **passes** are also available in Britain to nationals and foreign visitors alike, for those under 26, over 60 or travelling with children. For more details, and links to sites where you can book online, visit ⊛www.nationalrail.co.uk.

If you're travelling up from London it's definitely worth considering taking one of the **Caledonian Sleepers**, run by First ScotRail from London Euston (daily except Sat) to Glasgow, Edinburgh, Aberdeen, Inverness and Fort William. A sample return fare to Edinburgh or Glasgow is £89 if booked in advance. Sleeper cabins contain two beds, so you may have to share (with someone of the same sex) unless you pay a supplement; first-class customers automatically enjoy the luxury of a single-berth cabin. Otherwise, there's the budget option of a relatively comfortable reclining seat, starting at £40 return; while hardly the lap of luxury, this is still a more attractive option than the rather grim overnight bus journey (which is only slightly less expensive). You can usually board the train an hour before departure and leave half an hour or so after it arrives.

Train information

First ScotRail ☎0845/755 0033, ⓦwww .firstgroup.com/scotrail
GNER ☎0845/722 5225, ⓦwww.gner.co.uk
National Rail enquiries ☎0845/748 4950, ⓦwww.nationalrail.co.uk
Virgin ☎0845/722 2333, ⓦwww.virgintrains .co.uk

By road from England and Wales

Inter-town bus services (known as **coaches** throughout Britain) duplicate many train routes, often at half the price or less. The frequency of service is usually comparable to the train, and in some instances the difference in journey time isn't that great; buses are also reasonably comfortable, and on longer routes often have drinks and sandwiches available on board. The main operators are **National Express** (☎0870/580 8080, ⓦwww.nationalexpress .com) and its sister company **Scottish Citylink** (☎0870/550 5050, ⓦwww.citylink .co.uk). Buses run direct from most British cities to Edinburgh, Glasgow, Aberdeen and Inverness. Typical **fares** from London to Glasgow or Edinburgh (overnight journeys take around 8hr; daytime journeys nearer 10hr) are around £40 return; from Cardiff £50; from Manchester £30. If you book in advance, you can save £10 or so. There are also various discount **passes** available, detailed on the websites.

The two main **driving** routes to Scotland from the south are via the east of England on the A1, or via the west using the M6, A74(M) and M74. The A1, which passes by Peterborough, Doncaster, Newcastle and Berwick-upon-Tweed, gives you the option of branching off onto the A68, which takes the hilly but scenic route over the border at Carter Bar and adds an hour or so to the journey time; the M6 route, which goes around Birmingham, between Manchester and Liverpool and on to Carlisle, offers at least dual-carriageway

driving the whole way. Either way, it takes around 8hr to get from London or Cardiff to Edinburgh or Glasgow, barring roadwork delays; 2hr less from Birmingham.

From Ireland

Travel **from Ireland** is quickest by plane, with reasonable choice of flights from both Belfast and Dublin. There are also good ferry links with Northern Ireland, so taking the train or driving to Scotland is pretty straightforward.

Flying from **Dublin**, the best airfares are with Ryanair, which flies to Glasgow Prestwick for as little as €20 return, depending on availability. A fully flexible fare with Aer Lingus can cost five or six times that amount, but will allow you to change your ticket or claim a refund. From **Belfast** International, easyJet has return flights to Edinburgh or Glasgow from around £40; British Airways fares from Belfast or **Derry** to Glasgow start from £60 return (including tax).

Airlines in Ireland

Aer Arann Northern Ireland ☎0800/587 2324, Republic of Ireland ☎0818/210 210, ⓦwww .aerarann.com
Aer Lingus Northern Ireland ☎0845/084 4444, Republic of Ireland ☎0818/365 000, ⓦwww .aerlingus.ie
bmi Northern Ireland ☎0870/607 0555, ⓦwww .flybmi.com
British Airways Northern Ireland ☎0870/850 9850, Republic of Ireland ☎1800/626 747, ⓦwww.ba.com
easyJet Northern Ireland ☎0871/750 0100, ⓦwww.easyjet.com
Flybe Northern Ireland ☎0870/889 0908, Republic of Ireland ☎1890/925 532, ⓦwww.flybe.com
KLM Northern Ireland ☎0870/507 4074, ⓦwww .klmuk.com
Ryanair Northern Ireland ☎0871/246 0000, Republic of Ireland ☎0818/303 030, ⓦwww .ryanair.com

Flight agents in Ireland

ebookers Dublin ☎01/488 3507, ⓦwww .ebookers.ie. Low fares on an extensive selection of scheduled flights and package deals.
Joe Walsh Tours Dublin ☎01/676 0991, ⓦwww .joewalshtours.ie. Long-established general budget fares and holidays agent.
USIT Belfast ☎0870/240 1010, ⓦwww .usitcampus.co.uk; Dublin ☎01/602 1600,

@ www.usitnow.ie. Student, youth and independent travel specialists.

By ferry from Ireland

P&O Irish Sea runs several **sea** crossings daily from **Larne** to Cairnryan (takes 1hr 45min by ferry, or 1hr by jetliner) and Troon, just outside Ayr (1hr 50min). Stena Line operates conventional ferries and a high-speed service (HSS) daily from **Belfast** to Stranraer (takes between 1hr 45min and 3hr 15min). One day it is hoped that the ferry service from **Ballycastle** to Campbeltown will be resumed.

Fares for a small car and driver are pretty complex, and depend on the time, day and month of sailing, on whether you take the fast or slow services, on whether you book in advance and on how long you're staying over in Scotland. Peak period standard returns can cost over £250, though you can save around £50 by booking in advance, and another £50 by travelling off-peak. Passenger-only fares work out at around £50 return.

Ferry companies in Ireland

P&O Irish Sea UK ☎ 0870/242 4777, @ www .poirishsea.com

Stena Line Northern Ireland ☎ 028/9074 7747, Republic of Ireland ☎ 01/204 7777, @ www .stenaline.co.uk

By ferry from mainland Europe

Ferries run by Superfast go overnight from **Zeebrugge** in Belgium to Rosyth (daily; 18hr), near Edinburgh. Off-peak return fares start at around €110, plus €165 for a car, and another €50 for a cabin berth. Smyril Line runs summer ferries to Shetland from Norway, **Denmark**, the **Faroe Islands** and **Iceland** (mid-May to early Sept only). The most direct route is from **Bergen** (Norway) to Lerwick (1 weekly; 12hr), with the option of continuing on to Aberdeen (daily; 12hr) on Northlink Ferries. Peak period through-fares from Bergen to Aberdeen cost around 1700kr return per person, or 3000kr with a car.

There's a greater choice of ferry services from Europe to ports in England, the most convenient being those to **Newcastle**, less than an hour's drive south of the Scottish border. DFDS Seaways sails twice weekly to Newcastle from **Kristiansand** in Norway (18hr) and from **Gothenburg** in Sweden (26hr), as well as daily from **IJmuiden** near Amsterdam (16hr). Fjord Line sails three times a week to Newcastle from **Bergen**, **Haugesund** and **Stavanger** (18–25hr). Fares on all routes vary according to the time of year, time and type of crossing and number travelling; Direct Ferries (☎ 0871/222 3312, @ www.directferries.ie) has a very useful website that compares all the options.

Ferry companies

DFDS Seaways Netherlands ☎ 0255/54 66 66, Norway ☎ 21 62 13 40, Sweden ☎ 031/650680, UK ☎ 0870/252 0524, @ www.dfdsseaways.com

Fjord Line Norway ☎ 81 53 35 00, UK ☎ 0870/143 9669, @ www.fjordline.com

Northlink Ferries UK ☎ 0845/600 0449, @ www .northlinkferries.co.uk

Smyril Line Norway ☎ 55 59 65 20, UK ☎ 01595/690845, @ www.smyril-line.com

Superfast Ferries Belgium 02/226 4060, UK ☎ 0870/234 0870, @ www.superfast.com

Visas and red tape

B

BASICS | Visas and red tape

Citizens of most European countries can enter the UK with just a passport; EU citizens can stay indefinitely, other Europeans can stay up to three months. US, Canadian, Australian and New Zealand citizens can stay for up to six months, providing they have a return ticket and adequate funds to cover their stay. Citizens of most other countries require a visa, obtainable from the British consular or mission office in the country of application.

For current details about entry and **visa requirements**, consult the UK Foreign and Commonwealth Office's visa website: ⓦwww.ukvisas.gov.uk. Citizens of EU countries who want to stay in the UK other than as a short-term visitor or tourist can apply for a **residence permit**. Non-EU citizens can apply to extend their visas, though this must be done before the current visa expires. In both cases, you should first contact the **Immigration and Nationality Directorate**, Lunar House, 40 Wellesley Rd, Croydon CR9 2BY ⓉT0870/606 7766, ⓦwww.ind .homeoffice.gov.uk.

US, Canadian, Australian and New Zealand citizens who want to stay longer than six months will need an **entry clearance certificate**, available from the British consular office at the embassy/high commission in their own country. An independent charity, the **Immigration Advisory Service** (IAS), based on the 3rd Floor of County House, 190 Great Dover St, London SE1 4YB (ⓉT020/7967 1200, ⓦwww.iasuk.org), offers free and confidential advice to anyone applying for entry clearance into the UK. Consulates of foreign countries in Scotland are detailed in the listings sections for Edinburgh, Glasgow, Kirkwall and Lerwick.

UK embassies abroad

Australia British High Commission, Commonwealth Ave, Yarralumla, Canberra, ACT 2600 ⓉT02/6270 6666, ⓦwww.britaus.net

Canada British High Commission, 80 Elgin St, Ottawa, ON K1P 5K7 ⓉT613/237-1530, ⓦwww .britainincanada.org

Ireland British Embassy, 29 Merrion Rd, Ballsbridge, Dublin 4 ⓉT01/205 3700, ⓦwww .britishembassy.ie

New Zealand British High Commission, 44 Hill St, Thorndon, Wellington ⓉT04/924 2888, ⓦwww .britain.org.nz

US British Embassy, 3100 Massachusetts Ave NW, Washington DC 20008 ⓉT202/588-6500, ⓦwww .britainusa.com

Customs and tax

Travellers coming into Britain directly **from another EU country** can bring almost as many cigarettes and as much wine or beer into the country as they can carry. The guidance levels are 10 litres of spirits, 90 litres of wine and 110 litres of beer – any more than this and you'll have to provide proof that it's for personal use only. The general guidelines for tobacco are 3200 cigarettes, 400 cigarillos, 200 cigars or 3kg of loose tobacco – note that the limits from some new EU member countries are lower than this.

If you're travelling to or from a non-EU country, you can still buy **duty-free goods**, but within the EU, this perk no longer exists. The duty-free allowances are:

Tobacco 200 cigarettes; or 100 cigarillos; or 50 cigars; or 250 grammes of loose tobacco.

Alcohol 2 litres of still wine plus 1 litre of drink over 22 percent alcohol; or 2 litres of alcoholic drinks not over 22 percent.

Perfumes 60ml of perfume plus 250ml of toilet water.

Other goods to the value of £145.

If you need any clarification on British import regulations, contact **HM Revenue and Customs** (ⓉT0845/010 9000 or +4420/8929 0152 for international callers; ⓦwww.hmrv.gov.uk).

Pets from countries participating in the Pet Travel Scheme (PETS) are allowed into Britain without quarantine, providing their owners follow certain procedures; for more information, phone the helpline ☎0870/241 1710 or check the government website (ⓦwww.defra.gov.uk).

Most goods in Britain, with the chief exceptions of books and food, are subject to 17.5 percent **Value Added Tax** (VAT), which is included in the marked price of goods. Visitors from non-EU countries can save a lot of money through the **Retail Export Scheme** (tax-free shopping), which allows a refund of VAT on goods to be taken out of the country. (Savings will usually be minimal for EU nationals because of the rates at which the goods will be taxed upon import to the home country.) Note that not all shops participate in this scheme (those doing so will display a sign to this effect), and that you cannot reclaim VAT charged on hotel bills or other services.

Costs, money and banks

Scotland, like the rest of the UK, is a relatively expensive place to visit. Transport, accommodation and restaurant prices are all above average compared with the rest of the EU. The UK has not changed over to the euro, and for the foreseeable future looks unlikely to do so (for more information, visit ⓦ www.euro.gov.uk).

Currency and exchange

The basic unit of currency in the UK is the **pound sterling** (£), divided into 100 pence (p). Coins come in denominations of 1p, 2p, 5p, 10p, 20p, 50p, £1 and £2. Bank of England £5, £10, £20 and £50 banknotes are legal tender in Scotland; in addition the Bank of Scotland (now HBOS), the Royal Bank of Scotland and the Clydesdale Bank issue their own banknotes in all the same denominations, plus a £100 note. All Scottish notes are legal tender throughout the UK, no matter what shopkeepers south of the border might say. In general, few people use £50 or £100 notes, and shopkeepers are likely to treat them with suspicion, since forgeries are widespread. At the time of going to press, £1 was worth around $1.80, €1.50, C$2.10, A$2.35 and NZ$2.60. For the most up-to-date exchange rates, check the useful website ⓦwww.xe.com.

There are **no exchange controls** in Britain, so you can bring in as much cash as you like and change travellers' cheques up to any amount. In every sizeable town in Scotland, and in some surprisingly small places too, you'll find a branch of at least one of the big Scottish high-street **banks**: HBOS (Halifax Bank of Scotland), Royal Bank of Scotland, Clydesdale and Lloyds TSB Scotland. However, on some islands, and in remoter parts, you may find there is only a **mobile bank** that runs to a timetable (usually available from the local post office).

General **banking hours** are Monday to Friday from 9 or 9.30am to 4 or 5pm, though some branches are open until slightly later on Thursdays. Almost everywhere, banks are the best places in which to change money and travellers' cheques. Outside banking hours, you can change cheques or cash at **post offices** (locations are detailed in the guide) and **bureaux de change** – the latter tend to be open longer hours and are found in most city centres, and at major airports and train stations.

Carrying money

Credit/debit cards are by far the most convenient way to carry your money. Most hotels, shops and restaurants in Scotland accept the major credit cards, although

Service charges and tipping

Some restaurants levy a "discretionary" or "optional" **service charge** of ten or 12.5 percent. If they've done this, it should be clearly stated on the menu and on the bill. However, you are not obliged to pay the charge, and certainly not if the food or service wasn't what you expected.

Otherwise, although there are no fixed rules for **tipping**, a ten to fifteen percent tip is anticipated by restaurant waiters and expected by taxi drivers. It is not normal to leave tips in pubs, but the bar staff are sometimes offered drinks, which they may accept in the form of money. The only other occasions when you'll be expected to tip are in hairdressers, and in upmarket hotels where porters, bellboys and table waiters rely on being tipped to bump up their often dismal wages.

plastic is less useful in rural areas; smaller establishments all over the country, such as B&Bs, will often accept cash only. You can usually withdraw cash on your credit or debit card from **ATMs** (widely known as cash machines). Be warned, however, that cash machines can be few and far between in the Highlands and Islands. You can also get cash at most **supermarkets** when you make a purchase, and at some petrol stations.

Though a lot more hassle, old-fashioned **travellers' cheques** are still the safest way to carry your money. If the cheques are lost or stolen, the issuing company will expect you to report the loss immediately; most companies claim to replace lost or stolen cheques within 24 hours. Note that in the UK you are unlikely to be able to use your travellers' cheques as cash – you'll always have to cash them first, making them an unreliable source of funds in more remote areas.

Costs

The minimum **expenditure**, if you're cycling or hitching, preparing most of your own food and camping, is in the region of £30 a day, rising to around £40 a day if you're staying at hostels, using some public transport and eating the odd meal out. Couples staying at budget B&Bs, eating at unpretentious restaurants and visiting a fair number of tourist attractions, are looking at around £50

each per day; if you're renting a car, staying in comfortable B&Bs or hotels and eating well, you should reckon on at least £100 a day per person. If you're visiting Edinburgh, which can be pricey, allow at least an extra £10 or so a day.

Discounts and concessions

Concessionary rates for **senior citizens** (over 60) and **children** (from 5 to 16) apply almost everywhere, from fee-paying attractions to public transport, and typically give around fifty percent discount; you'll need official identification as proof of age. The unemployed and full-time students are often entitled to discounts too, and the under-5s are rarely charged.

Full-time students are eligible for the **International Student ID Card** (ISIC; ⑭www .isiccard.com), which entitles them to special air-, rail and bus fares and discounts at museums, theatres and other attractions. The **International Youth Travel Card** provides similar benefits for under-26s, while teachers qualify for the **International Teacher Card**. Several other travel organizations and accommodation groups (including the youth hostel organization, IYHF) have their own cards providing various discounts. Specialist travel agencies in your home country (including STA worldwide) can provide more information and application forms

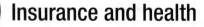

Insurance and health

Visitors are advised to take out an insurance policy before travelling to cover against theft, loss and illness or injury. A typical policy will provide cover for loss of baggage, tickets and – up to a certain limit – cash or travellers' cheques, as well as cancellation or curtailment of your journey. Most exclude so-called dangerous sports unless an extra premium is paid: in Scotland this can mean most water-sports, rock climbing, scuba diving, windsurfing and skiing, though probably not hiking and kayaking.

Medical coverage is strongly advised, though beforehand you should always ascertain whether benefits will be paid as treatment proceeds or only after you return home, and whether there is a 24-hour medical emergency number. When securing **baggage cover**, make sure that the per-article limit will cover your most valuable possession. If you need to make a claim, you should keep receipts for medicines and medical treatment, and in the event of having anything stolen you must obtain an official statement from the police – we've noted the contact details for police stations in all major towns and cities.

Health

No vaccinations are required for entry to the UK. EU citizens are entitled to free medical treatment at National Health Service hospitals on production of an **EHIC** card (which replaces the old **E111** form). Australia, New Zealand and several non-EU European countries have reciprocal health-care arrangements with the UK. Citizens of other countries will be charged for all medical services except those administered by Accident and Emergency (A&E) units at National Health Service hospitals. In other words, if you've just been hit by a car, you would not be charged if the injuries simply required stitching and setting in the emergency unit, but would were admission to a hospital ward be necessary. Health insurance is therefore extremely advisable for all non-EU nationals.

Pharmacists (known as chemists in Scotland) can dispense only a limited range of drugs without a doctor's prescription. Most are open standard shop hours, though in large towns some may close as late as 10pm; local newspapers carry lists of late-opening pharmacies, or you can contact the local police for current details. **Doctors' (GPs') surgeries** tend to be open from about 9am to noon and then for a couple of hours in the evening; outside surgery hours, you can turn up at the 24-hour casualty (A&E) department of the local **hospital** (detailed in our main city and town accounts). In an **emergency**, call an ambulance on ☎999.

Information, websites and maps

If you want to do a bit of research before arriving in Scotland, it's a good idea to visit some of the websites listed in this section (and throughout the main text of this book). You could also contact VisitBritain – the UK's tourist authority – which has offices worldwide, or the main office of VisitScotland, the Scottish tourist board. Either will send you a wealth of free literature, useful maps, city guides, event calendars and accommodation brochures.

Tourist offices

Tourist offices (often called Visitor or Tourist Information Centres, or even "TICs") exist in virtually every Scottish town; you'll find their phone numbers (see box) and opening hours in the relevant sections throughout this book. **Opening hours** are frequently confusing and vary from place to place and month to month. Note that many offices close completely in the winter, and, more often than not, phone enquiries are now directed to a central call centre in Livingstone, where the staff have no knowledge of local information other than what appears on their computer screen. Consequently, we've only given telephone numbers in the guide for tourist offices where you can be sure (at the time of going to print) of getting through to that specific office.

As well as being stacked full of souvenirs and other gifts, most TICs have a decent selection of leaflets, displays, maps and books relating to the local area. The staff are usually helpful and will do their best to help with enquiries about accommodation, local public transport, attractions and restaurants, although it is worth being aware that they are reluctant to divulge information about local attractions or accommodation which are not paid-up members of the Tourist Board – and a number of perfectly decent guesthouses and the like choose not to pay the fees. Some offices may make a small charge for a town guide with an accompanying street plan, or an accommodation list, and most will charge a fee of around £3 if they book accommodation for you (see p.45).

British Tourist Authority

ⓦ **www.visitbritain.com**
Australia ☎ 02/9021 4400 or 1300/858589, ⓦ www.visitbritain.com/au
Canada ☎ 1-888/847 4885, ⓦ www.visitbritain.com/ca
Ireland ☎ 01/670 8000, ⓦ www.visitbritain.com/ie
New Zealand ☎ 0800/700 741, ⓦ www.visitbritain.com/nz
US ☎ 1-800/462 2748, ⓦ www.visitbritain.com/us

Scottish Tourist Board

ⓦ **www.visitscotland.com**
Information ☎ 0845/225 5121. In Scotland: 23 Ravelston Terrace, Edinburgh EH4 3EU. In England: 19 Cockspur St, London SW1Y 5BL.

Regional tourist boards

Aberdeen and Grampian ☎ 01224/288828, ⓦ www.agtb.org
Angus and Dundee ☎ 01382/527527, ⓦ www.angusanddundee.co.uk
Argyll, the Isles, Loch Lomond, Stirling and Trossachs ☎ 01786/445222, ⓦ www.visitscottishheartlands.com
Ayrshire and Arran ⓦ www.ayrshire-arran.com
Dumfries and Galloway ☎ 01387/253862, ⓦ www.dumfriesandgalloway.co.uk
Edinburgh and the Lothians ⓦ www.edinburgh.org
Greater Glasgow and Clyde Valley ☎ 0141/566 0800, ⓦ www.seeglasgow.com
Highlands of Scotland ☎ 01997/421160, ⓦ www.host.co.uk
Kingdom of Fife ☎ 01334/472021, ⓦ www.standrews.co.uk
Orkney ☎ 01856/872856, ⓦ www.visitorkney.com
Perthshire ☎ 01738/627958, ⓦ www.perthshire.co.uk

Scottish Borders ℡01750/20555, ⓦwww
.scot-borders.co.uk
Shetland ℡01595/693434, ⓦwww.visitshetland
.com
Western Isles ℡01851/703088, ⓦwww
.visithebrides.com

Websites

Throughout the guide, we've included **websites** for specific accommodation, museums, galleries, transport, entertainment venues and other attractions. If you're looking for more general information about Scotland, or just a different take on things, then the list below is a useful starting point.

Guides and news

ⓦ**www.aboutscotland.com** Useful for accommodation, easy to use and linked to holiday activities.

ⓦ**adventure.visitscotland.com** Run in association with the tourist board, this is a rundown of various Scottish adventure holiday options, everything from pony trekking to all-night partying. Well worth a look if you need inspiration.

ⓦ**www.ceolas.org/ceolas.html** A very informative Celtic music site, both historical and contemporary, with lots of music to listen to.

ⓦ**www.geo.ed.ac.uk/home/scotland/ scotland.html** Produced by the Geography Department of Edinburgh University – an introduction to all things Scottish in the way of history, geography and politics. Excellent background information with a myriad of links.

ⓦ**www.hebrides.com** Beautiful black-and-white photographic journey courtesy of Sam Maynard through the Outer Hebrides (aka the Western Isles).

ⓦ**www.highlanderweb.co.uk** Styled as a magazine aimed primarily at businesses, but with a mixture of radio, music, products and more.

ⓦ**www.rampantscotland.com** Index of links to everything Scottish; well worth going to if you're searching for something specific.

ⓦ**www.scotland-info.co.uk** A big Internet guide to the country, with a commercial bent – lots of links to shops, hotels and so on – but good on information for individual areas.

ⓦ**www.scotland.org.uk** Exhaustive directory of Scottish websites.

ⓦ**www.travelscotland.co.uk** Run in association with the tourist board, this is a lively magazine-format site, full of news, features and reviews, but perhaps less useful for arranging a holiday.

ⓦ**www.undiscoveredscotland.co.uk** Great online guide to the country, with everything from features, maps and recipes to lists of boat charters and links to loads of local sites.

Peculiarly Scottish

ⓦ**www.hogmanay.net** Where to go and what to sing on Scotland's biggest night out.

ⓦ**www.met-office.gov.uk** The nation's favourite topic, the weather, discussed in detail with full regional (and shipping) forecasts.

ⓦ**www.rabbie-burns.com** All you need to know to organize the perfect Burns Night.

ⓦ**www.scotsclans.com** Join a clan, sort out your tartan and buy yourself a kilt.

ⓦ**www.sol.co.uk/d/dickwall/munroes.htm** A comprehensive list of Scotland's Munros (mountains over 3000ft) with pop-up maps to locate them all.

ⓦ**www.stonepages.com/scotland** Strangely compelling website for those hooked on cairns and stone circles.

ⓦ**www.strathspey.org** How to bluff your way in Scottish country dancing (in case you're asked to an obscure cousin's wedding).

Maps

The most comprehensive maps of Scotland are produced by the **Ordnance Survey** or OS (ⓦwww.ordsvy.gov.uk), renowned for their accuracy and clarity. Scotland is covered by 85 maps in their 1:50,000 (pink) Landranger series which shows enough detail to be useful for most walkers and cyclists. There's more detail still in the full-colour 1:25,000 (orange) Explorer series, which covers Scotland in around 170 maps. The full Ordnance Survey range is only available at a few big-city stores or online, although in any walking district of Scotland you'll find the relevant maps in local shops or tourist offices. If you're planning a walk of more than a couple of hours in duration, or intend to walk in the Scottish hills at all, it is strongly recommended that you carry the relevant OS map and familiarize yourself with how to navigate using it.

Virtually every service station in Scotland stocks at least one large-format **road atlas**, covering all of Britain at around three miles to one inch, and generally including larger-scale plans of major towns. For an overview of the whole of Scotland on one map, Estate Publications' *Scotland* (1:500,000) is produced in cooperation with various local tourist boards and is designed to highlight places of interest. They also produce regional maps that mark all the major tourist sights as well as youth hostels and campsites, perfect if you're driving or cycling round one particular region. These are available from just about every tourist office in Scotland.

Map websites

ⓦ **www.multimap.com** Town plans and area maps with scales up to 1:10,000, plus address search, traffic info and more.

ⓦ **www.streetmap.co.uk** Type in the address or postcode you want and this site will locate it for you in seconds.

ⓦ **www.visitmap.com** The Britain Visitor Atlas has a clickable A–Z of town and city maps.

Map outlets

UK and Ireland

Stanfords 12–14 Long Acre, London WC2E 9LP ☏ 020/7836 1321, ⓦ www.stanfords.co.uk. Also at 39 Spring Gardens, Manchester ☏ 0161/831 0250, and 29 Corn St, Bristol ☏ 0117/929 9966.

National Map Centre Ireland 34 Aungier St, Dublin ☏ 01/476 0471, ⓦ www.mapcentre.ie

US and Canada

Longitude Books 115 W 30th St #1206, New York, NY 10001 ☏ 1-800/342-2164, ⓦ www .longitudebooks.com

World of Maps 1235 Wellington St, Ottawa, ON, K1Y 3A3 ☏ 1-800/214-8524 or ☏ 613/724-6776, ⓦ www.worldofmaps.com

Australia and New Zealand

Map World (Australia) 371 Pitt St, Sydney ☏ 02/9261 3601, ⓦ www.mapworld.net.au. Also at 900 Hay St, Perth ☏ 08/9322 5733, Jolimont Centre, Canberra ☏ 02/6230 4097 and 1981 Logan Road, Brisbane ☏ 07/3349 6633.

Map World (New Zealand) 173 Gloucester St, Christchurch ☏ 0800/627 967, ⓦ www.mapworld .co.nz

Getting around

The majority of Scots live in the central belt, with Glasgow in the west and Edinburgh in the east. Public transport in this region is efficient and most places are easily accessible by train and bus. Further south and north it can be a different story: off the main routes, public transport services are few and far between, particularly in more remote parts of the Highlands and Islands. With careful planning, however, practically everywhere is accessible and you'll have no trouble getting to the main tourist destinations. And in most parts of Scotland, especially if you take the scenic back roads, the low level of traffic makes driving wonderfully unstressful.

By train

Scotland has a modest **rail** network, at its densest in the central belt, at its most skeletal in the Highlands, and all-but-nonexistent in the Islands. **First ScotRail** runs the majority of train services, reaching all the major towns, sometimes on lines rated as among the great scenic routes of the world.

You can buy train **tickets** at most stations, from major travel agents or over the phone and online with a credit card. If the ticket office at the station is closed, you may buy your ticket on board from the inspector using cash or a credit card. The cost of tickets varies enormously, but the earlier you book, the cheaper your ticket will be, and avoiding peak periods can also save you money.

National rail passes are available only in Britain itself, to locals and to visitors. These include the **Young Person's Railcard** (£20), available to full-time students and those aged between 16 and 25, and **Senior Railcard** for people over 60 (£20), both of which give a third off most fares. You can buy the passes at most UK stations – take along two passport photographs and proof of age or status. In addition, those with children in tow can buy a **Family Railcard** (£20), which entitles up to four adults to a 33 percent discount, and up to four children to a sixty percent reduction of the child's full fare. No photos are needed and adults and children need not be related.

In addition, First ScotRail offers several travel passes worth considering. The most flexible is the **Freedom of Scotland Travelpass**, which gives unlimited train travel within Scotland. It's also valid on all CalMac ferries, Glasgow Underground and on various buses in the remoter regions. Various versions of the pass are available, starting at £92 for four days' travel in an eight-day period, with discounts for national rail card holders. The **Highland Rover** is more limited in scope, allowing unlimited travel on trains within the Highland region, plus the West Highland Line, travel between Aberdeen and Aviemore and a few connecting bus routes; it costs £60 for four out of eight consecutive days. Lastly, there's a **Central Scotland Rover**, which gives unlimited travel on lines between Glasgow, Edinburgh, Stirling and Fife; it costs £30 for three out of seven consecutive days. Much less tempting are the various national rail passes which allow unlimited travel in Scotland, England and Wales. The only one that can be bought in the UK is the **All-Line Rover**, which starts at a whopping £355 for seven consecutive days' travel (with discounts for national rail card holders).

BritRail passes (ⓦwww.acprailnet.com/britrail) are only available for purchase before you leave your home country. The pass is available in a wide variety of types, with first- and second-class versions, discounted Youth Passes (second-class only) and Senior Passes (first-class only). The BritRail Consecutive Pass, which allows unlimited travel over a certain period (eight days costs US$299); and the BritRail Flexipass, which allows a set number of days' free travel within a two-month period (eight days costs

US$385). However, before you consider buying the BritRail Scottish Freedom Pass (US$214 for four days' travel in eight), it's worth checking to see if it wouldn't be cheaper instead to buy the Freedom of Scotland Travelpass when you reach Scotland. Any good travel agent or tour operator can supply up-to-date information, or consult ⓦwww.raileurope.com (North America), ⓦwww.railplus.com.au (Australia) or ⓦwww.railplus.co.nz (New Zealand).

If you've been resident in a European country other than the UK for at least six months, an **InterRail** pass, allowing unlimited train travel within Britain might be a cost-effective way to travel, if Scotland is part of a longer European trip. For more details, visit ⓦwww.raileurope.co.uk/inter-rail. Note that **Eurail** passes (ⓦwww.eurail.com) are not valid in the UK.

On most ScotRail routes **bicycles** are carried free, but since there are only between two and six bike spaces available, it's essential that you reserve ahead.

Useful rail contacts

First ScotRail ☎0845/755 0033, ⓦwww .firstgroup.com/scotrail. For booking tickets and seats on all trains within Scotland, and sleeper trains from London to Scotland.
National Rail Enquiries ☎0845/748 4950, ⓦwww.nationalrail.co.uk. Gives details of timetables, fares and other information on rail travel throughout the UK.
ⓦwww.seat61.com The world's finest train travel website. Amazingly comprehensive, with more detail than you ever wanted to know about train travel in the UK (and worldwide), but full of incredibly useful tips and links.

By coach and bus

All Scotland's major towns and cities are served by long-distance bus services, known across Britain as **coaches**, the majority of which are run by the national operator, **Scottish Citylink** (☎0870/550 5050, ⓦwww .citylink.co.uk). On the whole, coaches are cheaper than the equivalent train journey and, as a result, are very popular, so for busy routes and travel at weekends and holidays it's advisable to book ahead, rather than just turn up.

There are various **discount cards** on offer for those with children, those under 26 or over

50 and full-time students: contact Scottish Citylink for more on these. Overseas passport holders can buy a **Brit Xplorer** pass (in 7-, 14- or 28-day versions) in the UK, from National Express travel shops or at major ports and airports; the seven-day pass costs £79, though you'd have to do a lot of bus travelling to make it pay. Another option is a National Express **Tourist Trail Pass** (℡0870/580 8080, ⓦwww.nationalexpress.com), which gives you unlimited travel throughout Britain on National Express and Scottish Citylink coaches.

Local bus services are run by a bewildering array of companies, many of which change routes and timetables frequently. As a general rule, the further away from urban areas you get, the less frequent and more expensive bus services become. On the most remote routes the only service will be the school bus, running at roughly 8.30am and 3.30pm, but only during term times.

Some rural areas, particularly in the Highlands and Islands, are only served by the **postbus** network, which operates numerous minibuses carrying mail and three to ten fare-paying passengers. They set off early in the morning, usually around 8am from the main post office, and collect mail (or deliver it) from/to the hinterland. It's a sociable, though often excruciatingly slow, way to travel, and may well be the only means of reaching hidden-away B&Bs and the like. You can get a booklet of routes and time-tables from the Royal Mail Customer Service Centre (℡0845/774 0740, ⓦwww.royalmail .com/postbus), while details of relevant local services are available at tourist offices.

For comprehensive travel information for buses, as well as trains and ferries, including departure times and timetables, the publicly funded **Traveline Scotland** (℡0870/608 2608, ⓦwww.travelinescotland.com) provides a reliable service both online and by phone.

By car

In order to drive in Scotland you need a current full driving licence. If you're bringing your own vehicle into the country you should also carry your vehicle registration, owner-ship and insurance documents at all times.

In Scotland, as in the rest of the UK, you drive on the left. **Speed limits** are 20–40mph in built-up areas, 70mph on motorways and dual carriageways (freeways) and 60mph on most other roads. As a rule, assume that

---

Minibus tours

If you're backpacking or don't have your own transport, a cheap, flexible and fun way of getting a flavour of Scotland is to join one of the popular **minibus tours** that operate out of Edinburgh and head off into the Highlands. The current leading operator, **Haggis** (℡0131/557 9393, ⓦwww.haggisadventures.com), has bright yellow minibuses setting off daily on whistlestop tours of various parts of Scotland lasting between one and six days. In the company of a live-wire guide, the tours aim to show backpackers a mix of classic highlights with a few well-chosen spots off the tourist trail, with an emphasis on keeping the on-board atmosphere lively. A three-day round-trip from Edinburgh starts from £85 (food and accommodation not included).

Several other companies offer similar packages, including **Macbackpackers** (℡0131/558 9900, ⓦwww.macbackpackers.com), which runs tours linking up their own hostels round the country as well as a jump-on-jump-off service, and **Wild in Scotland** (℡0131/478 6500, ⓦwww.wild-in-scotland.com), which takes in the Outer Hebrides or Orkney during their tours. The popular **Rabbie's Trail Burners** tours (℡0131/226 3133, ⓦwww.rabbies.com) don't aim squarely at the backpacker market and have a rather more mellow approach.

Other tours offering different slants on the Scottish experience are **Heart of Scotland** (℡0131/558 8855, ⓦwww.heartofscotlandtours.co.uk), which specialize in one-day tours to the Highlands, Fife or Perthshire, and **Walkabout Scotland** (℡0131/661 7168, ⓦwww.walkaboutscotland.com), a company specializing in hill-walking day-trips from Edinburgh.

in any area with street lighting, the limit is 30mph. **Speed cameras** are increasingly used as a deterrent to speeding; if you're caught by one of these, the owner (or renter) of the vehicle will have to pay a fine. Also, don't underestimate the Scottish **weather** – snow, ice, fog and wind cause havoc every year, and driving conditions on motorways as much as in rural areas can deteriorate quickly. Local radio stations usually feature constantly updated traffic bulletins.

In the Highlands and Islands, there are still plenty of **single-track roads** with passing places; in addition to allowing oncoming traffic to pass at these points, you should also let cars behind you overtake. In remoter regions, the roads are dotted with sheep which are entirely oblivious to cars, so slow down and edge your way past; should you kill or injure one, it is your duty to inform the local farmer. In the cities, be wary of complex (and expensive) **parking** arrangements, as you can be fined £40 or more for transgressing the rules.

The AA (Automobile Association; ⊛www .theaa.com, ☎0800/887766), RAC (Royal Automobile Club; ⊛www.rac.co.uk, ☎0800/092 2222) and Green Flag (⊛www .greenflag.co.uk, ☎0800/051 0636) all operate **24-hour emergency breakdown** services, as well as other motoring and leisure facilities (including useful online route plans). You may be entitled to free assistance through a reciprocal arrangement with a motoring organization in your home country – check with your own association before setting out. You can make use of these emergency services if you are not a member of the organization, but you will need to join at the roadside and will incur a hefty surcharge too. In remote areas, particularly in the Highlands and Islands, you may have a long wait for assistance. Look into their **home-relay** policies, since most standard policies will only get you to the nearest garage, where you can find yourself stranded for days until the part you need is sent from Inverness or Glasgow.

Renting a car

Renting a car in Scotland is expensive, and is usually cheaper arranged in advance from home through one of the large multinational chains (Avis, Budget, Hertz, Holiday Autos,

National or Thrifty, for example). Over the counter, most firms charge £25–40 per day, £50 for a weekend or around £140 a week. The budget car rental firm, easyCar, offers web fares of under £15 per day. if you book far enough in advance, though there are only one or two small models on offer. Otherwise, small **local agencies** often undercut the major chains, who, with the exception of Arnold Clark, are mostly confined to the big cities – we've highlighted some in the accounts of certain places. Remember, too that **fuel** in Scotland is expensive – petrol (gasoline) and diesel cost around £1 per litre.

Automatics are rare at the lower end of the price scale – if you want one, you should book well ahead. Few companies will rent to drivers with less than one year's experience and most will only rent to people between 21 and 75 years of age.

UK car rental companies

Arnold Clark ☎0845/607 4500, ⊛www .arnoldclarkrental.co.uk
Avis ☎0870/010 0287, ⊛www.avis.co.uk
Budget ☎08701/539 170, ⊛www.budget.co.uk
easyCar ☎0906/333 3333, ⊛www.easycar.com
Europcar ☎0845/607 5000, ⊛www.europcar .co.uk
Hertz ☎0870/844 8844, ⊛www.hertz.co.uk
Holiday Autos ☎0870/400 0099, ⊛www .holidayautos.co.uk
National ☎0870/536 5365, ⊛www.nationalcar .co.uk
Suncars ☎0870/500 5566, ⊛www.suncars.com
Thrifty ☎01494/751600, ⊛www.thrifty.co.uk

By ferry

Scotland has over sixty inhabited islands, and nearly fifty of them have scheduled **ferry** links. Most ferries carry cars and vans, and the vast majority can – and should – be booked as far in advance as possible.

Caledonian MacBrayne (abbreviated by most people, and throughout this book, to **CalMac**) has a virtual monopoly on services on the River Clyde and to the Hebrides, sailing to 22 islands and four peninsulas. They aren't quick – no catamarans or fast ferries – or cheap, but they do have two types of reduced-fare pass. If you're taking more than one ferry, it's worth asking about the discounted **Island Hopscotch** tickets. If you're going to be taking a lot of ferries, you might be better off with an **Island Rover**, which entitles you to eight or fifteen consecutive days' unlimited ferry travel. It does not, however, guarantee you a place on any ferry, so you still need to book ahead. Prices for the eight-day/fifteen-day pass are £48.50/£71 for passengers and £234/£350 for cars.

Car ferries to Orkney and Shetland from Aberdeen and from Scrabster near Thurso are run by **Northlink Ferries**. **Pentland Ferries** runs a car ferry from Gill's Bay, near John O'Groats, to Orkney, and **John O'Groats Ferries** runs a summer-only passenger ferry from John O'Groats to Orkney. The various Orkney islands are linked to each other by services run by **Orkney Ferries**; Shetland's inter-island ferries are run in conjunction with the local council, so the local tourist board is your best bet for information. There are also numerous small operators round the Scottish coast that run day-excursion trips and even the odd scheduled service; their contact details are given in the relevant chapters of this guide.

Ferry companies

Caledonian MacBrayne ☎ 0870/565 0000, ⓦ www.calmac.co.uk
John O'Groats Ferries ☎ 01955/611353, ⓦ www.jogferry.co.uk
Northlink Ferries ☎ 0845/600 0449, ⓦ www .northlinkferries.co.uk

Orkney Ferries ☎ 01856/872044, ⓦ www .orkneyferries.co.uk
Pentland Ferries ☎ 01856/831226, ⓦ www .pentlandferries.co.uk

By plane

Apart from the three major airports of Glasgow, Edinburgh and Aberdeen, Scotland has numerous minor airports, many of them on the islands, some of which are little more than gravel airstrips. Internal **flights** are pretty expensive on the whole – a single fare from Glasgow to Islay will set you back around £80, and there are very few discounted tickets available – but the time saving may make it worthwhile. Another good option is British Airways' **Highland Rover**, which costs just £189, and allows you to take any five flights within seven days; flights to and between Orkney and Shetland are covered, but not inter-island flights within them. Most flights within Scotland are operated by British Airways or Loganair (a BA subsidiary), and the majority should be booked directly through British Airways (☎ 0870/850 9850, ⓦ www .ba.com). For inter-island flights in Shetland (excluding Fair Isle), you need to book direct through Loganair (☎ 01595/840246, ⓦ www .loganair.co.uk). Competition is, however, beginning to emerge, with Highland Airways (☎ 0845/450 2245, ⓦ www.highlandairways .co.uk) currently offering flights from Inverness to Shetland and the Western Isles.

Accommodation

In common with the rest of Britain, accommodation in Scotland is expensive. Budget travellers are well catered for with numerous hostels, often in picturesque surroundings and those with money to spend will relish the more expensive hotels, many of which are converted feudal seats. In the middle ground, however, the standard of many B&Bs, guesthouses and hotels is often disappointing, and it can be hard work finding places with the standards of taste, originality, efficiency and value which you might expect from a country with as well developed a tourist market as Scotland. Welcoming, comfortable, well-run places do, of course, exist in all parts of the country – but there are just not enough of them to go round.

Hotels, guesthouses and B&Bs

Visit Scotland operates a nationwide system for grading **hotels**, **guesthouses** and **B&Bs**, which is updated annually. Although they cover a huge amount of accommodation, not every establishment participates, and you shouldn't assume that a particular B&B is no good simply because it's not on Visit Scotland's lists. The tourist board uses **star awards**, from one to five, which are supposed to reflect the quality of welcome, service and hospitality – though you can be sure that anywhere that doesn't have all en-suite rooms, stick a TV in every room, have matching fabrics or provide a trouser press will be marked down.

Hotels come in all shapes and sizes. At the upper end of the market, they can be huge country houses and converted castles offering a very exclusive and opulent experience. Most will have a licensed bar and offer both breakfast and dinner, and often lunch as well. In the cities the increasing prevalence of modern **budget hotels** and travel lodges run by national (and international) chains may not do much for aesthetics or diversity, but they are competitively priced and for the most part meet criteria for clean, smart, serviceable accommodation. Also making a bit of a comeback are **inns** (in other words, pubs) or their modern equivalent, "restaurants with rooms". These will often only have a handful of rooms but their emphasis on creating an all-round convivial atmosphere, as well as serving up top-quality food in a dinner, bed and breakfast package, often make them worth seeking out.

Guesthouses and **B&Bs** offer the widest and most diverse range of accommodation. Visit Scotland uses the term "guesthouse"

Accommodation price codes

Throughout this book, accommodation prices have been graded with the **codes** below, corresponding to the cost of the least expensive double room in high season. The bulk of our recommendations fall in categories ❷ to ❺; those in the highest categories are limited to places that are especially attractive. Bear in mind that many of the chain hotels slash their tariffs at the weekend, and that a cheaper establishment may also have a selection of more expensive rooms. Price codes are not given for **campsites**, most of which charge less than £10 per person. Almost all **hostels** and **bunkhouses** charge between £8 and £15 per person per night; the few exceptions to this rule have their prices quoted in the review.

❶ Under £40	❹ £60–69	❼ £110–149
❷ £40–49	❺ £70–89	❽ £150–199
❸ £50–59	❻ £90–109	❾ Over £200

for a commercial venture that has four or more rooms, at least some of which are en suite, reserving "B&B" for a predominantly private family home that has only a few rooms to let. In reality, however, the different names reflect the pretensions of the owners and the cost of the rooms more than differences in service: in general, guesthouses cost more than B&Bs. Having said that, there's often a great deal of overlap: a small hotel might be indistinguishable in price and quality from an upmarket guesthouse, while a modest guesthouse might be surpassed in terms of service and price by a superbly run B&B. While some guesthouses and B&Bs can seem stuck in a time warp with garish fabrics, mismatching furniture, gaudy trinkets and insipid pictures, others make the most of compensating features such as a great location, an insight into the local way of life and advice about what's worth seeing in the area. The majority now offer **en-suite** toilets and showers, although often the conviviality of a communal lounge has been sacrificed in order to put a TV in the room, along with the ubiquitous mini-kettle and basket containing sachets of instant coffee and long-life milk.

At the bottom end of the **price scale** (though not necessarily the quality scale), B&Bs tend to charge £40–50 for a double room, while guesthouse prices can be £70 or more. Hotels, on the other hand, will rarely charge less than £50 a double, with £70 more like the average; an established, award-winning hotel might charge anything between £110 and £150.

Many B&Bs, even the pricier ones, have only a few rooms, so **advance booking** is recommended, especially in the Islands – most places now have a website and/or email. You might also want to book in for dinner, bed and breakfast (not to mention packed lunch), as many islands have limited, or no, eating and drinking options. Bear in mind, too, that outside the main towns and cities many places are only open for the **tourist season**, roughly from Easter to October: you'll always find somewhere to stay outside this period, but the choice may be limited.

Most **tourist offices** will help you find accommodation, either by offering you a brochure listing the local options, or by booking a room directly, for which they normally charge a flat fee or a percentage which is then deducted from your first night's bill. If you take advantage of this service, it's worth being clear as to what kind of place you'd prefer, as the tourist office quite often selects for you randomly across the whole range of their membership. The majority of tourist offices also operate a "Book-a-Bed-Ahead" service, whereby you can reserve accommodation in your next port of call for a fee of £3 per booking.

Hostels

There's an ever-increasing number of **hostels** in Scotland to cater for travellers – youthful or otherwise – who are unable or unwilling to pay the often exorbitant rates charged by hotels, guesthouses and B&Bs. Many hostels are well equipped, clean and comfortable, sometimes offering doubles and even singles as well as dormitory accommodation. Others concentrate more on keeping the price as low as possible, simply providing a roof over your head and a few basic facilities. Whatever type of hostel you stay in, expect to pay £8–15 per night.

There are eighty or so "official" hostels run by the **Scottish Youth Hostels Association** (☏0870/155 3255, ⓦwww.syha.org.uk), referred to throughout the guide as "SYHA hostels". While these places often occupy handsome buildings, and have moved well away from the ethic of former days (when you had to perform chores before leaving), many retain an institutionalized air. Bunk-bed accommodation in single-sex dormitories, lights out before midnight and no smoking/ no alcohol policies are the norm outside the big cities. Breakfast is not normally included in the price, though most hostels have self-catering facilities.

In order to stay in an SYHA hostel, you must be a member of one of the hostelling organizations affiliated to **Hostelling International (HI)**. If you aren't a member in your home country, you can join at any SYHA hostel for a £6 fee. You can also choose to pay the fee in £1 instalments over your first six nights, meaning that you can avoid the full whack if you end up staying only a couple of nights in hostels. Particularly in the popular city hostels, **advance booking** is recommended, and just about essential at Easter, Christmas and from May to August. You can book by post, phone and sometimes fax, and your bed will be held until 6pm on the day of arrival. If you have a credit card, you can book beds as far as six months in advance via the SYHA website or over the phone.

The Gatliff Hebridean Hostels Trust or **GHHT** (ⓦwww.gatliff.org.uk) is a charitable organization allied to the SYHA that runs four simple croft hostels in the Western Isles. Accommodation is basic, and you can't book ahead, but it's unlikely you'll be turned away. Elsewhere in the Highlands and Islands, these places tend to be known as "**bothies**" or "**bunkhouses**", and are usually independently run. In Shetland, camping böds, operated by the **Shetland Amenity Trust** (ⓦwww.camping-bods.co.uk), offer similarly plain accommodation: you need all your usual camping equipment to stay at one (except, of course, a tent). For more details about Gatliff hostels and camping böds, see the relevant chapters in the guide.

Many **independent hostels** now compete with the SYHA hostels. These are usually laid-back places with no membership, fewer rules, mixed dorms and no curfew, housed in buildings ranging from croft houses to converted churches. These are detailed in the annually updated **Independent Hostel Guide** (ⓦ www.independenthostelguide.co.uk). Many of them are also affiliated to the **Independent Backpackers Hostels of Scotland** (ⓦwww.hostel-scotland.co.uk), which has a programme of inspection and lists members in their free "Blue Guide".

Camping and self-catering

There are hundreds of **caravan and camping parks** around Scotland, most of which are open from April to October. The most expensive sites charge about £10 to pitch a tent, and are usually well equipped, with shops, a restaurant, a bar and, occasionally, sports facilities. Most of these, however, are principally aimed at caravans, trailers and motorhomes, and generally don't offer the tranquil atmosphere and independence that those travelling with a tent are seeking.

That said, informal sites of the kind **tent campers** relish do exist, and are described throughout this guide, though they are few and far between. Many hostels allow camping, and farmers will usually let folk camp on their land for free or for a nominal sum. Scotland's relaxed trespass law allows you the freedom to **camp wild** in open country, though most outdoor enthusiasts who make use of this emphasize the importance of being discreet and responsible, ensuring that you camp well away from private residences, livestock and cultivated land, and that you remove all signs of your presence when you leave.

The great majority of **caravans** are permanently moored nose-to-tail in the vicinity of some of Scotland's finest scenery; others are positioned singly in back gardens or amidst farmland. Some can be booked for self-catering, and with prices hovering around £100 a week, this can work out as one of the cheapest options if you're travelling with kids in tow.

If you're planning to do a lot of camping at official camping and caravanning sites, it might be worthwhile joining the **Camping and Caravanning Club** (☏024/7669 4995,

ⓦ www.campingandcaravanningclub.co.uk). Membership costs around £35 and entitles you to pay only a per-person fee, not a pitch fee, at CCC sites. Those coming from abroad can get the same benefits by buying an inter-national camping carnet, available from home motoring organizations or a CCC equivalent.

Self-catering

A **self-catering** cottage or apartment is a good way to cut down on costs. In most cases, however, and particularly during summer, the minimum period of let is a week, and therefore isn't a valid option if you're aiming to tour round the country. The least you can expect to pay in the high season is around £200 per week for a place sleeping four, but something special – such as a well-sited coastal cottage – might cost £500 or more. Such is the number and vari-ety of self-catering places on offer that we've mentioned only a few in the guide; the prices given are weekly summer rates, which tend to fall dramatically out of season. A good source of information is Visit Scotland's self-catering guide, updated annually and listing over 1200 properties.

Country Holidays ☎08700/781200, from overseas ☎01282/846137, ⓦwww.country-holidays.co.uk. Hundreds of reasonably priced properties all over Scotland.

Ecosse Unique ☎01835/870779, ⓦwww .uniquescotland.com. Carefully selected cottages across mainland Scotland, plus a few of the Inner Hebrides.

Forest Holidays ☎0131/314 6100, ⓦwww .forestholidays.co.uk. Purpose-built cabins sleeping five or six people, in beautiful woodland areas in Strathyre near Callander.

Highland Hideaways ☎01631/563901, ⓦwww .highlandhideaways.co.uk. A range of self-catering properties, mainly in Argyll and its islands, which range from a former bank in Oban to a converted boathouse on Loch Awe.

Landmark Trust ☎01628/825925, ⓦwww .landmarktrust.org.uk. A very select number of unforgettable, upmarket historical properties in Scotland; first, however, you must buy the brochure (£11, refundable on first booking).

Mackay's Agency ☎0870/429 5359, ⓦwww .mackays-self-catering.co.uk. A whole range of properties in every corner of Scotland (except Shetland), from chalets and town apartments to remote stone-built cottages.

National Trust for Scotland ☎0131/243 9331, ⓦwww.nts.org.uk. The NTS lets around forty of its converted historic cottages and houses.

Scottish Country Cottages ☎0870/078 1100, ⓦwww.scottish-country-cottages.co.uk. Superior cottages with lots of character scattered across the Scottish mainland, plus Skye and Mull.

Scottish Holiday Cottages ☎01463/224707, ⓦwww.scottish-holiday-cottages.co.uk. Fifty or so properties mainly in the Highlands and Islands; everything from castles to bothies.

Campus accommodation

A different, equally cheap, self-catering option, especially if you're staying a week or more in one of the cities, is **campus accommodation**. The universities of Glasgow, Strathclyde, Edinburgh, Stirling, St Andrews and Dundee all open their halls of residence to overseas visitors during the summer break, and some also offer rooms during the Easter and Christmas vacations. Accommodation varies from tiny single rooms in long, lonely corridors to relatively comfortable places in small shared apart-ments. Prices start at around £15 per night, not always including breakfast. All the useful university details are given in the guide, but if you want a list of everything that's on offer, contact the Summer Village (☎0870/712 5002, ⓦwww.thesummervillage .com) or Venuemasters (☎0114/249 3090, ⓦwww.venuemasters.co.uk).

Food and drink

Scotland isn't known for its culinary heritage, and the country's poor health records aren't exactly indicative of a healthy relationship with food. Yet Scottish produce – particularly its beef, fish, shellfish and game – can be outstanding, and in whisky the country lays almost complete claim to one of the world's most popular and sophisticated drinks. With only a limited range of traditional foods and recipes to draw on, Scottish cuisine has welcomed a host of foreign influences, from classic French cooking to the Italian, Indian and Asian ideas brought by immigrants. In what is generally described as Modern Scottish cooking, these influences join forces with fresh, well-sourced local produce, with results that can be a lot more impressive than visitors expect.

What to eat

In most hotels and B&Bs you'll be offered a **Scottish breakfast**, similar to its English counterpart of sausage, bacon and egg, but typically with the addition of local favourites such as black pudding (blood sausage) and potato scones. Porridge is another likely option, but despite its place at the heart of the traditional fare of Scots the quality is often variable: it's properly made with oatmeal and water and cooked with a pinch of salt, then eaten with a little milk, though some folk like to add honey, fruit or sugar as well. You may also be offered strongly flavoured kippers (hot-smoked herring) or more delicate **"Arbroath smokies"** (smoked haddock). Oatcakes (plain, slightly salty oatmeal biscuits) and a "buttery" – a butter-enriched bread related to the French croissant and popular in the northeast of Scotland – might feature. Scotland's staple drink, like England's, is **tea**, made from dubious teabags and drunk strong and with milk, though **coffee** is just as readily available everywhere. However, while designer coffee shops are now a familiar feature in the cities, and decent coffee is available in more and more places across the country, execrable versions of espressos and cappuccinos, as well as instant coffee, are still all too familiar.

The quintessential Scots dish is **haggis**, a type of rich sausage meat made from spiced liver, offal, oatmeal and onion and cooked inside a bag made from a sheep's stomach. Though more frequently found on tourist-oriented menus than the dining tables of Scots at home, it's surprisingly tasty and satisfying, particularly when eaten with its traditional accompaniments: "bashed neeps" (mashed turnips) and "chappit tatties" (mashed potatoes). The humble haggis has become rather trendy in recent years, appearing in swanky restaurants wrapped in filo pastry or drizzled with berry sauce, and a vegetarian version is widely available. Other traditional dishes which you may well encounter include **stovies**, a tasty mash of onion and fried potato heated up with minced beef, or various forms of meat pie: a **Scotch pie** has mince inside a circular hard pastry case, while a **bridie**, famously associated with the town of Forfar, has mince and onions inside a flaky pastry crescent. In this cold climate, home-made

---

Meal times

Unfortunately, in many parts of Scotland outside the cities, inflexible and unenlightened **meal times** mean that you have to keep a close eye on your watch if you don't want to miss out on eating. B&Bs and hotels will frequently serve breakfast only until 9am at the latest, lunch is usually over by 2pm, and, despite the long summer evenings, pub and hotel kitchens often stop serving dinner as early as 8pm.

soup is often welcome; try **Scots broth**, made with combinations of lentil, split pea, mutton stock or vegetables and barley. A more refined delicacy is **Cullen skink**, a rich soup made from smoked haddock, potatoes and cream.

Scots **beef** is delicious, especially the Aberdeen Angus breed, though Highland cattle are also rated for their depth of flavour. Scots farmers, aware of the standards their produce has reached, have preciously guarded their stock from the recent troubles associated with BSE and foot and mouth disease. **Venison**, the meat of the red deer, also features large – low in cholesterol and very tasty, it's served roasted or in casseroles, often cooked with juniper and red wine. Other forms of **game** are quite often encountered, including grouse, which when cooked properly is strong, dark and succulent; pheasant, a lighter meat; pigeon and rabbit.

Scottish **fish and shellfish** are the envy of Europe, with a vast array of different types of fish, prawns, lobster, mussels, oysters, crab and scallops found round the extensive Scottish coastline. Fresh fish is normally available in most coastal towns, as well as the big cities, where restaurants have well-organized supply lines. Elaborate dishes are sometimes concocted, though frankly the best seafood dishes are frequently the simplest. The prevalence of fish farming, now a significant industry in the Highlands and Islands, means that the once-treasured **salmon** is widespread and relatively inexpensive – its pale pink flesh is still delicious, though those concerned about the environment make sure to search out organic salmon, and connoisseurs keep an eye out for the more delicately flavoured (and more expensive) wild salmon. Both salmon and **trout**, another commonly farmed fish, are frequently smoked and served cold with bread and butter. **Herring**, once the staple fish in Scotland, is still popular in some parts fried in oatmeal or "soused" (pickled).

Another local product to enjoy an upsurge in popularity recently is **cheese**, which you'll find in a number of specialist shops and delis, while many classier restaurants make a point of serving only Scottish cheeses after dinner. The types on offer cover a wide

spectrum: look out in particular for Isle of Mull, a tangy farmhouse cheddar; Dunsyre Blue, a Scottish Dolcelatte; and Howgate, a Camembert made in Perthshire.

Scotland is notorious for its sweet tooth, and **cakes and puddings** are taken very seriously. Bakers with extensive displays of iced buns, cakes and cream-filled pastries are a typical feature of any Scottish high street, while home-made shortbread, scones or tablet (a hard, crystalline form of fudge) are considered great treats. Among traditional desserts, "clootie dumpling" is a sweet, stodgy fruit pudding soaked in a cloth for hours, while the rather over-elaborate Cranachan, made with toasted oatmeal steeped in whisky and folded into whipped cream flavoured with fresh raspberries, or the similar Atholl Brose, are considered more refined. In the summer months, Scottish berries, in particular raspberries and strawberries, are particularly tasty.

One Scottish institution that refuses to die out is **high tea**, consisting of a cooked main course and a plethora of cakes, washed down with lots of tea and eaten between about 5 and 6.30pm.

As for **fast food**, fish and chips are as popular as in England, and chip shops, or "**chippies**", abound, the best often found in coastal towns within sight of the fishing boats tied up in harbour. Deep-fried battered fish is the standard choice – when served with chips it's known as a "fish supper", even if eaten at lunchtime – though everything from hamburgers to haggis suppers is normally on offer, all deep-fried, of course. Scotland is even credited with inventing the **deep-fried Mars bar** (a caramel-chocolate bar coated in batter and fried in fat) as the definitive badge of a nation with the worst heart-disease statistics in Europe. For alternative fast food, the major towns feature all the usual **pizza**, **burger** and **baked potato** outlets, as well as Chinese, Mexican and Indian takeaways.

Where to eat

For budget eating, you'll find **cafés** ranging from the most basic "greasy spoon" diners to French-style **brasseries**, where, if you're lucky, you'll get a wide-ranging menu and decent, interesting meals. For snacks and light lunches, **tearooms** are a common feature of tourist attractions and villages; it's generally not advisable to go into one with high expectations, though you may often find decent home baking.

Some of the cheapest places to eat out are the **pubs** or **hotel bars** – indeed, in the smallest villages these might be your only option. Bar menus generally have a standard line-up of filling but unambitious options including soup, filled sandwiches, scampi and chips or steak pie and chips, with vegetarians in particular suffering from a paucity of choice. Having said that, some bar food is very satisfying, with freshly prepared, filling food that equals the à la carte dishes served in the adjacent hotel restaurant. Bar meals, or "pub grub" as it's sometimes described, are normally served at tables in the pub itself or a simple adjoining dining room, and will generally be available for slightly longer periods at lunchtime and in the evening than restaurants.

As for **restaurants**, standards vary enormously, but Scotland has an ever-increasing number of top-class chefs producing superb dishes with a Scottish slant that certainly rival their English and European counterparts. Small, independent restaurants using good-quality local produce and carving out a local reputation are found in many parts of Scotland, not just the big cities, and are well worth seeking out. Less predictable are hotel restaurants, including those which serve non-residents. Some have the budget to employ talented chefs, but in others the food can be very ordinary despite the high-faluting descriptions on the à la carte menu. Either way, you could easily end up paying £30–40 a head for a meal with wine.

In central Scotland, particularly in Edinburgh and Glasgow, you can find restaurants offering a range of **international** styles including Japanese, Thai, Caribbean and Turkish, as well as the more common and familiar Indian, Chinese and Italian establishments. Glasgow, in particular, considers itself one of Britain's **curry** capitals, while Edinburgh's restaurant scene is expanding rapidly, with a particular strength in its **seafood** and **vegetarian** restaurants.

When it comes to buying food, most Scots get the majority of their supplies from super-

markets, but the upsurge in interest in sourcing good-quality produce means that you're increasingly likely to come across good delis and specialist **food shops** around Scotland. Many of these make a point of stocking local produce alongside imported delicacies, as well as organic fruit and veg, specialist drinks such as locally brewed beer, freshly baked bread and sandwiches and other snacks for takeaway. Look out too for **farmers' markets** (🌐 www.scottishfarmersmarkets.co.uk), which take place on Saturday and Sunday mornings in town squares or other public spaces; local farmers and small producers from pig farmers to small smokeries set up stalls to sell their specialist lines.

There's no doubt that, as with the rest of the UK, eating out in Scotland is expensive. Our restaurant listings include a mix of high-quality and budget establishments. To help give an idea of costs, each place we've reviewed is placed in one of three **price categories**: inexpensive (under £10 per person for a standard two courses, excluding alcohol), moderate (£10–20) or expensive (£20–30). **Wine** in restaurants is marked up strongly, so you'll often pay £15 for a bottle selling for £5 in the shops; house wines generally start around the £10 mark. Bring your own bottle (BYOB) restaurants aren't all that common, but finding one can significantly keep down the cost of a meal.

Drinking

As in the rest of Britain, Scottish **pubs**, which originated as travellers' hostelries and coaching inns, are the main social focal points of any community. Pubs in Scotland vary hugely, from old-fashioned inns with open fires and a convivial atmosphere, to raucous theme pubs with jukeboxes and satellite TV. Out in the islands, pubs are few and far between, with most drinking taking place in the local hotel bar. In Edinburgh and Glasgow, by contrast, you'll find traditional pubs supplemented by upbeat, trendy café-bars.

The national drink is **whisky** (for more on which, see box opposite), though you might not guess it from the prodigious amount of "alcopops" (bottles of sweet fruit drinks laced with vodka or gin) and ready-made mixers consumed on a Friday and Saturday night.

Similarly, Scotland produces some exceptionally good cask-conditioned real ales, yet lager is much more popular. In our listings, we've tended to steer folk towards those pubs that take their beer and whisky seriously, rather than those hell-bent on getting their punters drunk as quickly as possible.

Scotland has very relaxed licensing laws compared with the traditional pattern in England and Wales. Pub **opening hours** are generally 11am to 11pm, but in the cities and towns, or anywhere where there is demand, places stay open much later. Whatever time the pub closes, "last orders" will be called by the bar staff about fifteen minutes before closing time to allow a bit of "drinking-up time". In general, you have to be 16 to enter a pub unaccompanied, though some places are easy about having folk with children in, or have special family rooms and beer gardens where the kids can run free. The legal drinking age is 18.

Whisky

Whisky – *uisge beatha*, or the "water of life" in Gaelic – has been produced in Scotland since the fifteenth century, but only really took off in popularity after the 1780 tax on claret made wine too expensive for most people. The taxman soon caught up with whisky distilling, however, and drove the stills underground. Today, many distilleries operate on the site of simple cottages that once distilled the stuff illegally. In 1823, Parliament revised its Excise Laws, in the process legalizing whisky production, and today the drink is Scotland's chief export. As with all spirits in Scotland, a standard single measure is 25ml, though some places serve 35ml.

There are two types of whisky: single malt, made from malted barley, and grain whisky, which is made from maize and a little malted barley in a continuous still – relatively cheap to produce, it was only introduced into Scotland in the 1830s. **Blended whisky**, which still accounts for more than ninety percent of all sales, is a mixture of the two types. Grain whisky forms about seventy percent of the average bottle of blended whisky, but each brand's distinctive flavour comes from the malt whisky which is added to the grain in different quantities: the more expensive the blend, the higher the proportion of skilfully chosen and aged malts that have gone into it. Johnnie Walker, Bells, Teachers and The Famous Grouse are some of the best-known blended whiskies. All have a similar flavour, and are drunk neat or with water, sometimes with mixers such as soda or lemonade.

Making malt whisky

Malt whisky is made by soaking barley in **steeps** (water cisterns) for two or three days until it swells, after which it is left to germinate for around seven days, during which the starch in the barley seed is converted into soluble sugars – this process is known as **malting**. The malted barley or "green malt" is then dried in a **kiln** over a furnace, which can be oil-fired, peat-fired or, more often than not, a combination of the two. Only a few distilleries still do their own malting and kilning in the traditional pagoda-style kilns; the rest simply have their malted barley delivered from an industrial maltings. The first process in most distilleries is therefore **milling**, which grinds the malted barley into "grist". Next comes the **mashing**, during which the grist is infused in hot water in mashtuns, producing a sugary concoction called "wort". After cooling, the wort passes into the washbacks, traditionally made of wood, where it is fermented with yeast for two to three days. During **fermentation**, the sugar is converted into alcohol, producing a brown foaming liquid known as "wash". **Distillation** now takes place, not once but twice: the wash is steam-heated, and the vapours siphoned off and condensed as a spirit. This is the point at which the whisky is poured into oak casks – usually ones which have already been used to store bourbon or sherry – and left to age for a minimum of three years. The average **maturation** period for a single malt whisky, however, is ten years; and the longer it matures, the more expensive it is, because two percent evaporates each year. Unlike wine, as soon as the whisky is bottled, maturation ceases.

Despite the dominance of the blended whiskies, **single malt whisky** is infinitely superior, and, as a result, a great deal more expensive. Despite the snobbishness which surrounds the subject, malt whisky is best drunk with a splash of water to release its distinctive flavours. Single malts vary enormously depending on the amount of peat used for drying the barley, the water used for mashing and the type of oak cask used in the maturing process (for more on which, see box on p.51). Traditionally they are divided into four distinct groups: Highland, Lowland, Campbeltown and Islay. However, with Campbeltown down to just two distilleries, and new distilleries springing up all over the country, there is a strong case for dispensing with the old labels.

The two most important whisky regions are **Speyside** (see p.566), which produces famous varieties such as Glenlivet, Glenfiddich and Macallan, and **Islay** (see p.394), which produces distinctively peaty whiskies such as Laphroaig, Lagavulin and Ardbeg. Many distilleries have a highly developed nose for PR and offer guided tours that range from slick and streamlined to small and friendly; details of some of the best are given in the main text of the guide. All of them offer visitors a "wee dram" as a finale, and those distilleries that charge an entrance fee often give you your money back if you buy a bottle at the end – though prices are no lower at source than in the shops (between £20 and £30 for the average 70cl bottle).

Beer

Traditional Scottish beer is a thick, dark ale known as **heavy**, served at room temperature in pints or half-pints, with a full head. Quite different in taste from English "bitter", heavy is a more robust, sweeter beer with less of an edge. Scottish beers are graded by the shilling in a system used since the 1870s to indicate the level of potency: the higher the shilling mark (/-), the stronger or "heavier" the beer. A pint costs anything from £1.70 to £2.70, depending on the brew and the locale of the pub.

Both of Scotland's biggest-name breweries, McEwan's and Tennents, produce standard own-name lagers as well as a selection of heavies: McEwan's Special and Tennent's Velvet are varieties of a 70/- ale, while the stronger, tastier 80/- varieties are slightly less widespread but do qualify as "real ales".

However, if you really want to discover how good Scottish beer – once renowned throughout the world for its strength – can be, look out for the products of the small **local breweries**. Edinburgh's Caledonian Brewery makes nine good cask beers, and operates from Victorian premises using much of their original equipment, including the only direct-fired coppers left in Britain. Others names to look out for are Belhaven, brewed in Dunbar; Greenmantle, brewed by Broughton Ales in the Borders; and Fraoch, mostly available in bottles, a very refreshing, light ale made from heather according to an ancient recipe. Small local micro-breweries are beginning to spring up all over the country; depending where you are, the produce of the breweries at Aviemore, the Black Isle, Arran, Skye, Orkney or Shetland might be available. Your best chance of uncovering these beers is to head for pubs promising "real" or "cask-conditioned" ales – these are often pointed out in the guide, though for a more comprehensive list covering the whole of the UK get hold of a copy of the *Good Beer Guide*, published annually by the Campaign for Real Ale (Ⓦwww.camra.org.uk).

Water and soft drinks

Scotland produces a prodigious amount of **mineral water**, which is mainly exported, as the tap water tends to be chill and clean. In addition, Scotland has the distinction of being the only country in the world where neither Coke nor Pepsi is the most popular fizzy drink. That accolade belongs to **Irn-Bru**, a fizzy orange, sickly sweet concoction sold in just about every shop in the country.

Communications

Communications are pretty modern and reliable in Scotland, although out in the more remote parts of the country, and particularly in the Highlands and Islands, you'll encounter difficulties: mobile phone coverage may well be patchy, though you'll usually find a payphone within easy walking distance. Internet cafés exist in most major towns and cities, and you'll often find computer access available in rural shops, cafés and guesthouses. It's worth keeping in mind that many public libraries offer free Internet access.

Post

Most **post offices** In towns and cities are open Monday to Friday 9am to 5.30pm and Saturday 9am to 12.30 or 1pm. However, in small communities you'll find sub-post offices operating out of a shop, shed or even a private house. In remote regions, the post office will often keep extremely restricted hours, even if the shop in which the post office counter is located keeps longer hours.

Stamps can be bought at post-office counters, from vending machines outside or from many newsagents and shops. Domestic UK postage costs 30p first-class, 21p second-class. Airmail letters are 42p to Europe, 47p worldwide, or you can buy a pre-stamped airletter for 42p (from post offices only). Postcard stamps cost 42p to Europe, 47p worldwide. Royal Mail can answer all enquiries (☎0845/774 0740, Ⓦwww.royalmail.com).

Phones

If you're travelling from overseas and want to use your **mobile phone** in Scotland, it's worth checking before you leave that it's compatible with the UK's GSM (Ⓦwww.gsmworld.com) technology. To save yourself money and hassle, it might be worth simply picking up a "pay-as-you-go" mobile once you've arrived in Britain. All the main UK networks cover Scotland; in general terms Vodaphone has the most reliable signal in Scotland, though you'll still find places in among the hills or out on the islands where there's no signal at all. If you're in a rural area and having trouble with reception, simply ask a local where the strongest signals are found nearby.

Most public **payphones** in Scotland are operated by British Telecom, known as BT (Ⓦwww.bt.com) and, in towns, at least, are widespread. Many BT payphones take all coins from 10p upwards, with a minimum charge of 30p. Most accept credit and debit cards.

Throughout this guide, every phone number is prefixed by the area code, which is separated from the number by an oblique slash. You don't have to dial the code if you're calling from within the same area, unless you're using a mobile phone. Any number with the prefix ☎0800 is toll-free; ☎0845 numbers are charged at local rate; ☎0870 at long-distance rate; and all ☎09 numbers at expensive premium rates. Most numbers beginning ☎07 are mobile phones.

Useful numbers

UK operator ☎100
British Telecom directory enquiries ☎118 500
Emergency number: ☎999 or ☎112
International operator ☎155
International directory enquiries ☎118 505

Phoning home

To the US or Canada ☎001 + area code + number
To Ireland ☎00353 + area code without the zero + number
To Australia ☎0061 + area code without the zero + number
To New Zealand ☎0064 + area code without the zero + number

Telephone charge cards

One of the most convenient ways of phoning home from abroad is with a **telephone charge card**. Using a toll-free UK access code and a PIN number, you can make calls from most hotel, public and private phones that will be charged to your own account. While rates are always cheaper from a residential phone at off-peak rates, that's normally not an option when you're travelling. You may be able to use the card to minimize hotel phone surcharges, but don't depend on it. However, the benefit of calling cards is mainly one of convenience, as rates aren't necessarily cheaper than calling from a public phone while abroad and can't compete with discounted off-peak times many local phone companies offer. But since most major charge cards are free to obtain, it's certainly worth getting one at least for emergencies.

AT&T, MCI, Sprint, Canada Direct and other **North American** long-distance companies all enable their customers to make credit-card calls while overseas. Call your company's customer service line to find out what the toll-free access code is in the UK. Calls made from Scotland will automatically be billed to your home number, although you can also choose to make a collect call via the operator. Elsewhere, charge cards such as Telstra Telecard or Optus Calling Card in **Australia**, and Telecom NZ's Calling Card in **New Zealand**, can be used to make calls abroad, which

are charged back to a domestic account or credit card. Apply to Telstra (☎1800/038 000), Optus (☎1300/300 937) or Telecom NZ (☎04/801 9000).

Calling Scotland from abroad

First dial your **international access code** (00 from Ireland and New Zealand; 011 from the US and Canada; 0011 from Australia), followed by **44** for the UK, then the Scottish area code minus its initial zero, then the number.

Email

An easy way to keep in touch while travelling is to sign up for a free Web **email** address that can be accessed from anywhere, for example YahooMail (🌐www.yahoo.com) or Hotmail (🌐www.hotmail.com). Once you've set up an account, you can use these sites to pick up and send mail from any café, library or hotel with Internet access. Internet cafés are most common in the big cities and towns, though a few are now appearing around the Highlands and Islands. That said, the tourist office should be able to tell you of somewhere you can get online for a nominal fee; sometimes the tourist office itself will have an access point, and public libraries often provide cheap or free access. The site 🌐www.kropla.com gives useful details of how to plug in your lap-top when abroad, phone country codes around the world and information about electrical systems in different countries.

Opening hours, public holidays and admission fees

Traditional shop hours in Scotland are Monday to Saturday 9am to 5.30 or 6pm. In the bigger towns and cities, many places now stay open on Sundays and late at night (often on Thursdays or Fridays). Large supermarkets typically stay open till 8pm and sometimes as late as 10pm. However, in the Highlands and Islands, you'll find precious little open on a Sunday, with many small towns also retaining an "early closing day" – often Wednesday – when shops close at 1pm.

Many shops and businesses will close on **bank** (or **public**) **holidays**, although few tourist-related businesses will observe these, particularly in the summer months. The main holidays include January 1 and 2; the Friday before Easter; the first and last Monday in May; Christmas Day (Dec 25); and Boxing Day (Dec 26); in addition, all Scottish towns and cities have one-day holidays in spring, summer and autumn – dates vary from place to place but normally fall on a Monday.

Admission to museums and monuments

Apart from the big city sights and a number of major attractions on the busier parts of the tourist trail, Scotland's **tourist season** runs from Easter to October, and outside this period many indoor attractions are shut, though ruins, parks and gardens are normally accessible year-round. We've given full details of opening hours and adult admission charges in the guide. Note that last entrance can be an hour (or more) before the published closing time.

Many of Scotland's most treasured sights – from castles and country houses to islands, gardens and tracts of protected landscape – come under the control of the privately run **National Trust for Scotland** (✆0131/243 9300, ✇www.nts.org.uk) or the state-run **Historic Scotland** (✆0131/668 8800, ✇www.historic-scotland.gov.uk); we've quoted "**NTS**" or "**HS**" respectively for each site reviewed in this guide. Both organizations charge an admission fee for most places, and these can be quite high, especially for the more grandiose NTS estates. If you think you'll be visiting more than half a dozen NTS properties, or more than a dozen

HS ones, it's worth taking annual membership, which costs £34 (HS) or £35 (NTS), and allows free admission to their properties. In addition, both the NTS and HS offer short-term passes: the **National Trust Discovery Ticket**, which costs between £12 for an adult ticket lasting three days to £42 for a family ticket lasting fourteen days; and the HS's **Explorer Pass**, ranging from £17 for three days to £56 for a family for ten days.

A lot of Scottish stately homes remain in the hands of the landed gentry, who tend to charge around £5–7 for admission to edited highlights of their domain. Many other old buildings, albeit rarely the most momentous structures, are owned by local authorities; admission is often cheap and sometimes free. Municipal art galleries and museums are usually free, too, as are most of the state-owned museums, although "voluntary" donations may be solicited.

The majority of fee-charging attractions in Scotland give 25–50 percent **reductions** for senior citizens, the unemployed, full-time students and children under 16, with under-5s being admitted free almost everywhere. Proof of age will be required in most cases. Family tickets are often available if you're travelling with kids.

A further option, open to non-UK citizens only, is the **Great British Heritage Pass** (✇www.visitbritain.com/heritagepass), which gives free entry to some 600 sites throughout Britain, including NTS or HS sites and many which are not run by either organization. Costing from £39/US$75 for seven days, it can be purchased online, through most travel agents at home, on arrival at any large UK airport or from major tourist offices across Britain.

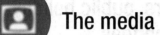

The media

In general, the Scots dismiss the UK's so-called "national media" as London-based and London-biased, and prefer to listen to Scottish radio programmes, read Scottish newspapers, and – albeit to a much lesser extent – watch Scottish TV. Local papers are also avidly consumed, with the weekly papers in places like Orkney and Shetland read by virtually the entire adult population.

The press

The **Scottish press** centres on two serious **dailies** – *The Scotsman*, now published in tabloid format and based in Edinburgh, and *The Herald*, a broadsheet published in Glasgow. Both of them offer good coverage of the current issues affecting Scotland, along with British and foreign news, sport, arts and lifestyle pages. Scotland's biggest-selling daily is the downmarket *Daily Record*, a tabloid from the same stable as the *Daily Mirror*. Meanwhile, many of Britain's national daily tabloid **newspapers** – from the reactionary *Sun* to the vaguely left-leaning *Daily Mirror* – appear in specific Scottish editions, although the "quality" press, ranging between the right-wing *Daily Telegraph* and the left-of-centre *Guardian*, are justifiably seen in Scotland as being London papers.

The provincial daily press in Scotland is more widely read than its English counterpart, with the two biggest-selling regional titles being Aberdeen's famously parochial *Press and Journal*, widely read in the north-east, Orkney and Shetland, and the right-wing *Dundee Courier*, mostly sold in Perth, Angus, Tayside and Fife. The **weekly** *Oban Times* gives an insight into life in the Highlands and Islands, but is staid compared with the radical, campaigning weekly *West Highland Free Press*, printed on Skye; both carry articles in Gaelic as well as English. Further north, the lively *Shetland Times* and sedate *Orcadian* are essential weekly reads.

Many national **Sunday newspapers** have a Scottish edition, although again Scotland has its own offerings – *Scotland on Sunday*, from the *Scotsman* stable, and the *Sunday Herald*, complementing its eponymous daily. Far more fun and widely read is the anachronistic *Sunday Post*, published by Dundee's mighty D.C. Thomson publishing group. It's a wholesome paper, uniquely Scottish, and has changed little since the 1950s, since which time its two long-running cartoon strips, *Oor Wullie* and *The Broons*, have acquired something of a cult status.

Scottish **monthlies** include the glossy *Scottish Field*, a parochial version of England's *Tatler*, covering countryside interests along with local travel and fashion, and the widely read *Scots Magazine*, an old-fashioned middle-of-the-road publication which promotes family values and lots of good fresh air. For visitors to Glasgow and Edinburgh, the fortnightly **listings magazine** *The List* is a must, covering all events in both cities and featuring lively interviews and articles. Another useful publication is the lively *Big Issue*, a weekly magazine with a Scottish edition, which contains listings, features and a focus on homelessness, the "issue" of the title; it's only available from official street vendors, who are themselves homeless, and to whom a large proportion of the cover price goes.

USA Today and the *International Herald Tribune* are the most widely available **North American papers**, though only the larger newsagents will stock them; you can also find *Time* and *Newsweek* in quality bookshops and newsagents.

TV and radio

In Scotland there are five main (sometimes called "terrestrial") **TV channels**: the state-owned BBC1 and BBC2, and the independent commercial channels, ITV1, Channel 4 and Five. The **BBC** continues to maintain its worldwide reputation for in-house quality productions, ranging from expensive costume dramas to intelligent documentaries, split between the avowedly mainstream BBC1 and the more rarefied fare of BBC2. **BBC Scotland** produces news programmes and a regular crop of local-interest lifestyle, current affairs, drama and comedy shows which slot into the schedules of both BBC channels. The commercial channel **ITV1** is divided between three regional companies: the populist STV, which is received in most of southern Scotland and parts of the West Highlands; Grampian, based in Aberdeen; and Border, which transmits from Carlisle. These are complemented by the quirkier **Channel 4**, and eclectic **Five**, which still can't be received in some parts of Scotland. A plethora of satellite and, in the cities, cable channels are also available; most prominent in this realm is Rupert Murdoch's **Sky** organization, which offers, among other channels, blanket sports coverage that plays wall-to-wall in pubs the length of the country.

The **BBC radio** network broadcasts six main channels in Scotland, five of which are national stations originating largely from London: Radio 1 (pop and dance music), Radio 2 (mainstream pop, rock and light music), Radio 3 (classical music), Radio 4 (current affairs, arts and drama) and Radio 5 Live (sports, news and live discussions and phone-ins). Only the award-winning BBC Radio Scotland offers a Scottish perspective on news, politics, arts, music, travel and sport, as well as providing a Gaelic network in the Highlands with local programmes in Shetland, Orkney and the Borders.

A web of local **commercial radio** stations covers the country, mostly mixing rock and pop music with news bulletins, but a few tiny community-based stations such as

Lochbroom FM in Ullapool – famed for its daily midge count – transmit documentaries and discussions on local issues. The most populated areas of Scotland also receive UK-wide commercial stations such as Classic FM, Virgin Radio and TalkSport. With a special DAB **digital radio**, you can get all the main stations crackle-free along with a range of other digital-only ones, most of which can also be picked up on cable or satellite-equipped TVs.

Some Scottish radio stations

BBC Radio Scotland 92–95FM, 810MW ⊛ www .bbc.co.uk/radioscotland. Nationwide news, sport, music, current affairs and arts.
Clyde 1 102.5FM ⊛ www.radioclyde.com. Glasgow's main contemporary rock and pop station. The slightly mellower Clyde 2 is at 1152MW.
Lochbroom FM 102.2 & 96.8FM ⊛ www .lochbroomfm.co.uk. One of Britain's smallest radio stations, broadcasting to the northwest coast from Ullapool.
Moray Firth 97.4FM, 1107MW ⊛ www.mfr .co.uk. Mainstream rock and pop for the youth of the Inverness area.
Nevis Radio 96.6 & 102.3FM ⊛ www.nevisradio .co.uk. From the slopes of Ben Nevis, all that's happening in Fort William and surrounds.
North Sound 96.9FM, 1035MW ⊛ www .northsound.co.uk. Pumps out the latest tunes to Aberdeen.
Radio Forth 97.3FM ⊛ www.radioforth.com. Rock and pop for Edinburgh and around. Forth 2 at 1548MW is their easier-listening stablemate.
Radio Tay 96.4 & 102.8FM, 1161 & 1584MW ⊛ www.radiotay.co.uk. Dundee's local radio.
Real Radio 100–101FM, ⊛ www.realradiofm.com. Mainstream pop and shock-jocks for the central belt.
SIBC 96.2FM ⊛ www.sibc.co.uk. Shetland's own independent station.

Crime and personal safety

For the most part the Scottish police are approachable and helpful to visitors. If you're lost in a major town, asking a police officer is generally the quickest way to get help; alternatively, you could ask a traffic warden, a much-maligned species of law enforcer responsible for parking restrictions and other vehicle-related matters.

As with any country, Scotland's major towns and cities have their danger spots, but these tend to be inner-city housing estates where no tourist has any reason to roam. The chief urban risk is **pickpocketing**, so carry only as much money as you need, and keep all bags and pockets fastened. Out in the Highlands and Islands, crime levels are very low. Should you have anything stolen or be involved in some incident that requires reporting, go to the local police station (addresses in the major cities are listed in this guide); the ☎999 (or ☎112) number should only be used in dire emergencies.

Emergencies

To call out the **police**, **fire service**, **ambulance** and/or, in certain areas, mountain rescue or the coastguard, dial ☎**999**.

Events and spectator sports

Scotland offers a huge range of organized annual events, reflecting both vibrant contemporary culture and well-marketed heritage. Many tourists will want to home straight in on Highland Games (for more details about the Games, see *Festivals* colour section) and other tartan-draped theatricals, but it's worth bearing in mind that there's more to Scotland than this: numerous regional celebrations perpetuate ancient customs, and the fabulous Edinburgh Festival is an arts celebration unrivalled in size and variety in the world. A few of the smaller, more obscure events, particularly those with a pagan bent, are in no way created for tourists, and indeed do not always welcome the casual visitor; local tourist offices always have full information.

The tourist board publishes a weighty list of all Scottish events twice a year: it's free and you can get it from area tourist offices or direct from their headquarters. Full details are at ⓦwww.visitscotland.com.

Events calendar

Dec 31 and Jan 1 Hogmanay and Ne'er Day. Traditionally more important to the Scots than Christmas, the occasion is known for the custom of "first-footing", when groups of revellers troop into neighbours' houses at midnight bearing gifts. More popular these days are huge and highly organized street parties, most notably in Edinburgh (ⓦwww .edinburghshogmanay.org), but also in Aberdeen, Glasgow and other centres.

Jan 1 Stonehaven fireball ceremony. Locals swing fireballs on long sticks to welcome New Year and ward off evil spirits. Also Kirkwall Boys' and Men's Ba' Games, Orkney: mass, drunken football game through the streets of the town, with the castle and the harbour the respective goals. As a grand finale the players jump into the harbour.

Jan 11 Burning of the Clavie, Burghead, Moray ⓦwww.hogmanay.net/scotland/burghhead.shtml. A burning tar barrel is carried through the town and then rolled down Doorie Hill. Charred fragments of the Clavie offer protection against the evil eye.

Mid- to late Jan Celtic Connections, Glasgow ⓦwww.celticconnections.co.uk. A major celebration of Celtic and folk music held in venues across the city.

Last Tues in Jan Up-Helly-Aa, Lerwick, Shetland ⓦwww.visitshetland.com/uphellyaa. Norse fire festival culminating in the burning of a specially built Viking longship. Visitors will need an invite from one of the locals, or you can buy a ticket for the Town Hall celebrations.

Jan 25 Burns Night. Scots worldwide get stuck into haggis, whisky and vowel-grinding poetry to commemorate Scotland's greatest poet, Robert Burns.

Feb Scottish Curling Championship ⓦwww .royalcaledoniancurlingclub.org, held in a different (indoor) venue each year.

Feb–March Six Nations Rugby tournament, between Scotland, England, Wales, Ireland, France and Italy ⓦwww.6nations.net. Scotland's home games are played at Murrayfield stadium in Edinburgh.

March 1 Whuppity Scourie, Lanark. Local children race round the church beating each other with home-made paper weapons in a representation (it's thought) of the chasing away of winter or the warding off of evil spirits.

April Scottish Grand National, Ayr ⓦwww .ayr-racecourse.co.uk. Not quite as testing as the English equivalent steeplechase, but an important event on the Scottish racing calendar. Also Rugby Sevens (seven-a-side tournament; ⓦwww .melrose7s.com) in the Borders, plus the acclaimed Shetland Folk Festival (ⓦwww.shetlandfolkfestival. com) and the non-boffin-friendly Edinburgh Science Festival (ⓦwww.sciencefestival.co.uk).

April 6 Tartan Day. Over-hyped celebration of ancestry by North Americans of Scottish descent on the anniversary of the Declaration of Arbroath in 1320. Ignored by most Scots in Scotland, other than journalists.

Early May Spirit of Speyside Scotch Whisky Festival (ⓦwww.spiritofspeyside.com), and Isle of Bute Jazz Festival.

May Scottish FA Cup Final. Scotland's premier football event, played in Glasgow.

Late May Atholl Highlanders Parade at Blair Castle, Perthshire ⓦwww.blair-castle.co.uk. The annual parade and inspection of Britain's last private army by their colonel-in-chief, the Duke of Atholl, on the eve of their Highland Games.

Early June Week-long festivities in Lanark culminating in the crowning of the Lanimer Queen, a ceremony dating back to the fifteenth century.

June–Aug Riding of the Marches. In the border towns of Hawick, Selkirk, Annan, Dumfries, Duns, Peebles, Jedburgh, Langholm and Lauder. The Ridings originated to check the boundaries of common land owned by the town and also to commemorate warfare between the Scots and the English. Nowadays individual Ridings have their own special ceremonies, though they all start with a parade of pipes and brass bands.

June Beginning of the Highland Games season across the Highlands, northeast and Argyll. St Magnus Festival, Orkney (ⓦwww.stmagnusfestival .com), is a classical and folk music, drama, dance and literature festival celebrating the islands.

Late June Royal Highland Agricultural Show, at Ingliston near Edinburgh ⓦwww.rhass.org.uk. Old wooden boats and fishing craft gather for the Traditional Boat Festival at Portsoy on the Moray Firth coast (ⓦwww.scottishtraditionalboatfestival.co.uk).

Early July Glasgow International Jazz Festival (ⓦwww.jazzfest.co.uk), and T in the Park (ⓦwww .tinthepark.com). The latter is Scotland's biggest outdoor music event, held at Balado near Kinross with a star-studded line-up of contemporary bands.

July Scottish Open Golf Championship. Held each year at Loch Lomond golf course, just before the British Open tournament, which is played in Scotland at least every alternate year.

Late July The Wickerman Festival of alternative music is held near Kirkcudbright (ⓦwww .thewickermanfestival.co.uk).

Aug Edinburgh Festival ⓦwww.edinburghfestivals .com. One of the world's great arts jamborees, described in full on p.147. The Edinburgh Military Tattoo (ⓦwww.edinburgh-tattoo.co.uk) features floodlit massed pipe bands and drums on the castle esplanade. There's also the World Pipe Band Championship at Glasgow, and plenty more Highland Games.

Early Sept Ben Nevis Race (for amateurs). Held on the first weekend in the month, running to the top of Scotland's highest mountain and back again. Also Shinty Camanachd Cup Final ⓦwww.shinty .com. The climax of the season for Scotland's own stick-and-ball game, normally held in one of the main Highland towns.

Late Sept Doors Open Day. The one weekend a year when many public and private buildings are open to the public; actual dates vary. Also another Spirit of Speyside Whisky Festival (®www .spiritofspeyside.com), the Scottish Book Town Festival in Wigtown (®www.wigtown-booktown .co.uk) and various food festivals and events under the banner of Scottish Food Fortnight (®www .scottishfoodfortnight.co.uk).

Oct The National Mod, held over nine days at a different venue each year. It's a competitive festival and features all aspects of Gaelic performing arts (®www.the-mod.co.uk).

Nov 30 St Andrew's Day. Celebrating Scotland's patron saint. The town of St Andrews hosts a week of events leading up to it (®www.standrewsweek .co.uk).

Football

Football (soccer) is far and away Scotland's most popular spectator sport, and one of the areas of Scottish life that has remained truly independent from the English. A potent source of pride for Scots everywhere, the national team (always accompanied by its distinctive and vocal supporters, known as the "Tartan Army") has consistently managed to hold its own in international competitions, qualifying frequently for World Cup finals but at the same time cornering the market in gallant failure by failing to progress far on every occasion.

Scotland was one of the first countries in the world to establish a national domestic league, in 1874, but today most of the teams which play in it are little known beyond the boundaries of Scotland. The exceptions are the two massive Glasgow teams which dominate the Scottish scene, **Rangers** and **Celtic** (known collectively as the "Old Firm"; see p.309). The sectarian, and occasionally violent, rivalry between these two is one of the least attractive aspects of Scottish life, and their stranglehold over the **Scottish Premier League** or SPL (®www.scotprem. com) has arguably been just as damaging. Although the 1980s saw Dundee United and Aberdeen break the deadlock, the old pattern reasserted itself during the 1990s, with the title all but guaranteed to end up on one or other side of Glasgow each year. During the past few seasons, calls have been mounting for the Old Firm to join either the English Premiership or a pan-European league, which would give them tougher opposition on a more regular basis. However, it's fairly claimed that the loss of the two flagship clubs would leave the Scottish league without a credible European contender, and serve an undeserved deathblow to the nation's rich footballing tradition.

With a couple of exceptions (notably Jock Stein's legendary Celtic sides of the late 1960s and early 1970s), Scottish soccer has traditionally been renowned less for its great teams than for its outstanding individuals – **players** such as Denis Law of Manchester United, Kenny Dalglish of Celtic and Liverpool, Billy Bremner at Leeds and Graeme Souness in the famous Liverpool side of the early 1980s, as well as **managers** of near-mythical status like Jock Stein, Matt Busby, Bill Shankly and, of course, Alex Ferguson of Manchester United. These days, as in England, foreign players have flooded the league, to the extent that home-grown players are the exception rather than the rule in the Rangers and Celtic teams. However, talented local players still have a stage on which to perform, and the new blend of continental sophistication mixed with Scottish passion and ruggedness makes for a distinctive spectacle which will appeal to soccer enthusiasts, who should definitely take in a game or two while they're here.

The **season** begins in early August and ends in mid-May, with matches on Saturday afternoons at 3pm, and also often on Sunday afternoons and Wednesday evenings. **Tickets** range from £10 to £25 for big games; the major clubs operate telephone credit-card booking services (see the relevant city's listings section for details). For a quick overview, ®www.scotprem.com features details of every Scottish club, with news and match-report archives.

Rugby

Rugby gets its name from Rugby public school in England, where the game mutated from football in the nineteenth century. A rugby match may at times look like a bunch of weightlifters grappling each other in the mud – as the old joke goes, rugby is a hooligan's game played by gentlemen, while football is a gentleman's game played by hooligans – but it is in reality highly tactical and athletic.

Although rugby has always lived under the shadow of football in Scotland, it ranks as one of the country's major sports, and the national team performs at a creditable level on the international stage. Weekends when the national team is playing a home international at **Murrayfield** stadium in Edinburgh are colourful occasions, with kilted masses filling the capital's pubs and lining the streets leading to the ground. Internationals take place in the spring, when Scotland take on the other "home nations", along with France and Italy, in the annual Six Nations tournament, although there are always fixtures in the autumn against international touring teams such as New Zealand, Australia and South Africa. Tickets for big games are hard to come by; contact the Scottish Rugby Union (☎0131/346 5000, ⊛www.sru.org .uk) for an indication of where and when tickets are available for any particular fixture.

The **club rugby** scene in Scotland is in a certain amount of disarray, with many of the country's top players finding better offers to play in England or France. The one area where the tradition runs deepest, however, is in the Borders, where towns such as Hawick, Kelso and Galashiels can be gripped by the fortunes of their local team on a Saturday afternoon. The Borders are also the home of **seven-a-side rugby**, an abridged version of the game which was invented in Melrose in the 1890s and is now played around the world, most notably at the glamorous annual event in Hong Kong. The Melrose Sevens is still the biggest tournament of the year in Scotland, although you'll find events at one or other of the Border towns through the spring, most going on right through an afternoon and invoking a festival atmosphere in the large crowd.

Shinty

Played throughout Scotland but with particular strongholds in the West Highlands and Strathspey, the game of **shinty** (the Gaelic *sinteag* means "leap") arrived from Ireland around 1500 years ago. Until the latter part of the nineteenth century, it was played on an informal basis and teams from neighbouring villages had to come to an agreement about rules before matches could begin. However, in 1893, the **Camanachd Association** – the Gaelic word for shinty is *camanachd* – was set up to formalize the rules, and the first Camanachd Cup Final was held in Inverness in 1896. Today, shinty is still fairly close to its Irish roots in the game of hurling, with each team having twelve players including a goalkeeper, and each goal counting for a point. The game, which bears similarities to an undisciplined version of hockey, isn't for the faint-hearted; it's played at a furious pace, with sticks – called camans or cammocks – flying alarmingly in all directions. Support is enthusiastic and vocal, and if you're in the Highlands during the season, which has recently changed to run from March to October to avoid the perils of midwinter, it's well worth trying to catch a match: check with tourist offices or the local paper to see if there are any local fixtures, or go to ⊛www .shinty.com.

Curling

The one winter sport which enjoys a strong Scottish identity is **curling** (⊛www .royalcaledoniancurlingclub.org), occasionally still played on a frozen outdoor rink, or "pond", though most commonly these days seen at indoor ice rinks. The game, which involves gently sliding smooth-bottomed 18kg discs of granite called "stones" across the ice towards a target circle, is said to have been invented in Scotland, although its earliest representation is in a sixteenth-century Flemish painting. Played by two teams of four, it's a highly tactical and skilful sport, enlivened by team members using brushes to furiously sweep the ice in front of a moving stone to help it travel further and straighter. The sport received a massive boost in profile when a team from Scotland won gold in the women's event at the 2002 Winter Olympics. If you're interested in seeing curling being played, go along to the ice rink in places such as Perth, Pitlochry or Inverness on a winter evening.

Outdoor pursuits

Scotland boasts a landscape that, weather conditions apart, is extremely attractive for outdoor pursuits at all levels of fitness and ambition. Recent legislation enacted by the Scottish Parliament has ensured a responsible right of access to hills, mountains, lochs and rivers at a level unrivalled elsewhere in the British Isles. Within striking distance of its cities are two national parks, remote wilderness areas and vast stretches of glens and moorland, while with thousands of miles of rugged but beautiful coastline Scotland can be a paradise for the sea-kayaker, sailor and surfer.

Walking and climbing

The whole of Scotland offers superb opportunities for **hill walking** and the freedom to roam responsibly in wilder parts of the countryside, with some of the finest Highland climbing areas in the ownership of bodies such as the National Trust for Scotland and the John Muir Trust (ⓦwww.jmt. org); both permit year-round access. Bear in mind, though, restrictions may be in place during lambing and deerstalking seasons. It's worthwhile picking up the booklet *Hill Phones* published by the Mountaineering Council of Scotland (MCofS), which provides walkers with detailed information for hiking safely during the stalking season. In addition, the green signposts of the Scottish Rights of Way Society point to established paths and routes all over the country.

There are several **Long-Distance Footpaths** (LDPs), such as the well-known West Highland Way, which take days to walk, though you can, of course, just do a section of them. Paths are generally well signposted and well supported, with a range of services from bunkhouses to baggage-carrying services, and are a great way to respond to the challenge of walking in Scotland without taking on the dizzy heights.

Numerous short walks (from accessible towns and villages) and several major walks are touched on in this guide and the *Great Outdoors* colour section. However, you should only use our notes as general outlines, and always in conjunction with a good map. Where possible, we have given details of the best maps to use – in most cases one of the excellent and reliable Ordnance Survey (OS) series (see p.38), usually available from local tourist offices, which can also supply other local maps, safety advice and guidebooks/leaflets. We've listed a number of the good walking **guidebooks** in the "Books" section of Contexts (p.851). These, as well as a wide range of maps, are available from most of the good **outdoor** stores scattered around the country (most notably Tiso and Nevisport), which are normally staffed by experienced climbers and walkers, and are a good source of candid advice about the equipment you'll need and favourite hiking areas.

For relatively gentle walking in the company of knowledgeable locals, look out for **guided walks** offered by rangers at many National Trust for Scotland, Forest Enterprise and Scottish Natural Heritage sites. These often focus on local wildlife, and the best can lead to some special sightings, such as a badger's sett or a golden eagle's eyrie.

Useful contacts for walkers

General information

ⓦ**www.hillphones.info** Daily information for hill walkers about deerstalking activities (July–Oct).

ⓦ**www.outdooraccess-scotland.com** All you need to know about the Scottish Outdoor Access Code.

ⓦ**www.walkingwild.com** Smart official site from Visitscotland, with good lists of operators, information on long-distance footpaths and details of deerstalking restrictions and contact phone numbers.

ⓦ**www.walkscotland.com** Comprehensive site with lists of specific walks, mountain routes, news, gear and even a few shaggy dog stories.

Midges and ticks

Despite being only just over a millimetre long, and enjoying a life span on the wing of just a few weeks, the midge (*Culicoides*) – a tiny biting fly prevalent in the Highlands (mainly the west coast) and Islands – is considered to be second only to the weather as the major deterrent to tourism in Scotland. There are more than thirty varieties of midge, though only half of these bite humans. Ninety percent of all midge bites are down to the female *Culicoides impunctatus* or Highland midge (the male does not bite), which has two sets of jaws sporting twenty teeth each; she needs a good meal of blood in order to produce eggs.

These persistent creatures can be a nuisance, but some people also have a violent allergic reaction to midge bites. The easiest way to avoid midges is to visit in the winter, since they only appear between April and October. Midges also favour still, damp, overcast or shady conditions and are at their meanest around sunrise and sunset, when clouds of them can descend on an otherwise idyllic spot. Direct sunlight, heavy rain, noise and smoke discourage them to some degree, though wind is the most effective means of dispersing them. If they appear, cover up exposed skin and get your hands on some kind of repellent. Recommendations include Autan, Eureka, Jungle Formula (widely available from pharmacists) and the herbal remedy citronella. An alternative to repellents for protecting your face, especially if you're walking or camping, is a midge net, a little like a bee-keeper's hat; although they appear ridiculous at first, you're unlikely to care as long as they work. The latest deployment in the battle against the midge is a gas-powered machine called a "midge magnet" which sucks up the wee beasties and is supposed to be able to clear up to an acre; each unit costs £300 and upwards, but there's been a healthy take-up by pubs with beer gardens and campsite owners.

If you're anywhere near woodland, there's a possibility you may receive attention from ticks, tiny parasites no bigger than a pin head, which bury themselves into your skin. Removing ticks by dabbing them with alcohol, butter or oil is now discouraged; the medically favoured way of extracting them is to pull them out carefully with small tweezers. There is a very slight risk of catching some very nasty diseases, such as encephalitis, from ticks. If flu-like symptoms persist after a tick bite, you should see a doctor immediately.

Clubs and associations

Mountain Bothies Association ⓦwww
.mountainbothies.org.uk. Charity dedicated to maintaining huts and shelters in the Scottish Highlands.
Mountaineering Council of Scotland ☎01738
/638227, ⓦwww.mountaineering-scotland.org.uk.
The representative body for all mountain activities, with detailed information on access and conservation issues.
Ramblers Association Scotland ⓦwww.
ramblers.org.uk/scotland. Campaigning organization with network of local groups and news on events and issues.
Scottish Mountaineering Club ⓦwww.smc.org.
uk. The largest mountaineering club in the country. A well-respected organization which publishes a popular series of mountain guidebooks.

Tour operators

Adventure Scotland ☎08702/402676, ⓦwww
.adventure-scotland.com. Highly experienced

operator providing a wide range of courses and one-day adventures, from telemark skiing to climbing, kayaking and biking.
Bespoke Highland Tours ☎01854/612628,
ⓦwww.scotland-inverness.co.uk/bht-main.htm.
Offers five–twelve-day self-led treks with a detailed itinerary along routes such as the Great Glen Way and West Highland Way, organizing baggage transfer and accommodation en route.
Cape Adventure International ☎01971/521006,
ⓦwww.capeventure.co.uk. From wonderfully remote northwest location near Kinlochbervie, Cape offers day, weekend and week-long individual and family adventure experiences including wilderness trips, climbing, sea-kayaking and walking.
C-N-Do Scotland ☎01786/445703, ⓦwww
.cndoscotland.com. Prides itself on offering the "best walking holidays in Scotland". Munro-bagging for novices and experts with qualified leaders.
G2 Outdoor ☎07946 285612, ⓦwww.g2outdoor
.co.uk. Personable, highly qualified adventure

specialists offering gorge, hill walking, rock climbing, canoeing and telemark skiing in the Cairngorms.

Glenmore Lodge ☎01479/861256, 🖥www .glenmorelodge.org.uk. Based within the Cairngorm National Park, and internationally recognized as a leader in outdoor skills and leadership training.

Hebridean Pursuits ☎01631/563594, 🖥www .hebrideanpursuits.com. Established in 1989, offering hill walking, winter and rock climbing in the Hebrides and West Highlands, as well as surf-kayaking and sailing trips.

North-West Frontiers ☎01854/612628, 🖥www .nwfrontiers.com. Based in Ullapool, offering guided mountain trips with small groups in the northwest Highlands, Hebrides and even the Shetland Islands. April to Oct.

Rua Reidh Lighthouse Holidays
☎01445/771263, 🖥www.ruareidh.co.uk. From its spectacular northwest location, this company, offers guided walks highlighting wildlife, rock climbing courses and week-long treks into the Torridon hills.

Vertical Descents ☎01855/821593, 🖥www .activities-scotland.com. Ideally located for the Glencoe and Fort William area, activities and courses include canyoning, funyakking (a type of rafting) and climbing.

Walkabout Scotland ☎0131/661 7168, 🖥www .walkaboutscotland.com. A great way to get a taste of hiking in Scotland, from exploring Ben Lomond to the Isle of Arran. Guided day and weekend walking from Edinburgh with all transport included.

Wilderness Scotland ☎0131/625 6635, 🖥www .wildernessscotland.com. Guided, self-guided and customized adventure holidays and trips that focus on exploring the remote and unspoiled parts of Scotland by foot, sea-kayak, yacht and even ski mountaineering.

Winter sports

Skiing and **snowboarding** take place at five different locations in Scotland – Glen Coe, the Nevis Range beside Fort William, Glen Shee, the Lecht and the Cairngorms near Aviemore – but as none of these can offer anything even vaguely approaching an alpine experience it is as well not to come with high expectations. The resorts can go for months on end through the winter with insufficient snow, then see the approach roads suddenly made impassable by a glut of the stuff. That said, when the conditions are good, Scotland's ski resorts have piste and off-piste areas that will challenge even the most accomplished alpine skier or tele-marker.

Expect to pay up to £25 for a standard day pass at one of the resorts, or £100 for a five-day pass; rental of skis or snowboard comes in at around £16 per day, with reductions for multiday rents. At weekends, in good weather with decent snow, expect the slopes to be packed with trippers from the central belt, although midweek usually sees queues dissolving. For a comprehensive rundown of all the resorts, including ticket prices and conditions, visit the Snowsports link at 🖥www.scottishsport.co.uk.

Telemark skiing is becoming increasingly popular in the hills around Braemar near Glenshee and the Cairngorms. The best way to get started or to find out about good routes is to contact an outdoor

Staying safe in the hills

Beguiling though the hills of Scotland can seem, you have to be properly prepared before venturing out onto them. Due to rapid weather changes, the mountains are potentially extremely dangerous and should be treated with respect. Every year, in every season, climbers and walkers lose their lives in the Scottish hills.

❏ Wear sturdy, ankle-supporting footwear and wear or carry with you warm, brightly coloured and waterproof layered clothing, even for what appears to be an easy expedition in apparently settled weather.

❏ Always carry adequate maps, a compass (which you should know how to use), food, water and a whistle. If it's sunny, make sure you use sun protection.

❏ Check out a weather forecast before you go. If the weather looks as if it's closing in, get down from the mountain fast.

❏ Always leave word with someone of your route and what time you expect to return, and remember to contact the person again to let them know that you are back.

❏ In an emergency, call mountain rescue on ☎999.

pursuits company that offers telemark or Nordic rental and instruction; in the Aviemore area try Adventure Scotland (✆www .adventure-scotland.com, ☎08702/402676) or G2 Outdoor ☎07946/285612, ✆www .g2outdoor.co.uk). Also check out the Huntly Nordic and Outdoor Centre in Huntly, Aberdeenshire (☎01466/794428, ✆www.huntly .net/hnoc). For equipment hire, sales or advice contact Braemar and Cairngorm Mountain Sports (✆www.braemarmountainsports.com, ☎01339/741242 or 01479/810903).

Pony trekking and horse riding

There are approximately sixty **pony-trekking** or **riding centres** across the country, all of them approved by either the Trekking and Riding Society of Scotland (TRSS, ✆www .ridinginscotland.com) or the British Horse Society (BHS, ✆www.bhs.org.uk). As a rule, any centre will offer the option of pony trekking (leisurely ambles on sure-footed Highland ponies), **hacking** (for experienced riders who want to go for a short ride at a fastish pace) and **trail riding** (over longer distances, for riders who feel secure at a canter). In addition, a network of special horse-and-rider B&Bs means you can ride independently on your own horse.

A four-day route – the **Buccleuch Country Ride** – was recently inaugurated in the Borders region, using private tracks, open country and quiet bridleways. For more information about this, and the B&B network for riders, contact the Scottish Borders Tourist Board (see p.38), or the TRSS.

Cycling and mountain biking

Although cycle touring is a great way to see some parts of Scotland, **road cyclists** are still treated with notorious neglect by many motorists and by the people who plan the country's traffic systems. Very few of Scotland's towns have proper cycle routes, but if you're hellbent on tackling the congestion, pollution and aggression of city traffic, get a **helmet** and a secure **lock**. Out in the countryside, it can be tricky finding spare parts: anything more complex than inner tubes or tyres can be very hard to come by.

The Forestry Commission has recently established 1150 miles of excellent off-road routes for **mountain biking** all over the country, which are detailed in numerous "Cycling in the Forest" leaflets (available from Forest Enterprise offices listed below, and from most tourist offices). Waymarked and graded, these are best attempted on mountain bikes with multi-gears, although many of the gentler routes may be tackled on hybrid and standard road cycles.

For up-to-date information on **long-distance routes**, including The Great Glen Cycle Way, along with a list of publications detailing specific routes, contact the cyclists campaigning group Sustrans (✆www .sustrans.co.uk), as well as some of the organizations listed on p.66.

Another option is to shell out on a **cycling holiday package**. Britain's biggest cycling organization, the **Cycle Touring Club**, or CTC, provides lists of tour operators and rental outlets in Scotland, and supplies members with touring and technical advice, as well as insurance. As a general introduction, Visit Scotland's "Cycling in Scotland" brochure is worth getting hold of, with practical advice and suggestions for itineraries around the country. The tourist board's "Cyclists Welcome" scheme gives guesthouses and B&Bs around the country a chance to advertise that they're cyclist-friendly, and able to provide such things as an overnight laundry service, a late meal or a packed lunch.

Transporting your bike by train is a good way of getting to the interesting parts of Scotland without a lot of hard pedalling. Bikes are allowed free on mainline GNER and Virgin Intercity trains, as well as ScotRail trains, but always subject to available space, so you should book the space as far in advance as possible. Bus and coach companies, including National Express and Scottish Citylink, rarely accept cycles unless they are dismantled and boxed; one notable exception is the excellent service operated by Dearman coaches (✆www.timdearmancoaches.co.uk, ☎01349/883585) between Inverness and Durness via Ullapool (May–Sept, 1 daily, Mon–Sat). If you don't bring your own wheels with you, most large towns and tourist centres will offer **bike rental**. Expect to pay

£10–20 per day; most outlets also give good discounts for multiday rents.

Useful contacts for cyclists

Cyclists' Touring Club ☏01483/417217, ⓦwww.ctc.org.uk. Britain's largest cycling organization, and a good source of general advice; their handbook has lists of cyclist-friendly B&Bs and cafés in Scotland. Annual membership £25.

Forest Enterprise ☏0845/3673787, ⓦwww .forestry.gov.uk. The best source of information on Scotland's extensive network of forest trails – ideal for mountain biking at all levels of ability.

Full On Adventure ⓦwww.fullonadventure .co.uk. Among its many offerings, provides fully guided mountain-bike tours of Highland trails.

The Hub in the Forest ☏01721/721736, ⓦwww.thehubintheforest.co.uk. One of Scotland's most established mountain-bike centres with a huge network of trails for all abilities in Glentress Forest.

Nevis Range ☏01397/705825, ⓦwww .nevisrange.co.uk. The home of Scotland's World Cup downhill and cross-country tracks (May–Oct) outside Fort William, with a gondola lift system and bike hire.

North Sea Cycle Route ⓦwww.northsea-cycle .com. Signposted 3725-mile (6000-km) route round seven countries fringing the North Sea, including 1242km in Scotland along the east coast and in Orkney and Shetland.

Scottish Cycle Safaris ☏0131/556 5560, ⓦwww.cyclescotland.co.uk. Fully organized cycle tours at all levels, from camping to country-house hotels, with a good range of bikes available for rent, from tandems to children's bikes.

Scottish Cycling ☏0131/652 0187, ⓦwww .scottishcycling.com. Produces an annual handbook and calendar of cycling events (£8) – mainly road, mountain-bike and track races.

Spokes ☏0131/313 2114, ⓦwww.spokes.org.uk. Active Edinburgh cycle campaign group with plenty of good links and news on events and cycle-friendly developments.

WolfTrax Mountain Bike Centre ☏01528/544786. Based just outside Laggan, this year-round mountain-bike facility has miles of trail for every level of rider and a café to revive weary legs.

Air sports

Scotland has its fair share of fine sunny days, when it's hard to beat scanning majestic mountain peaks, lochs and endless forests from the air. Whether you're a willing novice or an expert **paraglider** or **sky-diver**, there are centres just outside Glasgow, Edinburgh and Perth which will cater to your needs.

There are also opportunities to try **ballooning**, **gliding** and **hang-gliding**. The following are just a selection of operators who will help you spread your wings.

British Gliding Association ☏0116/2531051, ⓦwww.gliding.co.uk. Governing body for gliding enthusiasts and schools across the UK with information on where to find many clubs in Scotland.

Cloudbusters ☏07899/878509, ⓦwww .cloudbusters.co.uk. Highly reputable paragliding school which runs taster and fully accredited paragliding courses in the Lanarkshire hills outside Glasgow each weekend of the year.

Flying Fever ☏01770 820292, ⓦwww .flyingfever.net. Based on the stunning Isle of Arran, forty miles southwest of Glasgow. Fully accredited paragliding courses and tandem flights can be enjoyed for as little as £95.

Skydive St Andrews ☏01334/880678, ⓦwww .skydivestandrews.co.uk. Year-round, highly professional, fully accredited parachute school that offers tandem, solo "static" line and "accelerated free-fall courses" over the Fife countryside. Tandem jump from around £200.

Skydive Strathallan ☏01764 662572, ⓦwww .skydivestrathallan.co.uk. Located just outside Auchterarder, this non-commercial school operates year-round. Tandem jump from around £200.

Golf

There are over 400 **golf courses** in Scotland, where the game is less elitist and more accessible than anywhere else in the world. Golf in its present form took shape in the fifteenth century on the dunes of Scotland's east coast, and today you'll find some of the oldest courses in the world on these early coastal sites, known as "links". It's often possible just to turn up and play, though it's sensible to phone ahead; booking is essential for the championship courses.

Public courses are owned by the local council, while private courses belong to a club. You can play on both – occasionally the **private** courses require that you are a member of another club, and the odd one asks for introductions from a member, but these rules are often waived for overseas visitors and all you need to do is pay a one-off fee. The cost of a round will set you back around £10 on a small nine-hole course, and more than £40 for many good-quality eighteen-hole courses. Renting a caddie car will add a few pounds to the cost.

Scotland's **championship** courses, which often host the British Open, are renowned for their immaculately kept greens and challenging holes and, though they're favoured by serious players, anybody with a valid handicap certificate can enjoy them. **St Andrews** is the top destination for golfers: it's the home of the Royal and Ancient Golf Club, the worldwide controlling body that regulates the rules of the game. Ⓦwww.scotlands-golf-courses.com has contacts, scorecards and maps of signature holes for most main courses.

If you're coming to Scotland primarily to play golf, it's worth shelling out for a ticket which gives you access to a number of courses in any one region. There's more information at Ⓦwww.scottishgolf.com and Ⓦwww.visitscotland.com/golf.

Fishing

Scotland's serrated coastline – with the deep sea lochs of the west, the firths of the east and the myriad offshore islands – ranks among the cleanest coasts in Europe. Combine this with an abundance of **salmon**, **sea trout**, **brown trout** and **pike**, acres of open space and easy access, and you have a wonderful location for game-, coarse- or sea-fishing,

No licence is needed to fish in Scotland, although nearly all land is privately owned and its fishing therefore controlled by a landlord/lady or his/her agent. Permission, however, is usually easy to obtain: **permits** can be bought without hassle at local tackle shops, or through fishing clubs in the area – if in doubt, ask at the nearest tourist office. The other thing to bear in mind is that salmon and sea trout have strict **seasons**, which vary between districts but usually stretch from late August to late February. Once again, individual tourist offices will know the precise dates, or you can try to get hold of Visit Scotland's excellent "Fish Scotland" brochure (Ⓦwww.visitscotland.com/outdoor). More useful information and contacts can be found at the comprehensive website Ⓦwww.fishing-uk-scotland.com.

Sailing, windsurfing and kite-surfing

Opportunities for **sailing** are outstanding, tainted only by the unreliability of the weather. However, even in summer, the full force of the North Atlantic can be felt, and changeable conditions combined with tricky tides and rocky shores demand good sailing and navigational skills.

Yacht charters are available from various ports, either bareboat or in yachts run by a skipper and crew; contact Sail Scotland (Ⓦwww.sailscotland.co.uk) or the Associated Scottish Yacht Charters (Ⓦwww.asyc.co.uk).

An alternative way to enjoy Scotland under sail is to spend a week at one of the **sailing schools** around the country. Many schools, as well as small boat rental operations dotted along the coast, will rent sailing dinghies by the hour or day, as well as **windsurfers**, though the chilly water means you'll always need a wet suit. Scotland's top spot for windsurfing is Tiree (Ⓦwww.tireewindsurfing.com). Variations on a windy theme include **kite-surfing** – Ⓦwww.kitesurfing.org has a list of accredited schools, and Blo-karting – Ⓦwww.blokart.co.uk fills you in on where to find it around the country.

Beaches

Scotland is ringed by fine **beaches** and bays, most of them clean and many of them deserted even in high summer – perhaps hardly surprising, given the bracing winds and chilly water which often accompany them. Few people come to Scotland for a beach holiday, but it's worth sampling a beach or two, even if you keep your sweater on. Bizarrely enough, given the low temperature of the water, the beaches in the northeast are beginning to figure on surfers' itineraries, attracting enthusiasts from all over Europe (see the *Great Outdoors* colour section). Perhaps the most beautiful beaches of all are to be found on Scotland's islands: endless, isolated stretches that on a sunny day can be paradise.

The Marine Conservation Society (Ⓦwww.goodbeachguide.co.uk) monitors bathing-water quality, and in 2005 recommended fifty beaches in Scotland.

Sea-kayaking and surfing

In recent years **sea-kayaking** has witnessed an explosion in popularity, with a host of operators offering sea-kayaking lessons and expeditions across the country. Canoe Scotland (www.canoescotland.org.uk) can offer useful advice, while Glenmore Lodge (www.glenmorelodge.org.uk), Canoe Hebrides (www.canoehebrides.com) and Skyak Adventures (www.skyakadventures.com) are highly reputable for either training or tours.

In addition to sea-kayaking, Scotland is fast gaining a reputation as a **surfing** destination. However, Scotland's northern coastline lies on the same latitude as Alaska and Iceland, so the water temperature is very low: even in midsummer it rarely exceeds 15°C, and in winter can drop to as low as to 7°C. The one vital accessory, therefore, is a good wet suit (ideally a 5/3mm steamer), wet-suit boots and, outside summer, gloves and a hood, too.

Many of the best spots are surrounded by stunning scenery, and you'd be unlucky to encounter another surfer for miles. However, this isolation – combined with the cold water and big, powerful waves – means that, in general, much of Scottish surf is best left to **experienced surfers**. If you're a beginner, get local advice before you go in, and be aware of your limitations.

The popularity of surfing in Scotland has led to a spate of **surf shops** opening up, all of which rent or sell equipment and provide good information about the local breaks and events on the surfing scene (Clan Surf and Momentum can also organize surfing lessons). Two further sources of information are *Surf UK* by *Rough Guide* author Wayne "Alf" Alderson (Fernhurst Books; £13.95), with details on over 400 breaks around Britain, and the British Surfing Association (www.britsurf.co.uk).

Surf information, shops and schools

Adventure Sports 13 High St, Dunbar ☎01368/869734, www.c2cadventure.com. Year-round surfing lessons and surf safaris across Scotland.

Boardwise 1146 Argyle St, Glasgow ☎0870/750 4423; 4 Lady Lawson St, Edinburgh ☎0870/750 4420. Surf gear, clothes and short-term rental.

Clan Surf 45 Hyndland St, Partick, Glasgow ☎0141/339 6523. Combined surf, skate and snowboard shop. Lessons available.

ESP 5–7 Moss St, Elgin ☎01343/550129. Sales and rental only.

Granite Reef 45 The Green, Aberdeen ☎01224/252752. Sales, hire and lessons.

Thurso Surf Treehouse, Halkirk, Caithness ☎01847/831866 or 0774/836 2397, www.thursosurf.com. Lessons, April–Sept.

Wild Diamond Watersports Isle of Tiree, ☎0771/215 9205, www.tireewindsurfing.com. Instruction and hire for surfing, windsurfing, kite-surfing and kayaking.

Gay and lesbian travellers

Both Glasgow and Edinburgh have reasonably prominent gay and lesbian communities, with a well-established network of bars, cafés, nightclubs, support groups and events.

In Edinburgh, the area around Broughton Street is the heart of the city's "pink triangle", while in Glasgow the scene is mostly found in the Merchant City area; our entertainment listings for both cities include a number of gay bars and clubs. Elsewhere in Scotland, there are one or two gay bars in both Aberdeen and Dundee, with support and advice groups dotted around the country. Details for these, and many other aspects of the gay scene in Scotland, can be found on the website for the the monthly *Scotsgay* newspaper (www.scotsgay.co.uk). The Glasgow Lesbian, Gay, Bisexual & Transgender Centre website (☎0141/221 7203, www.glgbt.org.uk) also has a good list of useful links.

Contacts for gay and lesbian travellers

UK

@ **www.gaytravel.co.uk** Online gay and lesbian travel agent, offering good deals on all types of holiday. Also lists gay- and lesbian-friendly hotels.

North America

gaytravel.com ☏ 1-800/GAY-TRAVEL, @ www .gaytravel.com. The premier site for trip planning, bookings and general information about international gay and lesbian travel.
International Gay & Lesbian Travel Association ☏ 1-800/448-8550 or 954/776-2626, @ www.iglta.org. Trade group that can provide a list of gay- and lesbian-owned or -friendly travel agents, accommodation and other travel businesses.

Australia and New Zealand

Gay and Lesbian Tourism Australia @ www .galta.com.au. Directory and links for gay and lesbian travel in Australia and worldwide.
New Zealand Gay and Lesbian Tourism Association @ www.nzglta.org.nz. Organization devoted to enhancing the New Zealand travel experience for gay, lesbian and bisexual visitors.
Parkside Travel ☏ 08/8274 1222, @ parkside@herveyworld.com.au. Gay travel agent associated with local branch of Hervey World Travel; all aspects of gay and lesbian travel worldwide.
Silke's Travel ☏ 1800/807 860 or 02/8347 2000, @ www.silkes.com.au. Long-established gay and lesbian specialist, with the emphasis on women's travel.
Tearaway Travel ☏ 1800/664 440 or 03/9510 6644, @ www.tearaway.com. Gay-specific business dealing with international and domestic travel.

Travellers with specific needs

Travellers with disabilities

Scottish attitudes towards **travellers with disabilities** still lag behind advances towards independence made in North America and Australia. Access to many public buildings has improved recently, with recent legislation ensuring that all new buildings have appropriate facilities. It's worth keeping in mind, however, that installing ramps, lifts, wide doorways and disabled toilets is impossible or inappropriate in many of Scotland's older and historic buildings. Most trains in Scotland have wheelchair lifts and assistance is, in theory, available at all manned stations – for more, go to @ www.firstscotrail.com and click on "Special needs". Wheelchair users and blind or partially sighted people are automatically given 30–50 percent reductions on train fares, and people with other disabilities are eligible for the **Disabled Persons Railcard** (£14 per year; @ www.disabledpersons-railcard.co.uk), which gives a third off most tickets. There are no bus discounts for the disabled, and of the major **car-rental** firms only Hertz offers

models with hand controls at the same rate as conventional vehicles, and even these are only available in the more expensive categories. It's the same story for **accommodation**, with modified suites for people with disabilities available only at higher-priced establishments and perhaps the odd B&B.

Contacts for travellers with disabilities

UK and Ireland

All Go Here ☏ 01923/840 463, @ www.allgohere .com. Provides information on accommodation suitable for disabled travellers throughout the UK, including Northern Ireland.
Capability Scotland ☏ 0131/313 5510, @ www .capability-scotland.org.uk. The leading disability organization in Scotland. A well-run, well-connected outfit covering all local disability issues and information.
Equal Adventure Developments ☏ 01479/861372, @ equaladventure.co.uk. Specialist consultancy focusing on outdoor activities and adventure sports for disabled people. Based at Glenmore Lodge near Aviemore.
Holiday Care ☏ 0845/124 9971; @ www .holidaycare.org.uk. Provides free lists of accessible

accommodation in the UK. Information on financial help for holidays available.

Irish Wheelchair Association ℡01/818 6400, Ⓦwww.iwa.ie. Useful information provided about travelling abroad with a wheelchair.

RADAR (Royal Association for Disability and Rehabilitation) ℡020/7250 3222, Ⓦwww.radar .org.uk. A good source of advice on holidays and travel in the UK. They produce an annual holiday guide called *Holidays in Britain and Ireland* for £13 in the UK, £15 to Europe and £18 to other overseas destinations (includes postage), and have a dedicated accommodation website for Britain and Ireland, Ⓦwww.radarsearch.org.

Tripscope ℡0845/758 5641, Ⓦwww.tripscope .org.uk. This registered charity provides a national telephone information service offering free advice on UK and international transport for those with a mobility problem.

North America

Access-Able Ⓦwww.access-able.com. Online resource for travellers with disabilities.

Directions Unlimited 123 Green Lane, Bedford Hills, NY 10507 ℡1-800/533-5343 or 914/241-1700. Travel agency specializing in bookings for people with disabilities.

Mobility International USA 451 Broadway, Eugene, OR 97401 ℡541/343-1284, Ⓦwww .miusa.org. Information and referral services, access guides, tours and exchange programmes. Annual membership $35 (includes quarterly newsletter).

Society for the Advancement of Travelers with Handicaps (SATH) 347 5th Ave, New York, NY 10016 ℡212/447-7284, Ⓦwww.sath.org. Non-profit educational organization that has actively represented travellers with disabilities since 1976.

Wheels Up! ℡1-888/38-WHEELS, Ⓦwww .wheelsup.com. Provides discounted airfare, tour and cruise prices for disabled travellers, also publishes a free monthly newsletter and has a comprehensive website.

Australia and New Zealand

ACROD (Australian Council for Rehabilitation of the Disabled) ℡02/6282 4333, Ⓦwww.acrod .org.au. Provides lists of travel agencies and tour operators for people with disabilities.

Disabled Persons Assembly ℡04/801 9100, Ⓦwww.dpa.org.nz. New Zealand resource centre

with lists of travel agencies and tour operators for people with disabilities.

Senior travellers

Senior citizens, whether resident in the UK or not, are usually eligible for some kind of discount at sights all over Scotland, so it's always worth asking. Those aged 60 or over might also consider buying a **Senior Railcard** (Ⓦwww.senior-railcard.co.uk), which costs £20 and gives a third off standard rail fares. On the coaches, Scottish Citylink has "Senior Special" fares on certain routes. For all sorts of services aimed at the 50-plus age group, including holidays, insurance and even a radio station, contact Saga (℡0800/414525, Ⓦwww.saga.co.uk).

Travelling with children

Scottish attitudes to those **travelling with children** can be discouraging, particularly if you've experienced the more indulgent approach of the French or Italians. Restaurateurs would basically prefer it if parents and carers left the kids at home. Inevitably, cafés and bistros are more likely than more formal restaurants to cater for kids by providing high chairs and other facilities. It's in these more relaxed establishments, too, that more enlightened children's menus are starting to appear. Pubs have traditionally had to obtain a special licence to admit children under 16 after a certain time (often 7pm), although these laws are currently being revised. Out in rural areas, particularly in the Islands, attitudes are much more relaxed, and the sight of kids in the hotel lounge bar is not so unusual. However, most families with young children opt for self-catering cottages (see p.47) precisely to avoid the hassle of trying to eat out with kids. It's always worth asking about discounted "family tickets" when visiting any attractions or sight. If you're travelling on public transport, it's definitely worthwhile buying a **Family Railcard** (Ⓦwww .family-railcard.co.uk), which gives you sixty percent off kids' fares and thirty percent off adult train fares.

Directory

Electricity The current is 240v AC. North American appliances need a transformer and adapter; Australasian appliances need only an adapter.

Gaelic In some areas of Scotland, particularly in the Highlands and Hebrides, road signs are bilingual English–Gaelic. Throughout the guide, where appropriate, we've given the Gaelic translation (in italics and parentheses) the first time any village or island is mentioned, after which the English name is used. The main exception to this rule is in the Western Isles, where signposting is almost exclusively in Gaelic; we've reflected this by giving the Gaelic first and putting the English in parentheses, and thereafter using the Gaelic (except for the islands and ferry ports, which are more familiar in the English form they're given on ferry timetables).

Genealogy Many visitors to Scotland, particularly from North America and Commonwealth countries, have an interest in tracing family connections. Searches can involve days at registrars' offices looking through historical records or speculative wanderings through graveyards. The main official website relating to genealogy in Scotland is ⓦwww .scotlandspeople.gov.uk; you have to register and pay a small fee, but the database is one of the world's largest resources of genealogical information, with a searchable index of Scottish births (1553–1904), marriages (1553–1929) and deaths (1855–1954), as well as census data from 1871 to 1901.

Laundry Coin-operated laundries are found in nearly all Scottish cities and towns, and are open about twelve hours a day from Monday to Friday, less on weekends. A wash followed by a spin or tumble dry costs about £3; a "service wash" (having your laundry done for you in a few hours) costs about £2 extra. In the remoter regions of Scotland, you'll have to rely on hostel and campsite laundry facilities.

Smoking In 2005 the Scottish Parliament passed legislation that outlaws smoking in all enclosed public spaces. While smoking has been outlawed from just about all public buildings and on public transport for a number of years, in 2006 the ban was extended to all restaurants, bars, pubs and on clubs. Breaches of the law will see fines imposed on anyone caught smoking and on the proprietors of premises they are in. In effect, smokers are restricted to smoking outdoors or in private homes. Hotel owners may designate certain rooms as smoking bedrooms, but they are not obliged to do this.

Time From late October to late March, Scotland is on Greenwich Mean Time (GMT), which is five hours ahead of US Eastern Standard Time and ten hours behind Australian Eastern Standard Time. Over the summer, clocks go forward an hour for British Summer Time (BST).

Toilets Public loos are found at all train and bus stations and signposted on town high streets; a fee of 10p or 20p is sometimes charged.

DRESSING FOR DINNER IS OPTIONAL AT SMARTCITY

At **smartcityhostel** in Edinburgh we try to cater for everyone - you can have a snack in the TV lounge or dine in style in the bar/bistro whichever you prefer. You set the style, we set the table - and dressing for dinner is definitely a non-starter (unless of course you want to).

smartcityhostel is 5 star standard hostel which means a hotel style experience at hostel prices. You can eat, sleep, drink. chill out, have fun - all in-house. You can also take advantage of the great location and see the sights or take in the nightlife - in fact anything you want to do and be sure of somewhere warm and safe to crash out.

Booking Hotline 0870 892 3000
Book online www.smartcityhostels.com

smartcityhostels [ED]
EDINBURGH
THE ULTIMATE URBAN RESORT EXPERIENCE

50 Blackfriars Street, Old Town, Edinburgh, EH1 1NE T: 0870 892 3000
e:info@smartcityhostels.com   www.smartcityhostels.com

Guide

Guide

Edinburgh and the Lothians

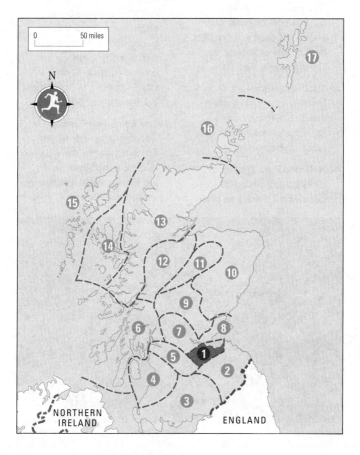

CHAPTER 1 # Highlights

✳ **The Old Town** The evocative heart of the historic city, with its tenements, closes, courtyards, ghosts and catacombs cheek-by-jowl with many of Scotland's most important buildings. **See p.90**

✳ **Edinburgh Castle** Perched on an imposing volcanic crag, the castle dominates Scotland's capital, its ancient battlements protecting the Crown Jewels. **See p.91**

✳ **Scottish Parliament** Enric Miralles' quirky yet thrilling design is a dramatic new presence in Holyrood's royal precinct. **See p.108**

✳ **Holyrood Park** Wild moors, rocky crags and an 800-foot peak (Arthur's Seat), all slap in the middle of the city. **See p.111**

✳ **Museum of Scotland** The treasures of Scotland's past housed in a dynamic and superbly conceived building. **See p.113**

✳ **Café Royal Circle Bar** In a city filled with fine drinking spots, there are few finer pubs in which to sample a pint of local 80 shilling beer; order six oysters (once the city's staple food) to complete the experience. **See p.141**

✳ **The Edinburgh Festival** The world's biggest arts festival, which transforms the city every August. Bewildering, inspiring, exhausting and endlessly entertaining. **See p.147**

△ Edinburgh Castle

Edinburgh and the Lothians

Venerable, dramatic **EDINBURGH**, the showcase capital of Scotland, is a historic, cosmopolitan and cultured city. The setting is wonderfully striking: perched on a series of extinct volcanoes and rocky crags which rise from the generally flat landscape of the Lothians, with the sheltered shoreline of the Firth of Forth to the north. "My own Romantic town", Sir Walter Scott called it, although it was another native author, Robert Louis Stevenson, who perhaps best captured the feel of his "precipitous city", declaring that "No situation could be more commanding for the head of a kingdom; none better chosen for noble prospects."

The centre has two distinct parts, divided by **Princes Street Gardens**, which run roughly east–west under the shadow of **Edinburgh Castle**, in the very heart of the city. To the north, the dignified, Grecian-style **New Town** was immaculately laid out in the eighteenth century during the Age of Reason, after the announcement of a plan to improve conditions in the city. The **Old Town**, on the other hand, with its tortuous alleys and tightly packed closes, is unrelentingly medieval, associated in popular imagination with the city's underworld lore of body snatchers Burke and Hare and of schizophrenic Deacon Brodie, inspiration for Stevenson's *Dr Jekyll and Mr Hyde*. Indeed, Edinburgh's ability to capture the literary imagination has recently seen it dubbed a "World City of Literature" by **UNESCO**, the same organization which previously conferred World Heritage Site status on a large section of the centre covering both Old and New towns.

Set on the hill which sweeps down from the fairy-tale Castle and east to the royal **Palace of Holyroodhouse**, the Old Town preserves all the key reminders of its role as a historic capital, augmented now by the dramatic and unusual new **Scottish Parliament building**, opposite the palace. A few hundred yards away immediately beyond here, a tantalizing glimpse of the wild beauty of Scotland's scenery can be had in **Holyrood Park**, an extensive area of open countryside dominated by **Arthur's Seat**, the largest and most impressive of the volcanoes.

In August and early September, around a million visitors flock to the city for the **Edinburgh Festival**, which is in fact a series of separate festivals that make up the largest arts extravaganza in the world. Among Edinburgh's many museums, the exciting **National Museum of Scotland** houses 10,000 of

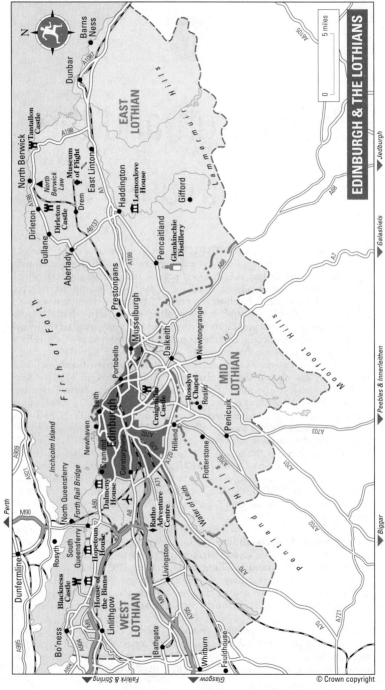

EDINBURGH & THE LOTHIANS

0   5 miles

N

Berwick-upon-Tweed

Barns Ness

Dunbar

EAST LOTHIAN

Tantallon Castle

North Berwick

North Berwick Law

Dirleton Castle

Dirleton

Gullane

Aberlady

Museum of Flight

Drem

East Linton

Haddington

Lennoxlove House

Gifford

L a m m e r m u i r   H i l l s

Pencaitland

Glenkinchie Distillery

F i r t h   o f   F o r t h

Prestonpans

Musselburgh

Portobello

Dalkeith

Newtongrange

MID LOTHIAN

Rosslyn Chapel

Roslin

Penicuik

Flotterstone

Hillend

M o o r f o o t   H i l l s

Leith

Newhaven

Edinburgh

Cramond

Corstorphine

Craigmillar Castle

Inchcolm Island

North Queensferry

Forth Rail Bridge

South Queensferry

Dalmeny House

Hopetoun House

Ratho Adventure Centre

W a t e r   o f   L e i t h

Livingston

P e n t l a n d   H i l l s

Perth

M90

Dunfermline

Rosyth

Bo'ness

Blackness Castle

House of the Binns

Linlithgow

WEST LOTHIAN

Bathgate

Whitburn

Fauldhouse

Falkirk & Stirling

Glasgow

Biggar

Peebles & Innerleithen

Galashiels

Jedburgh

A1

A198

A1087

A6105

A68

A7

A199

A6137

A702

A720

A71

A8

A90

A921

A909

A985

A904

A905

A801

M8

A705

A70

A721

A703

A701

A7

© Crown copyright

Scotland's most precious artefacts, while the **National Gallery of Scotland** and its offshoot, the **Scottish National Gallery of Modern Art**, house two of Britain's finest collections of paintings.

On a less elevated theme, the city's distinctive howffs (pubs), allied to its brewing and distilling traditions, make it a great **drinking** city. Its three **universities**, plus several colleges, mean that there is a youthful presence for most of the year – a welcome corrective to the stuffiness which is often regarded as Edinburgh's Achilles heel. Beyond the city centre, the most lively area is **Leith**, the city's medieval port, whose seedy edge is softened by a series of great bars and upmarket seafood restaurants, along with the presence of the former royal yacht **Britannia**, now open to visitors. The wider rural hinterland of Edinburgh, known as the **Lothians**, mixes rolling countryside and attractive country towns with some impressive historic ruins. In East Lothian, blustery cliff-top paths lead to the romantic battlements of **Tantallon Castle**, while nearby North Berwick, home of the **Scottish Seabird Centre**, looks out to the gannet-covered Bass Rock. The most famous sight in Midlothian is the mysterious fifteenth-century **Rosslyn Chapel**, while West Lothian boasts the towering, roofless **Linlithgow Palace**, thirty minutes from Edinburgh by train. To the northwest of the city, the dramatic steel geometry of the **Forth Rail Bridge** is best seen by walking across the parallel road bridge, starting at **South Queensferry**.

Some history

It was during the **Dark Ages** that the name Edinburgh – at least in its early forms of Dunedin or Din Eidyn ("fort of Eidyn") – first appeared. The strategic fort atop the Castle Rock volcano served as the nation's **southernmost border post** until 1018, when King Malcolm I established the River Tweed as the permanent frontier. In the reign of Malcolm Canmore in the late eleventh century the Castle became one of the main seats of the court, and the town, which was given privileged status as a **royal burgh**, began to grow. In 1128 King David established Holyrood Abbey at the foot of the slope, later allowing its monks to found a separate burgh, known as **Canongate**.

Robert the Bruce granted Edinburgh a **new charter** in 1329, giving it jurisdiction over the nearby port of Leith, and during the following century the prosperity brought by foreign trade enabled the newly fortified city to establish itself as the permanent **capital of Scotland**. Under King James IV, the city enjoyed a short but brilliant **Renaissance era**, which saw not only the construction of a new palace alongside Holyrood Abbey, but also the granting of a **royal charter** to the College of Surgeons, the earliest in the city's long line of academic and professional bodies.

This period came to an abrupt end in 1513 with the calamitous defeat by the English at the Battle of Flodden, which led to several decades of political instability. In the 1540s King Henry VIII's attempt to force a royal union with Scotland led to the sack of Edinburgh, prompting the Scots to turn to France: French troops arrived to defend the city, while the young queen Mary was dispatched to Paris as the promised bride of the Dauphin, later (briefly) François II of France. While the French occupiers succeeded in removing the English threat, they themselves antagonized the locals, who had become increasingly sympathetic to the ideals of the **Reformation**. When the radical preacher John Knox returned from exile in 1555, he quickly won over the city to his Calvinist message.

James VI's rule saw the foundation of the University of Edinburgh in 1582, but following the **Union of the Crowns** in 1603 the city was totally upstaged by London: although James promised to visit every three years, it was not until

1617 that he made his only return trip. In 1633 Charles I visited Edinburgh for his coronation, but soon afterwards precipitated a crisis by introducing episcopacy to the Church of Scotland, in the process making Edinburgh a bishopric for the first time. Fifty years of religious turmoil followed, culminating in the triumph of **Presbyterianism**. Despite these vicissitudes, Edinburgh grew throughout the seventeenth century but, constrained by its city walls, was forced to build both upwards and inwards.

The **Union of the Parliaments** of 1707 dealt a further blow to Edinburgh's political prestige, though the guaranteed preservation of the national Church and the legal and educational systems ensured that it was never relegated to a purely provincial role. On the contrary, it was in the second half of the eighteenth century that Edinburgh achieved the height of its intellectual influence, led by an outstanding group, including David Hume and Adam Smith. Around the same time, the city began to expand beyond its medieval boundaries, laying out a **New Town**, a masterpiece of the Neoclassical style.

Industrialization affected Edinburgh less than any other major city in the nation, and it never lost its white-collar character. Nevertheless, the city underwent an enormous **urban expansion** in the course of the nineteenth century, annexing, among many other small burghs, the large port of Leith.

In 1947 Edinburgh was chosen to host the great **International Festival** which served as a symbol of the new peaceful European order; despite some hiccups, it has flourished ever since, in the process helping to make tourism a mainstay of the local economy. In 1975 the city carried out another territorial expansion, moving its boundaries westwards as far as the old burgh of South Queensferry and the Forth bridges. Four years later, an inconclusive referendum on Scottish devolution delayed Edinburgh's revival of its role as a governmental capital, and Glasgow, previously the poor relation but always a tenacious rival, began to challenge the city's status as a cultural centre.

However, while the 1990s saw Glasgow establish a clear lead in driving Scotland's contemporary arts scene, they also marked the return of power and influence to Edinburgh. In 1997 the Scottish people voted resoundingly in favour of re-establishing its own **parliament** with control over a large part of the domestic agenda. Inevitably, the early years of the parliament have seen petty squabbling mixed with rather dizzying constitutional manoeuvring, but with debates, decisions and demonstrations about crucial aspects of the government of Scotland now taking place in Edinburgh, there has been a notable upturn in the sense of importance of the city. It has continued to assert itself as a significant centre for finance, research and arts, not just in Britain, but also Europe, although what many had hoped to be the crowning achievement of the age, the inspiring new parliament building which opened its doors in 2004 is for the moment tarnished by its spectacularly overblown budget and ongoing rows about design and management. There is little doubt, however, that this highly stylized design, which sits opposite the ancient Palace of Holyroodhouse at the foot of the Royal Mile, will in time establish itself as the contemporary emblem of an historic city.

Arrival, information and transport

Although Edinburgh occupies a large area relative to its population – less than half a million people – most places worth visiting lie within the compact city centre, which is easily explored on foot. This is divided clearly and unequivocally between the maze-like **Old Town**, which lies on and around the crag linking the Castle and the Palace, and the **New Town**, laid out in a symmetrical pattern on the undulating ground to the north.

Edinburgh International Airport (☎0870/040 0007, ⓦwww.baa.com) is at Turnhouse, seven miles west of the city centre, close to the start of the M8 motorway to Glasgow. Airlink shuttle buses (#100; journey time 30min; £3) connect to Waverley Station in the centre of town; services depart every ten or twenty minutes between 5am and midnight, and at least hourly through the night. **Taxis** charge around £15-20 for the same journey.

Conveniently situated at the eastern end of Princes Street right in the heart of the city, **Waverley Station** (timetable and fare enquiries ☎0845/748 4950, ⓦwww.nationalrail.co.uk) is the arrival point for all mainline trains. The **bus and coach** terminal for local and intercity services is located on the east side of St Andrew Square, two minutes' walk from Waverley Station.

There's a second mainline train stop, **Haymarket Station**, just under two miles west on the lines from Waverley to Glasgow, Fife and the Highlands, although this is only really of use if you're staying nearby.

Information

Edinburgh's main **tourist office** is found on top of Princes Mall near the northern entrance to the train station (April & Oct Mon–Sat 9am–6pm, Sun 10am–6pm; May, June & Sept Mon–Sat 9am–7pm, Sun 10am–7pm; July & Aug Mon–Sat 9am–8pm, Sun 10am–8pm; Nov–March Mon–Wed 9am–5pm, Thurs–Sat 9am–6pm, Sun 10am–5pm; ☎0845/225 5121, ⓦwww.edinburgh .org). Although inevitably hectic at the height of the season, it's reasonably effi-cient, with scores of free leaflets and a bank of computers available if you want to search for information on the Web. The much smaller **airport branch** is in the main concourse, directly opposite Gate 5 (daily: April–Oct 6.30am–10.30pm; Nov–March 7.30am–9.30pm). For backpacker-related information head to the **Haggis Office** at 60 High St (Mon, Wed–Sat 8am–6pm; Tues 10am–6pm; also Sun 8am–6pm Aug; ☎0131/557 9393, ⓦwww.haggisadventures.com). Although their main function is to run minibus tours of Scotland, they're a good source of general information about the backpacker scene around Scotland, and you can book hostels and intercity coaches from here, as well as change money. For up-to-date maps of the city head for one of the major bookstores: Waterstone's, 13–14 Princes St, is the nearest to Waverley Station.

Despite the compactness of the city centre, open-top **bus tours** are big business in Edinburgh, with three rival companies taking largely similar routes around the main sights. All three cost much the same, depart from Waverley Bridge and allow you to get on and off at leisure. The most entertaining of the three are MacTours (£8.50; ☎0131/556 2244, ⓦwww.mactours.co.uk), which uses a fleet of characterful vintage buses. Several companies along the Royal Mile offer **walking tours** of the street, including Auld Reekie Tours (☎0131/557 4700, ⓦwww.auldreekietours.co.uk) and Mercat Tours (☎0131/557 6464, ⓦwww.mercat-tours.co.uk). These two companies also offer night-time ghost tours around the Old Town, as do the entertaining Witchery Tours (☎0131/225 6745, ⓦwww.witcherytours.com) and the spine-tingling City of the Dead graveyard tour (☎0131/225 9044, ⓦwww.blackhart.uk.com). Other specialist outings include the **Edinburgh Literary Pub Tour** (☎0131/226 6665, ⓦwww .edinburghliterarypubtour.co.uk), which mixes a pub crawl with extracts from local authors acted out along the way; **Geowalks** (☎0131/555 5488, ⓦwww.geowalks .demon.co.uk), which offers guided walks up Arthur's Seat in the company of a qualified geologist; **Rebustours** (☎07866/536752, ⓦwww.rebustours.com), whose knowledgeable guides trace the footsteps of Inspector Rebus, hero of Ian Rankin's bestselling detective novels (see p.844); and Tim Bell's **Trainspotting** tour (☎0131/555 2500, ⓦwww.leithwalks.co.uk) which takes you round some of the scenes famous from Irvine Welsh's novels. Advance booking is recommended for all the above, the specialist tours in particular.

City transport

Most of Edinburgh's **public transport** services terminate on or near Princes Street, the city's main thoroughfare, which divides the Old Town from the New Town, with the main **bus station** located just north of here on St Andrew Square. The city is generally well served by **buses**; the white and maroon ones operated by Lothian Buses (timetables and passes from offices on Waverley Bridge, Shandwick Place or Hanover Street; enquiry line ☎0131/555 6363; ⓦwww .lothianbuses.co.uk) provide the most frequent and comprehensive coverage of the city. Note that all buses referred to in the text are run by Lothian unless otherwise stated. Usefully, every bus stop displays diagrams indicating which services pass by and the routes they take; some also have digital displays indicating when buses are next due. A good investment, especially if you're staying far out or want to explore the suburbs, is the Ridacard £12 **pass** allowing a week's unlimited travel on Lothian buses; you'll need a passport-sized photo. You can also buy a Lothian day pass for £2.30 (or £4.20 including an airport bus single) or, of course, tickets from the driver, for which you'll need exact change – the most common fare is 80p, which will get you from one side of the city centre to the other, with a longer journey to the suburbs costing £1.

The predominantly white, single-decker buses of First Edinburgh (enquiry line ☎0870/872 7271, ⓦwww.firstgroup.com) also run services on a number of the main routes through town, but are better for outlying towns and villages. They have their own system of tickets and day-tickets, similar in structure to Lothian Buses. Most services depart from or near the main bus station.

Edinburgh is well endowed with **taxi** ranks, and you can also hail black cabs on the street. Costs are reasonable – from the city centre to Leith, for example, will cost around £6. If you want to call a taxi, try one of the following: Computer Cabs (☎0131/272 8000), Central Radio Taxis (☎0131/229 2468) and City Cabs (☎0131/228 1211).

It is emphatically not a good idea to take a **car** into central Edinburgh: despite the presence of several expensive multistorey car parks, finding somewhere to park involves long and often fruitless searches. Traffic calming has been introduced in several key areas – Princes Street is now closed to all except buses, taxi and cycles from 7am to 8pm and George Street and Charlotte Square are pedestrian priority zones – and there is a growing network of green-painted bus lanes called "greenways", which must be left clear during rush hours. In addition, Edinburgh's street parking restrictions are famously draconian: residents' zone parking areas and double yellow lines are no-go areas at all times, while cars left for more than five minutes on single yellow lines or overdue meter-controlled areas are very likely to be fined £60 by one of the swarms of inspectors who patrol day and night. In some cases cars may be towed away, with a retrieval fee of £105. Most ticket and parking meter regulations don't apply after 6.30pm Monday to Saturday and all day Sunday.

Edinburgh is a reasonably cycle-friendly city – although hilly – with several **cycle paths**. The local cycling action group, Spokes (☎0131/313 2114, ⓦwww .spokes.org.uk), publishes an excellent map of the city. For rental, try

Biketrax, 13 Lochrin Place (☎0131/228 6333, ⓦ www.biketrax.co.uk), in Tollcross, or Cycle Scotland & Rent-a-Bike, 29 Blackfriars St (☎0131/556 5560, ⓦ www .cyclescotland.co.uk), just off the Royal Mile.

Accommodation

As befits its status as a busy tourist city and important commercial centre, Edinburgh has a greater choice of **accommodation** than any other place in Britain outside London. **Hotels** (and large backpacker **hostels**) are essentially the only options you'll find right in the heart of the city, but within relatively easy reach of the centre the selection of **guesthouses**, **B&Bs**, **campus accommodation** and even **campsites** broadens considerably.

Prices here are significantly higher than elsewhere in Scotland, with double rooms starting at £60 per night. Budget hotel chains offer the best value if you want basic accommodation right in the centre, with rooms available for £60–80; £80–100 per night will get you something more stylish. Bear in mind that many of the guesthouses and small hotels are located in Georgian and Victorian townhouses, over three or more floors, and usually have no lift so are not ideal if stairs are a problem. It's worthwhile making advance **reservations** at any time of year, though it's strongly recommended for stays during the Festival and around Hogmanay when places can often get booked out months ahead. The Scottish tourist board operates a booking centre for accommodation all over the country, including Edinburgh; call ☎0845 2255121 or go to ⓦ www .visitscotland.com. There's a £3 fee for this service, waived if you book online. Accommodation options are shown on the maps on pp.84–85 and pp.92–93.

Hotels

In the centre of Edinburgh there aren't many independent hotels left: almost all, whether grand and traditional, no-frills budget or part of the new breed of stylish contemporary places, are either part of a recognizable chain or an international marketing group. Anywhere boasting historic grandeur or the latest in high design is at the upper end of the market, but you will find a few places which balance style and reasonable prices. In addition, the abundance of establishments in the city centre means that you can often find good deals in quieter periods, and it's always worth looking out for special offers advertised by all the chains. Below we've selected a range of the more interesting, characterful and well placed across all categories. Note that smaller hotels have generally been included in the guesthouse section below.

Old Town

Apex International Hotel 31–35 Grassmarket ☎0845/608 3456, ⓦ www.apexhotels.co.uk. This ex-university building turned 175-bed business-oriented hotel has comfortable rooms, some with views over to the Castle. The street-level *Metro* brasserie looks out through plate-glass windows onto the bustling Grassmarket. Along the same road is the linked *Apex City Hotel* (at no. 61). ⑥
Ibis Edinburgh Centre 6 Hunter Square ☎0131/240 7000, ⓦ www.accorhotels.com. Probably the best-located chain hotel cheapie in the

Old Town, within sight of the Royal Mile; rooms are modern and inexpensive, but there are few facilities other than a rather plain bar. ⑤
Point Hotel 34–59 Bread St ☎0131/221 5555, ⓦ www.point-hotel.co.uk. Having been treated to a radical contemporary makeover, the former department store is now one of Edinburgh's most stylish and individual modern hotels. There's a popular cocktail bar and a decent restaurant at street level. ⑥
The Scotsman Hotel 20 North Bridge ☎0131/556 5565, ⓦ www.thescotsmanhotel.co.uk. The plush

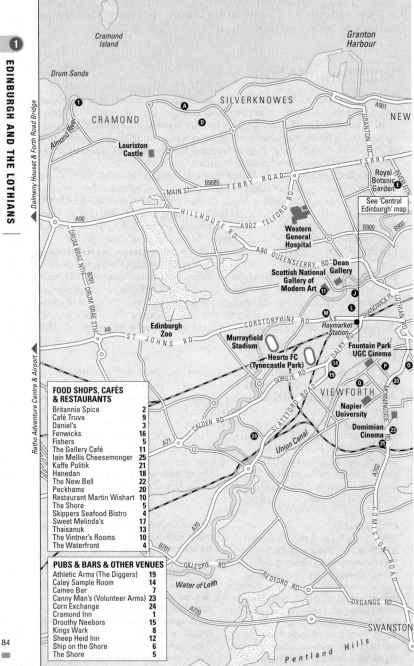

FOOD SHOPS, CAFÉS & RESTAURANTS

Britannia Spice	2
Café Truva	9
Daniel's	3
Fenwicks	16
Fishers	5
The Gallery Café	11
Iain Mellis Cheesemonger	25
Kaffe Politik	21
Hanedan	18
The New Bell	22
Peckhams	20
Restaurant Martin Wishart	10
The Shore	5
Skippers Seafood Bistro	4
Sweet Melinda's	17
Thaisanuk	13
The Vintner's Rooms	10
The Waterfront	4

PUBS & BARS & OTHER VENUES

Athletic Arms (The Diggers)	19
Caley Sample Room	14
Cameo Bar	7
Canny Man's (Volunteer Arms)	23
Corn Exchange	24
Cramond Inn	1
Drouthy Neebors	15
Kings Wark	8
Sheep Heid Inn	12
Ship on the Shore	6
The Shore	5

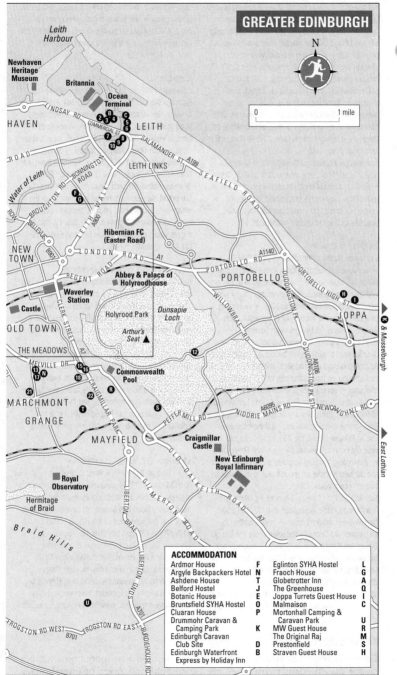

GREATER EDINBURGH

N

0   1 mile

Leith Harbour

Newhaven Heritage Museum

Britannia

Ocean Terminal

LINDSAY RD

HAVEN

COMMERCIAL ST

LEITH

SALAMANDER ST   A199

LEITH LINKS

SEAFIELD ROAD

ROAD

Water of Leith

BONNINGTON ROAD

BROUGHTON RD

BELLEVUE

LEITH WALK   A900

Hibernian FC (Easter Road)

NEW TOWN

LONDON ROAD

A1

PORTOBELLO RD   A1140

PORTOBELLO HIGH ST

PORTOBELLO

DUDDINGSTON PK

JOPPA

REGENT ROAD

Abbey & Palace of Holyroodhouse

Waverley Station

Castle

OLD TOWN

Holyrood Park

Dunsapie Loch

Arthur's Seat ▲

WILLOWBRAE RD

DUDDINGSTON PK STH

& Musselburgh

East Lothian

THE MEADOWS

MELVILLE DR

CLERK STREET

A7

Commonwealth Pool

A6106

NEWCRAIGHALL RD

MARCHMONT

GRANGE

CRAIGMILLAR PARK

PEFFER MILL RD

NIDDRIE MAINS RD   A6095

MAYFIELD

Craigmillar Castle

OLD DALKEITH ROAD

New Edinburgh Royal Infirmary

Royal Observatory

Hermitage of Braid

LIBERTON BRAE

GILMERTON ROAD

A7

Braid Hills

LIBERTON GDNS

BRIDGEHOUSE RD

FROGSTON RD WEST   B701   FROGSTON RD EAST

▼ Flotterstone

ACCOMMODATION

Ardmor House	F	Eglinton SYHA Hostel	L
Argyle Backpackers Hotel	N	Fraoch House	G
Ashdene House	T	Globetrotter Inn	A
Belford Hostel	J	The Greenhouse	Q
Botanic House	E	Joppa Turrets Guest House	I
Bruntsfield SYHA Hostel	O	Malmaison	C
Cluaran House	P	Mortonhall Camping &	
Drummohr Caravan &		Caravan Park	U
Camping Park	K	MW Guest House	R
Edinburgh Caravan		The Original Raj	M
Club Site	D	Prestonfield	S
Edinburgh Waterfront		Straven Guest House	H
Express by Holiday Inn	B		

© Crown copyright

but non-stuffy new occupant of the grand old offices of the *Scotsman* newspaper is one of Edinburgh's headline hotels. It's five-star stuff with modern gadgets and fittings, but the marble staircase and walnut panelled lobby have been retained, and you can sleep in the editor's old office; rooms from £260. ❾
Tailors Hall Hotel 139 Cowgate ☎0131/622 6801, ⊛www.festival-inns.co.uk. Stylish and modern en-suite rooms in a recently converted seventeenth-century trades hall and brewery in otherwise dingy Cowgate. In the same building is the lively, late-night mock-Gothic *Three Sisters Bar* (and beer garden). ❺
Travelodge Edinburgh Central 33 St Mary's St ⊛0870/191 1637, ⊛www.travelodge.co.uk. There's more than a hint of concrete brutalism about the look of this chain hotel, but it's well priced, and centrally located, 100 yards from the Royal Mile opposite a clutch of decent restaurants. ❺

New Town
Balmoral Hotel 1 Princes St ☎0131/556 2414, ⊛www.roccofortehotels.com. This elegant Edinburgh landmark is the finest grand hotel in the city, with nearly two hundred plush rooms (many with good views), full business facilities, a swimming pool and gym and two highly rated restaurants. ❼
Bonham Hotel 35 Drumsheugh Gardens ☎0131/623 9301, ⊛www.thebonham.com. One of Edinburgh's most stylish boutique hotels, cheekily hiding behind a grand West End Victorian facade and offering an interesting mix of fine period and chic contemporary design throughout. ❽
Caledonian Hotel Cnr Princes St and Lothian Rd ☎0131/222 8888, ⊛www.hilton.co.uk. Occupying a red-stone building and lording it over the west end of Princes Street, the 251-room hotel has recently been taken over by the Hilton Group, and is undergoing a rolling upgrade programme which should help it make up ground lost to its competitors in recent years. ❽
Edinburgh City Centre Express by Holiday Inn Picardy Place, Broughton ☎0131/558 2300, ☎www.hieedinburgh.co.uk. A great location in an elegant old Georgian tenement near the top of Broughton Street, with 160 rooms featuring neat but predictable chain-hotel decor and facilities. ❻
The Glasshouse Hotel 2 Greenside Place, Broughton ☎0131/525 8200, ⊛www.theetoncollection.com. Incorporating the castellated facade of the former Lady Glenorchy's Church, this

ultra-hip newcomer has 65 chi-chi rooms with push-button curtains and sliding doors opening onto a huge, lush roof garden scattered with Philippe Starck furniture. Perfect if you're in town for a weekend of flash indulgence. ❽

Leith
Edinburgh Waterfront Express by Holiday Inn Britannia Way, Ocean Drive ☎0870/744 2163, ⊛www.hiex-edinburgh.com. Purpose-built budget hotel that's a good mid-price option in the Leith area. In walking distance of Leith's best local restaurants and the Ocean Terminal shopping centre, and an easy bus ride (#1, #11, #22 or #35) into town. ❻
Malmaison 1 Tower Place ☎0131/468 5000, ⊛www.malmaison.com. Chic, modern hotel set in the grand old seamen's hostel just back from the wharf-side. Bright, bold original designs in each room, as well as CD players and cable TV. Also has a gym, room service, Parisian brasserie and café-bar serving lighter meals. ❻

South of the centre
Bruntsfield Hotel 69 Bruntsfield Place, Bruntsfield ☎0131/229 1393, ⊛www.thebruntsfield.co.uk. Now part of the Best Western group of independent hotels, this large, comfortable and peaceful, if somewhat traditional, hotel overlooks Bruntsfield Links, a mile south of Princes Street. ❽
Prestonfield Priestfield Road, Bruntsfield ☎0131/225 7800, ⊛www.prestonfield.com. This seventeenth-century mansion set in its own park below Arthur's Seat was recently taken over by the *Witchery* team (see opposite), and its extravagant baroque makeover has helped make it one of Edinburgh's most lavish and over-the-top places to stay. ❾

West of the centre
The Original Raj Hotel 6 West Coates ☎0131/346 1333, ⊛www.rajempire.com. Imaginatively conceived and pleasantly executed, this town-house hotel has seventeen rooms themed on India and the splendour of the Raj. Jump on bus #12, #26 or #31 (journey time 10–15min). ❺
Premier Travel Inn Edinburgh City Centre 1 Morrison Link, Haymarket ☎0870/238 3319, ⊛www.premiertravelinn.com. No-frills chain hotel in a fairly mundane location near Haymarket station; it's fairly inexpensive, however, and only about fifteen minutes' walk from Princes Street. ❹

Guesthouses

Generally offering much better value for money and a far more homely experience than the larger city hotels are Edinburgh's vast range of **guesthouses**, small hotels and bed & breakfast establishments. A few of these, command-ing a premium rate, can be found in the very centre of the city, but areas such as the edges of the New Town and the inner suburbs of Bruntsfield and the Grange offer a perfect balance of accessibility and good value. Elsewhere, almost all suburbs are well served by regular buses.

Old Town

Bank Hotel 1 South Bridge ☎0131/622 6800, ⓦwww.festival-inns.co.uk. Notable location in a 1920s bank at the crossroads of the Royal Mile and South Bridge, with *Logie Baird's Bar* downstairs and nine unusually decorated but comfortable rooms upstairs on the theme of famous Scots. ❻

The Witchery Apartments Castlehill, Royal Mile ☎0131/225 5613, ⓦwww.thewitchery.com. Seven riotously indulgent suites grouped around this famously spooky restaurant just downhill from the Castle; expect antique furniture, big leather armchairs, tapestry-draped beds, oak panelling and huge roll-top baths, as well as ultra-modern sound systems and complimentary bottles of champagne. Top of the range, unique and memorable. ❾

New Town

Ardenlee Guest House 9 Eyre Place, New Town ☎0131/556 2838, ⓦwww.ardenleeguesthouse .com. Welcoming non-smoking guesthouse at the foot of the New Town, with original Victorian features and nine reasonably spacious rooms, seven of which are en suite and some suitable for families. ❺

Castle View Guest House 30 Castle St ☎0131/226 5784, ⓦwww.castleviewgh.co.uk. A lot of stairs (and no lift), and the Castle view is sideways-on (and only from certain rooms), but the eight en-suite rooms are pleasant and include a few suitable for families, and its location is central, right in the heart of the New Town's shops and restaurants. ❻

Christopher North Hotel 6 Gloucester Place ☎0131/225 2720, ⓦwww.christophernorth.co.uk. Elegant and comfortable town-house hotel located on a typical New Town terrace. Decor is modern, opulent and striking, though it can feel a little overwhelming. ❻

Davenport House 58 Great King St, New Town ☎0131/558 8495, ⓦwww.davenport-house.com. A grand, regally decorated guesthouse in an attrac-tive Georgian town house; a well-priced and inti-mate alternative to some of the nearby hotels. ❺

Galloway Guest House 22 Dean Park Crescent, Stockbridge ☎0131/332 3672, Ⓔgalloway_ theclarks@hotmail.com. Friendly, family-run option with ten rooms in elegant Stockbridge, within walk-ing distance of the centre. Traditional in style but neat and well priced. ❸

Gerald's Place 21b Abercromby Place, New Town ☎0131/558 7017, ⓦwww.geraldsplace.com. A real taste of homely New Town life at an upmarket but wonderfully hospitable and comfy basement B&B. ❻

7 Gloucester Place 7 Gloucester Place ☎0131/225 2974, ⓦwww.aboutscotland.com /edin/gloucester.html. Elegant, well-cared-for B&B, with three bedrooms on the upper floor of a Geor-gian terrace house. The best of the double rooms has graceful garden views and use of a classic 1930s bathroom. ❺

Melvin House Hotel 3 Rothesay Terrace ☎0131/225 5084, ⓦwww.melvinhouse.co.uk. One of Edinburgh's grandest Victorian terraced houses, with exquisite internal wood panelling and a galler-ied library. The rooms are rather less memorable, though some have outstanding views over Dean village and the city skyline. ❻

11 Moray Place 11 Moray Place ☎0131/226 4997, ⓦwww.morayplace.co.uk. An old-fashioned B&B on a street lined with houses that rank among some of the New Town's finest architectural splendours. Rooms are on the upper floors (no lift) and look out either over Moray Place gardens or north to Fife. ❻

Regent House Hotel 3 Forth St, Broughton ☎0131/556 1616, ⓦwww.regenthousehotel.co.uk. A small hotel over four floors that makes up for its lack of glamour with a great location; right in the heart of Broughton on a quiet side street. Some rooms are big enough to accommodate 3–5 people. Large rooms from £30 per person. Doubles ❺

Rick's Restaurant with rooms 55a Frederick St, New Town ☎0131/622 7800, ⓦwww .ricksedinburgh.co.uk. Ten much sought-after rooms at the back of the popular New Town bar and restaurant. Beautifully styled with beds fitted with walnut headboards and plush fabrics, plus DVD player, they look out onto a cobbled lane behind. ❻

Six Mary's Place Raeburn Place, Stockbridge ☎0131/332 8965, ⓦwww.sixmarysplace.co.uk. A collectively run alternative-style guesthouse with eight smart, fresh-looking rooms, a no-smoking policy and excellent home-cooked vegetarian breakfasts served in a sunny conservatory. ❺

South of the centre

Ashdene House 23 Fountainhall Rd, Grange ☎0131/667 6026, ⓦwww.ashdenehouse.com. Well-run, environmentally friendly, non-smoking guesthouse, furnished in traditional Victorian style and located in the quiet southern suburbs. Bus #42 stops a few minutes' walk away. ⑤

Cluaran House 47 Leamington Terrace, Viewforth ☎0131/221 0047, ⊛www.cluaran-house -edinburgh.co.uk. Tasteful and welcoming B&B with lots of original features and paintings. Serves good traditional and vegetarian breakfasts. Close to Meadows with bus links (including #11 & #23) from nearby Bruntsfield Place. ⑤

The Greenhouse 14 Hartington Gardens, Viewforth ☎0131/622 7634, ⊛www.greenhouse-edinburgh .com. A fully vegetarian/vegan guesthouse, right down to the soaps and duvets, though a relaxed rather than right-on atmosphere prevails. The rooms are neat and tastefully furnished, with fresh fruit and flowers in each. Min. stay two nights. Buses #11 & #23 from Bruntsfield Place. ⑤

MW Guest House 94 Dalkeith Rd, Newington ☎0131/662 9265, ⊛www.mwguesthouse.co.uk. One of only a few guesthouses in town with a fresh, contemporary design – think muted tones and blonde wood. As it's set in a Victorian villa, every room is a bit different: those at the back are a bit quieter. If you're driving, the public parking here is easier than some other Southside choices. The linked *MW Townhouse* (11 Spence St) just round the corner is equally well presented. ④

The Stuarts B&B 17 Glengyle Terrace, Bruntsfield ☎0131/229 9559, ⊛www.the-stuarts.com. A five-star B&B, with three comfortable and well-equipped rooms in a basement beside Bruntsfield Links. ⑥

North Edinburgh

Ardmor House 74 Pilrig St, Pilrig ☎0131/554 4944, ⊛www.ardmorhouse .com. Victorian town house with some lovely

original features combined with smart contemporary decor. Gay-owned, straight-friendly and located halfway between town and Leith. ⑤

Botanic House Hotel 27 Inverleith Row, Inverleith ☎0131/552 2563, ⊛www.botanichousehotel .com. A small but smart family-run hotel with fresh and bright decor that nicely echoes the Botanic Gardens, which can be seen over the garden wall. There's a cosy but stylish bar in the basement that also serves food. Buses #23 and #27 go into town. ⑤

Fraoch House 66 Pilrig St, Pilrig ☎0131/554 1353, ⊛www.fraochhouse.com. A relaxing six-bedroom guesthouse with a slick, modern look created by its young owners. It's a ten- to fifteen-minute walk from both Broughton Street and the heart of Leith. ⑤

Inverleith Hotel 5 Inverleith Terrace, Inverleith ☎0131/556 2745, ⊛www.inverleithhotel.co.uk. Pleasant option near the Botanic Gardens, with twelve rooms of various sizes in a Victorian terraced house; all are en suite and tastefully decorated with wooden floors, antiques and tapestries. ⑤

East of the centre

Joppa Turrets Guest House 1 Lower Joppa, Joppa ☎0131/669 5806, ⊛www.joppaturrets .demon.co.uk. The place to come if you want an Edinburgh holiday by the sea: a quiet establishment on the beachfront in Joppa, five miles east of the city centre (buses #15 & #26). ④

Straven Guest House 3 Brunstane Rd North, Joppa ☎0131/669 5580, ⊛www .stravenguesthouse.com. Neat, friendly place near the beach with a no-smoking policy and environmentally friendly approach; vegetarian and vegan breakfast available. No children under 12. ④

Self-catering apartments and campus accommodation

Custom-built **self-catering serviced apartments** are popular with business travellers, but with no minimum let are a viable alternative to guesthouses. They're also well worth considering for longer stays, for example during the Festival. For a brochure of self-catering options contact the tourist board, and we've listed some of the best below. **Campus accommodation** is available in the city during the summer months, though it's neither as useful or cheap as might be expected.

Canon Court Apartments 20 Canonmills ☎0131/474 7000, ⊛www.canoncourt.co.uk. A block of smart, comfortable self-catering one- and two-bedroom apartments not far from Canonmills Bridge over the Water of Leith at the northern edge

of the New Town. Studio apartments from £74 per night.

Gladstone's Land 477b Lawnmarket, c/o National Trust for Scotland, 5 Charlotte Square ☎0131/243 9331, ⊛www.nts.org.uk. Two classic Old Town apartments on the fourth floor of the historic Gladstone's Land (see p.100). Set up for self-catering, both sleep two (twin beds), and there's a minimum stay of three nights. £435 per week.

Holyrood Aparthotel Nether Bakehouse Close, Holyrood ☎ 0131/524 3200, ⓦ www .holyroodaparthotel.com. A block of two-bedroom self-catering apartments near the Scottish Parliament. The location has lots of Old Town atmosphere, and the accommodation is slick and modern with most mod cons. Apartments from £120 (two people sharing).

Royal Garden Apartments York Buildings, Queen St ☎ 0131/625 1234, ⓦ www.royal-garden.co.uk.

Superbly equipped, comfortable modern one- and two-bedroom serviced apartments very centrally located opposite the National Portrait Gallery. Prices start at £155 per night.

University of Edinburgh Pollock Halls of Residence 18 Holyrood Park Rd, Newington ☎ 0131/651 2007, ⓦ www.edinburghfirst.com. Unquestionably the best setting of any of the city's university accommodation, right beside the Royal Commonwealth Pool and Holyrood Park, and with a range of accommodation from single rooms (£28), twins (£56) and en-suite doubles (£72) to self-catering flats (from £350 per week). Available Easter and June to mid-Sept only.

Hostels

Edinburgh is one of the UK's most popular backpacker destinations, and there are a large number of hostels in and around the city centre, ranging in size, atmosphere and quality. Competition is fierce, so be prepared for a bit of enthusiastic marketing when you make an enquiry.

Argyle Backpackers Hotel 14 Argyle Place, Marchmont ☎ 0131/667 9991, ⓦ www .argyle-backpackers.co.uk. Quiet, less intense version of the typical backpackers' hostel, pleasantly located in three adjoining town houses near the Meadows in studenty Marchmont. It's walking distance to town, but you can get bus #41 from the door. The small dorms have single beds, and there're a dozen or so double/twin rooms (❶), as well as a pleasant communal conservatory and garden at the back.

Belford Hostel 6–8 Douglas Gardens, West End ☎ 0131/225 6209, ⓦ www.hoppo.com. Housed in a converted Arts and Crafts church, just west of the centre close to St Mary's Cathedral and the Gallery of Modern Art. The dorms are in box rooms with the vaulted church ceiling above; a variety of twin and double rooms (❶) also available, including some en suite. Facilities include resident-only bar, pool table and lounge with DVD and widescreen TV.

Brodies 1 12 High St, Old Town ☎ 0131/556 6770, ⓦ www.brodieshostels.co.uk. Tucked down a typical Old Town close, with four fairly straightforward dorms sleeping up to a dozen and limited communal areas. It's smaller than many hostels, and a little bit more homely as a result.

Brodies 2 93 High St, Royal Mile ☎ 0131/556 2223, ⓦ www.brodieshostels.co.uk. The mellow atmosphere at this smart new hostel is even more marked than at its sister property across the road. Smaller dorms (mostly six- or eight-bed) as well as doubles (❷).

Bruntsfield SYHA Hostel 7 Bruntsfield Crescent, Bruntsfield ☎ 0870/004 1114, ⓦ www.syha.org.uk.

Overlooking the leafy Bruntsfield Links a mile south of Princes Street, with accommodation mostly in dorms sleeping six to ten – some of these are partially screened-off "pod rooms" which offer a bit more privacy and security than standard dorms. Non-smoking, and Internet access available.

Castle Rock Hostel 15 Johnston Terrace, Old Town ☎ 0131/225 9666, ⓦ www.scotlands-top -hostels.com. Tucked below the Castle ramparts, with 200 or so beds arranged in large, bright dorms, as well as triple and quad rooms and some doubles (❷). The communal areas include a games room with pool and table tennis.

Cowgate Tourist Hostel 96 Cowgate, Old Town ☎ 0131/226 2153, ⓦ www.hostelsaccommodation .com. Basic but central accommodation in small three-, four- and five-bedroom apartments with kitchens, in the heart of the Old Town.

Edinburgh Backpackers Hostel 65 Cockburn St, Old Town ☎ 0131/220 2200, ⓦ www.hoppo .com. Very central, with large but bright dorms and a decent number of doubles (❷) in a tall Old Town building. The communal areas are pretty standard, though there are a bar and café at street level.

Eglinton SYHA Hostel 18 Eglinton Crescent, Haymarket ☎ 0870/004 1116, ⓦ www.syha.org .uk. Situated in a characterful town house west of the centre, and popular amongst groups (communal areas can feel overrun with them) and families. Dorms are large, sleeping up to fourteen and non-smoking. Internet access available. Ten-minute walk to Princes Street or choice of buses from Haymarket.

Globetrotter Inn 46 Marine Drive, Cramond ☎ 0131/336 1030, ⓦ www.globetrotterinns.com.

A big departure from the buzzy city-centre hostels, in a sylvan parkland setting four miles from the centre with lovely views of the Firth of Forth. The 350-plus beds are mostly bunks with privacy curtains and individual reading lights, but there are also doubles (❷). There's access to a gym and sauna, lots of parking and an hourly shuttle service into town, as well as regular buses (#42). Families and kids are not encouraged.
High Street Hostel 8 Blackfriars St, Old Town ☎0131/557 3984, ⊛www.scotlands-top-hostels .com. Lively and popular hostel in an attractive sixteenth-century building just off the Royal Mile. Dorms only, but good communal facilities, which are shared by those staying at the *Royal Mile Backpackers* (see below) just up the road.

Royal Mile Backpackers 105 High St, Old Town ☎0131/557 6120, ⊛www.scotlands-top-hostels .com. Small, friendly hostel popular with longer-term residents, with limited communal areas but shared facilities with the nearby *High Street Hostel*.
St Christopher's Inns 9–13 Market St, Old Town ☎0131/226 1446, ⊛www.st-christophers.co.uk. Huge and a little corporate but very much in the modern hostel style – dorms are of varying size, and have en-suite bathrooms; some with TVs and there are a few double rooms (❸). There's a small communal area but no kitchen; the ground-floor bar serves food, though it's known more for its noisy party atmosphere and screenings of antipodean rugby games. Slightly more expensive than most other hostels.

Campsites

Drummohr Caravan and Camping Park Leven-hall, Musselburgh ☎0131/665 6867, ⊛www .drummohr.org. A large, pleasant site in this coastal satellite town to the east of Edinburgh, with excellent transport connections to the city, including buses #15, #26, #30 and #44. Open March–Oct.
Edinburgh Caravan Club Site Marine Drive, Silverknowes ☎0131/312 6874. Caravan-domi-nated site in a pleasant location close to the shore in the northwestern suburbs, with a handy bus service (#42) into town. Camping May–Sept only.
Mortonhall Camping & Caravan Park 38 Mortonhall Gate, Frogston Rd ☎0131/664 1533, ⊛www.meadowhead.co.uk/mortonhall. A good site, five miles south of the centre, near the Braid Hills; take bus #11 from Princes Street. Closed Feb.

The Old Town

The **OLD TOWN**, although only about a mile long and 300 yards wide, represents the total extent of the twin burghs of Edinburgh and Canongate for the first 650 years of their existence, and its general appearance and character remain indubitably medieval. Containing as it does the majority of the city's most famous tourist sights, it makes by far the best starting point for your explorations.

In addition to the obvious goals of the **Castle** and the **Palace of Holyrood-house** at either end of the famous **Royal Mile**, you'll find scores of historic buildings along the length of the street. Inevitably, much of the Old Town is sacrificed to hard-sell tourism, and can be uncomfortably crowded throughout the summer, especially during the Festival. Yet the area remains at the heart of Edinburgh, with important daily business being conducted in the law courts, city chambers and, of course, the new **Scottish Parliament**, housed in a radical and controversial collection of buildings at the foot of the Royal Mile. It's well worth extending your explorations to the area immediately to the south of the Royal Mile, and in particular to the engaging **National Museum of Scotland**.

The Old Town is compact enough to allow a brief glance at the highlights in the course of a single day, but a thorough visit requires several days. No matter how pressed you are, make sure you spare time for the wonderfully varied scenery and breathtaking vantage points of **Holyrood Park**, an extensive tract of open countryside on the eastern edge of the Old Town that includes Arthur's Seat, the peak of which rises so distinctively in the midst of the city.

The Castle

The history of Edinburgh, and indeed of Scotland, is indissolubly bound up with its **Castle** (daily: April–Oct 9.30am–6pm; Nov–March 9.30am–5pm, last entry 45 min before closing; £9.80; ⓦwww.historic-scotland.gov.uk), which dominates the city from its lofty seat atop an extinct volcanic rock. It requires no great imaginative feat to comprehend the strategic importance that underpinned the Castle's, and hence Edinburgh's, importance in Scotland: from Princes Street, the north side rears high above an almost sheer rock face; the southern side is equally formidable; the western, where the rock rises in terraces, only marginally less so. Would-be attackers, like modern tourists, were forced to approach the Castle from the narrow ridge to the east on which the Royal Mile runs down to Holyrood.

The disparate styles of the fortifications reflect the change in its role from defensive citadel to national monument, and today, as well as attracting more visitors than anywhere else in the country, the Castle is still a military barracks and home to Scotland's Crown Jewels. The oldest surviving part of the complex is from the twelfth century, while the most recent additions date back to the 1920s. Nothing remains from its period as a seat of the Scottish court in the reign of Malcolm Canmore; indeed, having been lost to (and subsequently recaptured from) the English on several occasions, the defences were dismantled by the Scots themselves in 1313, because of the problems that ensued when they were in the wrong hands, and they weren't rebuilt until 1356 when the return of King David II from captivity introduced a modicum of political stability. Thereafter, it gradually developed into Scotland's premier castle, with the dual function of fortress and royal palace. It last saw action in 1745, when Bonnie Prince Charlie's forces, fresh from their victory at Prestonpans, made a half-hearted attempt to storm it. Subsequently, advances in weapon technology diminished the Castle's importance, but under the influence of the Romantic movement it came to be seen as a great national monument.

Though you can easily take in the views and wander round the Castle yourself, you might like to join one of the somewhat overheated **guided tours** (every 15min in high season; 25min; free), with their talk of war, boiling oil and the roar of the cannon. Alternatively, **audio guides** (£3) are available from a booth just inside the gatehouse.

The Esplanade

The Castle is entered via the **Esplanade**, a parade ground laid out in the eighteenth century and enclosed a hundred years later by ornamental walls. For most of the year it acts as a coach park, though in July and August huge grandstands are erected for the Edinburgh Military Tattoo (see p.153), which takes place every night during August, coinciding with the Edinburgh Festival. A shameless and spectacular pageant of swinging kilts and massed pipe bands, the tattoo makes full use of its dramatic setting.

Dotted around the esplanade are several military monuments, including an equestrian **statue of Field Marshal Earl Haig**, the controversial Edinburgh-born commander of the British forces in World War I, whose trench warfare strategy of sending men "over the top" led to previously unimaginable casualties. Entry to the Esplanade is free, and if you don't have time to do the Castle justice, or don't want to pay the pricey entry fee, it does offer a taste of the precipitous location and eye-stretching views. If you are set on looking round the Castle, head straight to the booth located on the esplanade by the gatehouse.

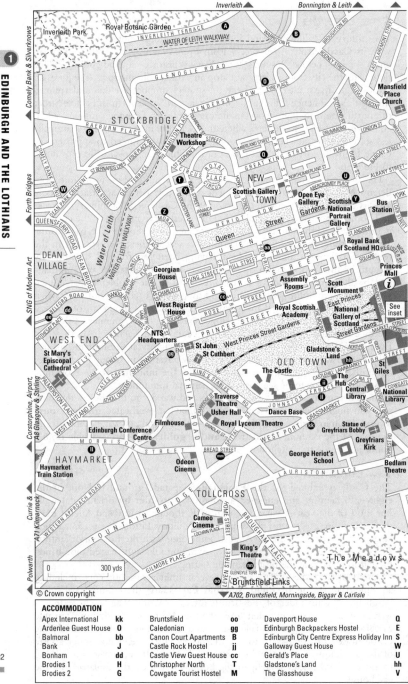

© Crown copyright

0   300 yds

Inverleith   Bonnington & Leith

A702, Bruntsfield, Morningside, Biggar & Carlisle

ACCOMMODATION

Apex International	**kk**	Bruntsfield	**oo**	Davenport House	**Q**
Ardenlee Guest House	**O**	Caledonian	**gg**	Edinburgh Backpackers Hostel	**E**
Balmoral	**bb**	Canon Court Apartments	**B**	Edinburgh City Centre Express Holiday Inn	**S**
Bank	**J**	Castle Rock Hostel	**jj**	Galloway Guest House	**W**
Bonham	**dd**	Castle View Guest House	**cc**	Gerald's Place	**U**
Brodies 1	**H**	Christopher North	**T**	Gladstone's Land	**hh**
Brodies 2	**G**	Cowgate Tourist Hostel	**M**	The Glasshouse	**V**

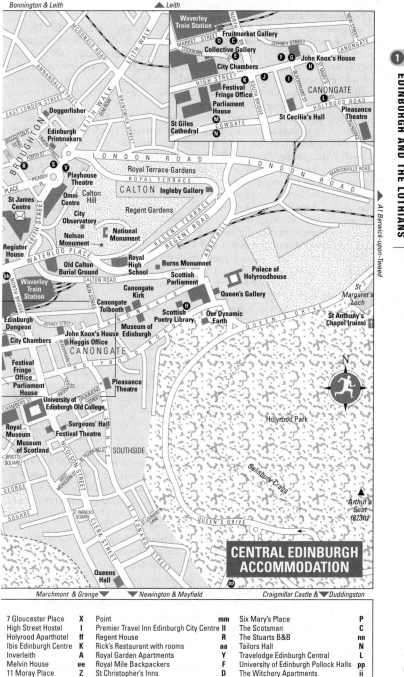

CENTRAL EDINBURGH ACCOMMODATION

7 Gloucester Place	X	Point	mm	Six Mary's Place	P
High Street Hostel	I	Premier Travel Inn Edinburgh City Centre	II	The Scotsman	C
Holyrood Aparthotel	ff	Regent House	R	The Stuarts B&B	nn
Ibis Edinburgh Centre	K	Rick's Restaurant with rooms	aa	Tailors Hall	N
Inverleith	A	Royal Garden Apartments	Y	Travelodge Edinburgh Central	L
Melville House	ee	Royal Mile Backpackers	F	University of Edinburgh Pollock Halls	pp
11 Moray Place	Z	St Christopher's Inns	D	The Witchery Apartments	ii

The lower defences

The **gatehouse** is a Romantic-style addition to the castle of the 1880s, complete with the last drawbridge ever built in Scotland. It was later adorned with appropriately heroic-looking statues of Sir William Wallace and Robert the Bruce. Standing guard by the drawbridge are real-life soldiers, members of the regiment in residence at the Castle; while their presence in full dress uniform is always a hit with camera-toting tourists, it's also a reminder that the Castle is still a working military garrison.

Rearing up behind is the most distinctive and impressive feature of the Castle's silhouette, the sixteenth-century **Half Moon Battery**, which marks the outer limit of the actual defences. Once through the gatehouse, continue uphill along Lower Ward, passing through the **Portcullis Gate**, a handsome Renaissance gateway of the same period as the battery above, marred by the addition of a nineteenth-century upper storey equipped with anachronistic arrow slits rather than gunholes. Beyond this the wide main path is known as Middle Ward, with the six-gun **Argyle Battery** to the right. The battery was built in the eighteenth century by Major-General Wade, whose network of military roads and bridges still forms an essential part of the transport infrastructure of the Highlands. Further west on **Mill's Mount Battery**, a well-known Edinburgh ritual takes place – the daily firing of the **one o'clock gun**. Originally designed for the benefit of ships in the Firth of Forth, these days it's an enjoyable ceremony for visitors to watch and a useful time signal for city-centre office workers. There's an interesting little exhibition about the history of the firing of the gun in a room immediately below Mill's Mount Battery. Both batteries offer wonderful panoramic views over Princes Street and the New Town to the coastal towns and hills of Fife across the Forth.

National War Museum of Scotland

Located in the old hospital buildings, down a ramp between the café/restaurant immediately behind the one o'clock gun and the Governor's House, the **National War Museum of Scotland** (free), part of the collection of the National Museums of Scotland, is a recently refurbished exhibition covering the last four hundred years of Scottish military history. Scots have been fighting for much longer than that, of course, but the slant of the museum is very definitely towards the soldiers who fought *for* the Union, rather than against it (or against themselves). While the various rooms are packed with uniforms, medals, paintings of heroic actions and plenty of interesting memorabilia, the museum manages to convey a reflective, human tone. Just as delicate is the job of showing no favouritism to any of the Scottish regiments, each of which has strong traditions more forcefully paraded in the various regimental museums found in regions of Scotland – the Royal Scots and the Scots Dragoon Guards, for instance, both have displays in other parts of Edinburgh Castle.

Back on Middle Ward, the **Governor's House** is a 1740s mansion whose harled masonry and crow-stepped gables are archetypal features of vernacular Scottish architecture. It now serves as the officers' mess for members of the garrison, while the governor himself lives in the northern side wing. Behind stands the largest single construction in the Castle complex, the **New Barracks**, built in the 1790s in an austere Neoclassical design. From here a cobbled road then snakes round towards the enclosed citadel at the uppermost point of Castle Rock, entered via **Foog's Gate**.

St Margaret's Chapel

At the eastern end of the citadel, **St Margaret's Chapel** is the oldest surviving building in the Castle, and probably also in Edinburgh itself. Although once believed to have been built by the saint herself, and mooted as the site of her death in 1093, its architectural style suggests that it actually dates from about thirty years later, and was thus probably built by King David I as a memorial to his mother. Used as a powder magazine for three hundred years, this tiny Norman church was rediscovered in 1845 and was eventually rededicated in 1934, after sympathetic restoration. Externally, it is plain and severe, but the interior preserves an elaborate zigzag archway dividing the nave from the sanctuary.

The battlements in front of the chapel offer the best of all the Castle's panoramic views. Here you'll see the famous fifteenth-century siege gun, **Mons Meg**, which could fire a 500-pound stone nearly two miles. A seventeenth-century visitor, the London poet, John Taylor, commented: "It is so great within, that it was told me that a child was once gotten there." In 1754 Mons Meg was taken to the Tower of London, where it stayed till Sir Walter Scott persuaded George IV, on the occasion of his 1822 state visit to Scotland, to return it. The battlements are interrupted by the **Lang Stairs**, which provide an alternative means of access from the Argyle Battery via the side of the Portcullis Gate. Just below the battlements there's a small **cemetery**, the last resting place of the **soldiers' pets**: it is kept in immaculate condition, particularly when contrasted with the dilapidated state of some of the city's public cemeteries. Continuing eastwards, you skirt the top of the Forewall and Half Moon Batteries, passing the 110-foot **Castle Well** en route to **Crown Square**, the highest, most important and secure section of the entire complex.

The Palace

The eastern side of Crown Square is occupied by the **Palace**, a surprisingly unassuming edifice built round an octagonal stair turret heightened in the nineteenth century to bear the Castle's main flagpole. Begun in the 1430s, the

The Stone of Destiny

Legend has it that the **Stone of Destiny** (also called the Stone of Scone) was "Jacob's Pillow", on which he dreamed of the ladder of angels from earth to heaven. Its real history is obscure, but it is known to have been moved from Ireland to Dunadd by missionaries, and thence to Dunstaffnage, from where Kenneth MacAlpine, king of the Dalriada Scots, brought it to the abbey at Scone, near Perth, in 838. There it remained for almost five hundred years, used as a coronation throne on which all kings of Scotland were crowned.

In 1296 an over-eager Edward I stole what he believed to be the Stone and installed it at Westminster Abbey, where, apart from a brief interlude in 1950 when it was removed by Scottish nationalists and hidden in Arbroath for several months, it remained for seven hundred years. All this changed in December 1996 when, after an elaborate ceremony-laden journey from London, the Stone returned to Scotland, in one of the doomed attempts by the Conservative government to convince the Scottish people that the Union was a good thing. Much to the annoyance of the people of Perth and the curators of Scone Palace (see p.471), and to the general indifference of the people of Scotland, the Stone was placed in Edinburgh Castle.

However, speculation surrounds the authenticity of the Stone, for the original is said to have been intricately carved, while the one seen today is a plain block of sandstone. Many believe that the canny monks at Scone palmed this off onto the English king (some say that it's nothing more sacred than the cover for a medieval septic tank), and that the real Stone of Destiny lies hidden in an underground chamber, its whereabouts a mystery to all but the chosen few.

Palace owes its Renaissance appearance to King James IV, though it was remodelled for Mary, Queen of Scots and her consort Henry, Lord Darnley, whose entwined initials (MAH), together with the date 1566, can be seen above one of the doorways. This gives access to a few historic rooms, the most interesting of which is the tiny panelled bedchamber at the extreme southeastern corner, where Mary gave birth to James VI.

Another section of the Palace has recently been refurbished with a detailed audiovisual presentation on the nation's **Crown Jewels**, properly known as the **Honours of Scotland**; the originals of which are housed in the Crown Room at the very end of the display. Though you might be put off by the slow-moving, claustrophobic queues that shuffle past the displays, they still serve as one of the most potent images of Scotland's nationhood. They were last used for the Scottish-only coronation of Charles II in 1651, before being locked away in a chest following the Union of 1707. For over a century they were out of sight and eventually presumed lost, before being rediscovered in 1818 as a result of a search initiated by Sir Walter Scott.

Of the three pieces comprising the Honours, the oldest is the **sceptre**, which bears statuettes of the Virgin and Child, St James and St Andrew, rounded off by a polished globe of rock crystal: it was given to James IV in 1494 by Pope Alexander VI, and refashioned by Scottish craftsmen for James V. Even finer is the **sword**, a swaggering Italian High Renaissance masterpiece by the silver-smith Domenico da Sutri, presented to James IV by the great artistic patron Pope Julius II. Both the hilt and the scabbard are engraved with Julius's personal emblem, showing the oak tree and its acorns, the symbols of the Risen Christ, together with dolphins, symbols of the Church. The jewel-encrusted **crown**, made for James V by the Scottish goldsmith James Mosman, incorporates the gold circlet worn by Robert the Bruce and is surmounted by an enamelled orb and cross.

The glass case containing the Honours has recently been rearranged to create space for its newest addition: the **Stone of Destiny** (see box on p.95). This remarkably plain object now lies incongruously next to the opulent Crown Jewels.

Around Crown Square

The south side of **Crown Square** is occupied by the **Great Hall**, built under James IV as a venue for banquets and other ceremonial occasions. Until 1639 the meeting place of the Scottish Parliament, it later underwent the indignity of conversion and subdivision, first into a barracks, then a hospital. During this time, its hammer beam roof – the earliest of three in the Old Town – was hidden from view. It was restored towards the end of the nineteenth century, when the hall was decked out in the full-blown Romantic manner.

In 1755, the castle church of St Mary on the north side of the square was replaced by a barracks, which in turn was skilfully converted into the quietly reverential **Scottish National War Memorial** in honour of the 150,000 Scots who fell in World War I.

The rest of the complex

From Crown Square, you can descend to the **Vaults**, a series of cavernous chambers erected by order of James IV to provide level surface for the buildings above. They were later used as a prison for captured foreign nationals, who bequeathed a rich legacy of graffiti. Directly opposite the entrance to the Vaults is the **Military Prison**, built in 1842, when the design and function of jails was a major topic of public debate. The cells, though designed for solitary confinement, are less forbidding than might be expected.

△ The Royal Mile

The Royal Mile

The **Royal Mile**, the name given to the ridge linking the Castle with Holyrood, was described by Daniel Defoe, in 1724, as "the largest, longest and finest street

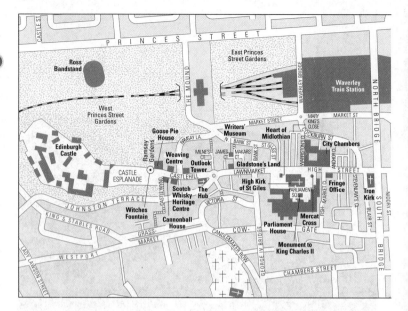

for Buildings and Number of Inhabitants, not in Bretain only, but in the World". Almost exactly a mile in length, it is divided into four separate streets – Castlehill, Lawnmarket, High Street and Canongate. From these, branching out in a herringbone pattern, are a series of tightly packed closes and steep lanes entered via archways known as "pends". After the construction of the New Town, in the eighteenth and nineteenth century much of the housing along the Royal Mile degenerated into a notorious slum, but has since shaken off that reputation, becoming once again a highly desirable place to live. Although marred somewhat by rather too many tacky tourist shops and the odd misjudged new development, it is still among the most evocative parts of the city, and one that particularly rewards detailed exploration.

Castlehill

The narrow uppermost stretch of the Royal Mile is known as **Castlehill**. The first building on the northern side of the street as you leave the Castle esplanade is the former reservoir for the Old Town, which has been converted into the **Edinburgh Old Town Weaving Centre** (daily: May–Oct 9am–6.30pm; Nov–April 9am–5.30pm). Very much a commercial enterprise, the centre contains various large shops selling kilts, rugs and other tartan adornments while noisy looms rhythmically churn the stuff out on the floors below.

On the corner of the wall of the Weaving Centre facing the Castle, a pretty Art Nouveau **Witches' Fountain** commemorates the three hundred or more women burnt at the spot on charges of sorcery, the last of whom died in 1722. Rising up behind is **Ramsay Gardens**, surely some of the most picturesque city-centre flats in the world. The oldest part is the octagonal Goose Pie House, home of the eighteenth-century poet Allan Ramsay, author of *The Gentle Shepherd* and father of the better-known portrait painter of the same name, while the rest dates from the 1890s and was the brainchild of Patrick Geddes, a pioneer of

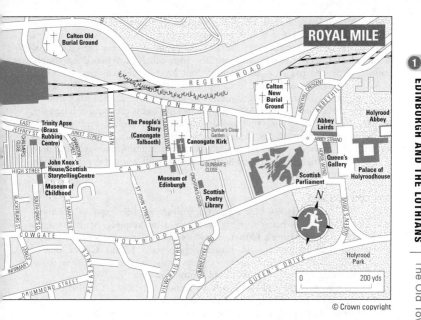

© Crown copyright

the modern town-planning movement, who created these desirable apartments in an attempt to regenerate the Old Town.

Opposite the Weaving Centre, the **Scotch Whisky Heritage Centre** (daily: June–Sept 9.30am–7pm; Oct–May 10am–6pm; last tour 90min before closing; £8.50; ⓦ www.whisky-heritage.co.uk) mimics the kind of tours offered at distilleries in the Highlands, and while it can't match the authenticity of the real thing, the centre does offer a thorough introduction to the "water of life" (*uisge beatha* in Gaelic). Tours start off with a dram (measure) of whisky, then move through a scale model of a distillery and an entertaining tutorial on the specialized art of blending, and conclude with a gimmicky ride in a moving "barrel" car through a series of uninspiring historical tableaux. On the ground floor, a well-stocked shop gives an idea of the sheer range and diversity of the drink, while downstairs there's a pleasant whisky bar and restaurant, *Amber* (see p.131).

Across the street, housed in the domed black-and-white turret atop the **Outlook Tower** (daily: April–Oct 9.30am–6pm, July & Aug open till 7.30pm; Nov–March 10am–5pm; £6.50; ⓦ www.camera-obscura.co.uk), Edinburgh's camera obscura has been a tourist attraction since 1853, providing an intriguing bird's-eye view of a city going about its business. The "camera" consists of a small darkened room with a white wooden table onto which a periscope reflects live images of prominent buildings and folk walking on the streets below.

The imposing black church at the foot of Castlehill is **The Hub** (Tues–Sat 9.30am–11pm, Sun & Mon 9.30am–6pm; ☏0131/473 2010, ⓦ www.eif.co.uk /thehub), also known as "Edinburgh's Festival Centre". Although the Festival only takes place for three weeks every August and early September, The Hub is open year-round, providing performance, rehearsal and exhibition space, a ticket centre and a café. The building itself was constructed in 1845 to designs by James Gillespie Graham and Augustus Pugin, one of the co-architects of the Houses of Parliament in London – a connection obvious from the superb neo-Gothic detailing and the sheer presence of the building, whose spire is the highest in Edinburgh. It was built as an Assembly Hall for the Church of Scotland, and became a parish church, the Tolbooth Kirk, when the assembly moved across the road. On the ground-floor level is the *Hub Café* (Tues–Sat 9.30am–11pm, Sun & Mon 9.30am–6pm), which serves drinks, coffees and a small selection of tasty snacks and meals in a vivid yellow interior space and on the large terrace area outside. Also worth checking out is the main hall upstairs, where the original neo-Gothic woodwork and high-vaulted ceiling is enlivened with a fabulous fabric design in Rastafarian colours. Permanent works of art have been incorporated into the centre, including over two hundred delightful foot-high sculptures by Scottish sculptor Jill Watson, depicting Festival performers and audiences.

Lawnmarket

Below the Hub, the Royal Mile opens out into the broader expanse of **Lawnmarket**, which, as its name suggests, was once a marketplace. At its northern end is the entry to **Milne's Court**, whose excellently restored tenements now serve as student residences, and immediately beyond, **James Court**, one of Edinburgh's most fashionable addresses prior to the advent of the New Town, whose previous residents include David Hume and James Boswell.

Back on Lawnmarket itself, **Gladstone's Land** (daily: April–Oct 10am–5pm, July–Aug 10am–7pm; NTS; £5) is the Royal Mile's best surviving example of a typical seventeenth-century tenement. The tall, narrow building – not unlike a canalside house in Amsterdam – would have been home to various families living in cramped conditions: the well-to-do Gledstanes, who built it in 1620, are thought to have occupied the third floor. The National Trust for Scotland has carefully restored the rooms, filling them with period furnishings and fittings; in each a prim guide is on hand to answer questions and pass out a sheet detailing what's on show. The arcaded and wooden-fronted ground floor is home to a reconstructed cloth shop; pass through this and you encounter a warren of tight little staircases, tiny rooms, creaking floorboards and peek-hole windows. The finest room, on the first floor immediately above the arcade, has a marvellous painted ceiling, some fine old dark furniture and an array of attractive rugs and Dutch paintings. The upper floors contain apartments which are rented to visitors (see p.88).

A few paces further on, steps lead down to Lady Stair's Close, in which stands the **Writers' Museum** (Mon–Sat 10am–5pm; also Sun noon–5pm during the Festival; free; @ www.cac.org.uk), housed in Lady Stair's House – a Victorian embellishment of a seventeenth-century residence set to one side of an open courtyard. Dedicated to Scotland's three greatest literary lions, Sir Walter Scott, Robert Louis Stevenson and Robert Burns, the museum has a slightly lacklustre collection of portraits, manuscripts and showcases filled with odd knick-knacks and relics associated with the writers – Scott's walking stick and a plastercast of Burns's skull among them. The house itself holds as much interest as the exhibits, its tight, winding stairs and poky, wood-panelled rooms offering a flavour of the medieval Old Town. Continuing the literary theme, the courtyard outside, known as the Makars' Court after the Scots word for the "maker" of poetry or prose, has a series of paving stones inscribed with quotations from Scotland's most famous writers and poets.

On the south side of Lawnmarket is **Brodie's Close**, named after the father of one of Edinburgh's most morbid characters, Deacon William Brodie, burglar by night and apparent pillar of society by day. Following his eventual capture, he managed to escape to Holland, but was betrayed, brought back to Edinburgh and hanged in 1788 on gallows of his own design. His ruse of trying to cheat death by secretly wearing an iron collar under his shirt failed. You can visit the popular *Deacon Brodie's Tavern* on the corner of the Lawnmarket and Bank Street and ruminate over a beer on the connections between Brodie, Robert Louis Stevenson's similarly themed tale *Dr Jekyll and Mr Hyde* and the various split personalities of Edinburgh itself, not least its Old Town and New Town.

High Street and the High Kirk of St Giles

Across the junction with George IV Bridge is the third section of the Royal Mile, known as the **High Street**, which occupies two blocks either side of the intersection between North Bridge and South Bridge. The dominant building of the southern side of the street is the **Kirk of St Giles** (May–Sept Mon–Fri 9am–7pm, Sat 9am–5pm, Sun 1–5pm; Oct–April Mon–Sat 9am–5pm, Sun 1–5pm; free; ⓦwww.stgilescathedral.org.uk), the original sole parish church of medieval Edinburgh, from where John Knox (see box on p.104) launched and directed the Scottish Reformation. St Giles is often referred to as a cathedral, although it has only been the seat of a bishop on two brief and unhappy occasions in the seventeenth century. According to one of the city's best-known legends, the attempt in 1637 to introduce the English prayer book, and thus episcopal government, so incensed a humble stallholder named Jenny Geddes that she hurled her stool at the preacher, prompting the rest of the congregation to chase the offending clergy out of the building. A tablet in the north aisle marks the spot from where she let rip.

△ High Kirk of St Giles

The location and historical significance of St Giles mean that it is often used for high-profile religious services, such as when the Queen is in town or at the opening of Parliament, though in fact it is strictly still an ordinary parish church with a regular congregation. The resplendent **crown spire** of the kirk is formed from eight flying buttresses and dates back to 1485, while **inside**, the four massive piers supporting the tower were part of a Norman church built here around 1120. In the nineteenth century, St Giles was adorned with a whole series of funerary monuments on the model of London's Westminster Abbey; around the same time it acquired several attractive Pre-Raphaelite stained-glass windows designed by Edward Burne-Jones and William Morris. A more recent addition was the great **west window**, whose dedication to Robbie Burns in 1985 caused enormous controversy – as a hardened drinker and womanizer, the national bard was far from being an upholder of accepted Presbyterian values. Look out, also, for an elegant bronze relief of Robert Louis Stevenson on the south side of the church.

At the southeastern corner of St Giles, the **Thistle Chapel** was built by Sir Robert Lorimer in 1911 as the private chapel of the sixteen knights of the Most Noble Order of the Thistle, the highest chivalric order in Scotland. Self-consciously derivative of St George's Chapel in Windsor, it's an exquisite piece of craftsmanship, with an elaborate ribbed vault, huge drooping bosses and extravagantly ornate stalls showing off Lorimer's bold Arts and Crafts styling.

Parliament Square

St Giles is surrounded on three sides by **Parliament Square**, which itself is dominated by the continuous Neoclassical facades of the **Law Courts**, originally planned by Robert Adam (1728–92), one of four brothers in a family of architects (their father William Adam designed Hopetoun House; see p.173) whose work helped imbue the New Town with much of its grace and elegance. Because of a shortage of funds and consequent delays, the present exteriors were built to designs by Robert Reid (1776–1856), the designer of the northern part of New Town, who faithfully quoted from Adam's architectural vocabulary without matching his flair. Reid's elevated Ionic columns and Classical statuary are typical of Edinburgh's grand Georgian style, but in fact the location is really too cramped for such flourishes to work effectively. On the west side of the square is William Stark's flamboyant **Signet Library** (ⓦwww.signetlibrary .co.uk), with one of the most beautiful interiors in Edinburgh, its sumptuous colonnaded hall a perfect embodiment of the ideals of the Age of Reason. It can only be seen on very occasional open days.

Around the corner, facing the southern side of St Giles, is **Parliament House**, built in the 1630s for the Scottish Parliament, a role it maintained until the Union. After the move to Westminster in 1707, Parliament House was incorporated into the law courts, and its main feature, the impressive 122-foot long main hall, today acts as a grandiose lobby for the courtrooms beyond. As the courts are open to the public, it's possible to get inside to look at the hall (Mon–Fri 9am–5pm; free), with its extravagant hammer beam roof and delicately carved stone corbels. In the far corner a small exhibition details the history of the building and courts, but it's more fun simply to watch everyday business going on in the hall, with solicitors and bewigged advocates in hushed conferrals, often following the time-honoured tradition of pacing up and down to prevent their conversation being overheard. Most of the court rooms have public galleries, which you can sit in if you're interested – ask one of the attendants in the lobby to point you in the right direction.

Outside on the square, an imposing equestrian **monument to King Charles II** depicts him in fetching Roman garb. Back on the High Street, between the entrance to St Giles and a bloated memorial to the fifth Duke of Buccleuch, the pattern set in the cobblestones is known as the **Heart of Midlothian**, a nickname for the Edinburgh Tolbooth, which stood on this spot and was regarded as the heart of the city. The prison attached to the Tolbooth was immortalized in Scott's novel of the same name, and you may still see locals spitting on the cobblestone heart, a continuation of the tradition of spitting on the door of the prison to ward off the evil contained therein. At the other end of St Giles, public proclamations (such as the announcement of the dissolution of parliament) have traditionally been read from the **Mercat Cross**. The present structure, adorned with coats of arms and topped by a sculpture of a unicorn, looks venerable enough, but most of it is little more than a hundred years old, a gift to the city from nineteenth-century prime minister William Ewart Gladstone.

Upper High Street

On the opposite side of the Royal Mile from Parliament Square, the first building after the intersection of George IV Bridge and Bank Street is the High Court of Justiciary, Scotland's highest criminal court, outside which is a statue of **David Hume**, the philosopher and one of Edinburgh's greatest sons, who looks decidedly wan and chilly dressed in nothing but a Roman toga. A little further on, opposite the Mercat Cross, the U-shaped **City Chambers** were designed by John Adam, brother of Robert, as the Royal Exchange. Local traders never warmed to the exchange, however, so the town council established its headquarters there instead. Beneath the City Chambers lies **Mary King's Close**, one of Edinburgh's most unusual attractions. When work on the chambers began in 1753, the tops of the existing houses on the site were simply sliced through at the level of the High Street and the new building constructed on top of them. Because the tenements had been built on a steep hillside, this process left parts of the houses together with the old streets (or closes) which ran alongside them intact but entirely enclosed among the basement and cellars of the City Chambers. You can visit this rather spooky subterranean "lost city" on **tours** led by costumed actors (daily: every 20min April–Oct 10am–9pm; Nov–March 10am–4pm; 1hr; £7.25; ⓦ www.realmarykingsclose.com), who take you round the cold, dark stone shells of the houses where various scenes from the Close's history have been recreated. As you'd expect blood, plague, pestilence and ghostly apparitions are to the fore, though there is an acknowledgement of the more prosaic side of medieval life in the archeological evidence of an urban cow byre. The tour ends with a stroll up the remarkably well-preserved Mary King's Close itself. A little further down the High Street is **Anchor Close**, site of the printing works of William Smellie, who published the first ever edition of the *Encyclopaedia Britannica* there in 1768.

Across the road you'll find the seventeenth-century **Tron Kirk**, a parish church until 1952. It was then closed for forty years, during which time excavations revealed sections of another old close, Marlin's Wynd. Various ambitious plans for the building are regularly mooted, but for the moment the building houses the **Old Town Information Centre** (daily; 10am–5pm, open till 7pm in summer), where you can peruse information boards on the buildings of the Old Town and look down from raised walkways on the Marlin's Wynd excavations.

Lower High Street

Beyond the intersection of North Bridge and South Bridge back on the northern side of High Street is **Paisley Close**, above whose entrance is a bust of

John Knox

The Protestant reformer **John Knox** has been alternately credited with, or blamed for, the distinctive national culture that emerged from the Calvinist Reformation, which has cast its shadow over Scottish history and the Scottish character right up to the present.

Little is known about Knox's early years: he was born between 1505 and 1514 in East Lothian, and trained for the priesthood at St Andrews University. Ordained in 1540, Knox then served as a private tutor, in league with Scotland's first significant Protestant leader, **George Wishart**. After Wishart was burnt at the stake for heresy in 1546, Knox became involved with the group who had carried out the revenge murder of the Scottish primate, Cardinal David Beaton, subsequently taking over his castle in St Andrews. The following year this was captured by the French, and Knox was carted off to work as a galley slave.

He was freed in 1548, as a result of the intervention of the English, who invited him to play an evangelizing role in the spread of their own Reformation. Following successful ministries in Berwick-upon-Tweed and Newcastle upon Tyne, Knox turned down the bishopric of Rochester, less from an intrinsic opposition to episcopacy than from a wish to avoid becoming embroiled in the turmoil he guessed would ensue if the Catholic Mary Tudor acceded to the English throne. When this duly happened in 1553, Knox fled to the Continent, ending up as minister to the English-speaking community in Geneva, which was then in the grip of the theocratic government of the Frenchman **Jean Calvin**.

In exile, Knox was much preoccupied with the question of the influence wielded by political rulers, believing that the future of the Reformation in Europe was at risk because of the opposition of a few powerful sovereigns. This prompted him to write his infamous treatise, *The First Blast of the Trumpet Against the Monstrous Regiment of Women*, a specific attack on the three Catholic women then ruling Scotland, England and France, which has made his name synonymous with misogyny ever since.

When Knox was allowed to return to Scotland in 1555, he took over as spiritual leader of the Reformation, becoming minister of St Giles in Edinburgh, where he established a reputation as a charismatic preacher. However, the establishment of Protestantism as the official religion of Scotland in 1560 was dependent on the forging of an alliance with Elizabeth I, which Knox himself rigorously championed: the swift deployment of English troops against the French garrison in Edinburgh dealt a fatal blow to Franco–Spanish hopes of re-establishing Catholicism in both Scotland and England. Although the return of Mary, Queen of Scots the following year placed a Catholic monarch on the Scottish throne, Knox was reputedly always able to retain the upper hand in his famous disputes with her.

Before his death in 1572, Knox began mapping out the organization of the Scots Kirk, sweeping away all vestiges of episcopal control and giving lay people a role of unprecedented importance. He also proposed a nationwide education system, to be compulsory for the very young and free for the poor, though lack of funds meant this could not be implemented in full. His final legacy was the posthumously published *History of the Reformation of Religion in the Realm of Scotland*, a justification of his life's work.

For all his considerable influence, Knox was not responsible for many of the features which have created the popular image of Scottish Presbyterianism – and of Knox himself – as austere and joyless. A man of refined cultural tastes, he did not encourage the iconoclasm that destroyed so many of Scotland's churches and works of art: indeed, much of this was carried out by English hands. Nor did he promote unbending Sabbatarianism, an obsessive work ethic or even the inflexible view of the doctrine of predestination favoured by his far more fanatical successors. Ironically, though, by fostering an irrevocable rift in the "Auld Alliance" with France, he did more than anyone else to ensure that Scotland's future was to be linked with that of England.

a youth with the inscription "Heave awa' chaps, I'm no' dead yet", uttered in 1861 by a boy trapped by rubble following the collapse of a tenement in the close, and who was subsequently dug out by rescue workers.

In Chalmers Close, just to the west, **Trinity Apse** is a poignant reminder of the fifteenth-century Holy Trinity Collegiate Church, formerly one of Edinburgh's most outstanding buildings, but demolished in 1848 to make way for an extension to Waverley Station. The stones were carefully numbered and stored on Calton Hill so that it could be reassembled at a later date, but many were pilfered before sufficient funds became available, and only the apse could be reconstructed on this new site. It's now home to a **Brass Rubbing Centre** (Mon–Sat 10am–4.30pm, also Sun noon–5pm during Aug; last rubbing sold 1hr before closing; free; ⓦ www.cac.org.uk), where you can rub your own impressions from Pictish crosses and medieval church brasses from £1.50 upwards.

On the other side of High Street, the noisy **Museum of Childhood** (Mon–Sat 10am–5pm, also June–Aug Sun noon–5pm; free; ⓦ www.cac.org.uk) has an odd history, having been founded in 1955 by a bachelor local councillor who heartily disliked children. In today's digital age the collection of dolls' houses, teddy bears, train sets and marionettes may be regarded as a little dull for some children, although their nostalgic charm often touches a chord with parents.

Across the street and just a little way downhill, jutting out into the street from the main line of buildings, is the fifteenth-century **John Knox's House** (Mon–Sat 10am–6pm, Sun noon–6pm; £3; ⓦ www.scottishstorytellingcentre .co.uk). With its distinctive external staircase, clustered high chimneys and timber projections, the building is a classic representation of the Royal Mile in its medieval heyday. Inside the house is a museum about the building and in particular John Knox (see opposite), the minister who led the Reformation in Scotland and established Calvinist Presbyterianism as the dominant religious force in the country. John Knox's House is linked to the Scottish Storytelling Centre, which is due to reopen in 2006 after a major redevelopment. The complex will include a theatre, café, storytelling garden and indoor storytelling court, with regular performances and events.

Canongate

For over seven hundred years, the district through which the eastern section of the Royal Mile, the **Canongate**, runs, was a burgh in its own right, officially separate from the capital, which was entered through the Netherbow Port. A notorious slum area even into the 1960s, it has been the subject of some of the most ambitious **restoration** programmes in the Old Town, though the lack of harmony between the buildings renovated in different decades can be seen fairly clearly. For such a central district, it's interesting to note that most of the buildings here are residential, and by no means are they all bijou apartments. The most dramatic slice of the redevelopment, however, is in the Holyrood area at its lower end where the new Parliament building has brought a radical contemporary slant to the look and feel of the whole area. As you wander down the Canongate, you might be diverted by one or two of an eclectic range of shops, which include a gallery of historic maps and sea charts, an old-fashioned whisky bottler and a genuine bagpipe maker.

Dominated by a turreted steeple and an odd external box clock, the late sixteenth-century **Canongate Tolbooth** on the north side of the street, has served both as the headquarters of the burgh administration and as a prison. It now houses **The People's Story** (Mon–Sat 10am–5pm, also Sun noon–5pm during Aug; free; ⓦ www.cac.org.uk), which contains a series of display cases, dense information boards and rather old-fashioned tableaux dedicated to the everyday life and work of Edinburgh's population down the centuries. This isn't one of Edinburgh's essential museums, but it does have a down-to-earth reality often missing from places dedicated to high culture or famous historical characters. Next door, **Canongate Kirk** was built in the 1680s to house the congregation expelled from Holyrood Abbey when the latter was commandeered by James VII (James II in England) to serve as the chapel for the Order of the Thistle. The kirk has a modesty rarely seen in churches built in later centuries, with a graceful curved facade, a mixture of arched and round windows and a bow-shaped gable to the rear. The airy interior has an odd light-blue colour scheme, as well as various crests and flags that highlight the kirk's continuing royal and military connections. The surrounding churchyard provides an attractive and tranquil stretch of green in the heart of the Old Town and affords fine views of Calton Hill; it also happens to be one of the city's most exclusive cemeteries – well-known internees include the political economist Adam Smith, Mrs Agnes McLehose (better known as Robert Burns's "Clarinda") and Robert Fergusson, regarded by some as Edinburgh's greatest poet, despite his death at the age of 24. Fergusson's headstone was donated by Burns, a fervent admirer, and a statue has recently been erected on the Royal Mile just outside the gates of the kirk.

Opposite the church, the **Museum of Edinburgh** in Huntly House (Mon–Sat 10am–5pm, also Sun noon–5pm during Aug; free; Ⓦwww.cac .org.uk) is the city's principal collection devoted to local history, though the museum is as interesting for the labyrinthine network of wood-panelled rooms within as for its rather quirky array of artefacts. These do, however, include a number of items of real historical significance, in particular the National Convention, the petition for religious freedom drawn up on a deerskin parchment in 1638, and the original plans for the layout of the New Town drawn by James Craig (see p.117), chosen by the city council after a competition in 1767.

Among the intriguing series of closes and entries on this stretch of Canongate, look out for **Dunbar's Close**, on the north side of the street, which has a beautiful seventeenth-century walled garden tucked in behind the tenements. Opposite this is the entry to Crichton's Close, through which you'll find the **Scottish Poetry Library** (Mon–Fri 11am–6pm, Sat 1pm–5pm; free; Ⓦwww .spl.org.uk), a small island of modern architectural eloquence amid a cacophony of large-scale developments. The building incorporates a section of an old city wall, and the attractive, thoroughly contemporary design harmoniously incorporates brick, oak, glass, Caithness stone and blue ceramic tiles. The library contains Scotland's most comprehensive collection of native poetry, and visitors are free to read the books, periodicals and leaflets found on the shelves, or listen to recordings of poetry in English, Scots and Gaelic. Readings and events are organized throughout the year.

At the very foot of the street, the entrance to the residential **Whitehorse Close** was once the site of the inn from where stagecoaches began the journey to London. Stridently quaint, it drips with the characteristic features of Scottish vernacular architecture: crow-stepped gables, dormer windows, overhanging upper storeys and curving outside stairs.

Holyrood

At the foot of Canongate lies **Holyrood**, for centuries known as Edinburgh's royal quarter, with its ruined thirteenth-century **abbey** and the **Palace of**

Holyroodhouse. In recent years, however, the area has been transformed by the addition of Enric Miralles' dazzling but highly controversial new Scottish Parliament, which was deliberately landscaped to blend in with the cliffs and ridges of Edinburgh's most dramatic natural feature, the nearby **Holyrood Park** and its slumbering peak, Arthur's Seat.

The **legend** of Holyrood goes back to 1128, when King David I, son of Malcolm Canmore and St Margaret, went out hunting one day and was suddenly confronted by a stag who threw him from his horse and seemed ready to gore him. In desperation, the king tried to protect himself by grasping its antlers, but instead found himself holding a crucifix, whereupon the animal ran off. In a dream that night, he heard a voice commanding him to "make a house for Canons devoted to the Cross"; he duly obeyed, naming the abbey Holyrood ("rood" being an alternative name for a cross). A more prosaic explanation is that David, the most pious of all Scotland's monarchs, simply acquired a relic of Christ's Cross and decided to build a suitable home for it.

Holyrood soon became a favoured **royal residence**, its situation in a secluded valley making it far more agreeable than the draughty Castle. At first, monarchs lodged in the abbey's monastic guesthouse, to which a wing for the exclusive use of the court was added during the reign of James II. This was transformed into a full-blown palace for James IV, which in turn was replaced by a much larger building for Charles II, although he never actually lived there. Indeed, it was something of a white elephant until Queen Victoria started travelling to Scotland frequently enough to establish an official residence.

The Palace of Holyroodhouse

In its present form, the **Palace of Holyroodhouse** (daily: April–Oct 9.30am–6pm; Nov–March 9.30am–4.30pm; last admission 1hr before closing; £8.50; ⓦ www.royal.gov.uk) is largely a seventeenth-century creation, planned for Charles II. However, the tower house of the old palace was skilfully incorporated to form the northwestern block, with a virtual mirror image of it erected as a counterbalance at the other end.

Tours of the palace move through a series of royal **reception rooms** featuring some outstanding encrusted plasterwork, each more impressive than the last – an idea Charles II had picked up from his cousin Louis XIV's Versailles – while on the northern side of the internal quadrangle, the **Great Gallery** extends almost the full length of the palace and is dominated by portraits of 96 Scottish kings, painted by Jacob de Wet in 1684 to illustrate the lineage of Stewart royalty: the result is unintentionally hilarious, as it is clear that the artist's imagination was taxed to bursting point by the need to paint so many different facial types without having an inkling as to what the subjects actually looked like. Leading from this into the oldest part of the palace, known as James V's tower, the formal, ceremonial tone gives way to dark medieval history, with a tight spiral staircase leading to the

Admission to Holyroodhouse

Compared with most royal palaces, visitor access to Holyroodhouse is extensive. However, the Queen still makes fairly regular visits and for this reason, the palace is normally closed in mid-May, late June and mid-November, and occasionally at other times if a state function is taking place.

chambers used by Mary, Queen of Scots. These contain various relics, including jewellery, associated with the queen, though the most compelling viewing is a tiny supper room, from where in 1566 Mary's Italian secretary, David Rizzio, was dragged by conspirators, who included her jealous husband, Lord Darnley, to the outer chamber and stabbed 56 times; a brass plaque on the wall points out what are rather optimistically identified as the bloodstains on the wooden floor.

Holyrood Abbey

Immediately adjacent to the palace are the evocative ruins of **Holyrood Abbey** (free access as part of Holyroodhouse tour), some of which date to the thirteenth century. Various invading armies paid little respect to the building over the years, and although it was patched up for Charles I's coronation in 1633 it was gutted in 1688 by an anti-Catholic mob. The roof finally tumbled down in 1768, but the melancholy scene has inspired artists down the years, among them Felix Mendelssohn, who in 1829 wrote: "Everything is in ruins and mouldering . . . I believe I have found the beginning of my Scottish Symphony there today." Adjacent to the abbey are the formal palace gardens, open to visitors during the summer months and offering some pleasant strolls.

The Queen's Gallery

Essentially an adjunct to Holyrood Palace, the **Queen's Gallery** (April–Oct 9.30am–6pm; Nov–March 9.30am–4.30pm; last admission 1hr before closing; £5 or £11 joint ticket with Holyroodhouse; Ⓦ www.royal.gov.uk) is located in the shell of a former church directly between the palace and the parliament. With just two principal viewing rooms, it's a compact space, but has an appealing contemporary style which manages to remain sympathetic to the older elements of the building. It's used to display changing exhibitions from the Royal Collection, a vast array of art treasures held by the Queen on behalf of the British nation. Because the pieces are otherwise exhibited only during the limited openings of Buckingham Palace and Windsor Castle, the exhibitions here tend to draw quite a lot of interest. Recent displays have included a priceless collection of drawings by Leonardo da Vinci and a glittering array of jewellery by Russian goldsmith Carl Fabergé.

The Scottish Parliament

For all its grandeur and size, Holyrood Palace is in danger of being upstaged by the striking buildings which make up the new **Scottish Parliament** (for visiting details, see box on p.110) By far the most controversial public building to be erected in Scotland since World War II, it houses the country's directly elected assembly, which was reintroduced into the British political scene in 1999 – previously, Scotland had no parliament of its own after 1707, when it joined the English assembly at Westminster as part of the Union of the two nations.

Made up of various linked elements rather than one single building, the unique design of the complex was the vision of Catalan architect **Enric Miralles**, whose death in 2000, halfway through the building process, caused more than a few ripples of uncertainty as to whether the famously whimsical designer had in fact set down his final draft. Initial estimates for the cost of the building were tentatively put at £40 million; by the time the Queen cut the ribbon in October 2004, the final bill was in the region of £450 million. A major public inquiry into the overspend blamed costing failures

△ Debating chamber, Scottish Parliament

early in the project and criticized the spendthrift attitude of politicians and civil servants alike, yet the building is still an impressive – if imperfect – testament to the ambition of Miralles and the man who championed him, Scotland's First Minister, Donald Dewar, who also died before the project was completed. Indeed, the building has won over the majority of the general architectural community, scooping numerous prizes including, in 2005, the most prestigious in Britain, the Royal Institute of British Architects (RIBA) Stirling Prize.

Visiting the Scottish Parliament

There's free access into the entrance lobby of the Parliament, entered from Horse Wynd, opposite the palace, where you'll find a small exhibition providing some historical, political and architectural background. If parliament is in session, it's normally possible to watch proceedings in the debating chamber from the public gallery – again, access is free, though you have to get a pass from the front desk in the lobby. To see the rest of the interior properly you'll need to join one of the regular **guided tours** (45min; £3.50; bookings not essential; ☎0131/348 5200), well worth the fee for a more detailed appreciation of the quality and features of the building's design.

There's action in the debating chamber only on "Business days" (Tues–Thurs 9am–7pm when Parliament is sitting), but tours don't tend to be as extensive on these days. On "Non-business days" (Mon & Fri when Parliament is sitting, or Mon–Fri if Parliament is in recess), the doors are open Apr–Oct 10am–6pm, Nov–Mar 10am–4pm, as well as Sat and Sun 10am–4pm throughout the year. For further details see ⓦwww.scottish.parliament.uk.

There are six interlinked structures within the complex, among them **Queensberry House**, which dates back to 1681, now home to the offices of the Presiding Officer, and the rather more modernistic towers housing offices and committee rooms. From the outside the Parliament building can appear cluttered, hemmed in by Holyrood Palace and haphazard tenements, and there's much to be said for taking a walk up the path under Salisbury Crags to get an overview of the site. Miralles had a conviction that "the Parliament sits in the land", which helps explain the leaf or petal-shaped design of the central buildings, as well as the landscaping which ties together the long grass banks of the Parliament's gardens with the wildness of the parkland beyond.

One of the most memorable features of the building is the fanciful motifs and odd architectural signatures running through the design, including the anvil-shaped cladding which clads the exterior and the extraordinary windows of the offices for MSPs (Members of the Scottish Parliament), shaped like the profile of a mountain or a section of the Forth Rail Bridge and said to have been inspired by a monk's contemplative cell. The stark concrete of the new building's interior may not be to all tastes, but several of the staircases and passageways remain evocative of the country's medieval castles, lending a sense of security and solidity in what often feels like a disorienting layout.

While some parts of the design are undoubtedly experimental and over-elaborate, there are moments where grace and boldness convene. One example is the **Garden Lobby**, an airy, bright meeting place in the heart of the campus with a fascinating roof of glass panels forming the shape of an upturned boat.

The main **debating chamber** itself is grand yet intimate and undoubtedly modern, with light flooding in through high windows and a complex network of thick oak beams, lights and microphone wires. The "European-style" layout is a deliberate move away from the confrontational Westminster model, though detractors of the parliament have been quick to point out that while the traditional inter-party insults still fly, the quality of the parliamentarians' rhetoric rarely matches that of their soaring new arena.

Our Dynamic Earth

The Scottish Parliament Building is by no means the only newcomer to this historic area. On the Holyrood Road, beneath a pincushion of white metal struts which make it look like a miniature version of London's Millennium Dome, **Our Dynamic Earth** (April–Oct daily 10am–5pm; July–Aug daily 10am–6pm; Nov–March Wed–Sun 10am–5pm; last admission 1hr 10min before closing; £8.95; ⓦ www.dynamicearth.co.uk), is a hi-tech attraction based on the theme of the wonders of the natural world and aimed at families with kids between 5 and 15. Although James Hutton, the Edinburgh-born "Father of Geology", lived nearby in the eighteenth century, there are few specific links to Edinburgh or Scotland. Inside, you are taken in a "time machine" elevator which whisks you off to the creation of the universe, fifteen billion years ago, which is described using impressive wide-screen video graphics, eerie music and a deep-throated commentary. Subsequent galleries cover the formation of the earth and continents with crashing sound effects and a shaking floor, while the calmer grandeur of glaciers and oceans are explored through magnificent large-screen landscape footage; further on, the polar regions – complete with a real iceberg – and tropical jungles are imaginatively recreated, with interactive computer screens and special effects at every turn. Outside, the dramatic **amphitheatre**, which incorporates the steps leading up to the main entrance, serves as a great venue for outdoor theatre and music performances, most notably during the Festival.

Holyrood Park, Arthur's Seat and Duddingston

Holyrood Park – or Queen's Park – a natural wilderness in the very heart of the modern city, is unquestionably one of Edinburgh's greatest assets. Packed into an area no more than five miles in diameter is an amazing variety of landscapes – hills, crags, moorland, marshes, glens, lochs and fields – representing something of a microcosm of Scotland's scenery. While old photographs of the park show crops growing and sheep grazing, it's now most heavily used by walkers, joggers, cyclists and other outdoor enthusiasts. A single tarred road, the **Queen's Drive**, loops through the park, enabling many of its features to be seen by car – however you need to get out and stroll around to appreciate it fully. You can pick up a map of suggested walks, as well as weekly ranger-led walks, from the Royal Parks Constabulary caravan in the car park situated between the palace and Salisbury Crags.

Two of the most rewarding walks begin from this point: one, along a pathway nicknamed the "Radical Road", traverses the ridge immediately below the **Salisbury Crags**, one of the main features of the Edinburgh skyline. This is arguably a finer walk than the sharper climb to the top of Arthur's Seat: note that climbing is not allowed on the crags, and that there's no continuous path along the top; any exploration here is dangerous, particularly in wet, windy or misty conditions. A better looped walk of about an hour's duration from Holyrood is to follow the "Volunteer's Walk" up the glen behind the Crags, then back along the Radical Road.

The usual starting point for the ascent of **Arthur's Seat**, which at 823ft above sea level easily towers over all of Edinburgh's numerous high points, is Dunsapie Loch, reached by following the tarred Queen's Drive in a clockwise direction from the palace gates. Part of a volcano which last saw action 350 million years ago, its connections to the legendary Celtic king are fairly sketchy: the name is likely to be a corruption of the Gaelic *Ard-na-said*, or "height of arrows". From Dunsapie Loch it's a twenty-minute climb up grassy slopes to the rocky summit. On a clear day, the views might just stretch to the English border and the Atlantic Ocean; more realistically, the landmarks which dominate are Fife, a few Highland peaks and, of course, Edinburgh laid out on all sides.

Queen's Drive continues round beneath the summit to meet itself again at a roundabout near the southern point of the Salisbury Crags. At a second roundabout the first exit leads out of the park past **Duddingston Loch**, a bird sanctuary (free access) with swans, herons and grebes often seen around its reedy fringes. Perched above the loch, just outside the park boundary, Duddingston Kirk dates back in part to the twelfth century and lies at the heart of **Duddingston Village**, an unspoilt corner of the city with cobbled lanes, cute cottages and, inevitably, high price tags. The *Sheep Heid Inn* here (see p.143) is one of Edinburgh's oldest pubs and a great waypoint if you're exploring the park; out at the back of the pub there's a traditional skittle alley, still very much in working order.

Cowgate and the Grassmarket

At the bottom of the valley immediately south of the Royal Mile, and following a roughly parallel course from the Lawnmarket to St Mary's Street, is the **Cowgate**. One of Edinburgh's oldest surviving streets, it was also formerly one of the city's most prestigious addresses. However, the construction of the great **viaducts** of George IV Bridge and South Bridge entombed it below street level, condemning it to decay and neglect and leading the nineteenth-century writer, Alexander Smith, to declare: "the condition of the inhabitants is as little known to respectable Edinburgh as are the habits of moles, earthworms, and the mining population." In the last decade or so the Cowgate has experienced something of a revival, with various nightclubs and Festival venues establishing themselves, though few tourists venture here and the contrast with the neighbouring Royal Mile remains stark.

The Grassmarket

At the western end of the Cowgate is an open, partly cobbled area girdled by tall tenements known as the **Grassmarket**, which was used as the city's cattle market from 1477 to 1911. Despite the height of many of the surrounding buildings, it offers an unexpected view up to the precipitous walls of the Castle and, come springtime, it's sunny enough for cafés to put tables and chairs along the pavement. Such continental aspirations are a bit misleading, however, as the Grassmarket is best remembered as the location of Edinburgh's public gallows – the spot is marked by a tiny garden. It was also the scene of the city's best-known civic uprising, in 1736, when the Captain of the Town Guard, John Porteous, was dragged from the Tolbooth and lynched by a mob upset that he had escaped punishment after ordering the Guard to shoot into a potentially restless execution crowd; nine citizens were killed. The notorious bodysnatching duo William Burke and William Hare had their lair in a now-vanished close just off the western end of the Grassmarket, and for a long time before its relatively recent gentrification there was a seamy edge to the place, with brothels, drinking dens and shelters for down-and-outs. Tucked away in the northwest corner is the award-winning modern architecture of **Dance Base** (℡0131/225 5525, @www.dancebase.co.uk), Scotland's National Centre for Dance, which holds classes, workshops and shows. Elsewhere, the Grassmarket's row of pubs has become a focus for many of the stag and hen parties which descend on Edinburgh, and there's also a series of interesting shops, in particular the string of offbeat, independent boutiques on curving **Victoria Street**, an unusual two-tier thoroughfare, with arcaded shops below and a pedestrian terrace above. This sweeps up to **George IV Bridge** and the **National Library of Scotland**, a looming, windowless facade adorned with allegorical figures by Scottish sculptor Hew Lorimer. This is Scotland's largest library and one of the UK's copyright libraries (it holds a copy of every book published in the country), and you have to apply for a reader's ticket to gain access to the collection. However, there is an interesting and well-researched small exhibition on the subject of books, printing and the written word mounted in a side gallery on the ground floor (usually Mon–Sat 10am–5pm, Sun 2–5pm, later during the Festival; free; ⓦ www.nls.uk).

Greyfriars and around

The **statue of Greyfriars Bobby** at the southwestern corner of **George IV Bridge** must rank as Edinburgh's most sentimental tourist attraction. Bobby was a Skye terrier acquired as a working dog by a police constable named John Gray. When Gray died in 1858, Bobby was found a few days later sitting on his grave, a vigil he maintained until his death fourteen years later. In the process, he became an Edinburgh celebrity, fed and cared for by locals who gave him a special collar to prevent him being impounded as a stray. The statue was modelled from life and erected soon after his death. Bobby's legendary dedication easily lent itself to children's books and was eventually picked up by Disney, whose 1960 feature film hammed up the story and ensured that streams of tourists have paid their respects ever since.

The grave Bobby mourned over is in the **Greyfriars Kirkyard**, which has a fine collection of seventeenth-century gravestones and mausoleums, including one to the Adam family of architects. The kirkyard is visited regularly by ghost tours (see p.81) and was known for grave-robbing long before Burke and Hare became the city's most notorious exponents of the crime. More significantly, the kirkyard was the setting, in 1638, for the signing of the National Covenant, a dramatic act of defiance by the Presbyterian Scots against the attempts of Charles I to impose an episcopal form of worship on the country. In an undemocratic age, thousands of townsfolk as well as important nobles signed the original at Greyfriars; copies were then made and sent around the country with some 300,000 names being added.

Greyfriars Kirk itself was built in 1620 on land which had belonged to a Franciscan convent, though little of the original late-Gothic style building remains. A fire in the mid-nineteenth century led to significant rebuilding and the installation of the first organ in a Presbyterian church in Scotland; today's magnificent instrument, by Peter Collins, arrived in 1990.

At the western end of Greyfriars Kirkyard is one of the most significant surviving portions of the **Flodden Wall**, the city fortifications erected in the wake of Scotland's disastrous military defeat of 1513. When open, the gateway beyond offers a short-cut to **George Heriot's Hospital**, otherwise approached from Lauriston Place to the south. The impressive four-turreted building, often mistaken for Holyrood Palace, is now one of Edinburgh's most prestigious fee-paying schools. Founded as a home for poor boys by "Jinglin' Geordie" Heriot, James VI's goldsmith, its array of towers, turrets, chimneys, carved doorways and traceried windows is one of the finest achievements of the seventeenth-century Scottish Renaissance. While you can't go inside, it's possible to enter the grounds during school holidays and take a stroll around the outside of the building and the interior quadrangle to admire the architectural finery from up close.

National Museum of Scotland

Immediately opposite Greyfriars Bobby, on the south side of Chambers Street, stands the striking honey-coloured sandstone **National Museum of Scotland**

(Mon–Sat 10am–5pm, Tues 10am–8pm, Sun noon–5pm; free; ⓦwww.nms .ac.uk). Scotland's premier museum displays many of the nation's most important historical artefacts as a means of telling the nation's history from earliest man to the present day. Custom-built in the 1990s, the National's modern lines and imaginatively designed interior offer a fresh – but still respectful – perspective on the nation's story and its historic treasures.

The most obvious feature of the exterior is the cylindrical entrance tower, which breaks up the angular, modern lines of the building and deliberately echoes the shape of the Half Moon Battery of Edinburgh Castle. The collection is generally, though not strictly, laid out in chronological order over seven different levels. The labyrinthine feel of the rooms and stairways is a little disorienting at first, though the unexpected views of different parts of the museum above and below are a deliberate effect by the architect to emphasize the interconnected layers of Scotland's history.

The main entrance is at the base of the tower (although it is also possible to enter through the neighbouring Royal Museum; see opposite). The information desk is located just before you get to **Hawthornden Court**, the central atrium of the museum and a useful orientation point; on this level you'll also find the shop and access to the Royal Museum café. The glossy **brochure** on sale (£2.50) is more a photographic souvenir than a guidebook; alternatively, free **guided tours** on different themes take place throughout the day, and **audio headsets** (free) give detailed information on the displays.

Beginnings and Early People

To get to the first section, **Beginnings**, take the lift or stairs from Hawthornden Court down to Level 0. Here, Scotland's story before the arrival of man is presented with audiovisual displays, artistic recreations and a selection of rocks and fossils, including some Lewisian gneiss, the oldest rock in Europe, and "Lizzie" (*Westlothiana lizziae*), the oldest known fossil reptile in the world.

The second section, **Early People**, also on Level 0, covers the period from the arrival of the first people to the end of the first millennium AD. This, in many ways, is the most engrossing section of the entire museum, an eloquent testament to the remarkable craftsmanship, artistry and practicality of Scotland's early people. The best way to approach this section is from the doors of the main lift, where you are confronted by eight giant bronze figures in the distinctive post-industrial style of Edinburgh-born sculptor **Sir Eduardo Paolozzi**. His trademark incorporation of geometric shapes into the human form allows the figures to "wear" different artefacts such as prehistoric bracelets and necklaces in small display compartments. The innovative use of contemporary art is continued with installations by the environmental artist **Andy Goldsworthy**, who shapes natural materials into sinuously beautiful geometrical patterns. Look out for *Hearth*, created from pieces of wood found on the construction site of the new museum, and *Enclosure*, four curved walls of slate roof tiles and four panels of cracked clay. Among the artefacts on display, highlights are the **Trappain treasure** hoard, 20kg of silver plates, cutlery and goblets found buried in East Lothian; the **Cramond Lioness**, a sculpture from a Roman tombstone found recently in the Firth of Forth; and the beautifully detailed gold, silver and amber **Hunterston brooch**, dating from around 700 AD.

The Kingdom of the Scots

The **Kingdom of the Scots** on Level 1 covers the period between Scotland's development as a single independent nation and the Union with England in 1707. Many famous Scots are represented here, including Robert the Bruce,

Mary, Queen of Scots and her son James VI, under whom the crowns of Scotland and England became united in 1603. Star exhibits include the **Monymusk reliquary**, an intricately decorated box said to have carried the remains of St Columba; the **Lewis chessmen**, exquisitely idiosyncratic twelfth-century pieces carved from walrus ivory; and the "**Maiden**", an early form of the guillotine. The section on the Church is of interest not only for the craftsmanship of some of the objects, most notably the silver-gilt **St Fillan's crozier**, but also because just outside the window you can glimpse Greyfriars Kirkyard, where the National Covenant was signed in 1638 (see p.113).

Scotland Transformed

Level 3 shows exhibits under the theme **Scotland Transformed**, covering the century or so following the Union of Parliaments in 1707. This was the period which saw the last of the Highland uprisings under Bonnie Prince Charlie (whose silver travelling canteen is on display), yet also witnessed the expansion of trade links with the Americas and developments in industries such as weaving and iron and steel production. Dominating the floor is a reconstructed steam-driven **Newcomen engine**, which was still being used to pump water from a coal mine in Ayrshire in 1901. Alongside it, in contrast, is part of a thatched, cruck-frame house of the 1720s of a type in which many Scots still lived during this time.

Industry and Empire

Following the early innovations of steam and mechanical engineering, Scotland went on to pioneer many aspects of heavy engineering, with ship and locomotive production to the fore. Largest of the exhibits in **Industry and Empire** on Level 4 is the steam locomotive *Ellesmere*. As well as industrial progress, other fields are covered too, including domestic life, leisure activities and the influence of Scots around the world, both as a result of emigration and through such luminaries as James Watt, Charles Rennie Mackintosh and Robert Louis Stevenson.

The Twentieth Century Gallery

For the **Twentieth Century Gallery** on Level 6, a range of Scots, from schoolchildren to celebrities, were asked to pick a single object to represent the twentieth century. Choices are intriguing, controversial and unexpected, from computers to football strips, cans of Irn Bru to a black Saab convertible. Tony Blair, who went to Fettes school in Edinburgh, chose a guitar, and former Edinburgh "milkie" Sean Connery a milk bottle. The obvious challenge is implicitly made: what would you choose, and why? Other features worth taking in here include a small **cinema** showing black-and-white documentary films about life in Scotland in the 1930s, and the **roof garden**, accessed by a lift. Up here, sweeping views open out to the Firth of Forth, the Pentland hills and across to the Castle and Royal Mile skyline. Other fine views can be enjoyed from the museum's stylish *Tower* restaurant (see p.131).

Royal Museum of Scotland

Interlinked with the National Museum, though also with its own entrance, is the Royal Museum of Scotland (same hours), a dignified Venetian-style palace with a cast-iron interior modelled on that of the former Crystal Palace in London. Intended as Scotland's answer to the museum complex in London's South Kensington, the Royal Museum has been an Edinburgh institution for over one hundred years and is a wonderful example of Victorian Britain's fascination with antiquities and natural history. Its exhibits are extraordinarily eclectic, from butterfly collections to colonial loot from around the world, and range through many different aspects of science, history, design and nature.

The wonderfully airy **Great Hall**, framed in cast iron, holds sculpture from Classical Greece and Rome alongside Buddhas from Japan, a totem pole from British Columbia and the bizarre Millennium Clock, a ten-metre tall, Heath-Robinson-style contraption which clicks and whirls into motion at 11am, noon, 2pm and 4pm. Rooms leading off from here hold collections of stuffed animals and birds, including the full skeleton of a blue whale. The more specialized collections on the upper floors include Egyptian mummies, ceramics from ancient Greece to the present day and a splendid selection of European decorative art.

The University of Edinburgh and around

Immediately alongside the Royal Museum is the earliest surviving part of the **University of Edinburgh**, variously referred to as Old College or Old Quad, although nowadays it houses only a few university departments; the main campus colonizes the streets and squares to the south. Founded as the "Tounis College" in 1583 by James VI (later James I of England), the university is now the largest in Scotland, with nearly 20,000 students.

The Old College was designed by Robert Adam, but was built after his death in a considerably modified form by William Playfair (1789–1857), one of Edinburgh's greatest architects. Playfair built just one of Adam's two quadrangles (the dome, topped by a golden "Youth", was not added until 1879) and his magnificent Neoclassical Upper Library is now mostly used for ceremonial occasions. The small **Talbot Rice Art Gallery** (Tues–Sat 10am–5pm, also Mon 10am–5pm & Sun 2pm–5pm during the Festival; free; Ⓦ www.trg.ed.ac.uk), housed in the southwest corner of the Old College, displays in rather lacklustre fashion part of the University's large art and bronze collection, including a number of twentieth-century works by Scots Joan Eardley and William McTaggart. The best part of the gallery, worth navigating the complex entrance route to find, is the rooms given to touring and temporary avant-garde exhibitions which are mounted here on a regular basis – the show held during the Festival is normally of a high standard.

A little further up Nicolson Street, the southern extension of South Bridge, is the glass-fronted **Festival Theatre** (see p.145), a refurbished music hall which opened in 1994, giving the city a long-awaited venue for presenting opera and dance on a large scale. Opposite this is the stately facade of **Surgeons' Hall**, a handsome Ionic temple built by Playfair as the headquarters of the Royal College of Surgeons. Inside is one of the city's most unusual and morbidly compelling **museums** (Mon–Fri noon–4pm; free; Ⓦ www.rcsed.ac.uk). In the eighteenth and nineteenth century Edinburgh developed as a leading centre for medical and anatomical research, nurturing world-famous pioneers such as James Young Simpson, founder of anaesthesia, and Joseph Lister, the father of modern surgery. The history of surgery takes up one part of the museum, with intriguing exhibits ranging from early surgical tools to a pocketbook covered with the leathered skin of bodysnatcher William Burke (see p.112). Another room has an array of gruesome instruments illustrating the history of dentistry, while nearby is a small display dedicated to a past president of the college, Joseph Bell, whose diagnostic prowess was infamously immortalized by one of his students, Arthur Conan Doyle. The third and most remarkable part of the museum, the elegant **Playfair Hall**, contains an array of specimens and jars from the college's anatomical and pathological collections dating back to the eighteenth century.

Lothian Road and around

The area immediately **west** and **southwest** of the Old Town was formerly known as **Portsburgh**, a theoretically separate burgh outside the city walls that was nonetheless a virtual fiefdom of Edinburgh. Since the 1880s and the construction of the **Royal Lyceum Theatre** on Grindlay Street, the area has gradually developed into something of a theatre district, with the Usher Hall, Traverse Theatre and Filmhouse cinema, along with a collection of good restaurants and bars, all within a few hundred yards of each other.

Lothian Road heads south to **Tollcross** – marked by a clock in the middle of a busy crossroads; this area is lively at night, and features the intimate art-house cinema The Cameo, off Home Street. Beyond Tollcross to the south, the open parkland areas of the Meadows and Bruntsfield Links mark the transition to Edinburgh's genteel Victorian villa suburbs. The streets closest to the meadows in the suburbs of Newington, Marchmont and Bruntsfield are dominated by students' flats. Further south again is **Morningside**, whose prim and proper outlook was immortalized in Muriel Spark's *The Prime of Miss Jean Brodie;* it remains a favourite target of stand-up comics at the Festival.

The New Town

The **NEW TOWN**, itself well over two hundred years old, stands in total contrast to the Old Town: the layout is symmetrical, the streets are broad and straight, and most of the buildings are Neoclassical. Originally intended to be residential, the entire area, right down to the names of its streets, is something of a celebration of the Union, which was then generally regarded as a proud development in Scotland's history. Today the New Town is the bustling hub of the city's professional, commercial and business life, dominated by shops, banks and offices.

The existence of the New Town is chiefly due to the vision of **George Drummond**, who made schemes for the expansion of the city soon after becoming Lord Provost in 1725. Work began on the draining of the Nor' Loch below the Castle in 1759, a job that was to last some sixty years. The North Bridge, linking the Old Town with the main road leading to the port of Leith, was built between 1763 and 1772 and, in 1766, following a public competition, a plan for the New Town by 22-year-old architect **James Craig** was chosen. Its gridiron pattern was perfectly matched to the site: central **George Street**, flanked by showpiece squares, was laid out along the main ridge, with parallel **Princes Street** and **Queen Street** on either side below, and two smaller streets, Thistle Street and Rose Street, in between the three major thoroughfares providing coach houses, artisans' dwellings and shops. Princes and Queen streets were built up on one side only, so as not to block the spectacular views of the Old Town and Fife. Architects were accordingly afforded a wonderful opportunity to play with vistas and spatial relationships, particularly well exploited by Robert Adam, who contributed extensively to the later phases of the work. The First New Town, as the area covered by Craig's plan came to be known, received a whole series of extensions in the early decades of the nineteenth century, all carefully in harmony with the Neoclassical idiom.

In many ways, the layout of the greater New Town is its own most remarkable sight, an extraordinary grouping of squares, circuses, terraces, crescents and parks with a few set pieces such as **Register House**, the north frontage of **Charlotte Square** and the assemblage of curiosities on and around **Calton Hill**. However, it also contains assorted Victorian additions, notably the **Scott Monument** on

Princes Street, the **Royal Botanic Garden** on its northern fringe, as well as two of the city's most important public collections – the **National Gallery of Scotland** and, further afield, the **Scottish National Gallery of Modern Art**.

Princes Street

Although only allocated a subsidiary role in the original plan of the New Town, **Princes Street** had developed into Edinburgh's principal thoroughfare by the middle of the nineteenth century, a role it has retained ever since. Its unobstructed views across to the Castle and the Old Town are undeniably magnificent. Indeed, without the views, Princes Street would lose much of its appeal; its northern side, dominated by ugly department stores, is almost always crowded with shoppers, and few of the original eighteenth-century buildings remain.

The East End

With its dignified Corinthian pillars and dome, **Register House** (Mon–Fri 9am–4.45pm; free) is the most distinguished building on Princes Street. It's best seen on the approach from North Bridge – the same perspective is hard to achieve close up, which is why it's routinely ignored by the streams of shoppers squeezing past. Unfortunately, the majesty of the setting is marred by the **St James Centre** to the rear, a covered shopping arcade now regarded as the city's worst-ever planning blunder. Register House was designed in 1774 by Robert Adam as a custom-built home for Scotland's historic records, a function it has maintained ever since, today acting as the home for the National Archives of Scotland. Its elegant interior is centred on a glorious Roman rotunda, lavishly decorated with plasterwork and antique-style medallions. Searches into family history are normally best begun at the adjacent **New Register House**. Home of the General Register Office for Scotland (Ⓦwww.gro-scotland.gov.uk) it contains records of births, deaths and marriages. A dedicated Scottish Family History Centre, which will act as a single point of access for those researching genealogical records, is due to open within Register House in 2006.

Opposite is one of the few buildings on the south side of Princes Street, the **Balmoral Hotel**, built as a railway hotel in the early 1900s. For much of the century it was known as the *North British Hotel*, though by the 1980s the use of the imperial "North Britain" as the alternative name for Scotland didn't impress too many locals. The 188-room, five-star establishment is one of the grandest hotels in the city, though it maintains its close association with the railway: the timepiece on its chunky clocktower always kept two minutes fast in order to encourage passengers to catch their trains at neighbouring Waverley Station. Downstairs in the hotel is a Michelin-starred restaurant, *Number One* (see p.135); a meal in *Hadrian's* or tea at the *Palm Court* (see p.134) are more affordable ways to get a taste of the place.

On the other side of Waverley Station from Princes Street, the **Edinburgh Dungeon** (daily: April–Oct 10am–5pm, July & Aug 10am–7pm; Nov–March 11am–4pm; £9.95; Ⓦwww.thedungeons.com) is an unashamedly OTT horror-themed attraction where you'll encounter various scenes using actors and gruesome special effects to ham up Edinburgh's associations with blood and gore of all varieties, from sixteenth-century witchhunts to the bodysnatchers Burke and Hare.

Princes Street Gardens

It's hard to imagine that the **gardens** (dawn to dusk; free) which flank nearly the entire length of Princes Street were once the stagnant, foul-smelling Nor'

△ Princes Street Gardens

Loch, into which the effluent of the Old Town flowed for centuries. The railway has since replaced the water and today a sunken cutting carries the main lines out of Waverley Station to the west and north. The gardens, split into East and West sections, were originally the private domain of Princes Street residents and their well-placed acquaintances, only becoming a public park in 1876. These days, the swathes of green lawn, colourful flower beds and mature trees are a green lung for the city centre: on sunny days local office workers appear in their droves at lunchtime, while in the run-up to Christmas the gardens' eastern section is home to a ice rink (late Nov to early Jan daily 10am–10pm; £6.50) and a towering ferris wheel (same times; £2). The larger and more verdant western section has a floral clock and the Ross Bandstand, a popular Festival venue.

The Scott Monument

Facing the Victorian shopping emporium Jenners, and set within East Princes Street Gardens, the 200ft-high **Scott Monument** (April–Sept Mon–Sat 9am–6pm, Sun 10am–6pm; Oct–March Mon–Sat 9am–3pm, Sun 10am–3pm; £3) was erected in memory of prolific author and patriot Sir Walter Scott within a few years of his death. The largest monument in the world to a man of letters, the elaborate Gothic spire was created by George Meikle Kemp, a carpenter and joiner whose only building this is; while it was still under construction, he stumbled into a canal one foggy evening and drowned. The architecture is closely modelled on Scott's beloved Melrose Abbey (see p.190), while the rich sculptural decoration shows sixteen Scottish writers and 64 characters from Scott's famous *Waverley* novels. On the central plinth at the base of the monument is a **statue** of Scott with his deerhound Maida, carved from a thirty-ton block of Carrara marble.

Inside the recently restored memorial, a tightly winding spiral staircase climbs to a narrow platform near the top: from here, you can enjoy some inspiring – if vertiginous – vistas of the city below and hills and firths beyond.

The National Gallery of Scotland

Princes Street Gardens are bisected by the **Mound**, one of only two direct road links between the Old and New Towns (the other is North Bridge). Its name is an accurate description: it was formed in the 1780s by dumping piles of earth and other waste brought from the New Town's building plots. At the foot of the mound on the Princes Street level are two grand Neoclassical buildings; the **National Gallery of Scotland** (daily: 10am–5pm, until 7pm Thurs; free, entrance charge for some temporary exhibitions; ⓦ www.natgalscot.ac.uk) and the **Royal Scottish Academy** (same hours). Both were designed by William Henry Playfair (1790-1857), though the exterior of the National Gallery is considerably more austere than its bold Athenian counterpart.

The recently completed **Weston Link**, Edinburgh's answer to I.M. Pei's Louvre pyramid in Paris, established a new entrance to both galleries with an underground passageway joining the two buildings. Built in tandem with the multi-million pound refurbishment of the Royal Scottish Academy, the entry

---

The National Gallery of Scotland is devoted to pre-twentieth century European art. Other works of the National Galleries' collection are on display at the Scottish National Portrait Gallery (see p.125), the Scottish National Gallery of Modern Art (p.128) and its neighbour the Dean Gallery (p.129). A **free bus** service (daily: 10.45am–5pm; every 45 min) connects all four buildings.

point from Princes Street Gardens East is perhaps not as discreet as originally intended (its facade is couched in pompously large classach stone slabs), but the basement extension offers improved access to both institutions as well as a lecture theatre, café, restaurant and shop.

Built as a "temple to the fine arts" in 1850, the National Gallery's collection is not as big as those found elsewhere in Europe, though it is no less worthy, housing Scotland's finest array of European and Scottish art from the early 1300s to the late 1800s, with an outstanding clutch of works ranging from High Renaissance to Post-Impressionism. Its modest size makes it a manageable place to visit in a couple of hours and affords a pleasantly unrushed atmosphere.

Entering from either Weston Link via Princes Gardens East or the entrance porticos at the northern end of the National Gallery building, you are immediately confronted with the vividly coloured walls and the double-decked arrangement of paintings. Under the instruction of the gallery's flamboyant director, Timothy Clifford, this interior was controversially transformed in the 1980s from its pale minimalist walls to the deep claret red that follows the plans of Playfair's interior decorator. Two small, late nineteenth-century works in Room 12 – one anonymous, the other by A.E. Moffat – offer a glimpse of how the gallery was decorated and hung at the time, with pictures tiling every available surface. In addition to this, a muddled collection of works including busts, bronzes, objets d'art and period furniture is carefully orchestrated within the rooms, creating a warm atmosphere that encourages visitors to take a relaxed wander through the collection rather than submit to the usually gruelling gallery-crawl.

The gallery follows a symmetrical arrangement that progresses more or less chronologically, starting in the upper rooms above the entrance, and continuing clockwise around the ground floor. Individual works are rotated regularly, and the gallery's programme of small temporary exhibitions may mean that some of the paintings described below will not be on display.

Early Netherlandish and German works

Among the Gallery's most valuable treasures are **Hugo van der Goes**'s *Trinity Panels*, on a long-term loan from the Queen, which consist of the remaining parts of the only surviving pre-Reformation altarpiece made for a Scottish church. Painted in the mid-fifteenth century, they were commissioned by Provost Edward Bonkil for the Holy Trinity Collegiate Church, which was later demolished to make way for Edinburgh's Waverley Station. Bonkil can be seen amidst the company of organ-playing angels in the finest and best preserved of the four panels, while on the reverse sides are portraits of James III, his son (the future James IV) and Queen Margaret of Denmark. The characterization of their faces is more humble than those of the patron saints, and were modelled from life by an unknown local painter after the altar had been shipped to Edinburgh. The panels are turned by the gallery every half-hour. Of the later Netherlandish works, **Gerard David** is represented by the touchingly anecdotal *Three Legends of St Nicholas*, while the *Portrait of a Man* by Quentin Massys is an excellent example of northern European assimilation of Italian Renaissance forms and techniques.

Italian Renaissance works

The Italian section includes a small but exquisite array of Renaissance masterpieces. One of the most recent additions is a superb painting by **Botticelli**, *The Virgin Adoring the Sleeping Christ Child* which, along with **Raphael**'s graceful tondo *The Holy Family with a Palm Tree*, has undergone careful restoration to reveal their striking luminosity and depth of colour.

Of the four mythological scenes by **Titian**, the sensuous *Three Ages of Man* is one of his most accomplished early compositions, while *Diana and Acteon* and its pendant *Diana and Calisto*, painted for Philip II of Spain, illustrate the highly impressionistic freedom of his late style. Many of the gallery's collection of Titians (as well as works by Poussin, Raphael and Rembrandt) have been on loan since 1945 from the Duke of Sutherland. This arrangement was jeopardized with the death of the sixth Duke in 2000 with his family selling Titian's *Venus Anadyomene* to pay inheritance tax. However, honouring a gentleman's agreement, the gallery was offered first refusal, and the work was swiftly bought up into the national collection, while the remaining works have been promised to the gallery for the lifetime of the present duke. Alongside the Titians, **Bassano**'s truly regal *Adoration of the Kings* and a dramatic altarpiece, *The Deposition of Christ*, by **Tintoretto**, as well as several other works by **Veronese**, complete the fine Venetian section.

Seventeenth-century southern European works

El Greco's *A Fable* was painted during his early years in Italy, this being the best of the three versions of the composition, though the artist's subject matter remains tantalizingly ambiguous. Indigenous Spanish art is represented by **Velázquez**'s *An Old Woman Cooking Eggs*, an amazingly assured work by the artist at the tender age of 19, and by **Zurbaran**'s *The Immaculate Conception*, part of his ambitious decorative scheme for the Carthusian monastery in Jerez. There are also two small copper panels by the short-lived but influential Rome-based German painter **Adam Elsheimer**.

Poussin's *Seven Sacraments* are proudly displayed in their own room, the floor and central octagonal bench of which repeat some of the motifs in the series. Based on the artist's extensive research into biblical times, this series marks the first attempt to portray scenes from the life of Jesus realistically, rather than images dictated by artistic conventions. The result is profoundly touching, with a numerous imaginative and subtle details.

Seventeenth-century Flemish and Dutch works

Rubens' *The Feast of Herod* is an archetypal example of his sumptuously grand manner. Its gory subject matter is overshadowed by the gaudy depiction of the delights of the table, and was recently enlivened by meticulous restoration. Like all his large works, it was executed with extensive studio assistance, whereas the three small *modellos* are all from his own hand. The trio of large upright canvases by **Van Dyck** date from the artist's early Genoese period; of these, *The Lomellini Family* shows his mastery in creating a definitive dynastic image. Among the four canvases by **Rembrandt** are a poignant *Self-Portrait Aged 51* and the ripely suggestive *Woman in Bed*, which is thought to represent the biblical figure of Sarah on her wedding night, waiting for her husband Tobias to put the devil to flight. *Christ in the House of Martha and Mary* is the largest and probably the earliest of the thirty or so surviving paintings by **Vermeer**.

European works of the eighteenth and nineteenth centuries

Of the large-scale eighteenth-century works, **Tiepolo**'s *The Finding of Moses* stands out as a gloriously bravura fantasy, with the Pharaoh's daughter and her attendants appearing in sixteenth-century garb. The canvas was cut in the early 1800s, losing a substantial section from the right-hand side that included another figure with a dog. By way of contrast, the gems of the French section are the smaller panels, in particular **Watteau**'s *Fêtes Vénitiennes*, a lively Rococo idyll, and **Chardin**'s *Vase of Flowers*. One of the gallery's most recent major purchases is **Canova**'s 1817 statue *The Three Graces* – saved at the last minute from the hands of the J. Paul Getty Museum in California.

There's also a superb group of early Impressionist works such as **Camille Pissarro**'s *Kitchen Garden L'Hermitage*. Other Impressionist masters have a strong showing, including a collection of **Degas**' sketches, paintings and bronzes, **Monet**'s *Haystacks (Snow)* and **Renoir**'s *Woman Nursing Child*. Representing the Post-Impressionists are three exceptional examples of **Gauguin**'s work, including *Vision After the Sermon*, set in Brittany; **Van Gogh**'s *Olive Trees*, and **Cézanne**'s *The Big Trees* – a clear forerunner of modern abstraction.

Scottish and English works

On the face of it, the gallery's Scottish collection, ambitiously covering the entire gamut from seventeenth-century portraiture to the Arts and Crafts movement, is a bit of an anticlimax. To their detriment, most works are hung in the rather drab basement, where space and access are cramped. There are, however, a few significant works displayed within a broad European context. Both **Gavin Hamilton**'s *Achilles Mourning the Death of Patroclus*, painted in Rome, and **Allan Ramsay**'s *Portrait of a Lady* are finer examples of arresting Scottish art.

Of Sir **Henry Raeburn**'s large portraits, the swaggering masculinity of *Sir John Sinclair in Highland Dress* shows the artist's technical mastery, though he was equally confident when working on a smaller scale for one of the gallery's most popular pictures, *The Rev Robert Walker Skating on Duddingston Loch*. The gallery also owns a brilliant array of watercolours by **Turner**, faithfully displayed

Contemporary art in Edinburgh

In addition to the contemporary art collections in the city's National Galleries there are a number of smaller, independent galleries around the city that are well worth discovering.

The Collective Gallery 22–28 Cockburn St ☏0131/220 1260. Tends to focus on young local artists, and doesn't flinch from showing experimental modern work.

doggerfisher 11 Gayfield Square ☏0131/558 7110, ⊛www.doggerfisher.com. A converted tyre garage where you can see small-scale single shows of avant-garde contemporary artists.

Edinburgh Printmakers 23 Union St ☏0131/557 2479, ⊛www.edinburgh -printmakers.co.uk. A highly respected studio and gallery dedicated to contemporary printmaking.

Fruitmarket Gallery 45 Market St ☏0131/225 2383, ⊛www.fruitmarket.co.uk. The stylish modern design of this dynamic and much-admired art space is the capital's first port of call for top-grade international artists – recent years have seen shows by the likes of Jeff Koons and Bill Viola.

Ingleby Gallery 6 Carlton Terrace ☏0131/556 4441, ⊛www.inglebygallery.com. An elegant Edinburgh town house containing the most impressive small private art gallery in town, where you'll encounter changing exhibitions by international contemporary artists including many of Scotland's premier stars such as Alison Watt, Craigie Aitchison and Callum Innes.

Open Eye Gallery 34 Abercromby Place ☏0131/557 1020, ⊛www.openeyegallery .co.uk. One of the city's best commercial galleries which features a number of Scotland's top contemporary artists.

Scottish Gallery 16 Dundas St ☏0131/558 1200, ⊛www.scottish-gallery.co.uk. One of a number of small galleries on this New Town street; often some of the most striking works here are in the basement area dedicated to applied art.

each January when damaging sunlight is at its weakest, though visitors at other times of year can enjoy two of his fine Roman views displayed in one of the darker galleries.

George Street

The street parallel to Princes Street to the north is **George Street**, rapidly changing its role from a thoroughfare of august financial institutions to a highbrow version of Princes Street, where the big deals these days are done in designer-label shops. George Street was designed to be the centrepiece of the First New Town, joining two grand squares. At its eastern end lies **St Andrew Square**, in the middle of which is the Melville Monument, a statue of Lord Melville, Pitt the Younger's Navy Treasurer. Rather going against its dignified role, St Andrew Square is home to both Edinburgh's bus station and the city's newest shopping mall, outlet for Harvey Nichols and other designer stores. Beside this on the eastern side stands a handsome eighteenth-century town mansion, designed by Sir William Chambers. Headquarters of the Royal Bank of Scotland since 1825, the palatial mid-nineteenth-century banking hall is a symbol of the success of the New Town.

Charlotte Square

At the western end of George Street, **Charlotte Square** was designed by Robert Adam in 1791, a year before his death. For the most part, his plans were faithfully implemented, an exception being the domed and porticoed church of St George, simplified on grounds of expense. Its interior was gutted in the 1960s and refurbished as **West Register House**; like its counterpart at the far end of Princes Street, it holds various historic records and features changing documentary exhibitions (Mon–Fri 9am–4.45pm; free; Ⓦwww.nas .gov.uk). Generally regarded as the epitome of the New Town's elegant simplicity, the square was once the most exclusive residential address in Edinburgh, and though much of it is now occupied by offices, the imperious dignity of the architecture is still clear to see. Indeed, the north side, the finest of Adam's drawings, is once again the city's premier address, with the official residence of the First Minister of the Scottish Executive at number 6 (Bute House), the Edinburgh equivalent of 10 Downing Street. In August each year the gardens in the centre of the square are colonized by the temporary tents of the Edinburgh Book Festival (see p.152).

Restored by the National Trust for Scotland, the lower floors of neighbouring no. 7 are open to the public under the name of the **Georgian House** (daily: March & Nov 11am–3pm; April–Oct 10am–5pm; July & Aug 10am–7pm; last entry 30min before closing; NTS; £5; Ⓦwww.nts.org.uk), the interior of which provides a revealing sense of well-to-do New Town living in the early nineteenth century. Though a little stuffy and lifeless, the rooms are impressively decked out in period furniture – look for the working barrel organ which plays a selection of Scottish airs – and hung with fine paintings, including portraits by Ramsay and Raeburn, seventeenth-century Dutch cabinet pictures and the beautiful *Marriage of the Virgin* by El Greco's teacher, the Italian miniaturist Giulio Clovio. In the basement are the original wine cellar, lined with roughly made bins, and a kitchen complete with an open fire for roasting and a separate oven for baking; video reconstructions of life below and above stairs are shown in a nearby room.

The love affair of the NTS with the square continues on the south side, most of which it occupies as its main **headquarters** in Scotland; the buildings have been superbly restored over the past few years to something approaching their Georgian grandeur. It's well worth paying a visit to no. 28 to peer at the sumptuous interior. One floor up, a small **gallery** (Mon–Fri 11am–3pm; free) shows a collection of twentieth-century Scottish art, including a number of attractive examples of the work of the Scottish Colourists, while two adjoining rooms offer an introduction to the Trust in general, with a video showing highlights of their properties around Scotland. Downstairs, there's a **shop** selling National Trust books and souvenirs, as well as a very pleasant **café**, authentically decked out with severe Georgian family portraits.

Queen Street

Queen Street, the last of the three main streets of the First New Town, is bordered to the north by gardens, and commands sweeping views across to Fife. Occupied mostly by offices, it's the best preserved of the area's three main streets, although it's principally notable for the striking late nineteenth-century home of the National Portrait Gallery.

The Scottish National Portrait Gallery

At the eastern end of Queen Street, just to the north of St Andrew Square, is the **Scottish National Portrait Gallery** (Fri–Wed 10am–5pm, Thurs 10am–7pm; free, entrance charge for some temporary exhibitions). A fantastic medieval Gothic palace in red sandstone, the Portrait Gallery makes an extravagant contrast to the New Town's prevailing Neoclassicism. The exterior of the building is encrusted with statues of famous national heroes, a theme reiterated in the stunning two-storey entrance hall by William Hole's tapestry-like frieze depicting notable figures from Scotland's past. Unlike the more global outlook of its sister National Galleries (see p.120), the portrait gallery devotes itself to images of famous Scots – a definition stretched to include anyone with the slightest connection to the country. Taken as a whole, it's an engaging procession through Scottish history, with familiar faces from Bonnie Prince Charlie and Mary, Queen of Scots to Alex Ferguson and Sean Connery appearing along the way. The permanent collection is located on the two upper floors; though the paintings on display are rotated frequently, there's normally a healthy representation of works by Scotland's best portraitists, from Allan Ramsay and Sir Henry Raeburn to contemporary luminaries such as David Mach and John Bellany. Temporary exhibitions are displayed in the galleries on the ground floor; elsewhere on this floor are the shop and a pleasant café.

Calton Hill

Edinburgh's longstanding tag as the "Athens of the North" is nowhere better earned than on **Calton Hill**, the volcanic peak which rises up above the eastern end of Princes Street. Numerous architects homed in on it as a showcase for their most ambitious and grandiose buildings and monuments, the presence of which emphasizes Calton's aloof air and sense of detachment today. But the hill and its odd collection of buildings aren't just for looking *at*: this is also one of the best viewpoints from which to appreciate the city as a whole, with its tightly knitted suburbs, landmark Old and New Town buildings and the sea beyond – much closer to Edinburgh than many visitors expect.

Waterloo Place forms a ceremonial way from Princes Street to Calton Hill. On its southern side is **Old Calton Burial Ground**, tucked in behind a line of high, dark, forbidding walls. The picturesque assembly of mausoleums and gravestones within, some at a jaunty angle and others weathered with age, make for an absorbing wander. Notable among the monuments is the cylindrical memorial by Robert Adam to the philosopher David Hume, one of Edinburgh's greatest sons, and a piercing obelisk commemorating various political martyrs. Hard up against the cemetery's eastern wall, perched above a sheer rockface, is a picturesque castellated building which many visitors arriving at Waverley Station below imagine to be Edinburgh Castle itself. In fact, it's the only surviving part of the **Calton Gaol**, once Edinburgh's main prison, most of which was demolished in the 1930s to make way for the looming Art Deco **St Andrew's House**, today occupied by civil servants.

Further on, set majestically on the slopes of Calton Hill looking towards Arthur's Seat, sits one of Edinburgh's greatest buildings, the **Old Royal High School**. With its bold central portico of Doric columns and graceful symmetrical colonnaded wings, Thomas Hamilton's elegant building of 1829 is regarded by many as the epitome of Edinburgh's Athenian aspirations. The capital's high school was based here between 1829 and 1968, at which point the building was converted to house a debating chamber and became Scotland's parliament-in-waiting. However, soon after the re-establishment of a Scottish parliament had been confirmed in 1997 the building was controversially rejected as too small for the intended assembly, with a brand-new building at Holyrood favoured instead. Currently used as offices by the city council, the latest plan is to convert it into a museum of the history of photography, based around the work of 1840s photographic pioneers David Octavius Hill and Robert Adamson, whose studio, Rock House, was located on Calton Hill below the Observatory. Across the road, Hamilton also built the **Burns Monument**, a circular Corinthian temple modelled on the Monument to Lysicrates in Athens, as a memorial to the national bard.

Robert Louis Stevenson reckoned that Calton Hill was the best place to view Edinburgh, "since you can see the Castle, which you lose from the Castle, and Arthur's Seat, which you cannot see from Arthur's Seat". Though the panoramas from ground level are spectacular enough, those from the top of the **Nelson Monument** (April–Sept Mon 1pm–6pm, Tues–Sat 10am–6pm; Oct–March Mon–Sat 10am–3pm; £3), perched near the summit of Calton Hill, are even better. Each day at 1pm, a white ball drops down a mast at the top of the monument; this, together with the one o'clock gun fired from the Castle battlements (see p.94), once provided a daily check for the mariners of Leith, who needed accurate chronometers to ensure reliable navigation at sea.

Alongside, the **National Monument** is often referred to as "Edinburgh's Disgrace", yet many locals admire this unfinished and somewhat ungainly attempt to replicate the Parthenon atop Calton Hill. Begun as a memorial to the dead of the Napoleonic Wars, the project's shortage of funds led architect William Playfair to ensure that even with just twelve of the massive columns completed, the folly would still serve as a striking landmark. It's one of those constructions which is purposeless yet still magnetic; with a bit of effort and care you can climb up and around the monument, sit and contemplate from one of the huge steps or meander around the base of the mighty pillars. New schemes for the development of the National Monument and its Calton Hill neighbours, either grandiose or foolish (or both), are regularly proposed – one of these may some day be carried out.

Designed by Playfair in 1818, the **City Observatory** is the largest of the buildings at the summit of Calton Hill. Because of pollution and the advent of street lighting, which impaired views of the stars, the observatory proper had to be relocated to Blackford Hill before the end of the nineteenth century, but the equipment here continues to be used by students. At the corner of the curtain walls is the castellated Observatory House, one of the few surviving buildings by James Craig, designer of the New Town. The complex isn't open to the public, but a stroll around its perimeter does offer a broad perspective over the city, with views out to the Forth bridges and Fife.

The Northern New Town

The **Northern New Town** was the earliest extension to the First New Town, begun in 1801, and today roughly covers the area north of Queen Street between India Street to the west and Broughton Street to the east, and as far as Fettes Row to the north. This has survived in far better shape than its predecessor: with the exception of one street, almost all of it is intact, and it has managed to preserve a predominantly residential character.

One of the area's most intriguing buildings is the neo-Norman **Mansfield Place Church**, on the corner of Broughton and East London streets, designed in the late nineteenth century for the strange, now defunct Catholic Apostolic sect. Having lain redundant and neglected for three decades, it has suddenly acquired cult status, its preservation the current obsession of local conservation groups. The chief reason for this is its cycle of **murals** by the Dublin-born **Phoebe Anna Traquair**, a leading light in the Scottish Arts and Crafts movement. Covering vast areas of the walls and ceilings of the main nave and side chapels, the wonderfully luminous paintings depict biblical parables and texts, with rows of angels, cherubs flecked with gold and worshipping figures painted in delicate pastel colours. The dilapidation of the church by the early 1990s prompted a campaign to save and protect the murals, which are recognized as the city's finest in-situ art treasure. The building now houses offices for Scottish voluntary groups and viewing of the murals is restricted to one Sunday afternoon each month, although more regular opening is normally arranged during the Festival. For more details see ⓦ www.mansfieldtraquair.org.uk.

The Royal Botanic Garden

Just beyond the northern boundaries of the New Town, with entrances on Inverleith Row and Arboretum Place, is the seventy-acre site of the **Royal Botanic Garden** (daily: March & Oct 10am–6pm; April–Sept 10am–7pm; Nov–Feb 10am–4pm; free; ⓦ www.rbge.org.uk). Filled with mature trees and a huge variety of native and exotic plants and flowers, the "botanics" (as they're commonly called) are most popular simply as a place to stroll and lounge around on the grass. Towards the eastern side of the gardens, a series of ten glasshouses (entry £3.50), including the elegant 1850s Palm House, shows off a steamy array of palms, ferns, orchids, cycads and aquatic plants, including some huge circular water lilies. Elsewhere, different themes are highlighted: the large Chinese-style garden, for example, has a bubbling waterfall and the world's biggest collection of Asian wild plants outside China, while in the northwest corner there's a Scottish native woodland which very effectively evokes the wild unkemptness of parts of the Scottish Highlands and west coast. Art is also a strong theme within the botanics, with a gallery showing changing contemporary exhibitions in the attractive eighteenth-century Inverleith House at the centre of the gardens, while scattered all around are a number of outdoor sculptures, including a giant pine cone by landscape artist Andy Goldsworthy and the striking stainless-steel east gate, designed in the form of stylized rhododendrons. Parts of the garden are also notable for some great vistas: the busy *Terrace Café* (see p.136) beside Inverleith House offers one of the city's best views of the

Castle and Old Town's steeples and monuments. **Guided tours** (£4) leave from the West Gate on Arboretum Place at 11am and 2pm (April–Sept).

① Stockbridge and Dean Village

Between the New Town and the Botanic Gardens, the busy suburb of **Stockbridge** grew up around the Water of Leith ford (and its seventeenth-century bridge) over which cattle were driven to market in Edinburgh. The hamlet was essentially gobbled up in the expansion of the New Town, but a few charming buildings and an independent character prevail in the district today. The area is a popular quarter for young professionals who can't afford the soaring property prices in the New Town proper, and as a result there's a good crop of bars, boutiques and places to eat along both Raeburn Place, the main road, and St Stephen's Street, long one of Edinburgh's more offbeat side streets and a great place for some shopping or bite to eat.

Less than half a mile from Stockbridge, linked by a riverside path which forms part of the **Water of Leith Walkway** (ⓦwww.waterofleith.org.uk), is the old milling community of **Dean Village**, one of central Edinburgh's most picturesque – yet unexpected – corners, its atmosphere of decay arrested by the conversion of numerous granaries and tall mill buildings into designer flats. Nestling close to the river, with steep banks rising up on both sides, the Victorian community has a self-contained air, its surviving features including the school, clocktower and communal drying green, while high above the Dean Village is **Dean Bridge**, a bravura feat of 1830s engineering by Thomas Telford, which carries the main road over 100ft above the river.

The West End

The western extension to the New Town was the last part to be built, deviating from the area's overriding Neoclassicism with a number of Victorian additions, including the city's principal Episcopal church, the huge Early English Gothic-style **St Mary's Cathedral**. With its proximity to the city centre, the West End is now mostly used for offices, with a decent clutch of bars and restaurants, though there is some elegant terraced housing towards its outer edges. Here, enjoying some green space and a dignified setting are two compelling collections of contemporary art, the well-established **Scottish National Gallery of Modern Art** and its newer neighbour, the **Dean Gallery**, both of which regularly host worthwhile seasonal and touring exhibitions.

The Scottish National Gallery of Modern Art

Set in spacious wooded grounds at the far northwestern fringe of the New Town, about ten minutes' walk from either the cathedral or Dean Village, the **Scottish National Gallery of Modern Art** on Belford Road (Fri–Wed 10am–5pm, Thurs 10am–7pm; free, entrance charge for some temporary exhibitions; ⓦwww.natgalscot.ac.uk), was established as the first collection in Britain devoted solely to twentieth-century painting and sculpture. It operates in tandem with Dean Gallery across the road (see opposite); both galleries are located in impressive Neoclassical buildings which have been superbly converted into pleasant, relaxing viewing spaces, and they also have excellent cafés – if it's a sunny day head for the one at the Gallery of Modern Art, which has a pleasant outdoor terrace. The extensive wooded grounds of the galleries serve as a sculpture park, featuring works by Jacob Epstein, Henry Moore, Barbara Hepworth and, most strikingly, Charles Jencks, whose prize-winning *Landform*, a swirling mix of ponds and grassy mounds, dominates the area in front of the Gallery of Modern Art. In contrast, there are few permanent works inside – one exception is Douglas Gordon's *List of Names (Random)*, an examination of "how our heads function", which lists in plain type on a white wall everyone the artist can remember meeting. Otherwise, the display space is divided between temporary exhibitions and selections from the gallery's own holdings; the latter are arranged thematically, but are almost constantly moved around. The collection starts with early twentieth-century Post-Impressionists, then moves through the Fauves, German Expressionism, Cubism and Pop Art, with works by Lichtenstein and Warhol establishing a connection with the extensive holdings of Paolozzi's work in the Dean Gallery. There's a strong section on living British artists, from Francis Bacon and Gilbert & George to Britart exponents such as Damien Hirst and Rachel Whiteread, while modern Scottish art ranges from the Colourists – whose works are attracting ever-growing posthumous critical acclaim – to the distinctive styles of contemporary Scots including John Bellany, a portraitist of striking originality, and the poet–artist–gardener Ian Hamilton Finlay.

The Dean Gallery

Opposite the Modern Art Gallery on the other side of Belford Road is the latest addition to the National Galleries of Scotland, the **Dean Gallery** (same hours; free; ⓦwww.natgalscot.ac.uk), housed in an equally impressive Neoclassical building completed in 1833. The interior of the gallery, built as an orphanage and later an education centre, has been dramatically refurbished specifically to make room for the work of Edinburgh-born sculptor **Sir Eduardo Paolozzi**, described by some as the father of Pop Art. The collection was partly assembled from a bequest by Gabrielle Keiller, and partly from a gift of the artist himself which included some three thousand sculptures, two thousand prints and drawings and three thousand books.

There's an awesome introduction to Paolozzi's work in the form of the huge *Vulcan*, a half-man, half-machine which squeezes into the Great Hall immediately opposite the main entrance – view it both from ground level and the head-height balcony to appreciate the sheer scale of the piece. No less persuasive of Paolozzi's dynamic creative talents are the rooms to the right of the main entrance, where his London studio has been expertly re-created, right down to the clutter of half-finished casts, toys and empty pots of glue. Hidden amongst this chaos is a large part of his bequest, with incomplete models piled four or five deep on the floor and designs stacked randomly on shelves. Elsewhere in the gallery, a selection of his sculptures and drawings are exhibited in a more traditional manner.

The ground floor also holds the Roland Penrose Gallery's world-renowned collection of **Dada** and **Surrealist** art; Penrose was a close friend and patron of many of the movements' leading figures, and Marcel Duchamp, Max Ernst and Man Ray are all represented. Look out also for Dali's *The Signal of Anguish* and

Approaches to the Modern Art and Dean galleries

The most pleasant way of getting to the neighbouring Modern Art and Dean galleries is on foot along the **Water of Leith Walkway**, which can be joined at Stockbridge or the Dean Village. Alternatively, a **free bus** runs every 45 min (Mon–Sat 10.45am–5pm, Sun noon–5pm) from outside the National Gallery on the Mound, stopping at the National Portrait Gallery on the way. The only regular **public transport** running along Belford Road is bus #13, which leaves from the western end of George Street.

Magritte's *Magic Mirror* along with work by Miró and Giacometti – all hung on crowded walls with an assortment of artefacts and ethnic souvenirs gathered by Penrose and his artist companions while travelling. The rooms upstairs are normally given over to special and touring exhibitions, which usually carry an entrance charge.

Eating

The last decade has seen a marked upsurge in style, sophistication and good taste in Edinburgh's cafés and restaurants. **Café culture** has hit the centre of the city, with tables spilling onto the pavements in the summer, and this has been matched by the rise of a clutch of original, upmarket and stylish **restaurants**, many identifying their cuisine as **contemporary** or **modern Scottish** and championing top-quality local meat, game and fish. As with most large cities in Britain, there's a well-padded mid-market populated by familiar chains and long-established Chinese, Indian and Mexican places, as well as more interesting outposts of Thai, North African and Spanish cuisine.

Generally, small **diners** and **bistros** predominate, many adopting a casual French style and offering good-value set menus. Traditional **Scottish cooking** can still be found at some of the more formal restaurants, and inevitably some tourist-oriented places offer haggis and other classic clichés. Edinburgh has a number of first-rate **vegetarian** restaurants, including a couple of classic Indian vegetarian places, and it's a excellent place if you like **fish and shellfish**, which have long been a speciality of the **Leith** waterfront, though you'll now also find a number of great seafood bistros in the centre of town.

Most of Edinburgh's restaurants serve from noon to 2.30pm and 6pm to 10pm, and many are closed at least one day a week – it's worth checking before heading out on a Sunday or Monday. During the **Festival** the majority of restaurants keep longer hours, but they are also much busier. Many **pubs** (see p.140) also serve food, either in the bar itself or an attached restaurant.

Cafés and restaurants are shown on the maps on pp.84–85 and pp.132–133.

Royal Mile and around

Generally, the cafés and restaurants of the **Royal Mile** are less obviously tourist traps than the shops of the ancient thoroughfare, and you can find plenty of places brimming with character and imagination. Many are tucked away down the lanes and closes of the Old Town, or located in unusual and interesting buildings. In summer, this is the busiest part of town, so it's advisable to book a table for an evening meal.

Bistros, cafés and diners

Always Sunday 170 High St ☏0131/622 0667. Proof that there's room for a bit of real food even on the tourist-thronged Royal Mile, this pleasantly positive independent café serves healthy lunches, home-made cakes, fresh smoothies and Fairtrade coffee. Open daily till 6pm. Inexpensive.

Café Hub Castlehill ☏0131/473 2067. Colourful, well-run café in the Edinburgh Festival centre, with light modern meals served right through the day and evening. Teas, coffees, snacks and drinks also

served. The large terrace is a good spot for watching the world passing on sunny days. Inexpensive.

Elephant House 21 George IV Bridge ☏0131/220 5355. Extolled as one of the places where J.K. Rowling, then a hard-up single mum, nursed her cups of coffee while penning the first Harry Potter novel, this is a decent daytime and evening café with a terrific room at the back full of philosophizing students and visitors peering dreamily at the views of the Castle. Daily 8am–11pm. Inexpensive.

Fruitmarket Gallery Café 45 Market St ☎0131/226 1843. This attractive café feels like an extension of the gallery space, its airy, reflective ambience enhanced by the wall of glass onto the street. Stop in for soups, coffees or a caesar salad. Mon–Sat 11am–5.30pm, Sun noon–4.30pm. Inexpensive.

The Outsider 15–16 George IV Bridge ☎0131/226 3131. Style-conscious, arty modern restaurant open right through from lunch to late evening and permanently filled with beautiful young things. The food, which leans towards fish, salads and healthier options, is fresh, modern, informal and, surprisingly, not overpriced. Moderate.

Plaisir du Chocolat 251–253 Canongate ☎0131/556 9524. Classy Parisian tearoom and chocolatier serving delicious, if pricey, lunches, luxurious patisserie treats, an array of gourmet teas and real hot chocolates. Open daily 10am–6pm. Moderate.

Spoon 15 Blackfriars St ☎0131/556 6922. Down a side road off the High Street, and a world away from modern café blandness. The approach is simple, with short menus of imaginative soups, expertly crafted sandwiches and a daily special such as farmhouse cheddar tart or *boudin noir* salad. Good coffee and cakes, too. Mon–Sat 8am–6pm. Inexpensive.

French

Café Marlayne 7 Old Fishmarket Close, off High St ☎0131/225 3838. A great location – in a series of old, low barrel-roofed cellars off a cobbled lane near Parliament Square – where you'll find moderately priced French home cooking. There's another branch at 76 Thistle St in the New Town. Moderate.

La Garrigue 31 Jeffrey St ☎0131/557 3032, ⓦwww.lagarrigue.co.uk. A place of genuine charm and quality, with a menu and wine list dedicated to the produce and traditions of the Languedoc region of France. The care and honesty of the cooking shine through in dishes such as cassoulet or bream with chard. Moderate.

Indian

Namaste 15 Bristo Place ☎0131/225 2000. A simple Indian diner in student-land with attractive Indian furniture and artefacts. The menu is (unusually) limited to two sides of paper, and dishes such as minty pudini chicken are light, tasty and beautifully cooked in a traditional brass pot. Closed Sat & Sun lunch. Moderate.

Suruchi 14a Nicolson St ☎0131/556 6583, ⓦwww.suruchirestaurant.co.uk. Popular establishment serving genuine South Indian dishes – bizarrely, the menu is written in broad Scots. Look

out for cross-cultural specials such as tandoori trout. Moderate.

Italian

Prego 38 St Mary's St ☎0131/557 5754, ⓦwww.prego-restaurant.com. Classy but not overpriced Italian place with a short, confident seasonal menu (no pizza) and knowledgeable service. It's a bit like eating in Italy, which is a rare find in Britain. Closed Sun. Moderate.

Mexican

Viva Mexico 41 Cockburn St ☎0131/226 5145, ⓦwww.viva-mexico.co.uk. Long one of Edinburgh's best Mexican restaurants, offering well-executed staples in a friendly, easygoing atmosphere. Moderate.

Scottish

Amber Scotch Whisky Heritage Centre, 354 Castlehill ☎0131/477 8477, ⓦwww.amber-restaurant.co.uk. Neat, contemporary-styled place serving a good choice of light food such as potted shrimp at lunchtime, and more substantial and expensive dishes in the evenings (Fri & Sat only), when there's a "whisky sommelier" on hand to suggest the best drams to accompany your honey-roast rack of Highland lamb or saddle of Balmoral venison. Expensive.

The Grain Store 30 Victoria St ☎0131/225 7635, ⓦwww.grainstore-restaurant.co.uk. Often missed by passers-by, this unpretentious restaurant is a relaxing haven amongst the bustle of the Old Town, serving fairly uncomplicated but top-quality modern Scottish food such as saddle of venison with beetroot fondant or toasted goat's cheese with caramelized walnuts. Reasonable lunchtime and set-price options. Expensive.

Reform Restaurant 267 Canongate ☎0131/558 9992, ⓦwww.reformrestaurant.com. One of the first places in Edinburgh to draw strongly on the ideas of Pacific Rim fusion food, this is a fresh, imaginatively run place which mixes the dignity of the Old Town with a sense of gastronomic adventure. Expect dishes such as steamed snapper fillet or barbecued ostrich steak with pear chutney. Moderate.

Tower Museum of Scotland, Chambers St ☎0131/225 3003, ⓦwww.tower-restaurant.com. Unique setting on Level 5 of the new Museum of Scotland; at night you are escorted along the empty corridors to the restaurant, where spectacular views to the floodlit Castle are revealed. Excellent modern Scottish food such as shellfish and expensive chargrilled Aberdeen Angus steaks in a self-consciously chic setting. Expensive.

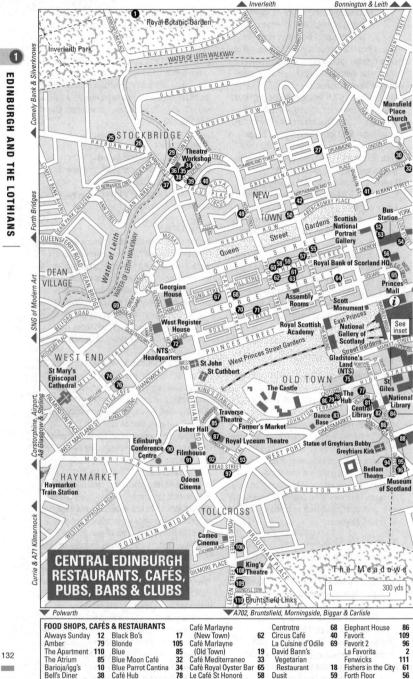

CENTRAL EDINBURGH
RESTAURANTS, CAFÉS,
PUBS, BARS & CLUBS

0   300 yds

FOOD SHOPS, CAFÉS & RESTAURANTS				
Always Sunday	12	Black Bo's	17	Café Marlayne (New Town) 62
Amber	79	Blonde	105	Café Marlayne (Old Town) 19
The Apartment	110	Blue	85	Café Mediterraneo 33
The Atrium	85	Blue Moon Café	32	Café Royal Oyster Bar 65
Barioja/igg's	10	Blue Parrot Cantina	34	Le Café St Honoré 58
Bell's Diner	38	Café Hub	78	

Centrotre	68	Elephant House	86
Circus Café	40	Favorit	109
La Cuisine d'Odile	69	Favorit 2	96
David Bann's Vegetarian Restaurant	18	La Favorita	2
		Fenwicks	111
Dusit	59	Fishers in the City	61
		Forth Floor	56

132

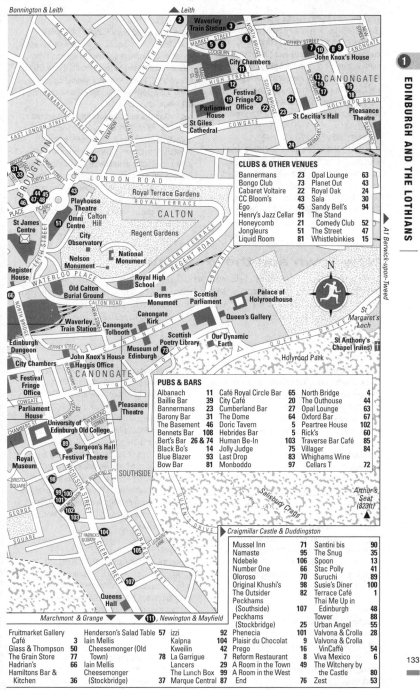

Bonnington & Leith

Leith

Waverley Train Station

City Chambers

John Knox's House

CANONGATE

Festival Fringe Office

Parliament House

St Giles Cathedral

St Cecilia's Hall

Pleasance Theatre

A1 Berwick-upon-Tweed

CLUBS & OTHER VENUES

Bannermans	23	Opal Lounge	63
Bongo Club	73	Planet Out	43
Cabaret Voltaire	22	Royal Oak	24
CC Bloom's	43	Sala	30
Ego	45	Sandy Bell's	94
Henry's Jazz Cellar	91	The Stand	
Honeycomb	21	Comedy Club	52
Jongleurs	51	The Street	47
Liquid Room	81	Whistlebinkies	15

Playhouse Theatre

Royal Terrace Gardens

ROYAL TERRACE

CALTON

Regent Gardens

St James Centre

Omni Centre

City Observatory

Nelson Monument

National Monument

Register House

Old Calton Burial Ground

Burns Monumnet

Scottish Parliament

Palace of Holyroodhouse

N

Waverley Train Station

Canongate Tolbooth

Canongate Kirk

Queen's Gallery

St Margaret's Loch

Edinburgh Dungeon

City Chambers

John Knox's House

Haggis Office

Scottish Poetry Library

Museum of Edinburgh

Our Dynamic Earth

St Anthony's Chapel (ruins)

CANONGATE

Holyrood Park

St Anthony's Chapel (ruins)

Festival Fringe Office

Parliament House

University of Edinburgh Old College

Pleasance Theatre

PUBS & BARS

Albanach	11	Café Royal Circle Bar	65	North Bridge	4
Baillie Bar	39	City Café	20	The Outhouse	44
Bannermans	23	Cumberland Bar	27	Opal Lounge	63
Barony Bar	31	The Dome	64	Oxford Bar	67
The Basement	46	Doric Tavern	5	Peartree House	102
Bennets Bar	108	Hebrides Bar	5	Rick's	60
Bert's Bar	26 & 74	Human Be-In	103	Traverse Bar Café	85
Black Bo's	14	Jolly Judge	75	Villager	84
Blue Blazer	93	Last Drop	83	Whighams Wine	
Bow Bar	81	Monboddo	97	Cellars T	72

Surgeon's Hall

Royal Museum

Festival Theatre

SOUTHSIDE

Salisbury Crags

Arthur's Seat (823ft)

GEORGE SQUARE

Craigmillar Castle & Duddingston

Queens Hall

Mussel Inn	71	Santini bis	90
Namaste	95	The Snug	35
Ndebele	106	Spoon	13
Number One	66	Stac Polly	41
Oloroso	70	Suruchi	89
Original Khushi's	98	Susie's Diner	100
The Outsider	82	Terrace Café	1
Peckhams		Thai Me Up in	
(Southside)	107	Edinburgh	48
Peckhams		Tower	88
(Stockbridge)	25	Urban Angel	55
Phenecia	101	Valvona & Crolla	28
Plaisir du Chocolat	9	Valvona & Crolla	
Prego	16	VinCaffè	54
Reform Restaurant		Viva Mexico	6
A Room in the Town	49	The Witchery by	
A Room in the West		the Castle	80
End	76	Zest	53

Marchmont & Grange

Newington & Mayfield

Fruitmarket Gallery		Henderson's Salad Table	57	izzi	92
Café	3	Iain Mellis		Kalpna	104
Glass & Thompson	50	Cheesemonger (Old		Kweilin	42
The Grain Store	77	Town)	78	La Garrigue	7
Hadrian's	66	Iain Mellis		Lancers	29
Hamiltons Bar &		Cheesemonger		The Lunch Box	99
Kitchen	36	(Stockbridge)	37	Marque Central	87

Plaisir du Chocolat	9		

133

The Witchery by the Castle 352 Castlehill
☎0131/225 5613, ⓦwww.thewitchery.com. A
fine dining restaurant that only Edinburgh could
create, set in magnificently over-the-top medieval
surroundings full of Gothic panelling, tapestries and
heavy stonework, all a mere broomstick-hop from
the Castle. The rich fish and game dishes are pricey,
but you can steal a sense of it all with a lunch or
pre- or post-theatre set menu (£12.50). Expensive.

Spanish

Barioja 19 Jeffrey St ☎0131/557 3622. Open
right through the day and good for a lunchtime
bocadillos sandwich or late-afternoon drink and
snack, this Spanish-owned bar makes a decent
stab at tapas in a metropolitan setting. Inexpensive.
The more upmarket *Igg's*, a Spanish-Scottish
hybrid, is next door.

Vegetarian

Black Bo's 57-61 Blackfriars St ☎0131/557
6136, ⓦwww.blackbos.co.uk. Inventive diner with
an earthy atmosphere and friendly service. Long
established as a vegetarian favourite, it now offers
a short meat menu for unreconstituted carnivores
in the party. Open evenings daily and lunch Fri &
Sat. Moderate.

David Bann's Vegetarian Restaurant
56–58 St Mary's St ☎0131/556 5888,
ⓦwww.davidbann.com. Thoroughly modern
vegetarian restaurant, open long hours and offering a wide choice of interesting, unconventional
dishes such as courgette and sweetcorn fritters
or celeriac and sweet potato roulade. The prices
are very reasonable and the overall design is
stylish and classy – not an open-toed sandal in
sight. Moderate.

New Town and the West End

For eating places, as well as clubs and bars, the **New Town** and the **West End**
are the happening part of town. Many nationwide chains have restaurants on
and around Princes and George streets, but it's worth exploring some of the
side streets and back lanes such as Thistle Street to find more authentic, home-
grown places.

Bistros, cafés and diners

Glass & Thompson 2 Dundas St ☎0131/557
0909. Tasteful, upmarket café-deli with huge bowls
of olives and an irresistible glass counter filled with
delicious food; scattered tables and chairs mean
you can linger over a made-to-order sandwich
or top-notch cake and coffee. Closed evenings.
Inexpensive.

Hadrian's 2 North Bridge ☎0131/557 5000.
Although it's strictly part of the upmarket *Balmoral
Hotel*, this brasserie is usefully open daily for lunch
and dinner and isn't too overpriced. The elegance
of the design and atmosphere, along with good-
quality modern British cooking, make it worth
seeking out. Moderate.

Urban Angel 121 Hanover St ☎0131/225
6215. Right-on but easygoing subterranean
bistro with a diverse and flexible blackboard menu
using lots of organic and Fairtrade produce. Closed
Sun eve. Moderate.

Chinese

Kweilin 19–21 Dundas St ☎0131/557 1875,
ⓦwww.kweilin.co.uk. One of the most
reliable Chinese restaurants in town, serving
Cantonese and Szechuan dishes in a pleasant
atmosphere. Slightly more expensive than some.
Moderate.

French

Le Café St Honoré 34 Thistle St Lane ☎0131/226
2211, ⓦwww.cafesthonore.com. A little piece
of Paris discreetly tucked away in a New Town
back lane. Fairly traditional top-quality French fare
– grilled oysters, warm duck salad and *tarte tatin*.
Closed Sun. Moderate.

La Cuisine d'Odile 13 Randolph Crescent, West
End ☎0131/225 5685. Genuine lunch-only French
home cooking in a basement under the French
Institute. There's a really authentic feel to the food,
with lots of inexpensive terrines, flans, game dishes
and some superb desserts, including a signature
"Choc'Odile" chocolate tart. Closed Sun, Mon &
July. Inexpensive.

Italian

Centrotre 103 George St ☎0131/225 1550,
ⓦwww.centotre.com. Slick but welcoming bar,
café and restaurant in an ornate former bank,
offering unfussy, top-quality Italian food from fresh
pastries and coffee to interesting pizzas or a simple
but blissful plate of gorgonzola served with a ripe
pear. All accompanied by a seriously impressive
drinks list. Moderate.

Valvona & Crolla VinCaffè 11 Multrees Walk
☎0131/557 0088, ⓦwww.valvonacrolla.com.
Suave sister venue to the famous Leith Walk deli,

with an espresso bar and takeaway downstairs and classy Italian snacks, meals and wines by the glass upstairs. Moderate to expensive.

Scottish

Forth Floor Harvey Nichols, 30–34 St Andrew Sq ℡0131/524 8350, ⊛www.harveynichols .com. While the rooftop views don't quite match its rivals *Oloroso* and the *Tower*, there's a confidence to Harvey Nic's approach which makes it a real contender among the city's fine modern Scottish options – including seared scallops with fig salsa, perhaps, or pot-roast pork. The restaurant gets the glass frontage; the brasserie with its simpler risottos and grills is less pricey but less memorable. Closed Sun & Mon eve. Moderate to expensive.

Number One 1 Princes St ℡0131/557 6727, ⊛www.thebalmoralhotel.com/restaurant1.html. Chef Jeff Bland is one of only two Michelin-star holders in Edinburgh; what's on offer is haute cuisine served in an overtly upmarket subterranean dining space within the five-star *Balmoral Hotel*. Lunches are (just about) affordable for a taste of the artistry; or for a bravura performance there's a six-course tasting menu, with dishes such as foie gras poached in port, for £60.

Oloroso 33 Castle St ℡0131/226 7614, ⊛www.oloroso.co.uk. Edinburgh's most glamorous upmarket dining space, with a rooftop location giving views to the Castle and the Forth. The menu features strong flavours such as chump of lamb or roast salmon, followed by playful puddings – try the deep-fried jam sandwich with ice cream. Eating (or drinking) from the more convivial bar is the cost-effective way to enjoy the setting, but the best views are from the balcony. Expensive.

A Room in the Town 18 Howe St ℡0131/225 8204, ⊛www.aroomin.co.uk/thetown. Manages to combine a couthy, relaxed atmosphere with decent, Scottish-slanted seasonal food. BYOB keeps the bills down. Sister restaurant *A Room in the West End* is below ground at 26 William St. Moderate.

Stac Polly 29–33 Dublin St ℡0131/556 2231, ⊛www.stacpolly.co.uk. Regularly trotted out as a classic example of a "Scottish" restaurant, *Stac*

Polly narrowly avoids the kitsch with some classy touches, atmospheric surroundings and a hearty menu of game, fish and meat dishes. Closed lunchtimes Sat & Sun. Expensive.

Seafood

Café Royal Oyster Bar 17a W Register St ℡0131/556 4124. An Edinburgh classic, with its splendidly ornate Victorian interior (featured in *Chariots of Fire*), stained-glass windows, marble floor and Doulton tiling. Time-honoured seafood dishes, including freshly caught oysters, served in a civilized, chatty setting. Very expensive.

Fishers in the City 58 Thistle St ℡0131/225 5109, ⊛www.fishersbistros.co.uk. New Town incarnation of Leith's best-loved seafood bistro. This one has a sleek modern interior, great service and some stunning seafood. Expensive.

Mussel Inn 61–65 Rose St ℡0131/225 5979, ⊛www.mussel-inn.com. After feasting on a kilo of mussels and a basket of chips for under £10 you'll realize why there's a demand to get in here. Owned by two west coast shellfish farmers, which ensures that the time from sea to stomach is minimal. Closed Sun. Moderate.

Thai

Dusit 49a Thistle St, West End ℡0131/220 6846, ⊛www.dusit.co.uk. The bold but effective blend of Thai flavours and well-sourced Scottish ingredients here brings a bit of originality and refinement to the often predictable Thai dining scene. The moderately priced specialities include guinea fowl with red curry sauce or vegetables stir-fried with a dash of whisky.

Vegetarian

Henderson's Salad Table 94 Hanover St ℡0131/225 2131, ⊛www.hendersonsofedinburgh .co.uk. A much-loved Edinburgh institution, this self-service basement vegetarian restaurant offers freshly prepared hot dishes plus a decent choice of salads, soups and cakes. The slightly antiquated cafeteria feel can be off-putting, but the food is honest, reliable and always tasty. Light live jazz every evening. Open Mon–Sat 8am–10.30pm. Inexpensive to moderate.

Broughton and Leith Walk

On the eastern edge of the New Town, the area around **Broughton Street** is young, trendy and less upmarket than the very centre of the city. The city's gay community is an obvious influence here, and you'll find a strong Italian presence, including *Valvona & Crolla*, Edinburgh's outstanding deli. The restaurants at the top of **Leith Walk** may not be the most sophisticated in town, but many are open into the small hours.

Bistros, cafés and diners

Blue Moon Café 1 Barony St ☎0131/557 0911. One of the best-known beacons of Edinburgh's gay scene, this easygoing, straight-friendly café-bar serves decent coffee, hearty breakfasts and light meals right through to 11pm. Moderate.

Café Mediterraneo 73 Broughton St ☎0131/557 6900. A friendly little place with a deli counter and a small dining space, serving inexpensive Italianish food in unpretentious style – not a red-checked table cloth to be seen. Open daytime Sun–Thurs, and till 10pm Fri and Sat. Moderate.

Indian

Zest 15 North St Andrew St ☎0131/556 5028. A welcome burst of contemporary decor and style in the Indian restaurant scene. The menu keeps up, with subtle northern Indian flavours and fine seafood curries. Moderate.

Italian

La Favorita 325–331 Leith Walk ☎0131/554 2430 @www.la-favorita.com. Among Edinburgh's best pizzerias, thanks to its flavour-enhancing wood-fired ovens; the place itself has a swanky, modern, North Italian feel with slick service. Inexpensive to moderate.

Valvona & Crolla 19 Elm Row, Leith Walk ☎0131/556 6066, @www.valvonacrolla .com. The café at the back of this Italian deli – arguably Britain's finest – serves authentic and delicious breakfasts, lunches and snacks. The best advert for the café is the walk through the shop – which has food stacked from floor to ceiling, with display cabinets full of sublime olives, meats and cheeses. V&C also has a new wine bar and restaurant in the New Town (see p.134). Open Mon–Sat 8am–5pm. Moderate.

Thai

Thai Me Up in Edinburgh 4 Picardy Place ☎0131/558 9234, @www.tmeup.com. Not the most convincing of names, but the Thai cooking is fresh, dynamic and colourful. The menu is short and to the point, with specialities including steamed fish and beef in red curry sauce, and the "authentic" Thai artefacts are subtle enough to allow the food to take centre stage. Moderate.

Stockbridge and around

The northern fringe of the New Town, **Stockbridge** is the home of many of the city's young professionals, and the eating scene here is straightforward and pleasant.

Bistros, cafés and diners

Bell's Diner 7 St Stephen St, Stockbridge ☎0131/225 8116. An unpretentious front-room restaurant with a simple menu of home-made burgers, decent steaks and pancakes. It's only open in the evenings (plus Saturday lunch) and is a longstanding local favourite, so tables aren't easy to come by. Moderate.

Circus Café 15 North West Circus Place, Stockbridge ☎0131/220 0333. An ultra-chic bank conversion with impeccable foodie credentials: a deli and wine shop in the basement, and an upstairs café that's open until 11pm and makes use of the best of the produce with platters, salads and reasonably priced main dishes. Moderate.

The Gallery Café Scottish National Gallery of Modern Art, Belford Rd, Dean Village ☎0131/332 8600. Far more than a standard refreshment stop for gallery visitors, the cultured setting (which includes a lovely outside eating area) and appealing menu of hearty soups, healthy salads and filled croissants pulls in reassuring numbers of locals. Open daily 10am–4.30pm. Moderate.

Hamiltons Bar & Kitchen 18 Hamilton Place, Stockbridge ☎0131/226 4199. One of the city's few self-proclaimed "gastro-pubs", where the food is of equal importance to the booze. Expect blonde wood fittings and sea bass with your chips. Food served daily at lunch and dinner. Moderate.

Terrace Café Royal Botanic Garden, Inverleith ☎0131/552 0616. A great location right in the middle of the garden, with outside tables offering stunning views of the city skyline, but the food isn't that memorable and it can be busy (and noisy) with families. Inexpensive.

Indian

Lancers 5 Hamilton Place, Stockbridge ☎0131/332 3444. A reliable old-school Indian restaurant serving mostly rich, filling Bengali and Punjabi curries. Moderate.

Mexican

Blue Parrot Cantina 49 St Stephen's St, Stockbridge ☎0131/225 2941. Cosy, quirky, basement Mexican restaurant, with a frequently changing evening menu that makes a decent effort to deviate from the predictable clichés; house specialities include *pescado baja* (haddock with a creamy lime sauce). Evenings only. Moderate.

Scottish

The Snug 33a St Stephen's St, Stockbridge
℡0131/225 9397. Tiny but friendly wee place

tucked into a basement room where dishes involve reasonably imaginative combos of classic local produce such as salmon and beef. Moderate.

Lothian Road and Tollcross

This is Edinburgh's theatre district, featuring sophisticated, lively places to eat and drink, and good-value pre- and post-theatre deals. **Lothian Road** is another of the city's popular late-night stops, while **Tollcross**, a bit closer to the student areas of the Southside, is an up-and-coming area with a growing number of attractive cafés and restaurants.

Bistros, cafés and diners

blue 10 Cambridge St ℡0131/221 1222. With minimalist modern decor, this impressive café/bistro hits the spot in terms of standards of food and service. It's handy for a quality pre- or post-theatre bite, with tasty modern dishes such as sea bass and baby onion *tatin* or confit duck leg with black pudding mash for under £10, and is one of the city's more sophisticated child-friendly options. Closed Sun. Moderate.

Ndebele 57 Home St ℡0131/221 1141. Colourful African café offering sandwiches with lots of alternative fillings, salads and *biltong* for homesick South Africans. Open daily till 10pm. Inexpensive.

Chinese

izzi 119 Lothian Rd ℡0131/466 988,8 ⓦwww. izzi-restaurant.co.uk. Set among the bright lights and late-night revelry of Lothian Road, this is a slick, contemporary restaurant offering both Chinese and Japanese cuisine, including some of the better sushi around. Moderate.

Italian

Santini bis 8 Conference Square ℡0131/221 7788. A slice of Milanese sophistication in this thoroughly modern dining space in a rather out-of-the-way location on the ground floor of the *Sheraton* hotel. Split into two parts, the "bis" is more informal, while the restaurant is for high rollers only. Closed Sun. Moderate.

Scottish and seafood

The Atrium 10 Cambridge St ℡0131/228 8882, ⓦwww.atriumrestaurant.co.uk. One of the most consistently impressive of Edinburgh's top-end restaurants. Quirky, arty design including features such as railway-sleeper tables, while the food focuses on high-quality Scottish produce including Buccleuch beef *carpaccio*, or warm berries served with mascarpone sorbet. Closed Sun. Expensive.

Marque Central 30b Grindlay St ℡0131/229 9859, ⓦwww.marquecentral.co.uk. Right next door to the Lyceum Theatre and Usher Hall, it's a good spot for pre- and post-theatre deals. At any time a place for imaginative modern Scottish food. Closed Sun & Mon. Moderate to expensive.

Southside

As the student quarter of the city, the **Southside** boasts plenty of good-value eating, but you'll also find an appealing number of ambitious, attractive restaurants staked out here on the fringe of the more expensive city centre.

Bistros, cafés and diners

The Apartment 7–13 Barclay Place, Bruntsfield ℡0131/228 6456. Hugely popular, highly fashionable modern diner, with IKEA-style furniture, sisal flooring and abstract modern art on the walls. Their "Chunky, Healthy Lines" feature filling kebabs of meat, fish or vegetables. Closed lunch Mon–Fri. Moderate.

Blonde 75 St Leonards St ℡0131/668 2917. Pleasant neighbourhood bistro, serving intriguing global combos such as salmon with black olive

noodles and venison with cardamom and bitter chocolate. Closed Mon lunch. Moderate.

Favorit 30–32 Leven St, Bruntsfield ℡0131/221 1800. Thoroughly modern café-diner dishing up coffees, fruit shakes, cakes and big sandwiches, as well as drinks, right through to 12.30am. The branch at 19–20 Teviot Place is open even later.

Kaffe Politik 146 Marchmont Rd, Marchmont ℡0131/446 9873. Café culture hits the student fiefdom of deepest Marchmont, in a relaxed and stylish venue serving coffees and impressive lunchtime and evening light meals such as toasted focaccia and creamy chicken laksa. Closed Sun eve. Inexpensive.

Indian

Kalpna 2–3 St Patrick's Square, Newington ☎0131/667 9890. Outstanding vegetarian restaurant serving authentic Gujarati dishes. Four set meals, including a vegan option, stand alongside the main menu. Moderate.

The Lunch Box Edinburgh Central Mosque, 50 Potterrow, Newington. Basic but filling and very cheap curries served from a tiny kitchen behind the mosque; the only seating is outside under a large awning. Popular with students and on sunny days. Inexpensive.

Original Khushi's 26–30 Potterrow, Newington ☎0131/667 0888, ⊛www.khushis.com. The latest incarnation of Edinburgh's (and one of Britain's) oldest curry houses; now it's a slick, friendly, modern curry café serving some excellent food and lip-smacking lassis. No corkage on BYOB. Moderate.

North African

Phenecia 55–57 W Nicolson St, Newington ☎0131/662 4493. A basic, easygoing joint beside the main university campus, serving mostly Tunisian food but drawing on a variety of Mediterranean cuisines; the three-course lunch for under £5 is very good value. Moderate.

Scottish and seafood

Fenwicks 15 Salisbury Place, Newington ☎0131/667 4265 ⊛www.fenwicks-restaurant .co.uk. One of the better places to eat in this part of town, this is a pleasant chef-owned operation serving dishes based around good Scottish produce. Moderate

The New Bell 233 Causewayside ☎0131/668 2868 ⊛www.thenewbell.com. A cosy, pleasant restaurant located above (but separate from) a pub, serving tasty meat and fish dishes such as seared tuna or roast guinea fowl. They're followed by crowd-pleasing desserts such as banana *tarte tatin*. Moderate.

Sweet Melinda's 11 Roseneath St, Marchmont ☎0131/229 7953. A smart seafood restaurant in a single, timber-panelled room with a friendly neighbourhood feel. It's edging towards the expensive side, but it's worth shelling out for dishes such as mackerel served with chorizo, or exquisitely fried squid. Closed Sun & lunchtime Mon. Moderate to expensive.

Thai

Thaisanuk 21 Argyle Place, Marchmont ☎0131/228 8855. Tiny diner offering inexpensive sit-in meals as well as some of the best takeaway/ delivery around. There are dishes from Malaysia and Vietnam alongside the Thai classics, but clean, rich, authentic flavours prevail, and you can bring your own alcohol to help keep the costs down. Open daily 6–11pm. Moderate.

Turkish

Hanedan 41 W Preston St, Newington ☎0131/667 4242. Another small and relatively simple BYOB. There's an authenticity to the kebabs, moussaka and *dolmates* which makes this place an interesting alternative to cheaper Italian or bistro fare. Closed Mon. Moderate.

Vegetarian

Susie's Diner 51 W Nicolson St, Newington ☎0131/667 8729. Popular café serving inventive soups, savouries and puddings, and a range of vegan food, to crowds of students. Inexpensive.

Leith

The area around the cobbled Shore of **Leith**, along the edge of the Water of Leith just as it reaches the sea, is the best-known dining quarter in Edinburgh, and lives up to its billing with good-quality, laid-back seafood bistros.

Bistros, cafés and diners

Café Truva 77 The Shore. Surprisingly, café culture hasn't really made it to Leith, but this Turkish-owned place just back from the water serves up decent daytime sandwiches and snacks, as well as coffee made both in the Italian and the Turkish way. Inexpensive.

Daniel's 88 Commercial St ☎0131/553 5933. Likeable, well-run bistro in an attractive setting on the ground floor of a converted warehouse. Food is

heartily French, with many dishes from the Alsace; the *tarte flambée*, one of the house specialities, is a simple but delicious onion and bacon pizza. Open daily 10am–10pm. Moderate.

French

Restaurant Martin Wishart 52 The Shore ☎0131/553 3557, ⊛www.martin-wishart.co.uk. One of only two Michelin-starred restaurants in Edinburgh, this place wows the gourmets with

△ Restaurant Martin Wishart

highly accomplished, French-influenced Scottish food (three-course lunch for around £20, five-course evening tasting menu at £55). The food is incredible, though the decor is rather beige. Reservations recommended. Closed Sat lunch, Sun & Mon. Very expensive.

The Vintner's Rooms 87 Giles St ☎0131/554 6767 ⓦwww.thevintnersrooms.com. Splendid restaurant in a seventeenth-century warehouse; the small but ornate Rococo dining room is a marvel and the food – from seafood to game – isn't bad either. Closed Sun eve & Mon. Expensive.

Indian

Britannia Spice 150 Commercial St ☎0131/555 2255, ⓦwww.britanniaspice.co.uk. The decor has a nautical theme, the food is prepared by specialist chefs from the subcontinent and the awards for this ambitious Indian restaurant have been piling up. Moderate.

Seafood

Fishers 1 The Shore ☎0131/554 5666, ⓦwww .fishersbistros.co.uk. One of the first wave of seafood bistros which put Leith's dining scene on the map. The menu here has an appealing range of expensive and fancy fish dishes, but there are also impressive bar-style snacks such as fishcakes and chowder. Reservations recommended. Moderate.

The Shore 3–4 The Shore ☎0131/553 5080. A well-lived-in bar/restaurant with huge mirrors, wood panelling and aproned waiters who serve up good fish dishes and decent wines. Live jazz, folk and hubbub floats through from the adjoining bar. Moderate.

Skippers Seafood Bistro 1a Dock Place ☎0131/554 1018, ⓦwww.skippers.co.uk. More relaxed than it looks from the outside, with a vaguely nautical atmosphere and a tempting menu based around Scottish fish and shellfish. Moderate.

The Waterfront 1c Dock Place ☎0131/554 7427 ⓦwww.waterfrontwinebar.co.uk. Housed in the former lock-keeper's cottage, you can eat in the wonderfully characterful wine bar or waterside conservatory. Again, fish dishes dominate. Moderate.

Specialist food shops

As in any other city in Britain, supermarkets dominate day-to-day food shopping in Edinburgh, but there are plenty of examples of good delis and specialist food retailers if you're prepared to seek them out. Most venerated of all is **Valvona & Crolla**, 19 Elm Row, Leith Walk, where you encounter a mouthwatering array of top-notch Italian produce, much of it delivered directly by a weekly truck from Milan's markets. If you want to discover some locally grown produce, there's a **Farmers' Market** on Castle every Saturday morning (9am–2pm). **Iain Mellis Cheesemonger** has three shops around town (30a Victoria St, 330 Morningside Rd and 6 Baker's Place, Stockbridge), all of which focus on expertly conditioned farmhouse and artisan cheeses from Britain and Ireland. For a decent range of general deli items, sold in shops which are open until late at night, look out for one of the **Peckhams** stores at 155–159 Bruntsfield Place, 49 South Clerk St, Southside and 48 Raeburn Place, Stockbridge.

Pubs and bars

Many of Edinburgh's **pubs**, especially in the Old Town, have histories that stretch back centuries, while others, particularly in the New Town, are unaltered Victorian or Edwardian period pieces. Add a plentiful supply of trendy modern **bars**, and there's enough to cater for all tastes. The standard licensing hours are 11am–11pm (12.30–11pm on Sundays), but many honest howffs stay open later and, during the Festival especially, it's no problem to find bars open till at least 1am.

Edinburgh has a long history of brewing beer, though only one working **brewery** remains in the city itself, the small Caledonian Brewery in the western reaches of town. Owned by multinational Scottish & Newcastle, it still uses old techniques and equipment to produce some of the best specialist beers in Britain. Tours (£7.50) of the brewery can be organized – call ☎0131/337 1286 or see ⓦwww.Caledonian-brewery.co.uk for details. For more on Scottish beer, see p.52.

Once upon a time Edinburgh's main drinking strip was the near-legendary **Rose Street**, a pedestrianized lane tucked between Princes and George streets in the New Town: the ultimate Edinburgh pub crawl was to take a drink in each of its dozen or so establishments. Things are a bit more sophisticated these days, with **George Street** itself taking a lead: various former financial institutions have been converted into bars, with a predictable invasion of suits by day and style by night. On the outer fringes of the New Town, **Stockbridge** features pleasant drinking establishments, whereas the **Broughton** area is one of the city's liveliest, as well as the established meeting point for the gay community.

While many of the **Royal Mile**'s pubs aren't ashamed to make the most of local historical connections to draw in the tourists, you don't have to travel far to find some lively places, notably the busy pubs in and around the **Grassmarket**, with a further batch on the studenty **Southside**. **Leith** has a range of bars, from rough spit-and-sawdust places to polished pseudo-Victoriana, though we've also listed a number of characterful places further away from the centre.

A fun way to explore Edinburgh's pubs is to take the **Edinburgh Literary Pub Tour**, a pub crawl with culture around Old and New Town watering holes. Led by professional actors, the tour introduces you to the scenes, characters and words of the major figures of Scottish literature, including Burns, Scott and MacDiarmid. The tour starts from the *Beehive Inn*, 18–20 Grassmarket (for contact details, see p.81).

The Royal Mile and around

Albanach 197 High St. A contemporary take on the Scottish theme bar: traditional elements such as bare stone and wood mix with hints of the Highlands colouring, but there's nothing old-fashioned about the place. Young trendies mix with tourists chuffed they've found somewhere without looped bagpipe music. Standard bar food served.

Bannermans 212 Cowgate. Once the best pub in the street, now the late-night live music can be a bit intrusive. Still atmospheric, however – a former vintner's cellar, it has a labyrinthine interior deep under the Old Town and good beer on tap. Open daily till 1am.

Black Bo's 55 Blackfriars St. No music and no decent ales, but a good example of how to stay trendy without going minimalist, with church pews and candles alongside original art and DJ decks. Just fifty yards from the Royal Mile, but well off the tourist trail. Vegetarian restaurant a couple of doors away (see p.134).

Bow Bar 80 West Bow. Wonderful old wood-panelled bar that won an award as the best drinkers' pub in Britain a few years back. Choose from among nearly 150 whiskies or a changing selection of first-rate Scottish and English cask beers.

City Café 19 Blair St. Longstanding but determinedly trendy bar on the street linking the Royal Mile to the clubbers' hub along the Cowgate. The blue pool tables are always popular and you can buy candies behind the American-style bar.

Doric Tavern 15 Market St. Long-established upstairs wine bar (open till 1am) is a favoured watering hole of journalists and artists. The brasserie beside the wine bar serves reliably good-quality Scottish food.

Hebrides Bar 17 Market St. Home from home for Edinburgh's Highland community; there's a ceilidh atmosphere with lots of jigs, strathspeys and reels, but no tartan kitsch.

Jolly Judge 7a James Court. Atmospheric, low-ceilinged bar in a close just down from the Castle. Cosy in winter and pleasant outside in summer.

Last Drop 74–78 Grassmarket. The "Drop" refers to the Edinburgh gallows, which were located out front, and whose former presence is symbolized in the red paintwork of the exterior. Cheapish pub food and, like its competitors in the same block, patronized mainly by students. Open till 1am.

North Bridge 20 North Bridge. Plush cocktail bar and brasserie of *The Scotsman Hotel* (see p.83), with its slick glass island bar contrasting with ornate pillars and original panelling. Decent food is served at intimate tables for two on the encircling balcony.

Villager 49–50 George IV Bridge. The bar of the moment in this part of town, so expect the local glitterati and lots of designer clothing in amongst the chocolate-brown sofas and teetering bar stools.

New Town and West End

Café Royal Circle Bar 17 W Register St. As notable as the *Oyster Bar* restaurant next door, the *Café Royal* is worth a visit just for its Victorian decor, notably the huge elliptical island bar and the tiled portraits of renowned inventors. More than that, the beer and food are good, too.

Cumberland Bar 1 Cumberland St. One of the few pubs in this part of the New Town, this mellow, cultured, old-fashioned place full of wood panelling and cosy nooks is a delightful find, and serves excellent cask-conditioned ales.

The Dome 14 George St. Opulent conversion of a massive New Town bank, thronging with well-dressed locals. Probably the most impressive bar interior in Edinburgh, though the ultra-chic atmosphere can be a bit intense. Sun–Thurs open till 11.30pm, Fri & Sat till 1am.

Opal Lounge 51 George St. A much-talked about, low-ceilinged bar with a faintly oriental theme, loud music and a long cocktail list. Over-dressed twentysomethings flock here for a glimpse of local celebrities, but usually have to stand in a queue and squeeze past the bouncers to get in.

Oxford Bar 8 Young St. An unpretentious, unspoilt, no-nonsense city bar – which is why local crime writer Ian Rankin and his Inspector Rebus like it so much. Fans duly make the pilgrimage, but fortunately not all the regulars have been scared off. Open until 1am.

Rick's 55a Frederick St. One of the most popular "scene" bars in the city centre, filled with suits after work and glad rags later on. There's good food from their bistro, and rooms (see p.87) as well. Open till 1am.

Whighams Wine Cellars 13 Hope St, Charlotte Square. One of the more sophisticated venues in the city centre, with an impressive wine list and some gloomy subterranean cubby holes. Recent expansion has added a stylish edge, and there's good seafood available, too.

Broughton and Leith Walk

The Barony Bar 81–85 Broughton St. A fine old-fashioned bar which manages to be big and lively without being spoilt. Chainification has blunted a bit of its appeal, but there's still real ale and a blazing fire.

The Basement 10a Broughton St. This dimly lit, grungy drinking hole has long been a favourite of the Bohemian Broughton Street crowd, with odd furniture made from old JCBs and filling food served by Hawaiian-shirted staff. Open till 1am.

The Outhouse 12a Broughton Street Lane. Busy pre-club bar tucked away down a cobbled lane off Broughton Street, with a lively beer garden and funky music. Open till 1am.

Stockbridge

Baillie Bar 2 St Stephen St. The best of the district's traditional pubs, with English and Scottish ales as well as reasonable pub grub. Open Sun–Thurs till midnight, Fri & Sat till 1am.

Bert's Bar 2–4 Raeburn Place, Stockbridge (also 29 William St, West End). Popular locals' pubs with a lived-in feel, despite their relatively recent arrival. Both serve excellent beer, tasty pies and strive to be authentic, non-theme-oriented venues, though the telly rarely misses any sporting action.

Lothian Road and Tollcross

Bennets Bar 8 Leven St, Tollcross. Edwardian pub with mahogany-framed mirrors and Art Nouveau stained glass; gets packed in the evening, particularly when there's a show at the King's Theatre next door. Mon–Sat serves lunch and opens till midnight.

Blue Blazer 2 Spittal St. This traditional Edinburgh howff with an oak-clad bar and church pews serves as good a selection of real ales as you'll find anywhere in the city. Open till 1am.

Monboddo 36 Bread St. Stylish modern bar on the street level of the chic *Point Hotel* (see p.83). Serves fine food at lunchtimes and beer in tall glasses by evening.

Traverse Bar Café Traverse Theatre, 10 Cambridge St. Much more than just a theatre bar, attracting a lively, sophisticated crowd who dispel any notion of a quiet interval drink. Good food available. One of *the* places to be during the Festival.

The Southside

Drouthy Neebors Causewayside, Newington. What a Scottish theme bar will look like when it's exported around the world to countries bored with Irish theme bars. Popular with students, and often lively. Open till 1am.

Human Be-In 2–8 West Crosscauseway, Newington. One of the trendiest student bars around, with huge plate-glass windows to admire the beautiful people and tables outside for summer posing. Good food too. Open till 1am.

Peartree House 36 W Nicolson St, Newington. Fine bar in an eighteenth-century house with old sofas and a large courtyard – one of central Edinburgh's very few beer gardens. Serves budget bar lunches. Open Mon–Wed & Sun until midnight, Thurs–Sat until 1am.

Leith

Cameo Bar 23 Commercial St. Relaxed place with different nooks and crannies, odd art and an astroturf putting green out the back.

Kings Wark 36 The Shore. Real ale in an atmospheric restored eighteenth-century pub right in the heart of Leith, with bar meals chalked up on the rafters. Open till midnight Fri & Sat.

Ship on the Shore 24–26 The Shore. The homeliest and least expensive of the waterfront bar-brasseries, serving fish-oriented meals and a changing range of cask ales.

The Shore 3–4 The Shore. Atmospheric traditional bar with an adjacent restaurant (see p.140). There's regular live jazz or folk music as well as real ales and good bar snacks.

Elsewhere in the city

Athletic Arms (The Diggers) 1–3 Angle Park Terrace, Polwarth. Known to all as *Diggers* after the spade-wielding employees of the cemetery across the road, this is a place of pilgrimage if you're into sport (Murrayfield and Hearts' Tyncastle ground are just along the road) and real ale, with the Caledonian Brewery's beers well represented. Open Mon–Thurs till midnight, Fri & Sat till 1am, Sun till 6pm.

Caley Sample Room 58 Angle Park Terrace, Polwarth. Showcase pub for the cask ales of the nearby Caledonian Brewery, though it gets fearsomely thronged when there's a big game at Murrayfield. Open Mon–Thurs & Sun till midnight, Fri & Sat till 1am.

Canny Man's (Volunteer Arms) 237 Morningside Rd, Morningside. Atmospheric and idiosyncratic pub-cum-museum adorned with anything that can

be hung on the walls or from the ceiling. Local ales and over 200 whiskies on offer, as well as snacks.

Cramond Inn Cramond Village. This old inn by the riverside at Cramond is the perfect place for a drink or a pub meal after a stroll along the coastal path.

Sheep Heid Inn 43 The Causeway, Duddingston. One of Edinburgh's best-known historic pubs, the building has barely survived various predictable makeovers, but despite this, remains an attractive spot. Decent meals are available at the bar, and there's an old-fashioned skittle alley out the back.

Nightlife and entertainment

Inevitably, Edinburgh's **nightlife** is at its best during the Festival (see p.147), which can make the other 49 weeks of the year seem like an anticlimax. However, at any time the city has plenty to offer, especially in the realm of **theatre** and **music**.

The **nightclub** scene is lively, with some excellent venues hosting a changing selection of one-nighters. In the bigger establishments, you may find different clubs taking place on each floor. Most of the city-centre clubs stay open till around 3am. While you can normally hear **live jazz**, **folk** and **rock** every evening in one or other of the city's pubs, for the really big rock events, ad hoc places – such as the Castle Esplanade or Murrayfield Stadium – are sometimes pressed into service. The city has permanent venues large enough to host large touring **orchestras** and **ballet** companies; elsewhere you can also uncover a lively **comedy** club and a couple of excellent arthouse **cinemas**.

Edinburgh has a dynamic **gay** culture, for years centred round the top of Leith Walk and Broughton Street, where the first gay and lesbian centre appeared in the 1970s. Since the start of the 1990s, more and more gay enterprises, especially cafés and nightclubs, have moved into this area, now dubbed the "Pink Triangle".

Hogmanay

One way of celebrating **Hogmanay** is to join one of the street parties which are held in the middle of towns and cities, often centred around a prominent clockface which rings out "the bells" at midnight. These days, the largest New Year's Eve street party in Europe takes place in Edinburgh, with around 100,000 people on the streets of the city enjoying the culmination of a week-long series of events. On the night itself, stages are set up in different parts of the city centre, with big-name rock groups and local ceilidh bands playing to the increasingly inebriated masses. The high point of the evening is, of course, midnight, when hundreds of tons of fireworks are let off into the night sky above the Castle, and Edinburgh joins the rest of the world singing "**Auld Lang Syne**", an old Scottish tune with lyrics by Robert Burns, Scotland's national poet.

For more details about the background to Hogmanay, see *Festivals* colour section. For information about celebrations in Edinburgh, and how to get hold of tickets for the street party, go to ⓦwww.edinburghshogmanay.org.

The best way to find out **what's on** is to pick up a copy of *The List*, a fortnightly listings magazine covering both Edinburgh and Glasgow (£2.20). Alternatively, get hold of the *Edinburgh Evening News*, which appears daily except Sunday: its listings column gives details of performances in the city that day, hotels and bars included. Information on nightclubs can be found on posters and piles of leaflets distributed to most of the pre-club bars around town. Box offices of individual halls and theatres are likewise liberally supplied with promotional leaflets about forthcoming music and theatre, and some are able to sell tickets for more than one venue.

Nightclubs

The Bongo Club Moray House, Holyrood Rd ☎0131/558 7604, ⊛www.thebongoclub.co.uk. Legendary Edinburgh club with a new venue; its line-up is eclectic but always worth checking out. Look out for the mighty dub and reggae Messenger Sound System twice monthly on Saturdays.

Cabaret Voltaire 36–38 Blair St ☎0131/220 6176. A nightclub in the atmospheric setting of the Old Town's underground vaults. Head here for some fine R&B and hip-hop at weekends, as well as live acoustic sets in the week.

Ego 14 Picardy Place ☎0131/478 7434. A former casino, this big venue hosts Wiggle, which plays to a gay and mixed crowd monthly on Saturdays, and the epic party night Vegas.

Honeycomb 15–17 Niddrie St ☎0131/530 5540, ⊛www.the-honeycomb.com. In amongst the vaults and hidden passageways under the Old Town, hosting big drum'n'bass night Manga and the free Motherfunk nights on Tuesdays.

The Liquid Room 9c Victoria St ☎0131/225 2564, ⊛www.liquidroom.com. One of the best of the larger venues, with nights including cabaret-cum–disco Snatch (Thurs), gay-friendly Taste (Sun) and Colours (Sat), a monthly house/techno club drawing big-name DJs.

Opal Lounge 51 George St ☎0131/226 2275, ⊛www.opallounge.co.uk. See and be-seen bar in the New Town with DJs funking things up later on. Always has a quota of suits who didn't make it home.

Gay clubs and bars

CC Bloom's 23–24 Greenside Place ☎0131/556 9331. Edinburgh's only uniquely gay club, with a big dance floor, stonking rhythms and a young, friendly crowd.

Planet Out 6 Baxter's Place ☎0131/524 0061. Trendy, friendly bar down from the Playhouse Theatre.

Sala 60 Broughton St ☎0131/478 7069. Fresh food, light Spanish snacks and drinks in a relaxed atmosphere at the Edinburgh Gay, Lesbian and Bisexual Centre. Open 11am–11pm. Closed Mon.

The Street 2 Picardy Place ☎0131/556 4272. Located at the top of Broughton Street, and therefore at the "gateway" to the Pink Triangle, this mainstream, gay-friendly bar is a sociable spot and good for watching the world (and talent) pass by.

Live music venues

Bannermans 212 Cowgate ☎0131/556 3254, ⊛www.bannermansgigs.co.uk. The best place in central Edinburgh to discover local indie bands hoping for a big break.

Corn Exchange 11 Newmarket Rd, Slateford ☎0131/477 3500, ⊛www.ece.uk.com. Once a slaughterhouse, now it's a 3000-capacity venue for big-name contemporary pop and rock acts, though the location, three miles west of the centre, is a bit off-putting.

Henry's Jazz Cellar 8 Morrison St, off Lothian Rd ☎0131/467 5200. Edinburgh's premier jazz and hip-hop venue, with live music every night and regular top performers.

The Liquid Room 9c Victoria St ☎0131/225 2564, ⊛www.liquidroom.com. Good-sized venue frequented by visiting indie and local R&B bands.

Queen's Hall 89 Clerk St ☎0131/668 2019, ⊛www.queenshalledinburgh.co.uk. Converted Georgian church which now operates as a concert hall; it's used principally by the Scottish Chamber Orchestra and Scottish Ensemble, and much favoured by jazz, blues and folk groups.

Royal Oak 1 Infirmary St ☎0131/557 2976, ⊛www.royal-oak-folk.com. A traditional pub hosting regular informal folk sessions and the "Wee Folk Club" on Sundays.

Sandy Bell's 25 Forrest Rd ☎0131/225 2751. A friendly bar and a good bet for folk music most nights of the week.

Usher Hall Cnr Lothian Rd and Grindlay St ☎0131/228 1155, ⊛www.usherhall.co.uk. Edinburgh's main civic concert hall, seating over 2500. Excellent for choral and symphony concerts, but less suitable for solo vocalists. The upper circle seats are cheapest and have the best acoustics, but the sound quality is overall much improved after a recent refurbishment.

Whistlebinkies 4–6 South Bridge ☎0131/557 5114, ⓦwww.whistlebinkies.com. One of the most reliable places to find live music every night of the week – often it's rock and pop covers, though there are some folk evenings. Daily till 3am.

Theatre and dance

Assembly Rooms 54 George St ☎0131/228 1155, ⓦwww.assemblyroomsedinburgh.co.uk. Varied complex of small and large halls. Used all year, but really comes into its own during the Fringe, featuring large-scale drama productions and mainstream comedy.

Bedlam Theatre 2a Forrest Rd ☎0131/225 9893, ⓦwww.bedlamtheatre.co.uk. Housed in a converted Victorian church and used predominantly by student productions of varying quality and impact, it does raise its game during the Festival.

Dance Base 14–16 Grassmarket, ☎0131/225 5255, ⓦwww.dancebase.co.uk. Scotland's sparkling new National Centre for Dance is used mostly for modern dance workshops and classes, but also hosts occasional performances.

Festival Theatre Nicolson St ☎0131/529 6000, ⓦwww.eft.co.uk. The largest stage in Britain, principally used for Scottish Opera and Scottish Ballet's appearances in the capital, but also for everything from the children's show *Singing Kettle* to Engelbert Humperdinck.

King's Theatre 2 Leven St ☎0131/529 6000. Stately Edwardian civic theatre that majors in pantomime, touring West End plays and the occasional major drama or opera performance.

Playhouse Theatre 18–22 Greenside Place ☎0870/606 3424, ⓦwww.eft.co.uk. The most capacious theatre in Britain, formerly a cinema. Recently refurbished, and used largely for extended runs of popular musicals and occasional rock concerts.

Royal Lyceum Theatre 30 Grindlay St ☎0131/248 4848, ⓦwww.lyceum.org.uk. Fine Victorian civic theatre with a compact auditorium. The leading year-round venue for mainstream drama.

Theatre Workshop 34 Hamilton Place ☎0131/226 5425, ⓦwww.theatre-workshop .com. Enticing programmes of international innovative theatre and performance art. Strong in the Festival and over Christmas, but fewer shows at other times.

Traverse Theatre 10 Cambridge St ☎0131/228 1404, ⓦwww.traverse.co.uk. Unquestionably one of Britain's premier venues for new plays and avant-garde drama from around the world. Going from strength to strength in its new custom-built home beside the Usher Hall, with a great bar downstairs and the popular *blue* café-bar upstairs.

Comedy

Jongleurs Omni Centre, Greenside Place ☎0870/787 0707, ⓦwww.jongleurs.com. An Edinburgh link in a national chain located in a huge glass-fronted cinema complex at the foot of Calton Hill. Fairly reliable for a year-round chance to encounter popular Festival stand-up acts and national stars.

The Stand Comedy Club 5 York Place ☎0131/558 7272 ⓦwww.thestand.co.uk. The city's top comedy spot, with a different act on every night and some of the UK's top comics headlining at the weekends. The bar is worth a visit in itself.

Cinemas

Cameo 38 Home St, Tollcross ☎0131/228 2800, ⓦwww.picturehouses.co.uk; bookings ☎0131/228 4141. A treasure of an art-house cinema; screens more challenging mainstream releases and cult late-nighters. Tarantino's been here and thinks it's great.

Dominion 18 Newbattle Terrace, Morningside ☎0131/447 4771, ⓦwww.dominioncinemas.net. A reminder of how cinemas were before multiplexes, the Dominion is still family-owned, and battling on with its screenings of popular new releases.

Filmhouse 88 Lothian Rd ☎0131/228 2688, ⓦwww.filmhousecinema.com. Three screens showing an eclectic programme of independent, art-house and classic films. Their café is a hangout for the city's dedicated film buffs.

Odeon 118 Lothian Rd ☎0131/221 1477, ⓦwww.odeon.co.uk; info and bookings ☎0870/224 4007. Central four-screen cinema showing the latest releases.

Ster Century Ocean Terminal, Ocean Drive, Leith ☎0131/553 0700, ⓦwww.stercentury.co.uk. Big multiplex in the docklands with plenty of bars and restaurants nearby.

UGC Fountainpark Dundee St, Fountainbridge ☎0871/200 2000, ⓦwww.ugccinemas.co.uk. Big, reasonably central multiplex not far from Tollcross and Bruntsfield.

Warner Village Omni Omni Centre, Greenside Place ☎0871/224 0240, ⓦwww.warnervillage .co.uk. Most central of the big new multiscreen venues, tucked under Calton Hill at the top of Leith Walk.

Shopping

Despite the relentless advance of the big chains, it's still possible to track down some characterful and unusual shops in central Edinburgh. **Princes Street**, one of Britain's most famous shopping streets, is all but dominated by standard chain outlets, though no serious shopper should miss out on a visit to Edinburgh's venerable department store, Jenners, at 48 Princes St, opposite the Scott Monument. More fashionable upmarket shops and boutiques are to be found on and around parallel **George Street**, including a newly created shopping area on the east side of St Andrew Square. There's nothing compelling about central Edinburgh's two big shopping malls, **Princes Mall** and the **St James Centre**, which are dominated by the big names.

For more original outlets, head for **Cockburn Street**, south of Waverley Station, a hub for trendy clothes and record shops, while on **Victoria Street** and in and around the **Grassmarket** you'll find an eclectic range of antique, crafts, food and book shops. Along and around the **Royal Mile** there are several distinctly offbeat places among the tacky souvenir sellers.

Books Waterstones is the major bookselling presence in Edinburgh, with large stores at 128 Princes St (℡0131/226 2666), 13–14 Princes St (℡0131/556 3034) and 83 George St (℡0131/225 3436). Ottakars at 57 George St (℡0131/225 4495) is the main city-centre alternative, with a Blackwells' store at 53–59 South Bridge (℡0131/662 8222) providing a strong general/academic presence near the university. There's a good selection of antiquarian bookshops in the city: Peter Bell, 68 West Port ℡0131/229 0562; McFeely's, 30 Buccleuch St ℡0131/662 8570; McNaughtan's Bookshop, 3a–4a Haddington Place, Leith Walk ℡0131/556 5897; and West Port Books, 147 West Port ℡0131/229 4431. Most of these sell a wide range of secondhand books: for shelves of cheap secondhand paperbacks also try Broughton Books, 2a Broughton Place (℡0131/557 8010), and Second Edition, 9 Howard St (℡0131/556 9403).

Clothes (new) Some of the more interesting clothes shops in town include: Corniche, 2–4 Jeffrey St ℡0131/556 3707 (ladies' and men's designer labels); Cruise, 80 George St ℡0131/226 3524 (men's fashion); Fabhatrix, 13 Cowgatehead ℡0131/225 9222 (contemporary hats); Harvey Nichols, 30–34 St Andrew Square ℡0131/524 8388 (expensive designer labels); Helen Bateman Shoes, 16 William St ℡0131/220 4495 (women's designer shoes); Ness, 367 High St ℡0131/226 5227 (contemporary Scottish knitwear and accessories).

Clothes (secondhand) Wm Armstrong, 81–83 Grassmarket ℡0131/220 5557, also at 64 Clerk St ℡0131/667 3056; Herman Brown, 151 West Port ℡0131/228 2589; Paddy Barras, 15 Grassmarket ℡0131/226 3087; and Flip, 60–62 South Bridge ℡0131/556 4966.

Crafts Anta, 91–93 West Bow, Victoria St ℡0131/226 4616; Just Scottish, 6 North Bank St ℡0131/226 4807; National Museum of Scotland Shop, Chambers St ℡0131/247 4422.

Maps Carson Clark, 181–183 Canongate (℡0131/556 4710), sells antique maps, charts and globes. Street maps can be found in all the main bookshops (see above) and the tourist information centre. Ordnance Survey maps for hill walking are available from good outdoor stores.

Music Check out Avalanche, 17 West Nicolson St (℡0131/668 2374), 28 Lady Lawson St (℡0131/228 1939) and 63 Cockburn St (℡0131/225 3939) for indie music; Coda, 12 Bank St (℡0131/622 7246) for contemporary Scottish folk and roots music; McAlister Matheson Music, 1 Grindlay St (℡0131/228 3827) for classical and jazz; Fopp, 55 Cockburn St (℡0131/220 0133) for a wide range of CDs; Underground Solu'shun, 9 Cockburn St (℡0131/226 2242) for house, garage, techno and drum'n'bass vinyl; and Vinyl Villains, 5 Elm Row (℡0131/558 1170) for secondhand records, tapes and ephemera.

Outdoors Tiso, 123–125 Rose St ℡0131/225 9486.

Tartan Kinloch Anderson, cnr Commercial and Dock streets, Leith (℡0131/555 1390), has a large showroom; Geoffrey Tailor, 57–59 High St (℡0131/557 0256) is one of the largest and most respected retailers on the Royal Mile – as well as traditional tartan they sell a line of "21st-century kilts" in materials including leather, plain tweed and camouflage pattern.

Whisky Royal Mile Whiskies, 379–381 High St ℡0131/225 3383; William Cadenhead, 172 Canongate ℡0131/556 5864.

Woollen goods Bill Baber Knitwear, 66 Grassmarket (℡0131/225 3249), has garments designed and made on the premises; Ragamuffin, 278 Canongate (℡0131/557 6007), features Skye knitwear.

The Edinburgh Festival

The **Edinburgh Festival** is actually an umbrella term which encompasses different festivals taking place at around the same time in the city. The principal events are the **Edinburgh International Festival** and the much larger **Edinburgh Festival Fringe**, but there are also **Film**, **Book**, **Jazz and Blues** and **Television** festivals, the **Military Tattoo** on the Castle Esplanade and the **Edinburgh Mela**, an Asian festival held over a weekend in late August/early September. For details about the background of the Edinburgh Festival, see *Festivals* colour section.

Doing the Festival

For the visitor, the sheer volume of the Festival's output can be bewildering: virtually every branch of arts and entertainment is represented somewhere, and world-famous stars mix with pub singers in the daily line-up. It can be a struggle to find **accommodation**, get hold of the tickets you want, book a table in a restaurant or simply get from one side of town to another; you can end up seeing something truly dire, or something mind-blowing; you'll inevitably try to do too much, stay out too late or spend too much money – but then again, most Festival veterans will tell you that if you don't experience these things then you haven't really done the Festival.

Note that dates, venues, names, star acts, happening bars and burning issues change from one year to the next. This unpredictability is one of the Festival's greatest charms, however, so while the following information will help you get to grips with it, be prepared for – indeed, enjoy – the unexpected. If you want up-to-the-minute information at any time of year, ⓦ **www.edinburghfestivals .co.uk** has links to the home pages of most of Edinburgh's main festivals.

The Edinburgh International Festival

The legacy of Rudolf Bing's Glyndebourne connections ensured that, for many years, the **Edinburgh International Festival** (sometimes called the "Official Festival") was dominated by opera. Although in the 1980s international theatre, ballet, dance and classical music were introduced, it's still very much a highbrow event, and forays into populist territory remain rare.

Edinburgh's other festivals

Quite apart from August's Edinburgh Festival, the city is now promoting itself as a year-round festival venue, with a number of different events well established. The **Science Festival** in April (☏0131/558 7666, ⓦwww.sciencefestival.co.uk) incorporates hands-on children's events as well as numerous lectures on a vast array of subjects. There's also a **Puppet and Animation Festival** in March (☏01786/467155, ⓦwww.puppetanimation.org), and a **Children's Festival** in late May (☏0131/225 8050 ⓦwww.imaginate.org.uk), with readings, magicians and specialist children's drama.

During December, **Edinburgh's Christmas** (ⓦwww.edinburghchristmas.com) draws together various seasonal events, most prominently the installation of a huge ferris wheel beside the Scott Monument and an outdoor skating rink nearby. At the turn of the year, **Edinburgh's Hogmanay** (see box on p.143) is one of the world's largest New Year street parties, involving torchlight processions, folk and rock concerts and fireworks galore. There's more revelry on the night of April 30 at **Beltane** (ⓦwww .beltane.org), an ancient Celtic fire festival celebrating the arrival of spring, which has a New-Agey feel to it with lots of painted flesh, beating drums and huge bonfires.

Finding out what's on

In addition to each festival's own programme, various publications give information about what's on day by day during the Festival. Every day the Fringe Office publishes **The Guide**, giving a chronological listing of virtually every Fringe show scheduled for that day. It's available free from the Office and hundreds of other spots around Edinburgh, as well as with the **Guardian** newspaper's Scottish edition. Of the local newspapers, the best coverage is in the **Scotsman**, which issues a dedicated daily Festival supplement. Their reviews and star-rating system carry a lot of weight. The **Herald**, published in Glasgow, also has good if slightly detached coverage. Most London-based newspapers print daily festival news and reviews, notably the **Guardian** and **The Times**. For a local view, the **Edinburgh Evening News** provides a no-nonsense round-up of news and festival issues. **The List**, a locally produced arts and entertainment guide, comes out weekly during the Festival and manages to combine comprehensive coverage with a reliably on-the-pulse sense of what's hot and what's not. Various freebie newspapers are also available at venues and bars around town – the best of them is **Fest**, which mixes news with pithy reviews and yet more listings.

The International Festival attracts truly international stars, along with some of the world's finest orchestras and opera, theatre and ballet companies. Performances take place at the city's larger venues such as the Usher Hall and the Festival Theatre and, while ticket prices run to over £40, it is possible to see shows for £10 or less if you're prepared to queue for the handful of tickets kept back until the day.

The most popular single event in the Festival is the dramatic **Fireworks Concert**, held late at night on the final Saturday of the International Festival: the Scottish Chamber Orchestra belts out pop classics from the Ross Bandstand in Princes Street Gardens, accompanied by a spectacular fireworks display high up above the ramparts of the Castle. Unless you want a seat right by the orchestra you don't need a ticket for this event: hundreds of thousands of people view the display from various vantage points throughout the city, the prime spots being Princes Street, Northbridge, Calton Hill or Inverleith Park and the Botanic Garden by Stockbridge.

The International Festival's year-round headquarters are located at **The Hub** (see p.99); you can contact them for further **information**, including the annual programme, which is released in April.

The Edinburgh Festival Fringe

Even standing alone from its sister festivals, the **Edinburgh Festival Fringe** is easily the world's largest arts gathering. Each year sees over 15,000 performances from over 700 companies, with more than 12,000 participants from all over the world. There are something in the region of 1500 shows every day, round the clock, in 200 venues around the city. While the headlining names at the International Festival reinforce the Festival's cultural credibility, it is the dynamism, spontaneity and sheer exuberance of the Fringe which dominate Edinburgh every August, giving the city its unique atmosphere.

For the first three decades of its existence, the Fringe was a fairly intimate affair, dominated by drama, and peopled largely by graduating Oxbridge students and talent-spotting producers (often Oxbridge graduates themselves). The burgeoning of the Fringe began in earnest in the late 1970s as other forms of entertainment established themselves, notably new comedy, which over the

△ Street performance, Edinburgh Festival

next quarter of a century became almost synonymous with the Edinburgh Fringe.

The first **Fringe Programme** appeared in 1951, the bright idea of a local printer. A single sheet of paper then, it's now a fat magazine crammed with information on most, though not all, participating shows. In 1959 the **Fringe Society** was founded by participants to provide basic marketing and coordination between events. Crucially, no artistic control was imposed on those who wanted to produce a show, a defining element of the Fringe which continues to this day – anyone who can afford the registration fee can take part. This means that the shows range from the inspired to the diabolical and ensures a highly competitive atmosphere, in which one bad review in a prominent publication means box-office disaster. Many unknowns rely on self-publicity, taking to the streets to perform highlights from their show, or pressing leaflets into the hands of every passer-by. Performances go on round the clock: if so inclined, you could sit through twenty shows in a day.

The full Fringe **programme** is usually available in June from the Festival Fringe Office (℡0131/226 0000, ⓦwww.edfringe.com). Postal and telephone **bookings** for shows can be made immediately afterwards, while during the Festival, tickets are sold at the Fringe box office (daily 10am–9pm), the venue itself or through the website.

Ticket prices for most Fringe shows start at £5, and average from £8 to £14 at the main venues, with the better-known acts going for even more. Although some theatre and music acts can be longer, most performances are scheduled to run for an hour, which means that you can easily spend £40–50 on admission alone in the course of a hard day's festivalling.

The International Festival and the Fringe don't quite coincide: the former tends to run over the last two weeks of **August** and the first week of **September**, whereas the latter starts a week earlier, culminating on the last weekend in August, traditionally an English (but, confusingly, not a Scottish) Bank Holiday weekend.

Theatre

Comedy grabs more headlines, but **theatre** still makes up the bulk of the Fringe. Right from the start, innovative, controversial, wonderful and sometimes downright ghastly productions have characterized the Fringe's drama content. Content ranges from Molière to Berkoff, from Shakespeare to Beckett (someone, somewhere, always puts on *Krapp's Last Tape*). There are numerous student productions, as well as the appearance of Scottish favourites, such as playwright Liz Lochhead or actor Russell Hunter. Unusual venues add spice to some productions: Inchcolm Island in the Firth of Forth has been used to stage *Macbeth*; *2001: A Space Odyssey* was performed to an audience sitting in a Hillman Avenger car; while current favourite venues include the back-room café at *Valvona & Crolla's* Italian deli on Elm Row and the Royal Botanic Garden in Inverleith.

One way of saving money on tickets is to look out for two-for-one ticket offers, usually advertised at venue box offices or in newspapers.

Comedy

Comedy is the Fringe's big success story. Until the 1970s the Festival was a rite of passage from the Cambridge Footlights or Oxford Revue to the BBC or the London stage, with teams such as those responsible for *Beyond the Fringe* and *Monty Python* appearing in Edinburgh before making their big break on TV. Although this still happens, the arena opened out in the 1980s with an explosion of talent and opportunities for selling it, and the Fringe became a hothouse for a generation of new comics once known as "alternative" and now mostly working for the BBC or Channel 4 – performers such as Stephen Fry, Jeremy Hardy, Steve Coogan and Eddie Izzard. Plenty of well-known names still come to Edinburgh, while most of the rest of the comedy acts are chasing the Perrier

Making it big at the Festival

There's hardly a serious **entertainer** worth their salt who hasn't played the Edinburgh Festival at some time. Best known are the satirists of *Beyond the Fringe*, the 1960 Edinburgh revue which launched the careers of Peter Cook, Jonathan Miller, Alan Bennett and Dudley Moore. Miller and Cook had come fresh from their student dramatic society, the Cambridge Footlights; other Footlighters have included the entire casts of *Monty Python* and *The Goodies*, David Frost, Germaine Greer, Richard Harris, Douglas Adams, Clive James, Griff Rhys-Jones, Stephen Fry and Emma Thompson. From Oxford came Rowan Atkinson and Mel Smith, while Manchester University graduates Ben Elton, Rik Mayall and Adrian Edmondson were first seen in Edinburgh in a revue called *Twentieth Century Coyote*. They teamed up with a duo called The Outer Limits (Nigel Planer and Peter Richardson) to form *The Young Ones*.

Other celebs who got their break at the Fringe include Paul Merton, Jo Brand, Steve Coogan, Frank Skinner and drag queen Lily Savage, while various soap stars have arrived in Edinburgh to reinvent themselves, including Nigel Pivaro (*Coronation Street*), Tom Watt (*Eastenders*), Dannii Minogue (*Home and Away*) and Mark Little (*Neighbours*).

Fringe venues

In addition to the many tiny and unexpected auditoriums, the four **main Fringe venues** are The Assembly Rooms, The Pleasance, The Gilded Balloon and a relative newcomer known as "C". Venue complexes rather than single spaces, the last three colonize clusters of different-sized spaces for the duration of the Festival. If you're new to the Fringe, these are all safe bets for decent shows and a bit of starspotting.

The atmosphere at the **Pleasance** (60 The Pleasance ☎0131/556 6550, 🌐www .pleasance.co.uk) is usually less frenetic than at the other venues, with classy drama and whimsical appearances by panellists on Radio 4 game shows. The **Assembly Rooms** (50 George St ☎0131/226 2428, 🌐www.assemblyrooms.com) provide a slick, grand setting for top-of-the-range drama and big-name music and comedy acts. The Fringe's premier comedy venue, **The Gilded Balloon** (Teviot Row House, Bristo Square ☎0131/668 1633, 🌐www.gildedballoon.co.uk), lost its long-standing home in a fire in early 2003, but was up and running in various new venues around town by the time the Festival came along. The disparate locations of **C** (☎0870/701 5105, 🌐www.cthefestival.com) have the most varied programme of the big four, and in recent years have been known to stage controversial productions that other venues might be too wary to promote.

While it's nothing like as large as the venues above, you shouldn't ignore the pro-gramme put on at the **Traverse Theatre**'s (see p.145) three stages. Long a champion of new drama, the "Trav" combines the avant-garde with professional presentation and its plays are generally among the Fringe's most acclaimed.

Comedy award, given to the outstanding up-and-coming stand-up or comedy cabaret, and there's no doubt that the Fringe is *the* place to catch new talent before it becomes famous.

Aside from a few variety artists, the entire UK comedy scene – plus many international acts – can be found in Edinburgh at some point during the Fringe season. The bigger names are booked by the Assembly Rooms, Pleasance or Gilded Balloon, while Edinburgh's own comedy club, The Stand, has become an increasingly viable alternative. Look out for "Best of the Fest" shows, held at the main venues, featuring a selection of the year's big names.

Music

The Fringe offers a wealth of reasonably priced **recitals** and other **concerts** to choose from. Near-professional standards are reached by the Rehearsal Orchestra, which performs a two-week season of classical music concerts; possibly the oldest Fringe music event, it has run since 1956. Established for top amateur musicians, the orchestra often plays the same pieces that are being performed in the Inter-national Festival – hence the name "Rehearsal" Orchestra. The annual Festival of Youth Orchestras at Tollcross, featuring groups from around the world, also sets high standards. A recent Fringe sensation is the Really Terrible Orchestra which brings together music-loving amateur players – often lawyers and doctors – who are given the chance to live out their dream of taking to the concert stage.

Fans of **folk**, **roots**, **world** and **alternative** music are not overlooked, although in recent years they've struggled to find a regular venue. In recent years, the Famous Spiegeltent (a wooden Victorian circus tent) has set up in George Square at the heart of the university campus, hosting gigs in an inspiring mix of genres, from serious instrumental groups to light-hearted, banjo-strum-ming duos, along with some risqué burlesque shows.

Jazz and blues, despite having their own festival early on in August (see p.152), do still feature around the Fringe, while **rock and pop** acts also try to muscle in on the action with events such as T on the Fringe drawing some big names.

Elsewhere at the Fringe

Dance and **physical theatre** make up a small but entertaining section of the Fringe programme, ranging from easy-watching box-office smashes like *Tap Dogs* or *Gumboots* to shock acts such as Jim Rose's *Circus*, which blurred the line between physical theatre, drama, circus and comedy. **Visual art** at the Fringe has traditionally taken a back seat, with surprisingly few special festival exhibitions. **Children's shows** at the Fringe take in puppetry, clowns, pantomime, musicals, magic and straightforward drama, and are staged mostly in the mornings.

Edinburgh International Film Festival

The **Edinburgh International Film Festival** runs for the last two weeks of August, normally finishing at around the same time as the Fringe. It's the longest continually running film festival in the world, having begun, like the International Festival and Fringe, in 1947. It can also claim a distinguished history at the cutting edge of cinema, premiering American blockbusters from directors like Steven Spielberg and Woody Allen, discovering low-budget smashes such as *My Beautiful Laundrette* and *Strictly Ballroom*, and introducing serious contenders such as *Mrs Brown* and *The Blair Witch Project*.

The Film Festival is a chance to see some of the year's big cinema hits before they go on general release, along with a varied and exciting bill of reissued movies. For those in the industry, it is also a vital talking shop, with debates, seminars and workshops, spiced up by the attendance of Hollywood stars at the succession of glittering parties which accompany the launches. **Tickets and information** are available from the main venue, the Filmhouse, 88 Lothian Rd, EH3 9BZ ☏0131/228 2688, ⓦwww.edfilmfest.org.uk.

Edinburgh International Book Festival

Begun in 1983, the annual **Edinburgh International Book Festival**, which takes place in the last two weeks of August, is the largest celebration of the written word worldwide. It's held in a tented village in the douce setting of Charlotte Square and offers talks, readings and signings by a star-studded line-up of visiting authors, as well as panel discussions and workshops. Well-known local authors such as Iain Banks, Ian Rankin and A.L. Kennedy are good for an appearance most years, while visitors from further afield have included Doris Lessing, Louis de Bernières, Ben Okri, John Updike and Salman Rushdie. In addition, there are cook-ups by celebrity chefs promoting their latest tomes and a dedicated programme of children's activities and book-related events. An on-site café and, of course, a bookshop, ensure that all the participants' needs are met.

Tickets (generally £7–8) often sell out quickly, particularly for the big-name events. For tickets and info during the Festival, contact the ticket office at Charlotte Square (☏0131/624 5050, ⓦwww.edbookfest.co.uk).

Edinburgh International Jazz and Blues Festival

The **Edinburgh International Jazz and Blues Festival**, which used to run concurrently with the other festivals, now runs immediately prior to the

Fringe in the first week in August, easing the city into the festival spirit with a full programme of gigs in many different locations. Like all the other festivals, this one has grown over the years from a concentrated international summer camp to a bigger, more modern affair, reflecting the panoply of generations and styles which appear under the banner of jazz and blues. Scotland's own varied and vibrant jazz scene is always fully represented, and late-night clubs with atmosphere complement major concerts given by international stars. Past visitors have included B.B. King, Bill Wyman, Dizzy Gillespie, Dave Brubeck, Van Morrison, Carol Kidd and the Blues Band. Highlights include **Jazz On A Summer's Day**, a musical extravaganza in Princes Street Gardens, and a colourful New Orleans-style **street parade**.

The **programme** is available at the end of May from the office at 29 St Stephen's St, EH3 5AN ☎0131/225 2202, ⓦwww.jazzmusic.co.uk. Tickets range in price from £5 for small pub gigs to £20 for a seat in a big venue, and are available from The Hub (☎0131/473 2000, ⓦwww.hubtickets.co.uk).

The Military Tattoo

Staged in the spectacular stadium of the Edinburgh Castle Esplanade, the **Military Tattoo** is an unashamed display of pomp and military pride. The programme of choreographed drills, massed pipe bands, historical tableaux, energetic battle re-enactments, national dancing and pyrotechnics has been a feature of the Festival for fifty years, the emotional climax provided by a lone piper on the Castle battlements. Followed by a quick firework display (longer and more splendid on Saturdays), it's a successful formula barely tampered with over the years.

Tickets (£10–30 depending on seat location) need to be booked well in advance, and it's advisable to take a cushion and rainwear. Tickets and information are available from the Tattoo Office, 32 Market St, EH1 1QB ☎0131/225 1188, ⓦwww.edintattoo.co.uk.

The Edinburgh Mela

A festival within a festival, the **Edinburgh Mela** is held in Pilrig Park on the fringes of Leith over the first weekend in September, coinciding with the finale of the International Festival. Truly a people's event, it was introduced to Edinburgh in the mid-1990s by the capital's Asian community. The word "Mela" is a Sanskrit term meaning "gathering", and is used to describe many different community events and festivals on the Asian subcontinent. In Edinburgh, the Mela is about cultural diversity, and the family-oriented programme is designed to celebrate the many different cultures in the city. Music, dance, foods, carnivals, fashion shows, sports, children's events, crafts and a two-day careers fair for school-leavers see the festival season out with a bang rather than a whimper. Further **details** from The Edinburgh Mela, 14 Forth St ☎0131/557 1400, ⓦwww.edinburgh-mela.co.uk.

Listings

Airlines British Airways ☎0870/551 1155; British Midland (bmi) ☎0870/607 0555; easyJet ☎0871/750 0100; KLM ☎0870/507 4074. **American Express** 69 George St ☎0131/718 2501.

Banks Barclays, 1 St Andrew Square ☎0845/755 5555; Clydesdale, 20 Hanover St ☎0131/456 4560; HBOS (Halifax-Bank of Scotland), 7–9 North Bank St (head office), 38 St Andrew Square ☎08457/801801; HSBC, 76 Hanover St

ⓣ0845/740 4404; Lloyds TSB, 28 Hanover St ⓣ0845/072 3333; Royal Bank of Scotland, 36 St Andrew Square ⓣ0131/556 8555.

Bike rental Biketrax, 11 Lochrin Place ⓣ0131/228 6633, ⓦwww.biketrax.co.uk; Edinburgh Cycle Hire, 29 Blackfriars St ⓣ0131/556 5560, ⓦwww.cyclescotland.co.uk.

Car rental Arnold Clark, Lochrin Place ⓣ0131/228 4747 or 0845/607 4500; Avis, 5 West Park Place ⓣ0870/153 9103; Budget, Edinburgh Airport ⓣ0131/333 1926; Europcar, Waverley Station ⓣ0870/607 5000; Hertz, 10 Picardy Place ⓣ0870/846 0013; Thrifty Car Rental, 42 Haymarket Terrace ⓣ0131/337 1319.

Consulates Australia, 69 George St ⓣ0131/624 3333; Denmark, 48 Melville St ⓣ0131/220 0300; France, 11 Randolph Crescent ⓣ0131/225 7954; Germany, 16 Eglington Crescent ⓣ0131/337 2323; Italy, 32 Melville St ⓣ0131/226 3631; Netherlands, 1–2 Thistle St ⓣ0131/220 3226; Norway, 86 George St ⓣ0131/226 5701; Poland, 2 Kinnear Rd ⓣ0131/552 0301; Spain, 63 N Castle St ⓣ0131/220 1843; Sweden, 22 Hanover St ⓣ0131/220 6050; US, 3 Regent Terrace ⓣ0131/556 8315.

Dentist Call the NHS Helpline (ⓣ0800/224488) for details of your nearest dental surgery. Chalmers Dental Centre, 3 Chalmers St (Mon–Fri 9am–4.30pm; ⓣ0131/536 4800) has a walk-in centre for emergency dental work if you're not registered locally, as well as an out-of-hours service.

Exchange Post offices will exchange currency commission-free; Thomas Cook, 28 Frederick St ⓣ0131/465 7700; currency exchange bureaus in the main tourist office (Mon–Wed 9am–5pm, Thurs–Sat 9am–6pm, Sun 10am–5pm) and beside platform 1 at Waverley Station (Sept–June Mon–Sat 7.30am–9pm, Sun 8.30am–9pm; July–Aug Mon–Sat 7am–10pm, Sun 8am–10pm). To change money after hours, try one of the upmarket hotels – but expect to pay a hefty commission charge.

Football Edinburgh has two Scottish Premier Division teams, which are normally at home on alternate weekends: Heart of Midlothian (known as Hearts) play at Tynecastle Stadium, Gorgie Rd (ⓣ0131/200 7201), a couple of miles west of the centre; Hibernian (or Hibs) play at Easter Rd Stadium (ⓣ0131/661 1875), a similar distance northeast of the centre. Between them, the two clubs dominated Scottish football in the 1950s, but neither has won more than the odd trophy since, though one or the other periodically threatens to make a major breakthrough. Tickets start around £15.

Gay and lesbian contacts Gay & Lesbian Switchboard (ⓣ0131/556 4049) Edinburgh LGBT Centre,

60 Broughton St (ⓣ0131/620 5138).

Genealogical research General Register Office for Scotland ⓣ0131/334 0380, ⓦwww .scotlandspeople.gov.uk; Scottish Genealogy Society, 15 Victoria Terrace ⓣ0131/220 3677; Scottish Roots, 22 Forth St ⓣ0131/477 8214.

Golf Edinburgh is awash with fine golf courses, but most of them are private. The best public courses are the two on the Braid Hills (ⓣ0131/447 6666); others are Carrick Knowe (ⓣ0131/337 1096), Craigentinny (ⓣ0131/554 7501) and Silverknowes (ⓣ0131/336 3843).

Hospital Royal Infirmary, Little France (ⓣ0131/536 1000), has a 24hr casualty department. There's also a minor injuries clinic at the Western General, Crewe Rd North (8am–9pm; ⓣ0131/537 1330), and a casualty department for children at the Sick Kid's hospital, Sciennes Rd (ⓣ0131/536 0000). NHS24 (ⓣ08454/242424) offers health advice and clinical assessment over the phone; it essentially covers periods when doctors' surgeries aren't open, but is available 24 hours.

Internet Terminals where you can access the Internet for free are increasingly common around town, as are Wi-Fi hotspots. Dedicated Internet cafés include Bytes & Slices, 3 Waverley Steps (Mon–Fri 8am–9.30pm, Sat & Sun 10am–8pm; ⓣ0131/557 8887); Double Dutch, 27–29 Marshall St (Mon–Fri 8am–8pm, Sat & Sun 10am–8pm; ⓣ0131/667 9997); Internet Café, 98 West Bow (daily 10am–11pm; ⓣ0131/226 5400).

Laundry Bendix Self-Service Laundrette, 348 Morningside Rd (ⓣ0131/447 5453); Canonmills Laundrerette, 7–8 Huntly St (ⓣ0131/556 3199); Tarvit Launderette, 7–9 Tarvit St, Tollcross (ⓣ0131/229 6382).

Left luggage Counter by platform 1 at Waverley Station; £5 per item (daily 7am–11pm; ⓣ0131/550 2333).

Libraries Central Library, George IV Bridge (Mon–Thurs 10am–8pm, Fri 10am–5pm, Sat 9am–1pm; ⓣ0131/242 8000). In addition to the usual departments, there's a separate Scottish section, plus an Edinburgh Room which is a mine of information on the city. The National Library of Scotland, George IV Bridge (Mon–Fri 9.30am–8.30pm, Sat 9.30am–1pm; ⓣ0131/226 4531), a magnificent copyright library, is for research purposes only and accreditation is necessary to use the facilities. There is freer access to an annex which contains the Map Room, 33 Salisbury Place (Mon–Fri 9.30am–5pm, Sat 9.30am–1pm).

Lost property Edinburgh Airport ⓣ0131/333 1000; Edinburgh Police HQ ⓣ0131/311 3141 (lost property found in taxis is sent here); Lothian Buses ⓣ0131/554 4494; Network Rail ⓣ0131/550 2333.

Motoring organizations AA, 18–22 Melville St ☎0870/587 7151; RAC, 35 Kinnaird Park ☎0800/550550.

Pharmacy Boots, 48 Shandwick Place (Mon–Fri 7.30am–8pm, Sat 7.30am–6pm, Sun 10am–5pm; ☎0131/225 6757) has the longest opening hours.

Police In an emergency call 999. Otherwise contact Lothian and Borders Police HQ, Fettes Ave ☎0131/311 3131; or the local police stations at Gayfield Square, Broughton ☎0131/556 9270; Queen Charlotte St, Leith ☎0131/554 9350; St Leonard's St, Southside ☎0131/662 5000; or Torphichen Place, West End ☎0131/229 2323.

Post office 8–10 St James Centre (Mon & Wed–Sat 9am–5.30pm, Tues 9.30am–5.30pm; ☎0845/722 3344).

Rape crisis centre ☎0131/557 6757.

Rugby Scotland's international fixtures are played at Murrayfield Stadium, a couple of miles west of the city centre. Visit ⓦwww.scottishrugby.org or phone ☎0131/346 5000 for information on ticket sales, but be warned tickets can be very hard to come by for the big games.

Sports stadium Meadowbank Sports Centre and Stadium, 139 London Rd (☎0131/661 5351), is Edinburgh's main venue for most spectator and participatory sports. Facilities include an athletics track, a velodrome and indoor halls.

Swimming pools The city has one Olympic-standard modern pool, the Royal Commonwealth Pool, 21 Dalkeith Rd (☎0131/667 7211); and a number of considerably older pools at Caledonian Crescent, Dalry (☎0131/313 3964); Glenogle Rd, Stockbridge (☎0131/343 6376); 15 Bellfield St, Portobello (☎0131/669 6888) and 6 Thirlestane Rd, Marchmont (☎0131/447 0052).

Taxis Central Radio Taxis ☎0131/229 2468; City Cabs ☎0131/228 1211.

Travel agents Edinburgh Travel Centre (student and youth specialist) 3 Bristo Square ☎0131/668 2221; STA, 27 Forest Rd ☎0131/226 7747.

Out from the centre

There's a great deal to be discovered beyond the compact centre of Edinburgh, in particular along the Firth of Forth coastline to the north and towards the Pentland Hills to the south. Just over a mile northeast of the city centre is **Leith**, the historic port of Edinburgh, a fascinating mix of cobbled streets and new developments, run-down housing and some of the city's top restaurants. Nearby you can find a flavour of the city's maritime and fishing heritage at the atmospheric harbour of **Newhaven**, while the long beach at **Portobello** is still a popular spot on a sunny day. To the north and west of the city are Edinburgh's long-established **zoo** and the placid charms of the old Roman village of **Cramond**, as well as the country mansions **Lauriston Castle** and **Dalmeny House**.

In the southeast suburbs of the city, the imposing fifteenth-century **Craigmillar Castle** is incongruously set amid a rather grim housing estate, but there is also a rural aspect to the area, with various hills, parks and, on the southern edge of the city, the **Pentland Hills** which offer some wild walking country and terrific views.

Leith and around

Although **LEITH** is generally known as the port of Edinburgh, it developed independently of the city up the hill, its history bound up in the hard graft of fishing, shipbuilding and trade. The presence of sailors, merchants and continental traders also gave the place a cosmopolitan – if slightly rough – edge, which is still obvious today in Leith's fascinating mix of cobbled streets and flash new housing, container ships and historic buildings, ugly council flats and trendy waterside bistros. While the stand-alone attractions are few, Leith is an intriguing place to explore, worth visiting not just for the contrasts to central Edinburgh, but also for its nautical air and the excellent eating and drinking scene, which majors on seafood but also includes haute cuisine and well-worn, friendly pubs.

Leith's initial revival from down-and-out port to characterful waterfront began in the 1980s around the area known as the **Shore**, the old harbour at the mouth of the Water of Leith. More recently, the massive dock areas beyond that are being transformed at a rate of knots, with landmark developments including a vast building housing civil servants from the Scottish Executive and the new Ocean Terminal, a shopping and entertainment complex, beside which the former royal yacht **Britannia** has settled into her retirement.

To reach Leith from the city centre, take one of the many buses going down Leith Walk, which connects with the eastern end of Princes Street and Queen Street.

Around the port

The best way to absorb Leith's history and seafaring connections is to take a stroll along **The Shore**, a tenement-lined road running alongside the Water of Leith. Until the mid-nineteenth century this was a bustling and cosmopolitan harbour, visited by ships from all over the world, but as vessels became increasingly large, they moored up instead at custom-built docks built beyond the original quays; these days, The Shore has only a handful of boats permanently moored alongside. Instead, the focus is on the numerous **pubs and restaurants** that line the street, many of which spill tables and chairs out onto the cobbled pavement on sunny days. The historic buildings along this stretch include the imposing Neoclassical Custom House, still used as offices by the harbour authority (though not open to the public); the round signal tower above *Fishers* restaurant (see p.139), which was originally constructed as a windmill; and the turrets and towers of the Sailors' Home, built in Scots Baronial style in the 1880s as a dosshouse for seafarers, and now home to the rather swankier digs of the *Malmaison* hotel (see p.86).

A little further south on Kirkgate, **Trinity House** (℡0131/554 3289, ⓦwww .historic-scotland.gov.uk; £3) is the only one of the port's grand buildings open to the public, but even here access is limited – all visits must be pre-booked, but if you're interested in maritime history, it's well worth the effort. Home of the Incorporation of Masters and Mariners of Leith, the present Neoclassical villa dates from 1816 and has some impressive original interiors and plasterwork, as well as a significant collection of maritime memorabilia including paintings and ships' models.

Leith Links is an area of predominantly flat parkland on the eastern side of Leith; documentary evidence from 1505 suggests that James IV used to "play at gowf at Leithe", giving rise to Leith's claim as the birthplace of the sport. In 1744 the first written rules of golf were drawn up here by the Honourable Company of Edinburgh Golfers, ten years before they were formalized in St Andrews. However, fans keen to pay homage to the spot may be a little disappointed: other than an informal practice sessions by locals, there's no golf played on the Links these days.

Britannia

A little to the west of The Shore, moored alongside **Ocean Terminal**, a huge shopping and entertainment centre designed by Terence Conran, is one of the world's most famous ships, **Britannia** (daily: April–Sept 9.30am–6pm; Oct–March 10am–5pm, last entry 90min before closing; £9; ⓦwww.royaly achtbritannia.co.uk). Launched in 1953 at John Brown's shipyard on Clydeside, *Britannia* was used by the royal family for 44 years for state visits, diplomatic functions and royal holidays. Leith acquired her following decommission in

1997, against the wishes of many of the royal family, who felt that scuttling would have been a more dignified end.

Visits to *Britannia* begin in the **visitor centre**, within Ocean Terminal, where royal holiday snaps and video clips of the ship's most famous moments, which included the evacuation of Aden and the British handover of Hong Kong in 1997, are shown. An audio handset is then handed out and you are allowed to roam around the yacht: the **bridge**, the **admiral's quarters**, the **officers' mess** and a large part of the **state apartments**, including the state dining and drawing rooms and the (separate) cabins used by the Queen and the Duke of Edinburgh, viewed through a glass partition. The ship has been largely kept as she was when in service, with a well-preserved 1950s dowdiness which the audio guide loyally attributes to the Queen's good taste and astute frugality in the lean postwar years. Certainly the atmosphere is a far cry from the opulent splendour which many expect.

The guide's commentary also reveals quirkier aspects of *Britannia*'s history: a full Marine Band was always part of the 300-strong crew; hand signals were used by the sailors to communicate orders as shouting was forbidden; and a special solid mahogany rail was built onto the royal bridge to allow the Queen to stand on deck as the ship came into port, without fear of a gust of wind lifting the royal skirt.

To get to Ocean Terminal from the city, jump on one of the tour buses that leave from Waverley Bridge; otherwise, make use of buses #11, #22 or #34 from Princes Street, or #35 from the Royal Mile.

Newhaven

To the west of Leith lies the old village (now suburb) of **NEWHAVEN**, established by James IV at the start of the sixteenth century as an alternative shipbuilding centre to Leith: his massive warship, the *Great Michael*, capable of carrying 120 gunners, 300 mariners and 1000 troops, and said to have used up all the trees in Fife, was built here. Newhaven has also been a ferry station and an important fishing centre, landing some six million oysters a year at the height of its success in the 1860s. Today, the chief pleasure here is a stroll around the stone harbour, which still has a pleasantly salty feel, with a handful of boats tied up alongside or resting gently on the tidal mud. You might want to make a brief stop at the small **Newhaven Heritage Museum** (daily: noon–4.45pm; free; ⓦ www.cac.org.uk), which has a fairly homespun series of exhibits about the district's history of fishing and seafaring. From the harbour itself, the *Maid of the Forth* heads out to the ruined abbey of Inchcolm Island (see p.173; April–Oct selected days; £13; ⓣ0131/331 5000, ⓦ www.maidoftheforth.co.uk) and the high-speed inflatable boats of **Seafari Adventures** (same phone number; ⓦ www.seafari.co.uk) tour the Forth Islands and South Queensferry (see p.172) on trips to view bird and sea life.

Portobello

Among Edinburgh's least expected assets is its **beach**, most of which falls within **PORTOBELLO**, the suburb to the southeast of Leith. Once a lively **seaside resort** it's now a forlorn kind of place, its funfairs and amusement arcades decidedly down at heel. Nonetheless, it retains a certain faded charm, and – on hot summer weekends at least – the beach can be a mass of swimmers, sunbathers, surfers and pleasure boats. A walk along the promenade is a pleasure at any time of the year. Portobello is about three miles east of the centre of town, and can be reached by a direct route on buses #15, #19 or #26.

△ Edinburgh Zoo

Edinburgh Zoo

A couple of miles due west of the city centre, **Edinburgh Zoo** (daily: April–
Sept 9am–6pm; March & Oct 9am–5pm; Nov–Feb 9am–4.30pm; £9, family
ticket from £28; Ⓦ www.edinburghzoo.org.uk) is set on an eighty-acre site on
the slopes of Corstorphine Hill (buses #12, #26, #31 and #100 from town).
Established in 1913, the zoo has a reputation for preserving rare and endan-
gered species, with the general emphasis moving away from bored animals in
cages to imaginatively designed habitats and viewing areas. The latter are best
seen by taking a **hilltop safari** (daily 10am–3.30pm/4.30pm; 30min), a regular shuttle trip to the top of Corstorphine Hill in a Landrover-pulled trailer,
passing large enclosures of camels and llamas. Once at the top, you can admire
the city views, then get out and wander back down past zebra and antelope
grazing in fields and a row of glass-walled pens containing tigers and lions.
The place is permanently packed with kids, and the zoo's most famous attraction is its **penguin parade** (daily 2.15pm April–Sept, and sunny days March
& Oct), when rangers encourage a bunch of the flightless birds to leave their
pen and waddle around a short circuit of pathways lined with admiring and
amused spectators.

Lauriston Castle and Cramond

Lauriston Castle (April–Oct 11.20am, 12.20pm, 2.20pm, 3.20pm, 4.20pm,
closed Fri; Nov–March Sat & Sun 2.20pm & 3.20pm; 50min guided tour;
£4.50; Ⓦ www.cac.org.uk) is a country villa set in its own parkland on the

fringes of Edinburgh's northwest urban sprawl, accessible from the city centre by bus #24.

On first sight a neo-Jacobean riot of pointy turrets, crow-stepped gables and tall, thin chimneys, the "castle" is in fact a late sixteenth-century tower house with extensive domestic additions from the 1820s and 1870s. At the turn of the twentieth century the house and its contents were gifted to Edinburgh Council by a prosperous local cabinet-maker, and they've been preserved as a time capsule of that era ever since, with the exception of a few mod cons such as hot and cold running water, central heating and double glazing. The mature grounds include a series of croquet lawns from where there are pleasantly sylvan views out over the Firth of Forth.

One mile further northwest, **CRAMOND** is one of the city's most atmospheric – and poshest – old villages. The enduring image of Cramond is of step-gabled whitewashed houses rising uphill from the waterfront, though it also boasts the foundations of a Roman fort, and a tower house, church, inn and mansion, all from the seventeenth century. The best reason to come here is to enjoy a stroll around and a bit of fresh air: the **walk** along the wide promenade which follows the shoreline, offers great views of the Forth; or head out across the causeway to the uninhabited bird sanctuary of Cramond Island – though be aware that the causeway disappears as high tide approaches and can leave you stranded if you get your timings wrong. For tide times, either check the noticeboard on shore or call the Coastguard (☏01333/450666). Inland of Cramond, there's another pleasant walk along a tree-lined path leading upstream along the River Almond, past former mills and their adjoining cottages towards the sixteenth-century Old Cramond Bridge. These walks should take around an hour each.

Craigmillar Castle

Situated around five miles southeast of Edinburgh's centre, amidst green belt, **Craigmillar Castle** (April–Sept daily 9.30am–6.30pm; Oct–March 9.30am–4.30pm, closed Thurs & Fri; last entry 30min before closing; HS; £3), is one of the best-preserved ruined medieval fortresses in Scotland. Before Queen Victoria set her heart on Balmoral, it was considered her royal castle north of the border, a possibility which seems somewhat odd now, given its proximity to the ugly council housing scheme of Craigmillar, one of Edinburgh's most deprived districts. That said, the immediate setting feels very rural and Craigmillar Castle enjoys splendid views back to Arthur's Seat and Edinburgh Castle. The oldest part of the complex is the L-shaped tower house, which dates back to the early 1400s – this remains substantially intact, and the great hall, with its resplendent late Gothic chimneypiece, is in good enough shape to be rented out for functions. The tower house was surrounded in the 1500s by a quadrangular wall with cylindrical corner towers and was used on occasion by Mary, Queen of Scots. It was abandoned to its picturesque decay in the mid-eighteenth century, and today the peaceful ruins and their adjoining grassy lawns make for a great place to explore, with kids in particular loving the run of their very own castle.

Take **bus** #30, #33 or #82, from North Bridge to Little France, from where the castle is a ten-minute walk along Craigmillar Castle Road.

The southern hills

The **hills** of Edinburgh's southern suburbs offer good, not overly demanding, walking opportunities, with plenty of sweeping panoramic views. The **Royal Observatory** (only open to the public for occasional evening talks and weekly stargazing sessions; ☏0131/668 8404, ⓦwww.roe.ac.uk) stands at the top of Blackford Hill, just a short walk south of Morningside or Newington; at the foot of the hill, the bird sanctuary of Blackford Pond is the starting point for one of the many trails running through the **Hermitage of Braid** local nature reserve, a lovely shady area along the course of the Braid Burn. The castellated eighteenth-century mansion along the burn, after which the reserve is

Robert Louis Stevenson

Though **Robert Louis Stevenson** (1850–94) is sometimes dismissed for his straight-up writing style, he was undoubtedly one of the best-loved writers of his generation, and one whose travelogues, novels, short stories and essays remain enormously popular over a century after his death.

Born in Edinburgh into a distinguished family of lighthouse engineers, Stevenson was a sickly child, with a solitary childhood dominated by his governess, Alison "Cummie" Cunningham, who regaled him with tales drawn from Calvinist folklore. Sent to the university to study engineering, Stevenson rebelled against his upbringing by spending much of his time in the lowlife howffs and brothels of the city. He later switched his studies to law, and although called to the bar in 1875, by then he had decided to channel his energies into literature: while still a student, he had already made his mark as an **essayist**, and eventually had over a hundred essays published, ranging from light-hearted whimsy to trenchant political analysis. A set of topographical pieces about his native city was later collected together as *Edinburgh: Picturesque Notes*, which conjure up nicely its atmosphere, character and appearance – warts and all.

Stevenson's other early successes were two **travelogues**, *An Inland Voyage* and *Travels with a Donkey in the Cevennes*, kaleidoscopic jottings based on his journeys in France, where he went to escape Scotland's weather, which was damaging his health. It was there that he met Fanny Osbourne, an American ten years his senior, who was estranged from her husband and had two children in tow. His voyage to join her in San Francisco formed the basis for his most important factual work, *The Amateur Emigrant*, a vivid first-hand account of the great nineteenth-century European migration to the United States.

Having married the now-divorced Fanny, Stevenson began an elusive search for an agreeable climate that led to Switzerland, the French Riviera and the Scottish Highlands. He belatedly turned to the novel, achieving immediate acclaim in 1881 for **Treasure Island**, a highly moralistic adventure yarn that began as an entertainment for his stepson and future collaborator, Lloyd Osbourne. In 1886 his most famous short story, **Dr Jekyll and Mr Hyde**, despite its nominal London setting, offered a vivid evocation of Edinburgh's Old Town: an allegory of its dual personality of prosperity and squalor, and an analysis of its Calvinistic preoccupations with guilt and damnation. The same year saw the publication of the historical romance **Kidnapped**, an adventure novel which exemplified Stevenson's view that literature should seek above all to entertain.

In 1887 Stevenson left Britain for good, travelling first to the United States where he began one of his most ambitious novels, *The Master of Ballantrae*. A year later, he set sail for the South Seas, and eventually settled in **Samoa**; his last works include a number of stories with a local setting, such as the grimly realistic *The Ebb Tide* and *The Beach of Falesà*. However, Scotland continued to be his main inspiration: he wrote *Catriona* (a passage from which can be found on p.834) as a sequel to *Kidnapped*, and was at work on two more novels with Scottish settings, *St Ives* and *Weir of Hermiston*, a dark story of father and son confrontation, at the time of his sudden death from a brain haemorrhage in 1894. He was buried on the top of Mount Vaea overlooking the Pacific Ocean.

named, now serves as a visitor centre (Mon–Thurs 2–5pm, Fri 2–4pm, Sun noon–5pm; ⓦwww.cecrangerservice.demon.co.uk). Immediately to the south are the **Braid Hills**, largely occupied by two golf courses, which are closed on alternate Sundays in order to allow access for walkers.

Further south are the **Pentland Hills**, a chain some eighteen miles long and five wide, which dominate most views south of Edinburgh and offer walkers and mountain bikers a thrilling taste of wild Scottish countryside just a few miles beyond the city suburbs. Numerous bike trails and walks, from gentle strolls along well-marked paths to a ten-mile traverse of the hills and moors, are outlined in a free pamphlet available from the Regional Park Information Centre at **FLOTTERSTONE**, ten miles south of the city centre on the A702. There's been an inn here since the seventeenth century; the present *Flotterstone Inn* is a good spot for a drink or a pub meal after your exertions.

SWANSTON is a good entry point to the Pentland Hills from within Edinburgh. It's an unspoiled, highly exclusive hamlet of whitewashed thatched roof dwellings separated from the rest of the city by almost a mile of farmland; **Robert Louis Stevenson** (see box opposite) spent his boyhood summers in Swanston Cottage, the largest of the houses, immortalizing it in the novel *St Ives*. The simplest way to get a taste of the scenery of the Pentlands is to set off from the car park by the ski centre at **Hillend** at the northeast end of the range; take the path up the right-hand side of the dry ski slopes, turning left shortly after crossing a stile to reach a prominent point with outstanding views over Edinburgh and Fife. If you're feeling energetic, the vistas get even better higher up. Hillend is connected with the city centre by buses #4 and #15, but only the infrequent McEwans coach #100 passes Flotterstone.

East Lothian

East Lothian consists of the coastal strip and hinterland immediately east of Edinburgh, bounded by the Firth of Forth to the north and the Lammermuir Hills to the south. All of it is within easy day-trip range from the capital, though there are places you can stay overnight if you're keen to explore it properly. Often mocked as the "home counties" of Edinburgh, there's no denying its well-ordered feel, with prosperous farms and large estate houses dominating the scenery. The most immediately attractive part of the area is the coastline, extending from **Musselburgh**, all but joined onto Edinburgh, round to **Dunbar**. There's something for most tastes here, including the wide sandy beaches by **Aberlady**, the famous golf courses of **Gullane**, the enjoyable Seabird Centre at **North Berwick**, dramatic cliff-top ruins at **Tantallon** and the supersonic draw of **Concorde** at the Museum of Flight. The inland region is often ignored in favour of the coast, or by traffic speeding along the main A1 road from Edinburgh which cuts through the region before turning south towards England. At the foot of the Lammermuirs is the county town of **Haddington**, a pleasant enough place, though the attractions nearby of Gifford, a neat village deeper into the hills, or Edinburgh's "local" whisky distillery by Pencaitland, are always likely to be a stronger draw.

Musselburgh to Dirleton

Though strictly the largest town in East Lothian, with a long history connected to the development of mussel beds at the mouth of the River Esk, **MUSSEL-BURGH** is a place you're unlikely to linger long in, if only for the feeling that you've hardly shaken off the dust of Edinburgh. There is, however, a **race course** here, one of the busiest in Scotland, with a regular programme of decent quality National Hunt and Flat meetings. For details of what's on, contact the course on ☎0131/665 2859, ⓦwww.musselburgh-racecourse.co.uk.

Bypassing the chimneys of the Cockenzie power station, the East Lothian coastline takes a turn for the better by **ABERLADY**, an elongated conservation village of Gothic-style cottages and mansions just sixteen miles east of Edinburgh. The village served as Haddington's port until its river silted up in the sixteenth century, the costly stained-glass windows of the honey-coloured medieval church acting as a reminder of more affluent times. The salt marshes and sand dunes of the adjacent **Aberlady Bay Nature Reserve**, a bird-watchers' haven, mark the site of the old harbour. On the main street, *Duck's at Aberlady* (☎01875/870682, ⓦwww.kilspindie.co.uk; ⑥) is a pleasant restaurant with rooms and is handy for somewhere to stop over.

From the nature reserve, it's a couple of miles to **GULLANE** (pronounced "Gillin"), the location of the famous shoreline links of **Muirfield Golf Course**, home of the grandly named Honourable Company of Edinburgh Golfers and occasional venue for the Open Championship. If golf isn't your thing (there are three other courses around Gullane, not to mention dozens more around East Lothian), you might prefer the fine sandy **beaches** of Gullane Bay or the chance to explore the genteel hamlet of **DIRLETON**, two miles east of Gullane, which huddles around **Dirleton Castle** (daily: April–Sept 9.30am–6.30pm; Oct–March 9.30am–4.30pm, last admission 30min before closing; £3.30; ⓦwww.historic-scotland.gov.uk), a romantic thirteenth-century ruin with gardens. Scrambling round the castle is fun, and if the weather's good you can take the mile-long path from the village church to the sandy, rock-framed beach at **Yellowcraigs**, which overlooks **Fidra Island**, a large lump of basalt that's home to thousands of (noisy) seabirds.

Near the beach, the *Yellowcraig Caravan Club Site* (☎01620/850217; April–Oct), with pleasant woodland walks to the shore, is the only budget place to **stay**; the splendid *Open Arms Hotel*, opposite the castle (☎01620/850241, ⓦwww.openarmshotel.com; ⑥), on the other hand, has every luxury, including a **restaurant** serving good, moderate to expensive food. Other eating options include the excellent if modest-looking *La Potinière* restaurant (☎01620/843214, ⓦwwwla-potiniere.co.uk; closed Mon & Tues) in Gullane, offering expensive set-price dinners, or upmarket **picnic fare** from Gullane Delicatessen at 40c High Street.

Museum of Flight

A few miles south of Dirleton, located on an old military airfield by East Fortune, the **Museum of Flight** (April–Oct daily 10am–5pm; Nov–March Sat & Sun 10am–4pm; £5, Concorde boarding pass £3 extra, pre-booking essential; ☎0870/421 4299, ⓦwww.nms.ac.uk/flight) is now home to *Alpha Alpha*, the first **Concorde** to fly in British Airways colours. One of the icons of the twentieth century, Concorde was the world's first supersonic passenger jet and was able to zip over the Atlantic in just under three hours. Now installed in a custom-built hangar, *Alpha Alpha*, one of only twenty planes built, has been reassembled to show how she looked when decommissioned in 2003. Despite its exclusive tag, space wasn't one of the luxuries available aboard the plane known to its crew as "the toothpick", and a visit onboard is restricted to a slightly stooped wander through the forward half of the aircraft, with the chance to look at the cockpit through a perspex partition. Elsewhere in the hangar, a short film tells the story of *Alpha Alpha*, including footage of its unusual journey by barge and road trailer to East Fortune, while information boards and display cabinets allow you to follow the Concorde project as a whole, from its early days of Anglo-French bickering to the tragic Paris crash of 2000. In and around the other, older hangars on the site you can see over fifty vintage aircraft including a Vulcan bomber, a Comet airliner, a Spitfire and a Tigermoth. To get to the museum by public transport, catch **First Bus** #131 from North Berwick and Drem, both of which have train connections from Edinburgh.

North Berwick

NORTH BERWICK has a great deal of charm and a somewhat faded, old-fashioned air, its guesthouses and hotels extending along the shore in all their Victorian and Edwardian sobriety. The town's small harbour is set on a headland which cleaves two crescents of sand, providing the town with an attractive coastal setting, though it is the two nearby volcanic heaps, the **Bass Rock** and **North Berwick Law**, which are the town's defining physical features. The Bass Rock is home to some 100,000 nesting gannets in summer, which can be observed closely from North Berwick's principal attraction, the **Scottish Seabird Centre**, located by the harbour.

Scottish Seabird Centre and the Bass Rock

Housed in an attractively designed new building by the harbour, the **Scottish Seabird Centre** (April–Oct daily 10am–6pm; Nov–March Mon–Fri 10am–4pm, Sat & Sun 10am–5.30pm; till 5pm Mon–Fri Feb & March; £6.95; Ⓦ www.seabird.org) offers an introduction to all types of seabird found around the Scottish coast, particularly the 100,000-plus gannets and puffins which nest on the Bass Rock every summer. Such is the connection between the rock and its annual visitors that the gannet, once known as the solan goose, takes its Latin name, *Morus bassana*, from the Bass Rock. Among the interactive exhibits and kids-oriented displays there's a live link from the centre to cameras mounted on the volcanic island, which show close-up pictures of the birds in their nesting grounds. The cameras are mounted in different locations, depending on the movement of birds – in winter, for example, the gannets aren't around so it's more interesting to watch the shore birds or some peregrine falcons which have nested on Fidra Island.

Resembling a giant molar, the **Bass Rock** rises 350ft above the sea some three miles east of North Berwick. This massive chunk of basalt has had an interesting history, having served as a prison, a fortress and a monastic retreat. The last lighthouse keepers left in 1988, leaving it, quite literally, to the birds – it's Scotland's second-largest gannet colony after St Kilda but also hosts razorbills, terns, puffins, guillemots and fulmars. If you're not content with viewing the birds on the video link-up in the Seabird Centre, there are, weather permitting, **boat trips** from North Berwick harbour – Jewels of the Forth (Ⓣ01620/890202, Ⓦ www.jewelsoftheforth.co.uk) has exclusive landing rights on the rock, while Aquatrek (Ⓣ01620/893952, Ⓦ www.aquatrek.co.uk) offers cruises around the rock and past some of the other nearby islands.

North Berwick Law

The other volcanic monolith, 613ft-high **North Berwick Law**, which dominates the Lothian landscape for miles around, is about an hour's walk from the beach (take Law Road off High Street and follow the signs). On a clear day, the views out across the Firth of Forth, Fife and the Lammermuir Hills make the effort worthwhile, and at the top you can see the remains of a Napoleonic watchtower and an arch made from the jawbone of a whale.

Practicalities

North Berwick is served by a regular half-hourly **train** from Edinburgh Waverley, with special travel and entry deals available for those heading for the Seabird Centre (ask at Waverley ticket office or call ℡08457/550033). From the station it's a ten-minute walk east to the town centre. **Buses** from Edinburgh (every 30min) run along the coast via Aberlady, Gullane and Dirleton and stop on High Street, while the hourly service from Haddington and Dunbar terminates outside the **tourist office** (April–June & Sept Mon–Sat 9am–6pm, Sun 11am–4pm, closed Tues April & May; July Mon–Sat 9am–7pm, Sun 11am–6pm; Aug Mon–Sat 9am–8pm, Sun 11am–6pm; Oct Mon–Sat 9am–5pm; ℡01620/892197), on Quality Street.

As befits a well-to-do holiday resort, there are several excellent **B&Bs**, including *Chestnut Lodge*, at 2a Ware Rd (℡01620/894256; ❸), a half-timber chalet run by keen golfers; and *Glebe House*, Law Road (℡01620/892608, ⓦwww .glebehouse-nb.co.uk; ❹), a grander eighteenth-century manse in secluded grounds overlooking the sea. Of the **guesthouses**, *Beach Lodge*, 5 Beach Rd (℡01620/892257, ⓦwww.beachlodge.co.uk; ❸), is near the main street and harbour and has some great views out to sea. The nearest **campsite**, *Tantallon Caravan Park* (℡01620/893348, ⓦwww.meadowhead.co.uk/tantallon; closed Feb), occupies a prime cliff-top location a couple of miles east of the centre.

One of the best **cafés** in town is at the Seabird Centre, which has panoramic views over the beach. For a daytime snack or coffee in town, try *Zanzibar* at 81 High St or the *Bass Rock Bistro* (℡01620/890875, ⓦwww.bassrockcafe.co.uk), at 37–39 Quality St, which also does evening meals on Friday and Saturday nights. *The Grange* at 35 High St (℡01620/893344; closed Sun) is a slightly more upmarket restaurant, serving moderately priced, mainstream Scottish dishes.

Tantallon Castle

The melodramatic ruins of **Tantallon Castle** (April–Sept daily 9.30am–6.30pm; Oct–March 9.30am–4.30pm Mon–Wed, Sat & Sun; HS; £3.30), three miles east of North Berwick on the A198, stand on the precipitous cliffs facing the Bass Rock. With a sheer drop down to the sea on three sides and a sequence of moats and ditches on the fourth, the castle's desolate invincibility is daunting, especially when the wind howls over the remaining battlements and the surf crashes on the rocks far below. Built at the end of the fourteenth century, the castle was a stronghold of the Douglases, the Earls of Angus, one of the most powerful noble families in Scotland.

Besieged several times, the castle was finally destroyed by Cromwell in 1651 after a twelve-day bombardment. The ruins, including a seventeenth-century dovecote left untouched by Cromwell's men, enjoy a wonderfully photogenic setting, with the Bass Rock and the Firth of Forth in the background. You can reach Tantallon Castle from North Berwick by the Dunbar **bus** (#120; Mon–Sat 6 daily, Sun 2 daily), which takes fifteen minutes, or you can walk there from town along the cliffs in around an hour.

Dunbar

Twelve miles further along the coast lies **DUNBAR**, which bears some resemblance to North Berwick with its wide, recently spruced-up High Street graced by several grand old stone buildings. One of the oldest is the **Town House** (April–Oct daily 12.30–4.30pm; free), formerly a prison and now home to a small archeology room and local history centre. Of greater significance is the three-storey **John Muir Birthplace**, 126 High St (April–Oct Mon–Sat 10am–5pm, Sun 1–5pm; Nov–March Wed–Sat 10am–5pm, Sun 1–5pm; free; ⓦwww .jmbt.org.uk), first home of the explorer and naturalist who created the United States national park system. Recently refurbished, the house now acts as an engaging interpretative and education centre about the pioneer's life and legacy. Inspiring though the centre is, a more appropriate tribute, in some respects, is the **country park** also named in Muir's honour, where an easy three-mile walk west of the harbour takes you along a rugged stretch of coast to the sands of Belhaven Bay.

The delightfully intricate double **harbour** at Dunbar merits a stroll, with its narrow channels, cobbled quays and roughened rocks, set beside the shattered remains of the castle. The town's one other claim to fame is as the home of **Belhaven beers**, which are still made on the original site of the monks' brewery, signposted off the Edinburgh road (guided tours by appointment Mon–Fri; £3; ⓣ01368/869200, ⓦwww.belhaven.co.uk).

The **tourist office**, 143a High St (April, May, Sept & Oct Mon–Sat 9am–5pm; June Mon–Sat 9am–6pm, Sun 11am–4pm; July Mon–Sat 9am–7pm, Sun 11am–6pm; Aug Mon–Sat 9am–8pm, Sun 11am–6pm; ⓣ01368/863353), will help with **accommodation**; try the non-smoking *Woodside* B&B, 13 North St (ⓣ01368/862384, ⓦwww.dunbarwoodside.co.uk; April–Sept; ❸), or one of the neat en-suite rooms at *The Rocks* (ⓣ01368/862287; ❹) on Marine Road, which is also one of the best places to **eat** in town, with a good bar menu and fine-dining options. An alternative is the *Creel* (ⓣ01368/863279, ⓦwww .creelrestaurant.co.uk), which serves bistro-style meals near the old harbour. The nearest **campsite** is *Belhaven Bay Caravan and Camping Park*, in the John Muir Park, just off the A1087 (ⓣ01368/865956, ⓦwww.meadowhead.co.uk /belhaven; closed Feb).

Haddington

The East Lothian gentry keep a watchful eye on **HADDINGTON**, their favourite country town. Its compact centre preserves an intriguing ensemble of seventeenth- to nineteenth-century architectural styles where everything of any interest has been labelled and plaqued. Yet the town's staid appearance belies a long history of innovation. During the early 1700s, Haddington became a byword for modernization as its merchants supplied the district's progressive landowners with all sorts of new-fangled equipment, stock and seed, and in only a few decades utterly transformed Lothian agriculture.

The Town

Haddington's centre is best approached from the west, where tree-trimmed **Court Street** ends suddenly with the soaring spire, stately stonework and dignified Venetian windows of the **Town House**, designed by William Adam in 1748.

Heading east from the town centre along High Street, it's a brief walk down Church Street – past the hooped arches of **Nungate Bridge** – to the hulking mass of **St Mary's Church** (Easter–Sept Mon–Sat 11am–4pm, Sun 2–4.30pm; free), Scotland's largest parish church. Built close to the reedy River Tyne, the church dates from the fourteenth century, but it's a real hotchpotch of styles, the squat grey tower uneasy above clumsy buttressing and pinkish-ochre stone walls. Inside, on the **Lauderdale Aisle**, a munificent tomb features the best of Elizabethan alabaster carving, moustached knights and their ruffed ladies lying beneath a finely ornamented canopy. In stark contrast, a plain slab in the choir is inscribed with Thomas Carlyle's beautiful tribute to his wife, Jane, who grew up in the town: "Suddenly snatched away from him, and the light of his life as if gone out." The church also offers brass rubbing, has a good tearoom and in the summer hosts internationally acclaimed concerts organized by the Lamp of Lothian Collegiate Trust (call ☎01620/823738). At nearby Haddington House, on Sidegate, the seventeenth-century medicinal gardens of **St Mary's Pleasance** (open during daylight hours; free) merit a brief stroll.

Practicalities

Fast and frequent **buses** connect Haddington with Edinburgh, fifteen miles to the west, and with North Berwick on the east coast, with all services stopping on High Street. There's no **tourist office**, but orientation is easy and *A Walk Around Haddington* (£1), detailing every building of any conceivable consequence, is available from local newsagents.

The *Plough Tavern*, 11 Court St (☎01620/823326; ❸), is a welcoming traditional **inn** right in the town centre. Alternatively, try the more luxurious *Brown's Hotel*, 1 West Rd (☎01620/822254, ⓦwww.browns-hotel.com; ❻), occupying a fine Regency town house. *Monks' Muir Caravan Park* (☎01620/860340), which takes its environmental credentials very seriously, is on the eastern edge of town by the A1, and also takes tents.

For **daytime snacks** and lovely deli lunch platters, the place to seek out is *Jaques & Lawrence* at 37 Court St, opposite the post office. For an **evening meal**, the *Waterside Bistro* (☎01620/825674), on the far side of Nungate Bridge, is popular for its convivial atmosphere and hearty meat dishes, while *Bonars Brasserie* (☎01620/822100) in nearby Poldrate, a settlement on the southeastern fringes of Haddington, serves accomplished, well-cooked meals in a more contemporary setting. Real-ale fans should head to *The Pheasant* also in Poldrate, rumoured to serve the best pint in East Lothian.

Around Haddington

A thorough exploration of Haddington will only take two or three hours, but there are other attractions in its vicinity.

Four miles south along the B6369 on the edge of the Lammermuir Hills, the pretty hamlet of **GIFFORD**, whose eighteenth-century estate cottages flank a trim whitewashed church, was the birthplace (in 1723) of the Reverend John Witherspoon, a signatory of the American Declaration of Independence. The hamlet makes a good base for walkers, with several footpaths setting out across the surrounding red-soiled farmland for the Lammermuir Hills, while longer trails connect with the Southern Upland Way. If you want **to stay**, try the traditional *Tweeddale Arms* (☎01620/810240, ⓦwww.tweeddalearmshotel.co.uk; ❸), which has a reasonable **restaurant**, or *Eaglescairnie Mains* (☎01620/810491, ⓦwww.eaglescairnie.com; ❸), a substantial farmhouse with open fires and a tennis court.

Glenkinchie Distillery

Six miles west of Gifford, and about the same distance from Haddington along the A6093, the village of Pencaitland is the closest place to Edinburgh where malt whisky is made. Set in a peaceful dip in the rolling countryside about two miles outside Pencaitland, the **Glenkinchie Distillery** (Easter–Oct Mon–Sat 10am–5pm, Sun noon–5pm; Nov daily noon–4pm; Dec–Easter Mon–Fri noon–4pm; last tour 1hr before closing; £5) is one of only a handful found in the Lowlands of Scotland. Here, of course, they emphasize the qualities which set Glenkinchie, a lighter, drier malt, apart from the peaty, smoky whiskies of the north and west. Also in the tour, there's an impressive scale model of a distillery, allowing you to place all the different processes in context, and a room where the art of blending is explained.

Midlothian

Immediately south of Edinburgh lies the old county of **MIDLOTHIAN**, once called Edinburghshire. It's one of the hilliest parts of the Central Lowlands, with the Pentland chain running down its western side, and the Moorfoots defining its boundary with the Borders to the south. Though predominantly rural, it contains a belt of former mining communities, which are struggling to come to terms with the recent decline of the industry. Such charms as it has are mostly low-key, with the exception of the riotously ornate chapel at **Roslin**, no longer a hidden gem thanks to its role in the book and film *The Da Vinci Code*.

Dalkeith and around

Despite its Victorian demeanour, **DALKEITH**, eight miles southeast of central Edinburgh – to which it is linked by regular buses (#3/3A, #49 or First Bus #86) – grew up in the Middle Ages as a baronial burgh under the successive control of the Douglases and Buccleuchs. Today it's a bustling shopping centre, with an unusually broad High Street at its heart and a large **country park** (April–Sept daily 10am–5.30pm; £3; Ⓦ www.dalkeithcountrypark.com) with walks and a large woodland playground.

A mile or so south of Dalkeith is the Lady Victoria Colliery at **NEWTON-GRANGE**, now open to the public as the **Scottish Mining Museum** (daily: Feb–Oct 10am–5pm; Nov–Jan 11am–3pm; £4.45; Ⓦ www.scottishmining museum.com). Staffed in large part by former miners, the museum mixes coal-mining heritage and artefacts with hands-on exhibits for kids and the chance to see some of the key working parts of the colliery, including the largest steam engine in Scotland, which powered the winding tower above a 1625-foot deep shaft. A great place for kids, visitors are kitted out with "magic helmets" (audio tour headphones built into old miners' hats), which allow them to take a virtual-reality tour of conditions below ground.

Roslin

The tranquil village of **ROSLIN** lies seven miles south of the centre of Edinburgh, from where it can be reached by bus #15A (Mon–Fri) or First Bus #141 (Sat) from St Andrew Square. An otherwise nondescript place, the village has two unusual claims to fame: it was near here, at the Roslin Institute, that the world's first cloned sheep, Dolly, was created in 1997, and it's also home to the mysterious, richly decorated late Gothic **Rosslyn Chapel** (Mon–Sat 9am–6pm, Sun noon–4.45pm; £6; Ⓦ www.rosslynchapel.org. uk). The chapel was intended to be a huge collegiate church dedicated to St Matthew, but construction halted soon after the founder's death in 1484,

△ Apprentice Pillar, Rosslyn Chapel

and the vestry built onto the facade nearly four hundred years later is the sole subsequent addition. After a long period of neglect, a massive restoration project has recently been undertaken, with a rigid, semi-permanent canopy constructed over the chapel in order to dry out the saturated ceiling and walls.

Visitors are free to look around both inside and out: Rosslyn's exterior bristles with pinnacles, gargoyles, flying buttresses and canopies, while inside the

Scotland's
architecture

Scotland's history is, of course, one of the country's most compelling subjects, and more often than not it's the buildings that tell the story. From brochs to bridges, crofts to castles and tenements to titanium, Scotland's social, military and artistic heritage is wrapped up in a range of unique architecture, shaped and refined by an often hostile climate, centuries of feuding, mind-boggling aristocratic wealth, enlightened engineering and a rich legacy of craft and design.

Crannog, Loch Tay

Early constructions

Orkney and Shetland are home to some of Europe's best-preserved Stone Age houses. The Neolithic stone village of **Skara Brae**, for example, is so well preserved that you can still see the stone beds, while recent loch-side excavations have shed light on semi-defensive Bronze Age dwellings called **crannogs**, timber huts built on artificial islands.

The most distinctive legacy of Iron Age Scotland are sturdy circular dry-stone constructions called **brochs**, now predominantly found in ruins along the coast of the islands and northwest Highlands, with Shetland's **Broch of Mousa** the finest vestige, thanks in large part to its isolated location.

The Middle Ages

The great **Border abbeys**, with their European influences, found in places such as Jedburgh, Dryburgh and Melrose, display a transitional style between Romanesque and Gothic, but their location left them vulnerable to attack from the English and today they stand as evocative ruins.

The Reformation aided the destruction of many **church** buildings, and with much of the church land sold off to nobles, aspirant landowners focused on strategically unimportant **tower houses**, and the Scottish Baronial style, characterized by crow-stepped gables and conical roofs, took flight – the most dramatic example, with its fairy-tale towers and turrets, is the pink-hued **Craigievar Castle**, west of Aberdeen, built in 1626.

Melrose Abbey

Scotland's finest castle?

The sturdy, picturesque castle is surely the icon of Scottish architecture, with the title of the finest castle in the country a straight fight between **Edinburgh** and **Stirling**, both perched on volcanic crags and both still military garrisons. The epitome of the romantic Highland castle, on the other hand, is **Eilean Donan** on Loch Duich, near Skye, though the present building is predominantly an early twentieth-century reconstruction. Rivalling it for scene stealing are **Castle Stalker**, north of Oban, and **Duart Castle**, guarding the Sound of Mull. There are plenty of contenders, too, for the prize for Scotland's moodiest ruins: **Dunottar Castle** near Aberdeen with its sheer cliffs on three sides, mournful **Castle Urquhart** on Loch Ness-side or spooky **Kilchurn Castle** in Loch Awe. The most disappointing castle? Surely **Balmoral** – still used by the Royals as a Highland retreat, it's a squat, uninspiring nineteenth-century imitation hidden away in the Deeside woodland.

Stirling Castle

The eighteenth and nineteenth centuries

Wide, symmetrical streets and elegant houses characterize the **Neoclassical** architecture of Edinburgh's New Town, which compared to the higgledy-piggledy, medieval Old Town signalled a new approach to civilized urban living.

In Glasgow, the industrial revolution brought with it slums and **tenement** flats, while some of Glasgow's finest architecture came as the result of shipbuilding wealth. The industrial age also gave birth to great feats of engineering. **Thomas Telford** constructed roads, bridges and canals throughout Scotland; the **Stevenson** family pioneered some remarkable lighthouses around the coast; and Benjamin Baker and John Fowler dreamed up the gigantic cantilevered girders of the **Forth Railway Bridge**, which spans more than a mile, took seven years to build and required 50,000 tons of steel.

St Magnus Cathedral, Kirkwall

Contemporary architecture

With the exception of Mackintosh, great architecture didn't abound in early twentieth-century Scotland and it wasn't until late in the century that a new wave of notable buildings started to appear. Glasgow's year as UK City of Architecture and Design in 1999 reminded everyone of the city's rich architectural heritage, and in the wake of it came Sir Norman Foster's **Armadillo** and the titanium-clad **Glasgow Science Centre** on opposite banks of the Clyde. Dundee, too, had its cultural renaissance expressed, in Richard Murphy's inspiring **DCA** (Dundee Contemporary Arts) building and Frank Gehry's tiny but moving **Maggies cancer care centre** at Ninewells Hospital. Industrial architecture still has its place in Scotland with the intriguing **Falkirk Wheel** proving a twenty-first century equivalent of the Forth Rail Bridge. Overshadowing them all, however, is the new **Scottish Parliament** building in Edinburgh, based on designs by the late Catalan architect Enric Miralles. It's a controversial project, not least because of the cost to the public purse, while its unconventional, freethinking architecture, laden with totemic imagery and references to centuries of vernacular building, ultimately brings a refreshing edge to historic Edinburgh and Scotland's aspirations as a modern European nation.

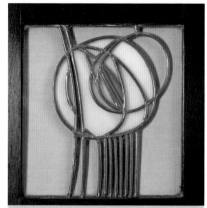

Charles Rennie Mackintosh

Historians may disagree over whether **Charles Rennie Mackintosh** was a forerunner of the Modernist movement or merely represented the sunset of Victorianism, but he nonetheless undoubtedly created buildings of great beauty, idiosyncratically fusing Scots Baronial with Gothic, Art Nouveau and modern design. Born in 1868, Mackintosh attended Glasgow School of Art, where he became part of a new artistic language, using extended vertical design, stylized forms and muted colours. However, it was architecture that truly challenged the artist, and his big break came in 1896, when he won the competition to design a new home for the Glasgow School of Art. This building remains the archetypal Mackintosh work, but there are many other examples around Glasgow including tearooms, a church, a school and the distinctive Hill House in his home town of Helensburgh. Strangely, the building which arguably displays Mackintosh at his most flamboyant was one he never saw built, the House for an Art Lover, which was constructed in Bellahouston Park in 1996, 95 years after plans for it were submitted to a German architectural competition.

Scottish Parliament, Edinburgh

stonework is, if anything, even more intricate. The foliage carving is particularly outstanding, with botanically accurate depictions of over a dozen different leaves and plants. Among them are cacti and Indian corn, compounding the legend that the founder's grandfather, the daring sea adventurer Prince Henry of Orkney, did indeed set foot in the New World a century before Columbus. The rich and subtle figurative sculptures have given Rosslyn the nickname of "a Bible in stone", though they're more allegorical than literal, with portrayals of the Dance of Death, the Seven Acts of Mercy and the Seven Deadly Sins.

The greatest and most original carving of all is the extraordinary knotted **Apprentice Pillar** at the southeastern corner of the Lady Chapel. According to local legend, the pillar was made by an apprentice during the absence of the master mason, who killed him in a fit of jealousy on seeing the finished work. A tiny head of a man with a slashed forehead, set at the apex of the ceiling at the far northwestern corner of the building, is popularly supposed to represent the apprentice, his murderer the corresponding head at the opposite side. The entwined dragons at the foot are symbols of Satan, and were probably inspired by Norse mythology.

The imagery of carvings such as the floriated cross and five-pointed star, together with the history of the family, the St Clairs of Rosslyn, which owns the chapel, leave little doubt about its links to the Knights Templar and freemasonry. Two members of the St Clair family, for example, were allegedly grand masters of the Prieuré de Sion, the shadowy order linked to the Templars, while the Masonic connection was said to have saved the chapel from the armies of Oliver Cromwell, himself a freemason, which destroyed the surrounding area but spared Rosslyn. More intriguing still are claims that, because of such connections, Rosslyn Chapel has been the repository for items such as the lost Scrolls of Solomon's Temple in Jerusalem, the true Stone of Scone and, most famously, the Holy Grail. This particular conspiracy theory led to the chapel appearing in the climax of Dan Brown's best-selling book *The Da Vinci Code*, and subsequently the film of it starring Tom Hanks, which has ensured a flood of visitors to the chapel in recent years.

West Lothian

To many, West Lothian is a poor relative to the rolling, rich farmland of East and Midlothian, with a landscape dominated by motorways, industrial estates and giant hillocks of ochre-coloured mine waste called "bings". However, in the ruined royal palace at **Linlithgow**, the area boasts one of Scotland's more magnificent ruins. There's some interesting industrial heritage, too, including the prettiest stretch of the recently upgraded **Union Canal**, and the restored railway at **Bo'ness**, a popular family attraction. Although strictly no longer part of West Lothian, the village of **South Queensferry** is only a few miles east of Bo'ness. It lies under the considerable shadow of the **Forth rail and road bridges**, though it's an interesting enough place in its own right, with a historic high street and the notable stately homes **Dalmeny** and Hopetoun nearby.

Linlithgow

Roughly equidistant (fifteen miles) from Falkirk, to the west, and Edinburgh is the ancient royal burgh of **LINLITHGOW**. The town itself has largely kept its medieval layout, but development since the 1960s has sadly stripped it of some fine buildings, notably close to the **Town Hall** and **Cross** – the former marketplace – on the long High Street.

Though hidden from the main road, **Linlithgow Palace** (daily: April–Sept 9.30am–6.30pm; Oct–March 9.30am–4.30pm; last admission 45min before closing; £4), is a splendid fifteenth-century ruin romantically set on the edge of Linlithgow Loch and associated with some of Scotland's best-known historical figures – including Mary, Queen of Scots, who was born here on December 8, 1542 and became queen six days later. A royal manor house is believed to have existed on this site since the time of David I, though James I began construction of the present palace, a process that continued through two centuries and the reign of no fewer than eight monarchs. From the top of the northwest tower, Queen Margaret looked out in vain for the return of James IV from the field of Flodden in 1513 – indeed, the views from her bower, six giddy storeys up from the ground, are exceptional. The ornate octagonal **fountain** in the inner courtyard, with its wonderfully intricate figures and medallion heads, flowed with wine for the wedding of James V and Mary of Guise. Bonnie Prince Charlie visited during the 1745 rebellion, and a year later the palace was burnt, probably accidentally, while occupied by General Hawley's troops.

This is a great place to take children: the elegant, bare rooms echo with footsteps and there's a labyrinthine network of spiral staircases and endless nooks and crannies. The galleried **Great Hall** is magnificent, as is the adjoining kitchen, which has a truly cavernous fireplace.

St Michael's Church, adjacent to the palace, is one of Scotland's largest pre-Reformation churches, consecrated in the thirteenth century. The present building was completed three hundred years later, with the exception of the hugely incongruous aluminium spire, tacked on in 1946.

Running through Linlithgow is part of the **Union Canal**, the 31-mile artery opened in 1822, which together with the Forth & Clyde Canal linked Edinburgh with Glasgow. At Falkirk, ten miles west of here, the incredible Falkirk Wheel (see p.419) transfers boats from one canal to the other. The Linlithgow Union Canal Society runs short trips on the *Victoria* (Easter–Sept Sat & Sun 2–5pm, July & Aug daily 2-5pm; £2.50; Ⓦ www.lucs.org.uk), a diesel-powered replica of a Victorian steam packet boat, and longer trips to the splendid Avon Aqueduct on the *St Magdalene*, an electric canal boat (Easter–Sept Sat & Sun 2pm, trip returns at 4.30pm; £6; same website). The boats depart from the Manse Road canal basin, uphill from the train station at the southern end of town, where the small Linlithgow Canal Centre (Easter–Oct Sat & Sun 2–5pm, July & Aug daily 2–5pm; free) is also located. An eighteen-mile walk along the canal towpath leads eventually to the centre of Edinburgh.

Practicalities

Frequent **buses** between Stirling and Edinburgh stop at the Cross, and the town is on the main **train** routes from Edinburgh to both Glasgow Queen Street and Stirling; the **train station** lies at the southern end of town. The **tourist office** is in the Town Hall building at the Cross (Easter–Oct daily 10am–5pm; ℡01506/844600), between the Palace and the High Street.

For **accommodation** try *The Star and Garter Hotel*, 1 High St (℡01506/846362, Ⓦ www.starandgarterhotel.com; ④), at the east end of town, a comfortable old coaching inn that serves inexpensive bar meals. Otherwise, on the outskirts

of town at Belsyde, there's smart *Arden House* (℡01506/670172, Ⓦwww
.ardenhouse-scotland.co.uk; ❹) and friendly *Belsyde Farm* (℡01506/842098,
Ⓦwww.belsydehouse.co.uk; ❸), a late eighteenth-century house on a sheep and
cattle farm beside the Union Canal.

There are a few decent places to **eat** in Linlithgow: for good pub food try
The Four Marys, opposite the Cross on High Street, which also has real ales or,
for more expensive Scottish cuisine, *Livingston's* (℡01506/846565, Ⓦwww
.livingstons-restaurant.co.uk), through an arch at 52 High St, which serves
upmarket meals in a small garden observatory. *Marynka* (℡01506/840123,
Ⓦwww.marynka.com), also on the High Street at number 57, is a brighter,
more modern bistro-style place. Best of the lot is a place just outside Linlithgow
on the way to Blackness called the *Champany Inn* (℡01506/834532, Ⓦwww
.champany.com), which serves delicious steaks and seafood.

The only official **campsite** in the area is at *Beecraigs Caravan Park*
(℡01506/844516, Ⓦwww.beecraigs.com), about four miles south of town and
part of the larger Beecraigs Country Park. There are only 36 pitches, however,
so get there early or phone first.

Around Linlithgow

The small hillside town of **BO'NESS**, roughly four miles north of Linlithgow
– which has traditionally looked down its nose at its pint-sized neighbour –
sprawls in a less than genteel fashion down to the Forth. On a clear day there are
good views across the Forth to Culross (see p.455). The **Bo'ness and Kinneil
Railway**, whose headquarters are in the old station at the eastern end of the
waterfront road, incorporates the recently expanded Scottish Railway Exhibition (11.30am–5pm on train service days only; £1), Scotland's largest dedicated railway exhibition with half a dozen sheds full of locomotives, carriages,
wagons and so on. In summer (April–Oct Sat & Sun, July & Aug Tues–Sun;
℡01506/822298, Ⓦwww.srps.org.uk) it runs lovingly kept steam trains to
Birkhill, just over three miles away (£4.50 return). Here you can wander along
the wooded Avon Gorge, or take a guided tour through the **Birkhill Fireclay
Mine** (4 tours a day coincide with train times; £3), where 300 million-year-old
fossils line the walls.

Along the coast from Bo'ness and four miles northeast of Linlithgow is
the village of **BLACKNESS**, once Linlithgow's seaport and location of the
dramatic fourteenth-century **Blackness Castle** (April–Sept daily 9.30am–
6.30pm, Oct–March Sat–Wed 9.30am–4.30pm; last admission 30min before
closing; HS; £3), which, after the Treaty of Union in 1707, was one of only
four castles in Scotland to be garrisoned. Built in the shape of a galleon jutting
out into the river Forth, the castle, which was used as one of the location shots
for Mel Gibson's film version of *Hamlet*, offers grand views of the Forth bridges
from the narrow gun slits in its northern tower.

General Tam Dalyell, the seventeenth-century Scottish royalist, spent part of
his youth at the **House of the Binns** (house June–Sept 2–5pm, closed Fri;
grounds daily April–Oct 10am–7pm, Nov–March 10am–4pm; last admission
30min before closing; NTS; £8), which occupies a fine hill-top site about a
mile inshore from Blackness and three miles east of Linlithgow. Today it's the
home of the former Labour MP Tam Dalyell, a regular thorn in the flesh of
governments of all hues and the man who first articulated the West Lothian
Question, which has troubled politicians in Edinburgh and London ever since.
Inside you can see ornate plaster ceilings, paintings, period furniture and family
relics not much changed since (the original) Tam's day.

Ratho Adventure Centre

One of Scotland's most exciting modern developments, the **Ratho Adventure Centre** (Mon–Fri 8am–10.30pm, Sat & Sun 9.30am–8pm; free, times and charges for activities vary; ☎0131/333 6333, Ⓦwww.adventurescotland.com) incorporates the world's largest indoor climbing arena, with a remarkable 2400 square metres of artificial climbing wall. Opened in 2003 at a cost of over £24 million, the spectacular vision of its architect founders was to enclose (and roof) a disused quarry, creating a giant area that's now used for international climbing competitions as well as classes (from £20 for an hour-long taster session) for climbers of all levels, including beginners and kids. Above the centre, just under the glass roof, is the SkyRide (£8), a stomach-churning aerial obstacle course 100ft off the ground, which you take on secured into a sliding harness. Elsewhere in this multi-faceted facility are a state-of-the-art gym, mountain bike routes, accommodation and a decent restaurant-café which looks out over the climbing arena.

At the time of going to press, a **bus** service to the centre from central Edinburgh is planned (see the website for updates); if you're driving, follow the signs from the Newbridge roundabout on the A8, not far from the airport.

South Queensferry and around

Eight miles northwest of the city centre of Edinburgh is the small town of **SOUTH QUEENSFERRY**, best known today for its location at the southern end of the two mighty **Forth bridges** – for more on these, see p.460. Named after the saintly wife of King Malcolm Canmore, Margaret, who would often use the ferry here to travel between the royal palaces in Dunfermline and Edinburgh, it's an attractive old settlement, with a narrow, cobbled High Street lined with tightly packed old buildings, most of which date from the seventeenth and eighteenth centuries. Only one row of houses separates the High Street from the water; through the gaps between these there's a great perspective of the two Forth bridges, an old stone harbour and a curved, pebbly beach, the scene each New Year's Day of the teeth-chattering "Loony Dook", when a gaggle of hung-over locals (along with some foolhardy tourists) charge into the sea for the quickest of dips. The small **museum**, 53 High St (Mon & Thurs–Sat 10am–1pm & 2.15–5pm, Sun noon–5pm; free), contains relics of the town's history and information on the building of the two bridges which loom over the village. A dedicated museum to the bridge can be found in North Queensferry (see p.459), while the best way to get a good view of the magnificent Rail Bridge is to walk (or cycle) across the Road Bridge.

South Queensferry has a couple of excellent spots to **eat**. 🍴 *The Boathouse* (☎0131/5429; closed Mon) at 19b High St – it's actually down a flight of stairs leading to the beach – serves moderately expensive but classy local seafood and has great views out to the bridges; a few doors away at no. 17, *Orocco Pier* (☎0131/331 1298, Ⓦwww.oroccopier.co.uk) is more ostentatiously slick and contemporary, but is a good spot for a drink with a view, some pleasant bistro food or a comfy bed for the night (Ⓖ).

Dalmeny House

Set on a two thousand-acre estate between South Queensferry and Cramond, **Dalmeny House** (July & Aug Mon, Tues & Sun 2pm–5.30pm; last entry 1hr before closing; £5; Ⓦwww.dalmeny.co.uk), is not the prettiest country seat you'll encounter in Scotland, its Tudor-Gothic style giving rather too much prominence to castellations, towers and chimney stacks. As it's the seat and residence of the Earl of Rosebery, entry is quite restricted, with viewing via tours only (generally on the hour and half-hour), but the quality of the items on show combined with the intriguing history of the family make it a fascinating place to visit. The fifth earl (1847–1929), a nineteenth-century British Prime Minister, married the heiress Hannah de Rothschild, and their union is the principal reason why Dalmeny boasts some the finest baroque and Neoclassical furniture produced for Louis XIV, Louis XV and Louis XVI during the hundred years before the French Revolution. Also in the collection are a very rare set of tapestries made from cartoons by Goya, and portraits by Raeburn, Reynolds, Gainsborough and Lawrence as well as a valuable collection of memorabilia relating to Napoleon Bonaparte.

Hopetoun House

Sitting in its own extensive estate on the south shore of the Forth, just to the west of South Queensferry, **Hopetoun House** (April–Sept daily 10am–5.30pm; last admission 1hr before closing; £7 house and grounds, £3.50 grounds only; ⓦ www.hopetounhouse.com) ranks as one of the most impressive stately homes in Scotland. The original house was built at the turn of the eighteenth century for the first Earl of Hopetoun by Sir William Bruce, the architect of Holyroodhouse. A couple of decades later, William Adam carried out an enormous extension, engulfing the structure with a curvaceous main facade and two projecting wings – superb examples of Roman Baroque pomp and swagger. The scale and lavishness of Adam's interiors, most of whose decoration was carried out by his sons after he died, make for a stark contrast with the intimacy of those designed by Bruce – the Red and Yellow Drawing Rooms, with their splendid ceilings by the young Robert Adam, are particularly impressive. Hopetoun's architecture is undoubtedly its most compelling feature, but the furnishings aren't completely overwhelmed, with some impressive seventeenth-century tapestries, Meissen porcelain and a distinguished collection of paintings, including portraits by Gainsborough, Ramsay and Raeburn. The house's grounds include a long, regal driveway and lovely walks along woodland trails and the banks of the Forth, as well as plenty of places for a picnic. If the weather's not favourable, the *Stables Tearoom* makes a classy alternative indoor venue for lunch or afternoon tea.

Inchcolm

From South Queensferry's Hawes Pier, just west of the rail bridge, the *Maid of the Forth* (April & Oct Sat & Sun; May, June & Sept Sat–Sun & some weekdays; July & Aug daily; £13; confirm sailing times in advance on ☏0131/331 5000, ⓦ www.maidoftheforth.co.uk) heads out in the direction of the island of **Inchcolm**, located about five miles northeast of South Queensferry near the Fife shore. The island is home to the best-preserved medieval **abbey** in Scotland, founded in 1235 after King Alexander I was stormbound on the island and took refuge in a hermit's cell. Although the structure as a whole is half-ruined today, the tower, octagonal chapterhouse and echoing cloisters are intact and well worth exploring. The hour and a half you're given ashore by the boat timetables also allows time for a picnic on the abbey's lawns or the chance to explore Inchcolm's old military fortifications and its extensive bird-nesting grounds. If you're lucky, dolphins and porpoises are sometimes sighted from the boat crossing to the island. The *Maid of the Forth* also makes occasional sailings to Inchcolm from Newhaven harbour, near Leith (see p.157).

Travel details

Trains

Edinburgh to: Aberdeen (hourly; 2hr 20min); Birmingham (4 daily; 5hr 30min); Dunbar (8 daily; 30min); Dundee (hourly; 1hr 45min); Falkirk (every 15min; 25min); Fort William (change at Glasgow, 3 daily; 4hr 55min); Glasgow (2–4 hourly; 50min); Inverness (5 daily direct; 3hr 50min); London (hourly; 4hr 30min); Manchester (direct, 4 daily; 4hr; change at Preston, 7 daily; 4hr); Newcastle upon Tyne (hourly; 1hr 30min); North Berwick (hourly; 30 min); Oban (2–3 daily, change at Glasgow; 4hr 10min); Perth (6 daily; 1hr 15min); Stirling (every 30min; 45min); York (hourly; 2hr 30min).

Buses

Edinburgh (St Andrew Square) to: Aberdeen (hourly; 3hr 50min); Birmingham (3 daily; 6hr 50min); Dundee (hourly; 1hr 45min–2hr); Fort William (4 daily direct; 4hr); Glasgow (every 15min; 1hr 10min); Inverness (hourly; 3–4hr); London (6 daily; 7hr 50min); Newcastle upon Tyne (2 daily; 3hr 15min); Oban (3 daily, change at Tyndrum or Perth; 5hr); Perth (hourly; 1hr 20min); York (1 daily; 5hr).

Flights

Edinburgh to: Belfast (Mon–Fri 8 daily; Sat & Sun 4 daily; 55min); Cardiff (2 daily; 1hr 10min); Dublin (Mon–Fri 4 daily, Sat & Sun 3 daily; 1hr); Kirkwall (Mon–Fri 2 daily, Sat & Sun 1 daily; 1hr 55min); Lerwick (1 daily; 1hr 30min); London City (Mon–Fri 12 daily, Sat 1, Sun 4 daily; 1hr 15min); London Gatwick (Mon–Fri 14 daily, Sat & Sun 6 daily; 1hr 15min); London Heathrow (Mon–Fri 18 daily, Sat & Sun 11–15 daily; 1hr); London Luton (Mon–Fri 6 daily, Sat & Sun 4 daily; 1hr 20min); London Stansted (Mon–Fri 6 daily, Sat & Sun 4–6 daily; 1hr 10min); Stornoway (Mon–Fri 3 daily, Sat 2, Sun 1; 1hr 10 min); Wick (Mon–Fri 1 daily; 1hr 10min).

The Borders

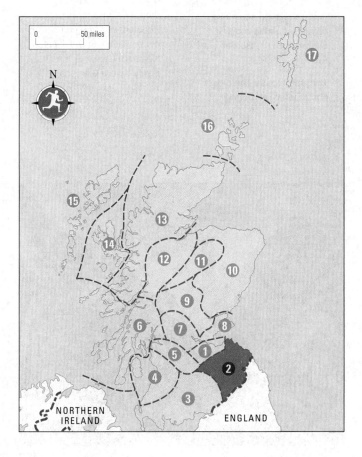

CHAPTER 2 # Highlights

✳ **St Abb's Head** Easily accessible, spectacular coastal scenery with sea stacks and nesting seabirds galore. **See p.180**

✳ **Melrose Abbey** The Border abbey with the best-preserved sculptural detail, set within most charming of the Border towns. **See p.190**

✳ **Traquair House** The oldest continuously inhabited house in Scotland, virtually unchanged since the fifteenth century. **See p.196**

✳ **Walking and cycling around Peebles** The banks of the Tweed are at their most scenic around Peebles, and you can cycle or walk to medieval Neidpath Castle or the lovely Kailzie Gardens. **See p.198**

△ Melrose Abbey

The Borders

S andwiched between the Cheviot Hills on the English border and the Pentland and Moorfoot ranges to the south of Edinburgh, the **Borders** (Ⓦ www.scot-borders.co.uk) is a region made up from the old shire counties of Berwick, Roxburgh, Selkirk and Peebles. If you've travelled from the south across the bleak moorland of neighbouring Northumberland, you'll be struck by the green lushness of **Tweeddale**, whose river is the pivotal feature of the region's geography. Yet the Borders also incorporate some of the wildest stretches of the Southern Uplands, with their bare, rounded peaks and weather-beaten heathery hills.

The Borders' most famous sights are its **ruined abbeys**, founded during the reign of King David I (1124–53), whose policy of encouraging the monastic orders had little to do with spirituality. The bishops and monks David established at Kelso, Melrose, Jedburgh and Dryburgh were the frontiersmen of his kingdom, helping to advance his authority in areas of doubtful allegiance. This began a long period of relative stability across the Borders which enabled its abbeys to flourish until the Wars of Independence with England, which erupted in 1296.

From the first half of the sixteenth century, until the Act of Union, the Borders again experienced turbulent times, bloodily fought over by the English and the Scots, and plagued by endless clan warfare and Reivers' raids (see box on p.187). Consequently, the countryside is strewn with ruined castles and keeps, while each major town celebrates its agitated past in the **Common Ridings**, when locals – especially the "callants", the young men – dress up in period costume and ride out to check the burgh boundaries. It's a boisterous, macho business, performed with pride and matched only by the local love of **rugby union**, which reaches a crescendo with the **Melrose Sevens** tournament in April.

Tweeddale is the Borders at its best, with the finest section between **Melrose** and **Peebles**, where you'll find a string of attractions, from the eccentricities of Sir Walter Scott's mansion at **Abbotsford** to the intriguing Jacobite past of **Traquair House**, along with the aforementioned ruined abbeys. The valley widens to the east to form the **Merse** basin, an area of rich arable land that boasts a series of grand stately homes, principally **Floors Castle**, **Manderston**, **Paxton** and **Mellerstain House**, all featuring the Neoclassical work of the Adam family – William and two of his four sons, John and Robert.

To the west, the Borders have a much wilder aspect, where a series of narrow valleys lead up to the border with Dumfriesshire: remote **Liddesdale**, southwest of Jedburgh; **Teviotdale**, to the north, which passes through Hawick and carries the A7 down to Carlisle; Ettrick Water, which takes you over into Eskdale; and **Yarrow Water** which connects Selkirk with Moffat in

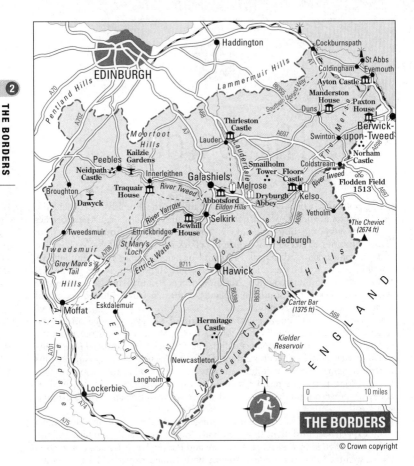

© Crown copyright

Dumfriesshire. Choose any of these four routes for the scenery. North of the Tweed, the **Lammermuir Hills**, a narrow band of foothills, forms the southern edge of Lothian and the central belt. Further to the east in **Berwickshire**, especially around **St Abb's Head**, the coastline becomes more rugged, its cliffs and rocky outcrops harbouring a series of desolate ruined castles, while inland, the flatness of the terrain is interrupted by the occasional extinct volcano.

Transport

The only **train** line in the Borders runs along the east coast, though the Scottish executive is committed to rebuilding at least part of the Waverley Line which used to run from Edinburgh to Carlisle via Galashiels. Travelling around the region by **bus** takes some planning – pick up timetables from any tourist office and plot your connections closely, as it's often difficult to cross between valleys.

This is excellent **walking** country, with lots of short walks and two marked treks for the ambitious hiker: the **St Cuthbert's Way**, which follows a sixty-mile trail from Melrose, where St Cuthbert started his ministry, to Lindisfarne (the Holy Isle), south of the English border, where he died; and the **Southern**

Upland Way, a 212-mile coast-to-coast hike from Portpatrick in the west to Cockburnspath in the east.

The combination of rolling landscape and quiet backroads also makes the region good for **cyclists**: many of the forested hills have mountain-biking tracks and rental centres, while the 88-mile **Tweed Cycleway** runs through attractive countryside from Biggar to Berwick-on-Tweed. Detailed maps of all cycle trails are available from any tourist office.

Berwickshire

The bleak Lammermuir Hills, on the border of **Berwickshire** and Lothian, are not going to top anyone's Scottish holiday itinerary, though there are plenty of decent walks to be had in amongst them. In truth, of course, Berwickshire, Scotland's easternmost county, lost its natural focus and centre when the English finally captured the town of Berwick-upon-Tweed in 1482 – in its place, unassuming **Duns** had to fill in as the old county town. The brief Borders coastline is bracing rather than beguiling, and has more in common with East Lothian, to the north, than the rest of the Borders. The chief settlement is the fishing port of **Eyemouth**, and the main attraction the dramatic cliff scenery around **St Abbs**.

The Lammermuir Hills and Lauder

What physically separates Scotland and England is not so much the gentle River Tweed, which marks the border here, but the **Lammermuir Hills**, setting for Scott's *Bride of Lammermoor*, which in turn was inspiration for Donizetti's opera *Lucia di Lammermoor*. A slender east–west chain, the flat-topped summits and quiet streams are crisscrossed with footpaths, some of which follow ancient carting and droving trails as they slice from north to south. The hills are a favourite haunt of Edinburgh-based ramblers, as well as those completing the **Southern Upland Way**, which tracks along the body of the Lammermuirs between Lauder in the west and Cockburnspath on the coast. If you're keen to sample a portion, follow the minor road to Abbey St Bathans, a hamlet beside the Whiteadder Water (pronounced "whitta-der") for a pretty and undemanding ten-mile stretch of the trail which leads down to the sea. Alternatively, you could carry on north to Gifford (see p.166) in East Lothian, on the other side of the Lammermuirs.

It is also easy to join the Southern Upland Way on the western edge of the Lammermuir Hills in **LAUDER** (pronounced "lorder"), a grey market town 25 miles or so southeast of Edinburgh on the A68. Nearby **Thirlestane Castle** (Easter & May–June & Sept Wed–Fri, Sun 10.30am–3.30pm; July & Aug daily except Sat; £5.50; guided tours until 2.30pm; grounds only £2; ⓦwww .thirlestanecastle.co.uk) is an imposing Scots Baronial pile on the eastern edge of town; the main entrance is half a mile south of Lauder, but pedestrians can take the signposted footpath from the main square about halfway along High Street. Begun by John Maitland in the late sixteenth century, when he became Lord Chancellor of Scotland, and still owned by the family, the castle has been refashioned and remodelled on several occasions, but its impressive reddish turrets and castellated towers nevertheless appear as a cohesive whole. The somewhat undistinguished interior is redeemed by the extravagant plasterwork of the Restoration ceilings and a wealth of domestic detail from the Victorian period, including a wonderland of children's toys. There's also an adventure playground for those with children, and a woodland walk for those who wish to avoid them. In Lauder, the *Flat Cat Gallery & Coffee Shop* on the market square is a stylish **café** serving decent coffee and snacks, and the *Black Bull Hotel* has award-winning bar meals.

St Abbs and around

Flanked by jagged cliffs, the remote fishing village of **ST ABBS** (Ⓦ www.stabbs .com) has a rugged setting, with old fishermen's cottages tumbling down to the tiny, surf-battered harbour. The village is named after Abba, a seventh-century Northumbrian princess who struggled ashore here after being shipwrecked – and promptly founded a nunnery. From the harbour, you can take sea-angling, sub-aqua-diving, bird-watching and regular sightseeing **boat trips** with a local guide (Ⓣ 01890/771681). There are a couple of places to **stay**: the excellent *Castle Rock Guest House*, Murrayfield (Ⓣ 01890/771715, Ⓦ www .castlerockbandb.co.uk; mid-Feb to mid-Nov; ❷), a Victorian manse whose spick-and-span bedrooms and gingerbread woodwork look out along the sea cliffs; and *Springbank Cottage* B&B, a fisherman's cottage right on the harbour (Ⓣ 01890/771477, Ⓔ davemac55@hotmail.com; closed Jan; ❷).

The main reason to come to this stretch of the coastline is to visit **St Abb's Head National Nature Reserve**, reached from the tearoom and car park half a mile back along the road, where there's a small **visitor centre** (April–Oct daily 10am–5pm) and the Kittiwake Gallery, with an adjacent coffee shop which also does packed lunches. Owned by the NTS, the reserve comprises 200 acres of wild and rugged coastline with sheer, seabird-nesting cliffs rising

△ St Abbs

300ft above the water. An easy-to-follow walking trail ends at the Stevensons' lighthouse, a mile or so from the car park, but you only need to follow it for half a mile and you'll already be rewarded with a spectacular view of the rugged Berwickshire coast – especially at high tide on a stormy day.

To the south of St Abbs is **COLDINGHAM BAY**, where intrepid surfers gather. This pint-sized place has a fine sandy beach and an SYHA **hostel** (℡0870/004 1111, ⓦwww.syha.org.uk; April–Sept) in a large Victorian villa on a hill overlooking the seashore. For a luxurious bed for the night, along with the option of fine Scottish food, go for the *Dunlaverock House* **hotel** (℡01890/771450; ❺). For **camping**, the *Scoutscroft Holiday Centre* (℡01890/771338; ⓦwww.scoutscroft.co.uk; March–Nov) is just off the St Abbs road, very close to the beach at Coldingham Sands, and has a full range of facilities plus a **dive shop** for equipment rental and courses, should you wish to take advantage of one of the east coast's best diving locations.

Eyemouth and around

Almost the entire 3500 population of **EYEMOUTH** (ⓦwww.eyemouth.com), a few miles south of St Abbs – and accessible via a pleasant two-hour coastal walk – is dependent on the fishing industry, started by the thirteenth-century Benedictine monks of Coldingham Priory. Eyemouth's tiny centre is drearily modern, despite the town's medieval foundation, but the long, slender harbour remains very much the focus of activity, its waters packed with deep-sea and inshore fleets and its quay strewn with tatters of old net, discarded fish and fish crates. You can also see *Bertha*, the oldest working steamboat in existence, built by Isambard Kingdom Brunel in the 1840s, set to form the basis of a new maritime museum. Eyemouth boasts three annual fishy events, the week-long **Herring Queen Festival** in July, the weekend **Seafood Festival** on the second weekend in June and the **Lifeboat Gala** in August.

The **Eyemouth Museum**, in the Auld Kirk on the Market Place (April–June & Sept Mon–Sat 10am–5pm, Sun noon–3pm; July & Aug Mon–Sat 9.30am–6pm, Sun noon–6pm; Oct Mon–Sat 10am–4pm; £2) is just about worth a visit for the vast **Eyemouth Tapestry**, a recent composition commemorating the east-coast fishing disaster of 1881 when a freak storm destroyed most of the inshore fleet: 129 local men were lost, a tragedy of extraordinary proportions for a place of this size. The elegant **Gunsgreen House**, standing alone on the far side of the harbour, was designed in the 1750s by James Adam, one of the famous family of architects. Despite its respectable appearance – in keeping with its present use by the golf club – the house was once used by smugglers, with secret passages and underground tunnels leading back into town. This illicit trade in tobacco and booze peaked in the late eighteenth century, with local fishermen using their knowledge of the coast regularly to outwit the excise.

There is nowhere worth staying in Eyemouth itself, but there is somewhere good to eat: *Oblò Bar & Bistro*, a pleasant café-restaurant at 20 Harbour Rd. The pubs in Eyemouth are pretty dismal; for fish and chips and home-made ice cream, try the celebrated *Giacopazzi's*, 18 Harbour Rd. At weekends in season you can buy freshly caught shellfish at the end of the pier. Underwater enthusiasts should head to the Eyemouth Diving Centre on Fort Road (℡01890/751202), which rents out **dive equipment**, charters boats and runs diving courses. For **boat trips** contact 01890/771676 or ⓦwww.marine-quest.co.uk.

Paxton House

Built for Patrick Home in 1758, **Paxton House** (April–Oct daily 11.15am–5pm; grounds same days 10am–sunset; £6; ⓦwww.paxtonhouse.com), located eight miles south of Eyemouth and five miles west of Berwick-upon-Tweed, was the last act of a would-be matrimonial fiasco. Sent to the University of Leipzig, the young Scot quickly became a great success at the court of Frederick the Great in Berlin, even seducing the Queen's lady-in-waiting, Sophie de Brandt. The affair became public and Home was compelled to leave Berlin, but not before the lovers "plighted their troth". Forced to return to England on the murder of his mother – apparently, the butler did it – he built Paxton for his intended bride, but, sadly, they were never to meet again.

The building, designed by John and James Adam, is a modest Palladian mansion, with a carefully contrived facade, whose imposing centrepiece comprises columns rising two storeys to an impressive pediment. This geometrical simplicity is continued inside, where the guided tour, which lasts about an hour, leads you through a succession of rooms displaying the delights of the Adam brothers' style. Also on display is a stunning collection of Chippendale furniture, commissioned by the cousin to whom the broken-hearted Patrick sold the house on the death of Sophie. Finally, the expansive **Picture Gallery**, completed in the 1810s, blends aspects of earlier Neoclassicism into a more austere design, with most of the plasterwork moulded to look like masonry. The National Gallery of Scotland uses this room as an outstation, displaying some of its lesser works here and changing the exhibits frequently.

The **grounds**, eighty acres of mixed parkland and woodland abutting the Tweed, laid out by an assistant of Capability Brown, boast gentle footpaths, a croquet lawn, an army-built adventure playground, a tearoom, Highland cattle, Shetland ponies, a Victorian boathouse housing a salmon-netting museum and a hide, from where you can spy on red squirrels and woodpeckers.

Duns and around

Heading inland from Eyemouth, the B6355 and then the A6105 cross the fertile farmland of the Merse to **DUNS**, the tiny, former county town of Berwickshire (Berwick itself lying over the border in England). Duns gets few visitors nowadays, though it has a very pleasant little market square. A few folk come to pay their respects at the **Jim Clark Room**, 44 Newtown St (April–Sept Mon–Sat 10.30am–1pm & 2–4.30pm, Sun 2–4.30pm; Oct Mon–Sat 1–4pm; £1.30), dedicated to a local farmer-turned-motor-racing ace, twice world champion, whose brilliant career ended in death on the track at Hockenheim in Germany in 1968. Duns is also the (disputed) birthplace of **John Duns Scotus** (c.1265–1308), a medieval scholar, vehemently opposed to modern theology, whose followers were known as "Scotists" or "Dunses", hence the word "dunce" for someone who is slow to learn.

Duns is well connected by **bus** to all the major settlements of the east Borders, and has a couple of excellent **B&Bs**: the central *St Albans* (T01361/883285, Wwww.scotlandbordersbandb.co.uk; ❹), a former eighteenth-century manse, situated on an unlikely sounding street called Clouds, off Preston Road; and *Wellfield House* (T01361/883189; ❸), a rather grand Georgian house on Preston Road, with a library/billiard room and real fires. The wooden bar of the venerable *Whip and Saddle* on the market square is the best place for a **drink** and traditional bar **food**. Local **walks** are detailed in the leaflet "Walks Around Duns", available from *The Cherry Tree*, an attractive café serving light meals on the market square.

Two places near Duns raise the tone significantly. **SWINTON**, an ordinary-looking village six miles southeast, boasts the award-winning *Wheatsheaf* (T01890/860257, Wwww.wheatsheaf-swinton.co.uk; ❺), a **restaurant** whose rather twee dining room, overlooking the rectangular village green, nevertheless offers traditional Scottish dishes sourced locally and served with finesse; there are six nicely furnished rooms up above. Set in its own grounds to the east of **CHIRNSIDE** village, seven miles northeast of Duns, is *Chirnside Hall* (T01890/818219, Wwww.chirnsidehallhotel.co.uk; G), more of a full-blown **country-house hotel**, with a splendid restaurant attached. While you're passing through the village, cast a glance at the striking Art Deco primary school.

Manderston House

Manderston House (mid-May to Sept Thurs & Sun 1.30–5pm; £7, gardens only £3.50; Wwww.manderston.co.uk), two miles east of Duns on the A6105, is the very embodiment of Edwardian Britain. Between 1871 and 1905, the Miller family spent most of their herring and hemp fortune on turning their Georgian home into a prestigious country house, with no expense spared as architect John Kinross added entire suites of rooms in the Neoclassical style of Robert Adam. It's certainly a staggering sight, from the intricate plasterwork ceilings to the inlaid marble floor in the hall and the extravagant silver staircase, the whole lot sumptuously furnished with trappings worthy of a new member of the aristocracy: James Miller married Eveline Curzon, the daughter of Lord Scarsdale, in 1893. The house is currently the home of Lord and Lady Palmer, of Huntley & Palmers biscuits fame – there's a Biscuit Tin Museum in the house to prove it. When you've finished inside the house, stroll round the fifty or so acres of **gardens**, noted for their courtyard stables (where you can have an Edwardian cream tea), cloistered marble dairy, mock tower house and rhododendrons and azaleas.

Tweeddale

Rising in the hills far to the west, the **River Tweed** (Wwww.visittweeddale .com) snakes its way across the Borders until it reaches the North Sea at Berwick-upon-Tweed, most of its final stretch forming the boundary between Scotland and England. This is the area known as the **Merse**, a beguiling, gentle, rural landscape of rich farmland and wooded riverbanks where the occasional military ruin, usually on the south side of the border, serves as a reminder of more violent days. The **Border abbeys** – perhaps the best reason for visiting the region – also lie in ruins, not because of the Reformation, but because they were burnt to the ground by the English, for whom the lower Tweed was the obvious point at which to cross the border into Scotland: time and again they launched themselves north, destroying everything in their way. Indeed, the English turned Berwick-upon-Tweed into one of the most heavily guarded frontier towns in northern Europe, and its massive Elizabethan fortifications survive today.

On the Scottish side, the lower Tweed has just one town of note, **Kelso**, a busy agricultural centre distinguished by its proximity to **Floors Castle** and **Mellerstain House**, and by the Georgian elegance of its main square. Kelso is also visited for its abbey, though the ruins of the colossal twelfth-century foundation, whose abbots claimed precedence over St Andrews, are easily upstaged by those at **Melrose** and **Dryburgh**, further upstream. Melrose makes a great base for exploring the middle reaches of the Tweed Valley. The rich, forested scenery inspired Sir Walter Scott, whose own purpose-built creation, **Abbotsford House**, stands a few miles outside Melrose. Perhaps fortunately, Scott died before

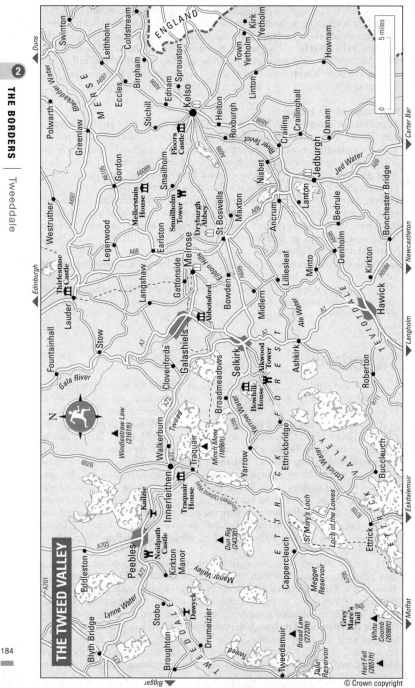

THE TWEED VALLEY

© Crown copyright

The Battle of Flodden

The Borders region witnessed one of the most devastating of sixteenth-century battles when possibly the largest Scots army ever to invade England was decimated by the English at **Flodden Field** in 1513. For once, it wasn't English aggression which brought the two sides to battle, but the "Auld Alliance" between Scotland and France.

James IV's brother-in-law, the English king Henry VIII, had invaded France, and the Scots opted to stand by their French allies. The Scots army, under James's command, took the English strongholds of Norham, Etal, Ford and Wark before being confronted to the south of the village of Branxton, three miles southeast of Coldstream, by an English force of roughly equal size under the Earl of Surrey. However, the English artillery was lighter and more manoeuvrable, and forced the Scots to come down off their advantageous position on Branxton Hill. Subsequently, the heavily armoured Scottish noblemen got stuck in the mud, and their over-long pikes and lances proved no match for the shorter and sturdier English halberds. English losses were heavy, but the Scots lost as many as ten thousand men, including the king himself, fighting at the head of his troops, along with his son (an archbishop), nine earls, fourteen lords and even the chiefs of many of the great Highland clans. After the battle was over, James's body was taken to his brother-in-law, but Henry denied it burial and no one knows what became of it.

If Bannockburn was Scotland's greatest victory over the English, and Bonnie Prince Charlie's last stand at Culloden their most noble defeat, Flodden was simply an unmitigated disaster. It became the subject of numerous songs and ballads and remains a painful memory for Scots even today. The English, meanwhile, have forgotten all about it.

the textile boom industrialized parts of the Tweed Valley, turning his beloved **Selkirk** and **Galashiels** into mill towns. The Tweed is at its most beguiling in the stretch between Melrose and the pleasant country town of **Peebles**, when it winds through the hills past numerous stately homes, most notably **Traquair House**. Public transport is no problem, with frequent buses travelling along the valley. Just west of Peebles, the Tweed curves south towards Tweedsmuir, from where it's just a few miles further to Moffat in Dumfriesshire (see p.217).

Coldstream

The tiny border town of **COLDSTREAM**, which sits tight against the Tweed, is famous for its association with the Second Regiment of the Foot Guards, popularly known as the **Coldstream Guards,** the oldest continuously serving regiment in the British Army. Formed in 1650 from Cromwell's New Model Army by General George Monck in order to fight the Scottish Presbyterians, they switched sides along with their general in 1660 and marched on London for Charles II. Monck's regiment was thereafter recognized as the "Coldstream Guards" and the general became the first Duke of Albemarle – a handsome payoff for his timely change of heart. Oddly enough, in the sort of detail beloved of military historians, the Coldstreamers still sport the crownless tunic buttons they first wore as part of Cromwell's Model Army. The regiment's deeds are recorded in the **Coldstream Museum** (April–Sept Mon–Sat 10am–4pm, Sun 2–4pm; Oct Mon–Sat 1–4pm; free), on the rather desolate little Market Square, hidden away off the High Street.

Coldstream has long been an important border crossing, but the town's ford was replaced only in 1766 by the handsome five-arched **Smeaton's Bridge** you now see across the Tweed. Like Gretna Green (see p.213), Coldstream issued "irregular marriages" to runaway English couples, in this case from the Toll House at the far end of the bridge (where three English Lord Chancellors were married). You might suspect the huge fluted **column** near the bridge to be dedicated to the local regiment, but in fact it celebrates the victory of the local MP following the Reform Act in 1832. Coldstream's long High Street forms part of the trunk road linking Newcastle and Edinburgh, now the A697, and as such is busy with traffic most days. If you want to stretch your legs, you're best off walking along the **Nun's Walk** which gives fine views over the Tweed into England and as far the Cheviots. To reach the path, head for the pocket-size **Henderson Park**, opposite the tourist office, which also boasts an aromatic garden for the blind with signs in braille.

Slightly further afield, on the western side of Coldstream, you can visit the 3000-acre **Hirsel Country Park**. Hirsel House, home to the Douglas-Home family (of Tory prime minister fame), is not open to the public, but you can walk around the attractive grounds, complete with lake, picnic area and rhododendron woods, which are particularly resplendent in early summer. The **Homestead Museum** (daily 10.30am–5pm; free), housed in the old outhouses, shows the workings of the estate, past and present.

Practicalities

Coldstream's **tourist office** (April–Oct Mon–Sat 10am–5pm, Sun 10am–2pm), roughly halfway down the High Street, has a comprehensive supply of brochures and booklets on the Borders. There's a handful of **B&Bs** in the town, but you're probably better off pushing on to Kelso or Melrose; if you're looking for a bit of luxury, head for the *Wheatsheaf* in nearby Swinton (see p.182). Your best bet for a **drink** and a bite to **eat** is the cosy *Besom Inn*, in the High Street, its tiny series of bars decked out with a sprinkling of militaria. For a decent **tearoom**, head into the Hirsel estate (see above).

Kelso and around

KELSO, eight miles upstream from Coldstream, at the confluence of the Tweed and Teviot, grew up in the shadow of its now-ruined Benedictine **Abbey** (daily; free), once the richest and most powerful of the Border abbeys. Unfortunately, the English savaged Kelso three times in the first half of the sixteenth century: the last (and by far the worst) assault was part of the "Rough Wooing" led by the Earl of Hertford when the Scots refused to ratify a marriage treaty between Henry VIII's son and the infant Mary, Queen of Scots. Such was the extent of the devastation – compounded by the Reformation – that less survives of Kelso than any of the Border abbeys. Nevertheless, at first sight, it looks pretty impressive, with the heavy Norman west end of the abbey church almost entirely intact. Beyond, little remains, though it is possible to make out the two transepts and towers which gave the abbey the shape of a double cross, unique in Scotland. Just across the leafy cemetery from the abbey stands the **Old Parish Church**, constructed in 1773 by a local man to an octagonal design that excited universal execration. "It is," wrote one contemporary, "a misshapen pile, the ugliest Parish Church in Scotland, but it is an excellent model for a circus." While you're in the vicinity, pop into the **Kelso Pottery** (Tues–Sat 10am–1pm & 2–5pm), close by at The Knowes, to see ceramics fired in a large outdoor pit kiln.

Kelso town managed to rebuild itself and is now centred on the **Square**, an unusually large cobbled expanse presided over by the honey-hued Ionic

The Border Reivers

From the thirteenth to the early seventeenth centuries, the wild, inhospitable border country stretching from the Solway Firth in the west to the Tweed Valley in the east, well away from the power bases of both the Scottish and English monarchs, was overrun by outlaws known as the **Border Reivers**, *reive* being a Scots word for plunder. As George MacDonald Fraser put it in his book *The Steel Bonnets*, "The great border tribes of both Scotland and England feuded continuously among themselves. Robbery and blackmail were everyday professions; raiding, arson, kidnapping, murder and extortion were an accepted part of the social system." This, then, was no cross-border dispute, but an open struggle for power among the tribes of the region. Those who "shook loose the Border" included people from all walks of life – agricultural labourers, gentleman farmers, smallholders, even peers of the realm – for whom theft, raiding, tracking and ambush became second nature.

The source of this behaviour was the destruction and devastation wrought upon the region by virtually continual warfare between England and Scotland, and the "slash and burn" policy of the era. With many residents no longer able to find sustenance from the land, crime became the only way to survive. Cattle-rustling, blackmail and kidnapping led to an anarchical mindset, where feuding families would wreak havoc and devastation on each other almost as a way of life.

The legacy of the Border Reivers can still be seen today in the fortified farms and churches of the region's architecture; in the **Common Riding** traditions of many border towns; in the language (the words "blackmail" and "bereaved" have their roots in the destructive behaviour that was so characteristic of this period); and in the great family names such as Armstrong, Graham, Kerr and Nixon, which once filled the hearts of Borderers with dread.

columns, pediment and oversized clock belltower of the elegant **Town Hall**. To one side stands the imposing *Cross Keys Hotel*, with its distinctive rooftop balustrade, and a supporting chorus of three-storey eighteenth- and nineteenth-century pastel buildings on every side. Leaving the Square along Roxburgh Street, take the alley down to the **Cobby Riverside Walk**, where a brief stroll leads to Floors Castle (see p.188). En route, but hidden from view by the islet in the middle of the river, is the spot where the Teviot meets the Tweed. This bit of river, known as The Junction, has long been famous for its **salmon fishing**, with permits – costing thousands – booked years in advance. Permits for fishing other, less expensive reaches of the Tweed and Teviot are available from Tweedside Tackle, 36 Bridge St (☎01573/225306). Details of last-minute fishing lets are available from the Tweedline on ☎0906/583412; for fishing catches and prospects, phone ☎0906/583410.

Practicalities

With good connections to Melrose and Jedburgh to the west and a less regular service to Coldstream and Duns, Kelso **bus station** on Roxburgh Street is a brief walk from The Square, where you'll find the **tourist office** in the Town Hall (Mon–Sat 10am–5pm, Sun 10am–2pm).

Other than during Kelso's main **festivals** – the Border Union Dog Show in late June, the Border Union Agricultural Show in late July, the Kelso Rugby Sevens in early September, the Ram Sales a week or so later, or when Kelso races are on – **accommodation** is not a problem. One of the best B&Bs in town is *Abbey Bank*, near Kelso Pottery on The Knowes (☎01573/226550, ⓔ diah@abbeybank.freeserve.co.uk; ➌), a Georgian house with large double beds and a lovely south-facing garden. Another good choice is the *Ednam*

House Hotel (☎01573/224168, ⓦwww.ednamhouse.com; ⑤), a splendid Geor-gian mansion set back off Bridge Street, with antique furnishings and fittings and gardens that abut the Tweed; make sure, though, that you're not put in the modern extension. Lastly, there's the *Roxburghe Hotel* (☎01573/450331, ⓦwww.roxburghe.net; ⑥), a luxury hotel two miles south of Kelso on the A698 at Heiton, owned by the duke and duchess of Roxburghe, which also boasts an eighteen-hole championship golf course.

Most **eating** places are just off The Square: the *Cobbles Inn* restaurant is housed in a former pub just up Bowmont Street – check the specials menu for the best dishes – and the *Cross Keys* in the square specializes in local produce. *Oscar's Wine Bar* in Horsemarket is popular in the evenings and open daily, or try Gary Moore's excellent ☆ *Queen's Bistro* (ⓦwww.garymoorerestaurants.com) in the *Queen's Head Hotel* in Bridge Street for more gourmet fare such as venison with black pudding or lamb shank with rosemary and pear. For a snack, there's *Le Jardin*, next to the Kelso Pottery (closed Mon). If you're looking to pick up picnic food in the area, head for the *Teviot Smokery*, on the A698 five miles south of Kelso, where you can also enjoy a river walk, a stroll through the water gardens or a snack in the café.

Floors Castle

If you stand on Kelso's handsome bridge over the Tweed, you can easily make out the pepperpot turrets and castellations of **Floors Castle** (Easter–Oct daily 10am–4.30pm; £6, grounds & garden only £3; ⓦwww.floorscastle.com), a mile or so northwest of the town. The bulk of the building was designed by William Adam in the 1720s for the first Duke of Roxburghe and, picking through the Victorian modifications, the interior still demonstrates his uncluttered style, while the superb views from the windows give the place an airy feel. The eighth duke followed the *fin-de-siècle* trend by marrying American money: the castle's star feature are **paintings** by Matisse, Augustus John and Odilon Redon which the duchess carried off from her family home – she also brought the fine Brussels and Gobelin tapestries. However, you won't see much of the house, as just ten rooms and a basement are open to the public. Floors remains privately owned, home of the tenth duke of Roxburghe, whose imperious features can be seen in a variety of portraits and photos. There's an above-average **café** and you can wander down to the Tweed and see the holly tree which marks the spot where James II was killed by an exploding cannon during the siege of Roxburgh Castle. His son, also James, was crowned James III at the age of nine at Kelso Abbey.

Kirk Yetholm and Town Yetholm

Yetholm, perched on the edge of the Cheviot Hills six miles southeast of Kelso along the B6352, is actually two separate places, **KIRK YETHOLM** and **TOWN YETHOLM**, lying a quarter of a mile apart. The villages, accessible by bus from Kelso, lie at the northern end of the **Pennine Way**, a long-distance footpath which travels the length of northern England finishing at the Kirk Yetholm SYHA **hostel** (☎0870/004 1132, ⓦwww.syha.org.uk; April–Sept). The hostel also marks the end of the second leg of **St Cuthbert's Way** (see p.178). Walkers who have completed the Pennine Way clutching a copy of Wainwright's guidebook to the long-distance footpath are entitled to a celebratory free half-pint at the *Border Hotel* (☎01573/420237, ⓦwww .theborderhotel.com; ③) in Kirk Yetholm, which serves good food including local lamb and fish dishes.

Mellerstain House

Six miles northwest of Kelso off the A6089, **Mellerstain House** (guided tours: Easter & May–Sept daily except Tues 12.30–5pm; Oct Sat & Sun only; £5.50; Ⓦ www.mellerstain.com) represents the very best of the Adams' brothers' work: William designed the wings in 1725, and his son Robert the castellated centre fifty years later. Inside, it has an elegant, domestic air, lacking in pomposity. Robert Adam's love of columns, delicate roundels and friezes culminates in a stunning sequence of plaster-moulded, pastel-shaded ceilings, which still preserve the original colours; the **library** is the high point of the tour for Adam lovers, with four unusual long panels in plaster relief of classical scenes relegating the books to second place. Perhaps the most intriguing Adam's creation is the charming but freezing bathroom in the basement, the only one known to have been designed by him. There are also some interesting paintings by Constable, Gainsborough, Ramsay and Veronese. The house remains the home of the thirteenth earl and countess of Haddington, descendants of the Baillie family who acquired the estate in 1642. After a visit you can wander the formal Edwardian gardens, which slope down to the lake, or venture further afield to the Fairy Glen.

Smailholm Tower

In marked contrast to Mellerstain is the craggy **Smailholm Tower** (April–Sept daily 9.30am–6.30pm, Oct–March Sat 9.30am–4.30pm, Sun 2–4.30pm; HS; £2.50), perched on a rocky outcrop a few miles to the south. A remote and evocative fastness recalling Reivers' raids and border skirmishes, the fifteenth-century tower was designed to withstand sudden attack. The rough rubble walls average six feet in thickness and both the entrance – once guarded by a heavy door plus an iron yett (gate) – and the windows are disproportionately small. These were necessary precautions: on both sides of the border, clans were engaged in endless feuds, a violent history that stirred the imagination of a "wee, sick laddie" who was brought here to live in 1773. The boy was Walter Scott, and his epic poem *Marmion* resounds to the clamour of Smailholm's ancient quarrels:

[The forayers], home returning, fill'd the hall
With revel, wassel-rout, and brawl.
Methought that still with trump and clang,
The gateway's broken arches rang;
Methought grim features, seam'd with scars,
Glared through the window's rusty bars.

Inside, ignore the inept costumed models and press on up to the roof, where two narrow **wall-walks**, jammed against the barrel-vaulted roof and the crow-stepped gables, provide panoramic views. On the north side the watchman's seat has also survived, stuck against the chimney stack for warmth and with a recess for a lantern.

Dryburgh Abbey

Hidden away in a U-bend in the Tweed, ten miles upstream from Kelso, the remains of **Dryburgh Abbey** (Easter–Sept daily 9.30am–6.30pm; Oct–Easter Mon–Sat 9.30am–4.30pm, Sun 2–4.30pm; HS; £3.30) occupy an idyllic position against a hilly backdrop, with ancient cedars, redwoods, beech and lime trees and wide lawns flattering the pinkish-red hues of the stonework. The

Premonstratensians, or White Canons, founded the abbey in the twelfth century, but they were never as successful – or apparently as devout – as their Cistercian neighbours in Melrose. Their chronicles detail interminable disputes about land and money: one story relates how a fourteenth-century canon called Marcus flattened the abbot with his fist. Later, the abbey attained its own folklore: Scott's *Minstrelsy* records the tale of a woman who lived in the vaults with a sprite called Fatlips. She only came out after dark to beg from her neighbours and was variously thought mad or demonic.

The romantic setting is second to none, but the ruins of the **Abbey Church** are much less substantial than, say, at Melrose or Jedburgh. Virtually nothing survives of the nave, but the transepts have fared better, their chapels now serving as private burial grounds for, among others, Sir Walter Scott and Field Marshal Haig, the World War I commander whose ineptitude cost thousands of soldiers' lives. The night stairs, down which the monks stumbled in the early hours of the morning, survive in the south transept, and lead even today to the monks' dormitory. Leaving the church via the east processional door in the south aisle, with its dog-tooth decoration, you enter the cloisters, the highlight of which is the barrel-vaulted **Chapter House**, complete with low stone benches and blind interlaced arcading.

Next door to the abbey is the *Dryburgh Abbey Hotel* (℡01835/822261, Ⓦwww.dryburgh.co.uk; ❼), a sprawling red-sandstone **hotel** that's a hunting, shooting, fishing kind of place. You can enjoy the indoor pool, or simply have a cup of tea or a drink in the bar. Dryburgh is not easy to get to by **public transport**, though it's only a mile's walk north from St Boswell's on the A68, and a pleasant three or four miles from Melrose. Drivers and cyclists should approach the abbey via the much-visited **Scott's View**, to the north on the B6356, overlooking the Tweed Valley, where the writer and his friends often picnicked and where Scott's horse stopped out of habit during the writer's own funeral procession. The scene inspired Joseph Turner's *Melrose 1831*, now on display in the National Gallery of Scotland (see p.120).

Melrose

Tucked in between the Tweed and the gorse-backed Eildon Hills, minuscule **MELROSE** is the most beguiling of towns, its narrow streets trimmed by a harmonious ensemble of styles, from pretty little cottages and tweedy shops to high-standing Georgian and Victorian facades. Its chief draw is its ruined abbey, by far the best of the Border abbeys, but it's also perfectly positioned for exploring the Tweed Valley. Most of the year it's a sleepy little place, but as the birthplace in 1883 of the **Rugby Sevens** (seven-a-side games), it swarms during Sevens Week (second week in April), and again in early September when it hosts the **Melrose Music Festival**, a popular weekend of traditional music attracting folkies from afar.

The Town and abbey

To the north of the town square, the pink- and red-tinted stone ruins of **Melrose Abbey** (April–Sept daily 9.30am–6.30pm; Oct–March Mon–Sat 9.30am–4.30pm, Sun 2–4.30pm; HS; £4) soar above their riverside surroundings. Founded in 1136 by King David I, Melrose was the first Cistercian settlement in Scotland and grew rich selling wool and hides to Flanders, but its prosperity was fragile: the English repeatedly razed Melrose, most viciously under Richard II in 1385 and the Earl of Hertford in 1545. Most of the present remains date from the intervening period, when extensive rebuilding abandoned the original Cistercian austerity for an elaborate, Gothic style inspired by the abbeys of northern England, though it seems likely that the abbey was never fully finished before the Reformation. The sculptural detailing at Melrose is of the highest quality, but it's easy to miss if you don't know where to look, so taking advantage of the free audioguide, or buying yourself a guidebook, is a good idea.

The site is dominated by the **Abbey Church**, which has lost its west front, and whose nave is reduced to the elegant window arches and chapels of the south aisle. Amazingly, however, the stone **pulpitum** (screen), separating the choir monks from their lay brothers, is preserved. Beyond, the **presbytery** has its magnificent perpendicular window, lierne vaulting and ceiling bosses intact, with the capitals of the surrounding columns sporting the most intricate of curly kale carving. In the **south transept**, another fine fifteenth-century window sprouts yet more delicate, foliate tracery and the adjacent cornice is enlivened by angels playing musical instruments, though these figures are badly weathered. This kind of finely carved detail is repeated everywhere you look in Melrose. Outside, the exterior sculpture on the south transept is even more impressive, lower niche-corbels are decorated with crouching figures holding scrolls bearing inscriptions such as "He suffered because he willed it". Elsewhere, look for the statue of the Virgin and Child, high on the south side of the westernmost surviving buttress, the Coronation of the Virgin on the east end gable and the numerous mischievous **gargoyles**, from peculiar crouching beasts to the pig playing the bagpipes on the roof on the south side of the nave.

Legend has it that the heart of **Robert the Bruce** is buried here (his body having been buried at Dunfermline Abbey), and in 1997, when a heart cask was publicly exhumed, this theory received an unexpected boost. However, the burial location was not in accordance with Bruce's own wishes. In 1329, the dying king told his friend, Sir James Douglas, to carry his heart on a Crusade to the Holy Land in fulfilment of an old vow: "Seeing therefore, that my body cannot go to achieve what my heart desires, I will send my heart instead of my body, to accomplish my vow." Douglas tried his best, but was killed fighting the Moors in Spain – and Bruce's heart ended up in Melrose. A new commemorative stone marks its current resting place in the chapter house, to the north of the sacristy.

The paltry ruins of the old monastic buildings edge the church to the north and lead over the road to the **Commendator's House** (same hours as the abbey), a lovely red sandstone building converted into a private house in 1590 by the abbey's last Commendator, and now housing a modest collection of ecclesiastical bric-a-brac. Beyond the house is the mill-lade, where water used to flow in order to power the abbey's mills, and was also diverted to flush the monks' latrines. Back towards the town, to the south of the abbey, you could pop into the tiny, delightful **Priorwood Garden** (Easter–Christmas, Mon–Sat 10am–5pm, Sun 1–5pm; NTS; £3), whose compact walled precincts are given over to an orchard and flowers that are suitable for drying; there's a dried flower shop, too.

Melrose's other museum, the **Trimontium Exhibition**, just off Market Square (April–Oct Mon–Fri 10.30am–4.30pm, Sat & Sun 10.30am–1pm & 2–4.30pm; ⓦwww.trimontium.net; £1.50), is a quirky little centre that merits a browse. Its displays include Celtic bronze axe-heads excavated from the Eildon Hills, dioramas, models and the odd archeological find outlining the three Roman occupations of the region. For further Roman adventures, the four-mile circular **Trimontium Walk** (April–June, Sept & Oct Thurs 1.30–5.15pm; July & Aug Tues & Thurs 1.30–5.15pm; £3) visits various Roman sites in the

Walking in the Eildons and St Cuthbert's Way

Ordnance Survey Explorer map No. 338

From the centre of Melrose, it's a vigorous three-mile walk to the top of the **Eildon Hills**, whose triple volcanic peaks are the Central Borders' most distinctive landmark. The tourist office sells a leaflet detailing the hike, which begins about ninety yards south of – and up the hill from – Market Square, along the B6359 to Lilliesleaf. The path is signposted to the left and leads to the saddle between the North and Mid Hills. To the right of the saddle are **Mid Hill**, the highest summit at 1385ft, and further south, **West Hill**; to the left, **North Hill** is topped by the scant remains of an Iron Age fort and a Roman signal station. There are several routes back to town; one heading down from the northeast picks up a path to Newstead and you can return to Melrose by the river.

The hills have been associated with all sorts of legends, beginning with tales of their creation by the wizard-cum-alchemist Michael Scott (1175–1230) who, in the words of Sir Walter Scott, "cleft the Eildon Hills in three". It was here that the mystic **Thomas the Rhymer** received the gift of prophecy from the Faerie Queen, and Arthur and his knights are reckoned to lie asleep deep within the hills, victims of a powerful spell. The ancient Celts, who revered the number three, also considered the site a holy place and maintained their settlements on the slopes long after the Romans' departure.

Melrose is also the starting point for the popular **St Cuthbert's Way**, a sixty-mile walk which finishes at Lindisfarne (Holy Island of Northumberland) on the east coast. The tourist office can give details of the walk, though the trail is well marked by yellow arrows from the abbey up over the Eildons to the pretty village of **Bowden**, where you can make a detour to see a twelfth-century kirk, half a mile down the hill from the square, and browse secondhand books and get a really good, home-made tea at *The Old School*.

area (although there's not much left on the ground), including the Leaderfoot viaduct, and the most northerly amphitheatre in the Roman Empire.

Practicalities

Buses to Melrose stop in Market Square, from where it's a brief walk north to the abbey ruins and the **tourist office** opposite (Mon–Sat 10am–5pm, Sun 10am–2pm).

Melrose has a clutch of **hotels**, with prices generally higher than you might expect. The best of the bunch is ⚜ *Burt's*, a smartly converted old inn on Market Square (☎01896/822285, ⊛www.burtshotel.co.uk; ❻); rooms are small, but very comfortable. Across the street is the ten-bedroom *Townhouse* (☎01896/822645, ⊛www.thetownhousemelrose.co.uk; ❺), recently smartened up and owned by the same family as *Burt's*. It's among Melrose's simple **B&Bs**, however, that you'll get the real flavour of the place, most notably at the easygoing and comfortable *Braidwood*, on Buccleuch Street (☎01896/822488, ⊛www.braidwoodmelrose.co.uk; ❷), a stone's throw from the abbey, and the equally agreeable *Dunfermline House* (☎01896/822411, ⊛www.dunmel.freeserve.co.uk; ❷) opposite – advance booking is recommended at both during the summer. The town also has an SYHA **hostel** (☎0870/004 1141, ⊛www.syha.org.uk; March–Oct) in a sprawling Georgian villa overlooking the abbey from beside the access road into the bypass. The *Gibson Caravan Park* **campsite** (☎01896/822969) is in the town centre, just off the High Street, opposite the Greenyards rugby grounds.

Melrose offers a good choice of **eating** options. *Marmion's Brasserie* (℡01896/822245), housed in a spacious Victorian house on Buccleuch Street, serves well-prepared imaginative meals, as does the award-winning restaurant run by Gary Moore in the *Station Hotel* on the square. *Burt's* does excellent bar meals and, if you're feeling energetic, walk 500 yards past the abbey and across the old suspension bridge to Gattonside, where the *Hoebridge Inn* (℡01896/823082; closed Mon), once a bobbin mill and now one of the Borders' best restaurants, serves home-made Scottish food in relaxed, low-key surroundings. If you want a light lunch or snack, head to *Russell's* (closed Thurs), a popular, very traditional tearoom on Market Square; or *Haldane's Fish & Chip Shop* (closed Wed), next door.

For **pubs**, try the popular *King's Arms* on the High Street, or the *Ship Inn*, on East Port at the top of the square, the liveliest in town, especially during the Folk Festival and on Saturday afternoons when the Melrose rugby team have played at home. Be sure to check out what's on at *The Wynd* (℡01896/823854, Ⓦwww.thewynd.com), Melrose's very own pint-sized **theatre**, tucked away down the alleyway, north off the main square, which shows films and puts on gigs as well as live drama.

Abbotsford

Abbotsford (mid-March to Oct Mon–Sat 9.30am–5pm, March, April, May & Oct Sun 2–5pm; June–Sept Sun 9.30am–5pm; £4.75), a stately home three miles up the Tweed from Melrose, was designed to satisfy the Romantic inclinations of **Sir Walter Scott**, who lived here from 1812 until his death twenty years later. Built on the site of a farmhouse Scott bought and subsequently demolished, Abbotsford (as Scott chose to call it) took twelve years to evolve, with the fanciful turrets and castellations of the Scots Baronial exterior incorporating copies of medieval originals: the entrance porch imitates that of Linlithgow Palace and the screen wall in the garden echoes Melrose Abbey's cloister. Scott was proud of his *folie de grandeur*, writing to a friend, "It is a kind of conundrum castle to be sure [which] pleases a fantastic person in style and manner." That said, it was undoubtedly one of the chief causes of Scott's subsequent bankruptcy.

Despite all the exterior pomp, the interior is surprisingly small and poky, with just six rooms open for viewing on the upper floor. Visitors start in the wood-panelled **study**, with its small writing desk made of salvage from the Spanish Armada, at which Scott churned out the Waverley novels at a furious rate. The heavy wood-panelled **library** boasts Scott's collection of more than nine thousand rare books and an extraordinary assortment of memorabilia, the centrepiece of which is Napoleon's pen case and blotting book, but which also includes Rob Roy's purse and *skene dhu* (knife), a lock of Nelson's hair and of Bonnie Prince Charlie's plus the latter's *quaich* (drinking cup), Flora Macdonald's pocketbook, the inlaid pearl crucifix that accompanied Mary, Queen of Scots to the scaffold and even a piece of oatcake found in the pocket of a dead Highlander at Culloden. You can also see Henry Raeburn's famous portrait of Scott in the **drawing room**, and all sorts of weapons – notably Rob Roy's sword, dagger and gun – in the **armoury**. In the barbaric-looking **entrance hall**, hung with elk and wild cattle skulls, and spoils gathered from the battlefield of Waterloo by Scott himself, is a model of the skull of Robert the Bruce and some of Scott's dandyish clothes.

△ Sir Walter Scott's Armoury, Abbotsford

The fast and frequent Melrose–Galashiels **bus** provides easy access to Abbotsford: ask for the Tweedbank island on the A6091, from where the house is a ten-minute walk up the road.

Galashiels

It's hard to avoid **GALASHIELS** (Ⓦ www.galashiels.bordernet.co.uk), or "Gala" as it's known locally, a hard-working textile town four miles west of

Sir Walter Scott

Walter Scott (1771–1832) was born in Edinburgh to a solidly bourgeois family whose roots were in Selkirkshire. As a child he was left lame by polio and his anxious parents sent him to recuperate at his grandfather's farm in Smailholm, where the boy's imagination was fired by his relatives' tales of derring-do, the violent history of the Borders retold amidst the rugged landscape that he spent long summer days exploring. Scott returned to Edinburgh to resume his education and take up a career in law, but his real interests remained elsewhere. Throughout the 1790s he transcribed hundreds of old Border ballads, publishing a three-volume collection entitled *Minstrelsy of the Scottish Borders* in 1802. An instant success, *Minstrelsy* was followed by Scott's own *Lay of the Last Minstrel*, a narrative poem whose strong story and rose-tinted regionalism proved very popular.

More poetry was to come, most successfully *Marmion* (1808) and *The Lady of the Lake* (1810), not to mention an eighteen-volume edition of the works of John Dryden and nineteen volumes of Jonathan Swift. However, despite having two paid jobs, one as the sheriff-depute of Selkirkshire, the other as clerk to the Court of Session in Edinburgh, his finances remained shaky. He had become a partner in a printing firm, which put him deeply into debt, not helped by the enormous sums he spent on his mansion, Abbotsford. From 1813, Scott was writing to pay the bills and poured out a veritable flood of historical novels using his extensive knowledge of Scottish history and folklore. He produced his best work within the space of ten years: *Waverley* (1814), *The Antiquary* (1816), *Rob Roy* and *The Heart of Midlothian* (both 1818), as well as two notable novels set in England, *Ivanhoe* (1819) and *Kenilworth* (1821). In 1824 he returned to Scottish tales with *Redgauntlet*, the last of his quality work.

A year later Scott's money problems reached crisis proportions after an economic crash bankrupted his printing business. Attempting to pay his creditors in full, he found the quality of his writing deteriorating with its increased speed, and the effort broke his health. His last years were plagued by illness, and in 1832 he died at Abbotsford and was buried within the ruins of Dryburgh Abbey.

Although Scott's interests were diverse, his historical novels mostly focused on the Jacobites, whose loyalty to the Stuarts had riven Scotland since the "Glorious Revolution" of 1688. That the nation was prepared to be entertained by such tales was essentially a matter of timing: by the 1760s it was clear the Jacobite cause was lost for good and Scotland, emerging from its isolated medievalism, had been firmly welded into the United Kingdom. Thus its turbulent history and independent spirit was safely in the past, and ripe for romancing – as shown by the arrival of King George IV in Edinburgh during 1822 decked out in Highland dress. Yet, for Sir Walter the romance was tinged with a genuine sense of loss. Loyal to the Hanoverians, he still grieved for Bonnie Prince Charlie; he welcomed a commercial Scotland but lamented the passing of feudal ties, and so his heroes are transitional, fighting men of action superseded by bourgeois figures searching for a clear identity.

Melrose whose workers' terraces of grey-green spread along the valley of the Gala Water near its junction with the Tweed. It occupies a pivotal position in the Borders, and has the region's principal **bus station**, situated close to (and north of the river from) the town centre. The main street runs parallel with the river, its eastern end cheered by a melodramatic equestrian statue of a Border Reiver above the town's war memorial. You could while away half an hour at the sixteenth-century **Old Gala House** (April–June & Sept Tues–Sat 10am–4pm;

July & Aug Mon–Sat 10am–4pm, Sun 2–4pm; Oct Tues–Sat 1–4pm; free), the town's oldest house and now the local museum, up St John's Street and then left down Scott Crescent. The long-demolished New Gala House, a mansion that stood at the top of the town, was taken over during World War II by an Edinburgh girls' school, **St Trinnean's**; the artist Ronald Searle met two of the pupils in 1941, inspiration for the unruly schoolgirls in his St Trinian's novels. Galashiels doesn't have a tourist office as such, though there are plenty of leaflets available at the **Lochcarron Visitor Centre** (Mon–Sat 9am–5pm; June–Sept also Sun noon–5pm; £2.50; ⓦwww.lochcarron.com), a woollen mill on Huddersfield Street that offers guided tours of its factory, which specializes in cashmere.

Innerleithen and around

If you're driving west and want to avoid Galashiels, then simply follow the Tweed instead of the main road. Whichever way you go, you'll eventually pass through **INNERLEITHEN**, a rural village which gained prominence in the eighteenth century as a mill town and spa centre. Aside from its main attraction, wonderful Traquair House (see below), the town boasts **Robert Smail's Printing Works** (Easter & June–Sept Mon, Thurs, Fri & Sat noon–5pm, Sun 2–5pm; NTS; £5), a working museum on the main street, with original nineteenth-century machinery where you can try your hand at type-setting. Ten to fifteen minutes' walk north of the main street are the quaint **St Ronan's Wells** (Easter to mid-Oct Mon–Fri 10am–1pm & 2–5pm, Sat & Sun 2–5pm; free), where Walter Scott used to imbibe the sulphur waters, and where you can still taste them from a tap under the porch (or buy the stuff bottled from Pearce & Sons on Miller Street). The current building is a Victorian reconstruction of the original 1828 pump room, with its striking peacock-blue and white weatherboarding and its pepperpot towers sporting thistle finials. This was built to accommodate the tourists drawn here by the success of Scott's novel *St Ronan's Well*.

Most visitors make Peebles their base, but you could **stay** in Innerleithen at the central *Traquair Arms Hotel*, on Traquair Road (☎01896/830229, ⓦwww.traquair-arms-hotel.co.uk; ❹), a cosy old inn that's also a great place for a pint, a cup of tea and some filling bar food. Alternatively, there's *Caddon View* (☎01896/830208, ⓦwww.caddonview.co.uk; ❸), a comfortable and spacious double-fronted Victorian villa at 14 Pirn Rd. For either place, you'll need to book early during the Traquair Fair in August. Campers should head for the *Tweedside Caravan Park* **campsite** (☎01896/831271; April–Oct), by the river down Montgomery Street; it has laundry facilities and a games room. **Bike rental** is available from Bike Sport on Peebles Road (☎01896/830880), should you feel like checking out the many graded cycle routes through Glentress, Cardrona, or the Elibank and Traquair forests.

Traquair House

Peeping out from the trees a mile or so south of Innerleithen on the B709, **Traquair House** (daily: April, May & Sept noon–5pm; June–Aug 10.30am–5pm; Oct 11am–4pm; £5.80, grounds only £2.50; ⓦwww.traquair.co.uk) is the oldest continuously inhabited house in Scotland, with the present owners – the Maxwell Stuarts – having lived here since 1491. The first laird of Traquair (pronounced "tra-quare"), inherited an elementary fortified tower, which his powerful descendants gradually converted into a mansion, visited, it is said, by 27 monarchs, including Mary, Queen of Scots. Persistently Catholic, the family paid for its principles: the Jacobite fifth earl spent two years in the Tower of London; Protestant mill-workers repeatedly attacked their property; and by 1800 little remained of the family's once enormous estates – certainly not enough to fund any major rebuilding.

Consequently, Traquair's main appeal is in its ancient shape and structure. The whitewashed facade is strikingly handsome, with narrow windows and trim turrets surrounding the tiniest of front doors – an organic, homogeneous edifice that's a welcome change from other grandiose stately homes. Inside, you can see the original vaulted cellars, where locals once hid their cattle from raiders; the twisting main staircase as well as the earlier medieval version, later a secret escape route for persecuted Catholics; a carefully camouflaged priest's hole; and even a **priest's room** where a string of resident chaplains lived in hiding until the Catholic Emancipation Act freed things up in 1829. Of the furniture and fittings, it's not any particular piece that impresses, but rather the accumulation of family possessions and revealing letters that give a real insight into the Maxwell Stuarts' revolving-door fortunes and eccentricities. In the **museum room** there is a wealth of treasures, including a fine example of a Jacobite Amen glass, a rosary and crucifix owned by Mary, Queen of Scots and the cloak worn by the earl of Nithsdale during his dramatic escape from the Tower of London, where he was under sentence of death for his part in the Jacobite Rising of 1715. (The earl was saved by his wife who got his jailers drunk and smuggled him out disguised as a maid in spite of his red beard.)

It's worth sparing time for the surrounding **gardens** where you'll find a **hedge maze**, several craft workshops and the **Traquair House Brewery** dating back to 1566, which was revived in 1965 and claims to be the only British brewery that still ferments totally in oak. You can learn about the brewery and taste the ales in the Brewery Shop. There's an attractive café serving snacks in an estate cottage on the redundant avenue which leads to the locked **Bear Gates**; Bonnie Prince Charlie departed the house through the gates, and the then owner promised to keep them locked till a Stuart should ascend the throne.

If you're really taken by the place, you can stay in one of its three double guest **rooms** (℡01896/830323; ❽), decked out with antiques and four-posters, on a bed-and-breakfast basis only.

Peebles

Fast, wide, tree-lined and fringed with grassy banks, the Tweed looks at its best at **PEEBLES**, a handsome royal burgh that sits on the north bank, seven miles upstream from Innerleithen. The town itself has a genteel, relaxed air, its wide, handsome High Street bordered by houses in a medley of architectural styles, mostly dating from Victorian times. The soaring crown spire of the **Old Parish Church** (daily 10am–4pm) rises up at the western end of the High Street and, inside, the church has some unusual features in its elegant oak, bronze and engraved-glass entrance screen and 22 modern oil paintings illustrating the scriptures. Suspended from the ceiling are tattered Napoleonic flags, emblems of 1816, the year the Peeblesshire Militia disbanded.

Further down the High Street is the **Tweeddale Museum & Gallery** (Mon–Fri 10am–noon & 2–5pm, April–Oct also Sat 10am–1pm, 2–4pm; free), housed in the Chambers Institute, which is heralded by two wonderfully ornate wrought-iron street lamps painted up in magenta and silver. William Chambers, a local worthy, presented the building to the town in 1859, complete with an

Walks around Peebles

A series of footpaths snake through the hills surrounding Peebles with their rough-edged burns, bare peaks and deep woods. The five-mile **Sware Trail** is one of the easiest and most scenic, weaving west along the north bank of the river and looping back to the south. On the way, it passes **Neidpath Castle** (bank holidays & mid-June to Aug Mon–Sat 10.30am–4.30pm, Sun 12.30–4.30pm; £3), a gaunt medieval tower house perched high above the river on a rocky bluff. It's a superb setting, and the interior possesses a pit prison and a great hall bedecked with stunning batik wall-hangings depicting the life of Mary, Queen of Scots. The walk also goes by the splendid skew rail bridge, part of the Glasgow line which was finished in 1850. Other, longer footpaths follow the old drove roads, like the thirteen-mile haul to **St Mary's Loch** or the fourteen-mile route to Selkirk via Traquair House (see p.196). For either of these, you'll need an Ordnance Survey map, a compass and proper hiking gear (see p.64). A more gentle stroll is the 2.5-mile amble to the privately owned **Kailzie Gardens** (daily: April–Oct 10am–5.30pm; Nov–March 11am–5pm; £3), whose fifteen acres include a walled garden, trout pond (fly-fishing tackle is available for rent) and a pleasant wood-panelled tearoom; it's also one of the places (the other being Glentress Forest), where you can see live CCTV pictures of the ospreys which have been successfully introduced into the nearby forest.

art gallery dedicated to the enlightenment of his neighbours. He stuffed the place with casts of the world's most famous sculptures and, although most were lost long ago, today's "Secret Room", once the Museum Room, boasts two handsome friezes: one a copy of the Elgin marbles taken from the Parthenon; the other of the Triumph of Alexander, originally cast in 1812 to honour Napoleon.

Practicalities

Buses to Peebles from Selkirk, Galashiels and Edinburgh stop outside the post office, a few doors down from the well-stocked **tourist office** on the High Street (Mon–Sat 9am–5pm, Sun 11am–4pm).

Peebles boasts a vast number of **B&Bs**: try *Rowanbrae,* a trim, pint-sized Victorian place on a quiet cul-de-sac on Northgate, off the east end of High Street (☎01721/721630, ✉john@rowanbrae.freeserve.co.uk; ❶); or *Viewfield,* 1 Rosetta Rd (☎01721/721232, ✉mmitchell38@yahoo.com; ❶), an attractive detached Victorian house a ten-minute walk west of the bridge, with rooms overlooking a lovely garden – take the Old Town road (the A72) and follow it round, turning right up Young Street. For upmarket **hotels** you have to head out of town: *Castle Venlaw Hotel* (☎01721/720384, ⓦwww.venlaw.co.uk; ❼) is a Scots Baronial house set in its own grounds on the edge of town up the Edinburgh Road; the *Cringletie House Hotel* (☎01721/725750, ⓦwww.cringletie.com; ❽) is a still more splendid Baronial pile a couple of miles further up the Edinburgh Road; and finally, there's the *Peebles Hotel Hydro* (☎01721/720602), ⓦwww.peebleshotelhydro.co.uk; ❽), a massive Edwardian purpose-built hotel, which prides itself on welcoming families with kids and/or grandparents in tow. Of the two **campsites** on the edge of town, the *Rosetta Caravan Park* (☎01721/720770; April–Oct) is the quieter, set in a field surrounded by mature woods, a fifteen-minute walk north of the High Street (directions as for *Viewfield* B&B).

The best place to **eat** is the *Sunflower* (☎017221/722420), a tiny, brightly coloured restaurant at 4 Bridgegate, just off Northgate, which does sandwiches

Mountain biking in Glentress Forest

Glentress Forest, two miles east of Peebles on the A72, has some of the best mountain biking to be had in Scotland. Not only are there five superb, carefully crafted, purpose-built trails, there's a fantastic bike centre at the entrance to the forest called **The Hub** (☎01721/721736, ⓦwww.thehubintheforest.co.uk), a mecca for mountain bikers with changing rooms and showers, a café and a shop filled with spares that stays open late. You can choose from a whole range of excellent MTBs for all ages and there are even occasional training weekends so you can improve your technique.

at lunch time, and more adventurous (and slightly pricier) evening meals, for which it's advisable to book. *The Halcyon Restaurant* in Eastgate (above Ville-neuve's Wines) does an upmarket designer menu in formal, elegant surroundings at quite a moderate price. You can also munch on a baguette and get a good coffee at the café in the Eastgate Theatre, a state-of-the-art church conversion (ⓦwww.eastgatearts.com) on Eastgate. The *Tatler Café*, on the High Street, provides basic fried fare, though it also serves good coffee. As for **pubs**, the *Crown Hotel* on the High Street, is a cosy place to hunker down; the *Tontine Hotel*, opposite, is a grander place with views south over the Tweed, and a standard hotel menu. For really good pub food, try one of the bar meals at the *Castle Venlaw Hotel*, or you could pick up a picnic at *Central Baguette* in the High Street.

Tweeddale

Upstream from Peebles, the Tweed valley is more commonly known as **Tweeddale**. The valley sides gradually narrow as the road follows the river upstream and south to the source of the Tweed, at the border with Dumfries and Galloway. Eight miles southwest of Peebles, near Strobo, the Tweed passes **Dawyck Botanic Garden** (daily: late Feb & late Nov 10am–4pm; March & Oct 10am–5pm; April–Sept 10am–6pm; £3.50; ⓦwww.rbge.org .uk), an arboretum outstation of the Royal Botanic Garden in Edinburgh, which specializes in rare trees and shrubs, but also has an impressive display of rhododendrons and azaleas.

Two miles west of Dawyck stands the village of **BROUGHTON**, home of the excellent Broughton Ales. Inside the old Free Church, the **John Buchan Centre** (Easter & May to mid-Oct daily 2–5pm; £1.50) commemorates John Buchan, first Baron Tweedsmuir (1875–1940), author and diplomat, who spent his childhood holidays in the district. Three miles down a dead-end road in pretty, secluded **Holmswater Glen**, the *Glenholm Centre* (☎01899/830408, ⓦwww.glenholm.co.uk; closed Jan; ❸) is a working farm with a cosy four-room guesthouse, the perfect base for exploring the surrounding hills.

Ten miles or so further south on the A701, the Tweed eventually reaches tiny **TWEEDSMUIR**, en route passing *The Crook Inn* (☎01899/880272; ❹), one-time watering hole of Robbie Burns and a good base for climbing **Broad Law** (2723ft), the Southern Uplands' second highest hill. Behind the hotel, there's a small workshop and craft centre, where you can watch glass-blowing displays. At Tweedsmuir, you can either head over the pass to the Devil's Beef Tub and Moffat (see p.217), or east over the **Tweedsmuir Hills** to St Mary's Loch (see opposite). The eleven-mile single-track road to St

Mary's Loch, inaccessible in winter, climbs at a twenty percent gradient past **Talla Reservoir**, where many men lost their lives constructing a water supply for Edinburgh in 1905. Fishing permits for Talla and the neighbouring Megget Reservoir are available from *Tibbie Shiels Inn* at St Mary's Loch (see p.202).

Selkirk and around

Just south of the River Tweed, some five miles southwest of Melrose, lies the royal burgh of **SELKIRK**. The old town sits high up above Ettrick Water; down in the valley by the riverside, the town's imposing greystone woollen mills are mostly boarded up now, an eerie reminder of a once prosperous era. There's precious little reason to linger in Selkirk itself, though the town sits on the edge of some lovely countryside, and serves as the gateway to the picturesque, sparsely populated valleys of Yarrow Water and Ettrick Water, to the west.

At the centre of Selkirk, at one end of the High Street, you'll find the tiny **Market Square**, where you should pop into *Grieve's Snack Attack* and purchase the local "Selkirk Bannock", a sort of fruit cake. While munching it, you can admire Selkirk's statues, the most prominent being that of Sir Walter Scott, which stands outside the former Town House, now dubbed **Sir Walter Scott's Courtroom** (April–Sept Mon–Fri 10am–4pm, Sat 10am–2pm; May–Aug also Sun 10am–2pm; Oct Mon–Sat 1–4pm; free), where he served as sheriff for 33 years. At the other end of the High Street is a rather more unusual statue of **Mungo Park**, the renowned explorer and anti-slavery advocate, born in the county in 1771. The base displays two finely cast bas-reliefs depicting his exploits along the River Niger, which came to an end with his accidental drowning in 1805; his son, who died searching for his father's body in 1827, is also commemorated. The bronze life-size African mourners, *Peace, War, Slavery* and *Home Life in the Niger,* were added in 1913, after several petitions and newspaper editorials demanded that Park be further commemorated.

Just off Market Square to the south is **Halliwell's House Museum** (April–Sept Mon–Sat 10am–5pm, Sun 10am–noon; July & Aug Mon–Sat 10am–5.30pm, Sun 10am–1pm; Oct Mon–Sat 10am–4pm; free), an old-style hardware shop and an informative exhibit on the industrialization of the Tweed Valley, while the adjacent Robson Gallery hosts a series of temporary exhibitions of paintings and ceramics. Down by the river at the junction of the A7 with the B7014, **Selkirk Glass** (Mon–Sat 9am–5pm, Sun 11am–5pm; free) is a thriving craft industry that stands in stark contrast to the neighbouring mills. Visitors arrive by the coachload to sit in the café and watch glass-blowers making intricate paperweights and the like.

If you want to see the **salmon** for which the local rivers are famous, head west along the A708 and stop at the restored watermill from which a path leads to the weir where there's a salmon ladder – the fish are counted as they leap up-river in May and June.

The **tourist office** (same hours as Halliwell's House) is in Halliwell's House off Market Square, and can help with **accommodation**. First choice for those with an unlimited budget is the upmarket ⚑ *Philipburn House Hotel* (☎01750/720747, ⓦwww.philipburnhousehotel.co.uk; ⑥), an unusual eighteenth-century house set in its own grounds a mile west of the town centre; the hotel offers expensive but excellent Scottish cuisine. Slightly more modest in price, but still full of character is the *Heatherlie House Hotel* (☎01750/721200, ⓦwww.heatherlie.freeserve.co.uk; ⑤), a Victorian mansion a sharp left turn up from the road to Ettrick at Heatherlie Park. **Camping** is possible beside the river, next to the swimming pool at *Victoria Park* (℡01750/720897; April–Oct), though the campsites in the Ettrick Valley are far more scenic.

Bowhill House

Three miles west of Selkirk off the A708, **Bowhill House** (July daily 1–5pm; £6) is the property of the duke of Buccleuch and Queensberry, a seriously wealthy man. Beyond the grandiose mid-nineteenth-century mansion's facade of dark whinstone is an outstanding collection of French antiques and European **paintings**: in the dining room, for example, there are portraits by Reynolds and Gainsborough and a Canaletto cityscape, while the drawing room boasts Boulle furniture, Meissen tableware, paintings by Ruysdael, Leandro Bassano and Claude Lorraine, as well as two more family portraits by Reynolds. Look out also for the Scott Room, which features another splendid portrait of Sir Walter by Henry Raeburn, and the Monmouth Room, commemorating James, Duke of Monmouth, the illegitimate son of Charles II, who married Anne of the Buccleuchs. After several years in exile, Monmouth returned to England when his father died in 1685, hoping to wrest the crown from James II. He was defeated at the Battle of Sedgemoor in Somerset and subsequently sent to the scaffold; among other items, his execution shirt is on display.

The wooded hills of **Bowhill Country Park** adjoining the house (Easter–June & Aug daily except Fri 11am–5pm; July daily noon–5pm; £2) are criss-crossed by scenic footpaths and cycle trails: you can rent **mountain bikes** from the visitor centre. Getting to Bowhill by **public transport** is difficult. The Peebles bus, leaving Selkirk daily at 2pm, will drop you at General's Bridge (takes 10min), from where it's a mile or so's walk through the grounds to the house.

Yarrow Water

The A708, which passes by Bowhill, follows **Yarrow Water** upstream towards Dumfriesshire. A couple of miles west of Bowhill there's the Broadmeadows SYHA **hostel** near Yarrowford (℡0870/004 1107, ⓦwww.syha.org.uk; April–Sept) – the SYHA's first hostel, opened in 1931 – which serves as a convenient starting point for some good hill walks. From here, you can reach the hill-top cairns of **The Three Brethren**, whose 1530-foot summit offers excellent views over the Borders. You can also link up with stretches of the Southern Upland Way by heading east down through Yair Forest, or by following an old drove road west to the Cheese Well at Minchmoor (so called because of offerings left by travellers for the faerie folk), and ending up at Traquair House near Innerleithen (see p.196).

Eight miles further west, the A708 is crossed by the B709 going north through the hills to Innerleithen and southeast to Hawick. The junction is marked by the **Gordon Arms Hotel** (℡01750/82232; ➋), reputedly the last meeting place of Walter Scott and James Hogg, the "Shepherd Poet of Ettrick", where framed fragments of letters from Scott are on display in an otherwise basic bar serving meals and real ale. From the hotel, which offers a transport service and a cheap **bunkhouse** for walkers, you can follow the course of the lovely Yarrow Water further east for about seventeen miles to Selkirk (see opposite). Buses along the Yarrow Valley take you only as far as the *Gordon Arms Hotel* and then turn north to Traquair and Peebles.

A couple of miles further up the A708 at the top of Yarrow Water lies a pair of icy lakes: **St Mary's Loch**, and its diminutive neighbour, **Loch of the Lowes**, separated by a slender isthmus and magnificently set beneath the surrounding hills. This spot was popular with the nineteenth-century Scottish literati, especially Scott and Hogg, who eulogized "the bosom of the lonely Lowes". The pair gathered to chew the fat at ✠ **Tibbie Shiels Inn** on the isthmus, which takes its name from Isabella Shiel, a formidable and, by all accounts, amusing woman who ruled the place till her death in 1878 at the age of 96. Today, the inn is a famous watering hole on the Southern Upland Way; it provides bar meals, specializing in veggie menu, but has only limited opening in the winter (to check, phone ☎01750/42231). On the last Sunday in July the **Blanket Preaching** takes place here – an open-air service recalling a time when preachers were barred from the church. For a short and enjoyable walk, follow the footpath from the inn along the east side of St Mary's Loch into **Bowerhope Forest**. Alternatively, the Southern Upland Way heads across the moors north to Traquair House and south to the valley of the **Ettrick Water**, both strenuous hikes that require an Ordnance Survey map, a compass and proper clothing (see p.64).

Teviotdale and Liddesdale

To the south of the Tweed, **Teviotdale** is an altogether gentler valley, stretched between Teviothead, in the western hills, and Kelso, where the river joins the Tweed. The chief draw here is the best preserved of all the Border abbeys, at **Jedburgh**, which lies on a tributary of the Teviot called Jed Water. The main town on the Teviot itself is **Hawick**, famous for its knitwear factories, but hardly a must on most people's itinerary. From Hawick the busy A7 tracks up the most dramatic section of Teviotdale towards Langholm in Dumfriesshire. The alternative is to head down **Liddesdale** along the B6399, or – if you're coming straight from Jedburgh – the B6357, both slower but even more picturesque, remote roads flanked by dense forests, barren moors and secluded heaths. If you do come this way, stop off at solitary **Hermitage Castle**.

The Galashiels to Carlisle **bus** travels along much of Teviotdale via Hawick, where buses connect with Jedburgh.

Jedburgh

Just ten miles north of the border with England, **JEDBURGH** (ⓦwww .jedburgh.org.uk) nestles in the lush valley of Jed Water near its confluence with the Teviot out on the edge of the wild Cheviot Hills. During the interminable Anglo-Scottish Wars, Jedburgh was the quintessential frontier town, a heavily garrisoned royal burgh incorporating a mighty castle and abbey. Though the castle was destroyed by the Scots in 1409 to keep it out of the hands of the English, its memory has been kept alive by stories: in 1285, for example, King Alexander III was celebrating his wedding feast in the great hall when a ghostly apparition predicted his untimely death and a bloody civil war; sure enough, he died in a hunting accident shortly afterwards and chaos ensued. Today, Jedburgh is the first place of any size that you come to on the A68, having crossed over Carter Bar from England, and as such gets quite a bit of passing tourist trade. The ruined **abbey** is the main event, though a stroll round Jedburgh's old town centre is a pleasant way to while away an hour or so.

The abbey and town

Despite its ruinous state, **Jedburgh Abbey** (May–Sept daily 9.30am–6.30pm; Oct–April Mon–Sat 9.30am–4.30pm, Sun 2–4.30pm; HS; £4) still dominates

△ Jedburgh Abbey

the town, particularly when you approach from the south. Founded in the twelfth century as an Augustinian priory by King David I, it's the best preserved of all the Border abbeys, its vast church towering over a sloping site right in the centre of town, beside Jed Water. Built in red, yellow and grey sandstone, the abbey church can appear by turns gloomy, calm or richly warm, depending on the weather and the light. The abbey was burnt and badly damaged on a number of occasions, but by far the worst destruction was inflicted by the English in the 1540s. By this time, the contemplative way of life had already fallen prey to corruption and only a few canons remained living in the ruins of the abbey, until it was finally closed in 1560. The abbey church remained the parish kirk for another three centuries and as a result has survived particularly well preserved.

Entry is through the bright **visitor centre** at the bottom of the hill, which has an optional fifteen-minute audiovisual show on the ground floor and a viewing room overlooking the site upstairs (a useful retreat if it's raining). Here, too, you'll see Jedburgh's most treasured archeological find, the **Jedburgh Comb**, carved around 1100 from walrus ivory and decorated with a griffin and a dragon. All that remains of the conventual buildings where the canons lived are the foundations and basic ground plan, but then Jedburgh's chief glory is really its **Abbey Church**, which remains splendidly preserved. As you enter via the west door, the three-storey nave's perfectly proportioned parade of columns and arches lies before you, a fine example of the transition from Romanesque to Gothic design, with pointed window arches surmounted by the round-headed arches of the triforium, which, in turn, support the lancet windows of the clerestory. Be sure you climb up the narrow staircase in the west front to the balcony overlooking the nave, where you can contemplate how the place must have looked all decked out for the marriage of Alexander III to Yolande de Dreux in 1285.

It's a couple of minutes' walk from the abbey round to the small square **Market Place**, surrounded by soft oatmeal-coloured houses and centred on the Jubilee Fountain, a red sandstone column erected in 1889 and topped by a unicorn. Up the hill from here, at the top of Castlegate, stands **Jedburgh Castle Jail** (Easter–Oct Mon–Sat 10am–4.30pm, Sun 1–4.30pm; £2), an impressive castellated nineteenth-century pile built on the site of the old royal castle, which is well worth a visit. As well as detailed information about the history of Jedburgh, there's a fascinating insight into conditions in jail, deportations, crime and punishment (discover what happened to 9-year-olds who threw stones at ducks). The cells themselves are, for the period, remarkably comfortable, reflecting the influence of reformer John Howard.

Back down near the Market Place, signs will guide you to **Mary, Queen of Scots' House** (March–Nov Mon–Sat 10am–4.30pm, Sun 11am–4.30pm; £3). Despite the name, it seems unlikely that Mary ever actually stayed in this particular sixteenth-century house, though she did visit the town in 1566 for the Assizes staying at a place owned by her protector, Sir Thomas Kerr, ancestor of the present Lord Lothian of Ferniehurst Castle. The attempt to unravel her complex life is cursory, the redeeming features being a copy of Mary's death mask and one of the few surviving portraits of the Earl of Bothwell. One curious feature of all Kerr houses is that the staircases spiral to the left for ease of sword-drawing, giving rise to the Scottish term for left-handedness, "kerry haunded" or "kerry fisted". Just north of the town are **Monteviot House Gardens** (April–Oct noon–5pm; £2.50) which slope down to the Teviot and include stunning water gardens, herbaceous borders and roses in season.

Jedburgh festivals

Jedburgh is at its busiest during the town's two main festivals. The **Common Riding**, or Callants' Festival, takes place in late June or early July, when the young people of the town – especially the lads – mount up and ride out to check the burgh boundaries, a reminder of more troubled days when Jedburgh was subject to English raids. In similar spirit, early February sees the day-long **Jedburgh Hand Ba'** game, an all-male affair between the "uppies" (those born above Market Place) and the "doonies" (those born below). In theory the aim of the game is to get a hay-stuffed leather ball – originally representing the head of an Englishman – from one end of town to the other, but there's more at stake than that: macho reputations are made and lost during the two two-hour games.

Practicalities

Jedburgh is the starting point for a wide range of services around the Borders, with **coaches** picking up and dropping off at Canongate near the town centre. Yards away on Murray's Green is the **tourist office** (Mon–Sat 9.30am–5pm, Sun 10am–5pm).

There are several **B&Bs** among the pleasant and antique row of houses of Castlegate, one of the finest being *Meadhon House*, at no. 48 (☎01835/862504; ❷), which has a conservatory round the back overlooking a lovely garden. There's also a Georgian hotel in Castlegate, *Glenbank House Hotel* (☎01835/862258, ⓦwww.glenbankhotel.co.uk; ❸). Another great choice is *Hundalee House* (☎01835/863011, ⓦwww.accommodation-scotland.org; March–Oct; ❷), a seventeenth-century mansion house in open grounds, a mile south of town on the A68. Of the two **campsites** nearby, the *Jedwater Caravan Park* (☎01835/869595; ⓦwww.jedwater.co.uk; March–Oct) is cheaper and more secluded, in a pleasant riverside site four miles south of town on the A68. For **horse riders**, there are both stables and accommodation at *Ferniehurst Mill Lodge*, two miles south of Jedburgh on the A68 (☎01835/863279; ❷), from where experienced riders can venture out into the Cheviot Hills, and you can hire bikes and tandems from Tandem & Bike Hire (☎01835/830326).

There's a shortage of good **eating** places, but probably the best place is *Simply Scottish*, 6–8 High St (☎01835/864696), a smart but relaxed bistro-style café/restaurant serving inexpensive Scottish meals, as well as pasta dishes and the usual snacks. Try the local speciality Jethart Snails, sticky boiled sweets invented by a French POW in the 1700s and on sale everywhere. Further out of town, south on the A68, the comfortable *Jedforest Hotel* (☎01835/840222, ⓦwww.jedforesthotel.com; ❻) has a restaurant with an excellent reputation and set menus from £10–20 for three courses.

Hawick

Fourteen miles southwest of Jedburgh, **HAWICK** (pronounced "hoyk") is the largest town in the Borders. Despite being a busy, working mill town, Hawick fairly swarms with visitors, the majority of whom are drawn here in search of bargains from its woollen knitwear factory outlets. The town's heyday as the centre of the region's knitwear and hosiery industry was in the late nineteenth century, yet companies like Pringle, Lyle & Scott and Peter Scott continue to produce quality cashmere knitwear here. Followers of the yarn can satiate themselves at the **Hawick Cashmere Visitor Centre** (Mon–Sat 9.30am–5pm, Sun 11am–4pm; ☎01450/371221, ⓦwww.hawickcashmere.com), on Arthur Street, east of the town centre off the A698, which has a viewing gallery overlooking the frames at work. You can also take a guided tour of a couple of the **mills**: Peter Scott & Co, 11 Buccleuch St (Mon–Fri 10am–5pm, Sat 10am–4pm; free), centrally located just west of the tourist office, and the more traditional Wrights of Trowmill (Mon–Thurs 9am–4pm, Fri 9–11.30am; free), a couple of miles east of the town centre off the A698.

Hawick's handsome, wide **High Street** suffers from a surfeit of charity shops, though its Victorian architecture reflects the confident prosperity of the late nineteenth century, particularly the Scots Baronial town hall halfway down the street. At the southwestern end of the street stands **Drumlanrig Tower** (March Sat 10am–5pm, Sun noon–3pm; April–Sept Mon–Sat 10am–5pm, Sun noon–3pm; Oct Mon–Sat 10am–5pm; £2.50), not a tower at all, but a former inn and hotel. However, it started out in life as a medieval fortified keep, and now houses an interesting exhibition on local history, spread out over three floors; you can even climb out onto the roof, from which you get a good view of the nearby medieval motte. Hawick's other formal attraction is the **Hawick Museum & Scott Art Gallery** (April–Sept Mon–Fri 10am–noon & 1–5pm, Sat & Sun 2–5pm; Oct–March Mon–Fri 1–4pm, Sun 2–4pm; free), a mile or so west of the town centre in Wilton Lodge Park. The museum has displays reflecting the manufacturing life of the area and a special section on Jimmie Guthrie, a local motorcycle ace who died during the German Grand Prix in 1937. There's also a gallery housing nineteenth- and twentieth-century Scottish art; more exciting, though, are the regular travelling exhibitions which Hawick manages to attract.

The **tourist office** is on the ground floor of Drumlanrig Tower (same hours as Hawick Museum). A good choice for **accommodation** is the *Kirklands Hotel* (T01450/372263; ❹), a genuinely friendly, unpretentious place, which serves reasonably priced bar and restaurant meals. Hawick's most celebrated annual event is its **Common Riding**, which is held in early June, and commemorates a skirmish in 1514 when the local Hawick callants defeated a small English force and captured their banner. Another date for the diary is the Borders **festival of jazz and blues**, which takes place in Hawick in early September (Wwww.borderevents.com/annual).

Liddesdale

Either forming the border with England, or sticking close to it, **Liddesdale** is the only valley in the Borders whose river flows westwards. It's best approached via the hamlet of Bonchester Bridge, which sits on the A6088 from Hawick to Carter Bar. From here, the B6357 cuts south through Wauchope Forest before reaching Liddesdale.

The valley's wild beauty is at its most striking between Saughtree and Newcastleton, where there's a turning to **Hermitage Castle** (April–Sept daily 9.30am–6.30pm; HS; £2.50), a bleak and forbidding fastness bedevilled by all sorts of horrifying legends: one owner, William Douglas, starved his prisoners to death, whilst Lord de Soulis, another occupant, engaged the help of demons to fortify the castle in defiance of the king, Robert the Bruce. Not entirely trusting his demonic assistants, Soulis also drilled holes into the shoulders of his vassals, the better to yoke them to sledges of building materials. Bruce became so tired of the complaints that he exclaimed, "Boil him if you please, but let me hear no more of him." Bruce's henchmen took him at his word and ambushed the rebellious baron. Convinced, however, that Soulis had a pact with his demonic familiar, Redcap, that made him difficult to kill ("ropes could not bind him, nor steel weapons touch"), they bound him with ropes of sifted sand, wrapped him in lead and boiled him slowly. From the outside, the castle remains an imposing structure, its heavy walls topped by stepped gables and a tidy corbelled parapet. However, the apparent homogeneity is deceptive: certain features were invented during a Victorian restoration, a confusing supplement to the ad hoc alterations that had already transformed the fourteenth-century original. The ruinous interior is a bit of a letdown, but look out for the tight Gothic doorways and gruesome dungeon.

It's a short journey on to **NEWCASTLETON**, a classic estate village built for the hand-loom weavers of the third duke of Buccleuch in 1793. The gridiron streets fall either side of a long main road that connects three geometrically arranged squares, with the largest, Douglas Square, as the centrepiece. You can have a **drink**, sample some local trout or pheasant or even **stay** the night at the *Liddesdale Hotel* (T01387/375255; ❺), a family-run inn on Douglas Square itself. Book ahead if you plan to stay during the hugely popular **Newcastleton Folk Festival** in July. There are no buses along the length of Liddesdale.

Travel details

Trains

Edinburgh to: Berwick-upon-Tweed (every 1–2hr; 40–45min).

Buses

Berwick-upon-Tweed to: Duns (5–9 daily; 25min); Eyemouth (hourly; 15min); Galashiels (5–9 daily; 1hr 45min); Melrose (5–7 daily; 1hr 20min).
Duns to: Eyemouth (Mon–Sat 4 daily; 40min); Kelso (Mon–Fri 2 daily; 50min).
Edinburgh to: Coldingham (Mon–Sat every 2hr, 3 on Sun; 1hr 30min); Eyemouth (Mon–Sat 6 daily, 3 on Sun; 1hr 40min); Galashiels (Mon–Sat hourly; 2hr); Hawick (hourly; 2hr); Jedburgh (Mon–Fri hourly, 9 on Sat, 5 on Sun; 1hr 40min); Kelso (4–6 daily; 2hr); Lauder (Mon–Sat 7 daily, 4 on Sun; 1hr 10min); Melrose (hourly; 2hr 15min); Peebles (hourly; 1hr); Selkirk (hourly; 1hr 40min).
Galashiels to: Hawick (Mon–Sat hourly, 4 on Sun; 45min); Langholm (Mon–Sat 8–9 daily, 4 on Sun; 1hr 15min); Kelso (Mon–Sat 7–9 daily, 5 on Sun; 1hr); Melrose (Mon–Sat hourly, 7 on Sun; 15min); Peebles (Mon–Sat hourly, 9 on Sun; 45min); Selkirk (Mon–Sat every 30min, Sun hourly; 15min).
Hawick to: Jedburgh (Mon–Sat every 30min–1hr; 25min); Kelso (hourly; 1hr); Langholm (Mon–Sat hourly, 4 on Sun; 30min); Newcastleton (Mon–Fri 3–4 daily, 2 on Sat; 45min); Selkirk (Mon–Sat hourly, 4 on Sun; 25min).
Jedburgh to: Kelso (Mon–Sat 5–7 daily; 25min); Lauder (3–4 daily; 45min); Melrose (Mon–Sat 1–2 hourly, 7 on Sun; 30min).
Kelso to: Coldstream (Mon–Sat every 1–2hr; 20min); Kirk Yetholm (Mon–Sat 6 daily; 20min); Lauder (4–6 daily; 45min); Melrose (Mon–Sat 7–9 daily, 5 on Sun; 30–40min).
Melrose to: Duns (Mon–Sat 5–7 daily, 3 on Sun; 50min); Galashiels (Mon–Sat hourly, 7 on Sun; 15min); Hawick (Wed, Fri & Sat 2 daily; 40min); Jedburgh (Mon–Sat 1–2 hourly, 7 on Sun; 30min); Kelso (Mon–Sat 8–12 daily, 4 on Sun; 30min); Peebles (Mon–Sat hourly, 6 on Sun; 1hr 10min); Selkirk (Mon–Sat hourly, 2 on Sun; 20min).
Newcastleton to: Carlisle (Mon–Sat 2–5 daily; 50min); Hawick (Mon–Fri 3–4 daily, 2 on Sat; 45min); Langholm (Mon–Sat 3–4 daily; 40min).
Selkirk to: Ettrick (Mon–Fri 2 daily; 50min); Hawick (Mon–Sat hourly, Sun every 2hr; 20min); Langholm (Mon–Sat 6–7 daily, 3 on Sun; 1hr).

Dumfries and Galloway

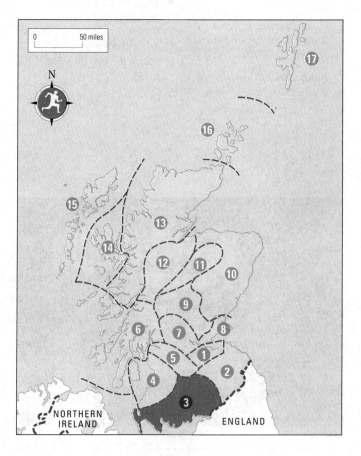

CHAPTER 3   # Highlights

* **Samye Ling Monastery**
  Eskdalemuir's golden Tibetan
  monastery is an arresting
  sight, especially when set
  against the bleak backdrop
  of the Southern Uplands. **See
  p.216**

* **Caerlaverock** One of
  Scotland's most photogenic
  moated castles, beside a
  superb site for waterfowl and
  waders. **See p.223**

* **Kirkcudbright** One-time
  artists' colony, and the best-

looking town in the "Scottish
Riviera". **See p.231**

* **Galloway Forest Park** Go
  mountain-biking along remote
  forest tracks, or hiking on the
  Southern Upland Way. **See
  p.237**

* **Mull of Galloway** Picture-
  postcard headland, with
  Stevenson lighthouse, cliffs
  full of seabirds and views
  across the Irish Sea. **See
  p.244**

△ Kirkcudbright

Dumfries and Galloway

The southwest corner of Scotland, now known as **Dumfries and Galloway**, (Ⓦ www.dumfriesandgalloway.co.uk) is a region set apart. A lot of people heading north from England might pause to explore the Borders region, but few bother to exit the main Carlisle–Glasgow motorway. Yet Dumfries and Galloway have stately homes, deserted hills and ruined abbeys to compete with the best of the Borders. They also have something the Borders don't have, and that's the Solway coast, a long, indented coastline of sheltered sandy coves that's been dubbed the "Scottish Riviera" – an exaggeration perhaps, but it's certainly Scotland's warmest, southernmost stretch of coastline. Also, being off the beaten track, and not crossed by any motorways Galloway, in particular, suffers little of the tourist crush familiar further north.

The region has a fascinatingly diverse heritage. Originally inhabited by southern Picts, it has at various times been overrun by Romans, Anglo-Saxons from Northumberland and Celts from Ireland: the name Galloway means the "land of the stranger Gaels". It was an unruly land, where independent chieftains maintained close contacts with the Vikings rather than the Scots, right up until medieval times. Gradually, this autonomy was whittled away, and the area was swallowed up by the Scottish crown, though Galloway, in particular, has continued to be a fiercely independent region, typified by local hero, Robert the Bruce. Later, Galloway became a stronghold of the Covenanters, and suffered terribly during the "Killing Times" following the Restoration, when the government forces came to impose Episcopalianism. From around the seventeenth century, the ports of the Solway coast prospered with the expansion of local shipping routes over to Ireland. The region subsequently experienced economic decline as trade routes changed, turning busy ports into sleepy backwaters, and these days southwest Scotland is one of the most agreeably laid-back areas of the country.

Dumfries is the obvious gateway to the region, a pleasant enough town that's only really a must for those on the trail of **Robert Burns**, who spent the last part of his life here. More compelling is the nearby coast, overlooking the Solway Firth, the shallow estuary wedged between Scotland and England, famed for its wildlife and for the nearby red sandstone ruins of **Caerlaverock Castle** and **Sweetheart Abbey**. Edged by tidal marsh and mudbank, much

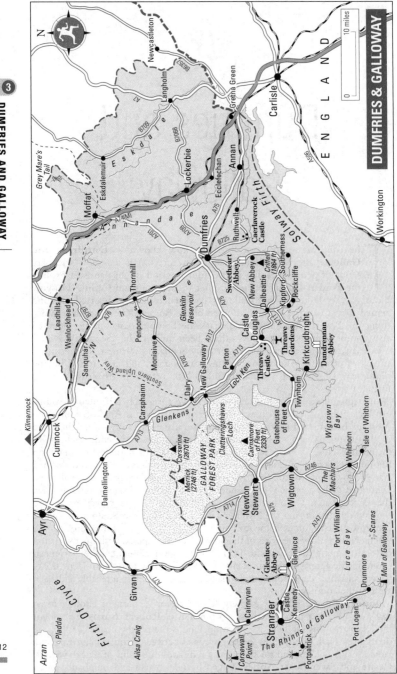

DUMFRIES & GALLOWAY

0   10 miles

© Crown copyright

of the Solway shoreline is flat and eerily remote, but there are also some fine rocky bays sheltering beneath wooded hills, most notably along the **Colvend coast**. Further along the coast is **Kirkcudbright**, once a bustling port thronged with sailing ships, later an artists' retreat and now a tranquil, well-preserved little eighteenth- and early nineteenth-century town. Like Kirkcudbright, **Threave Garden and Castle**, just outside Castle Douglas, are popular with – but not crowded by – tourists.

Contrasting with the essentially gentle landscape of the Solway coast, is the brooding presence of the **Galloway Hills** to the north, their beautiful moors, mountains, lakes and rivers centred on the 150,000-acre **Galloway Forest Park**, a seriously underused hill-walking and mountain-biking paradise. Continuing west into what used to be Wigtownshire, the landscape becomes flatter and more relentlessly agricultural. The three main points of interest here are **Whithorn**, where St Ninian introduced Christianity to Scotland; the attractive seaport of **Portpatrick** on the hammer-headed Rhinns of Galloway; and the **Mull of Galloway**, Scotland's southernmost point, and a nesting site for thousands of seabirds.

Travelling the region by **bus** presents few problems; in addition, there's a **train** line up Annandale from Carlisle to Glasgow and one up Nithsdale via Dumfries. It's also easy to travel on from southwest Scotland by **ferry** to Northern Ireland, from Stranraer to Belfast and from Cairnryan to Larne. The combination of rolling landscape and quiet back roads makes the region good for **cyclists**: five of the **7stanes** (Ⓦwww.7stanes.gov.uk) purpose-built mountain-bike routes are in the forested hills of Dumfries and Galloway. This is also excellent **walking** country, featuring the **Southern Upland Way** (Ⓦwww.dumgal.gov.uk/southernuplandway or Ⓦwww.southernuplandway .com), a 212-mile coast-to-coast hike from Portpatrick in the west to Cockburnspath in the east.

Annandale

Cutting through **Annandale**, the A74(M) and the main railway line connect Carlisle with Glasgow. This is the fastest route for crossing southern Scotland but it's a fairly bleak landscape and an unpleasantly busy motorway, jam-packed with trucks and lorries. If you simply need to break your journey, then the market town of **Moffat**, thirty miles or so north of the border (and bypassed by the railway and motorway), is the best choice – it's also a feasible base for exploring the surrounding Southern Uplands. Alternatively, if you're heading east into the Borders, you could leave the motorway earlier, either at **Lockerbie** and head up via **Eskdalemuir**, or even before that, and head towards Teviotdale, via **Langholm**.

Gretna Green and around

Ten miles north of Carlisle, just over the border from England, **GRETNA GREEN** is synonymous with elopements and quick **weddings**, thanks to a historic anomaly between the English and Scottish legal systems (see box on p.214). Gretna still makes its money from the marriage charade, which is fair enough given that there's not much else going for the place. A steady stream of cars and coaches roll up at the **World Famous Old Blacksmith's Shop Centre**, a vast complex of tartan and whisky shops, arts gallery, café, restaurant, toilets and museum, all to the backdrop hum of the nearby A74(M). Not to

Gretna Green marriages

Up until 1754 English couples could buy a quick and secret wedding at London's Fleet Prison, bribing imprisoned clerics with small amounts of money. The **Hardwicke Marriage Act** brought an end to this seedy wheeze, enforcing the requirement of a licence and a church ceremony. However, in Scotland, a marriage declaration made before two witnesses remained legal. The consequences of this difference in the law verged on farce: hundreds of runaway couples dashed north to Scotland, their weddings witnessed by just about anyone who came to hand – ferrymen, farmers, tollgate keepers and even self-styled "priests" who set up their own "marriage houses".

Gretna Green, due to its position beside the border on the main turnpike road to Edinburgh, became the most popular destination for the fugitives. In their rush, many people tied the knot at the first place to hand after dismounting from the stagecoach, which happened to be a **blacksmith's shop** situated at the crossroads, though the better-off maintained class distinctions, heading for the staging post at Gretna Hall. The association with blacksmiths was strengthened by one of the first "priests", the redoubtable Joseph Paisley, a 25-stone Goliath who – in business from 1754 to 1812 – gave a certain style to the ceremony by straightening a horseshoe, a show of strength rather than a symbolic act. His melodramatic feat led to stories of Gretna Green weddings being performed over the blacksmith's **anvil**, and later "priests" were more than happy to act out the rumour. Gretna Green boomed until the marriage laws were further amended in 1856, but some business continued right down to 1940, when marriage by declaration was made illegal.

The only marriages that take place in Gretna Green nowadays, however, are for couples taken in by the "romance" of the name – over 4000 annually – and English couples under 18, who want to get married without the permission of their parents (Ⓦ www.gretnaweddings.com).

be outdone, the *Gretna Hall Hotel*, on the other side of the motorway, has built itself a rival blacksmith's and also runs its own museum. There's no conceivable reason to stop at either place, although there is a useful **tourist office** (daily: April–June, Sept & Oct 10am–4pm; July & Aug 10am–5pm; Ⓣ01461/337834), opposite the blacksmith's.

During World War I, the nearby settlement of **GRETNA** (Ⓦ www.gretna-area .co.uk) was built from scratch, along with **EASTRIGGS**, some four miles west, to house the 30,000 women and men who worked in HM Factory Gretna. The munitions factory was once the largest in the world, stretching for over nine miles, with 125 miles of its own railway track, its own power station and even its own state-owned pubs. The factory's fascinating story is told in the exhibition **The Devil's Porridge** (Easter weekend & May–Oct Mon–Sat 10am–4pm, Sun noon–4pm; £1.50; Ⓦ www.devilsporridge.co.uk), housed in St John's Church, Dunedin Road, in Easteriggs, off the A75. The exhibition takes its name from the explosive paste, which was mixed by hand in large vats, and was described as "the devil's porridge" by Sir Arthur Conan Doyle when he visited the factory in 1918.

Ecclefechan

It's about nine miles from the border to the tidy hamlet of **ECCLEFECHAN**, birthplace of the historian and essayist **Thomas Carlyle** (1795–1881). Born into a strongly Calvinist family, Carlyle wrote a highly successful account of the French Revolution (1837), seting out his theory of history as "Divine Scripture": the French aristocracy had reaped the rewards of their corruption and indulgence. However, with no clearly defined political ideology his radicalism soon began to wane, reinforced by the failure of contemporary activist movements to live up to his idealistic expectations. Disillusioned, Carlyle was eventually to become the strongest voice for the moral concerns of the Victorian bourgeoisie and, as such, a litmus paper for his age. His long marriage was turbulent, but when his wife died in 1866 he never recovered and was a semi-recluse for many years before his death. His old home, the whitewashed **Arched House** (May–Sept Mon, Fri & Sat 1–5pm; NTS; £5), a typical two-storey house with a central pend (passage), was built by his father and uncle, and is now a tiny museum, featuring among the personal memorabilia a bronze cast of his hands, old smoking caps and his cradle. The family moved from the Arched House while Thomas was in his infancy; in 1828, he moved to Craigenputtock, thirteen miles northwest of Dumfries, and from 1834 until his death, he lived in London. He's buried in the local churchyard.

The double bay-fronted Victorian *Cressfield Country House Hotel*, on Townfoot (☎01576/300281; ❸), designed by Carlyle's father, is a good choice for **accommodation**; to get there, follow the signs to the nearby *Cressfield Caravan Park* **campsite** (☎01576/300702), a pristinely kept site set within a country park.

Lockerbie and around

The quiet country town of **LOCKERBIE**, halfway between the border and Moffat, was catapulted into the headlines on Wednesday, December 21, 1988, when a 747 jumbo jet, on Pan-Am flight 103 from Frankfurt to New York via London Heathrow, was blown up at 31,000ft by a terrorist bomb concealed in a transistor radio. All 259 crew and passengers died, plus eleven residents of Lockerbie where the plane's fuselage landed. This event caused terrible trauma in Lockerbie, both physically and psychologically, and continues to do so even now, more than seventeen years later. A memorial was set up, and links were forged with the families of the US victims, but there was also a strong suspicion among the victims' groups of a cover-up by the powers that be.

Jim Swire, a doctor from the English Midlands, who lost his 24-year-old daughter in the crash, was instrumental in pressing for those responsible to be brought to trial, and for the truth to be told about the whole incident. He even went as far as visiting Libya, meeting with relatives of those who were killed in the revenge air attacks launched by the US, and personally asking Colonel Gaddafi (who lost his own 2-year-old daughter in one of the raids) to allow the two Libyans charged with the crime to stand trial. Eventually, more than ten years after the event, a trial was held under Scottish law in a specially created court in the Netherlands, and resulted in the conviction of one of the two suspects, a Libyan intelligence officer called Megrahi. Following the trial, Libya finally agreed $2.7 billion in compensation for the victims' families, in return for the lifting of UN sanctions. More recently, however, anomalies in the evidence used to convict Megrahi have been uncovered, and the case is set to be reviewed. Many believe the true suspects were, in fact, members of the Syrian-led Popular Front for the Liberation of Palestine-General Command (PFLP-GC). Meanwhile Jim Swire continues to press for a public inquiry into the many unanswered questions, not least why various intelligence warnings prior to the bombing were ignored (for more on this, visit ⓦ www .lockerbietruth.com).

A couple of miles south of Lockerbie, along the road to Dalton is the **Hallmuir POW Chapel** (daily; free), built out of a corrugated iron hut by Ukrainian POWs, several hundred of whom were sent here from Italy in 1947, rather than handed over to the Russians. Lavishly decorated with paintings and artefacts made from any scraps they could gather, the chapel is a remarkable sight and Greek Catholic services are still held here on a regular basis.

Langholm and around

While not strictly in Annandale, **LANGHOLM** (ⓦ www.langholm-online .co.uk) is on the road from Carlisle and Gretna Green to the Borders. A quiet, stone-built mill town at the confluence of the Esk, Ewes and Wauchope waters, Langholm flourished during the eighteenth-century textile boom, and is still dominated by the industry. This was the birthplace of the poet **Hugh MacDiarmid** (1892–1978), a key player in the Scottish nationalist literary renaissance between the two world wars. A cofounder of the Scottish National Party and later a Communist Party member, he was expelled from each in turn. MacDiarmid, born Christopher Murray Grieve, looked to the hard Scots language of the Border ballads and medieval poets such as Dunbar and Henryson, but had little time for what he saw as the naive sentimentality of Burns, and the Tory politics of Scott, heaping scorn on the local anglicized gentry. This didn't go down well with some of the burghers of Langholm, who, when MacDiarmid died at the age of 86, tried to prevent him being buried in the local churchyard.

A generation on, and how times have changed: the local tourist board now hands out a leaflet on the "MacDiarmid Trail", tracing the roots of "Scotland's greatest twentieth-century poet". Even if you've no interest in MacDiarmid, it's worth heading out to the striking **MacDiarmid Memorial**, a giant rusting metal book on a hill two miles up the road to Newcastleton, off the A7. The path past the sculpture continues up the hill to an earlier monument, the **Malcolm Memorial**, commemorating another local boy, albeit a rather more conventional one, Sir John "Boy" Malcolm (1769–1833), an ambitious, reactionary colonialist who became governor of Bombay; the views from his monument are terrific.

Eskdalemuir

Three roads lead out of Langholm into the Borders, the most stunning being the narrow country lane that snakes its way east over the empty hills to Newcastleton in Liddesdale (see p.206), followed by the far slower trip northwest up Eskdale for Selkirk and the Tweed Valley (see p.200). Thirteen miles up Eskdale, the fluttering prayer flags, scarlet-robed Buddhists and golden temple of the **Tibetan Monastery** (☏ 01387/373232, ⓦ www .samyeling.org) make a surreal sight against the bleak backdrop of the barren hills above the tiny village of **ESKDALEMUIR**. Visitors are welcome to look round the incredibly ornate and very gold interior of the Samye Ling temple, and to attend courses on Buddhist meditation and Eastern philosophy. **Accommodation** and a basic vegetarian canteen are available for people staying on retreats or attending courses, and there's a small shop and Tibetan-style café which serves toasties, coffees and so on for passing visitors.

Moffat and around

Encircled by hills and dales, **MOFFAT** (Ⓦ www.visitmoffat.co.uk) is an old market town whose heyday was during the eighteenth century, when it was briefly a modish spa, its sulphur springs attracting the rich and famous. One disappointed customer suggested they smelt of bilge water, but they were good enough for Robbie Burns and James Boswell, who came to "wash off the scurvy spots". Moffat is no longer so fashionable; its shops now sell tartan and tat, and its hotels and inns have all seen better days. Nevertheless, the wide **High Street** has a pleasingly eclectic mixture of buildings, from the *Victorian Star Hotel*, "famous" as Britain's narrowest free-standing hotel, to the Neoclassical town hall, on the opposite side of the street. The most obvious reminder of Moffat's halcyon period is the John Adam-designed **Moffat House Hotel**, a three-storey greystone house, with characteristic red sandstone trim around the windows, flanked by matching outbuildings. Inside, only the central oval staircase hints at former days, the rest of the place resembling every other hotel run by the multinational Best Western chain. Back on the High Street, don't miss the nearby **Colvin Fountain**, whose sturdy bronze ram was accidentally cast without any ears.

For details of the town's history as a spa, among other topics, and as a retreat from bad weather, pop into the **Moffat Museum** (Easter & Whitsun–Sept Mon, Tues & Thurs–Sat 10.30am–5pm, Sun 2.30–5pm; £1), in an old bakehouse at Church Gate, at the bottom of the High Street. A little way further south along the road to Dumfries is the giant **Moffat Woollen Mill** (daily 9am–5pm; free), where you can watch weaving demonstrations and visit the inevitable clan tartan centre and whisky shop. In sunny weather, those with small children might like to take them to **Moffatasia** (May–Sept Mon–Sat 10am–8pm, Sun 1–7pm; free), an outdoor water-feature playground where the little ones can soak themselves under various mushroom jets, fountains and water cannon.

Moffat is also a good base for **walking** in the surrounding countryside. The tourist office has a helpful compendium of local walks, one of the best being the short but brisk hike up to the top of Gallow Hill, from where there are great views out over Annandale (allow a couple of hours). For a more gentle stroll round the outskirts of the town by the River Annan, follow the "waterside walk" sign opposite Station Park. More strenuous walking is within reach in the Lowther Hills (see p.227), and nearby Beattock marks the midway point of the Southern Upland Way.

Practicalities

Despite the proximity of the railway line, the nearest station is sixteen miles away in Lockerbie; **buses** drop passengers off on the High Street, in the town centre. The **tourist office** (April, May, Sept & Oct Mon–Sat 10am–5pm, Sun noon–4pm; June–Aug daily 9.30am–6.30pm; ℡01683/220620) is hidden away in a corner of the large car park of the Moffat Woollen Mill to the south of the town centre. There is no shortage of **accommodation**, though you're much better off avoiding the hotels that line the High Street, all of which have seen better days. Instead, head off into the quiet backstreets to the east of the High Street and try an attractive Victorian mansion like *Craigie Lodge* (℡01683/221769, Ⓦ www.craigielodge.co.uk; ❷) on Ballplay Road, or *Kirkland House* (℡01683/221133, Ⓦ www.kirkland-house.co.uk; ❷), the town's former manse, and *Burnside* (℡01683/221900, Ⓦ www.burnsidemoffat .co.uk; ❸), both on Well Road. Moving up the price range, there's the large, double-fronted *Well View Hotel* (℡01683/220184, Ⓦwww.wellview.co.uk; ❺), on Ballplay Road on the eastern edge of Moffat, which also has an excellent restaurant. The fourteen-acre *Hammerland's Farm* **caravan** and **camping** site (℡01683/220436; March–Oct) is a short walk from the centre of town, near the tourist office.

Apart from the *Well View Hotel*, the most imaginative **food** to be had is from *The Limetree* (℡01683/221654, Ⓦwww.limetree-restaurant.co.uk), a small place at the top of the High Street, opposite the *Moffat House Hotel*. Otherwise, head for *Claudio's* (℡01683/220958), a popular, cosy Italian restaurant housed in the attractive Victorian former police station on Burnside. For snacks and decent coffee, go to *Ariete* **café** on the High Street; for a drink, penetrate the dark shadows of the *Black Bull*, (Ⓦwww.blackbullmoffat.co.uk), at the bottom of the High Street on Churchgate, a **pub** which once quartered John Graham of Claverhouse as he planned his persecution of the Covenanters on behalf of Charles II, and was a favourite haunt of Burns.

Around Moffat

From Moffat, there are two beautiful routes you can take through the most dramatic parts of the Southern Uplands and into the Borders region. Of the two, the finer is the A708, which heads northeast up Moffat Water over to Selkirk in the Borders (see p.200). On the way, the 200-foot **Grey Mare's Tail Waterfall** (NTS), which tumbles down a rocky crevasse, provides one of Dumfriesshire's best-known beauty spots. The base of the falls is approached by a precipitous footpath along the left side of the stream, a ten-minute clamber each way from the road. There's a longer hike, too, up the steep right-hand bank, past the head of the falls and on to the remote **Loch Skeen**, where you can fish without permits. Further northeast, in the Borders, St Mary's Loch gives easy access to an especially stimulating section of the Southern Upland Way (see p.200).

The second route, to the west, uses the A701, which ascends the west side of Annandale to skirt the impressive box canyon at its head, and cuts down Tweeddale towards Peebles (see p.197). Best viewed from the road about six miles from town, the gorge – the **Devil's Beef Tub** – takes its name from the days when rustling Reivers hid their herds here. Walter Scott described the place aptly: "It looks as if four hills were laying their heads together to shut out daylight from the dark hollow place between them." The gorge was also a suitably secret hideaway for persecuted Covenanters during Charles II's "Killing Times".

Travelling these routes by **bus** remains difficult, with just an infrequent summer service along the A708 from Moffat to Selkirk on three days of the week.

Dumfries and around

Situated on the wide banks of the River Nith a short distance inland from the Solway Firth, **DUMFRIES** is by far the largest town in southwest Scotland, with a population of more than thirty thousand. Long known as the "Queen of the South" (as is its football club), the town flourished as a medieval seaport and trading centre, its success attracting the attention of many English armies. The invaders managed to polish off most of the early settlement in 1448, 1536

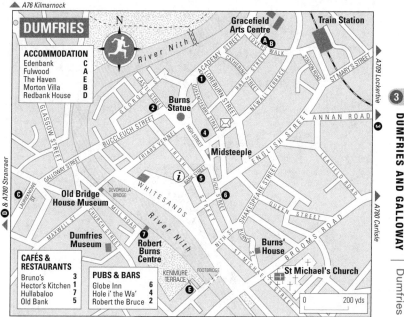

DUMFRIES

N

River Nith

Gracefield Arts Centre

Train Station

ACCOMMODATION
Edenbank   C
Fulwood   A
The Haven   E
Morton Villa B
Redbank House D

Burns Statue

Midsteeple

ⓘ

Old Bridge House Museum

DEVORGILLA BRIDGE

W H I T E S A N D S

River Nith

Dumfries Museum

Robert Burns Centre

CAFÉS & RESTAURANTS
Bruno's   3
Hector's Kitchen 1
Hullabaloo   7
Old Bank   5

PUBS & BARS
Globe Inn   6
Hole i' the Wa'   4
Robert the Bruce 2

KENMURE TERRACE

FOOTBRIDGE

Burns' House

St Michael's Church

0   200 yds

© Crown copyright

and again in 1570, but Dumfries survived to prosper with its light industries and port supplying the agricultural hinterland. The town planners of the 1960s badly damaged the place, but enough remains of the warm red sandstone buildings that distinguish Dumfries from other towns in the southwest to make it worth at least a brief stop. It also acts as a convenient base for exploring the Solway coast, to the east and west, and is second only to Ayr for its associations with Robbie Burns, who spent the last five years of his life here employed as an exciseman.

The Town

Orientation around Dumfries is easy, with the railway to the east, and the river to the north and west. The pedestrianized **High Street** runs roughly parallel to the Nith; at its northern end, presiding over a floral roundabout, is the **Burns Statue**, a sentimental piece of Victorian frippery in white Carrara marble, featuring the great man holding a posy in one hand while the other clutches at his heart. His faithful hound, Luath, lies curled around his feet – though it doesn't look much like a Scots collie (as Luath was). Further down the High Street, Burns's body lay in state at the town's most singular building, the **Midsteeple**, an appealingly wonky hotchpotch of a building, built in 1707 to fulfil the multiple functions of town prison, clocktower, courthouse and arsenal.

If you're on Burns's trail, make sure you duck down the alleyway to the **Globe Inn** (Ⓦ www.globeinndumfries.co.uk), just past the ornate red and gold Victorian fountain, a little further down the High Street. This white-washed inn, with its own suntrap courtyard, is Burns's most famous "howff"

△ Midsteeple, Dumfries

(pub), headquarters of the local Burns society and one of the town's few surviving seventeenth-century buildings. Burns had a fling with Annie Park, a barmaid at the Globe Inn, and the resultant child was taken into the Burns household by the long-suffering Jean Armour, who apparently opined that "our Robbie should have had twa wives".

Southeast of the High Street, in what was once Mill Vennel and is now, inevitably, Burns Street, stands **Burns House** (April–Sept Mon–Sat 10am–5pm, Sun 2–5pm; Oct–March Tues–Sat 10am–1pm & 2–5pm; free), a simple sandstone building where the poet died of rheumatic heart disease in 1796 aged 37, a few days before the birth of his last son, Maxwell. Burns lived here just three years before he died, though his wife, Jean Armour, stayed on until her own death, some 38 years later. Inside, there's the usual collection of Burns memorabilia – manuscripts, letters, his nutmeg grater and the like – while one of the bedroom windows bears his signature, scratched with his diamond ring. As a member of the Dumfries Volunteers, Burns was given a military funeral, before being buried nearby in a simple grave by **St Michael's Church** (Mon–Fri 10am–4pm; free), a large red sandstone church, built in 1745, with a slightly ill-fitting Gothic tower. In 1815 Burns was dug up and moved across the graveyard to a purpose-built **Mausoleum**, a bright white Neoclassical eyesore, which houses a slightly ludicrous statue of him being accosted by the poetic Muse. The rest of the graveyard is packed full of large red sandstone tombstones, including many of the poet's friends, all architecturally plain, but inscribed with the most wonderfully verbose epitaphs.

From the church, head down to the Nith, which is shallow and fast-running, especially as it rushes down the weir. This side of the river, known as **Whitesands**, was once busy with timberyards, tanneries, breweries, boats and the local cattle market; nowadays, it serves as the town's main car park, and is architecturally a bit of a mess. More impressive is the pedestrian-only **Devorgilla Bridge**, a little further upstream, built in 1431 and one of the oldest bridges in Scotland. Attached to its southwestern end is the town's oldest house, built in 1660, now housing the tiny **Old Bridge House Museum** (April–Sept Mon–Sat 10am–5pm, Sun 2–5pm; free), stuffed full of Victorian domestic bric-a-brac, including a teeth-chattering range of Victorian dental gear.

Downstream from the Old Bridge House, an old watermill has been converted into the **Robert Burns Centre**, or RBC (April–Sept Mon–Sat 10am–8pm, Sun 2–5pm; Oct–March Tues–Sat 10am–1pm & 2–5pm; free), with an optional twenty-minute slide show (£1.55) and a simple exhibition on the poet's years in Dumfries upstairs. On the hill above the RBC stands the **Dumfries Museum** (April–Sept Mon–Sat 10am–5pm, Sun 2–5pm; Oct–March Tues–Sat 10am–1pm & 2–5pm; free), from which there are great views over the town. The museum is housed partly in an eighteenth-century windmill, which was converted into the town's observatory in the 1830s and features a **camera obscura** on its top floor (April–Sept; £1.80), well worth a visit on a clear day. Outside the museum, don't miss the statuary that shelters within a Neoclassical mausoleum, featuring Robert Paterson, the model for Scott's "Old Mortality", lounging around by his pony.

Back on the other side of the river, up Academy Street, is the **Gracefield Arts Centre** (Tues–Sat 10am–5pm; free), which puts on changing exhibitions drawn from its collection of nineteenth- and twentieth-century Scottish paintings by the likes of Hornel, the Faeds, Elizabeth Blackadder and Alan Davey, to name but a few, as well as sculpture by local boy Andy Goldsworthy.

Anyone interested in sculpture should also check out the private collection that is dotted about the landscape around the remote **Glenkiln Reservoir**, some eight miles west of Dumfries (ask at the tourist office for directions and for an information sheet). A naked *John the Baptist* by Jacob Epstein welcomes visitors to the car park – this is one of five startling sculptures set in the landscape, including a Rodin and two Henry Moores.

Slightly out of the centre (signposted off the A76 to Kilmarnock and through a housing estate), the attractive ruins of the red sandstone **Lincluden Collegiate Church** are seldom visited, though the south transept and choir are well preserved, as are a range of domestic buildings to the north. It was built by Archibald, third Earl of Douglas, in the early fifteenth century on the site of a Benedictine nunnery, who clearly employed a master mason, most probably from Melrose. The best surviving work is in the choir, which harbours the splendidly ornate tomb of Archibald's widow, Princess Margaret, eldest daughter of Robert III; the sedilia and piscina, opposite, are of similar craftsmanship.

Practicalities

Dumfries **train** station is five minutes' walk east of the town centre, while **buses** drop you off at Whitesands beside the River Nith. The **tourist office** (June–Sept Mon–Sat 9.30am–6pm, Sun noon–5pm; Oct–May Mon–Sat 10am–5pm; ☏01387/253862) is also on Whitesands; it stocks a "Burns trail" leaflet for the afflicted, and houses a small exhibition and film on the area.

Dumfries abounds in handsome sandstone villas, several of which have been turned into **guesthouses** and **B&Bs**. For value and convenience, you can't beat *Morton Villa*, 28 Lovers Walk (☏01387/255825; ❷), a large Victorian house with a pleasant garden, or the very welcoming *Fulwood Hotel* (☏01387/252262; ❷), next door at no. 30, both near the station. For a more distinctive setting, try *The Haven*, 1 Kenmure Terrace (☏01387/251281; ❶), where guests have their own kitchens; it's situated on a short block of attractive old houses overlooking the Nith from beside the suspension footbridge below the RBC. If you're looking for a bona fide **hotel**, head for Laurieknowe Street, a five- to ten-minute walk west of Devorgilla Bridge, where you'll find the welcoming, family-run *Edenbank* (☏01387/252759, Ⓦwww.edenbankhotel.co.uk; ❹) at no.17. *Redbank House* (☏01387/247034, Ⓦwww.redbankhouse.co.uk; ❸) is a pristine red-brick mansion set within its own wooded garden at the edge of town on the A710, boasting a sauna, snooker room and gym.

By far the best option for **food** is ✴ *Hullabaloo* (☏01387/259679; Ⓦwww.hullabaloorestaurant.co.uk; closed Mon & Sun eve), a stylish restaurant on the top floor of the RBC, with a summer terrace overlooking the river. Lunchtimes are for wraps, bagels and ciabatta sandwiches; in the evening, when it's advisable to book, there are moderately expensive Mediterranean-influenced dishes on offer. Another good option is *Hector's Kitchen*, a much smaller place at 20 Academy St (closed Sun), which offers toasties, baguettes, nachos and crepes for lunch, and more substantial fare in the evening. The *Old Bank*, a tearoom on Irish Street, has a more predictable menu, plus a wide selection of cream cakes. There are lots of Italian restaurants; one of the best is the family-friendly *Bruno's* (☏01387/255757; closed Tues) on Balmoral Road that's become a Dumfries institution, with the equally popular *Balmoral* chippie round the side which justifiably claims to sell the best chips in the southwest.

Two of Burns's favourite drinking places are still in operation: the *Hole i' the Wa'* **pub**, down an alley opposite Woolworth's on High Street, serves the usual bar food, but for somewhere with a bit more atmosphere, make for the smoky, oak-panelled *Globe Inn* (Ⓦwww.globeinndumfries.co.uk) on the High Street, which is crammed with memorabilia connected with the poet but is otherwise little changed since his time. The *Robert the Bruce* pub, with its Neoclassical portico at the top of Buccleuch Street, is a typical and very popular church conversion by the J.D. Wetherspoons chain. **Films** are regularly shown at the RBC (Tues–Sat; ☎01387/264808, Ⓦwww.rbcft.co.uk). Grierson and Graham, 10 Academy St (☎01387/259483), offers **bike rental**, useful for reaching the nearby Solway coast.

Around Dumfries

Dumfries itself might be short on top-drawer sights, but the countryside immediately around it, within easy reach, more than makes up for the lack. To the north, **Ellisland Farm**, where Burns made his final stab at running his own farm, is much more atmospheric than any of the Burns sights in Dumfries. To the southeast, the medieval ruins of **Caerlaverock Castle** are simply magnificent, as is the adjacent nature reserve and the early Christian cross at nearby **Ruthwell**. On the west bank of the Nith estuary, the star attraction is **Sweetheart Abbey**, the best preserved of the trio of Cistercian abbeys in Dumfries and Galloway. Regular **buses** run to all these sights, with timetables available from the Dumfries tourist office.

Ellisland Farm

North of Dumfries, the A76 passes **Ellisland Farm** (April–Sept Mon–Sat 10am–5pm, Sun 2–5pm; Oct–March Tues–Sat 10am–5pm; Ⓦwww.ellislandfarm.co.uk; £2.50), built by Robert Burns in 1788 as a family home and working farmhouse. His three years at Ellisland were very productive: Burns wrote over 130 poems and songs, including *Tam o' Shanter* and *Auld Lang Syne*. The farm, though, didn't prosper – "a ruinous affair", Burns called it – due to the boggy soil, and eventually Burns got a salaried post as an exciseman. Ellisland remains a working farm, though it also houses a museum, where you can see Burns's fishing rod and flute, the original range installed by the poet for his wife and many of the agricultural implements Burns used, not to mention his pistol and sword – essential possessions when carrying out the unpopular job of levying taxes.

Caerlaverock Castle and around

Caerlaverock Castle, eight miles southeast of Dumfries (daily: April–Sept 9.30am–6.30pm; Oct–March 9.30am–4.30pm; HS; £4), is a picture-perfect ruined castle. Not only is it moated, it's built from the rich local red sandstone, is triangular in shape and has preserved its mighty double-towered gatehouse. Built in the late thirteenth century, it clearly impressed medieval chroniclers. During the siege of 1300 by Edward I, a contemporary bard commented: "In shape it was like a shield, for it had but three sides round it, with a tower at each corner ... and good ditches filled right up to the brim with water. And I think you will never see a more finely situated castle." Caerlaverock sustained further damage in 1312, this time from the Scots, and again in 1356–7 from the English, forcing numerous rebuilding programmes. Close inspection of the main gatehouse reveals several phases of construction: the fifteenth-century machicolations of the gatehouse top earlier towers that are themselves studded with wide-mouthed gunports from around 1590. The most surprising addition, however, lies inside, where you're confronted by the ornate Renaissance facade of the **Nithsdale Lodging**, erected in the 1630s by the first earl of Nithsdale.

③

The decorated tympana above the windows feature lively mythological and heraldic scenes in what was clearly the latest style. Sadly, Nithsdale didn't get much value for money: just six years later he and his royal garrison were forced to surrender after a thirteen-week siege and bombardment by the Covenanters, who proceeded to wreck the place. It was never inhabited again.

Caerlaverock Castle makes for a popular family day out; it has a siege-engine playground, a tearoom and an exhibition and video on the siege of 1300, where kids can do their own heraldry – a useful wet-weather retreat. There are also various **walks** marked out along the edge of the neighbouring national nature reserve, including one leading to the earthworks of the old castle which preceded Caerlaverock; en route, you should look out for the rare natterjack toad.

Three miles further east, at Eastpark, is the **Caerlaverock Wildfowl and Wetlands Trust Centre** (daily 10am–5pm; £4.40; ⑩ www.wwt.org.uk/visit/ caerlaverock), 1350 acres of protected salt marsh and mudflat edging the Solway Firth. The centre is equipped with screened approaches that link the main observatory to a score of well-situated bird-watchers' hides. It's famous for the 25,000 or so barnacle geese which winter here between September and April. The rest of the year, when the geese are away nesting in Svalbard, there's plenty of other flora and fauna to look out for, as well as the aforementioned natterjack toad. Throughout the year the wild whooper swans have a daily feeding time and the wardens run free wildlife safaris; call ☎ 01387/770200 for up-to-date details. You can **camp** or stay in one of the **rooms** in the centre's converted farmhouse (✉ info.caerlaverock@wwt.org.uk; ③), which has its own observation tower, plus a kitchen and washing machine for guests' use. Both the castle and the centre are reached along the B725; this is the route the bus takes, mostly terminating at the castle but sometimes continuing to the start of the two-mile lane leading off the B725 to the centre.

The Ruthwell Cross

From Caerlaverock, it's about seven miles east along the B725 to the village of **RUTHWELL**, whose modest country church houses the remarkable eighteen-foot **Ruthwell Cross** (the keys are kept at one of the houses at the foot of the lane; look out for the information notice). An extraordinary early Christian monument from the early or mid-eighth century when Galloway was ruled by the Northumbrians, the cross was considered idolatrous during the Reformation, smashed to pieces and buried. Only in the nineteenth century was it finally reassembled and given its own purpose-built semicircular apse. The decoration on the cross reveals a strikingly sophisticated style and iconography, probably derived from the eastern Mediterranean. The main inscriptions are in Latin, but running round the edge is a poem written in the Northumbrian dialect in runic figures. However, it's the biblical carvings on the main face that really catch the eye, notably Mary Magdalene washing the feet of Jesus. While you're in the village, you might fancy popping into the **Savings Bank Museum** (Tues–Sat 10am–4pm; free; ⑩ www.savingsbanksmuseum.co.uk) that celebrates the world's first-ever savings bank, a community self-help project established in 1810.

Your best bet for **accommodation** is the comfortable *Kirklands Country House Hotel* (☎ 01387/250677, ⑩ www.kirklandscountryhousehotel.co.uk; ④), the old manse right next to the church.

New Abbey and around

NEW ABBEY is a tidy little one-street village, eight miles south of Dumfries, that originally evolved in order to service its giant neighbour, **Sweetheart**

Abbey (April–Sept daily 9.30am–6.30pm; Oct–March Mon–Wed, Sat & Sun 9.30am–4.30pm; HS; £2), which now lies romantically ruined to the east. The abbey takes its unusual name from its founder, Devorgilla de Balliol, Lady of Galloway, who carried the embalmed heart of her husband, John Balliol (of Oxford college fame) around with her for the remaining 22 years of her life – she is buried, with the casket, in the presbytery. The last of the Cistercian abbeys to be founded in Scotland, in 1273, Sweetheart is dominated by the red sandstone ruins of the abbey church, which remains intact, albeit minus its roof. Standing in the grassy nave, flanked by giant compound piers supporting early Gothic arches, and above them a triforium, it's easy to imagine what the completed church must have looked like. The central square tower is a massive, brutal structure fitted with battlements, and looks as if it was built more for defence than for the glory of God. However, the elaborate tracery in some of the windows and the flamboyant corbelling below the central tower clearly marks a change from the austere simplicity of earlier Cistercian foundations. The rest of the conventual buildings are revealed only in the outline of the foundations, with the exception of the precinct wall, to the north and east of the abbey. This massive structure – up to ten feet high and four feet wide in places – is made from rough granite boulders, and is the most complete of its kind in the country.

The *Abbey Cottage* **tearoom** is renowned for its good coffee, teas and home-made cakes, and enjoys an unrivalled view over the abbey. At the centre of the village, two **pubs** face one another across a cobbled square: the *Abbey Arms* (☎01387/850489, ✉enquiries@abbeyarms.netlineuk.net; ❸), and the *Criffel Inn* (☎01387/850244, ⓦwww.criffelinn.com; ❸); both have seats outside, serve pub food and do B&B. Just beyond the pubs, but before the bridge, is the eighteenth-century water-powered **New Abbey Corn Mill** (times as for abbey; HS; £3). Try and time your visit to coincide with one of the daily demonstrations (noon & 3pm), when the custodian puts the mill machinery through its paces. The mill pond, above the mill, is a lovely spot for a picnic.

Around New Abbey

Just outside New Abbey on the Dumfries road lies **Shambellie House** (April–Oct daily 10am–5pm; ⓦwww.nms.ac.uk/costume; £3), a Scots Baronial pile designed by David Bryce in 1856, but only completed after a great deal of wrangling between architect and client. William Stewart, who built the house, clearly had big ideas, but was endlessly trying to reduce his costs – in the end, he fell out with everyone involved in the project, and paid out more than he had saved on legal fees. The house isn't, in fact, all that grand inside, so it's only worth visiting if you want to see the dummies who now inhabit the rooms, dressed to the nines in a variety of costumes from the Victorian era to the 1920s, all collected by William Stewart's great-grandson. There's also a tearoom, with tables outside overlooking the house's lawn, garden and wooded grounds.

One and a half miles south of New Abbey, Ardwell Mains Farm marks the start of the walk up **Criffel** (1864ft), a hump-backed whale of a hill – the biggest for miles around – which offers great views of the Borders and the Lake District. A couple of miles further on, at Kirkbean, a small turning on the left leads to **John Paul Jones Museum** (April–June & Sept Tues–Sun 10am–5pm; July & Aug daily 10am–5pm; ⓦww.jpj.demon.co.uk; £2), where the "father of the US Navy" was born into extreme poverty in 1747. Jones was seen by the British at the time as a pirate, but he is revered by Americans. Here, you can learn about his eventful and varied naval career, which began when he went to sea at the age of 13, and which, interestingly enough, included a spell in the Russian navy.

Nithsdale

North of Dumfries, the A76 and the railway line to Kilmarnock travel the length of **Nithsdale**, whose gentle slopes and old forests hide one major attraction: the massive, many-turreted seventeenth-century mansion of **Drumlanrig Castle** near **Thornhill**, just one of three substantial country seats owned by the duke of Buccleuch. At the opposite end of the class system were the miners working the lead mines in the neighbouring Lowther Hills, to the east, commemorated in the intriguing **Museum of Lead Mining** in Wanlockhead.

Thornhill and Moniaive

Fourteen miles north of Dumfries, the A76 passes through **THORNHILL**, whose exceptionally wide, straight and leafy main street is lined with handsome, prosperous Victorian villas, all built in the local red sandstone. Unfortunately, since the main street is also the A76 Dumfries–Kilmarnock trunk road, the peace is usually shattered by traffic. One positive reason for stopping is to pop into the *Buccleuch and Queensberry Hotel* (℡01848/330215, ⓦwww.buccleuchhotel .co.uk; ❸), a hunting, shooting and fishing **inn** built in pink sandstone at the main crossroads, whose plush, comfortable bar serves a whole range of superb real ales and very good pub food. For **accommodation**, head south down the A76 for a couple of miles to the *Trigony House Hotel* (℡01848/331211, ⓦwww. trigonyhotel.co.uk; ❺), an ivy-clad, pink sandstone former shooting lodge, with a very pleasant, warm atmosphere and a good, moderately expensive Scottish **restaurant**.

For a more peaceful setting, head west along the A702 through the village of **PENPONT**, home to the studio of artist **Andy Goldsworthy**, who uses the flotsam and jetsam of nature to create his works of art, one of which, a cairn, can be seen on the left as you enter the village from the south. After eight miles, you'll come to the conservation village of **MONIAIVE**, a tiny settlement of narrow streets and antiquated cottages, which nestles between several glens and offers lovely walks and cycle rides. The *Green Tea House* (closed Mon), in a former bank, can provide organic home-made snacks. Further west still lies the wilderness of the Galloway Forest Park (see p.236).

Drumlanrig Castle

Three miles north of Thornhill, **Drumlanrig Castle** (May & June daily except Fri noon–4pm; July & Aug daily noon–4pm; ⓦwww.buccleuch.com; £7; gardens and country park only £3) is not a castle at all, but the grandiose stately home of the Duke of Buccleuch and Queensberry, one of the country's wealthiest men. Visitors approach via an impressive driveway that sweeps up an avenue of lime trees to the pink sandstone house with its forest of cupolas, turrets and towers. The front is graced by a charming horseshoe-shaped stair-way – a welcome touch of informality to the stateliness of the structure behind. The highlights of the richly furnished interior are really the paintings in the oak-panelled staircase hall. The castle's most famous works are **Rembrandt**'s *Old Woman Reading*, an extremely sensitive composition dappling the shadow of the subject's hood against her white surplice, and **Hans Holbein**'s formal portrait of Sir Nicholas Carew, Master of the Horse to Henry VIII; the *Madonna with the Yarnwinder* by **Leonardo da Vinci** was, sadly, stolen in 2003. Other artists to look out for, amidst the innumerable family portraits, include Joost van Cleef, Murillo, Jan Gossaert and Van Dyck. Also be sure to check out the striking 1950s portrait of the present duchess, all debutante coiffure and high-society décolletage, by John Merton in the morning room, and, in the serving room, John Ainslie's *Joseph Florence, Chef*, a sharply observed and dynamic portrait much liked by Walter Scott.

As well as the house, Drumlanrig offers a host of other attractions, including formal **gardens** and a forested **country park** (April–Sept daily 11am–5pm). The old stableyard beside the castle contains a visitor centre, a few shops, the inevitable tearoom and also a useful **bike rental** outlet, as the park is criss-crossed by footpaths and cycle routes. There's also a **cycle museum** filled with every type of bike from MTBs to a replica of the first-ever pedal bike, invented in 1839 by local boy Kirkpatrick MacMillan. Before you go for a stroll round the gardens, pick up the tree trail leaflet, which will point out significant trees, such as the red oak planted by Neil Armstrong – and don't miss out on the Victorian **Heather Hut**, either. If you're heading here by bus from Dumfries or Ayr, bear in mind it's a one-and-a-half-mile walk from the road to the house.

Sanquhar and the Lowther Hills

Leaving Drumlanrig, the A76 slips through the wooded hills of Nithsdale, passing the turning to Wanlockhead (see below) en route to **SANQUHAR**, a trim market town and the first stop on the railway line north from Dumfries. Like Thornhill, it suffers from having the main Dumfries–Kilmarnock trunk road pass right through it. Jutting out into the main street is Sanquhar's most notable building, the **Tolbooth** (April–Sept Tues–Sat 10am–1pm & 2–5pm, Sun 2–5pm; free), a handsome Georgian town house with a pedimented facade, a double-side forestair, a square clocktower and finished off with an octagonal cupola; now a museum, it features the unique and world-famous black-and-white knitting of the region. Sanquhar's other claim to fame is the bow-windowed shop at 39–41 High St, which claims to be the oldest working **post office** in Britain, dating from 1712.

Instead of continuing north into Ayrshire from Sanquhar, you could head east into the nearby **Lowther Hills**, which separate Nithsdale from the M74. This wild landscape of tightly clustered peaks, bare until the heather blooms, hides fast-flowing burns and narrow valleys – a dramatic terrain once known as "God's Treasure House" on account of its gold and silver ores. These mineral deposits were much sought after by the impoverished kings of Scotland, who banned their export and claimed a monopoly – draconian measures that only encouraged smuggling. There was **lead** here too, mined from Roman times right up to the 1950s, and used in the manufacture of pottery and glass. The only way to reach Leadhills and Wanlockhead by public transport is on the once- or twice-daily service from Sanquhar.

Wanlockhead

Remote and windswept **WANLOCKHEAD**, at 1500ft, is the highest village in Scotland, and is now home to the fascinating open-air **Museum of Lead Mining** (daily: April–June, Sept & Oct 11am–4.30pm; July & Aug 10am–5pm; Ⓦ www.leadminingmuseum.co.uk; £5), which deserves a good hour or two of your time. After a brief foray into the spruce visitor centre, which traces the development of the industry and its workforce, you should don your hard hat and go on a guided tour of the underground **Lochnell Mine**. The site's heritage trail takes you past a rare example of a wooden beam engine and all sorts of industrial bits and pieces, mostly dating from the late 1950s when government grants sponsored a brief revival in lead mining; the earlier workings were closed

△ Miners' cottages, Leadhills

in the 1930s. You should also visit the remarkable eighteenth-century **Miners' Library**, its 3000-plus volumes purchased from the voluntary subscriptions of its members, and try your hand at gold panning (Wanlockhead hosts the national gold-panning championships and runs courses on gold panning).

Most weekends, you can travel from Wanlockhead to the neighbouring mining village of Leadhills on the **Leadhills & Wanlockhead Railway** (Easter–Sept Sat & Sun 11am–5pm; ⓦ www.leadhillsrailway.co.uk; £3), Britain's highest adhesion railway. The terraced cottages of this classic "company town" were built by the mine owners for their employees, but the boom years ended in the 1830s, since when the village has been left pretty much to itself. Untouched by the heritage industry, Leadhills has an authentic, disconsolate air, born of its wilderness surroundings. Wanlockhead straddles the Southern Upland Way, and is thus blessed with an SYHA **hostel** (ⓣ0870/004 1157, ⓦwww.syha.org.uk; April–Sept), sited in the old mine surgeon's house.

The Colvend coast and beyond

The **Colvend coast**, twenty miles or so southwest of Dumfries, is probably one of the finest stretches of coastline along the so-called "Scottish Riviera". The best approach is via the A710, which heads south through New Abbey (see p.224), before cutting across a handsome landscape of rolling farmland to the aptly named **SANDYHILLS**, little more than a scattering of houses dotted around a sandy bay overlooking the tidal mudflats of the Solway Firth. There's a very well-equipped **campsite**, the *Sandyhills Leisure Park* (ⓣ01387/780257; April–Oct), down by the beach, plus a couple of lovely **guesthouses** with stunning views over the bay: *Craigbittern* (ⓣ01387/780247, ⓦwww.smoothhound.co.uk; ❸), an imposing greystone pile, and the nearby Edwardian villa of *Cairngill House* (ⓣ01387/780681, ⓦwww.cairngill.co.uk; March to mid-Nov; ❸).

A mile or so further west, a side road leads down to **ROCKCLIFFE**, a beguiling little place of comfortable villas sheltered beneath wooded hills and nestled around a beautiful rocky, sand and shell bay. Excellent B&B **accommodation** and self-catering is available at *Millbrae House* (☎01556/630217; March–Oct; ❷), a whitewashed cottage a short stroll from the bay. For **camping**, the *Castle Point Caravan Site* (☎01556/630248; March–Oct) is in a secluded spot, just south of the village, a stone's throw from the seashore. The *Garden House* tearoom (closed Mon & Tues), at the entrance to the village, can give you simple sustenance and has a garden at the back.

For vehicles, Rockcliffe is a dead end, but it's the start of a pleasant half-hour walk along the Jubilee Path to neighbouring **KIPPFORD**, a tiny, lively yachting centre strung out along the east bank of the Urr estuary. En route, the path passes the Celtic hill fort of the **Mote of Mark**, a useful craggy viewpoint. At low tide you can walk over the Rough Firth causeway from the shore below across the mudflats to **Rough Island**, a humpy twenty-acre bird sanctuary owned by the National Trust for Scotland – it's out of bounds in May and June when the resident terns and oystercatchers are nesting. The reward for your gentle stroll is a drink and a bite to eat at the ever-popular *Anchor Hotel* (☎01556/620205; ❸), on Kippford's waterfront, which serves tasty **bar meals** – be sure to check the specials board. If you need to stay the night, though, you might find it more peaceful at the *Rosemount* (☎01556/620214; ⓦwww .rosemountguesthouse.com; Feb–Nov; ❷), an excellent **guesthouse** close by on the seafront.

Dalbeattie and around

Beyond Kippford, the A710 heads north to **DALBEATTIE**, an old-fashioned town that sees few tourists, though you'll find a reasonable range of shops and supermarkets. What is distinctive about Dalbeattie is the grey granite, used throughout the town, which is now the subject of an annual **Festival of Granite** in mid-September. From Dalbeattie, you can continue along the attractive though circuitous coastal road, the A711, to Kirkcudbright (see p.231), taking a brief signposted detour en route down a narrow country lane to see the evocative remains of **Orchardton Tower** (free), a mid-fifteenth-century fortified tower house, whose circular design is unique in Scotland, but common across the water in Ireland.

A little further on, just before you enter the village of **AUCHENCAIRN** (ⓦwww.auchencairn.org.uk), a side road leads off down the coast to the award-winning *Balcary Bay Hotel* (☎01556/640217, ⓦwww.balcary-bay-hotel.co.uk; ❽), a whitewashed pile with sky-blue trimmings, typical of the area, which enjoys a stunning location at the water's edge overlooking Hestan Island, once a notorious smugglers' hideout. The restaurant has won several awards, but its lunches are reasonably priced; dinner is more expensive. Alternatively, for a fraction of the price, you can **stay** nearby at the more modest *Balcary Mews* (☎01556/640276; ❸), just before you reach the hotel, or at *Bluehill*, a beautiful farmhouse B&B just west of Auchencairn (☎01556/640228; ❷), and have a drink in the *Old Smugglers Inn*, in the centre of the village.

Another five miles or so west along the A711 are the greystone ruins of **Dundrennan Abbey** (April–Sept daily 9.30am–6pm; Oct Mon–Wed, Sat & Sun 9.30am–4.30pm; Nov–March Sat & Sun 9.30am–4.30pm; HS; £2), hidden in the village of the same name. Founded in 1142, Dundrennan was the mother house of the local Cistercian abbeys of Sweetheart and Glenluce, and was clearly the grandest of the lot, even though it's now reduced to just its transepts. The surviving windows show the classic transition from the rounded arches of the Romanesque period to the pointed arches of the early Gothic. The chief treasures of the abbey are the chapter house's finely carved cusped portal, and the medieval effigy of a tonsured abbot in the northwest corner of the nave; he was murdered – hence the faded dagger in his chest – and the figure being trampled at his feet is thought to be his assassin, in the process of being disembowelled. **Bus** #501 connects Dundrennan with Kirkcudbright (not Sun).

Castle Douglas and around

The man responsible for the late eighteenth-century grid-plan streets of **CASTLE DOUGLAS**, (ⓦwww.castledouglas.net), eighteen miles southwest of Dumfries, was William Douglas, a local lad who made a fortune trading in the West Indies. Douglas had ambitious plans to turn his town into a prosperous industrial and commercial centre, but, like his scheme to create an extensive Galloway canal system, it didn't quite work. Still, thanks to Douglas, the town now has a distinctive, dead-straight main street, **King Street**, that slopes down past the landmark clocktower, built in a mixture of red sandstone and grey granite that's typical of the town. Most folk come here simply to visit the nearby attractions of Threave Garden and Castle (see below), and there's no real need to linger any longer than you have to in the town itself – though it's pleasant enough – unless you wish to go on a guided tour of the independent **Sulwath Micro-brewery** (Mon–Sat 10am–4pm; ⓦwww.sulwathbrewers.co.uk; £3.50), hidden down an alleyway at 209 King St; you can also sample their beers on draught at the nearby *Douglas Arms Hotel*.

The **tourist office** (April–June, Sept & Oct Mon–Sat 10am–4.30pm, Sun 11am–4pm; July & Aug Mon–Sat 10am–6pm, Sun 11am–5pm; ⓣ01556/502611) is at the top end of King Street. All the old coaching inns on King Street offer **accommodation**, but you're better off trying one of the well-built Victorian guesthouses out on Ernespie Road, such as *Albion House* (ⓣ01556/502360; March–Oct; ❷), at no. 49; just to the south of Castle Douglas, the *Smithy House* (ⓣ01556/503841, ⓦwww.smithyhouse.co.uk; ❸) is a nicely converted smiddy overlooking Loch Carlinwerk. Campers should make for the *Lochside* **campsite** (ⓣ01556/502949; Easter–Oct), beside Loch Carlingwark, a short walk from the bottom of King Street down Marle Street. The best place to grab a bite **to eat** is *Designs* (ⓦwww.designsgallery.co.uk; closed Sun), a café at the back of an arts and crafts shop and gallery at 179 King St, with a lovely conservatory and garden and serving great ciabattas and bruschettas and decent coffee. For a picnic, you can get the most delicious ciabatta rolls from Purdies Delicatessen at 173 King St. **Bike rental** – useful for getting out to Threave – is available from the Castle Douglas Cycle Centre on Church St (ⓣ01556/504542; closed Thurs & Sun). For weekend **entertainment**, find out what's on at the Lochside Theatre (ⓣ01556/504506, ⓦwww.lochsidetheatre.co.uk), housed in the former Church of St Andrew, two blocks east of King Street down Marle Street; the theatre hosts gigs and shows films.

Threave Garden

Threave Garden (daily 9.30am to sunset; NTS; £5), the premier horticultural sight in Dumfries and Galloway, is a pleasant mile or so's walk or cycle south of Castle Douglas, along the shores of Loch Carlingwark. The garden features a magnificent spread of flowers and woodland, sixty acres subdivided into more than a dozen areas, from the old-fashioned herbaceous borders of the Walled Garden to the brilliant banks of rhododendrons in the Woodland Garden and the ranks of primula, astilbe and gentian in the Peat Garden. In springtime, thousands of visitors turn up for the flowering of more than two hundred types of daffodil.

The **visitor centre** (daily: April–Oct 9.30am–5.30pm; Feb, March, Nov & Dec 10am–4pm) has maps of and an exhibition about the garden and the surrounding estate (also NTS property), though the restaurant's fruit pies and outdoor terrace are more immediately appealing. Threave is also home to the School of Practical Gardening, whose postgraduate students occupy one floor of **Threave House**, a hulking Scots Baronial mansion built by the Gordon family in 1872, and now restored to its 1938 condition; it can be visited on a guided tour (daily 11am–4pm; joint house and garden ticket £9).

Threave Castle

The nicest way of reaching **Threave Castle** (April–Sept daily 9.30am–6.30pm; HS; £3), a mile or so north of the gardens, is to walk through the estate. However you decide to get there, you should follow the signs to the Open Farm (which has the *Bothy* tearoom serving soup and sandwiches), from where it's a lovely fifteen-minute walk down to the River Dee, where you ring a brass bell for the boat to take you over to the flat and grassy island on which the stern-looking tower house stands. Built for one of the Black Douglases, Archibald the Grim, first Lord of Galloway and third Earl of Douglas, in around 1370, the fortress was among the first of its kind, a sturdy, rectangular structure completed shortly after the War of Independence when clan feuding spurred a frenzy of castle building. During the reign of James II, there was a sustained campaign to crush the Black Douglases: the 9-year-old king was present at the Black Dinner in Edinburgh Castle when the sixth earl of Douglas was executed. Some years later, in Stirling, after another dinner, the king personally murdered the eighth earl.

The rickety curtain wall to the south and east is all that remains of the **artillery fortifications**, hurriedly constructed in the 1450s by the ninth earl in a desperate – and unsuccessful – attempt to defend the castle against James II's new-fangled cannon. The castle fell to the English in 1545 and 1588, but a royalist garrison withstood a thirteen-week siege by the Covenanters in 1640, only surrendering after orders from the king. As at Caerlaverock, the castle was then partially dismantled, but enough remains of the interior to make out its general plan, beginning with the storage areas and spitefully gloomy **prison** in the basement. Up above, the entrance level was once reached from the outside by removable timber stairs, while inside a spiral staircase ascended to the upper floors; you can still make out its course. The **roof** was flat to accommodate stone-throwing machinery, and had a projecting wooden gallery to enable the defenders to drop nasty objects onto the heads of the attackers: from the outside you can clearly see the holes where the timber supports were lodged.

Kirkcudbright and around

KIRKCUDBRIGHT – pronounced "kir-coo-bree" (@ www.kirkcudbright .co.uk) – hugging the muddy banks of the River Dee ten miles southwest of Castle Douglas, is the only major town along the Solway coast to have retained a working harbour. In addition, it has a ruined castle and the most attractive of

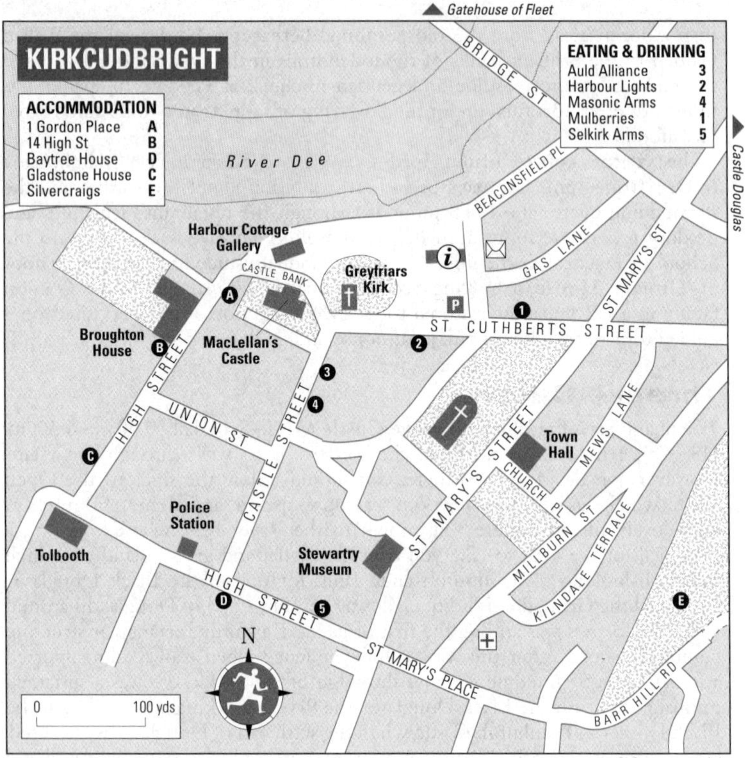
Gatehouse of Fleet
KIRKCUDBRIGHT
ACCOMMODATION
1 Gordon Place A
14 High St B
Baytree House D
Gladstone House C
Silvercraigs E
EATING & DRINKING
Auld Alliance 3
Harbour Lights 2
Masonic Arms 4
Mulberries 1
Selkirk Arms 5
Castle Douglas
River Dee
BRIDGE ST
BEACONSFIELD PL
GAS LANE
ST MARY'S ST
Harbour Cottage Gallery
CASTLE BANK
Greyfriars Kirk
ST CUTHBERTS STREET
Broughton House
MacLellan's Castle
HIGH STREET
UNION ST
CASTLE STREET
ST MARY'S STREET
Town Hall
MEWS LANE
CHURCH PL
MILLBURN ST
KILNDALE TERRACE
Police Station
Tolbooth
Stewartry Museum
HIGH STREET
ST MARY'S PLACE
BARR HILL RD
N
0
100 yds
© Crown copyright

town centres, a charming medley of simple two-storey cottages with medieval pends, Georgian villas and Victorian town houses, all built in a mixture of sandstone, granite and brick, and attractively painted, with their windows and quoins picked out. It comes as little surprise, then, to find that Kirkcudbright became something of a magnet for Scottish artists from the late nineteenth century onwards. It may no longer live up to the tourist board's "artists' town" label, but it does have a rich artistic heritage that's easy and enjoyable to explore.

The Town

The most surprising sight in Kirkcudbright is **MacLellan's Castle** (April–Sept daily 9.30am–6pm; HS; £2.50), a pink-flecked sixteenth-century tower house that sits at one end of the High Street by the harbourside. Part fortified keep and part spacious mansion, the castle was built in the 1570s for the then Provost of Kirkcudbright, Sir Thomas MacLellan of Bombie, when a degree of law and order permitted the aristocracy to relax its former defensive preoccupations and satisfy its increasing desire for comfort and domestic convenience. As a consequence, chimneys have replaced battlements at the wall-heads and windows begin at the ground floor. Nevertheless, the walls remain impressively thick, and there are a handful of wide-mouthed gun loops, though these are haphazard affairs designed to deter intruders rather than beat off an invading army. The interior is well preserved from the kitchen (complete with bread oven), and vaulted storerooms in the basement, to the rabbit warren of well-appointed domestic apartments above. Keep an eye out for the spyhole known as the "**laird's lug**", behind the fireplace of the Great Hall. MacLellan's son, Robert, rose to even greater social heights than his father, but amassed so many debts that on his death in 1639, the house had to be sold off along with most of the family's estate, and from then on the place was more or less abandoned. Sir Thomas MacLellan is buried in the neighbouring **Greyfriars Kirk** (currently closed for major refurbishment), where his tomb is an eccentrically crude attempt at Neoclassicism; it even incorporates parts of someone else's gravestone.

Near the castle, on the L-shaped High Street, is **Broughton House** (daily: Easter, July & Aug 10am–5pm; April–June, Sept & Oct noon–5pm; Feb & March garden only daily 11am–4pm; NTS; £8), a smart Georgian town house set back from, and elevated above, the surrounding terraces. This is the former home of the artist, **Edward Hornel** (1863–1933), an important member of the late nineteenth-century Scottish art scene, who spent his childhood a few doors down the street, and returned in 1900 to establish an artists' colony in Kirkcud-bright with some of the "Glasgow Boys" (see p.302). Hornel bought Broughton House in 1901 and added a studio and a vast, glass-roofed, mahogany-panelled gallery at the back of the house. The gallery, now filled with the mannered, vibrantly coloured and rather formulaic paintings of girls at play, which he churned out in the latter part of his career, also features a scaled-down plaster cast of the Elgin Marbles decorating the cornice (which determined the size of the room). Note, too the model of the extraordinary war memorial which stands outside MacLellan's Castle, and which Hornel helped to choose. The best example of his work in the house is the early portrait, *Man in a Red Tunic*, which hangs in the dining room (which served as the town library in the 1950s). A trip to Japan in 1893 imbued Hornel with a life-long affection for the country, and his surprisingly large, densely packed, wonderful jewel box **gardens** have a strong Japanese influence.

Before visiting Broughton House, to give you some background information on Kirkcudbright, you should really pay a visit to the town's imposing, church-like **Tolbooth**, with its stone-built clocktower and spire. Built in the 1620s, it used to serve as town council, courthouse, debtors' prison, water supply and town hall: outside on the forestair, you also see the mercat cross and a pair of cast-iron "jougs", in which felons were publicly displayed. Unfortunately, the interior has much less character, but it does house the **Tolbooth Art Centre** (May–Sept Mon–Sat 10am–6pm, Sun 2–5pm; Oct–April Mon–Sat 11am–4pm; £1.50), which has, on the upper floor, a small permanent display of works by some of Kirkcudbright's erstwhile resident artists, including Hornel's striking *Japanese Girl* and S.J. Peploe's Colourist view of the Tolbooth. The ten-minute video gives you a good, succinct overview of Kirkcudbright's artistic heritage. The town's artistic connections are furthered by its several art galleries, includ-ing the picturesque **Harbour Cottage Gallery**, near the castle, which hosts a variety of temporary exhibitions (March–Nov Mon–Sat 10.30am–12.30pm & 2–5pm, Sun 2–5pm; £1).

Don't miss the **Stewartry Museum** on St Mary Street (June–Sept Mon–Sat 10am–5pm, Sun 2–5pm; Oct–May Mon–Sat 11am–4pm; free), where, packed into a purpose-built Victorian building, hundreds of local exhibits illuminate the life and times of the Solway coast. It's an extraordinary collection: cabinets crammed with anything from glass bottles, weaving equipment, pipes, pictures and postcards to stuffed birds, pickled fish and the tricornered hats once worn by town officials. There are also examples of book jackets designed by Jessie King and E.A. Taylor, two of Hornel's coterie. Incidentally, the "Stewartry" is the old name for the former county of Kirkcudbrightshire, as for centuries it was ruled by a royal steward appointed by the Balliol family.

Around Kirkcudbright

There are a few minor sights just outside Kirkcudbright where you could while away bad weather and/or entertain the kids. The most interesting is the **Tongland Power Station** (late May to mid-Sept Mon–Sat 10am–5pm; July & Aug also Sun; £2.50), whose hydroelectric turbines and generators are housed in a fine Art Deco building a couple of miles up the River Dee. More appealing to children is the local **Wildlife Park** (Jan & Dec Sat & Sun 10am–4pm; Feb–Nov daily 10am–dusk; ⓦwww.gallowaywildlife.co.uk; £4.50), a mile or so up the B727 east of Kirkcudbright. Lesser pandas, collared peccaries and Scottish wildcats are just some of the animals you can expect to see, and you can feed the goats, deer and llama – and have an encounter with a snake.

Practicalities

Buses to Kirkcudbright stop by the harbour car park, next to the **tourist office** (April–June, Sept & Oct Mon–Sat 10am–5pm, Sun noon–4pm; July & Aug Mon–Sat 9.30am–6pm, Sun 10am–5pm; ☎01557/330494), where you can get help finding a place to stay, a service you will probably need in high season. If you fancy a view of Kirkcudbright from the water, there are daily **boat trips** from the slipway near Broughton House.

The town has some excellent **accommodation** choices, worth booking in advance: one of the best is *14 High St* (☎01557/330766, ⓔ14highstreet@kirk cudbright.co.uk; April–Sept; ❸), next door to Broughton House, with a garden overlooking the river, followed by *Baytree House*, at no. 110 (☎01557/330824, ⓦwww.baytreehouse.net; ❹), another Georgian house with comfortable rooms, good cooking and a beautiful garden with sundeck, or *Gladstone House* (☎01557/331734, ⓔhilarygladstone@aol.com; ❹), yet another Georgian house set back slightly from the street; cheaper B&B can be had from *1 Gordon Place* (☎01557/330472, ❷), at the castle end of the High Street. The *Silvercraigs* caravan and **campsite** (☎01557/330123; Easter to late Oct) is five or ten minutes' walk from the centre down St Mary's Street and Place, on a bluff overlooking town. Alternatively, you could head to the *Seaward* caravan and campsite at Brighouse Bay (☎01557/331079, ⓦwww.gillespie-leisure.co.uk; March–Oct), six miles southwest of town, offering the full range of facilities in a new leisure complex.

Kirkcudbright is strangely limited when it comes to **restaurants**. Top choice is the *Auld Alliance*, 5 Castle St (☎01557/330569), a superior, if pricey, restaurant offering an old-fashioned fusion of French and Scottish cuisine, where you need to book ahead. Otherwise, there's the usual bar food at the Best Western-run *Selkirk Arms Hotel* on the High Street, which boasts a large garden out the back. There are also several decent daytime **cafés**: try *Mulberries*, on St Cuthbert Street, or, for more substantial fare, *Harbour Lights*, further up the street (open Fri & Sat eve in season). For a **drink**, the busy *Masonic Arms*, on Castle Street, pulls a reasonable pint of real ale. Kirkcudbright has a small **jazz festival** in mid-June and a host of **summer festivities** in the middle of August.

Gatehouse of Fleet

Like Castle Douglas, **GATEHOUSE OF FLEET** (ⓦwww.gatehouse-of -fleet.co.uk), ten miles west of Kirkcudbright, has a distinctive long, straight main street. However, the quiet streets of Gatehouse have none of the life and bustle of Castle Douglas. By contrast, in the late eighteenth and early nineteenth century, the town was a thriving industrial centre with cotton mills, shipbuilding and a brewery. The man who made all this happen (and made himself immeasurably rich in the process) was the local laird James Murray (1727–99). Yorkshire mill owners provided the industrial expertise, imported engineers designed aqueducts to improve the water supply, and dispossessed crofters – and their children – contributed the labour. Between 1760 and 1790, Murray achieved much success, but his custom-built town failed to match its better-placed rivals. By 1850 the boom was over, the town was bypassed by the railway, the mills slipped into disrepair, and nowadays tiny Gatehouse is sustained by tourism and forestry.

It's the country setting that sets Gatehouse apart, rather than any particular sight. As at Castle Douglas, the sloping whitewashed High Street has a landmark clocktower, in this case an incongruous free-standing one, built in grey granite and topped by strange mitre-shaped crenellations. More picturesque is Ann Street, beside the tower, at the end of which you can gain access to the wooded grounds of **Cally House Gardens** (Easter–Sept Tues–Fri 2–5.30pm, Sat & Sun 10am–5.30pm; Ⓦwww.callygardens.co.uk; £1.50). A palatial Neoclassical country mansion (now the *Cally Palace Hotel*), Cally House was built in the 1760s, and is proof positive of the fortune already owned by the Murray family, even before James Murray began his cotton enterprise. Back in town, the **Mill on the Fleet** (April–Oct daily 10.30am–5pm; £1.50), opposite the car park by the river at the bottom of the High Street, traces the economic and social history of Gatehouse and Galloway from inside a restored grey granite bobbin mill; its café has an attractive terrace overlooking the river.

Perched on a hill a mile southwest of Gatehouse stands **Cardoness Castle** (April–Sept daily 9.30am–6.30pm; Oct Mon–Wed, Sat & Sun 9.30am–4.30pm; Nov–March Sat & Sun 9.30am–4.30pm; HS; £2.50), a classic late fifteenth-century fortified tower house. It once edged the Water of Fleet river, but this was canalized long ago and today Cardoness overlooks the minor road linking Gatehouse with the busy A75, nearby. Ancient seat of the McCullochs, it was mortgaged and bought by the Gordon family in 1622, a state of affairs that was unacceptable to some of the McCullochs, who subjected the Gordons to extreme acts of violence on more than one occasion. Inside, it has some fashionably decorated fireplaces and plenty of en-suite latrines. The views out to Fleet Bay in the distance are excellent, though, of course, they're even better from the monument at the top of the hill behind the castle.

Also worth a visit are the ruins of **Anwoth Church**, a couple of miles west of Gatehouse. The centre of the old nave is occupied by the ornate seventeenth-century sarcophagus of the Gordon family, decorated with some wonderful wordy, stirring epitaphs, as is the table-top grave of some Covenanter martyrs, to the west of the church, in the atmospheric graveyard.

Practicalities

The **tourist office** (mid-March to June, Sept & Oct Mon–Sat 10am–4.30pm, Sun 11am–4pm; July & Aug Mon–Sat 10am–5.30pm, Sun 10.30am–4.30pm; Ⓣ01557/814212) is situated by the car park by the river. The place to stay is the sumptuous *Cally Palace* **hotel** (Ⓣ01557/814341, Ⓦwww.callypalace .co.uk; closed Jan; ❼), though make sure you're placed in the old house rather than the ugly modern extension, and be sure to take a jacket and tie if you're going to eat there; the *Cally* boasts its own leisure centre, tennis courts and eighteen-hole golf course. **B&B** in Gatehouse itself is available at the terraced *Bobbin Guest House*, 36 High St (℡01557/814229; ❷), or at the *Murray Arms Hotel* (℡01557/814207, Ⓦwww.murrayarms.com; ❺), the old coaching inn next to the clocktower, where Robbie Burns wrote *Scots wha hae*. For good **pub food**, head for the bar or the conservatory of the welcoming *Masonic Arms*, just up Ann Street. For the ultimate array of whiskies, head for the *Anwoth Hotel*, at the bottom of the High Street. The *Gatehouse* **café**, inside the original "Gatehouse", the oldest (and once the only) house in town, serves takeaways and snacks all day, washed down with Sulwath ales from Castle Douglas.

Galloway Forest Park and around

The strange thing about Galloway is that while the area around the coast is all rolling farmland, stately homes, sandy coves and estuarine mudflats, you only have to head north ten or twenty miles and you're transported to the entirely different landscape of the Galloway Hills, an environment of glassy lochs, wooded hills and bare, rounded peaks. Much of this landscape is now incorporated into the **Galloway Forest Park**, Britain's largest forest park, which stretches all the way from the southern part of Ayrshire right down to Gatehouse of Fleet, laid out on land owned by the Forestry Commission. Few people actually live here, but the park is a major draw for hikers and mountain bikers, who are both well catered for with lots of trails clearly marked out. Accommodation is thin on the ground in the park itself, except for the Forestry Commission campsite in Glen Trool, though **Newton Stewart**, to the southwest, and **New Galloway**, in the **Glenkens** to the east; both places have hostels and B&Bs and are feasible to use as bases for exploring the park.

Newton Stewart

NEWTON STEWART, (Ⓦwww.newtonstewart.org), famous for its salmon and trout fishing, is an unassuming market town on the west bank of the River Cree, which used to form the county boundary between Kirkcudbrightshire and Wigtownshire. As the largest town within easy reach of the Galloway Forest Park, with some good accommodation choices and bus connections, it's a popular choice as a base for hikers and cyclists. Originally known as Fordhouse of Cree, it was renamed in the seventeenth century by the local laird, William Stewart. A hundred years later, the estate was bought by William Douglas (of Castle Douglas fame), who preferred Newton Douglas, though neither the name, nor the cotton and carpet industry he established lasted long.

Newton Stewart's most intriguing sight is on the eastern riverbank in what used to be the separate village of Minnigaff, where, a mile or so up Millcroft Road, the big Victorian **Monigaff church** (July & Aug Mon & Fri 2–4.30pm; free) houses three eleventh-century carved grave-slabs. Otherwise, the town's attractions are pretty much confined to the local **museum** (April–Sept daily 2–5pm; £1), situated in the deconsecrated Church of St Andrew, to the west of the main street. There's also a remarkable collection of over fifty dolls' houses on display at **Sophie's Puppenstube and Dolls' House Museum** (Easter–Oct Mon–Sat 10am–4pm; Nov–Easter Tues–Sat 10am–4pm; £2.75; Ⓦwww.sophiesdollshouse.co.uk), located at 29 Queen St, on the road heading west from the main square.

Practicalities

On the main square itself, by the bus station, you'll find the local **tourist office** (April & Oct Mon–Sat 10am–4.30pm; May–Sept Mon–Sat 10am–5pm, Sun 10.30am–4pm; ☎01671/402431), which has plenty of helpful literature. The finest **hotel** is the warm and friendly ⚓ *Creebridge House Hotel* (☎01671/402121, ⊛www.creebridge.co.uk; ❻), in an appealing eighteenth-century granite hunting lodge near the main bridge. It's a haunt of serious anglers and can arrange fishing permits, personal gillies (guides), and even tackle (March to mid-Oct). A cheaper option is to go for one of the substantial red sandstone Victorian villa **B&Bs**, such as *Rowallan House* (☎01671/402520, ⊛www.rowallan.co.uk; ❸), on Corsbie Road, west of the main street up Church Lane, or *Flowerbank* (☎01671/402629, ⊛www.flowerbankgh.com; ❷), a lovely house by the river, on the road to Monigaff church. There's also an SYHA **hostel** (☎0870/004 1142; ⊛www.syha.org.uk; April–Sept) in an old school in Minnigaff, up Millcroft Road from the bridge.

The best place **to eat** is the *Creebridge*, which has a wonderful but pricey restaurant as well as serving great pub food with its real ales. Another, more formal option is to eat at the restaurant at the *Kirroughtree Hotel* (☎01671/402141, ⊛www.kirroughtreehouse.co.uk; mid-Feb to Dec; ❽), a whitewashed mansion surrounded by beautiful gardens of azaleas and rhododendrons on the south-eastern outskirts of town near the A75/A712 junction. It's worth knowing (and somewhat surprising) that Newton Stewart has a **cinema**, known as The Cinema (☎01671/403333, ⊛www.nscinema.co.uk), on the main street.

Galloway Forest Park

The only tarmacked road to cross the **Galloway Forest Park** (⊛www.forestry .gov.uk/gallowayforestpark) is the desolate twenty-mile stretch of the A712 from Newton Stewart east to New Galloway, known as the **Queen's Way**, which cuts through the southern half of the park. Travelling this road, you'll pass all sorts of hiking trails, some the gentlest of strolls, others long-distance treks. For a short walk, stop at the **Grey Mare's Tail Bridge**, about seven miles east of Newton Stewart, where the Forestry Commission has laid out various trails, all delving into the pine forests beside the road, crossing gorges, waterfalls and burns. A mile or so further up the road, you can take a guided tour of the park's **Red Deer Range** (July & Aug Tues & Thurs 11am & 2pm, Sun 2.30pm; £3.50), and a few more miles on, you'll come to **Clatteringshaws Loch**, a reservoir surrounded by pine forest, with a fourteen-mile footpath running right round the loch. This runs past the **Bruce's Stone**, a huge boulder where Robert the Bruce is supposed to have rested after victory over the English. The trail also connects with the Southern Upland Way as it meanders north towards the **Rhinns of Kells**, the bumpy hill range marking the park's eastern boundary. Heading southeast from Clatteringshaws is the **Raiders Road**, a ten-mile-long former drovers' road, now a forest drive popular with cyclists, but sadly also open to cars (April–Oct; £2).

Many hikers aim for **Glen Trool**, at the western edge of the park, about ten miles north of Newton Stewart, where a narrow lane twists the five miles over to **Loch Trool**. Halfway up the loch stands another **Bruce Stone**, this one marking the spot where Robert the Bruce ambushed an English force in 1307 after routing the main body of the army at Solway Moss. From here, there's a choice of magnificent hiking trails, including access to **Merrick** (2746ft), the highest hill in the southwest, as well as lesser tracks laid out by the Forestry Commission. Several longer routes curve round the grassy peaks and icy lochs of the Awful Hand and Dungeon ranges, while another includes part of the Southern Upland Way, which threads through the Minnigaff hills to Clatteringshaws Loch (see above).

Practicalities

There are three **visitor centres** (April–Oct daily 10.30am–5pm; ℡01671/402420, ⓦwww.forestry.gov.uk) in the forest park: at Clatteringshaws by the loch, Glentrool and Kirroughtree, off the A75 east of Newton Stewart. The visitor centres each has a tearoom, several waymarked walks and lots of information on activities and events; you can also pick up a leaflet about the various works of art strewn about the forest park. There are just a few **accommodation** choices around Glentrool: the small *House O'Hill Hotel* (℡01671/840243; ❷), shortly after you turn off the A714, provides basic accommodation, beer, food and, occasionally, great music, or there's the *Glentrool* **campsite** (℡01671/840280, ⓦwww.glentroolholidaypark.co.uk; March–Oct) a little further up the road before you get to Glentrool village.

The Glenkens

At the eastern edge of the forest park is the river valley of the **Glenkens**, which extends south as far as Castle Douglas along Loch Ken, and north along the Water of Ken as far as Carsphairn, a desolate hamlet surrounded by wild moors near the border with Ayrshire. The wooded banks of **Loch Ken** are particularly stunning in autumn, and the area is a haven for the watersports fans. For sailing, windsurfing, kayaking and other outdoor activities, head for the Galloway Sailing Centre (℡01644/420626, ⓦwww.lochken.co.uk), which can organize half-day, full-day and week-long packages; for waterskiing, contact the Loch Ken Waterski School (℡0705/009 2792) further down the loch. To the south of Loch Ken, off the B795 near Laurieston, is Bellymack Hill Farm which has a **Kite Feeding Station** (daily 2pm; £2; ⓦwww.gallowaykitetrail.com), where you're guaranteed a spectacular view of at least a dozen red kites tucking in. The village of **PARTON**, halfway up the loch, is home to the **Scottish Alternative Games** (ⓦwww.scottish-alternative-games.com), which usually take place on the first Sunday in August and feature lots of frivolous and obscure games such as the world "gird'n'cleek" championships, "spinnin' the peerie", "hurlin' the curlin' stane" and snail racing.

　　NEW GALLOWAY, nineteen miles east of Newton Stewart, is a smart little one-street town of stone-built whitewashed cottages at the northern tip of Loch Ken. The *Smithy* **tearoom** (March–Oct; closed Wed), at the bottom of the high street, is a good source of local information, while *Kitty's Tearoom* is excellent for snacks. The award-winning *Cross Keys Hotel* in the High Street is a good place for a pint of real ale. New Galloway's accommodation is undistinguished, and you're better off heading north a few miles to the neighbouring village of St John's Town of Dalry, more commonly known simply as **DALRY**. Its main street has a more spacious feel than New Galloway's, with the Southern Upland Way actually passing through it. The *Lochinvar Hotel* (℡01644/430210, ⓦwww.lochinvarhotel.com; ❷) is an old-fashioned, creeper-clad inn on the road in from New Galloway, while the nearest SYHA **hostel** is a simple barn-like structure at **KENDOON** (℡0870/004 1130, ⓦwww.syha.org.uk; April–Sept), five miles north of Dalry along the B7000. The hostel is about twenty minutes' very pleasant walk through the woods from the A713 to the west; if you're travelling there on the Castle Douglas–Ayr bus, ask the driver to tell you when to get off.

The Machars

The Machars is the name given to the triangular peninsula of rolling farmland and open landscapes south of Newton Stewart. Its title comes from the Gaelic *machair*, which is the name for the low-lying sandy grasslands by the coast. It's a neglected part of the coastline, a bit out on a limb, and with a somewhat disconsolate air. However, you could easily while away an hour or two in **Wigtown**'s various bookshops and, as the birthplace of Scottish Christianity, **Whithorn** is well worth a visit.

Wigtown

Seven miles south of Newton Stewart, **WIGTOWN** (ⓦwww.wigtown -booktown,co,uk) is a tiny place, considering it was once the county town

△ Wigtown "Book Town"

of Wigtownshire. Despite its modest size, it has a remarkable main square, a vast, triangular-shaped affair, its layout unchanged since medieval times. Overlooking and dominating the square and its central bowling green are the gargantuan, rather exotic-looking **County Buildings**, built in French Gothic style, and now home to the town's library. Wigtown has since reinvented itself as "Scotland's National Book Town" (ⓦ www.wigtown-booktown.co.uk), with ten to fifteen **bookshops** occupying some of the modest houses which line the square, and more elsewhere in the vicinity; for a map of their locations, head for the information centre (Mon–Fri 9am–noon & 1–5pm), on the main square. Most are closed on Sundays, the one notable exception being *Readinglasses*, which also has a small **café**. The town also hosts a **literary festival** of some note in late September. It's a five-minute walk from the square down Harbour Street to the tidal flats below, where a simple stone post commemorates two **Covenanter martyrs**, Margaret McLachlan (aged 63) and Margaret Wilson (aged 18), who in 1685 were tied to stakes on the flats and drowned by the rising tide; their tombstones lie in the local churchyard, smothered in stirring epitaphs.

If you're looking for somewhere to eat or sleep, the best thing to do is to head to **BLADNOCH**, a little village by the river a mile or so southwest. Here, by the bridge you'll find a pretty little cottage **B&B**, *The Old Coach House* (ⓣ01988/402316, ⓦ www.bladnoch-guesthouse.co.uk; ❷). Across the road stands the greystone **Bladnoch distillery** (ⓣ01988/402605, ⓦ www .bladnoch.co.uk), Scotland's southernmost whisky distillery, and the only one in the southwest. Resurrected in 2000, having been closed for seven years, Bladnoch offers frequent **guided tours** from its visitor centre daily from 10am, at the end of which you'll get the traditional generous dram (phone first to check times).

Whithorn and around

Fifteen miles south of Wigtown is **WHITHORN** (ⓦ www.whithorn .com), a one-street town which nevertheless occupies an important place in Scottish history, for it is thought that here in 397 **St Ninian** founded the first Christian church north of Hadrian's Wall. According to the Venerable Bede, Ninian built a church in "a manner to which the Britons were not accustomed", and it became known as *Candida Casa*, "a bright and shining place", translated by the southern Picts he had come to convert as "Hwiterne" (White House) – hence Whithorn. No one can be sure where the *Candida Casa* actually stood, and very little is known about Ninian's life, but his tomb at Whithorn soon became a popular place of pilgrimage and, in the twelfth century, a Premonstratensian priory was established to service the shrine. For generations the rich and the royal made the trek here, the last being Mary, Queen of Scots in 1563, but then came the Reformation and the prohibition of pilgrimages in 1581.

These days, it takes a serious leap of the imagination to envisage Whithorn as a medieval pilgrimage centre. For this reason, it's a good idea to start by watching the audiovisual show at the **Whithorn Story** (Easter–Oct daily 10.30am–5pm; £2.70; HS members £1.90), to the right of the pend (arched house) on the main street, which leads to the remains of the priory. In the excellent adjacent exhibition, there's a handful of archeological finds including a lead Viking cat-skinning trough, a carved oak statue of St Ninian, a gold pontifical ring and a copper-gilt crozier; the upstairs Discovery Centre, meanwhile, is aimed primarily at kids and school groups. Heading outside, the dig site is pretty uninspiring, as are the nearby ruins of the nave of **Whithorn Priory**, though the latter does have a couple of finely carved thirteenth-century south-facing doorways. The most compelling early Christian relics found in the vicinity – a whole series of standing crosses and headstones – are housed in the onsite **Whithorn Museum**. The best preserved is the tenth-century Monteith Cross, decorated with interlaced patterns, and displayed immediately as you enter; the oldest is the Latinus stone (labelled no. 1) from the mid-fifth century, the earliest Christian stone in Scotland; while the Petrus stone (labelled no. 2), with its *chi-rho* symbol and Latin inscription "the place of Peter the Apostle", dates from the mid-seventh century. Should you be picnic-less, grab a snack at the Whithorn Dig's *Pilgrims' Tearoom*.

The pilgrims who crossed the Solway to visit St Ninian's shrine landed at the **ISLE OF WHITHORN**, four miles south of Whithorn, no longer an island, but an antique and picturesque little seaport. If you continue to the end of the harbour, you'll pick up signs to the minuscule remains of the thirteenth-century **St Ninian's Chapel**, which some believe was the site of the original *Candida Casa*. You can still follow in the pilgrims' footsteps by walking, cycling or riding the marked **Pilgrim Way** in a hundred-mile round-trip, starting from Glenluce and winding along paths and quiet roads to the Isle of Whithorn. For the less energetic, there's a pleasant twelve-mile round-walk between Whithorn and the Isle of Whithorn, which takes in **St Ninian's Cave**, three miles to the west, where the saint allegedly first put foot on Scottish soil. If you want to **stay**, try the unassuming *Steam Packet Inn* (☎01988/500334, ⓦwww.steampacketinn .com; ❸), right on the quay in Isle of Whithorn; it does pub food that's above average in quality and price, and has a moderately expensive **restaurant**.

The Rhinns of Galloway

West of the Machars, the hilly, hammer-shaped peninsula at the end of the Solway coast, known as the **Rhinns of Galloway**, encompasses two contrasting towns: the grimy port of **Stranraer**, from where there are regular ferries to Northern Ireland, and the beguiling seaside resort of **Portpatrick**. At either end of the peninsula are two lighthouses: one stands above Corsewall Point, and is now home to a luxury hotel, the other stands on the **Mull of Galloway**, a windswept headland at the southwest tip of Scotland, which is home to a vast array of nesting seabirds.

Stranraer and around

No one can say that **STRANRAER** (ⓦwww.stranraer.org) is beautiful, and if you're heading to (or coming from) Ireland, there's really no reason to linger longer than you have to. If you find yourself with time to kill, head for the town's one specific attraction, the **Castle of St John** (Easter to mid-Sept Mon–Sat 10am–1pm & 2–5pm; free), a ruined four-storey tower house built around 1500, which now stands on its own little green halfway down the main street, one block inland from the harbourfront. Inside, several videos trace the history of the castle, which was notorious in the 1680s as the headquarters of Graham of Claverhouse, sheriff of Wigtown and known as "bloody Clavers" for his brutal campaigns against the local Covenanters. Later, the tower was used as a police station and prison, and still retains the old exercise yard on the roof, from which you get great views over the port. If you've yet more time on your hands, pop into the local **Stranraer Museum**

(Mon–Fri 10am–5pm, Sat 10am–1pm & 2–5pm; free), in the Old Town Hall, a distinctive building in vanilla and pistachio colours a short distance west along George Street.

Practicalities

The **train station** is right by the Stena Line **ferry** terminal (℡0870/570 7070, Ⓦwww.stenaline.co.uk) on the East Pier, from where boats depart for Belfast. A couple of minutes' walk away, on Port Rodie, is the **bus station**. Stena Line's fast HSS **catamarans** depart for Belfast from the West Pier on the other side of the harbour. P&O Irish Sea ferries (℡0870/2424 777, Ⓦwww.poirishsea.com) to and from Larne, arrive not in Stranraer, but at the port of **CAIRNRYAN**, some five miles north; note, though, that bus services to Cairnryan are infrequent and aren't integrated with the ferry times.

Stranraer's **tourist office** is at 28 Harbour St (April–Oct 9.30am–5.30pm, Sun 10.30am–4.30pm; Nov–March Mon–Sat 10am–4pm; ℡01776/702595) between the two piers. Should you need **accommodation**, head for the *Harbour Guest House* (℡01776/704626, Ⓦwww.harbourguesthouse.com; ❸), a decent **B&B** on the seafront on Market Street, just a short stroll from either pier. You'll have few problems **eating out** if you're after fish and chips, pizzas or pub grub. *L'Aperitif* on London Road (℡01776/702991) is a friendly Italian restaurant or there's the moderately expensive restaurant of the *North West Castle Hotel* (℡01776/704413, Ⓦwww.northwestcastle.co.uk; ❻), the vast, whitewashed crenellated pile next to the police station on Port Rodie. Built in 1820 as a double bay-fronted house for the Arctic explorer Sir John Ross, who tried in vain to discover the Northwest Passage, and later went in search of Sir John Franklin, the whole place has been vastly extended since then to provide a slightly dowdy, but grandiose place in which to hide away from the rest of Stranraer – it even has its very own indoor curling rink (Oct–April). For **campers**, *Aird Donald Caravan Park* (℡01776/702025, Ⓦwww.aird-donald .co.uk) is ten minutes' walk east of the town centre along London Road, though there are much nicer sites elsewhere on the Rhinns.

A better bet, if you want to splash out on a posh hotel with a wonderful view, is to head out to **Corsewall Point**, eleven miles north of Stranraer, at the northern tip of the Rhinns of Galloway, where the (still functioning) 1815 lighthouse has been incorporated into the luxury ⚲ *Corsewall Lighthouse Hotel* (℡01776/853220, Ⓦwww.lighthousehotel.co.uk; including champagne breakfast ❻). If you don't have your own transport, the owners will collect you from Stranraer, as long as you book in advance.

Castle Kennedy Gardens

The approach to **Castle Kennedy Gardens** (April–Sept daily 10am–5pm; Ⓦwww.castlekennedygardens.co.uk; £4), three miles east of Stranraer, is splendid, passing along a tree-lined avenue which frames the ruined medieval fortress of Castle Kennedy beyond, and then across a palm-fringed canal. The castle forms the centrepiece of the gardens, on a hill squeezed between two lochs, though its ruins can no longer be visited. The 75-acre landscaped gardens, which include a lovely walled garden, stretch west as far as nearby Lochinch Castle, seat of the earl of Stair (and also inaccessible), via a giant lily pond and a stupendous avenue of one hundred-year-old monkey puzzle trees.

Glenluce Abbey

Seven miles east of Castle Kennedy, along the A75, you'll pick up signs for **Glenluce Abbey** (April–Sept daily 9.30am–6.30pm; Oct Mon–Wed, Sat

& Sun 9.30am–4.30pm; Nov–March Sat & Sun 9.30am–4.30pm; HS; £2), whose ruins lie in a gentle valley by the railway, a couple of miles north of the main road. Founded in 1192 as a daughter-house of Dundrennan, Glenluce is the most ruinous of the trio of Cistercian monasteries in the southwest. However, it does have one surviving gem: the fifteenth-century **Chapter House**, which has survived pretty much intact, its ribbed-vault ceiling generating the clearest of acoustics; opera singers practise here and so should you. Notice, too, the green man motif carved into the corbels and ceiling bosses. Popularized in the twelfth century, these grotesques have human or cat-like faces, with large, glaring eyes, frowning foreheads and prominent teeth or fangs. All have greenery sprouting from their faces, a feature that originated with pagan leaf masks and the Celtic concept of fertility. The one other remarkable relic at Glenluce is the monks' water-supply system, whose clay pipes (and even a lidded junction box), can be seen in and around the cloisters. Glenluce is also known for the wizard and alchemist **Michael Scott** who lived here in the thirteenth century, supposedly luring the plague into a secret vault where he promptly imprisoned it. Scott, one-time magician to the court of the Emperor Frederick in Sicily, appears in Dante's *Inferno*.

If you wish **to stay** the night or grab a bite **to eat**, head for the *Kelvin House Hotel* (T01581/300528, Wwww.kelvin-house.co.uk; ❷), a small hotel in the centre of the village, with a convivial bar. Glenluce also has a lovely **campsite** (T01581/300412, Wwww.glenlucecaravan.co.uk; March–Oct) right in the village. Note that there are no direct **buses** to the abbey, but the Glenluce–Newton Stewart bus will drop you off along the main road and you can walk the mile or so from there.

Portpatrick and around

Situated roughly halfway along the west shore of the Rhinns, **PORTPATRICK** has an attractive pastel-painted seafront that wraps itself round a small rocky bay, sheltered by equally rocky cliffs. Until the mid-nineteenth century, when sailing ships were replaced by steamboats, Portpatrick was a thriving seaport, serving as the main embarkation point for Northern Ireland, with coal, cotton and British troops heading in one direction, Ulster cattle and linen in the other. Nowadays, it's a quiet, comely resort enjoyed for its rugged scenery, sea-angling and coastal hikes, including the twenty-minute stroll along the sea cliffs to the shattered ruins of **Dunskey Castle**, an L-shaped tower house dating from the early sixteenth century (take the steep steps near the garages beyond the lighthouse, then follow the public footpath). Walkers can also tackle the first stretch of the 212-mile coast-to-coast **Southern Upland Way** (Wwww.southernuplandway.com), which starts at the quayside.

Practicalities

Portpatrick has several good **hotels** and **guesthouses**, the best of which is the lilac-painted *Waterfront Hotel* (T01776/810800, Wwww.waterfronthotel.co.uk; ❹), which has a refreshingly contemporary look inside. Cheaper choices include the comfortable Victorian *Carlton Guest House*, also on the harbour at 21 South Crescent (T01776/810253; ❷), or the *Knowe Guest House* (T01776/810441, Wwww.theknowe.co.uk; ❶), a bright, white B&B overlooking the harbour, which runs a tearoom in its conservatory. Another option, if you're on an unlimited budget, is *Knockinaam Lodge* (T01776/810471, Wwww.knockinaamlodge.com; ❾), a rather self-consciously exclusive small country-house hotel hidden away in its own private cove a couple of miles south of Portpatrick.

There are several caravan and **campsites** in a row on the hill overlooking Portpatrick and Dunskey Castle, quite a distance from town (and the sea), but accessed by a pleasant walk along the disused railway and cliff-top trail; *Sunnymeade* (℡01776/810293; March–Oct) has the better facilities, but *Castle Bay* (℡01776/810462; March–Oct) has the more informal atmosphere.

Portpatrick's pubs can get pretty lively on the weekend, and all of them offer fairly standard bar meals. The *Crown* on the seafront is probably the cosiest, though the adjacent *Harbour Inn* has real ale. For something more formal and slightly pricier, head to the *Waterfront Bistro* next door. Portpatrick has an annual **folk festival** in the first weekend of September (call ℡01776/810717 or visit Ⓦwww.stranraer.org for more details).

Port Logan

The remoter reaches of the Rhinns of Galloway, extending about twenty miles south from Portpatrick, consist of gorse-covered hills and pastureland crossed by narrow country lanes and dotted with farming hamlets. Of the two shorelines, the west has a sharper, rockier aspect and it's here, just north of the village of **PORT LOGAN**, you'll find the **Logan Botanic Garden** (March–Oct daily 10am–6pm; Ⓦwww.rbge.org.uk; £3.50), a peaceful little outpost of Edinburgh's Royal Botanic Garden. The Gulf Stream keeps the Rhinns almost completely free of frost, allowing subtropical species to grow, including plants from South and Central America, southern Africa, Australasia and the Mediterranean. Be sure to check out the primeval giant Brazilian rhubarb in the Gunnera Bog, and take a wander in the woods to the south, but most of all, you should head for the absolutely enormous walled gardens, where you'll find a water garden, a peat garden (the first ever), and a massive twenty-foot-high beech hedge. A door in the north end of the walled garden leads through into what remains of the privately owned **Logan House Gardens** (March–Aug daily 9.30am–5.30pm; £2), which are about the same size again as the botanic garden, though nothing like as exceptional. Incidentally, the Discovery Centre, back near the entrance, is an excellent wet-weather retreat, with lots of books and natural artefacts to examine under the microscope, and the garden's salad bar is a good place to grab a snack.

On the north side of the bay, on which Port Logan sits, a rough track leads to a castellated fishkeeper's house, where you'll find the **Logan Fish Pond** (daily: Feb–Sept 10am–5pm; Oct 10am–4pm; Ⓦwww.loganfishpond.co.uk; £3.50), created as a fish larder in 1800 by the local laird (from Logan House) by adapting a natural tidal pool created by a blow hole formed during the Ice Age. The water level is now carefully controlled to enable visitors to take a look at the trout, turbot, plaice, eels and rays and feed the coleys; you can also handle starfish and admire the plants. As you leave, be sure to take a look at the nearby bathing hut and pool which was built around the same time as the fish pond.

Mull of Galloway

From Port Logan to the **Mull of Galloway** (Ⓦwww.mull-of-galloway .co.uk), it's another twelve miles, but it's well worth the ride. This precipitous headland, crowned by a classic whitewashed Stevenson lighthouse, from which on a clear day you can see the Isle of Man, as well as the coasts of Ireland and England, really feels like the end of the road. It is, in fact, the southernmost point in Scotland, further south even than Hartlepool in England. It's also a favourite nesting spot for guillemots, razorbills, kittiwakes, shag, fulmar and even a few puffin; skeins of gannets fish here, too, from their gannetry on the Scares, clearly visible to the east. The headland is also an RSPB reserve – good for linnets and twite – with a **visitor centre** (Easter–Sept daily 10.30am–5pm) in a building near the **lighthouse**, which can be climbed on summer weekends (April–Sept Sat & Sun 10am–3.30pm; £2). Just below the car park, perched on the cliff-edge and roofed with turf, is an excellent 🍴 **café**, serving hot meals and snacks (Nov–March closed Wed & Thurs), whose terrace provides armchair bird-watching.

Travel details

Trains

Dumfries to: Carlisle (Mon–Sat 14 daily, 5 on Sun; 40min); Glasgow Central (Mon–Sat 8 daily, 2 on Sun; 1hr 50min); Kilmarnock (Mon–Sat 10 daily, 2 on Sun; 1hr 5min); Sanquhar (Mon–Sat 10 daily, 2 on Sun; 25min); Stranraer (Mon–Sat 2 daily; 3hr).
Stranraer to: Ayr (Mon–Sat 7 daily, 2 on Sun; 1hr 20min); Dumfries (Mon–Sat 2 daily; 3hr); Girvan (Mon–Sat 7 daily, 3 on Sun; 50min); Glasgow (Mon–Sat 7 daily, 2 on Sun; 2hr 10min).

Buses

Castle Douglas to: Dalbeattie (Mon–Sat hourly, Sun every 2hr; 30min); Dalry (Mon–Sat 6 daily, 1 on Sun; 40min); Dumfries (Mon–Sat hourly, Sun every 2hr; 45min); Dundrennan (Mon, Wed & Fri 1 daily; 35min); Kirkcudbright (Mon–Sat hourly, 6 on Sun; 20min); New Galloway (Mon–Sat 6 daily, 1 on Sun; 30min).
Dumfries to: Ayr (Mon–Sat every 2hr; 2hr 10min); Caerlaverock (Mon–Sat every 2hr, 2 on Sun; 30min); Carlisle (Mon–Sat hourly, Sun every 2hr; 1hr 25min); Castle Douglas (Mon–Sat hourly, 4 on Sun; 30–45min); Dalry (Mon–Sat 1–2 daily; 50min); Edinburgh Mon–Sat 4 daily, 2 on Sun; 2hr 40min); Gatehouse of Fleet (Mon–Sat 8 daily, 3 on Sun; 55min–1hr 25min); Gretna (Mon–Sat hourly, Sun every 2hr; 1hr); Kirkcudbright (Mon–Sat hourly, 6 on Sun; 1hr 10min); Moffat (Mon–Sat 8 daily, 4

on Sun; 45min); New Abbey (Mon–Sat hourly, 4 on Sun; 15min); New Galloway (Mon–Sat 1–2 daily; 55min); Newton Stewart (Mon–Sat 8 daily, 2 on Sun; 1hr 30min); Rockcliffe (5 daily; 1hr); Stranraer (Mon–Sat 8 daily, 2 on Sun; 2hr 10min); Thornhill (Mon–Sat hourly, 8 on Sun; 25min).
Gatehouse of Fleet to: Kirkcudbright (Mon–Sat 8–10 daily, 5 on Sun; 20min); Newton Stewart (Mon–Sat 10–12 daily, 3 on Sun; 25min); Stranraer (Mon–Sat every 2hr, 3 on Sun; 1hr 20min).
Kirkcudbright to: Dundrennan (Mon–Sat 6 daily; 10min).
Newton Stewart to: Ayr (Mon–Sat 4–5 daily, 2 on Sun; 2hr 45min); Castle Kennedy (Mon–Sat 15 daily, 5 on Sun; 10min); Glenluce (Mon–Sat 15 daily, 5 on Sun; 15min); Glentrool (Mon–Sat 7 daily, 4 on Sun; 20min); Stranraer (Mon–Sat 15 daily, 5 on Sun; 45min); Whithorn (Mon–Sat hourly, 4 on Sun; 50min); Isle of Whithorn (Mon–Sat hourly, 4 on Sun; 1hr); Wigtown (Mon–Sat hourly, 6 on Sun; 15min).
Sanquhar to: Leadhills (Mon–Sat 5–6 daily; 30min); Wanlockhead (Mon–Sat 5–6 daily; 25min).
Stranraer to: Port Logan (Mon–Sat 6–8 daily, 3 on Sun 3; 45min); Portpatrick (Mon–Sat 7 daily, 3 on Sun; 25min).

Ferries (summer timetable)

Cairnryan to: Larne (7–9 daily; 1hr–1hr 45min).
Stranraer to: Belfast (7–8 daily; 1hr 45min–3hr 15min).

Ayrshire and Arran

CHAPTER 4

Highlights

* **Alloway** The village where poet Robert Burns was born, and the best of many Burns pilgrimage spots in the region. **See p.253**

* **Culzean Castle** Stately home with a fabulous cliff-edge setting, surrounded by acres of gardens and woods reaching down to the shore. **See p.257**

* **Ailsa Craig** Watch baby gannets learn the art of flying and diving for fish. **See p.259**

* **Goat Fell, Arran** Spectacular views over north Arran's craggy mountain range and the Firth of Clyde. **See p.270**

△ Culzean Castle

Ayrshire and Arran

The rolling hills and rich soil of **Ayrshire** make for prime farming country and, as such, are not really top of most visitors' Scottish itinerary. **Ayr**, the county town and birthplace of Robert Burns, is handsome enough, but won't keep you long, and workaday **Kilmarnock**, the largest place in the region, sees virtually no tourists. However, with Ireland only a short ferry ride away, and Glasgow a short train ride away, Ayrshire still gets plenty of visitors. Most wisely stick to the coastline, attracted by the wide, flat, sandy **beaches** and the region's vast number of **golf** courses. South of Ayr, the most obvious points of interest are **Culzean Castle**, with its Robert Adam interior and extensive wooded grounds, and the offshore islands of **Ailsa Craig**, home to the world's second-largest gannetry. North of Ayr, where the towns benefited from the industrialization of Glasgow, there are even fewer places to detain you, with the exception of **Irvine**, home to the fascinating Scottish Maritime Museum.

Ayrshire is divided into three separate counties: South Ayrshire (which includes Ayr), East Ayrshire (which includes Kilmarnock) and North Ayrshire (from Irvine northwards). The last also includes the **Isle of Arran**, without doubt the most alluring destination in Ayrshire, its jagged outline visible across the Firth of Clyde. Arran is often described as "Scotland in miniature", and it certainly is a great place to get a quick taste of the Highlands in the barren north of the island, or relax in the Edwardian seaside resorts to the south.

Ayrshire is home to the misleadingly named Glasgow Prestwick **airport**, which lies, in fact, just outside Ayr. Both Prestwick and Ayr are served by frequent **trains** from Glasgow Central, and there's a useful train line from Ayr down the coast to Stranraer, and north to Largs. From Troon, just north of Ayr, fast **ferries** depart to Larne, and from the port of Ardrossan, further north still, you can cross to the Isle of Arran, from where you can hopscotch on to Kintyre and the Hebrides in summer.

Ayr and around

With a population of around fifty thousand, **AYR** is by far the largest town on the Firth of Clyde coast. It was an important seaport and trading centre for many centuries, and rivalled Glasgow in size and significance right up until the late seventeenth century. In recognition, Cromwell made it a centre of his administration and built an enormous fortress here, long since destroyed. With the relative decline of its seaborne trade, Ayr reinvented itself in the nineteenth

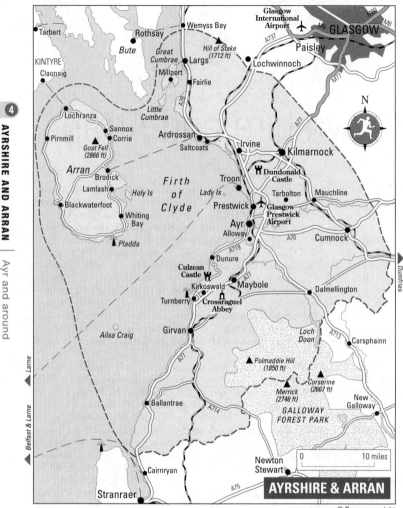

© Crown copyright

century as an administrative centre and a popular resort for middle-class Victorians. Nowadays, the town won't detain you long, though its prestigious **racecourse** (Ⓦwww.ayr-racecourse.co.uk), venue for the Scottish Grand National and the Scottish Derby, pulls in huge crowds, and the local tourist industry continues to do steady business out of the fact that Robbie Burns was born in the neighbouring village of **Alloway** (see p.253).

Ayr is one of many towns on this stretch of coast, and along the Firth of Clyde, visited in July and August by the *Waverley*, the last seagoing **paddle steamer** in the world; look out for Waverley advertisements, call ☎0845/130 4647 or visit Ⓦwww.waverleyexcursions.co.uk for exact details.

Ayr **train** station is ten minutes' walk southeast of the town centre, while the **bus** station is in the centre at the foot of Sandgate; nearby is the **tourist office**,

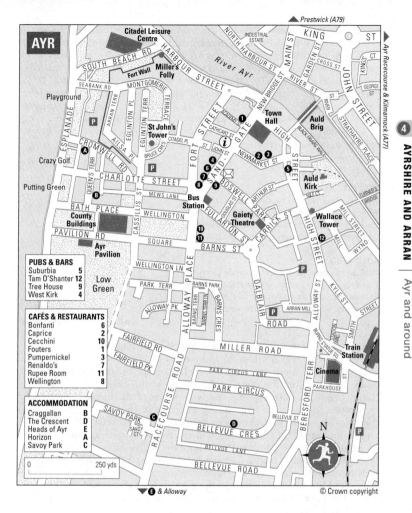

PUBS & BARS

Suburbia	**5**
Tam O'Shanter	**12**
Tree House	**9**
West Kirk	**4**

CAFÉS & RESTAURANTS

Bonfanti	**6**
Caprice	**2**
Cecchini	**10**
Fouters	**1**
Pumpernickel	**3**
Renaldo's	**7**
Rupee Room	**11**
Wellington	**8**

ACCOMMODATION

Craggallan	**B**
The Crescent	**D**
Heads of Ayr	**E**
Horizon	**A**
Savoy Park	**C**

at 22 Sandgate (July & Aug Mon–Sat 9am–6pm, Sun 10am–5pm; Oct–June Mon–Sat 9am–1pm & 2–5pm; ☎01292/290300), which can help with accommodation, a particularly useful service during big race meetings. For details of what to do if you're arriving at nearby Glasgow Prestwick airport, see p.260.

Accommodation

Ayr has a vast choice of **accommodation**, the best of which is found in the leafy streets to the south of the town centre: try *The Crescent*, a lovely spacious Victorian house with a four-poster suite available, at 26 Bellevue Crescent (☎01292/287329, ⓦwww.26crescent.freeserve.co.uk; ④), or the luxurious *Savoy Park Hotel*, 16 Racecourse Rd (☎01292/266112, ⓦwww.savoypark .com; ⑥), a splendid red sandstone Scots Baronial building, with a lovely garden complete with gazebo and swings; the public rooms are suitably grand and the bedrooms have all mod cons.

The cheapest accommodation is clustered in the streets between the town centre and the Esplanade. Of the numerous choices on Queen's Terrace, head for *Craggallan* (℡01292/264998, Ⓦwww.craggallan.com; ❸), a friendly little guesthouse with a dining table that converts into a billiards table. Alternatively, there's the *Horizon Hotel* (℡01292/264384, Ⓦwww.horizonhotel.com; ❺), a purpose-built modern hotel, and the only one (almost) on the seafront. Those wishing to camp should head for the *Heads of Ayr* caravan and **campsite** (℡01292/442269; March–Oct), three miles south of town along the coastal A719, beside the popular Heads of Ayr Farm Park (Easter–Oct daily 10am–5pm; Ⓦwww.headsofayrfarmpark.co.uk; free).

The Town

NEW BRIG
Will your poor narrow foot-path of a street,
Where twa wheel-barrows tremble when they meet,
Your ruin'd formless bulk o' stane and lime,
Compare wi' bonnie brigs o' modern time?...

AULD BRIG
Conceited gowk! puff'd up wi' windy pride!
This mony a year I've stood the flood an' tide;
And tho' wi' crazy eild I'm sair forfairn,
I'll be brig, when ye're a shapeless cairn!

The Brigs of Ayr by Robbie Burns

Burns' words proved prophetic, since Ayr's New Bridge, designed by none other than Robert Adam himself, and erected in 1787, was pulled down and replaced by the current structure in 1877. By contrast, the cobbled, four-arched **Auld Brig** survived the threat of demolition in the early twentieth century, thanks largely to Burns's poem, and is now one of the oldest stone bridges in Scotland, having been built during the reign of James IV (1488–1513). A short stroll upstream from the bridge stands the much restored **Auld Kirk**, the church funded by Cromwell as recompense for the one he incorporated into his stronghold. At the lych gate, look out for the coffin-shaped mort-safe (heavy grating) on the walls; placed over newly dug graves, these mort-safes were an early nineteenth-century security system, meant to deter bodysnatchers at a time when dead bodies were swiftly bought up by medical schools with no questions asked. The church's dark and gloomy interior retains the original pulpit (call ℡01292/262580 for access).

The rest of Ayr's busy town centre, wedged between Sandgate and the south bank of the treacly River Ayr, was rebuilt by the Victorians, and is now busy most days with shoppers from all over the county. The most conspicuous landmark is the big, grey, rather ugly, castellated **Wallace Tower**, erected in 1828 at the southern end of the High Street. It stands on what is thought to have been the site of Edward I's barracks, which were set alight by Wallace in 1297. At the junction of the High Street and Sandgate sits the rather more impressive Neoclassical **Town Hall**, completed in 1832, whose spectacular 226-foot spire is guarded by griffins, eagles and a Triton.

All you can see of Cromwell's zigzag **Citadel**, built to the west of the town centre in 1650s, is a small section of the old walls – the area was built over, for the most part, in Victorian times, but is still known locally as "the Fort". The best-preserved section of the fortifications lies on South Harbour Street, though the one surviving corbelled corner turret is, in fact, a Victorian addition known as **Miller's Folly** after its eccentric former owner. Another survivor from the distant past is the **St John's Tower** (call ☎01292/286385 to arrange access), which stands on its own in a walled garden at the heart of the old citadel, and is all that remains of the medieval church where the Scottish parliament met after the Battle of Bannockburn in 1315 to decide the royal succession, and which Cromwell later used as an armoury.

To the south of the citadel are the wide, gridiron streets of Ayr's main Georgian and Regency residential development. **Wellington Square**, whose first occupants were "Gentlemen of Rich Fortune and Retired Army Officers", is the area's showpiece, its trim gardens and terraces overlooked by the **County Buildings**, a vast, imposing Palladian pile from 1820. The opening of the Glasgow-to-Ayr train line in 1840 brought the first major influx of holidaymakers to the town, but today only a few hardy types take a stroll along Ayr's bleak, long **Esplanade** and beach, which look out to the Isle of Arran. The one building of note is the distinctive whitewashed **Ayr Pavilion**, built in 1911 with its four tall corner towers – it now houses the suitably tacky Pirate Pete's indoor adventure playground.

Eating, drinking and nightlife

Ayr is blessed when it comes to **eating** options. Arguably the town's best restaurant is *Fouters*, 2a Academy St (☎01292/261391, ⓦwww.fouters.co.uk; closed Mon & Sun), a cellar bistro off Sandgate – its short but imaginative menu features fresh local seafood, beef and lamb; main courses are over £15 in the evening, but lunch is a better deal. During the day, the *Pumpernickel* deli (closed Sun out of season) on pedestrianized Newmarket Street, does tasty, continental-style toasties and other snacks; *Caprice* (☎01292/610916), a smart French-style place further along the same street, serves slightly pricier, more substantial bistro food, including mussels. There are quite a few good Italian places in town, like the long-established *Bonfanti* (☎01292/266577), at the top of Sandgate, or *Cecchini* (☎01292/263607, ⓦwww.cecchinis.com; closed Sun), an inexpensive family-run pizza and pasta joint on the eastern side of Wellington Square. A few doors up is the *Rupee Room* (☎01292/283002), a popular Indian restaurant, decked out with modern minimalist furnishings. You can have eat-in or takeaway fish and chips from *Wellington*, a long-established chippie at the corner of Sandgate and Fort Street, next door to which is *Renaldo's*, renowned for its authentic Italian ice cream and Ayr rock.

Ayr's **pubs** are heaving most weekends. The most historic pub in town is the thatched *Tam o' Shanter*, on the High Street, though it's no museum piece. For a quiet pint of real ale, head for the *West Kirk*, a music-free J.D. Wetherspoon church to pub conversion on Sandgate, with wooden balconies held up by pistachio-coloured fluted pillars. Younger folk head for the *Tree House* also on Sandgate, where you can watch live sports, or Ayr's newest pub, *Suburbia*, on the High Street, with three bars laid out over two floors, thumping dance music and plenty of action.

Alloway

ALLOWAY, formerly a small village but now on the southern outskirts of Ayr, is the birthplace of Robert Burns (1759–96), Scotland's national poet. There are several places in Alloway associated with Burns, all gathered under the grandly titled Burns National Heritage Park (ⓦwww.burnsheritagepark.com), and you can get a joint "passport" for the lot lasting three days for £5. Your first port of call, however, should be the **Burns Cottage and Museum** (daily: April–Sept

△ Burns Monument, Alloway

9.30am–5.30pm; Oct–March 10am–5pm; £3), opposite the village post office and shop. The poet's birthplace, a low, whitewashed, thatched cottage where animals and people lived under the same roof, with a separate section for grain storage, was quite modern in its day. Much altered over the years, you can nevertheless gain an impression of what the place must have been like when Burns, the first of seven children, was born in the box bed in the only room in the house. The nearby two-room museum boasts all sorts of memorabilia: the giant family Bible, letters and manuscripts, the pistol he carried while an exciseman, a lock of his hair, plus lots of kitsch Burnsiana through the centuries.

Robert Burns

The first of seven children, **Robert Burns** (ⓦ www.robertburns.org), the national poet of Scotland, was born in Alloway on January 25, 1759. His father, William, was employed as a gardener until 1766, when he became a tenant farmer at Mount Oliphant, near Alloway, moving to Lochlie farm, Tarbolton, eleven years later. A series of bad harvests and the demands of the landlord's estate manager bankrupted the family, and William died almost penniless in 1784. These events had a profound effect on Robert, leaving him with an antipathy towards political authority and a hatred of the land-owning classes.

With the death of his father, Robert became head of the family and they moved again, this time to a farm at Mossgiel, near Mauchline. Burns had already begun writing **poetry** and **prose** at Lochlie, recording incidental thoughts in his *First Commonplace Book*, but it was here at Mossgiel that he began to write in earnest, and his first volume, *Poems Chiefly in the Scottish Dialect*, was published in Kilmarnock in 1786. The book proved immensely popular, celebrated by ordinary Scots and Edinburgh literati alike, with the satirical trilogy *Holy Willie's Prayer*, *The Holy Fair* and *Address to the Devil* attracting particular attention. The object of Burns's poetic scorn was the kirk, whose ministers had obliged him to appear in church to be publicly condemned for fornication – a commonplace punishment in those days.

Burns spent the winter of 1786–7 in the capital, lionized by the literary establishment. Despite his success, however, he felt trapped, unable to make enough money from writing to leave farming. He was also in a political snare, fraternizing with the elite, but with radical views and pseudo-Jacobite nationalism that constantly landed him in trouble. His frequent recourse was to play the part of the unlettered ploughman-poet, the noble savage who might be excused his impetuous outbursts and hectic womanizing.

He had, however, made useful contacts in Edinburgh and as a consequence was recruited to collect, write and rearrange two volumes of songs set to traditional Scottish tunes. These volumes, James Johnson's *Scots Musical Museum* and George Thomson's *Select Scottish Airs*, contain the bulk of his **songwriting**, and it's on them that Burns's international reputation rests, with works like *Auld Lang Syne*, *Scots, Wha Hae*, *Coming Through the Rye* and *Green Grow the Rushes, O*. At this time, too, though poetry now took second place, he produced two excellent poems: *Tam o' Shanter* and a republican tract, *A Man's a Man for a' That*.

Burns often boasted of his sexual conquests, and he fathered several illegitimate children, but in 1788, he eventually married **Jean Armour**, a stonemason's daughter from Mauchline, with whom he already had two children, and moved to Ellisland Farm, near Dumfries (see p.223). The following year he was appointed excise officer and could at last leave farming, moving to Dumfries in 1791. Burns's years of comfort were short-lived, however. His years of labour on the farm, allied to a rheumatic fever, damaged his heart, and he died in Dumfries on July 21, 1796, aged 37.

Burns's work, inspired by a romantic nationalism and tinged with a wry wit, has made him a potent symbol of "Scottishness". Ignoring the anglophile preferences of the Edinburgh elite, he wrote in Scots vernacular about the country he loved, an exuberant celebration that filled a need in a nation culturally colonized by England. Today, Burns Clubs all over the world mark every anniversary of the poet's birthday with the Burns Supper, complete with Scottish totems – haggis, piper and whisky bottle – and a ritual recital of Burns's *Ode to a Haggis*.

Ten minutes' walk down the road from the cottage are the plain, roofless ruins of **Alloway Kirk**, where Robert's father William is buried. Burns set much of *Tam o' Shanter* here. Tam, having got drunk in Ayr, passes "by Alloway's auld haunted kirk" and stumbles across a riotous witches' dance. Down the road from the church, the **Brig o' Doon**, the picturesque thirteenth-century hump-backed bridge over which Tam is forced to flee for his life, still stands, curving gracefully over the river. High above the river and bridge, in a small carefully manicured garden, towers the **Burns Monument** (daily: April–Sept 9am–5pm; Oct–March 10am–4pm; free), a striking, slightly ludicrous Neoclassical rotunda, topped by a scalloped cornice and a miniature copper-gilt baldachin. You can climb to the top for views over to the Brig, and, in the nearby **Statue House**, admire some eighteenth-century stone statues of Tam, Soutar and Nanse, which are, in fact, portraits of Burns's friends. To enter the garden, you need to approach from the nearby **Tam o' Shanter Experience** (daily: April–Sept 10am–5.30pm; Oct–March 10am–5pm; £1.50), on the opposite side of the road from Alloway Kirk. Don't bother with the "Experience" itself, however, as its low-budget audiovisual presentation of *Tam o' Shanter* fails to do justice to Burns's poem.

True Burns junkies might want to eat, drink and stay at the pricey *Brig o' Doon* **hotel** on the banks of the River Doon (℡01292/442466, ⓦwww.brigadoon .com; ❼), reputed to be another of Burns's drinking haunts. The inn retains its modest and ancient facade, though the interior has been totally refurbished with knick-knackery, and massively extended down to the river. Nevertheless, it's a comfortable place to spend the night, with great views over the River Doon, and Burns quotes all over the building. As there are only five rooms it's advisable to book ahead. To reach Alloway from Ayr town centre, **buses #1 and #57** set off from Sandgate (Mon–Sat hourly) and go right to the Tam o' Shanter Experience; otherwise, you can catch bus #58 or #60 from the bus station to Alloway.

South of Ayr

Fifty miles from top to bottom, the **South Ayrshire coastline** between Ayr and Stranraer is largely unblemished by modern industry or major seaside developments. Glasgow is that much further away, which deters day-trippers, and the sandy beaches are frequently interspersed with coastal cliffs. Apart from to play golf, the two main reasons visitors venture here are to visit **Culzean Castle**, Robert Adam's Neoclassical mansion on the cliffs between Ayr and Girvan, and to take a boat trip to see the gannets on **Ailsa Craig**, the giant muffin-shaped island in the Firth of Clyde. The A77 stays away from the coast until just before **Girvan**, a low-key seaside resort where boats depart for Ailsa Craig. If you keep to the main road, however, you'll pass by the area's most overlooked sight, the medieval ruins of **Crossraguel Abbey**. As for public transport, there's a good **bus** service along the coast, particularly between Ayr and Culzean, plus a **train** line from Ayr to Girvan and on to Stranraer.

Dunure

Typical of the south Ayrshire coastline is **DUNURE**, the first place you come to, six miles after leaving Ayr on the coastal A719. It's a tiny little settlement of fifty or so houses clinging to a sloping hill looking out across the sea to the Isle of Arran. The harbour shelters a few boats, the rocky shoreline attracts a few holidaying families, and overlooking the whole scene is the bleak ruined medieval **castle** that was once the ancient seat of the Kennedys of Carrick (as the local region is known). It was here in the castle's "black vault" in 1570 that Allan Stewart, the commendator of nearby Crossraguel Abbey, was stripped, put on a spit and roasted until he gave up his lands to the family. Unfortunately, the castle is in a scandalous state inside, though it's still worth having a peek at the perfectly preserved late-medieval doocot, situated close by. The local **pub**, *The Anchorage*, serves decent food, and the place of choice for **accommodation** is *Dunduff House* (☎01292/500225, Ⓦwww.gemmelldunduff.co.uk; ❸), 400 yards south past the village school, an old country house with stunning sea views from all three of its double bedrooms.

Culzean Castle

Sitting on the edge of a sheer cliff, looking out over the Firth of Clyde to Arran, **Culzean Castle** (Easter–Oct daily 10.30am–5pm; NTS; £12) couldn't have a more impressive situation. Given its strategic position, it's hardly surprising that the Kennedy family maintained a castle at Culzean (pronounced "cullane") from the twelfth century onwards. The current castle is actually a grand, late-eighteenth-century stately home, designed by the Scottish Neoclassical archi-tect **Robert Adam** for the tenth earl of Cassillis (pronounced "cassles"), as the Kennedys had by then become. Since passing into the hands of the National Trust for Scotland in 1945, Culzean, and in particular its surrounding 560-acre country park (daily 9.30am to dusk; park only £8), has become one of Ayrshire's top tourist attractions.

The best place to start is at the **visitor centre** (Easter–Oct daily 9.30am–5.30pm; Nov–Easter Sat & Sun 11am–4pm) in the modernized Home Farm buildings. Here you can watch an audiovisual show on the house, and pick up **free maps** – as well as wildlife leaflets – that help you get your bearings,

On the Burns trail

The number of memorials, museums, pubs and places across the region associated with **Robert Burns** is quite staggering, especially given the brevity of his life. If you've only a passing interest in the poet, then you're best off visiting either his birthplace in **Alloway**, near Ayr (see p.253), or the town where he died and is buried, **Dumfries** (see p.221). However, the dedicated Burns fan can also visit a few more minor Burns sights in Ayrshire.

The **Bachelors' Club** (Easter–Sept Mon, Tues & Fri–Sun 1–5pm; NTS; £2.50) is a wee thatched house in the tiny village of Tarbolton, some six miles northeast of Ayr. It was here in the upstairs room – the largest in the village at the time – that the 20-year-old Burns attended dancing classes, set up a debating society and became a freemason.

In Kirkoswald, fourteen miles southwest of Ayr, is **Souter Johnnie's Cottage** (April–Sept Mon, Tues & Fri–Sun 11.30am–5pm; NTS; £2.50), the simple thatched house that was once the home of John Davidson, the boon companion of Robert Burns and the original of Souter (cobbler) Johnnie in *Tam o' Shanter*. To the rear of the house, the restored alehouse has life-size stone figures of Johnnie, Tam himself (called after his boat, Shanter being his farm) and other Burnsian characters, all of whom are buried in the nearby graveyard.

Scotland's largest monument to Burns is slowly disintegrating in Kilmarnock (see p.261), where his first poems were published, but there's an equally impos-ing one in Mauchline, eleven miles east of Ayr. The **National Burns Memorial Tower**, erected in 1897 on the centenary of the poet's death, stands just by the A76 to the northwest of the town centre, and can be climbed by prior arrange-ment (☎01292/550633). You can also visit the **Burns House Museum** (Tues–Sat 11am–5pm; £1), on Castle St, where Burns lived at the time of his marriage to Jean Armour, a local stonemason's daughter. As well as the usual Burnsiana, there's a large display of local box ware and an exhibition on curling stones, which are manufactured locally from Ailsa Craig granite.

the layout of the place being rather confusing. The visitor centre's self-service **restaurant** is good, though you might prefer to head over to the Old Stables **coffee house** beside the castle, a quieter spot with table service.

From the visitor centre, it's a few minutes' walk through Adam's mock-ruined arch to the **Castle** itself, which overlooks the pristine lawn and herbaceous borders of the Fountain Court on one side, with the high sea cliffs on the other. Begun in 1777, Culzean's exterior preserves a medieval aspect, with its arrow slits and battlements; the interior, however, exemplifies the delicate, harmonious Neoclassical designs Adam loved – look out for the dolphins and swans (emblems of the Kennedy family) and the rams' heads (Adam's own favourite motif).

The most brilliantly conceived work by Adam is the **Oval Staircase**, where tiers of classical columns lead up to a huge glazed cupola allowing light to stream down. After admiring the portrait of Napoleon by Lefèvre, you pass through to the impressive circular **Saloon**, whose symmetrical flourishes deliberately contrast with the natural land and seascapes on view through the windows. Further on, there's a superb Chippendale four-poster bed, a great book-shaped tin bath, a painting of an Aesop fable by Snyders and a great boat-shaped cradle in the boudoir, created by the local shipbuilders. A small exhibition celebrates **President Eisenhower** and his rather bizarre association with Culzean: the castle's top floor was gifted to him out of the blue in 1945 by the Kennedy family, for his lifetime, and the president duly visited four times before his death in 1969.

Many folk come here purely to stroll and picnic in the woods, mess about by the beach or simply have tea and cakes, rather than admire the interior of the castle, and it's certainly worth leaving enough time for an exploration of the **country park**. You can also **stay** at Culzean (℡01655/884455, ⓦwww.culzeancastle.net; April–Oct; ⓞ), on the top floor, where six double bedrooms have been done out in a comfortably genteel style. Guests eat together in the shared dining room and the chef comes in to do breakfast as well. Although it's hard to imagine a more distinctive setting, it comes at a price: the smallest rooms start at £250 per night for bed, breakfast, afternoon tea and complimentary drinks; dinner is an extra £60 a head (including wine). The National Trust also has four much cheaper **self-catering** cottages (℡0131/243 9300) in the grounds, and there's the well-maintained ⚑ *Culzean Castle* **campsite** (℡01655/760627; March–Oct), located in the woods by the castle entrance, with great views across to Arran.

Crossraguel Abbey

The substantial remains of **Crossraguel Abbey** (Easter–Sept daily 9.30am–6.30pm; HS; £2.50), three miles inland from Culzean, right by the A77, are mostly overlooked – something of a surprise considering their singularity. Founded in 1250 as a Cluniac monastery – one of only two in Scotland – Crossraguel benefited from royal patronage, with its abbots holding land "for ever in free regality". The Cluniac order was famous for its elaborate ritual, which kept the choir monks busy all day long, but the abbots took the temporal side of their work just as seriously and became powerful local lords. By the early sixteenth century, they had constructed an extensive and well-fortified private compound complete with a massive gatehouse and sturdy tower house, both of which still stand.

The best place to start is in the choir of the **abbey church**, where only the ornate carving over the piscina and sedilia, in the polygonal apse, gives any indication of the quality of architecture that once must have existed throughout the building. Better still is the fifteenth-century **sacristy**, which has kept its vaulted ceiling and its decorative capitals, corbels and bosses, embellished with various images: squirrels, lions and other creatures, plus a triple-faced head and a green man. Next door, off the cloisters, the vaulted **chapter house** is also intact, with stone benches on every side and a fancy canopied seat for the abbot; it also boasts the most wonderful acoustics. The **tower house**, tacked onto the eastern end of the complex, was built around 1480 to provide the kind of luxury accommodation more in keeping with the abbot's high status in the outside world, and clearly illustrates the corruption of the monastic ideal that spurred the Reformation. On the opposite side of the abbey, the **gatehouse** is equally grand and has been restored, so that you can climb right up to the cap house and walk out onto the battlements. Clearly visible nearby is the abbey's well-preserved dovecote, a beehive-shaped affair that was a crucial part of the abbey's economy; the monks not only ate the doves but also relied on them for eggs.

Turnberry

Beyond Crossraguel, the A77 eventually reaches the coast at the village of **TURNBERRY**, a vast purpose-built Edwardian golfing resort, which has recently been massively expanded to make room for the Colin Montgomerie Links Golf Academy. Turnberry's links courses are occasional home to the Open Championship, and wealthy golfers tend to head for the luxurious *Westin Turnberry Resort* (☎01655/331000, ⓦturnberry.co.uk; ⑨). Visible out on the rocks on the point to the north of the village are a lighthouse and the ruined **castle** where Robert the Bruce was born in 1274, and which was in all likelihood left to fall into rack and ruin in 1307, after Bruce himself attacked and routed the English troops garrisoned within.

Girvan and around

Set beneath a ridge of grassy hills, **GIRVAN**, five miles south of Turnberry, is at its best round the busy harbour, a narrow slit beside the mouth of the Girvan Water. Here, overlooked by old stone houses, the fishing fleet sets about its business, and, for a moment, it's possible to ignore the run-down nature of the rest of the town. The long beaches around Girvan's otherwise rugged coastline are great for seaside strolls, though clambering down the cliff to the caves where the legendary Sawney Bean and his cannibal family lived is not recommended. Girvan has a helpful, privately run **visitor centre** (July & Aug daily 8am–8pm; shorter hours out of season; ⓦwww.girvan-online.net), on Bridge Street, between the harbour and the train station. One of the nicest **places to stay** is *Southfield House* (☎01465/714222, ⓦwww.southfieldhotel.co.uk; ④), a handsome whitewashed hotel on The Avenue, which also does bar meals and has a more formal and moderately expensive **restaurant**.

Ailsa Craig

The best reason for visiting Girvan is to take the boat excursion to the island of **Ailsa Craig**, which lies ten miles off the coast in the middle of the Firth of Clyde. The island's name means "Fairy Rock" in Gaelic, though it looks more like an enormous muffin than a place of enchantment. It would certainly have been less than enchanting for the persecuted Catholics who escaped here during the Reformation. The island's granite has long been used for making what many consider to be the finest curling stones – a company in nearby

Mauchline still has exclusive rights and sporadically collects a few boulders. In the late nineteenth century 29 people lived on the island, either working in the quarry or at the Stevenson lighthouse. With its volcanic, columnar cliffs and 1114-foot summit, Ailsa Craig is now a **bird sanctuary** that's home to some 40,000 gannets. The best time to make the trip is at the end of May and in June when the fledglings are trying to fly. Several companies **cruise** round the island, but only Mark McCrindle, who also organizes sea-angling trips, is licensed to land (May to late Sept 1–2 daily; ☎01465/713219, ⓦwww.ailsacraig.org.uk). It takes about an hour to reach the island, so you've enough time to walk up to the summit of the rock and watch the birds, weather permitting. The exact timings and prices depend on the length of trip, tides and weather; booking ahead is essential.

Dunaskin Open Air Museum

Twelve miles southeast of Ayr down the A713, the **Dunaskin Open Air Museum** (April–Oct daily 10am–5pm; £4.50; ⓦwww.dunaskin.co.uk), is a popular school outing and a genuinely interesting slice of industrial heritage. In 1848 the Dalmellington Iron Company set up an ironworks here, using local coal deposits to make "pig iron", with eight furnaces working day and night, employing around 1400 people at its zenith. After a brief introductory video, you're free to wander, with your audioguide, round the site, which is pretty vast, ranging from the ornate sandstone Blowing Engine House to Ardoon House, in the woods above the mine, where the owner used to live. At set times throughout the day, you can don a hard hat and go on a pretend trip down a mine, or visit one of the workers' rather spacious terraced cottages from 1914. On Sundays in July and August the local rail enthusiasts usually get one of the old steam engines going for brief rides down the surviving tracks. In 1921 the company switched to producing bricks, eventually closing down in 1976, although there's a modern open-cast coal mine closer to Dalmellington – hence the rail freight line beside the museum.

North of Ayr

The Ayrshire coast extends some thirty miles or so north of Ayr. A train line and the busy coastal road, the A78, cut across this disparate shoreline, where rolling farmland is interrupted by the pockmarks of industrialization, interspersed with moribund seaside resorts and internationally famous links golf courses. One place that is worth a visit is **Irvine**, home to the excellent Scottish Maritime Museum. The northernmost town on the Ayrshire coast, and also easily the area's most agreeable seaside resort, is **Largs**, from where you can catch a ferry across to the nearby island of **Great Cumbrae**, a low-key but justifiably popular holiday spot.

Public transport is pretty good, with frequent **buses** and a **train** line reaching as far as Largs. In addition, fast ferries depart from **Troon** to Belfast and Larne, and dour **Ardrossan** is the departure point for CalMac ferries to the Isle of Arran (see p.265).

Prestwick and Troon

Leaving Ayr, the A78 trims the outskirts of **PRESTWICK**, best known for **Glasgow Prestwick airport** (☎0871/223 0700, ⓦwww.gpia.co.uk), which lies just to the northeast of the town, and has regular transport to Ayr and Glasgow. The airport has its own **train station** (alight at Prestwick Airport not Prestwick Town station), with trains (every 30min) taking 45 minutes to reach Glasgow and 20 minutes to reach Ayr; there's also an express **bus** #X77 to Glasgow's Buchanan Street station (hourly; 50min).

Prestwick's golf club initiated the Open Championship in 1860, and the old links course was the competition's exclusive venue for the first decade of the competition. Unless you're a golf fan, however, Prestwick can be happily bypassed, as can **TROON**, another uninspiring seaside resort and port three miles further north, which boasts no fewer than six golf courses surrounding the town on every side and fast ferries to Larne with P&O (Ⓦwww.poirishsea.com).

Kilmarnock

Twelve miles northeast from Ayr, **KILMARNOCK** is, by and large, a shabby and depressed manufacturing town, known principally for being the home of Johnnie Walker whisky. The town planners of the 1960s and 1970s didn't do the place any favours, saddling it with some terrible shopping centres and a grim one-way road system. Yet "Killie" as the locals call it, isn't a bad-looking town in parts, thanks to the local red sandstone, and it does have one or two sights.

One of the town's most handsome buildings is the **Dick Institute** (Tues–Sat 11am–5pm; free), a splendid edifice with a Corinthian portico flanked by monkey-puzzle trees, just off the B7073 London Road. Opened in 1901, and completely rebuilt ten years later after a disastrous fire, the institute was paid for with money donated by local boy James Dick, who made his fortune in gutta-percha (a type of rubber used in shoemaking). On the ground floor is the town library, and a space for temporary exhibitions; upstairs is the local museum, an endearingly old-fashioned place piled high with fossils, stuffed fauna, model boats and a lace loom. Also on display is a selection of the institute's artworks, which include a couple of top-notch Pre-Raphaelite paintings by Alma-Tadema and Millais, and several works by Edward Hornel.

To the north of the Dick Institute, beyond Kilmarnock College and the railway, is Kay Park, site of the largest **Burns Monument** in Scotland, a Scots Baronial monstrosity erected in 1879. It currently stands rather forlorn at the highest point in the town, closed up and surrounded by security fencing. More uplifting is **Dean Castle** (April–Oct Wed–Sun 11am–5pm; Nov–March Sat & Sun noon–4pm; free; Ⓦwww.deancastle.com), set in beautiful wooded grounds a mile or so to the north up Kilmarnock Water, with a mini-farm, aviaries and adventure playground. The castle keep dates back to around 1360, while the adjacent palace was built a hundred years later, though both were accidentally burnt to the ground in 1735. The whole complex was restored and lived in by the eighth lord Howard de Walden in the early part of the twentieth century, before being gifted to the local council in 1975. The highlights of the castle interior include several fifteenth- and sixteenth-century Brussels tapestries, plus a collection of musical instruments and a large armoury from the same period.

Practicalities

Kilmarnock's **train station** lies at the north end of John Finnie Street, which is lined with impressive red sandstone Victorian buildings and runs parallel with the much less attractive main shopping drag, King Street, to the east. If you need a place to **stay**, *Dean Park Guest House* (Ⓣ01563/572794; ❷) is a decent family-run place at 27 Wellington St, just behind the train station, or you could cocoon yourself in the modern fifty-bed *Park Hotel* (℡01563/522952, Ⓦwww .burnsidehotel.co.uk; ❺), in Rugby Park, just southwest of the centre, off the A759. If you need to **eat or drink**, J.D. Wetherspoon have kindly provided the eminently civilized, though entirely modern, *Wheatsheaf* pub, just up from The Cross, at the northern end of King Street.

Irvine

IRVINE, twelve miles north of Ayr, was once the principal port for trade between Glasgow and Ireland, and later for coal from Kilmarnock, its halcyon days recalled by a branch of the **Scottish Maritime Museum** (April–Oct daily 10am–5pm; Ⓦwww.scottishmaritimemuseum.org; £3), which is spread across several locations down at the town's carefully restored old harbour. The best place to start is in the **Linthouse Engine Shop**, on Harbour Road, a late-nineteenth-century hangar-like building held up with massive iron girders, moved here brick by brick from Govan in Glasgow in 1990. Inside, the ad hoc displays include everything from old sailing dinghies, yachts and canoes to a giant ship's turbines. Free guided tours set off roughly four times a day round the nearby **Shipyard Worker's Tenement Flat**, which has been restored to something like its appearance in 1910, when a family of six to eight would have occupied its two rooms and scullery (and rented one of them out to a lodger). Moored at the **pontoons** on Harbour Street is an assortment of craft, which you can board, including a tug, a trawler, a "puffer" boat, a yacht driven by a wind turbine and the SY *Carola*, the oldest seagoing steam yacht in the country. At the nearby **Boatshop** kids can learn morse code and semaphore and you can find out more about the SV *Carrick*, the world's oldest colonial clipper, originally built in 1864 to ship cargo and passengers between Australia and London, and currently in a parlous state just upriver.

The **old town** of Irvine lies a mile or so to the east of the harbour, separated by railway lines and the gargantuan **Riverfront Shopping Mall**, an abomination through which you must walk to reach the High Street. Here and there a couple of narrow streets hint at the town's antiquity, amid the prevailing architectural gloom. The cobbled street of Glasgow Vennel, south of the High Street, features the **Vennel Gallery** (Fri–Sun 10am–1pm & 2–5pm; free), which exhibits contemporary art and crafts and shows a video on Burns, who stayed here for six months at the age of 22, while learning the trade of flax-combing in the thatched "heckling shop" round the corner. He didn't enjoy it much, falling ill with pleurisy, though he did manage to taste his first whisky there, and lose his virginity. The most atmospheric street is **Seagate**, another cobbled affair, this time off the north end of the High Street, boasting ancient cottages and the remains of **Seagate Castle**, a sixteenth-century fortified house.

Practicalities

Arriving at Irvine's adjacent **train** or **bus stations**, you'll find yourself exactly halfway between the harbour to the west, and the Riverfront carbuncle and old town to the east. Kilwinning Road, heading north out of Irvine, has several inexpensive **B&Bs**: *Laurelbank Guest House*, a whitewashed Victorian villa, is set back from the road at no. 3 (℡01294/277153, Ⓔlaurelbankguesthouse @hotmail.com; ❷); should you wish to pamper yourself a bit more, head for *Annfield House*, 6 Castle St (℡01294/278903, Ⓦwww.annfieldhousehotel .co.uk; ❺), a big Victorian mansion overlooking the river at the end of Sandgate, which has spacious bedrooms.

If you fancy a swim (and the sea's too cold) head for the far end of the harbour where you'll find **Magnum** (Ⓦ www.naleisure.co.uk), Scotland's largest leisure centre and swimming pool. And if you're in town on a Wednesday, check to see if the **Irvine Folk Club** (Ⓦ www.irvinefolkclub.co.uk) is meeting up at the Golf Hotel on Kilwinning Road, as it puts on some excellent gigs. Irvine's busiest time of the year is August, when the **Marymass Festival** (Ⓦ www .marymass.org) takes place: ten days of dog shows, flower shows and folk music, culminating in a horse-drawn procession through the town.

Largs and around

Nineteen miles north of Irvine, tucked in between the hills and the sea, **LARGS** remains the most traditional of Ayrshire's family resorts, its guesthouses and B&Bs spreading out behind an elongated seaside promenade. Largs also conceals one real gem: **Skelmorlie Aisle** (June–Aug Mon–Sat 2–5pm; keys from the museum next door; free), a slice of the Renaissance hidden away beside the old graveyard off Main Street – to get there, enter the yard opposite the WHSmith newsagent. Once the north transept of a larger church (long since gone), and now standing alone in the graveyard, the aisle was converted in 1636 into a mausoleum by Sir Robert Montgomerie, a local bigwig, in memory of his wife who died tragically from a horse-riding accident. Carved by Scottish masons following Italian patterns, the tomb is decorated with Montgomerie's coat of arms as well as symbols of mortality such as the skull, winged hourglass and inverted torch. Up above, the intricate paintwork of the barrel-vaulted ceiling includes the signs of the zodiac, biblical figures and texts and – in tiny detail on the painted corbels – the legendary coats of arms of the tribes of Israel.

Largs' chief historical claim to fame is the **Battle of Largs**, which took place in 1263. The battle was actually an accident, forced on King Haakon's Vikings when their longships were blown ashore by a gale. The invaders were attacked by the Scots as they struggled through the surf and, although both sides claimed victory, the Norwegians retreated north and abandoned their territorial claims to the Hebrides three years later. The battle provides a historical link for **Vikingar!** (April–Sept daily 10.30am–5.30pm; March & Oct daily 10.30am–3.30pm; Nov–Feb Sat & Sun 10.30am–3.30pm; £4; Ⓦ www.naleisure.co.uk), a light-hearted Viking-themed extravaganza housed in a purpose-built leisure complex, swimming pool and cinema, five minutes' walk north of the pier. A Viking guide talks you round an exhibition of the history of the Vikings in Scotland, aided by dramatic mood music, dioramas and interactive fun and games. Largs also holds a week-long **Viking Festival** (Ⓦ www.largsvikingfestival.com) at the end of October, which includes a costumed re-enactment of the famous skirmish.

The Battle of Largs is also commemorated by the distinctive **Pencil Monument**, a modern obelisk a mile south of the town centre, close to the marina, and opposite the **Kelburn Castle and Country Centre** (Easter–Oct daily 10am–6pm; £6.50; Ⓦ www.kelburncountrycentre.com), seat of the earls of Glasgow (aka the Boyle family) since the twelfth century, and now a very popular tourist attraction. The castle itself, which dates back to 1581, but has been much altered since, is no great shakes inside and is only open in July and August with a guided tour (£2). Much more enticing are the castle grounds, which feature a steep gorge and waterfall, one-thousand-year-old yew trees, an Adam monument and some lovely, relatively informal, gardens. There's also plenty for kids to do, including an adventure course, a secret forest playground (open from noon), a pets' corner, pony-riding and lots of one-off events.

Practicalities

Largs' **bus** and **train station** are both just south of Main Street, a short stroll east of the pier, and there's a tiny **tourist office** (April Mon–Sat 9am–1pm & 2–5pm; May, June, Sept & Oct Mon–Sat 9am–5pm, Sun 11am–3pm; July & Aug Mon–Sat 9am–6pm, Sun 10am–5pm; ☎01475/689962) inside the train station. Caledonian MacBrayne operates a regular **ferry service** to Great Cumbrae (every 15min in summer; ☎01475/674134, ⓦwww.calmac.co.uk) from Largs' pier. The old **paddle steamer**, the *Waverley*, also visits regularly during the summer (☎0845/130 4647, ⓦwww.waverleyexcursions.co.uk), as do Clyde Marine of Greenock (☎01475/721281, ⓦwww.clyde-marine.co.uk; June–Aug).

Being a holiday town, Largs has no shortage of **guesthouses** and **B&Bs**. There's a cluster along Aubery Crescent, a quiet street overlooking the curving bay, ten minutes' walk north of the pier – head for the *Old Rectory* at no. 2 (☎01475/674405, ⓦwww.oldrectorylargs.co.uk; Feb–Nov; ❸) or the *Carlton* (☎01475/672313, ⓦwww.carltonguesthouse.co.uk; ❷), both with excellent views over to Cumbrae and Arran. A cheaper option still is *Biscayne House* (☎01475/672851, ⓦwww.biscayneguesthouse.co.uk; ❷), up the hill by the main road, which offers B&B as well as self-catering accommodation for backpackers. *South Whittlieburn Farm* **campsite** (☎01475/675881) lies on a working sheep farm in a peaceful glen about three miles northeast of town.

As for **food**, fish and chips is the staple diet of most visitors, and there are plenty of places to choose from. Largs is best known for *Nardini's*, an Italian ice-cream parlour housed in a wonderful L-shaped Art Deco building on the Promenade, just north of the pier, but the place is currently closed due to a family dispute. As an alternative, head up Nelson Street for a take-away foccacia from *Silvano's*.

Great Cumbrae

Immediately offshore from Largs lies **Great Cumbrae**, a plump, hilly and wonderfully peaceful little island roughly four miles long and half as wide. The only settlement of any size is **MILLPORT**, which curves around a lovely wide bay on the south coast, overlooking the privately owned neighbouring island of Little Cumbrae (on the market for £3 million in 2005). The seafront is one long parade of Victorian seaside villas and terraces, interrupted only by **The Garrison**, a distinctive building with castellated gables, set back from the road. Originally built as a barracks for customs men in the early nineteenth century to keep an eye on the island's smugglers, it was gifted to the town by the marquess of Bute, only to be damaged by fire in 2001. When the building has been repaired, the tiny **Museum of the Cumbraes** (Easter–Oct Tues, Thurs & Fri 11am–1pm & 2–4.30pm; free) will once more have a permanent home; in the meantime, it's housed in a temporary hut in the grounds.

Hidden from view in the woods above the town is the Episcopal **Cathedral of Argyll & the Isles** (Mon–Sat 11am–4pm; ⓦwww.argyll.anglican.org), completed in 1851 to a design by William Butterfield, one of the leading High Victorian Gothic architects. It's pretty modest by Butterfield standards, with only the polychromatic tiling in the chancel giving any hint of his usual exuberance. However, with a nave measuring just 40ft by 20ft, though some 50ft in height, it does have the distinction of being Britain's smallest cathedral (it is in fact a co-cathedral along with Oban in Argyll), with seating for just a hundred worshippers. Just out of Millport, to the east, overlooking the Hunterston nuclear power station and iron-ore terminal back on the mainland, is the University Marine Biological Station, originally established by a Glasgow merchant who was an amateur enthusiast and now run jointly by Glasgow and London universities. Its west wing contains the **Robertson Museum & Aquarium** (Mon–Fri 9am–12.15pm & 1.45–4.45pm; June–Sept also Sat 10am–1pm & 2–4.45pm; £1.50), which has a laudably ecological exhibition on the local marine environment, and an old-fashioned aquarium displaying all manner of sea creatures from giant whelks and starfish to dogfish, conger eels and cod.

The CalMac **ferry** over from Largs is very frequent (every 15min in summer), and takes just ten minutes to reach the island's northeast tip, near the Scottish National Centre for watersports (Ⓦwww.sportscotland.org.uk), with a connecting **bus** to Millport. The most popular activity on Great Cumbrae is **cycling**: a circuit of the island takes no more than two hours even at a very leisurely pace, the road is very quiet, and there are a couple of good red sandstone beaches on the west coast overlooking Bute. Several **bike rental** outfits in Millport offer very reasonable rates: Bremner's (Ⓣ01475/530707), 17 Cardiff St, just up from the bus stop, has a huge range, including kids' bikes, helmets, trailers, the lot.

Cheap cafés and fish and chips abound in Millport, plus one Indian and one Chinese restaurant. The only **eating** place that rises slightly above the ordinary is *K2*, at the east end of the seafront on Kelburne Street, which serves toasties, fajitas, salads and wraps as well as the usual fare. The island is at its most peaceful once the day-trippers have gone home, and the most atmospheric and tranquil place **to stay** is the *College of the Holy Spirit* (Ⓣ01475/530353, Ⓦwww .argyll.anglican.org/retreats; ❷), an Anglican retreat house adjacent to the cathedral, which provides accommodation and food in a very peaceful setting. If you want a more conventional bed for the night, head for the *Millerston* (Ⓣ01475/530480; ❸), a double bay-fronted villa with modern furnishings at 29 West Bay Rd. If you have any questions, head for Millport's voluntary-run, seasonal **information office** (Ⓦwww.millport.org) in a caravan opposite the post office on the seafront.

The Isle of Arran

Shaped like a kidney bean and occupying centre stage in the Firth of Clyde, **Arran** (Ⓦwww.visitarran.net) is the most southerly (and therefore the most accessible) of all the Scottish islands. The Highland–Lowland dividing line passes right through its centre – hence the cliché about it being like "Scotland in miniature" – leaving the northern half sparsely populated, mountainous and bleak, while the lush southern half enjoys a much milder climate. The population of around five thousand – many of whom are incomers – tends to stick to the southeastern quarter of the island, leaving the west and the north relatively undisturbed.

There are two big crowd-pullers on Arran: **geology** and **golf**. The former has fascinated rock-obsessed students since Sir James Hutton came here in the late eighteenth century to confirm his theories of igneous geology. A hundred years later, Sir Archibald Geikie's investigations were a landmark in the study of Arran's geology, and the island remains a popular destination for university and school field-trips. As for golf, Arran boasts seven courses, including three of the eighteen-hole variety at Brodick, Lamlash and Whiting Bay, and a unique twelve-hole course at Shiskine, near Blackwaterfoot; an Arran Golf Pass is available for £80, giving you a round on each course.

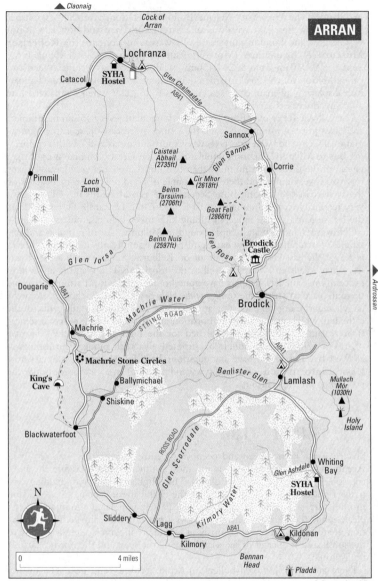

ARRAN

Claonaig
Cock of
Arran
Lochranza
SYHA
Hostel
Catacol
Glen Chalmadale
A841
Sannox
Pirnmill
Loch
Tanna
Caisteal
Abhail
(2735ft)
Glen Sannox
Corrie
Cir Mhor
(2618ft)
Beinn
Tarsuinn
(2706ft)
Goat Fell
(2866ft)
Beinn Nuis
(2597ft)
Glen Rosa
Brodick
Castle
Glen Iorsa
Dougarie
A841
Ardrossan
Machrie Water
STRING ROAD
Brodick
Machrie
Machrie Stone Circles
Benlister Glen
Lamlash
King's
Cave
Ballymichael
Mullach
Mór
(1030ft)
Shiskine
ROSS ROAD
Holy
Island
Blackwaterfoot
Glen Scorrodale
Kilmory Water
Glen Ashdale
Whiting
Bay
SYHA
Hostel
N
Sliddery
Lagg
A841
Kildonan
Kilmory
Bennan
Head
Pladda

0   4 miles

© Crown copyright

Although **tourism** is now by far its most important industry, Arran, at twenty miles in length, is large enough to have a life of its own. While the island's post-1745 history and the Clearances (set in motion by the local lairds, the dukes of Hamilton) are as depressing as elsewhere in the Highlands, in recent years Arran's population has actually increased, in contrast with more remote islands. **Transport** on Arran itself is pretty good: daily buses circle the island (Brodick tourist office has timetables and an Arran Rural Rover day-ticket costs just £4) and link in with the two ferry services: a year-round one from Ardrossan in Ayrshire to Brodick, and a smaller ferry from Claonaig on the Kintyre peninsula to Lochranza in the north (April–Oct).

Brodick

Although the resort of **BRODICK** (from the Norse *breidr vik*, "broad bay") is a place of only moderate charm, it does at least have a grand setting in a wide, sandy bay set against a backdrop of granite mountains. Its development as a tourist resort was held back for a long time by its elitist owners, the dukes of Hamilton, though nowadays, as the island's capital and main communication hub, Brodick is by far the busiest town on Arran.

Brodick's shops and guesthouses are spread out along the south side of the bay, along with the tourist office and the CalMac pier. However, Brodick's tourist sights, such as they are, are clustered on the west and north side of the bay, a couple of miles from the ferry terminal. First off, on the road to the castle, there's the **Arran Heritage Museum** (April–Oct daily 10.30am–4.30pm; £2.50; Ⓦ www.arranmuseum.co.uk), housed in a whitewashed eighteenth-century crofter's farm, and containing an old smiddy and a Victorian cottage with box bed and range. In the old stables there are lots of agricultural bits and bobs, plus material on Arran's wartime role, its intriguing geology and a Neolithic skull found on the island. Other wet-weather options in the **Arran Visitor Centre**, in neighbouring Home Farm, include the Island Cheese Company, where you can see the soft, round crottins of goat's cheese being made and taste Brodick and Glenshant blues; Arran Aromatics where you can watch natural soapmaking; and *Creelers* smokehouse which offers succulent seafood. Round the corner in Cladach, right by the castle, you can also visit the **Arran Brewery** (Ⓦ www.arranbrewery.com) and take a guided tour or simply quaff some of its award-winning beers.

Brodick Castle

Even if you're not based in Brodick, it's worth coming here in order to visit **Brodick Castle** (daily: April–Sept 11am–4.30pm; Oct 11am–3.30pm; NTS; £10), former seat of the dukes of Hamilton on a steep bank on the north side of the bay. The bulk of the castle was built in the nineteenth century, giving it a domestic rather than military look, and the **interior** – once you've fought your way past the 87 stags' heads on the stairs – is comfortable but undistinguished. Don't miss the portrait of the eleventh duke's faithful piper, who injured his throat on a grouse bone, was warned never to pipe again, but did so and died. Probably the most atmospheric room is the copper-filled Victorian kitchen, which conjures up a vision of the sweated and sweating labour required to feed the folk upstairs.

Much more attractive, however, are the walled **gardens** (daily 9.30am–dusk; gardens and country park only £5) and extensive grounds, a treasury of exotic plants and trees (including one of Europe's finest collections of rhododendrons) enjoying the favourable climate, and commanding a superb view across the bay. There is an adventure playground for kids, but the whole area is a natural playground with waterfalls, a giant pitcher plant that swallows thousands of midges daily and a maze of paths. Buried in the grounds is a bizarre Bavarian-style **summerhouse** lined entirely with pine cones, one of three built by the eleventh duke to make his wife, Princess Marie of Baden, feel at home. For the energetic there is also a **country park** with eleven miles of scenic

△ Brodick Castle, Isle of Arran

trails, starting from a small informative, hands-on nature centre. The excellent castle **tearoom** serves traditional food with a local flavour and is highly recommended.

Practicalities

Brodick's **tourist office** (May–Sept Mon–Thurs & Sat 9am–5pm, Fri 9am–7.30pm, Sun 10am–5pm; Oct–April Mon–Sat 9am–5pm) is by the CalMac pier, and has reams of information on every activity from pony trekking to paragliding. Unless you've got to catch an early-morning ferry, however, there's little reason to stay in Brodick, though there's a decent choice should you need to. The best **rooms** close to the ferry terminal are at the excellent *Dunvegan Guest House* on Shore Road (℡01770/302811, ✉dunveganhouse1@hotmail.com; ❹), or *Carrick Lodge* (℡01770/302550; March to mid-Nov; ❸), a spacious sandstone manse south of the pier on the Lamlash road. Closer to the castle is the peaceful sandstone farmhouse of *Glencloy* (℡01770/302351, ✉glencloyfarm@aol.com; ❷), which has real fires and a warm welcome. Finally, the luxury option is the tasteful *Kilmichael Country House Hotel* (℡01770/302219, ⓦwww .kilmichael.com; ❺), originally built in the seventeenth century and still retaining lots of period features; dinner here is very expensive and very formal, but it's one of the best you'll get on the island. The nearest **campsite** is *Glenrosa* (℡01770/302380), a lovely, but very basic, farm site (cold water only and no showers), two miles from town off the B880 to Blackwaterfoot.

For **food**, apart from dinner at the aforementioned *Kilmichael*, the only place that really stands out is the expensive seafood restaurant *Creelers* (℡01770/302797, ⓦwww.creelers.co.uk; Easter–Oct), which has its own smokehouse, by the museum on the road to the castle. Nearer to the ferry terminal, the bar snacks (lunch only) at *Mac's Bar* in the *McLaren Hotel* make a cheaper option and there's real ale too. The Good Food Shop, on the corner of Auchencrannie Road, bakes fresh wholemeal bread and has a self-service **laundrette** next door. If you want to find out about any other events taking place on Arran, pick up a copy of the island's **weekly newspaper**, the *Arran Banner*.

The south

The **southern half of Arran** is less spectacular and less forbidding than the north; it's more heavily forested and the land is more fertile, and for that reason the vast majority of the population lives here. The tourist industry has followed them, though with considerably less justification.

Lamlash, Holy Island and Whiting Bay

With its distinctive Edwardian architecture and mild climate, **LAMLASH**, four miles south of Brodick, epitomizes the sedate charm of southeast Arran. The best reason for coming to Lamlash is to visit the slug-shaped hump of **Holy Island**, which shelters the bay. The island is owned by a group of **Tibetan Buddhists**, who have established a long-term retreat at the lighthouse on the island's southern tip and built a Peace Centre at the north end of the island. Providing you don't dawdle, it's possible to scramble up to the top of Mullach Mór (1030ft), the island's highest point, and still catch the last ferry back. En route, you might well bump into the island's most numerous residents: feral goats, Eriskay ponies, Soay sheep and rabbits. The Holy Island ferry runs more or less hourly (☎01770/600998; £8 return), and you can stay at the Peace Centre (☎01387/373232, ⓦwww.holyisland.org; full board ❹), where they put on a range of courses on yoga, meditation and relaxation throughout the season.

If you want to **stay** in Lamlash, head for the comfortable *Lilybank* (☎01770/600230, ⓦwww.smoothhound.co.uk/hotels/lilybank; Easter–Oct; ❸), overlooking the bay and offering good home-made food. Another option is the *Aldersyde Bunkhouse* (☎01770/600959) a basic, purpose-built **hostel** south of the pier behind the *Aldersyde Hotel*. You can also **camp** at the fully equipped *Middleton Camping Park* (☎01770/600255; April–Oct), just five minutes' walk south of the centre. The best food option is the **bar meals** at the *Pier Head Tavern*, on the main street, or at the friendly *Drift Inn*, which has tables by the shore.

An established Clydeside resort for over a century, **WHITING BAY**, four miles south of Lamlash, is spread out along a very pleasant bay, though it doesn't have quite the distinctive architecture of Lamlash. It's a good base for walking, with the gentle hike up to the **Glenashdale Falls** probably the most popular excursion; the waterfall can be reached via a pretty woodland walk that sets off from beside the SYHA hostel (2hr return). Whiting Bay also has some excellent **places to stay**, including *Argentine House Hotel*, run (confusingly) by a multilingual Swiss couple (☎01770/700662, ⓦwww .argentinearran.co.uk; ❹), on Shore Road, or *Mingulay* (☎01770/700346; ❷), a smaller, but equally comfortable B&B on Middle Road. The afore-mentioned SYHA **hostel** (☎0870/004 1158; April–Oct) is situated at the southern end of the bay, but was closed for refurbishment at the time of going to press so phone ahead to check. The **food** is very good at the *Burlington Hotel* on Shore Road, and at the nearby *Argentine House Hotel*, though both are expensive. Otherwise, head for 🦌 *Joshua's*, a café bang on the seafront offering snacks and home-made cakes, or try the simple bistro fare at the *Pantry* (closed Sun eve) opposite the post office, with views over the bay. For **bike rental**, enquire at the *Coffee Pot* (☎01770/700382), further south on the seafront.

Kildonan to Lagg

Access to the sea is tricky along the south coast, but worth the effort, as the sandy beaches here are among the island's finest. One place where you can get down to the sea is at **KILDONAN**, an attractive small village south of Lamlash. It's set slightly off the main road, with a good sandy beach which you share with the local wildlife and views out to the tiny flat island of **Pladda**, with its distinctive lighthouse and, in the distance, the great hump of Ailsa Craig (see p.259). Kildonan has a nice **campsite** (℡01770/820320) right by the sea next to the newly refurbished *Kildonan Hotel* (℡01770/820207, Ⓦwww.kildonanhotel .co.uk; ❺).

KILMORY, four miles west of Kildonan, is the home of the prizewinning **Torrylinn Creamery** (Mon–Thurs 8.30am–2pm, Fri 8.30am–3.30pm; free), which produces a cheddary cheese called Arran Dunlop, and where you can watch the whole process from a viewing window. Next door to Kilmory is the picturesque village of **LAGG**, nestling in a tree-filled hollow by Kilmory Water. The friendly village stores has an excellent **tearoom**; those feeling flush should **stay** at the comfortable ⚑ *Lagg Inn* (℡01770/870255,www.arran Ⓦwww .lagghotel.com; ❻), an old-fashioned eighteenth-century inn beside the main road, with real fires and good food.

Blackwaterfoot and Machrie

BLACKWATERFOOT, at the western end of the String Road, which bisects the island, is dominated, not to say somewhat spoilt, by the presence of the island's largest hotel, the *Kinloch Hotel*. In every other way, Blackwaterfoot is a beguiling little place, boasting the only twelve-hole golf course in the world. A gentle two-mile walk north along the coast will bring you to the **King's Cave**, one of several where Robert the Bruce is said to have encountered the famously persistent arachnid while hiding during his final bid to free Scotland in 1306. If you want **to stay**, the late Victorian *Blackwaterfoot Lodge* (℡01770/860202, Ⓦwww.blackwaterfoot-lodge.co.uk; Easter–Oct; ❸) is a good place to hole up, though there are also a couple of great B&Bs: *Lochside Guest House* (℡01770/860276, Ⓔbannatyne@lineone .net; ❷), just half a mile south along the main road, is set beside its very own trout loch.

North of Blackwaterfoot, the wide expanse of **Machrie Moor** boasts a wealth of Bronze Age sites. No fewer than six **stone circles** sit east of the main road, and, although many of them barely break the peat's surface, the tallest surviving monolith is over eighteen feet high. The most striking configuration is at Fingal's Cauldron Seat, with two concentric circles of granite boulders; legend has it that Fingal tied his dog to one of them while cooking at his cauldron. If you're feeling peckish, the Machrie golf course **tearoom** (April to mid-Oct) is a welcome oasis in this sparsely populated area.

The north

The **north half of Arran** – effectively the Highland part – features wonderful bare granite peaks, the occasional golden eagle and miles of unspoilt scenery, within reach only of those prepared to do some hiking. Arran's most accessible peak is also the island's highest, **Goat Fell** (2866ft) – take your pick from the Gaelic, *goath*, meaning "windy", or the Norse, *geit-fjall*, "goat mountain" – which can be ascended in just three hours from Brodick or from Corrie (return journey 5hr), though it's a strenuous hike (for the usual safety precautions, see p.64).

Corrie and Sannox

Arran's prettiest little seaside village is **CORRIE**, six miles north of Brodick, where a procession of pristine cottages lines the road to Lochranza and wraps itself around an exquisite little harbour and pier. If you want to use Corrie as a base for hiking, book ahead at the *North High Corrie Croft*, a **bunkhouse** (☎01770/302310), ten minutes' steep climb above the village on a raised beach; it has one large room for group bookings, and an annexe with eight beds. The red sandstone *Corrie Hotel*, at the centre of the village, does bar **meals**, and the tearoom in the *Corrie Golf Club*, confusingly in Sannox, offers good-value food all day in summer.

At **SANNOX**, two miles north, the road leaves the shoreline and climbs steeply, giving breathtaking views over to the scree-strewn slopes around Caisteal Abhail (2735ft). If you make this journey around dusk, be sure to pause in **Glen Chalmadale**, on the other, northern side of the pass, to catch a glimpse of the red deer that come down to pasture by the water. Another possibility is to turn off to North Sannox, where you can park and walk along the shore to the **Fallen Rocks**, a major rock-fall of Devonian sandstone.

Lochranza

On fair Lochranza streamed the early day,
Thin wreaths of cottage smoke are upward curl'd
From the lone hamlet, which her inland bay
And circling mountains sever from the world.

The Lord of the Isles by Sir Walter Scott

The ruined castle which occupies the mudflats of the bay and the brooding north-facing slopes of the mountains which frame it make for one of the most spectacular ensembles on the island – yet **LOCHRANZA**, despite being the only place of any size in this sparsely populated area, attracts far fewer visitors than Arran's southern resorts. The castle is worth a brief look inside, but Lochranza's main tourist attraction now is the island's modern **distillery** (mid-March to Oct daily 10am–6pm; Nov & Dec phone ☎01770/830264, ⓦwww.arranwhisky .com; £3.50), a pristine complex distinguished by its pagoda-style roofs at the south end of the village. The tours are entertaining and slick and end with a free sample of the island's newly emerging single malt.

The finest **accommodation** is to be had at the superb ⚑ *Apple Lodge* (☎01770/830229; ❹), the old village manse where you'll get excellent home cooking, or at the equally welcoming *Lochranza Hotel* (☎01770/830223, ⓦwww.lochranza.co.uk; ❷), whose bar is the centre of the local social scene. Lochranza also has a friendly SYHA **hostel** (☎0870/004 1140; March–Oct), situated halfway between the distillery and the castle, and a well-equipped **campsite** (☎01770/830273, ⓦwww.arran.net/lochranza; April–Oct), beautifully placed by the golf course on the Brodick road, where deer come to graze in the early evening.

The distillery **café** offers salads, pasta dishes, baguettes and Scottish specialities during the day; in the evening, your only option is **bar meals** at the *Lochranza*. If you're just passing through, there's the take-away *Sandwich Station*, situated close to the CalMac terminal.

Catacol and Pirnmill

An alternative to staying or drinking in Lochranza is to continue a mile or so southwest along the coast to **CATACOL**, and stay or drink at the friendly

Catacol Bay Hotel (☎01770/830231, Ⓦwww.catacol.co.uk; ❷), which serves basic pub grub (with several veggie options) and real ale. There's a small adjoining **campsite**, seals and shags to view on the nearby shingle and occasional live music.

Just past the pub there is a row of striking black-and-white cottages, known as the **Twelve Apostles**, built by the eleventh duke of Hamilton, and intended to house tenants displaced to make way, not for sheep, but for deer (thanks to Queen Victoria's passion for stalking them), though no one could be persuaded to live in them for two years.

From here to the String Road it's very bleak, but ideal for spotting wildlife, on the hillside and at sea. The next village of any size is neat and tidy **PIRNMILL**, so called because they used to make "pirns", or bobbins, for the mills of Paisley here (until they ran out of trees).

Travel details

Trains

Ayr to: Girvan (Mon–Sat 12 daily, 2 on Sun; 25min); Glasgow Central (every 30min; 50min); Irvine (every 30min; 15min); Kilmarnock (Mon–Sat 7 daily; 30min); Prestwick Airport (every 30min; 7min); Stranraer (Mon–Sat 7 daily, 2 on Sun; 1hr 20min).

Glasgow Central to: Ardrossan Harbour (4–5 daily; 50min); Ayr (every 30min; 55min); Irvine (every 30min; 35min); Kilmarnock (hourly; 40min); Largs (hourly; 1hr); Prestwick Airport (every 30min; 45min); Stranraer (Mon–Sat 4 daily, Sun 2 daily; 2hr).

Buses

Ayr to: Ardrossan (Mon–Sat every 30min, Sun every 2hr; 55min); Cairnryan (4–7 daily; 1hr 50min); Culzean Castle (Mon–Sat hourly, Sun every 2hr; 30min); Dalmellington (Mon–Sat every 15–25min, Sun hourly; 1hr); Dunure (hourly; 30min); Girvan (Mon–Sat hourly, Sun every 2hr; 1hr); Glasgow (hourly; 55min); Kilmarnock (Mon–Sat every 30min, Sun hourly; 1hr 10min); Largs (Mon–Sat

every 30min, Sun every 2hr; 1hr 20min); New Galloway (Mon–Sat 2 daily; 1hr 20min); Portpatrick (Mon–Sat 6 daily; 2hr 25min); Stranraer (4–6 daily; 2hr); Wemyss Bay (Mon–Sat every 30min, Sun every 2hr; 1hr 30min).

Brodick (Arran) to: Blackwaterfoot (Mon–Sat 12 daily, Sun 6 daily; 30min); Corrie (4–6 daily; 20min); Kildonan (3–5 daily; 40min); Lagg (3–5 daily; 50min); Lamlash (Mon–Sat 14–16 daily, Sun 4 daily; 10–15min); Lochranza (Mon–Sat 6 daily, Sun 3 daily; 45min); Pirnmill (4–6 daily; 1hr); Whiting Bay (Mon–Sat 14–16 daily, Sun 4 daily; 25min).

Ferries (summer timetable)

Ardrossan to: Brodick, Isle of Arran (4–6 daily; 55min).

Cairnryan to: Larne (7–9 daily; 1hr–1hr 45min).

Largs to: Great Cumbrae (every 15min; 10min).

Lochranza to: Claonaig (8–9 daily; 30min).

Stranraer to: Belfast (7–8 daily; 1hr 45min–3hr 15min).

Troon to: Larne (2 daily; 1hr 50min).

5

Glasgow and the Clyde

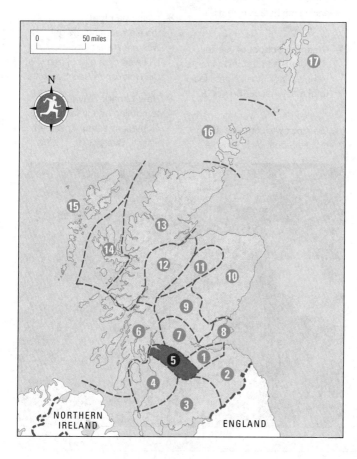

NORTHERN
IRELAND

ENGLAND

CHAPTER 5

Highlights

* **Gallery of Modern Art** Idiosyncratic but populist collection of contemporary artworks, bang in the heart of the city. **See p.288**

* **Necropolis** Elegantly crumbling graveyard on a city-centre hill behind the ancient cathedral, with great views. **See p.296**

* **Glasgow School of Art** Take a student-led tour of Charles Rennie Mackintosh's architectural masterpiece. **See p.297**

* **Clydeside** The river that made Glasgow: walk or cycle along it, take a boat on it, cross a bridge over it, or get a view of it from the futuristic Science Centre. **See p.304**

* **Burrell Collection** An inspired and eclectic art collection displayed in a purpose-built museum in Pollok Park. **See p.308**

* **"Glaesga nightlife"** Sample the glamour and the grit with cocktails at the *Rogano* followed by a pint of heavy at the *Horseshoe Bar*. **See p.317**

* **New Lanark** Stay for next to nothing at this fascinating eighteenth-century planned village. **See p.331**

△ Necropolis

Glasgow and the Clyde

Rejuvenated, upbeat **Glasgow**, Scotland's largest city, has not traditionally enjoyed the best of reputations. Set on the banks of the mighty River Clyde, this former industrial giant can still initially seem a grey and depressing place, with the M8 motorway screeching through the centre and dilapidated housing estates on its outskirts. However, the effects of Glasgow's remarkable overhaul, set in motion in the 1980s by the "Glasgow's Miles Better" campaign and crowned by the awarding of the title of European City of Culture in 1990, are still much in evidence, even if the momentum has slowed. Glasgow's image of itself has changed irrevocably, and few visitors will be left in any doubt that the city is, in its own idiosyncratic way, a cultured and dynamic place well worth getting to know.

The city has much to offer, including some of the best-financed and most imaginative museums and galleries in Britain – among them the showcase **Burrell Collection** of art and antiquities – nearly all of which are free. Glasgow's **architecture** is some of the most striking in the UK, from the restored eighteenth-century warehouses of the **Merchant City** to the hulking Victorian prosperity of George Square. Most distinctive of all is the work of local luminary Charles Rennie Mackintosh, whose elegantly streamlined Art Nouveau designs appear all over the city, reaching their apotheosis in the stunning **School of Art**. Recent development of the old shipyards of the Clyde, notably in the space-age shapes of the new **Glasgow Science Centre**, hint at yet another string to the city's bow: combining design with innovation. The metropolis boasts thriving live-music venues, distinctive places to eat and drink, busy theatres, concert halls and an opera house. Above all, the feature that best defines the individualism and peculiar attraction of the city is its **people**, whether rough-edged comedians on the football terraces or bright young things dressed to the nines in the trendiest of bars.

Despite all the upbeat hype, Glasgow's gentrification has passed by deprived inner-city areas such as the **East End**, home of the **Barras market** and some staunchly change-resistant pubs. This area, along with isolated housing schemes such as Castlemilk and Easterhouse, needs more than a face-lift to resolve its complex social and economic problems, and has historically been the breeding ground for the city's much-lauded **socialism**, celebrated in the wonderful **People's Palace** social-history museum. Indeed, even in the more stylish

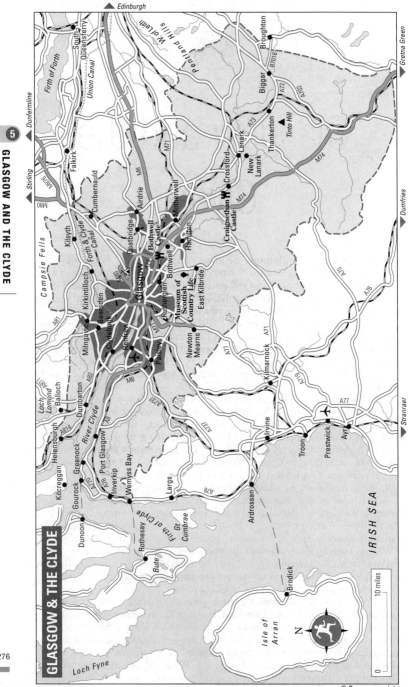

GLASGOW & THE CLYDE

© Crown copyright

quarters of Glasgow, there's a gritty edge that's never far away, reinforcing a peculiar mix of grime and glitz which the city seems to have patented.

Quite apart from its own attractions, Glasgow makes an excellent base from which to explore the **Clyde Valley and coast**, made easily accessible by a reliable train service. Chief among the draws is the remarkable eighteenth-century **New Lanark** mills and workers' village, a World Heritage Site, while other daytrips might take you to the **National Museum of Scottish Country Life** near East Kilbride or on a boat heading "doon the watter" towards the scenic Argyll sea lochs, past the old shipbuilding centres on the Clyde estuary.

Glasgow

GLASGOW's earliest history, like so much else in this surprisingly romantic city, is obscured in a swirl of myth. The city's name is said to derive from the Celtic *Glas-cu*, which loosely translates as "the dear, green place" – a tag that the tourist board is keen to exploit as an antidote to the sooty images of popular imagination. It is generally agreed that the first settlers arrived in the sixth century to join Christian missionary **Kentigern** – later to become St Mungo – in his newly founded monastery on the banks of the tiny Molendinar Burn.

William the Lionheart gave the town an official charter in 1175, after which it continued to grow in importance, peaking in the mid-fifteenth century when the **university** – the second in Scotland after St Andrews – was founded on Kentigern's site. This led to the establishment of an archbishopric, and hence city status, in 1492, and, due to its situation on a large, navigable river, Glasgow soon expanded into a major industrial **port**. The first cargo of tobacco from Virginia offloaded in Glasgow in 1674, and the 1707 Act of Union between Scotland and England – despite demonstrations against it in Glasgow – led to a boom in trade with the colonies until American independence. Following the **Industrial Revolution** and James Watt's innovations in steam power, coal from the abundant seams of Lanarkshire fuelled the ironworks all around the Clyde, worked by the cheap hands of the Highlanders and, later, those fleeing the Irish potato famine of the 1840s.

The **Victorian** age transformed Glasgow beyond recognition. The population boomed from 77,000 in 1801 to nearly 800,000 at the end of the century, and new tenement blocks swept into the suburbs in an attempt to cope with the choking influxes of people. Two vast and stately **International Exhibitions** were held in 1888 and 1901 to showcase the city and its industries to the outside world, necessitating the construction of huge civic monoliths such as the Kelvingrove Art Gallery and the Council Chambers in George Square. At this time Glasgow revelled in the title of the "Second City of the Empire" – an unexpected epithet for a place that rarely acknowledges second place in anything.

By the turn of the twentieth century, Glasgow's industries had been honed into one massive **shipbuilding** culture. Everything from tugboats to transatlantic liners were fashioned out of sheet metal in the yards that straddled the Clyde from Gourock to Rutherglen. In the harsh economic climate of the 1930s, however, unemployment spiralled, and Glasgow could do little to

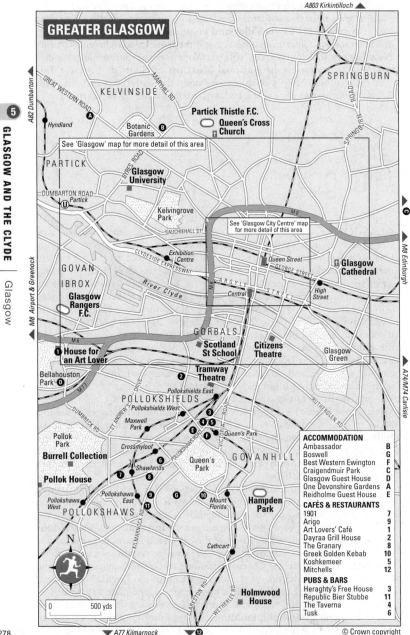

GREATER GLASGOW

A803 Kirkintilloch

A82 Dumbarton

GREAT WESTERN ROAD

KELVINSIDE

MARYHILL RD

SPRINGBURN

SPRINGBURN ROAD

Hyndland

A

Botanic Gardens

B

Partick Thistle F.C.

Queen's Cross Church

See 'Glasgow' map for more detail of this area

M8 Airport & Greenock

PARTICK

Byres Road

Glasgow University

DUMBARTON ROAD

Partick

U

Kelvingrove Park

SAUCHIEHALL ST

See 'Glasgow City Centre' map for more detail of this area

M8

C

M8 Edinburgh

GOVAN

Exhibition Centre

Queen Street

GEORGE STREET

Glasgow Cathedral

IBROX

CLYDESIDE EXPRESSWAY

River Clyde

ARGYLE STREET

Central

High Street

Glasgow Rangers F.C.

M8

GORBALS

Scotland St School

Citizens Theatre

Glasgow Green

A74/M74 Carlisle

1 House for an Art Lover

Bellahouston Park

D

M77

2 Tramway Theatre

RUTHERGLEN RD

DUMBRECK RD

ST ANDREW'S DRIVE

POLLOKSHIELDS

Pollokshields East

Pollokshields West

3

Maxwell Park

POLLOKSHAWS ROAD

4 5

E

F

Queen's Park

VICTORIA ROAD

GOVANHILL

Pollok Park

Burrell Collection

Crossmyloof

6

Shawlands

7 8

Queen's Park

Pollok House

Pollokshaws East

9

6

10

Mount Florida

Hampden Park

Pollokshaws West

POLLOKSHAWS

11

KILMARNOCK RD

KILMARNOCK RD

Cathcart

N

Holmwood House

0   500 yds

A77 Kilmarnock

12

CLARKSTON RD

WETHERLE RD

© Crown copyright

ACCOMMODATION
Ambassador	B
Boswell	G
Best Western Ewington	F
Craigendmuir Park	C
Glasgow Guest House	D
One Devonshire Gardens	A
Reidholme Guest House	E

CAFÉS & RESTAURANTS
1901	7
Arigo	9
Art Lovers' Café	1
Dayraa Grill House	2
The Granary	8
Greek Golden Kebab	10
Koshkemeer	5
Mitchells	12

PUBS & BARS
Heraghty's Free House	3
Republic Bier Stubbe	11
The Taverna	4
Tusk	6

counter its popular image as a city dominated by inebriate violence and (having absorbed vast numbers of Irish emigrants) sectarian tensions. The **Gorbals** area in particular became notorious as one of the worst slums in Europe. The city's image has never been helped by the depth of animosity between its two great rival football teams, Catholic **Celtic** and Protestant **Rangers**.

Shipbuilding, and many associated industries, died away almost completely in the 1960s and 1970s, leaving the city depressed, jobless and directionless. Then, in the 1980s, the self-promotion campaign began, snowballing towards the 1988 Garden Festival and year-long party as European City of Culture in 1990. Glasgow then beat off competition from Edinburgh and Liverpool to become **UK City of Architecture and Design** in 1999, an event which strove valiantly to showcase the city's rich architectural heritage and highlight the role of design in modern everyday living. These various titles have helped to reinforce the impression that Glasgow, despite its many problems, has successfully broken the industrial shackles of the past and evolved into a city of stature and confidence.

Arrival, orientation and information

Glasgow International airport (℡0870/040 0008, Ⓦwww.glasgowairport .com) is at Abbotsinch, eight miles southwest of the city – not to be confused with Glasgow Prestwick airport, which is thirty miles south near Ayr. From the international airport, the Glasgow Airport Link bus (£3.30) runs from bus stops 1 or 2 into the central Buchanan Street bus station every ten to fifteen minutes during the day; the journey takes 25 minutes. Airport taxis charge around £17.

From **Glasgow Prestwick** airport (℡0871/223 0700, Ⓦwww.gpia.co.uk), the simplest way to get to Glasgow is by **train**: there's a station right by the terminal (alight at the airport, not Prestwick Town), with trains taking 45 minutes to reach Glasgow Central station (Mon–Sat every 30min, Sun hourly). Tickets are half-price (around £2.50) for all air passengers, though some airlines have deals which allow free train travel. **Buses** to Glasgow depart from directly outside the terminal: there's an express bus #X77 every half an hour (£4.20; 50min) to Glasgow's Buchanan Street bus station.

Nearly all **trains** from England come into **Central station**, which sits over Argyle Street, one of the city's main shopping thoroughfares. Bus #398 from the front entrance on Gordon Street shuttles every ten minutes to **Queen Street station**, at the corner of George Square, terminus for trains serving Edinburgh and the north. The walk between the two takes about ten minutes. Bus #398 also stops at **Buchanan Street bus station**, arrival point for regional and inter-city **coaches**.

Orientation

Glasgow is a sprawling place, built on some punishingly steep hills, and with no really obvious focus, although, as most transport services converge on the area around **Argyle Street** and, 200 yards to the north, **George Square**, this pocket is the most obvious candidate for city-centre status. However, with the renovated, upmarket **Merchant City** immediately to the east and the main business and commercial areas to the west, the centre, when the term is used, actually refers to a large swathe from **Charing Cross** and the M8 in the west through to **Glasgow Green** in the run down **East End**.

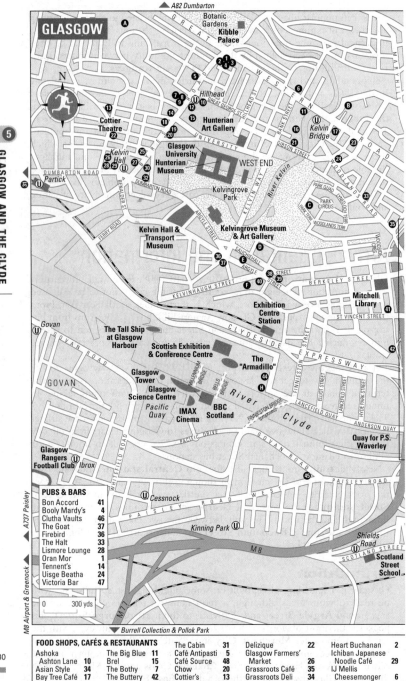

GLASGOW

A82 Dumbarton

Botanic
Gardens
Kibble
Palace

WEST END

Hunterian
Art Gallery

Cottier
Theatre

Hillhead

Kelvin
Hall

Glasgow
University
Hunterian
Museum

Partick

Kelvingrove
Park

River Kelvin

Park
Circus

Kelvin
Bridge

Kelvin Hall &
Transport
Museum

Kelvingrove Museum
& Art Gallery

Mitchell
Library

Exhibition
Centre
Station

Govan

The Tall Ship
at Glasgow
Harbour

Scottish Exhibition
& Conference Centre

The
"Armadillo"

GOVAN

Glasgow
Tower

Glasgow
Science Centre

Pacific
Quay

IMAX
Cinema

BBC
Scotland

River Clyde

Quay for P.S.
Waverley

Glasgow
Rangers
Football Club Ibrox

Cessnock

Kinning Park

Shields
Road

Scotland
Street
School

PUBS & BARS

Bon Accord	41
Booly Mardy's	4
Clutha Vaults	46
The Goat	37
Firebird	36
The Halt	33
Lismore Lounge	28
Oran Mor	1
Tennent's	14
Uisge Beatha	24
Victoria Bar	47

0   300 yds

280

GLASGOW AND THE CLYDE

M8 Airport & Greenock ◄ A737 Paisley ◄

▼ Burrell Collection & Pollok Park

FOOD SHOPS, CAFÉS & RESTAURANTS

Ashoka		The Big Blue	11	The Cabin	31	Delizique	22	Heart Buchanan	2
Ashton Lane	10	Brel	15	Café Antipasti	5	Glasgow Farmers'		Ichiban Japanese	
Asian Style	34	The Bothy	7	Café Source	48	Market	26	Noodle Café	29
Bay Tree Café	17	The Buttery	42	Chow	20	Grassroots Café	35	IJ Mellis	
				Cottier's	13	Grassroots Deli	34	Cheesemonger	6

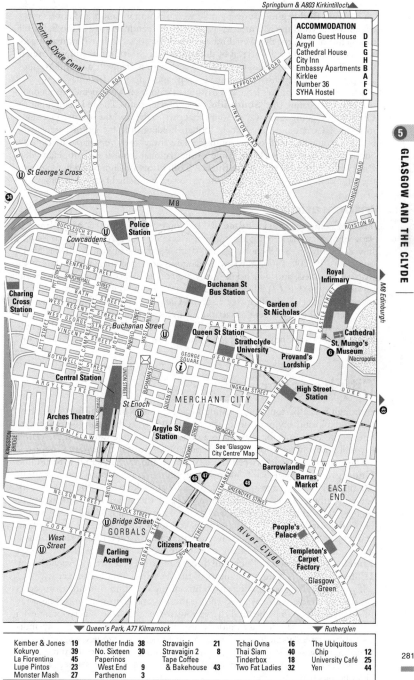

Springburn & A803 Kirkintilloch ▲

ACCOMMODATION

Alamo Guest House	**D**
Argyll	**E**
Cathedral House	**G**
City Inn	**H**
Embassy Apartments	**B**
Kirklee	**A**
Number 36	**F**
SYHA Hostel	**C**

Forth & Clyde Canal

POSSIL ROAD

GARSCUBE ROAD

KEPPOCHHILL ROAD

PINKSTON ROAD

SPRINGBURN ROAD

Ⓤ St George's Cross

34

M8

ROYSTON RD.

◀ M8 Edinburgh

BUCCLEUCH ST
Ⓤ **Police Station**
Cowcaddens

Royal Infirmary

CASTLE STREET

RENFREW STREET
SAUCHIEHALL STREET
BATH STREET
WEST REGENT STREET
WEST GEORGE STREET
VINCENT STREET
BOTHWELL STREET
ARGYLE STREET

PITT STREET
PITT STREET
BLYTHSWOOD STREET
WEST CAMPBELL STREET
HOPE STREET
RENFIELD STREET
WEST NILE STREET

Charing Cross Station

Buchanan St Bus Station

Garden of St Nicholas

Cathedral

St. Mungo's Museum
Ⓖ

Necropolis

Buchanan Street
Queen St Station
Ⓤ

CATHEDRAL STREET

Strathclyde University

Provand's Lordship

Central Station

UNION STREET

BUCHANAN ST

GEORGE SQUARE

GEORGE STREET

INGRAM STREET

DUKE ST

High Street Station

✉

ⓘ

St Enoch
Ⓤ

QUEEN ST

M E R C H A N T   C I T Y

HIGH STREET

Arches Theatre

BROOMIELAW

Argyle St Station

TRONGATE

GALLOWGATE

See 'Glasgow City Centre' Map

Barrowland

Barras Market

EAST END

KINGSTON BRIDGE

43

NELSON STREET

BRIDGE ST

NORFOLK STREET

COOK STREET

46 **47**

48

GREENDYKE STREET

SALTMARKET

LONDON RD

West Street
Ⓤ

Ⓤ Bridge Street
GORBALS

People's Palace

River Clyde

CROWN STREET

GORBALS STREET

Carling Academy

Citizens' Theatre

Templeton's Carpet Factory

THE GREEN

BALLATER STREET

Glasgow Green

▼ Queen's Park, A77 Kilmarnock

▼ Rutherglen

Kember & Jones	**19**	Mother India	**38**	Stravaigin	**21**	Tchai Ovna	**16**	The Ubiquitous	
Kokuryo	**39**	No. Sixteen	**30**	Stravaigin 2	**8**	Thai Siam	**40**	Chip	**12**
La Fiorentina	**45**	Paperinos		Tape Coffee		Tinderbox	**18**	University Café	**25**
Lupe Pintos	**23**	West End	**9**	& Bakehouse	**43**	Two Fat Ladies	**32**	Yen	**44**
Monster Mash	**27**	Parthenon	**3**						

© Crown copyright

The **West End** begins just over a mile west of Central station, and covers most of the area beyond the M8 motorway. In the nineteenth century, as the East End tumbled into poverty, the West End ascended the social scale with great speed, a process crowned by the arrival of the **university**. Today, this is still very much the student quarter of Glasgow, exuding a decorous air, with graceful avenues and parks, and inexpensive, interesting shops and cafés.

While the Clyde figures large in Glaswegian identity, it has generally had a divisive effect, relegating the "**Southside**" to secondary status. The redevelopment of **Clydeside** is going some way to adjust that perspective, and the southern ex-slum suburbs of Govan and the Gorbals, though holding little for visitors, are slowly becoming desirable. Parts of the Southside have always been very pleasant: the leafy enclaves of **Queen's Park** are home to the national football stadium, Hampden Park, while **Pollok Park** and the **Burrell Collection** are undisputed highlights of the city. All these Southside attractions can be easily reached by train or bus.

Information

The city's efficient **tourist office**, at 11 George Square (April & May Mon–Sat 9am–6pm, Sun 10am–6pm; June & Sept Mon–Sat 10am–7pm, Sun 10am–6pm; July & Aug Mon–Sat 9am–8pm, Sun 10am–6pm; rest of year Mon–Sat 9am–6pm; ☎0141/204 4400, ⓦ www.seeglasgow.com), provides a wide array of maps and leaflets, and will hook into VisitScotland's accommodation-booking service for you (fee £3). They also sell travel passes and theatre tickets and organize car rental. Pick up their free *Essential Guide to Glasgow*, a chunky brochure with details of every tourist attraction for miles around.

There's also a branch of the tourist office in the **airport's** international arrivals hall (daily 7.30am–5pm, except Oct–April Sun 8am–3.30pm; ☎0141/848 4440).

City transport

Although it can be tough negotiating Glasgow's steep hills, **walking** is the best way of exploring any one part of the city. However, as the main sights are scattered – the West End, for example, is a good thirty-minute walk from the centre – you'll probably need to use the comprehensive **public transport** system.

The best way to get between the city centre and the West End is to use the **Underground** (Mon–Sat 6.30am–11pm, Sun 11am–5.30pm), whose stations are marked with a large orange U. Affectionately known as the "Clockwork Orange" (there's only one, circular route and the trains are a garish bright orange), the service is extremely easy to use. There's a flat fare of £1, or you can buy a **day ticket** (called a Discovery Ticket) for £1.90 (Mon–Sat after 9.30am and all day Sun). The main stations are **Buchanan Street**, near George Square and connected to Queen Street train station by a moving walkway, and **St Enoch**, at the junction of Buchanan Street pedestrian precinct and Argyle Street. **Hillhead** station is bang in the heart of the West End, near the university.

If you're travelling beyond the city centre or the West End, or to the main sights on the Southside, you may need to use the bus and train networks. The array of different **bus** companies and the various routes they take is perplexing even to locals, and there's no easy guide to using them other than picking up individual timetables at the Travel Centre on St Enoch's Square (see opposite). The main operator is First Glasgow (ⓦ www.firstgroup.com); Arriva (ⓦ www.arriva .co.uk) also operates many services. Information on relevant services is given at some bus stops.

City tours

City Sightseeing (April–Oct daily 9.20am–4.40pm; £8.50) run tours of the sights by **open-top bus**, which leave every half-hour from George Square on a continuous circuit of all the major attractions in the city centre and West End, allowing you to get on and off as you please. You can combine this with a **river taxi** trip (£5.50 extra) on the Clyde, a route also plied by the fast **powerboat rides** offered by Seaforce (from £6 for 30min; ☎0141/221 1070, ⓦwww.seaforce.co.uk), based at Glasgow Harbour near the SECC. Back on dry land, Journeyman Tours (☎0800/093 9984, ⓦwww .journeymantours.co.uk; Oct–April tours by booking only) lead you **on foot** round the Merchant City (Sun–Thurs 7.30pm) or on a **pub and ceilidh** tour (Fri & Sat 7pm). Mercat Tours also offers a guided **ghost tour** round some of the spookier parts of the city (for details and bookings contact ☎0141/586 5378 or 07761 092948, ⓦwww .mercat-glasgow.co.uk).

The suburban **train** network is swift and convenient. Suburbs south of the Clyde are connected to Central station, either at the mainline station or the subterranean low-level station, while trains from Queen Street (which also has mainline and low-level stations) head into the northeast suburbs. There are two grim but functional **cross-city lines**: the one running through Central station connects to southeastern districts as far out as Lanark, while the Queen Street line links to the East End and points east. Trains on both lines go through **Partick** station, near the West End, which is also an underground stop; beyond Partick, the trains are an excellent way to link to points west and northwest of Glasgow, including Milngavie (for the start of the West Highland Way), Dumbarton and Helensburgh.

You can hail a black **taxi** from anywhere in the city centre, day or night. There are also taxi ranks at Central and Queen Street train stations and Buchanan Street bus station. Fares are very reasonable; from the city centre to the West End costs £4–5, or the three-mile journey from Central station to Pollok Park and the Burrell Collection costs £8–10.

As for **driving**, the M8 motorway runs right through the heart of Glasgow, making the centre very accessible; once you're there, however, the grid of one-way streets and pedestrian precincts can be frustrating to navigate. You'll find plenty of parking meters and there are many **car parks** dotted around the city centre, though the charges can mount up if you're parked in one all day.

Transport passes and information

Various **public transport passes** are available if you plan to do lots of travelling on one day or are in the city for more than a few days. For train and underground travel the **Roundabout Glasgow** ticket (£4.50; available Mon–Fri after 9am, and all day Sat & Sun) gives unlimited travel for a day. The simplest of a complicated system of **Zonecards**, covering train, underground, buses and ferries, costs around £13 and gives travel for a week in central Glasgow, including Partick in the west and the Burrell Collection in the south. Both of the main bus companies offer tickets for all-day travel on their buses, which are cheaper after 9.30am on weekdays.

To help demystify the system, and get detailed information on local public transport, make for the neo-Gothic hut of the **Travel Centre** (Mon–Sat 8.30am–5.30pm), located a couple of hundred yards southwest of the tourist office above St Enoch underground station, where you can pick up sheaves of maps, leaflets and bus timetables. There are smaller Travel Centres at Buchanan

Street bus station and Hillhead underground station. For information on all transport within the city and further afield, call the fairly efficient national Traveline ☎0870/608 2608, ⓦwww.travelinescotland.com.

503 2476

Accommodation

There's a good range of **accommodation** in Glasgow, from a large, well-run youth hostel through to some highly fashionable (and not over-priced) designer hotels in the centre. The majority of the best guesthouses and B&Bs can be found in the West End or in the southern suburb of Queen's Park. In general, prices are significantly lower than in Edinburgh, and given that many hotels are business-oriented, you can often negotiate good deals at weekends.

Hotels and guesthouses

It's worth booking ahead at **hotels and guesthouses** to ensure a good room, especially in summer. If you're prepared to sacrifice character, ambience and home comforts, you'll often find the cheapest rooms in the city at the **budget chain hotels** found throughout the city centre. Big players include Ibis (☎0141/225 6000, ⓦwww.ibishotel.com), Travel Inn (☎0870/238 3320, ⓦwww.travelinn.co.uk) and Express by Holiday Inn (☎0141/548 5000, ⓦwww.hiexpressglasgow.co.uk) – the latter two also have hotels in a handy position near Glasgow International Airport.

City centre

Adelaide's 209 Bath St ☎0141/248 4970, ⓦwww.adelaides.co.uk. Eight simple, functional rooms in a beautifully restored church building, run by pleasant staff as part of a broad-thinking, approachable Baptist church community. Breakfast excluded. ❸

Bewley's 110 Bath St ☎0141/353 0800, ⓦwww.bewleyshotels.com. Angular, glass-fronted new central hotel, part of the famous Irish chain, with rooftop views from the upper floors and double, triple and family rooms at a year-round flat rate. ❹

The Brunswick 106 Brunswick St ☎0141/552 0001, ⓦwww.brunswickhotel.co.uk. A small, independent and individual designer hotel in the heart of the Merchant City; fashionable but good value with minimalist furniture and a smart bar and restaurant. ❸

Cathedral House 28 Cathedral Squqare ☎0141/552 3519, ⓦwww.cathedralhouse.com. In the oldest part of the city near the cathedral, this free-standing red sandstone Victorian building with turrets and high chimney stacks has comfortable modern rooms and a popular downstairs bar and bistro. ❺

Langs 2 Port Dundas Place ☎0141/333 1500, ⓦwww.langshotels.co.uk. Big, sassy, classy but refreshingly independent modern hotel with a spa, trendy restaurants and lots of mod cons. ❻

Malmaison 278 West George St ☎0141/572 1000, ⓦwww.malmaison.com. Glasgow's version of the sleek, chic mini-chain, an austere Grecian-temple frontage masking a superbly comfortable designer hotel. ❼

The Old School House 194 Renfrew St ☎0141/332 7600, ⓔoschoolh@hotmail.com. Attractive stand-alone villa with seventeen well-equipped and keenly priced rooms right next to a rather gruesome annexe of the School of Art. ❸

Pipers' Tryst 30–34 McPhater St ☎0141/353 5551, ⓦwww.thepipingcentre.co.uk. Eight fortunately soundproofed, hotel-grade rooms attached to the bagpiping centre; a café on the ground floor (Mon–Sat) serves breakfasts and evening meals. ❹

Radisson SAS 301 Argyle St ☎0141/204 3333, ⓦwww.radisson.com. Huge place by Central station with 250 rooms, a health centre and a decent brasserie – it's also one of the more dramatic pieces of modernist architecture in the city centre. ❻

Saint Judes 190 Bath St ☎0141/352 8800, ⓦwww.saintjudes.com. Elegant contemporary boutique hotel with six rooms and some exquisite designer touches. ❻

West End and Clydeside

Alamo Guest House 46 Gray St ☎0141/339 2395, ⓦwww.alamoguesthouse.com. Good-value, family-run boarding house next to Kelvingrove Park. Small but comfortable rooms. ❷

Ambassador 7 Kelvin Drive ☎0141/946 1018, @www.glasgowhotelsandapartments.co.uk. A standard but comfortable small hotel in lovely surroundings next to the River Kelvin and Botanic Gardens. ⑤

Argyll 973 Sauchiehall St ☎0141/337 3313, @www.argyllhotelglasgow.co.uk. Lots of tartan trimmings, but this well-run hotel near Kelvingrove Museum and Art Gallery has neat rooms and friendly staff. ⑤

City Inn Finnieston Quay ☎0141/240 1002, @www.cityinn.com. One of the better of the chain hotels made interesting by its riverside location right under the Finnieston crane; stylish rooms and decent rates. ⑥

Kirklee 11 Kensington Gate ☎0141/334 5555, @www.kirkleehotel.co.uk. Characterful West End B&B in an Edwardian town house, with antique furniture and walls crammed with paintings and etchings. ⑤

Number 36 36 St Vincent Crescent ☎0141/248 2086, @www.no36.co.uk. Neat, comfortable guesthouse in a lovely crescent well located for Kelvingrove, the SECC and transport links to the city centre. ④

One Devonshire Gardens 1 Devonshire Gardens, Great Western Rd ☎0141/339 2001, @www.onedevonshiregardens.com. Glasgow's most exclusive and exquisite small hotel, a ten-minute walk up the Great Western Road from the Botanic Gardens. Good chance it's where visiting pop and film stars will stay. ⑦

Southside

Best Western Ewington 132 Queen's Drive ☎0141/423 1152, @www.ewingtonhotel.co.uk. A grand, upmarket hotel with a nice outlook onto Queen's and a subterranean restaurant. Prices can drop dramatically at weekends. ⑤

Boswell Hotel 27 Mansionhouse Rd ☎0141/632 9812. Informal, relaxing hotel in an old Queen's Park villa with a popular locals' bar and conservatory restaurant. ④

Glasgow Guest House 56 Dumbreck Rd ☎0141/427 0129, @get-me.to/glasgowguest-house. Pleasant if subdued four-room guesthouse with some antique furniture, good disabled facilities and handy transport links into the city centre. ②

Reidholme Guest House 36 Regent Park Square ☎0141/423 1855, @reidholm@fish.co.uk. Small, friendly guesthouse in a quiet side street, designed by Alexander "Greek" Thomson (see p.292). ③

Hostels, campsites and self-catering

Glasgow doesn't have nearly as many **hostels** as Edinburgh, though it isn't short of bed space, thanks to the bright-pink liveried, seven-storey *Euro Hostel* smack in the centre of the city at 318 Clyde St (☎0141/222 2828, @www.euro-hostels.com), which tries to bridge the gap between backpacker hostel and budget hotel. Its 360 beds are all bunks but they're in smart en-suite rooms sleeping two, four, six or more – some of which have great views. Bed and continental breakfast is from £13.75. The popular and recently upgraded SYHA hostel, 7–8 Park Terrace (☎0870/004 1119, @www.syha.org.uk), is located in a large town house in one of the West End's grandest terraces. It's a ten-minute walk south of Kelvinbridge underground station; bus #11 or #44 from the city centre leaves you with a short stroll west up Woodlands Road.

Campsite

The only **campsite** within a decent distance of Glasgow is *Craigendmuir Park*, Campsie View, Stepps (☎0141/779 4159, @www.craigendmuir.co.uk), four miles northeast of the centre, about fifteen minutes' walk from Stepps train station. It has adequate facilities with showers, a laundry and a shop, but there are only ten pitches.

Self-catering

Low-priced **self-catering** rooms and flats are available at the University of Glasgow (☎0141/330 4116, @www.cvso.co.uk) from June to mid-September, mostly located in the West End, with prices starting at around £15 per person per night. The University of Strathclyde (☎0141/553 4148, @www.rescat.strath.ac.uk) has various sites available during the same period, most of which are gathered around the cathedral: B&B in single rooms is available near the main campus in Cathedral Street starting at £25 per person per night, though you can pick up four-bed rooms for as little as £60.

Embassy Apartments, at 8 Kelvin Drive (☎0141/946 6698, Ⓦ www.glasgowhotelsandapartments.co.uk; ❹), have useful self-catering apartments located near Byres Road and the Botanic Gardens, available on a nightly basis.

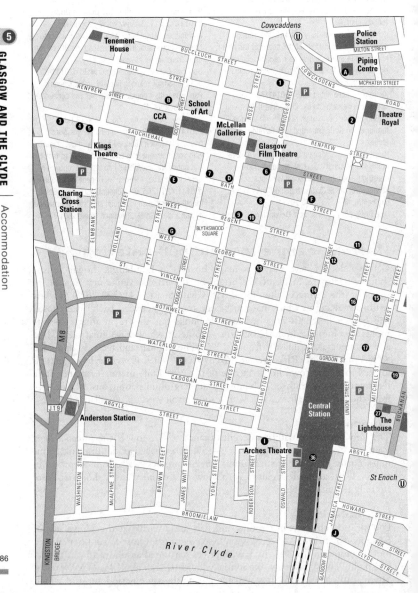

The City Centre

Glasgow's large **City Centre** is ranged across the north bank of the River Clyde. At its geographical heart is **George Square**, a nineteenth-century municipal showpiece crowned by the enormous **City Chambers** at its eastern end. Behind this lies one of the greatest marketing successes of the 1980s, the

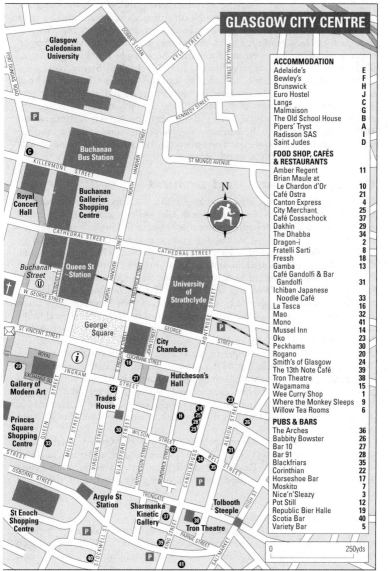

GLASGOW CITY CENTRE

ACCOMMODATION
Adelaide's	E
Bewley's	F
Brunswick	H
Euro Hostel	J
Langs	C
Malmaison	G
The Old School House	B
Pipers' Tryst	A
Radisson SAS	I
Saint Judes	D

FOOD SHOP, CAFÉS & RESTAURANTS
Amber Regent	11
Brian Maule at Le Chardon d'Or	10
Café Ostra	21
Canton Express	4
City Merchant	25
Café Cossachock	37
Dakhin	29
The Dhabba	34
Dragon-i	2
Fratelli Sarti	8
Fressh	18
Gamba	13
Café Gandolfi & Bar Gandolfi	31
Ichiban Japanese Noodle Café	33
La Tasca	16
Mao	32
Mono	41
Mussel Inn	14
Oko	23
Peckhams	30
Rogano	20
Smith's of Glasgow	24
The 13th Note Café	39
Tron Theatre	38
Wagamama	15
Wee Curry Shop	1
Where the Monkey Sleeps	9
Willow Tea Rooms	6

PUBS & BARS
The Arches	36
Babbity Bowster	26
Bar 10	27
Bar 91	28
Blackfriars	35
Corinthian	22
Horseshoe Bar	17
Moskito	7
Nice'n'Sleazy	3
Pot Still	12
Republic Bier Halle	19
Scotia Bar	40
Variety Bar	5

0 — 250yds

© Crown copyright

Merchant City, an area which blends magnificent Victorian architecture with yuppie conversions. The grand buildings and trendy cafés cling to the borders of the rundown **East End**, a strongly working-class district that chooses to ignore its rather showy neighbour. The oldest part of Glasgow, around the **Cathedral**, lies immediately north of the East End.

Called by poet John Betjeman "the greatest Victorian city in the world", Glasgow's commercial core spreads west of George Square, and is mostly built on a large grid system – possibly inspired by Edinburgh's New Town – with ruler-straight roads soon rising up severe hills to grand, sandblasted buildings. The same style was copied by many North American cities, and indeed parts of Glasgow have been pressed into service as nineteenth-century New York in films such as *House of Mirth*. The main shopping areas here are **Argyle Street**, running parallel to the river, and **Buchanan Street**, which links Argyle Street to the pedestrianized shopping thoroughfare, **Sauchiehall Street**. Just to the northwest of here is Charles Rennie Mackintosh's famous **Glasgow School of Art**. Lying between the commercial bustle of Argyle and Sauchiehall streets, and to the immediate west of Buchanan Street, are the contours of an Ice Age drumlin (one of three main drumlins in the area), now known as **Blythswood Hill**. In comparison with the bustling shopping parades surrounding it on three sides, this area is remarkably quiet and reserved, with streets of Georgian buildings crowned by neat Blythswood Square.

George Square and around

Now hemmed in by the city's grinding traffic, the imposing architecture of **George Square** reflects the confidence of Glasgow's Victorian age. The wide-open plaza almost has a continental airiness about it, although there isn't much subtlety about the eighty-foot column rising up at its centre. It's topped by a statue of Sir Walter Scott, even though his links with Glasgow are, at best, sketchy. Haphazardly dotted around the great writer's plinth are a number of dignified statues of assorted luminaries, ranging from Queen Victoria to Scots heroes such as James Watt and wee Robbie Burns. The florid splendour of the **City Chambers**, opened by Queen Victoria in 1888, occupies the entire eastern end of the square. Built from wealth gained by colonial trade and heavy industry, it epitomizes the aspirations and optimism of late-Victorian city elders. Its intricately detailed facade includes high-minded friezes typical of the era: the four nations which then comprised the United Kingdom (England, Scotland, Wales and Ireland) at the feet of the throned queen, the British colonies and allegorical figures representing Religion, Virtue and Knowledge. You can head inside and wander around the ground floor, where you'll see domed mosaic ceilings and two mighty Italian marble stairwells, but to get any further join in one of the free **guided tours** of the labyrinthine interior (Mon–Fri 10.30am & 2.30pm).

Equally opulent is the **Merchant's House** opposite Queen Street station (appointment only; ☎0141/221 8272; free), where the grand Banqueting Hall and silk-lined Directors' Room are highlights. Even if you don't get inside, look out for the golden square-rigged ship on a globe perched on the top of the building.

The Gallery of Modern Art

Queen Street leads south from George Square to **Royal Exchange Square**, where the focal point is the graceful mansion built in 1775 for tobacco lord William Cunninghame. This was the most ostentatious of the Glasgow merchants' homes and, having served as the city's Royal Exchange and central library, now houses the **Gallery of Modern Art** (Mon–Wed & Sat 10am–5pm, Thurs 10am–8pm, Fri & Sun 11am–5pm; free). Surrounded by controversy from the day it opened in 1996, GOMA (as the gallery is often referred to) has tended to please the punters more than the critics, who have damned the place for emphasizing presentation over content. However, what it lacks in critical approbation it more than makes up for in popularity, not least with Glaswegians, giving the place a down-to-earth, populist feel lacking in many of the country's grander art collections.

The mirrored reception area leads you straight into the spacious ground-floor gallery, a striking room with elaborate gold leaf fringing its barrelled ceiling, rows of Corinthian pillars and huge windows. It's principally used for temporary exhibitions, though large-scale socially committed works by the "New Glasgow Boys" – Peter Howson, Adrian Wisniewski, Ken Currie and Steven Campbell – are often included. Look out too for the kinetic sculpture *Titanic* by Russian émigré Eduard Bersudsky, made of scrap metal and old junk, but symbolizing freedom of movement and expression.

Down in the basement there's an art library and café, while the smaller galleries on the two upper floors are either linked together for larger exhibitions or used to show smaller themed shows by contemporary artists from around the world. It's worth exploring the various nooks and crannies which lead off the main galleries, where there's a chance you'll stumble upon pieces from the permanent collection including a gruesome row of guillotined heads in baskets by Scottish conceptual artist Ian Hamilton Finlay as well as the mischievous *Peep Hole* in chunky, sinuous wood by Tim Stead.

Along Buchanan Street

Buchanan Street runs north–south one block west of George Square, defining Glasgow's main shopping district. At the southern end of the street is **Princes Square**, one of the most stylish and imaginative shopping centres in the country, hollowed out of the innards of a soft sandstone building. The interior, all recherché Art Deco and ornate ironwork, has lots of pricey, highly fashionable shops, the whole place set to a soothing background of classical music. A short walk south is the **St Enoch Shopping Centre**, sandwiched between Argyle and Howard streets – a lofty glass pyramid built around a redundant train station.

Glaswegians' voracious appetite for shopping is fed further at the northern end of Buchanan Street, just beyond the underground station, where the **Buchanan Galleries** is a bewilderingly vast shopping mall of some 600,000 square feet stuffed with most of the predictable chain stores. Next door is the anonymous £30-million **Royal Concert Hall**, with

△ Princes Square

only three huge flagpoles protruding to proclaim that this is, in fact, a building of note. The showpiece hall does, however, have an excellent auditorium which plays host to world-class musical events, from touring orchestras to rock acts, while the lobbies are used for temporary art exhibitions. Standing outside the Concert Hall is a statue of **Donald Dewar**, Scotland's First Minister until his untimely death in 2000, looking rather dour and serious in a plain suit and tie, though it's testament to his self-depreciating humour and enjoyment of Glasgow life that the statue was placed among the shopping throngs and late-night revellers rather than the civic dignitaries of George Square.

The Lighthouse

At 11 Mitchell Lane, an otherwise nondescript alleyway between Buchanan Street and Union Street, is **The Lighthouse** (Mon & Wed–Sat 10.30am–5pm, Tues 11am–5pm, Sun noon–5pm; £3; Ⓦwww.thelighthouse.co.uk), a spectacularly converted Charles Rennie Mackintosh building which has found new life as Scotland's Centre for Architecture, Design and the City. The 1895 building was Mackintosh's first public commission, and housed the offices of the *Glasgow Herald* newspaper; despite glass and sandstone additions by architects Page & Park, it retains many original features, including the distinctive tower from which the building takes its name. The venue played a central role in Glasgow's reign as City of Architecture and Design in 1999, and acts as a permanent legacy of that year, mounting temporary exhibitions on design and architecture alongside the permanent **Mackintosh Interpretation Centre**, a great place to learn more about the man and his work. It features plans, models, photographs, original objects and computer and video displays which explore many of Mackintosh's unique buildings and interiors, while both the viewing platform and Lighthouse Tower itself gives fantastic views out over the city skyline to a number of his important buildings, including the School of Art and Scotland Street School.

The Merchant City

The grid of streets that lies immediately east of the City Chambers is known as the **Merchant City** (Ⓦwww.glasgowmerchantcity.net), an area of eighteenth-century warehouses and homes once bustling with cotton, tobacco and sugar traders, which in the last two decades has been sandblasted and swabbed clean with greater enthusiasm and municipal money than any other part of Glasgow in an attempt to bring residents back into the city centre. The expected flood of yuppies, however, was more like a trickle, and the latest efforts to woo them centre on New York-style loft conversions. Yet the expensive designer shops, style bars and bijou cafés continue to flock here, giving the area a pervasive air of sophistication and chic. A Merchant City Trail leaflet, which guides you around a dozen of the most interesting buildings in the area, is normally available at the tourist office or from the attractions in the area.

At the junction of Ingram and John streets is the delicate white spire of **Hutcheson Hall**, the long-standing regional headquarters for the National Trust for Scotland (Mon–Sat 10am–5pm; free). It's possible that they'll be forced to move elsewhere sometime during 2006 or 2007, but if not, it's worth a visit to look around the ground-floor shop which displays some attractive work by contemporary designers and craftsmen. Upstairs, there's a particularly fine, ornately decorated hall.

Almost opposite in the other direction, a little way down Glassford Street, the Robert Adam-designed **Trades Hall** (April–Oct Mon–Fri 10am–5pm, Sat

10am–2pm, Sun noon–5pm; Nov–March Sun noon–5pm or by appointment; ☎0141/552 2418, ⓦwww.tradeshallglasgow.co.uk; £3.50) is easily distinguished by its neat, green copper dome. Purpose-built in 1794, it still functions as the headquarters of the Glasgow trade guilds. Its history can be traced back to 1605 when fourteen societies of well-to-do city merchants, who were the forerunners of the trade unions, first incorporated. These included a Bakers' Guild, and societies for Hammermen, Gardeners, Bonnet-Makers, Wrights and Weavers, although today they have limited connections to their respective trades and act as charitably minded associations from all sections of Glasgow's business community (mostly male). The former civic pride and status of the guilds is still evident, however, from the rich assortment of carvings and stained-glass windows, with a lively pictorial representation of the different trades in the silk frieze around the walls of the first-floor banqueting hall.

Glasgow Cross

Before 1846, **Glasgow Cross** – the junction of Trongate, Gallowgate and the High Street, at the southeastern corner of the Merchant City – was the city's principal intersection, until the construction of the new train station near George Square shifted the city's emphasis west. The turreted seventeenth-century **Tolbooth Steeple** still stands here, although the rest of the building has long since disappeared, and today the stern tower is little more than a traffic hazard at a busy junction.

Sharmanka Kinetic Gallery

Tucked away on the second floor of 14 King St, an extension of Candleriggs on the south side of the Trongate, is Glasgow's most unusual art gallery. Founded by Russian émigrés Eduard Bersudsky and Tatyana Jakovskaya, the **Sharmanka Kinetic Gallery** (ⓦwww.sharmanka.co.uk) is like a mad inventor's magical workshop, with hundreds of carved figures mounted on moving contraptions made from old wheels, levers, lights and scrap metal. A unique art form, Sharmanka (Russian for barrel organ or hurdy gurdy) is at once hypnotic, playful and deeply poignant, with its mechanical figures imprisoned in their relentless routine, while choreographed lighting draws you from one part of the show to the next and rather sinister fairground-style music plays in the background. It takes an hour for the sculptures to "perform", so the full programmes are only run a few times during the week (Thurs 7pm, Sun 3pm & 7pm; £4), although shorter shows can be organized if you call ☎0141/552 7080 to make arrangements. Note that the gallery is due to relocate to a nearby space for a period during 2006–7 while the original building is renovated. Phone or check the website for the latest.

The East End

East of Glasgow Cross, down Gallowgate beyond the train lines, lies the **East End**, the district that perhaps most closely corresponds to the old perception of Glasgow. Hemmed in by Glasgow Green to the south and the old university to the west, this densely packed industrial area essentially created the city's wealth. The Depression caused the closure of many factories, leaving communities stranded in an industrial wasteland. Today isolated pubs, tatty shops and cafés sit amidst this dereliction, in sharp contrast to the gloss of the Merchant City only a few blocks to the west. Walking around here you definitely get the sense that you're off the tourist trail, but unless you're here after dark it's not as threatening as it may feel, and there's no doubt that the area offers a rich flavour of working-class Glasgow.

Glasgow, founded on religion, built on trade and now well established as a cultural centre, has become recognized for its architectural riches, from the medieval cathedral to the modern glass-lined galleries of the Burrell Collection. Most dominant is the legacy of the **Victorian age**, when booming trade and industry allowed merchants to commission the finest architects of the day. The celebrated work of **Charles Rennie Mackintosh** (see box on p.298) took Glasgow architecture to the forefront of early twentieth-century design, a final flowering of homespun genius before economic conditions effectively stopped the architectural trade in its tracks, its revival only really taking hold in the 1980s and 1990s.

The city's expansion: 1750–1850

Glasgow's great expansion was initiated in the eighteenth century by wealthy tobacco merchants who built the grand edifices of public and municipal importance that still make up much of the **Merchant City**. One of the finest Merchant City views is down Garth Street, which frames the Venetian windows and Ionic columns of the **Trades Hall**, designed by Robert Adam in 1791, while nearby **Hutcheson Hall** boasts an elegant tower that moves from a square through octagonals to a drum – an early nineteenth-century architectural nod to the Renaissance by the architect David Hamilton.

Further west, **Royal Exchange Square** is one of the best examples of a typical Glasgow square: treeless, bare and centred around a building of importance, the 1829 **Royal Exchange**, now housing the Gallery of Modern Art. As workers piled into the centre of Glasgow in the early nineteenth century, filling up the already crowded tenements, wealthy residents began moving west to the gridded streets that line **Blythswood Hill** (mostly developed after 1820) with two- or three-storey terraces, their porches and heavy cornices providing textural relief to the endless sandstone monotony. The dignified proportions and design of **Blythswood Square** are a highlight of this area; at no. 5 the later Art Nouveau doorway designed by Charles Rennie Mackintosh sits incongruously amongst the Georgian solidity. Above all, the long streets provide a beautiful selection of open-ended views, one moment leading into the heart of the city, the next filled with distant hills and sky.

Desiring to surround themselves with trees and fields, the well-to-do continued their migration west; in the early 1830s, the Woodlands Hill development was completed beyond Charing Cross – a leafy parkland area in contrast to the treeless town squares of the city centre. Here **Woodside Crescent**, leading into Woodside Terrace, is a severe line of buildings with splendid Doric porches and neatly organized gardens. **Park Circus**, on the other hand, is a parade of uninterrupted Georgian magnificence, with delicate detail – such as narrow window slots on either side of the doors – enhancing the dignified crescent. It's an excellent example of grand planning which, having changed from residential to commercial use, is rapidly being transformed again into upmarket designer apartments.

"Greek" Thomson and the Victorians

Long since overshadowed by Charles Rennie Mackintosh, the design of **Alexander "Greek" Thomson**, in the latter half of the nineteenth century, though well respected in its time, has been sadly neglected. As his nickname suggests, his work took the principles of Greek architecture, but reprocessed them in a highly unique manner. Energetic and talented, he designed buildings from lowly

Three hundred yards down either London Road or Gallowgate is **The Barras**, Glasgow's largest and most popular weekend market (Sat & Sun 10am–5pm; ⓦwww.glasgow-barrowland.com). Red iron gates announce its tenements to grand suburban villas. The 1857 **St Vincent Street Church**, his best work, has a massive simplicity and serenity lightened by the use of exotic Egyptian and Hindu motifs, particularly in the tower with its decorated egg-shaped dome. This fusion of the Classical and the Eastern stands out for its originality at a time when Gothic Revival or Renaissance work was all the rage. Thomson's buildings are now coming to the prominence they deserve, though some were tragically torn down in the municipal clearances of the 1970s. Most recently, the National Trust has opened his finest domestic dwelling, **Holmwood House**, on the Southside, to the public (see p.311).

West from Park Circus lies **Glasgow University** (1866–86), its Gothic Revivalism – the work of Sir George Gilbert Scott – representing everything that Greek Thomson despised; he called it "sixteenth-century Scottish architecture clothed in fourteenth-century French details". Scottish features abound, such as crow-stepped gables, round turrets with conical caps and the top-heavy central tower. Inside, cloisters and quadrants sum up a suitably scholastic severity.

Originally conceived as a convenient way to house the influx of workers in the late 1800s, the Glasgow **tenement** design became more refined as the wealthy middle classes began to realize its potential. Mainly constructed between 1860 and 1910, tenements have three to five storeys with two or three apartments per floor. Important rooms are picked out with bay windows, middle storeys are emphasized by architraves or decorated panels below sill or above lintel, and street junctions are given importance by swelling bay windows, turrets and domes. A fascinating example of the style of these buildings, as well as the typical style of life inside them, can be seen at the **Tenement House** (see p.300), while west of the university the streets off **Byres Road** are lined with similarly grand tenement buildings, in particular the Baronial red sandstone of Great George Street.

From World War I to the present

World War I put an end to the glorious century of Glasgow building, and the Depression years did little to enhance the city. However, since World War II bombing was targeted on the shipbuilding district of Clydebank, west of the centre, most of the city's legacy of fine sandstone buildings survived intact.

Glassy office buildings have sprung up in recent years, their mirrored walls basking in the reflected glory of the surrounding buildings to disguise their banality of design. Modern domestic architecture has proved relentlessly utilitarian, with the exception of the experimental **Homes for the Future** complex on the north side of Glasgow Green, conceived as part of Glasgow's Year of Architecture and Design in 1999 to introduce practical prototypes of urban living in the twenty-first century. However, the 1980s onwards have seen the return of the grand public building as inheritor of architectural innovation. Beginning with the imaginative **Burrell Collection**, the theme has been taken up by the titanium-clad behemoths of Clydeside: the unmistakeable Clyde Auditorium, better known as the "**Armadillo**", the curvaceous **Science Centre** and its new neighbour, the glass shoe-box of BBC Scotland's new HQ. This is not to ignore the poverty of artistry which went into great works such as the Kingston Bridge and Royal Concert Hall, but few could argue that Glasgow has failed to open itself to innovation and ideas. Above all, the city can be credited with involving its citizens in an awareness that everyone is influenced, as well as represented, by the buildings around them.

official entrance, but boundaries are breached as the stalls – selling household goods, bric-a-brac, secondhand clothes and records, none of it of particularly high quality – spill out into the surrounding cobbled streets. The fast-talking traders, lively atmosphere and entertaining vignettes of Glasgow life make it an offbeat diversion from shopping-mall banality.

Between London Road and the River Clyde are the wide and tree-lined spaces of **Glasgow Green**. Reputedly the oldest public park in Britain, the Green has been common land since at least 1178, when it was first mentioned in records. Glaswegians hold it very dear, considering it to be an immortal link between themselves and their ancestors, for whom a stroll on the Green was a favourite Sunday afternoon jaunt. It has also been the site of many of the city's major political demonstrations – the Chartists in the 1830s and Scottish republican campaigners in the 1920s – and was the traditional culmination of the May Day marches until the 1950s, when the celebrations were moved to Queen's Park. Various memorials (some in bad states of disrepair) are dotted around the lawns: the 146-foot **Nelson Monument**; the ornate but derelict terracotta **Doulton Fountain**, rising like a wedding cake to a pinnacle where a forlorn Queen Victoria oversees her crumbling Empire; and the stern monument extolling the evils of drink and the glory of God that was erected by the nineteenth-century **Temperance movement** – now quite a meeting place for local drunks. On the northeast side of the Green, just beyond the People's Palace, it's worth taking a look at the extraordinary **Templeton's Carpet Factory**, a massive brick edifice of turrets, arched windows, mosaic-style patterns and castellated grandeur designed in the style of the Doge's Palace in Venice and built in 1892. Following its days as a carpet factory it has been a small business centre and a health centre, but is now disused.

The People's Palace

Opposite the Templeton's carpet factory on Glasgow Green you can still see some poles erected to hang out washing, recalling the days when the Green was very much a public space in daily use. Beside these, the **People's Palace** (Mon–Thurs & Sat 10am–5pm, Fri & Sun 11am–5pm; free) houses a wonderfully haphazard evocation of the city's history. This squat, red sandstone Victorian building, with a vast semicircular glasshouse tacked on the back, was purpose-built as a museum back in 1898 – almost a century before the rest of the country caught onto the fashion for social-history collections. Many of the displays are designed to instill a warm glow in the memories of older locals: the museum is refreshingly unpretentious, with visitors are almost always outnumbered by Glaswegian families.

On the **top floor**, glowing murals by local artist Ken Currie powerfully evoke the spirit of radical Glasgow, from the Carlton Weavers strike in 1787 to the Red Clydesiders of the 1920s (a radical Independent Labour Party formed during the post-World War I economic slump), and look down upon a potted history of Glasgow's social and economic development. Decorated by Suffragette flags and trade-union banners, the room contains a host of memorabilia, including the desk of John MacLean, who became consul to the Russian Bolshevik government in 1918. The **west wing** looks at famous Glasgow products through history, with displays of everything from cast-iron railings and biscuit wrappers to a giant portrait of Billy Connolly. In the **East Gallery**, an entertaining sound-and-light show reconstructs a "single-end" or one-roomed house, a typical setting for the daily life of hundreds of thousands of Glasgow people through the years. Downstairs, various themes with a particular resonance in Glasgow are explored, including alcohol, the traditional holiday excursion "doon the watter" by steamer to various Clyde coastal resorts and some guidance to understanding "the Patter", Glaswegians' idiosyncratic version of the Queen's English.

The glasshouse at the back of the palace contains the **Winter Gardens**, with a café, water garden, twittering birds and assorted tropical plants and shrubs.

The cathedral area

Rising north up the hill from the Tolbooth Steeple at Glasgow Cross is Glasgow's **High Street**. In British cities, the name is commonly associated with the busiest central thoroughfare, and it's a surprise to see how forlorn and dilapidated Glasgow's version is, long superseded by the grander thoroughfares further west. The High Street leads up to the **Cathedral**, on the site of Glasgow's original settlement.

Glasgow Cathedral

Built in 1136, destroyed in 1192 and rebuilt soon after, stumpy-spired **Glasgow Cathedral** (April–Sept Mon–Sat 9.30am–6pm, Sun 2–5pm; Oct–March Mon–Sat 9.30am–4pm, Sun 2–4pm; free; ⓦ www.glasgowcathedral.org.uk) was not completed until the late fifteenth century, with the final reconstruction of the chapter house and the aisle designed by Robert Blacader, the city's first archbishop. Thanks to the intervention of the city guilds, it is the only Scottish mainland cathedral to have escaped the hands of religious reformers in the sixteenth century. The cathedral is dedicated to the city's patron saint and reputed founder, St Mungo, about whom four popular stories are frequently told – they even make an appearance on the city's coat of arms. These involve a bird that he brought back to life, the bell with which he summoned the faithful to prayer, a tree that he managed to make spontaneously combust and a fish that he caught with a repentant adulterous queen's ring on its tongue.

Because of the sloping ground on which it is built, at its east end the cathedral is effectively on two levels, the crypt being part of the lower church. On entering, you arrive in the impressively lofty nave of the **upper church**, with the lower church entirely hidden from view. Most of this upper church was

△ Glasgow Cathedral

completed under the direction of Bishop William de Bondington (1233–58), although later design elements came from Blacader. Either side of the nave, the narrow **aisles** are illuminated by vivid stained-glass windows, most of which date from the last century. Threadbare Union flags and military pennants hang listlessly beneath them, serving as a reminder that the cathedral is very much a part of the Unionist Protestant tradition. Beyond the nave, the **choir** is hidden from view by the curtained stone pulpit, making the interior feel a great deal smaller than might be expected from the outside. In the choir's northeastern corner, a small door leads into the gloomy **sacristy**, in which Glasgow University was first founded over five hundred years ago. Wooden boards mounted on the walls detail the alternating Roman Catholic and Protestant clergy of the cathedral, testimony to the turbulence and fluctuations of the Church in Scotland.

Two sets of steps from the nave lead down into the **lower church**, where you'll see the dark and musty **chapel** surrounding the tomb of St Mungo. The saint's relics were removed in the late Middle Ages, although the tomb still forms the centrepiece. The chapel itself is one of the most glorious examples of medieval architecture in Scotland, best seen in the delicate fan vaulting rising up from the thicket of cool stone columns. Scots designer Robert Stewart was commissioned in 1979 to produce a tapestry detailing the four myths of St Mungo, which can be illuminated using the button at the bottom of the north-side stairs to reveal its swirl of browns and oranges. Also in the lower church, the spaciously light **Blacader Aisle** was originally built as a two-storey extension; today only this lower section survives, where the bright, and frequently gory, medieval ceiling bosses stand out superbly against the simple whitewashed vaulting.

The Necropolis

Rising up behind the Cathedral, the atmospheric **Necropolis** is a grassy mound covered in a fantastic assortment of crumbling and tumbling gravestones, ornate urns, gloomy catacombs and Neoclassical temples. Inspired by the Père Lachaise cemetery in Paris, developer John Strong created a garden of death in 1833, and it quickly became a fitting spot for the great and the good of wealthy nineteenth-century Glasgow to indulge their vanity. Various paths lead through the rows of eroding, neglected graves, and from the summit, next to the column topped with an indignant John Knox, there are superb **views** which capture the city and its trademark mix of grit and grace – the steaming chimneys of the Tennants brewery, the traffic on the M8 motorway, the crowded city-centre offices, the serene cathedral itself and a wide cityscape of spires and high-rise blocks to the south and east. Glasgow City Council has recently started running free tours of the cemetery, lasting around one hour (phone ℡0141/552 1142 for details).

Cathedral Square

Back in Cathedral Square, the **St Mungo Museum of Religious Life and Art** (Mon–Thurs & Sat 10am–5pm, Fri & Sun 11am–5pm; free), housed in a late twentieth-century pastiche of a Scots medieval town house, focuses on objects, beliefs and art from Christianity, Buddhism, Judaism, Islam, Hinduism and Sikhism. In addition to the main exhibition there is a small collection of photographs, papers and archive material looking at religion in Glasgow, the power and zealotry of the nineteenth-century Temperance movement and Christian missionaries (local boy David Livingstone in particular). Outside is Britain's only permanent "dry stone" Zen Buddhist garden, with slabs of rock, white gravel and moss arranged to suggest the forms of land and sea.

Across the square, the oldest house in the city, the **Provand's Lordship** (same times; free) dates from 1471, and has been used, among other things, as an ecclesiastical residence and an inn. Inside, the re-creations of life in the fifteenth century aren't particularly arresting unless you've an interest in period furniture. As a reminder of the manse's earthier history, the upper floor contains pictures of assorted lowlife characters, such as the notorious drunkards and prostitutes of eighteenth- and nineteenth-century Glasgow.

Behind the Provand's Lordship lies the small **Garden of St Nicholas**, a herb garden contrasting medieval and Renaissance aesthetics and approaches to medicine, with muddled clusters of herbs amid stone carvings of the heart and other organs, and a controlled arrangement of plants around a small ornate fountain. The garden, bordered by sandstone walkways where you can sit, is an aromatic and peaceful haven away from the High Street.

Sauchiehall Street and around

Glasgow's most famous street, **Sauchiehall Street**, runs in a straight line west from the northern end of Buchanan Street, past some unexciting shopping malls to a few of the city's most interesting sights. Charles Rennie Mackintosh fans should head for the **Willow Tea Rooms** (W www.willowtearooms.co.uk), not all that easy to spot at first, above Henderson the Jeweller at 217 Sauchiehall St. This is a faithful reconstruction (opened in 1980 after more than fifty years of closure) on the site of the 1904 original, which was created for Kate Cranston, one of Rennie Mackintosh's few contemporary supporters in the city. Ask for a table in the Salon de Lux (it would have cost a penny extra for tea here a century ago), where everything, from the fixtures and fittings right down to the teaspoons and menu cards, was designed by Mackintosh. Taking inspiration from the word *Sauchiehall*, which means "avenue of willow", he chose the willow leaf as a theme to unify the whole structure from the tables to the mirrors and the ironwork. The motif is most apparent in the stylized linear panels of the bow window which continues into the intimate dining room as if to surround the sitter, like a willow grove, and is echoed in the distinctively high-backed silver and purple chairs. These elongated forms were used to enhance the small space and demonstrate Mackintosh's superb ability to fuse function with decoration. Tea is served here Mon–Sat 9.30am until 4.30pm, and noon–3.30pm on Sundays in summer (for a review, see p.313).

A few blocks further west at no. 350, it's usually worth wandering into the **CCA** (Centre for Contemporary Arts; ☎0141/352 4900, W www.cca-glasgow .com), where eclectic exhibitions of international and home-grown modern art, combined with a well-designed atrium bar and café, consistently make this one of the city's trendiest cultural hotspots.

The Glasgow School of Art

Rising above Sauchiehall Street to the north is one of the city centre's steepest hills, with Dalhousie and Scott streets veering up to Renfrew Street, where you'll find Charles Rennie Mackintosh's **Glasgow School of Art**, 167 Renfrew St (guided tours April–Sept daily 10.30, 11am, 11.30am, 1.30pm, 2pm & 2.30pm; Oct–March Mon–Sat 11am & 2pm; booking advised; £6; ☎0141/353 4526, W www.gsa.ac.uk). This is one of the most prestigious art schools in the country, with such notable alumni as Robert Colquhoun and Robert Macbryde and, more recently, Steven Campbell, Ken Currie and actor Robbie Coltrane. Widely considered to be the pinnacle of Mackintosh's work, the school is a characteristically angular building of warm sandstone which, due

Charles Rennie Mackintosh

The work of the architect **Charles Rennie Mackintosh** (1868–1928), has come to be synonymous with the image of Glasgow. Historians may disagree over whether his work was a forerunner of the Modernist movement or merely the sunset of Victorianism, but he undoubtedly created buildings of great beauty, idiosyncratically fusing Scots Baronial with Gothic, Art Nouveau and modern design. Though the bulk of his work was conceived at the turn of the twentieth century, since the postwar years Mackintosh's ideas have become particularly fashionable, giving rise to a certain amount of ersatz **"Mockintosh"** in his home city, with his distinctive lettering and small design features used time and again by shops, pubs and businesses. Fortunately, there are also plenty of examples of the genuine article, making the city something of a pilgrimage centre for art and design students from all over the world. A one-day **Mackintosh Trail Ticket** (£12) is available, the price including entry to twelve principal Mackintosh buildings as well as unlimited Underground and bus travel. These are available at the tourist office, any of the attractions on the trail or from ⓦ www.crmsociety.com.

Although his family did little to encourage his artistic ambitions, as a young child Mackintosh began to cultivate his interest in drawing from nature during walks in the countryside, taken to improve his health. This talent was to flourish when he joined the Glasgow School of Art in 1884, where the vibrant new director, Francis Newbery, encouraged his pupils to create original and individual work. Here he met Herbert MacNair and the sisters Margaret and Frances MacDonald, whose work seemed to be sympathetic with his, fusing the organic forms of nature with a linear, symbolic Art Nouveau style. Nicknamed **"The Spook School"**, the four created a new artistic language, using extended vertical design, stylized abstract organic forms and muted colours, reflecting their interest in Japanese design and the work of Whistler and Beardsley. However, it was architecture that truly challenged Mackintosh, allowing him to use his creative artistic impulse in a three-dimensional and cohesive manner.

His big break came in 1896, when he won the competition to design a new home for the **Glasgow School of Art** (see p.297). This is his most famous work, but a number of smaller buildings created during his tenure with the architects Honeyman and Keppie, which began in 1889, document the development of his style. One of his earliest commissions was for a new building to house the *Glasgow Herald* on Mitchell Lane, off Argyle Street. A massive tower rises up from the corner, giving the building its popular name of **The Lighthouse**; it now houses the Mackintosh Interpretation Centre (see p.290).

In the 1890s Glasgow went wild for tearooms, where the middle classes could play billiards and chess, read in the library or merely chat. The imposing Miss Cranston, who dominated the Glasgow teashop scene and ran the most elegant establish-

to financial constraints, had to be constructed in two sections (1897–99 and 1907–09). There's a clear change in the architect's style from the earlier severity of the mock-Baronial east wing to the softer lines of the western half.

The only way to see the school is to take one of the student-led **guided tours**, the extent of which are dependent on curricular activities. You can, however, be sure of seeing key examples of Mackintosh's dynamic and inspired touch and a handful of the most impressive rooms. All over the school, from the roof to the stairwells, Mackintosh's unique touches recur – light oriental reliefs, tall-backed chairs and stylized Celtic illuminations. Even before entering the building up the gently curving stairway, you cannot fail to be struck by the soaring height of the north-facing windows, which light the art studios and were designed, characteristically, to combine aesthetics with practicality.

ments, gave Mackintosh great freedom of design, and in 1896 he started to plan the interiors for her growing business. Over the next twenty years he designed articles from teaspoons to furniture and, finally, as in the case of the **Willow Tea Rooms** (see p.297), the structure itself.

Mackintosh designed few **religious buildings**: Queens Cross Church of 1896, still at the junction of Garscube and Maryhill roads in the northwest of the city, is the only completed example standing. Hallmarks include the sturdy box-shaped tower and asymmetrical exterior with complex heart-shaped floral motifs in the large chancel window. To give height to the small and peaceful interior, he used an open-arched timber ceiling, enhanced by carved detail and an oak pulpit decorated with tulip-form relief. It isn't the most unified of structures, but shows the flexibility of his distinctive style. It is now home to the **Charles Rennie Mackintosh Society** (Mon–Fri 10am–5pm, also Sun 2–5pm March–Oct; £2; ☏0141/946 6600, ⊛www.crmsociety.com).

The spectre of limited budgets was to haunt Mackintosh throughout his career, and he never had the chance to design and construct with complete freedom. However, these constraints didn't manage to dull his creativity, as demonstrated by the **Scotland Street School** of 1904, just south of the river (see p.307). Here, the two main stairways that frame the entrance are lit by glass-filled bays that protrude from the building. It is his most symmetrical work, with a whimsical nod to history in the Scots Baronial conical tower roofs and sandstone building material. Mackintosh's forceful personality and originality did not endear him to construction workers: he would frequently change his mind or add details at the last minute, often overstretching a budget. This lost him the support of local builders and architects, despite his being admired on the continent, and prompted him to move to Suffolk in 1914 to escape the "philistines" of Glasgow and to re-evaluate his achievements. Indeed, the building which arguably displays Mackintosh at his most flamboyant was one he never saw built, the **House for an Art Lover** (see p.308), constructed in Bellahouston Park in 1996, 95 years after plans for it were submitted to a German architectural competition.

Having moved away from Glasgow, Mackintosh made use of his natural ability to draw flora and fauna, often in botanical detail and coloured with delicate watercolour washes. While living in 1923–27 in Port Vendres, on the Mediterranean coast of southwestern France, he produced a series of still lifes and landscape works which express something of his architectural style: houses and rocks are painted in precise detail with a massive solidity and geometric form, and bold colours unite the patterned texture of the landscape, within an eerie stillness unbroken by human activity. These are a final flowering of his creative talent, a delicate contrast to the massive legacy of stonework left behind in the city that he loved.

In the main entrance hall, the school shop sells tour tickets and a good selection of Mackintosh books, posters and cards. Hanging in the hall stairwell is the artist's highly personal wrought-iron version of the legend of St Mungo represented on the city's coat of arms. Above this, the **Gallery**, the largest space in the school, is a classic example of the architect's use of contrasts, with light flooding in from a skylight yet dark beams lowering the perceived space to create a degree of intimacy. Forbidding wrought-iron work gives the sense of a Highland castle, while half-hidden alcoves with unexpected windows look out over the city. The **Furniture Gallery**, tucked up in the eaves, shelters an Aladdin's cave of designs that weren't able to be housed elsewhere in the school – numerous tall-backed chairs, a semicircular settle designed for the Willow Tea Rooms, domino tables, a chest of drawers with highlighted silver panels and two bedroom suites. Below this is the school's most spectacular room, the glorious two-storey **Library**. Designed to give the sense of a clearing in a forest, sombre oak panelling is set against angular lights adorned with primary colours, dangling down in seemingly random clusters. The dark bookcases sit precisely in their fitted alcoves, while, of the furniture, the most unusual feature is the central periodical desk, whose oval central strut displays perfect and quite beautiful symmetry.

The school also puts on various **exhibitions** through the year, which you can view without going on a tour. For details, contact the school or check up-to-date listings.

The Tenement House

Just a few hundred yards north of the School of Art – on the other side of a sheer hill – is the **Tenement House**, 145 Buccleuch St (March–Oct daily 1–5pm; NTS; £5). This is a typical tenement block still lived in on most floors, except for the ground and first floors, where you can see the perfectly preserved home of Agnes Toward, who moved here with her mother in 1911, changing nothing and throwing very little out until she was hospitalized in 1965. On the ground floor, the National Trust for Scotland has constructed a fascinating display on the development of the humble tenement block as the bedrock of urban Scottish housing, with a display of relics – ration books, letters, bills, holiday snaps and so forth – from Miss Toward's life. Upstairs, you have to ring the doorbell to enter the flat, which gives every impression of still being inhabited, with a cluttered hearth and range, kitchen utensils, recess beds, framed religious tracts and sewing machine all untouched. The only major change since Miss Toward left has been the reinstallation of the flickering gas lamps she would have used in the early days. Tenement flats were home for the vast majority of Glaswegians for much of the twentieth century, and as such developed a culture and vocabulary all of their own: the "hurley", for example, was the bed on castors which was kept below the box bed in an alcove off the kitchen.

The Piping Centre

Behind the hulking Royal Scottish Academy for Music and Drama, a short way east of the Tenement House, the **National Piping Centre**, at 30–34 McPhater St, prides itself on being an international centre for the promotion of the bagpipe. Equipped with rehearsal rooms, performance halls, conference centre, accommodation (see p.284), museum and an attractive café, it is a meeting place for fans and performers from all over the world. For the casual visitor, the single-room **museum** (Mon–Sat 9am–5pm, also Sun 10am–4pm in summer months; £3; ⓦ www.thepipingcentre.co.uk) is of most interest, with a collection of instruments and related artefacts from the fourteenth century to the present day. Headsets provide a taped commentary with musical examples at relevant stages and the museum shop contains a stack of related material, from tapes and videos to manuscripts and piping accessories.

The West End

The urbane **West End** seems a world away from Glasgow's industrial image and the hustle and bustle of the city centre. In the 1800s the city's wealthy merchants established huge estates away from the soot and grime of city life, and in 1870 the ancient university was moved from its cramped home near the cathedral to a spacious new site overlooking the River Kelvin. Elegant housing swiftly followed, the Kelvingrove Art Gallery and Museum was built to house the 1888 International Exhibition, and, in 1896, the Glasgow District Subway – today's Underground – started its circuitous shuffle from here to the city centre.

The hub of life in this part of Glasgow is **Byres Road**, running between Great Western Road and Dumbarton Road past Hillhead underground station. Shops, restaurants, cafés, some enticing pubs and hordes of roving young people, including thousands of students, give the area a sense of style and vitality. Glowing red sandstone tenements and graceful terraces provide a suitably upmarket backdrop to this cosmopolitan district.

The main sights straddle the banks of the cleaned-up River Kelvin, which meanders through the gracious acres of the **Botanic Gardens** and the slopes, trees and statues of **Kelvingrove Park**. Overlooked by the Gothic towers and turrets of **Glasgow University**, Kelvingrove Park and its immediate vicinity are home to the nostalgia-rich **Transport Museum** and the pride of Glasgow's civic collection of art and artefacts, **Kelvingrove Museum and Art Gallery**, off Argyle Street, fresh from a major refurbishment.

The Transport Museum

Twin-towered **Kelvin Hall** opposite the Kelvingrove Museum is home to both an international indoor sports arena and, for now at least, the engaging **Transport Museum** (Mon–Thurs & Sat 10am–5pm, Fri & Sun 11am–5pm; free). Here you'll find an enormous collection of trains, cars, trams, bikes and any other form of transport with a Glasgow connection, including the March 701 racing car in which Jackie Stewart won the Spanish Grand Prix in 1970. In general, the displays aren't particularly sophisticated, and there's a slightly tatty edge to the place ahead of its proposed relocation to a custom-built new home on the banks of the Clyde in 2008, but in the packed rows of cars and hulking locomotives there's a sense of nostalgia at every turn. Cobbled "Kelvin Street", lined with old cars, is a re-created 1938 street featuring an old Italian coffee shop, a butcher (complete with plastic meat joints dangling in the window), a bakery and an old-time underground station. A cinema shows fascinating films – including reels of old Glasgow life, with crackly footage of Sauchiehall Street packed solid with trams and shoppers and hordes of pasty-faced Glaswegians setting off for their annual jaunts down the coast. Upstairs, the large Clyde Room displays hundred of scale models of ships forged in Glasgow's yards, everything from tiny schooners to ostentatious ocean liners such as the *QE2*.

Kelvingrove Art Gallery and Museum

Founded on donations from the city's industrialists Victorian, the huge, red sandstone fantasy castle of **Kelvingrove Art Gallery and Museum** is a brash statement of Glasgow's nineteenth-century self-confidence. The current building opened at an international fair held in 1901, Kelvingrove (as it's popularly known) is intricate and ambitious both in its riotous outside detailing and within, where a superb galleried main hall running the depth of the building gives way to attractive upper balconies and small, interlinked display galleries.

Following a massive, three-year refurbishment, the art gallery and museum is due to reopen in the summer of 2006. There's little doubt that Kelvingrove will very quickly re-establish itself as one of Glasgow's – and indeed Scotland's – most popular attractions. As with many of the city's collections of art and artefacts, the affection of, and use by, the local citizenry is as important as tourist numbers.

In the 1870s a group of Glasgow-based painters formed a loose association that was to imbue Scottish art with a contemporary European flavour far ahead of the rest of Britain. Dominated by five men – Guthrie, Lavery, Henry, Hornel and Crawhall – "**The Glasgow Boys**" came from very different backgrounds, but all violently rejected the eighteenth-century conservatism which spawned little other than sentimental, anecdotal renditions of Scottish history peopled by "poor but happy" families. They dubbed these paintings "**gluepots**" for their use of megilp, an oily substance that gave the work the brown patina of age, and instead began to experiment with colour, liberally splashing paint across the canvas. The content and concerns of the paintings, often showing peasant life and work, were as offensive to the art establishment as their style: until then most of Glasgow's public art collections had been accrued by wealthy tobacco lords and merchants, who had a taste for Classical style and noble subjects.

Sir James Guthrie, taking inspiration from the *plein air* painting of the Impressionists, spent his summers in the countryside, observing and painting everyday life. Instead of happy peasants, his work shows individuals staring out of the canvas, detached and unrepentant, painted with rich tones but without undue attention to detail or the play of light. Typical of his finest work during the 1880s, *A Highland Funeral* was hugely influential for the rest of the group, who found inspiration in its restrained emotional content, colour and unaffected realism. Seeing it persuaded **Sir John Lavery**, then studying in France, to return to Glasgow. Lavery was eventually to become an internationally popular society portraitist, his subtle use of paint revealing his debt to Whistler, but his earlier work, depicting the middle class at play, is filled with fresh colour and figures in motion.

Rather than a realistic aesthetic, an interest in colour and decoration united the work of friends **George Henry** and **E.A. Hornel**. The predominance of colour, pattern and design in Henry's *Galloway Landscape*, for example, is remarkable, while their joint work *The Druids* (both part of the Kelvingrove collection; see p.301), in thickly applied impasto, is full of Celtic symbolism. In 1893 both artists set off for Japan, funded by Alexander Reid and later William Burrell, where their work used vibrant tone and texture for expressive effect and took Scottish painting to the forefront of European trends.

Newcastle-born **Joseph Crawhall** was a reserved and quiet individual who combined superb draughtsmanship and simplicity of line with a photographic memory to create watercolours of an outstanding naturalism and freshness. Again, William Burrell was an important patron, and a number of Crawhall's works reside at the Burrell Collection (see p.308).

The Glasgow Boys school had reached its height by 1900 and did not outlast World War I, but the influence of their work cannot be underestimated, shaking the foundations of the artistic elite and inspiring the next generation of Edinburgh painters, who became known as the "**Colourists**". Samuel John Peploe, John Duncan Fergusson, George Leslie Hunter and Francis Cadell shared an understanding that the manipulation of colour was the heart and soul of a good painting. All experienced and took inspiration from the avant garde of late nineteenth-century Paris as well as the landscapes of southern France. **J.D. Fergusson**, in particular, immersed himself in the bohemian, progressive Parisian scene, rubbing shoulders with writers and artists including Picasso. Some of his most dynamic work, such as *Rhythm* (1911) displays elements of Cubism, yet is still clearly in touch with the Celtic imagery of Henry, Hornel and, indeed, Charles Rennie Macintosh. The influence of post-Impressionists such as Matisse and Cézanne is obvious in the work of all four, with their seascapes, society portraits and still lifes bursting with fluidity, unconventionality and, above all, manipulation of colour and shape. The work of the Scottish Colourists has become highly fashionable and valuable over the last couple of decades, with galleries and civic collections throughout the country featuring their work prominently.

Although the displays are set to include a World War II Spitfire suspended from the roof of the West Court, the most compelling aspect of the museum is likely to remain the paintings, which include Salvador Dali's stunning *St John of the Cross*. The focus of huge controversy when it was purchased by the city in 1952 for what was regarded as the vast sum of £9200, it has returned to Kelvingrove following a prolonged period at the St Mungo Musuem of Religious Life and Art. Other favourites include Rembrandt's calm *A Man in Armour*, Constable's *Hampstead Heath* and some notable paintings by Pissarro, Monet and Renoir. You can also acquaint yourself with significant Scottish art by Charles Rennie Mackintosh, the Glasgow Boys and the Scottish Colourists (see box opposite).

The **opening hours** for the reopened museum and art gallery are likely to reflect those of other Glasgow City Council Museums, namely Mon–Thurs & Sat 10am–5pm, Fri & Sun 11am–5pm, with free admission. Updates are available at Ⓦ www.glasgowmuseums.com.

Glasgow University and the Hunterian bequests

Dominating the West End skyline, the gloomy turreted tower of **Glasgow University** (Ⓦ www.gla.ac.uk), designed by Sir George Gilbert Scott in the mid-nineteenth century, overlooks the glades edging the River Kelvin. Access to the main buildings and museums is from University Avenue, running east from Byres Road. In the dark neo-Gothic pile under the tower you'll find the **University Visitor Centre & Shop** (Mon–Sat 9.30am–5pm) which, as well as giving information for potential students, has a small café and distributes leaflets about the various university buildings and the statues around the campus. From May to September **historical tours** of the campus are run from here (phone ☎0141/330 5511 for details). It's possible to join a tour up the sky-piercing university **tower** (May–Sept Fri 2pm; free), climbing 226 narrow spiral-staircase steps to some heady views; places, though, are limited to twenty people, with tickets available only in person that morning from the Visitor Centre.

Beside the Visitor Centre is the **Hunterian Museum** (Mon–Sat 9.30am–5pm; free), Scotland's oldest public museum, dating back to 1807. The collection was donated to the university by ex-student William Hunter, a pathologist and anatomist whose eclectic tastes form the basis of a fairly diverting zoological and archeological jaunt. Exhibitions include Scotland's only dinosaur, a look at the Romans in Scotland – the furthest outpost of their massive empire – and a vast numismatic collection (coins, in other words).

The Hunterian Art Gallery

Opposite the university, across University Avenue, is Hunter's more frequently visited bequest, the **Hunterian Art Gallery** (Mon–Sat 9.30am–5pm; free), best known for its wonderful works by James Abbott McNeill Whistler: only Washington DC has a larger collection. The most compelling part of the display is Whistler's portraits of women, which give his subjects a resolute strength in addition to their fey and occasionally winsome qualities: look out especially for the trio of full-length portraits, *Harmony of Flesh Colour* and *Black, Pink and Gold – The Tulip* and *Red and Black – The Fan*.

The gallery's other major collection is of nineteenth- and twentieth-century Scottish art, including the quasi-Impressionist Scottish landscapes of William McTaggart, a forerunner of the Glasgow Boys movement, itself represented here by Guthrie and Hornel. Taking the aims of this group one step further, the monumental dancing figures of J.D. Fergusson's *Les Eus* preside over a small collection of work by the Scottish Colourists, including Peploe, Hunter and Cadell, who left a vibrant legacy of thickly textured, colourful landscapes and portraits. A small selection of French Impressionism includes works by Boudin and Pissarro, with Corot's soothing *Distant View of Corbeil* being a highlight from the Barbizon school.

A side gallery leads to the **Mackintosh House** (£2.50, free after 2pm Wed), a re-creation of the interior of the now-demolished Glasgow home of Margaret MacDonald and Charles Rennie Mackintosh. An introductory display contains photographs of the original house sliding irrevocably into terminal decay, from where you are led into an exquisitely cool interior that contains over sixty pieces of Mackintosh furniture on three floors. Among the highlights are the studio drawing room, whose cream and white furnishings are bathed in expansive pools of natural light, and the Japanese-influenced guest bedroom in dazzling, monochrome geometrics. In addition, a permanent Mackintosh exhibition gallery shows a selection of his two-dimensional work, from watercolours to architectural drawings.

The Botanic Gardens

At the northern, top end of Byres Road, where it meets the Great Western Road, is the main entrance to the **Botanic Gardens** (daily 7am–dusk; free). The best-known glasshouse here, the hulking, domed **Kibble Palace** (closed for refurbishment until 2006), was built in 1863 for wealthy landowner John Kibble's estate on the shores of Loch Long, where it stood for ten years before he decided to transport it into Glasgow, drawing it up the Clyde on a vast raft pulled by a steamer. For over two decades it was used not as a greenhouse but as a Victorian pleasure palace, before the gardens' owners put a stop to the drunken revels that wreaked havoc with the lawns and plant beds. Today the palace is far more sedate, housing a damp, musty collection of swaying palms from around the world. Nearby, the **Main Range Glasshouse** (same times) is home to lurid flowers and plants luxuriating in the humidity, including stunning orchids, cacti, ferns and tropical fruit. Between the two in the old curator's house is a small **visitor centre** (daily 11am–4pm; free) with art exhibitions and computer games aimed at younger visitors.

In addition to the area around the main glasshouses, there are some beautifully remote paths in the gardens that weave along the closely wooded banks of the deep-set River Kelvin, linking up with the walkway which runs alongside the river all the way down to Dumbarton Road, near its confluence with the Clyde.

Clydeside

"The **Clyde** made Glasgow and Glasgow made the Clyde" runs an old saw, full of sentimentality for the days when the river was the world's premier shipbuilding centre, and when its industry lent an innovation and confidence which made Glasgow the second city of the British Empire. Despite the hardships heavy industry brought, every Glaswegian would follow the progress of the skeleton ships under construction in the riverside yards, cheering them on their way down the Clyde as they were launched. The last of the great liners to be built on **Clydeside** was the *QE2* in 1967, yet such events are hard to visualize today, with the banks of the river all but devoid of any industry: shipbuilding is now restricted to a couple

The Waverley

One of Glasgow's best-loved treasures is the **Waverley**, the last seagoing paddle steamer in the world, which spends the summer cruising "doon the watter" to various ports on the Firth of Clyde and the Ayrshire coast from its base at Anderson Quay between Finnieston and the Kingston Bridge. Built on Clydeside as recently as 1947, she's an elegant vessel to look at, not least when she's thrashing away at full steam with the hills of Argyll or Arran in the background. Call the booking office on ☎ 0845/130 4647 or check ⊛ www.waverleyexcursions.co.uk for her sailing times and itinerary.

of barely viable yards, as derelict warehouses, crumbling docks and overgrown wastelands crowd the river's flanks.

Glasgow is often accused of failing to capitalize on its river, and it's only in the last few years, with a flurry of construction activity, that it's once again becoming a focus of attention. Striking buildings including the titanium-clad "**Armadillo**" concert hall and **Glasgow Science Centre** have become icons of the city's forward-thinking image, though the shipbuilding heritage is not forgotten, with attractions such as the **Tall Ship at Glasgow Harbour** and **Clydebuilt** striving to recreate the river's heyday.

The easiest way to reach the cluster of Clydeside attractions is to **walk** the mile or so west along the riverside footpath from the city centre. Otherwise, jump on a **train** from Glasgow Central low-level station to the Exhibition Centre station. Two footbridges cross the river to the Science Centre on the south bank, also served by Arriva buses #23 or #24 from Renfield Street.

The north bank

On Clydeside immediately south of the West End, just over a mile west of the city centre, is the harshly re-landscaped Scottish Exhibition and Conference Centre, or **SECC**. It was built on a reclaimed dock in 1985 to kick-start the revival of the riverbank: two vast adjoining red and grey sheds that make a dutifully utilitarian venue for travelling fairs, mega-concerts and anonymous bars and cafés. Although the huge **Finnieston Crane**, retained as an icon of shipbuilding days, stands alongside the SECC, the site was rescued from bland obscurity by the arrival in 1997 of a supplementary concert hall officially entitled the Clyde Auditorium but universally nicknamed "**the Armadillo**" for its rounded exterior of armour-plating. It's like a poor man's Sydney Opera House but has quickly established itself as one of the city's architectural landmarks.

A few hundred yards downstream on the north bank of the river, the masts and rigging of the huge square-rigger *Glenlee* draw you to an attraction known as the **Tall Ship at Glasgow Harbour** (daily: March–Oct 10am–5pm; Nov–Feb 11am–4pm; £4.95; ⊛ www.glenlee.co.uk). A 245-foot-long, three-masted barque, the *Glenlee* was launched on the river in 1896 and is now one of only five large sailing vessels built on Clydeside still afloat. Although the lovingly careful restoration project of the Clyde Maritime Trust is ongoing, you're able to snoop around most of the ship, including three main decks and the hold. The sheer scale of the *Glenlee* is her most impressive feature, though various parts of the ship are imaginatively set up to offer an insight into life aboard when she was a hard-working merchant vessel carrying cargo round Cape Horn. In the Pump-house Visitor Centre, on the quay alongside, changing exhibitions highlight different aspects of the ship's links to Glasgow and the city's maritime history.

The Glasgow Science Centre

On the south bank of the river, linked to the SECC by pedestrian Bell's Bridge, are the three space-age, titanium-clad constructions which make up the **Glasgow Science Centre** (Science Mall or IMAX £6.95, both £9.95; ⓦwww.gsc.org .uk). Of the three buildings, the largest is the curvaceous, wedge-shaped **Science Mall** (daily 10am–6pm). Behind the vast glass wall which faces the river are four floors of interactive exhibits ranging from lift-your-own-weight pulleys to high-tech thermograms. Described as "hands-on info-tainment for the genome generation", it's like all your most enjoyable school science experiments packed into one building, with in-house boffins demonstrating chemical reactions and pensioners and toddlers equally captivated by cockroach colonies and jigsaw puzzles of human organs. The centre covers almost every aspect of science, from simple optical illusions to cutting-edge computer technology, including a section on moral and environmental issues – lots of good fun, although weekends and school holidays are busy and noisy. Within the mall, an impressive planetarium and 3-D virtual science theatre put on regular shows through the day.

Alongside the Science Mall is the bubble-like **IMAX theatre**, which shows a range of mostly science- and nature-based documentaries on its giant screen, with programmes changing regularly. Also on the site is the 417-foot **Glasgow Tower**, the tallest free-standing structure in Scotland, built with an aerofoil-like construction to allow it to rotate to face into the prevailing wind. Glass lifts ascend to the viewing cabin at the top, offering suitably panoramic views, but it has been dogged with technical difficulties since it opened, preventing visitor access on a reliable schedule.

Clydebuilt at Braehead

Three miles downriver (west) from the Science Centre, a further tribute to the Clyde shipbuilding legacy can be found at **Clydebuilt** (Mon–Sat 10.30am–5.30pm, Sun 11am–5pm; £4.25), a small outpost of Irvine's Scottish Maritime

△ Glasgow Science Centre, Clydeside

Museum (see p.262). The attraction, a single building with a couple of retired working boats moored alongside, is completely overwhelmed by the massive **Braehead** shopping centre which surrounds it, though the fact that a **water-bus** (6 daily; 30min; £4 single) runs here from beside King George V Bridge in Glasgow city centre – one of the few opportunities that exists to travel on the river – makes a visit more appealing. The museum takes a look at Glasgow's rise as a trading port and shipbuilding centre, with a series of displays, reconstructions and films, the old Clyde puffer tied up to the pontoon beside it offering the most tangible sense of the past.

The Southside

The section of Glasgow south of the Clyde is generally described as the **Southside**, though within this area there are a number of districts with recognizable names, including the notoriously deprived Gorbals and Govan, which are sprinkled with new developments but still obviously derelict and tatty in many parts. There's little reason to venture here unless you're making your way to the Science Centre (see above), the famously innovative Citizens' Theatre (see p.321) or one of the revived architectural gems of Charles Rennie Mackintosh, the **Scotland Street School** and the **House for an Art Lover**.

Moving further south, inner-city decay fades into altogether gentler and more salubrious suburbs, including Queen's Park, home to Scotland's national football stadium, **Hampden Park**; Pollokshaws and the rural landscape of Pollok Park, which contains two of Glasgow's major museums, the **Burrell Collection** and **Pollok House**; and Cathcart, location of Alexander "Greek" Thomson's **Holmwood House**.

Southside attractions are fairly widely spread. The **Underground** will get you to Scotland Street School and the House for an Art Lover, while a **train** from Central station is best for Hampden Park (Mount Florida station) and Holmwood House (Cathcart station). For Pollok Park either take the train to Pollokshaws West station (not to be confused with Pollokshields West), or **bus** #45, #47 or #57 to Pollokshaws Road, or a **taxi** (£8–10 from the centre). From the park gates a **free minibus** runs every half-hour between 10am and 4.30pm to both the Burrell Collection and Pollok House.

Scotland Street School Museum of Education

Opposite Shields Road underground station is the **Scotland Street School Museum of Education** (Mon–Thurs & Sat 10am–5pm, Fri & Sun 11am–5pm; free), another of the city's Charles Rennie Mackintosh treasures. Opened as a school in 1906 to Mackintosh's distinctively angular design, it closed in 1979, since when it has been entertainingly refurbished to house a fascinating collection of memorabilia related to classroom life. There are reconstructed classrooms from the Victorian and Edwardian eras, World War II and the 1960s, as well as changing rooms, a primitive domestic science room and re-creations of the school matron's sanatorium and a janitor's lair. If you visit on a weekday during term time, you may stumble on a period lesson, local schoolkids struggling with their ink blotters, gas masks and archly unsympathetic teachers, the faint smell of antiseptic conjuring up memories of scuffed knees and playground tantrums.

House for an Art Lover

West of Scotland Street School, tucked just inside Bellahouston Park, is Charles Rennie Mackintosh's **House for an Art Lover** (April–Sept Mon–Wed 10am–4pm, Thurs–Sun 10am–1pm; Oct–March Sat & Sun 10am–1pm but closed occasionally for functions; £3.50; ☎0141/353 4770, ⊛www.housefor anartlover.co.uk). Designed in 1901 for a German competition, it was not until 1996, after years of detailed research, that the building was actually constructed and opened as a centre for Glasgow School of Art postgraduate students, with a limited number of rooms open to the public.

It's all quintessential Mackintosh, the exquisitely stylish and original nature of the design making it hard to imagine it suffering the wear and tear of day-to-day life. On the upper floor, you can watch a video giving a detailed account of the building's history, then pass into the delicate **Oval Room**, intended for women to retire to after dinner. From here, a small corridor leads into the main **hallway**, where massive windows cast a cool light upon an area designed for large parties. In direct contrast, the dazzling white **Music Room** has bow windows opening out to a large balcony, though the garden view is marred by an artificial ski slope. The **Dining Room** is decorated with darkened stained wood and enhanced by some beautiful gesso tiles.

On the ground floor, the **café** (☎0141/353 4779) is particularly popular with locals on Sunday mornings; there's an attractive menu, and it's open every day (even if the rest of the house is closed to the public) and sometimes also in the evenings.

Hampden Park and the Scottish Football Museum

Two and a half miles due south of the city centre, just to the west of the tree-filled Queen's Park, the floodlights and giant stands of Scotland's national football stadium, **Hampden Park**, loom over the surrounding suburban tenements and terraces. Home of Queen's Park Football Club (these days not one of Scotland's more esteemed outfits despite the grandeur of their home turf), the fact that it's the venue for Scotland's international fixtures and major cup finals makes it a place of pilgrimage for the country's football fans. Regular **guided tours** (daily 10.30am–3.30pm; £6, or £8 including entry to the museum; ⊛www .hampdenpark.co.uk) offer the chance to see the changing rooms, warm-up areas and inside the stadium itself, complete with anecdotes of players past and the story of the ground and its recent renovation (which almost bankrupted the Scottish Football Association). Also here is the engaging **Scottish Football Museum** (Mon–Sat 10am–5pm, Sun 11am–5pm; £5), with extensive collections of memorabilia, video clips and displays covering almost every aspect of the game. On view is the Scottish Cup, the world's oldest footballing trophy, and a re-creation of the old changing room at Hampden, though there's also a light-hearted side to the museum, with one of the more bizarre exhibits a life-size reconstruction of various Dutch defenders floundering in the wake of Archie Gemmill as he slots home the most famous goal in Scottish footballing history during the otherwise embarrassing 1978 World Cup campaign in Argentina.

The Burrell Collection

Located in Pollok Park some six miles southwest of the city centre, the outstanding **Burrell Collection** (Mon–Thurs & Sat 10am–5pm, Fri & Sun

Football in Glasgow

Football, or *fitba'* as it's pronounced locally, is one of Glasgow's great passions – and one of its great blights. While the city can claim to be one of Europe's premier footballing centres, it's known above all for one of the most bitter rivalries in any sport, that between **Celtic** and **Rangers**. Two of the largest clubs in Britain, with weekly crowds regularly topping 60,000, the Old Firm, as they're collectively known, have dominated Scottish football for a century, most notably in the last fifteen years as they have lavished vast sums of money on foreign talent in an often frantic effort both to outdo each other and to stay in touch with the standards of the top English and European teams.

The roots of Celtic, who play at Celtic Park in the eastern district of Parkhead (T0141/551 8653, Wwww.celticfc.co.uk), lie in the city's immigrant Irish and **Catholic** population, while Rangers, based at Ibrox Park in Govan on the Southside (T0870/600 1993, Wwww.rangers.co.uk), have traditionally drawn support from local **Protestants**. As a result, sporting rivalries have been enmeshed in a sectarian divide which many argue would not have remained so long, nor so deep, had it been divorced from the footballing scene: although Catholics do play for Rangers, and Protestants for Celtic, sections of supporters of both clubs seem intent on perpetuating the feud. While large-scale violence on the terraces and streets has not been seen for some time – thanks in large measure to canny policing – Old Firm matches often seethe with bitter passions, and sectarian-related assaults do still occur in parts of the city.

However, there is a less intense side to the game, found not just in the fun-loving "Tartan Army" which follows the (often rollercoaster) fortunes of the Scottish national team, but also in Glasgow's smaller clubs, who actively distance themselves from the distasteful aspects of the Old Firm and plod along with homegrown talent in the lower reaches of the Scottish league. **Queen's Park**, residents of Hampden (T0141/632 1275, Wwww.queensparkfc.co.uk), **St Mirren**, the Paisley team (T0141/889 2558, Wwww.stmirrenfc.co.uk), and the much-maligned **Partick Thistle**, who play at Firhill Stadium in the West End (T0141/579 1971, Wwww.ptfc.co.uk), offer the best chances of experiencing the more down-to-earth side of Glaswegian football – along with all-important reminders that it is, in the end, only a game.

11am–5pm; free), the lifetime collection of shipping magnate Sir William Burrell (1861–1958), is, for some, the principal reason for visiting Glasgow. Unlike many other art collectors, Sir William's only real criterion for buying a piece was whether he liked it or not, enabling him to buy many "unfashionable" works, which cost comparatively little but subsequently proved their worth. He wanted to leave his 9000-piece collection of art, sculpture and antiquities for public display, but stipulated in 1943 that they should be housed "in a rural setting far removed from the atmospheric pollution of urban conurbations, not less than sixteen miles from the Royal Exchange".

For decades, these conditions proved too difficult to meet, with few open spaces available and a pall of industrial smoke ruling out any city site. However, by the late 1960s, after the nationwide Clean Air Act had reduced pollution, and vast **Pollok Park** had been donated to the city, plans began for a new, purpose-built gallery, which finally opened in 1983. Today the simplicity and clean lines of the Burrell building are its greatest assets, with large picture windows giving sweeping views over woodland and serving as a tranquil backdrop to the objects inside. The major part of the collection, including the sculpture and antiques, are arranged in a fairly fluid style on the **ground floor**, while a **mezzanine** above displays most of the paintings.

The courtyard

On entering the building, head past the information desk and shop to an airy covered **courtyard** where the most striking piece, by virtue of sheer size, is the **Warwick Vase**, a huge bowl containing fragments of a second-century AD vase from Emperor Hadrian's villa in Tivoli. Next to it is a series of sinewy and naturalistic bronze casts of **Rodin sculptures**, among them *The Age of Bronze*, *A Call to Arms* and the famous *Thinker*. On three sides of the courtyard, a trio of dark and sombre panelled rooms have been re-erected in faithful detail from the Burrells' Hutton Castle home, their heavy tapestries, antique furniture and fireplaces displaying the same eclectic taste as the rest of the museum.

The ground floor

From the courtyard, go through the massive sandstone portal and door from Hornby Castle, incorporated into the building, to the start of the **Ancient Civilizations** collection – a catch-all title for Greek, Roman and earlier artefacts – which includes an exquisite mosaic Roman cockerel from the first century BC and a 4000-year-old Mesopotamian lion's head. The bulk of it is Egyptian, however, with rows of inscrutable gods and kings. Nearby, also illuminated by enormous windows, the **Oriental Art** collection forms nearly a quarter of the whole display, ranging from Neolithic jades through bronze vessels and Tang funerary horses to cloisonné. The earliest piece, from around the second century BC, is a loveable earthenware watchdog from the Han Dynasty, but most dominant is the serene fifteenth-century *Lohan* (disciple of Buddha), who sits cross-legged and contemplative against the background of a glass wall and the trees of Pollok Park. Near Eastern art is also represented, in a dazzling array of turquoise- and cobalt-decorated jugs and a swathe of intricate carpets.

Burrell considered his **Medieval and Post-Medieval European Art**, which encompasses silverware, glass, textiles and sculpture, to be the most valuable part of his collection. Ranged across a maze of small galleries, the most impressive sections are the sympathetically lit stained glass – note the homely image of a man warming his toes by the fire – and the numerous tapestries, among them the riotous fifteenth-century *Peasants Hunting Rabbits with Ferrets*. Among the church art and reliquary are simple thirteenth-century Spanish wooden images and cool fifteenth-century English alabaster, while a trio of period interiors spans the period from the Gothic era to the eighteenth century. This is interrupted by a selection from Burrell's vast art collection, the highlight of which is one of Rembrandt's evocative early self-portraits.

The mezzanine

Upstairs, the cramped and comparatively gloomy **mezzanine** is probably the least satisfactory section of the gallery, not the best setting for its sparkling array of paintings. The range of works on show does change, but it can make incongruous leaps from a small gathering of fifteenth-century religious works to Géricault's darkly dynamic *Prancing Grey Horse* and Degas's thoughtful and perceptive *Portrait of Émile Duranty*. Pissarro, Manet, Cézanne and Boudin are also represented, along with some exquisite watercolours by Glasgow Boy Joseph Crawhall, revealing his accurate and tender observations of the animal world.

Pollok House

Within Pollok Park, a quarter of a mile down rutted tracks west of the Burrell Collection, lies the lovely eighteenth-century **Pollok House** (daily 10am–5pm; NTS; April–Oct £8, rest of year free; café and gardens free year-round), the manor of the Pollok Park estate and once home of the Maxwell family, local lords and owners of most of southern Glasgow until well into the last century. Designed by William Adam in the mid-1700s, the house is typical of its age: graciously light and sturdily built, it looks out onto the pristine raked and parterre gardens, whose stylized daintiness contrasts with the heavy Spanish paintings inside, among them two El Greco portraits and works by Murillo and Goya.

The house recently came under the management of the National Trust for Scotland – a happy reunion, as it was in the upstairs smoking room in 1931 that the then owner, Sir John Stirling Maxwell, held the first meetings with the 8th Duke of Atholl and Lord Colquhoun of Luss that led to the formation of the NTS. The Trust has made a deliberate effort to return the house to the layout and style it enjoyed when the Stirling Maxwells were living here in the 1920s and 1930s. As a result, the **paintings** range from the Spanish masterpieces in the morning room and some splendid Dutch hunting scenes in the dining room to Sir John's own worthy but noticeably amateur efforts which line the upstairs corridors. Generally, the rooms have the flavour of a well-to-do but unstuffy country house, with the odd piece of attractive furniture and some pleasant rooms, but little that can be described as outstanding. The servants' quarters downstairs, however, do capture the imagination – the virtually untouched labyrinth of tiled Victorian parlours and corridors includes a good **tearoom** in the old kitchen. Free tours of the house are available from the front desk, or you can wander around at your own pace.

Holmwood House

Four miles south of the city centre in the suburb of Cathcart, **Holmwood House** (April–Oct daily noon–5pm; NTS; £5), the finest domestic design by rediscovered Glasgow architect Alexander "Greek" Thomson, has recently been restored and opened to the public. A commission by James Couper, co-owner of a paper mill on the nearby River Carth, the house shows off Thomson's bold Classical concepts, with exterior pillars on two levels and a raised main door, as well as his detailed and highly imaginative interiors. The restoration is ongoing, as you'll see from the patches of exquisite stencilling revealed beneath the wallpaper, and the fact that the rooms are unfurnished.

A free audioguide provides some background information and explanation in each of the rooms. One room upstairs is given over to a series of displays about Thomson and the history of the house. Also on the upper floor is the **drawing room** – look for the white marble fireplace and the night-time star decorations on the ceiling, which contrast with a black marble fireplace and sunburst decorations in the room immediately underneath on the downstairs level, the **parlour**, which also boasts a delightful round bay window. Across the corridor, the **dining room** has a frieze of scenes from the *Iliad*, along with a skylight at the back of the room designed to allow the Greek gods to peer down on the feasts being consumed inside. One unusual feature not designed by Thomson is the small hatch cut in the interconnecting door between the dining room and the butler's pantry; the house was last occupied by a sisterhood of nuns, who used the dining room as a chapel and created the small hatch for use as a confessional.

Eating

Glasweigans have always enjoyed going out, and while this has traditionally implied an evening of drinking and dancing, dining out now fits comfortably into the social agenda. There's a fairly adventurous side to Glasgow's **restaurant** scene, which sometimes sees the latest trendy eating place folding within a year of opening, but it also ushers in new and ambitious ventures. **Contemporary Scottish** cuisine featuring fresh west-coast seafood or locally reared meat, often cooked with French and other international influences, is a particular strength in Glasgow, and in recent years the positive attitude to Scottish, seasonal and wholesome food has filtered down to more affordable bistros, diners and cafés. The sheer number of **Italian** eating options betrays the continuing popularity of the pizza-pasta option, though among imported cuisine it's **Indian** food which is most commonly associated with Glasgow, long established as one of Britain's curry capitals. Beyond these, the **ethnic range** is global, with the opportunity to dine out on Kurdish, Russian, Middle Eastern and Korean food alongside the usual suspects. The number of dedicated **vegetarian** restaurants is not huge, but practically every restaurant in the city does serve meat-free options. By April 2006, restaurants will be completely non-smoking by law.

The city's more casual bar/diners and bistros frequently are **open** from 11am right through the day and evening. Most of the more formal restaurants typically serve lunch between noon and 2.30pm and dinner from 5–6pm to about 10.30pm. Many places are not open at all on Sundays, and Monday is another common day off. Most places to eat are concentrated in the commercial hub and **Merchant City** district of the **city centre**, as well as in the trendy **West End**. We have indicated if they are closed on particular days or where the hours diverge from the norm.

For comprehensive listings and reviews of cafes and restaurants, buy the *List Eating & Drinking Guide* at newsagents and larger bookshops. If you're travelling on a budget, note that many restaurants have excellent pre-theatre or early dining deals – it's worth logging onto the restaurant-booking website Ⓦwww.5pm.co.uk, which lists Glasgow restaurants offering special lunch and early evening deals.

Cafés, diners and café-bars

For inexpensive to moderately priced food, **cafés** and **café-bars** – in addition, of course, to local **diners**, fast-food outlets and that perennial fall-back, the fish and chip shop – are the best bets, serving filling snacks all day and often into the evening. The best of these are concentrated in districts where younger folk and students congregate: the West End, particularly on Byres Road, and the Merchant City.

City centre and the Merchant City

Café Gandolfi and Bar Gandolfi 64 Albion St ℡0141/552 6813, Ⓦwww.cafegandolfi .com. This bona fide landmark was one of the first to test the waters in the Merchant City. Designed with distinctive wooden furniture that its creator, the late Tim Stead, called "sculpture in disguise", *Gandolfi* serves up Scottish staples (including great black pudding), soups, salads, fish dishes and Continental cuisine. The bar upstairs is more contemporary in feel but the food's still good. Moderate.

Café Ostra 15 John St ℡0141/552 4433, Ⓦwww.cafeostra.com. More casual sister to *Gamba* (see p.315), this seafood café is not the cheapest option on this list, but it serves good fresh food right through the day, has excellent wines and offers the added lure of outdoors seating. Moderate.

Café Source 1 St Andrews Square ℡0141/548 6020, Ⓦwww.cafesource.co.uk. In the basement of an eighteenth-century church, patterned on the St Martin in the Fields and now a folk music and Scottish dance centre. The café serves up Scottish favourites with mostly local produce. Frequent live jam sessions. Inexpensive.

Fressh 51–53 Cochrane St ℡0141/552 5532, Ⓦwww.fressh.com. Not a typo, but the intentionally misspelled name of this fresh fruit and smoothies specialist café near the City Chambers. Food is limited to sandwiches and soup. Inexpensive.

Tron Theatre Chisholm St off the Trongate ☎0141/552 8587, ⓦwww.tron.co.uk. Another arty hangout (see p.321), this time for writers and theatrical types in either the contemporary streetside café-bar or the Victorian pub/restaurant inside. Moderate.

Where the Monkey Sleeps 182 West Regent St ☎0141/226 3406, ⓦwww.wherethemonkeysleeps .com. Owned by gregarious art-school graduates who acquired their barista skills between classes, this hip home-grown café doubles as a gallery. Food options focus on soups and sandwiches, and the espresso is superb. Usually closes at 7pm. Inexpensive.

Willow Tea Rooms 217 Sauchiehall St ☎0141/332 0521, ⓦwww.willowtearooms .co.uk. An authentic landmark on the Charles Rennie Mackintosh trail, the first-floor dining room here offers tea with scones and midday meals. A similarly themed branch is at 97 Buchanan St (☎0141/204 5242). Closes before 5pm. Moderate.

West End

Bay Tree Café 403 Great Western Rd ☎0141/334 5898. Middle Eastern flavours dominate this simple café, which offers a lot of vegetarian options with some meat dishes (prepared separately), as well. Counter service. Inexpensive.

Brel 39–43 Ashton Lane ☎0141/342 4966. Popular with students, post-grads and profs, offering a smattering of Belgian food (*moules et frites*) and beers (Leffe). A rear conservatory opens onto a secluded grassy knoll. Frequent live music or DJs playing ambient sounds. Moderate.

Kember & Jones 134 Byres Rd ☎0141/337 3851, ⓦwww.kemberandjones.co.uk. Opened in 2004, this café and deli quickly became a popular spot in an already competitive market. No hot food, but good freshly made salads and sandwiches made from what's sold at the deli counter. Inexpensive.

Monster Mash 41Byres Rd ☎0141/339 3666, ⓦwww.monstermashcafe.co.uk. Fancy some classic bangers and mash? This is place for you, with a range of top-quality sausages (including meat-free options) and selection of mash potatoes, plus hearty portions of chicken pie or macaroni cheese. Inexpensive.

Stravaigin 2 8 Ruthven Lane ☎0141/334 7165, ⓦwww.stravaigin.com. A popular diner/bistro that serves excellent burgers alongside an innovative menu similar to the award-wining modern Scottish *Stravaigin* restaurant (see p.316). Moderate.

Tchai Ovna 42 Otago Lane ☎0141/357 4524, ⓦwww.tchaiovna.com. A low-key bohemian hangout near the Kelvin River with cakes, snacks and a selection of teas from around the world. Tobacco is forbidden but the house water-pipe with dried fruit serves as a substitute. Inexpensive.

Tinderbox 189 Byres Rd ☎0141/339 3108. A modern espresso café-bar offering an array of lattes, cappuccinos and the like as well as designer looks. Even in trendy Glasgow, it remains amazingly successful. Inexpensive.

University Café 87 Byres Rd ☎0141/339 5217. A bona fide institution adored by at least three generations of students and West End residents. Formica tables in snug booths, glass counters and original Art Deco features, where the favourites are fish'n'chips or mince'n'tatties rounded off with an ice-cream cone. Sometimes closes in afternoon. Inexpensive.

Southside

1901 1534 Pollokshaws Rd ☎0141/632 0161. Once known as the *Stoat & Ferret*, this Frenchinfluenced bistro/pub near Pollok Country Park is a lesser-known gem serving hearty Mediterranean food. Moderate.

Dayraa Grill House 105 Albert Drive ☎0141/424 1116. Not far from the Tramway contemporary arts centre, this casual Indo-Pakistani eatery and takeaway offers some of the best marinated and char-grilled meats in the city. No alcohol allowed. Inexpensive.

The Granary 10–16 Kilmarnock Rd ☎0141/649 0594. At Shawlands Cross, in the commercial heart of the Southside, this bar/bistro serves an international selection of food and satisfying desserts. Moderate.

Koshkemeer 271 Pollokshaws Drive ☎0141/423 9494. New in 2004, this welcoming and unpretentious place offers Kurdish cuisine – the only we know of in Scotland. Especially good is the mixed grill and the flat breads served with almost every meal. Unlicensed, but OK to BYOB. Inexpensive.

Restaurants

Despite the rash of chain restaurants and bars, not to mention multinational fast-food outlets, Glasgow still boasts a fairly high percentage of independent and locally owned establishments. Near the heart of things, the Merchant City (southeast of George Square) combines hip bars and good restaurants – literally wall-to-wall on **Candleriggs** – amid warehouse conversions, new flats and a few cool shops. Two other city-centre hotbeds of dining and drinking activity are **Bath Street** and more famous **Sauchiehall Street**, especially in the Charing Cross neighbourhood of the latter. The West End boasts an attractive selection of bars, cafés and restaurants, thanks to the local university population and the area's perennially young, affluent and creative vibe. The focus of activity is around the Hillhead underground station on **Byres Road**, with nearby cobbled **Ashton Lane** and its chock-a-block restaurants and pubs always a lively patch. The Southside is quieter, more residential and less intense, featuring some family-run restaurants with a welcoming ambience.

City centre and Merchant City restaurants

Chinese and Far East

Amber Regent 50 West Regent St ☎0141/331 1655, ⓦwww.amberregent.com. Refined service, restrained ambience and quality Chinese food. The Cantonese menu offers half-price main courses early evening on weekdays. Closed Sun. Moderate/expensive.

Canton Express 407 Sauchiehall St ☎0141/332 0145. Cheap eats near the many bars and clubs of Sauchiehall Street. Counter service and nothing fancy but it is reliable. Open late. Inexpensive.

Dragon-i 311–313 Hope St ☎0141/332 7728, ⓦwww.dragon-i.co.uk. Intriguing mix of Chinese and Far East influences in the dishes at this restaurant across from the Theatre Royal; good pre-theatre menu. Moderate.

Ichiban Japanese Noodle Café 50 Queen St ☎0141/204 4200, ⓦwww.ichiban.co.uk. Japanese-style informal eating, with long benches and tables shared by diners. Bowls (or plates) of noodles and sushi are specialities here; service is efficient. There's a second branch in the West End (see p.316). Inexpensive.

Mao 84 Brunswick St ☎0141/564 5161, ⓦwww.cafemao.com. Bright café-bar in the Merchant City with a range of Asian cuisine, including spicy Korean and Indonesian dishes. Moderate.

Oko 68 Ingram St ☎0141/572 1500, ⓦwww.okorestaurants.com. Locally owned restaurant bringing freshly prepared sushi on colour-coded plates and a Yo!Sushi style conveyor belt to the Merchant City. Not open for lunch Sun & Mon. Moderate.

Wagamama 93–107 West George St ☎0141/229 1468, ⓦwww.wagamama.com. The first Scottish branch of this London chain of Japanese-style noodle bars. No bookings. Moderate.

Yen 28 Tunnel St ☎0141/847 0110, ⓦwww.yenrotunda.com. Near the Clydeside hotels and the exhibition centre, Yen has a moderately priced café on the first floor as well as an expensive tepanyaki restaurant where the food's "barbecued" at the table. Moderate/expensive.

European

Brian Maule at Le Chardon d'Or 176 West Regent St ☎0141/248 3801, ⓦwww.lechardondor.com. Owner/chef Maule once worked with the Roux brothers at Le Gavroche restaurant in London. Fancy but not pretentious French-influenced food. Closed Sun (& Mon bank holidays). Expensive.

Café Cossachok 10 King St ☎0141/553 0733, ⓦwww.cossachok.com. Hearty Slavic-style dishes accompanied by Russian musicians on occasion and plenty of chilled vodka. There's a gallery on the mezzanine. Closed Mon. Moderate.

Fratelli Sarti 133 Wellington St or 121 Bath St ☎0141/204 0440, ⓦwww.fratellisarti.com. The Sarti brothers' flagship Italian café and restaurant: authentic and popular. The formal dining space is accessed from the Bath Street entrance; the more atmospheric café round the corner opens in the mornings Mon–Sat. Moderate.

La Tasca 39–43 Renfield St ☎0141/204 5188. Not the most authentic Spanish tapas ever devised in the UK, but moderately priced and delivered to tables with panache in a convenient city-centre location right through the day. Inexpensive/moderate.

Smith's of Glasgow 109 Candleriggs ☎0141/552 6539. Owner/chef Michael Smith recreates Parisian brasserie style in the Merchant City, with seasonally changing menus and complimentary aperitifs. Closed Sun. Moderate.

Indian

Dakhin 89 Candleriggs ☎0141/553 2585, ⓦwww.dakhin.com. Opened in 2004 and owned by the same brothers as the Dhabba (see below), this first-floor restaurant (above Bar 91) specializes in South Indian cuisine. Be sure and try a rice dosa. Moderate/expensive.

The Dhabba 44 Candleriggs ☎0141/553 1249, ⓦwww.thedhabba.com. This is not your typical Glasgow curry house. Prices are higher, portions

△ Fratelli Sarti

are smaller but the menu has some truly interesting options and fresh ingredients which put it a few steps above others. Moderate/expensive.

Wee Curry Shop 7 Buccleuch St ℡ 0141/353 0777. Tiny place near the Glasgow Film Theatre and Sauchiehall Street shops, serving home-made bargain meals to compete with the best in town. BYOB. Closed Sun. Inexpensive.

Scottish and seafood

The Buttery 652 Argyle St ℡ 0141/221 8188. Located near the shadow of the M8 flyover, this atmospheric, Victorian-era fine-dining restaurant offers complex but deftly handled dishes. Book ahead, and don't be surprised if the cabbie thinks the place is long gone. Closed Sun & Mon. Expensive.

City Merchant 97 Candleriggs ℡ 0141/553 1577, ⓦ www.citymerchant.co.uk. Popular brasserie that blazed the Merchant City trail which plenty of others have followed. Fresh Scottish produce from Ayrshire lamb to the house speciality: west-coast seafood. Closed Sun. Expensive.

Gamba 225a West George St ℡ 0141/572 0899, ⓦ www.gamba.co.uk. This modern basement restaurant offers probably the best meal in Glasgow. Continental contemporary sophistication prevails, with dishes such as

sashimi of fresh fish or roast halibut served with lobster. If you love fish, come here. Closed Sun. Expensive.

Mussel Inn 157 Hope St ℡ 0141/572 1405, ⓦ www.mussel-inn.com. Like the Edinburgh flagship, this branch concentrates on simply prepared pots of fresh mussels, grilled scallops and other delights from the sea in relaxed, buzzy environs. Moderate.

Rogano 11 Exchange Place ℡ 0141/248 4055, ⓦ www.rogano.co.uk. An Art Deco fish restaurant and Glasgow institution, decked out in 1935 in the style of the *Queen Mary* ocean liner. *Café Rogano*, in the basement, is cheaper. Or just have some oysters at the bar. Expensive.

Vegetarian

Mono 12 King's Court ℡ 0141/553 2400, ⓦ www .gomono.com. This places combines a fully vegan restaurant, Fairtrade food shop, bar and indie CD shop. Lots of space and home-made organic drinks. Inexpensive.

The 13th Note Café 50–60 King St ℡ 0141/553 1638, ⓦ www.13thnote.co.uk. Vegetarian and vegan fare with Greek and other Mediterranean influences in one of Glasgow's hipper drinking and indie/experimental music haunts on arty King Street. Inexpensive.

Chinese and Far East

Asian Style Chinese & Malaysian Restaurant
185–189 St Georges Rd ☎0141/332 8828. Unpretentious and honest Chinese cuisine at extremely reasonable prices, just south of St George's Cross underground along the M8 slip roads. Open evenings. Inexpensive.

Chow 98 Byres Rd ☎0141/334 9818. Proof that Chinese restaurants can be modern and non-kitsch. This bijou diner with extra tables upstairs offers excellent value-for-money meals. Moderate. A second outlet trades at 52 Bank St (☎0141/357 6682).

Ichiban Japanese Noodle Café 184 Dumbarton Rd ☎0141/334 9222, ⓦwww.ichiban.co.uk. Similar to the city-centre sister restaurant, offering a good selection of noodle bowls, sushi and other Japanese dishes such as bento boxes. Moderate.

Kokuryo 1138 Argyle St ☎0141/334 5566. Opened in late 2004, a Korean restaurant in a tiny space but with lots of big flavours on your plate, whether spiced *kimchi* or sizzling pork and beef. Inexpensive/moderate.

Thai Siam 1191 Argyle St ☎0141/229 1191, ⓦwww.thaisiamglasgow.com. A friendly neighbourhood ambience with the city's only Thai-born chefs. New owners in 2003 haven't changed the formula. Moderate.

European

The Big Blue 445 Great Western Rd ☎0141/357 1038. A casual Italian restaurant and bar with outdoor tables overlooking the River Kelvin. Good for pizza. Inexpensive/moderate.

Café Antipasti 337 Byres Rd ☎0141/337 2737. A busy Italian bistro serving tasty and well-priced pastas and salads. No bookings are taken, so expect a queue on busy nights. Second outlet in town at 305 Sauchiehall St (☎0141/332 9002). Inexpensive.

Parthenon 725 Great Western Rd ☎0141/334 6265. Cypriot-influenced Greek food with expected staples – moussaka, for example – and some surprises such as grilled monkfish. Moderate.

Paperino's West End 227 Byres Rd ☎0141/334 3811, ⓦwww.laparmigiana.co.uk. Owned by the same family which runs the nearby and respected *La Parmigiana* (477 Great Western Rd), this is a second branch for this modern Italian trattoria with pizza, pasta and few meaty mains, opened in 2005. Moderate. The original outlet in city centre is at 283 Sauchiehall St (☎0141/332 3800).

Indian

Ashoka Ashton Lane 19 Ashton Lane ☎0141/337 1115, ⓦwww.harlequingroup.net. Lively curry house in the Harlequin chain which has franchises across the west of Scotland; all offer consistent quality. Other *Ashoka* restaurants are at 1284 Argyle St (☎0141/339 3371), and on the Southside at 268 Clarkston Rd (☎0141/637 0711). Moderate.

🏃 **Mother India** 28 Westminster Terrace, off Sauchiehall St ☎0141/221 1663. This is one of the best Indian restaurants in Glasgow. Home cooking with some original specials as well as the old favourites at affordable prices in laid-back surroundings. Moderate. Also very much worth trying if you're on a budget is the nearby spin-off: *Mother India's Café* at 1355 Argyle St (☎0141/339 9145). Inexpensive.

Mexican

Cottier's 93–95 Hyndland St ☎0141/357 5825. Not pure Mexican, as it takes in Latin American and Caribbean. With a welcoming West End vibe, it's located on the top floor of a church annexe adjacent to Cottier's Theatre. Moderate.

Scottish and seafood

The Bothy 11 Ruthven Lane ☎0141/334 4040, ⓦwww.bothyrestaurant.co.uk. The menu is a bit of a laugh with its broad Scots vernacular, but the trad Scottish food is largely accomplished – especially given the reasonable prices of most dishes. Moderate.

The Cabin 996 Dumbarton Rd ☎0141/569 1036. Unique in Glasgow. One seating per night for three courses of upmarket Scottish food with a hint of Irish influence. Memorable post-meal entertainment is provided by host/chanteuse Wilma, who belts out a series of classic songs. Best for parties of four or more. Book in advance; deposit sometimes requested. Closed Mon. Expensive.

No. Sixteen 16 Byres Rd ☎0141/339 2544. A local favourite, with daily menus of Scottish produce, from pigeon to fillet of sea bream. Moderate.

🏃 **Stravaigin** 28–30 Gibson St ☎0141/334 2665, ⓦwww.stravaigin.com. Scottish meats and fish are given an international makeover using a host of unexpected ingredients, offering unusual flavour combinations. Adventurous fine dining in the basement restaurant and an exceptional-value menu in the street-level bar-café. Restaurant closed Mon. Moderate upstairs, expensive downstairs.

Two Fat Ladies 88 Dumbarton Rd ☎0141/339 1944. Perhaps the second-best fish restaurant in Glasgow, after *Gamba* (see p.315). Intimate space with the kitchen right up front. Moderate to expensive. A new outlet has recently opened at 118a Blythswood St (☎ 0141/847 0088) in the city centre.

The Ubiquitous Chip 12 Ashton Lane ☎ 0141/334 5007, ⒲ www.ubiquitouschip.co.uk. Opened in 1971, *The Chip* led the way in headlining Scotland's quality fresh produce at the heart of a contemporary, upmarket dining experience. Some say it's living on its reputation, but it's still up there. Expensive, but less pricey options upstairs in the bistro.

Vegetarian

Grassroots Café 93 St Georges Rd ☎ 0141/333 0534, ⒲ www.grassroots.co.uk. Although the competition is not especially stiff, this vegetarian outlet (just cross the M8 motorway from the city centre) has the best reputation for meat-free fare in Glasgow. Fresh, creative cooking and a relaxed atmosphere. Inexpensive/moderate.

Southside restaurants

European

Arigo 67 Kilmarnock Rd ☎ 0141/636 6616, ⒲ www.arigorestaurants.com. A charming local favourite in the heart of the Southside's retail district where meals are made fresh to order. Moderate.

Greek Golden Kebab 34 Sinclair Drive ☎ 0141/649 7581. The longest-running Greek restaurant in Glasgow hasn't changed its rustic cooking in probably thirty years. Worth seeking out near Queens Park. Closed Mon–Wed. Moderate.

La Fiorentina 2 Paisley Rd West ☎ 0141/420 1585, ⒲ www.la-fiorentina.com. A critical favourite that also tops popular surveys, this Tuscan-oriented restaurant has become an institution. Not far from the Glasgow Science Centre in Govan. Moderate

Scottish

Art Lovers' Café In House for an Art Lover (see p.308), Bellahouston Park, 10 Dumbreck Rd ☎ 0141/353 4779. The dining room, looking onto a charming garden in this showcase house based on unfinished Mackintosh designs, offers sublime lunches. Closed eves. Moderate.

Mitchell's 107 Waterside Rd, Carmunock ☎ 0141/644 2255. This restaurant began near the Mitchell library in the city centre, but now runs on the southern, nearly rural, city fringes, serving good-value Scottish and Continental cooking. Closed Mon & Tues. Moderate/expensive.

Specialist food shops

There are a host of specialist outlets around Glasgow where you can stock up on good food. Heart Buchanan Fine Food & Wine, 380 Byres Rd, has excellent pre-prepared meals, as well as **deli**, dry goods and wine. I.J. Mellis, 492 Great Western Rd, is a wonderful, old-fashioned **cheesemonger** specializing in farmhouse cheeses from the British Isles, though they also keep a selection of the best from the Continent. Also in the West End, Delizique, 66 Hyndland St, offers more first-class deli and pre-cooked foods. Nearby in Mansfield Park, just off Dumbarton Road, Glasgow's **farmers' market** takes place on the second and fourth Saturday of every month from about 10am. Grassroots, 93 Woodlands Rd, is the best **vegetarian** and Fairtrade food shop in the city, while those missing Mexican, American and Asian treats should visit Lupe Pintos at 313 Great Western Rd.

In the city centre, the Peckhams chain has a late-opening branch at 65 Glassford St in the Merchant City; it's a reliable upmarket deli with an impressive range including lots of tasty takeaway options and a full wine cellar. If you're willing to travel slightly further afield, go to Dennistoun (1/2 mile east of Glasgow Cathedral) and sample **organic** bakery goods from Tapa Coffee & Bakehouse at 21 Whitehill St.

Drinking

Glasgow's mythical tough-guy image has been linked with its **pubs**, mistakenly believed by a few to be no-go areas for visitors. Today, however, the city is much changed, and many of the once windowless, nicotine-stained working men's taverns have been converted into airy modern bars. Most drinking dens in the **city centre**, the adjoining **Merchant City** and the fashionable **West End** are places to experience real Glaswegian bonhomie.

If you tire of trendier wine bars and pre-club pubs, set out for the slightly edgier **Saltmarket** district near the Clyde, where the local spit-and-sawdust establishments offer a welcome change. The liveliest area for nightlife is still the West End, with students mixing with locals around Byres Road, as well as in the nearby Woodlands and Kelvingrove districts. Decent pubs are more widely scattered across the more suburban **Southside**, but you'll find a handful of pleasant spots, ranging from stylish hangouts to historic locals.

As for **opening hours**, Glasgow's licensing regulations generally give bars and pubs more freedom than they have had historically. From Sunday to Thursday, many pubs and bars often keep serving until midnight, although some outside the centre close at 11pm during the week. On Friday and Saturday, you'll often find bars open until 1am – and occasionally later. After closing time, your option is to head to a nightclub (see opposite), some of which don't close until 5am. By April 2006, bars will be completely non-smoking by law.

City centre and Merchant City pubs and bars

The Arches 253 Argyle St. The basement bar is a focal point in this contemporary arts centre under Central station. Decent pub grub and an arty clientele.

Babbity Bowster 16–18 Blackfriars St, off High St. Lively place with an unforced and kitsch-free Scottish feel that features spontaneous folk sessions at the weekend. Good beer and wine, tasty food and some outdoor seating.

Bar 10 10 Mitchell St. Across from the Lighthouse architecture centre, and considered the grand-daddy of Glasgow style bars. Still popular and suitably chic.

Bar 91 91 Candleriggs. This Merchant City style bar tends to be friendlier, less pretentious and draws a more diverse crowd than most.

Blackfriars 36 Bell St. Excellent beer selection (both imported and hand-pulled UK ales) in suitably worn environment. There are often jazz or comedy performances in the basement space.

Corinthian 191 Ingram St. A remarkable renovation of a florid early Victorian Italianate bank. Three distinct bars, one restaurant and a private club: dress smartly.

Horseshoe Bar 17 Drury St. A must for pub aficionados. An original "Gin Palace" with the longest continuous bar in the UK, this is reputedly Glasgow's busiest drinking hole; karaoke upstairs.

Moskito 200 Bath St. Less full of posing youth than some but nonetheless hip and stylish, with inexpensive food and ambient tunes.

Nice'n'Sleazy 421 Sauchiehall St. Better known for its indie rock performance space (see p.320), the ground-floor bar has the feel of New York's

East Village, with slightly tatty booths and the best jukebox in the city.

Pot Still 154 Hope St. Whisky galore! At least 500 different single malts are found in this traditional pub, which has a decent ale selection as well.

Republic Bier Halle 9 Gordon St. Chunky modern industrial design using shuttered concrete and blocks of stone in subterranean setting. Serves 130 different beers.

Variety Bar 401 Sauchiehall St. Featuring faded faux Art Nouveau decor, this place is frequented by nearby Glasgow Art School students. Located near clubs.

Saltmarket pubs and bars

Clutha Vaults 167 Stockwell St. Slightly more scrubbed and less atmospheric than the *Scotia* (see below) but host to a similar line-up of free live music.

Scotia Bar 112 Stockwell St. Billy Connolly began his career here, telling jokes between singing folk songs; today it's a place for semi-pro live blues, folk and skiffle sessions.

Victoria Bar 157–159 Bridgegate. Time-honoured, basic pub serving a selection of real ales and hosting a range of live music, with monthly bluegrass and even Morris dancers.

West End pubs and bars

Bon Accord 153 North St. At the eastern edge of the West End, adjacent to the M8, this pub began the real-ale revival in Glasgow, and often hosts UK beer festivals.

Booly Mardy's 28 Vinicombe St. An anagram of Bloody Marys, this modern, stylish bar specializes

5

in cocktails, with decent daytime food and south-facing pavement-seating on a street with no through traffic.

Firebird 1321 Argyle St. Airy modern drinking spot near the Kelvingrove Art Gallery, with a wood-stoked pizza oven producing some tasty snacks plus DJs to keep the pre-clubbing crowd entertained.

The Goat 1287 Argyle St. Occupying a large corner location, this two-floor pub has modern sensibilities and is geared to a slightly more grown-up bunch of West End cool cats.

The Halt 106 Woodlands Rd. A good beer and whisky selection in this relaxed, un-modernized pub, where live rockin' music is played in the adjoining lounge.

Lismore Lounge 206 Dumbarton Rd. Decorated with specially commissioned stained-glass panels depicting the Highland Clearances, this bar is a meeting point for the local Gaels, who come here to chat, relax and listen to the impromptu music sessions.

Oran Mor Byres Rd cnr Great Western Rd ☎0141/357 6200. Arguably the most impressive addition in many years to the nightlife scene, with a big bar, club venue and performance space/auditorium (plus two different dining rooms) all within the tastefully – and expensively – restored Kelvinside parish church.

Tennent's 191 Byres Rd. No-nonsense, beery pub that offers a refreshing antidote to designer-driven bars nearby. Large and popular, with real ale and a no-music policy.

Uisge Beatha 232 Woodlands Rd. An unexceptional frontage belies an eclectic interior, with lots of sofas and ironic Scots kitsch. Barmen wear kilts and keep the atmosphere lively. The name is Gaelic for "the water of life" – that is, whisky.

Southside pubs and bars

Heraghty's Free House 708 Pollokshaws Rd. Authentic Irish pub that prides itself on pouring the perfect pint of Guinness. Still living down its history of not having a women's loo: one's been installed for several years now.

Republic Bier Stube 87 Kilmarnock Rd. *Stube* means "local" in German and this sister operation to the city-centre *Republic* (see opposite) is quite neighbourly in its welcome and ambience, with better food than the flagship.

The Taverna 778 Pollokshaws Rd. A favourite of many who stay in this neck of the Southside, in a bright, light corner location with potted palms and a selection of real ales.

Tusk 18 Moss Side Rd. Operated by the same company behind the *Corinthian* (see opposite), *Tusk* is almost as flamboyant, with a giant Buddha as the focal point of decoration.

Nightlife and entertainment

Glasgow offers a thriving **contemporary music** community, with loads of new bands emerging practically every year, Franz Ferdinand being the best-known recently. There are clutch of venues, from the famous Barrowlands to King Tut's Wah Wah Hut, where you've a good chance of catching a live act. Additionally, the city's **clubbing scene** has long been rated among the best in the UK, with the city attracting top DJs from around the world and also breeding a good deal of local talent. Establishments are pretty mixed and an underground scene thrives, while some mega-discos still have dress codes. Opening hours hover between 11pm to 3am, though some stay open until 5am. Cover charges are variable: expect to pay around £5 during the week and up to £20 at the weekend. Drinks are usually about thirty percent more expensive than in the pubs.

On the **performing arts** scene, Glasgow is no slouch either: it's home to Scottish Opera, Scottish Ballet and the Royal Scottish National Orchestra. All told, the city's cultural programme offers a range of **music**, from contemporary to heavyweight classical, plus **dance**, **theatre** (both mainstream and experimental/performance art), as well as **cinema**. Most of the larger theatres, cinema multiplexes and concert halls are in the city centre; the West End is home to just one or two venues while the Southside can boast two theatres noted for cutting-edge drama, the Citizens' and Tramway.

For detailed **listings** on what's on, pick up the comprehensive fortnightly magazine *The List* (£2.20), which also covers Edinburgh, or consult Glasgow's

Herald or *Evening Times* newspapers. To book **tickets** for theatre productions or big concerts, try Tickets Scotland, 239 Argyle St, under Central station (Mon–Wed, Fri & Sat 9am–6pm, Thurs 9am–7pm, Sun 11.30am–5.30pm; ℡0141/204 5151), or Way Ahead (℡0141/339 8383).

Clubs

Archaos 25 Queen St ℡0141/204 3189. Massive, multi-level venue with designer decor and a music policy that emphasizes hard house, R&B and party.
The Arches 30 Midland St, off Jamaica St ℡0141/221 4001, ⓦwww.thearches.co.uk. In converted railway arches under Central station, the club portion of this arts venue offers an eclectic array of music: hard house, trance, techno and funk.
Fury Murry's 96 Maxwell St, behind the St Enoch Centre ℡0141/221 6511, ⓦwww.furyslive.co.uk. Student-oriented and lively, with music spanning the 1960s to recent indie and chart favourites.
The Garage 490 Sauchiehall St ℡0141/332 1120. Medium-sized club that also hosts gigs across the rock'n'roll spectrum.
Glasgow School of Art 167 Renfrew St ℡0141/332 0691. Blissfully unadorned space for hipsters, with music that ranges widely from obscure house to electronica, epitomized by Saturday's Eskrima.
Sub Club 22 Jamaica St ℡0141/248 4600, ⓦwww.subclub.co.uk. Near-legendary venue and base for the noteworthy Subculture and Optimo clubs, the home of house and techno in Scotland.
The Tunnel 84 Mitchell St ℡0141/204 1000. Contemporary and progressive house music club with arty decor (dig the gents' cascading waterfall walls) and fairly strict dress codes.

Gay clubs and bars

Bennett's 90 Glassford St, Merchant City ℡0141/552 5761. Glasgow's longest-running gay club (reopened recently after a fire): predominantly male, fairly traditional and with commercially oriented music.
Delmonica's 68 Virginia St ℡0141/552 4803. One of Glasgow's liveliest gay bars, in a popular area, with a mixed, hedonistic crowd and some kind of entertainment or event nightly.
LGBT Centre 11 Dixon St ℡0141/221 7203, ⓦwww.glgbt.org.uk. Licensed café in addition to more institutional support such as information and reading rooms.
Merchant's Pride 20 Candleriggs ℡0141/564 1285. Formerly the *Candle Bar*. Relaxed and unpretentious, with DJs, karaoke and quiz nights.
Polo Lounge 84 Wilson St, off Glassford St ℡0141/553 1221. Original Victorian decor – marble tiles and open fires – and gentleman's club atmosphere upstairs, with dark, pounding

nightclub underneath which attracts a gay and gay-friendly crowd.
Revolver 6a John St ℡0141/553 2456. Geared more towards the art of conversation than dance, although the jukebox is tops; welcomes men and women.

Live-music venues

ABC 300–330 Sauchiehall St ℡0141/332 2232. Opened in 2005 and more proof that Glasgow's a gig-hungry town, this small- to medium-size hall offers an intimate setting to see bands.
Barfly 260 Clyde St ℡0141/221 0414, ⓦwww.barflyclub.com. Part of a British chain, big with UK indie bands, underground and avant-garde DJs.
Barrowland 244 Gallowgate ℡0141/552 4601, ⓦwww.glasgow-barrowland.com. Legendary East End ballroom that hosts some of the sweatiest and best gigs you may ever encounter. With room for a couple of thousand, it mostly books bands securely on the rise but still hosts some big-time acts who return to it as their favourite venue in Scotland.
Carling Academy Eglington St ℡0870/771 2000, ⓦwww.glasgow-academy.co.uk. Owned by the same people behind London's famous Brixton Academy, this renovated theatre south of the River Clyde has stolen a bit of the Barrowland's thunder since opening in 2002.
The Garage 490 Sauchiehall St ℡0141/332 1120. Nightclub which converts to a medium-size venue for bands that are just about to make it big.
King Tut's Wah Wah Hut 272a St Vincent St ℡0141/221 5279, ⓦwww.kingtuts.co.uk. Famous as the place where Oasis were discovered, and still presenting one of the city's best live-music programmes. Also has a good bar, with an excellent jukebox.
Nice'n'Sleazy 421 Sauchiehall St ℡0141/333 0900, ⓦwww.nicensleazy.com. Alternative and indie-oriented acts play most nights in the appropriately dingy performance space below this city-centre bar (see p.318).
Queen Margaret Union 22 University Gardens ℡0141/339 9784, ⓦwww.qmu.org.uk. Once an indie showcase but now likely to feature dance-oriented acts as well.

Theatres and comedy venues

Arches Theatre 253 Argyle St ℡0141/565 1023, ⓦwww.thearches.co.uk. Home to its own avant-garde theatre company, reviving old classics and introducing new talent in this hip subterranean venue.

Citizens' Theatre 119 Gorbals St ☎0141/429 0022, ⓦwww.citz.co.uk. The "Citz" has evolved from its 1960s working-class roots into one of the most respected and innovative contemporary theatres in Britain. Three stages, concession rates for students and free preview nights.

Cottier Theatre 93–95 Hyndland St ☎0141/357 3868, ⓦwww.thecottier.com. This performance space in the old Dowanhill church hosts touring shows, dance and music gigs. An adjoining bar with beer garden is a favourite on warm summer evenings.

Jongleurs Cineworld Building, Renfrew St ☎0870/787 0707, ⓦwww.jongleurs.com. Big mainstream acts and some of the best in British/ international comedy.

King's Theatre 297 Bath St T0141/240 1111, ⓦwww.kings-glasgow.co.uk Gorgeous interiors within an imposing red sandstone Victorian building; the programmme is good quality, if mainstream.

Ramshorn Theatre 98 Ingram St ☎0141/552 3489. Another church conversion, this Merchant City venue features student and other productions at bargain prices.

The Stand 333 Woodlands Rd ☎0870/600 6055, ⓦwww.thestand.co.uk. Sister to the first-rate comedy club in Edinburgh, booking local, national and international acts.

Theatre Royal 282 Hope St ☎0141/332 9000, ⓦwww.theatreroyalglasgow.com. This late-nineteenth-century playhouse was revived in the mid-1970s as the opulent home of Scottish Opera, whose recent productions include an acclaimed *Ring* cycle. It also plays regular host to visiting theatre groups, including the Royal Shakespeare Company, as well as orchestras.

Tramway 25 Albert Drive, off Pollokshaws Rd ☎0141/330 3501, ⓦwww.tramway.org. Based in a converted tram terminus, whose lofty proportions qualified it as the only suitable UK venue for Peter Brook's famous production of the *Mahabharata* in 1998. Premier avant-garde venue for experimental theatre, dance and music, as well as art exhibitions.

Tron Theatre 63 Trongate ☎0141/552 4267, ⓦwww.tron.co.uk. Varied repertoire of some mainstream and, more importantly, challenging productions from itinerant companies, such as Glasgow's Vanishing Point. Folk music performances in theatre bar.

Concert halls

Glasgow Royal Concert Hall 2 Sauchiehall St ☎0141/353 8000, ⓦwww.grch.com. One of Glasgow's less memorable modern buildings, this is the venue for big-name touring orchestras and the home of the Royal Scottish National Orchestra. Also features major rock and R'n'B stars, and middle-of-the-road music hall acts.

Scottish Exhibition and Conference Centre, and Clyde Auditorium Finnieston Quay ☎0870/040 4000, ⓦwww.secc.co.uk. The SECC is a gigantic airplane hangar-like space with dreadful acoustics that, unfortunately, is the only indoor venue in Scotland for world-touring megastars from Bob Dylan to 50 Cent. The adjacent Clyde Auditorium – better known as the Armadillo – is smaller but more melodic.

Cinemas

Cineworld 7 Renfrew St ☎0870/907 0789. Formerly the UGC, this is a gigantic multistorey cinema with first-run Hollywood and a few art films as well.

Glasgow Film Theatre 12 Rose St ☎0141/332 8128, ⓦwww.gft.org.uk. Dedicated art, independent and repertory cinema house. Its in-house *Café Cosmo* is an excellent place for pre-show drinks.

IMAX Theatre Glasgow Science Centre, 50 Pacific Quay ☎0141/420 5000, ⓦwww.glasgowsciencecentre.org. 3-D and super-screen documentaries and features.

Odeon City Centre 56 Renfield St ☎0871/224 4007, ⓦwww.odeon.co.uk. Multiscreen cinema with the latest releases. Another Odeon complex is across the river at Springfield Quay, Paisley Rd.

Grosvenor Ashton Lane ☎0141/339 8444, ⓦwww.grosvenorcinema.co.uk. Renovated two-screen neighbourhood film house with bar – and sofas you can reserve for screenings of mostly mainstream films.

Shopping

Glasgow's **shopping** is reckoned to be the second best in the UK – after London, of course. While the city's gritty industrial reputation doesn't, on the face of it, sit all that obviously with its status as an oasis of retail therapy, the local population has long enjoyed dressing up to go out. The main area for spending in the city centre is formed by the Z-shaped and mostly pedestrianized route of **Argyle, Buchanan and Sauchiehall streets**. Along the way you'll find Princes Square, the city's poshest malls (see p.289), plus major department stores such as M&S, Debenhams and John Lewis and branches of upmarket chains such as Hugo Boss, Gap, Karen Millen and Urban Outfitters. The Buchanan Galleries, a bland complex built around John Lewis, features some high-fashion budget stores.

Otherwise, make for the **West End** – or the **Merchant City**, with its chichi and pricey Italian Centre for some imported glamour or home-grown Cruise for designerwear on Ingram Street. In general the Merchant City and West End have more eccentric and individual offerings – the latter is the only district in the city with secondhand and antiquarian **book shops**.

For more on delis and specialist **food** shopping in the city, see p.317.

Books The biggest, most central shop is Borders, 98 Buchanan St (℡0141/222 7700), with a selection of international newspapers and magazines. Waterstone's has an almost equally large outlet at 153 Sauchiehall St (℡0141/332 9105). For secondhand try Caledonian Bookshop, 483 Great Western Rd (℡0141/334 9663) or Oxfam Bookshop, 330 Byres Rd (℡0141/334 7669).

Camping and outdoors gear Try Tiso, 129 Buchanan St (℡0141/248 4877) and Couper St, north of Buchanan bus terminal (℡0141/559 5450), which features an ice-climbing wall, a waterfall (to test cagoules) and 100m walking-boot test track. Less grand but useful is Blacks at 211 Sauchiehall St (℡0141/353 2344) and 28 Union St (℡0141/221 2295).

Clothes Dr Jives, 113 Candleriggs (℡0141/552 5451) features cutting-edge style. Urban Outfitters, 157 Buchanan St (℡0141/248 9203) offers US city and retro gear. Cruise, 180 Ingram St (℡0141/572 3232), is in label-land with Prada, Armani and so on.

Clothes (secondhand) Go to Starry Starry Night, 19 Dowanside Lane, near Byres Rd (℡0141/337 1837); Flip, 15 Bath St, near Buchanan St (℡0141/353 1634); or the Barras market, 244

Gallowgate (Sat & Sun 10am–5pm), which has clothes and a whole lot more at its raft of stalls.

Music One of the better shops for local, indie and secondhand is the tiny Avalanche branch, 34 Dundas St, near Queen St station (℡0141/332 2099). Also good for contemporary CDs is Fopp, 19 Union St (℡0141/222 2128) and 358 Byres Rd (℡0141/357 0774). For mainstream, there are two Virgin outlets, on Argyle and Buchanan streets, and three HMVs: 72 Union St, 1850 Argyle St and 154 Sauchiehall St.

Novelties/souvenirs Highland Trading, St Enoch Centre (℡0141/248 1506), has a wide selection of souvenirs. Hutcheson's Hall, 158 Ingram St (℡0141/552 8391), houses the Scottish National Trust's excellent shop featuring "Glasgow Style" and work from local designers. Shops in the Gallery of Modern Art and the Lighthouse (see p.288 & p.290) are also well stocked with tasteful gifts and original design items.

Shoes Soletrader, 164 Buchanan St, and Schuh, 9 Sauchiehall St, are reliable for fresh treads.

Tartan/woollen Places to select your tweeds and tartans are James Pringle Weavers of Inverness, 130 Buchanan St; Hector Russell Kiltmakers, 110 Buchanan St; and Geoffrey (Tailor) Kiltmakers and Weavers, 309 Sauchiehall St.

Listings

American Express 115 Hope St (Mon–Fri 8.30am–5.30pm, except Wed 9.30am–5.30pm, Sat 9am–noon; ℡0141/222 1401).

Banks and exchange Bank of Scotland/Halifax, 110 Queen St; Clydesdale Bank, 30 St Vincent Place; Royal Bank of Scotland, 130 George St. English banks in Glasgow include Barclays, 90 St Vincent St and Lloyds/TSB, 52–60 St Vincent St. Post offices in Hope and St Vincent streets operate bureaux de change as does Glasgow Tourist

Information Centre, 11 George Square (℡0141/204 4400). Thomas Cook is in Central train station ℡0141/207 3400.

Bike rental and routes A good selection can be found at West End Cycles, 16 Chancellor St (℡0141/357 1344), which is located close to the start of the Glasgow to Loch Lomond route, one of a number of cycle routes which radiate out from the city. For further details, check ⊛ www.sustrans .co.uk.

5

Bus and coach information Buchanan Street bus station (℡0141/333 3708); Citylink coaches ℡0870/550 5050; First Glasgow (local services; ℡0141/423 6600, ⑩www.firstglasgow.co.uk). The comprehensive Traveline ℡0870/608 2608 has full information.

Car rental Arnold Clark, multiple branches (℡0845/607 4500); Avis, 70 Lancefield St (℡0141/221 2827); Budget, 101 Waterloo St (℡0141/243 2047). Car hire at the airport includes Budget (℡0141/889 1479) and Hertz (℡0870/846 0007).

Dentist National Health Service line (℡0800/224488) lists local and emergency dentists. Glasgow Dental Hospital, 378 Sauchiehall St (℡0141/211 9600).

Flight information Glasgow International airport (℡0141/887 1111, ⑩www.baa.com /Glasgow). Glasgow Prestwick International airport (℡0871/223 0700, ⑩www.gpia.co.uk).

Football Glasgow is home to two of the biggest clubs in the UK as well as Scotland's National Stadium, Hampden Park (℡0141/620 4000), where there's a national football museum (see p.308). Celtic FC (℡0141/556 2611, ⑩www .celticfc.net); Partick Thistle FC (℡0141/632 1275, ⑩www.ptfc.co.uk); Queens Park FC (℡0141/632 1275, ⑩www.queensparkfc.co.uk); Rangers FC (℡0870/600 1972, ⑩www.rangers.co.uk).

Gay and lesbian contacts Strathclyde Lesbian and Gay Switchboard (℡0141/847 0447); Glasgow Lesbian, Gay, Bisexual and Transgender (LGBT) Centre, 11 Dixon St (℡0141/221 7203, ⑩www .glgbt.org.uk).

Golf The city operates several inexpensive munici-pal courses. One of the best-maintained and longest is Littlehill, Auchinairn Rd (℡0141/772 1916).

Hospital 24hr casualty department at the Royal Infirmary, 84 Castle St near Glasgow Cathedral (℡0141/211 4000).

Internet EasyEverything is at 57–61 St Vincent St (℡0141/222 2365). Most libraries also offer access.

Laundry Harvey's, 161 Great Western Rd; Majestic Laundrette, 1110 Argyle St.

Left luggage Buchanan Street bus station and lockers at Central train station.

Libraries Mitchell Library, North St (℡0141/287 2999), is the largest public reference library in Europe.

Pharmacies Boots, Buchanan Galleries (Mon–Sat 9am–6pm, Thurs until 8pm, Sun 11am–5pm; ℡0141/333 9306) and branches throughout the city.

Police Strathclyde Police HQ, Pitt St (℡0141/532 2000). For emergencies, dial 999.

Post office General information (℡0845/722 3344). Main office at 47 St Vincent St (Mon–Fri 8.30am–5.45pm, Sat 9am–5.30pm); other city centre offices at 87–91 Bothwell St and 228 Hope St.

Swimming pools At city-run leisure centres in the Gorbals (℡0141/418 6400); Scotstoun (℡0141/959 4000); Tollcross (Olympic size; ℡0141/763 2345).

Taxis Glasgow Wide TOA (℡0141/429 7070); Glasgow Private Hire (℡0141/774 3000).

Train information National Rail enquiries (℡0845/748 4950, ⑩www.nationalrail.co.uk).

Travel agents Clifford International Ltd, 20–22 Cambridge St (℡0141/332 9990); STA Travel Ltd, 184 Byres Rd (℡0141/ 338 6000).

The Clyde

The **River Clyde** is the dominant physical feature of Glasgow and its environs, an area which comprises the largest urban concentration in Scotland, with almost two million people living in the city and satellite towns. Little of this immediate hinterland can be described as beautiful, with crisscrossing motor-ways and relentlessly grim housing estates dominating much of the landscape. However, there are pockets of interest, many related to the river itself or the industries which grew up from it. Beyond the urban sprawl, rolling green hills, open expanses of water and attractive countryside eventually begin to dominate, not always captivating initially, but holding promises of wilder country beyond.

West of the city, regular trains and the M8 motorway dip down from the southern bank of the Clyde to **Paisley**, where the distinctive cloth pattern gained its name, before heading back up to the edge of the river again as it broadens into the **Firth of Clyde**. Here the former shipbuilding towns of **Port Glasgow**, **Greenock** and **Gourock** look out over the water to the lochs and hills of Argyll, a prospect which also serves as a backdrop to two towns on the north bank of the firth – the ancient Strathclyde capital of **Dumbarton**, and **Helensburgh**, birthplace of architect Charles Rennie Mackintosh and television pioneer John Logie Baird.

North of Glasgow lies some wonderful upland countryside. Trains terminate at tiny Milngavie (pronounced "Mill-guy"), which makes great play of its status as the start of Scotland's best-known long-distance footpath, the **West Highland Way** (for more about this, see p.426). Nearby, the rolling beauty of the Campsie Fells provides excellent walking and stunning views down onto Glasgow and the glinting river that runs through it.

Heading southeast out of Glasgow, the industrial landscape of the **Clyde Valley** eventually gives way to a far more attractive scenery of gorges and towering castles. Here lie the stoic town of **Lanark**, where eighteenth-century philanthropists built their model workers' community around the mills of **New Lanark**, and the spectacular **Falls of Clyde**, a mile upstream. Even further beyond, deep into the rolling countryside of South Lanarkshire where the Clyde is little more than a widening stream, the market town of **Biggar** with its unusual clutch of museums serves as a useful orientation point for the hill-farming country of the Scottish Borders beyond.

The Firth of Clyde – south bank

The swift journey from Glasgow along the M8, coupled with the proximity of the international airport, can belie the fact that **Paisley** is not a suburb of Glasgow but a town in its own right, with a long and distinctive history, particularly in the textile trade. Further west, the motorway and train line rejoin the Clyde by the **Erskine Bridge**, a huge concrete parabola which carries cars between the two banks of the river. As the estuary widens, the former shipbuilding centres of Port Glasgow and **Greenock** crowd the riverbank, followed by the old-fashioned seaside resort of **Gourock**, and eventually **Wemyss Bay**, jumping-off point for the ferry to Rothesay on Bute. Of the four, Greenock is by far the most interesting, with an excellent town museum that examines the life and achievements of local boy James Watt.

Paisley

Founded in the twelfth century as a monastic settlement around an abbey, **PAISLEY** expanded rapidly after the eighteenth century as a linen-manufacturing town, specializing in the production of highly fashionable imitation Kashmiri shawls. Paisley quickly eclipsed other British centres producing the cloth, eventually lending its name to the swirling pine-cone design.

South of the train station, down Gilmour or Smithills streets, lies the bridge over the White Cart Water and the burgh's ponderous **Town Hall**, seemingly built back to front as its municipal clock and mismatched double towers loom incongruously over the river instead of facing onto the town. Opposite the town hall, the **Abbey** (Mon–Sat 10am–3.30pm; free) was built on the site of the town's original settlement and was massively overhauled in the Victorian age. The unattractive, fat grey facade of the church does little justice to the renovated interior, which is tall, spacious and elaborately decorated; the elongated choir, rebuilt extensively throughout the last two centuries, is illuminated by jewel-coloured stained glass from a variety of ages and styles. The abbey's oldest monument is the tenth-century Celtic cross of St Barochan, which lurks like a gnarled old bone at the eastern end of the north aisle.

Paisley's bland pedestrianized **High Street** leads westwards from the town hall towards two churches that make far more of an impression on the town's skyline than the modest abbey. The steep cobbles of Church Hill rise away from the High Street up to the grand steps and five-stage spire of the **High Church**, while beyond the civic museum at the bottom of the High Street stands the **Thomas Coats Memorial Church**, a Victorian masterpiece of hugely over-stated grandeur. Between the two churches, Paisley's civic **Museum and Art Gallery** (Tues–Sat 10am–5pm, Sun 2–5pm; free) shelters behind pompous Ionic columns that face the grim buildings of Paisley University. Inside, it's a reason-ably attractive civic building, with grand domes and staircases. The main reason for coming here is to see the Shawl Gallery, which deals with the growth and development of the Paisley pattern and shawls, showing the familiar pine-cone (or teardrop) pattern from its simple beginnings to elaborate later incarnations. Paisley's identity as a centre for craftsmanship is also celebrated in displays of the work of contemporary local artisans, found on the balcony overlooking the entrance hall, and alongside these a number of working looms are looked after by a weaver-in-residence. Leading on from this is the largest gallery, mixing local social history with blown-up photos of locals (or "buddies", as inhabitants of Paisley like to be known) selecting their favourite exhibits in the museum. The Upper Gallery houses a small art collection including works by Glasgow Boys Hornel, Guthrie and Lavery (see box on p.302), as well as one or two paintings by local boy John Byrne, artist and playwright best known for his plays *The Slab Boys* and *Tutti Frutti*.

On Oakshaw Street, which runs along the crest of the hill above the Art Gallery, the **Coats Observatory** (Tues–Sat 10am–5pm, Sun 2–5pm; free) has recorded astronomical and meteorological information since 1884. Today it houses a ten-inch telescope under its dome, and a couple of small exhibition areas display seismic recorders that documented the cataclysmic San Francisco earthquake of 1906. The telescopes are used for public viewing on Thursday evenings from the last Thursday in October until the last Thursday in March (7.30–9.30pm, weather permitting).

To bring you back down to earth, the harsh reality of eighteenth-century life is re-created in the **Sma' Shot Cottages** (April–Sept Wed & Sat noon–4pm; free) in George Place, off New Street. These old houses contain perfect re-creations of eighteenth- and nineteenth-century daily life, complete with bone cutlery and ancient looms. The nineteenth-century artisan's home is filled with artefacts, from ceramic hot-water bottles to period wallpaper, and leads you into a cosy tearoom where you can enjoy some home baking.

Practicalities

Regular **trains** from Glasgow Central run to Paisley's Gilmour Street station in the centre of town, and they're a faster, more convenient option than **buses** #9 (First), #36, #38 or #39 (all Arriva) from Glasgow city centre. Buses leave Paisley's Gilmour Street forecourt every ten minutes for Glasgow International airport, two miles north of the town. The **tourist office** is right in the centre at 9a Gilmour St (April–Sept Mon–Sat 9.30am–5.30pm, Sun noon–5pm; Oct–March Mon–Sat 10am–5pm; ℡0141/889 0711).

Few people bother to **stay** in Paisley; *Ardgowan House*, 92 Renfrew Rd (℡0141/889 4763, ⓦwww.ardgowanhouse.com; ❷), has a hotel and cheaper guesthouse alongside each other, while a homely B&B can be found at *Greenhill House*, 111 Greenhill Rd (☎0141/889 6752, ⓦwww.greenhillhouse.co.uk; ❸). For **food** the Paisley Arts Centre has a small bar, daytime café and outside seating, while most of the pubs in the centre, including the *Last Post* in the old Post Office building in County Square, serves a range of bar meals. *Aroma Room* is a more modern spot right opposite the Museum and Art Gallery, which serves coffees, snacks and lunches; not far away, both *Cardosi's* on Storie Street and *Raeburn's Bistro and Grill* on New Street have decent evening menus.

❺ Greenock and around

GREENOCK, west of Glasgow, was the site of the first dock on the Clyde, founded in 1711, and the community has grown on the back of shipping ever since. Despite its ranks of anonymous tower blocks and sterile shopping centres, the town still retains a few features of interest. To get there, you'll pass through **Port Glasgow**, a small fishing village until 1688, when the burghers of Glasgow bought it and developed it as their main harbour. As you come into the town, look out for sturdy fifteenth-century **Newark Castle** right on the banks of the river (April–Sept daily 9.30am–6.30pm; HS; £2.50), but much of the rest of Port Glasgow is fairly grim, with nothing to detain you.

The train line splits at Port Glasgow, one branch heading west along the industrialized coast to Greenock and its neighbour Gourock, the other heading inland before curving round to the ferry port at Wemyss Bay. From the Central train station in Greenock (also served by hourly Citylink buses from Glasgow's Buchanan Street station), it's a short walk down the hill to **Cathcart Square**, where an exuberant 245-foot Victorian tower looms high over the elegant Council House. There's no tourist office in Greenock – the best you'll do is the small selection of leaflets and maps available at the central library opposite the Council House (Mon, Tues, Thurs & Fri 10am–8pm, Wed & Sat 10am–1pm). On the dockside, reached by crossing the dual carriageway behind the square, the Neoclassical **Custom House** is Greenock's finest building, splendidly located looking out over the river. Now the principal office for HM Revenue & Customs in Scotland, there's an informative **museum** (Mon–Fri 10am–4pm; free) inside which covers the work of the Revenue & Customs departments, with displays on illicit whisky distilleries as well as more modern contraband. From the dock in front, tens of thousands of nineteenth-century emigrants departed for the New World. These days, **Clyde Marine Cruises** (June to Aug; ☎01475/721281, ⓦwww.clyde-marine.co.uk) operates from Victoria Harbour, a few minutes from Central Station; it operates chartered cruises, as well as a planned ferry link to Loch Long and Loch Goil in the Loch Lomond and Trossachs National Park.

Greenock's town centre has been disfigured by astonishingly unsympathetic developments. More attractive, and indicative of the town's wealthy past, is the western side of town, with its mock-Baronial houses, graceful churches and quiet, tree-lined avenues. This area can be reached either via Greenock West station, or by taking a ten-minute walk up the High Street from the Council House. A hundred yards from the well-proportioned **George Square**, close to Greenock West station, the **McLean Museum and Art Gallery** in Union Street (Mon–Sat 10am–5pm; free) contains pictures and contemporary records of the life and achievements of Greenock-born James Watt, prominent eighteenth-century industrialist and pioneer of steam power, as well as featuring exhibits on the shipbuilding industry and other local trades. The upper gallery houses a curious exhibition that purports to show the district's internationalism through its trading links, with a random selection of oddments from, among others, Japan, Papua New Guinea, India, China and Egypt. The small art gallery on the ground floor contains work by Glasgow Boys Hornel and Guthrie plus Colourists Fergusson, Cadell and Peploe.

Accommodation is particularly scarce in Greenock, so it's advisable to book ahead. *The Tontine Hotel* in Ardgowan Square, a few minutes' walk west of the Art Gallery, is smart but expensive (☎01475/723316, ⓦ www.tontine-hotel .co.uk; ❺); the smaller and more intimate former sugar-baron's mansion *Lindores Manor Hotel* lies further west, at 61 Newark St (☎01475/783075, ⓦ www .lindores.co.uk; ❹). The *James Watt Halls of Residence* (☎01475/731360, ⓦ www .jameswatt.ac.uk; ❷) on Customhouse Quay, overlooking the river, offer clean and tidy en-suite twin rooms all year round. Greenock's eating options are restricted to predictable high-street cafés and takeaways, or the pricey restaurant at *Lindores Manor* for something more upmarket. Neighbouring Gourock has a slightly better selection, including *Café Continental* on Kempock Street which serves bar/bistro food and has views across the Clyde.

Gourock

On the train line west of Greenock, Fort Matilda station perches below **Lyle Hill**, an invigorating 450-foot climb that is well worth the effort for the astounding views over the purple mountains of Argyll and the creeks and lochs spilling off the Firth of Clyde. West of here lies the dowdy old resort of **GOUROCK**, once a holiday destination for generations of Glaswegians, but today only of significance as a **ferry** terminal: both CalMac (enquiries ☎01475/650100, sales ☎0870/5650000, ⓦ www.calmac.co.uk) and the more frequent Western Ferries (☎01369/704452, ⓦ www.western-ferries.co.uk) ply the twenty-minute route across the Firth of Clyde to Dunoon on the Cowal peninsula (see p.343), while a passenger-only ferry runs year-round to Kilcreggan and Helensburgh on the north bank of the Clyde (check ⓦ www.spt.co.uk for details). By the seafront there's a heated outdoor **swimming pool** (May–Sept Mon, Wed & Fri 9.30am–8.30pm, Tues & Thurs 8.30am–8.30pm, Sat & Sun 10am–4.30pm; £2.40) with a spectacular backdrop of the Argyll mountains, which can be seen in their full glory from Tower Hill, reached from John Street past the health centre; it's a steep climb but the view makes the effort worthwhile.

Wemyss Bay

There's not much south of Gourock apart from a gruesome power-station chimney and large yacht marina at **Inverkip**, until you reach **WEMYSS** (pron. "Weems") **BAY**, the terminus of the southern branch of the train line from Port Glasgow, which clips the edge of Greenock before curling around the mountains and moors, playing a game of peek-a-boo with the Clyde estuary. The most memorable part of the journey is the arrival at the rather grand and old-fashioned Wemyss Bay station, an impressive wrought-iron and glass palace which serves as a reminder of the great glory days when thousands of Glaswegians would alight for their steamer trip "doon the watter". Today the only steamer connection is the rather prosaic CalMac **ferry** over to Rothesay, capital of the Isle of Bute (see pp.345–346).

The Firth of Clyde – north bank

Heading west out of Glasgow, the A82 road and the train tracks both follow the north bank of the river, passing through Clydebank, another ex-shipbuilding centre, and Bowling, the western entry point of the newly reopened Forth & Clyde canal (see p.419). At **Dumbarton**, an ancient regional capital, the main road swings north towards Loch Lomond (see p.423), while the railway and A814 carry on along the shores of the Firth of Clyde to wealthy **Helensburgh**, before themselves turning north along the shores of Gare Loch and Loch Long to Arrochar, which marks the beginning of Argyll (see p.341).

Dumbarton

Founded in the fifth century, the town of **DUMBARTON** today is for the most part a brutal concrete sprawl, fulfilling every last cliché about postwar planning and architecture. Its few attractive Victorian buildings are mostly overshadowed by industrial warehouses and grim modern shopping developments, so avoid the town itself – though Talking Heads fans might be interested to know that David Byrne was born here – and head a mile southeast to **Dumbarton Castle** (April–Sept daily 9.30am–6.30pm; Oct–March Sat–Wed 9.30am–4.30pm; £3), which sits atop a twin outcrop of volcanic rock surrounded by water on three sides. First founded as a Roman fort, the structure was expanded in the fifth century by the Damnonii tribe, and remained Strathclyde's capital until its absorption into the greater kingdom of Scotland in 1034. The castle then became a royal seat, from which Mary, Queen of Scots sailed for France to marry Henri II's son in 1548, and to which she was attempting to escape when she and her troops were defeated twenty years later at the Battle of Langside. Since the 1600s, the castle has been used as a garrison and artillery fortress to guard the approaches to Glasgow; most of the current buildings date from this period.

The solid eighteenth-century **Governor's House** lies at the base of the rock, from where you enter the castle complex proper by climbing the steep steps up into the narrow cleft between the two rocks, crowned by the oldest remaining structure in the complex, a fourteenth-century **portcullis arch**. Vertiginous steps ascend to each peak: to see both you must climb more than five hundred steps. The **eastern rock** is the higher, with a windy summit that affords excellent views over the lochs and mountains of the Firth of Clyde.

Dumbarton is also home to a quirky but fascinating piece of industrial heritage relating to the glory days of Clyde shipbuilding, housed on Castle Street, between the castle and the town centre. The **Denny Tank** (Mon–Sat 10am–4pm; £2), an outpost of the Scottish Maritime museum, houses the world's oldest working ship-model experiment tank, at around 110yd long. It's still used to test scale models of ships prior to the expensive business of construction, and explanatory panels cover the whole process from wax modelling up to the experiments themselves.

For the most part, however, Dumbarton is just a waypoint for those heading into the Loch Lomond and the Trossachs National Park, either via Helensburgh and the coast or more directly through Balloch (see p.425). If you need to get hold of information or book accommodation there's a **tourist office** (daily: April, May & Oct 10am–5pm; June–Sept 10am–6pm) situated a couple of miles east of town by the side of the main A82 road.

Helensburgh

HELENSBURGH, twenty miles or so northwest of Glasgow, is a smart, Georgian grid-plan settlement overlooking the Clyde estuary. In the eighteenth century it was a well-to-do commuter town for Glasgow and also a seaside resort, whose bathing-master, **Henry Bell**, invented one of the first steamboats, the *Comet*, to transport Glaswegians "doon the watter". Today, Helensburgh is a stop on the route of the paddle steamer **Waverley** (see box on p.305), and in addition, there's a passenger-only **ferry** service across the Clyde to Kilcreggan and Gourock (see p.327); pick up timetables for both services from the **tourist office**, on the ground floor of the old Italianate church tower by the Clyde (daily: Easter–June 10am–5pm; July & Aug 10am–6pm; Oct 10am–4.30pm).

The inventor of TV, John Logie Baird, was born here, as was Charles Rennie Mackintosh, who in 1902 was commissioned by the Glaswegian publisher Walter Blackie to design **Hill House** on Upper Colquhoun Street (April–Oct daily 1.30–5.30pm; NTS; £8). You may have to join a queue to get in: the house is so popular it can barely cope with the tide of visitors, and the number of people who can be in the house at any one time is restricted. Without doubt the best surviving example of Mackintosh's domestic architecture, the house is stamped with his very personal, elegant interpretation of Art Nouveau – right down to the light fittings and fire irons – characterized by his sparing use of colour and stylized floral patterns. The effect is occasionally overwhelming – it's difficult to imagine actually living in such an environment – yet it is precisely Mackintosh's attention to detail that makes the place so special. Various upstairs rooms are given over to interpretative displays on the architect's use of light, colour, form and texture, while changing exhibitions on contemporary domestic design from around Britain are a testament to Mackintosh's ongoing influence and inspiration. After exploring the house, head for the **tearoom** in the kitchen quarters, or wander round the beautifully laid-out **gardens**.

Practicalities

Hill House is a good twenty-minute walk up Sinclair Street from Helensburgh Central **train** station, or just five minutes from Helensburgh Upper train station (where trains to and from Oban and Fort William stop). There's not a lot of choice when it comes to **hotels**: the purpose-built *Commodore*, 112–117 West Clyde St (℡01436/676924; ❻), overlooking the Clyde, is probably the first choice. The town's **B&Bs** are a better bet: the antique-filled, non-smoking *Lethamhill*, 20 West Dhuhill Drive (℡01436/676016, ⓦwww.lethamhill.co.uk; ❹), is set in the attractive, leafy villa district near Helensburgh Upper, while Ravenswood (℡01436/672112, ⓦwww.stayatlochlomond.com/ravenswood; ❷), 32 Suffolk St, also non-smoking, is in the western part of town. Helensburgh isn't short of tearooms and coffee shops; for evening **meals** the choice isn't inspired but there are one or two places along the sea-facing West Clyde Street, including the *Upper Crust* Scottish restaurant (℡01436/678035; closed Sun, Mon), at number 88a.

The Clyde valley

The journey southeast of Glasgow into Lanarkshire, while mostly following the course of the Clyde upstream, is dominated by endless suburbs, industrial parks and wide strips of concrete highway. The principal road here is the M74, though you'll have to get off the motorway to find the main points of interest, which tend to lie on or near the banks of the river. Less than ten miles from central Glasgow, **Bothwell Castle** lies about a mile northeast of the **Blantyre** millworkers' tenement in which the explorer David Livingstone was born. Five miles west of Blantyre, on the outskirts of the new town of East Kilbride, the **National Museum of Scottish Country Life**, set on a historic farm, offers an in-depth look at the history of agriculture in Scotland.

From here, the Clyde winds through lush market gardens and orchards before passing beneath the sturdy little town of **Lanark**, probably the best base from which to explore the valley. **New Lanark**, on the riverbank, is a remarkable eighteenth-century planned village. Ten miles further upstream, the country town of **Biggar** is a pleasant spot with a surprising number of rather quirky museums, and marks the transition from the industrial central belt to rolling Border country.

Blantyre and around

BLANTYRE, now a colourless suburb of Hamilton, was a remote hamlet based around a mill on the banks of the Clyde when explorer and missionary David Livingstone was born there in 1813. First Bus's **bus** #267 from Glasgow (Buchanan St) to Hamilton runs via Blantyre, or there are frequent **trains** from Glasgow Central's lower level.

A separate tenement block set in a quiet country park near the river houses the **David Livingstone Centre** (April–Dec Mon–Sat 10am–5pm, Sun 12.30–5pm; NTS; £5). In 1813, the block consisted of 24 one-room tenements, each occupied by an entire family of mill-workers. Today, one room shows the claustrophobic conditions under which Livingstone was brought up; all the others feature slightly defensive exhibitions on the missionary movement, with tableaux of scenes from his life in Africa, including his "discovery" of the Victoria Falls and the famous meeting with Henry Stanley (who greeted the explorer with the words, "Dr Livingstone, I presume?"). The displays indicate the extent to which Livingstone was a much-feted hero of nineteenth-century Britain, and the fact that his belief that "commerce and Christianity" would offer an alternative to slavery and poverty in Africa were behind his intrepid, if somewhat self-concerned, adventures into the continent.

A mile or so north of Blantyre, **Bothwell Castle** (April–Sept daily 9.30am–6.30pm; Oct–March Sun–Wed 9.30am–4.30pm; HS; £2.50) is one of Scotland's most dramatic citadels, its great red sandstone bulk looming high above a loop in the river. The oldest section is the solid donjon, or circular tower, built by the Moray family in the late thirteenth century to protect themselves against the English king Edward I during the Scottish wars of independence. Edward only succeeded in capturing it after ordering the construction and deployment of a massive siege engine, wheeled in from Glasgow in order to lob huge stones at the castle walls. Over the next two centuries, the castle changed hands numerous times and was added to by each successive owner; despite its jigsaw construction, today the overwhelming impression is of the near-impenetrable strength of the fortress, its solid red towers – whose walls stand almost sixteen feet thick in places – holding firm centuries after their construction. First Bus operates **bus** #255 from Glasgow (Buchanan St) to Motherwell, which will drop you off on the Bothwell Road near the castle entrance. By car, it is best approached from the B7071 Bothwell–Uddingston road.

National Museum of Scottish Country Life

On the edge of **EAST KILBRIDE** new town, five miles west of Blantyre and seven miles southeast of Glasgow centre, the **National Museum of Scottish Country Life** (daily 10am–5pm; NTS; £4) is a slightly unexpected union of historic farm and modern museum. The site of the museum, **Kittochside**, is a 170-acre farm which avoided the intensive farming which came to dominate agriculture in Britain after World War II, and it has been retained as a working model farm showcasing traditional methods of farming.

The custom-built, £6-million museum building on the edge of the farm was opened in 2001, and while it has all the charm of a small factory from the outside, the interior uses space and light creatively to show displays about Scots' relationship with the land over centuries, how farmers and their families have lived and the farm equipment they have used, from early ploughs to the combine harvester. For tractor aficionados, there's a room full of various vintages.

What really makes the museum, however, is its contextual setting. A tractor and trailer shuttle visitors the half-mile up to the eighteenth-century **farmhouse**, which is furnished much as it would have been in the 1950s, the crucial decade just before traditional methods using horses and hand-tools were replaced by tractors and mechanization. There are **paths** leading from the farmhouse around the surrounding fields, and you're encouraged to wander along these, not just to get a sense of the wider farm, but also to see and experience the farm in use.

Transport isn't straightforward if you don't have your own vehicle. **Bus** #31 from Glasgow's St Enoch Centre to East Kilbride takes you past the museum (Stewartfield Way), or you can get the **train** from Glasgow Central, and then take a taxi for the final three miles to the museum.

Lanark and New Lanark

The neat little market town of **LANARK** is an old and distinguished burgh, sitting in the purple hills high above the River Clyde, its rooftops and spires visible for miles around. Beyond the **world's oldest bell**, cast in 1130 and on show in the Georgian church of St Nicholas, there's little to see in town unless you are around during the lively **Lanimer** celebrations in early June, one of Scotland's oldest ceremonies of riding the marches or boundaries, which goes back to 1140. Most people head straight on for the village of **NEW LANARK** (Ⓦ www.newlanark.org), a mile below the main town on Braxfield Road, whose importance as a centre of social and industrial innovation has recently been recognized by UNESCO, which has included it on its list of World Heritage Sites.

Although New Lanark is served by an hourly **bus** from Lanark train station, it's well worth the steep downhill walk to get there. The first sight of the village, hidden away down in the gorge, is unforgettable: large broken curving walls of honeyed warehouses and tenements, built in Palladian style, are lined up along the turbulent river's edge. The community was founded by David Dale and Richard Arkwright in 1785 to harness the power of the Clyde waterfalls in their cotton-spinning industry, but it was Dale's son-in-law, Robert Owen, who revolutionized the social side of the experiment in 1798, creating a "village of unity". Believing the welfare of the workers to be crucial to industrial success, Owen built adult educational facilities, the world's first day nursery and playground, and schools in which dancing and music were obligatory and there was no punishment or reward.

While you're free to wander around the village, which rather unexpectedly for such a historic site is still partially residential, to get into any of the **exhibitions** (all daily 11am–5pm) you need to buy a passport ticket (£5.95; various discount tickets are available, including an all-in ticket covering admission and the return train and bus trip from Glasgow). The Neoclassical building which now houses visitor reception was opened by Owen in 1816 under the utopian title of **The Institute for the Formation of Character**. These days, it houses the **New Millennium Experience**, which whisks visitors on a chairlift through a social history of the village, conveying Robert Owen's vision not just for the idealized life at New Lanark, but also what he predicted for the year 2000. With a plethora of special effects, the ten-minute journey offers an intriguing glimpse

△ New Lanark

of Owen's social vision. Other exhibits in the adjoining mill buildings include working weaving looms and a massive steam engine.

Other parts of New Lanark village prove just as fascinating: everything, from the cooperative store to the workers' tenements and workshops, was built in an attempt to prove that industrialism need not be unaesthetic. You can wander through the 1820s shop, and find out how the workers lived in the **New Buildings**, then poke around the domestic kitchen, study and living areas of **Robert Owen's House**. In the **School for Children** there's a clever cinematic show giving an unsentimental picture of village life through the imaginary perspective of a young mill girl. Situated in the Old Dyeworks, the **Scottish Wildlife Trust Visitor Centre** (daily Jan & Feb daily noon–4pm; March–Dec 11am–5pm; free) provides information about the history and wildlife of the area, with evening trips organized to view bats or a local badger sett. Beyond the visitor centre, a riverside path leads you the mile or so to the major **Falls of the Clyde**, where, at the stunning tree-fringed Cora Linn, the river plunges ninety feet in three tumultuous stages.

Practicalities

Lanark is the terminus of **trains** from Glasgow Central. The town's **tourist office** (May–Sept daily 10am–5pm; Oct–April Mon–Sat 10am–5pm; ☏01555/661661) is housed in the Horsemarket, next to Somerfields supermarket, a hundred yards west of the station.

By far the most original **accommodation** options in the area, at both ends of the market, make use of reconstructed mill buildings in New Lanark: the SYHA **hostel** (℡0870/004 1143, Ⓦwww.syha.org.uk) has two-, four- and five-bed rooms in the cutely named Wee Row on Rosedale Street, while the *New Lanark Mill* (℡01555/667200, Ⓦwww.newlanark.org; Ⓖ) is a four-star **hotel** with good views and lots of character. Elsewhere are the spectacular wooded surroundings of the *Cartland Bridge Hotel* on the town's edge just off the A73 Glasgow road (℡01555/664426, Ⓦwww.cartlandbridge.co.uk; Ⓖ), while the best of the **B&Bs** are a little out of town: try Mrs Findlater at Jerviswood Mains Farm (℡01555/663987, Ⓦwww.jerviswoodmains.com; Ⓔ). There are plenty of cheap **cafés** and takeaways on the High Street, as well as some more pricey Indian and Italian **restaurants** along Wellgate, while the unpretentious *Crown Tavern*, a quiet drinking haunt in Hope Street, does reasonable food until 9.30pm.

Biggar and around

On the journey upstream, you leave industrial Lanarkshire behind and come instead to the gentle undulations of the Border hills. **BIGGAR**, twelve miles from Lanark, has the sense of being slightly adrift, formally in Lanarkshire but more a Border town, as close to Edinburgh as it is to Glasgow but with no strong connection to either. An old market town, its wide main street is still lined with rather dated shops, and with a mix of old and new houses it struggles to exert much charm. For a town of its size, Biggar has an inordinate number of museums; none could be described as essential, though each has its own quirky appeal. The most general is the **Moat Park Heritage Centre** (May–Sept Mon–Sat 11am–4.30pm, Sun 2–4.30pm; £2), which occupies a grand neo-Romanesque church near the foot of Kirkstyle (off High Street). Inside, the geological and archeological history of Upper Clydesdale is traced, while elsewhere you can take your pick from a display of extraordinary table covers by local tailor Menzies Moffat and a collection of four thousand thimbles. Staff can give details of **Brownsbank Cottage**, the former home of poet Hugh MacDiarmid and his wife, which is located three miles from Biggar on the Edinburgh road. Filled with books and artefacts from MacDiarmid's life, it is normally home to a writer-in-residence, and can only be visited by appointment.

Tucked in behind the High Street, the **Gladstone Court Museum** (May–Sept Mon–Sat 11am–4.30pm, Sun 2–4.30pm; £2) has a re-created street of Victorian shops, including a telephone exchange, bank and cobbler. Alongside this is the **Albion Museum** (April–Sept Sat & Sun 11am–5pm; free), a collection of old vehicles commemorating the local Albion Motors firm. Returning to Kirkstyle, walk over the hill to the footpath beside Biggar burn; to the right is the **Greenhill Covenanters' Museum** (May–Sept Sat & Sun 2–4.30pm; Mon–Fri by appointment; £1), which explores the development of the Covenanting movement and the religious conflicts that ensued. To the left along the burn lies **Biggar Gasworks Museum** (June–Sept daily 2–4.30pm; £1), which has the appearance of a Lilliputian power station. Built in 1839, it is the only coal-based gasworks still standing; most were demolished in the 1970s when the North Sea gas grid was developed. Finally, on Broughton Road near the country park, the **Biggar Puppet Theatre** (daily 10am–4.30pm, depending on performances scheduled; call ℡01899/220631 or go to Ⓦwww.purvespuppets.com for details of shows), stages regular shows and workshops for children in its Victorian building. Tours of its museum and backstage cost £2.50, but require a minimum of five people.

Regular **bus** services to Biggar arrive from a wide range of towns; from Lanark, take bus #191, but there are also services from Edinburgh, Peebles,

Moffat, Dumfries and more. They stop on High Street, near the **tourist office** (May–Aug daily 10am–5pm, April & Sept Mon–Sat 10am–5pm; ☏01899/221066). There's a **B&B**, *Daleside*, a few doors down at 165 High St (☏01899/220097; ❷), and **camping** at *Biggar Caravan Park* on Broughton Road (☏01899/220319; April–Oct). For **food**, *Restaurant 55* at 55 High St (☏01899/231555) serves modern Scottish cuisine in relaxed, contemporary surroundings, while the *Elphinstone Hotel* and the *Crown*, both also on High Street, serve up hearty pub grub. For a friendly cup of tea and good home baking make for the Gillespie Centre in Biggar Kirk, facing the two hotels; it's volunteer-run but the conservatory looks out on the comings and goings of the main street and is child-friendly.

Around Biggar

Six miles west of Biggar along the A72/73, near the village of Thankerton, the solitary peak of **Tinto Hill**, or "hill of fire" was the site of Druidic festivals in honour of the sun-god Baal, or Bel. It's relatively easy to walk the footpath up to the 2320ft summit, from where the views are splendid – you'll also see a druidic circle and a Bronze Age burial cairn on the summit. Regular **buses** between Biggar and Lanark stop at Thankerton.

Travel details

Trains

Glasgow Central to: Ardrossan for Arran ferry (every 30min; 45min); Ayr (every 30min; 50min); Birmingham (7 daily; 4hr); Blantyre (every 30min; 20min); Carlisle (hourly; 1hr 25min); East Kilbride (every 30min; 30min); Gourock (every 30min; 50min); Greenock (every 30min; 40min); Lanark (every 30min; 50min); Largs (hourly; 1hr); London (every 1–2hr; 5–6hr); Paisley (every 10min; 10min); Queen's Park (every 15min; 6min); Stranraer (5 daily; 2hr 10min); Wemyss Bay (hourly; 50min); York (7 daily; 3hr 30min).

Glasgow Queen St to: Aberdeen (hourly; 2hr 35min); Aviemore (3 daily; 2hr 40min); Balloch (every 30min; 45min); Dumbarton (every 20min; 35min); Dundee (hourly; 1hr 20min); Edinburgh (every 15min; 50min); Fort William (Mon–Sat 3 daily, Sun 1–2 daily; 3hr 40min); Helensburgh (every 30min; 40min); Inverness (3 daily; 3hr 25min); Mallaig via Fort William (Mon–Sat 3 daily, Sun 1–2 daily; 5hr 15min); Milngavie (every 30min; 25min); Oban (Mon–Fri 3 daily, Sat 4 daily, Sun 1–3 daily; 3hr); Perth (hourly; 1hr); Stirling (hourly; 30min).

Buses

Glasgow Buchanan St to: Aberdeen (every 2hr; 3hr 20min); Aviemore (every 2hr; 3hr 30min); Campbeltown (3 daily; 4hr 20min); Dundee (hourly; 1hr 45min); Edinburgh (every 15min; 1hr 10min); Fort William (3 daily; 3hr); Glen Coe (3 daily; 2hr 30min); Inverness (every 2hr; 4–5hr); Kyle of Lochalsh (3 daily; 5hr); Loch Lomond (hourly; 45min); London (5 daily; 8hr); Oban (3 daily; 3hr); Perth (hourly; 1hr 35min); Pitlochry (every 2hr; 2hr 20min); Portree (3 daily; 6hr); Stirling (hourly; 45min).

Flights

Glasgow International to: Barra (2 daily; 1hr 5min); Belfast (Mon–Fri 8 daily; Sat & Sun 3 daily; 45min); Benbecula (Mon–Sat 2 daily; Sun 1 daily; 1hr); Campbeltown (Mon–Fri 2 daily; 40min); Dublin (4 daily; 1hr); Islay (Mon–Fri 2 daily, Sat 1 daily; 45min); Kirkwall (1 daily; 2hr); Lerwick (Mon–Fri 2 daily, Sat & Sun 1 daily; 1hr 30min–3hr); London City (Mon–Fri 3 daily, Sun 1 daily; 1hr 30min); London Gatwick (Mon–Fri 6 daily, Sat & Sun 4 daily; 1hr 30min); London Heathrow (Mon–Fri 20 daily, Sat & Sun 12 daily; 1hr 30min); London Luton (Mon–Fri 7 daily, Sat 3 daily, Sun 4 daily; 1hr 15min); London Stansted (Mon–Fri 5 daily, Sat 3 daily, Sun 4 daily; 1hr 30min); Stornoway (Mon–Fri 4 daily, Sat 2 daily, Sun 1 daily; 1hr 10min); Tiree (Mon–Sat 1 daily; 50min).

Glasgow Prestwick to: Bournemouth (1 daily; 1hr 35min); Cardiff (Mon–Fri 2 daily, Sat & Sun 1 daily; 1hr 10min); Dublin (Mon–Fri 3 daily, Sat & Sun 2 daily; 45min); London Stansted (5 daily; 1hr 10min).

Argyll and Bute

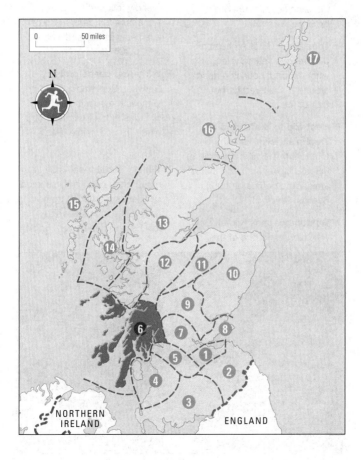

CHAPTER 6   # Highlights

＊**Loch Fyne Oyster Bar, Cairn-dow** Dine in or take away at Scotland's finest smokehouse and seafood outlet. See p.342

＊**Mount Stuart, Bute** Explore this architecturally overblown mansion set in magnificent grounds. See p.347

＊**Tobermory, Mull** Archetypal picturesque fishing village, with colourful houses ranged around a sheltered harbour. See p.360

＊**Boat trip to Staffa and the Treshnish Isles** Take the boat to see the "basalt cathedral" of Fingal's Cave, and then picnic amidst the puffins on Lunga. See p.361

＊**Golden beaches** Kiloran Bay on Colonsay is one of the most perfect sandy beaches in Argyll, but there are plenty more on Islay, Coll and Tiree. See p.377

＊**Isle of Gigha** The perfect island escape: sandy beaches, friendly folk and the azaleas of Achamore Gardens – you can even stay at the laird's house. See p.386

＊**Wintering geese on Islay** Between September and April witness the spectacular sight of thousands of barnacle and white-fronted geese. See p.391

＊**Whisky distilleries, Islay** With eight, often beautifully situated distilleries to choose from, Islay is the ultimate whisky lover's destination. See p.394

△ Tobermory, Mull

Argyll and Bute

C ut off for centuries from the rest of Scotland by the mountains and sea lochs that characterize the region, **Argyll** remains remote, its scatter of offshore islands forming part of the Inner Hebridean archipelago (the remaining Hebrides are dealt with in Chapters 14 & 15). Geographically as well as culturally, this is a transitional area between Highland and Lowland, boasting a rich variety of scenery, from lush, subtropical gardens warmed by the Gulf Stream to flat and treeless islands on the edge of the Atlantic. It's in the folds and twists of the countryside, the interplay of land and water and the views out to the islands that the strengths and beauties of mainland Argyll lie. The one area of man-made sights you shouldn't miss, however, is the cluster of **Celtic** and **prehistoric sites** in mid-Argyll near Kilmartin.

Overall, the population is tiny (less than 100,000); even **Oban**, Argyll's chief ferry port, has just eight thousand or so inhabitants, while the prettiest settlement, **Inveraray**, boasts only five hundred. Much of mainland Argyll is comprised of remote peninsulas separated by a series of long sea lochs. The first peninsula you come to from Glasgow is **Cowal**, cut off from the rest of Argyll by a set of mountains including the Arrochar Alps. Nestling in one of Cowal's sea lochs is the **Isle of Bute**, whose capital, Rothesay, is probably the most appealing of the old Clyde steamer resorts. **Kintyre**, the long finger of land that stretches south towards Ireland, is less visually dramatic than Cowal, though it does provide a stepping stone for several Hebridean islands, as well as Arran (covered in Chapter 4).

Of the islands covered in this chapter, mountainous **Mull** is the most visited, though it is large enough to absorb the crowds, many of whom are only passing through en route to the tiny isle of **Iona**, a centre of Christian culture since the sixth century, or to **Tobermory**, the island's impossibly picturesque port (aka "Balamory"). **Islay**, best known for its distinctive malt whiskies, is fairly quiet even in the height of summer, as is neighbouring **Jura**, which offers excellent walking opportunities. And, for those seeking further solitude, there's the island of **Colonsay**, with its beautiful golden sands, and the windswept islands of **Tiree** and **Coll**, which also boast great beaches and enjoy more sunny days than anywhere else in Scotland.

History

The region's name derives from *Aragaidheal*, which translates as "Boundary of the Gaels", the Irish Celts who settled here in the fifth century AD, and whose **kingdom of Dalriada** embraced much of what is now Argyll. Known to the Romans as *Scotti* – hence "Scotland" – it was the Irish Celts who promoted Celtic Christianity, and whose Gaelic language eventually became the national

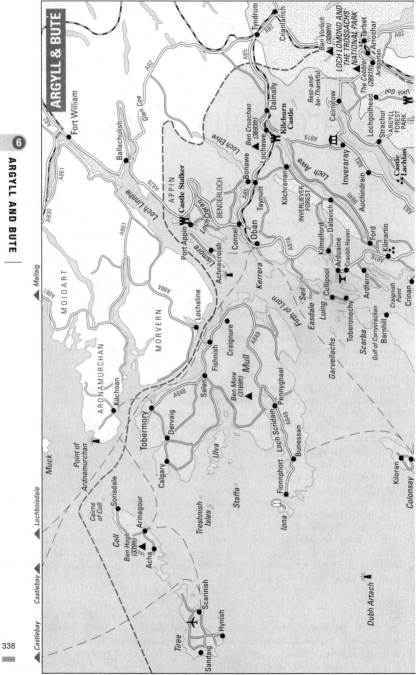

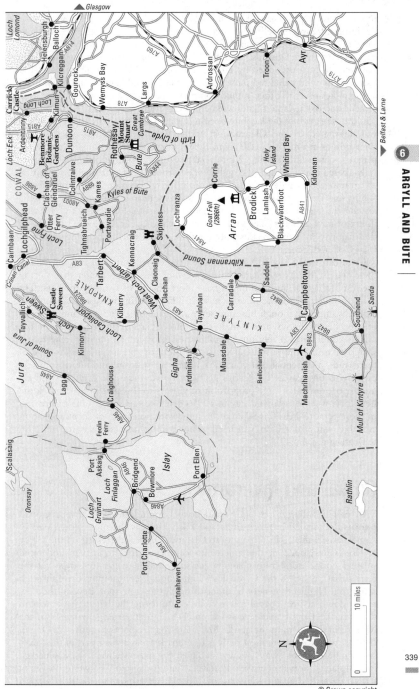

▲ Glasgow

▼ Belfast & Larne

© Crown copyright

tongue. After a period of Norse invasion and settlement, the islands (and the peninsula of Kintyre) fell to the immensely powerful Somerled, who became king of the Hebrides and lord of Argyll in the twelfth century. Somerled's successors, the MacDonalds, established Islay as their headquarters in the 1200s, but were in turn dislodged by Robert the Bruce. Of Bruce's allies, it was the **Campbells** who benefited most from the MacDonalds' demise and eventually, as the dukes of Argyll, they gained control of the entire area – even today, they remain one of the largest landowners in the region.

In the aftermath of the Jacobite uprisings, Argyll, like the rest of the Highlands, was devastated; by the **Clearances**, with thousands of crofters evicted from their homes in order to make room for profitable sheep-farming – "the white plague" – and cattle-rearing. More recently, forestry plantations have dramatically altered the landscape of Argyll, while purpose-built marinas have sprouted all around the heavily indented coastline. Today the traditional industries of fishing and farming are in deep crisis, as is the modern industry of fish-farming, leaving the region ever more dependent on tourism, EU grants and a steady influx of new settlers to keep things going, while Gaelic, once the language of the majority in Argyll, retains only a tenuous hold on the outlying islands of Islay, Coll and Tiree.

If you can, avoid July and August, when the crowds on Mull and Iona are at their densest; there's no guarantee the weather will be any better than during the rest of the year, and you might have more chance of avoiding the persistent Scottish midge (for more on which, see p.385). **Public transport** throughout Argyll is minimal, though buses do serve most major settlements, and the train line reaches all the way to Oban. In the remoter parts of the region and on the islands you'll have to rely on a combination of walking, hitching, bike rental, shared taxis and the postbus. If you're planning to take a car across to one of the islands, it's essential that you book both your outward and return journeys as early as possible, as the ferries get very booked up. And lastly, a word on **accommodation**: a large proportion of visitors to this part of Scotland come here for a week or two and stay in self-catering cottages. On some islands and in more remote areas this is often the most common form of accommodation available – in peak season, you need to book months in advance (for more on self-catering, see p.47).

Cowal and Inveraray

West of Helensburgh (see p.328) and Loch Lomond, the claw-shaped **Cowal peninsula**, formed by Loch Fyne and Loch Long, is the most-visited part of Argyll, largely due to its proximity to Glasgow. The seaside resorts on the Clyde sea lochs developed in the nineteenth century thanks to regular and rapid steamer connections from Glasgow. It's still quicker to get to Cowal via the ferries that ply across the Clyde; it's a long, though exhilarating, drive through some rich Highland scenery in order to reach the same spot. Beyond the now rather down-at-heel coastal towns such as **Dunoon**, the largest settlement in the area, the Cowal landscape is extremely rich and varied, ranging from the Munros of the north to the gentle, low-lying coastline of the southwest. One of the best ways to explore it properly is to embark upon at least part of the forty-seven-mile **Cowal Way** (Ⓦwww.colglen.org.uk/cowalway), a waymarked long-distance footpath between Portavadie and Ardgartan. The western edge of Cowal is marked by the long, narrow Loch Fyne, famous for both its kippers (smoked herring) and, more recently, oysters. The main settlement on the loch-side is **Inveraray**, a small but dignified town beside Inveraray Castle, the home of the powerful dukes of Argyll.

Arrochar to Inveraray

The boundaries of Loch Lomond and the Trossachs National Park extend quite a long way into Cowal, incorporating the **Argyll Forest Park** which stretches west from the village of Arrochar along the shores of Loch Fyne and south as far as Holy Loch. The area has the most grandiose scenery on the peninsula, including the ambitiously named **Arrochar Alps**, whose peaks offer some of the best climbing in Argyll: Ben Ime (3318ft) is the tallest of the range, while Ben Arthur or "The Cobbler" (2891ft), named after the anvil-like rock forma-tion at its summit, is easily the most distinctive. All are for experienced walkers only, although at the other end of the scale there are several gentle forest walks clearly laid out by the Forestry Commission, and helpful leaflets are available from tourist offices.

Arrochar and around

Approaching by road from Glasgow, Helensburgh or Loch Lomond, the entry point to Cowal is **ARROCHAR**, at the head of Loch Long. The village itself is ordinary enough, but the setting is dramatic, and it makes a convenient base for exploring the nearby Alps and forests. There's a **train station** a mile or so east, just off the A83 to Tarbert (see p.385), and numerous **hotels** and **B&Bs**; try the very friendly *Lochside Guest House* on the main road (℡01301/702467, ⓦwww.stayatlochlomond.com/lochside; ❸), or *Fascadail* (℡01301/702344, ⓦwww.fascadail.com; ❸), a guesthouse with a glorious garden situated in the quieter southern part of the village. If you want a bite **to eat**, head for the *Village Inn* (℡01301/702279, ⓦwww.villageinnarrochar.com), which has tables outside overlooking the loch as well as a cosy real-ale bar and en-suite rooms (❹).

Two miles west of Arrochar at **ARDGARTAN**, there's a well-main-tained lochside Forestry Commission **campsite** (℡01301/702293, ⓦwww.forestholidays.co.uk; April–Oct), and, a little further down the road, in the Ardgartan Visitor Centre is a **tourist office** (daily: July & Aug 10am–6pm; April–June, Sept & Oct 10am–5pm; ℡01301/702432), which doubles as a forestry office and has occasional organized walks. There are also waymarked **walks and bike trails** starting from here.

Heading west from Arrochar to Inveraray or the rest of Cowal, you're forced to climb **Glen Croe**, a strategic hill pass whose saddle is called – for obvious reasons – **Rest-and-be-Thankful**. Here the road forks, with the single-track B828 heading down to isolated-feeling **LOCHGOILHEAD**, overlooking Loch Goil. From the village, a road tracks the west side of the loch, petering out after five miles at the picturesque ruins of **Carrick Castle**, a classic tower-house castle built around 1400 and used as a hunting lodge by James IV. Facing this across the water is a hilly peninsula known as **Argyll's Bowling Green** – no ironic nickname, but an English corruption of the Gaelic *Baile na Greine* (Sunny Hamlet).

Cairndow and around

If you'd rather skip Lochgoilhead, continue west towards Inveraray along the A83 via Glen Kinglas to **CAIRNDOW**, at the head of Loch Fyne. Just behind the village, off the main road, you'll find the **Ardkinglas Wood-land Garden** (daily during daylight hours; £3; ⓦwww.ardkinglas.com), which contains exotic rhododendrons, azaleas and a superb collection of conifers, some of which rise to over 200ft. The *Cairndow Stagecoach Inn* (℡01499/600286, Ⓦwww.cairndowinn.com; ❹), in the village itself, is good for a pint and inexpensive pub food, with views over the loch from some of the (mainly small) bedrooms, but for something a bit special continue a mile or so further along on the A83 to the famous ⚓**Loch Fyne Oyster Bar and Shop** (℡01499/600236, Ⓦwww.loch-fyne.com), which sells more oysters than anywhere else in the country, plus lots of other fish and seafood treats. You can easily assemble a gourmet picnic in the shop here or stock up on provisions for the week, and the moderately expensive **restaurant** (daily 9am–9pm) is excellent, though booking is advisable at busy times.

Inveraray

A classic example of an eighteenth-century planned town, **INVERARAY** was built on the site of a ruined fishing village in 1745 by the third duke of Argyll, head of the powerful Campbell clan, in order to distance his newly rebuilt castle from the hoi polloi in the town and to establish a commercial and legal centre for the region. Today Inveraray, an absolute set piece of Scottish Georgian architecture, has a truly memorable setting, the brilliant white arches of Front Street reflected in the still waters of **Loch Fyne**, which separate it from the Cowal peninsula.

The Town

Squeezed onto a promontory some distance from the duke's new castle, there's not much more to Inveraray's New Town than its distinctive **Main Street** (set at a right angle to Front Street), flanked by whitewashed terraces, whose window casements are picked out in black. At the top of the street, the road divides to circumnavigate the town's Neoclassical church, originally built in two parts: the southern half served the Gaelic-speaking community, while the northern half – still in use and worth a peek for its period wood-panelled interior – served those who spoke English.

East of the church is **Inveraray Jail** (daily: April–Oct 9.30am–6pm; Nov–March 10am–5pm; £5.95; Ⓦwww.inverarayjail.co.uk), whose attractive Georgian courthouse and grim prison blocks ceased to function in the 1930s. The jail is now an imaginative and thoroughly enjoyable museum, which graphically recounts prison conditions from medieval times up until the nineteenth century – and even brings it up to date by including a picture of life in Glasgow's Barlinnie Prison. You can also sit in the beautiful semicircular courthouse and listen to a re-enactment of the trial of a farmer accused of fraud.

Moored at the town pier is the **Arctic Penguin** (daily: April–Oct 10am–6pm; Nov–March 10am–5pm; £3.80), a handsome, triple-masted schooner built in Dublin in 1911. It has some nautical knick-knacks and displays on the maritime history of the Clyde, but is only really worth exploring if you're a naval enthusiast or wet weather inhibits town wanderings. Also based at the pier, an old-time Clyde puffer runs short **boat trips** on the loch.

Inveraray Castle

A ten-minute walk north of the New Town, the neo-Gothic **Inveraray Castle** (June–Sept Mon–Sat 10am–5.45pm, Sun 1–5.45pm; April–May & Oct Mon–Thurs & Sat 10am–1pm & 2–5.45pm, Sun 1–5.45pm; £5.90; Ⓦwww.inveraray-castle.com) remains the family home of the duke of Argyll. Built in 1745 by the third duke, it was given a touch of the Loire in the nineteenth century with the addition of dormer windows and conical roofs. Inside, the most startling feature is the armoury hall, whose displays of weaponry – supplied to the Campbells by the British government to put down the Jacobites – rise through several storeys; look out for Rob Roy's rather sad-looking sporran and dirk handle (a dirk being a dagger, traditionally worn in Highland dress).

Practicalities

Inveraray's **tourist office** is on Front Street (April, Sept & Oct Mon–Sat 9am–5pm, Sun noon–5pm; May & June Mon–Sat 9am–5pm, Sun 11am–5pm; July & Aug daily 9am–6pm; Nov–March Mon–Fri 10am–3pm, Sat & Sun 11am–3pm; ℡01499/302063), as is the town's chief **hotel**, the historic *Argyll* (℡01499/302466, ⓦwww.the-argyll-hotel.co.uk; ❺), now part of the Best Western group but formerly the *Great Inn*, where Dr Johnson and Boswell once stayed. A cheaper, but equally well-appointed alternative is the Georgian *Fernpoint Inn* (℡01499/302170; ❸), round by the pier, which has a nice pub garden and well-appointed rooms; otherwise, there's the **B&B** *Creag Dhubh* (℡01499/302430, ⓦwww.creagdhubh.com; March–Nov; ❷), set in a large garden overlooking Loch Fyne down the A83 to Lochgilphead. The SYHA **hostel** (℡0870/004 1125, ⓦwww.syha.org.uk; mid-March to Sept) is in a modern building a short distance north on the A819 Dalmally road, while the old Royal Navy base, two miles down the A83 to Lochgilphead, has been converted into the excellent, fully equipped *Argyll Caravan Park* (℡01499/302285, ⓦwww.argyllcaravanpark.com; April–Oct). The **bar** of the central *George Hotel* is the town's liveliest spot, and also serves fine bar **food**; for tea and cakes head for *The Poacher* round by the *Fernpoint Inn*. The best place to sample Loch Fyne's delicious fresh fish and seafood is the superb, moderately priced restaurant of the *Loch Fyne Oyster Bar* (see opposite), six miles northeast back up the A83 towards Glasgow.

Dunoon

The second principal entry point into Cowal from the Glasgow area, though this time by sea, is **DUNOON**, the largest town in Argyll, with 13,000 inhabitants. In the nineteenth century it grew from a mere village to a major Clyde seaside resort and favourite holiday spot for Glaswegians. Nowadays, tourists tend to arrive by ferry from Gourock but while Dunoon is a great position to watch the comings and goings on the Firth of Clyde, it's no longer a thriving place and there's little to tempt you to stay, particularly with attractive country-side beckoning just beyond.

The centre of town is dominated by a grassy lump of rock known as **Castle Hill**, crowned by Castle House, built in the 1820s by a wealthy Glaswegian and the subject of a bitter dispute with the local populace over closure of the common land around his house. The people eventually won, and the grounds remain open to the public to this day, as does the house, which is now home to the **Castle House Museum** (Easter–Oct Mon–Sat 10.30am–4.30pm, Sun 2–4.30pm; £1.50; ⓦwww.castlehousemuseum.org.uk). There's some good hands-on nature stuff for kids and an excellent section on the Clyde steamers as well as more about "Highland Mary", betrothed to Robbie Burns (despite the fact that he already had a pregnant wife), who died of typhus before the pair could see through their plan to elope to the West Indies.

With an hour or so to spare, you could visit the **Cowal Bird Garden** (April–Oct daily 10.30am–6pm; £4), located in woodland one mile northwest along the A885 to Sandbank, or, if the weather's fine, take the **Ardnadam Heritage Trail**, a forty-minute walk located a mile further up the road, which leads to the wonderful Dunan viewpoint looking out to the Firth of Clyde.

Practicalities

Dunoon's **tourist office**, the principal one in Cowal, is located on Alexandra Parade (Mon–Fri 9am–5.30pm, Sat & Sun 10am–5pm; ☎01369/703785). There are two **ferry** crossings across the Clyde from Gourock to Dunoon; the shorter, more frequent service is half-hourly on Western Ferries to Hunter's Quay, a mile north of the town centre; CalMac's boats, though, arrive at the main pier, and have better transport connections if you're on foot.

There's an enormous choice of **B&Bs**, none of them outstanding. You're better off heading out of town or persuading the tourist office to help you, since availability in summer is the biggest problem. Worth considering are the welcoming *Abbot's Brae* half a mile from the pier above West Bay (☎01369/705021, ⓦwww.abbotsbrae.co.uk; ❺), or the smart *Dhailling Lodge* (☎01369/701253, ⓦwww.dhaillinglodge.com; ❹), closer to town on Alexandra Parade. A cheaper and cheery alternative is the traditional *Cot House Hotel* (☎01369/840260, ⓦwww.cothousehotel.com; ❷), about ten minutes' drive north at Kilmun. Immediately beside the hotel is a caravan and **campsite** (☎01369/840351; closed Nov & Feb).

Chatters, 58 John St (☎01369/706402; Wed–Sat only; closed Jan & Feb), is Dunoon's best **restaurant**, offering delicious Loch Fyne seafood and Scottish beef. For something a bit less pricey, you could do worse than the simple **café** serving soups, sandwiches and light meals run by the Baptist church right next door to the tourist office; there's also a vast Italian menu at *La Cantina* (☎01369/703595) in Argyll Street. For **bike rental**, head for the Highland Stores on Argyll Street. For **pony trekking**, contact the Velvet Path Riding and Trekking Centre (☎01369/830580) at Inellan, four miles south of town. Dunoon boasts a two-screen **cinema** (a rarity in Argyll) on John Street, but the town's most famous entertainment is the **Cowal Highland Gathering** (ⓦwww.cowalgathering.com), the largest of its kind in the world, held here on the last weekend in August, and culminating in the awesome spectacle of the massed pipes and drums of more than 150 bands marching through the streets.

Holy Loch and Loch Eck

Immediately north of Dunoon lies **Holy Loch**, the former site of a US nuclear submarine base which closed in 1992. Just three miles north of Holy Loch along the A815 is **Loch Eck**, a narrow freshwater loch squeezed between steeply banked woods, which is a favourite spot for trout fishing. At the loch's southern tip are the beautifully laid-out **Benmore Botanic Gardens** (daily: March & Oct 10am–5pm; April–Sept 10am–6pm; £3.50), an offshoot of Edinburgh's Royal Botanic Gardens. Occupying 140 acres of lush hillside, the mild, moist climate of Argyll allows a vast range of unusual plants to grow here, with different sections devoted to rainforest species native to places as exotic as China, Chile and Bhutan. The gardens boast 250 species of rhododendrons and a memorably striking avenue of great redwoods, planted in 1863 and now over 150ft high. There's a pleasant, inexpensive **café** by the entrance, open in season, with an imaginative menu. It's easy to combine a visit with one of the local **forest walks**, the most popular being a leisurely stroll up the rocky ravine of **Puck's Glen** (1hr 30min round-trip), which begins from the car park a mile south of the gardens.

Halfway along Loch Eck, the shore-side *Coylet Inn* (☎01369/840426, ⓦwww.coylet-locheck.co.uk; ❺), a sympathetically renovated coaching inn, makes for a lovely place to eat or **stay**. The family-oriented *Stratheck Country Park* **campsite** at the southern end of Loch Eck (℡01369/840472, Ⓦwww .stratheck.co.uk; March–Oct) enjoys a good location, surrounded by wooded slopes, and has caravans for rent – just make sure you've come armed with effective midge repellent.

Southwest Cowal

The mellower landscape of **southwest Cowal**, which stands in complete contrast to the bustle of Dunoon or the Highland grandeur of the Argyll Forest Park, is immediately apparent as soon as you head into the area, either over the hill from Dunoon or down the A886 from Glen Kinglas.

There are few more beautiful sights in Argyll than the **Kyles of Bute**, the slivers of water that separate Cowal from the bleak bulk of the Isle of Bute and constitute some of the best sailing territory in Scotland. **COLINTRAIVE**, on the eastern Kyle, marks the narrowest point in the area – barely more than a couple of hundred yards across – and is the place from which the small CalMac car ferry departs to Bute. The most popular spot from which to appreciate the Kyles is along the A8003 as it rises dramatically above the sea lochs before descending to the peaceful, lochside village of **TIGHNABRUAICH**, best known for its excellent **sailing school** (℡01700/811717, Ⓦwww.tssargyll.co.uk), which offers week-long courses from beginners to advanced. Boat trips, including the Waverley paddlesteamer (see box on p.305), still call at the pier and the village can be a pleasant place to stay: the impressive 🕭 *Royal Hotel* (℡01700/811239, Ⓦwww .royalhotel.org.uk; ❻), by the waterside, serves exceptionally good bar meals, and has wonderful views over the Kyles; not quite so grand, but justifiably popular with sailors and walkers, is the *Kames Hotel* (℡01700/811489, Ⓦwww .kames-hotel.com; ❺) in neighbouring **KAMES**. You can get B&B at *Ardeneden Guest House* (℡01700/811354; ❸), run by the same people who look after the inexpensive *Burnside Bistro* in the village, while there's camping at *Carry Farm* (℡01700/811717, Ⓦwww.carryfarm.co.uk), a few miles south of Kames. If you're driving to Kintyre, Islay or Jura, you can avoid the long haul around Loch Fyne – some seventy miles or so – by using the **ferry** to Tarbert from **Portavadie**, three miles southwest of Kames.

The Kyles can get busy in July and August, but it's possible to escape the crowds by heading for Cowal's deserted west coast, overlooking Loch Fyne. The road meets the loch shore at **OTTER FERRY**, which has a small shingle beach, a wonderful pub and an oyster restaurant, *The Oystercatcher*, with outside tables in good weather. There was once a ferry link to Lochgilphead from here, though the "otter" part is not derived from the furry creature but from the Gaelic *an oitir* (sandbank), which juts out a mile or so into Loch Fyne. If you're continuing north you'll come to the romantic ruin of **Castle Lachlan**. Overlooking it, there's another excellent restaurant, *Inver Cottage* (℡01369/860537, Ⓦwww.invercottage.co.uk), a contemporary and relaxed place which serves good coffee through the day, light lunches and evening meals based around local produce. For somewhere to stay nearby, try the small roadside B&B, *Balnacarry* (℡01369/860212; March–Oct; ❸).

Isle of Bute

The island of **BUTE** (Ⓦwww.isle-of-bute.com) is in many ways simply an extension of the Cowal peninsula, from which it is separated by the narrow

Kyles of Bute. Thanks to its consistently mild climate and its ferry link with Wemyss Bay, Bute has been a popular holiday and convalescence spot for Clydesiders – particularly the elderly – for over a century. Its chief town, **Rothesay**, rivals Dunoon as the major seaside resort on the Clyde, easily surpassing it thanks to some splendidly over-the-top Victorian architecture, excellent accommodation and eating options and the chance to visit **Mount Stuart**, one of Scotland's singular aristocratic piles. Most of Bute's inhabitants live around the two wide bays on the east coast of the island, which resembles one long seaside promenade. Consequently, it's easy enough to escape the crowds by heading for the sparsely populated west coast, which, in any case, has the sandiest beaches.

Rothesay

Bute's only town, **ROTHESAY** is a handsome Victorian resort, set in a wide, sweeping bay, backed by green hills, with a classic palm-tree promenade and 1920s pagoda-style pavilion originally built to house the Winter Gardens. Though often busy with day-trippers from Glasgow, there's plenty that's attractive about the place, with some handsome buildings, a prominent Art Deco pavilion and occasional flourishes of wrought-ironwork.

Rothesay also boasts the militarily useless, but architecturally impressive, moated ruins of **Rothesay Castle** (April–Sept daily 9.30am–6.30pm; Oct–March Sat–Wed 9.30am–4.30pm; HS; £3), hidden amid the town's backstreets but signposted from the pier. Built around the twelfth century, it was twice captured by the Vikings in the 1200s; such vulnerability was the reasoning behind the unusual, almost circular, curtain wall, with its four big drum towers, only one of which remains fully intact.

On the fringes of Rothesay, heading east along the coast, not far from Craigmore Pier, you'll come to **Ardencraig Gardens** (May–Sept Mon–Fri 10.30am–4.30pm, Sat & Sun 1–4.30pm; free), a small riot of colour in summer, with a series of Victorian hothouses and an aviary full of exotic birds surrounding a lovingly tended hillside garden. More horticultural delights are to be found out along the road to Mount Stuart (see opposite) at the **Ascog Fernery and Garden** (April to mid-Oct Wed–Sun 10am–5pm; £3), an unusual Victorian fernery that has been lovingly restored and boasts an ancient fern, reputed to be a thousand years old.

Rothesay's lovely lavvy

Whether you need to go or not, it's still worth spending a few pennies on a visit to Rothesay's ornate **Victorian toilets** (daily: Easter–Sept 8am–9pm; Oct–Easter 9am–5pm; 15p), located in a red-brick building on the ferry pier. Built in 1899 and fitted out by bathroom enamel manufacturers Twyfords, the interior is as much a museum piece as a public convenience. The toilets were saved and restored in the 1990s, and there's a genuine pride in the highly polished copper pipework and gleaming mosaic floor. A central, "island" urinal in the men's has a well-tended flower pot on top, while each WC has a wonderfully solid, large wooden seat, and emits a long, low grumble after you pull the chain as the water builds up for its energetic, gushing flush. The Victorians didn't tend to make provision for ladies' conveniences, so this half is a modern add-on, but if the coast is clear the attendant – attired in a neat burgundy waistcoat – will allow ladies a tour of the gents.

Practicalities

Rothesay's **tourist office** (April–June & Sept daily 10am–5pm; July & Aug Mon–Fri 10am–6pm, Sat & Sun 9.30am–5pm; Oct–March Mon–Fri 10am–5pm, Sat & Sun 11am–4pm; ☎01700/502151) is in a "Discovery Centre", which occupies the refurbished Winter Gardens alongside the pier, and has some well-presented displays on the life and times of Bute. Staff can also help with **accommodation**, though there's no shortage of B&Bs all along the seafront from Rothesay north to Port Bannatyne. One of the more attractive hotels is *Cannon House* (☎01700/502819, ⓦwww.cannonhousehotel .co.uk; ❹), occupying a Georgian house close to the pier on Battery Place, while the nearby *Commodore* (☎01700/502178, ⓦwww.commodorebute .com; ❷) at no. 12, is a more modest but equally accommodating guesthouse. Alternatively, *The Boat House* (☎01700/502696, ⓦwww.theboathouse-bute .co.uk; ❹) at no. 15 is a stylish "boutique B&B" with classy contemporary furnishings and decor. Further out, in Ascog, the B&B at *Ascog Farm* (☎01700/503372; ❷) is exceptionally good value, while *Chandlers Hotel* (☎01700/505577, ⓦwww.visitchandlers.com; ❻) offers a more decadent retreat, with smart modern rooms in an attractive red sandstone villa, and has a good bar and restaurant.

The best **food** option in Rothesay is *The Bistro* in the Winter Gardens, which offers a good-value restaurant menu and a superb view of the bay. If you're prepared to travel a short way, try the highly original and engaging *Port Royal Hotel* in Port Bannatyne, which describes itself as a "Waterfront Russian Tavern" and serves fresh local seafood alongside dishes such as blini, and has a terrific array of real ales. Alternatively, *The Pier at Craigmore* (☎01700/502867), on the coast road out of Rothesay on the way to Mount Stuart, is open through the day for coffee, home-baked cakes and light snacks, and for evening meals in summer. For Rothesay's finest fish and chips, head for the *West End Café* on Gallowgate. The small but stylish café, *Musicker*, just across from the castle has good coffee, and you can also listen to some music and browse through their book selection.

Bute holds its own **Highland Games** on the third weekend in August, an international **folk festival** on the third weekend in July, and a (mainly trad) **jazz festival** over May Bank Holiday (ⓦwww.butejazz.com). There are several golf courses in the area; **pony trekking** at Kingarth Trekking Centre near Kilchattan Bay (☎01700/831673, ⓦwww.kingarthtrekkingcentre.co.uk); and **bike rental** from Rob Cycles (☎01700/500602; April–Sept). An open-topped **tour bus** goes around the southern half of the island (May–Sept 11am, 1pm and 3pm; £6) in about an hour and a half if you want to check out the lay of the land. You can also use this service to get to and from Mount Stuart (£2.50 return).

Mount Stuart

One very good reason for coming to Bute is to visit **Mount Stuart** (May–Sept Sun–Fri 11am–5pm, Sat 10am–1.30pm; tours £7, gardens only £3.50; ⓦwww .mountstuart.com), a fantasy Gothic house set amidst acres of lush woodland gardens overlooking the Firth of Clyde four miles south of Rothesay. Setting for the glamorous wedding in 2003 of Sir Paul McCartney's daughter, Stella, Mount Stuart is the ancestral home of the seventh marquess of Bute, also known as Johnny Bute or, in his younger days as a Formula One racing driver, as Johnny Dumfries. The building was created by the marvellously eccentric third marquess and architect Sir Robert Rowand Anderson after a fire in 1877 had destroyed

△ Horoscope Room, Mount Stuart

the family seat. With little regard for expense, the marquess shipped in tons of Italian marble, building a railway line to transport it down the coast and employing craftsmen who had worked with the great William Burges on the marquess's earlier medieval concoctions at Cardiff Castle.

A **bus** runs from Rothesay approximately every forty-five minutes to the gates of Mount Stuart, while the house itself is a pleasant fifteen-minute walk through the gardens from the unexpectedly sleek **visitor centre**, an award-winning piece of contemporary architecture which contains a gallery, shop and excellent 🍴 **café/restaurant** which serves interesting lunches using produce from the Mount Stuart kitchen garden and other parts of the island; if it's raining it might be worth taking the shuttle service provided.

To see the inside of Mount Stuart itself you'll have to join one of the guided tours. The showpiece is the columned **Marble Hall**, its vaulted ceiling and stained-glass windows decorated with the signs of the zodiac, reflecting the marquess's taste for mysticism. He was equally fond of animal and plant imagery; hence you'll find birds feeding on berries in the dining-room frieze and monkeys reading (and tearing up) books and scrolls in the library. Look out also for the unusual heraldic plaster ceiling in the drawing room. After all the heavy furnishings, seek aesthetic relief in the **Marble Chapel**, built entirely out of dazzling white Carrara marble, with a magnificent cosmati floor pattern. Upstairs is less interesting, with the notable exception of the **Horoscope Room**, where you can see a fine astrological ceiling and adjacent observatory.

Although the sumptuous interior of Mount Stuart is not to everyone's taste, it's still worth coming here to explore the wonderfully mature **gardens** (daily 10am–6pm), established in the eighteenth century by the third earl of Bute, who had a hand in London's Kew Gardens. A leaflet outlines various paths crisscrossing the three hundred acres of mixed woodland, lawn and shoreline; quiet nooks, neat vegetable patches and a solidly built children's adventure playground are all incorporated within the grounds.

Around Bute

The Highland–Lowland dividing line passes through the middle of Bute, which is all but sliced in two by the freshwater Loch Fad. As a result, the northern half of the island is hilly, uninhabited and little visited, while the southern half is made up of Lowland-style farmland.

A site well worth visiting is **St Blane's Chapel**, a twelfth-century ruin beautifully situated in open countryside amidst the foundations of an earlier Christian settlement established in the sixth century by St Catan, uncle to the local-born St Blane. Passing the chapel is the route of the thirty-mile **West Island Way**, a waymarked footpath which starts at Kilchattan Bay and stretches the length of the island. It can be done in two long (or three more leisurely) days, though you can of course tackle shorter sections of it. Maps of the Way are available at Rothesay's tourist office.

A good base in the south of the island is the recently renovated *Kingarth Hotel* (☎01700/831662, ⓦwww.kingarthhotel.com; ❸), which has a convivial bar serving top-notch pub grub, as well as decent rooms.

Bute's finest sandy beach is further north at **Ettrick Bay**, which has a tearoom (April–Oct) and basic camping site at its north end. To get a proper feel for the countryside of rural Bute, you can stay in a remote spot on the west coast at *Glecknabae Farmhouse* (☎01700/505655, ⓦwww.isleofbuteholidays.com; ❹), a B&B with a lovely garden and great views over the water.

Oban and around

The solidly Victorian resort of **OBAN** (ⓦwww.oban.org.uk) enjoys a superb setting – the island of Kerrera to the southwest providing its bay with a natural shelter – distinguished by a bizarre granite amphitheatre, dramatically lit at night, on the hilltop above the town. Despite a population of just 8000, it's by far the largest port in northwest Scotland, the second-largest town in Argyll and the main departure point for ferries to the Hebrides. If you arrive late, or are catching an early boat, you may have to spend the night here (there's no real need otherwise); if you're staying elsewhere, it's a useful location for wet-weather activities and shopping, and it's a great place to eat fresh seafood, although it does get uncomfortably crowded in the summer.

Oban lies at the centre of the coastal region known as Lorn, named after the Irish Celt Loarn, who, along with his brothers Fergus and Oengus, settled here around 500 AD. Given the number of tourists that pass through or stay in the area, it's hardly surprising that a few out-and-out tourist attractions have developed. The mainland is very picturesque, although its beauty is no secret – to escape the crowds, head off and explore the nearby islands, like **Lismore** or **Kerrera**, just offshore.

Arrival and information

Arriving in Oban **by car** can be a bit of a nightmare in the summer, when traffic chokes the main drag. If you're heading straight for the ferry, make sure you leave an extra hour to allow for sitting in the tailbacks. If you're just coming into town to look around, use one of the non-central or supermarket car parks. The CalMac **ferry terminal** (☎01631/566688, ⓦwww.calmac.co.uk) for the islands is on Railway Pier, a stone's throw from the train station, which is

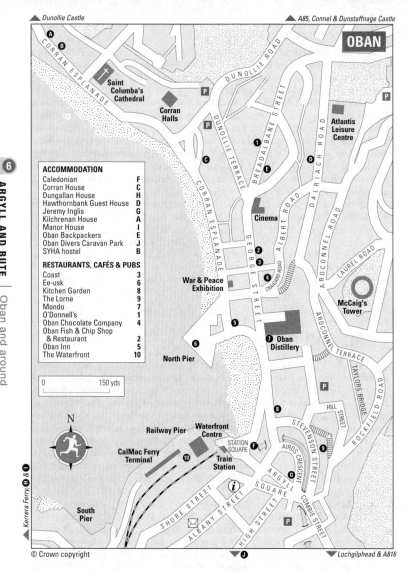

OBAN

▲ Dunollie Castle

CORRAN ESPLANADE

Ⓐ
Ⓑ

Saint
Columba's
Cathedral

Ⓟ

DUNOLLIE ROAD

Corran
Halls

Ⓟ

DUNOLLIE TERRACE

BREADALBANE STREET

Ⓟ

Atlantis
Leisure
Centre

❶

DALRIACH ROAD

ⒸⒸ

Ⓔ

CORRAN ESPLANADE

ALBERT ROAD

LAUREL ROAD

Cinema

ARDCONNEL ROAD

GEORGE STREET

❷
❸

CRAIGARD ROAD

McCaig's
Tower

War & Peace
Exhibition

❹

ARDCONNEL TERRACE

TAYLORS BRIDGE

❺

ROCKFIELD ROAD

North Pier

❻

❼ Oban
Distillery

Oban
Distillery

ACCOMMODATION

Caledonian	F
Corran House	C
Dungallan House	H
Hawthornbank Guest House	D
Jeremy Inglis	G
Kilchrenan House	A
Manor House	I
Oban Backpackers	E
Oban Divers Caravan Park	J
SYHA hostel	B

RESTAURANTS, CAFÉS & PUBS

Coast	3
Ee-usk	6
Kitchen Garden	8
The Lorne	9
Mondo	7
O'Donnell's	1
Oban Chocolate Company	4
Oban Fish & Chip Shop & Restaurant	2
Oban Inn	5
The Waterfront	10

0 ⊢————————————⊣ 150 yds

N

❽

HILL STREET

STEVENSON STREET

❾

Railway Pier

Waterfront
Centre

STATION
SQUARE

Ⓕ

AIRDS CRESCENT

CalMac Ferry
Terminal

❿

Train
Station

ARGYLL

ⓖ

COMBIE STREET

South
Pier

SHORE STREET

ⓘ

SQUARE

ALBANY STREET

HIGH STREET

Ⓟ

© Crown copyright

▼Ⓙ

▼ *Lochgilphead & A816*

◀ *Kerrera Ferry, ⒽⒽ & ⓘ*

Ⓖ

⑥

ARGYLL AND BUTE | Oban and around

itself adjacent to the bus stops on Station Square. The **tourist office** (April
Mon–Fri 9am–5pm, Sat & Sun 10am–5pm; May to mid-June Mon–Sat 9am–
5.30pm, Sun 10am–5pm; mid- to late June & Sept Mon–Sat 9am–6.30pm,
Sun 10am–5pm; July & Aug Mon–Sat 9am–8pm, Sun 9am–7pm; late Sept
to Oct Mon–Sat 9am–5.30pm, Sun 10am–4pm; Nov–March Mon–Fri
9.30am–5pm, Sat 10am–4pm, Sun noon–4pm; ☎01631/563122) is housed
in a converted church on Argyll Square, and has heaps of leaflets and books
as well as Internet access.

Accommodation

Oban is positively heaving with **hotels** and **B&B**s, most of them very reasonably priced and many on or near the quayside. Although it's easy enough to search out a vacancy, in high season it might be wise to pay the fee (£3) charged by the tourist office for finding you a room. It's also worth considering the options a little way out of town, in quieter spots such as Connel and Benderloch (see p.355).

Hotels and B&Bs

Caledonian Hotel Station Square ☎0871/222 3415, ⓦwww.go2oban.com. Large old station hotel overlooking the ferry pier, with recently refurbished stylish and contemporary rooms. Economy rooms ❺, luxury "Captains' Rooms" ❼
Corran House Hotel 1 Victoria Crescent ☎01631/566040, ⓦwww.corranhouse.co.uk. A good budget option, with a decent en-suite double and family rooms as well as bunk rooms above the popular *Markie Dan*'s pub. ❶
Dungallan House Hotel Gallanach Rd ☎01631/563799, ⓦwww.dungallanhotel-oban. co.uk. Solid Victorian villa hotel with a dozen rooms set in its own woodland grounds, hidden away on the Gallanach Road, with great views across the Sound of Kerrera. Closed Jan & Feb. ❼
Hawthornbank Guest House Dalriach Rd ☎01631/562041, ⓦwww.smoothhound .co.uk/hotels/hawthorn.html. Decent traditional guesthouse in the lower backstreets of Oban, just across the road from the swimming pool. ❸
Kilchrenan House Corran Esplanade ☎01631/562663, ⓦwww.kilchrenanhouse.co.uk. Tasteful, hospitable guesthouse located near the cathedral, with ten rooms, most of which have sea views. ❹
Manor House Hotel Gallanach Rd ☎01631/562087, ⓦwww.manorhouseoban.com.

Beautiful eighteenth-century manor house, peacefully located on the fringes of town by the shores of the Sound of Kerrera, with a top-notch restaurant attached. ❻

Hostels and campsites

Jeremy Inglis 21 Airds Crescent ☎01631/565065. Halfway between a hostel and a B&B, with an eccentric proprietor who also runs *McTavish's Kitchens*. Shared rooms, doubles or family rooms available, plus kitchen facilities; breakfast included.
Oban Backpackers Breadalbane St ☎01631/562107, ⓦwww.scotlands-top-hostels .com. Friendliest, cheapest and most central of Oban's hostels, with a pool table, real fire and Internet access. March–Oct & Christmas–New Year.
Oban Divers Caravan Park Glenshellach Rd ☎01631/562755, ⓦwww.obandivers.co.uk. Pleasant site with lots of camping space situated a mile and a half from Oban up a pretty glen. Open April–Oct.
SYHA hostel Corran Esplanade ☎0870/004 1144, ⓦwww.syha.org.uk. Converted Victorian house, with a quieter, modern annexe behind, both a fair trek with a backpack from the ferry terminal along the Corran Esplanade, just beyond the Catholic Cathedral. Two-, three- and four-bed en-suite rooms available.

The Town

Through the summer months, an **open-topped tour bus** offers a basic introduction to the town and surrounds (May–Sept daily 11am & 2pm; £6). Apart from the setting and views, however, the only truly remarkable sight in Oban is the town's landmark, **McCaig's Tower**, a stiff ten-minute climb from the quayside. Built in imitation of Rome's Colosseum, it was the brainchild of a local businessman a century ago, who had the twin aims of alleviating off-season unemployment among the local stonemasons and creating a museum, art gallery and chapel. Originally, the plan was to add a 95-foot central tower, but work never progressed further than the exterior granite walls before McCaig died. In his will, McCaig gave instructions for the lancet windows to be filled with bronze statues of the family, though no such work was ever undertaken. Instead, the folly has been turned into a sort of walled garden which is a popular rendezvous for Oban's youth after dark, but for the rest of the time simply provides a wonderful seaward panorama, particularly at sunset.

Down in the centre of town, you can pass a few hours admiring the boats in the harbour and looking out for scavenging seals in the bay. If the weather's bad, the best option is to sign up for one of the excellent guided tours around **Oban Distillery** (April–Oct Mon–Sat 9.30am–5pm; July–Sept also open until 7.30pm Mon–Fri and Sun noon–5pm; Nov & March Mon–Fri 10am–5pm; Dec & Feb Mon–Fri 12.30–4pm; £5, with £3 redeemable against the cost of a bottle), slap in the centre of town off George Street. The tour ends with a generous dram of Oban's lightly peaty malt. Another refuge is the **War and Peace Exhibition** (Mon–Sat 10am–4pm; free) in the old *Oban Times* building beside the Art Deco *Regent Hotel* on the Esplanade; stuffed full of memorabilia and staffed by enthusiasts, it tells the story of the intriguing wartime role of the area around Oban as a flying-boat base, mustering point for Atlantic convoys and as a training centre for the D-day landings.

A host of private tour operators can be found around the harbour, on the North, South and Railway piers: their all-inclusive ferry, coach and/or boat **trips and tours** – to Mull, Iona, Staffa, Seal Island and the Treshnish Isles – are worth considering, particularly if you're pushed for time, or have no transport. For a rundown of the best of these trips, see the box on p.361. For a fast and furious alternative which sticks to the local area, Puffin Dive Centre (see below) uses a powerful RIB to head out into the Sound of Mull on the lookout for wildlife on sea and land.

Bike rental is available from Oban Cycles, 29 Lochside St (☎01631/566996), and **car rental** from Flit on Glencruitten Road (☎01631/566553, ⓦwww .selfdrive.me.uk). If you fancy taking the plunge and trying your hand at some **diving**, Puffin Dive Centre is based a mile south of Oban at Port Gallanach (☎01631/566088, ⓦwww.puffin.org.uk), though it also has a booking office in town opposite the cinema.

Eating, drinking and nightlife

If you're only here to catch a ferry, you might as well grab a quick langoustine sandwich or dressed fresh crab from John Ogden's excellent **takeaway** seafood shack near the CalMac terminal. Nearby, D. Watt's fishmonger is good for smoked fish and fresh seafood. For sit-down snacks, there's a **café** on the mezzanine above the impressive *Kitchen Garden* deli on George Street, while the *Oban Chocolate Company* at 9 Craigard Rd is a friendly little shop and café serving coffee, hot chocolate and lovely handmade chocolate treats. It was once nearly impossible to get good fresh seafood in Oban, despite the rows of fishing boats at the pier, but things have changed for the better with the arrival of two top fish **restaurants**: on the North Pier the swanky designer *Ee-usk* (☎01631/565666) serves glistening seafood platters, fresh fish dishes and lighter alternatives such as Thai fish cakes; while in the rather less glamorous setting of the old seaman's mission on the CalMac pier is *The Waterfront* (☎01631/563110), which has an open kitchen rustling up impressive dishes using scallops, langoustine and the best of the daily catch. *Coast* (☎01631/569900), a Scottish contemporary bistro, or the cheap, cheerful and more youthful *Mondo*, both on George Street, are alternatives, and, of course, there's always fish and chips from *Oban Fish & Chip Shop & Restaurant*, at 116 George St.

The best **pub** in town is the *Oban Inn* opposite the North Pier, with a classic dark-wood, flagstone and brass bar downstairs and lounge bar with stained glass upstairs. The town's nightlife doesn't bear thinking about (though you can read all about it in the *Oban Times*). It's worth noting, however, that Oban is one of the few places in Argyll with a **cinema**, confusingly known as The Highland Theatre (T01631/562444), at the north end of George Street. You should be able to catch some **live music** at the weekend at *O'Donnell's* Irish pub, underneath a restaurant called *The Gathering*, on Breadalbane Street, or in *The Lorne*, a popular bar on Stevenson Street which also serves real ales.

Isle of Kerrera

One of the best places to escape from the crowds that plague Oban is the low-lying island of **Kerrera**, which shelters Oban Bay from the worst of the westerly winds. Measuring just five miles by two, the island is easily explored on foot and often crawling with geology students in the holidays. The island's most prominent landmark is the **Hutcheson's Monument**, best viewed, appropriately enough, from the ferries heading out of Oban, as it commemorates David Hutcheson, one of the Victorian founders of what is now Caledonian MacBrayne. The most appealing panoramas, however, are from Kerrera's highest point, **Càrn Breugach** (620ft), over to Mull, the Slate Islands, Lismore, Jura and beyond.

The ferry lands roughly halfway down the east coast, at the north end of **Horseshoe Bay**, where King Alexander II died in 1249. If the weather's fine and you feel like lazing by the sea, head for the island's finest sandy beach, **Slatrach Bay**, on the west coast, one mile northwest of the ferry jetty. Otherwise, there's a very rewarding trail down to **Gylen Castle**, a cliff-top ruin enjoying a majestic setting on the south coast, built in 1582 by the MacDougalls and burnt to the ground by the Covenanter General Leslie in 1647. You can head back to the ferry via the Drove Road, where cattle from Mull and other islands were once herded to be swum across the sound to the market in Oban.

The passenger and bicycle **ferry** crosses regularly (roughly every 30min in summer 8.45am–6pm; every 1–2 hours in winter 8.45am–5pm; £3.50 return T01631/563665) through the day from the mainland two miles down the Gallanach road from Oban. In summer, **bus** #431 (departs 10.20am, returns 4.10pm) from Oban Railway Station connects with the ferry. Kerrera has a total population of fewer than thirty – and no shop – so if you're day-tripping make sure you bring enough supplies with you. Alternatively, you can eat home-made, often organic, veggie **snacks** at the *Kerrera Teagarden* (April–Sept Wed–Sun 10.30am–4.30pm), located in a nice spot at Lower Gylen, a 45-minute walk from the ferry. Right beside this is the *Kerrera Bunkhouse* (T01631/570223, Wwww.kerrerabunkhouse.co.uk; open all year, but booking advised), a converted eighteenth-century stable building which sleeps seven. For simple **B&B** or self-catering accommodation enquire at *Ardentrive Farm* (T01631/570938, Edavid@ardentrive.fsnet.co.uk; ❶), at the north of the island.

East of Oban

Just beyond the northern satellite suburbs of Oban, on a strategic promontory overlooking the important water crossroads at the mouth of Loch Etive, lie the ruins of **Dunstaffnage Castle** (April–Sept daily 9.30am–6.30pm; Oct–March Mon–Wed, Sat & Sun 9.30am–4.30pm; HS; £2.50). Originally built as a thirteenth-century MacDougall fort, the castle was captured by Robert the Bruce in 1309, and remained in royal hands until it was handed over to the Campbells in 1470. Garrisoned by government forces during the 1745 rebellion, it served as a temporary prison for Flora MacDonald, and was eventually destroyed by fire in 1810.

A couple of miles further up the A85, at **CONNEL**, you can't fail to admire the majestic steel cantilever **Connel Bridge**, built in 1903 to take the old branch railway line across the sea cataract at the mouth of Loch Etive, north to Fort William. The name "Connel" comes from the Gaelic *conghail* (tumultuous flood), which refers to the falls, or rapids, created by tidal streams rushing over a ledge of rock. Known as the Falls of Lora, this is one of the few tidal waterfalls in the country and looks as menacing as it does spectacular. These days the bridge is used by road transport, with the A828 now crossing it to take you on to Benderloch. If you want to stay out here in Connel as a mellower alternative to Oban, *Ards House* (☎01631/710255, ⓦwww.ardshouse.com; ④), a whitewashed Victorian villa by the main road overlooking the water, is a pleasant option, while a good place to admire the kayakers tackling the tidal falls is *Strumhor* guesthouse (☎01631/710167, ⓦwww.strumhor.co.uk; ②), whose proprietors run sea-kayaking courses from beginners upwards (ⓦwww.seafreedomkayak.co.uk). There are also rooms at the *Wide-Mouthed Frog* (☎01631/567005, ⓦwww.widemouthedfrog.com; mid-Feb to Dec; ④), at Dunstaffnage Marina, a popular hangout for "yotties" which also serves pub grub and has tables outside with views over to the castle. In Connel itself, you can get pub meals and seafood at the *Oyster Inn*, tucked underneath the bridge.

Taynuilt and Loch Etive

TAYNUILT, seven miles east of Connel, at the point where the River Awe flows into the sea at **Loch Etive**, is a small but sprawling village, best known for its iron-smelting works. To reach this industrial heritage site, follow the signpost off the A85 to **Bonawe Iron Furnace** (April–Sept daily 9.30am–6.30pm; HS; £3), which was originally founded by Cumbrian ironworkers in 1753. A whole series of buildings in various states of repair are scattered across the factory site, which employed six hundred people at its height, and eventually closed down in 1876.

From the pier beyond the iron furnace, **boat cruises** (mid–April to Sept Sun–Fri noon & 2pm; £6/2hr, £11/3hr) check out the local seals and explore the otherwise inaccessible reaches of Loch Etive; phone Loch Etive Cruises (☎01866/822430) for more details. A mile or so east up the A85 from Taynuilt, a sign invites you to visit the tucked-away **Inverawe Fisheries and Smokery** (Easter–Oct & Dec daily 8.30am–5pm, open till 6pm June–Aug; Nov Sat & Sun 8.30am–5pm), where you can buy lots of lovely local food including traditionally smoked fish and mussels, eat the same in their café, check out the exhibition on traditional smoking techniques, learn how to fly-fish or go for a stroll down to nearby Loch Etive with your picnic.

Loch Awe

Legend has it that **Loch Awe** – at more than 25 miles in length, the longest stretch of fresh water in the country – was created by a witch and inhabited by a monster even more gruesome than the one at Loch Ness. Most travellers only encounter the north end of the loch as they speed along its shores by car or train on the way to Oban. This part of the loch has several tiny islands sporting picturesque ruins. Fifteenth-century **Kilchurn Castle**, strategically situated on a rocky spit – once an island – at the head of the loch and formerly a Campbell stronghold, has been abandoned to the elements since being struck by lightning in the 1760s, and is now one of Argyll's most photogenic lochside ruins. The only way to see the castle properly is to join one of the hour-long steamboat cruises (☎01838/200440) that set off during summer months from the pier at the small village of **LOCHAWE**, right by the village's train station (where there's also a small tearoom in a parked railway carriage).

The main attraction on the shores of Loch Awe is, however, rather less picturesque. **Cruachan Power Station** (Easter–Oct daily 9.30am–5pm; Nov–March Mon–Fri 10am–4pm; £4) is actually constructed inside mighty Ben Cruachan (3693ft), which looms over the head of Loch Awe; it was built in 1965 as part of the hydroelectric network which generates around ten percent of Scotland's electricity. Half-hour guided tours set off every hour from the **visitor centre** by the loch, taking you to a viewing platform above the generating room deep inside the "hollow mountain". The whole experience of visiting an industrial complex hidden within a mountain is very James Bond, and it certainly pulls in the tour coaches, so if you're keen to go, make sure you get there before the queues start to form, particularly in summer.

There aren't many decent places to stay around Loch Awe, with the exception of two particularly luxurious hotels on the peaceful northwestern shores, reached by a back road from Taynuilt to the hamlet of Kilchrenan. The *Taychreggan Hotel* (☎01866/833211, ⓦwww.taychregganhotel.co.uk; ❼) is an old drovers' inn by the loch now plumped up into an upmarket retreat, while the *Ardanaiseig Hotel* (☎01866/833333, ⓦwww.ardanaiseig .com; closed Jan; ❼) is a wonderfully secluded, romantic escape set in a palatial Scottish Baronial pile four miles to the northeast down a dead-end track. Both these hotels have superb, though expensive, restaurants, and the *Ardanaiseig* also has its own glorious **gardens** (daily 9.30am–dusk), home of rare species of azaleas and rhododendrons, worth visiting even if you're not staying here.

North of Oban

On the north side of the Connel Bridge lies the hammerhead peninsula of **Benderloch** (from *beinn eadar da loch*, "hill between two lochs"), which has little to distinguish it other than the fact that it's the location for three of Argyll's most interesting **places to stay**. Standing on its own, right above the beach just west of the village of Benderloch, ⚓ *Dun Na Mara* (☎01631/720233, ⓦwww.dunnamara.com; ❺) is a fine Arts and Crafts-style holiday home where highly stylish contemporary decor is complemented by the warm hospitality (including imaginative breakfasts) of its two young architect owners. A contrast in style can be found on the northern side of the peninsula at **Barcaldine Castle**, an early seventeenth-century Campbell tower house. Bought as a ruin in 1896 and restored, it is now run as a B&B by the current heir, London-born and -bred Roderick, and his wife Caroline. There are no real treasures here, but the castle is fun to explore, with dungeons and hidden staircases and it makes a fairly memorable place to stay (☎01631/720598, ⓦwww .freewebs.com/barcaldinecastle; Oct–March minimum stay 2 nights; ❺). If you have an unlimited budget you might like to stay at the area's most exclusive hotel, the *Isle of Eriska*, a luxury, turreted, Scottish Baronial place with a spa, pool and upmarket dining room. It's run by the Buchanan-Smiths on their own three-hundred-acre island off the northern point of Benderloch (☎01631/720371, ⓦwww .eriska-hotel.co.uk; ❾).

Since the weather in this part of Scotland can be bad at almost any time of the year, it's as well to know about the **Scottish Sea Life & Marine Sanctuary** (daily: 10am–5pm, open till 6pm July & Aug; £9.50), which is to be found on the A828, along the southern shores of Loch Creran. Here you can see loads of sea creatures at close quarters, touch the (non-)stingrays, do a bit of rockpool dipping, keep a look out for the resident otters and learn about how common seal orphan pups are rescued and returned to the wild.

Appin

With the new Creagan Bridge in place – the old wrought-iron railway bridge sadly having been demolished – there's no need to circumnavigate Loch Creran in order to reach the district of **Appin**, best known as the setting for Robert Louis Stevenson's *Kidnapped*, a fictionalized account of the "Appin Murder" of 1752, when Colin Campbell was shot in the back, allegedly by one of the disenfranchised Stewart clan.

The name Appin derives from the Gaelic *abthaine*, meaning "lands belonging to the abbey", in this case the one on the island of Lismore (see opposite), which is linked to the peninsula by passenger ferry from **PORT APPIN**, a pretty little fishing village at the peninsula's westernmost tip. Overlooking a host of tiny little islands dotted around Loch Linnhe, with Lismore and the mountains of Morvern and Mull in the background, this is, without doubt, one of Argyll's most picturesque spots. The *Pierhouse Hotel* (℡01631/730302, ⓦwww .pierhousehotel.co.uk; ➎), nicely situated right by the ferry, has a popular bar and an expensive seafood restaurant. If you're wandering around the village, take time to look at the display beside the village hall about the lighthouse on nearby Sgeir Bhuidhe (Yellow Skerry), which one night in 2001 was painted pink with yellow spots by protesters campaigning against its removal.

Framed magnificently as you wind along the single-track road to Port Appin is one of Argyll's most romantic ruined castles, the much-photographed **Castle Stalker**, which occupies a tiny rocky island to the north of Port Appin. Built by the Stewarts of Appin in the sixteenth century and gifted to King James IV as a hunting lodge, it inevitably fell into the hands of the Campbells after 1745. The current owners open the castle to the public for very short periods each year, and all visits are by appointment only; ring ℡01631/730354, check ⓦwww .castlestalker.com or ask at Oban tourist office for opening times. Open all year, however, and offering one of the best outlooks over the castle, the pleasant, modern Castle Stalker View **café** (March–Oct daily 9.30am–5.30pm; Nov–Feb Wed–Sun 10am–4pm) is located a little way up the main road north towards

△ Castle Stalker, Appin

Ballachullish. **Bike rental** is available from Port Appin Bikes (℡01631/730391) and it's worth noting that bicycles travel for free on the passenger ferry to Lismore (see below). For other **outdoor pursuits**, head for the Linnhe Marine Water Sports Centre (℡07721/503981; May–Sept) in Lettershuna (just north of Castle Stalker), which rents out boats of all shapes and sizes, offers sailing and windsurfing lessons, not to mention water-skiing, clay-pigeon shooting and even pony trekking.

Isle of Lismore

Lying in the middle of Loch Linnhe, to the north of Oban, and barely rising above a hillock, the narrow island of **LISMORE** (Ⓦwww.isleoflismore.com) offers wonderful gentle walking and cycling opportunities, with unrivalled views, in fine weather, across to the mountains of Morvern, Lochaber and Mull. Legend has it that St Columba and Moluag both fancied the skinny island as a missionary base, but as they raced towards it Moluag cut off his finger and threw it ashore ahead of Columba, claiming the land for himself. Of Moluag's sixth-century foundation nothing remains, but from 1236 until 1507 the island served as the seat of the bishop of Argyll. It was a judicious choice, as Lismore is undoubtedly one of the most fertile of the Inner Hebrides – its name, coined by Moluag himself, derives from the Gaelic *lios mór*, meaning "great garden" – and before the Clearances (see p.804) it supported nearly 1400 inhabitants; the population today is around a tenth of that figure, half of them over 60.

Lismore is about eight miles long and one mile wide, and the ferry from Oban lands at **ACHNACROISH**, roughly halfway along the eastern coastline. To get to grips with the history of the island and its Gaelic culture (and have a cup of tea), follow the signs for the nearby **Comann Eachdraidh Lios Mór**, or Lismore Historical Society (May–Sept Mon, Tues, Thurs–Sat 11am–4pm; £2). When you're there, ask if you can pay a visit to a cottar's (landless tenant's) cottage, **Tigh Iseabail Dhaidh**, restored by the Historical Society to the way it would have been in the nineteenth century, with traditionally built stone walls, birch roof timbers and thatched roof. The island post office and shop are along the main road between Achnacroish and **CLACHAN**, a couple of miles northeast, where the diminutive, whitewashed former **Cathedral of St Moluag** stands. All that remains of the fourteenth-century cathedral is the choir, which was reduced in height and converted into the parish church in 1749; inside you can see a few of the original seats for the upper clergy, a stone basin in the south wall and several medieval doorways. Due east of the church – head north up the road and take the turning signposted on the right – the circular **Tirefour Broch**, over 2000 years old, occupies a commanding position and boasts walls almost ten feet thick in places. West of Clachan are the much more recent ruins of **Castle Coeffin**, a twelfth-century MacDougall fortress once believed to have been haunted by the ghost of Beothail, sister of the Norse prince Caiffen. A few other places worth exploring are **Sailean**, an abandoned quarry village further south along the west coast, with its disused kilns and cottages; the ruins of **Achanduin Castle**, in the southwest, where the bishops are thought to have resided; and Barr Mór (416ft), the island's highest point.

Two **ferries** serve Lismore: a small CalMac car ferry from Oban to Achnacroish (Mon–Sat 2–5 daily; 50min), and a shorter passenger- and bicycle-only crossing from Port Appin to the island's north point (daily every 2hr; 5min). Only one bus a day connects Oban all the way through to Port Appin, departing from the train station at 7.20am. On the island itself, a **postbus** does a daily round (Mon–Sat; pick up a timetable from Oban tourist office or check route 202 at ⓦwww.postbus.royalmail.com). **Accommodation** on the island is extremely limited: try the budget B&B at the *Schoolhouse* (☎01631/760262; ❷), north of Clachan, which also serves evening meals. **Bike rental** is available from Island Bike Hire (☎01631/760213) for around £10 a day – they'll deliver to the ferry if you make prior arrangements.

Isle of Mull

The second largest of the Inner Hebrides, **MULL** (ⓦwww.holidaymull.org .uk) is by far the most accessible: just forty minutes from Oban by ferry. As so often, first impressions largely depend on the weather – it is the wettest of the Hebrides (and that's saying something) – for without the sun the large tracts of moorland, particularly around the island's highest peak, Ben More (3169ft), can appear bleak and unwelcoming. There are, however, areas of more gentle pastoral scenery around **Dervaig** in the north and **Salen** on the east coast, and the indented west coast varies from the sandy beaches around **Calgary** to the cliffs of Loch na Keal. The most common mistake is to try and "do" the island in a day or two: flogging up the main road to the picturesque capital of **Tobermory**, then covering the fifty-odd miles between there and Fionnphort, in order to visit **Iona**. Mull is a place that will grow on you only if you have the time and patience to explore.

Historically, crofting, whisky distilling and fishing supported the islanders (*Muileachs*), but the population – which peaked at 10,000 – decreased dramatically

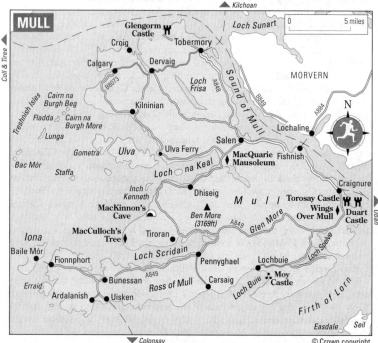

© Crown copyright

in the late nineteenth century due to the Clearances and the 1846 potato famine. On Mull, it is a trend that has been reversed, mostly owing to the large influx of settlers from elsewhere in the country, which has brought the current population up to over 2500. One of the main reasons for this resurgence is, of course, tourism – more than half a million visitors come here each year – although, oddly enough, there are very few large hotels or campsites. Mull makes particular efforts to draw visitors to **special events** through the year: these annual events include a wildlife week in May, the Mendelssohn on Mull Festival in July, which commemorates the composer's visit here in 1829, and a rally car event around the island's winding roads in October.

Craignure is the main entry point to Mull, with a frequent daily **car ferry** link to Oban; if you're taking a car over, it's advisable to book ahead for this service. A much smaller and less expensive car ferry crosses daily from Lochaline on the Morvern peninsula (see p.616) to the slipway at Fishnish, six miles northwest of Craignure. Another even smaller car ferry connects Kilchoan on the Ardnamurchan peninsula (see p.618) with Tobermory, 24 miles northwest of Craignure. Both of these two smaller ferries run on a first-come, first-served basis. **Public transport** on Mull is not too bad on the main A849, but there's more or less no service along the west coast (for more information, visit Ⓦwww.mict.co.uk/travel). If you're **driving**, note that the roads are still predominantly single-track, with passing places, which can slow journeys down considerably, particularly during the busier months of summer.

Craignure and around

CRAIGNURE is little more than a scattering of cottages, though there is a small shop, a bar, some toilets and a CalMac ticket and **tourist office** – the only one on the island open all year round – situated opposite the pier (April–June & Sept Mon–Fri 8.30am–5.15pm, Sat 9am–6.30pm, Sun 10.30am–5.30pm; July & Aug Mon–Fri 8.30am–7.30pm, Sat 9am–6.30pm, Sun 10am–7pm; Oct–March Mon–Sat 9am–5pm, Sun 10.30am–noon, 3.30–5pm; ℡01680/812377). The old-style, whitewashed *Craignure Inn* (℡01680/812305, Ⓦwww.craignure-inn.co.uk; ❺), just a minute's stroll up the road towards Fionnphort, is a snug **pub** to hole up in, with decent rooms and food. Along the side road leading to Mull Rail, there's also a well-equipped **campsite** run by Shieling Holidays (℡01680/812496, Ⓦwww.shielingholidays.co.uk; April–Oct) set above a shingle beach with good views over to the Morvern shore. The campsite offers the usual pitches, plus hostel and self-catering accommodation in "shielings" (essentially large, furnished, hard-top tents), and has boats, canoes and bikes for rent. Another pleasant place to camp is the well-equipped *Balmeanach Park* site (℡01680/300342; April–Oct), five miles up the A849 at Fishnish, which has a small tearoom attached. There are several B&Bs in the area, but the best **guesthouse** is the *Old Mill Cottage* (℡01680/812442, Ⓦwww.oldmill.mull.com; ❹), a sensitively converted mill, three miles south on the A849 in Lochdon; it also has a small and highly recommended restaurant attached (dinner only; bookings essential).

Buses to the Iona ferry at Fionnphort (Mon–Sat 3–4 daily, Sun 1 daily; 1hr 15min) and Tobermory (Mon–Sat 4–5 daily, Sun 2 daily; 50min) don't necessarily connect with every ferry sailing, so check the timetables carefully before you leave Oban. The other method of transport available at Craignure is the diminutive, narrow-gauge Mull & West Highland Railway, commonly known as **Mull Rail** (Easter to mid-Oct; £4 return; ☎01680/812494, ⓦwww.mullrail.co.uk), built in the 1980s and the only working railway in the Scottish islands. The Craignure station is situated beyond the Shieling Holidays campsite, and the line stretches southeast for about a mile and a half to Torosay Castle (see below). If you prefer to take the train one way only, it's a lovely thirty-minute walk along the coast (with the possibility of spotting an otter). The company uses diesel and steam locomotives, so ring ahead if you want to be sure of a steam-driven train.

Torosay and Duart castles

Two castles lie immediately southeast of Craignure. The first, a mile-long walk or short train ride from Craignure, is **Torosay Castle** (April to mid-Oct daily 10.30am–5.30pm; £5.50; ⓦwww.torosay.com), a full-blown Scottish Baronial creation. The house itself is stuffed with memorabilia relating to the present owners, the Guthries, all of it amusingly captioned but of no great importance, with the possible exception of the belongings of the late David Guthrie-James, who made a daring escape from a POW camp in Germany during World War II. Torosay's real highlight, however, is the magnificent **gardens** (daily: summer months 9am–7pm, winter during daylight hours; £4.50) with their avenue of eighteenth-century Venetian statues, a Japanese section and views up Loch Linnhe.

Very different in style is **Duart Castle** (April Sun–Thurs 11am–4pm; May–Oct daily 10.30am–5.30pm; £4.50; ⓦwww.duartcastle.com), a couple of miles east of Torosay, which is perched on a rocky promontory sticking out into the Sound of Mull, making it a striking landmark from the Oban–Craignure ferry. If you're arriving off the ferry, look out for the Duart Coach, which meets the boats arriving at 10.45am, 12.45pm and 2.45pm (10.15am, 12.15pm and 2.15pm on Sat) for the ten-minute ride to the Castle. Duart was headquarters of the once-powerful MacLean clan from the thirteenth century, but was burnt down by the Campbells and confiscated after the 1745 rebellion. In 1911 the 26th clan chief, Fitzroy MacLean (1835–1936) – not to be confused with the Scottish writer of the same name – managed to buy it back and restore it. Buffeted by winds and weather, the castle is by no means a luxurious country seat: you can peek at the dungeons, climb up to the ramparts, study the family photos and learn about the world scout movement (the 27th clan chief became Chief Scout in 1959). After your visit, you can enjoy home-made cakes and tea at the castle's friendly tearoom (May–Sept).

Wings Over Mull

A short way past Torosay Castle, a turn-off leads to **Wings over Mull** (mid-Feb to Oct 10.30am–5.30pm; £4.50; ⓦwww.wingsovermull.com), a conservation centre and sanctuary devoted to birds of prey. While keen bird-watchers coming to Mull have an excellent chance of seeing some of Britain's finest birds of prey in the wild, the visitors' centre here, based in a converted steading, has lots of background information about all kinds of owls, hawks, falcons and eagles, as well as details about the work done at the centre to rescue and preserve these species. More memorably, you can take a close look at around forty different birds housed in cages and pens nearby. They're not cooped up all the time, however, with flying displays taking place at noon, 2pm and 4pm each day.

Tobermory

Mull's chief town, **TOBERMORY** (ⓦwww.tobermory.co.uk), at the northern tip of the island, is easily the most attractive fishing port on the west coast of

Festivals

There's a bewildering diversity of annual events in Scotland, with just about every town celebrating with a big shindig at least once a year. The cultural extravaganza of the Edinburgh Festival stands head and shoulders above the rest, but there are one or two peculiarly Scottish celebrations, such as Hogmanay and Burns Night, that stand out. Highland Games, large and small, are ubiquitous over the summer, and should definitely be sampled, as should one of the country's more esoteric gatherings listed here.

Edinburgh Festival

The **Edinburgh Festival** began in 1947, when, driven by a desire for postwar reconciliation and escape from austerity, the Viennese-born former manager of the Glyndebourne Opera, Rudolf Bing, brought together a host of distinguished musicians from the war-ravaged countries of central Europe. At the same time, eight theatre groups turned up in Edinburgh, uninvited, performing in an unlikely variety of local venues; the next year a critic dubbed their enterprise "the fringe of the official festival drama", and the name and the spirit of the Fringe was born. Since then, the Festival and its **Fringe** have grown out of all proportion so that for the best part of August, Scotland's capital is totally dominated by the world's largest celebration of the arts. Every available performance space – from the city's grandest concert halls to pub courtyards – plays host to everything from high drama to base comedy. The streets fill with buskers, hustlers, circus acts and craft stalls, and the population doubles. Pubs and restaurants stay open later, posters plaster every vertical space and the atmosphere in town takes on a slightly surreal, vital buzz. For more on how to "do the festival", see p.147.

Street performer at Edinburgh Festival

Hogmanay

Hogmanay is the name Scots give to New Year's Eve, a celebration they have made all their own with a unique mix of tradition, hedonism, sentimentality and enthusiasm. The roots of the Hogmanay are in ancient pagan festivities based around the winter solstice, which in most places gradually merged with Christmas. When hardline Scottish Protestant clerics in the sixteenth century abolished Christmas for being a Catholic mass, the Scots, not wanting to miss out on a mid-winter knees-up, instead put their energy into greeting the New Year. Houses were cleaned from top to bottom, debts were paid and quarrels made up, and, after the bells of midnight were rung, great store was laid by welcoming good luck into your house. This still takes the form of the tradition of "first-footing" – visiting your neighbours and bearing gifts. The ideal first-foot is a tall dark-haired male carrying a bottle of whisky; women or redheads, on the other hand, bring bad luck – though to be honest no one carrying a bottle of whisky tends to be turned away these days, whatever the colour of their hair. All this neighbourly greeting means a fair bit of partying, and no one is expected to go to work the next day or, indeed, the day after. Even today, January 1 is a public holiday in the rest of the UK, but only in Scotland does the holiday extend to the next day too. In fact, right up to the 1950s Christmas was a normal working day for many people in Scotland, and Hogmanay was widely regarded as by far the more important celebration.

Highland Games

Hogmanay celebrations, Edinburgh

Despite their name, **Highland Games** are held all over Scotland, not just in the Highlands. The Games probably originated in the fourteenth century as a means of recruiting the best fighting men for the clan chiefs, and were popularized by Queen Victoria to encourage the traditional dress, music, games and dance of the Highlands; indeed various royals still attend the Games at Braemar.

Apart from Braemar, the most famous games take place at Oban and Cowal, but the smaller events, held throughout the summer, are often more fun – like a sort of Highland version of a school sports day, with running races and high jump (without a mat) as well as **piping** and **dancing** competitions. There's money to be won, too, so the Games are usually pretty competitive. The most distinctive events are known as the "**heavies**" – tossing the caber (pronounced "kabber"), putting the stone, and tossing the weight over the bar – all of which require prodigious strength and skill and the wearing of a kilt. Tossing the caber is the most spectacular, when the athlete must lift an entire tree trunk up, cupping it in his hands, before running with it and attempting to heave it end over end.

Highland Games competitor tossing the caber

Burns Night

Far more than St Andrew's Day, **Burns Night** is the Scottish annual national holiday. To celebrate the birthday of the country's best-known poet, Rabbie Burns (1759–96), Scots all over the world gather together for a **Burns Supper** on January 25. Whatever the scale and formality of the event, a Burns Night includes at least one or two of the following key elements. Strictly speaking, a piper should greet the guests until everyone is seated ready to hear the first bit of Burns' poetry, *The Selkirk Grace*:

Some hae meat and canna eat,
and some wad eat that want it,
but we hae meat and we can eat,
and sae the Lord be thankit.

At this point the star attraction of the
evening, the **haggis**, is piped in on a
silver platter, after which someone reads
out Burns's Ode to a Haggis, beginning
with the immortal line, "*Fair fa' your
honest, sonsie face/Great chieftain o'
the pudding-race!*". During the recitation,
the reader raises a knife ("*His knife
see Rustic-labour dight*"), pierces the
haggis, allowing the tasty gore to spill
out ("*trenching its gushing entrails*"),
and then toasts the haggis with the final
line ("*Gie her a Haggis!*"). After everyone
has tucked into their haggis, tatties and
neaps, someone gives a paean to the life
of Burns along with more of his poetry. A
male guest then has to give a speech in
which women are praised (often ironically)
through selective quotations from Burns,
ending in a **Toast to the Lassies**. This is
followed by a (usually scathing) reply
from one of the Lassies, again through
judicious use of Burns quotes. Finally,
there's a stirring rendition of Burns' poem,
Auld Lang Syne, to the familiar tune.

Haggis

The Weird
and Wonderful

If the organized mayhem of the
likes of the Edinburgh Festival and the
Highland Games don't excite you, then
you can always look up one of Scotland's
smaller-scale, more unusual festivals. In
Orkney, the folk of Kirkwall spend most of
Christmas Day and New Year's Day taking
part in the traditional ball game known
as **The Ba'**, in which the "Uppies"
and the "Doonies" spend hours
stuck in a heaving, steaming
scrum. Shetlanders, meanwhile greet
the new year with **Up Helly-Aa**, dressing up as
helmeted Vikings and setting fire to their carefully
constructed longships. Further south, in Burghead,
on the Moray Firth, an equally dramatic fire
ceremony takes place, known as the **Burning of
the Clavie**. On New Year's Day, according to the
old Julian calendar (January 11), a burning tar
barrel is carried around the town, before being
rolled into the sea. On March 1, to usher in the
spring and ward away evil spirits, the lads and
lassies of Lanark chase each other round the
local church swinging a ball of paper in an event
known as the **Whuppity Scoorie**. More recently
established oddities include the World Stone
Skimming Championships on the Hebridean island
of Easdale; the World Porridge Championships
in Carrbridge, Invernesshire; and the national
Gold Panning Championships in Wanlockhead,
Dumfriesshire.

6

Trips and tours by land and sea around Mull, Staffa and Iona

Mull, Staffa and Iona offer such a concentrated range of experiences, from exploring peaceful ruins to seeing killer whales, that it's little surprise that a wide choice of trips and tours is available around the islands. Mull is perhaps second only to Skye when it comes to the number of **coach tours** that clog up the island's single-track roads. Many of these are operated by Bowman's (℡01680/812313, ⊛www.bowmanstours.co.uk), who offer whistle-stop (if sometimes exhausting) day-tours taking in either Iona and a boat trip to Staffa or Tobermory and a bit of Mull scenery. If you start from Oban, tours begin at around £25; from Craignure, they start at just £20. These trips are organized in conjunction with CalMac (℡01631/562244) and Gordon Grant Marine (see below), both of whom you can use to book. A more intimate way to explore Mull is on a specialized land-based **wildlife tour**; most of these head off in pursuit of the island's three most elusive creatures, the otter, the sea eagle and the golden eagle. Try Island Encounter (℡01680/300441, ⊛www.mullwildlife.co.uk), or Isle of Mull Wildlife Expeditions (℡01688/500121, ⊛www.torrbuan.com), which both offer a full day's outing, with food, for around £30.

 Boat trips, which leave from many different places around Mull, tend to offer a mix of sightseeing and wildlife, with prices ranging from around £15 for a two-hour cruise to £50 for a full day **whale-watching**. Sea Life Surveys (℡01688/302916, ⊛www.sealifesurveys.com), which is linked to the research being done by the Hebridean Whale and Dolphin Trust, focuses on seeking out the whales (minke and even killer whales are the most common), porpoises, dolphins and basking sharks that spend time in the waters around the Hebrides. Based in Tobermory, the same outfit also operates Ecocruz, which sticks to coastal waters rather than heading for the open sea, and is particularly good for families. Rather more sedate are the wildlife cruises on the solid gaff-rigged ketch *Solais Na Mara* (⊛www.hebrideanadventure.co.uk; book through the CalMac office in Tobermory ℡01688/302017), which heads out of Tobermory harbour under sail, weather permitting, for three-hour trips during the day as well as a two-hour sunset cruise. Finally, you can combine a wildlife cruise with a trip to the island of Rùm (see p.688) on the dive-charter boat *Silver Swift* (℡01688/302390, ⊛www.silverswift.co.uk), which goes to the Small Isles on Wednesdays throughout summer (and other days, depending on weather and demand).

 Elsewhere on Mull, Turus Mara (℡0800/085 8786, ⊛www.turusmara.com), based at Ulva Ferry, sets out in the direction of Staffa and the Treshnish Isles, where the birdlife, including puffins, is prodigious. They also include Iona in some of their trips. Otherwise, dedicated excursions to Staffa mostly run from Fionnphort and Iona: try Iolaire (℡01681/700358, ⊛www.staffatrips.f9.co.uk) or Gordon Grant Marine (℡01681/700338, ⊛www.staffatours.com) – trips run twice daily (weather permitting) between April and October and cost around £18, and there's usually a chance to get onto the island to visit Fingal's Cave.

Scotland, its clusters of brightly coloured houses and boats sheltering in a bay backed by a steep bluff. Founded in 1788 by the British Society for Encouraging Fisheries, it never really took off as a fishing port and only survived due to the influx of crofters evicted from other parts of the island during the Clearances. With a population of more than eight hundred, it is the most important settlement on Mull, and if you're staying any length of time on the island you're bound to want to visit, not least because it has a Womble named after it (or, if you're under 10, because it's the setting for the children's TV show *Balamory*).

Information and accommodation

The **tourist office** (April Mon–Fri 9am–5pm, Sat & Sun noon–5pm; May & June Mon–Fri 9am–5pm, Sat & Sun 11am–5pm; July & Aug Mon–Sat

9am–6pm, Sun 10am–5pm; Sept & Oct Mon–Sat 10am–5pm, Sun noon–5pm; ☎01688/302182) is in the same building as the CalMac ticket office on the pier at the far end of Main Street. If you want to **rent a bike**, head to Archibald Brown, the endearingly old-fashioned ironmongers on Main Street (☎01688/302020, Ⓦwww.browns-tobermory.co.uk).

The tourist office can book you into a **B&B** for a small fee – not a bad idea in high season, when the places on Main Street tend to get booked up fast, and the rest are a stiff climb from the harbour. The small, friendly SYHA **hostel** is on Main Street (☎0870/004 1151, Ⓦwww.syha.org.uk; March–Oct) and has Internet and laundry facilities. The nearest **campsite** is *Newdale* (☎01688/302624, Ⓦwww.tobermory-campsite.co.uk; April–Oct), nicely situated one and a half miles uphill from Tobermory on the B8073 to Dervaig.

The Town

The harbour – known as **Main Street** – is one long parade of multicoloured hotels, guesthouses, restaurants and shops, and you could happily spend an hour or so meandering around: Mull Pottery and the Mull Silver Company are both worth a browse, as is the **Hebridean Whale and Dolphin Trust** (April–Oct daily 10am–4pm; Nov–March Mon–Fri 11am–5pm; free; Ⓦwww.hwdt.org), run by a welcoming bunch of enthusiasts. The small office has lots of information on how to identify marine mammals, and on recent sightings. They're very child-friendly, too, and will keep kids amused for an hour or so with computer marine games, word searches and a bit of artwork. Note that you can't book whale-watching trips here – to do this you should contact one of the operators listed in the box on page 361.

Another good wet-weather retreat is the **Mull Museum** (Easter to mid-Oct Mon–Fri 10am–4pm, Sat 10am–1pm; £1), further along Main Street, which packs a great deal of information and artefacts – including a few objects salvaged from the *San Juan* – into one tiny room. Alternatively, there's the minuscule **Tobermory Distillery** (Easter–Oct Mon–Fri 10am–5pm; £2.50) at the south end of the bay, founded in 1795 but closed down three times since then. Today, it's back in business and offers a pretty desultory guided tour, rounded off with a dram.

A stiff climb up Back Brae will bring you to the island's main arts centre, **An Tobar** (Tues–Sat 10am–4pm; June–Aug also Sun 1–4pm; free; Ⓦwww.antobar.co.uk), housed in a converted Victorian schoolhouse. The small but attractive centre hosts exhibitions and a variety of live events, and contains a

6

café with comfy sofas set before a real fire. The rest of the upper town, laid out on a classic grid plan, merits a stroll, if only for the great views over the bay.

If you've got transport, or are prepared to walk a mile or so uphill out of town, pay a visit to **Sgriob–ruadh Farm** (daily 10am–4pm; free; ℡01688/302235, ⓦwww.isleofmullcheese.co.uk) on the Glengorm road, where one of Scotland's finest artisan cheeses, the tangy, Cheddar-like "Isle of Mull", is produced. You can usually see some aspect of the cheese-making process going on through viewing windows and if staff are available there's always the chance to find out more about the different types made here, including a tour to the cellars. You can also buy cheese directly from the farm. Four miles further out along the same road are the towers and turrets of **Glengorm Castle** (ⓦwww.glengormcastle.co.uk), a Scots Baronial pile overlooking the sea which offers accommodation (see opposite) and also has an attractively converted steading, which incorporates a modern café, well-stocked farm shop and art gallery (Easter to mid-Oct daily 10am–5pm; for winter opening, phone ℡01688/302321). You can walk around their attractive walled garden or take on longer forest and coastal trails.

Eating and drinking

Main Street heaves with **places to eat**, including a highly rated fish and chip van on the old pier which will serve up scallops and chips alongside more traditional fish suppers. The best of the bunch on this street is probably *The Water's Edge* in the *Tobermory Hotel*, which makes a good effort to emphasize local produce, particularly seafood, while for something more exotic, *Javier's Restaurant* (℡01688/302350) above *MacGochan's* (see below) serves hearty Argentinian/Hispanic cuisine. A good option for imaginatively prepared meals using local produce is the pleasant upstairs café/bistro at the *Mull Pottery* at Ballinsgate, just on the edge of town (℡01688/302592), while *Ulva House* (℡01688/302044, ⓦwww.mull-shellfish.co.uk), located above the bay between An Tobar and the prominent *Western Isles Hotel*, is another notch up, serving uncomplicated but very well-prepared meals based around a platter of the island's finest seafood. Fine **picnic** fodder, fresh bread and goodies can be found at the excellent Island Bakery, also on the harbourfront.

The lively bar of the *Mishnish Hotel* has been the most popular local **drinking** hole for many years, and features live music at the weekend. Unfortunately, the place lost much of its character (and some of its custom) after a facelift, no doubt prompted by the arrival of *MacGochan's*, a purpose-built, though pleasant enough, pub, which also offers occasional live music, on the opposite side of the harbour near the distillery.

If you want to know what there is in the way of **entertainment** in Tobermory (or anywhere else on Mull), be sure to pick up the free monthly newsletter *Round & About*, and/or buy a copy of *Am Muileach*, the monthly island newspaper. It's worth checking the programme at An Tobar for concerts by touring musicians, while the Mull Theatre (℡01688/302828, ⓦwww.mulltheatre.com) uses various venues around the island for its widely acclaimed productions. If you want to watch a film, look out for the *Screen Machine* (ⓦwww.screenmachine .co.uk; bookings on ℡01463/720890, ⓦwww.thebooth.co.uk) which often pulls into town: a mobile cinema squeezed into the back of a specially converted articulated lorry, it can seat up to eighty people and shows fairly recent releases.

Dervaig and Calgary

The gently undulating countryside west of Tobermory, beyond the freshwater Mishnish lochs, provides some of the most beguiling scenery on the island.

Added to this, the road out west, the B8073, is exceptionally dramatic, with fiendish switchbacks much appreciated during the annual Mull Rally, which takes place each October. Loch Frisa, a long slash in the landscape south of the road, is a well-known nesting place for some of the island's **white-tailed (or sea) eagles**. There's a well-placed hide which has close-up, live CCTV pictures of the nest; if you're here between April and July, when the birds are nesting, guided access to the hide is available through the RSPB (£3; bookings on ☎01688/302038)

The only village of any size on this side of the island is **DERVAIG**, which nestles beside narrow Loch Chumhainn, just eight miles southwest of Tobermory, distinguished by its unusual pencil-shaped church spire and single street of dinky whitewashed cottages and old corrugated-iron shacks. Signposted off the main road a little beyond Dervaig, the **Old Byre Heritage Centre** (Easter–Oct Wed–Sun 10.30am–6.30pm; £3) shows a video on the island's history and has a gift-festooned tearoom.

Dervaig has a wide choice of **places to stay**. At the upper end of the scale, Victorian *Druimard Country House* (☎01688/400345, ⓦwww.druimard .co.uk; ❻), located on the fringe of Dervaig, is a pleasant, comfy place serving good dinners. There's also fine local food served at the *Druimnacroish Hotel* (☎01688/400274, ⓦwww.druimnacroish.co.uk; March–Nov; ❺), a lovely country house in a rural setting two miles out on the Salen road. There are several pleasant B&Bs, including the excellent *Cuin Lodge* (☎01688/400346, ⓦwww.cuin-lodge.mull.com; ❷), an old shooting lodge overlooking the loch, to the northwest of the village. There's also a **bunkhouse** (☎01688/400492) right in the centre of the village, with bedding provided and disabled facilities.

The road continues cross-country to **CALGARY**, once a thriving crofting community, now a quiet glen which opens out onto Mull's finest sandy bay, backed by low-lying dunes and machair, with wonderful views over to Coll and Tiree. A few hundred yards back from the beach is a cluster of buildings grouped around the delightful *Calgary Hotel* (☎01688/400256, ⓦwww.calgary .co.uk; March–Nov; ❺), one of the island's most pleasant hotels, with an art gallery, daytime café and the excellent, moderately priced *Dovecote* restaurant. Down by the beach itself, there's a small but spectacular spot for **camping** rough; the only facilities are the public toilets.

Salen and around

SALEN, on the east coast halfway between Craignure and Tobermory, lies at the narrowest point on Mull. There's not a great deal to the place, though a pair of beached fishing boats and the ivy-covered ruins of Gylen Castle might catch your eye as you pass through. There are, however, several decent places to stay in the vicinity, ranging from the **hostel**-style accommodation of *Arle Lodge* (☎01680/300299, ⓦwww.arlelodge.co.uk; ❷), with twin and family rooms four miles north of Salen on the road to Tobermory, to the pretty, Victorian *Gruline Home Farm* **B&B** (☎01680/300581, ⓦwww.gruline.com; dinner, bed & breakfast ❽), a non-working farmhouse four miles to the southwest near the shores of Loch Na Keal, which serves up extra special dinners (non-residents must reserve). Simpler, less expensive B&B is available next door at *Barn Cottage* (☎01680/300451, ⓦwww.holidaymull.org/barncottage; ❷). Salen itself has a very pleasant place to **eat**, *Mediterranea* (☎01680/300200, ⓦwww .mullonthemed.com), which mixes engaging Scottish hospitality with Sicilian cooking. You can also **rent bikes** here from *On Yer Bike* (☎01680/300501), which has mountain bikes, hybrids and child trailers to rent.

The Isle of Ulva

Ulva's (@www.ulva.mull.com) population peaked in the nineteenth century at a staggering 850, sustained by the huge quantities of kelp which were exported for glass and soap production. That was before the market for kelp collapsed and the 1846 potato famine hit, after which the remaining population was brutally evicted. Nowadays barely thirty people live here, and the island is littered with ruined crofts, not to mention a church, designed by Thomas Telford, which would once have seated over three hundred parishioners. It's great walking country, however, with several clearly marked paths crisscrossing the native woodland and the rocky heather moorland interior – and you're almost guaranteed to spot some of the abundant wildlife: at the very least deer, if not buzzards, golden eagles and even sea eagles, with seals and divers offshore. If you like to have a focus for your wanderings, head for the ruined crofting villages and basalt columns similar to those on Staffa along the island's southern coastline; for the island's highest point, Beinn Chreagach (1027ft); or along the north coast to Ulva's tidal neighbour, Gometra, off the west coast.

To **get to Ulva**, which lies just a hundred yards or so off the west coast of Mull, follow the signs for "Ulva Ferry" west from Salen or south from Calgary – if you've no transport, a postbus can get you there, but you'll have to make your own way back. From **Ulva Ferry**, a small bicycle/passenger-only ferry (£5 return) is available on demand (Mon–Fri 9am–5pm; June–Aug also Sun; at other times by arrangement on ☎01688 500226). *The Boathouse*, near the ferry slip on the Ulva side, serves as a licensed **tearoom** selling soup, cakes, snacks, Guinness and Ulva oysters. You can learn more about the history of the island from the **Heritage Centre** exhibition upstairs, and pop into the newly restored thatched smiddy nearby, housing **Sheila's Cottage**, which has been restored to something like its former state when islander Sheila MacFadyen used to live there in the first half of the last century. There's no accommodation, but with permission from the present owners (☎01688/500264, @ulva@mull.com) you can **camp** rough overnight.

The Isle of Staffa and the Treshnish Isles

Five miles southwest of Ulva, **Staffa** is the most romantic and dramatic of Scotland's many uninhabited islands. On its south side, the perpendicular rock-face features an imposing series of black basalt columns, known as the Colonnade, which have been cut by the sea into cathedralesque caverns, most notably **Fingal's Cave**. The Vikings knew about the island – the name derives from their word for "Island of Pillars" – but it wasn't until 1772 that it was "discovered" by the world. Turner painted it, Wordsworth explored it, but Mendelssohn's *Die Fingalshöhle* (the lovely "Hebrides" overture), inspired by the sounds of the sea-wracked caves he heard on a visit here in 1829, did most to popularize the place – after which Queen Victoria gave her blessing, too. Geologists say these polygonal basalt organ pipes were created some sixty million years ago by a massive subterranean explosion. A huge mass of molten basalt burst forth onto land and, as it cooled, solidified into what are, essentially, crystals. Of course, confronted with such artistry, most visitors have found it difficult to believe that their origin is entirely natural – indeed, the various Celtic folk tales, which suggest that the Giant's Causeway in Ireland reached all the way here before being destroyed by rival giants, are certainly more appealing. To **get to Staffa**, you can join one of the many boat trips from Fionnphort, Iona, Ulva Ferry, Dervaig or even Oban (see box on p.361 for full details).

△ Fingal's Cave, Staffa

Several operators also offer **boat trips** around the archipelago of uninhabited volcanic islets that make up the **Treshnish Isles** northwest of Staffa. None of the islands is more than a mile or two across, the most distinctive being **Bac Mór**, shaped like a puritan's hat and popularly dubbed the Dutchman's Cap. Most trips include a stopover on **Lunga**, the largest island, and a nesting place for hundreds of seabirds, in particular guillemots, razorbills (mid-May to July) and puffins (late April to mid-Aug), as well as a breeding ground for common seals (June) and Atlantic greys (early Sept). The two most northerly islands, **Cairn na Burgh More** and **Cairn na Burgh Beag**, have the remains of ruined castles, the first of which served as a lookout post for the Lords of the

Isles and was last garrisoned in the Civil War; Cairn na Burgh Beag hasn't been occupied since the 1715 Jacobite uprising.

Ben More and the Ardmeanach peninsula

From the southern shores of Loch na Keal, which almost splits Mull in two, rise the terraced slopes of **Ben More** (3169ft) – literally "big mountain" – a mighty extinct volcano, and the only Munro in the Hebrides outside of Skye. It's most easily climbed from Dhiseig, halfway along the loch's southern shores, though an alternative route is to climb up to the col between Beinn Fhada and A'Chioch, and approach via the mountain's eastern ridge. Further west along the shore the road carves through spectacular overhanging cliffs before heading south past the Gribun rocks which face the tiny island of **Inch Kenneth**, where Unity Mitford lived until her death in 1948. There are great views out to Staffa and the Treshnish Isles as the road leaves the coast behind, climbing over the pass to Loch Scribain, where it eventually joins the equally dramatic Glen More road (A849) from Craignure.

If you're properly equipped for walking, however, you can explore the **Ardmeanach peninsula**, to the west of the road, on foot. The area, which features a large sea cave and a fossilized tree, is NTS-owned and there is a car park just before *Tiroran House* (☎01681/705232, ⓦwww.tiroran.com; ❼), a beautiful secluded **hotel** with six rooms, cosy lounges, good home cooking and a lovely, lush, south-facing garden. They've also got a more affordable room (❺) for hikers tackling nearby Ben More.

The Ross of Mull

Stretching for twenty miles west as far as Iona is Mull's rocky southernmost peninsula, the **Ross of Mull**, which, like much of Scotland, appears blissfully tranquil in good weather, and desolate and bleak in bad. Most visitors simply drive through the Ross en route to Iona, but if you have the time it's definitely worth considering exploring, or even staying, in this little-visited part of Mull.

The most scenic spots on the Ross are hidden away on the south coast. If you're approaching the Ross from Craignure, the first of these (to Lochbuie) is signposted even before you've negotiated the splendid Highland pass of Glen More, which brings you to the Ross itself. The road to **LOCHBUIE** skirts Loch Spelve, a sheltered sea loch, followed by the freshwater Loch Uisg, which is fringed by woodland, before emerging, after eight miles, on a fertile plain beside the sea. The bay here is rugged and wide, and overlooked by the handsome peak of Ben Buie (2352ft), to the northwest. Hidden behind a patch of Scots pine are the ivy-strewn ruins of **Moy Castle**, an old MacLean stronghold; in the fields to the north is one of the few **stone circles** in the west of Scotland, dating from the second century BC, the tallest of its stones about 6ft high. The best accommodation in the vicinity is at *Barrachandroman* (☎01680/814220, ⓦwww.barrachandroman.co.uk; ❸), a converted stone barn in Kinlochspelve, overlooking the sea loch. A popular and fairly easy walk is the five-mile hike west along the coastal path to Carsaig (see p.368).

The main A849 road, single-track (for the most part) and plagued by the large number of coaches that steam down it en route to Iona, hugs the northern coastline of the Ross. The first sign of civilization after Glen More is the small pub, the *Kinloch Hotel*, with an adjoining shop, followed a mile or so later by the tiny settlement of **PENNYGHAEL**, home to the *Pennyghael Hotel* (☎01681/704288, ⓦwww.pennyghaelhotel.com; ❼), which has a good restaurant serving local meat and seafood.

A rickety single-track road heads south for four miles from Pennygael to **CARSAIG**, which enjoys an idyllic setting, looking south out to Colonsay, Islay and Jura. Carsaig is home to the Inniemore School of Painting, but most folk come here either to walk east to Lochbuie (see p.367), or west under the cliffs, to the **Nuns' Cave**, where nuns from Iona are alleged to have hidden during the Reformation, and then, after four miles or so, at Malcolm's Point, the spectacular **Carsaig Arches**, formed by eroded sea caves, which are linked to basalt cliffs.

Meanwhile, the main road continues for another eleven miles to **BUNESSAN**, the largest village on the peninsula, roughly two-thirds of the way along the Ross. Bunessan has a few useful shops, and a pub and a tearoom, but is otherwise pretty undistinguished.

If the weather's good, it might be worth heading off from Bunessan to the sandy bays of the south coast. There's a car park near the *Ardachy House Hotel* (T01681/700505, Wwww.ardachy.co.uk; March–Oct; ➎) – so remote that there's no TV reception – which overlooks the wide expanse of **Ardalanish Bay**, or you can continue to the more sheltered bay of sand and granite outcrops at neighbouring **UISKEN**, a mile to the east. Overlooking the latter is *Uisken Croft* (T01681/700307; March–Oct; ➋), a welcoming, modern B&B, a stone's throw from the beach, where you can camp. From Uisken, the Lorn Ferry Service (April to mid-Oct; T01951/200320) runs a **passenger-only ferry** to Colonsay (Tues & Sat), though you should phone ahead to check times and book your journey.

The road ends at **FIONNPHORT**, facing Iona, probably the least attractive place to stay on the Ross, though it has a nice sandy bay backed by pink granite rocks to the north of the ferry slipway. Partly to ease congestion on Iona, and to give their neighbours a slice of the tourist pound, Fionnphort was chosen as the site for the **Columba Centre** (Easter–Sept daily 10.30am–1pm & 2–5.30pm; free); inside, a small exhibition outlines Iona's history, tells a little of Columba's life (for more on which, see box opposite), and has a few facsimiles of the illuminated manuscripts produced by the island's monks.

If you're in need of a **B&B** in Fionnphort (keeping in mind that it's limited on Iona itself), try the granite *Seaview* (T01681/700235, Wwww.seaview-mull .co.uk; ➋) or the whitewashed *Staffa House* (T01681/700677, Wwww .staffahouse.co.uk; ➌), both of which are close to the ferry and the local pub, the *Keel Row*, which serves reasonable meals. Just out of Fionnphort (no bad thing), there's also *Achaban House* (T01681/700205, Wwww.achabanhouse.co.uk; ➌), an old manse with some character overlooking Loch Pottie. The basic *Fidden Farm* **campsite** (T01681/700427; April–Sept), a mile south along the Knockvologan road by Fidden beach, is the nearest to Iona. Fidden beach looks out to the **Isle of Erraid**, where Robert Louis Stevenson is believed to have written *Kidnapped* while staying in one of the island's cottages. **Bikes** for exploring the quiet roads of the Ross can be rented from *Seaview* B&B.

Isle of Iona

Ross: Where is Duncan's body?
Macduff: Carried to Colme-kill,
The sacred storehouse of his predecessors,
And guardian of their bones.

William Shakespeare, Macbeth (Act II, Scene 4)

Less than a mile off the southwest tip of Mull, **IONA** (Wwww.isle-of-iona .com) – just three miles long and not much more than a mile wide – has been

St Columba

Legend has it that **St Columba** (Colum Cille), born in Donegal some time around 521, was a direct descendant of the semi-legendary Irish king, Niall of the Nine Hostages. A scholar and soldier priest, who founded numerous monasteries in Ireland, he is thought to have become involved in a bloody dispute with the king when he refused to hand over a copy of *St Jerome's Psalter*, copied illegally from the original owned by St Finian of Moville. This, in turn, provoked the Battle of Cúl Drebene (Cooldrumman) – also known as the **Battle of the Book** – at which Columba's forces won, though with the loss of over three thousand lives. The story goes that, repenting this bloodshed, Columba went into exile with twelve other monks, eventually settling on Iona in 563, allegedly because it was the first island he encountered from which he couldn't see his homeland. The bottom line, however, is that we know very little about Columba, though he undoubtedly became something of a cult figure after his death in 597. He was posthumously credited with miraculous feats such as defeating the Loch Ness monster – it only had to hear his voice and it recoiled in terror – and casting out snakes (and, some say, frogs) from the island. He is also famously alleged to have banned women and cows from Iona, exiling them to Eilean nam Ban (Woman's Island), just north of Fionnphort, for, as he believed, "where there is a cow there is a woman, and where there is a woman there is mischief."

a place of pilgrimage for several centuries, and a place of Christian worship for more than 1400 years. For it was to this flat Hebridean island that St Columba fled from Ireland in 563 and established a monastery which was responsible for the conversion of more or less all of pagan Scotland as well as much of northern England. This history and the island's splendid isolation have lent it a peculiar religiosity; in the much-quoted words of Dr Johnson, who visited in 1773, "that man is little to be envied . . . whose piety would not grow warmer among the ruins of Iona." Today, however, the island can barely cope with the constant flood of day-trippers, so to appreciate the special atmosphere and to have time to see the whole island, including the often overlooked west coast, you should plan on staying at least one night.

Some history

Whatever the truth about Columba's life (see box above), in the sixth and seventh centuries Iona enjoyed a great deal of autonomy from Rome, establishing a specifically **Celtic Christian** tradition. Missionaries were sent out to the rest of Scotland and parts of England, and Iona quickly became a respected seat of learning and artistry; the monks compiled a vast library of intricately **illuminated manuscripts** – most famously the *Book of Kells* (now on display in Trinity College, Dublin) – while the masons excelled in carving peculiarly intricate crosses. Two factors were instrumental in the demise of the Celtic tradition: a series of Viking raids, the worst of which was the massacre of 68 monks on the sands of Martyrs' Bay in 806; and relentless pressure from the established Church, beginning with the Synod of Whitby in 664, which chose Rome over the Celtic Church, and culminated in its suppression by King David I in 1144.

In 1203, Iona became part of the mainstream Church with the establishment of an **Augustinian nunnery** and a **Benedictine monastery** by Reginald, son of Somerled, Lord of the Isles. During the Reformation, the entire complex was ransacked, the contents of the library burnt and all but three of the island's 360 crosses destroyed. Although plans were drawn up at various times to turn the abbey into a Cathedral of the Isles, nothing came of them until in 1899, when the (then) owner, the eighth duke of Argyll, donated the abbey buildings to the **Church of Scotland**, who restored the abbey church for worship over the course of the next decade. Iona's modern resurgence began in 1938, when **George MacLeod**, a minister from Glasgow, established a group of ministers, students and artisans to begin rebuilding the remainder of the monastic buildings. What began as a mostly male, Gaelic-speaking, strictly Presbyterian community is today a lay, mixed and ecumenical retreat. The entire abbey complex has been successfully restored, and is now looked after by Historic Scotland, while the island, apart from the church land and a few crofts, is in the care of the NTS.

Baile Mór

The passenger ferry from Fionnphort drops you off at the island's main village, **BAILE MÓR** (literally "Large Village"), which is in fact little more than a single terrace of cottages facing the sea. Just inland lie the extensive pink granite ruins of the **Augustinian nunnery**, disused since the Reformation. A beautifully maintained garden now occupies the cloisters, and if nothing else

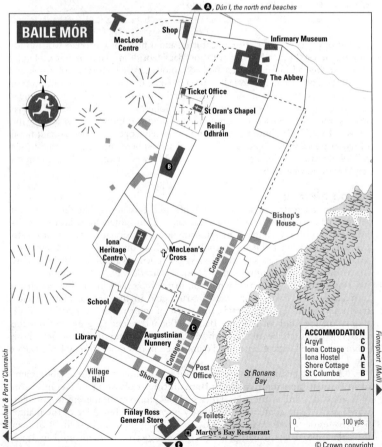

BAILE MÓR

A, Dún I, the north end beaches

MacLeod Centre

Shop

Infirmary Museum

The Abbey

Ticket Office

St Oran's Chapel

Reilig Odhráin

Bishop's House

Iona Heritage Centre

MacLean's Cross

Cottages

School

Library

Augustinian Nunnery

Village Hall

Shops

Post Office

St Ronans Bay

Finlay Ross General Store

Toilets

Martyr's Bay Restaurant

Machair & Port a'Clunraich

Fionnphort (Mull)

ACCOMMODATION
Argyll — C
Iona Cottage — D
Iona Hostel — A
Shore Cottage — E
St Columba — B

0   100 yds

© Crown copyright

the complex gives you an idea of the state of the present-day abbey before it was restored. Across the road to the north, housed in a manse built, like the nearby parish church, by the ubiquitous Thomas Telford, is the **Iona Heritage Centre** (Easter–Oct Mon–Sat 10.30am–4.30pm; £2), with displays on the social history of the island over the last two hundred years, including the Clearances, which nearly halved the island's population of five hundred in the mid-nineteenth century. At a bend in the road, just south of the manse and church, stands the fifteenth-century **MacLean's Cross**, a fine late medieval example of the distinctive, flowing, three-leaved foliage of the Iona school.

Iona Abbey

No buildings remain from Columba's time: the present **abbey** (daily: April–Sept 9.30am–6.30pm; Oct–March 9.30am–4.30pm; HS; £3.30) dates from the arrival of the Benedictines in around 1200; it was extensively rebuilt in the fifteenth and sixteenth centuries, and restored virtually wholesale last century. Iona's oldest building, the plain-looking **St Oran's Chapel**, lies south of the abbey, to your right, and boasts an eleventh-century door. Legend has it that the original chapel could only be completed through human sacrifice. Oran apparently volunteered to be buried alive, and was found to have survived the ordeal when the grave was opened a few days later. Declaring that he had seen hell and it wasn't all bad, he was promptly reinterred for blasphemy.

Oran's Chapel stands at the centre of Iona's sacred burial ground, **Reilig Odhráin** (Oran's Cemetery), which is said to contain the graves of sixty kings of Norway, Ireland, France and Scotland, including Duncan and Macbeth. The best of the early Christian gravestones and medieval effigies which once

△ Cloisters, Iona Abbey

lay in the Reilig Odhráin have unfortunately been removed to the Infirmary Museum, behind the abbey, and to various other locations within the complex. The graveyard is still used as a cemetery by the island, however, and also contains the grave of the short-lived leader of the Labour Party, **John Smith** (1938–94), who was a frequent visitor to Iona, though he himself was born in the town of Ardrishaig.

Approaching the abbey itself, from the ticket office, you cross an exposed section of the evocative medieval **Street of the Dead**, whose giant pink granite cobbles once stretched from the abbey, past St Oran's Chapel, to the village. Beside the road stands the most impressive of Iona's Celtic high crosses, the eighth-century **St Martin's Cross**, smothered with figural scenes – the Virgin and Child at the centre, Daniel in the lions' den, Abraham sacrificing Isaac and David with musicians in the shaft below. The reverse side features Pictish serpent-and-boss decoration. Standing directly in front of the abbey are the base of St Matthew's Cross (the rest of which is in the Infirmary Museum) and, to the left, a concrete cast of the eighth-century **St John's Cross**, decorated with serpent-and-boss and Celtic spiral ornamental panels. Before you enter the abbey, take a look inside **St Columba's Shrine**, a small steep-roofed chamber to the left of the main entrance. Columba is believed to have been buried either here or under the rocky mound to the west of the abbey, known as Tórr an Aba.

The **Abbey** itself has been simply and sensitively restored to incorporate the original elements. You can spot many of the medieval capitals in the south aisle of the choir and in the south transept, where the white marble effigies of the eighth duke of Argyll and his wife, Ina, lie in a side-chapel – an incongruous piece of Victorian pomp in an otherwise modest and tranquil place. The finest pre-Reformation effigy is that of John MacKinnon, the last abbot of Iona, who died around 1500, and now lies on the south side of the choir steps. For reasons of sanitation, the **cloisters** were placed, contrary to the norm, on the north side of the church (where running water was available); entirely reconstructed in the late 1950s, they now shelter lots of medieval grave slabs, a useful historical account of the abbey's development. There are free daily guided tours of the abbey (the times are posted up at the ticket office).

The rest of the island

Not many day-visitors get further than the village and abbey, but it's perfectly possible to walk to the stunning sandy beaches and turquoise seas at the **north end** of the island, or up to the highest point, **Dún I**, a mere 328ft above sea level but with views on a clear day to Skye, Tiree and Jura. Alternatively, it takes about half an hour to walk over to the **machair**, or common grazing land, on the west side of Iona, which lies adjacent to the evocatively named Bay at the Back of the Ocean, a crescent of pebble and shell-strewn sand with a spouting cave to the south. Those with more time (2–3hr) might hike over to the **south** of the island, where Port a' Churaich ("Bay of the Coracle", also known as St Columba's Bay), the saint's traditional landing place on Iona, is filled with smooth round rocks and multicoloured pebbles and stones.

Practicalities

There's no **tourist office** on Iona, and as demand far exceeds supply you should organize **accommodation** well in advance. Of the island's two **hotels**, the stone-built *Argyll* (☎01681/700334, ⓦwww.argyllhoteliona.co.uk; ⓞ), in the village's terrace of cottages overlooking the Sound of Iona, is by far the nicer, although the larger alternative, the *St Columba Hotel* (℡01681/700304, Ⓦwww.stcolumba-hotel.co.uk; ❻), has been improving recently. As for **B&Bs**, try *Iona Cottage* (℡01681/700579, Ⓔck@ionacottage.freeserve.co.uk; ❷), which overlooks the jetty, or *Shore Cottage* (℡01681/700744, Ⓦwww.shorecottage.co.uk; Jan–Oct; ❷), a short walk south. **Camping** is not permitted on Iona, but there is a terrific ⚑ **hostel** (℡01681/700781, Ⓦwww.ionahostel.co.uk) at the north of the island, where the main room is filled with lovely wooden furniture and huge picture windows look out to the Treshnish Islands. If you want to stay with the **Iona Community** (℡01681/700404, Ⓦwww.iona.org.uk), either in the abbey itself or the *MacLeod Centre* (popularly known as "The Mac"), you must book well in advance and be prepared to participate fully in the daily activities, prayers and religious services. **Eating** options aren't bad: the restaurant at the *Argyll* is notable for its home-grown vegetables and organic produce, though it's worth booking ahead to confirm there's a table; the *St Columba* has more space for lunches and dinners, and the pub grub at the bar adjoining the *Martyr's Bay Restaurant* by the jetty is reasonable too, often serving up locally caught seafood. For something lighter during the day, head for the basic tearoom beside the Heritage Centre (Mon–Fri 11am–3.30pm), which serves home-made soup and tasty cakes.

Visitors are not allowed to bring cars onto the island, but **bikes** can be rented in Fionnphort (see p.368) or from the Finlay Ross general store in the village (℡01681/700357). There's also a taxi on the island. Some of the Mull-based **boat trips** (see box on p.361) include Iona and Staffa on their itinerary, while a couple of local operators, Iolaire and Gordon Grant Marine, do the majority of the trips to Staffa. Also based on Iona, Mark Jardine's Alternative Boat Hire (℡01681/700537, Ⓦwww.boattripsiona.com) takes the lovely wooden gaff-rigged sailing boat *Freya* on short trips to some of the less-visited spots around the Sound of Iona and Erraid.

Coll and Tiree

Coll and **Tiree** are among the most isolated of the Inner Hebrides, and if anything have more in common with the outlying Western Isles than with their closest neighbour, Mull. Each is roughly twelve miles long and three miles wide, both are low-lying, treeless and exceptionally windy, with white sandy beaches and the highest sunshine records in Scotland. Like most of the Hebrides, they were once ruled by Vikings, and didn't pass into Scottish hands until the thirteenth century.

In the 1830s Coll's population peaked at 1440, Tiree's at a staggering 4450, but both were badly affected by the Clearances, which virtually halved their populations in a generation. Coll was fortunate to be in the hands of the enlightened MacLeans, but they were forced to sell in 1856 to the Stewart family, who sold two-thirds of the island to a Dutch millionaire in the 1960s. Tiree was ruthlessly cleared by its owner, the duke of Argyll, who sent in the marines in 1885 to evict the crofters. After the passing of the Crofters' Act the following year, the island was divided into crofts, though it remains a part of the duke of Argyll's estate. Both islands have strong Gaelic roots, but the percentage of English-speaking newcomers is rising steadily.

The CalMac **ferry** from Oban calls at Coll (2hr 40min) daily except Thursdays and Fridays, and at Tiree daily (3hr 40min); in winter, the ferry calls at both islands on Tuesdays, Thursdays and Saturdays. On Thursdays – though the day may change – the ferry continues on to Barra in the Western Isles, and calls in at Tiree on the way back, making it possible to visit on a **day-trip from Oban**; a minibus tour of the island is thrown in as part of the package. Tiree also has an **airport** with daily flights (Mon–Sat) to and from Glasgow. The majority of visitors on both islands stay for at least a week in self-catering accommodation (see opposite), though there are B&Bs and hotels on the islands. Choice is limited, however, so it's as well to book as far in advance as possible (and that goes for the ferry crossing, too).

Isle of Coll

The fish-shaped rocky island of **Coll** (ⓌWww.isleofcoll.org), with a population of around a hundred, lies less than seven miles off the coast of Mull. The CalMac ferry drops off at Coll's only real village, **ARINAGOUR**, whose whitewashed cottages line the western shore of Loch Eatharna, a popular safe anchorage for boats. Half the island's population lives in the village, and it's here you'll find the island's hotel and pub, post office, churches and a couple of shops; two miles northwest along the Arnabost road, there's even a golf course. The island's petrol pump is also in Arinagour, and is run on a volunteer basis – it's basically open when the ferry arrives.

On the southwest coast there are two edifices, both confusingly known as **Breachacha Castle**, and both built by the MacLeans. The older, at the head of Loch Breachacha, is a fifteenth-century tower house with an additional curtain wall, now used by Project Trust overseas aid volunteers. The less attractive "new castle", to the northwest, is made up of a central block built around 1750 and two side pavilions added a century later, and is used as holiday cottages. It was here that Dr Johnson and Boswell stayed in 1773 after a storm forced them to take refuge en route to Mull – Johnson considered the place to be "a mere tradesman's box". Much of the area around the castles is now owned by the RSPB, in the hope of protecting the island's precious corncrake population. At Totronald, north of the castles, there is a small RSPB information point, and the warden does guided walks on a Wednesday. A vast area of **giant sand dunes** lies to the west of the castles, with two glorious golden sandy bays stretching for over a mile on either side. At the far western end, is *Caolas*, where you can get a cup of tea and home-baked goodies – you can also stay there (see opposite).

For an overview of the whole island, and a fantastic Hebridean panorama, you can follow in Johnson and Boswell's footsteps and take a wander up **Ben Hogh** – at 339ft, Coll's highest point – two miles west of Arinagour, close to the shore. On the summit is a giant boulder known as an "erratic", perilously perched on three small boulders. The island's northwest coast boasts some of the finest sandy beaches in the Hebrides, which take the full brunt of the Atlantic winds. When the Stewart family took over the island in 1856, and raised the rents, the island's population moved wholesale from the more fertile southeast, to this part of the island. However, overcrowding led to widespread emigration; a few of the old crofts in Bousd and Sorisdale, at Coll's northernmost tip, have more recently been restored. From here, there's an impressive view over to the headland, the Small Isles and the Skye Cuillin beyond.

Practicalities

In Arinagour, the small, family-run *Coll Hotel* (Ⓣ01879/230334, ⓌWww .collhotel.co.uk; ❸) provides excellent **accommodation**. Otherwise, there are a couple of B&Bs to choose from: *Tigh-na-Mara* (Ⓣ01879/230354; ❷), a purpose-built guesthouse near the pier, and *Achamore* (☎01879/230430; ❶), a traditional nineteenth-century farmhouse B&B, just north of Arinagour. Or, if you really want to get away from it all, book in at *Caolas* (☎01879/230438, 🖥 www .caolas.net; full board ❺), a restored farmhouse on the remote western side of the island – phone ahead and your friendly hosts will pick you up and drive you across the sand; you can also stay at their nice, compact **self-catering** bothy (❸) and bikes and boats are available for guests. *Garden House* (☎01879/230374), down a track on the left before the turn-off for the castles, runs a **campsite** in the shelter of what was formerly a walled garden; wild camping is also possible on Coll – your best bet is to contact the hotel. The *Coll Hotel* doubles as the island's social centre, does excellent **meals** and has a dining-room overflow. Another good eating option is the *First Port of Coll* café, in the old harbour stores overlooking the bay, which offers hot meals all day. For **bike rental**, go to Taigh Solas (☎01879/230216), opposite the post office.

Isle of Tiree

Tiree (🖥 www.isleoftiree.com), as its Gaelic name *tir-iodh* (land of corn) suggests, was once known as the breadbasket of the Inner Hebrides, thanks to its acres of rich machair. Nowadays crofting and tourism are the main sources of income for the resident population of around 750. One of the most distinctive features of Tiree is its architecture, in particular the large numbers of "pudding" or "spotty" houses, where only the mortar is painted white. In addition, there are numerous "white houses" (*tigh geal*) and traditional "blackhouses" (*tigh dubh*). Wildlife lovers can also have a field day on Tiree, with lapwings, wheat-ears, redshank, greylag geese and large, laid-back brown hares in abundance. And, with no shortage of wind, Tiree's sandy beaches attract large numbers of windsurfers for the Tiree Wave Classic (🖥 www.tireewaveclassic.com) every October.

The CalMac ferry calls at Gott Bay Pier, now best known for **An Turas** (The Journey), Tiree's award-winning "shelter", which features two parallel white walls connected via a black felt section to a glass box which punctures a stone dyke and frames a seaview. As a shelter, it's a bit of a non-starter, and as a contemplative space with a good view, it is in direct competition with the CalMac waiting room. Just up the road from the pier is the village of **SCARINISH**, home to a post office, some public toilets, a supermarket, the butcher's and the bank, with a petrol pump back at the pier. Also in Scarinish you'll find **An Iodhlann** (June–Sept Tues–Fri noon–5pm; Oct–May Mon–Fri 10.30am–3.30pm; £3; 🖥 www.tireearchive.com) – meaning "haystack" in Gaelic – the island's two-roomed archive which puts on occasional summer exhibitions.

To the east of Scarinish, **Gott Bay** is backed by a two-mile stretch of sand, and just one mile to the north is Vaul Bay, on the north coast, where the well-preserved remains of a dry-stone broch, **Dun Mor** – dating from the first century BC – lie hidden in the rocks to the west of the bay. From here it's another two miles west along the coast to the Clach a'Choire or **Ringing Stone**, a huge glacial boulder decorated with mysterious prehistoric mark-ings, which when struck with a stone gives out a metallic sound, thus giving rise to the legend that inside is a crock of gold. The story goes that, should the Ringing Stone ever be broken in two, Tiree will sink beneath the waves. A mile further west you come to the lovely **Balephetrish Bay**, where you can watch waders feeding in the breakers, and look out to sea to Skye and the Western Isles.

△ Windsurfing, Tiree

The most intriguing sights, however, lie in the bulging western half of the island, where Tiree's two landmark hills rise up. The higher of the two, **Ben Hynish** (463ft), is unfortunately occupied by a "golf-ball" radar station, which tracks incoming transatlantic flights; the views from the top, though, are great. Below Ben Hynish, to the east is **HYNISH**, with its recently restored **harbour**, designed by Alan Stevenson in the 1830s to transport building materials for the magnificent 140-foot-tall **Skerryvore Lighthouse**, which lies on a seaswept reef some twelve miles southwest of Tiree. The harbour features an ingenious reservoir to prevent silting, and up on the hill behind, beside the row of lighthouse keepers' houses, a stumpy granite signal tower. The tower, whose signals used to be the only contact the lighthouse keepers had with civilization, now houses a **museum** telling the history of the herculean effort required to erect the lighthouse; weather permitting, you can see the lighthouse from the tower's viewing platform.

On the other side of Ben Hynish, a mile or so across the golden sands of Balephuil Bay, is the spectacular headland of **Ceann a'Mhara** (pronounced "kenavara"), home to thousands of seabirds, including fulmars, kittiwakes, guillemots, razorbills, shags and cormorants, with gannets and terns feeding offshore. In the scattered west coast settlement of **SANDAIG**, to the north of Ceann a'Mhara, three thatched white houses in a row have been turned into the **Taigh Iain Mhoir** (June–Sept Mon–Fri 2–4pm; free), which gives an insight into how the majority of islanders lived in the nineteenth century.

Practicalities

If you're arriving at the **airport**, about three miles west of Scarinish, you should arrange for your hosts to collect you (most will). Tiree has a Ring'n' Ride **minibus** service (Mon–Sat 7am–6pm, Tues until 10pm; (℡01879/220419) which will take you anywhere on the island; **bike rental** (℡01879/220428) or MacLennans **car rental** (℡01879/220555) are the

other options, not to mention **pony trekking** (☎01879/220881, ⓦwww
.tireeonhorseback.co.uk).

The island has two **hotels**: the newly refurbished *Scarinish* (☎01879/220308,
ⓦwww.tireescarinishhotel.com; ❹), overlooking the old harbour, and the *Tiree
Lodge* (☎01879/220368; ❷), a mile or so east of Scarinish along Gott Bay. Other
options include the *Kirkapol House* (☎01879/220729, ⓦwww.kirkapoltiree.
co.uk; ❸), a friendly **B&B** in a tastefully converted kirk beyond the *Tiree Lodge*,
and *Glebe House* (☎01879/220758; ❺), the renovated former manse overlooking
the pier in Scarinish. Good **hostel** accommodation is available at the *Millhouse*
(☎01879/220435, ⓦwww.tireemillhouse.co.uk), near Loch Bhasapol, in the
northwest of the island, either in bunks or twins (❶). There's no official campsite,
but **camping** is allowed with the local crofter's permission.

As for **eating**, the bar meals at both the *Scarnish* and *Tiree Lodge* are good, and
there are unpretentious snacks and meals available at the pine-clad *Rural Centre*
café by the airport. For a **map** of the island and the daily papers, you need to
go to the supermarket at Crossapol.

Isle of Colonsay

Isolated between Mull and Islay, the **Isle of Colonsay** (ⓦwww.colonsay.org
.uk) – eight miles by three at its widest – is nothing like as bleak and windswept
as Coll or Tiree. Its craggy, heather-backed hills even support the occasional
patch of woodland, plus a bewildering array of plant and birdlife, wild goats and
rabbits, and one of the finest quasi-tropical gardens in Scotland. The population
is currently around a hundred, down from a pre-Clearance peak of just under a
thousand. With no camping allowed, only one hotel and infrequent ferry links
with the mainland, there's no fear of mass tourism taking over.

The CalMac ferry terminal is at **SCALASAIG**, on the east coast, where
there's a post office/shop, a petrol pump, a restaurant and the island's hotel.
Right by the pier, the old waiting room now serves as the island's heritage
centre and is usually open when the ferry docks. Two miles north of Scalasaig,
inland at **KILORAN**, is **Colonsay House**, built in 1722 by Malcolm MacNeil.
In 1904, the island and house were bought by Lord Strathcona, who made his
fortune building the Canadian Pacific Railway (and whose descendants still own
the island). He was also responsible for the house's lovely woodland **gardens**
(April–Sept Wed & Fri), which are slowly being restored to their former glory.
The outbuildings are now holiday cottages and you're free to wander round the
woodland garden to the south, and inspect the strange eighth-century **Riasg
Buidhe Cross**, to the east of the house, decorated with an unusually lifelike
mug shot (possibly of a monk).

To the north of Colonsay House, where the road ends, you'll find the island's
finest sandy beach, the breathtaking **Kiloran Bay**, where the breakers roll in
from the Atlantic. There's another unspoilt sandy beach backed by dunes at
Balnahard, two miles northeast along a rough track; en route, you might spot
wild goats, choughs and even a golden eagle.

Isle of Oronsay

Whilst on Colonsay, most folk take a day out to visit the **Isle of Oronsay** (sometimes written as Oranasay), which lies half a mile to the south and contains the
ruins of an Augustinian priory. The two islands are separated by "The Strand",
a stretch of tidal mudflats which act as a causeway for two hours either side

of low tide (check locally for timings); you can drive over to the island at low tide, though mostly people park their cars and walk across. Although legends (and etymology) link SS Columba and Oran with both Colonsay and Oronsay, the ruins actually only date back as far as the fourteenth century. Abandoned since the Reformation and now roofless, you can, nevertheless, still make out the original church and tiny cloisters. The highlight is the **Oronsay Cross**, a superb example of late medieval artistry from Iona which, along with thirty or so beautifully carved grave slabs, can be found in the restored side chapel. It takes about an hour to walk from the tip of Colonsay across the Strand to the priory (wellington boots are a good option).

Practicalities

CalMac **ferries** call daily except Tuesday and Saturday from Oban (2hr 15min); once a week from Kennacraig via Islay (Wed; 3hr 35min), when a day-trip is possible, giving you around six hours on the island. There's also the passenger/bicycle-only Lorn Ferry Service (April to mid-Oct; ☎01951/200320), which runs timetabled services to Uisken on the Ross of Mull (Tues & Sun), Tarbert on Jura (Tues & Fri), and Bunnahabhainn and Port Askaig on Islay (Mon), though you should phone ahead to check times and book your journey.

The island's only **hotel**, the *Isle of Colonsay* (☎01951/200316, ✉reception@thecolonsay.com; ❻), is a cosy eighteenth-century inn at heart, within easy walking distance of the pier in Scalasaig; it serves very decent bar snacks and acts as the island's social centre. The best alternative is to stay at the superb ☆ *Seaview* **B&B** (☎01951/200315; April–Oct; ❸), run by the charming Lawson family in Kilchattan on the west coast – it's well worth booking in for dinner, too. Camping is not normally permitted on the island so the budget option is to sleep at the *Keepers' Lodge* in Kiloran (☎01951/200312), a very comfortable **hostel** with a real fire. Most people who visit the island, however, stay in **self-catering accommodation**, the majority of which is run by the Colonsay Estate (phone as for hostel), who offer a whole range of cottages. It's also possible to book self-catering places at the aforementioned *Seaview* or, for short or long lets, you can book one of the lodges behind the hotel run by *Isle of Colonsay Lodges* (☎01951/200320).

An alternative to **eating out** at the hotel bar is *The Pantry*, above the pier in Scalasaig, which offers simple home-cooking as well as teas and cakes (ring ahead if you want to eat in the evening; ☎01951/200325). If you fancy the famous Colonsay oysters or wildflower honey, contact Andrew Abrahams at Pollgorm (☎01951/200365). All accommodation (and ferry crossings) need to be booked well in advance for the summer; self-catering cottages tend to be booked from Friday to Friday, because of the ferries. A **bus** meets the Wednesday ferry and will take folk around the island, and there's a limited **postbus** service. The hotel, *Seaview* and Archie McConnel (☎01951/200355) will rent out **bikes**. If you need a map or any books on the Highlands and Islands, go to the very well-stocked **bookshop** next door to the hotel.

Mid-Argyll

Mid-Argyll is a vague term which loosely describes the central wedge of land south of Oban and north of Kintyre. **Lochgilphead**, on the shores of Loch Fyne is the chief town in the area, though it has little to offer beyond its practical uses – it has a tourist office, a good supermarket, several banks and is the regional transport hub, though, on the whole, public transport is thin on the ground. The highlights of this gently undulating scenery lie along the sharply indented west coast. Closest to Oban are the melancholy former slate mining settlements of Seil, Easdale and Luing, known collectively as the **Slate Islands**. Further south, **Arduaine Gardens** are among Argyll's most celebrated horticultural attractions, while the rich Bronze Age and Neolithic remains in the **Kilmartin** valley comprise one of the most important prehistoric sites in Scotland. Just to the south, separating Kilmartin Glen from the **Knapdale** peninsula, is the **Crinan Canal**, a short cut for boats disinclined to round the Mull of Kintyre, which ends in the pint-sized, picturesque port of **Crinan**.

The Slate Islands

Just eight miles south of Oban, a road heads off the A816 west to a small group of islands commonly called the **Slate Islands** (Ⓦwww.slate.org.uk), which at their peak in the mid-nineteenth century quarried over nine million slates annually. Today many of the old slate villages are sparsely populated, and an inevitable air of melancholy hangs over them, but their dramatic setting amid crashing waves makes for a rewarding day-trip.

Isle of Seil

The most northerly of the Slate Islands is **Seil**, a lush island, now something of an exclusive enclave. It's separated from the mainland only by the thinnest of sea channels and spanned by an elegant humpback **Clachan Bridge**, built in 1793 and popularly known as the "Bridge over the Atlantic". The pub next door to the bridge is the *Tigh na Truish* (House of the Trousers), where kilt-wearing islanders would change into trousers to conform to the post-1745 ban on Highland dress. The nearby *Willowburn Hotel* (☎01852/300276, Ⓦwww .willowburn.co.uk; March–Nov; ❼) is the **accommodation** of choice on Seil; a peaceful and very comfortable hotel overlooking Seil Sound, with an excellent restaurant to boot – all rates include dinner, bed and breakfast.

The main village on Seil is **ELLENABEICH**, its neat white terraces of workers' cottages – featured in the film *Ring of Bright Water* – crouching below black cliffs on the westernmost tip of the island. This was once the tiny island of Eilean a'Beithich (hence Ellenabeich) separated from the mainland by a slim sea channel until the intensive slate quarrying succeeded in silting it up. Confusingly, the village is often referred to by the same name as the nearby island of Easdale, since they formed an interdependent community based exclusively around the slate industry. The **Scottish Slate Islands Heritage Centre** (April–Oct daily 10.30am–5pm; £2) is housed in one of the little white cottages. The best feature of the exhibition is the model of the slate quarry as it would have been at the height of its fame in the nineteenth century.

For a good range of snacks, including locally caught **fish and seafood**, pop inside the *Oyster Brewery* (☎01852/300121, Ⓦwww.oysterbrewery.com; restaurant open lunch & dinner) on the way to the ferry, which also brews its own ale. High-adrenalin **boat trips** are offered by Sea.fari Adventures (☎01852/300003, Ⓦwww.seafari.co.uk), who are based at the Ellenabeich jetty; the boats are rigid inflatables (RIBs) and travel at some speed round the offshore islands and through the Corryvreckan Whirlpool (see box on p.380).

Isle of Easdale

Easdale remains an island, though the few hundred yards that separate it from Ellanabeich have to be dredged to keep the channel open. Up to the eve of a great storm on November 23, 1881, Easdale supported an incredible 452 inhabitants, despite being less than a mile across at any one point. That night, waves engulfed the island and flooded the quarries. The island never really recovered; slate quarrying stopped in 1914, and by the 1960s the population was reduced to single figures.

Recently many of the old workers' cottages have been restored: some as holiday homes, others sold to new families (the present population is now approaching sixty). One of the cottages houses the interesting **Easdale Folk Museum** (daily: April–Oct 10.30am–5.30pm; £2), near the main square, selling a useful historical map of the island, which you can walk round in about half an hour. The **ferry** from Ellenabeich runs on demand (press the buttons in the ferry shed or phone ℡01586/552056), and there's *The Puffer* **bar/restaurant** (℡01852/300579, ⊛www.pufferbar.com; closed Mon, Wed & Sun eves) if you've failed to put together a picnic.

With lots of wonderfully flat stones freely available, Easdale makes the perfect venue for the annual **World Stone Skimming Championships** (⊛www.stoneskimming.com), held on the last Sunday of September.

Isle of Luing

To the south of Seil, across the narrow, treacherous Cuan Sound lies **Luing** (⊛www.isleofluing.co.uk) – pronounced "Ling" – a long, thin, fertile island renowned for its beef and for the chocolate-brown crossbreed named after it. A council-run car **ferry** (Mon–Sat 7.30am–6pm; Sun 11am–6am mid-June to Aug also Mon–Sat 6.30–10pm) crosses the Cuan Sound every half-hour or so, though foot passengers can cross until later in the evening (Mon–Thurs 8am–10pm, Fri & Sat 8am–11.30pm, Sun 11am–6pm). There's a decent **postbus** service on Luing itself (Mon–Sat).

CULLIPOOL, the pretty main village with its post office and general store, lies a mile or so southwest; quarrying ceased here in 1965. Luing's only other village, **TOBERONOCHY**, lies on the more sheltered east coast, three miles southeast of Cullipool, its distinctive white cottages built by the slate company in 1805. The only **accommodation** available on the island is self-catering cottages, or one of the static caravans at the tiny *Sunnybrae Caravan Park* (℡01852/314274, ⊛www.sunnybrae-luing.co.uk; March–Oct) close to the ferry, which also offers **bike rental**.

The Gulf of Corryvreckan

Scarba is the largest of the islands around Luing, a brooding 1500-foot hulk of slate, not much more than a couple of miles across, inhospitable and wild – most of the fifty or so inhabitants who once lived here had left by the mid-nineteenth century. To the south, between Scarba and Jura, the raging **Gulf of Corryvreckan** is the site of one of the world's most spectacular whirlpools, thought to be caused by a rocky pinnacle below the sea. It remains calm only for an hour or two at high and low tide; between flood and half-flood tide, accompanied by a southerly or westerly wind, water shoots deafeningly some 20ft up in the air. Inevitably there are numerous legends about the place – known as *coire bhreacain* (speckled cauldron) in Gaelic – concerning *Cailleach* (Hag), the Celtic storm goddess. The best place from which to view it is the northern tip of Jura (see p.399).

If you're interested in taking a **boat trip** to Scarba, Corryvreckan or the nearby Garvellach islands, contact Gemini Cruises (℡01546/830238, ⊛www.gemini-crinan.co.uk), who operate from Crinan (see p.384), or Sea.fari (℡01852/300003, ⊛www.seafari.co.uk), who have a base at Easdale.

Arduaine and Craignish

Probably the finest spot at which to stop and have a picnic on the main road from Oban to Lochgilphead is in **Arduaine Garden** (daily 9.30am–dusk; NTS; £5), which enjoys views over Asknish Bay and out to the islands of Shuna, Luing, Scarba and Jura. Gifted to the National Trust as recently as 1992, the gardens are stupendous, particularly in May and June, and have the feel of an intimate private garden, with pristine lawns, lily-strewn ponds, mature woods and spectacular rhododendrons and azaleas. The gardens' disgruntled former owners, the Wright brothers, still live next door and have an impressive rhododendron display of their own. The best **accommodation** in the area is about three miles back up the road to Oban at *Cnoc na Ceardaich* (☎01852/200348, Ⓦfreespace.virgin.net/tom .kilmelford; Easter–New Year; ❸), an absolutely delightful Victorian former manse offering B&B in spacious, beautifully decorated rooms, just off the A816.

A couple of miles south, on the far side of Asknish Bay, is the slightly surreal **CRAOBH HAVEN**, a purpose-built holiday village and yacht marina, whose street of pastel-coloured "traditional" cottages is reminiscent of a set for a soap opera. However, there is a range of self-catering and B&B **accommodation** close by, in the rambling Baronial pile of *Lunga* (☎01852/500237, Ⓦwww .lunga.com; ❸), run by an eccentric laird. For **food** try either the *Lord of the Isles* pub or the *Cabin* bistro café opposite.

There's a fine walk to be had from Craobh Haven along the spine of the **Craignish peninsula** to the southernmost tip some five miles away. Alternatively, you can simply head over to **ARDFERN**, on the sheltered shores of Loch Craignish, a favourite anchorage for visiting yachts. Ardfern is everything Croabh Haven isn't and boasts a real pub, the *Galley of Lorne* (☎01852/500284, Ⓦwww.galleyoflorne.co.uk) with a rather more upmarket restaurant attached. Opposite the pub is *The Crafty Kitchen* ((☎01852/500303; closed Mon), a small popular restaurant (and craftshop) specializing in inexpensive locally sourced and vegetarian food.

Kilmartin Glen

The chief sight on the road from Oban to Lochgilphead is **Kilmartin Glen**, the most important prehistoric site on the Scottish mainland. The most remarkable relic is the **linear cemetery**, where several cairns are aligned for more than two miles, to the south of the village of Kilmartin. These are thought to represent the successive burials of a ruling family or chieftains, but nobody can be sure. The best view of the cemetery's configuration is from the Bronze Age **Mid–Cairn**, but the Neolithic **South Cairn**, dating from around 3000 BC, is by far the oldest and the most impressive, with its large chambered tomb roofed by giant slabs.

Close to the Mid-Cairn, the two **Temple Wood stone circles** appear to have been the architectural focus of burials in the area from Neolithic times to the Bronze Age. Visible to the south are the impressively cup-marked **Nether Largie standing stones** (no public access), the largest of which looms over 10ft high. **Cup- and ring-marked rocks** are a recurrent feature of prehistoric sites in Kilmartin Glen and elsewhere in Argyll. There are many theories as to their origin: some see them as Pictish symbols, others as primitive solar calendars. The most extensive markings in the entire country are at **Achnabreck**, off the A816 towards Lochgilphead.

Kilmartin

Situated on high ground to the north of the cairns is the tiny village of **KILMARTIN**, where the old manse adjacent to the village church now

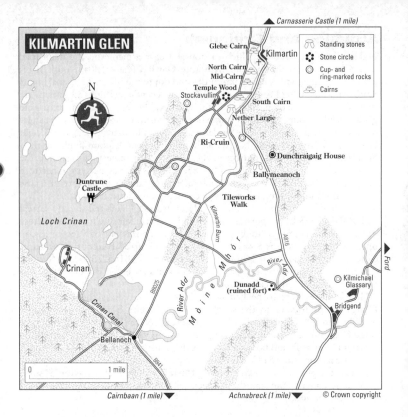

KILMARTIN GLEN

Glebe Cairn ✚Kilmartin

North Cairn
Mid-Cairn

Temple Wood
Stockavullin ∴
South Cairn

Nether Largie

Ri-Cruin

⊙Dunchraigaig House

Ballymeanoch

Duntrune
Castle

Tileworks
Walk

Loch Crinan

N

Crinan

Dunadd
(ruined fort)

○ Kilmichael
Glassary

Bridgend

Ford ▶

Bellanoch

River Add

Móine Mhór

Crinan Canal

B8025

B841

0   1 mile

	Standing stones
	Stone circle
○	Cup- and ring-marked rocks
	Cairns

houses a **Museum of Ancient Culture** (daily 10am–5.30pm; £4.50; Ⓦwww .kilmartin.org), which is both enlightening and entertaining. Not only can you learn about the various theories concerning prehistoric crannogs, henges and cairns, but you can practise polishing an axe, examine different types of wood and fur, and listen to a variety of weird and wonderful sounds (check out the Gaelic bird imitations).

Nearby **Kilmartin church** is worth a brief reconnoitre, as it shelters several richly sculptured graves and crosses, while a separate enclosure in the graveyard houses a large collection of medieval grave slabs of the Malcolms of Poltalloch. Kilmartin's own castle is ruined beyond recognition; head instead for the much less ruined **Carnasserie Castle**, on a high ridge a mile up the road towards Oban. The castle was built in the 1560s by John Carswell, an influential figure in the Scottish Church, who published the first-ever book in Gaelic, *Knox's Liturgy*, which contained the doctrines of the Presbyterian faith. Architecturally, the castle is interesting, too, as it represents the transition between fully fortified castles and later mansion houses, and has several original finely carved stone fireplaces and doorways, as well as numerous gun-loops and shot holes.

For something to eat, head for the museum **café**, with home-baked produce on offer, which you can wash it down with heather beer – it's open in the early evening too (Thurs–Sat). The nearest **B&B** is at *Dunchraigaig House* (☏01546/605209, ⓔdunchraig@aol.com; ❸), a large detached Victorian house situated opposite the Ballymeanoch standing stones.

Mòine Mhór and Dunadd

To the south of Kilmartin, beyond the linear cemetery, lies the raised peat bog of **Mòine Mhór** (Great Moss), now a nature reserve and home to remarkable plant, insect and birdlife. To get a close look at the sphagnum moss and wetlands, head for the newly laid-out Tileworks Walk, just off the A816, which includes a short boardwalk over the bog.

Mòine Mhór is best known as home to the Iron Age fort of **Dunadd**, one of Scotland's most important Celtic sites, occupying a distinctive 176-foot-high rocky knoll once surrounded by the sea but currently stranded beside the winding River Add. It was here that Fergus, the first king of Dalriada, established his royal seat, having arrived from Ireland in around 500 AD. Its strategic position, the craggy defences and the view from the top are all impressive, but it's the **stone carvings** (albeit now fibreglass copies) between the twin summits that make Dunadd so remarkable: several lines of inscription in ogham (an ancient alphabet of Irish origin), the faint outline of a boar, a hollowed-out footprint and a small basin. The boar and the inscriptions are probably Pictish, since the fort was clearly occupied long before Fergus got there, but the footprint and basin have been interpreted as being part of the royal coronation rituals of the kings of Dalriada. It is thought that the Stone of Destiny was used at Dunadd before being moved to Scone Palace (see box on p.471).

Lochgilphead

The unlikely administrative centre of Argyll and Bute, **LOCHGILPHEAD** (Ⓦ www.lochgilphead.info), as the name suggests, lies at the head of Loch Gilp, an arm of Loch Fyne. It's a planned town in the same vein as Inveraray, though nothing like as picturesque. If you're staying in the area, however, you're bound to find yourself here at some point, as Lochgilphead has the only bank and supermarket (not to mention swimming pool) for miles. The **tourist office**, 27 Lochnell St (April–Oct Mon–Sat 10am–5pm, Sun noon–5pm; longer hours in summer; Ⓣ 01546/602344), can help find you **accommodation** in the area. If you need a place in Lochgilphead itself, try *Cairnsmore House* (Ⓣ 01546/602885 Ⓦ www.cairnsmorehouse.co.uk; ❸), an attractive Victorian villa with light airy rooms in the quiet backstreet of Manse Brae, or *Allt-na-Craig* (Ⓣ 01546/603245, Ⓦ www.allt-na-craig.co.uk; ❺), a very handsome, stylish, detached Victorian guesthouse set back from the road to Ardrishaig. You can also **camp** at the pristinely maintained *Lochgilphead Caravan Park*, a short distance west of town in Bank Park (Ⓣ 01546/602003, Ⓦ www.lochgilpheadcaravanpark.co.uk; April–Oct); bike rental is available, too. As for **food**, the best place in town is *Pinto's* (Ⓣ 01546/602547; closed Sun), a modern veggie restaurant that offers lunch for a fiver, as well as wraps, soup and sandwiches, and a slightly more expensive menu (mains under £10) in the evening (Thurs–Sat only). *The Smiddy*, on Smithy Lane (closed Sun), does simple café fare. For high-class picnic provisions, call in at *Cockles*, a smart deli on the main street that also sells fresh and smoked fish and delicious home-made bread.

Knapdale

Forested **Knapdale** – from the Gaelic *cnap* (hill) and *dall* (field) – forms a buffer zone between the Kintyre peninsula and the rest of Argyll, bounded to the north by the Crinan Canal and to the south by West Loch Tarbert and consisting of three fingers of land, separated by Loch Sween and Loch Caolisport.

Crinan Canal

The nine-mile-long **Crinan Canal** opened in 1801, linking Loch Fyne, at Ardrishaig south of Lochgilphead, with the Sound of Jura, thus cutting out the long and treacherous journey around the Mull of Kintyre. John Rennie's original design, although an impressive engineering feat, had numerous faults, and by 1816 Thomas Telford was called in to take charge of the renovations. The canal runs parallel to the sea for quite some way before cutting across the bottom of Mòine Mhór and hitting a flight of locks either side of **CAIRNBAAN** (there are fifteen in total); a walk along the towpath is both picturesque and pleasantly unstrenuous. A useful pit stop can be made at the excellent *Cairnbaan Hotel* (℡01546/603668, ⓦwww.cairnbaan.com; ❻), a very comfortable, eighteenth-century coaching inn overlooking the canal; it also has a decent restaurant and bar meals featuring locally caught seafood – to whip up an appetite you can nip up to the cup- and ring-marked stone behind the hotel.

There are usually one or two yachts passing through the locks, but the most relaxing place from which to view the canal in action is **CRINAN**, the pretty little fishing port at the western end of the canal. Crinan's tiny harbour is, for the moment at least, still home to a small fishing fleet; a quick burst up through Crinan Wood to the hill above the village will give you a bird's-eye view of the sea-lock and its setting. Every room in the *Crinan Hotel* (℡01546/830261, ⓦwww.crinanhotel.com; ❽) looks across Loch Crinan to the Sound of Jura – one of the most beautiful (and expensive) views in Scotland, especially at sunset, when the myriad islets and the distinctive Paps of Jura are reflected in the waters of the loch. If the *Crinan* is beyond your means, try the secluded **B&B** *Tigh-na-Glaic* (℡01546/830245; ❸), perched above the harbour, also with views out to sea, or the superb *Bellanoch House* (℡01546/830149, ⓦwww.bellanochhouse.co.uk; ❺), a grand, old schoolhouse with stripped pine floors and lots of character, right on the canal, a mile or so before Crinan.

Bar **meals** at the *Crinan* are moderately expensive, but utterly delicious. Down on the lockside there is a cheaper, cheerful **café** called the *Coffee Shop* (Easter–Oct), serving mouthwatering home-made cakes and wonderful clootie dumplings. The **boat trips** organized by Gemini Cruises (℡01546/830238, ⓦwww.gemini-crinan.co.uk) leave from Crinan's other harbour, half a mile further down the coast, though they will pick up from other points along the coast; from here the waymarked three-mile **Crinan Walk** takes you through the nearby Forestry Commission plantation, with excellent views out to sea.

Knapdale Forest and Loch Sween

Continuing down the western finger of Knapdale you come to the village of **TAYVALLICH** (ⓦwww.tayvallich.com), with its attractive horseshoe bay, after which the peninsula splits again. The western arm leads eventually to the medieval **Chapel of Keills**, which houses a display of late medieval carved stones. The other arm, the **Taynish peninsula** has one of the largest remaining oak forests in Britain, boasting over twenty species of butterfly. If you want to eat or drink round here, then head for the *Tayvallich Inn* (℡01546/870282, ⓦwww.tayvallich.com), in the village of the same name, for very good local food.

Six miles south of Achanamara, on the eastern shores of **Loch Sween**, is the "Key of Knapdale", the eleventh-century **Castle Sween**, the earliest stone castle in Scotland, but in ruins since 1647. The tranquillity and beauty of the setting are spoilt by the nearby caravan park, an eyesore which makes a visit pretty depressing. You're better off continuing south to the thirteenth-century **Kilmory Chapel**, also ruined but with a new roof protecting the medieval grave slabs and the well-preserved MacMillan's Cross, an eight-foot fifteenth-century Celtic cross showing the Crucifixion on one side and a hunting scene on the other.

The easternmost finger of Knapdale is isolated and fairly impenetrable, but it's worth persevering the fourteen miles of single-track road in order to reach **KILBERRY**, where you can **camp** at the *Port Ban Caravan Park* (☎01880/770224, Ⓦwww.portban.com; March–Oct), and enjoy the fantastic sunsets and views over Jura, or **stay the night** in comfort and style at the ⚲ *Kilberry Inn* (☎01880/770223, Ⓦwww.kilberryinn.com; April–Oct; ❺); the inn's **food** is superb (Tues–Sun) and uses fresh local produce. There's also a church worth viewing in Kilberry and a small collection of carved medieval grave slabs.

Kintyre

But for the mile-long isthmus between West Loch Tarbert and the much smaller East Loch Tarbert, the little-visited peninsula of **KINTYRE** (Ⓦwww.kintyre .org) – from the Gaelic *ceann tire*, "land's end" – would be an island. Indeed, in the eleventh century, when the Scottish king, Malcolm Canmore, allowed Magnus Barefoot, king of Norway, to lay claim to any island he could circumnavigate by boat, Magnus succeeded in dragging his boat across the Tarbert isthmus and added the peninsula to his Hebridean kingdom. During the Wars of the Covenant, population and property were almost entirely wiped out by a combination of the 1646 potato blight and the destructive attentions of the earl of Argyll. Kintyre remained a virtual desert until the earl began his policy of transplanting Gaelic-speaking Lowlanders to the region. They probably felt quite at home here, as the southern half of the peninsula lies on the Lowland side of the Highland Boundary Fault.

There are regular daily **buses** from Glasgow to Campbeltown, via Tarbert and the west coast, and even a skeleton service down the east coast. Bear in mind, though, if you're driving, that the new west coast road is extremely fast, whereas the single-track east coast road takes more than twice as long. There's a **ferry** to Tarbert from Portavadie on the Cowal peninsula, and Campbeltown has an airport, with daily flights from Glasgow, which is only forty miles away by air, compared to over 120 miles by road.

Tarbert

A distinctive rocket-like church steeple heralds the fishing village of **TARBERT** (in Gaelic *An Tairbeart*, meaning "isthmus"), sheltering an attractive little bay backed by rugged hills. Tarbert's herring industry was mentioned in the Annals of Ulster as far back as 836 AD, though right now the local fishing industry is down to its lowest level ever. Ironically, it was local Tarbert fishermen, who, in the 1830s, pioneered the method of herring-fishing known as trawling, seining or ring-netting, which eventually wiped out the Loch Fyne herring stocks. Tourism is now an increasingly important source of income, though there's nothing much to see in Tarbert itself. Most people pass through or come during the last week in May, when the yacht races of the famous Scottish Series take place, and in the first weekend in July when traditional boats and a seafood festival hit town.

Tarbert's **tourist office** (April–Oct Mon–Sat 10am–5pm, Sun noon–5pm; longer hours in summer; ☎01880/820429) is on the harbour. If you need to **stay**, there's no shortage of B&Bs, though none is outstanding – try *Springside* on Pier

Road (☎01880/820413, ✉marshall.springside@virgin.net; ❷), which overlooks the harbour. Tarbert's luxury option is *Stonefield Castle Hotel* (☎01880/820836, ⓦwww.innscotland.com; ❸), two miles up the A83 to Lochgilphead, a handsome, grandiose Scots Baronial mansion set in magnificent grounds overlooking Loch Fyne; all bookings are for dinner, bed and breakfast.

The *Ca'Dora* is the caff to head for on the seafront, while *The Anchor* pub, also overlooking the harbour, is a good option for a seafood lunch. The best **food** is to be had courtesy of the French chef at the evening-only ✣ *Corner House Bistro* (☎01880/820263), just by the side of the *Corner House* pub, or at the more expensive, but equally excellent *Anchorage* (☎01880/820881; Oct–March eve only), on south side of the harbour.

Isle of Gigha

Gigha (ⓦwww.gigha.org.uk) – pronounced "Geeya", with a hard "g" – is a low-lying, fertile island, just three miles off the west coast of Kintyre, reputedly occupied for five thousand years. The island's Ayrshire cattle produce over a quarter of a million gallons of milk a year, though since the closure of Gigha's creamery in the 1980s, the island's distinctive (occasionally fruit-shaped) cheese has been produced on the mainland. Like many of the smaller Hebrides, Gigha was bought and sold numerous times after its original lairds, the MacNeils, sold up, and was finally bought by the 130 or so inhabitants themselves in 2002.

The ferry from Tayinloan, 23 miles south of Tarbert, deposits you at the island's only village, **ARDMINISH**, where you'll find the post office and shop and the all-denominations island church with some interesting stained-glass windows, including one to Kenneth MacLeod, composer of the well-known ditty *Road to the Isles*. The main attraction on the island is the **Achamore Gardens** (daily 9am–dusk; £4), a mile and a half south of Ardminish. Established by the first postwar owner, Sir James Horlick of hot-drink fame, their spectacularly colourful display of azaleas are best seen in early summer. To the southwest of the gardens, the ruins of the thirteenth-century **St Catan's Chapel** are floored with weathered medieval gravestones; the ogham stone nearby is the only one of its kind in the west of Scotland. The real draw of Gigha, however, apart from the peace and quiet, are the white sandy beaches – including one at Ardminish itself – that dot the coastline.

Gigha is small – six miles by one mile – and most visitors come here just for the day. However, it's a great place to **stay** too: for simple B&B, try the old *Post Office House* (☎01583/505251, ⓦwww.gighastores.co.uk; ❷) or the newly-built *Tighnavinish* (☎01583/505378, ⓦwww.gigha.net; March–Oct; ❸), half a mile to the north; if you want to stay in style, head for *Achamore House* (☎01583/505400, ⓦwww.achamorehouse.com; ❺), the beautiful house in the midst of Achamore Gardens; if you're interested in **camping**, you should contact the *Gigha Hotel* (☎01583/505254), the very pleasant social centre of the island just south of the post office. The licensed *Boathouse*, by the pier, is the place to go for delicious **food**, and, occasionally, live music. **Bike rental** is available from the shop (open daily), and there's a nine-hole **golf course**.

The west coast

Kintyre's bleak **west coast** ranks among the most exposed stretches of coastline in Argyll. Atlantic breakers pound the rocky shoreline, while the persistent westerly wind forces the trees against the hillside. However, when the weather's fine and the wind not too fierce, there are numerous deserted sandy beaches to enjoy, with great views over to Gigha, Islay, Jura and even Ireland.

There are several **campsites** to choose from along the stretch of coast around **TAYINLOAN**, ranging from the big *Point Sands Caravan Park* (℡01583/441263; April–Oct), two miles to the north, set back a long way from the main road near a long stretch of sandy beach, to the smaller, more informal *Muasdale Holiday Park*, three miles to the south (℡01583/421207, ⓦ www.muasdaleholidays.com; Easter–Oct), squeezed between the main road and April beach. **Accommodation** along the coast includes the *Balinakill Country House* (℡01880/740206, ⓦ www.balinakill.com; ❺), a capacious late-Victorian hotel with lots of period touches, set in its own grounds near Clachan north of Tayinloan; the kitchen produces decent bar food until 7pm, and much more expensive à la carte after that. Further south at **BELLOCHANTUY**, the *Argyll Hotel* (℡01583/421212, ⓦ www.argyllhotel.co.uk; ❹) is a welcoming roadside pub serving pub food in its conservatory or on outside tables overlooking the sand and sea – you can also camp next door. Another **food** option along the coast is *North Beachmore*, signposted off the A83, just south of Tayinloan, a restaurant boasting panoramic views out to Gigha, and serving straightforward snacks, lunches and evening meals (reservations advisable at the weekend; ℡01583/421328).

The only major development along the entire west coast is **MACHRIHANISH**, at the southern end of Machrihanish Bay, the longest continuous stretch of sand in Argyll. There are two approaches to the **beach**: from Machrihanish itself, or from Westport, at the north end of the bay, where the A83 swings east towards Campbeltown; either way, the sea here is too dangerous for swimming. Machrihanish itself was once a thriving salt-producing and coal-mining centre – you can still see the miners' cottages at neighbouring Drumlemble – but now survives solely on tourism. The main draw, apart from the beach, is the exposed championship **golf links** between the beach and Campbeltown airport on the nearby flat and fertile swath of land known as the Laggan.

Several of the imposing, detached Victorian town houses overlooking the bay in Machrihanish, such as *Ardell House* (℡01586/810235; March–Oct; ❸), offer **accommodation**; there's also a large, fully equipped and very exposed **campsite** (℡01586/810366, ⓦ www.campkintyre.com; March–Sept) overlooking the golf links. In the evening, *The Beachcomber* bar is the liveliest place in Machrihanish.

Campbeltown

CAMPBELTOWN's best feature is its setting, in a deep bay sheltered by Davaar Island and the surrounding hills. With a population of around five thousand, it is also one of the largest towns in Argyll and, if you're staying in the southern half of Kintyre, its shops are by far the best place to stock up on supplies. Originally known as Kinlochkilkerran (*Ceann Loch Cill Chiaran*), the town was renamed in the seventeenth century by the earl of Argyll – a Campbell – when it became one of the main points for immigration from the Lowlands. As is evident from the architecture, Campbeltown's heyday was the Victorian era, when shipbuilding was going strong, coal was shipped by canal from Drumlemble, the fishing fleet was vast and Campbeltown Loch was said to be made of whisky. The decline of all its old industries has left the town permanently depressed, and unemployment and underemployment remain persistent problems, though hopes are once more pinned on the revival of the ferry link to Ballycastle in the Northern Ireland.

The Town

Nineteenth-century visitors to Campbeltown frequently found the place engulfed in a thick fog of pungent peat smoke from the town's 34 **whisky**

distilleries. Today, only Glen Scotia, Springbank and the former Glengyle distillery are left to maintain this regional subgroup of single malt whiskies (see p.51 for more on whisky), but you can buy a guide to Campbeltown's former distilleries from the tourist office. The deeply traditional, family-owned **Springbank**, off Longrow, is the only distillery in Scotland that does absolutely everything from malting to bottling, on its own premises, and they offer no-nonsense guided tours (Easter–Sept Mon–Thurs by appointment; £3; ☎01586/552085, ⓦwww.springbankdistillers.com). At the end, you get a voucher to exchange for a miniature at Eaglesome, on Longrow South, whose range of whiskies is awesome.

The town's one major sight is the **Campbeltown Cross**, a fourteenth-century blue-green cross with figural scenes and spirals of Celtic knotting, which presides over the main roundabout on the quayside. Back on the palm-tree-dotted waterfront is the **Wee Pictures**, a dinky little Art Deco cinema on Hall Street, built in 1913 and still going strong (daily except Fri; ☎01586/533657, ⓦwww.weepictures.co.uk). Next door is the equally delightful **Campbeltown Museum and Library** (Tues–Sat 10am–1pm & 2–5pm, Tues & Thurs also 5.30–7.30pm; free), built in 1897 in the local sandstone, crowned by a distinctive lantern and decorated on its harbourside wall with four relief panels depicting each of the town's main industries at the time. Inside, the museum itself provides a less than remarkable rundown on local history – for a more enlightening version, head to the Heritage Centre (described below). The library also hides one new, but little-known sight: the **Linda McCartney Memorial Garden**, which features a slightly ludicrous bronze statue of Linda holding a lamb, commissioned by the ex-Beatle, who spent many happy times with Linda and the kids on the farm he owns near Campbeltown.

The former Lorne Street Church, known locally as the "Tartan Kirk", partly due to its Gaelic associations and partly due to its stripy bell-cote and pinnacles, has now become the **Campbeltown Heritage Centre** (April–Sept Mon–Sat noon–5pm, Sun 2–5pm; £2). A beautiful wooden skiff from 1906 stands where the main altar once was, and there's plenty on the local whisky industry and St Kieran, the sixth-century "Apostle of Kintyre", who lived in a cave – which you can get to at low tide – not far from Campbeltown. A dedicated ascetic, he would only eat bread mixed with a third sand and a few herbs; he wore chains, had a stone pillow and slept out in the snow – unsurprisingly, at the age of 33, he died of jaundice.

Campbeltown's newest attraction is the **Scottish Owl Centre** (April to early Oct daily except Tues 1.30–4.30pm; £5; ⓦwww.scottishowlcentre.tk), sign-posted off the B842 to Machrihanish, five minutes' walk out of town. As well as being actively involved in conservation work, the centre has a huge collection of owls spread out in terraced aviaries, ranging from the tiny Scops Owl to the world's largest, the Eurasian Eagle Owl. Try and time your visit with the daily flight display at 2.30pm.

One of the most popular day-trips is to **Davaar Island**, linked to the penin-sula at low tide by a mile-long shoal, or *dóirlinn* as it's known in Gaelic. Check the times of the tides from the tourist office before setting out; you have around six hours in which to make the return journey from Kildalloig Point, two miles or so east of town. Davaar is uninhabited and used for grazing (hence no dogs are allowed); its main claim to fame is the cave painting of the Crucifixion executed in secret by local artist Archibald MacKinnon in 1887 and touched up by him after he'd owned up in 1934; a year later, aged 85, he died. The cave, on the south side of the island, is easy enough to find, but the story is better than the end product, and you're better off walking up to the island's high point (378ft) and enjoying the view.

Practicalities

Campbeltown's **tourist office** is on the Old Quay (April–Oct Mon–Fri 10am–5pm, Sun noon–4pm; Nov–March Mon–Fri 9am–4pm; ☎01586/552056), and will happily hand out a free map of the town. The **airport** (☎01586/552571) lies three miles west, towards Machrihanish; there's a bus connection, but you need to phone ahead to book it (☎01586/552319) – it's part of Campbeltown's **Ring'n'Ride** service, which also operates around the town and to Southend (pick up a bus timetable from the tourist office for more details). As for the **ferry** connection with Ballycastle in Northern Ireland, it should be resumed in the near future.

The best centrally located **accommodation** is the delightful family-run *Ardshiel Hotel*, on Kilkerran Road (☎01586/552133, ⓦwww.ardshiel.co.uk; ❺), situated on a lovely leafy square, just a block or so back from the ferry terminal, with a cosy bar, and a more expensive à la carte restaurant. On the north side of the bay, on Low Askomill, is *Craigard House* (☎01586/554242, ⓦwww.craigard-house.co.uk; ❻), a former whisky distiller's grandiose sandstone mansion with a hint of the Italian Renaissance. For an inexpensive, central B&B, head for *Westbank Guest House*, on Dell Road (☎01586/553660; ❷), off the B842 to Southend. Another place worth considering is ⚐ *Oatfield House* (☎01586/551551, ⓦwww.oatfield.org; ❸), a beautifully renovated laird's house set in its own grounds, three miles down the B842 to Southend.

As for **places to eat**, the *Palm Bistro* on the harbourfront serves up standard café cuisine and the best bar meals are to be found at the aforementioned *Ardshiel Hotel*, while the *Commercial Inn* on Cross Street is a good drinking hole. You can **rent bikes** at The Bike Shop, Longrow (☎01586/554443). If you're here in the middle of August, be sure to check out the **Mull of Kintyre Music & Arts Festival** (ⓦwww.mokfest.com), which features some great traditional Irish and Scottish bands.

Southend and the Mull of Kintyre

The bulbous, hilly end of Kintyre, to the south of Campbeltown, features some of the most spectacular scenery on the whole peninsula, mixed with large swathes of Lowland-style farmland. **SOUTHEND** itself, a bleak, blustery spot, comes as something of a disappointment, though it does have a golden sandy beach. Below the cliffs to the west of the beach, a ruined thirteenth-century chapel marks the alleged arrival point of St Columba prior to his trip to Iona, and on a rocky knoll nearby a pair of footprints carved into the rock are known as **Columba's footprints**, though only one is actually of ancient origin. Jutting out into the sea at the east end of the bay is **Dunaverty Rock**, where a force of 300 Royalists was massacred by the Covenanting army of the earl of Argyll in 1647, despite having surrendered voluntarily.

A couple of miles out to sea from Southend lies **Sanda Island**, which contains the remains of St Ninian's chapel, plus two ancient crosses, a holy well, an unusual lighthouse comprised of three sandstone towers and lots of seabirds, including Manx shearwaters, storm petrels and puffins. The island has its own **pub**, the *Byron Darnton*, named after a seven-thousand-ton vessel wrecked on Sanda in 1946 without any loss of life, as well as a bird observatory and several self-catering cottages; the farmhouse also offers **B&B** (☎01586/553511, ⓦwww.sanda-island.co.uk; ❹). Unless you've your own boat, you'll need to board the

Seren Las in Campbeltown to reach the island (£20 return; ☎01586/554667) or take a helicopter from Arran (see the website for more details).

Most people venture south of Campbeltown to make a pilgrimage to the **Mull of Kintyre** – the nearest Britain gets to Ireland, whose coastline, just twelve miles away, appears remarkably close on fine days. Although the Mull was made famous by the mawkish number-one hit by sometime local resident Paul McCartney, with the help of the Campbeltown Pipe Band, it's also infamous as the site of the RAF's worst peacetime accident when, on June 2, 1994, a Chinook helicopter on its way from Belfast to Inverness crashed, killing all 29 on board. A small memorial can be found on the hillside, not far from the **Gap** (1150ft) – where you must leave your car. There's nothing specifically to see in this godforsaken storm-racked spot, and the road down to the lighthouse, itself 300ft above the ocean waves, is terrifyingly tortuous. It's about a mile from the "Gap" to the lighthouse (and a long haul back up), though there's a strategic viewpoint just ten minutes' walk from the car park; the principal lightkeeper's cottage, known as *Hector's House*, is now a remote **self-catering** option (phone the NTS; ☎0131/243 9331).

Southend has a **pub**, the *Argyll Arms*, which is unremarkable except for the fact that it has a post office inside it. The derelict Art Deco *Keil Hotel* cuts a forlorn figure, set back from the bay, but there are a couple of excellent **B&Bs** in the surrounding area: *Ormsary Farm* (☎01586/830665, Ⓔormsaryfarm@tinyworld .co.uk; April–Sept; ❶), a small dairy farm up Glen Breakerie, and the nearby picturesque croft of *Low Cattadale* (☎01586/830205; March–Nov; ❷). **Camping** is possible in the field right by the beach, run by *Machribeg Farm* (☎01586/830249; Easter–Sept). If you're interested in **horse riding**, call the Mull of Kintyre Equestrian Centre at Homeston Farm (☎01586/552437; April–Oct), signposted off the B842 to Southend.

The east coast

The **east coast** of Kintyre is gentler than the west, sheltered from the Atlantic winds and in parts strikingly beautiful, with stunning views across to Arran. However, be warned that there's no bus service between Carradale and Skipness and, if you're driving the thirty or so miles up to Skipness on the slow, winding, single-track B842, you'll need a fair amount of time.

The ruins of **Saddell Abbey**, a Cistercian foundation thought to have been founded by Somerled in 1148, lie ten miles up the coast from Campbeltown, set at the lush, wooded entrance to Saddell Glen. The abbey fell into disrepair in the sixteenth century, and, though the remains are not exactly impressive, there's a good collection of medieval grave slabs decorated with full-scale relief figures of knights housed in a new shelter in the grounds. Standing by the privately owned shoreline there's a splendid memorial to the last Campbell laird to live at Saddell Castle, which he built in 1774.

Further north lies the fishing village of **CARRADALE**, the only place of any size on the east coast north of Campbeltown, and "popular with those who like unsophisticated resorts", as one 1930s guide put it. Carradale does have a couple of good wet-weather retreats. The village itself is rather drab, but the tiny, very pretty harbour with its small fishing fleet, and the wide, sandy beach to the south, make up for it. Outside the village, there's the small, but informative **Network Carradale Heritage Centre** (Easter to mid-Oct Mon–Sat 10.30am–5pm, Sun 12.30–5pm; free), by the car park, with good home baking to be had in the tearoom. A mile or so to the south, in the old laundry of the imposing Scots Baronial Torrisdale Castle, you'll find **Grogport Tannery** (daily 9am–6pm; free;

@www.torrisdalecastle.com), which produces naturally coloured, organically tanned, fully washable sheepskins (gloves and slippers, too).

Accommodation is available at the *Carradale Hotel* (☎01583/431223, @www.carradalehotel.com; ❸), whose bar is the hub of village social life (and whose food is good), and at *Dunvalanree* (☎01583/431226, @www.dunvalanree .com; ❹), the big Victorian house, overlooking the sheltered little bay of Port Righ, towards Carradale Point – it's beautifully decorated inside and is, in fact, a licensed hotel. There's also the well-equipped *Carradale Bay Caravan Park* **campsite** (☎01583/431665, @www.carradalebay.com; April–Sept), right by the sandy beach. Carradale boasts a real baker, too – try the treacle scones or cookie pudding (known as bread-and-butter pudding south of the border).

The B842 ends twelve miles north of Carradale at **CLAONAIG**, little more than a slipway for the small summer car ferry to Arran. Beyond here, a dead-end road winds its way along the shore a few miles further north to the tiny village of **SKIPNESS**, where the considerable ruins of the enormous thir-teenth-century **Skipness Castle** and a chapel look out across the Kilbrannan Sound to Arran. You can sit outside and admire both, whilst enjoying fresh oysters, delicious queenies (queen scallops), mussels and home-baked cakes from the excellent **seafood cabin** (late May to Sept) at Victorian *Skipness Castle*, which also offers **accommodation** in a family home (☎01880/760207, Ⓔsophie@skipness.freeserve.co.uk; ❻). There are several gentle **walks** laid out in the nearby mixed woodland, up the glen.

Isle of Islay

The fertile, largely treeless island of **ISLAY** (pronounced "eye-la"; @www .isle-of-islay.com) is famous for one thing – single malt **whisky**. The smoky, peaty, pungent quality of Islay whisky is unique, recognizable even to the untutored palate, and all eight of the island's distilleries will happily take visi-tors on a guided tour, ending with the customary complimentary tipple. Yet, despite the fame of its whiskies, Islay remains relatively undiscovered, especially compared with Mull or Skye. Part of the reason may be the expense of the two-hour ferry journey from Kennacraig on Kintyre, or perhaps the rela-tive paucity of luxury hotels or fancy restaurants. If you do make the effort, however, you'll be rewarded with a genuinely friendly welcome from islanders proud of their history, landscape and Gaelic culture.

In medieval times, Islay was the political centre of the Hebrides, with **Finlaggan**, near Port Askaig, the seat of the MacDonalds, Lords of the Isles. The picturesque, whitewashed villages you see on Islay today, however, date from the planned settlements founded by the Campbells in the late eighteenth and early nineteenth centuries. Apart from whisky and solitude, the other great draw is the **birdlife** – there's a real possibility of spotting a golden eagle or the rare crow-like chough, and no possibility at all of missing the scores of white-fronted and barnacle geese who winter here in their thousands. In late May/early June, the **Feis Ile**, or Islay Festival of Malt and Music (@www.feisile.org), takes place, with whisky tasting, piping recitals, folk dancing and other events celebrating the island's Gaelic roots.

Public transport, in the form of buses and postbuses, will get you from one end of the island to the other, but it's as well to know that there is one solitary bus on a Sunday; pick up an island transport guide from the Islay tourist office

△ Whisky barrels, Lagavulin, Islay

in **Bowmore**. The **airport**, which lies between Port Ellen and Bowmore, has regular flights to and from Glasgow, and the local bus or postbus will get you to either of the above villages. For a local point of view and news of upcoming events, pick up a copy of the fortnightly newspaper, *Ileach*, or visit their website (Ⓦ www.ileach.co.uk).

Port Ellen and around

Laid out as a planned village in 1821 by Walter Frederick Campbell, and named after his wife, **PORT ELLEN** is the chief port on Islay, with the island's largest fishing fleet, and main CalMac ferry terminal. The neat whitewashed terraces of Frederick Crescent, which overlook the town's bay of golden sand, are pretty

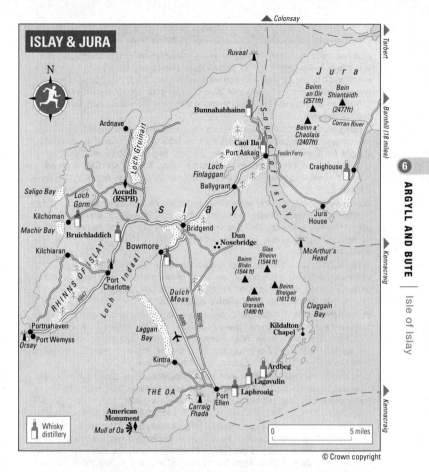

N

▲ Colonsay

► Tarbert

► Barnhill (18 miles)

6

ARGYLL AND BUTE | Isle of Islay

► Kennacraig

► Kennacraig

J u r a

Ruvaal ☀

Beinn
an Oir
(2571ft) ▲

Bein
Shiantaidh
(2477ft) ▲

Bunnahabhainn 🍾

Corran River

Beinn a'
Chaolais
(2407ft) ▲

Ardnave

Caol Ila 🍾

Port Askaig   • Feolin Ferry

Loch
Finlaggan

Craighouse 🍾

S o u n d   o f   I s l a y

Aoradh
(RSPB)

Saligo Bay

Loch
Gorm

Loch Gruinart

Ballygrant

Jura
House

I s l a y

Kilchoman

Bridgend

Dun
• Nosebridge

Machir Bay

Bruichladdich 🍾

McArthur's
Head

Bowmore 🍾

Glas
Bheinn
(1544 ft) ▲

Kilchiaran

Beinn
Bhàn
(1544 ft) ▲

Port
Charlotte

RHINNS OF ISLAY

Loch Indaal

Duich
Moss

Beinn
Uraraidh
(1490 ft) ▲

Beinn
Bheigeir
(1612 ft) ▲

Claggain
Bay

A847

Portnahaven

Laggan
Bay

Kildalton
Chapel

Orsay • Port Wemyss

A846

B8016

Kintra

THE OA

Ardbeg 🍾

Lagavulin 🍾

Carraig
Fhada

Port
Ellen

Laphroaig 🍾

American
Monument

Mull of Oa ☀

🍾 Whisky
distillery

0   5 miles

© Crown copyright

enough, but the strand to the north, up Charlotte Street, is dominated by the modern maltings, on the Bowmore road, whose powerful odours waft across the town. Arriving at Port Ellen by boat, it's impossible to miss the unusual, square-shaped **Carraig Fhada lighthouse**, at the western entrance to the bay, erected in 1832, in memory of Walter Frederick Campbell's aforementioned wife. Just beyond the lighthouse is the prettiest bay on the island's south coast, Traigh Bhán, or the **Singing Sands**, a perfect sandy beach, peppered with jagged rocky extrusions.

There's really not much point in basing yourself in Port Ellen. If you need a bite **to eat**, your best bet is actually the *Old Kiln Café* in Ardbeg distillery (see box on p.394), or the mobile *Nippy Chippy* (Fri & Sat only). For **accommodation** in Port Ellen itself, the best place is *Caladh Sona* (☎01496/302694, ⓔhamish .scott@lineone.net; March–Oct; ❷), a detached house at 53 Frederick Crescent, followed by the artistic *Carraig Fhada* B&B by the lighthouse (☎01496/302114, ⓔharry.underwood@talk21.com; ❶).

Another option is to head out of Port Ellen up the A846 towards the airport, to the excellent *Glenmachrie Farmhouse* (☎01496/302560, ⓦwww.glenmachrie .com; ❺), a whitewashed, family-run guesthouse, which does superb home

Islay has woken up to the fact that its whisky distilleries are a major tourist attraction. Nowadays, every distillery offers guided tours, traditionally ending with a generous dram, and a refund for your entrance fee if you buy a bottle in the shop – be warned, however, that a bottle of single malt is no cheaper at source, so expect to pay over £20 for the privilege. Phone ahead to make sure there's a tour running, as times do change frequently.

Ardbeg ☎01496/302244, ⓦwww.ardbeg.com. The ten-year-old Ardbeg is traditionally considered the saltiest, peatiest malt on Islay (and that's saying something). Bought by Glenmorangie in 1997, the distillery has been thoroughly overhauled and restored, yet it still has bags of character inside. The *Old Kiln Café* is excellent (Mon–Fri 10am–4pm; June–Aug daily 10am–5pm). Guided tours regularly 11.30am–2.30pm; £2.

Bowmore ☎01496/810671, ⓦwww.morrisonbowmore.com. Bowmore is the most touristy of the Islay distilleries, too much so for some. However, it is by far the most central distillery (with unrivalled disabled access), and also one of the few still doing its own malting and kilning. Guided tours Mon–Fri 10am, 11am, 2pm & 3pm, Sat by appointment; £2.

Bruichladdich ☎01496/850190. Bruichladdich was rescued in 2001 by a group of whisky fanatics and is the only independent distillery left on Islay. Regular guided tours take place (Easter–Oct Mon–Fri 10.30am, 11.30am & 2.30pm, Sat 10.30am & 2.30pm; Nov–Easter Mon–Fri 11.30am & 2.30pm, Sat 10.30am; £3).

Bunnahabhainn ☎01496/840646, ⓦwww.bunnahabhain.com. A visit to Bunnahabhain (pronounced "Bunna-have-in") is really only for whisky obsessives. The road from Port Askaig is windy, the whisky is the least characteristically Islay and the distillery itself is only in production for a few months each year. Guided tours April–Oct Mon–Fri 10.30am, 12.45pm, 2pm & 3.15pm; free.

Caol Ila ☎01496/302 760, ⓦwww.discovering-distilleries.com. Caol Ila (pronounced "Cul-eela"), just north of Port Askaig, is a modern distillery, the majority of whose lightly peaty malt goes into blended whiskies. No-frills guided tours are by appointment (April–Oct Mon–Thurs 9.30am, 10.45am & 1.45pm, Fri 9.30am & 10.45am; £3).

Kilchoman ☎01496/850011, ⓦwww.kilchomandistillery.com. The first new distillery on the island for over a century, Kilchoman is farm-based and aims to grow the barley, malt, distil, mature and even bottle its whisky on site. The distillery welcomes visitors (May, June & Sept Mon–Sat 10am–5.30pm; July & Aug daily; Oct–Dec Mon–Fri only), and there are regular guided tours (11am & 3pm; £3).

Lagavulin ☎01496/302730. Lagavulin probably is the classic, all-round Islay malt, with lots of smoke and peat. The distillery enjoys a fabulous setting and is extremely busy all year round. Phone ahead for details of the guided tours (Mon–Fri 9.30am, 11.15am & 2.30pm; £3), at the end of which you'll get a taste of the best-selling 16-year-old malt.

Laphroaig ☎01496/302418, ⓦwww.laphroaig.com. Another classic smoky, peaty Islay malt, and another great setting. One bonus at Laphroaig is that you get to see the malting and see and smell the peat kilns. There are regular guided tours (Mon–Fri 10.15am & 2.15pm; free), but phone ahead to book.

cooking, and fantastic breakfasts – the same family now also runs the nearby *Glenegedale House Hotel* (☎01496/302147; ❹), opposite the airport building. Alternatively, there's an independent **campsite** at the stone-built *Kintra Farm* B&B (☎01496/302051, ⓦwww.kintrafarm.co.uk; April–Sept; ❷), three miles northwest of Port Ellen, at the southern tip of Laggan Bay.

Along the coast to Kildalton

From Port Ellen, a dead-end road heads off east along the coastline, passing three distilleries in as many miles. First comes **Laphroaig**, a whitewashed distillery that enjoys a gorgeous setting by the sea. Laphroaig has the stamp of approval from Prince Charles, who famously paid a flying visit to the island in 1994, crashing an aircraft of the Queen's Flight in the process. A mile down the road lies **Lagavulin** distillery, beyond which stands **Dunyvaig Castle** (*Dún Naomhaig*), a romantic ruin on a promontory looking out to the tiny isle of Texa. Another mile further on, **Ardbeg** distillery sports the traditional pagoda-style kiln roofs, and has recently been brought back to life by Glenmorangie. In common with all Islay's distilleries, the above three offer guided tours (for more on which, see box opposite).

Six miles beyond Ardbeg, slightly off the road, the simple thirteenth-century **Kildalton Chapel** boasts a wonderful eighth-century Celtic ringed cross made from the local "bluestone", which is a rich blue-grey. The quality of the scenes matches any to be found on the crosses carved by the monks on Iona: the Virgin and Child are on the east face, with Cain murdering Abel to the left, David fighting the lion on the top, and Abraham sacrificing Isaac on the right; on the west side amidst the serpent-and–boss work are four elephant-like beasts.

The Oa

The most dramatic landscape on Islay is to be found in the nub of land to the southwest of Port Ellen known as **The Oa** (pronounced "O"), a windswept and inhospitable spot, much loved by illicit whisky distillers and smugglers over the centuries. The chief target for most visitors to the Oa, however, is the gargantuan **American Monument**, built in the shape of a lighthouse on the clifftop above the Mull of Oa. It was erected by the American National Red Cross in memory of those who died in two naval disasters that took place in 1918. The first occurred when the troop transporter, SS *Tuscania*, carrying over two thousand American army personnel, was torpedoed by a German U-Boat seven miles offshore in February 1918. As the lifeboats were being lowered, several ropes broke and threw the occupants into the sea, drowning 266 people. The monument also commemorates those who drowned when the *Otranto* was wrecked off Kilchoman (see p.397) in October of the same year. The memorial is inscribed with the unusual sustained metaphor: "On Fame's eternal camping ground, their silent tents are spread, while glory keeps with solemn round, the bivouac of the dead." If you're driving, you can park in a car park, just before Upper Killeyan farm, and follow the duckboards across the soggy peat (now in the hands of the RSPB). En route, look out for choughs, golden eagles and other birds of prey, not to mention feral goats and, down on the shore, basking seals; for a longer walk, follow the coast five miles round to or from Kintra.

Bowmore

At the northern end of seven-mile-long Laggan Bay, across the monotonous peat bog of Duich Moss, lies **BOWMORE**, Islay's administrative capital, with a population of around eight hundred. It was founded in 1768 to replace the village of Kilarrow, which was deemed by the local laird to be too close to his own residence. It's a striking place, laid out in a grid plan rather like Inveraray, with the whitewashed terraces of Main Street climbing up the hill in a straight line from the pier on Loch Indaal to the town's crowning landmark, the **Round Church** (@ www.theroundchurch.org.uk), whose central tower looks uncannily like a lighthouse. Built in the round, so that the devil would have no corners in which to hide, it has a plain, wood-panelled interior, with a lovely tiered balcony and a big central mushroom pillar. A little to the west of Main Street is **Bowmore distillery** (see box on p.394), the first of the legal Islay distilleries, founded in 1779, and still occupying its original whitewashed buildings by the loch. One of the distillery's former bonded warehouses is now the **MacTaggart Leisure Centre** (closed Mon), whose pool is partially heated by waste heat from the distillery; if you're camping or self-catering, it's as well to know that it has a very useful, minuscule laundrette.

Islay's only official **tourist office** is in Bowmore (April–Oct Mon–Sat 10am–5pm; May–Aug also Sun 2–5pm; Nov–March Mon–Fri noon–4pm; ☎01496/810254); it can help you find **accommodation** anywhere on Islay or Jura. Bowmore is central, but not necessarily the best place to stay on the island. If you choose to, however, head for the *Harbour Inn* (☎01496/810330, ⓦwww .harbour-inn.com; ❻) on Main Street, is Bowmore's cosiest and most central pub, or you could stay in one of the town's better B&Bs, such as *Lambeth House* (☎01496/810597; ❷), centrally located on Jamieson Street. **Bike rental** is available from the craft shop beside the post office on Main Street.

At the *Harbour Inn* on Main Street, you can warm yourself by a peat fire in the **pub**, or eat at the inn's outstanding **restaurant**: they make award-winning porridge for breakfast, offer a reasonably priced lunchtime menu, and serve more expensive evening meals. At the other end of the scale, there's an excellent **bakery** on Main Street, and, further up on the same side of the street, *The Cottage* (closed Sun), a cheap and friendly greasy spoon. Somewhat incredibly, there's no permanent fish-and-chip shop in Bowmore, only the mobile *Nippy Chippy* (Thurs only).

Loch Gruinart to Kilchoman

If you're visiting Islay between mid-September and the third week of April, it's impossible to miss the island's staggeringly large wintering population of **Greenland Barnacle** and **Greater White-fronted geese**. You can see the geese just about anywhere on the island – there are an estimated 15,000 white-fronted and 40,000 barnacles here (and rising) – though they are usually at their most concentrated in the fields between Bridgend and Ballygrant. In the evening, they tend to congregate in the tidal mud flats and fields around **Loch Gruinart**, which is an **RSPB nature reserve**. The nearby farm of Aoradh (pronounced "oorig") is run by the RSPB, and one of its outbuildings contains a **visitor centre** (daily 10am–5pm; free), housing an observation point with telescopes and a CCTV link with the mud flats; there's also a hide across the road looking north over the salt flats at the head of the loch, though you're more likely to see ducks than geese. Anyone interested in **birding** or **bushcraft** should get in touch with Islay Birding (☎01496/850010, ⓦwww .islaybirding.co.uk), based in Port Charlotte, who organize all sorts of outings and activities.

Without doubt the best sandy beaches on Islay are to be found on the isolated northwest coast, in particular, the lovely golden beach of **Machir Bay**, which is backed by great white-sand dunes. The sea here has dangerous undercurrents, however, and is not safe to swim in (the same goes for the much smaller Saligo Bay, to the north). At the nearby settlement of **KILCHOMAN**, set back from Machir Bay, beneath low rocky cliffs, where fulmars nest inland, the church is in a sorry state of disrepair. Its churchyard, however, contains a beautiful fifteenth-century cross, decorated with interlacing on one side and the Crucifixion on the other; at its base there's a **wishing stone** that should be turned sunwise when wishing. Across a nearby field towards the bay lies the **sailors' cemetery**, containing just 75 graves of the 400 or so who were drowned when the armed merchant cruiser SS *Otranto* collided with another ship in its convoy in a storm in October 1918.

Port Charlotte and the Rhinns of Islay

PORT CHARLOTTE, founded in 1828 by Walter Frederick Campbell and named after his mother, is generally agreed to be Islay's prettiest village. Known as the "Queen of the Rhinns" (derived from the Gaelic word for a promontory), its immaculate whitewashed cottages cluster around a sandy cove overlooking Loch Indaal. On the northern fringe of the village, in a whitewashed former chapel, the imaginative **Museum of Islay Life** (Easter–Oct Mon–Sat 10am–5pm, Sun 2–5pm; Nov–Easter Mon–Fri 10am–4pm, Sat 10am–4pm; £2) has a children's corner, quizzes, a good library of books about the island, and tantalizing snippets about eighteenth-century illegal whisky distillers. The **Wildlife Information Centre** (Easter–Oct daily except Sat 10am–3pm; July & Aug daily 10am–5pm; £2.50), housed in the former distillery warehouse, is also worth a visit for anyone interested in the island's fauna and flora. As well as an extensive library to browse, there's lots of hands-on stuff for kids: microscopes, a touch table full of natural goodies, a seawater aquarium, a bugworld and owl pellets to examine. Tickets are valid for a week, allowing you to go back and identify things that you've seen on your travels.

Port Charlotte is the perfect place in which to base yourself on Islay. The welcoming *Port Charlotte Hotel* (℡01496/850360, ⓦwww.portcharlottehotel .co.uk; ⑥) has the best **accommodation** – the seafood lunches served in the bar are very popular, and there's a good, though expensive restaurant. For B&B, you're actually better off going for the excellent *Octofad Farm* (℡01496/850594, ⓦwww.octofadfarm.com; April–Oct; ①), a few miles down the road beyond Nerabus, or *Coultorsay House* (℡01496/850298, ⓔwood .islay@virgin.net; ③), a lovely old farmhouse, halfway between Bruichladdich and Port Charlotte. Port Charlotte itself is also home to Islay's SYHA **hostel** (℡0870/004 1128, ⓦwww.syha.org.uk; April–Sept), housed in an old bonded warehouse next door to the Wildlife Information Centre. The *Croft Kitchen* (℡01496/850230; April–Oct), opposite the museum, serves simple **food**, such as sandwiches and cakes, as well as inexpensive seafood, during the day, and pricier, more adventurous fare in the evenings (except Wed). The **bar** of the *Port Charlotte* is very easygoing, while the crack (and occasional live music) goes on at the *Lochindaal Inn*, down the road, where you can also tuck into a very good local-bred steak. **Bike rental** is available from a house on Main Street (℡01496/850488), opposite the hotel.

The main coastal road culminates seven miles south of Port Charlotte at **PORTNAHAVEN**, a fishing and crofting community since the early nineteenth century. The familiar whitewashed cottages wrap themselves prettily around the steep banks of a deep bay, where seals bask on the rocks in considerable numbers; in the distance, you can see Portnahaven's twin settlement, **PORT WEMYSS**, a mile south. The communities share a little whitewashed church, located above the bay in Portnahaven, with separate doors for each village. For a drink, head for Portnahaven, which has a tiny *pub*, *an tigh seinnse*, where you can sit outside and enjoy the view in fine weather. A short way out to sea are two islands, the largest of which, Orsay, sports the **Rhinns of Islay Lighthouse**, built by Robert Louis Stevenson's father in 1825; ask around locally if you're keen to visit the island. Also worth a mention, just north of Portnahaven, is the island's groundbreaking wave energy generator, known as the **Limpet** (@www.wavegen.co.uk), which harnesses the power of the sea and turns it into electricity.

Finlaggan and Port Askaig

Just beyond Ballygrant, on the road to Port Askaig, a narrow road leads off north to **Loch Finlaggan**, site of a number of prehistoric crannogs (artificial islands) and, for four hundred years from the twelfth century, headquarters of the Lords of the Isles, semi-autonomous rulers of the Hebrides and Kintyre. The site is evocative enough, but there are, in truth, very few remains beyond the foundations. Remarkably, the palace that stood here appears to have been unfortified, a testament perhaps to the prosperity and stability of the islands in those days. Unless you need shelter from the rain, or are desperate to see the head of the commemorative medieval cross found here, you can happily skip the **information centre** (Easter & Oct Tues, Thurs & Sun 2–4pm; May–Sept daily except Sat 2.30–5pm; £2), to the northeast of the loch, and simply head on down to the site itself (access at any time), which is dotted with interpretive panels. Duckboards allow you to walk out across the reed beds of the loch and explore the main crannog, **Eilean Mor**, where several carved gravestones are displayed under cover in the chapel, all of which seem to support the theory that the Lords of the Isles buried their wives and children there, while having themselves interred on Iona. Further out into the loch is another smaller crannog, **Eilean na Comhairle**, originally connected to Eilean Mor by a causeway, where the Lords of the Isles are thought to have held meetings of the Council of the Isles.

Islay's other ferry connection with the mainland, and its sole link with Colonsay and Jura, is from **PORT ASKAIG**, a scattering of buildings which tumbles down a little cove by the narrowest section of the Sound of Islay or Caol Ila. The only real reason to come here is to catch one of the ferries or go to the hotel bar (see below); if you've time to kill, you can wander round the island's **RNLI lifeboat station** or through the nearby woods of Dunlossit House. Whisky fanatics might want to head half a mile north of Port Askaig to the distilleries of **Caol Ila** and **Bunnahabhainn**, a couple of miles further on; both enjoy idyllic settings, overlooking the Sound of Islay, though they are no beauties in themselves (see box on p.394 for details of their tours).

Easily the most comfortable **place to stay** is the lovely whitewashed *Kilmeny Farmhouse* (☎01496/840668, @www.kilmeny.co.uk; ❻), southwest of Ballygrant, a place which richly deserves all the superlatives it regularly receives, its rooms furnished with antiques and its dinners (Mon–Fri only) worth the extra £25 a head. The *Ballygrant Inn* is a good **pub** in which to grab a pint, as is the bar of the *Port Askaig Hotel*, which enjoys a wonderful position by the pier at Port Askaig, with views over to the Paps of Jura. For high-adrenalin **boat trips**, contact Islay Sea Safari (☎07768/450000, @www.islayseasafari.co.uk), which is based in Port Askaig and best known for whizzing round the distilleries in a rigid inflatable. It's also possible to take a **day-trip to Colonsay** (see p.377) on a CalMac ferry on Wednesday. In addition, the passenger-only Lorn Ferry Service (April to mid-Oct; ☎01951/200320) also runs timetabled services from Colonsay to Bunnahabhainn and Port Askaig on Islay (Mon), though you should phone ahead to check times and book your journey.

Isle of Jura

Twenty-eight miles long and eight miles wide, the long whale-shaped island of **Jura** is one of the wildest and most mountainous of the Inner Hebrides, its entire west coast uninhabited and inaccessible except to the dedicated walker. The distinctive **Paps of Jura** – so called because of their smooth breast-like shape, though there are in fact three of them – seem to dominate every view off the west coast of Argyll, their glacial rounded tops covered in a light dusting of quartzite scree. The island's name is commonly thought to derive from the Norse *dyr-oe* (deer island) and, appropriately enough, the current deer population of six thousand outnumbers the 180 humans 33:1; other wildlife to look out for include mountain hares and eagles. With just one road, which sticks to the more sheltered eastern coast of the island, and only one hotel and a couple of B&Bs, Jura is an ideal place to go for peace and quiet and some great walking.

If you're just coming over for the day from Islay, pop into the **Feolin Research Centre** (daily; free), near the ferry slipway, which has information and displays on the island, and then head off, five miles up the road, to the lovely wooded grounds of **Jura House** (daily 9am–5pm; ⓦ www .jurahouseandgardens.co.uk; £2), originally built by the Campbells in the early nineteenth century. Pick up a booklet at the entrance to the grounds, and follow the path which takes you down to the sandy shore, a perfect picnic spot in fine weather. Closer to the house itself, there's an idyllic **walled garden**, divided in two by a natural rushing burn that tumbles

---

George Orwell on Jura

In April 1946, Eric Blair (better known by his pen name of **George Orwell**), intending to give himself "six months' quiet" in which to complete his latest novel, moved to a remote farmhouse called **Barnhill**, at the northern end of Jura, which he had visited for the first time the previous year. He appears to have relished the challenge of living in Barnhill, fishing almost every night, shooting rabbits, laying lobster pots and even attempting a little farming. Along with his adopted 3-year-old son Richard, and later his sister Avril, he clearly enjoyed his spartan existence. The book Orwell was writing, under the working title *The Last Man in Europe*, was to become *1984* (the title was arrived at by simply reversing the last two digits of the year in which it was finished – 1948). During his time on Jura, however, Orwell was suffering badly from tuberculosis, and eventually he was forced to return to London, where he died in January 1950.

Barnhill, 23 miles north of Craighouse, is as remote today as it was in Orwell's day. The road deteriorates rapidly beyond Lealt, where vehicles must be left, leaving pilgrims a four-mile walk to the house itself. Alternatively, the Richardsons in Kinauachdrachd Farm (☎07899/912116) can organize a taxi and guided walk, should you so wish. Orwell wrote most of the book in the bedroom (top left window as you look at the house – at present, there is no public access). If you're keen on making the journey out to Barnhill, you might as well combine it with a trip to the nearby **Gulf of Corryvrechan** (see box on p.380), which lies between Jura and Scarba, to the north. Orwell nearly drowned in the **whirlpool** during a fishing trip in August 1947, along with his three companions (including Richard): the outboard motor was washed away, and they had to row to a nearby island and wait for several hours before being rescued by a passing fisherman. The best time to see the water whirling is between flood and half-flood tide, with a southerly or westerly wind, and the best place to view it from Jura is Carraig Mhor, seven miles from Lealt.

down in steps. The garden specializes in antipodean plants, which flourish in the frost-free climate; in season, you can buy some of the garden's organic produce or take tea in the tea tent (late May to Aug; closed Sat).

Anything that happens on Jura happens in the island's only real village, **CRAIGHOUSE**, eight miles up the road from Feolin Ferry. The village enjoys a sheltered setting, overlooking Knapdale on the mainland – so sheltered, in fact, that there are even a few palm trees thriving on the seafront. There's a shop/ post office, the island hotel and a tearoom, plus the tiny **Isle of Jura distillery** (℡01496/820240, Ⓦwww.isleofjura.com), which is very welcoming to visitors and offers free guided tours (Easter–Oct Mon–Fri 11am & 2pm; at other times by appointment).

The family-run *Jura Hotel* in Craighouse is the island's one and only **hotel** (℡01496/820243, Ⓦwww.jurahotel.co.uk; ❺), not much to look at from the outside, but warm and friendly within, and centre of the island's social scene. The hotel does moderately expensive bar meals, and has a shower block and laundry facilities round the back for those who wish **to camp** in the hotel gardens. For **B&B**, look no further than Mrs Boardman at 7 Woodside (℡01496/820379; April–Sept; ❹).

Very occasionally a **minibus** (℡01496/820314) meets the **car ferry** (℡01496/840681) from Port Askaig – phone ahead to check times. The ferry itself occasionally fails to run if there's a strong northerly or southerly wind, so bring your toothbrush if you're coming for a day-trip. Lorn Ferry Service (April–Sept; ℡01951/200320) also runs a timetabled **passenger/ bicycle-only ferry** from Colonsay to Tarbert, halfway up the west coast of Jura (Tues & Fri), though you should phone ahead to check times and book your journey. In addition, there's a **water taxi** service to or from Crinan, on the mainland, run by Gemini Cruises (℡01546/830208, Ⓦwww.gemini -crinan.co.uk). For a window on local life, look out for the *Jura Jottings*, the island's "newspaper".

Travel details

Trains

Glasgow (Queen St) to: Arrochar and Tarbert (Mon–Sat 3–4 daily, Sun 1–3 daily; 1hr 20min); Dalmally (Mon–Sat 3–4 daily, Sun 1–3 daily; 2hr 15min); Oban (Mon–Sat 3–4 daily, Sun 1–3 daily; 3hr).

Mainland buses (not postbuses)

Arrochar to: Carrick Castle (Mon–Sat 1–2 daily; 50min); Inveraray (3 daily, Sun 2 daily; 35min); Lochgilphead (3 daily; 1hr 30min); Lochgoilhead (Mon–Sat 1–2 daily; 40min).
Campbeltown to: Carradale (Mon–Sat 4–5 daily, Sun 2 daily; 45min); Machrihanish (Mon–Sat 9 daily, Sun 3 daily; 20–30min); Saddell (Mon–Sat 4–5 daily, Sun 2 daily; 25min); Southend (Mon–Sat 4–5 daily, Sun 2 daily; 23min).
Colintraive to: Dunoon (2 daily; 1hr); Tighnabruaich (Mon–Thurs 1–2 daily; 35min).

Dunoon to: Colintraive (2 daily; 1hr); Inveraray (Mon–Sat 3 daily, Sun 0–3 daily; 1hr 10min); Lochgoilhead (Mon–Sat 3 daily; 1hr).
Glasgow to: Arrochar (3–5 daily; 1hr 10min); Campbeltown (2–3 daily; 4hr 25min); Dalmally (Mon–Sat 4 daily, Sun 2 daily; 2hr 20min); Inveraray (4–6 daily; 1hr 45min); Kennacraig (Mon–Sat 2 daily, Sun 1 daily; 3hr 30min); Lochgilphead (2–3 daily; 2hr 40min); Oban (Mon–Sat 4 daily, Sun 2 daily; 3hr); Tarbert (2–3 daily; 3hr 15min); Taynuilt (Mon–Sat 4 daily, Sun 2 daily; 2hr 45min).
Inveraray to: Dalmally (Mon–Sat 3 daily, Sun 2 daily; 25min); Dunoon (Mon–Sat 3 daily, Sun 0–3 daily; 1hr 10min); Lochgilphead (2–3 daily; 40min); Oban (Mon–Sat 3 daily, Sun 2 daily; 1hr 5min); Tarbert (2–3 daily; 1hr 30min).
Kennacraig to: Claonaig (Mon–Sat 3 daily; 15min); Skipness (Mon–Sat 3 daily; 20min).
Lochgilphead to: Campbeltown (3–5 daily; 1hr 45min); Crinan (Mon–Sat 3–4 daily; 20min);

Kilmartin (Mon–Sat 2–5 daily; 15min); Tarbert (5–7 daily; 30min); Tayvallich (3–4 daily; 25min).

Oban to: Appin (Mon–Sat 3 daily, Sun 1 daily; 30min); Benderloch (6 daily; 20min); Kilmartin (Mon–Sat 2–4 daily; 1hr 20min); Lochgilphead (Mon–Sat 2–4 daily; 1hr 30min); Mallaig (daily April–Oct; 2hr 30min).

Tarbert to: Campbeltown (Mon–Sat 4 daily, Sun 2 daily; 1hr 15min); Claonaig (Mon–Sat 3 daily; 30min); Kennacraig (3–6 daily; 15min); Skipness (Mon–Sat 3 daily; 35min); Tayinloan (3–6 daily; 30min).

Tighnabruaich to: Portavadie (3–4 daily; 25min).

Island buses

Arran

Brodick to: Blackwaterfoot (Mon–Sat 12 daily, Sun 6 daily; 30min); Corrie (4–6 daily; 20min); Kildonan (3–5 daily; 40min); Lagg (3–5 daily; 50min); Lamlash (Mon–Sat 14–16 daily, Sun 4 daily; 10–15min); Lochranza (Mon–Sat 6 daily, Sun 3 daily; 45min); Pirnmill (4–6 daily; 1hr); Whiting Bay (Mon–Sat 14–16 daily, Sun 4 daily; 25min).

Bute

Rothesay to: Kilchattan Bay (Mon–Sat 4 daily, Sun 3 daily; 30min); Mount Stuart (every 45min; 15min); Rhubodach (Mon–Fri 1–2 daily; 20min).

Colonsay

Scalasaig to: Kilchattan (Mon–Fri 2–4 daily; 30min); Kiloran Bay (Mon–Fri 2–3 daily; 12min); The Strand (Mon–Fri 1 daily).

Islay

Bowmore to: Port Askaig (Mon–Sat 8–10 daily, Sun 1 daily; 30–40min); Port Charlotte (Mon–Sat 5–6 daily; 25min); Port Ellen (Mon–Sat 9–12 daily, Sun 1 daily; 20–30min); Portnahaven (Mon–Sat 5–7 daily; 50min).

Mull

Craignure to: Fionnphort (Mon–Sat 3–4 daily, Sun 1 daily; 1hr 10min); Fishnish (3 daily; 10min); Salen (4–6 daily; 20min); Tobermory (4–6 daily; 45min).

Tobermory to: Calgary (Mon–Sat 2 daily; 45min); Dervaig (Mon–Fri 3 daily, Sat 2 daily; 30min); Fishnish (2–4 daily; 40min).

Ferries

Car ferries

Summer timetable indicated.

To Arran: Ardrossan–Brodick (4–6 daily; 55min); Claonaig–Lochranza (8–9 daily; 30min).

To Bute: Colintraive–Rhubodach (frequently; 5min); Wemyss Bay–Rothesay (every 45min; 30min).

To Coll: Oban–Coll (daily except Thurs; 2hr 40min).

To Colonsay: Kennacraig–Colonsay (Wed 1 daily; 3hr 35min); Oban–Colonsay (1 daily except Tues & Sat; 2hr 15min); Port Askaig–Colonsay (Wed 2 daily; 1hr 15min).

To Dunoon: Gourock–Dunoon (hourly; 20min); McInroy's Point–Hunter's Quay (every 30min; 20min).

To Gigha: Tayinloan–Gigha (hourly; 20min).

To Islay: Colonsay–Port Askaig (Wed 2 daily; 1hr 15min); Kennacraig–Port Askaig (1–3 daily; 2hr); Kennacraig–Port Ellen (1–3 daily; 2hr 10min).

To Jura: Port Askaig–Feolin Ferry (Mon–Sat hourly, Sun 3 daily; 10min).

To Kintyre: Portavadie–Tarbert (hourly; 25min).

To Lismore: Oban–Lismore (Mon–Sat 2–5 daily; 50min).

To Luing: Cuan Ferry (Seil)–Luing (every 30min; 5min).

To Mull: Kilchoan–Tobermory (Mon–Sat 7 daily; June–Aug also Sun 5 daily; 35min); Lochaline–Fishnish (Mon–Sat every 50min, Sun hourly; 15min); Oban–Craignure (every 2hr; 45min).

To Tiree: Barra–Tiree (Wed 1 daily; 3hr 5min); Oban–Tiree (1 daily; 3hr 40min).

Passenger-only ferries

Summer timetable indicated

To Colonsay: Bunnahabhain (Islay)–Colonsay (Mon; 1hr 45min); Tarbert (Jura)–Colonsay (Tues & Fri; 2hr); Uisken (Mull)–Colonsay (Tues & Sun; 1hr 45min).

To Iona: Fionnphort–Iona (Mon–Sat frequently, Sun hourly; 5min).

To Kerrera: Gallanach–Kerrera (every 30min; 10min).

To Lismore: Port Appin–Lismore (every 2hr; 5min).

Flights

Glasgow to: Campbeltown (Mon–Fri 2 daily; 35min); Islay (Mon–Fri 2 daily, Sat 1 daily; 40min); Tiree (Mon–Sat 1 daily; 45min).

Stirling, Loch Lomond and the Trossachs

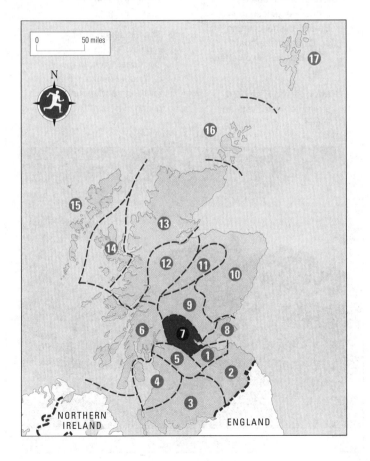

CHAPTER 7

Highlights

* **Stirling Castle** Impregnable, impressive and resonant with history. If you see only one castle in Scotland, make it this one. See p.410

* **Falkirk Wheel** The most remarkable piece of modern engineering in Britain, this fascinating contraption lifts boats 100ft between two canals. See p.419

* **Loch Leven** A moody stretch of water with an island castle ruin from where Mary, Queen of Scots made a daring escape. See p.422

* **Loch Lomond islands** Putter out on a mail boat to one of the wooded islands at the heart of Scotland's first national park. See p.427

* **The Trossachs** Pocket Highlands with shining lochs, wooded glens and noble peaks. Great for hiking and mountain biking. See p.429

△ Stirling Castle

Stirling, Loch Lomond and the Trossachs

T he central lowlands of Scotland were, for several centuries, the most strategically important area in Scotland. In 1250, a map of Britain was compiled by Matthew Paris, a monk of St Albans, which depicted Scotland as two separate land masses connected only by the thin band of Stirling Bridge; although this was a figurative interpretation, Stirling was once the only **gateway** from the fertile central belt to the rugged, mountainous north. For long periods of Scotland's history kings, queens, nobles, clan chiefs and soldiers wrestled for control of the area, and it's no surprise that today the landscape is not only littered with remnants of the past – well-preserved medieval towns and castles, royal residences and battle sites – but also coloured by the many romantic myths and legends that have grown up around it.

Lying at the heart of Scotland, **Stirling** and its fine castle, from where you can see both snowcapped Highland peaks and Edinburgh, are unmissable for anyone wanting to grasp the complexities of Scottish history. To the south of the city on the road to Edinburgh lies **Falkirk**, its industrial heritage now enlivened by the extraordinary Falkirk Wheel; to the east, the gentle **Ochil Hills**, where large flocks of sheep vital to the area's historical wool industry once grazed, run towards Fife, while the flat plain extending west, the **Carse of Stirling**, has the little-visited **Campsie Fells** on one side and the fabled mountains, glens, lochs and forests of the **Trossachs**, stretching west from **Callander** to Loch Lomond, to the north.

On the western side of the region, **Loch Lomond** is the largest – and most romanticized – stretch of fresh water in Scotland. Now at the heart of the **Loch Lomond and the Trossachs National Park**, the peerless scenery of the loch and its famously "bonnie banks" can be tainted by the sheer numbers of tourists and day-trippers who stream towards it in summer. It can get similarly clogged in the neighbouring Trossachs region, although, as with much of this area, there's plenty in the way of trips and attractions for families, as well as for those keen on **outdoor activities**: the area is traversed by the **Glasgow–Loch Lomond–Killin cycleway**; well-managed forest tracks are ideal for mountain biking; the hills of the Trossachs provide great walking country; while the **West Highland Way**, Scotland's premier long-distance footpath, winds along the length of Loch Lomond up to Fort William in the Highlands.

405

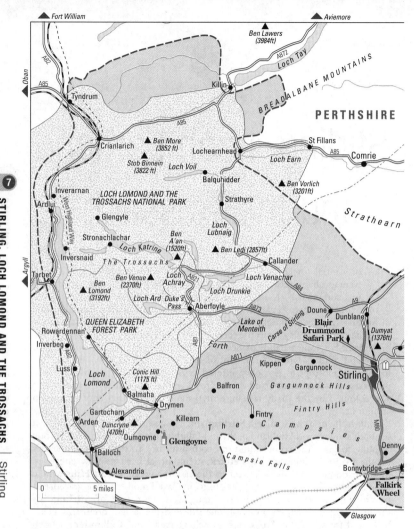

Fort William ▲

Aviemore ▲

Ben Lawers
(3984ft) ▲

Loch Tay

Killin

BREADALBANE MOUNTAINS

PERTHSHIRE

Tyndrum

Oban ◀

Crianlarich

Ben More
(3852 ft) ▲

Lochearnhead

St Fillans

Comrie

Loch Earn

Stob Binnein
(3822 ft) ▲

Loch Voil

Balquhidder

Ben Vorlich
(3201ft) ▲

Strathearn

Inverarnan

LOCH LOMOND AND THE
TROSSACHS NATIONAL PARK

Strathyre

Ardlui

West Highland Way

Glengyle

Loch
Lubnaig

Stronachlachar

Ben
A'an
(1520ft) ▲

Ben Ledi (2857ft) ▲

Inversnaid

The Trossachs

Loch Katrine

Callander

Tarbet ◀

Argyll

Ben Venue
(2370ft) ▲

Loch
Achray

Loch Venachar

Doune

Dunblane

Ben
Lomond
(3192ft) ▲

Loch Ard

Duke's
Pass

Loch Drunkie

Aberfoyle

A9

QUEEN ELIZABETH
FOREST PARK

Lake of
Menteith

Carse of Stirling

Blair
Drummond
Safari Park

Dumyat
(1376ft) ▲

Rowardennan

Inverbeg

Forth

Kippen

Gargunnock

Stirling

Luss

Loch
Lomond

Conic Hill
(1175 ft) ▲

Balfron

Gargunnock Hills

Balmaha

Drymen

Fintry Hills

Gartocharn

Killearn

The Campsies

Arden

Duncryne
(470ft) ▲

Dumgoyne

Fintry

Balloch

Glengoyne

Campsie Fells

Denny

Alexandria

Bonnybridge

Falkirk
Wheel

0   5 miles

Glasgow ▼

Stirling

Straddling the River Forth a few miles upstream from the estuary at Kincardine, **STIRLING** (ⓦ www.stirling.co.uk) appears at first glance like a smaller version of Edinburgh. With its crag-top castle, steep, cobbled streets and mixed community of locals, students and tourists, it's an appealing place, though it lacks the cosmopolitan edge of its near neighbours Edinburgh and Glasgow.

Stirling was the scene of some of the most significant developments in the evolution of the Scottish nation. It was here that the Scots under William Wallace defeated the English at the **Battle of Stirling Bridge** in 1297, only to fight – and win again – under Robert the Bruce just a couple of miles away at the **Battle of Bannockburn** in 1314. Stirling

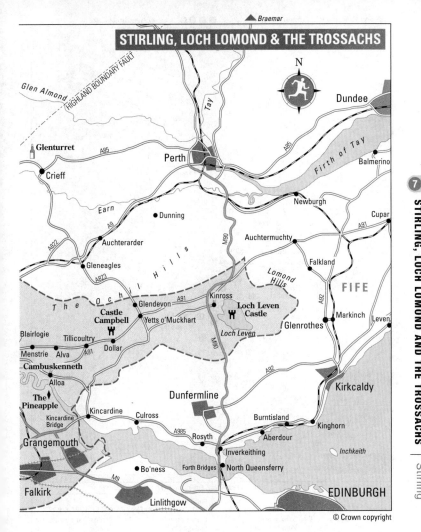

enjoyed its golden age in the fifteenth to seventeenth centuries, most notably when its castle was the favoured residence of the Stuart monarchy and the setting for the coronation in 1543 of the young Mary, future Queen of Scots. By the early eighteenth century the town was again besieged, its location being of strategic importance during the Jacobite rebellions of 1715 and 1745.

Today Stirling is known for its **castle** – arguably the best in Scotland, and certainly as atmospheric as Edinburgh's – and the lofty **Wallace Monument**, a mammoth Victorian monolith high on Abbey Craig to the northeast which has become a place of pilgrimage for admirers both of William Wallace and of Mel Gibson's Oscar-winning film epic *Braveheart*, based on Wallace's life.

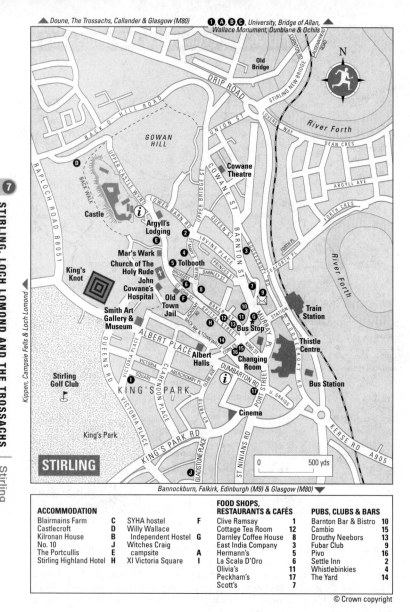

N

Old
Bridge

DRIP ROAD

STIRLING NEW BRIDGE

River Forth

OVERS WAY

BACK O HILL ROAD

UNION ST

DEAN CRES

GOWAN
HILL

RAPLOCH ROAD B8051

UPPER CASTLE WYND

BACK WALK

LOWER BARN RD

COWANE ST

ARGYLL AVE

FORTH CRES

Cowane
Theatre

UPPER BRIDGE ST

QUEEN ST

BARNTON ST

FORTH PL

River Forth

Castle

LOWER BARN RD

ⓘ

Argyll's
Lodging

❷

IRVINE PLACE

STUART ST

SEAFORTH PL

D

E

Mar's Wark

Church of The
Holy Rude

John
Cowane's
Hospital

❹

❺ Tolbooth

PRINCES ST

DARNLEY ST

❼

❾

King's
Knot

BROAD ST

❻

❽

FRIARS ST

BAKER ST

Smith Art
Gallery &
Museum

Old
Town
Jail

F

SPITTAL STREET

BACK WK & TOWN WALL

ACADEMY RD

❿

⓫

G

Train
Station

STATION RD

GOOSECROFT RD

MURRAY PL

ALBERT PLACE

⓬

⓭ Bus Stop

Thistle
Centre

QUEENS RD

VICTORIA PLACE

VICTORIA
SQUARE

CLARENDON PLACE

ABERCROMBY PL

COWANE ST

⓮

⓯

Albert
Halls

Changing
Room

PORT STREET

COW LN

KING ST

Bus Station

KING'S   PARK

Stirling
Golf Club

VICTORIA PLACE

ⓘ

DUMBARTON RD

BO 819

U GRAIGS

⓱

KERSE RD A905

King's Park

GLADSTONE PLACE

KING'S PARK RD

Cinema

ST NINIANS RD

0   500 yds

STIRLING

Ⓙ

ACCOMMODATION			FOOD SHOPS, RESTAURANTS & CAFÉS		PUBS, CLUBS & BARS	
Blairmains Farm	C	SYHA hostel F	Clive Ramsay	1	Barnton Bar & Bistro	10
Castlecroft	D	Willy Wallace	Cottage Tea Room	12	Cambio	15
Kilronan House	B	Independent Hostel G	Darnley Coffee House	8	Drouthy Neebors	13
No. 10	J	Witches Craig	East India Company	3	Fubar Club	9
The Portcullis	E	campsite A	Hermann's	5	Pivo	16
Stirling Highland Hotel	H	XI Victoria Square I	La Scala D'Oro	6	Settle Inn	2
			Olivia's	11	Whistlebinkies	4
			Peckham's	17	The Yard	14
			Scott's	7		

Arrival and information

The **train station** is near the centre of town on Station Road, just five minutes' walk from the **bus station** on Goosecroft Road. To reach the town centre from the train station, walk up Station Road and turn left at the mini-roundabout; from the bus station cut through the Thistle Shopping Centre to reach the main drag, pedestrianized Port Street/Murray Place.

The main **tourist office** is near the town centre at 41 Dumbarton Rd (April & May Mon–Sat 9am–5pm; June & Sept Mon–Sat 9am–6pm, Sun 10am–4pm; July & Aug Mon–Sat 9am–7pm, Sun 9.30am–6pm; Oct Mon–Sat 9.30am–5pm; Nov–March Mon–Fri 10am–5pm, Sat 10am–4pm, ☎01786/475019), and stocks a wide range of books, maps and leaflets and runs an accommodation booking service. The tourist centre outside the main castle entrance is equally frenetic (daily: April–Oct 9.30am–6pm; Nov–March 9.30pm–5pm; ☎01786/479901). Because Stirling is a compact town, sightseeing in the Old Town is best done **on foot**, though to avoid the steep hills or to reach the more distant attractions you can take the hop-on/hop-off City Sightseeing **bus tour** (every 30min April–Oct 9.30am–4.30pm; £7) which takes a circular route around the bus and train stations, the castle, the attractive satellite village of Bridge of Allan, the university, Wallace Monument and Smith Art Gallery. Actor-led **ghost walks** leave from the Old Town Jail during July & August (nightly Tues–Sat 8.30pm; 90min duration; £6; ☎01786/450050).

Accommodation

Between May and October, it's worth booking **accommodation** as far in advance as possible. Stirling has good options in most categories from backpacker hostels to large hotels, and is understandably popular both as a lower-key alternative to Glasgow or Edinburgh, and as a base for exploring central Scotland. For a fee, the tourist office will help you find somewhere to stay.

Hotels and B&Bs

Blairmains Farm Manor Loan, Blairlogie ☎01259/761338. Simple, friendly farmhouse B&B just three miles east of Stirling, adjacent to a farm shop and café. ❷

Castlecroft Ballengeich Rd ☎01786/474933, ⓦ www.castlecroft.uk.com. Modern guesthouse with six en-suite rooms on the site of the King's Stables just beneath the castle rock, with terrific views north and west. ❸

Kilronan House 15 Kenilworth Rd, Bridge of Allan ☎01786/831054, ⓦ www.kilronan.co.uk. A grand Victorian family house built in 1853 with spacious en-suite B&B rooms in the fine Victorian spa town of Bridge of Allan, just a couple of miles north of Stirling and easily reached by regular buses. ❷

No. 10 10 Gladstone Place ☎01786/472681, ⓦ www.cameron-10.co.uk. Modernized Victorian home with neat, uncluttered decor providing friendly and pleasant B&B accommodation close to the city centre. ❸

The Portcullis Castle Wynd ☎01786/472290, ⓦ www.theportcullishotel.com. Traditional hotel with four en-suite rooms in an imposing building built in 1787. Dramatic Old Town location adjacent to the castle. Cosy bar, open log fire and beer garden. ❺

Stirling Highland Hotel Spittal St ☎01786/272727, ⓦ www.paramount-hotels.co.uk. Upmarket if rather pretentiously genteel hotel in a handsome Victorian Gothic building that once

housed Stirling High School and still maintains an observatory on the top floor. It features comfortable en-suite rooms and has good leisure facilities, including a 15m pool and a gym. The location, in the Old Town just 500 yards from the castle, is excellent. ❽

XI Victoria Square 11 Victoria Square ☎01786/475545, ⓦ www.xivictoriasquare.com. Very stylish B&B in town with designer rooms, complimentary drams of malt whisky, great breakfasts and fine views of the Old Town. ❻

Hostel, campsite and campus accommodation

Willy Wallace Independent Hostel 77 Murray Place ☎01786/446773, ⓦ www .willywallacehostel.com. A welcoming, friendly place located 100 yards from the station in an old Victorian building; this is the liveliest budget option in town, with a big, bright common room, six dorms, a double and a twin (both ❶).

SYHA hostel St John St ☎0870/004 1149, ⓦ www.syha.org.uk. Located at the top of the town, a strenuous trek with a backpack, in a converted church with an impressive 1824 Palladian facade. All rooms have showers and toilets en suite, and facilities include a games room and Internet access.

Stirling University ☎01786/467141, ⓦ www .holidays.stir.ac.uk. Campus accommodation in single rooms in halls of residence a couple of miles north of the town centre. The hop-on/hop-off City Sightseeing tour bus passes through the campus, which is also served by regular buses #50, #53, #54, #58, #62 and #63 from Murray Place in the town centre. ❶ room only or ❷ B&B; June–early Sept. **Stirling Management Centre** Stirling University campus ☎01786/451712, ⓦwww.smc.stir.ac.uk.

Also on campus, but available year-round, the centre has hotel-standard en-suite rooms and residents have use of the university's pool and gym. ❽ **Witches Craig Campsite** Blairlogie ☎01786/474947. A pleasant spot three miles east off the A91 road to St Andrews. Take #62 bus from Stirling. April–Oct.

The Town

Stirling evolved from the top down, starting with its castle and gradually spreading south and east onto the low-lying flood plain. At the centre of the original **Old Town**, Broad Street was the main thoroughfare, with St John Street running more or less parallel, and St Mary's Wynd forming part of the original route to Stirling Bridge below. In the eighteenth and nineteenth centuries, as the threat of attack decreased, the centre of commercial life crept down towards the River Forth, with the modern town growing on the edge of the plain over which the castle has traditionally stood guard.

Stirling Castle

Stirling Castle (daily: April to end Sept 9.30am–6pm; Oct–March 9.30am–5pm; £8.50, includes entry to Argyll's Lodging) must have presented would-be invaders with a formidable challenge. Its impregnability is most daunting when you approach the town from the west, from where the sheer 250ft drop down the side of the crag is most obvious. The rock was first fortified during the Iron Age, though what you see now dates largely from the fifteenth and sixteenth centuries. Built on many levels, the main buildings are interspersed with delightful gardens and patches of lawn, while endless battlements, cannon ports, hidden staircases and other nooks and crannies make it thoroughly explorable and inspiring.

The souvenir-choked **visitor centre** is in a whitewashed cottage on one side of the esplanade car park (£2 for cars); unless you've got lots of time, don't bother with the introductory film giving a potted history of the castle. Free **guided tours** begin at the well in the lower square (every 30min July–Sept and at various times thereafter; ☎01786 431316). A comprehensive audio guide in six languages is also available for £2; while it allows you to go round at your own pace it does lack the personal touch.

From the esplanade, cross a bridge over the grassy moat to Guardroom Square. From here, you can head up through the much-modified but still imposing **Forework**, designed by James IV with classic round towers, arrow slits and battlements to underline his romantic view of royal authority. Through the archway is the **Outer Close**, the first of two main courtyard areas. Looming over it is the magnificently restored **Great Hall**, dating from 1501–3 and used as a barracks by the British army until 1964. The building stands out across Stirling for its controversially bright, creamy yellow cladding, added after the discovery during renovations of a stretch of the original sixteenth-century limewash behind a bricked-up doorway. Inside, the hall has been restored to its original state as the finest medieval secular building in Scotland, complete with five gaping fireplaces and an impressive hammer beam ceiling of rough-hewn wood. To one side of the Great Hall, displays in the restored castle **kitchens** make a lively attempt to re-create the preparations for the spectacular Renaissance banquet given by Mary, Queen of Scots for the baptism of the future James VI. Along with an audiovisual display describing how delicacies for the feast were procured, plus an abundance of stuffed animals (who, we are assured, died natural deaths) in various stages of preparation, the kitchens feature life-size models fussing over *faux* recipe books with delights such as sugar wineglasses, golden steamed custard and dressed peacock.

The exterior of the **Palace**, the largest building in the castle, dates from 1540–42 and is richly decorated with grotesque carved figures and Renaissance sculpture, including, in the left-hand corner, the glaring bearded figure of James V in the dress of a commoner. Inside in the royal apartments are the **Stirling Heads**, 56 elegantly carved oak medallions which once comprised the ceiling of the Presence Chamber, where visitors were presented to royalty. Otherwise the royal apartments are mostly bare, their emptiness emphasizing the fine dimensions and wonderful views. Note the ongoing restoration of the Palace (until 2009) means that different sections may occasionally be closed.

There's an internal courtyard known as the **Lion's Den** which had a small garden and was used for outdoor theatre; the name also indicates that it was the likely exercise area of a lion that James V is known to have received as a gift in 1537.

On the opposite side of the Inner Close, the sloping upper courtyard of the castle, the **Chapel Royal** was built in 1594 by James VI for the baptism of his son, to replace an earlier chapel that was deemed insufficiently impressive. The interior is charming, with a seventeenth-century fresco of elaborate scrolls and patterns. Alongside, the **King's Old Building**, at the highest point in the castle, now houses the museum of the Argyll and Sutherland Highlanders regiment, with its collection of well-polished silver and memorabilia, including a seemingly endless display of Victoria Crosses. While the regiment has a proud military history, the museum makes an effort to stay up to date, with material relating to the role of the regiment's soldiers in Northern Ireland and the Gulf War. Go through a narrow passageway between the King's Old Building and the Chapel Royal to get to the **Douglas Gardens**, reputedly the place where the eighth earl of Douglas, suspected of treachery, was thrown to his death by James II in 1452. It's a lovely, quiet corner of the castle, with mature trees and battlements over which there are splendid views of the rising Highlands beyond, as well as a bird's-eye view down to the **King's Knot**, a series of grassed octagonal mounds, which in the seventeenth century were planted with box trees and ornamental hedges.

The Old Town

Leaving the castle, head downhill into the old centre of Stirling, fortified behind the massive, whinstone boulders of the **town walls**, built in the mid-sixteenth century and intended to ward off the advances of Henry VIII, who had set his sights on the young Mary, Queen of Scots as a wife for his son, Edward. The walls now constitute some of the best-preserved town defences in Scotland, and can be traced by following the path known as **Back Walk**. This walkway was built in the eighteenth century and in the upper reaches leads right under the castle, taut along the edge of the crag. Though a little overgrown in places, it's a great way to take in the castle's setting, and in various places you'll catch panoramic views of the surrounding countryside.

At the top of Castle Wynd, **Argyll's Lodging** (daily: April–Sept 9.30am–6pm; Oct–March 9.30am–5pm; HS; £3.30) is a romantic Renaissance town house built by Sir William Alexander of Menstrie in the seventeenth century. Inside, an informative exhibition takes you through the history of the building in its various incarnations, from its period as the home of Alexander, the first earl of

Stirling, to its later uses as military hospital and youth hostel. The oldest part of the building, marked by low ceilings and tiny windows, is the Great Kitchen, whose enormous fireplace comes complete with a special recess for salt, while the Drawing Room, hung with lavishly decorated purple tapestries, contains the ninth earl's imposing chair of state. An adjoining smaller room for his wife, Anna, contains her personal chamber pot, an ornate affair in purple.

Further down Castle Wynd at the top of Broad Street, a richly decorated facade hides the dilapidated **Mar's Wark**, a would-be palace which the first Earl of Mar, regent of Scotland and hereditary Keeper of Stirling Castle, started in 1570. His dream house was never to be realized, however, for he died two years later and what had been built was left to ruin, its degeneration speeded up by extensive damage during the 1745 Jacobite rebellion. Behind here is the **Church of the Holy Rude** (May–Sept Mon–Sat 10am–5pm), a fine medieval structure, the oldest parts of which, including the impressive oak hammer beam ceiling, date from the early fifteenth century. It's not hard to imagine the lavish ceremony that was held here in 1567 for the coronation of the infant James VI – later the first monarch of the United Kingdom; the atmospheric graveyard alongside can conjure up ghosts of a different type if you're here to watch the sun set. Just south of the church on the edge of the crag, the grand E-shaped **John Cowane's Hospital** was built as a 1649 almshouse for "decayed [unsuccessful] members of the Guild of Merchants". Above the entrance, the wealthy merchant John Cowane, founder of the hospital, is commemorated in a statue which, it is said, comes alive at Hogmanay.

A short walk down St John Street, a sweeping driveway leads up to the impressive **Old Town Jail** (daily 10am–5pm; ☎01786/450050, Ⓦwww .oldtownjail.com). It was built by Victorian prison reformers as an alternative to the depravity of the medieval Tolbooth (see below). Subsequently used as a military jail, it was rescued from dereliction in 1994, with part of the building turned into offices and a substantial section used to create an entertaining visitor attraction. Telling the history of the building and prisons in general, tours are either self-led using an audio handset (£4.50) or taken by actors (April–Sept daily; Oct–March Sat & Sun; £5.75), who enthusiastically change costumes and character a number of times; among the features of the jail they'll introduce you to is a working example of the dreaded crank, a lever which prisoners had to turn 14,400 times per day for punishment. Take the glass lift up to the prison roof to admire spectacular views across Stirling and the Forth Valley. Opposite and just uphill from the entrance to the Old Town Jail on St John Street, look out for the **Boy's Club**, a 1929 conversion of the town's old butter market, with its encouraging little mottoes engraved above the door such as "Keep smiling" and "Quarrelling is taboo".

Directly opposite the Old Town Jail, between St John Street and Broad Street, is the original medieval prison, the **Tolbooth**, itself completely renovated in the form of the city's most inspirational music and arts centre (daily from 9am; ☎01786/274000, Ⓦwww.stirling.gov.uk/tolbooth). Originally built in 1705, the striking modern redevelopment received an architectural award in 2002 as the UK's best public building. It incorporates three separate medieval buildings, including the former town hall and courthouse (now the main auditorium) – during the renovations a secret staircase was discovered, as was a complete skeleton, thought to have been that of the last man publicly hanged in Stirling. Inside there's an airy café-bar, a restaurant for evening dining (see p.415), a top-floor viewing platform looking out over the Old Town rooftops and a box office where you can find out about the centre's diverse programme incorporating comedy, theatre, touring bands and the occasional festival.

Back on Broad Street, the town's former marketplace, there are various historical buildings and monuments including the stone **Mercat Cross** (the unicorn on top is known, inexplicably, as "the puggy") and **Darnley's House**, where Mary, Queen of Scots' husband is believed to have lodged while she lorded it up in the castle; it now houses a coffee shop (see p.415).

The Lower Town and around

The further downhill you go in Stirling's Lower Town, the more recent the buildings become. By the time the two main streets of the Old Town merge into King Street, austere Victorian facades block the sun from the cobbled road. Stirling's main **shopping** area is down here, along Port Street and Murray Place. Tucked in above the Crawford Arcade off King Street, the **Changing Room** (Wed–Sat noon–5pm; free; ☎01786/479361) is a dynamic contemporary art space linked to the Tolbooth, with various exhibitions and events throughout the year. The only other sight of note in the centre is the **Smith Art Gallery and Museum** (Tues–Sat 10.30am–5pm, Sun 2–5pm; free; ⓦ www.smithartgallery .demon.co.uk), a short walk west up Dumbarton Road near the King's Knot. Founded in 1874 with a legacy from local painter and collector Thomas Stuart Smith, it houses "The Stirling Story", a reasonably entertaining whirl through the history of the town, balancing out the stories of kings and queens with more social and domestic history. Among the exhibits is the world's oldest known football, made out of a pig's bladder; it was found in the rafters of the Queen's Chamber in the castle and is thought to date from the 1540s. The small art gallery includes changing displays of mostly local arts and crafts, contemporary art and photography, and there's a pleasant café inside.

The fifteenth-century **Old Bridge** over the Forth lies to the north on the edge of the town centre (a 20min walk from Murray Place). Although once the most important river crossing in Scotland – the lowest bridging point on the Forth until the new bridge was built in 1831 – it now stands virtually forgotten, an incidental reminder of Stirling's former importance. An earlier wooden **bridge** nearby, no trace of which survives, was the focus of the Battle of Stirling Bridge in 1297, where William Wallace defeated the English (see below).

The National Wallace Monument and Cambuskenneth

A mile and a half north of the Old Town over the new bridge, the prominent **National Wallace Monument** (daily: March–May & Oct 10am–5pm; June 10am–6pm; July & Aug 9.30am–6pm; Sept 9.30am–5pm; Nov–Feb 10.30am–4pm; £6, including a free audio-tour handset; ☎01786/472140) is a freestanding, five-storey tower built in the 1860s as a tribute to Sir William Wallace, the freedom fighter who led Scottish resistance to Edward I, the "Hammer of the Scots", in the late thirteenth century. A hero to generations of Scots, Wallace shot to international fame on the back of his depiction by Mel Gibson in the epic movie *Braveheart*. Though derided for its historical inaccuracies, the film was hugely popular not just in Scotland but around the world, and with the general lack of historic buildings closely associated with Wallace, the monument has become a focus for Wallace (and *Braveheart*) fans. The crag on which it is set was the scene of Wallace's greatest victory, when he sent his troops charging down the hillside onto the plain to defeat the English at the Battle of Stirling Bridge in 1297. Exhibits inside the tower include Wallace's long steel sword and the Hall of (Scottish) Heroes, a row of stern white marble busts featuring John Knox and Adam Smith, as well as a life-size "talking" model of Wallace, who tells visitors about his preparations for the battle. If you can manage the climb – up 246 spiral steps – to the top of the 220ft tower, you'll be rewarded with superb views across to Fife and Ben Lomond. Bus #62 or the Heritage Bus Tour will get you here.

About a mile south from the Wallace Monument lie the ruins of **Cambus-kenneth Abbey**, rather incongruously set right on the edge of a suburb of modern bungalows (daily April–Sept 9.30am–6.30pm; free). Founded in 1147 by David I on the site of an Augustinian settlement, the abbey is distinguished by its early fourteenth-century bell tower, though there's little else to see other than a graveyard and the stone foundations of what was obviously a substantial building. The Scots parliament met here in 1326 to pledge allegiance to Robert the Bruce's son David, and James III (1451–88) and his wife, Queen Margaret of Denmark, are both buried in the grounds, their graves marked by a nineteenth-century monument erected at the insistence of Queen Victoria.

Bannockburn

A couple of miles south of Stirling centre, on the A872, all but surrounded by suburban housing, the **Bannockburn Heritage Centre** (daily: April–Oct 10am–5.30pm; rest of the year 10.30am–4pm, closed Jan; NTS; £5) commemorates the most famous battle in Scottish history, when King Robert the Bruce won his mighty victory over the English at the **Battle of Bannockburn** on June 24, 1314. It was this battle, the climax of the Wars of Independence, which united the Scots under Bruce and led to independence from England sealed by the Declaration of Arbroath (1320) and the Treaty of Northampton (1328).

Within the centre there is an audiovisual presentation on the battle and the background to it, highlighting the brilliantly innovative tactics Bruce employed in mustering his army to defeat a much larger English force. Visitors can also hear "living history" talks from actors dressed in period costume and observe their use of ancient weaponry (daily noon). Outside, a concrete rotunda encloses a cairn which marks the spot said to have been Bruce's command post for an early phase of the fighting. Of the original stone, only a fragment remains, safely on display inside the visitor centre. Over-eager visitors used to chip pieces off, and the final straw came when a particularly zealous enthusiast attempted to blast enough of it away to make two curling stones. Pondering the scene is a stirring equestrian **statue** of Bruce, set against the skyline of Stirling Castle, the English army's approach to which he was intentionally blocking. The actual site

△ Robert the Bruce, Bannockburn

of the main battle is, oddly, still a matter of debate. Most agree that it didn't take place near the present visitor centre; a cogent theory argues that it took place on a boggy carse a mile or so to the west. Bus #56 leaves for Bannockburn from Murray Place every hour.

Eating

Stirling doesn't have a strong reputation for its **restaurants**, with venues struggling to hang around long enough to earn a good name. However, it is possible to find places serving quality contemporary Scottish cuisine and lighter **bistro**-style food, and inevitably there's a range of tearooms, cafés and pubs. Good **deli** food can be found in Stirling at *Scott's*, 22 Barnton St (Mon–Thurs 8am–8pm, Fri & Sat 8am–10pm, Sun noon–6pm), and at the well-stocked *Peckham's* chain at 52 Port St (daily 8am–midnight). In **Bridge of Allan**, knowledgeable foodies head straight for *Clive Ramsay's* delicatessen at 28 Henderson St (the main street), one of the best delis in Scotland, which also has a great **café**-restaurant (daily 8am–late; ☎01786 833903, ⓦwww.cliveramsay.com) serving everything from breakfast through to table d'hôte dinners at night.

Barnton Bar and Bistro Barnton St. Popular local bar with a hearty menu of pub staples, great coffee and an upbeat attitude. Moderate.

Cambio Cnr Corn Exchange and the top of King St. Popular, stylish bar serving bistro food and an intriguing selection of cocktails. Moderate.

Cottage Tea Room Spittal St. Upmarket tearoom serving traditional fare en route to the castle. Inexpensive.

Darnley Coffee House Bow St (the continuation of Broad St). A bit old-fashioned but with plenty of Old Town atmosphere and serving reasonably priced lunches and teas in an impressive barrel-vaulted interior. Inexpensive.

East India Company 7 Viewfield Place ☎01786/471330. Good Indian food, Raj-style decor and the friendliest service in town. Moderate.

Hermann's 58 Broad St ☎01786/450632. Set in the historic Mar Place House towards the top of the Old Town, with a downstairs brasserie open at lunchtime and upmarket Austrian-Scottish dining such as *jager schnitzel* (veal) or Scottish lamb with cheese potatoes in the evening. Expensive.

La Scala D'Oro Tolbooth, Jail Wynd ☎01786/274010. Contemporary dishes based on fusion of Scottish and Italian cuisine. Open for lunch and dinner including a pre-theatre menu. Moderate to expensive.

Olivia's 5 Baker St ☎01786/446277. Modern Scottish cooking in a reasonably smart but informal small restaurant. Mon–Fri eve only. Moderate.

Peckham's 52 Port St ☎01786/463222. Plain decor but tasty international modern dishes within the same building as a popular deli. Moderate.

Nightlife and entertainment

Nightlife in Stirling revolves around **pubs** and **bars** and is dominated by the student population. The lively *Barnton Bar and Bistro* (see above) serves a good selection of beers and food in a setting of wrought-iron and marble tables, while the *Settle Inn*, 91 St Mary's Wynd, Stirling's oldest alehouse (est. 1733), serves a wide range of Scottish real ales to an eclectic crowd. Nearby at no. 73, *Whistlebinkies* has regular folk music sessions and reasonable bar meals. The hipper modern bars in town include *Cambio*, located in an old bank at 1 Corn Exchange, and its next-door neighbour *Pivo*, a popular hangout with DJs playing regularly. *Drouthy Neebors* on Baker St, with its slate-clad bar, is another popular nightspot.

If you want to carry on after the pubs close, you could try *The Yard*, a trendy, three-bar **nightclub** on the Back Walk which gets particularly busy at weekends, or *Fubar Club* in Maxwell Place, off Murray Place, which is known for its lively student-oriented nights. For **live music**, head for the Tolbooth (see p.412), a popular venue for local and touring folk, rock and jazz acts. If you're here in summer, check local publicity for rock concerts sometimes held on the castle esplanade. The Tolbooth also has a regular **comedy** club, while the Albert Halls near the tourist office are used for small classical concerts.

The main venue for **theatre** and **film** is the excellent MacRobert Arts Centre (℡01786/466666, ⓦwww.macrobert.org) on the university campus, which shows a good selection of mainstream and art-house films, as well as occasional jazz and dance performances.

Around Stirling

Stirling's strategic position between the Highlands and Lowlands was not only important in medieval times, but as the Industrial Revolution grew across Scotland's central belt so the town's proximity to the Forth gave it renewed significance. To the north and west of Stirling, the historic aspect of the region is reflected in the cathedral at **Dunblane**, the imposing castle at **Doune** and the sedate settlements of the **Carse of Stirling**, while to the east and south, on either side of the Forth, the county of **Clackmannanshire** mill towns, at the foot of the **Ochil Hills**, and the area around **Falkirk** tell of a rich industrial heritage. An undoubted highlight of this hinterland is the massive **Falkirk Wheel**, a spectacular feat of modern engineering which transfers canal boats up and down a 100-foot drop at the interchange of the newly restored Forth and Clyde and Union canals.

Dunblane

Frequent trains, bus #58 and bus #358 in school term-time, make the journey five miles north of Stirling to **DUNBLANE**, a small, attractive place which has been an important ecclesiastical centre since the seventh century, when the Celts founded the church of St Blane here. **Dunblane Cathedral** (April–Sept Mon–Sat 9.30am–6pm, Sun 1.30pm–6pm; Oct–March Mon–Sat 9.30am–4pm, Sun 2–4pm; HS; free; ℡ 01786 823388) dates mainly from the thirteenth century, and restoration work carried out a century ago has returned it to its Gothic splendour. Inside, note the delicate blue-purple stained glass, and the exquisitely carved pews, screen and choir stalls, all crafted in the early twentieth century. Various memorials within the cathedral include a tenth-century Celtic cross-slab standing stone and a modern, four-sided standing stone by Richard Kindersley commemorating the tragic shooting in 1996 of sixteen Dunblane schoolchildren and their teacher by local man, Thomas Hamilton. The cathedral, praised in the highest terms by John Ruskin ("I know not anything so perfect in its simplicity, and so beautiful, in all the Gothic with which I am acquainted"), stands serenely amid a clutch of old buildings, among them the seventeenth-century Dean's House, which houses the small **Dunblane Museum** (May to early Oct Mon–Sat 10.30am–4.30pm; free) with exhibits on local history. Close by stands the **Leighton Library** (Wed–Fri 10am–12.30pm & 2pm–4.30pm; donation). Established in 1684, it's the oldest private lending library in Scotland and houses 4500 books in ninety languages printed between 1500 and 1840. Visitors can browse through some of the country's rarest books, including a first edition of Sir Walter Scott's *Lady of the Lake*.

Overlooking the cathedral in Cathedral Square is *Chimes House B&B* (℡0845/6442223, ⓦwww.bedandbreakfast-scotland.co.uk; ➌) with pleasant en-suite doubles and a good Scottish breakfast.

Doune and around

DOUNE, eight miles northwest of Stirling and three miles due west of Dunblane, is a sleepy village surrounding a stern-looking castle. The fourteenth-century **castle** (April–Sept daily 9.30am–6.30pm; Oct–March Mon–Wed & Sat 9.30am–4.30pm, Sun 2pm–4.30pm; £3; HS) is a marvellous semi-ruin standing on a small hill in a bend of the River Teith. Today the most prominent features of the castle are its mighty 95-foot gatehouse, with spacious vaulted rooms, and the kitchens, complete with medieval rubbish chute. Built by Robert, Duke of Albany, it ended up in the hands of the second earl of Moray, James Stewart – son of James V and half-brother of Mary, Queen of Scots – who was murdered in 1592 and immortalized in the ballad *The Bonnie Earl of Moray*; it has been in the hands of the Moray family ever since, though it was used as a prison by Bonnie Prince Charlie's army after the battle of Falkirk. The castle's greatest claim to fame today, however, is as the setting for the 1970s movie *Monty Python and the Holy Grail*. Despite the legions of Python fans who come here on pilgrimage, Historic Scotland is rather po-faced about the links, though the shop by the gatehouse does keep a scrapbook of stills from the film, as well as a small selection of souvenirs including bottles of the locally brewed Holy Grail Ale. Close to the castle, **accommodation** is available at the excellent *Glenardoch House*, Castle Road (☎01786/841489; May–Sept; ❸), an eighteenth-century country-house B&B with two comfortable en-suite rooms and a beautiful riverside garden.

Three miles south of Doune, families will find plenty to entertain them at the **Blair Drummond Safari Park** (mid-March–Sept daily 10am–5.30pm; £9.50; ⓦwww.blairdrummond.com), which attempts to re-create the African bush in the Scottish countryside with everything from big cats to rhinos and elephants. Take the regular #59 bus from Stirling bus station. Meanwhile, at the crest of the hill on the B824 between Doune and Dunblane, anyone interested in the modern history of the British Army is likely to be diverted by the **statue of Sir David Stirling**, the founder of the SAS who grew up on the nearby Keir estate, on a spot enjoying sweeping views of the Trossachs peaks.

The Carse of Stirling

West of Stirling, the wide flood plain of the Forth river is known as the Carse of Forth or **Carse of Stirling**, fertile farmland with, to the south, the Gargunnock and Fintry hills, which gradually blend into the **Campsie Fells**. To the north are the Trossachs (see p.429), which inevitably draw away many visitors, with the main road west of Stirling, the A811, connecting to Loch Lomond through the carse. There's some pleasant walking in the Campsies, including the **Campsie Fells Trail** (leaflets and information available at Stirling tourist office), which links villages such as **Fintry**, **Kippen** and **Gargunnock**, with forest and open-country paths. The hourly bus #12 from Stirling to Balfron goes through Gargunnock and Kippen.

Gargunnock and Kippen

Six miles west of Stirling and just off the A811, **GARGUNNOCK** has a mix of eighteenth-century cottages and modern bungalows with a seventeenth-century crow-stepped church at its centre. The village is home to the oldest **agricultural show** in Scotland, held here every summer since 1794 (check website for further details ⓦwww.gargunnockshow.co.uk). To the east of the village in rolling parkland is handsome **Gargunnock House**, ancestral home of the Stirlings, where Chopin is reputed to have spent two weeks improving the family's keyboard skills. Larger groups (up to sixteen) can stay here on a self-catering basis – contact the Landmark Trust (℡01628/825925, 𝖂www.landmarktrust.org.uk; see p.47). There is one **pub** in the centre of the village, the *Gargunnock Inn*, which serves real ale and better than average bar meals.

West from Gargunnock is the attractive village of **KIPPEN** with its distinctive red sandstone church tower. There is little to do in Kippen other than wander along its pretty cobbled street of eighteenth-century houses, which include a beautifully restored **smithy** (admission by arrangement with the NTS; ℡0141/6162266), and round the adjoining ruined church and graveyard. However, you can enjoy a good **meal** at *The Cross Keys*, an eighteenth-century pub on the main street, which also has two twin **rooms** (℡01786/870293; ❺). Across the road, the equally welcoming *The Inn at Kippen* (℡01786 871010) serves good food and has several contemporary rooms (❹).

Fintry and Drymen

The one settlement within the Campsies themselves is **FINTRY**, a picture-postcard village at the head of Strathendrick valley that is a regular winner of the "Best Kept Small Village in Scotland" award. There are a couple of **places to stay**: if you're feeling flush, try the wonderful *Culcreuch Castle Hotel* (℡01360/860228, 𝖂www.culcreuch.com; ❼), a fourteenth-century pile with thick walls and parapets which includes the atmospheric *Dungeon Bar*. In addition to hearty bar food, *Fintry Inn* (℡01360/860224; ❸) offers guests the opportunity to stay in a small self-contained flat within its white building on Main Street.

At the western end of the Campsie Fells, all roads (including the West Highland Way long-distance footpath – see box on p.426) meet at the small village of **DRYMEN**, an ancient ecclesiastical centre and stopover point for Highland drovers that sits peacefully in the hills overlooking the winding Endrick Water as it nears Loch Lomond. In the village square, the small seasonal **tourist office** (June–Sept Mon–Sat 9am–5pm, Sun 10am–4pm; ℡01360/660068) is adjacent to the basic *Winnock Hotel* (℡01360/660245, 𝖂www.winnockhotel.com; ❻), which has comfortable en-suite **rooms** and a reasonable restaurant. Nearby, the *Clachan Inn* (℡01360/660824; ❷) is an atmospheric spot for some **pub grub** or a pint. Established in 1734, it's reputed to be Scotland's oldest licensed public house. Across the road and popular with a more sedate clientele, *The Pottery* is great for lunch, mid-afternoon tea or dinner. Elsewhere in the area, moderately priced **meals** can be enjoyed at *The Beech Tree Inn* in Dumgoyne village, five miles south of Drymen, while in the well-heeled village of Killearn, *The Old Mill* dishes up great food and beer in a cosy atmosphere by a roaring open fire. Just one mile south of Dumgoyne, more drink is on offer at **Glengoyne Distillery** (tours on the hour Mon–Sat 10am–4pm, Sun noon–4pm; £4.50). It's the closest whisky distillery to Glasgow offering tours.

Falkirk and around

Southeast of Stirling along the south bank of the widening Forth Estuary, farmland gives way to industry, notably BP's gargantuan petrochemical plant nearby at Grangemouth. The lights and fires of the refineries are spectacular at night, and inspired Bertrand Tavernier to make his dour 1979 sci-fi film *Death Watch* in Scotland. Strangely, given its nondescript industrial surroundings, **FALKIRK** – located about halfway between Stirling and Edinburgh on the M9 motorway – has a good deal of visible history, going right back to the remains of the

Roman Antonine Wall. It was also the site of two major battles, one in 1298 when William Wallace's army fell victim to the English under Edward I, and the other in 1746, when Bonnie Prince Charlie's disintegrating force, retreating northwards, sent the Hanoverians packing in one of its last victories. Traditionally a livestock centre, Falkirk became better known for its industry, with the founding in 1759 of the now-redundant Carron Ironworks which manufactured "carronades" (small cannons) for Nelson's fleet. The town was further transformed later in the eighteenth century by the construction of first the Forth and Clyde Canal, allowing easy access to Glasgow and the west coast, and then the Union Canal, which continued the route through to Edinburgh. Just twenty years later, the trains arrived, and the canals gradually fell into disuse.

The town of Falkirk is a busy local shopping hub, whose only formal attraction, set in Callendar Park, is **Callendar House** (Mon–Sat 10am–5pm; April–Sept also Sun 2–5pm; £3; ⑩www.callendarhouse.org), which was owned by the staunchly Jacobite Livingston family. It's now an entertaining local history museum where trained staff in period costume guide you through a printer's and clockmaker's workshops, 1825 kitchens with gleaming utensils and a huge mechanized spits and a Georgian garden planted with traditional herbs and flowers. In the grounds, a small section of the Antonine Wall (see p.420) can be made out. In the oak-panelled Victorian library of the house, the **Historical Research Centre** (Mon–Fri 10am–12.30pm & 1.30–5pm; free) will gladly help you delve into local family history.

The Falkirk Wheel

While Falkirk's two canals were a very visible sign of the area's industrial heritage, it was only in recent years that their leisure potential was realized, thanks to British Waterway's £84.5 million **Millennium Link** project to restore the canals and re-establish a navigable link between east and west coasts. The icon of this project is the remarkable **Falkirk Wheel** (⑩www.thefalkirkwheel .co.uk), two miles west of Falkirk town centre. Opened in 2002, the giant grey wheel, the world's first rotating boat lift, scoops boats in two giant buckets, or caissons, the 115 feet between the levels of the two canals.

Previously, boats transferring between the Union and Forth and Clyde canals had to negotiate an exhausting flight of eleven locks, which could take a full day to complete. With the canals all but redundant, these locks were infilled in 1933, so the challenge of how to connect the two canals loomed large when the restoration project was first considered. The solution was this unique structure, built in concrete and steel by an international team of engineers and designers, which is capable of lifting some 600 tonnes of water extremely efficiently – it has been estimated that one turn of the wheel uses the same energy as eight toasters. The claw-like form of the wheel has an awkward, gangly kind of beauty, not least because it is an essentially simple engineering principle executed on a massive scale.

A **visitor centre** (daily: April–Oct 9am–6pm; Nov–March 9.30am–5pm; free) is located right underneath the wheel, and this is where to head for background information and to buy tickets for a **boat trip** (daily: April–Oct every 30mins 9.30am–5pm; Nov–March hourly 10am–3pm; £8), which involves a one-hour journey from the lower basin into the wheel, along the Union Canal for a short distance, then back down to the basin again via the wheel. However, the boat trip certainly isn't essential if you just want to see the wheel in action, which is arguably best done by **walking** around the basin and adjoining towpaths. From lock 16 on the Forth and Clyde canal, about halfway between the wheel and the centre of Falkirk, the *Bonny Barge* offers **cruises** (℡0772/0866397;

£9) along the canal, including an hourly shuttle up to the wheel. Bus #3 will take you to the wheel from Falkirk town centre; alternatively, it's a pleasant 20-minute walk along the Union Canal from Falkirk High train station.

Practicalities

Falkirk's centrally located **bus** station is at Callendar Riggs. Regular **trains** run from Edinburgh to Stirling via Falkirk **Grahamston Station**, while Falkirk **High Station**, which is further from the centre, is a stop on the Edinburgh–Glasgow line. From Grahamston Station it's a five-minute walk to the **tourist office**, 2–4 Glebe St (daily: June–Aug Mon–Sat 9.30am–5.30pm, Sun 12 noon–4pm; Sept & Oct Mon–Sat 10am–5pm; Nov–March Mon–Sat 10am–4pm; April & May Mon–Sat 10am–5pm; ☎01324/620244). Be sure to pick up the helpful Falkirk Heritage Trail leaflet if you want a look around the town centre. The best bet for **accommodation** is the elegant *Darroch House* B&B (☎01324/623041; ❸), on Camelon Road at the west end of town, with en-suite rooms and peaceful gardens. Rather different in style, *Beancross* (☎01324/718333, ⓦwww.beancross .co.uk; ❹) is a brightly coloured, modernized farm courtyard between Falkirk and junction 5 on the M9 motorway, with a mixture of stylish doubles and suites, plus a bar, bistro and family area.

The town has a reasonable selection of places to **eat** and **drink**. *Comma Bar Café*, 14 Lint Riggs, is a brasserie-style café and trendy bar, while *Behind the Wall* at 14 Melville St incorporates a microbrewery, café and restaurant – try a Falkirk 400 ale to accompany the Tex-Mex food. If you're strolling by the canal, call in at the three-storey *Union Inn* by lock 16, which dates from the days when bargemen would stop for a drink and to water their horses after a hard day's toil working the locks.

Around Falkirk

Unlikely as it might seem, **BONNYBRIDGE**, a largely nondescript settlement five miles west of Falkirk, claims more UFO sightings than anywhere else in Britain. Quite what attracts aliens to the area is a puzzle, as the only notable draw hereabouts is **Rough Castle**, one of the forts set up, at two-mile intervals, to defend the entire length of the Roman **Antonine Wall**. The most northerly frontier of the Roman Empire, it was built in 142 AD of turf rather than stone, stretching for 37 miles right across the country from the Forth to the Clyde. Assailed by skirmishing Picts and the grim Scottish weather, it didn't take long for the Romans to abandon the wall and retreat to Hadrian's Wall between the Solway and the Tyne, just south of Scotland's present border with England. The signposted site lies along a pot-holed back road, and though little more than a large grassy mound interpreted by a couple of information boards, the remains at Rough Castle are the best-preserved part of the Antonine Wall. If you're interested in tracking down further parts of it, pick up the booklet available at Falkirk tourist office.

The **Pineapple**, five miles north of Falkirk (turn off the A905 onto the B9124, or take bus #75), qualifies as one of Scotland's most exotic and eccentric buildings, a 45ft-high stone pineapple built as a garden folly in the 1770s for the fourth earl of Dunmore. The folly was an elaborate joke on Lord Dunmore's part; returning from a spell as governor of Virginia, where sailors would put a pineapple on a gatepost to announce their return, he chose to signal his homecoming on a grand scale. The grounds, with apple orchards and wildlife such as newts and bats, are run by the NTS and open to the public (daily 9.30am–dusk; free); the outhouse can be rented for holidays through the Landmark Trust (see p.47).

The Ochil Hills

The rugged **Ochil Hills** stretch for roughly forty miles northeast of Stirling, forming a steep-faced range which drops down to the flood plain of the Forth Valley and is sliced by a series of deep-cut, richly wooded glens. Tucked up against the southern slopes of the Ochils is a string of settlements known as the **Hillfoot villages**, which have been at the centre of Scotland's wool production for centuries, rivalled only by the Borders. By the mid-nineteenth century there were more than thirty mills in the tiny county of **Clackmannanshire**, a fifteen-mile stretch between the Ochils and the banks of the Forth, though recent times have seen the old family firms and hand-knitters unable to compete with modern technology, and only a handful remain. Some of the traditions are maintained through the **Mill Trail** that starts in **Alva**, though by and large this has become little more than a series of shops selling discount woollen products.

From the area the country's powerful families could keep abreast of developments at the royal court at Stirling, and a number of fortified tower houses can still be seen, notably at **Alloa** and **Castle Campbell** at Dollar, an atmospheric spot with some great walks nearby. Beyond Dollar the road runs east along the Devon Valley to **Kinross**, on the shores of Loch Leven, where you can take a boat out to wander round the ruins of a castle in which Mary, Queen of Scots was once imprisoned.

There are no trains to destinations in the Ochils, but the regular **bus** service between Stirling and St Andrews travels along the A91 through the Hillfoot villages.

The Hillfoot villages

Three miles or so northeast of Stirling, the first of a series of small settlements nestling into the steep south-facing side of the Ochils is **BLAIRLOGIE**, a small and appealing village which sits amidst orchards and gardens below a private castle; it also features an attractive campsite (see p.410). Beautifully sited by Logie Burn is **Logie Old Kirk**, a ruined church and graveyard dating from the late seventeenth century. Immediately to the rear looms **Dumyat** (pronounced "dum-eye-at"), which offers spectacular views from its 1376ft summit.

As well as a strong tradition of weaving, **ALVA**, six miles further east, was also known for its silver mining in the early eighteenth century – an industry long since gone. From here you can follow **Alva Glen**, a hearty mile-and-a-half walk dipping down through the hills, which takes in a number of waterfalls. There aren't actually any working mills left in Clackmannanshire, though you will see signs for the tourist board's **Mill Trail**, which starts from Glentana Mills, on Stirling Street, where the former workshops now sell piles of jerseys, scarves and other garments and where you'll also find a **tourist office** and **visitor centre** (daily: July & August 9am–5pm; Sept–June 10am–5pm; ☎01259/769696). The visitor centre (being upgraded during 2006 to include audiovisual displays on the history of the area) is the only part of the Mill Trail worth stopping at; most of the other former mill sites on the route are essentially dedicated clothing shops.

A few miles south of Alva on the A907, the nondescript town of **ALLOA**, once one of the country's main centres of brewing, is home to the beautifully restored **Alloa Tower** (April–Oct daily 1–5pm; NTS; £4). Ancestral home of the earls of Mar for four centuries, it's the largest surviving keep in Scotland, though it's now incongruously surrounded by housing estates. Inside, you'll find some portraits and silver owned by the earl of Mar, as well as an attractive oak-beamed ceiling; at the top, the parapet walk offers lovely views of the Forth.

Dollar and around

Nestling in a fold of the Ochils on the northern bank of the small River Devon, where mountain waters rush off the hills, affluent **DOLLAR** is known for its Academy, founded in 1820 with a substantial bequest from local lad John MacNabb, and now one of Scotland's most respected private schools; its pupils and staff account for around a third of the town's population. Above the town, the dramatic chasm of **Dollar Glen** is commanded by **Castle Campbell** (April–Sept daily 9.30am–6.30pm; Oct–March Mon–Wed, Sat & Sun 9.30am–4.30pm; HS; £3.30), formerly, and still unofficially, known as Castle Gloom – a fine and evocative tag but, prosaically, a derivation of "Gloume", an old Gaelic name. A one-and-a-half-mile road leads up from the main street, but becomes very narrow and very steep and stops short of the castle, with only limited parking at the top. There are a series of marked **walks** around the glen, taking in mossy crags, rushing streams and, if you strike out on the three-hour hike to the top of Dollar Hill, great views. There's a map showing the walks on a board on the way up to the castle, though it's advisable to buy the relevant OS map (Explorer 366) if you're setting off for the longer hike.

The castle came into the hands of the Campbells in 1481, who changed its name from Castle Gloom in 1489. John Knox preached here in 1556, although probably from within the castle rather than from the curious archway in the garden as is traditionally claimed. In 1654 the castle was partially burnt by Cromwell's troops; the remains of a graceful seventeenth-century loggia and a roofless hall bear witness to the destruction. However, the oldest part of the castle, the fine fifteenth-century tower built by Sir Colin Campbell, survived the fire; look out for the claustrophobic pit-prison just off the Great Hall and the latrines with their vertiginous views. You can also walk round the roof of the tower, where there's a wonderful vista of the hills behind the castle, and down the glen to Dollar.

The *Lorne Tavern*, 17 Argyll St (✆01259/743423; ❷), is a traditional inn offering simple **B&B**, or there's the comfortable *Castle Campbell Hotel* on Bridge Street (✆01259/742519; ❻). The *Strathallan Hotel* on Chapel Road is a good spot for a pub **lunch** with real ale and outside seating, while three miles east of town, on the Tillicoultry road, the *Harvieston Country Hotel and Restaurant* (✆01259/752522, ⓦwww.harviestouncountryhotel.com; ❺) offers reasonably priced Scottish food as well as the nicest rooms in this area.

Kinross and Loch Leven

Although by no means a large place, **KINROSS**, ten miles east of Dollar, has been transformed in the last couple of decades by the construction of the nearby M90 Edinburgh–Perth motorway. The old village is still there, at the southern end of the main street, but apart from the views of Loch Leven its charm has been eroded by amorphous splodges of modern housing, which threaten to nudge it into the loch itself.

Without doubt the most attractive part of Kinross is by the shores of trout-filled **Loch Leven**, signposted from the main street. The whole of the loch is a National Nature Reserve; it's a good place to see some interesting birds, including visiting geese and various types of duck, and you'll almost always find a number of fishermen casting from small boats. From the shore a small ferry chugs over to an island on which stands the ruined fourteenth-century **Loch Leven Castle** (April–Sept daily 9.30am–last ferry 5.15pm; HS; £4 including ferry trip), where Mary, Queen of Scots was imprisoned for eleven months in 1567–68. This isn't the only island fortress Mary spent time in, and it's easy to imagine the isolation of the tragic queen, who is believed to have miscarried twins while here. She managed to charm the 18-year-old brother of the castle's owner, Sir William Douglas, into helping her escape: he stole the castle keys, secured a boat in which to row ashore, locked the castle gates behind them and threw the keys into the loch – from where they were retrieved three centuries later.

If you're interested in the loch's natural life, head to the RSPB's **Vane Farm Reserve** (daily 10am–5pm; £3 for non-RSPB members) on the southern shore, where there's a visitor centre, coffee shop, bird hide and a number of interpretive walks.

Kinross's **tourist information centre** (April–June Mon–Sat 10am–5pm; July & Aug Mon–Sat 9.30am–5.30pm, Sun 11am–4pm; Sept & Oct Mon–Sat 9.30am–5pm; Nov–March Mon–Wed, Fri & Sat 10am–2pm; ☎01577/863680) is adjacent to the filling station on the outskirts of the town, and is most useful if you're heading north towards Perth on the motorway, though it also acts as an orientation point for those travelling west into the Trossachs or east into Fife. Not far from here is Balado Farm, location of the annual **T in the Park** (ⓦ www.tinthepark.com), one of the largest outdoor weekend music events in Britain, where in recent years bands such as Radiohead, REM, Pixies and Coldplay have made an appearance.

Loch Lomond

The largest stretch of fresh water in Britain (23 miles long and up to five miles wide), **Loch Lomond** is the epitome of Scottish scenic splendour,

△ Loch Lomond

thanks in large part to the ballad which fondly recalls its "bonnie, bonnie banks". The song was said to have been written by a Jacobite prisoner captured by the English, who, sure of his fate, wrote that his spirit would return to Scotland on the low road much faster than his living compatriots on the high road.

The **Loch Lomond and the Trossachs National Park** (Ⓦwww .lochlomond-trossachs.org), designated as Scotland's first national park in 2002, covers a large stretch of scenic territory from the lochs of the Clyde estuary (see p.323) to Loch Earn and Loch Tay, on the southwest fringes of Perthshire. The centrepiece of the park, however, is undoubtedly Loch Lomond, and the most popular gateway into the park is **Balloch**, the town at the loch's southern tip; with Glasgow city centre just 19 miles away, both Balloch and the southwest side of the loch around **Luss** are often packed with day-trippers and tour coaches. Many of these continue up the western side of the loch, though the fast A82 road isn't ideal for tourists who wish to enjoy a leisurely drive by the loch-side. On the loch itself, legislative moves are afoot to control the speed of motorboats that frequent the water on summer weekends and destroy the tranquillity which so impressed Queen Victoria and Sir Walter Scott.

Very different in tone, the eastern side of the loch, abutting the Trossachs, operates at a different pace, with wooden ferryboats puttering out to a scattering of tree-covered islands off the village of **Balmaha**. Much of the eastern shore can only be reached by boat or foot, although the West Highland Way long-distance footpath (see box on p.426) and the distinctive peak of **Ben Lomond** ensure that even these parts are well traversed in comparison with many other areas of the Highlands.

Taking the high road around Loch Lomond

Ordnance Survey Explorer Map nos. 347 & 364.

Ben Lomond (3192ft), the most southerly of the "Munros" (see p.12), is one of the most frequently climbed hills in Scotland, its commanding position above Loch Lomond affording amazing views of both the Highlands and Lowlands. You should allow five to six hours for the climb to the summit and back. The most popular route starts in Rowardennan, at the car park just beyond the *Rowardennan Hotel*. It rises through forest and crosses open moors to gain the southern ridge, which leads to the final pyramid. The path zigzags up, then edges the crags of the northeast corrie to reach the summit. You can return the same way or start off westwards, then south, to traverse the subsidiary top of Ptarmigan hill down to the youth hostel in Rowardennan and then along the track back to the start.

If you're looking for an easier climb, but an equally impressive view over Loch Lomond, consider climbing **Conic Hill** (1175ft), further to the south, instead. Start from the large public car park at Balmaha and walk up through the woods. The views open up as soon as you leave the trees behind, so you don't even need to make it all the way to the top. You should allow two to three hours for the walk to the summit and back.

Finally, for an even less strenuous overview of the loch and its islands, climb **Duncryne** (470ft), a small conical hill to the southeast of Gartocharn, on the south side of the loch. The forty-minute walk, which starts from the woods to the south of the village, begins with various cautionary signs erected at the side of the path by the landowner about responsible access, but the route up is undemanding and the view wonderfully rewarding.

Balloch

The main settlement on Loch Lomond-side is **BALLOCH** at the southwestern corner of the loch, where the water channels into the River Leven for its short journey south to the sea in the Firth of Clyde. Surrounded by housing estates and overstuffed with undistinguished guesthouses, Balloch has few redeeming features, and is little more than a suburb of the much larger factory town of Alexandria, to the south. However, Balloch's accessibility from Glasgow by both car and train ensured that it was chosen as the focal point of the national park with the siting of a huge multifaceted development, **Loch Lomond Shores** (Ⓦwww.lochlomondshores.com). Signposted from miles around, the complex contains the **National Park Gateway Centre** (daily 9.30am–6pm, extended hours in the summer; Ⓣ01389/722199 or 0845/345 4978), which has background on the park, tourist information and a leaflet outlining all transport links within the park, as well as Internet access and a "retail crescent" of shops including a branch of Edinburgh's venerable department store Jenners. Alongside the centre, **Drumkinnon Tower** is a striking, stone-built, cylindrical building which houses a giant-screen auditorium where films about the natural and cultural history of the area are shown, and the tower's top-floor lookout post and small café afford excellent views over the loch towards Ben Lomond. At the time of going to press there were plans to transform the lower half of the tower into an aquarium (Ⓣ01389/722406; Ⓦwww.lochlomondaquarium.co.uk).

There are a number of **activities** available, including nature walks, canoe, bike and even pedalo rental with Can You Experience (Ⓣ01389/602576, Ⓦwww.canyouexperience.com), based right beside Drumkinnon Tower, and loch **cruises** (including a 2–3hr trip to Luss) from the nearby slipway with Sweeney's Cruises (Ⓣ01389/752376, Ⓦwww.sweeney.uk.com). Also at the slipway, the partially restored 1950s **paddle steamer** *The Maid of the Loch* is permanently moored at the pier (daily Easter–Oct 11am–4pm, rest of the year weekends only); aboard you can find out about her glory days sailing the loch and have a cup of tea in the onboard café.

For a more edifying aspect to Balloch and the loch, head across the river to the extensive mature grounds of **Balloch Castle Country Park**. In addition to shore-side and sylvan walks, there's a **National Park Centre** (daily: April–June 10am–6pm; July & Aug 10am–6.45pm; Sept–March 10am–5.45pm; Ⓣ01389/722230) in the mock-Gothic castle, which also has information on various aspects of the national park.

Another nearby attraction is the Loch Lomond **Bird of Prey Centre** (Mon–Fri 9am–5pm, Sat & Sun 9am–6pm; £3.50; Ⓣ07751/862416, Ⓦwww.birdsofprey.org.uk), half a mile east of Balloch towards Gartocharn. Here you can eyeball a rare golden eagle, as well as buzzards, hawks and falcons, or, for £25 you can take a one-hour "hawk walk", which offers instruction on handling and flying the bird.

Practicalities

Balloch has a direct **train** connection with Glasgow Queen Street. Opposite the train station is a small **tourist office** (daily: May 10am–5pm; June & Sept 10am–5.30pm; July & Aug 9.30am–6pm; closed rest of year Ⓣ01389/753533) – a larger office can be found at the Loch Lomond Shores Gateway Centre (see above). There's really little point in basing yourself in Balloch, although there are one or two more appealing options on the outskirts, including one of Scotland's most impressive SYHA **hostels** (Ⓣ0870/004 1136, Ⓦwww.syha.org.uk; April–Oct);

the grand country house with turrets, stained-glass windows and walled gardens lies two miles northwest of Balloch train station, just off the A82; you can either walk there from Balloch, or if you're travelling by bus, ask the driver to drop you off close by. Also on the western side of Balloch, just off the A82 at the large round-about, is *Sheildaig Farm* (℡01389/752459, Ⓦwww.stayatlochlomond.com; ❹), a pleasant **B&B** with a good restaurant. In Gartocharn, a tiny village three miles east of Balloch, the 200-year-old former tollhouse, *Ardoch Cottage* (℡01389/830452; ❸) provides comfortable en-suite accommodation. In Balloch itself there's the year-round *Lomond Woods Holiday Park*, beside Loch Lomond Shores (℡01389/755000, Ⓦwww.holiday-parks.co.uk), an excellent **campsite**.

STIRLING, LOCH LOMOND AND THE TROSSACHS

Loch Lomond

7

The West Highland Way

Opened in 1980, the spectacular **West Highland Way** was Scotland's first long-distance footpath, stretching some 95 miles from Milngavie (pronounced "mill-guy"), six miles north of central Glasgow, to Fort William, where it reaches the foot of Ben Nevis, Britain's highest mountain. Today, it is by far the most popular such footpath in Scotland, and while for many the range of scenery, relative ease of walking and nearby facilities make it a classic route, others find it a little too busy in high season, particularly in comparison with the relative isolation which can be found in many other parts of the Highlands.

The route follows a combination of ancient **drove roads**, along which Highlanders herded their cattle and sheep to market in the lowlands, military roads built by troops to control the Jacobite insurgency in the eighteenth century, old coaching roads and disused railway lines. In addition to the stunning scenery, which is increasingly dramatic as the path heads north, walkers may see some of Scotland's rarer **wildlife**, including red deer, feral goats – ancestors of those left behind after the Highland clearances – and, soaring over the highest peaks, golden eagles.

Passing through the lowlands north of Glasgow, the route runs along the eastern shores of Loch Lomond, over the Highland Boundary Fault Line, then round Crianlarich, crossing open heather moorland across the **Rannoch Moor** wilderness area. It passes close to **Glen Coe**, notorious for the massacre of the MacDonald clan, before reaching **Fort William**. Apart from a stretch between Loch Lomond and Bridge of Orchy, when the path is within earshot of the main road, this is wild, remote country: north of Rowardennan on Loch Lomond, the landscape is increasingly exposed, and you should be well prepared for sudden and extreme weather changes.

Though this is emphatically not the most strenuous of Britain's long-distance walks – it passes below lofty mountain peaks, rather than over them – a moderate degree of fitness is required as there are some steep ascents. If you're looking for an added challenge, you could work a climb of Ben Lomond or Ben Nevis into your schedule. You might choose to walk individual sections of the Way (the eight-mile climb from Glen Coe up the Devil's Staircase is particularly spectacular), but to tackle the whole thing you need to set aside at least seven days; avoid a Saturday start from Milngavie and you'll be less likely to be walking with hordes of people, and there'll be less pressure on accommodation. Most walkers tackle the route from south to north, and manage between ten and fourteen miles a day, staying at hotels, B&Bs and bunk-houses en route. Camping is permitted at recognized sites.

Although the path is clearly waymarked, you may want to check one of the many maps or guidebooks published: the **official guide**, published by Mercat Press (£14.99), includes a foldout map as well as descriptions of the route, with detailed cultural, historical, archeological and wildlife information. Further details about the Way, including a comprehensive accommodation list, can be found at Ⓦwww .west-highland-way.co.uk, which also has links to tour companies and transport providers, who can take your luggage from one stopping point to the next.

The exclusive *Cameron House Hotel* (☎01389/755565, ⓦwww.cameronhouse .co.uk; ⑨), just north of Balloch, has three **restaurants**, including the upmarket *Georgian Room,* the *Drawing Room* (for afternoon tea) and the lochside *Marina Restaurant and Bar* which offers Mediterranean-style fare. At Loch Lomond Shores there are various daytime options, including the viewing gallery café at the top of Drumkinnon Tower. In Balloch, *Balloch House* is popular for **lunches** and snacks, while the *Tullie Inn*, next to the train station, and *The Dog House* are both reliable bets for **pub grub** and a chat with locals.

The eastern shore of Loch Lomond and the islands

The tranquil **eastern shore** is far better for walking and appreciating the loch's natural beauty than the overcrowded western side. The dead-end B837 from Drymen (see p.418) will take you halfway up the east bank, as far as you can get by car or bus (#309 from Balloch and Drymen runs to Balmaha every 2hr), while the West Highland Way sticks close to the shores for the entire length of the loch, beginning at the tiny lochside settlement of **BALMAHA**, which stands on the Highland Boundary Fault, the geological fault that separates the Highlands from the Lowlands. If you stand on the viewpoint above the pier, you can see the fault line clearly marked by the series of woody islands that form giant stepping stones across the loch. Many of the loch's 37 **islands** are privately owned, and rather quaintly an old wooden mail boat still delivers post to four of them. It's possible to join the **mail boat cruise**, which is run by MacFarlane & Son from the jetty at Balmaha (May, June & Sept Mon, Thurs & Sat 11.30am returns 2pm; July & Aug Mon–Sat 11.30am returns 2pm; Oct–April Mon & Thurs 10.50am returns 12.50pm; £8; ☎01360/870214; ⓦwww .balmahaboatyard.co.uk). In summer the timetable allows a one-hour stop on Inchmurrin Island, the largest and most southerly of the islands inhabited by just ten permanent residents; it has the ruins of a monastery and castle, and a bar in the *Inchmurrin Hotel* (☎01389/850245). If you're looking for an island to explore, however, a better bet is **Inchailloch**, the closest to Balmaha. Owned by Scottish Natural Heritage, there's a two-mile-long nature trail signposted round the island, which was extensively planted with oaks to provide bark for the local tanning industry. Along the way you'll encounter the ruins of a fourteenth-century nunnery and associated burial ground, and there's a picnic and camping site at Port Bawn on the southwestern side of the island, near a pleasant sandy beach. Until the mid-seventeenth century parishioners on the far (western) shore of Loch Lomond used to row across to Inchailloch for Sunday services at the church linked to the nunnery. It's possible to row here yourself using a boat hired from MacFarlane & Son (from £10/hr), or you can make use of their on-demand ferry service (£4 return).

Balmaha gets very busy in summer, not least with day-trippers on the West Highland Way. Beside the large car park is a **National Park Centre** (daily: April–Sept 10am–6pm) where you can find out about local forest walks and occasional wildlife workshops. You can **stay** at the well-run *Oak Tree Inn* (☎01360/870357, ⓦwww.oak-tree-inn.co.uk), set back from the boatyard, in one of their en-suite double rooms (④) or bunk-bed quads (③). There's also a convivial pub, and all-day **food** is served here. A cheaper option is the *Balmaha Bunkhouse Lodge* (☎01360/870084) just across the road. **Camping** is available two miles north, on the lochside at Milarrochy Bay (☎01360/870236; March–Oct) or, a couple of miles or so further up the road, at Cashel, a lovely, secluded Forestry Commission campsite (☎01360/870234, ⓦwww.forestholidays.co.uk; mid-March to Oct).

Public transport ends at Balmaha, but another seven miles north through the woods brings you to the end of the road at **ROWARDENNAN**, a scattered settlement which sits below Ben Lomond (see box on p.431). Passenger ferries (Easter–Sept 3 daily, contact *Rowardennan Hotel* to book) cross between Inverbeg and Rowardennan, where **accommodation** is available at the recently refurbished *Rowardennan Hotel* (℡01360/870273, Ⓦwww.rowardennanhotel .com; ❺), and, half a mile beyond, at a wonderfully situated SYHA **hostel** (℡0870/004 1148, Ⓦwww.syha.org.uk; March–Oct), a classic Scottish stone-built lodge with lawns running down to the shore.

Only walkers can continue further north up the lochside, where the only other settlement is seven miles north at **INVERSNAID**, made famous by a poem of the same name by Gerard Manley Hopkins about a frothing waterfall nearby ("This darksome burn, horseback brown,/His rollrock highroad roaring down . . ."). Though remote, the *Inversnaid Hotel* (℡01877/386223; ❹) by the shore is mainly used by coach tours, who arrive via the only road in, the remote B829 from Aberfoyle, though walkers can snap up any free rooms or grab a drink or bite to eat. Up the hill the *Inversnaid Lodge* (℡01877/386254, Ⓦwww .inversnaidphoto.com; ❹), once the hunting lodge of the duke of Montrose, is a photography centre with instruction and workshops from guest tutors; if space allows, the centre offers B&B to walkers on the West Highland Way. Situated in an old church on the B829, the ⚡ *Inversnaid Bunkhouse* (℡01301/702970) with its hot tub and licensed coffeeshop offers a free pick-up service from Inversnaid car park. A **ferry** (£4 one-way/£5 return) crosses to Inveruglas on the western shore but you'll have to phone the *Inversnaid Hotel* to make arrangements. The West Highland Way continues through the Inversnaid RSPB reserve (free access) to the head of the loch, five miles further north.

The western shore of Loch Lomond

Despite the roar of traffic hurtling along the upgraded A82, the **west bank** of Loch Lomond is an undeniably beautiful stretch of water and gives better views of the loch's wooded islands and surrounding peaks than the heavily wooded east side. The exclusive, US-owned **Loch Lomond golf course**, which obscures the view for part of the way, is the venue for the annual Scottish Open.

LUSS, setting for the Scottish TV soap *High Road*, is without doubt the prettiest village in the region, with its prim, identical sandstone and slate cottages garlanded in rambling roses, and its narrow sandy, pebbly strand. However, its charms are no secret, and its streets and beach can become unbearably crowded in summer. If you want to escape the crowds, pop into the parish **church**, which is a haven of peace and has a lovely ceiling made from Scots pine rafters and some fine Victorian stained-glass windows. There's a **National Park Centre** (April–May & Oct daily 10am–5pm; June–Sept daily 10am–6.30pm) adjacent to the massive village car park, which is often choked with coaches, busking bagpipers and souvenir stalls. The cheery *Coach House*, whose owner often sports a spiky blonde haircut and purple kilt, is located just off the main street towards the church, and serves up home-made soup, huge rolls, tea, coffee and cakes.

If you need a place to **stay**, you could do worse than the *Inverbeg Inn* (℡01436/860678, Ⓦwww.inverbeginn.co.uk; ❼), a few miles further north on the A82, which offers very good **bar food** as well as a few comfortable rooms. A passenger and bicycle **ferry** (Easter–Sept 3 daily; £5) links Inverbeg with Rowardennan on the east bank (see above). Seventeen miles north at **TARBET**, the West Highland **train** – the line from Glasgow to Fort William and Mallaig, with a branch line to Oban – reaches the shoreline at the point where the A83 heads off west into Argyll; the A82 continues north along the banks of the loch towards Crianlarich. Tarbet has a small **tourist office** (April–June & Sept–Oct 10am–5pm; July & Aug 10am–6pm; ☎01301/702260), close to which is a small tearoom with great cakes. At the pier near the *Tarbet Hotel* you can hop on an hour-long **loch cruise**, run by Cruise Loch Lomond (daily: March–Oct 8am–5.30pm; Nov–Feb 9am–5pm; from £5; ☎01301/702356). The same operator also offers trips to Inversnaid on the east side.

North of Tarbet, the A82 turns back into the narrow, winding road of old, making for slower but much more interesting driving. There's one more **train station** on Loch Lomond at **ARDLUI**, at the mountain-framed head of the loch, where you can have a pint at the *Ardlui Hotel*, and catch an on-demand ferry (9am–8pm; ask at the hotel for further details) to Ardleish on the other side. Also near here is a bistro/bar called *McGregor's Landing* (☎01301/704205, ⓦwww .mcgregorslanding.com; ❸), which offers comfortable hotel-style and backpacker accommodation. A couple of miles further north at **INVERARNAN**, there's a bridge over the river behind the ☩ *Drover's Inn* (☎01301/704234, ⓦwww .droversinn.co.uk; ❸), arguably, one of the most idiosyncratic **hotels** in Scotland. The bar has a roaring fire, barmen dressed in kilts, weary hill walkers sipping pints and bearded musicians banging out folk songs. Down the creaking corridors, past moth-eaten stuffed animals, are a number of supposedly haunted and resolutely old-fashioned rooms. The owners also run the more modern and plainer *Stagger Inn* directly opposite (☎01301/704274; ❸), which provides a rather better ordered but less traditional experience.

Crianlarich and Tyndrum

CRIANLARICH, some eight miles north of the head of Loch Lomond, is an important staging post on various transport routes, including the West Highland Railway which divides here, one branch heading due west towards Oban, the other continuing north over Rannoch Moor to Fort William. The West Highland Way long-distance footpath (see box on p.426) also trogs past. Otherwise there's little reason to stop here, unless you're keen on tackling some of the steep-sided hills that rise up from the glen.

Five miles further north from here on the A82/A85, the village of **TYNDRUM** owes its existence to a minor (and very short-lived) nineteenth-century gold rush, but today supports little more than a busy service station and several characterless hotels. However, five minutes' walk down a track there's a good campsite and small bunkhouse at *By The Way Hostel and Campsite* (☎01838 400333; ⓦwww.tyndrumbytheway.com), and for a refreshingly different roadside dining experience, it's well worth trying the airy *Real Food Café* (daily until 10pm) on the main road for fresh, fast food that's locally sourced and cooked to order. At Tyndrum the road divides, with the A85 heading west to Oban, and the A82 heading for Fort William via Glen Coe. The railway divides further south at Crianlarich, though the two branches run in parallel to Tyndrum: it's only a short walk from Tyndrum Lower station (on the Oban line) to Tyndrum Upper (on the Fort William line).

The Trossachs

Often described as the Highlands in miniature, the **Trossachs** area boasts a magnificent diversity of scenery, with dramatic peaks and mysterious, forest-covered slopes that live up to all the images ever produced of Scotland's wild land. It is country ripe for stirring tales of brave kilted clansmen, a role fulfilled by Rob Roy Macgregor, the seventeenth-century outlaw whose name seems to attach to every second waterfall, cave and barely discernible path. Strictly speaking, the name "Trossachs", normally translated as either "bristly country" or "crossing place", originally referred only to the wooded glen between **Loch Katrine** and Loch Achray, but today it is usually taken as being the whole area from **Callander** right up to the eastern banks of Loch Lomond, with which it has been grouped as part of Scotland's first national park.

The Trossachs' high tourist profile was largely attributable in the early days to Sir Walter Scott, whose novels *Lady of the Lake* and *Rob Roy* were set in and around the area. According to one contemporaneous account, after Scott's *Lady of the Lake* was published in 1810, the number of carriages passing Loch Katrine rose from fifty the previous year to 270. Since then, neither the popularity nor beauty of the region has waned, and in high season the place is jam-packed with coaches full of tourists as well as walkers and mountain-bikers taking advantage of the easily accessed richness of the scenery. Autumn is a better time to come, when the hills are blanketed in rich, rusty colours and the crowds are thinner. In terms of where to stay, **Aberfoyle** has a rather dowdy air while **Callander** feels rather overrun, and you're often better off seeking out one of the guesthouses or B&Bs tucked away in secluded corners of the region.

If you don't have your own transport, you could take advantage of the **Trossachs Trundler**, a useful minibus service which loops round Callander, Loch Katrine and Aberfoyle four times a day (10am–4pm) from late May to early Oct; helpfully for walkers, it stops on demand and can also cope with two bikes and wheelchairs. The bus is timed to connect with sailings of the SS *Sir Walter Scott* on Loch Katrine (see p.433), and costs £5 for a day pass or £12 for two adults and four children (for further details call ☏01786/451200).

Rob Roy

A member of the outlawed Macgregor clan, **Rob Roy** (meaning "Red Robert" in Gaelic) was born in 1671 in Glengyle, just north of Loch Katrine, and lived for some time as a respectable cattle farmer and trader, supported by the powerful duke of Montrose. In 1712, finding himself in a tight spot when a cattle deal fell through, Rob Roy absconded with £1000, some of it belonging to the duke. He took to the hills to live as a brigand, his feud with Montrose escalating after the duke repossessed Rob Roy's land and drove his wife from their house. He was present at the Battle of Sheriffmuir during the earlier Jacobite uprising of 1715, ostensibly supporting the Jacobites but probably as an opportunist: the chaos would have made cattle-raiding easier. Eventually captured and sentenced to transportation, Rob Roy was pardoned and returned to **Balquhidder**, northeast of Glengyle, where he remained until his death in 1734.

Rob Roy's status as a local hero in the mould of Robin Hood should be tempered with the fact that he was without doubt a notorious bandit and blackmailer. His life has been much romanticized, from Sir Walter Scott's 1818 novel *Rob Roy* to the 1995 film starring Liam Neeson, although the tale does serve well to dramatize the clash between the doomed clan culture of the Gaelic-speaking Highlanders and the organized feudal culture of lowland Scots, which effectively ended with the defeat of the Jacobites at Culloden in 1746. His **grave** in Balquhidder, a simple affair behind the ruined church, is one of the principal sights on the unofficial Rob Roy trail, though the peaceful graveyard is mercifully underdeveloped and free of the tartan trappings which has seen the Trossachs dubbed "Rob Roy Country".

Aberfoyle and the Lake of Menteith

Each summer the sleepy little town of **ABERFOYLE**, twenty miles west of Stirling, dusts itself down for its annual influx of tourists. Though of little appeal itself, Aberfoyle's position in the heart of the Trossachs is ideal, with **Loch Ard Forest** and **Queen Elizabeth Forest Park** stretching across to Ben Lomond and Loch Lomond to the west, the long curve of Loch Katrine and Ben Venue to the northwest, and Ben Ledi to the northeast.

Don't come here for lively nightlife or entertainment, but for a good, healthy blast of the outdoors. From Aberfoyle you might like to wander north of the village to **Doon Hill**: cross the bridge over the Forth, continue past the cemetery and then follow signs to the **Fairy Knowe** (knoll). A toadstool marker points you through oak and holly trees to the summit of the Knowe where there is a pine tree said to contain the unquiet spirit of the Reverend Robert Kirk, who studied local fairy lore and published his inquiries in *The Secret Commonwealth* (1691). Legend has it that, as punishment for disclosing supernatural secrets, he was forcibly removed to fairyland where he has languished ever since, although his mortal remains can be found in the nearby graveyard. This short walk should preferably be made at dusk, when it is at its most atmospheric.

Practicalities

Regular **buses** from Stirling pull into the car park on Aberfoyle's Main Street. The **tourist office** next door (daily: April–June, Sept & Oct 10am–5pm; July & Aug 9.30am–6pm; Nov–March Sat & Sun 10am–4pm only) has full details of local accommodation, sights and outdoor activities. The nearby **Scottish Wool**

Hiking and biking in the Trossachs

Despite the steady flow of coach tours taking in the scenic highlights of the area, the Trossachs are ideal for exploring **on foot** or on a **mountain bike**. This is partly because the terrain is slightly more benign than the Highlands proper, but much is due to the excellent management of the **Queen Elizabeth Forest Park**, a huge chunk of the National Park between Loch Lomond and Loch Lubnaig. The main visitor centre for the area, David Marshall Lodge (see 433), is just outside Aberfoyle, and is well worth a visit if you want to get some orientation on the region and learn about the local trees, geology and wildlife, which includes roe deer and birds of prey.

For **hillwalkers**, the prize peak is Ben Lomond (3192ft), best accessed from Rowardennan (see p.428). Other highlights include Ben Venue (2370ft) and Ben A'an (1520ft) on the shores of Loch Katrine, as well as Ben Ledi (2857ft), just northwest of Callander, which all offer relatively straightforward but very rewarding climbs and, on clear days, stunning views. Walkers can also choose from any number of waymarked routes through the forests and along lochsides; pick up a map of these at the visitor centre.

The area is also a popular spot for **mountain-biking**, with a number of useful rental shops, a network of forest paths and one of the more impressive stretches of the National Cycle Network cutting through the region from Loch Lomond to Killin. If you don't have your own bike, you can **rent** one from Wheels Cycling Centre (℡01877/331100), next to *Trossachs Backpackers* (see p.434) a mile and a half southwest of Callander, the best rental place in the area, with front or full suspension models available, as well as baby seats and children's cycles. Also well set up is Trossachs Cycles (℡01877/382614), at the *Trossachs Holiday Park* (see p.432) on the A81 two miles south of Aberfoyle, while more centrally located is Mounter Bikes (℡01877/331052) beside the visitor centre in Callander (see p.434).

Centre (daily: May–Sept 9.30am–6pm; Oct–April 10am–5pm; free) – a popular stop-off point with tour buses – is a glorified country knitwear shop selling all the usual jumpers and woolly toys as well as featuring daily shows of sheep-shearing and sheep-dog trials (£2.50).

Accommodation options in Aberfoyle itself aren't all that inspiring. Best of the B&Bs is *Creag-Ard House* (℡01877/382297, ⓦwww.creag-ard.co.uk; ❹; Easter–Oct), one mile west of Aberfoyle, where you'll leave in the morning satisfied with a large breakfast including locally sourced haggis. Further west, at the historic and friendly ⚓ *Altskeith Hotel* (℡01877/387266; ⓦwww.altskeith .com; ❹), there are delightful views over Loch Ard towards Ben Lomond, as well as warm hospitality and delicious evening meals. The **Lake of Menteith** (see below) is another beautiful place to stay: the *Lake of Menteith Hotel* (℡01877/385258, ⓦwww.lake-of-menteith-hotel.com; ❻) at Port of Menteith has a lovely waterfront setting next to the Victorian Gothic parish church, as well as a classy restaurant.

For **camping**, a couple of miles south of Aberfoyle, off the A81 and on the edge of Queen Elizabeth Forest Park, there's *Cobleland* (℡01877/382392, ⓦwww.forestholidays.co.uk; April–Oct), run by the Forestry Commission, which covers five acres of woodland by the River Forth (little more than a stream here). Further south, the excellent family-run *Trossachs Holiday Park* (℡01877/382614, ⓦwww.trossachsholidays.co.uk; March–Oct) is twice the size and has **bikes** for rent.

In Aberfoyle, the best of a limited range of **eating** options are the *Forth Inn* on the main street or the *Covenanters Inn* at the large, turreted *Inchrie Castle Hotel*, five minutes' walk from the centre; both serve bar food and smarter restaurant meals.

The Lake of Menteith

About four miles east of Aberfoyle towards Doune, the **Lake of Menteith** is a superb fly-fishing centre and Scotland's only lake (as opposed to loch), so named due to a historic mix-up with the word *laigh*, Scots for "low-lying ground", which applied to the whole area. To rent a **fishing boat** or a rod contact the Lake of Menteith Fisheries (℡01877/385664; April–Oct).

From the northern shore of the lake, you can take a little ferry out to the **Island of Inchmahome** (April–Sept daily 9.30am–6.30pm; HS; £4 including ferry) in order to explore the lovely ruined Augustinian abbey. Founded in 1238, **Inchmahome Priory** is the most beautiful island monastery in Scotland, its remains rising tall and graceful above the trees.

△ Lake of Menteith

The masons employed to build the priory are thought to be those who built Dunblane Cathedral (see p.416); certainly the western entrance there resembles that at Inchmahome. The nave of the church is roofless, but in the choir are preserved the graves of important families from the surrounding area. Most touching is a late thirteenth-century double effigy depicting Walter, the first Stewart earl of Menteith, and his countess, Mary, who, feet resting on lion-like animals, turn towards each other and embrace.

Also buried here is the adventurer and scholar Robert Bontine Cunninghame Graham, once a pal of Buffalo Bill's in Mexico, an intimate friend of the novelist Joseph Conrad, and first president of the National Party of Scotland. Five-year-old Mary, Queen of Scots was hidden at Inchmahome in 1547 before being taken to France, and there's a formal garden in the west of the island, known as Queen Mary's Bower, where legend has it she played. Traces remain of an orchard planted by the monks, but the island is thick now with oak, ash and Spanish chestnut. Visible on a nearby but inaccessible islet is the ruined castle of **Inchtalla**, the home of the earls of Menteith in the sixteenth and seventeenth centuries.

Aberfoyle to Callander

North of Aberfoyle, the A821 road to Loch Katrine winds its way into the Queen Elizabeth Forest, snaking up **Duke's Pass** (so called because it once belonged to the duke of Montrose). You can walk or drive the short distance to the park's excellent **visitor centre** at David Marshall Lodge (daily: March–June, Sept & Oct 10am–5pm; July & Aug 10am–6pm; Nov & Dec 10am–4pm; Jan Sat & Sun 10am–4pm; Feb Thurs–Sun 10am–4pm; car park £1; ℡01877/382258), where you can pick up maps of the walks and cycle routes in the forest, get background information on the flora and fauna of the area (there's a great video relay and plans for a live web-cam to the nests of local peregrine falcons and ospreys) or settle into the café with its splendid views out over the tree tops. Adjacent to the centre, there's an excellent adventure park for kids, and various marked paths wind through the forest, giving glimpses of the lowlands and surrounding hills. The only road in the forest open to cars is the **Achray Forest Drive**, just under two miles further on, which leads through the park and along the western shore of **Loch Drunkie** before rejoining the main road.

Loch Katrine

Heading down the northern side of the Duke's Pass you come first to **Loch Achray**, tucked under Ben A'an. Look out across the loch for the small **Callander Kirk** in a lovely setting alone on a promontory. At the head of the loch a road follows the short distance through to the southern end of **Loch Katrine** at the foot of Ben Venue (2370ft), from where the elegant Victorian passenger **steamer**, the SS *Sir Walter Scott*, has been plying the waters since 1900, chugging up to the wild country of Glengyle. It does two runs from the pier each day, the first departing at 11am and stopping off at Stronachlachar before returning almost two hours later (April–Oct daily; £7.25 return; ℡01877/376316); the one-hour afternoon cruise leaves at 1.45pm but doesn't make any stops (April–Oct daily; £6.25). A popular combination is to **rent a bike** from the Katrinewheels (℡01877/376316) hut by the pier, take the steamer up to Stronachlachar, then cycle back by way of the road around the north side of the loch.

From Loch Katrine the A821 heads due east past the tiny village of **Brig o'Turk**, where it's worth looking in on the *Byre Inn*, a tiny pub and restaurant set in an old stone barn with wooden pews and a welcoming open fire. The cosy, wooden clad *Brig o' Turk Tea-Room* (Easter–Sept 11am–4pm) is also a good place to refresh after a walk or cycle. Carry on along the shores of Loch Venacher to get to Kilmahog, where the road meets the A84 a short distance from Callander.

Callander and around

CALLANDER, on the eastern edge of the Trossachs, sits on the banks of the River Teith at the southern end of the **Pass of Leny**, one of the key routes into the Highlands. Significantly larger than Aberfoyle, eleven miles west, it is a popular summer holiday base and suffers in high season for being right on the main tourist trail from Stirling through to the west Highlands. Callander first came to fame during the "Scottish Enlightenment" of the eighteenth and nineteenth centuries, when the glowing reports of the Trossachs given by Sir Walter Scott and William Wordsworth prompted the first tourists to venture into the wilds by horse-drawn carriage. Development was given a boost when Queen Victoria chose to visit, and then by the arrival of the train line – long since closed – in the 1860s.

Tourists have arrived in throngs ever since, as the plethora of restaurants and tearooms, antique shops, secondhand bookshops and shops selling local woollens and crafts testifies. A typical day in summer sees visitors thronging the pavements and traffic crawling down the long main street; you'd be forgiven the desire to move on swiftly to more tranquil countryside beyond. The chief attraction in town is the **Rob Roy and Trossachs Visitor Centre** in a converted church at Ancaster Square on the main street (daily: March–May & Oct 10am–5pm; June–Sept 10am–6pm; Nov–Feb 11am–4pm; upstairs £3.60). Upstairs a hammed-up audiovisual display offers an entertaining and partisan account of the life and times of Rob Roy and those who have portrayed him in film and fiction.

Practicalities

Callander's **tourist office** is downstairs in the Rob Roy and Trossachs Visitor Centre (same times; ☎01877/330342), and can book **accommodation**. Wheels Cycling Centre (☎01877/331100, ⦿www.scottish-cycling.co.uk), part of *Trossachs Backpackers* (see below), offers excellent **bike rental** as well as advice on the best local routes.

Accommodation

Arden House Bracklinn Rd ☎01877/330235, ⦿www.ardenhouse.org.uk. A grand Victorian guesthouse in its own gardens with good views and woodland walks from the back door. Open April–Oct. ➎

Burnt Inn House Brig o'Turk, ☎01877/376212, ⦿www.burntinnhouse.co.uk. As an alternative to staying in Callander, this historic place offers simpler, farmhouse-style B&B right in the heart of the Trossachs countryside. ➌

Callander Meadows 24 Main St ☎01877/330181, ⦿www.callandermeadows.co.uk. Centrally located rooms in an attractive town house which boasts three comfortable en-suite rooms and an excellent restaurant. Full board available. ➌

The Conservatory Ballachallan ☎01877/339190, ⦿www.ballachallan.co.uk. Three pleasant, well-presented en-suite rooms in an eighteenth-century farmhouse, two miles southeast of town, and a fish restaurant in the conservatory. ➍

Roman Camp Country House Hotel Main St ☎01877/330003, ⦿www.roman-camp-hotel.co.uk. The upmarket option in town, a romantic, turreted seventeenth-century hunting lodge situated in twenty-acre gardens on the River Teith. ➐

Trossachs Backpackers Invertrossachs Rd ☎01877/331200, ⦿www.scottish-hostel.co.uk. A friendly, well-equipped and comfortable 32-bed hostel and activity centre with self-catering dorms and family rooms, located a mile southwest of town down a turn-off from the A81 to Port of Menteith. Bike rental available next door. ➊

Eating and drinking

Despite Callander's popularity, the town itself has few **restaurants** worth recommending. *Callander Meadows* (see opposite; restaurant closed Tues & Wed) serves up delicious, freshly cooked lunches and dinners. Its "Meadows **Wave**" option includes every dessert on the menu. *The Conservatory* fish restaurant at Ballachallan (see opposite; closed Mon & Tues), two miles from Callander along the Doune road, serves great Scottish seafood dishes at reasonable prices in a pleasant conservatory dining room. For good **pub food** try the convivial *Lade Inn* in Kilmahog, a mile west of Callander. For unbeatable fresh sandwiches, great coffee and a fine selection of breads, cheeses and other deli items head for *Deli Ecosse* adjacent to the visitor centre.

North of Callander

On each side of Callander, pleasant and untaxing walks wind west for a couple of miles through a wooded gorge to the **Falls of Leny** and north for a mile or so through forest to the **Bracklinn Falls**. Longer walks of varying degrees of exertion thread their way through the surrounding countryside, the most challenging being that to the summit of **Ben Ledi** (2857ft); set off from the public car park at the turn-off marked "Strathyre Forest Cabins".

North of town, you can walk or ride the scenic six-mile Callander to Strathyre (Route 7) Cycleway, which forms part of the network of cycleways between the Highlands and Glasgow. The route is based on the old Caledonian train line to Oban, which closed in 1965, and runs along the western side of Loch Lubnaig. At the head of the loch, the main road runs straight through **STRATHYRE**, though if you're looking for somewhere to stay it's worth turning off to *Creagan House* (℡01877/384638, ⓦwww.creaganhouse.co.uk; ⑥), an old farm steading less than half a mile north of Strathyre with cosy rooms and an excellent restaurant, well stocked with fine wines and malt whisky.

Just northwest of here is tiny **BALQUHIDDER** (#59 bus from Stirling), most famous as the site of the **grave of Rob Roy**, which you'll find in the small yard behind the ruined church. Refreshingly, considering the Rob Roy fever that plagues the region, his grave – marked by a rough stone carved with a sword, cross and a man with a dog – is remarkably underplayed. Small, professional classical **concerts** are held in the atmospheric 150-year-old church on six summer Sundays (late June to early Aug; ℡01877/384265), while the village's tiny wood-panelled library – built by the laird as an alternative distraction to the pub across the road – is now a tearoom (Easter–Oct daily 10am–5pm) serving freshly baked scones to passing cyclists and walkers. Avoid the plethora of Rob Roy-themed **accommodation** in Balquhidder, and drive six miles beyond the village to the award-winning ⅄ *Monachyle Mhor* hotel (℡01877/384622, ⓦwww.monachylemhor.com; ⑥), an eighteenth-century farmhouse with stylish modern rooms and a terrific restaurant (open to non-residents, but book ahead) specializing in locally sourced organic food and with the added bonus of lovely views over the hills surrounding Loch Voil. On the road to the hotel is the unexpected sight of the Dhanakosa Buddhist retreat centre (℡01877/384213 ⓦwww.dhanakosa.com) – details of weekend or week-long retreats here, with courses ranging from tai chi to hill walking, can be found on their website.

North of Balquhidder the busy A84 slides past Lochearnhead, at the western end of Loch Earn, and Killin, at the western end of Loch Tay, both of which are covered in the Perthshire chapter (see p.476 & p.481), before swinging west towards Crianlarich (see p.429) and the west coast.

Travel details

Trains

Balloch to: Glasgow (every 30min; 40min).
Crianlarich to: Fort William (4 Mon–Sat, 2 Sun; 1hr 50min); Glasgow Queen Street (3–4 Mon–Sat, 2 Sun; 1hr 50min); Oban (6 Mon–Sat, 3 Sun; 1hr 10min).
Falkirk to: Edinburgh (every 30min; 35min); Glasgow Queen Street (every 30min; 25min); Stirling (every 30min; 15min).
Stirling to: Aberdeen (hourly; 2hr 15min); Dundee (hourly; 1hr); Edinburgh (hourly; 1hr); Falkirk Grahamston (hourly; 30min); Glasgow Queen Street (hourly; 30min); Inverness (3–5 daily; 2hr 30min); Perth (hourly; 30min).

Buses

Aberfoyle to: Callander (June–Sept 4 Thurs–Tues; 25min); Port of Menteith (June–Sept 4 Thurs–Tues; 10min).
Balloch to: Balmaha (every 2hr; 25min); Luss (8–9 daily; 15min).
Callander to: Loch Katrine (June–Sept 4 daily; 55min).
Luss to: Tarbet (Mon–Sat 4 daily; 10min).
Stirling to: Aberfoyle (4 daily; 45min); Callander (hourly; 45min); Dollar (6 daily; 35min); Doune (hourly; 25min); Dunblane (hourly; 25min); Dundee (hourly; 1hr 30min); Edinburgh (hourly; 1hr 10min); Falkirk (every 40min; 30min); Glasgow (hourly; 50min); Inverness (every 2hr; 3hr 20min); Killin (3–4 daily; 1hr 30min); Perth (hourly; 40min); St Andrews (3 daily; 2hr).

Fife

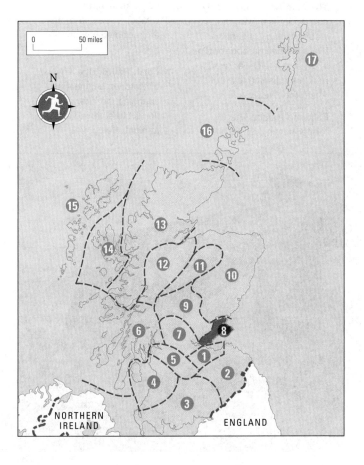

CHAPTER 8

Highlights

* **Himalayas putting green, St Andrews** The world's finest putting course right beside the world's finest golf course; a snip at £1 a round. See p.443

* **The East Neuk** Buy freshly cooked lobster from the wooden shack at Crail's historic stone harbour or dine in style at *The Cellar* restaurant in the fishing town of Anstruther. See p.448

* **Falkland Palace** The former hunting retreat of the Stuart kings, an atmospheric semi-ruin set in lovely gardens within a charming village. See p.452

* **Culross** Scotland's best-preserved historic village, all pantile roofs and cobbled wynds. See p.455

* **Forth Rail Bridge** An icon of Victorian engineering spanning the Firth of Forth, floodlit to stunning effect at night. See p.460

△ Forth Rail Bridge

8

Fife

The ancient Kingdom of **Fife**, designated as such by the Picts in the fourth century, is a small area barely fifty miles at its widest point, but one which has a definite identity, inextricably linked with the waters which surround it on three sides – the Tay to the north, the Forth to the south, and the cold North Sea to the east. Despite its small size, Fife encompasses several different regions, with a marked difference between the rural north and the semi-industrial south. Tourism and agriculture are the economic mainstays of the **northeast** corner of Fife, where the landscape varies from the gentle hills in the rural hinterland to the windswept cliffs, rocky bays and sandy beaches on which scenes from the film *Chariots of Fire* were shot. Fishing still has a role, but ultimately it is to **St Andrews**, Scotland's oldest university town and the home of the world-famous Royal and Ancient Golf Club, that most visitors are drawn. Development here has been cautious, and both the town itself and the surrounding area retain an appealing and old-fashioned feel. South of St Andrews, the tiny stone harbours of the fishing villages of the **East Neuk** are an appealing extension to any visit to this part of Fife.

Inland from St Andrews, the central Fife settlements of Glenrothes, an unremarkable postwar new town, and Cupar, a more interesting market town, are overshadowed by the absorbing village of **Falkland** with its impressive ruined palace. In the **south**, the closure of the coal mines over the last twenty years has left local communities floundering to regain a foothold, and the squeeze on the fishing industry may well lead to further decline. In the meantime, a number of the villages have capitalized on their unpretentious appeal and welcomed tourism in a way that has enhanced rather than degraded their natural assets; the perfectly preserved town of **Culross** is the most notable of these with its cobbled streets and collection of historic buildings. Otherwise, southern Fife is dominated by the town of **Dunfermline**, a former capital of Scotland, and industralized **Kirkcaldy**, with the **Forth Rail Bridge** and Road Bridge the most memorable sights of this stretch of coastline.

Transport

The main **road** into the region is the M90, which links the Forth Road Bridge northwest of Edinburgh with Perth, fringing Fife's western boundary. The A92 road cuts a swathe across the county, linking Dunfermline, Glenrothes and the Tay Road Bridge in the north. However, there are innumerable back-road alternatives throughout Fife, with the coastal roads inevitably the most attractive. The **train** line follows the coast as far north as Kirkcaldy and then cuts inland towards Dundee, stopping on the way at Cupar and Leuchars (from where buses run to St Andrews). Exploration by public transport of the eastern and

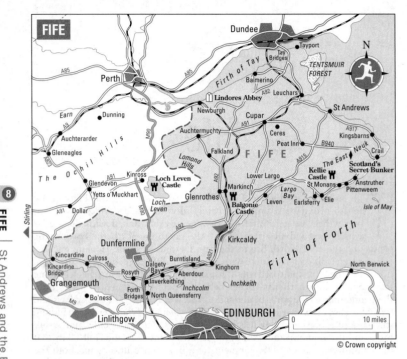

© Crown copyright

western fringes requires some planning as there is no train service and buses are few and far between. However, if you're planning on tackling a large chunk of Fife in one day, ask for an **Explorer ticket** from any bus driver; this costs £10 for a day and is valid on all Stagecoach Fife buses, including those connecting with Glasgow, Edinburgh, Dundee and Stirling. Fife's relatively flat terrain and network of quiet backroads have seen it marketed as great **cycling** country (Ⓦ www.fife-cycleways.co.uk), which holds true when the weather's fair, but it can be harder going with a cold wind whipping in off the North Sea.

St Andrews and the East Neuk

Confident, poised and well groomed, if a little snooty, **ST ANDREWS**, Scotland's oldest **university town** and a pilgrimage centre for **golfers** from all over the world, is situated on a wide bay on the northeastern coast of Fife. Of all Scotland's universities, St Andrews is the one most often compared to Oxford or Cambridge, both for the dominance of gown over town and for the intimate, collegiate feel of the place. Accentuating the comparison is the fact that the student population has a significant proportion of English undergraduates, among them, famously, Prince William, who spent four years studying here.

According to legend, the town was founded, pretty much by accident, in the fourth century. **St Rule** – or Regulus – a custodian of the bones of St Andrew in Patras in southwestern Greece, had a vision in which an angel ordered him to carry five of the saint's bones to the western edge of the world, where he

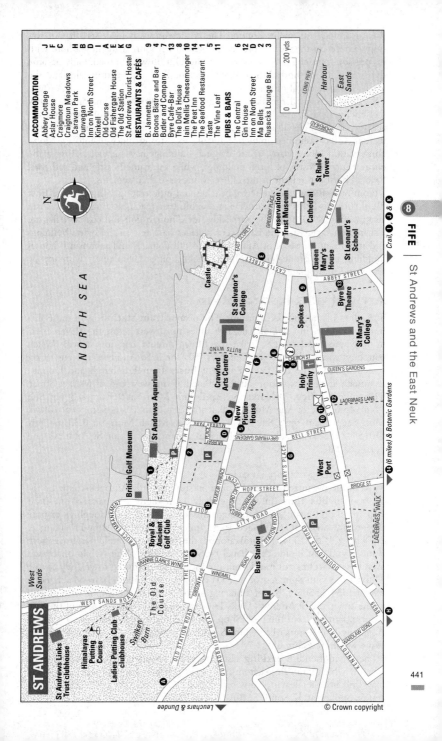

ST ANDREWS

West Sands

NORTH SEA

St Andrews Links
Trust clubhouse

Himalayas
Putting
Course

Ladies Putting Club
clubhouse

Swilken Burn

The Old Course

BRUCE EMBANKMENT

British Golf Museum

St Andrews Aquarium

Royal & Ancient
Golf Club

GRANNIE CLARK'S WYND

WEST SANDS ROAD

THE LINKS

GIBSON PLACE

WINDMILL

GUARDBRIDGE ROAD

OLD STATION ROAD

Bus Station

STATION ROAD

GOLF PLACE

PILMOUR TERRACE

PILMOUR LINKS

HOPE STREET

CITY ROAD

ABBOTSFORD CRESCENT

HOWARD PLACE

ST MARY'S PLACE

MURRAY PARK

MURRAY PLACE

THE SCORES

BUTTS WYND

Crawford
Arts Centre

New
Picture
House

GREYFRIARS GARDENS

BELL STREET

West Port

BRIDGE ST

St Salvator's
College

NORTH STREET

MARKET STREET

CHURCH ST

Holy
Trinity

SOUTH STREET

Spokes

QUEEN'S GARDENS

St Mary's
College

LADEBRAES LANE

QUEEN'S GARDENS

Byre
Theatre

ABBEY STREET

Queen Mary's
House

St Leonard's
School

PENDS ROAD

Cathedral

St Rule's
Tower

Preservation
Trust Museum

GREGORY PLACE

EAST SCORES

CASTLE STREET

Castle

SHOREHEAD

LONG PIER

Harbour

East
Sands

LADEBRAES WALK

ARGYLE STREET

DOUBLEDYKES ROAD

B988

WARDLAW GDNS

KENNEDY GARDENS

N

N O R T H   S E A

0   200 yds

Leuchars & Dundee

Crail, I, J & K

6 miles) & Botanic Gardens

ACCOMMODATION
Abbey Cottage   J
Aslar House   F
Craigmore   C
Craigtoun Meadows
 Caravan Park   H
Dunvegan   B
Inn on North Street   D
Kinkell   I
Old Course   A
Old Fishergate House   E
The Old Station   K
St Andrews Tourist Hostel G

RESTAURANTS & CAFÉS
B. Jannetta   9
Broons Bistro and Bar   4
Butler and Company   7
Byre Café-Bar   13
The Doll's House   8
Iain Mellis Cheesemonger   10
The Peat Inn   1
The Seafood Restaurant   14
Taste   5
The Vine Leaf   11

PUBS & BARS
The Central   6
Gin House   12
Inn on North Street   D
Ma Bells   2
Rusacks Lounge Bar   3

8

FIFE | St Andrews and the East Neuk

441

© Crown copyright

was to build a city in his honour. The conscientious courier set off, but was shipwrecked on the rocks close to the present harbour. Struggling ashore with his precious burden, he built a shrine to the saint on what subsequently became the site of the **cathedral**; St Andrew became Scotland's patron saint and the town its ecclesiastical capital.

St Andrews isn't a large place, with only three main streets and an open, airy feel encouraged by the long stretches of sand on either side of town and the acreage of golf links all around. Local residents are proud of their town, with its refined old-fashioned ambience. Thanks to a strong and well-informed local conservation lobby, many of the original buildings have survived. Almost the entire centre consists of listed buildings, while the ruined castle and cathedral have all but been rebuilt in the efforts to preserve their remains.

From St Andrews, the attractive beaches and little fishing villages of the **East Neuk** (*neuk* is Scots for "corner") are within easy reach, although the area can also be approached from the Kirkcaldy side. Though golf and coastal walks are a shared characteristic, the East Neuk villages have few of the grand buildings and important bustle of St Andrews, with old cottages and merchants' houses huddling round stone-built harbours in groupings fallen upon with joy by artists and photographers.

Arrival and information

St Andrews is not on the train line. The nearest **train station** is on the Edinburgh–Dundee line at Leuchars, five miles northwest across the River Eden, from where regular buses make the fifteen-minute trip into town. (When you buy your rail ticket to Leuchars, ask for a St Andrews rail-bus ticket which includes the bus fare.) Frequent **buses** from Edinburgh and Dundee terminate at the bus station on City Road at the west end of Market Street. The **tourist office**, 70 Market St (April–June Mon–Sat 9.30am–5.30pm, Sun 11am–4pm; July & Aug Mon–Sat 9.30am–7pm, Sun 10am–5pm; Sept & Oct Mon–Sat 9.30am–6pm, Sun 11am–4pm; Nov–March Mon–Sat 9.30am–5pm; ☎01334/472021), holds comprehensive information about St Andrews and northeast Fife.

Tours and getting around

Most of the organized tours take place in summer only. An open-topped hop-on/hop-off **bus tour** (July & Aug daily 11am–3pm; £6) takes a one-hour spin around the main sights, although the town is compact enough to explore thoroughly on **foot**. Guide-led tours (mid-June to Aug Mon–Fri 11am & 2.30pm; £4; ☎01334/462245) around the **university** buildings leave from Butt's Wynd, just beside the chapel by St Salvator's College, while on certain evenings a **witches tour** seeks out the spooky spots around town (July & Aug Thurs, Fri & Sun 8pm; rest of year Fri only 8pm or 7.30pm Nov–March; book on ☎01334/655057). To get a bracing introduction to the importance of **golf** to the town, the St Andrews Links Trust runs guided walking tours of the Old Course, starting from the Golf Shop just behind the eighteenth green (July & Aug daily 11am–4pm; May & June Sat & Sun same times; £2; ☎01334/466666, ⓦwww.standrews.org.uk).

The town's fiendish **parking** system requires vouchers (Mon–Sat 9am–5pm; 60p/hr) which you can get from the tourist office and some local shops – you may find it easier leaving your car in one of the free car parks fringing the centre. Spokes, at 37 South St (☎01334/477835), offers **bike rental**.

St Andrews **Royal and Ancient Golf Club** (or "R&A") is the international governing body for golf, and dates back to a meeting of 22 of the local gentry in 1754, who founded the Society of St Andrews Golfers, being "admirers of the ancient and healthful exercise of golf". The game itself has been played here since the fifteenth century. Those early days were instrumental in establishing Scotland as the home of golf, for the rules were distinguished from those of the French game by the fact that participants had to manoeuvre the ball into a hole, rather than hit an above-ground target. It was not without its opponents, however – particularly James II who, in 1457, banned his subjects from playing since it was distracting them from archery practice.

The approach to St Andrews from the west runs adjacent to the famous **Old Course**, one of seven courses in the immediate vicinity of the town. The R&A's strictly private **clubhouse**, a stolid, square building dating from 1854, is at the eastern end of the Old Course overlooking both the eighteenth green and the long strand of the West Sands. The British Open Championship was first held here in 1873, having been inaugurated in 1860 at Prestwick in Ayrshire, and since then it has been held at St Andrews regularly, pulling in enormous crowds. Pictures of golfing greats from Tom Morris to Tiger Woods, along with clubs and a variety of memorabilia donated by famous players, are displayed in the admirable **British Golf Museum** on Bruce Embankment, along the waterfront below the clubhouse (April–Oct Mon–Sat 9.30am–5.30pm, Sun 10am–5pm; Nov–March Mon–Sat 10am–4.30pm; £5). Guided walks of the Old Course are available (see opposite), though any golf aficionado will savour a stroll around the immediate environs of the golf courses, where there are numerous golf shops, including a couple selling and repairing old-fashioned hickory-shafted clubs.

Where to play

It is possible to **play** any of the town's courses, ranging from the nine-hole Balgove course (£10 per round) to the venerated Old Course itself – though for the latter you'll need a valid handicap certificate and must enter a daily ballot for tee times; if you're successful the green fees are £115 in summer. All this and more is explained at the clubhouse of the **St Andrews Links Trust** (🌐 www.standrews.org.uk), the organization which looks after all the courses in town, located alongside the fairway of the first hole of the Old Course. Arguably the best golfing experience in St Andrews, even if you can't tell a birdie from a bogey, is the **Himalayas** (April–Sept Mon–Sat 10.30am–6.30pm, Sun noon–6.30pm; £1), a fantastically lumpy eighteen-hole putting course in an ideal setting right next to the Old Course and the sea. Officially the Ladies Putting Club, founded in 1867, with its own clubhouse, the grass is as perfectly manicured as the championship course, and you can have all the thrill of sinking a six-footer in the most famous location in golf, all for £1 per round.

Accommodation

With St Andrews' wide-ranging appeal to visitors, there's no shortage of **accommodation** both in town and around, although average prices in all categories vie with Edinburgh's as the highest in Scotland. Upmarket **hotels** are thick on the ground, notably around the golf courses. What many take to be the finest hotel, the red sandstone building immediately behind the Royal & Ancient clubhouse and eighteenth green of the Old Course, is in fact Hamilton Hall, a student residence; however, B&B is sometimes available here in summer (see p.444). There are plenty of **guesthouses**, though rooms often get booked up in the summer, when you should definitely book in advance. For **camping**,

the nicest spot is *Craigtoun Meadows Caravan Park* (☎01334/475959, ⓦwww
.craigtounmeadows.co.uk; March–Oct), just over a mile west from the centre
of town.

In-town accommodation

Hotels

Dunvegan Hotel 7 Pilmour Place
☎01334/473105, ⓦwww.dunvegan-hotel.com.
Anywhere else this would be a typical, decent
Scottish hotel, but it's just along the road from the
Old Course and is run by golf fans, so one theme
predominates. The bar is popular with visiting
caddies, who sometimes drag along their more
famous employers. ❼

Inn on North Street 127 North St ☎01334/473387,
ⓦwww.theinnonnorthstreet.com. Appealing mid-
range option with a youthful feel and modern Gaelic
style: tasteful rooms, wooden floors, DVD players and
a lively bar and restaurant area (see p.447). ❻

Old Course Hotel ☎01334/474371, ⓦwww
.oldcoursehotel.co.uk. The best-known hotel in St
Andrews, located just a sliced two-iron from the
seventeenth tee. A large, luxurious resort complex
with all facilities including a spa. ❾

B&Bs, hostel and campus accommodation

Abbey Cottage Abbey Walk ☎01334/473727,
ⓦwww.abbeycottage.co.uk. Inexpensive B&B in a
cottage with a pretty garden south of the cathedral,
near the harbour. ❸

Aslar House 120 North St ☎01334/473460,
ⓦwww.aslar.com. A smart guesthouse in a three-
storey town house with an unusual round tower at
the back. ❺

Craigmore 3 Murray Park ☎01334/472142,
ⓦwww.standrewscraigmore.com. A neat, non-
smoking guesthouse with seven en-suite rooms in
a very central location. ❺

Old Fishergate House North Castle St
☎01334/470874, ⓦwww.oldfishergatehouse.
co.uk. Seventeenth-century town house in the
oldest part of town with two spacious twin rooms
full of period features. ❺

St Andrews Tourist Hostel St Mary's Place
☎01334/479911, ⓦwww.hostelsaccommodation
.com. Superbly located backpacker hostel in a
pleasantly converted town house right above *The
Grill House* restaurant with plenty of dorm beds,
but no doubles.

University of St Andrews ☎01334/462000,
ⓦwww.escapetotranquillity.com. Rents out rooms
in various student residences between June and
September, all on a B&B basis. Self-catering
houses also available. Single rooms from £27.50,
twin ❸

Out-of-town accommodation

🏃 **Kinkell** By Brownhills ☎01334/472003,
ⓦwww.kinkell.com. Countryside B&B in a
lovely family farmhouse near the beach, about two
miles south of town off the A917. ❺

The Old Station Stravithie Bridge
☎01334/880505, ⓦwww.theoldstation.co.uk. A

couple of miles south of the town on the B9131 to
Anstruther, you can stay in tasteful rooms in the
main house (based around a former station waiting
room) or in an imaginatively designed suite in an
old railway carriage parked alongside. Main house
❺, carriage ❼

The Town

The centre of St Andrews still follows its medieval layout. On the three main
thoroughfares, **North Street**, **Market Street** and **South Street**, which run west
to east towards the ruined Gothic cathedral, are several of the original university
buildings from the fifteenth century. Narrow alleys connect the cobbled streets,
attic windows and gable ends shape the rooftops and here and there you'll see
the old wooden doors with heavy knockers and black iron hinges.

St Andrews Cathedral and around

The ruin of the great **cathedral** (visitor centre: April–Sept daily 9.30am–
6.30pm; Oct–March 9.30am–4.30pm; HS; £3, joint ticket with castle £5;

grounds: year-round 9am–6.30pm; free), at the east end of town, gives only an idea of the importance of what was the largest cathedral in Scotland. Though founded in 1160, it was not finished and consecrated until 1318, in the presence of Robert the Bruce. On June 5, 1559, the Reformation took its toll, and supporters of John Knox, fresh from a rousing meeting, plundered the cathedral and left it to ruin. Stone was still being taken from the building for various local projects as late as the 1820s.

The cathedral site, above the harbour where the land drops to the sea, can be a blustery place, with the wind whistling through the great east window and down the stretch of turf that was once the central aisle. In front of the window a slab is all that remains of the high altar, where the relics of St Andrew were once enshrined. Previously, it is believed that they were kept in **St Rule's Tower**, the austere Romanesque monolith next to the cathedral, which was built as part of an abbey in 1130. From the top of the tower (a climb of 157 steps), there's a good view of the town and surroundings, and of the remains of the monastic buildings which made up the priory. Around the entire complex is a sturdy wall dating from the sixteenth century, over half a mile long and with three gateways.

Southwest of the cathedral enclosure lies **the Pends**, a huge fourteenth-century vaulted gatehouse which marked the main entrance to the priory, and from where the road leads down to the harbour, passing prim **St Leonard's**, once one of Scotland's leading private schools for girls, though now co-ed. The sixteenth-century, rubble-stonework building on the right as you go through the Pends is **Queen Mary's House**, where she is believed to have stayed in 1563. The house was restored in 1927 and is now used as the school library.

Down at the **harbour**, gulls screech above the fishing boats, keeping an eye on the lobster nets strewn along the quay. If you come here on a Sunday morning, you'll see students parading down the long pier, red gowns billowing in the wind, in a time-honoured after-church walk. The beach, **East Sands**, is a popular stretch, although it's cool in summer and bitterly cold in winter. A path leads south from the far end of the beach, climbing up the hill past the caravan site and cutting through the gorse; this makes a pleasant walk on a sunny day, taking in hidden coves and caves.

St Andrews Castle

Not far north of the cathedral, the rocky coastline curves inland to the ruined **castle** (same hours as cathedral; £3, joint ticket with cathedral £5; HS), with a drop to the sea on two sides and a moat on the inland side. Founded around 1200 and extended over the centuries, it was built as part of the palace of the bishops and archbishops of St Andrews and was consequently the scene of some fairly grim incidents at the time of the Reformation. There's not a great deal left of the castle, since it fell into ruin in the seventeenth century, and most of what can be seen dates from the sixteenth century, apart from the fourteenth-century Fore Tower.

Protestant reformer George Wishart was burnt at the stake in front of the castle in 1546, as an incumbent Cardinal Beaton looked on. Wishart had been a friend of John Knox's, and it wasn't long before fellow reformers sought vengeance for his death. Less than three months later, Cardinal Beaton was stabbed to death and his body displayed from the battlements before being dropped into the **bottle dungeon**, a 24-foot pit hewn out of solid rock which can still be seen in the Sea Tower. The perpetrators then held the castle for over a year, and during that time dug the secret passage which can be entered from the ditch in front. Outside the castle, the initials "GW" are carved in stone.

Around the university

A little way down North Street from the cathedral, housed in a picturesque sixteenth-century cottage with a low wooden door, the **St Andrews Preservation Trust Museum and Garden** (June–Sept daily 2–5pm; occasionally open by appointment at other times of year; free; ⓦ www.standrewspreservationtrust .co.uk) presents an intimate picture of the town's history and glamorous golf connections.

Further along North Street is the enclosed quadrangle of **St Salvator's College**, the oldest part of the scattered campus of the town's famous university. St Andrews University is the oldest in Scotland, founded in 1410 by Bishop Henry Wardlaw, although James I, to whom the bishop was tutor, is the nominal founder (and was a great benefactor of the university). The original building was on the site of the Old University Library and by the end of the Middle Ages three colleges had been built: St Salvator's (1450) on North Street, **St Leonard's** (1512) on The Pens and **St Mary's** (1538) on South Street. At the time of the Reformation, St Mary's became a seminary of Protestant theology, and today it houses the university's Faculty of Divinity. Its **quad** features beautiful gardens and some magnificent old trees, perfect for flopping under on a warm day. **Guided tours** (see p.442) of the university buildings start from St Salvator's Chapel, or you can wander freely around the buildings at your own pace. Almost all of the oldest and most attractive university buildings are found along North and South streets, with more recent parts of the campus dotted around the centre of town and further out.

The beaches, Botanic Gardens and Aquarium

St Andrews has two great **beaches**, the West Sands which stretch for two miles from just below the R&A Clubhouse, and the shorter more compact East Sands which curve round from the harbour. The West Sands are best known from the opening sequences of the Oscar-winning film *Chariots of Fire*; while it's still used by budding athletes, less energetic activities include sandcastle competitions, breath-taking dips in the North Sea and bird-watching at the lonely north end.

△ St Mary's Quad, St Andrew's University

The blustery winds which are the scourge of golfers and walkers alike do at least make the beach a great place to fly a kite – if you're keen to try, contact Wind and Water (☎07890/647227, ⓦwww.wind-and-water.co.uk), which offers a range of introductory tuition sessions.

Another way to escape the bustle of the town is to head to the **Botanic Gardens** on Canongate (daily 10am–7pm, Oct–April closes 4pm; glasshouses close 4pm; £2), a peaceful retreat just ten minutes' walk south of South Street.

If you've got children in tow you may want to visit the huge **St Andrews Aquarium** (daily: July & Aug 10am–6pm; rest of year 10am–5pm; £5.85; ☎01334/474786, ⓦwww.standrewsaquarium.co.uk) on The Scores, at the west end of town close to the golf museum. Here you can see and touch marine life of all shapes and sizes, and there are observation pools and daily feeding sessions with the resident seals.

Eating and drinking

St Andrews has no shortage of **restaurants** and **cafés**. There are a number of blow-out options, but given the local student population, there's also plenty of choice at the cheaper end of the market, as well as lots of good **pubs**. For **picnic** food, you won't fail to find some tempting deli treats at Butler and Company, 10 Church St, or Iain Mellis Cheesemonger, 149 South St. You'll also get a great ice cream at *B. Jannetta*, 31 South St – whose flavours include Scottish tablet and Irn Bru sorbet.

Restaurants and cafés

Broons Bistro and Bar 119 North St. Right beside the classic New Picture House cinema, a comfortable yet still young and fun café-bar-bistro with regular live music sessions. Moderate.

🏃 **Byre Café-Bar** Abbey St ⓦwww .byretheatre.com. One of the nicer spots in town for a leisurely coffee or light meal; interesting contemporary dishes include red snapper and venison steak. Moderate.

The Doll's House 3 Church Square ☎01334/477422, ⓦwww.dolls-house.co.uk. Stylish modern dishes based around top Scottish produce, with a continental feel to the outdoor tables and occasional jazz evening. Moderate to expensive.

The Peat Inn Cupar, six miles southwest of town ☎01334/840206, ⓦwww.thepeatinn.co.uk. The first Scottish restaurant to receive a Michelin star, when founding chef David Wilson established a great reputation based on local specialities with French influences. The dining area is intimate without being cramped, and a three-course meal – perhaps featuring lobster broth, venison or roast monkfish – will set you back at least £40 per head. Also has eight plush if pricey suites attached (❽). Closed Sun & Mon. Expensive.

🏃 **The Seafood Restaurant** The Scores ☎01334/479475, ⓦwww.theseafoodres taurant.com. Sister to its acclaimed namesake in St Monans (see p.450), this restaurant has an amazing location in a custom-built glass building on the

beach between the Aquarium and the Old Course. The venue has as much wow-factor as its fish-dominated menu. Expensive.

Taste 131 North St. A small but cultured coffee shop selling good brews and a few snacks but not much else; it's one of St Andrews' bona fide hip hangouts. Inexpensive.

The Vine Leaf 131 South St ☎01334/477497, ⓦwww.vineleafstandrews.co.uk. Plenty of gourmet temptations in a large menu encompassing bold seafood, beef, game and vegetarian dishes, served in a cosy, lived-in dining room with a convivial atmosphere. Closed Sun & Mon. Expensive.

Pubs and bars

The Central Market St. Old pub serving huge pies and a powerful beer brewed by Trappist monks.

Gin House 116 South St. Raucous spot and a current student favourite. Full of chrome and wood, with regular DJs playing and food served all day.

Inn on North Street 127 North St. Tends to attract slightly older students, but houses the popular *Lizard* basement nightclub Fri & Sat. Also has rooms (see p.444).

Ma Bells 40 The Scores. In the basement of the *St Andrews Golf Hotel*, a lively pub serving cheap food which is often thronged with students.

Rusacks Lounge Bar 16 Pilmour Links. Hotel bar with the best views of the Old Course; settle into one of their comfy chairs and watch golfers through huge windows as you sip pricey drinks.

Art and entertainment

As you'd expect of a university town, St Andrews has a healthy cultural scene. The best place for contemporary **arts and crafts** is the Crawford Arts Centre at 93 North St (Mon–Sat 10am–5pm, Sun 2–5pm; free; Ⓦwww.crawfordarts .free-online.co.uk), which hosts changing exhibitions. The other important arts venue in town is the **Byre Theatre** (Ⓦwww.byretheatre.com), which began life in an old cowshed in 1933 and now occupies a stylishly designed modern building including a pleasant café/bistro on Abbey Street. Productions range from important Scottish drama to populist musicals – to find out what's on contact the box office (Ⓣ01334/475000). There's also a small **cinema**, the New Picture House (Ⓣ01334/473509, Ⓦwww.nphcinema.co.uk), a few doors down from the Crawford Arts Centre.

The East Neuk

Extending south of St Andrews as far as Largo Bay, the **East Neuk** is famous for its series of quaint fishing villages, all crow-stepped gables and red pantiled roofs, the Flemish influence in the architecture indicating a history of strong trading links with the Low Countries. Inland, gently rolling hills provide some of the best farmland in Scotland, with quiet country lanes more redolent of parts of southern England than north of the border. Not surprisingly the area is dotted with windy **golf courses**, though if you prefer your walk unspoilt there are plenty of bracing coastal paths, including one out to Fife Ness, the "nose" of Fife sticking out into the North Sea, or along the waymarked **Fife Coastal Path** (see p.459), which traces the shoreline all the way between St Andrews and the Forth Rail Bridge, and is at its most scenic in the East Neuk stretch. **Bus** #95 runs from Leven around the coast to St Andrews.

Well patronized by holiday-makers and weekenders from the central belt, arts and crafts and good food are highlights of the area; the various **restaurants** of the East Neuk are well known for serving fresh seafood, often complemented by produce gleaned from the fertile Fife farmland.

Crail

CRAIL is the archetypally charming East Neuk fishing village, its maze of rough cobbled streets leading steeply down to a tiny stone-built harbour surrounded by piles of lobster creels, and with fishermen's cottages tucked into every nook and cranny in the cliff. Though often populated by artists at their easels and camera-toting tourists, it is still a working harbour, and if the boats have been out you can often buy fresh lobster and crab cooked to order from a small wooden shack right on the harbour edge. Above the harbour are perched the grander merchants' houses, as well as the twelfth-century **St Mary's Church**, where legend has it that the large blue stone by the gate was tossed there by the Devil, all the way from the offshore Isle of May. You can trace the history of the town at the **Crail Museum and Heritage Centre**, 62 Marketgate (Easter–Sept daily 10am–1pm & 2pm–5pm, Sun 2–5pm; free) which also doubles up as the town's **tourist office**. The **Crail Pottery**, 75 Nethergate (Mon–Fri 9am–5pm, Sat & Sun 10am–5pm), is worth a visit for its wide range of locally made pottery, while the **Jerdan Gallery**, 42 Marketgate South (daily 11am–5pm, closed Tues), displays an array of contemporary painting, sculpture and ceramics by top Scottish artists.

Accommodation choices include *Selcraig House*, 47 Nethergate (Ⓣ01333/450697, Ⓦwww.selcraighouse.co.uk; ③), a non-smoking guesthouse just along from the tourist office. Across the road from this, the *Marine Hotel*,

54 Nethergate South (℡01333/450207; ❸), is a traditional inn with sea views and a welcoming attitude. Also well worth considering is the upmarket B&B on offer at *Cambo House* (℡01333/450054, Ⓦwww.camboestate.com; ❻), a grand house set among some stunning parkland and beautifully tended gardens near the small village of Kingsbarns, between Crail and St Andrews. The *Sauchope Links Park* (℡01333/450460, Ⓦwww.sauchope.co.uk; March–Oct) is a very pleasant **campsite**, a few miles north of Crail. Tucked into a wee cottage on the way down to the harbour, *Crail Harbour Gallery and Tearoom* (daily 10.30am–5pm, closed Mon & Tues in winter) serves fresh **coffee** and toasted panini and has a terrace overlooking the Isle of May. Apart from that and 🍴 Mrs Riley's shack selling lobster and crab down at the harbour (mid-April to early Oct Tues–Sun noon–4pm), there's nowhere notable to sit down and **eat**, particularly in comparison with what's on offer elsewhere in the East Neuk. The various hotels in the village serve bar meals, and you can get fish and chips from *Borellas* on the High Street.

Anstruther and around

ANSTRUTHER is the largest of the East Neuk fishing harbours, but it too has an attractively old-fashioned air and no shortage of character in its houses and narrow streets. It is home to the wonderfully unpretentious **Scottish Fisheries Museum** (April–Oct Mon–Sat 10am–5.30pm, Sun 11am–5pm; Nov–March Mon–Sat 10am–4.30pm, Sun noon–4.30pm; £4.50). Set in an atmospheric complex of sixteenth- to nineteenth-century buildings with timber ceilings and wooden floors, it chronicles the history of the Scottish fishing and whaling industries with ingenious displays, including a whole series of exquisite ships models built on site by a resident model-maker. The museum incorporates the old Smith & Hutton boat-builder's yard, where you can see a number of complete old craft, including the last full-scale "Zulu", a stylish and practical wooden sailing ship which once dominated the Scottish herring industry. Anstruther's helpful **tourist office** (Easter–Sept Mon–Sat 10am–5pm, Sun 11am–4pm; Oct Mon–Sat 10am–4pm, Sun 11am–4pm; ℡01333/311073) is next to the museum.

Located on the rugged **Isle of May**, several miles offshore from Anstruther, is a lighthouse erected in 1816 by Robert Louis Stevenson's grandfather, as well as the remains of Scotland's first lighthouse, built in 1636, which burnt coals as a beacon. The island is now a nature reserve and bird sanctuary, and can be reached by boat from Anstruther (May–Sept once daily, no sailing Tues May & June; £15; ℡01333/310103, Ⓦwww.isleofmayferry.com). Between April and July the dramatic sea cliffs are covered with breeding kittiwakes, razorbills, guillemots and shags, while inland there are thousands of puffins and eider ducks. Grey seals also make the occasional appearance. Check in advance for departure times, as crossings vary according to weather and tide, and allow between four and five hours for a round trip: an hour each way, and a couple of hours on the island. You'll also need plenty of warm, waterproof clothing.

Anstruther has a decent choice of places to stay and eat. For **B&B**, try *The Spindrift* (℡01333/310573, Ⓦwww.thespindrift.co.uk; ❹), on Pittenweem Road, or the more contemporary rooms attached to the middle-of-the-road *Waterfront* restaurant on Shore Street (℡01333/312200, Ⓦwww.anstruther-waterfront.com; ❹). Tucked in beside the museum in one of the village's oldest buildings, once a cooperage and smokehouse, is the East Neuk's most impressive fish **restaurant**, 🍴 *The Cellar*, at 24 East Green (℡01333/310378; booking recommended). For decent fish and chips, head for the *Anstruther Fish Bar*, at 44 The Shore, a regular award winner.

Scotland's Secret Bunker

Four miles inland from Anstruther on the B940 towards St Andrews is **Scotland's Secret Bunker** (April–Oct daily 10am–5pm; £7.50), as idiosyncratic a tourist attraction as you are likely to find. Long a top-secret part of the military establishment, the bunker was opened to the public in 1994 following its decommissioning at the end of the Cold War. Above ground, all you can see is an innocent-looking farmhouse, although the various pieces of military hardware now parked outside and the rows of barbed wire fencing hint that something more sinister is afoot. From the farmhouse, you walk down a long ramp to the bunker, which comprises a vast subterranean complex of operations rooms 100ft below ground and encased in 15ft of reinforced concrete. In the event of a nuclear war this was to have become Scotland's new administrative centre with room for three hundred people; it has not been spruced up for tourists, and remains uncompromisingly spartan, with various rooms showing dormitories, radio rooms and kitsch James Bond-type control centres.

Pittenweem and around

West of Anstruther are more fishing villages, all undeniably attractive and rewarding if you have the time to stroll around and take in some of the coastline, or seek out one or two of the fine places to eat and drink. Two miles from Anstruther, **PITTENWEEM** has a busy harbour and fish market, as well as a number of small art galleries. The village has become something of an artists' colony, and its annual arts festival (Ⓦwww.pittenweemartsfestival.co.uk) in early August is a unique event, with dozens of locals turning their houses into temporary art galleries for the week. Three miles north of Pittenweem on the B9171, **Kellie Castle** (mid-April to Sept daily 1–5pm; £8; grounds year-round daily 9.30am–sunset; NTS; £3) has an unusual but harmonious mix of twin sixteenth-century towers linked by a seventeenth-century building. Abandoned in the early nineteenth century, it was discovered in 1878 by Professor James Lorimer, a distinguished political philosopher, who took on the castle as an "improving tenant". The wonderful **gardens**, where space is broken up by arches, alcoves and paths which weave between profuse herbaceous borders, were designed by the professor's son Robert, aged just 16. Later Sir Robert Lorimer, he became a well-known architect specializing in restorations and war memorials; among his restoration works is the Hill of Tarvit in Cupar (see p.453). Robert's son Hew, who also lived here, was one of Scotland's finest twentieth-century sculptors; an engaging exhibition on his life and work can be found in the converted castle stables.

St Monans

Pittenweem almost merges into **ST MONANS**, the smallest of the East Neuk fishing villages – if you take the coastal footpath between the two you'll encounter a reconstructed stone windmill, a reminder of the area's link with the Low Countries, standing above some old saltpans. St Monans is worth a visit for its splendid *Seafood Restaurant*, at the far end of the harbour (☎01333/730327), an older sister to its glamorous new namesake in St Andrews (see p.447). Beyond a dignified old bar is the smart restaurant perched right on the sea's edge with panoramic views out to sea; the sophisticated meals, while expensive, use the freshest local fish and crustaceans.

Elie

Three miles on from St Monans is **ELIE**, gathered round a curve of golden-brown sand twelve miles south of St Andrews, a popular escape for middle-class

Edinburgh families who come for the bracing air and golf courses. Once known as a popular bathing spot, east of Elie bay stands a tower built for Lady Janet Anstruther in the late eighteenth century as a summerhouse, with a changing room to allow her to bathe in a pool in the rocks below. The essential stop in Elie is the relaxed and convivial *Ship Inn*, overlooking the beach near the harbour, where you'll find great **bar food** and, come summer, lots of lively local banter in the beer garden. You can **stay** beside the pub at *Rockview Guesthouse* (℡01333/330246, ⒲www.ship-elie.com; ❺), and there's yet another excellent **restaurant** here, *Sangster's* (℡01333/331001, ⒲www.sangsters.co.uk) on the High Street. The sheltered bay is understandably popular for **watersports** – if you fancy a spin on a windsurfer or sailing dinghy, head for Elie Watersports (℡01333/330962, ⒲wwww.eliewatersports.com) at the harbour, which rents out various craft by the hour.

Lower Largo

There's not a great deal to **LOWER LARGO**, which clings to the shore of sandy Largo Bay halfway between Elie and Leven, the point where less glamorous, industrial Fife reappears. Largo also has nothing much notable in its history other than the fact that it was the birthplace in 1676 of one **Alexander Selkirk**, the "real" Robinson Crusoe. A navigator on a ship called *Cinque Ports*, he judged the ship unseaworthy and asked to be dropped off at the next island, Juan Fernandez, four hundred miles west of Chile. He led a solitary life on the island for over four years before being rescued, returning to Largo for some years and then going to sea again. His adventures were first published in 1713, but were immortalized by Daniel Defoe when he used them as the basis for his famous castaway in *Robinson Crusoe*, published in 1719. A small statue of Crusoe dressed in goatskins and peering out to sea stands in a recess in the wall of a house built on the site of the old Selkirk family home on Main Street. You can learn a bit more about his story in the tiny Selkirk Room at the *Crusoe Hotel* (℡01333/320759, ⒲www.crusoehotel.co.uk; ❺), a hundred yards away by the harbour.

Central Fife

The main A92 road cuts right through **Central Fife**, ultimately connecting the Forth Road Bridge on the southern coast of Fife with the Tay Road Bridge on the northern coast. Inland from Kirkcaldy, the old mining towns of Cowdenbeath, Kelty, Lochgelly and Cardenden huddle together, places that are routinely ignored by visitors shooting up to St Andrews on the coastal route or zooming along the M90 to Perth. Take the train, however, and you'll weave through this forlorn stretch as the line leaves the coast and heads inland. The main settlement of this inland region is **Glenrothes**, a new town created after World War II in old coal-mining territory. Generally the scenery in this part of the county is pleasant rather than startling, though it is worth making a detour to seek out **Falkland** and its magnificent ruined palace, and the sights around **Cupar**, the county town on the road to St Andrews.

Glenrothes and around

Ten miles inland from Kirkcaldy, **GLENROTHES** is a largely generic new town, best known for its microelectronics factories, part of "Silicon Glen" (Scotland's version of Silicon Valley), which has injected parts of the region with much-needed wealth and self-confidence. If you have even a passing interest in castles and their construction, try to visit **Balgonie Castle**, two miles east of Glenrothes on the B921 off the A911. Set above the River Leven, this splendid castle with its fourteenth-century keep and fine open courtyard has a somewhat unkempt and informal appearance from the outside; only a wooden plaque stating that it is home to the laird and lady of Balgonie suggests it's inhabited. Once inside, you are guaranteed a uniquely personal tour from the laird or a member of his family; the castle is open (roughly 10am–5pm; £3; appointments recommended on ☎01592/750119) except when the fourteenth-century chapel is being used for candlelit weddings.

Falkland

The **Howe of Fife**, north of Glenrothes, is a low-lying stretch of ground (or "howe") at the foot of the twin peaks of the heather-swathed **Lomond Hills** – West Lomond (1696ft) and East Lomond (1378ft). Nestling in the lower slopes of East Lomond, the narrow streets of **FALKLAND** are lined with fine and well-preserved seventeenth- and eighteenth-century buildings. The village grew up around **Falkland Palace** (March–Oct Mon–Sat 10am–6pm, Sun 1–5.30pm; £10, gardens only £5; NTS), which stands on the site of an earlier castle, home to the Macduffs, the earls of Fife. James IV began the construction of the present palace in 1500; it was completed and embellished by James V, and became a favoured country retreat for the royal court. Charles II stayed here in 1650 when he was in Scotland for his coronation, but after the Jacobite rising of 1715 and temporary occupation by Rob Roy the palace was abandoned, remaining so until the late nineteenth century when the keepership was acquired by the third marquess of Bute. He completely restored the palace, and today it is a stunning example of Early Renaissance architecture, complete with corbelled parapet, mullioned windows, round towers and massive walls. You can pick up an audio guide (free) which leads you round a cross-section of public and private rooms in the south and east wings. The former is better preserved and includes the stately drawing room, the Chapel Royal (still used for Mass) and the Tapestry Gallery, swathed with splendid seventeenth-century Flemish hangings. Outside, the **gardens** are also worth a look, their well-stocked herbaceous borders lining a pristine lawn. Don't miss the high walls of the oldest real (or royal) tennis court in Britain – built in 1539 for James V and still used.

Falkland is also a good base for **walks**, with several leading from the village; but for the more serious hikes to the summits of East and West Lomond, you have to start from Craigmead car park about two miles west of the village (follow the usual safety precautions; see p.64). The concentration of charming old cottages and historic buildings in the heart of Falkland also make it a particularly pleasant place to wander around.

Accommodation includes family-friendly *Burgh Lodge*, a newly renovated independent **hostel** on Back Wynd (☎01337/857710, ⓦwww.burghlodge .co.uk), with disabled facilities. Both the *Hunting Lodge Hotel*, on High Street, directly opposite the palace (☎01337/857226; ➋), and the *Covenanter Hotel* (☎01337/857224, ⓦwww.covenanterhotel.com; ➋ in separate cottage; ➌ in hotel), just up the road, are comfortable traditional inns, with great pubs as well as a couple of rooms upstairs. *The Greenhouse* (☎01337/858400; closed Mon & Tues), also on the High Street, is a small modern **restaurant** serving local organic food. Not far out of the village on the A912 there's a good little farm shop and café (daily 10am–6pm) at *Pillars of Hercules Organic Farm*.

Cupar and around

Straddling the small River Eden and surrounded by gentle hills, **CUPAR** is the capital of Fife, despite the fact that St Andrews' star is these days a fair bit brighter. In 1276 Alexander III held an assembly in Cupar, bringing together the Church, aristocracy and local burgesses in an early form of Scottish parliament. For his troubles he subsequently became the butt of Sir David Lindsay's *Ane Pleasant Satyre of the Thrie Estaitis* (1535), one of the first great Scottish dramas.

Situated at the centre of Fife's road network, Cupar's main street, part of the main road from Edinburgh to St Andrews, is plagued with traffic jams. The **Mercat Cross**, stranded in the midst of the lorries and cars which grind through the centre, now consists of salvaged sections of the seventeenth-century original, following its destruction by an errant lorry some years ago.

One of the best reasons for stopping off at Cupar is to visit the **Hill of Tarvit** (Easter–Sept daily 1–5pm; £8; gardens daily 9.30am–sunset; NTS; £3), an Edwardian mansion two miles south of town remodelled by Sir Robert Lorimer from a late seventeenth-century building. The house, formerly the home of the geographer and cartographer Sir John Scott, contains an impressive collection of eighteenth-century Chippendale and French furniture, Dutch paintings, Chinese porcelain and a restored Edwardian laundry. Also on the estate is a five-storey, late sixteenth-century **Scotstarvit Tower**, three-quarters of a mile west of the present house (keys available from the house during season only). Set on a little mound, Scotstarvit is a fine example of a Scots tower house, providing both fortification and comfort.

Practicalities

Cupar's **train station** is immediately south of the centre; **buses** from Dundee, Edinburgh, St Andrews and Stirling stop outside. If you want to **stay**, try Westfield House on Westfield Road (℡01334/655699; ⓦwww.standrews4 .freeserve.co.uk; ❻), an upmarket B&B set in a landscaped garden, or the simpler farmhouse B&B at Scotstarvit Farm (℡01334/653591, ⓦwww.scotstarvitfarm .co.uk; ❷), just south of Cupar, off the A916. There are some good **restaurants** in the area; try the excellent ⚐ *Ostler's Close*, 25 Bonnygate (℡01334/655574, ⓦwww.ostlersclose.co.uk), or follow the B940 east to the renowned *Peat Inn* (see p.447). During the day, you'll find a simple sandwich and home-baking at *Café Moka*, also tucked down a close at 29 Bonnygate.

Around Cupar

Near Cupar there are a couple of attractions particularly suitable for children. The **Scottish Deer Centre** (daily 10am–6pm; Nov–Easter closes 5pm; £4.50), three miles from Cupar on the A91, specializes in the rearing of red deer, and is also home to nine species including sika, fallow and reindeer. The tamer animals can be approached and there are falconry displays three times a day, as well as play and picnic areas and guided nature trails. Meanwhile, at Cairnie Fruit Farm just north of Cupar, a huge **maze**, designed by maze specialist Adrian Fisher is cut each summer (July–Sept 9.30am–6pm; £4) in about five acres of maize – , the corn grows to about eight feet, making it a serious navigational challenge. To refuel afterwards, the farm has lots of strawberries, raspberries and other soft fruit which you can pick yourself.

A couple of miles southeast of Cupar, **CERES**, set around a village green, is a pleasantly slow-paced hamlet which is home to the **Fife Folk Museum** (Easter & May–Sept daily 11.30am–4.30pm; £2.50). Occupying several well-preserved seventeenth- to nineteenth-century buildings, it exhibits all manner of historical farming and agricultural paraphernalia. The pillory that used to restrain miscreants on market days still stands at the entrance of the old burgh tolbooth, and at the village crossroads is an unusual seventeenth-century stone carving of a man in a three-cornered hat with a toothy grin and a beer glass on his knee, said to be a depiction of a former provost. Also in the village is **Griselda Hill Pottery** (daily 9am–5pm), where you can see brightly hand-painted pottery in a distinctive style known as Wemyss Ware – developed in Fife in the 1880s and highly prized by collectors – being made.

The Tay coast

North of Cupar, Fife's **Tay coast** is a tranquil wedge of rural hinterland on the edge of the River Tay looking across to Dundee and Perthshire. It offers little in the way of specific attractions, but a lot of undiscovered hideaways. Gentle hills fringe the shore, sheltering the villages that lie in the dips and hollows along the coast.

LEUCHARS, five miles north of St Andrews, is known for its RAF base, from where low-flying jets screech over the hills, appearing out of nowhere and sending sheep, cows and horses galloping for shelter. However, there is a beautiful twelfth-century church in the village, with fine Norman stonework. Northeast of Leuchars, **Tentsmuir Forest**, which occupies the northeasternmost point of the Fife headland, is a nature reserve with a good beach and peaceful woodland walks. The main road, however, is busy with traffic heading for the **Tay Road Bridge**, which links Fife with Dundee. A couple of miles to the west, the current Tay **rail bridge** is the second to span the river on this spot, the first having collapsed in a terrifying disaster during a storm on December 28, 1879, which claimed the lives of around a hundred people in a train crossing the bridge at the time. The event was recorded by the poet William McGonagall, who has gone down in history as being responsible for some of the most banal verse ever written, including a memorably trite rhyme about the disaster:

The storm Fiend did loudly bray,
Because ninety lives had been taken away,
On the last Sabbath day of 1879,
Which will be remember'd for a very long time.

There's a **camping** and **caravan** site (March–Oct; ☎01382/552334) at **TAYPORT**, a popular resort a couple of miles east of the road bridge, from where one of Scotland's oldest ferries once ran across the river. Here the "silvery Tay" more than justifies its traditional description, shimmering in the light whatever the season. There are good views across the river from most points along the banks of Tay on the Fife side, though there's little of note until you get to **Lindores Abbey**, a now-ruined Benedictine settlement dating back to the twelfth century which is associated with the first records of whisky production in Scotland, exchequer rolls from 1494 indicating that James IV had placed an order for eight bols (about 400 bottles) of "aquavitae" with the friars while staying at Falkland Palace. The west tower still stands, silhouetted against the sky, and there are views down to nearby **NEWBURGH**, stunning on a summer evening, with the setting sun lighting up the mudflats below and skimming across the Tay. Newburgh itself is a fairly quiet, slightly rough-edged place. Originally a fishing village, it evolved due to its proximity to the abbey, and is now known for the admirable **Laing Museum** (April–Sept daily noon–5pm; free). The collection, donated by the banker and historian Dr Alexander Laing in 1892, includes a fine array of antiques and geological specimens gathered in the area, including fossils, old prints and examples of the work of historic local craftsmen.

Southern Fife

Although the coast of **southern Fife** is predominantly industrial – with everything from cottage industries to the refitting of nuclear submarines – thankfully only a small part has been blighted by insensitive development. Even the old coal-mining areas, disused pits and left-over slag heaps have either been well camouflaged through landscaping or put to alternative use as recreation areas. Thanks to its proximity to the early coal mines, the charming village of **Culross** was once a lively port which enjoyed a thriving trade with Holland, the Dutch influence obvious in its lovely gabled houses. It was from nearby **Dunfermline** that Queen Margaret ousted the Celtic Church from Scotland in the eleventh century; her son, David I, founded an abbey here in the twelfth century, and Dunfermline remains the chief town and focus of the area. Southern Fife is linked to Edinburgh by the two **Forth bridges**, the red-painted girders of the rail bridge representing one of Britain's great engineering spectacles. East of the bridges are a string of historic coastal settlements dominated by the ancient royal burgh of **Kirkcaldy**, familiarly known as "The Lang Toun" for its four-mile-long esplanade which stretches the length of the waterfront. Still largely industrial, it's unlikely to keep you for long; from here you can either head east for the picturesque villages of the East Neuk (see p.448), or turn north along the main A92 road towards Central Fife (see p.451). Trains link the towns and villages of southern Fife, complemented by a good local bus service.

Culross

The A985 crosses the Forth Road Bridge, with unattractive views of the shipyard at Inverkeithing and the naval dock at Rosyth (now used as a port for ferry crossings to Zeebrugge in Belgium), before heading west along the Forth estuary to **CULROSS** (pronounced "Coorus"), one of Scotland's most picturesque settlements, all cobbled streets and squat cottages with crow-stepped gables. The town's development began in the fifth century with the arrival of St Serf on the northern side of the Forth at Cuileann Ros ("point where holly grows"), and is also said to have been the birthplace of St Mungo, founder of Glasgow cathedral. Culross today is the best-preserved seventeenth-century town in Scotland, thanks in large part to the work of the National Trust for Scotland, which has been renovating its whitewashed, pantiled buildings since 1932. **Bus** #14a between Dunfermline and Stirling passes through hourly.

For an excellent introduction to the burgh's history, head to the **National Trust Visitor Centre** (Easter–Sept daily noon–5pm; joint ticket for Town House, Palace and Study; NTS; £8), located in the **Town House** facing Sandhaven, where goods were once unloaded from ships. On the upper floor of the house, some of the four thousand witches executed in Scotland between 1560 and 1707 were tried and held while awaiting their fate in Edinburgh. Behind the ticket office is a tiny prison with built-in manacles. The most impressive building in the village is the nearby ochre-coloured **Culross Palace** (same hours), built by wealthy coal merchant George Bruce in the late sixteenth century; it's not a palace at all – its name comes from the Latin *palatium*, or "hall" – but a grand and impressive house, with lots of small rooms and connecting

△ Culross

passageways. Inside, well-informed staff point out the wonderful painted ceilings, pine panelling, antique furniture and curios; outside, dormer windows and crow-stepped gables dominate the walled court in which the house stands. The garden is planted with grasses, herbs and vegetables of the period, carefully grown from seed.

The charm of Culross is evident simply by wandering through its narrow streets looking for old inscriptions above windows or investigating crooked passageways with names such as "Wee Causeway" and "Stinking Wynd". Leading uphill from the Town House, a cobbled alleyway known as **Back Causeway**, complete with a raised central aisle formerly used by noblemen to separate them from the commoners, leads up to the **Study** (same hours as visitor centre) a restored house that takes its name from the small room at the top of the corbelled projecting tower, reached by a turnpike stair. Built in 1610, its Dutch Renaissance style oak panelling is further indication of the links with the Low Countries which are evident in much of Culross's architecture. There are very few **accommodation** options in Culross itself: one is *St Mungo's Cottage* (℡01383/882102, ✉martinpjackson@hotmail.com; ❶), which offers B&B and has views out to the Forth, while the *Dundonald Arms* (℡01383/882443, ⓦdundonaldarms.co.uk; ❸) on Mid Causeway has rooms as well as a convivial bar serving **food**.

Culross Abbey

Further up the hill from the Study lie the remains of **Culross Abbey**, founded by Cistercian monks on land given to the church in 1217 by the earl of Fife. The nave of the original building is a ruin, a lawn studded with great stumps of columns. Although it is difficult to get a sense of what the abbey would have looked like, the overall effect is of grace and grandeur. A ladder leads to a vaulted chamber, now exposed to the elements on one side, which feels as if it is suspended in mid-air. This adjoins the fine seventeenth-century **manse** and the choir of the abbey, which became the **Parish Church** in 1633. Inside, wooden panels detail the donations given by eighteenth-century worthies to the parish poor, and a tenth-century Celtic cross in the north transept is a reminder of the origins of the abbey (a Celtic church stood here in 450). Alabaster figures of Sir George Bruce, his lady, three sons and five daughters decorate a splendid family tomb, the parents lying in state and the children lined up and kneeling in devotion. A brass plaque tells the story of Edward, Lord Bruce of Kinloss, who was defeated by Sir Edward Sackville in a duel fought in Bergen in Holland in 1613. The luckless lord had been buried in Holland, but a persistent rumour that his heart had been taken back to Scotland was proved true when it was found during building work in the church in 1808, embalmed in a silver casket of foreign workmanship.

The **graveyard** of the church is fascinating. Many of the graves are eighteenth century, with symbols depicting the occupation of the person who is buried; the gravestone of a gardener has a crossed spade and rake as well as an hourglass with the sand run out. Note the Scottish custom, still continued, of marking women's graves with maiden names, even when they are buried with their husbands.

Dunfermline

Scotland's capital until the Union of the Crowns in 1603, **DUNFERMLINE** lies inland seven miles east of Culross, north of the Forth bridges. This "auld, grey toun" is built on a hill, dominated by the **abbey** and ruined **palace** at the top. In the eleventh century, Malcolm III (Malcolm Canmore) offered refuge here to Edgar Atheling, heir to the English throne, and his family, who were shipwrecked in the Forth while fleeing the Norman Conquest. Malcolm married Edgar's Catholic sister Margaret in 1067, and in so doing started a process of reformation that ultimately supplanted the Celtic Church. Until the late nineteenth century, Dunfermline was one of Scotland's foremost linen producers, as well as a major coal-mining centre, and today the town is a busy place, its ever-increasing sprawl attesting to a growing economy.

The Town

Dunfermline's **centre**, at the top of the hill around the abbey and palace, features narrow, cobbled streets, pedestrianized shopping areas and gargoyle-adorned buildings. One of the best of these, the **city chambers** on the corner of Bridge and Bruce streets, is a fine example of late nineteenth-century Gothic Revival style. Among the ornate porticoes and grotesques of dragons and winged serpents which adorn the exterior are the sculpted heads of Robert the Bruce, Malcolm Canmore, Queen Margaret and Elizabeth I. In summer, a **vintage bus** (free) leaves from outside the tourist information office on the hour (May–Sept daily 10am–5pm), offering a half-hour tour of the main sights in town.

The abbey and palace

The oldest part of **Dunfermline Abbey** (April–Sept daily 9.30am–6.30pm; Oct–March Mon–Wed & Sat 9.30am–4.30pm, Thurs 9.30am–12.30pm, Sun 2–4.30pm; HS; £2.50; ⓦ www.dunfermlineabbey.co.uk) is attributable to Queen Margaret, who began building a Benedictine priory in 1072, the remains of which can still be seen beneath the nave of the present church; her son, **David I**, raised the priory to the rank of abbey in the following century. In 1303, during the first of the **Wars of Independence**, the English king Edward I occupied the palace, had the church roof stripped of lead to provide ammunition for his army's catapults, and also appears to have ordered the destruction of most of the monastery buildings. **Robert the Bruce** helped rebuild the abbey, and when he died of leprosy was buried here 25 years later, although his body went undiscovered until building began on a new parish church in 1821. Inside, the stained glass is impressive, and the columns are artfully carved into chevrons, spirals and arrowheads. The enormous stonework graffiti at the top of the tower outside, "King Robert the Bruce", is attributable to an over-excited architect thrilled by the discovery of Bruce's remains. Malcolm and his queen, Margaret, who died of grief three days after her husband in 1093, have a shrine outside too.

The guesthouse of Margaret's Benedictine monastery, south of the abbey, became the **palace** in the sixteenth century under James VI, who gave both it and the abbey to his consort, Queen Anne of Denmark. Charles I, the last monarch to be born in Scotland, entered the world here in 1600. Today, all that is left of it is a long, sandstone facade, especially impressive when silhouetted against the evening sky.

Near the entrance to the abbey, pink-harled **Abbot House** (daily 10am–5pm; £3; Ⓦ www.abbothouse.co.uk), possibly fourteenth-century, has been used as an iron foundry, an art school and a doctor's surgery. Now a museum, it houses a rather haphazard array of exhibits and "experiences" designed to bring different parts of Dunfermline's past to life, from an audiovisual ghost to a 1960s living room. You can visit the witches'-coven-style café with a patio garden first to decide if you are willing to pay the entrance fee and see more.

Pittencrieff Park and around

Pittencrieff Park, known to locals as "the Glen", covers a huge area in the centre of Dunfermline, and is an attractive green haven. Bordering the ruined palace, the 76-acre park used to be owned by the lairds of Pittencrieff, whose 1610 estate house, built of stone pillaged from the palace, still stands within the grounds. In 1902, however, the entire plot was purchased by the local rags-to-riches industrialist and philanthropist Andrew Carnegie, who donated it to his home town. This was just as much sweet revenge as beneficent public-spiritedness: the young Carnegie had been banned from the estate, according to a former laird's edict that no Morrison would pass through the gates. Since his mother had been a Morrison, Carnegie could do little more than gaze through the bars on the one day a year that the estate was open to the rest of the public. Today **Pittencrieff House** (daily 11am–5pm; Oct–March closes 4pm; free) displays exhibits on local history, and the glasshouses are filled with exotic blooms. In the centre of the park by a small stream are the remains – little more than the foundations – of **Malcolm Canmore's Tower**, which may be the location of Malcolm's residence, known to have been somewhere to the west of the abbey. Dunfermline, meaning "fort by the crooked pool", takes its name from the tower's location: *dun* meaning hill or fort; *fearum* bent or crooked; and *lin* (or *lyne/line*) a pool or running water.

Just beyond the southeast corner of the park, the modest little cottage at the bottom of St Margaret Street is **Andrew Carnegie's Birthplace** (April–Oct Mon–Sat 11am–5pm, Sun 2–5pm; £2; Ⓦ www.carnegiebirthplace.com). The son of a weaver, Carnegie (1835–1919) lived as a child upstairs with his family, while the room below housed his father's loom shop. After the family emigrated to America in 1848, Carnegie worked first on the railroads and then in the iron and steel industries; he began acquiring steel-production firms in the 1870s and was so successful that by the time he retired in 1901 he was a multimillionaire – one of the richest men in the world. For the next eighteen years he devoted himself to giving the money away, endowing educational establishments and free libraries around the world, including some six hundred in Britain. Dunfermline's local theatre is Carnegie Hall, though not quite on the scale of its New York namesake. The cottage, preserved as it was at the end of the nineteenth century, and the adjacent Memorial Hall, describe his life and work.

Outside the park to the northeast, the Glen has been filled in to create a car park; this development entombed **St Margaret's Cave** (April–Sept daily 11am–4pm; free), where it's said Malcolm's wife came to pray. Eighty-seven steps lead down to the damp sandstone hollow, a site of pilgrimage for Catholics for the past century or so.

Practicalities

Trains from Edinburgh stop at Dunfermline's **train station**, halfway down the long hill of St Margaret's Drive, southeast of the centre. It's a fifteen-minute walk up the hill from here to the **tourist office** at 1 High St, immediately opposite the City Chambers (April–Sept Mon–Sat 9.30am–5.30pm, Sun 11am–4pm; Oct–March Mon–Sat 9.30am–5pm; ℡01383/720999). An hourly bus from Edinburgh comes in at the **bus station**, in the unprepossessing Kingsgate Centre, on the north side of town. For **accommodation**, try the comfortable *Davaar House Hotel*, 126 Grieve St (℡01383/721886, ⓦwww .davaar-house-hotel.com; ❻), in a tastefully furnished Victorian town house, or the more affordable *Hillview House*, 9 Aberdour Rd (℡01383/726278; ⓦwww .hillviewhousedunfermline.co.uk; ❸), a traditional, neat B&B. There are some good, well-priced **places to eat**, including the idiosyncratic modern *Town House Restaurant and Bistro* at 48 East Port (℡01383/432382); the stylish *Bar Café Brio* on the corner of Canmore and Guildhall streets; and the *Old Inn*, just down Kirkgate, which serves bar meals and has *The Creepy Wee Pub* right next door.

The Forth bridges to Kirkcaldy

Fife's **south coast** curves sharply north at the mouth of the Firth of Forth, exposing the towns and villages to an icy east wind that somewhat undermines the sunshine image of the beaches. The highlight of the coast is one of the largest man-made structures in Scotland, the impressive Forth Rail Bridge, which joins Fife at **North Queensferry**. East from here you'll find a straggle of Fife fishing communities such as **Aberdour**, **Burntisland** and **Kinghorn** which have depended on the sea for centuries, and now make popular, although not especially attractive, holiday spots as well as commuter belt for Edinburgh. The fast route from the Forth Road Bridge to Kirkcaldy and the rest of Fife is along the inland A92 dual carriageway; a pleasant but more time-consuming alternative route is along the A921 which follows the northern shore of the firth. Both the **train** line from Inverkeithing and twice-hourly **buses** #7 and #7a from Dunfermline stop at all towns, making it quite possible to take on a section of the 81-mile-long **Fife Coastal Path**, a waymarked walking trail which begins underneath the Forth Rail Bridge at North Queensferry and links every coastal settlement including Kirkcaldy, Crail and St Andrews, finishing up at the Tay Road Bridge at Newport-on-Tay (details and leaflets available from local tourist offices).

North Queensferry

Cowering beneath the Forth bridges, **NORTH QUEENSFERRY** is a small fishing village which, until the opening of the road bridge, was the northern landing point of the ferry from South Queensferry (see p.172) and a nineteenth-century bathing resort. Built on a rocky outcrop, the place is comparatively well preserved for somewhere which takes such a battering from the elements. Everything in North Queensferry is, however, quite literally overshadowed by the two great bridges, each about a mile and a half in length, which traverse the **Firth of Forth** at its narrowest point. The cantilevered **Forth Rail Bridge**, built from 1883 to 1890 by Sir John Fowler and Benjamin Baker, ranks among the supreme achievements of Victorian engineering. Some 50,000 tons of steel were used in the construction of a design that manages to express grace as well as might. Maintenance of the bridge is a challenge – the phrase "like painting the Forth Bridge" has entered the lexicon to express the dispiriting nature of a task that has to begin again the moment it is completed. However, recently they've started using a high-tech, long-lasting coating that should render the continuous painting process redundant.

Derived from American models, the suspension format chosen for the **Forth Road Bridge** alongside makes an interesting modern complement to the older structure. Erected between 1958 and 1964, it finally killed off the 900-year-old ferry, and now attracts such a heavy volume of traffic that a second road crossing is being considered.

The only way to cross the rail bridge is aboard a train heading to or from Edinburgh, though inevitably this doesn't allow much of a perspective of the spectacle itself. For the best **panorama** of the rail bridge, make use of the pedestrian and cycle lane on the east side of the road bridge. For some background to the construction of both structures, head to the **Forth Bridges Exhibition** (daily 9am–9pm; free), occupying a couple of rooms tacked onto the modern *Corus Hotel* (previously the *Queensferry Lodge Hotel*), accessed off the B981 road that leads from the A90 to North Queensferry, which has a series of storyboards, photographs, models and displays. Here you can contemplate various mind-boggling statistics such as the fact that there are six and a half million rivets in the rail bridge, and that a shower of rain adds around 100 tons to its weight.

Tucked underneath the mighty geometry of the rail bridge is **Deep-Sea World** (daily: April–Oct 10am–6pm; Nov–March 11am–5pm; £8.55; ℡01383/411880, ⊛www.deepseaworld.com), one of Scotland's most popular family attractions. Full of weird and wonderful creatures from sea horses to piranhas, the highlight is a huge aquarium that boasts the world's largest underwater viewing tunnel, through which you glide on a moving walkway while sharks, conger eels and all manner of fish from the deep swim nonchalantly past. You can see the sharks being fed by divers (Wed & Sat 1pm), or for a few more thrills, get into the tank alongside them. The two-hour session, which includes about twenty minutes in the water, costs £125. Bookings are essential, and it's for over 16-year-olds only, but full training and safety briefings are given and you don't need a dive qualification.

Aberdour and Burntisland

Four miles east of North Queensferry, **ABERDOUR** clings tight to the walls of its **castle** (April–Sept daily 9.30am–6.30pm; Oct–March Mon–Wed, Sat & Sun 9.30am–4.30pm; HS; £3) at the southern end of the main street. Once a Douglas stronghold, the castle is on a comparatively modest scale, with gently sloping lawns, a large enclosed seventeenth-century garden and terraces. The fourteenth-century tower is the oldest part of the castle, the other buildings having been added in the sixteenth and seventeenth centuries, including the well-preserved dovecote. Worth more perusal is **St Fillan's Church**, also in the castle grounds, which dates from the twelfth century, with a few sixteenth-century additions, such as the porch restored from total dereliction in the last century. There's little else to see here apart from the town's popular **silver sands** beach which, along with its watersports, golf and sailing, has earned Aberdour the rather optimistic tourist-board soubriquet the "Fife Riviera". Off Aberdour is **Inchcolm** island, known as "the Iona of the East", with a ruined abbey dating back to 1123; to get to the island you have to join a boat trip leaving from South Queensferry (see p.172).

A real gem for **accommodation** is ⚓ *Hawkcraig House*, Hawkcraig Point (☎01383/860335; ❸), a guesthouse in an old ferryman's residence overlooking the harbour, which offers excellent **evening meals** to residents. Alternatively, you could try the friendly *Aberdour Hotel*, 38 High St (☎01383/860325, ⓦwww.aberdourhotel.co.uk; ❹), which also has an inexpensive restaurant and real ale bar downstairs.

Three miles east of Aberdour is the large holiday resort of **BURNTISLAND** with its fine stretch of sandy beach. The busy High Street runs the length of the waterfront, hemmed in by buildings at the western end, where you'll find the unkempt **train station**. Offices now occupy **Rossend Castle**, a fifteenth-century tower beyond the west end of the street with sixteenth-century additions, sadly not open to the public. Good B&B is available at *Gruinard*, 148 Kinghorn Rd (☎01592/873877, ⓦwww.gruinardguesthouse.co.uk; ❸), a comfortable place featuring a log fire and conservatory, and offering pancakes for breakfast. **Eating** options include *The Smugglers Inn*, 14 Harbour Place, which does snacks and bar meals and has a good vegetarian selection.

Kinghorn

Shortly before reaching **KINGHORN**, the coastal road from Burntisland passes a **Celtic cross** commemorating Alexander III, the last of the Celtic kings, who plunged over the cliff near here one night in 1286 when his horse stumbled. The event was more than unfortunate for Scotland, as it threw the country from relative stability into a crisis of succession in which the English king Edward I was only too happy to play a role. The ancient settlement of Kinghorn is today a popular but not too crowded holiday centre, with few formal attractions, but a good beach. At the southern end of town, a hill lined with Spanish-style villas leads down to the waterfront and the beach at **Pettycur Bay**, where fishing boats cluster round the small harbour and brightly coloured lobster nets dot the sands. There's an interesting diversion inland by pretty Kinghorn Loch where Craigencalt Farm Ecology Centre is home to the UK's first **Earthship** (July & Aug Wed–Sun noon–5pm; rest of year generally Wed–Fri noon–3pm; tours £3; ☎01592/891884, ⓦwww.sci-scotland.org.uk), a house built into the hillside from recycled materials such as aluminium cans and old car tyres which provides its own heating, power, water and sewage treatment. Even if the Earthship isn't open, you can wander around the gardens beside it where polytunnels, a waterwheel, wind turbine, compost bins and beds of vegetables and wild flowers offer a healthy-looking vision of sustainable living.

Kirkcaldy

KIRKCALDY (pronounced "kir-coddy") doesn't hold a great deal of interest for the visitor, its charms largely obliterated by overdevelopment. The town's long esplanade was built in 1923 – not just to hold back the sea, but also to alleviate unemployment – and runs parallel for part of the way with the shorter High Street. If you're here in mid-April, you'll see the historic **Links Market**

(@www.linksmarket.org.uk), a week-long funfair that dates back to 1305 and is possibly the largest street fair in Britain. The town's history is chronicled in its **Museum and Art Gallery** (Mon–Sat 10.30am–5pm, Sun 2–5pm; free) in the colourful War Memorial Gardens between the train and bus stations, a short way uphill from the front. The museum covers everything from archeological discoveries to the tradition of the local Wemyss Ware pottery. Since its inception in 1925, the gallery has built up its collection to around three hundred works by some of Scotland's finest painters from the late eighteenth century onwards, including paintings by the portraitist Sir Henry Raeburn, the historical painter Sir David Wilkie, the Scottish Colourists, the Glasgow Boys and William McTaggart. For a town known primarily for linoleum production and with a reputation firmly rooted in the prosaic, the art gallery is an unexpected draw.

Just beyond the northern end of the waterfront, Ravenscraig Park is the site of the substantial ruin of **Ravenscraig Castle** (free access), a thick-walled, fifteenth-century defence post, which occupies a lovely spot above a beach. The castle looks out over the Forth, and is flanked on either side by a flight of steps – the inspiration, apparently, for the title of John Buchan's novel, *The Thirty-Nine Steps*. Sir Walter Scott also found this a place worthy of comment, using it as a setting for the story of "lovely Rosabella" in *The Lay of the Last Minstrel*.

On the eastern edge of Kirkcaldy lies the old suburb of **Dysart**, where tall ships once arrived bringing cargo from the Netherlands, and setting off again with coal, beer, salt and fish. Well restored, and retaining historic street names such as Hot Pot Wynd (after the hot pans used for salt evaporation), it's an atmospheric place of narrow alleyways and picturesque old buildings. In Rectory Lane, the birthplace of explorer John McDouall Stuart (who in 1862 became the first man to cross Australia from south to north) now holds the **John McDouall Stuart Museum** (June–Aug daily 2–5pm; free), giving an account of his emigration to Australia in 1838 and his subsequent adventures.

Incidentally, though there's little to show for it today, architect brothers **Robert and James Adam**, famous for some of the finest buildings in Edinburgh's New Town, Culzean Castle and the Trades Hall in Glasgow, were born in Kirkcaldy, as was the eighteenth-century scholar, philosopher and political economist **Adam Smith**, whose great 1776 work *The Wealth of Nations* established political economy as a separate science.

Practicalities

Kirkcaldy's **train** and **bus stations** are in the upper part of town – keep heading downhill to get to the centre, where you'll find the **tourist office** in the Merchant's House, 339 High St (April–Sept Mon–Sat 9.30am–5.30pm, Sun 11am–4pm; Oct–March Mon–Sat 9.30am–5pm; ☎01592/267775). There are very few places **to stay** in the centre, although the refined *Dunnikier House Hotel*, Dunnikier Way (☎01592/268393, @www.dunnikier-house-hotel.co.uk; ❻), serves fine local food and is set in pleasant grounds adjacent to the golf course. Otherwise, *Dunedin House*, 25 Townsend Place (☎01592/203874, @www.dunedinhouse.com; ❹), offers decent B&B in a relatively central location.

If you're after something to **eat**, try the *Old Rectory Inn*, West Quality Street (☎01592/651211; closed Mon & Sun eves), in Dysart. Otherwise, *Valente's*, 73 Overton Rd, Kirkcaldy, is an unprepossessing, hard-to-find but award-winning fish and chip shop much treasured by locals. (Overton Road is east of the centre, roughly parallel to St Claire Street which leads down to the front.)

There's a good **arts cinema** housed in the Adam Smith Theatre on Bennochy Road in the town centre (☎01592/412929); the small café here is best known for its **breakfasts** served to accompany morning movies.

Travel details

9

Perthshire

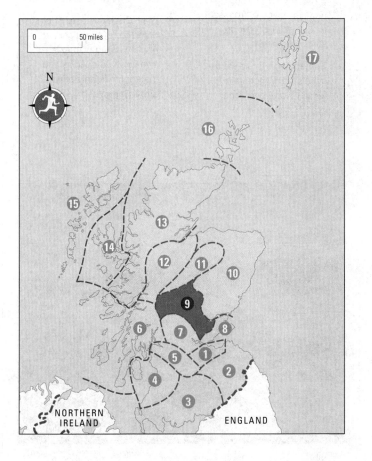

CHAPTER 9

Highlights

* **Folk music** Join in a session at the bar of the *Taybank Hotel* in the dignified town of Dunkeld. See p.478

* **Scottish Crannog Centre, Loch Tay** Engrossing reconstruction of Iron Age loch dwellings built on stilts. See p.481

* **Schiehallion** Scale Perthshire's "fairy mountain" for the views over lochs, hills, glens and moors. See p.486

* **Rannoch Moor** One of the most inaccessible places in Scotland, where hikers can discover a true sense of remote emptiness. See p.486

* **Blair Castle** A taste of the grand life of the Highland nobility, along with extensive forested policies and the country's only private army. See p.487

△ Scottish Crannog Centre, Loch Tay

Perthshire

Genteel, attractive **Perthshire** is, in many ways, the epitome of well-groomed rural Scotland. An area of gentle glens, mature woodland, rushing rivers and peaceful lochs, it's the long-established domain of Scotland's well-to-do country set. First settled over eight thousand years ago, it was ruled by the Romans and then the Picts before Celtic missionaries established themselves, enjoying the amenable climate, fertile soil and ideal defensive and trading location.

Occupying a strategic position at the mouth of the River Tay, the ancient town of **Perth** has as much claim as anywhere to be the gateway to the Highlands. Salmon, wool and, by the sixteenth century, whisky – Bell's, Dewar's and the Famous Grouse brands all hail from this area – were exported, while a major import was Bordeaux claret. At nearby **Scone**, Kenneth MacAlpine established the capital of the kingdom of the Scots and the Picts in 846. When this settlement was washed away by floods in 1210, William the Lion founded Perth as a royal burgh and it stood as Scotland's capital until the mid-fifteenth century.

Rural Perthshire is dominated by the gathering mountains of the Highlands, topography which inevitably determines transport routes, influences the weather and tolerates little development. There's plenty of good agricultural land, however,

---

Out and about in Perthshire

To many, Perthshire is a celebration of the great outdoors, with **activities** ranging from gentle strolls through ancient oak forests to white-knuckle rides down frothing waterfalls. The variety of landscapes and their relative accessibility from the central belt has also led to a significant number of operators being based in the area. Many of these are linked to the tourist board's Activity Line (℡01577/861186, www.adventureperthshire.co.uk), which can give advice and contacts for over thirty different outdoor operators who comply with the Adventure Perthshire Operators' Charter. For canyoning, cliff-jumping and an "activity" called "sphere-ing" which involves tumbling down a hillside inside a giant plastic ball, get in touch with adrenalin junkies Nae Limits (℡01350/727242, www.naelimits.co.uk), based in Dunkeld. For rafting on larger craft through the best rapids on the Tay at Grandtully try Splash (℡01887/829706, www.rafting.co.uk) or Freespirits (℡01887/829280, www.freespirits-online.co.uk), both based in or near Aberfeldy. Also in Aberfeldy is the National Kayak School (www.nationalkayakschool.com) and the rather more sedate Highland Adventure Safaris (℡01887/820071, www.highlandadventuresafaris.co.uk), which offers an inspiring introduction to wild Scotland in which you're taken by four-wheel-drive vehicle to search for golden eagle eyries, stags and pine martens.

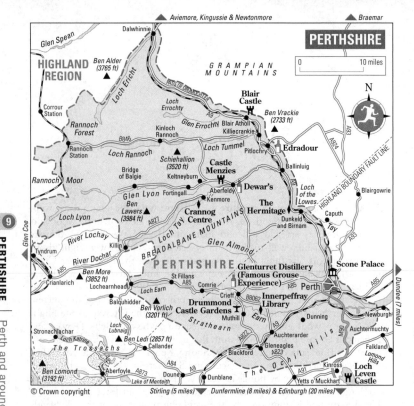

© Crown copyright Stirling (5 miles) ▼ Dunfermline (8 miles) & Edinburgh (20 miles) ▼

and the area is dotted with neat, confident towns and villages like **Crieff**, at the heart of the rolling Strathearn valley, **Dunkeld and Birnam**, with its mature trees and lovely ruined cathedral, and **Aberfeldy** set deep amid farmland east of Loch Tay. Among the wealth of historical sites in Perthshire is the grand **Scone Palace** outside Perth, the splendid Baronial **Blair Castle** north of Pitlochry and the impressive Italianate gardens at **Drummond Castle** near Crieff.

North and west of Perth, **Highland Perthshire** begins to weave its charms: mighty woodlands blend with gorgeously rich scenery, particularly along the banks of the River Tay, leading to **Loch Tay**, overlooked by **Ben Lawers**, the area's tallest peak. Further north, the countryside becomes more sparsely populated and more spectacular, with some wonderful walking country, especially around **Pitlochry**, **Blair Atholl** and the wild expanses of **Rannoch Moor** to the west.

Transport connections in the region are at their best if you head straight north from Perth, along the main A9 road and train line to Inverness, but buses – albeit often infrequent – also serve the more remote areas.

Perth and around

Surrounded by fertile agricultural land and beautiful scenery, the bustling market town of **PERTH** was Scotland's capital for several centuries. During

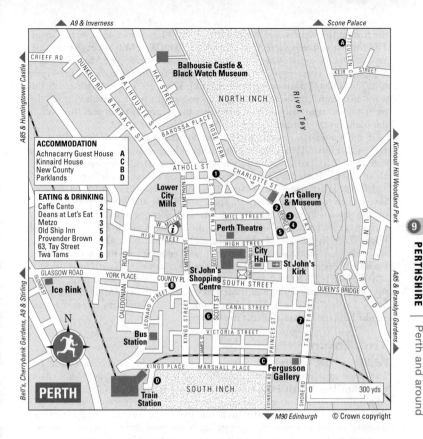

CRIEFF RD

Balhousie Castle &
Black Watch Museum

NORTH INCH

River Tay

ACCOMMODATION
Achnacarry Guest House   **A**
Kinnaird House   **C**
New County   **B**
Parklands   **D**

EATING & DRINKING
Caffe Canto   **2**
Deans at Let's Eat   **1**
Metzo   **3**
Old Ship Inn   **5**
Provender Brown   **4**
63, Tay Street   **7**
Twa Tams   **6**

Lower
City
Mills

Art Gallery
& Museum

Perth Theatre

City
Hall

St John's
Kirk

GLASGOW ROAD   YORK PLACE

Ice Rink

St John's
Shopping
Centre

Bus
Station

Ferguson
Gallery

PERTH

Train
Station

SOUTH INCH

0   300 yds

9

PERTHSHIRE | Perth and around

the reign of James I, parliament met here on several occasions, but its glory was short-lived: the king was murdered in the town's Dominican priory in 1437 by the traitorous Sir Robert Graham, who was captured in the Highlands and tortured to death in Stirling. During the Reformation, on May 11, 1559, John Knox preached a rousing sermon in St John's Kirk, which led to the destruction (by those Knox later condemned as "the rascal multitude") of the town's four monasteries, an event which quickened the pace of reform in Scotland. Despite decline in the seventeenth century, the community expanded in the eighteenth and has prospered ever since; today the whisky and insurance trades employ significant numbers, and Perth remains an important town. It has a long history in **livestock trading**, a tradition continued throughout the year, with regular Aberdeen Angus shows and sales from June to September, while its position at the heart of one of Scotland's richest food-producing areas encouraged Perth to pioneer the re-establishment of a regular **farmers' market**, which takes place on King Edward Street in the centre of town on the first Saturday of every month (9am–2pm; Ⓦwww.perthfarmersmarket.co.uk).

Arrival, information and accommodation

Perth is on the main train lines north from Edinburgh and Glasgow and is well connected by bus; the **bus** and **train stations** are on opposite sides of the road at the west end of town where Kings Place runs into Leonard Street. The **tourist office** is a five-minute walk north on West Mill Street (April–June, Sept & Oct Mon–Sat 9am–5pm, Sun 11am–4pm; July & Aug Mon–Sat 9am–6.30pm, Sun 10am–5pm; Nov–March Mon–Fri 9am–5pm, Sat 10am–4pm; ☎01738/450600, ⓦwww.perthshire.co.uk). While it's easy to walk to all the main attractions in the centre of Perth, you might want to make use of the open-topped **tour bus** (July & Aug) that loops around town and stops off at the sights on the outskirts, including Scone Palace (see p.472).

Of the numerous central **hotels**, aim for the fourteen-bedroom *Parklands Hotel* (☎01738/622451, ⓦwww.theparklandshotel.com; ❻) close to the train station at 2 St Leonards Bank, which has a touch of contemporary styling about it with flatscreen TVs and broadband in all rooms, or the equally central and freshly refurbished *New County Hotel* on County Place (☎01738/623355, ⓦwww.newcountyhotel.com; ❻). There are **B&Bs** and guesthouses on most of the approach roads into town. Marshall Place, overlooking the South Inch, is a good place to look right in the centre; *Kinnaird House*, 5 Marshall Place (☎01738/628021, ⓦwww.kinnaird-guesthouse.co.uk; ❸), offers a warm welcome in a lovely town house with well-equipped en-suite rooms. Along Pitcullen Crescent, on the east bank of the Tay, *Achnacarry Guest House*, at no. 3 (☎01738/621421, ⓦwww.achnacarry.co.uk; ❷), is a reasonable if plain alternative within walking distance of town. You can **camp** in pleasant surroundings by Scone Palace (☎01738/552323) on the outskirts of town, from where there are regular bus connections to Perth town centre.

The Town

Perth's compact **centre** occupies a small patch on the west bank of the Tay. Two large areas of green parkland, known as the North and South Inch, flank the centre. The **North Inch** was the site of the Battle of the Clans in 1396, in which thirty men from each of the Chattan and Quhele (pronounced "kay") clans clashed, while the **South Inch** was the public meeting place for witch-burning in the seventeenth century. Both are now used for more civilized public recreation, with sports pitches to the north and boating and putting to the south. The city's main shopping areas are **High Street** and **South Street**, as well as St John's shopping centre on King Edward Street.

Opposite the entrance to the centre, the imposing **City Hall** is used by Scotland's politicians for party conferences. Behind here lies the solid and attractive **St John's Kirk** (Mon–Sat 10am–4pm, Sun 12.30–2pm, except during services; free), surrounded by cobbled lanes and cafés. It was founded by David I in 1126, although the present building dates from the fifteenth century and was restored to house a war memorial chapel designed by Robert Lorimer in 1923–28. Perth was once known as "St John's Town", and the local football team takes the name **St Johnstone** rather than that of Perth.

Perth is at its most attractive along **Tay Street**, with a succession of grander buildings along one side and the attractively landscaped riverside embankment on the other. Look out for some quirky themed sculpture as well as boards with information on local history. On the corner of Tay Street and Marshall Place you'll come across the one essential place to visit, the **Fergusson Gallery** (Mon–Sat 10am–5pm; free), located in a striking round Victorian sandstone water tower. The gallery is home to an extensive collection of the work of J.D. Fergusson, the foremost artist of the Scottish Colourist movement (see p.302). Born in Leith, he lived and worked for long periods in France, where he was greatly influenced by Impressionist and post-Impressionist artists, creating a distinctive approach which marries both movements' freedom of style with bold use of colour and lighting – seen, for example in his portrait of Elizabeth Dryden entitled *The Hat with the Pink Scarf*. At the beginning of the twentieth century, Fergusson developed a more radical technique to paint some dramatic nudes such as the Matisse-inspired *At My Studio Window*, which mixes elements of an illuminated Celtic manuscript with his confident understanding of the female form. As well as oils, the collection includes sketches, notebooks and sculpture: among the latter, look out for *Eastre: Hymn to the Sun*, an exotic, radiant and almost sexy brass head dating from 1924. The building which houses the artwork is fascinating in itself; recently refurbished, the Neoclassical dome is constructed from 192 cast-iron panels. Typically, the three small galleries on two floors within the building show only a small selection of the whole collection, with themed exhibitions and changing displays of contemporary art alongside the principal Fergusson works.

More art is on show at the town's **Art Gallery and Museum**, 78 George St (Mon–Sat 10am–5pm; free), another of Perth's grand buildings, which has exhibits on local history, art, natural history, archeology and whisky, and gives a good overview of local life through the centuries.

North of the town centre off Hay Street, and adjacent to the North Inch, fifteenth-century Balhousie Castle, is home of the headquarters and **museum of the Black Watch** regiment (May–Sept Mon–Sat 10am–4.30pm; Oct–April Mon–Fri 10am–3.30pm; free; Ⓦ ww.theblackwatch.co.uk/museum). Originally the seat of the earls of Kinnoull, the castle sits incongruously in a peaceful residential area and has been restored in Scots Baronial style with turrets and crow-stepped gables. The Black Watch – whose name refers to the dark colour of their tartan – is the local regiment and one of the oldest in Scotland, having been formed in 1740. The museum chronicles its history through a good display of paintings, uniforms, documents, weapons and photographs.

Perth Ice Rink, in the Dewar's Centre, Glasgow Road, is one of the best places in the country to watch a game of **curling** (see p.61), a winter sport popular in Scotland, Canada and northern Europe but little known elsewhere.

Eating and drinking

Perth has some excellent **restaurants**. At the top end of the market is *63, Tay Street* (Ⓣ01738/441451, Ⓦwww.63taystreet.co.uk, closed Sun & Mon), serving classy and expensive modern Scottish fare in a designer setting; and *Deans at Let's Eat* restaurant at 77 Kinnoull St (Ⓣ01738/643377, Ⓦwww.letseatperth .co.uk, closed Sun & Mon), one of the country's better chefs uses top-quality local produce to create innovative dishes in a pleasantly homely environment. For more moderately priced fare try *Metzo* at 33 George St (Ⓣ01738/626016, Ⓦwww.metzorestaurant.co.uk), a relaxed bistro serving decent if familiar dishes with international influences, while *Caffe Canto* at 62–64 George St is a decent stop for coffee and inexpensive light snacks. Also on George Street, at no. 23, is Perth's best **deli**, *Provender Brown*. Of the many **pubs** in the town centre, *Twa Tams*, on Scott Street, has a good beer garden as well as regular live music, while near the High Street on Skinnergate, the long-established *Old Ship Inn* serves real ale and pub grub.

Around Perth

Almost as well known as Perth itself is **Scone**, one-time home of the Stone of Destiny and the first capital of a united Scotland. The present palace at Scone exudes graceful Scottish country living, and there are some pleasant walks in the grounds, while hints of the grander Perthshire countryside can be found at **Branklyn Gardens** and **Kinnoull Hill** nearby. To the west of Perth are the **Bell's Cherrybank Gardens**, a showcase for heather; beyond this **Huntingtower Castle** is the best of the relatively few fortified buildings on view in the Perthshire hinterland.

Scone Palace and around

Just a couple of miles north of Perth on the A93 (catch the open-topped tour bus, or bus #3 or #58) is **Scone Palace** (pronounced "skoon"; April–Oct daily 9.30am–5.30pm; £6.95, grounds only £3.50; ⓦ www.scone-palace .co.uk), one of Scotland's finest historical country homes. Owned and occupied by the Earl and Countess of Mansfield, whose family has held it for almost four centuries, the two-storey building on the eastern side of the Tay is stately but not overpowering, far more a home than an untouchable monument: the rooms, although full of priceless antiques and lavish furnishings, feel lived-in and used.

Restored in the nineteenth century, the palace today consists of a sixteenth-century core surrounded by earlier buildings, most built of red sandstone, complete with battlements and the original gateway. The abbey that stood here in the sixteenth century, where all Scottish kings until James IV were crowned, was one of those destroyed following John Knox's sermon in Perth. Long before that, Scone was the capital of Pictavia, and it was here that Kenneth MacAlpine brought the famous Coronation **Stone of Destiny**, or Stone of Scone, now to be found in Edinburgh Castle (see p.95) and ruled as the first king of a united Scotland. A replica of the (surprisingly small) stone can be found on Moot Hill, immediately opposite the palace. Moot Hill, as its name suggests, was the place where Scottish earls came to swear loyalty to their king and discuss the affairs of state in an early form of national parliament. In a symbolic gesture, oak trees from the estate were used in the construction of Scotland's most recent parliamentary accommodation at Holyrood in Edinburgh (see p.108).

Inside the palace, a good selection of sumptuous rooms is open, including the library, which houses one of the foremost collections of porcelain in the world, with items by Meissen, Sèvres, Chelsea, Derby and Worcester. Elsewhere, look out for some beautiful papier-mâché dishes, Marie Antoinette's writing desk and John Zoffany's exquisite eighteenth-century portrait, *Lady Elizabeth Murray* [daughter of the second earl] *with Dido*. Just as appealing are the **grounds**, where you'll find peacocks strutting in the gardens, a beech-hedge maze in the pattern of the heraldic family crest and avenues of venerable trees. Scone was the birthplace of botanist and plant collector **David Douglas**, and following the trail named after him you'll encounter a fragrant pinetum planted in 1848 with many of the exotics he discovered in California and elsewhere. Story-boards with yarns about his daring adventures can be found in a corridor of the basement of the palace near the coffee shop.

Branklyn Gardens and Kinnoull Hill

On the same side of the Tay, **Branklyn Gardens**, 116 Dundee Rd (Easter–Oct daily 10am–5pm; NTS; £5; ☎01738/625535), has a compact but impressive botanical collection, including alpine plants, dwarf rhododendrons, lilies and the Himalayan poppy, *Meconopsis*. Looking over the gardens from the north is **Kinnoull Hill**, which also offers splendid views of Perth, the Tay and the surrounding area from its 783ft summit (a 20min walk from the car park on Braes Road). Pick up a leaflet from Perth's tourist office for details of the hill's various woodland walks.

Bell's Cherrybank Gardens

A popular destination for coach tours is **Bell's Cherrybank Gardens** (March–Oct Mon–Sat 10am–5pm, Sun noon–5pm; Nov & Dec Mon–Sat 10am–4pm, Sun noon–4pm; Jan & Feb Thu–Sat 10am–4pm, Sun noon–4pm; £3.75; ⓦwww.thecalyx.co.uk), a mile west of Perth town centre by bus #7. Here, among eighteen acres of well-kept gardens, you'll find the largest collection of different types of heather in Britain, interspersed with lawns, pools and a small aviary. Over the next few years, this and a large swathe of adjoining land will be incorporated into *The Calyx*, an attraction incorporating various different pavilions and outdoor plots based around gardening and horticulture.

Huntingtower Castle

Nothing like as grand as Scone, but intriguing for its historical connections, is **Huntingtower Castle** (April–Sept daily 9.30am–6.30pm; Oct–March Sun–Wed & Sat 9.30am–4.30pm; HS; £3; ☎01738/627231), three miles northwest of Perth on the A85 (bus #13, #14 or #15 from Scott Street). Two three-storey towers formed the original fifteenth- and sixteenth-century tower house, and these were linked in the seventeenth century by a range to provide more room. Formerly known as Ruthven Castle, it was here that the Raid of Ruthven took place in 1582, when the 16-year-old James VI, at the request of William, fourth Earl of Ruthven, came to the castle only to be held captive by a group of conspirators demanding the dismissal of favoured royal advisers. The plot failed, and the young James was released ten months later. Today the castle's chief attractions are its splendid sixteenth-century painted ceilings – you'll see them in the main hall in the east tower.

Strathearn

Strathearn – the valley of the River Earn – stretches west of Perth for some forty miles to **Loch Earn**, a popular watersports spot located just to the north of the Trossachs. Agricola was here around two thousand years ago, trying to establish a foothold in the Highlands; later the area was frequented by Bonnie Prince Charlie and Rob Roy, both bound up in the north–south struggle between Highlands and Lowlands. Today the main settlement in the valley is the well-heeled town of **Crieff**, which despite its prosperous air has some hints of wilder Highland countryside close by, notably around the popular **Glenturret Distillery**.

Auchterarder and around

At the southern edge of Strathearn, twelve miles southwest of Perth on the A9, the large village of **AUCHTERARDER** (known as "the Lang Toun" – long town), is recognized mainly for its proximity to Scotland's finest five-star hotel, **Gleneagles** (☎01764/662231, ⓦwww.gleneagles.com; ❾), home to no fewer than three championship golf courses and location of the G8 summit of world leaders in 2005. Even if staying here is beyond your means, you might consider eating at the main restaurant, the refreshingly unstuffy *Andrew Fairlie at Gleneagles* (☎01764/694267; dinner only; not Sun); it is the finest in Scotland, with highly innovative, dynamic dishes created by Fairlie, an immensely talented Scottish chef who trained under Michel Guerard in France. At £60 for three courses, however, it's still a rare treat.

Just to the east of the hotel, the village of **BLACKFORD** is famous for its spring water – in 1488 James IV demanded beer made from the village's water to be served at his coronation, while these days it's bottled as Highland Spring mineral water, now one of Scotland's best-known international brand names. Not surprisingly, the local whisky distillery, Tullibardine, makes much of the benefits the quality of water adds to their product. You can take a distillery tour or stop in at the café at their new visitors centre (Mon–Sat 9am–6pm, Sun 10am–6pm; tours £3; ⓦwww.tullibardine.com) located on the edge of the village right beside the A9; alongside this, Baxters, famous for making tinned versions of traditional Scots fare such as cock-a-leekie soup, have a large shopping complex aimed at the tourist traffic passing on the A9.

The area's other main attraction is in the quiet village of **DUNNING**, five miles east of Auchterarder on the B8062, where **St Serf's** (April–Sept daily 9.30am–6.30pm; Oct–March access by arrangement; free; ⓣ01786/450000), a rugged church with a Norman tower and arch, houses the magnificent **Dupplin Cross**, reckoned to be the finest surviving carved Pictish stone. Dating from the early ninth century, it was made in honour of Constantine, the first king of the Picts also to reign over the Scots of Dalriada (Argyll). The combination of Pictish and Christian imagery – intricately carved Celtic-knot patterns, depictions of animals and warriors – illustrates the developing relationship between king and the Church. The nearby village of **Forteviot** was, in fact, once the capital of the Picts; that it looks today more like a quaint English garden village is thanks to the chairman of Dewar's Distillers, Lord Forteviot, who rebuilt it in the 1920s. Just west of Dunning is an extraordinary monument, a pile of stones surmounted by a cross, and scrawled with the words: "Maggie Wall, Burnt here, 1657". Maggie Wall was burnt as a witch, and the rumour is that local women replenish the white writing on the monument every year.

The local **tourist office**, roughly halfway along Auchterarder's extended High Street (April–June, Sept & Oct Mon–Sat 10am–5pm; July & Aug Mon–Sat 9.30am–5.30pm, Sun 11am–4pm; Nov–March Mon, Tues, Thurs–Sat 10am–2pm; ⓣ01764/663450) can point you in the right direction for transport links and accommodation. For a daytime coffee or bite to **eat**, try *inDulge* (closed Sun), on the High Street, at no. 22, a café that's also open on Thursday and Friday evenings.

Crieff

At the heart of Strathearn is the old spa town of **CRIEFF**, in a lovely position on a south-facing slope of the Grampian foothills. Cattle drovers used to come to a market, or "tryst", here in the eighteenth century, since this was a good location – between the Highlands and the Lowlands – for buying and selling livestock, but Crieff really came into its own with the arrival of the railway in 1856. Shortly after that, Morrison's Academy, a local private school, took in its first pupils, and in 1868 the grand *Crieff Hydro*, then known as the *Strathearn Hydropathic*, opened its doors to Victorian visitors seeking water-therapy cures. These days, Crieff values its respectability and has an array of fine Edwardian and Victorian houses, with a busy little centre which retains something of the atmosphere of the former spa town. The **Crieff Visitor Centre** (daily 10am–4.30pm; £2.50; ⓦwww.crieff.co.uk), at the bottom of the hill, is essentially a garden centre and gift shop with an exhibition about the cattle drovers. More engaging if you're interested in the town's history is the small "Stones, Stocks & Stories" exhibition downstairs from the **tourist office** (April–June, Sept & Oct Mon–Sat 9.30am–5pm, Sun 11am–3pm; July & Aug Mon–Sat 9.30am–6.30pm,

Sun 10am–4pm; Nov–March Mon–Sat 10am–4pm; ☎01764/652578) in the town hall on High Street.

The imposing *Crieff Hydro* (☎01764/655555, ⦿www.crieffhydro.com; ❼ for dinner, bed & breakfast) is still the grandest place to **stay** in town, despite the institutional atmosphere, and has splendid leisure facilities for families, including a pool and horse riding. Cheaper alternatives include the friendly *Galvelmore House* on Galvelmore Street (☎01764/655721, ⦿www.galvelmore.co.uk; ❷), with a lovely oak-panelled lounge, and *Kingarth Guest House* (☎01764/652060, ⦿www.kingarthguesthouse.com; ❹) on Perth Road. The *Muthill Village Hotel* (☎01764/681451, ⦿www.muthillvillagehotel.com; ❺), three miles south of Crieff on the A822, is a reasonable option, thanks mainly to its great bothy bar with regular live music, bar suppers and real ale. The one **hostel** in the area is *Comrie Croft Hostel* (☎01764/670140, ⦿www.comriecroft.com), a largish bunkhouse set on a working sheep farm halfway between Crieff and Comrie, with its own private fishing loch, mountain bike rental and network of paths and walks. Your best bet for fine **food** in town is the *Bank Restaurant* (☎01764/656575, ⦿www.thebankrestaurant.co.uk; closed Sun & Mon), immediately opposite the tourist office, serving relaxed bistro lunches and more upmarket dinners, while the *Red Onion Bistro* at 31 West High St offers lighter meals and snacks. Crieff also has an eclectic selection of old-fashioned and independent shops, including *McNee's*, a handy deli with good bread and cheese located near the tourist office.

Around Crieff

From Crieff, it's a short drive or a twenty-minute walk north to the **Famous Grouse Experience** (daily 9am–6pm; tours 9.30am–4.30pm; £6.95; ⦿www.famousgrouse.co.uk/experience), located at the venerable **Glenturret Distillery** just off the A85 to Comrie. To get there on public transport, catch any bus going to Crieff, Comrie or St Fillans and ask the driver to drop you at the bottom of the Glenturret Distillery road, from where it's a five-minute walk. Glenturret is Scotland's **oldest distillery**, established in 1775, and still one of the more attractive, with whitewashed buildings and pagoda roofs situated beside a gurgling stream. In recent years it has been designated by its large corporate owners as the home of the Famous Grouse blend, one of Scotland's best-known whisky brands. While a simple wander through the workings of the distillery is still part of the experience, the second half of the tour is a lot livelier than most, with a video about the Famous Grouse's light-hearted TV advertising campaign followed by a multimedia presentation which includes interactive games for kids and a "grouse-eye" view of Scotland's scenic highlights. The corporate edge may be hard to avoid, and the coach park often full, but this is one distillery that makes a decent effort to be family-friendly and to avoid much of the romanticized pomposity which comes with other parts of the malt whisky trail.

A complete contrast, certainly in terms of visitor numbers, is the delightfully hidden **Innerpeffray Library** (March–Oct Mon–Wed, Fri & Sat 10am–12.45pm & 2–4.45pm, Sun 2–4pm; Nov–Feb phone for appointment; £2.50; ☎01764/652819), four miles southeast of Crieff on the B8062 road to Auchterarder. Situated in an attractive eighteenth-century building right by the River Earn, beside an old stone chapel and schoolhouse, the serene and studious public library, originally founded in 1680, is the oldest in Scotland. It's a must for bibliophiles: its shelves containing some four thousand cloth and leather-bound books, mainly on theological and classical subjects, which visitors are allowed to browse through (it ceased to lend books out in 1968). You may come across books dating from each of the five centuries of the library's existence, though the most venerable and valuable are kept in display cabinets.

The most visually impressive of the attractions around Crieff are the magnificent **Drummond Castle Gardens** (May–Oct daily 1–6pm; £4; Ⓦwww.drummondcastlegardens.co.uk) near Muthill, two miles south of Crieff on the A822 (bus #47 from Crieff towards Muthill, then a mile and a half walk up the castle drive). The approach to the garden is impressive, up a splendid avenue of trees; crossing the courtyard of the castle to the grand terrace, you can view the garden in all its symmetrical glory. It was laid out by John Drummond, second Earl of Perth, in 1630, and shows clear French and Italian influence, although the central structural feature of the parterre is a St Andrew's cross. Italian marble statues punctuate the long lines of the cross, and the overall effect is of exceptional harmony and grace. Beyond the formal garden, everything from corn to figs and grapes grows in the Victorian greenhouse and kitchen garden. The castle itself (no public access) is a wonderful mixture of architectural styles, a blunt fifteenth-century keep on a rocky crag adjoining a much-modified Renaissance mansion house.

Comrie

COMRIE, a pretty conservation village another five miles from the turn-off to Glenturret along the River Earn, has the dubious distinction of being the location where more seismic tremors have been recorded than anywhere else in Britain, owing to its position on the Highland Boundary Fault. Earthquake readings are still taken at the curious **Earthquake House**, a tiny building set atop a mound all on its own in the middle of a field. If you walk up to the building you can read information panels outside, or peer through the windows at a model of the world's first seismometer, set up here in 1874, as well as some rather more up-to-date equipment. To find the house, follow the signs to Dalrannoch over the hump-backed stone bridge towards the western end of Comrie, then head 600yd or so along the road.

Loch Earn

At the western edge of Strathearn is **Loch Earn**, a gently lapping Highland loch dramatically edged by mountains. The A85 runs north along the loch shore from the village of **St Fillans**, at the eastern tip, to a slightly larger settlement, **LOCHEARNHEAD**, at the western end of the loch, where it meets the A84 linking the Trossachs to Crianlarich (see p.429). The wide tranquil expanse of Loch Earn is popular for **watersports**, particularly engine-based pursuits such as water-skiing, powerboating and jet-skiing. It's also one of the few stretches of inland waterway in the UK where you might see a float-plane landing. *Lochearnhead Watersports* (Ⓣ01567/830330, Ⓦwww.lochearnhead-water-sports.co.uk) incorporates an outfit offering water-skiing, wake-boarding and the like (including water-skiing for the disabled), as well as the licensed *Lochside Café*, where daytime meals, drinks and home baking can be had while you peer out through picture windows to the loch. For **accommodation**, try the *Lochearnhead Hotel* (Ⓣ01567/830229; Ⓦwww.lochearnhead-hotel.com; ❹), or the very friendly *Earnknowe* B&B (Ⓣ01567/830238, Ⓦwww.earnknowe.co.uk; ❸), both overlooking the water at Lochearnhead. Perhaps the best choice for this locale, though, is the chalet-like *Four Seasons Hotel* (Ⓣ01764/685333, Ⓦwww.thefourseasonshotel.co.uk; ❺) in St Fillans, with its wonderful waterside location. It's also the best place to **eat**; indeed, there are few other good options in the area.

Strath Tay to Loch Tay

Heading due north from Perth both the railway and main A9 trunk road carry much of the traffic heading into the Highlands, often speeding straight through some of Perthshire's most attractive countryside in its eagerness to get to the bleaker country to the north. Perthshire has been dubbed "**Big Tree Country**" by the tourist board in recognition of some magnificent woodland in the area, including a number of individual trees which rank among Europe's oldest, tallest and certainly most handsome specimens. Many of these are found around the valley – or "strath" – of the River Tay as it heads towards the sea from attractive **Loch Tay**, set up among the high Breadalbane mountains which include the striking peak of **Ben Lawers**, Perthshire's highest, and the hills which enclose the long, enchanting **Glen Lyon**. Studded around Loch Tay are remains of crannogs, ancient dwellings built on man-made islands, which are brought to life at the **Crannog Centre** beside the village of Kenmore. Not far downriver is the prosperous small town of **Aberfeldy**; from here the Tay drifts southeast between the unspoilt twin villages of **Dunkeld and Birnam** before meandering its way past Perth.

Dunkeld and Birnam

DUNKELD, twelve miles north of Perth on the A9, was proclaimed Scotland's ecclesiastical capital by Kenneth MacAlpine in 850. Its position at the southern boundary of the Grampian Mountains made it a favoured meeting place for Highland and Lowland cultures, but in 1689 it was burned to the ground by the Cameronians – fighting for William of Orange – in an effort to flush out troops of the Stuart monarch, James VII. Subsequent rebuilding, however, didn't intrude into the modern era, and as a result the town is one of the area's most pleasant communities, with handsome whitewashed houses, appealing arts and crafts shops and a charming cathedral. The **tourist office** is at The Cross in the town centre (April–June, Sept & Oct Mon–Sat 10am–5pm, Sun 11am–4pm; July & Aug Mon–Sat 9.30am–6.30pm, Sun 10am–5pm; Nov–March Mon, Tues, Fri–Sun 10am–4pm; ☎01350/727688).

Dunkeld's partly ruined **cathedral** (daily: May–Sept 9.30am–6.30pm; Oct–April 9.30am–4pm; free; ⊛www.dunkeldcathedral.org.uk) is on the northern side of town, in an idyllic setting amid lawns and trees on the east bank of the Tay. Construction began in the early twelfth century and continued throughout the next two hundred years, but the building was more or less ruined at the time of the Reformation. The present structure consists of the fourteenth-century choir and the fifteenth-century nave; the choir, restored in 1600 (and several times since), now serves as the parish church, while the nave remains roofless apart from the clocktower. Inside, note the leper's peep near the pulpit in the north wall, through which lepers could receive the sacrament without coming into contact with the congregation. Also look out for the great effigy of the **Wolf of Badenoch**, Robert II's son, born in 1343. The Wolf acquired his name and notoriety when, after being excommunicated for leaving his wife, he took his revenge by burning the towns of Forres and Elgin and sacking Elgin cathedral. He eventually repented, did public penance for his crimes and was absolved by his brother Robert III.

Birnam

Dunkeld is linked to its sister community, **BIRNAM**, by Thomas Telford's seven-arched bridge of 1809. This little village has a place in history thanks to

Shakespeare, for it was on Dunsinane Hill, to the southeast of the village, that Macbeth declared: "I will not be afraid of death and bane/Till Birnam Forest come to Dunsinane", only to be told later by a messenger "I look'd toward Birnam, and anon me thought/The wood began to move . . ."

The **Birnam Oak**, a gnarly old character propped up by crutches which can be seen on the waymarked riverside walk, is inevitably claimed to be a survivor of the infamous mobile forest. Several centuries after Shakespeare, another literary personality, Beatrix Potter, drew inspiration from the area, recalling her childhood holidays here when penning the Peter Rabbit stories. A Potter-themed exhibition and garden, aimed at both children and parents, can be found on the main road in the impressive barrel-fronted **Birnam Institute** (daily 10am–5pm; free; ⓦwww.birnaminstitute.com), a modern theatre, arts and community centre with a busy programme of events.

Practicalities

Dunkeld is well served by **public transport**: by train between Perth and Inverness, and bus from Perth #23 (Stagecoach) and #957 (Scottish City-link). There are several large **hotels** in Dunkeld and Birnam, including the *Royal Dunkeld*, Atholl Street (☎01350/727322, ⓦwww.royaldunkeldhotel.co.uk; ❺), which also has cheaper twin rooms in an annex (❸), and the looming Victorian Gothic *Birnam House Hotel* on Perth Road (☎01350/727462, ⓦwww.birnamhousehotel.co.uk; ❻). Most sumptuous of the lot is the *Dunkeld House Hilton* (☎01350/727771, ⓦwww.hilton.co.uk/dunkeld; ❼ for dinner, B&B), a vast country estate house on the banks of the Tay to the north of town which incorporates a spa, swimming pool and excellent facilities for outdoor pursuits. Much less grand, but full of personality is the central *Taybank Hotel* (☎01350/727340, ⓦwww.taybank.com; ❷), a real beacon for music fans who come for the regular live sessions in the convivial bar. The rooms are simple and inexpensive, and the rate includes a continental breakfast. Local **B&Bs** include the pleasant *Waterbury Guest House* (☎01350/727324, ⓦwww.waterbury-guesthouse.co.uk; ❸) on Murthly Terrace in Birnam, or the more luxurious *The Pend* (☎01350/727586, ⓦwww.thepend.com; ❺) just off the main street in Dunkeld. For **food**, try the decent bar meals at the *Taybank* (the stovies are particularly filling) or the *Tap Inn*, the wee pub beside the *Birnam House Hotel*, which also hosts regular folk and jazz sessions; during the day the *Foyer Café* in the Birnam Institute (see above) serves coffee, cakes and light meals, or you can pick up some delicious snacks and sandwiches at the Robert Menzies deli in Dunkeld.

Around Dunkeld

Dunkeld and Birnam are surrounded by some lovely countryside, both along the banks of the Tay and into the deep forests which seem to close in on the settlement. One of the most rewarding walks is a mile and a half from Birnam to **The Hermitage**, set in a grandly wooded gorge of the plunging River Braan. Here you'll find a pretty eighteenth-century folly, also known as Ossian's Hall, which was once mirrored to reflect the water – the mirrors were smashed by Victorian vandals and the folly was more tamely restored. The hall, appealing yet incongruous in its splendid setting, neatly frames a dramatic waterfall. Nearby you can crane your neck to look up at a Douglas fir which claims the title of tallest tree in Britain – measuring these behemoths isn't easy, but last time the tape was out it managed 212ft.

Two miles east of Dunkeld, the **Loch of the Lowes** is a nature reserve that offers a rare chance to see breeding **ospreys** and other wildfowl; the visitor centre (April–Sept 10am–5pm; £2; ☎01350/727337) has video relay screens and will point you in the direction of the best vantage points. If the surroundings seem appealing enough to warrant lingering a day or two, you could head for the mellow *Wester Caputh Independent Hostel* (☎01738/710449, ⓦwww .westercaputh.co.uk), four miles downstream along the Tay from Dunkeld with small dorms and doubles (❶), is a great base with a relaxing and welcoming atmosphere. For details about how to reach Wester Caputh village, phone the hostel direct.

Aberfeldy and around

From Dunkeld the A9 runs north alongside the Tay for eight miles to Ballinluig, a little place marking the turn-off along the A827 to **ABERFELDY**, a generally prosperous settlement of large stone houses and four-wheel-drive vehicles that acts as a service centre for the wider Loch Tay area. The enthusiastic **tourist office** at The Square in the town centre (April–June, Sept & Oct Mon–Sat 9.30am–5pm, Sun 11am–3pm; July & Aug Mon–Sat 9.30am–6.30pm, Sun 10am–4pm; Nov–March Mon–Sat 10am–4pm; ☎01887/820276) is good for advice on local accommodation and details of nearby walking trails. If you want to **rent a bike**, head to *Girvans* outdoor store (☎01887/820254), located behind the filling station on your way into town from the east.

Aberfeldy sits at the point where the Urlar Burn – lined by the silver birch trees celebrated by Robert Burns in his poem *The Birks of Aberfeldy* – flows into the River Tay. The Tay is spanned by the humpbacked, four-arch **Wade's Bridge**, built by General Wade in 1733 during his efforts to control the unrest in the Highlands, and one of the general's more impressive pieces of work. Overlooking the bridge from the south end is the **Black Watch Monument**, depicting a pensive, kilted soldier, erected in 1887 to commemorate the first muster of the Highland regiment commissioned to "watch upon the braes" and gathered as a peacekeeping force by Wade in 1740. The regiment, prominent in recent conflicts in Northern Ireland and Iraq, retains close ties with Perthshire, including a regimental museum in Perth (see p.471).

The main set-piece attraction in town is **Dewar's World of Whisky** at the Aberfeldy Distillery (April–Oct Mon–Sat 10am–6pm, Sun noon–4pm; Nov–March Mon–Sat 10am–4pm; £5; ⓦwww.dewarswow.com), which puts on an impressive show of describing the making of whisky – worthwhile if you haven't been given a similar lowdown at distilleries elsewhere. As with many of the distilleries these days, a connoisseurs' **tour** (£10) is available, giving a more in-depth look around the distillery and a chance to taste (or "nose") the whisky at different stages in its life. The rest of the small town centre is a busy mixture of craft and tourist shops, the most interesting by far being **The Watermill** on Mill Street (Mon–Sat 9am–5pm, Sun noon–5pm, ⓦwww.aberfeldywatermill .com), an inspiring bookshop, art gallery and café located in the town's superbly restored early nineteenth-century mill. Oatmeal was still produced here until a few years ago, and most of the old structure and internal workings have been left in place, lending a certain charm. If you've some time on your hands, it's worth wandering into the most venerable shop in Aberfeldy, Haggarts, located on the corner of Dunkeld Street and Moness Terrace, a classic old-time tweed tailors which sells stout tweed suits and deerstalker hats.

Practicalities

Accommodation in the middle-to-upper price bracket is impressively stylish: in town there's *Guinach House*, by the The Birks (☎01887/820251, www.guinachhouse.co.uk; ⑥), a tastefully decorated guesthouse in well-tended grounds; while a few miles away is *Farleyer* (☎01887/820332, Ⓦwww.farleyer.com; ⑥), a smart, contemporary restaurant just beyond Castle Menzies with nine tastefully decorated rooms. For B&B accommodation, try *Balnearn Guest House* (☎01887/820431, Ⓦwww.balnearnhouse.com; ❷), or *Mavisbank*, Taybridge Drive (☎01887/820223, Ⓔnancynunn@onetel.net; ❷; May–Sept), both attractive stone houses in town. There are two **bunkhouses** in the area, both in the settlement of Weem, half a mile from Aberfeldy on the north side of the Tay: *Glassie Farm* (☎01887/820265, Ⓦwww.thebunkhouse.co.uk) has a lovely location a mile or so up on the hillside above Weem, while *Adventurer's Escape* (☎01887/820498, Ⓦwww.adventurers-escape.co.uk) occupies an old house and steading right next to the *Weem Hotel* on the road to Castle Menzies. Both are worth contacting if you're interested in trying out the many adventure sports and outdoor pursuits which are available locally.

For something to **eat**, Aberfeldy isn't short on cafés and tearooms; best bet for a good cup of coffee or a bowl of soup at lunchtime is the relaxed café in *The Watermill*, or there are some decent places to buy picnic food, including Farm Fresh deli, 22 Dunkeld St, and the delicious meats, fish and cheese at *Tombuie Smokehouse*'s stall (March–Sept) beside the main road between town and the distillery. Decent bar meals can be found over the Wade Bridge in Weem at the *Ailean Chraggan Inn*; in town, there's reasonable casual dining at *Kiwi's* on The Square (☎01887/829229; closed Tue & Wed eve), or for something more upmarket, *Farleyer Restaurant* (see above) is a couple of miles out of town but well worth considering for both bistro-style and more formal modern Scottish dining.

Castle Menzies and around

One mile west of Aberfeldy, across Wade's Bridge, **Castle Menzies** (April to mid-Oct Mon–Sat 10.30am–5pm, Sun 2–5pm; £3.50; Ⓦwww.menzies.org) is an imposing, Z-shaped, sixteenth-century tower house which until the middle of the last century was the chief seat of the Clan Menzies (pronounced "Ming-iss"). With the demise of the line, the castle was taken over by the Menzies Clan Society, who since 1971 has been involved in the lengthy process of restoring it. Much of the interior is on view, most of it refreshingly free of fixtures and fittings, displaying an austerity which is much more true to medieval life than many grander, furnished castles elsewhere in the country.

Even if you pass the castle by, it's well worth stopping at **Castle Menzies Farm** next door, where an imaginative modern conversion has turned an old cow byre into the *House of Menzies* (Mon–Sat 10am–5pm, Sun 11am–5pm; Nov–Dec closed Mon; Jan–April closed Mon & Tues, Ⓦwww.houseofmenzies.com), which combines a specialist New World wine shop with a modern café and relatively tasteful gift shop.

A mile or so further along the road by the hamlet with the unfortunate name of **Dull** is Highland Adventure Safaris (☎01887/820071, Ⓦwww.highlandadventuresafaris.co.uk), where you can join Landrover trips into the heather-clad hills nearby in search of wildlife such as eagles, red deer and grouse. At the lodge you can try your hand at gold and mineral panning (£3), a big hit with kids; there's also a deer park, play area and café.

The road from here carries on either deep into the hills of Glen Lyon (see p.482), or connects north past the striking mountain Schiehallion to Loch Tummel (see p.485).

Loch Tay

Aberfeldy grew up around a crossing point on the River Tay, which leaves it slightly oddly six miles adrift of Loch Tay, a fourteen-mile-long stretch of fresh water which all but hooks together the western and eastern Highlands. Guarding the northern end of the loch is **KENMORE**, where whitewashed estate houses and well-tended gardens cluster around the gate to the extensive grounds of **Taymouth Castle**, built by the Campbells of Glenorchy in the early nineteenth century, and now undergoing extensive renovation to convert it into a top-class hotel and golf resort. The main attraction here is the **Scottish Crannog Centre** (mid-March to Oct daily 10am–5.30pm, Nov Sat & Sun 10am–4pm; £4.75; ⓦ www.crannog.co.uk), one of the best heritage museums in the country. Crannogs are Iron Age loch dwellings built on stilts over the water, with a gangway to the shore which could be lifted up to defy a hostile intruder, whether animal or human. Following extensive underwater archeological excavations in Loch Tay, the team here has superbly reconstructed a crannog, and visitors can now walk out over the loch to the thatched wooden dwelling, complete with sheepskin rugs, wooden bowls and other evidence of the way life was lived 2500 years ago.

Kenmore is a popular holidaying spot, and as a result there are a number of activity-based operations here. Best of the lot is Croft-na-Caber (☎01887/830588, ⓦ www.croftnacaber.com), an impressive **outdoor pursuits** complex situated next door to the Crannog Centre, where you can try various watersports on Loch Tay including water-skiing, fishing, canoeing and sailing. The nicest place to **stay** in town is the pleasant and well-run *Kenmore Hotel*, in the village square (☎01887/830205, ⓦ www.kenmorehotel.com; ❻), a descendant of Scotland's oldest inn (established here in 1572); alternatively, *Culdees*, four miles along the loch's north shore at Fearnan (☎01887/830519, ⓦ www.culdeesbunkhouse .co.uk; ❷), has family-friendly bunkhouse and B&B accommodation on a farm which aims to promote permaculture and spiritual values. For something to **eat**, head to *The Courtyard* (☎01887/830763; ⓦ www.taymouthcourtyard.com), an attractive new development beside the Kenmore golf course and caravan site comprising a smart, moderate to expensive restaurant, large bar and well-stocked deli/gift shop.

Dominating the northern side of Loch Tay is moody **Ben Lawers** (3984ft), Perthshire's highest mountain; from the top there are incredible views towards both the Atlantic and the North Sea. The ascent – which should not be tackled unless you're properly equipped for Scottish hillwalking (see p.64) – takes around three hours from the NTS visitor centre (May–Sept daily 10.30am–5pm; ☎01567/820397), located at 1300ft and reached by a winding hill road off the A827. The centre has an audiovisual show, slides of the mountain flowers – including the rare alpine flora found here – and a nature trail with accompanying descriptive booklet.

Killin

The **mountains of Breadalbane** (pronounced "bred–albin", from the Gaelic "braghaid Albin" meaning high country of Scotland) loom over the southern end of Loch Tay. Glens Lochay and Dochart curve north and south respectively from the small town of **KILLIN**, right in the centre of which the River Dochart comes rushing down over the frothy **Falls of Dochart** before disgorging into Loch Tay. A short distance west of Killin the A827 meets the A85, linking the Trossachs with Crianlarich (see p.429), an important waypoint on the roads to Oban, Fort William and the west coast.

There's little to do in Killin itself, but it makes a convenient base for some of the area's best walks. The **tourist office** is located in the ground floor of the old watermill by the falls (March–May & Oct daily 10am–5pm; June & Sept daily 10am–6pm; July & Aug daily 9.30am–6.30pm; ℡01567/820254); upstairs is the **Breadalbane Folklore Centre** (same times; £2.50). The centre explores the history and mythology of Breadalbane and holds the 1300-year-old "healing stones" of St Fillan, an early Christian missionary who settled in Glen Dochart.

Killin is littered with **B&Bs**, including *Fairview House*, halfway along Main Street (℡01567/820667, Ⓦwww.fairview-killin.co.uk; ❸), a Victorian villa with decent rooms and breakfasts. There's also an SYHA **hostel** (℡0870/004 1131, Ⓦwww.syha.org.uk; March–Oct), in a fine old country house just beyond the eastern end of the village, with views out over the loch. The place to grab a bite to **eat** is the *Falls of Dochart Inn*, which has an attractive stone-walled pub right above the famous rapids. If you're interested in **outdoor activities**, make for the helpful and enthusiastic Killin Outdoor Centre and Mountain Shop, on Main Street (℡01567/820652, Ⓦwww.killinoutdoor.co.uk), which rents out mountain bikes, canoes and tents, sells maps and guidebooks and normally has a local weather forecast chalked up on a blackboard.

Glen Lyon

North of Breadalbane, the mountains tumble down into **Glen Lyon** – at 34 miles long, the longest enclosed glen in Scotland – where, legend has it, the Celtic warrior Fingal built twelve castles. The narrow single track road through the glen starts at **Keltneyburn**, near Kenmore at the northern end of the loch, although a road does struggle over the hills past the Ben Lawers visitor centre (see p.481) to **Bridge of Balgie**, halfway down the glen, where the post office has an art gallery and does good tea and scones. Either way, it's a long, winding journey. A few miles on from Keltneyburn, the village of **FORTINGALL** is little more than a handful of pretty thatched cottages, although locals make much of their 5000-year-old yew tree – believed (by them at least) to be the oldest living thing in Europe. The venerable tree can be found in the churchyard, showing its age a little but well looked after, with a timeline nearby listing some of the events the yew has lived through. One of these, bizarrely, is the birth of Pontius Pilate, reputedly the son of a Roman officer stationed near Fortingall in the last years BC. If you're taken by the peace and remoteness of Glen Lyon, you might like to **stay** on a working sheep farm nearby, *Kinnighallen* (℡01887/830619, Ⓦwww.kinnighallen.co.uk; ❶), a pretty cottage on Duneaves Road not far outside Fortingall.

Highland Perthshire

North of the Tay Valley, Perthshire doesn't discard its lush richness immediately, but there are clear indications of the more rugged, barren influences of the Highlands proper. The principal settlements of **Pitlochry** and **Blair Atholl**, both just off the A9, are separated by the narrow gorge of Killiecrankie, a crucial strategic spot in times past for anyone seeking to control movement of cattle or armies from the Highlands to the Lowlands. Though there are reasons to stop in both places, inevitably the greater rewards are to be found further from the main drag, most notably in the winding westward road along the shores of **Loch Tummel** and **Loch Rannoch** past the distinctive peak of **Schiehallion**, which eventually leads to the remote wilderness of **Rannoch Moor**.

Pitlochry

PITLOCHRY has, on the face of it, a lot going for it, not least the backdrop of Ben Vrackie (see box on p.484) and the River Tummel slipping by. It's also undoubtedly a useful place to find somewhere to stay or eat en route to or from the Highlands. However, there's little charm to be found on the main street, filled with crawling traffic and seemingly endless shops selling cut-price woollens, knobbly walking sticks and glass baubles. The town has grown comfortable in its utilitarian, mass-market role and, given its self-appointed role as a "gateway to the Highlands", you'd be perfectly excused if you carried straight on through.

The one attraction with some distinction in the immediate vicinity is the **Edradour Distillery** (March–Oct Mon–Sat 9.30am–6pm, Sun 11.30am–5pm; Nov & Dec Mon–Sat 9.30am–5pm, Sun 11.30am–5pm; Jan & Feb Mon–Sat 10am–4pm, Sun noon–4pm; free; ⓦwww.edradour.co.uk), Scotland's smallest, set in an idyllic position tucked into the hills a couple of miles east of Pitlochry on the A924. Although the tour of the distillery itself isn't out of the ordinary, the lack of industralization and the fact that the whole traditional process is done on site and on a small scale give Edradour more personality than many of its rivals.

It's hard to say the same for Bells' **Blair Athol Distillery**, Perth Road (Easter–Sept Mon–Sat 9.30am–5pm, June–Sept also Sun noon–5pm; Oct Mon–Fri 10am–4pm; Nov–Easter Mon–Fri tours 11am, 1pm & 3pm; £4), at the southern end of the main street (Atholl Road leading to Perth Road) in Pitlochry, where a more modern visitor centre illustrates the process involved in making the Blair Athol malt, one of the key ingredients of the Bell's blend.

On the western edge of Pitlochry, just across the river, lies Scotland's renowned "Theatre in the Hills", the **Pitlochry Festival Theatre** (ⓣ01796/484626, ⓦwww.pitlochry.org.uk). Set up in 1951, the theatre started in a tent on the site of what is now the town curling rink, before moving to the banks of the river in 1981. A variety of productions – mostly mainstream theatre from the resident repertoire company, along with regular music events – are staged in the summer season (May–Oct) and during winter weekends (Nov–April). By day it's worth coming here to wander around **Explorers: the Scottish Plant Hunters' Garden** (daily April–June, Sept & Oct 10am–5pm; July & Aug 10am–7.30pm; £3; tours June–Sept Wed 10.30am & Sun 11.30am & 2.30pm; ⓦwww.explorersgarden.com), an extended garden and forest area which pays tribute to Scottish botanists and collectors who roamed the world in the eighteenth and nineteenth centuries in search of new plant species. Although many of the trees planted for the opening of the garden in 2003 are a long way from maturity, this is very much a modern rather than traditional garden, with carefully constructed, sinuous trails taking you past some attractive landscapes and features such as an open-air amphitheatre (sometimes used for outdoor performances), sculptures and the David Douglas pavilion, a soaring chamber beautifully constructed from Douglas fir.

A short stroll upstream from the theatre is the **Pitlochry Power Station and Dam**, a massive concrete wall that harnesses the water of the artificial Loch Faskally, just north of the town, for hydroelectric power. The **visitor centre** (April–June, Sept & Oct Mon–Fri 10.30am–5.30pm; July & Aug daily; £3) offers a pretty thorough rundown on how hydro schemes work, but what draws most attention, apart from the views up the loch, is the **salmon ladder**, a staircase of murky glass boxes through which you might see some nonplussed fish making their way upstream past the dam.

Ordnance Survey Explorer Map no. 368

Pitlochry is surrounded by good walking country. The biggest lure has to be **Ben Vrackie** (2733ft), which provides a stunning backdrop for the town and deserves better than a straight up-and-down walk; however, the climb should only be attempted in settled weather conditions, with the right equipment and following the necessary safety precautions (see p.64).

The direct route up the hill follows the course of the Moulin burn past the inn of the same name. Alternatively, a longer but much more rewarding circular route heads north out of Pitlochry, along the edge of attractive Loch Faskally, then up the River Garry to go through the **Pass of Killiecrankie**. This is looked after by the NTS, which has a visitor centre detailing the famous battle here as well as the abundant natural history of the gorge. From the NTS centre walk north up the old A9 and branch off on the small tarred road signposted **Old Faskally**, that twists up under the new A9. The route from here is signposted: continue up the hillside until you finally leave the cultivated land and join a track which zigzags up heathery pasture and then heads across open hillside to reach a saddle by **Loch a'Choire**. Here you join the track from Pitlochry/Moulin that crosses below the dam on the loch and heads directly up the peak. To get back to Pitlochry take the Moulin path back from the loch.

Other worthwhile walks in the area include the trip right round **Loch Faskally**, or you could follow the walk above but turn back from Killiecrankie. A lovely short hill walk from the south end of Pitlochry follows a path through oak forests along the banks of the **Black Spout** burn; when you emerge from the woods it's a few hundred yards further uphill to the lovely Edradour Distillery (see p.483).

Practicalities

Pitlochry is on the main **train** line to Inverness, and has regular **buses** running from Perth which stop near the train station on Station Road, five minutes' walk up the main street from the **tourist office**, 22 Atholl Rd (July–Sept Mon–Sat 9am–7pm, Sun 9.30am–6pm; April–June & Oct Mon–Sat 9am–6pm, Sun 10am–5pm; Nov–March Mon–Fri 10am–5pm, Sat 10am–4pm; ☎01796/472215). The office can sell you a guide to walks in the surrounding area (50p), and also offers an accommodation booking service. For **bike rental**, advice on local cycling routes, as well as general outdoor gear, try Escape Route at 3 Atholl Rd (☎01796/473859, ⓦwww.escape-route.biz).

As a well-established holiday town, Pitlochry is packed with grand houses converted into large- and medium-sized **hotels**. The *Moulin Hotel* (☎01796/472196, ⓦwww.moulinhotel.co.uk; ❹), at Moulin on the outskirts of Pitlochry along the A924, is a pleasant and popular old travellers' inn with a great bar and its own brewery, while *Craigatin House and Courtyard* (☎01796/472478, ⓦwww.craigatinhouse.co.uk; ❹) on the northern section of the main road through town, is an attractive, contemporary **B&B** with large beds, soothing decor and an pleasant garden. Otherwise, try *Ferryman's Cottage*, Port-na-Craig (☎01796/473681, ⓦwww.ferrymanscottage.co.uk; ❸), a small, more traditional, but very welcoming B&B in a beautiful position next to the River Tummel and the theatre. Right in the centre *Pitlochry Backpackers Hotel*, 134 Atholl Rd (☎01796/470044, ⓦwww.scotlands-top-hostels.com), is a **hostel** based in a former hotel and offers dorms along with around ten twin and double rooms (❶).

Pitlochry is the domain of the tearoom and you have to hunt to find the decent **places to eat**; *The Old Armoury* (☎01796/474281; ⓦwww.theoldar-mouryrestaurant.com) on a back road between the train station and dam is a civilized restaurant serving expensive taste-of-Scotland-style meals in the evening, with a secluded tea garden which is pleasant for simpler fare during the day. A more moderately priced contemporary bistro can be found in the *Strathgarry Hotel* in the centre of town; the same owners run the *Port-na-craig Inn* which has a beautiful riverside location near the theatre. The best bet for traditional **pub grub** is the *Moulin Inn*, handily placed at the foot of Ben Vrackie. For something a bit smarter altogether, it's worth considering the *Killiecrankie Hotel* (☎01796/473220, ⓦwww.killiecrankiehotel.co.uk; ❼ B&B, ❾ dinner, B&B) at Killiecrankie, three miles north of Pitlochry on the old A9, a lovely old manse which serves excellent bar meals and impressive, upmarket Scottish cuisine to both residents and non-residents.

Loch Tummel and Loch Rannoch

West of Pitlochry, the B8019/B846 makes a memorably scenic, if tortuous, traverse of the shores of **Loch Tummel** and then **Loch Rannoch**.

△ Rannoch Moor

These two lochs, celebrated by Harry Lauder in his famous song *The Road to the Isles*, and their adjoining rivers were much changed by the massive hydroelectric schemes built in the 1940s and 1950s, yet this is still a spectacular stretch of countryside and one which deserves leisurely exploration. **Queen's View** at the eastern end of Loch Tummel is an obvious vantage point, looking down the loch to the misty peak of **Schiehallion** (3553ft) from the Gaelic meaning "Fairy Mountain", one of the few freestanding hills in Scotland. It's a popular, fairly easy and inspiring mountain to climb, with views on a good day to both sides of Scotland and north to the massed ranks of Highland peaks; the path up starts at Braes of Foss, just off the B846 which links Aberfeldy with Kinloch Rannoch. Expect the climb to the top and back to take around 3–4 hours. At Queen's View, the Forestry Commission's **visitor centre** (April–Oct daily 10am–6pm) interprets the fauna and flora of the area, and also has a tearoom and information on a network of forest walks nearby. A few miles further on, about halfway along Loch Tummel, the cosy *Loch Tummel Inn* (℡01882/634272; ⑤) serves real ale, local venison and salmon and enjoys fine views out across the water and hills.

Beyond Loch Tummel, marking the eastern end of Loch Rannoch, the small community of **KINLOCH RANNOCH** doesn't see a lot of passing trade – fishermen and hillwalkers are the most common visitors. Otherwise, the only real destination here is Rannoch Station, a lonely outpost on the Glasgow–Fort William West Highland train line (see p.429), sixteen miles further on. The road goes no further. Here you can contemplate the bleakness of **Rannoch Moor** (see box below), a wide expanse of bog, heather and wind-blown pine tree which stretches right across to the imposing entrance to Glen Coe. A local bus service (#85) from Kinloch Rannoch and a postbus from Pitlochry (#223; departs 8am) provide connections to the railway station.

In Kinloch Rannoch, *Bunrannoch House* (℡01882/632407, ⓦwww.bunrannoch .co.uk; ③), a Victorian former shooting lodge, with lovely views, is a good bet for **accommodation** (they also serve evening meals); otherwise,

Rannoch Moor

Rannoch Moor occupies roughly 150 square miles of uninhabited and uninhabitable peat bogs, lochs, heather hillocks, strewn lumps of granite and a few gnarled Caledonian pines, all of it over one thousand feet above sea level. Perhaps the most striking thing about the moor is its inaccessibility: one road, between Crianlarich and Glen Coe, skirts its western side, while another struggles west from Pitlochry to reach its eastern edge at Rannoch Station. The only regular form of transport is the **West Highland Railway**, which stops at **Rannoch** and, a little to the north, Corrour Station, which has no road access at all. There is a simple tearoom in the station building at Rannoch, as well as a pleasant small hotel, the *Moor of Rannoch* (℡01882/633238, ⓦwww.moorofrannoch.co.uk; ⑤), but even these struggle to diminish the feeling of isolation. **Corrour**, meanwhile, stole an unlikely scene in *Trainspotting* when the four heroes headed here for a taste of the great outdoors; a SYHA hostel is located a mile away on the shores of **Loch Ossian** (℡0870/004 1139, ⓦwww.syha.org.uk; April–Oct), making the area a great place for hikers seeking somewhere genuinely off the beaten track. From Rannoch Station it's possible to catch the train to Corrour and walk the nine miles back; it's a longer slog west to the *Kingshouse Hotel* (see p.588) at the eastern end of Glen Coe, the dramatic peaks of which poke up above the moor's western horizon. Determined hill walkers will find a clutch of Munros around Corrour, including remote Ben Alder (3765ft), high above the forbidding shores of Loch Ericht.

dominating the main square of the village, the huntin', fishin' and shootin' *Dunalastair Hotel* (℡01882/632218, Ⓦwww.dunalastair.co.uk; ❻) has lots of rooms and a pricey restaurant. Though uncomplicated, the nearby community-run *Post Taste* tearoom is open every day all year round and is a cheery place for snacks, coffee, takeaway and evening **meals** (not Sun).

North of Pitlochry

Four miles north of Pitlochry, the A9 cuts through the **Pass of Killiecrankie**, a breathtaking wooded gorge which falls away to the River Garry below. This dramatic setting was the site of the **Battle of Killiecrankie** in 1689, when the Jacobites crushed the forces of General Mackay. Legend has it that one soldier of the Crown, fleeing for his life, made a miraculous jump across the eighteen-foot **Soldier's Leap**, an impossibly wide chasm halfway up the gorge. Queen Victoria, visiting here 160 years later, contented herself with recording the beauty of the area in her diary. Exhibits at the slick NTS **visitor centre** (daily: April–Oct 10am–5.30pm; ℡01796/473233; parking £2) recall the battle and examine the gorge in detail. The surroundings here are thick, mature forest, full of interesting plants and creatures – the local ranger often sets off on free **guided walks** which leave from the visitor centre and are well worth joining if you're around at the right time; the centre will let you know what's scheduled when.

Blair Atholl

Three miles north of Killiecrankie, the village of **BLAIR ATHOLL** makes for a much quieter and more idiosyncratic stop than Pitlochry. At the **Atholl Estates Information Centre** (April–Oct daily 9am–4.45pm; ℡01796/481646, Ⓦwww.athollestatesrangerservice.co.uk) you can get details of the extensive network of local walks and bike rides as well as interesting information on surrounding flora and fauna. Right beside this, the modest **Atholl Country Life Museum** (May–Sept daily 1.30–5pm, July & Aug opens 10am; £3; ℡01796/481232) offers a homespun and nostalgic look at the history of life in the local glens; in among the old photos and artefacts the star attraction is a stuffed, full-size Highland cow. The grand but reasonably priced *Atholl Arms Hotel* (℡01796/481205, Ⓦwww.athollarms.co.uk; ❹) is the best place in town for a drink or a bar meal; alongside it, in the old petrol station, is a secondhand bookshop called Atholl Browse (a pun on "Atholl Brose", a sickly sweet, whisky-laced dessert). Nearby, you can wander round the **Water Mill** on Ford Road (April–Oct daily 10.30am–5.30pm; £1.50), which dates back to 1613, and witness flour being milled; better still, you can enjoy home-baked scones and light lunches in its pleasant timber-beamed tearoom.

Blair Castle

By far the most important and eye-catching building in these parts, **Blair Castle** (April–Oct daily 9.30am–last admission 4.30pm; Nov–March Tues & Sat only 9.30am–12.30pm; £6.90, grounds only £2.20; Ⓦwww.blair-castle.co.uk) is reached by a driveway leading from the centre of Blair Atholl village. Seat of the Atholl dukedom, this whitewashed, turreted castle, surrounded by parkland and dating from 1269, presents an impressive sight as you approach up the drive. A piper may be playing in front of the castle, one of the Atholl Highlanders, a select group retained by the duke as his private army – a unique privilege afforded to him by Queen Victoria, who stayed here in 1844.

Thirty or so rooms are open for inspection, and display a selection of paintings, antique furniture and plasterwork that is sumptuous in the extreme.

Highlights are the soaring **entrance hall**, with every spare inch of wood panelling covered in weapons of some description; the **Tapestry Room**, on the top floor of the original Cumming's Tower, adorned with Brussels tapestries and containing an ostentatious four-poster bed, topped with vases of ostrich feathers which originally came from the first duke's suite at Holyrood Palace in Edinburgh; and the vast **ballroom**, with its timber roof, antlers and mixture of portraits.

As impressive as the castle's interior are its surroundings: Highland cows graze the ancient landscaped grounds and peacocks strut in front of the castle. There is a **riding stable** from where you can take treks, and formal woodland walks take you to various interesting parts of the castle grounds, including the neglected, walled water garden named after the statue of Hercules which overlooks it, and the towering giant conifers of Diana's Grove. There is also a busy but attractive caravan and **camping** park (℡01796/481263, ⓦwww.blaircastlecaravanpark .co.uk) in the grounds.

Drumochter and Dalwhinnie

A few miles north of Blair Atholl, insistent signs point the way to the House of Bruar, a sprawling emporium of tweeds, waxed jackets and tasty-looking foodstuffs which acts as the final outpost of the Perthshire country set before the A9 sweeps northward over the barren **Pass of Drumochter**, often affected by snow falls in winter. Beyond this the bleak little village of **DALWHINNIE** has a striking distillery with whitewashed buildings topped by copper pagoda "hats", but little else to draw you in. It lies at the northern end of **Loch Ericht**, around which are some of the most remote high hills in Scotland, including spooky Ben Alder. The scenery all the way is inspiring and desolate, in equal measure. Not far beyond Dalwhinnie you encounter the neighbouring villages of Kingussie and Newtonmore, the start of the Strathspey region (see p.564).

Travel details

Trains

Perth to: Aberdeen (hourly; 1hr 40min); Blair Atholl (3–7 daily; 40min); Dundee (hourly; 25min); Dunkeld (3–7 daily; 20min); Edinburgh (9 daily; 1hr 25min); Glasgow Queen St (hourly; 1hr 5min); Inverness (4–9 daily; 2hr); Pitlochry (4–9 daily; 30min); Stirling (hourly; 30min).
Rannoch to: Corrour (2–4 daily; 12min); Fort William (2–4 daily; 1hr); Glasgow Queen St (2–4 daily; 2hr 45min); London Euston (sleeper service; Sun–Fri daily; 11hr).

Buses

Aberfeldy to: Pitlochry (3 daily; 30min); Killin (5 daily; 1hr).
Crieff to: Stirling (8 daily; 50min).
Kinloch Rannoch to: Pitlochry (4 daily; 1hr); Rannoch Station (3 daily; 40min).
Perth to: Aberfeldy (10 daily; 1hr 15min); Crieff (hourly; 45min); Dundee (hourly; 45min); Dunkeld (hourly; 30min); Edinburgh (hourly; 1hr 20min); Glasgow (hourly; 1hr 35min); Gleneagles (hourly; 25min); Inverness (hourly; 2hr 45min); Oban (2 daily; 3hr); Pitlochry (hourly; 45min); Stirling (hourly; 50min).

Northeast Scotland

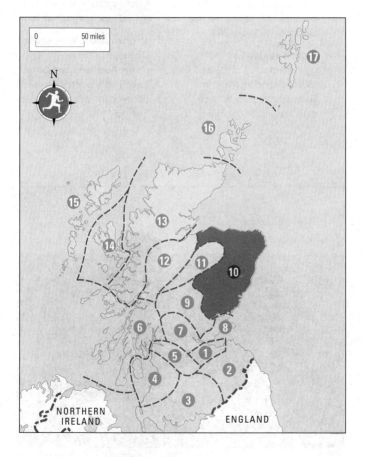

CHAPTER 10

Highlights

* **DCA** Arts centre/cinema/ café at the hip new heart of Dundee's up-and-coming cultural scene. See p.498

* **Arbroath smokie** A true Scottish delicacy: succulent haddock still warm from the oak smoker. See p.503

* **Pictish stones** Fascinating carved relics of a lost culture, standing alone in fields or in museums such as at Meigle. See p.508

* **Dunnottar Castle** The moodiest cliff-top ruin in the country. See p.532

* **Museum of Scottish Lighthouses** Lights, lenses and legends at one of the best small museums in the country, in Fraserburgh. See p.542

* **Pennan and Gardenstown** One-street fishing villages on the Aberdeenshire coast: there's no room for any more between the cliff and the sea. See p.543

△ Dunnottar Castle

Northeast Scotland

A large triangle of land thrusting into the North Sea, **northeast Scotland** comprises the area east of a line drawn roughly from Perth north to the fringe of the Moray Firth at Forres. The area takes in the county of Angus and the city of Dundee to the south and, beyond the Grampian Mountains, the counties of Aberdeenshire and Moray and the city of Aberdeen. Geographically diverse, the landscape in the south of the region is made up predominantly of undulating farmland, but, as you get further north of the Firth of Tay, this gives way to wooded glens, mountains and increasingly harsh land fringed by a dramatic coast of cliffs and long sandy beaches.

The northeast was the southern kingdom of the **Picts**, reminders of whom are scattered throughout the region in the form of numerous symbolic and beautifully carved stones found in fields, churchyards and museums, such as the one at **Meigle**. Remote, self-contained and cut off from the centres of major power in the south, the area never grew particularly prosperous, and a handful of feuding and intermarrying families, such as the Gordons, the Keiths and the Irvines, grew to wield disproportionate influence, building many of the region's **castles** and religious buildings and developing and planning its towns.

Many of the most appealing settlements are along the coast, but while the fishing industry is but a fondly held memory in many parts, a number of the northeast's ports have been transformed by the discovery of **oil** in the North Sea in the 1960s – particularly **Aberdeen**, Scotland's third-largest city. Despite its relative isolation in the Scottish context, Aberdeen remains a sophisticated city which, for the time being, still rides a diminishing wave of oil-based prosperity. At the same time, **Dundee**, the northeast's next-largest metropolis, is fast losing its depressed post-industrial image with a reinvigorated cultural scene and some heavily marketed tourist attractions, including *Discovery*, the ship of Captain Scott ("of the Antarctic"). A little way up the Angus coast lie the historically important towns of **Arbroath** and **Montrose** while, inland, the picturesque **Angus glens** cut into the Grampian mountains, offering a readily accessible taste of wild Highland scenery to both hikers and skiers.

North of the glens and west of Aberdeen, **Deeside** is a fertile yet ruggedly attractive area made famous by the Royal Family, who have favoured the estate at **Balmoral** as a summer holiday retreat ever since Queen Victoria fell in love with it back in the 1840s. Beyond Deeside and the similarly endowed although less visited **Don Valley** are the eastern sections of the **Cairngorm National Park**, while the northeast coast offers yet another aspect of a diverse region, with rugged cliffs, empty beaches and historic fishing villages tucked into coves and bays.

Northeast Scotland is well served by an extensive **road** network, with fast links between Dundee and Aberdeen, while the area north and east of Aberdeen

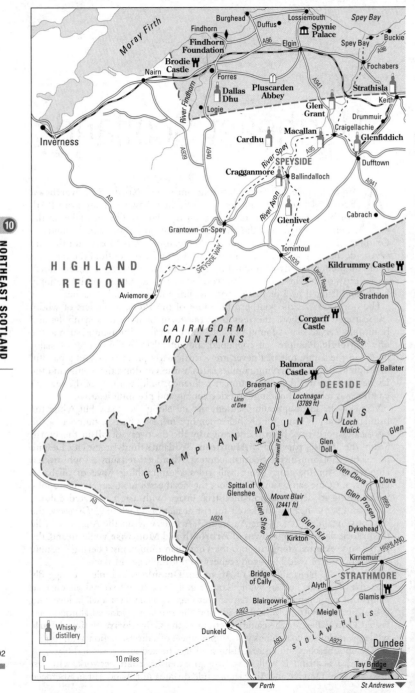

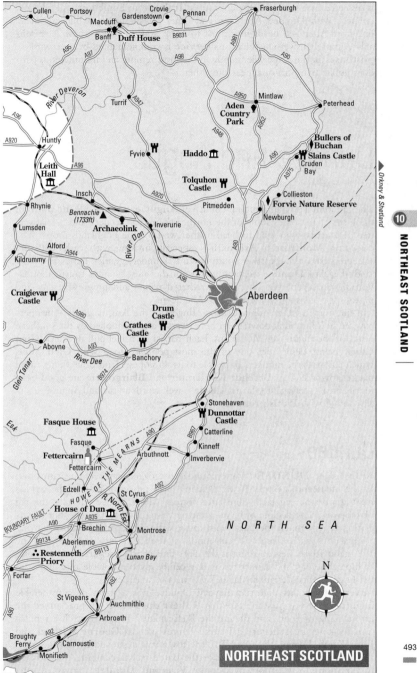

▲ Orkney & Shetland

NORTH SEA

N

NORTHEAST SCOTLAND

© Crown copyright

is dissected by a series of efficient routes. **Trains** from Edinburgh and Glasgow connect with Dundee, Aberdeen and other coastal towns, while an inland line from Aberdeen heads northwest to Elgin and on to Inverness. A reasonably comprehensive scheduled **bus service** is complemented by a network of **postbuses** in the Angus glens: only in the most remote and mountainous parts does public transport disappear altogether.

Dundee and Angus

The predominantly agricultural county of **Angus**, east of the A9 and north of the Firth of Tay, holds some of the northeast's greatest scenery and is relatively free of tourists, who tend to head further west for the Highlands proper. The coast from **Montrose** to **Arbroath** is especially inviting, with scarlet cliffs and sweeping bays, then, further south towards Dundee, gentler dunes and long sandy beaches. **Dundee** itself, although not the most obvious tourist destination, has in recent years become a rather dynamic and progressive city, and makes for a less snooty alternative to Aberdeen.

In the north of the county, the long fingers of the **Angus glens** – heather-covered hills tumbling down to rushing rivers – are overlooked by the southern peaks of the Grampian Mountains. Each has its own feel and devotees, **Glen Clova** being, deservedly, one of the most popular, along with **Glen Shee**, which attracts large numbers of people to its ski slopes. Handsome if uneventful market towns such as **Brechin**, **Kirriemuir** and **Blairgowrie** are good bases for the area, extravagant **Glamis Castle** is well worth a visit, and Angus is liberally dotted with **Pictish remains**.

Dundee

At first sight, **DUNDEE** (Ⓦ www.dundeecity.gov.uk) can seem a grim place. In the nineteenth century it was Britain's main processor of jute, the world's most important vegetable fibre after cotton, which earned the city the tag "Juteopolis". The decline of manufacturing wasn't kind to Dundee, but regeneration is very much the buzz word today, with some commentators drawing comparisons with Glasgow's reinvention of itself as a city of culture in the 1980s and 1990s. Less apparent is the city's international reputation as a centre of biotechnology and cancer research, recently given a notable monument in the Frank Gehry-designed Maggie's Centre for cancer care.

Even prior to its Victorian heyday, Dundee was a town of considerable importance. It was here in 1309 that **Robert the Bruce** was proclaimed the lawful King of Scots, and during the Reformation it earned itself a reputation for tolerance, sheltering leading figures such as **George Wishart** and **John Knox**. During the Civil War, the town was destroyed by the Royalists and Cromwell's army. Later, prior to the Battle of Killiecrankie, it was razed to the ground once more by Jacobite **Viscount Dundee**, known in song

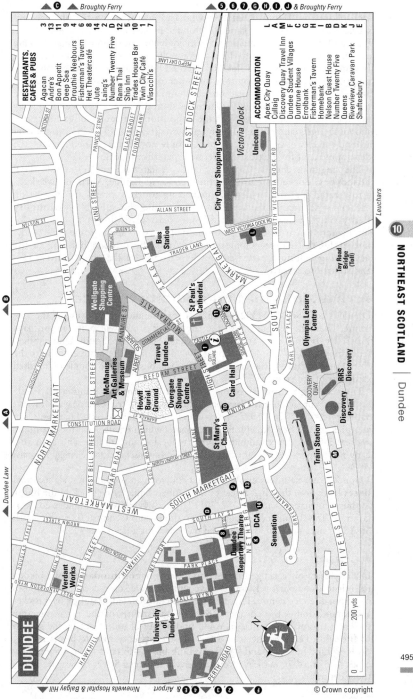

DUNDEE

RESTAURANTS, CAFÉS & PUBS

Agacan	3
Andre's	13
Bon Appetit	11
Deep Sea	9
Drouthie Neebours	4
Fisherman's Tavern	6
Het Theatercafé	8
Jute	14
Laing's	2
Number Twenty Five	12
Rama Thai	5
Ship Inn	10
Trades House Bar	1
Twin City Café	
Visocchi's	7

ACCOMMODATION

Apex City Quay	L
Cullaig	A
Discovery Quay Travel Inn	M
Dundee Student Villages	F
Duntrune House	C
Errolbank	G
Fisherman's Tavern	H
Homebank	I
Nelson Guest House	B
Number Twenty Five	D
Queens	K
Riverview Caravan Park	J
Shaftesbury	E

▲ **C** ▲ *Broughty Ferry*

▲ **5, 6, 7, G, H, I, J** & *Broughty Ferry*

▲ *Dundee Law*

◀ *Leuchars*

PEEP O'DAY LANE

EAST DOCK STREET

VICTORIA ST.

PRINCES STREET

BLACKSCROFT

FOUNDRY LANE

Victoria Dock

City Quay Shopping Centre

Unicorn

SOUTH VICTORIA DOCK RD

WEST VICTORIA DOCK RD

VICTORIA ROAD

NELSON ST.

KING STREET

ALLAN STREET

Bus Station

TRADER LANE

SEAGATE

QUEEN'S ST.

COWGATE

Wellgate Shopping Centre

PANMURE ST

WILFRAVEGATE

COMMERCIAL ST

St Paul's Cathedral

Tay Road Bridge (Toll)

BUNHOPE STREET

BELL STREET

McManus Art Galleries & Museum

ALBERT SQUARE

REFORM STREET

Travel Dundee

CASTLE ST

i

CITY SQUARE

SHORE TERR.

Caird Hall

EARL GREY PLACE

Olympia Leisure Centre

NORTH MARKETGAIT

CONSTITUTION ROAD

BARRACK ST

Howff Burial Ground

Overgate Shopping Centre

HIGH STREET

UNION ST.

DISCOVERY QUAY

RRS Discovery

Discovery Point

WEST BELL STREET

WARD ROAD

SOUTH WARD STREET

St Mary's Church

NORTH LINDSAY STREET

OVERGATE LANE

Train Station

WEST MARKETGAIT

SOUTH MARKETGAIT

BROWN STREET

SOUTH TAY ST

GREENMARKET

RIVERSIDE DRIVE

DOUGLAS STREET

MILN STREET

WEST PORT

NETHERGATE

Dundee Repertory Theatre

DCA

Sensation

PARK PLACE

Verdant Works

HAWKHILL

GUTHRIE STREET

HAWKHILL

MILN STREET

HENDERSON'S WYND

SMALLS WYND

University of Dundee

PERTH ROAD

▲ *Ninewells Hospital & Balgay Hill*

▼ **F** & *Airport*

▼ **2, 3** ▼ **4, 5** ▼ **9**

N

0 200 yds

© Crown copyright

and folklore as "Bonnie Dundee", who had been granted the place for his services to the Crown by James II. Dundee picked itself up in the 1800s, its train and harbour links making it a major centre for shipbuilding, whaling and the manufacture of **jute**. This, along with jam and journalism – the three Js which famously defined the city – has all but disappeared, with only local publishing giant D.C. Thomson, publisher of the timelessly popular *Beano* and *Dandy*, as well as a spread of other comics and newspapers, still playing a meaningful role in the city. As factories shut, the planners moved in, hardly helping Dundee's self-image with the imposition of a couple of garish central shopping malls and the seemingly endless spread of 1970s housing estates around the city edges, a legacy which is only now being pushed aside by the development of the cultural quarter and waterfront areas.

The major sight is Captain Scott's Antarctic explorer ship, **RRS Discovery**, docked underneath the Tay Road Bridge. **Verdant Works** is a re-created jute mill which has picked up tourism awards for its take on the city's distinctive industrial heritage, while the suburb of **Broughty Ferry** offers a distinct change of tone, particularly if you're looking for somewhere to eat or drink. You should also try to spend some time at the upbeat **DCA** (Dundee Contemporary Arts), the totemic building of the developing cultural quarter around which most of the city's lively artistic and social life revolves.

Arrival, information and city transport

Dundee's **airport** (☎01382/643242) is five minutes' drive west of the city centre. There are no buses into the centre, but a taxi will only set you back £2–3. By **train**, you'll arrive at Taybridge Station on South Union Street (enquiries ☎0845/748 4950), about 300yd south of the city centre near the river. Long-distance **buses** arrive at the Seagate bus station, a couple of hundred yards east of the centre.

The very helpful **tourist office** is right in the centre of things at 21 Castle St (June–Sept Mon–Sat 9am–6pm, Sun noon–4pm; Oct–May Mon–Sat 9am–5pm; ☎01382/527527, ⓦwww.angusanddundee.co.uk). Here you can also pick up the free *Accent* listings magazine, which details local theatre, music and exhibitions; ⓦwww.dundee.com has local listings online. The city's two daily newspapers are the morning *Courier & Advertiser* and the *Evening Telegraph & Post*.

Dundee's centre is reasonably compact and you can walk to most sights; **local buses** leave from the High Street or from Albert Square, one block to the north; for bus information, call ☎01382/201121, check ⓦwww.traveldundee.co.uk or go to the Travel Dundee Travel Centre, in the Forum Centre at 92 Commercial St. A Daysaver ticket, with unlimited bus travel for a day, costs £2.30.

Accommodation

In a city that's only just getting used to tourists, **accommodation** isn't plentiful, but it is comparatively inexpensive and there are some decent guesthouses out from the city centre. There isn't any recommended hostel or backpacker accommodation – the cheaper **B&B**s on the fringes of the city centre are the most reasonable alternative. You'll find plenty of rooms out by the suburb of Broughty Ferry, connected to the city by a twenty-minute bus ride (£1) on Red Line buses #7 and #8, Ferry Link buses #9x and #10x, or Strathtay buses #73 and #76 (all leave from either Commercial Street or Seagate in the town centre).

Hotels

Apex City Quay Hotel West Victoria Dock Rd ☎01382/202404, ⊛www.apexhotels.co.uk. Large, sleek and modern hotel in the redeveloping dockland area, incorporating a spa, pool and restaurant. ❼

Discovery Quay Premier Travel Inn Riverside Drive ☎01382/203240, ⊛www.premiertravelinn .com. Bland, modern chain hotel well positioned beside Discovery Point and the train station. ❸

Number Twenty Five 25 Tay St ☎01382/200399, ⊛www.g1group.co.uk. Right beside the action in the Cultural Quarter, with four designer rooms above a bar and restaurant (see p.501). ❻

Queens 160 Nethergate ☎01382/322515, ⊛www.queenshotel-dundee.com. Grand old hotel with refurbished rooms and a friendly welcome. Its location is good too, on the main road between the city and the university, and it has discount rates at the weekend. ❺

Shaftesbury 1 Hyndford St ☎01382/669216, ⊛www.shaftesbury-hotel.co.uk. A converted jute merchant's house in a residential area not far west of the centre, with a dozen comfortable rooms. ❺

Guesthouses and B&Bs

Cullaig Rosemount Terrace, Upper Constitution St ☎01382/322154, ⊛www.cullaig.co.uk. Victorian terraced guesthouse, within walking distance from town on the lower slopes of Dundee Law. ❷

Duntrune House Duntrune ☎01382/350239, ⊛www.duntrunehouse.co.uk. Three spacious rooms in a wing of a grand country house five miles northeast of Dundee. Lovely gardens and big sea views. ❹

Errolbank 9 Dalgleish Rd ☎01382/462118. Solid Victorian villa with good views of the Tay; all rooms are en suite. ❷

Fisherman's Tavern 12 Fort St, Broughty Ferry ☎01382/775941, ⊛www.fishermans-tavern -hotel.co.uk. Refurbished en-suite rooms above a cosy traditional pub with decent food, great real ales and malt whiskies. ❹

Homebank 9 Ellieslea Rd, Broughty Ferry ☎01382/477481, ⊛www.scotland2000.com /homebank. B&B in an elegant mansion house set in walled gardens, a good example of why Broughty Ferry was the suburb of choice for the wealthy. ❹

Nelson Guest House 8 Nelson Terrace ☎01382/225354. Inexpensive B&B with three twin rooms, located up the hill from the downtown area. ❶

Campus accommodation and camping

Dundee Student Villages ☎01382/573111, ⊛www.Scotland2000.com/seabraes. En-suite single or double rooms (❶) or exclusive use of flats sleeping up to 8, located at Seabraes, just west of the city centre. Also available is B&B in the West Park Conference Centre on Perth Rd (☎01382/647171, ⊛www.westparkcentre.com; ❸). Both July & Aug only.

Riverview Caravan Park Marine Drive, Monifieth ☎01382/535471. Well-run camping park in a suburb beyond Broughty Ferry, with an easy train link to Dundee. April–Oct.

The City and around

The best approach to Dundee is across the mile-and-a-half-long **Tay Road Bridge** from Fife. While the Tay bridges aren't nearly as spectacular as the bridges over the Forth near Edinburgh, they do offer a magnificent panorama of the city on the northern bank of the firth. The bridge, opened in 1966, has a central walkway for pedestrians and a £1 toll for cars. Running parallel half a mile upstream is the **Tay Rail Bridge**, opened in 1887 to replace the spindly structure which collapsed in a storm in December 1879 only eighteen months after it was built, killing the crew and 75 passengers on a train passing over the bridge at the time.

Dundee's city centre, dominated by large shopping malls filled with mundane chain stores, is focused on **City Square**, a couple of hundred yards north of the Tay. The attractive square, set in front of the city's imposing Caird Hall, has been much spruced up in recent years, with fountains, benches and extensive pedestrianization making for a relaxing environment.

The main street, which is pedestrianized as it passes City Square, starts as Nethergate in the west, becomes High Street in the centre, then divides into Murraygate (which is also pedestrianized) and Seagate. Opposite this junction is the mottled spire of **St Paul's Episcopal Cathedral** (hours vary; free), a rather gaudy Gothic Revival structure by George Gilbert Scott, notable for its vivid if sentimental stained glass and floridly gilded high altar. Immediately in front of the cathedral is a recently erected statue to one of the city's heroes, **Admiral Duncan of Camperdown**, who defeated a Dutch fleet not far offshore from Dundee during the Napoleonic Wars. Back where Reform Street meets City Square, look out for a couple of other statues to Dundee heroes: **Desperate Dan** and **Minnie the Minx**, both from the *Dandy* comic, which is produced a few hundred yards away in the D.C. Thomson building on Albert Square.

The **McManus Art Galleries and Museum** (ⓦ www.mcmanus.co.uk), Dundee's most impressive Victorian structure and the city's largest civic exhibition space, will be closed for renovation until 2008. Many of the key exhibits will be part of a touring exhibition, but few will be seen in Dundee itself. In the absence of the McManus, there isn't much in the way of tourist attractions in the heart of the city centre, though some visitors enjoy a snoop around the **Howff Burial Ground** (daily 9am–dusk), located across Ward Road from the museum, which has some great carved tombstones dating from the sixteenth to nineteenth centuries. Originally gardens belonging to a monastery, the land was given to Dundee for burials in 1564 by Mary, Queen of Scots.

Five minutes' walk west of here, on West Henderson Wynd in Blackness, an award-winning museum, **Verdant Works**, tells the story of jute from its harvesting in India to its arrival in Dundee on clipper ships (April–Oct Mon–Sat 10am–6pm, Sun 11am–6pm; Nov–March Wed–Sat 10.30am–4.30pm, Sun 11am–4.30pm; £5.95, joint ticket with Discovery Point £10.95; ⓦ www.verdant-works.co.uk). In the nineteenth century, Dundee's jute mills employed fifty thousand people and were responsible for the rapid industrialization and development of the city as a trading port. The museum, set in an old jute mill, makes a lively attempt to re-create the turn-of-the-century factory floor, the highlight being the chance to watch jute being processed on fully operational quarter-size machines originally used for training workers.

The Cultural Quarter

Immediately west of the city centre, High Street becomes Nethergate and passes into what is now being dubbed, with a fair amount of justification, Dundee's "**Cultural Quarter**". As well as the university and the highly respected Rep theatre, the area is also home to the best concentration of pubs and cafés in the city. Principal among the many arts venues is the hip and exciting **DCA**, or Dundee Contemporary Arts, at 152 Nethergate (Mon–Sat 10.30am–midnight, Sun noon–midnight; galleries Tues–Sun 10.30am–5.30pm, until 8.30pm Thurs, Sun noon–5.30pm; ☎01382/909252, ⓦ www.dca.org.uk), a stunningly designed complex which incorporates galleries, a print studio and an airy café-bar (see p.501). The centre, opened in 1999, was designed by Richard Murphy, who converted an old brick building which had been a garage and car showroom into an inspiring new space, given energy and confidence by its bright, sleek interior and distinctive ship-like exterior. It's worth visiting for the stimulating temporary and touring exhibitions of contemporary art, and an eclectic programme of art-house films and cult classics.

Tucked in behind DCA is another new building, **Sensation** (daily 10am–5pm; June–Aug closes 6pm; £6.50; ⓦ www.sensation.org.uk), best approached from Greenmarket, off Marketgate. Aimed squarely at families and schoolchildren, it's a fun-packed exploration of science, using sixty different interactive exhibits and participatory experiments.

The waterfront

Just south of the city centre, at the water's edge alongside the Tay Road Bridge, the domed **Discovery Point** is an impressive development centring on the Royal Research Ship *Discovery* (April–Oct Mon–Sat 10am–6pm, Sun 11am–5pm; Nov–March Mon–Sat 10am–5pm, Sun 11am–5pm; £6.45, joint ticket with Verdant Works £10.95; ⓦ www.rrs-discovery.co.uk). Something of an icon for Dundee's renaissance, *Discovery* is a three-mast steam-assisted vessel built in Dundee in 1901 to take Captain Robert Falcon Scott on his polar expeditions. A combination of brute strength and elegance, she has been beautifully restored, with polished wood panels and brass trimmings giving scant indication of the privations suffered by the crew. In the Antarctic, temperatures on board would plummet to -28°C and turns at having a bath came round every 47 days. As an introduction before stepping aboard you're led through a series of displays about the construction of the ship and Scott's journeys, including the chill-inducing "Polarama" about life in Antarctica.

In total contrast is the endearingly simple wooden frigate **Unicorn** (April–Oct daily 10am–5pm; Nov–March Wed–Fri noon–4pm, Sat & Sun 10am–4pm; £4), moored amidst some new dockland redevelopments in Victoria Dock on the other side of the road bridge (a footpath connects the two ships). Built in 1824, it's the oldest British warship still afloat and was in active service up until 1968. During its service years, over three hundred men would have lived and worked aboard. The fact that its 46 guns – eighteen-pounder cannons are still on display – were never fired in aggression probably accounts for its survival. Although the interior is sparse, the cannons, the splendid figureheads and the wonderful model of the ship in its fully rigged glory (the real thing would have featured over 23 miles of rope) are fascinating.

Out from the centre

A mile or so north of town, **Dundee Law** is the plug of an extinct volcano and, at 571ft, the city's highest point. Once the site of a seventh-century defensive hillfort, it's now an impressive lookout, with great views across the whole city and the Tay; the climb is steep and often windy. It takes thirty minutes to walk to the foot of the Law from the city centre, or you can take bus #4A from Albert Square.

△ Maggie's Centre, Dundee

The city's other volcanic outcrop sits a mile to the west of Dundee Law. **Balgay Hill** is skirted by the wooded **Lochee Park**, while on its summit sits the **Mills Observatory** (April–Sept Tues–Fri 11am–5pm, Sat & Sun 12.30–4pm; Oct–March Mon–Fri 11am–10pm, Sat & Sun 12.30–4pm; free), Britain's only full-time public observatory with a resident astronomer. The best time to go is after dark on winter nights; in summer there's little to be seen through the telescope, but well-explained, quirky exhibits and displays chart the history of space exploration and astronomy, and on sunny days you can play at being a human sundial and take in the fantastic views over the city through little telescopes. A **planetarium** has shows on the last Friday of every month (£1), while the observatory also has special opening times to coincide with eclipses and other astronomical events. Bus #2, #9 or #37 from Nethergate drops you in Balgay Road, at the entrance to the park.

Around a mile further west from Balgay Park is the sprawling Ninewells Hospital, not an obvious draw for fans of modern architecture. In the grounds of the hospital, however, is **Maggie's Centre**, designed by US architect Frank Gehry, best known for Bilbao's Guggenheim Museum. Gehry's first public commission in the UK, the building is one of a series of cancer-support centres established around Britain to offer a calm, inspiring environment for patients and their families, and features a distinctively freeform style with a wavy roof constructed from timber clad with stainless steel. The building is not open to the general public, and is operational through the week, but for anyone interested in seeing one of Gehry's visionary constructions up close it is possible to walk up to and around it at weekends. Buses #22 and #9x go to the hospital; if you're travelling by car use the main hospital car park.

Broughty Ferry and around

Four miles east of Dundee's city centre lies the seaside settlement of **BROUGHTY FERRY**, now engulfed by the city as a reluctant suburb. The ferry referred to in the name was a railway ferry, carrying carriages travelling between Edinburgh and Aberdeen, which was inevitably closed following the building of the ill-fated first Tay Rail Bridge. Comprising an eclectic mix of big villas built by jute barons up the hillside and small fishermen's cottages along the shoreline, "The Ferry", as it's known, has experienced a recent resurgence in popularity. Now a pleasant and relaxing spot with some good restaurants and pubs, it has none of Dundee's industrialization, and both the beach and the castle's "green", or grounds, are popular run-around spots for kids. The striking **Broughty Castle and Museum**, right by the seashore (Mon–Sat 10am–4pm, Sun 12.30–4pm; Oct–March Tues–Sat 10am–4pm, Sun 12.30–4pm; free), is worth a look. Built in the fifteenth century to protect the estuary, its four floors now house local-history exhibits, covering the story of Broughty Ferry as a fishing village and the history of whaling, as well as details of local geology and wildlife.

Just north of Broughty Ferry, at the junction of the A92 and B978, the chunky bricks of **Claypotts Castle** (limited opening hours; details on ✆01786/431324; free) constitute one of Scotland's most complete Z-shaped tower houses. Built between 1569 and 1588, its two round towers have stepped projections to support extra rooms, a sixteenth-century architectural practice that makes Claypotts look like it's about to topple.

Eating, drinking and nightlife

The west end of Dundee, around the main university campus and Perth Road, is the best area for **eating and drinking**; the city centre has a few good pubs and one or two decent restaurants tucked away. Broughty Ferry is a pleasant alternative, with a good selection of pubs and restaurants which get particularly busy on summer evenings.

Restaurants and cafés

Agacan 113 Perth Rd ☎01382/644227. Tiny Turkish restaurant with an unmistakeable colourful exterior, and rough-hewn walls inside; they serve up decent kebabs and stuffed pittas, and also do take-aways. Moderate. Closed lunchtimes & all day Mon.

Andre's 134a Nethergate ☎01382/224455. A cosy, endearing bastion of traditional French dining – expect coq au vin or moules marinière done just the way they should be. Moderate. Closed Mon.

Bon Appetit 22-26 Exchange St ☎01382/809000, Ⓦwww.bonappetit-dundee.com. Another decent French restaurant, with a modern Franco-Scots theme. Moderate. Closed Sun.

Deep Sea 81 Nethergate. The best of Dundee's fish-and-chips restaurants and takeaways, serving huge and tasty portions, but closes early (6.40pm). Inexpensive.

Het Theatercafé Dundee Repertory Theatre, Tay Square ☎01382/206699, Ⓦwww.het-theatercafe .co.uk. Popular, vibey spot with lots of options for coffee and cakes to interesting, Indonesian-influenced meals. Inexpensive–moderate. Closed Sun.

Jute Dundee Contemporary Arts (DCA), 152 Nethergate. Trendy spot occupying a large open-plan space on the lower level of this arts centre which works equally well for a coffee, lunch or pre-cinema snack. There's table service for the decent range of sandwiches and light meals, served until 9.30pm. Inexpensive.

Number Twenty Five 25 Tay St ☎01382/200399. Large, contemporary restaurant serving modern Scottish dishes, with a café-bar on the ground floor for cocktails and light snacks and a large bar below this with DJs at the weekend. Moderate.

Rama Thai 32–34 Dock St ☎01382/223366. Grand Thai restaurant with chunky carved furniture and a tasty, well-executed menu. Moderate.

Ship Inn 121 Fisher St, Broughty Ferry. A narrow pub with a warm atmosphere right on the water-front. The bistro upstairs has views over the Tay and serves big platefuls of great seafood. Moderate.

Twin City Café 4 City Square ☎01382/223662. Almost achieves a continental feel, with tables and chairs spilling out onto the square. Daytime only, with a fairly standard menu of light snacks.

Visocchi's 40 Gray St, Broughty Ferry. Authentic Italian fare served in an informal, popular ice-cream café. Inexpensive.

Pubs

Drouthie Neebours 142–146 Perth Rd. A cheerful bar with a Robbie Burns theme, lavish painted murals and a lively student clientele. Occasional live music.

Fisherman's Tavern 12 Fort St, Broughty Ferry. Best real-ale pub around, and plenty of seafood on the menu. Not quite on the sea, but tucked away in a low-ceilinged cottage.

Laing's 8 Roseangle, off Perth Rd. Usually packed on warm summer nights, thanks to its beer garden and great river views.

Trades House Bar 40 Nethergate. Probably the best pub in the centre of town, with nice wood fittings, stained-glass windows and some decent ales.

Nightlife

When it comes to post-pub **nightlife**, Dundee is muted to say the least. The main **nightclub** is *Fat Sam's* on South Ward Road, while **live music** venues include the *Reading Rooms* at 57 Blackscroft and the *Westport Bar* at 66 North Lindsay St.

Right at the heart of the Cultural Quarter on Tay Square, north of Nethergate, is the prodigious Dundee Repertory Theatre (☎01382/223530, Ⓦwww .dundeereptheatre.co.uk), an excellent place for indigenously produced contemporary **theatre** and the home of the only permanent repertory company in Scotland. The best venue for **classical** music, including visits by the Royal Scottish Orchestra and other bigwigs, is Caird Hall (☎01382/434451, Ⓦwww .cairdhall.co.uk), whose bulky frontage dominates City Square. For **movies**, DCA (☎01382/909900, Ⓦwww.dca.org.uk) has two comfy auditoriums showing an appealing range of foreign and art-house movies alongside the more challenging mainstream releases; otherwise you have to head a fair way out of the centre to the UGC/Cineworld multiplex at Camperdown Leisure Park (☎0870/902 0407; bus #4A/4B) or the Odeon at Douglasfield, east of the city (☎0870/5050007; bus #28 or 29).

Listings

Airport ☎01382/662200.

Banks Bank of Scotland, 2 West Marketgate; Clydesdale Bank, 96 High St; Royal Bank of Scotland, 3 High St.

Bike rental Easy Ride Cycles, off Wm Fitzgerald Way, Barns of Claverhouse ☎01382/505683.

Books Ottakars, 80 High St; Waterstone's, 34 Commercial St.

Bus information Scottish Citylink ☎0870/550 5050; Strathtay Scottish for regional buses ☎01382/228345; Traveline Scotland ☎0870/608 2608.

Car rental Arnold Clark, East Dock St ☎01382/225382; Alamo, 45–53 Gellatly St ☎01382/224037; Hertz, 18 West Marketgate ☎01382/223711.

Gay, lesbian and bisexual Switchboard ☎01382/202620 (Mon 7–10pm), ⓦwww.diversitay .org.uk.

Genealogical research There's a Genealogy Unit at Dundee City Registrar, 89 Commercial St ☎01382/435222, ⓦwww.dundeeroots.com. You could also try the Tay Valley Family History Society ☎01382/461845, ⓦwww.tayvalleyfhs.org.uk.

Internet Central Library, Wellgate Shopping Centre (Mon–Fri 9.30am–8.30pm, Sat 9.30am–4.30pm). The tourist office also has Internet access.

Library The Central Library is in the Wellgate Shopping Centre.

Medical facilities Ninewells Hospital in the west of the city has an Accident and Emergency department (☎01382/660111). NHS 24 ☎08454/242424. Boots pharmacy is at 49–53 High St (Mon–Sat 8.30am–6pm, Tue opens 9am, Thurs closes 7pm, Sun 12.30–5pm).

Police Tayside Police HQ, West Bell St ☎01382/223200.

Post office 4 Meadowside (Mon–Fri 9am–5.30pm, Sat 9am–12.30pm).

Sport The city has two leading football clubs, Dundee (☎01382/889966, ⓦwww.dundeefc .co.uk) and Dundee United (☎01382/833166, ⓦwww.dundeeunitedfc.co.uk), whose stadiums face each other across Tannadice St in the north of the city. Fortunes fluctuate for the teams, but one or the other is usually playing in the Premier League. There are public golf courses at Ashludie, Golf Ave, Monifieth (☎01382/535553); Caird Park (☎01382/438871); and Camperdown Country Park (☎01382/431820). Other courses along the Angus coast include Carnoustie (☎01241/853789, ⓦwww.carnoustie.org), a British Open venue. The Olympia leisure complex, beside Discovery Point, has a swimming pool (during school term: Mon–Fri noon–7.30pm, Sat & Sun 10am–5.30pm; during school holidays Mon–Sun 10am–5.30pm; ☎01382/432300).

Taxis There are taxi ranks on Nethergate, or call City Cabs ☎01382/203020; Handy Taxis ☎01382/225825; or, in Broughty Ferry, Discovery Taxis ☎01382/732111.

The Angus coast

Two roads link Dundee to Aberdeen and the northeast coast of Scotland. By far the more pleasant option is the slightly longer A92 coast road, which joins the inland A90 at Stonehaven, just south of Aberdeen. Intercity **buses** follow both roads, while the coast-hugging train line from Dundee is one of the most picturesque in Scotland, passing attractive beaches and impressive cliffs, and stopping in the old seaports of **Arbroath** and **Montrose**.

Arbroath and around

Since it was settled in the twelfth century, local fishermen have been landing their catches at **ARBROATH**, situated on the Angus coast where it starts to curve in from the North Sea towards the Firth of Tay, about fifteen miles northeast of Dundee. The name of the town stems from Aber Brothock, the burn which runs into the sea here, and although it has a great location, with long sandy beaches and stunning sandstone cliffs on either side of town as well as an attractive old working harbour, Arbroath – like Dundee – has suffered from short-sighted development, its historical associations all but subsumed by pedestrian walkways, a mess of one-way systems and ugly shopping centres.

The town's most famous product is the **Arbroath smokie** – line-caught haddock, smoke-cured over smouldering oak chips, and still made here in a number of family-run smokehouses tucked in around the harbour. One of the most approachable and atmospheric is M&M Spink's tiny whitewashed premises at 10 Marketgate; chef and cookery writer Rick Stein described the fish here, warm from the smoke, as "a world-class delicacy".

Down by the harbour, the elegant Regency **Signal House Museum** (Mon–Sat 10am–5pm, July & Aug also Sun 2–5pm; free) stands sentinel as it has since 1813 when it was built as the shore station for the Bell Rock lighthouse, improbably erected on a reef eleven miles offshore by Robert Stevenson. The interior is now given over to some excellent local history displays: a school room, fisherman's cottage and lighthouse kitchen have all been carefully re-created, with the addition of realistic smells.

Arbroath Abbey

By the late eighteenth century, chiefly due to its harbour, Arbroath had become a trading and manufacturing centre, famed for boot-making and sail-making (the *Cutty Sark's* sails were made here). The town's real glory days, however, came much earlier in the thirteenth century with the completion in 1233 of **Arbroath Abbey** (daily April–Sept 9.30am–6.30pm; Oct–March 9.30am–4.30pm; HS; £3.30), whose rose-pink sandstone ruins, described by Dr Johnson as "fragments of magnificence", stand on Abbey Street. Founded in 1178 but not granted abbey status until 1285, it was the scene of one of the most significant events in Scotland's history when, on April 6, 1320, a group of Scottish barons drew up the **Declaration of Arbroath**, asking the pope to reverse his excommunication of Robert the Bruce and recognize him as king of a Scottish nation independent from England. The wonderfully resonant language of the document still makes for a stirring expression of Scottish nationhood: "For so long as one hundred of us remain alive, we will never in any degree be subject to the dominion of the English, since it is not for glory, riches or honour that we do fight, but for freedom alone, which no honest man loses but with his life." It was duly dispatched to Pope John XXII in Avignon, who in 1324 agreed to Robert's claim.

Walks around Arbroath

There's not much to see in Arbroath besides the abbey and the smokehouses, but there are some great coastal **walks** in the vicinity. From the Signal House, you can wander east through the huddled cottages of the Fit o'the Toon, the harbour district where the smell of Arbroath smokies usually hangs heavy in the air. Beyond it, the seafront road heads into Victoria Park; at the far end of the road, a path climbs up over the red sandstone cliffs of **Whiting Ness**, stretching endlessly onto the horizon and eroded into a multitude of inlets, caves and arches that warrant hours of leisurely exploration. The *Arbroath Cliffs Nature Trail Guide*, free from the tourist office, picks out twenty good viewing points along the first mile and a half, and also gives details on the local flora and fauna; you may even see puffins. After four miles the path comes to the foot of the neat little fishing village of Auchmithie; a further four (very windy) miles north is the crest of Lunan Bay, a classic sweep of glorious sand crowned by the eerie ruins of Red Castle at the mouth of the Lunan Water.

The abbey was dissolved during the Reformation, and by the eighteenth century it was little more than a source of red sandstone for local houses. However, there's enough left to get a good idea of how vast the place must have been: the semicircular **west doorway** is more or less intact, complete with medieval mouldings, and the **south transept** has a beautiful round window, once lit with a beacon to guide ships. In the early 1950s, the **Stone of Destiny** had a brief sojourn here when it was stolen from London by a group of Scottish nationalists and appeared, wrapped in a Scottish flag, at the High Altar. It was duly returned to Westminster Abbey, where it stayed until its relatively recent move to Edinburgh Castle (see p.95). A radically designed new **visitor centre** at the Abbey Street entrance offers some in-depth background on these events and other aspects of the history of the building.

St Vigeans and Auchmithie

Although now little more than a northwestern dormitory of Arbroath, the pristine and peaceful hamlet of **ST VIGEANS** is a fine example of a Pictish site colonized by Christians: the church is set defiantly on a pre-Christian mound at the centre of the village. Many Pictish and earlier remains are housed in the wonderful little **museum** (only on request; collect the key from Arbroath Abbey; free), including the Drosten Stone, presumed to be a memorial. One side depicts a hunt, laced with an abundance of Pictish symbolism, while the other side bears a cross, which dates it to around 850 AD.

Four miles north of Arbroath by road or coastal footpath, the cliff-top village of **AUCHMITHIE** is the true home of the Arbroath smokie. However, the village didn't have a proper harbour until the nineteenth century – local fishermen, apparently, were carried to their boats by their wives to avoid getting wet feet – so Arbroath became the more important port and laid claim to the delicacy. Now an attractive little fishing village, Auchmithie's main attraction is the *But'n'Ben* **restaurant** (☎01241/877223; closed Tues), one of the best along this coast, which specializes in delicious, moderately priced Scottish dishes and seafood.

Practicalities

Arbroath's helpful **tourist office** is at Market Place right in the middle of town (April, May & Sept Mon–Fri 9am–5pm, Sat 10am–5pm; June–Aug Mon–Sat 9.30am–5.30pm, Sun 10am–3pm; Oct–March Mon–Fri 9am–5pm, Sat 10am–3pm; ☎01241/872609). Staff can recommend local walks and book accommodation. The **bus** station is on Catherine Street, about a five-minute walk south of the tourist office, while **trains** arrive at the station just across the road on Keptie Street.

For somewhere **to stay**, the *Five Gables House* (☎01241/871632, ⓦwww .fivegableshouse.co.uk; ❷) is a mile south of Arbroath on the A92; formerly a golf clubhouse, it has a great position overlooking the sea. Alternatively, try the appealing *Harbour Nights Guest House* (☎01241/434343, ⓦwww .harbournights-scotland.com; ❸), down by the harbour at 4 The Shore, which is also where you'll find the best **restaurants** and **pubs**. The best way to sample Arbroath smokies is while they're still warm, straight from one of the smokehouses. *The Old Brewhouse* (☎01241/879945) is a convivial and moderately priced restaurant-cum-pub by the harbour wall at the end of High Street – the bar here has gained a certain notoriety for selling smokie-flavoured vodka. For more conventional fish and chips, the locals' favourite is *Peppo's* by the harbour at 51 Ladybridge St.

Montrose and around

Here's the Basin, there's Montrose, shut your een and haud your nose.

As the old rhyme indicates, **MONTROSE**, a seaport and market town since the thirteenth century, can sometimes smell a little rich, mostly because of its position on the edge of a virtually landlocked two-mile-square lagoon of mud known as the Basin. But with the wind in the right direction, Montrose is a great little town to visit, with a pleasant old centre and an interesting museum. The Basin too is of interest: flooded and emptied twice daily by the tides, it's a nature reserve for the host of geese, swans and wading birds who frequent the ooze. On the south side of the Basin, a mile out of Montrose along the A92, the **Montrose Basin Wildlife Centre** (mid-March to mid-Nov daily 10.30am–5pm; mid-Nov to mid-March Fri–Sun 10.30am–4pm; £3; Ⓦ www .montrosebasin.org.uk) has binoculars, high-powered telescopes, bird hides and remote-control video cameras. In addition, the centre's resident ranger leads regular guided walks around the reserve.

Montrose locals are known as "Gable Endies", because of the unusual way in which the town's eighteenth- and nineteenth-century merchants, influenced by architectural styles they had seen on the continent, built their houses gable-end to the street. The few remaining original gabled houses line the wide **High Street**, off which are numerous tiny alleyways and quiet courtyards.

Two blocks behind the soaring kirk steeple at the lower end of High Street, the **Montrose Museum and Art Gallery** (Mon–Sat 10am–5pm; free), on Panmure Place on the western side of Mid Links park, is one of Scotland's oldest museums, dating from 1842. For a small-town museum, it has some particularly unusual exhibits, among them the so-called Samson Stone, a Pictish relic dating from 900 AD bearing a carving of Samson slaying the Philistines. In the local history section, look out for the mechanical paper sculpture of the town of Montrose, with a green train running along the top and yachts sailing by. On the upper floor, the maritime history exhibits include a cast of Napoleon's death mask and a model of a British man-of-war, sculpted out of bone by Napoleonic prisoners at Portsmouth. Most intriguing, however, is the message on a scrap of paper found in a bottle at nearby Ferryden beach in 1857, written by the chief mate of a brigantine eighty years earlier: "Blowing a hurricane lying to with close-reefed main topsails ship waterlogged. Cargo of wood from Quebec. No water on board, provisions all gone. Ate the dog yesterday, three men left alive. Lord have mercy on our souls. Amen."

Outside the museum entrance stands a winsome study of a boy by local sculptor William Lamb (1893–1951). More of his work can be seen in the moving **William Lamb Memorial Studio** on Market Street (July to mid-Sept daily 2–5pm; at other times, ask at the museum; free), including bronze heads of the Queen, Princess Margaret and the Queen Mother. The earnings from these pieces enabled him to buy the studio in the 1930s, which he donated to the town of Montrose on his death. A superbly talented but largely unheralded artist, Lamb is the more impressive because he taught himself to sculpt with his left hand, having suffered a war wound in his right. You can see another Lamb sculpture, *Whisper*, outside the library on the High Street. Opposite this, the castellated building which now houses the Job Centre has a long history: built on the site of Montrose Castle after it was demolished by William Wallace, it became the home of the Graham family. In front of the building is a statue of the family's most famous scion, James Graham, **Marquis of Montrose**, one of Scotland's most brilliant military strategists.

Finally, don't ignore the town's fabulous golden **seashore**. The beach road, Marine Avenue, across from the town museum, heads down through sand dunes and golf links to car parks fringing the fine, wide beach overlooked by a slender white lighthouse.

Around Montrose: the House of Dun

Across the Basin, four miles west of Montrose, is the Palladian **House of Dun** (April–June & Sept Wed–Sun 11.30am–5.30pm; July & Aug daily 11.30am–5.30pm; NTS; £8), accessible on the hourly Montrose–Brechin bus #30; ask the driver to let you off outside. Built in 1730 for David Erskine, Laird of Dun, to designs by William Adam, the house was opened to the public in 1989 after extensive restoration, and is crammed full of period furniture and *objets d'art*. Inside, the ornate relief plasterwork is the most impressive feature, extravagantly emblazoned with Jacobite symbolism. You can also see some gorgeous pieces of intricate needlework, stitched by the illegitimate child of King William IV, Lady Augusta, who married into the Dun family in 1827.

The buildings in the courtyard – a hen house, gamekeeper's workshop and potting shed – have been renovated, and include a tearoom and a craft shop.

Practicalities

Montrose **tourist office** is squeezed into a former public toilet next to the library, at the point where Bridge Street merges into the lower end of High Street (April–June & Sept Mon–Sat 10am–5pm; July & Aug Mon–Sat 9.30am–5.30pm; ☎01674/672000). Most **buses** stop in the High Street, while the **train** station lies a block back on Western Road. For B&B **accommodation**, try *36 The Mall*, in the northern section of the town (☎01674/673464, ⓦwww.36themall .co.uk; ❸) or, if you don't mind heading out of Montrose, make for *Woodston Fishing Station* (☎01674/850226, ⓦwww.woodstonfishingstation.co.uk; ❸), a neat, antique-filled house on the cliff-top at St Cyrus, a couple of miles north of town. Nearby, the simpler *Kirkside Bothy* (☎01674/830780, ⓦwww.kirksidebo thy.co.uk; ❷) is an isolated converted fishing bothy situated on the edge of the sand dunes by St Cyrus Nature Reserve.

For **eating**, the liveliest place in town is unquestionably *Roo's Leap*, a sports bar and restaurant by the golf club off the northern end of Traill Drive, with an unlikely, but decent mix of moderately priced Scottish, American and Australian cuisine. If you want a **drink**, the vitality of *Roo's Leap* is matched by *Sharky's*, a cavernous venue close to the centre of town at 21 George St, which also serves inexpensive pastas, burgers and so on. There's also a small tearoom at *Kirkside Bothy* (see above).

Strathmore and the Angus glens

Immediately north of Dundee, the low-lying Sidlaw Hills divide the city from the rich agricultural region of **Strathmore**, whose string of tidy market towns lies on a fertile strip along the southernmost edge of the heather-covered lower slopes of the Grampian Mountains. These towns act as gateways to the **Angus glens** (ⓦwww.angusglens.co.uk), a series of tranquil valleys penetrated by single-track roads and offering some of the most rugged and majestic landscapes in northeast Scotland. It's a rain-swept, wind-blown, sparsely populated area, whose roads become impassable with the first snows, sometimes as early as October, and where the summers see clouds of ferocious midges. Nevertheless, most of the glens, particularly **Glen Clova**, are well and truly on the tourist circuit, with the rolling hills and dales attracting hikers, bird-watchers and botanists in the summer, grouse shooters and deerhunters in autumn and a growing number of skiers in winter. The most useful road through the glens is the A93, which cuts through **Glen Shee**, linking Blairgowrie to Braemar on Deeside (see p.536). It's pretty dramatic stuff, threading its way over Britain's highest main-road pass, the **Cairnwell Pass** (2199ft).

Public transport in the region is limited: to get up the glens you'll have to rely on the **postbuses** from Blairgowrie (for Glen Shee) and Kirriemuir (for glens Clova and Prosen).

Blairgowrie and Glen Shee

The upper reaches of **Glen Shee**, the most dramatic and best known of the Angus glens, are dominated by its **ski fields**, ranged over four mountains above the Cairnwell mountain pass. During the season (Dec to March), ski lifts and tows give access to gentle beginners' slopes, while experienced skiers can try the more intimidating Tiger run. In summer it's all a bit sad, with lifeless chairlifts and bare, scree-covered slopes, although hang-gliders take advantage of the crosswinds between the mountains and there are some excellent hiking and mountain-biking routes.

To get to Glen Shee from the south you'll pass through the well-heeled little town of **BLAIRGOWRIE**, set among raspberry fields on the glen's southernmost tip and a good place to pick up information and plan your activities. Strictly two communities, Blairgowrie and **Rattray**, set on either side of the river Ericht, the town's modest claim to fame is that St Ninian once camped at Wellmeadow, a pleasant grassy triangle in the town centre. If you've time to kill here, wander up the leafy riverbank past a series of old mill buildings. Altogether more ambitious is the sixty-four-mile **Cateran Trail**, a long-distance footpath which starts in Blairgowrie then heads off on a long loop into the glens to the north following some of the drove roads used by caterans, or cattle thieves. It's a four- to five-day tramp, though of course it's possible to walk shorter sections of the way. You can get a map and more information from the tourist office, or by going to Ⓦwww.pkct.org/caterantrail.

Blairgowrie **tourist office** (April–June & Sept–Oct Mon–Sat 9.30am–5pm, Sun 11am–3pm; July & Aug Mon–Sat 9.30am–6.30pm, Sun 11am–4pm; Nov–March Mon–Sat 10am–4pm; Ⓣ01250/872960, Ⓦwww.perthshire.co.uk), on the high side of Wellmeadow, can help with **accommodation**. A number of Blairgowrie's grand houses offer B&B, among them the attractive *Duncraggan* (Ⓣ01250/872082; ❷) on Perth Road and *Heathpark House* (Ⓣ01250/870700, Ⓦwww.heathparkhouse.com; ❸) on the Coupar Angus Road. **Camping** is available at the year-round *Blairgowrie Holiday Park* on Rattray's Hatton Road (Ⓣ01250/876666), within walking distance of Wellmeadow.

Blairgowrie boasts plenty of places to **eat**: *Cargills* by the river on Lower Mill Street (Ⓣ01250/876735; closed Tues) is the best bet for a moderately priced formal meal or civilized coffee and cakes; for less elaborate food and takeaways, there's the inexpensive *Dome Restaurant*, just behind the tourist office, which has been run by two local Italian families since the 1920s. For a good local **pub** try the *Ericht Alehouse* on Wellmeadow, which serves real ale and plays real music, or head six miles north of town on the A93 to the welcoming *Bridge of Cally Hotel* (Ⓣ01250/886231, Ⓦwww.bridgeofcallyhotel.com; ❺) which serves food all day, plus real ale by an open fire. Back in Blairgowrie you can rent **bikes** from Crichton's Cycle Hire, 87 Perth St (Ⓣ01250/876100).

Skiing at Glen Shee

Scotland's **ski resorts** may not amount to much more than gentle training slopes in comparison with those of the Alps or North America, but any of them make for a fun day out for anyone from beginners to experienced skiers interested in experiencing the conditions. The strongest card of all the resorts is probably their scenic surroundings, and given that **Glen Shee** is both the most extensive and the most accessible of Scotland's ski areas, just over two hours from both Glasgow and Edinburgh, it's as good an introduction as any to the sport in Scotland.

For information, contact Ski Glenshee (☎013397/41320, ⓦwww.ski-glenshee .co.uk), which also offers ski rental and lessons. In addition, lessons, skis and boards are available from Cairnwell Mountain Sports (☎01250/885255, ⓦwww.cairnwell mountainsports.co.uk), at the Spittal of Glenshee. **Ski rental** starts at around £15 a day, while lessons are around £15 per half-day. **Lift passes** cost £22 per day or £88 for a five-day (Mon–Fri) ticket. For the latest snow and **weather conditions**, phone the centre itself or check out the Ski Scotland website (ⓦhttp://ski.visitscotland.com). Should you be more interested in **cross-country** skiing, there are some good touring areas in the vicinity; contact Cairnwell Mountain Sports (see above) or Braemar Mountain Sports (☎013397/41242, ⓦwww.braemarmountainsports.com) for information and equipment rental.

Nearly twenty miles north of Blairgowrie, the small settlement of **SPITTAL OF GLENSHEE** (the names derives from the same root as "hospital", indicating a refuge), though ideally situated for skiing, has little to commend it other than the busy *Gulabin Bunkhouse* on the A93, run by Cairnwell Mountain Sports (☎01250/885255, ⓦwww.cairnwellmountainsports.co.uk), which rents out skis and bikes and offers instruction in activities such as kayaking and mountaineering. Tucked away among the hills behind Spittal, *Dalmunzie House* (☎01250/885224, ⓦwww.dalmunzie.com; ❼) is a lovely Highland retreat on the theme of a sporting lodge. From Spittal the road climbs another five miles or so to the ski centre at the crest of the Cairnwell Pass.

Blairgowrie is well linked by hourly **bus** #57 to both Perth and Dundee. To travel up Glen Shee, you'll have to rely on the **postbus**, which leaves town at 7.30am (not Sun) and returns from the Spittal of Glenshee at 12.30pm.

Meigle and Glen Isla

Fifteen miles north of Dundee on the B954 lies the tiny settlement of **MEIGLE**, home to Scotland's most important collection of early Christian and Pictish inscribed stones. Housed in a modest former schoolhouse, the **Meigle Museum** (April–Sept daily 9.30am–6.30pm; HS; £2.20) displays some thirty pieces dating from the seventh to the tenth centuries, all found in and around the nearby churchyard. The majority are either gravestones that would have lain flat, or cross slabs inscribed with the sign of the cross, usually standing. Most impressive is the seven-foot-tall great cross slab, said to be the gravestone of Guinevere, wife of King Arthur, carved on one side with a portrayal of Daniel surrounded by lions, a beautifully executed equestrian group and mythological creatures including a dragon and a centaur. On the other side various beasts are surmounted by the "ring of glory", a wheel containing a cross carved and decorated in high relief. The exact meaning and purpose of the stones and their enigmatic symbols is obscure, as is the reason why so many of them were found at Meigle. The most likely theory suggests that Meigle was once an important ecclesiastical centre which attracted secular burials of prominent Picts.

Glen Isla

Three miles north of Meigle is **ALYTH**, near which, legend has it, Guinevere was held captive by Mordred. The sleepy village lies at the south end of **Glen Isla**, which runs parallel to Glen Shee and is linked to it by the A926. Dominated by Mount Blair (2441ft), Glen Isla is a lot less dramatic than its sister glens, and suffers from an excess of angular conifers alongside great bald chunks of hillside waiting to be planted. Heading north along the B954, the River Isla narrows and then plunges some 60ft into a deep gorge to produce the classically pretty waterfall of **Reekie Linn**, or "smoking fall", so called because of the water-mist produced when the fall hits a ledge and bounces a further 20ft into a deep pool known as the Black Dub. Just after this, a side road leads east to the pleasant Loch of Lintrathen, beside which is the *Lochside Lodge* (℡01575/560340, ⓦ www.lochsidelodge.com; ❺), a cosy bar set in a converted steading full of old pews and farming implements, with a noted restaurant alongside and bedrooms in the old hay loft. Heading back into the glen proper, you'll come on the tiny hamlet of **KIRKTON OF GLENISLA** ten miles or so up the glen. Here, the cosy ⚜ *Glenisla Hotel* (℡01575/582223, ⓦ www .glenisla-hotel.com; ❸) is great for classy home-made bar food and convivial drinking. There are some relatively easy **hiking** trails in the nearby Glenisla forest, while just before Kirkton, a turn-off on the right-hand side leads northeast up a long bumpy road to the unexpected *Glenmarkie Guesthouse Health Spa and Riding Centre* (℡01575/582295 ⓦ www.glenmarkie.co.uk; ❸), which offers both pedicures and pony trekking.

Transport connections into the glen are limited: Alyth is on the main bus routes linking Blairgowrie with Dundee and Kirriemuir, while hourly bus #57 from Dundee to Perth passes through Meigle. Transport up to Kirkton is limited to a postbus which leaves Blairgowrie at 7am (not Sun) and travels via Alyth (confirm on ℡01250/872766).

Forfar and around

Around fifteen miles north of Dundee on the main A90 lies **FORFAR**, Angus's county town and the ancient capital of the Picts. Old Pictish connections are still evident in Forfar's strong support for the Scottish National Party (SNP), with a profusion of Scottish flags and stirring messages on civic buildings. The wide High Street is framed by some impressive Victorian architecture and small old-fashioned shops. Midway along, at 20 West High St, the **Meffen Institute Museum and Art Gallery** (Mon–Sat 10am–5pm; free) exhibits Neolithic, Pictish and Celtic remains and a thoroughly enjoyable collection of re-created historical street scenes. The most disturbing examines the town's seventeenth-century passion for witch-hunting, with a taped re-creation of locals baying for blood. There is also a comprehensive interactive computer catalogue of all the Pictish stones in Angus, and an art gallery with good changing exhibitions.

A series of glacial lochs peters out in the west of the town at **Forfar Loch**, now surrounded by a pleasant country park with a visitor centre and three-mile nature trail. Two miles east and situated in the middle of farmland are the remains of **Restenneth Priory** (free access), approached along a hard-to-spot side road off the B9113. King Nechtan of the Picts was thought to have established a place of worship here in the eighth century, although the oldest parts of the present structure are from an Augustinian priory erected on the spot around 1100. The splayed foot spire, first seen beckoning from the road, was added in the fifteenth century. A little way south of this, off the B9128, a cairn in the village of **DUNNICHEN** commemorates a battle at nearby Nechtansmere in 685 in which the Picts unexpectedly defeated a Northumbrian army, thus preventing the Angles from extending their kingdom northwards.

Forfar's small **tourist office** (April–June & Sept Mon–Sat 10am–5pm; July & Aug Mon–Sat 9.30am–5.30pm; ☎01307/467876) is at 45 East High St, opposite the soaring steeple of the parish church. Numerous shops and bakers stock the famous **Forfar Bridie**, a semicircular folded pastry-case of mince, onion and seasonings, including Saddlers, a few doors down from the tourist office, and McLarens (the locals' favourite), at 8 West High St. Otherwise, all-day **food** and **drink** can be found at the *Royal Hotel* on Castle Street, by the Town Hall.

Glamis Castle

Bus #22 from Forfar runs regularly to Dundee via the pink sandstone **Glamis Castle** (mid-March to Oct daily 10am–6pm, last tour 4.30pm, Nov & Dec noon–4pm; £7, grounds only £3.50; ⓦwww.glamis-castle.co.uk), located a mile north of the picturesque village of **GLAMIS** (pronounced "glahms"). A wondrously over-the-top, L-shaped five-storey pile set in an extensive landscaped park complete with deer and pheasants, this is one of the most famous Scottish castles. Shakespeare chose it as a central location in *Macbeth*, and its **royal connections** (as the childhood home of the late Queen Mother and birthplace of Princess Margaret) make it one of the essential stops on every coach tour of Scotland, though for many visitors the Queen Mum gloss is laid on rather thick.

Approaching the castle down the long main drive, a riot of turrets, towers and conical roofs appears fantastically at the end of the sweeping avenue of trees, framed by the Grampian Mountains. The bulk of the current building dates from the fifteenth century, although many of the later additions (particularly from the seventeenth century) give it its startling Disneyesque appearance. Glamis began life as a comparatively humble hunting lodge, used in the eleventh century by the kings of Scotland. In 1372 King Robert II gave the property to his son-in-law, Sir John Lyon, who built the core of the present building. His descendants, the earls of Kinghorne and Strathmore, have lived here ever since.

△ Glamis Castle

Obligatory guided tours take visitors through the Victorian **Dining Room**, notable for its fine rose-and-thistle ceiling, then through a door in the wood panelling to the fifteenth-century **Crypt**, where the atmosphere changes dramatically. As the Lower Hall of the original tower house, the crypt's 12ft-thick walls enclose a haunted "lost" room, reputed to have been sealed with the red-bearded lord of Glamis and Crawford (also known as Beardie Crawford) inside, after he dared to play cards with the Devil one Sabbath. From here, the tour passes up a seventeenth-century staircase, whose hollow central pillar provided a primitive system of central heating, into the arch-roofed **Drawing Room**, with delightful wedding-cake plasterwork (dated 1621), and then to the family **Chapel**, completed in 1688. Artist Jacob de Wet was commissioned to produce the frescoes from the family Bible, although his depictions of Christ wearing a hat and St Peter in a pair of glasses have raised eyebrows ever since. The chapel is said to be haunted by the spectre of a grey lady, the ghost of the sixth Lady Glamis who was burnt as a witch on the order of James V. **King Malcolm's Room**, so called because it is believed he died nearby in 1034, is most notable for its carved wooden chimneypiece, on which many of the most decorative panels are made from highly polished leather.

From here, the tour passes into the **Royal Apartments**, where you can see the Queen Mother's delicate gilt four-poster bed, to **Duncan's Hall**, a fifteenth-century guardroom, the traditional – but inaccurate – setting for Duncan's murder by Macbeth (it actually took place near Elgin). The tour concludes with a random display of family artefacts that include the Queen Mother's old dolls' house.

Glamis' **grounds** are worth a few hours in their own right, holding lead statues of James VI and Charles I at the top of the main drive, a seventeenth-century Baroque sundial, a formal Italian garden and verdant walks out to Earl John's Bridge and through the woodland. In Glamis village, on the edge of the castle's grounds, the humble **Angus Folk Museum** (April–June & Sept Fri–Tues noon–5pm, Sun 1–5pm; July & Aug Mon–Sat 11am–5pm, Sun 1–5pm; NTS; £5), housed in six low-slung cottages in Kirk Wynd, has a bewildering array of local ephemera, including bizarrely named agricultural implements, a nineteenth-century horse-drawn hearse and a section on local bothies.

Aberlemno

Five miles east of Forfar, straddling the ridge-topping B9134, the hamlet of **ABERLEMNO** is home to a superb collection of open-air Pictish stones, unfortunately boxed out of sight in winter (Oct–April) in weatherproofed wood. In the churchyard, just off the main road, an eighth-century cross slab combines a swirling Christian Celtic cross with Pictish beasts on one side and an elaborate Pictish battle scene on the other, thought to commemorate victory over the Northumbrians in 685. Three other stones, bristling with Pictish and early Christian symbols, sit by the main road, overlooking huge sweeps of valley and mountain, though plans are afoot to move all the stones to a nearby indoor location to prevent further erosion. The Forfar–Brechin **bus** #21A stops in Aberlemno.

Kirriemuir and glens Prosen, Clova and Doll

The sandstone town of **KIRRIEMUIR**, known locally as Kirrie, is set on a hill six miles northwest of Forfar on the cusp of glens Clova and Prosen. Despite the influx of hunters up for the "season", it's still a pretty special place, a haphazard confection of narrow closes, twisting wynds and steep braes. The main cluster of streets have all the appeal of an old film set, with their old-fashioned bars, tiled butcher's shop, tartan outlets and haberdasheries somehow managing to avoid being contrived and quaint – although the recent recobbling of the town centre around a twee statue of Peter Pan undermines this somewhat.

Peter Pan's presence is justified, however, since Kirrie was the birthplace of his creator, **J.M. Barrie**. A local handloom-weaver's son, Barrie first came to notice with his series of novels about "Thrums", a village based on his home town, in particular *A Window in Thrums* and his third novel, *The Little Minister*. The story of Peter Pan, the little boy who never grew up, was penned by Barrie in 1904 – some say as a response to a strange upbringing dominated by the memory of his older brother, who died as a child. **Barrie's birthplace**, a plain little white-washed cottage at 9 Brechin Rd (April–June & Sept Sat–Wed noon–5pm; July & Aug Mon–Sat 11am–5pm, Sun 1–5pm; NTS; £5, includes entrance to the camera obscura), has been opened up as a visitor attraction, with a series of small rooms decorated as they would have been during Barrie's childhood, as well as displays about his life and works. The wash house outside – romantically billed as Barrie's first "theatre" – was apparently the model for the house built by the Lost Boys for Wendy in Never-Never Land. Despite being offered a prestigious plot at London's Westminster Abbey, Barrie chose to be buried in Kirrie, and the unassuming family grave can be seen in the town cemetery, a short walk from the **camera obscura** cricket pavilion (April–Sept daily noon–5pm depending on weather conditions; NTS; £3.50, or £5 combined ticket with Barrie's Birthplace), in the old cricket pavilion above town just off West Hill Road. This unexpected treasure was donated to the town in 1930 by Barrie, and offers splendid views of Strathmore and the glens. Another local son who attracts a handful of rather different pilgrims is **Bon Scott** of the rock band AC/DC, who was born and lived here before emigrating to Australia.

More on Scott, as well as other notable residents of the town, can be found Kirriemuir's **Gateway to the Glens Museum** (Mon–Wed, Fri & Sat 10am–5pm, Thurs 1–5pm; free), in the old Town House on the main square. The oldest building in Kirrie, it has seen service as a tolbooth, court, jail, post office, police station and chemist; these days you can find two floors of information and exhibits on the town and the Angus Glens, including scale models of Kirrie in 1604, the year the tolbooth was erected, and one of Glen Clova, showing the relief of the hills.

Kirrie's helpful **tourist office** is in Cumberland Close (July & Aug Mon–Sat 9.30am–5.30pm; April–June & Sept Mon–Sat 10am–5pm; ☎01575/574097), in the new development behind *Visocchi's* in the main square. **Accommodation** is available at the attractively upgraded *Airlie Arms*, St Malcolm's Wynd (☎01575/572847, ⓦwww.airliearms-hotel.co.uk; ❹), while on the edge of town, and offering a taste of the rolling countryside, is the working *Muirhouses Farm* (☎01575/573128, ⓦwww.muirhousesfarm.co.uk; ❸). *Visocchi's* is great for daytime **snacks** and ice cream, while the *Airlie* and *Hook's Hotel* on Bank Street both serve good food in the evening. Of the **pubs**, *Hook's Hotel* or, opposite the museum, *Three, Bellies Brae*, are the most lively.

Postbuses into glens Clova and Prosen leave from the main post office on Reform Street at 8.30am (not Sun). A second Glen Clova bus leaves at 3.10pm (Mon–Fri), but only goes as far as Clova village before returning to Kirriemuir. The hourly #20 bus runs from Kirriemuir High Street to Forfar and Dundee.

Glen Prosen

Five miles north of Kirrie, the low-key hamlet of **DYKEHEAD** marks the point where **Glen Prosen** and Glen Clova divide. A mile or so up Glen Prosen, you'll find the house where Captain Scott and fellow explorer Doctor Wilson planned their ill-fated trip to Antarctica in 1910–11, with a roadside **stone cairn** commemorating the expedition. From here on, Glen Prosen remains essentially a quiet wooded backwater, with all the wild and rugged splendour of the other glens but without the crowds. To explore the area thoroughly you need to go on foot, but a good road circuit can be made by crossing the river at the tiny village of **GLENPROSEN** and returning to Kirriemuir along the western side of the glen via Pearsie. Alternatively, the reasonably easy four-mile **Minister's Path** (so called because the local minister would walk this way twice every Sunday to conduct services) links Prosen with Clova. It is clearly marked and leaves from near the church in the village.

Glen Clova and Glen Doll

With its stunning cliffs, heather slopes and valley meadows, **Glen Clova** – which in the north becomes **Glen Doll** – is one of the loveliest of the Angus glens. Although it can get unpleasantly congested in peak season, the area is still remote enough to enable you to leave the crowds with little effort. Wildlife is abundant, with deer on the mountains, wild hares and even grouse and the occasional buzzard. The meadow flowers on the valley floor and arctic plants (including great splashes of white and purple saxifrage) on the rocks also make it something of a botanist's paradise.

Walks from Glen Doll

Ordnance Survey Explorer Maps nos. 388 & 387.
These **walks** are some of the main routes across the Grampians from the Angus glens to Deeside, many of which follow well-established old drovers' roads. A number of them cross the royal estate of Balmoral, and Prince Charles's favourite mountain – **Lochnagar** – can be seen from all angles. The walks all begin from the car park at the end of the tarred road where Glen Clova meets Glen Doll; all routes should always be approached with care, and you should make sure to follow the usual safety precautions.

Capel Mounth to Ballater (15 miles; 7hr). Head across the bridge from the car park turning right after a mile when the track crosses the Cald Burn. Out of the wood, the path zigzags its way up fierce slopes before levelling out on the moorland plateau. Soon descending, the path crosses a scree near the eastern end of Loch Muick. With the loch to your left, walk down along the scree till you reach the River Muick, crossing the bridge to take the quiet track along the river's northern bank to Ballater.

Capel Mounth round-trip (15 miles; 8hr). Follow the above route to Loch Muick, then take the path down to loch level and double back on yourself along the loch's southern shore. When the track crosses the Black Burn, either take the steep left fork or continue along the shore for another mile, heading up the dramatic Streak of Lightning path that follows Corrie Chash. Both paths meet at the ruined stables below Sandy Hillock. Just beyond, take the path to the left, descending rapidly to the waterfall by the bridge at Bachnagairn, where a gentle burn-side track leads the three miles back to Glen Doll car park.

Jock's Road to Braemar (14 miles; 7hr). Take the road north from the car park; after almost a mile, follow the signposted Jock's Road to the right, keeping on the northern bank of the burn. Pass a barn, Davey's Shelter, below Cairn Lunkhard and continue onto a wide ridge towards the path's summit at Crow Craigies (3018ft). From here, the path bumps down over scree slopes to the head of Loch Callater. Go either way round the loch, and follow the Callater Burn at the other end, eventually hitting the main A93 two miles short of Braemar.

The B955 from Dykehead and Kirriemuir divides at the Gella bridge over the swift-coursing River South Esk (unofficially, road traffic is encouraged to use the western branch of the road for travel up the glen, and the eastern side going down). Six miles north of Gella, the two branches of the road join up once more at the hamlet of **CLOVA**, little more than the hearty *Glen Clova Hotel* (☎01575/550350, ⓦwww.clova.com; ❺), which also has a refurbished bunkhouse (£11 per night) and a private fishing loch. Meals and real ale are available in the lively *Climbers' Bar* at the side of the hotel. An excellent, if fairly strenuous, four-hour walk from behind the old school at the back of the hotel leads up into the mountains and around the lip of **Loch Brandy**, which legend predicts will one day flood and drown the valley below.

North from Clova village, the road turns into a rabbit-infested lane coursing along the riverside for four miles to the car park, a useful starting point for numerous superb **walks** (see box on p.513). There are, however, no other facilities following the recent closure of both the campsite and SYHA hostel.

Brechin

Twelve miles or so northeast of Kirriemuir, **BRECHIN** is an attractive, confident town whose red sandstone buildings give it a warm, welcoming feel. The chief attraction is the old **Cathedral** on Bishop's Close, off the High Street. There's been a religious building of sorts here since the arrival of evangelizing Irish missionaries in 900 AD, and the red sandstone structure has become something of a hotchpotch of architectural styles. What you see today chiefly dates from an extensive rebuilding in 1900, with the oldest surviving part of the cathedral being the 106-foot round tower, one of only two in Scotland. The cathedral's doorway, built 6ft above the ground for protection against Viking raids, has some notable carvings, while inside you can see various Pictish stones, illuminated by the jewel-coloured stained-glass windows. Also in town, just off St Ninian Square, is the train station of the **Caledonian Railway** (talking timetable ☎01356/622992; information line ☎01561/377760, ⓦwww.caledonianrailway.co.uk), which operates steam trains on summer Sundays (as well as some Saturdays and bank holidays) along four miles of track from Brechin to the Bridge of Dun.

A mile from the town centre along the Forfar road in the Brechin Castle Park is **Pictavia** (April–Sept Mon–Sat 9.30am–5.30pm, Sun 10.30am–5.30pm; Oct–March Mon–Sat 9am–5pm, Sun 10am–5pm; £3.25; ⓦwww.pictavia.org.uk), a custom-built tourist attraction rather incongruously tacked onto a garden centre. Based on the history and heritage of the Picts, you'll find a typical modern blend of sound-and-light entertainments and distinctively designed displays, along with a handful of Pictish stones and fibreglass casts of stones. Overall, it's a bit lacking in substance, and is missing the slightly mystical atmosphere you can find at stones out in the wild in places such as nearby Aberlemno (see p.511) and throughout the northeast.

There is a **tourist office** desk at Pictavia (same hours; ☎01356/623050). Brechin is on main **transport** routes: bus #30 runs hourly to Montrose, nine miles east, and it's also served by regular Citylink coaches between Dundee and Aberdeen.

Edzell and Glen Esk

Travelling around Angus, you can hardly fail to notice the difference between organic settlements and planned towns built by landowners who forcibly rehoused local people in order to keep them under control, especially after the Jacobite uprisings. One of the better examples of the latter, **EDZELL**, five miles north of Brechin on the B966 (and linked to it by buses #21, #29C and #30), was cleared and rebuilt with Victorian rectitude a mile to the west of its original site in the 1840s. Through the Dalhousie Arch at the entrance to the village the long, wide and ruler-straight main street is lined with prim nineteenth-century buildings, now doing a roaring trade as genteel teashops and antiques emporia.

The original village (identifiable from the cemetery and surrounding grassy mounds) lay immediately to the west of the wonderfully explorable red sandstone ruins of **Edzell Castle** (April–Sept daily 9.30am–6.30pm; Oct–March Sun–Wed 9.30am–4.30pm; HS; £3.30), itself a mile west of the planned village. The main part of the old castle is a good example of a comfortable tower house, whose main priority became luxurious living rather than defence, with some intricate decorative corbelling on the roof, a vast fireplace in the first-floor hall and numerous telltale signs of building from different ages. However it's the **pleasance garden** overlooked by the castle tower that makes a visit to Edzell essential, especially in late spring and early to mid-summer. The garden was built by Sir David Lindsay in 1604, at the height of the optimistic Renaissance, and its refinement and extravagance are evident. The walls contain sculpted images of erudition: the Planetary Deities on the east side, the Liberal Arts (including a decapitated figure of Music) on the south and, under floods of lobelia, the Cardinal Virtues on the west wall. In the centre of the garden, low-cut box hedges spell out the family mottoes and enclose voluminous beds of roses.

Four miles southwest of Edzell, lying either side of the lane to Bridgend which can be reached either by carrying on along the road past the castle or by taking the narrow road at the southern end of Edzell village, are the **Caterthuns**, twin Iron Age hill forts that were probably occupied at different times. The surviving ramparts on the White Caterthun (978ft) – easily reached from the small car park below – are the most impressive, and this is thought to be the later fort, occupied by the Picts in the first few centuries AD. Views from both, over the mountains to the north and the plains and foothills to the south, are stunning.

Just north of Edzell, a fifteen-mile road climbs alongside the River North Esk to form **Glen Esk**, the most easterly of the Angus glens and, like the others, sparsely populated. Ten miles along the Glen, the excellent **Glenesk Folk Museum** (Easter–May Sat & Sun noon–6pm; June to mid-Oct daily noon–6pm; £2; entry arrangements subject to change once refurbishment is completed), brings together records, costumes, photographs, maps and tools from the Angus glens, depicting the often harsh way of life for the inhabitants. The museum is housed in a recently redeveloped shooting lodge known as The Retreat, and is run independently and enthusiastically by the local community. Inside there's also a gift shop and a noted tearoom – due reward for those who have endured the winding glen road. There are some excellent **hiking** routes further up the glen, including one to Queen Victoria's Well in Glen Mark and another up Mount Keen, Scotland's most easterly Munro.

In Edzell, *Alexandra Lodge*, Inveriscandye Road (T01356/648266, Wwww .alexandralodge.co.uk; April–Oct; ❸) is a decent **B&B**, while the most attractive of the **hotels** in town, the *Panmure Arms* (T01356/648950, Wwww .panmurearmshotel.co.uk; ❺), at the far end of the main street near the turn-off to the castle, has recently been smartened up and offers sizeable rooms and predictable bar meals. Further up the glen, one and a half miles north of the village, you can **camp** at the small, child-friendly *Glenesk Caravan Park* (☎01356/648565; April–Oct), while at **INVERMARK**, near the head of the Glen and a good jumping-off point for various hiking routes, is *The House of Mark* (☎01356/670315, ⓦwww.thehouseofmark.com; ➌), a former manse in a lovely setting, which can arrange evening meals featuring local game and home baking.

Aberdeenshire and Moray

Aberdeenshire and Moray cover a large chunk of northern Scotland – some 3500 square miles, much of it open and varied country dotted with historic and archeological sights, from neat NTS properties and eerie prehistoric rings of standing stones to quiet kirkyards and a rash of dramatic castles. Geographically, the counties break down into two distinct areas: the **hinterland**, once barren and now a patchwork of fertile farms, rising towards high mountains, sparkling rivers and gentle valleys; and the **coast**, a classic stretch of rocky cliffs, remote fishing villages and long, sandy beaches.

For visitors, the large city of **Aberdeen** is the obvious focal point of the region, and while it's not a place to keep you engrossed for long, it does boast some intriguing architecture, attractive museums and a lively social scene. From here, it's a short hop west to **Deeside**, annually visited by the Royal Family, where the trim villages of **Ballater** and **Braemar** act as a gateway to the spectacular mountain scenery of the Cairngorms National Park, which covers much of the upland areas in the west of this region. To the north lies the meandering **Don Valley**, a quiet area notable for **castles** such as Kildrummy and Corgarff, both situated in appealingly remote scenery. Further north, the dramatic **coast** is punctuated by picturesque fishing villages left almost unchanged by the centuries, and there's a handful of engaging sights including **Duff House**, an outpost of the National Galleries of Scotland, and the New Age community at **Findhorn**.

Aberdeen has an **airport**, and **trains** to Inverness and major points further south. **Buses** in the hinterland can be few and far between, often running on schooldays only, but the main centres are well served. By car, signposted **trails** set up by the tourist board make navigation around the northeast coast and castles a bit easier.

Aberdeen

The third-largest city in Scotland, **ABERDEEN** (ⓦwww.aberdeen-grampian .com), commonly known as the Granite City, lies 120 miles northeast of Edinburgh on the banks of the rivers Dee and Don, smack in the middle of the northeast coast. Based around a working harbour, it's a place that people either love or hate. Lewis Grassic Gibbon, one of the northeast's most eminent novelists, summed it up: "One detests Aberdeen with the detestation of a thwarted

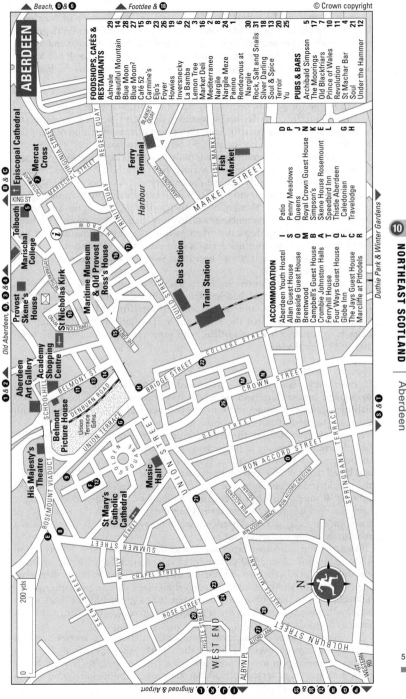

lover. It is the one hauntingly and exasperatingly lovable city of Scotland."
Certainly, while some extol the many tones and colours of Aberdeen's **granite**
buildings, others see only uniform grey and find the city grim, cold and unwelcoming. The weather doesn't help: Aberdeen lies on a latitude north of Moscow
and the cutting wind and driving rain (even if it does transform the buildings
into sparkling silver) can be tiresome.

Since the 1970s, **oil** has made Aberdeen a hugely wealthy and self-confident
place. Despite (or perhaps because of) this, it can seem a soulless city; there's a
feeling of corporate sterility and sometimes, despite its long history, Aberdeen
seems to exist only as a departure point for the transient population of some ten
to fifteen thousand who live on the 130 oil platforms out to sea.

That said, Aberdeen's **architecture** is undeniably striking – a granite cityscape
created in the nineteenth century by three fine architects: Archibald Simpson
and John Smith in the early years of the century and, subsequently, A. Marshall
Mackenzie. Classical inspiration and Gothic Revival styles predominate, giving
grace to a material once thought of as only good enough for tombs and paving
stones. In addition, it sometimes seems like every spare inch of ground has been
turned into **flower gardens**, the urban parks being some of the most beautiful in Britain. This positive floral explosion – Aberdeen was once barred from
"Britain in Bloom" competitions because it won too often – certainly cheers
up the general greyness.

Staying in such a prosperous place has its advantages. There are some
reasonable restaurants and hotels while certain sights, including Aberdeen's
splendid **Art Gallery** and the excellent **Maritime Museum**, are free.
Furthermore, the fact that the city is the bright light in a wide hinterland
helps it to sustain a lively **nightlife**, with some decent pubs and a colourful
arts and cultural scene.

Some history

In the twelfth century, Alexander I noted "Aberdon" as one of his principal
towns, and by the thirteenth century it had become a centre for **trade and
fishing**, a jumble of timber and wattle houses perched on three small hills, with
the castle to the east and St Nicholas's kirk outside the gates to the west.

It was here that **Robert the Bruce** sought refuge during the Scottish Wars
of Independence, leading to the garrison of the castle by Edward I and Balliol's
supporters. In a night-time raid in 1306, the townspeople attacked the garrison
and killed them all, an event commemorated by the city's motto "Bon Accord",
the watchword for the night. The victory was not to last, however, and in 1337
Edward III stormed the city, forcing its rebuilding on a grander scale. A century
later Bishop Elphinstone founded the Catholic university in the area north of
town known today as **Old Aberdeen**, while the rest of the city developed as a
mercantile centre and important port.

Industrial and economic expansion led to the Aberdeen New Streets Act in
1800, setting off a hectic half-century of development that almost led to financial disaster. Luckily, the city was rescued by a boom in trade: in the **shipyards**
the construction of Aberdeen clippers revolutionized sea transport, giving Britain supremacy in the China tea trade, and in 1882 a group of local businessmen
acquired a **steam** tugboat for trawl fishing. Sail gave way to steam, and fisher
families flooded in.

By the mid-twentieth century, Aberdeen's traditional industries were in
decline, but the discovery of **oil** in the North Sea transformed the place
from a depressed port into a boom town (see box on opposite). The oil-borne
prosperity may have served to mask the thinness of the region's other wealth

When **oil** was discovered in BP's Forties Field in 1970, Aberdonians rightly viewed it as a massive financial opportunity, and – despite fierce competition from other British ports, Scandinavia and Germany – the city succeeded in persuading the oil companies to base their headquarters here. Land was made available for housing and industry, millions were invested in the harbour and offshore developments, new schools opened and the airport expanded to include a heliport, which has since become the busiest in the world.

The city's **population** swelled by sixty thousand, and earnings escalated from fifteen percent below the national average to a figure well above it. Wealthy oil companies built prestigious offices, swish new restaurants, upmarket bars and shops. At the peak of production in the **mid-1980s**, 2.6 million barrels a day were being turned out, and the price had reached $80 a barrel. The effect of the 1986 slump – when oil prices dropped to $10 a barrel – was devastating: jobs vanished at the rate of a thousand a month, house prices dropped and Aberdeen soon discovered just how dependent on oil it was. The moment oil prices began to rise, crisis struck again with the loss of 167 lives when the **Piper Alpha oil rig** exploded, precipitating an array of much-needed but very expensive safety measures.

In recent years production levels have risen back up, though with assurances that this time the dangers of boom-and-bust policies have been heeded. Oil remains the cornerstone of Aberdeen's economy, keeping unemployment down to one of the lowest levels in Britain and driving up house prices in the city itself and an increasingly wide area of its rural hinterland. Predictions of the imminent decline in oil reserves and the end of Aberdeen's economic boom are heard frequently, but reliable indicators suggest that the black gold will be flowing well into the new millennium. Even so, business leaders are already looking to refocus existing expertise and make Aberdeen just as famous for the new game in town – renewable energy.

10

NORTHEAST SCOTLAND | Aberdeen

creators, but it has nonetheless allowed Aberdeen to hold its own as a cultural and academic centre and as a focus of the northeast's identity.

Arrival, information and city transport

Aberdeen's Dyce **airport**, seven miles northwest of town, is served by flights from most parts of the UK and a few European cities. Buses #10, #27, #307 and #737 all run to the city centre; a taxi costs £12–15. The main **train station** is on Guild Street, in the centre of the city (℡0845/748 4950), with the **bus** terminal right beside it (general route information ℡0870/608 2608; intercity buses ℡0870/550 5050 or ℡0870/580 8080).

Aberdeen is also linked to Lerwick in Shetland and Kickwall in Orkney by **ferry**, with regular crossings from Jamieson's Quay in the harbour; see p.727 for details.

Information

From the train and bus station it's a five-minute uphill walk to Union Street, Aberdeen's main thoroughfare. The **tourist office**, 23 Union St, is at the east end (July–Aug Mon–Sat 9am–6.30pm, Sun 10am–4pm; April–June & Sept–Oct Mon–Sat 9am–5.30pm; rest of year Mon–Sat 9am–4.30pm; ℡01224/288828). They'll book accommodation for you, charging ten percent of the stay plus a £3 booking fee, while Internet access is also available.

The tourist office also hands out the *What's On* leaflet, with details of upcoming events, art exhibitions and theatre. The local newspapers, the morning *Press and Journal* and the *Evening Express*, are both good for cinema and what's on that day. More esoteric information – anything from t'ai chi workshops to ceilidhs – is in the glossy bimonthly programme produced by the Lemon Tree, 5 West North St (℡01224/642230, ⓦwww.lemontree.org), a vibrant arts centre which serves as the city's cultural hub. For details of local gigs, consult ⓦwww.aberdeen-music.com.

City transport and tours

Aberdeen's centre is best explored on foot, but you might need to use **buses**, most of which pass along Union Street, to reach some sights. An all-day ticket covering all city routes costs £2.70 (£2.40 after 9.30am on weekdays), and you can get a weekly pass for £13. If you plan to use the buses a lot, you can buy a **Farecard** (in £5, £10 or £20 denominations) from the depot at 395 King St, branches of newsagent RS McColl or the travel centre at 47 Union St, which also hands out London Underground-style transport **maps**; each time you travel the fare is deducted from the card. Late-night services on Friday and Saturday – the last leaving at 3.15am – cost a flat fare of £2.10, and head to six separate destinations on the city's outskirts. For information on city bus services, call the Busline (℡01224/650065).

Taxis operate from ranks throughout the city centre, all of which attract long queues after the pubs and clubs empty at the weekend. If you don't manage to hail one, call ComCab (℡01224/353535).

Accommodation

As befits a high-flying business city, Aberdeen has a large choice of **accommodation** – much of it is characterless and expensive. Predictably, the best budget options are the **B&Bs** and **guesthouses**, many of which are strung along Bon Accord and Crown streets (served by buses #6 and #17 to and from Union Street), and Great Western Road (buses #18, #19 and #24). Cheapest of all are the **hostel** and **student halls** left vacant for visitors in the summer. The emphasis on business trade means weekday rates are often considerably more expensive than weekends; the price codes below are for the lowest rates quoted.

Hotels

Brentwood 101 Crown St ℡01224/595440, ⓦwww.brentwood-hotel.co.uk. Spick-and-span refurbished old hotel south of Union St. ❸

Ferryhill House 169 Bon Accord St ℡01224/590867, ⓦwww.ferryhillhousehotel.co.uk. A mansion set apart in its own grounds within walking distance of Union St. Its historic pub has real ale, a beer garden and decent food. ❸

Marcliffe at Pitfodels North Deeside Rd, Pitfodels ℡01224/861000, ⓦwww.marcliffe.com. Four miles west of the city centre, this forty-room hotel in its own grounds is by far the most luxurious and tasteful option in the area. There's a fine restaurant with a suitably upmarket ambience. ❼

Patio Beach Boulevard ℡01224/633339, ⓦwww.patiohotels.com. Business hotel near the beach with a pool, gym and all the familiar trappings of a chain hotel. ❺

Queens 49–53 Queens Rd ℡01224/209999, ⓦwww.the-queens-hotel.com. Cheerful medium-sized city-centre hotel, with a good culinary reputation. ❸

Simpson's 59–63 Queens Rd ℡01224/327777, ⓦwww.simpsonshotel.co.uk. Style-conscious boutique hotel in a former granite terrace house, with an excellent brasserie and good weekend rates. ❻

Speedbird Inn Argyll Rd, Dyce ℡01224/772884, ⓦwww.speedbirdinns.co.uk. Large, modern chain hotel at the airport. ❷

Thistle Aberdeen Caledonian 10–14 Union Terrace ℡01224/640233, ⓦwww.thistlehotels.com. Posh hotel in an impressive Victorian edifice just off Union St. ❺

Travelodge 9 Bridge St ℡01224/584555, ⓦwww.travelodge.co.uk. Typically bland budget option – but you can't beat the convenient location, right next to Union St and minutes from the stations. ❹

Guesthouses and B&Bs

Allan Guest House 56 Polmuir Rd
☏01224/584484, ⓦwww.theallan.co.uk. Tasteful and enthusiastically run guesthouse not far from Duthie Park. Filling meals or a light supper available if arranged in advance. ❹

Braeside Guest House 68 Bon Accord St
☏01224/571471, ⓔcheynemcmenal@amserve .net. Standard but inexpensive B&B within easy walking distance of the stations and city centre. ❷

Campbell's Guest House 444 King St
☏01224/625444, ⓦwww.campbellsguesthouse .com. Standard rooms but highly recommended breakfasts. One mile from the city centre and handy for the beach and Old Aberdeen. ❷

Four Ways Guest House 435 Great Western Rd
☏01224/310218. A converted manse in the West End, usefully positioned near main roads out of the city. ❷

Globe Inn 13–15 North Silver St ☏01224/624258. Easygoing city-centre inn with seven en-suite rooms above a bar that hosts live jazz, blues and traditional music. Rate includes continental breakfast. ❷

The Jays Guest House 422 King St
☏01224/638295, ⓦwww.jaysguesthouse.co.uk.

Well-run, non-smoking place near Old Aberdeen and the university. ❹

Penny Meadow 189 Great Western Rd
☏01224/588037, ⓔfrances@pennymeadow .freeserve.co.uk. Friendly guesthouse a short walk from the city centre, with an immaculately kept back garden for guests. ❹

Royal Crown Guest House 111 Crown St
☏01224/586461, ⓦwww.royalcrown.co.uk. Comfortable guesthouse within walking distance of stations and Union St. Non-smoking. ❷

Hostel, campus and self-catering accommodation

Aberdeen Youth Hostel 8 Queens Rd ☏0870/004 1100, ⓦwww.syha.org.uk. Rather soulless hostel with dorms for four to sixteen. Doors close at 2am but you can arrange to get in later. Bus #14 or #15 from Union St.

Crombie Johnston Halls College Bounds, Old Aberdeen ☏01224/273444, ⓦwww.abdn.ac.uk /hospitality. Private rooms in the best student halls, in one of the most interesting parts of the city. Available from early July to Sept, though some year-round accommodation also available. ❶

Skene House Rosemount 96 Rosemount Viaduct ☏01224/645971, ⓦwww.skene-house.co.uk. Serviced apartments with one to three rooms, all with TVs. Good central location. ❹

The City

Aberdeen divides neatly into five main areas. The **city centre**, roughly bounded by Broad Street, Union Street, Schoolhill and Union Terrace, features the opulent **Marischal College**, the colonnaded **Art Gallery** with its fine collection, the burgeoning nightlife of Belmont Street, and homes that pre-date Aberdeen's nineteenth-century town planning and have been preserved as **museums**. Union Street leads west to the schism of gentrified shopping and raucous nightlife that defines the **West End**. To the south, the **harbour** still heaves with boats serving the fishing and oil industries, while north of the centre lies attractive **Old Aberdeen**, a village neighbourhood presided over by **King's College** and **St Machar's Cathedral** and influenced by the large student population. The long sandy **beach** with its esplanade development, only a mile or so from the heart of the city, marks Aberdeen's eastern border.

The city centre

The centre of Aberdeen is dominated by mile-long **Union Street**, still the grandest and most ambitious single thoroughfare in Scotland – although these days its impressive architecture is sometimes lost among the shoppers and chain stores. The key to the early nineteenth-century city planners who conceived the street was the building of the ambitious **Union Street bridge**, spanning two hills and the Denburn gorge. The first attempt, a triple-span design by Glasgow architect David Hamilton, bankrupted the city and collapsed during construction. The famous Thomas Telford then proposed the single-arch structure that became an engineering wonder of its age. Since completion in 1805 the bridge has been widened twice, the second time, in 1963, adding a row of shops to the southern side which obscures the dramatic impact of the structure.

Castlegate and around

Any exploration of the **city centre** should begin at the open, cobbled **Castle-gate**, where Aberdeen's long-gone castle once stood. At its centre is the late seventeenth-century **Mercat Cross**, carved with a unique gallery of Stewart sovereigns alongside some fierce gargoyles. Castlegate was once the focus of city life but nowadays seems rather lifeless unless you dart along the easily missed lane to Peacock Visual Arts (℡01224/639539, Ⓦwww.peacockvisual arts.co.uk), at 21 Castle St, a hub for issue-based exhibitions often featuring rising international stars. The view up gently rising Union Street – a jumble of grey spires, turrets and jostling double-decker buses – is quintessential Aberdeen.

As Union Street begins you have to crane your neck to see the towering, turreted spire of the **Town House**, though the steely grey nineteenth-century exterior is in fact a facade behind which lurks the early seventeenth-century **Tolbooth** (July–Sept Tues–Sat 10am–4pm, Sun 12.30–3.30pm; phone for opening times during the rest of the year; free; ℡01224/621167), one of the city's oldest buildings. A jail for centuries, the Tolbooth now houses a museum of crime and imprisonment. Its steep and narrow staircase – there's no lift – means visits are not recommended to those with limited mobility.

Nearby, on King Street, the sandstone **St Andrew's Episcopal Cathedral** (mid-May to mid-Sept Mon–Sat 11am–4pm; free), where Samuel Seabury, America's first bishop, was ordained in 1784, offers welcome relief from the uniform granite. Inside, spartan whiteness is broken by florid gold ceiling bosses representing the (then) 48 states of the USA and 48 local families who remained loyal to the Episcopal Church during the eighteenth-century Penal Laws. Even more resplendent is the gilded baldachino canopy over the High Altar and the brightly coloured Seabury Centenary window in the Suther Chapel.

Heading west, Union Street brings you to Broad Street where, at 45 Guestrow, **Provost Skene's House** (Mon–Sat 10am–5pm, Sun 1–4pm; free) is Aberdeen's oldest-surviving private house, dating from 1545; it's hemmed in by ghastly modern office blocks which city planners have finally suggested knocking down. In the sixteenth century all the well-to-do houses in the area looked like this, with mellow stone and rounded turrets – yet it was only the intervention of the Queen Mother in 1938 which saved this sole survivor from demolition. The house is now a museum, with a costume gallery, archeological exhibits, period rooms and a café-bar. Don't miss the Painted Gallery, where a cycle of beautiful religious tempera paintings from the mid-seventeenth century show scenes from the life of Christ.

Marischal College and museum

On Broad Street stands Aberdeen's most imposing edifice, and the world's second-largest granite building after the Escorial in Madrid – exuberant **Marischal College**, whose tall, steely-grey pinnacled neo-Gothic facade is in absolute contrast to the hideously utilitarian concrete office blocks opposite. This spectacular building, with all its soaring, surging lines, has been painted and sketched more than any other in Aberdeen, and though not to everyone's taste – it was once described by a minor art historian as "a wedding cake covered in indigestible grey icing" – there's no escaping that it is a most extraordinary feat of sculpture. The college was founded in 1593 by the fourth Earl Mari-schal, and coexisted as a separate Protestant university from Catholic King's, just up the road, for over two centuries. It was long Aberdeen's boast to have as many universities as the whole of England, and it wasn't until 1860 that the two were united as the University of Aberdeen. In 1893, the central tower was more than doubled in height by A. Marshall Mackenzie and the profusion of spirelets added, though the facade, which fronts an earlier quadrangle designed by Archibald Simpson in 1837–41, was not completed until 1906.

Behind the tower, through the college entrance, the **Mitchell Hall**'s east window illustrates the history of the university in stained glass. You're unlikely to get a good view of this, however, since the university has all but moved from the college, and the building is largely closed to the public. What you can see is the **Marischal Museum** (Mon–Fri 10am–5pm, Sun 2–5pm; free) and its wealth of weird exhibits, many gathered by Victorian anthropologists and other collectors who roamed the world filling their luggage with objects. Sensitive to the cultural crassness this represents to modern tastes, the museum concentrates as much on the phenomenon of these collectors as what they brought back. But that's not to say that many exhibits – from a mummy case of a five-year-old Egyptian girl to a stomach-churning human foot preserved in brine – aren't intriguing. Look out too for a kayak, discovered off the coast of Aberdeen around 1700 with the preserved body of an Inuit fisherman inside. The "Encyclopaedia of the Northeast" – running alphabetically from Aberdeen through to Whisky – is an amusing and lively display pulling together the nature and character of this corner of Scotland.

St Nicholas Kirk

Between Upperkirkgate and Union Street stands **St Nicholas Kirk** (May–Sept Mon–Fri noon–4pm, Sat 1–3pm; Oct–April contact keyholder in church office; free; ☎01224/321451, ⓦwww.kirk-of-st-nicholas.org.uk). It's actually two churches in one, with a solid, central bell tower, from where the 48-bell carillon, the largest in Britain, regularly chimes. There's been a church here since 1157 or thereabouts, but as the largest kirk in Scotland it was severely damaged during the Reformation and divided into the West and the East Church, separated today by the transepts and crossing; only the north transept, known as Collinson's aisle, survives from the twelfth century. The Renaissance-style **West Church**, formerly the nave of St Nicholas, was designed in the mid-eighteenth century by James Gibbs, architect of St Martin in the Fields in London. The **East Church** was rebuilt over the groin-vaulted crypt of the restored fifteenth-century St Mary's Chapel (entered from Correction Wynd), which in the 1600s was a place to imprison witches: you can still see the iron rings to which they were chained. The green marble tombs and Baroque monuments of the large churchyard are an escape from bustling Union Street, popular with snacking workers and loafing teenagers.

The Aberdeen Art Gallery and around

A little further west up Schoolhill, Aberdeen's engrossing **Art Gallery** (Mon–Sat 10am–5pm, Sun 2–5pm; free) was purpose-built in 1884 to a Neoclassical design by Mackenzie. You enter via the airy **Centre Court**, dominated by Barbara Hepworth's central fountain and thick pillars running down from the upper balcony, each hewn from a different local marble. The walls highlight the policy of acquiring contemporary art, with British work to the fore, including one of Francis Bacon's *Pope* paintings – the artist was obsessed with this subject for some thirty years and the series is considered his most important work. Recent additions include the disturbing *Jesus is Condemned to Die*, part of a collaborative project between David Bailey and Damien Hirst based on

△ Centre Court, Aberdeen Art Gallery

the Stations of the Cross, and Kenny Hunter's *Feedback Loop*, a huge sculpted teenager created using propaganda posters from communist China. The **Side Court** contains *Jungled*, a garish, erotic spin on stained-glass windows by Gilbert and George, and works by YBAs (Young British Artists) gifted by the Saatchi collection, including Jordan Baseman's extraordinary *I Love You Still*, made from tree limbs and human hair. The **Memorial Court**, a calming, white-walled circular room under a skylit dome, serves as the city's principal war memorial. It also houses the Lord Provost's book of condolence for the 167 people who died in the 1988 Piper Alpha oil rig disaster.

The **upstairs** rooms house the main body of the gallery's painting collection. The permanent collection is occasionally moved around, and some rooms are given over to temporary exhibitions.

The sheer number of landscapes crowding the walls of **Room One** can be disconcerting, but closer inspection reveals a superb collection of Victorian narrative art. Pre-Raphaelite canvases by Rossetti and William Waterhouse are on display beside Queen Victoria's favourite painter, Aberdeen-born John Phillip (1817–67), so heavily influenced by Velázquez and Murillo that he became known as "Spanish Phillip"; look out for his anecdotal scenes of everyday Scottish life such as *The Scotch Fair* (1848) and *Baptism in Scotland* (1850). **Room Two** steps back in history, concentrating on eighteenth-century painters such as landscape artist Alexander Nasmyth and Scotland's famous portraitists, Henry Raeburn and Alan Ramsay.

Room Three and **Room Four** feature changing displays from the gallery's permanent collections, while **Room Six** and the adjoining balcony concentrate on British twentieth-century painting. Predictably popular is the Impressionist collection, including works by Boudin, Courbet, Sisley, Monet, Pissarro and a deliciously bright Renoir, *La Roche Guyon*. A fabulous, sinewy cast of a Rodin male torso is the sculptural highlight, and there's a Toulouse Lautrec sketch of fellow-artist Charles Conder. The strong connections between the French schools and the development of modernism in Scottish painting saw the emergence of the "Glasgow Boys" in the 1880s (see p.302), exemplified here by John Lavery's *The Tennis Party*. The Scottish Colourists are also in evidence: Peploe's *Landscape, Cassis* shows off his instinct for colour, with daringly angled foreground tree trunks in rich blue, chocolate and purple shadows. Superb works by British Impressionists and Modernists include Stanley Spencer's joyful portrait of the British seaside, *Southwold*, and Duncan Grant's *Back Window of Gordon Square*. You'll also find a good selection of modern Scottish artists, including Peter Howson and Joan Eardley, who captured the landscape around Catterline, a coastal village just south of Aberdeen, so memorably.

Opposite the gallery is a designer shopping arcade called **The Academy**, a gateway to Aberdeen's answer to a Bohemian quarter: cobbled Belmont and Little Belmont streets feature a number of the city's more interesting bars, shops and restaurants, and farmers' markets take place on the last Saturday of each month and some other dates. West of Belmont Street, across the Denburn gorge, spanned by the Union Bridge and Schoolhill viaduct, the sunken **Union Terrace Gardens** are a welcome relief from the hubbub of Union Street. From here there are views across to the three domes of the Central Library, St Mark's Church and His Majesty's Theatre, traditionally referred to as "Education, Salvation and Damnation". Outside the theatre stands a hulking statue of William "Braveheart" Wallace, erected in 1888. The crumbling red-brick spire at the other end of the viaduct tops **Triple Kirks**. Built in 1843 and one of Archibald Simpson's most famous creations, it was Scotland's only example of a single building hosting three churches for three denominations. Even so, developers are now advocating demolition.

The West End

The **West End**, the area around the westernmost part of Union Street, begins more or less at the great granite columns of the city's **Music Hall**. A block north is **Golden Square** – a misnomer, as the trim houses, pubs and restaurants surrounding the statue of the Duke of Gordon are uniformly grey. The city has invested much in gentrifying the area north of Union Street, resulting in neat cobbles, old-fashioned lamps, a growing restaurant scene and a string of somewhat stuffy designer boutiques around Thistle Street. Huntly Street, west of Golden Square, heads off towards the curiously thin spire of **St Mary's Catholic Cathedral** (Mon–Fri 8am–4pm, Sat 8am–8pm, Sun 8am–8.30pm), a typical example of Victorian Gothic church architecture.

To the south of Union Street, wedged between Bon Accord Street and Bon Accord Terrace, **Bon Accord Square** is a typical, charming Aberdeen square. A grassy centre surrounds a huge solid block of granite commemorating **Archibald Simpson**, architect of much of nineteenth-century Aberdeen. West of Bon Accord Terrace is Justice Mill Lane, a seedy area with a collection of rowdy bars and nightclubs.

The harbour

Old, cobbled Shiprow winds down from Castlegate at the east end of Union Street to the north side of the **harbour**. Just off this steep road, peering towards the harbour through a striking glass facade, is the **Maritime Museum** (Mon–Sat 10am–5pm, Sun noon–3pm; free), which combines a modern, airy museum with the aged labyrinthine corridors of **Provost Ross's House**. The museum is a thoroughly engrossing, imaginative tribute to Aberdeen's maritime traditions.

Just inside the front entrance you'll see blackboards, computer readouts and barometers showing everything from the time of high tide to the up-to-the-minute price of a barrel of crude oil. Suspended above the foyer and visible from five different levels is a spectacular 27ft-high model of an oil rig, which, along with terrific views over the bustling harbour, serves as a constant reminder that Aberdeen's maritime links remain very much alive. While large sections of the museum are devoted to North Sea oil and gas, the older industries of herring-fishing, whaling, shipbuilding and lighthouses also have their place, with well-designed displays and audiovisual presentations, many drawing heavily on personal reminiscences. Passages lead into Provost Ross's House, where intricate ship's models and a variety of nautical paintings and drawings are on display.

At the bottom of Shiprow the cobbles meet **Market Street**, which runs the length of the harbour. Brightly painted oil-supply ships, sleek cruise ships and peeling fishing boats jostle amid an ever-constant clatter and the screech of well-fed seagulls. With high fences, rushing traffic and a series of drab office blocks, it's not the most attractive part of the city, although you can encounter plenty of life and colour if you follow your nose to the **fish market**, off Market Street, best visited early (Mon–Fri opens 7.30am) when the place is in full swing. Be warned, however, that it's not set up for visitors and entry is not guaranteed. The current market building dates from 1982, but fish have been traded here for centuries: the earliest record, from 1281, shows that an envoy of Edward I was invoiced for 1000 barrels of sturgeon and 5000 salt fish.

At the north end of Market Street, Trinity Quay runs past industrial yards and down York Street towards **Footdee**, or Fittie (an easy walk or bus #14 or #15 from Union Street), a quaint nineteenth-century fishermen's village of higgledy-piggledy cottages backing onto the sea. Their windows and doors face inwards for protection from storms but also, so they say, to stop the devil sneaking in the back door. Here, in a great setting beside the lighthouse at the channel into the harbour, you'll find the *Silver Darling* (see p.528), one of the northeast's finest seafood restaurants.

From Market Street it's a twenty-minute walk or ten-minute bus ride (#6 from Market Street or #16 and #17 from Union Street) to **Duthie Park** (daily 9.30am–dusk; free), on the banks of the Dee at the end of Polmuir Road. The rose garden here, known as Rose Mountain due to its profusion of blooms, can be stunning in summer, but the real treat is the **Winter Gardens** (daily: April 9.30am–5.30pm; May–Sept 9.30am–7.30pm; Oct–March 9.30am–4.30pm; free), a steamy paradise of enormous cacti and exotic plants. Recently reintroduced outdoor concerts have also made the vintage bandstand a focal point. From the northwestern corner of Duthie Park, a great cycle and walkway, the **Old Deeside Railway Line**, heads west out of the city past numerous long-gone train stations.

Old Aberdeen

An independent burgh until 1891, tranquil **Old Aberdeen**, a ten-minute ride north of the city centre on bus #20 from Marischal College at Littlejohn Street, has maintained a village-like identity. Dominated by King's College and St Machar's Cathedral, its medieval cobbled streets, wynds and little lanes are beautifully preserved. Despite the tranquillity, the establishment of a single University of Aberdeen was a tempestuous affair. It finally came about in 1860 when Protestant Marischal College and sceptical King's College were merged, well over two hundred years after the first attempt. Rivalry between the two, though traditionally intense (and sometimes leading to well-charted brawls in the streets), has faded since all university functions other than graduation ceremonies were shifted from Marischal College.

The southern half of cobbled High Street is overlooked by **King's College Chapel** (Mon–Fri 8am–4pm; free), the first and finest of the college buildings, completed in 1495, with a chunky Renaissance spire. Named in honour of James IV, the chapel's west door is flanked by his coat of arms and that of his queen. It stands on the quadrangle, whose gracious buildings retain a medieval plan but were built much later; those immediately north were designed by Mackenzie early last century, with the exception of Cromwell Tower at the northeast corner, completed in 1658. The highlights of the interior, which, unusually, has no central aisle, are the ribbed arched wooden ceiling and the rare and beautiful examples of medieval Scottish woodcarving in the screen and the stalls. The remains of Bishop Elphinstone's tomb and the carved pulpit from nearby St Machar's are also here. From the college, High Street leads a short way north to **St Machar's Cathedral** on the leafy Chanonry (daily 9am–5pm, except during services; free; ☎01224/485988), overlooking Seaton Park and the River Don. The site was reputedly founded in 580 by Machar, a follower of Columba, when he was sent by the latter to find a grassy platform near the sea, overlooking a river shaped like the crook on a bishop's crozier. This setting fitted the bill perfectly, and the cathedral, a huge fifteenth-century fortified building, became one of the city's first great granite edifices. Inside, the stained-glass windows are a dazzling blaze of colour, and above the nave the heraldic oak ceiling from 1520 shows nearly fifty different coats of arms from Europe's royal houses and Scotland's bishops and nobles.

Also on the Chanonry, the **Cruickshank Botanic Gardens** (May–Sept Mon–Fri 9am–4.30pm, Sat & Sun 2–5pm; Oct–April irregular opening; free; ☎01224/272137), laid out in 1898, have pretty flowerbeds and lovely glimpses of the cathedral through the trees, but don't bother with the dreary zoological museum.

A wander through Seaton Park brings you to the thirteenth-century **Brig o'Balgownie**, which gracefully spans the River Don nearly a mile north of the cathedral. Still standing (despite Thomas the Rhymer's prediction that it would fall were it ever crossed by an only son riding a mare's only foal), the bridge is best visited at sunset; Byron, who spent much of his childhood in Aberdeen, remembered it as a favourite place. Across the bridge, at 79 Balgownie Rd, is a small museum celebrating **Thomas Blake Glover** (Mon–Fri, phone ☎01224/709303 to check hours in advance; £3), the "Scottish Samurai" who introduced railway locomotives to Japan, helped establish the Mitsubishi business empire and reputedly inspired Puccini's opera *Madame Butterfly*.

The beach

Aberdeen can surely claim to have the best sandy **beach** of all Britain's large cities. Less than a mile east of Union Street is a great two-mile sweep of clean sand, broken by groynes and lined all along with an esplanade, where most of the city's population seems to gather on sunny days. Towards the south is a concrete expanse of chain restaurants, a fairly tatty amusement park, a multiplex cinema and a vast leisure centre. Further north, most of the beach's hinterland is devoted to golf links. Bus #14 goes along the southern esplanade.

A little way inland, the city's old tram depot at 179 Constitution St, near the *Patio Hotel*, houses **Satrosphere** (Mon–Sun 10am–5pm; £5.50; ☎01224/640340, ⊚www.satrosphere.net), Aberdeen's entertaining and educational hands-on science exhibition aimed at kids.

Eating, drinking and nightlife

Aberdeen is not short of good **cafés** and **restaurants**, mostly around Union Street, though you'll find it pricier than elsewhere in northeast Scotland. Like most ports, Aberdeen caters for a transient population with a lot of disposable income and a desire to get drunk as quickly as possible. Although you'll find no shortage of loud, flashy **bars** catering to such needs, there are still a number of more traditional **pubs** which, though usually packed, are well worth a visit.

As far as **delicatessens** go, Terroir (℡01224/623262; Mon–Sat), at 22 Thistle St, is crammed with European and British produce unobtainable anywhere else in the city, while Mediterraneo, 40 St Andrew St (℡01224/639799; daily) has a good range of Italian and Spanish imports and surprisingly inexpensive takeaway sandwiches. Rocksalt and Snails, 40 St Swithin St (℡01224/200012; Mon–Sat) and the Market Deli, 39 Market St (℡01224/581297; Tues–Sat) are newer arrivals but are well located for Great Western Road's guesthouses and the city centre respectively.

Cafés and restaurants

Ashvale 44–48 Great Western Rd ℡01224 575842, ⓦwww.theashvale.co.uk. One of Scotland's finest, and biggest, fish-and-chip shops. Restaurant open daily until 11pm; takeaway until 1am. Inexpensive.

Beautiful Mountain 11 Belmont St 01224/645353. Welcoming daytime café and takeaway with staggering range of sandwiches, including ample vegetarian and organic options. Inexpensive.

Blue Moon 11 Holburn St ℡01224/589977, ⓦwww.bluemoon-aberdeen.com. The pick of Aberdeen's Indian restaurants: sleek surroundings and dozens of inventive dishes. A sister restaurant, *Blue Moon*[2] has opened at nearby 1 Alford Lane. Moderate.

Café 52 52 The Green ℡01224/590094, ⓦwww.cafe52.net Cosy, bohemian hangout by day that turns into a crowded restaurant by night, thanks to imaginative takes on popular dishes. Closed Sun evening and Mon daytime. Moderate.

Carmine's 32 Union Terrace ℡01224/624145. An Aberdeen institution, featuring an amazing three-course lunch menu of Italian staples for under a fiver. Also open early evening. Closed Sun. Inexpensive.

Eljo's 4 Rose St ℡01224/624626. Tiny café offering delicious tapas well into the evening (Mon lunchtime only) and welcome relief from the lunch-time hubbub of the west end of Union St. Lunch-time takeaways. Closed Sun. Inexpensive.

Foyer 82a Crown St ℡01224/582277, ⓦwww.foyerrestaurant.com. Top-notch contemporary bistro in a tastefully converted church, acting as commercial arm of a charity for disadvantaged young people and the homeless. Moderate.

Howies 50 Chapel St ℡01224/639500. Aberdeen outpost of an Edinburgh institution, serving modern Scottish cooking in a wecloming environment. Well-priced set meals and house wine. Moderate.

Inversnecky Beach Esplanade. Still the best beach café, despite the imposing chains nearby; great for hangover breakfasts and ice cream. Inexpensive.

La Bamba 21 Crown Terrace ℡01224/590088, ⓦwww.labamba.biz. Boisterous and unpretentious Mexican restaurant. There's a good selection of Asian eateries on the same side street. Moderate.

Lemon Tree 5 West North St ℡01224/621610, ⓦwwwlemontree.org/café. Easygoing daytime café inside the arts venue, serving snacks and meals – including good vegetarian and vegan options – to live music. Open Thurs–Sun. Inexpensive.

Nargile 77–79 Skene St ℡01224/636093. Much loved family-run Turkish restaurant. Closed Sun, although the newer west end sister restaurant in Forest Avenue, *Rendezvous at Nargile*, and the informal *Nargile Meze Bar* on Rose Street are open seven days. Moderate.

Panino 281 George St ℡01224/620116. Authentic Italian restaurant whose fresh pasta dishes change each week and ensure it's always busy, despite being in a neglected part of the city. Open daytime only Mon–Wed, closed Sun. Moderate.

Silver Darling Pocra Quay, North Pier ℡01224/576229. Attractively located at the harbour in Footdee, this impressive restaurant majors in sophisticated French seafood dishes. Closed Sat lunch & Sun. Expensive.

Soul & Spice 15–17 Belmont St ℡01224/645200. Entertaining and colourful café serving up fantastic African and Caribbean dishes. Open evenings Tues–Sat and lunchtime Sat. Moderate.

Yu 347 Union St ℡01224/580318, ⓦwww.yurestaurant.co.uk. Decent, central Chinese with good fish dishes. Moderate.

Pubs and bars

Archibald Simpson 5 Castle St. J.D. Wetherspoon chain-pub on the corner of Union St, an extravagant, ornate interior and plenty of economical food and drink.

The Moorings 2 Trinity Quay. A well-kept secret on Aberdeen's pub scene, this apparently typical harbourside drinking den hosts a friendly, alternative crowd, sipping absinthe and unusual ciders to the sounds of a rock-oriented jukebox.

Old Blackfriars 52 Castle St. A genuinely traditional pub that puts ersatz copyists to shame: cosy interior, great selection of beers and pub grub and a constant buzz of conversation.

Prince of Wales 7 St Nicholas Lane. The quintessential Aberdeen pub with a long bar and flagstone floor. With fine pub grub, renowned real ales and a Sunday evening folk session, it's little wonder that it's often crowded.

Revolution 25 Belmont St. Stylish bar with explosive cocktails and a perfect understanding of the vagaries of Scottish weather – there's a fire and comfy sofas as you go in, and rooftop alfresco drinking out back.

St Machar Bar 97 High St, Old Aberdeen. The medieval quarter's only pub, a poky, old-fashioned bar attracting an intriguing mix of King's College students and workers.

Soul Langstane Kirk, Union St. Affectedly trendy, but this converted church is one of the places to be seen in Aberdeen. The outdoor terrace is thronged during outbreaks of sun.

Under the Hammer 11 North Silver St. This snug little basement wine bar with a continental vibe is a popular refuge when icy winter winds hit the city.

Nightlife, live music and entertainment

A number of **nightlife** venues feature regular jazz, folk and rock **music sessions**, while the Lemon Tree Arts Centre has as good a selection of touring theatre, bands and workshops as anywhere of its size in Scotland. Don't expect too much from the city's **clubs**, though you'll find them lively at weekends. You can buy tickets for most events at Aberdeen's **theatres** and **concert halls** from the box office beside the Music Hall on Union Street (Mon–Sat 9.30am–6pm; ☎01224/641122).

Clubs, live music venues and concert halls

Aberdeen Exhibition and Conference Centre Off Ellon Rd at Bridge of Don ☎01224/824824, ⓦwww.aecc.co.uk. Huge hall hosting the biggest rock and pop acts.

The Blue Lamp 121 Gallowgate ☎01224/647472. A spacious bar featuring live bands, usually at weekends, and a Monday folk session; there's also a much smaller snug for relative peace and quiet.

Cowdray Hall Schoolhill ☎01224/523700. Classical music venue, often with visiting orchestras.

Drummonds 1 Belmont St. Unapologetically murky bar, providing a welcome contrast to more glossy neighbours, that has undergone a renaissance since putting the emphasis back onto live music; the intimate stage attracts upcoming talent and the occasional big name.

The Globe Inn 13–15 North Silver St ☎01224/624258. Pleasant city-centre inn with jamming sessions on Tuesdays and live jazz, blues and covers bands Thurs–Sun.

Lemon Tree 5 West North St ☎01224/642230, ⓦwww.lemontree.org. The fulcrum of the city's arts scene, with a great buzz and regular live music, club nights and comedy.

Music Hall Union St ☎01224/641122. Big-name comedy and music acts.

The Priory St Nicholas Hall, 33 Belmont St ☎01224/625555. Converted two-tier church pumping out chart sounds onto increasingly flash Belmont St; often packed to the rafters with a young crowd.

Snafu 5 Union St ☎01224/622660, ⓦwww.clubsnafu.com. Aberdeen's best dance club, attracting frequent visits from the hottest DJs around.

The Tunnels Carnegies Brae ☎01224/211121. Thriving live-music venue resembling Liverpool's Cavern, with an intriguing mix of rising young bands, open mic sessions and club nights with reggae, hip-hop, ska and Northern Soul to the fore. There's also a record shop drawing on the manager's vinyl collection, thought to be the biggest in Scotland.

Theatres and cinemas

Aberdeen Arts Centre 33 King St ☎01224/635208, ⓦwww.aberdeenartscentre.org.uk. Hosts a variety of theatrical productions, lectures and exhibitions.

Belmont Picture House 9 Belmont St ☎01224/343536, ⓦwww.picturehouses.co.uk. Art-house cinema showing the more cerebral new releases alongside classic, cult and foreign-language films. There's a comfortable café inside and some good places nearby for a bite before or after.

Cineworld Beach Esplanade ☎0871/200 2000. Huge multiplex cinema showing all the mainstream releases.

His Majesty's Rosemount Viaduct ☎0845/270 8200, ⓦwww.aberdeenperformingarts.com. Aberdeen's main theatre, in a beautiful Edwardian building, with a programme ranging from highbrow drama and opera to pantomime. A new extension, including a café and restaurant, aims to keep the cultural buzz going throughout the day.

Lemon Tree 5 West North St ☎01224/642230, ⓦwww.lemontree.org. Avant-garde events with off-the-wall comedians and plays, many coming hotfoot from the Edinburgh festivals.

Listings

Airport ☎08700/400006.

Banks Bank of Scotland, 201 or 501 Union St; Clydesdale Bank, 62 or 238 Union St; Royal Bank of Scotland, 78 Union St or 12 Golden Square.

Bike rental Alpine Bikes, 66–70 Holburn St ☎01224/211455; Anderson's Cycles ☎01224 641520.

Bookshops The largest are Waterstone's, 269–271 Union St, and Ottakar's, in the Mall Trinity, Union St. Winram's, 32–36 Rosemount Place, and The Old Aberdeen Bookshop, 140 Spital, are best for secondhand, while Books and Beans, 22 Belmont St, offers a more populist selection.

Bus information First Aberdeen Busline ☎01224/650065.

Car rental Arnold Clark, Girdleness Rd ☎01224/249159, Lang Stracht (airport pick-ups) ☎01224/663723; Budget, Wellheads Drive (airport pick-ups) ☎01224/793333; National, 16 Broomhill Rd ☎01224 595366 and airport ☎0870/400 4502.

Exchange Thomas Cook in the Bon Accord Centre (Mon, Tues, Fri, Sat 9am–5.30pm, Wed 10am–5.30pm, Thurs 9am–8pm, Sun noon–5pm; ☎01224/807100).

Ferry information ☎0845/600 0449, ⓦwww .northlinkferries.co.uk.

Genealogical research Aberdeen & North-East Family History Society, 158–164 King St ☎01224/646323, ⓦwww.anesfhs.org.uk.

Internet Free access in the Central Library on Rosemount Viaduct (Mon–Thurs 9am–8pm, Fri & Sat 9am–5pm). Otherwise, try the tourist office, 23 Union St, and *Costa Coffee* on Loch St, next to the Bon Accord Centre, or the Family History Society at 158–164 King St.

Left luggage Small lockers at the train station cost £2–4. It's supposedly a 24-hour service but you can struggle to find anyone to help at unsociable hours.

Lesbian and gay helpline PHACE Scotland (Mon–Fri 9am–5pm; ☎0845/241 2151).

Libraries Central Library, Rosemount Viaduct ☎01224/652500.

Medical facilities The Royal Infirmary, on Foresterhill, northeast of the town centre, has a 24hr casualty department (☎01224/681818). Boots pharmacy is at 161 Union St (Mon–Wed & Fri 7.45am–6pm, Thurs 7.45am–8pm, Sat 8.30am–6pm, Sun noon–5pm; ☎01224/211592). For late-night pharmacies phone ☎0845/456 6000.

Outdoor supplies Tiso, 26 Netherkirkgate (☎01224/634934), and Blacks, 135 George St (☎01224/622272), have everything for hiking and outdoor pursuits, including maps and tips on where to go.

Police Main station is on Queen St ☎0845/600 5700, including the lost property office.

Post office The central office is in the St Nicholas Centre, between Union St and Upperkirkgate (Mon, Wed–Fri 9am–5.30pm, Tues & Sat 9.30am–5.30pm), with another branch at 489 Union St (Mon, Wed–Fri 9am–5.30pm, Tues 9.30am–5.30pm, Sat 9.30am–12.30pm).

Sports The local football team, Aberdeen, struggles to live to up its golden era of the 1980s when then-manager Alex Ferguson brought home league titles and European trophies. Home fixtures take place at Pittodrie Stadium (☎087/1983 1903, ⓦwww.afc.co.uk), between King St and the beach. There are golf courses all over the northeast; the municipal King's Links (☎01224/641577, ⓦwww.kings-links .com) skirts the beach, while Murcar Golf Club (☎01224/704354, ⓦwww.murcar.co.uk), a testing links five miles north of Aberdeen, is only open to visitors at certain times, but has an attractive nine-hole course, Strabathie, beside it. Bon Accord Baths and Leisure Centre, Justice Mill Lane (☎01224/587920), has a 40-yard (36.6-metre), swimming pool; Beach Leisure Centre (☎ 01224 647647) on the Esplanade boasts a fun pool with flumes and slides.

Taxis ComCab ☎01224/353535.

Travel agents STA, 30 Upperkirkgate ☎01224/658222.

Stonehaven and the Mearns

South of Aberdeen, the A92 and the main train line follow the coast to **Stonehaven**, a pretty harbour town and base for nearby **Dunnottar Castle**, a stunningly moody ruin perched on the cliffs. The area to the south and west is known as the **Mearns**, an agricultural district of scattered population and gathering hills famous for its links to Scots author Lewis Grassic Gibbon.

Stonehaven is easily reached by **bus** or **train** from Aberdeen or Montrose, although public transport inland into the Mearns is virtually nonexistent.

Stonehaven and around

A busy, pebble-dashed town, **STONEHAVEN** attracts hordes of holiday-makers in the summer due to the sheltered Kincardine coastline, and in mid-July in particular because of its respected **folk festival**. The town itself is split into two parts, the picturesque working harbour area being most likely to detain you. On one side of the harbour, Stonehaven's oldest building, the **Tolbooth** (June–Sept Mon & Wed–Sun 1.30–4.30pm; free), built as a storehouse during the construction of Dunnottar Castle (see p.532), is now a museum of local history and fishing. On calm summer evenings, you can take **boat trips** from the harbour to the RSPB reserve at Fowlsheugh (late May–July daily except Wed 6pm & 7.30pm; £8; booking necessary on ℡01224/624824).

The old High Street, lined with some fine town houses and civic buildings, connects the harbour and its surrounding old town with the late eighteenth-century planned centre on the other side of the River Carron. On New Year's Eve, High Street is the location for the ancient ceremony of **Fireballs**, when locals parade its length swinging metal cages full of burning debris around their heads to ward off evil spirits for the coming year. The **new town** focuses on the market square, overlooked by a dusky-pink granite market hall with an impressive steeple. In the northern part of the new town is Stonehaven's wonderful open-air Art Deco **swimming pool** (June & early Sept Mon–Fri 1–7.30pm, Sat & Sun 10am–6pm; July–Aug Mon–Fri 10am–7.30pm, Sat & Sun 10am–6pm; £3; ☒www.stonehavenopenairpool.co.uk), opened in 1934 and always packed with locals on a sunny day. As well as regular daytime hours, it's open for midnight swims on Wednesdays (July & early Aug 10pm–midnight).

Practicalities

The **tourist office** is at 66 Allardice St, the main street past the square (April–June, Sept & Oct Mon–Sat 10am–1pm & 2–5pm; July & Aug Mon–Sat 10am–7pm, Sun 1–5.30pm; ℡01569/762806). For **B&B** accommodation, *Arduthie House* on Ann Street (℡01569/762381, ☒www.arduthieguest-house.com; ❸) and the non-smoking *Alexander Guest House* at 36 Arduthie Rd (℡01569/762265, ☒www.alexanderguesthouse.com; ❸), are both good bets, while a few miles south of town on the A92, *Dunnottar Mains Farm* (℡01569/762621, ☒www.dunnottarmains.co.uk; ❷) is a decent farmhouse B&B beautifully situated right beside Dunnottar Castle.

For **food**, try the compelling Art Deco surroundings of the smart *Carron Restaurant* at 20 Cameron St (℡01569/760460, ☒http://carron-restaurant.co.uk) or the moderately expensive *Tolbooth Seafood Restaurant* (℡01569/762287, ☒http://tolbooth-restaurant.co.uk; closed Mon), above the museum on the harbour. Another excellent option, four miles north of town at Netherley, *Lairhillock Inn* (℡01569/730001, ☒www.lairhillock.co.uk) serves imaginative, if expensive, modern Scottish food in an atmospheric old coaching inn. For cheaper **pub** food or just a drink, try the entertaining *Marine Hotel* or the attractive *Ship Inn*, both on the harbour.

Dunnottar Castle, Kinneff and Arbuthnott

Two miles south of Stonehaven (the tourist office sells a walking guide for the scenic amble), **Dunnottar Castle** (Easter–Oct Mon–Sat 9am–6pm, Sun 2–5pm; rest of year Fri–Mon 9.30am–4pm, Dec & Jan closes 3pm; £4) is one of the finest of Scotland's ruined castles, a huge ninth-century fortress set on a three-sided sheer cliff jutting into the sea – a setting striking enough to be chosen as the backdrop for Zeffirelli's movie version of *Hamlet*. Once the principal fortress of the northeast, the ruins are worth a good root around, and there are any number of dramatic views out to the crashing sea. Siege and bloodstained drama splatter the castle's past: in 1297 the whole English Plantagenet garrison were burnt alive here by William Wallace, while one of the more gruesome tales from the castle's history tells of the imprisonment and torture of 122 men and 45 women Covenanters in 1685 – an event, as it says on the Covenanters' Stone in the churchyard, "whose dark shadow is for evermore flung athwart the Castled Rock".

Four miles south of Dunnottar Castle, **CATTERLINE** is a cliff-top hamlet typical of those along this stretch of coast – worth a visit for the views and the delicious, well-priced shellfish at the cosy *Creel Inn* (☎01569/750254, ⊛www.thecreelinn.co.uk).

Four miles further south, the tiny village of **KINNEFF** lies among fields tumbling down to the sea. Its **church**, for the most part eighteenth-century, is a successor to the one in which the Scottish crown jewels were hidden as Cromwell marched on Scotland in 1651. Popular tradition has it that the wives of the Dunnottar garrison commander and the Kinneff parish minister hid the crown under an apron and carried the state sceptre, disguised as a distaff, with bundles of flax. The crown jewels were successfully hidden here for nine years. Memorials and interpretive boards inside the beautifully light and simple old church tell the story.

Some five miles inland, the straggling village of **ARBUTHNOTT** was the home of prolific local author, **Lewis Grassic Gibbon** (1901–35), whose romanticized realism perfectly encapsulates the spirit of the agricultural Mearns area. His descriptions were often quite awesome: Glasgow, for example, he neatly summed up as "the vomit of a cataleptic commercialism". *Sunset Song*, his most famous work, is an essential read for those travelling in this area (for an extract, see p.836). The community-run **Grassic Gibbon Centre** (April–Oct daily 10am–4.30pm; £2.50), on the B967 through the village, is a great introduction to this fascinating and self-assured man who died so young. He is buried (under his real name of James Leslie Mitchell) in the corner of the little village graveyard, overlooking the forested banks of the Bervie Water off the main road. The parish **church** itself, one of the few surviving intact in Scotland that pre-date the Reformation, is interesting for its Norman arch, unusual fifteenth-century circular bell tower and glorious thirteenth-century chancel.

Deeside

More commonly known as **Royal Deeside**, the land stretching west from Aberdeen along the River Dee revels in its connections with the Royal Family, who have regularly holidayed here, at **Balmoral**, since Queen Victoria bought the estate. Eighty thousand Scots turned out to welcome her on her first visit in 1848, but some weren't so charmed: one local journalist remarked that the area was about to be "desolated by cockneys and other horrible reptiles". Today, most locals are fiercely protective of the royal connection.

Many of Victoria's guests weren't as enthusiastic about Deeside as she was: Count von Moltke, then aide-de-camp to Prince Frederick William of Prussia, observed, "It is very astonishing that the Royal Power of England should reside amid this lonesome, desolate, cold mountain scenery", while Tsar Nicholas II whined, "The weather is awful, rain and wind every day and on top of it no luck at all – I haven't killed a stag yet." However, Victoria adored the place, and the woods were said to remind Prince Albert of Thuringia, his homeland.

Deeside is undoubtedly handsome in a fierce, craggy, Scottish way, and the royal presence has helped keep a lid on any unattractive mass development. The villages strung along the A93, the main route through the area, are well heeled and have something of an old-fashioned air. Facilities for visitors hereabouts are first-class, with a number of bunkhouses and hostels, some decent hotels and plenty of castles and grounds to snoop around. It's also an excellent area for **outdoor activities**, with hiking routes into both the Grampian and Cairngorm mountains, and good mountain-biking, horse riding and skiing.

Stagecoach Bluebird **bus** #201 from Aberdeen regularly chugs along the A93, serving most of the towns on the way to Braemar.

West of Aberdeen

West of Aberdeen, you'll pass through low-lying land of mixed farming, forestry and suburbs. Easily reached from the main road are the castles of **Drum** and **Crathes**, both interesting fortified houses with pleasant gardens, while the uneventful town of **Banchory** serves as gateway to the heart of Royal Deeside. Further west, **Glen Tanar** is a great example of the area's attractive blend of forest, river and mountain scenery.

Drum Castle and Crathes Castle

Ten miles west of Aberdeen on the A93, **Drum Castle** (daily: April, May & Sept 12.30–5.30pm; June–Aug 10am–5.30pm; grounds 9.30am–sunset all year; NTS; £8, grounds only £3) stands in a clearing in the ancient **woods of Drum**, made up of the splendid pines and oaks that covered this whole area before the shipbuilding industry precipitated mass forest clearance. The castle itself combines a 1619 Jacobean mansion with Victorian extensions and the original, huge thirteenth-century keep, which has been restored and reopened. Given by Robert the Bruce to his armour-bearer, William de Irvine, in 1323 for services rendered at Bannockburn, the castle remained in Irvine hands for 24 generations until the NTS took over in 1976. The main part of the house is Victorian in character, with grand, antique-filled rooms and lots of family portraits. The finest room is the library, within the ancient tower; you'll get an even better sense of the medieval atmosphere of the place by climbing up to the upper levels of the tower, with the battlements offering grand views out over the forest.

Further along the A93, four miles west of Drum Castle, **Crathes Castle** (daily: April–Sept 10am–5.30pm; Oct 10am–4.30pm; NTS; £10) is a splendid sixteenth-century granite tower house adorned with flourishes such as overhanging turrets, gargoyles and conical roofs. Its thick walls, narrow windows and tiny rooms loaded with heavy old furniture make Crathes rather claustrophobic, but it is still worth visiting for some wonderful painted ceilings, either still in their original form or sensitively restored; the earliest dates from 1602. The grounds include an impressive walled garden complete with yew hedges clipped into various shapes.

By the entrance to Crathes, a cluster of restored stone cottages house various **craft shops** and **galleries** as well as the *Milton* (℡01330/844566, ⓦwww .themilton.co.uk; closed Sun & Mon eve), an unexpectedly upmarket **restaurant** serving ambitious, expensive à la carte meals as well as a lighter all-day menu. Beside the cottages, two old railway carriages mark the base camp for a bunch of enthusiasts who are busy rebuilding a stretch of the old Royal Deeside **railway line** – in time, they hope to have a small stretch between here and Banchory open for trips.

Banchory

BANCHORY, meaning "fair hollow", is a one-street town which essentially acts as a gateway into rural Deeside. The small local **museum** on Bridge Street, behind High Street (April & Oct Sat 11am–1pm & 2–4.30pm; May–Sept Mon–Sat 11am–1pm & 2–4.30pm, plus July & Aug Sun 2–4.30pm; free), may warrant half an hour or so if you're a fan of local boy James Scott Skinner, renowned fiddler and composer of such tunes as *The Bonnie Lass o'Bon Accord*.

The **tourist office** in the museum (April–June & Sept Mon–Sat 9.30am–1pm & 2–5.30pm; July & Aug Mon–Fri 9.30am–6pm, Sat 9.30am–1pm & 2–6pm, Sun 1–6pm; Oct Mon–Sat 10am–1pm & 2–5pm; ℡01330/822000) can provide information on walking and fishing in the area. There are one or two places **to stay** in town, including the smart *Tor-Na-Coille Hotel* (℡01330/822242, ⓦwww.tornacoille.com; ❼), once a retreat for Charlie Chaplin and his family, though there's an understandable temptation to push on into the attractive Deeside countryside. If you do hang around, the *Burnett Arms Hotel*, a friendly former coaching inn at 25 High St (℡01330/824944, ⓦwww .burnettarms.co.uk; ❺), has standard rooms but does Banchory's best pub grub, and there are a couple of good delis, including the Dee Larder on Watson Lane, which leads off the main street.

Aboyne and Glen Tanar

Twelve miles west of Banchory on the A93, **ABOYNE** is a typically well-mannered Deeside village at the mouth of **Glen Tanar**, which runs southwest from here for ten miles or so deep into the Grampian hills. The glen, with few steep gradients and some glorious stands of mature Caledonian pine, is ideal for walking, mountain-biking or horse riding; the ranger information point two miles into the glen off the B976 has details of suitable routes, while the Glen Tanar Equestrian Centre (℡01339/886448) offers one- and two-hour horse rides. Aboyne has some handy retreats for **food** after a day's activity: the excellent *Black Faced Sheep* coffee shop just off the main road serves home baking and light lunches, while the *Boat Inn* on Charlestown Road right beside the bridge over the Dee does good-quality pub grub.

Ballater and Balmoral

Ten miles west of Aboyne is the neat and ordered town of **BALLATER**, attractively hemmed in by the river and fir-covered mountains. The town was dragged from obscurity in the nineteenth century when it was discovered that the local waters were useful in curing scrofula, and these days Ballater spring water is back in fashion and on sale around town.

It was in Ballater that Queen Victoria first arrived in Deeside by train from Aberdeen back in 1848; she wouldn't allow a station to be built any closer to Balmoral, eight miles further west. Although the line has long been closed, the town's rather self-important royalism is much in evidence at the restored **train station** in the centre (daily: June–Sept 9am–5.45pm; Oct–March 10am–4.45pm), where various video presentations and life-sized models relive the comings and goings of generations of royals (though trains have long since stopped running). The local shops, having provided Balmoral with groceries and household basics, also flaunt their connections, with oversized "By Appointment" crests sported above the doorways of most businesses from the butcher to the newsagent.

If you prefer to discover the fresh air and natural beauty that Victoria came to love so much, Ballater is an excellent base for local **walks and outdoor activities**. There are numerous hikes from Loch Muik (pronounced "mick"), nine miles southwest of town, including the Capel Mounth drovers' route over the mountains to Glen Doll (see p.513), and a well-worn but strenuous all-day trek up and around Lochnagar (3789ft), the mountain much painted and written about by the current Prince of Wales. Good-quality **bikes** can be rented from Cabin Fever (☎013397/54004), beside the station on Station Square, or Cycle Highlands (☎013397/55864) at 16 Bridge St. Other outdoor equipment, as well as local guidebooks, a full range of OS maps and good advice about heading to the surrounding hills, is available at the friendly Lochnagar Leisure outdoor shop on Station Square (daily 9am–5.30pm).

Practicalities

The **tourist office** is in the renovated train station (daily: July & Aug 9am–6pm; rest of year 10am–5pm; ☎013397/55306). Good-quality **bunkhouse** accommodation is available at the *Schoolhouse*, Anderson Road (☎013397/56333, Ⓦ www.theschool-house.com), where inexpensive evening meals are served, and there are plenty of reasonable **B&Bs** in town, including non-smoking *Inverdeen House* on Bridge Square (☎013397/55759, Ⓦ www.inverdeen.com; ❸), which offers a wide choice of breakfasts, most involving local produce and home baking. Other places to try include the welcoming *Deeside Hotel* (☎013397/55420, Ⓦ www.deesidehotel.co.uk; ❸), or the small *Green Inn Restaurant*, 9 Victoria Rd (☎013397/55701, Ⓦ www.green-inn.com; ❹), which has three very comfortable rooms. For **camping**, head for *Anderson Road Caravan Park* (☎013397/55727; Easter–Oct) down towards the river.

There are numerous **places to eat**, from smart hotel restaurants to bakers and coffee shops: the *Green Inn* is pricey but excellent with its French-influenced menu, while *La Mangiatoia* (☎013397/55999), on Bridge Square opposite the *Monaltrie Hotel*, is a cheaper and cheerful family pizza/pasta place. The *Station Restaurant*, next door to the tourist office in the Victorian station, serves home baking and lunches; a couple of miles east of Ballater on the A93 there's also the *Crannach Coffee Shop and Bakery* (closed Mon), a cultured spot offering good coffees, snacks and light meals, as well as superb cakes and bread from their in-house organic bakery. For **drinking** with locals and the opportunity to sample some real ales, try the back bar (entrance down Golf Street) of the *Prince of Wales*, which faces the main square.

Balmoral Estate and Crathie Church

Originally a sixteenth-century tower house built for the powerful Gordon family, **Balmoral Castle** (April–July daily 10am–5pm; also weekly guided tours Nov & Dec; £6; ☎013397/42534, Ⓦ www.balmoralcastle.com) has been a royal residence since 1852, when it was converted to the Scottish Baronial mansion that stands today. The Royal Family traditionally spend their summer holidays here each August, but despite its fame it can be something of a disappointment even for a dedicated royalist. For the three months when the doors are nudged open, the general riffraff are permitted to view only the ballroom, an exhibition room and the grounds; for the rest of the year it's not even visible to the paparazzi who have been known to snoop around with their long lenses. With so little of the castle on view, it's worth making the most of the grounds and larger estate by following some of the country walks, heading off on a Land Rover safari or joining a two-hour **pony trek** (April–July Mon–Wed & Fri–Sun 10am & 2pm; some riding experience required; call ☎013397/42534 for details; £30).

Opposite the castle's gates on the main road, the otherwise dull granite church of **Crathie**, built in 1895 with the proceeds of a bazaar held at Balmoral, is the royals' local church. A small **tourist office** operates in the car park by the church on the main road (daily: April–June, Sept & Oct 9.30am–5pm; July & Aug 9.30am–5.30pm; ☎013397/42414).

⑩ Braemar

Continuing westwards for another few miles, the road rises to 1100ft above sea level in the upper part of Deeside and the village of **BRAEMAR**, situated where three passes meet and overlooked by an unremarkable **castle** (July & Aug daily 10am–5pm; Easter–June & Sept–Oct closed Fri; £4). Signs as you enter Braemar boast that it's an "Award-Winning Tourist Village", which just about sums it up, as everything seems to have been prettified to within an inch of its life. That said, it's an invigorating, outdoor kind of place, well patronized by committed hikers, but probably best known for its Highland Games, the annual **Braemar Gathering**, on the first Saturday of September (ⓦwww.braemargathering.org). Since Queen Victoria's day, successive generations of royals have attended, and the world's most famous Highland Games have become rather an overcrowded, overblown event. You're not guaranteed to get in if you just turn up; the website has details of how to book tickets in advance.

A pleasant diversion from Braemar is to head six miles west to the end of the road and the **Linn of Dee**, where the river plummets savagely through a narrow rock gorge. From here there are countless walks into the surrounding countryside or up into the heart of the Cairngorms (see p.553), including the awesome Lairig Ghru pass which cuts all the way through to Strathspey. There's a very basic SYHA hostel just before the falls at Inverey (T0870/004 1126, Wwww.syha.org.uk; May–Sept). A postbus runs from Braemar to the Linn of Dee every day except Sunday at 1.20pm.

Practicalities

Braemar's **tourist office** is in the modern building known as the Mews, in the middle of the village on Mar Road (June & Sept daily 9am–5pm; July & Aug daily 9am–6pm; Oct Mon–Sat 9am–5pm, Sun 1–5pm; rest of year Mon–Sat 10.30am–1.30pm & 2–5pm, Sun 1–4pm; T013397/41600). **Accommodation** is scarce in Braemar in the lead-up to the Games, but at other times there's a wide choice. *Clunie Lodge Guest House*, Clunie Bank Road (T013397/41330, Wwww.clunielodge.com; **❷**), on the edge of town, is a good **B&B** with lovely views up Clunie Glen, and there's a large SYHA **hostel** at Corrie Feragie, 21 Glenshee Rd (T0870/004 1105, Wwww.syha.org.uk; mid-Dec to Oct). Cheery *Rucksacks*, an easygoing bunkhouse well equipped for walkers and backpackers, is just behind the Mews complex (T013397/41517), while the *Invercauld Caravan Club Park* (T013397/41373), just south of the village off Glenshee Road, has fifteen **camping** pitches – you should phone ahead to reserve one.

For **food**, avoid the large hotels, which tend to be filled with coach parties, and try either *Taste*, a coffee shop and moderately priced contemporary restaurant on the road out to the Linn of Dee, or *The Gathering Place*, a pleasant bistro with reasonably priced meat and game dishes in the heart of the village next door to Braemar Mountain Sports.

Advice on **outdoor activities**, as well as ski, mountain-bike and climbing equipment rental, is available from Braemar Mountain Sports (daily 8.30am–6pm).

The Don Valley

The quiet countryside around the **Don Valley**, once renowned for its illegal whisky distilleries and smugglers, lies at the heart of Aberdeenshire's prosperous agricultural region. From Aberdeen, the River Don winds northwest through **Inverurie**, where it takes a sharp turn west to **Alford**, then continues past ruined castles through the **Upper Don Valley** and the heather moorlands of the eastern Highlands. This remote and undervisited area is positively littered with ruined castles, Pictish sites, stones and hillforts.

Inverurie is served by the regular Aberdeen to Inverness **train** and various **bus** services up the A96. Stagecoach Bluebird buses #215 and #220 link Aberdeen with Alford, but getting any further by public transport is all but impossible.

Inverurie and around

Some seventeen miles northwest of Aberdeen, the prosperous – if largely unexciting – farming town of **INVERURIE** lies fairly central to the numerous relics and castles in the area. The **tourist office** (Mon–Sat 9am–5pm; July & Aug closes 5.30pm; T01467/625800) shares space with a bookshop at 18 High St, not far from the station; it's a good place to stop before setting off to find the local sites, many of which are tucked away and confusingly signposted.

Bennachie and Archaeolink

The granite hill **Bennachie**, five miles west of Inverurie, is possibly the site of Mons Graupius, Scotland's first-ever recorded battle, when the Romans defeated the Picts in 84 AD. At 1733ft, this is one of the most prominent tors in the region, with tremendous views, and makes for a stiff two-hour walk. The best route starts from the **Bennachie Centre** (Tues–Sun: April–Oct 10.30am–5pm; Nov–March 9.30am–4pm), a countryside ranger station and interpretation centre located two miles south of **Chapel of Garioch** (pronounced "geery"). A mile immediately west of Chapel of Garioch is one of the most notable Pictish standing stones in the region, the **Maiden Stone**, a ten-foot slab inscribed with marine monsters, an elephant-like beast and the mirror and comb for which it's named.

A further four miles northwest of Chapel of Garioch on the B9002 at Oyne, the **Archaeolink Prehistory Park** (daily: April–Oct 11am–5pm; Nov–March 11am–4pm; £4.75; ⓦ www.archaeolink.co.uk) gives an insight into the area's Pictish heritage. An ambitious modern attraction, it includes a reconstructed Iron Age farm, a hillside archeological site and an innovative grass-roofed building containing lively audiovisual displays and hands-on exhibits.

Fyvie Castle

Some thirteen miles north of Inverurie stands the huge, ochre mansion of **Fyvie Castle** (April–June & Sept Sat–Wed noon–5pm; July–Aug daily 11am–5pm; NTS; £8). Scottish Baronial to the hilt, Fyvie's fascinating roofscape sprouts five curious steeples, one for each of the families who lived here from the thirteenth to the twentieth century. In 1889 the castle was sold to the Forbes-Leiths, a local family who had made a fortune in America and were responsible for the grand Edwardian interior. The exquisite dining room is nowadays rented out for corporate entertaining by oil companies who hobnob among the Flemish tapestries, Delft tiles and the fine collection of paintings that includes feathery Gainsborough portraits and twelve works by Sir Henry Raeburn.

Alford and around

ALFORD (pronounced "aa-ford"), 25 miles west of Aberdeen, only exists at all because it was chosen, in 1859, as the terminus for the Great North Scotland Railway. A fairly grey little town now firmly within the Aberdeen commuter belt, it's still well worth making the trip here for the **Grampian Transport Museum** on Main Street (April–Sept daily 10am–5pm; Oct 10am–4pm; £5.20). Here you'll find a large, diverse display of transport through the ages, from tramcars to sleek designs which have won endurance events for ecofriendly designs. Mixing the bizarre with nostalgic, exhibits include the Craigevar Express, a strange, three-wheeled steam-driven vehicle developed by the local postman for his rounds, and that famous monument to British eccentricity and ingenuity, the Sinclair C5 motorized tricycle.

Practically next door is the terminus for the **Alford Valley Railway** (April, May & Sept Sat & Sun 1–4.30pm; June–Aug daily 1–4.30pm; ⓣ019755/62326), a narrow-gauge train that runs for about a mile from Alford Station through wooded vales to the wide open space of **Murray Park**; the return journey (£2) takes an hour. The station is also home to the neat **tourist office** (April–Sept Mon–Sat 10am–5pm, Sun 1–5pm; ⓣ019755/62052).

Craigievar Castle

Six miles south of Alford on the A980, **Craigievar Castle** (NTS; ⓣ013398/83635) is a fantastic pink confection of turrets, gables, balustrades

△ Craigievar Castle

and cupolas bubbling over from its top three storeys. It was built in 1626 by a Baltic trader known as Willy the Merchant, who evidently allowed his whimsy to run riot. The castle's massive popularity, however – it features on everything from shortbread tins to tea towels all over Scotland – has been its undoing, and the sheer number of visitors has caused interior damage which means that the castle will be closed to visitors until Easter 2007 for restoration work. However, you can still visit the well-kept **grounds** (all year 9.30am to sunset; £1).

The Upper Don Valley

Travelling west from Alford, settlements become noticeably more scattered and remote as the countryside takes on a more open, familiarly Highland appearance. Ten miles from Alford stand the impressive ruins of the thirteenth-century

Kildrummy Castle (April–Sept daily 9.30am–6.30pm; HS; £2.50), where Robert the Bruce sent his wife and children during the Wars of Independence. The castle blacksmith, bribed with as much gold as he could carry, set fire to the place and it fell into English hands. Bruce's immediate family survived, but his brother was executed and the entire garrison hanged, drawn and quartered. Meanwhile, the duplicitous blacksmith was rewarded for his help by having molten gold poured down his throat. The sixth earl of Mar used the castle as the headquarters of the ill-fated Jacobite risings in 1715, but after that, Kildrummy became redundant and it was abandoned as a fortress and residence and fell into ruin. Beside the ruins, the separate **Kildrummy Castle Gardens** (April–Oct daily 10am–5pm; £2.50) are quite a draw, boasting everything from swathes of azaleas in spring to Himalayan poppies in summer. A few miles before you reach the castle, *Frog Marsh Bed & Breakfast* has three tastefully decorated **B&B** rooms (℡019755/71355; ⓦwww.frogmarsh.com; ❹).

Ten miles further west, the A944 sweeps round into the parish of **STRATHDON**, little more than scattered buildings by the roadside. Four miles north of here, up a rough track leading into Glen Nochty, lies the unexpected **Lost Gallery** (Mon & Wed–Sun 11am–5pm; ⓦwww.lostgallery.co.uk), which shows work by some of Scotland's leading modern artists in a wonderfully remote and tranquil setting. Heading west again on the A944, you'll come to the walled grounds of Candacraig House, Highland retreat of comedian Billy Connolly. The house is private, but the old laundry on the other side of the main house, ⚥ *No. 3 Candacraig Square* (℡019756/51472, ⓦwww.candacraig .com; ❺) has been converted into a stylish **B&B** with wooden floors, piles of books and a promise of fresh fish for breakfast. A further eight miles west, just beyond the junction of the Ballater road, lies **Corgarff Castle** (April–Sept daily 9.30am–6.30pm; Oct–March Sat & Sun 9.30am–4.30pm; HS; £3.30), an austere tower house with an unusual star-shaped curtain wall – and an eventful history. Built in 1537, it was turned into a barracks by the Hanoverian government in 1748 in the aftermath of Culloden in order to track down local Jacobite rebels; a century later, English redcoats were stationed here with the unpopular task of trying to control whisky smuggling. Today the place has been restored to resemble its days as a barracks, with stark rooms and rows of hard, uncomfortable beds – authentic touches which extend to graffiti on the walls and peat smoke permeating the building from a fire on the upper floor. One unexpected bonus here if you're from far-flung parts is the chance to hear the history of the castle in one of the nineteen languages the keeper has recorded it in over the years, ranging from Thai to Icelandic.

Leading to the castle from the south is the old military road, which, unusually, hasn't been covered over by the present road and is fairly clear for about three miles. A mile or so along this from the castle, approached from the main road by the track beside Rowan Tree Cottage, is ⚥ *Jenny's Bothy* at Dellachuper (℡019756/51449; ⓦwww.upperdonside.org.uk/jenboth/), a beautifully remote and simple **bunkhouse**, surrounded by empty scenery and wild animals. You'll have to bring your own supplies if you're coming here, but it's a great base for hiking, cycling or skiing, or just detaching yourself from the madding crowd for a day or two. Another bunkhouse, along with standard **B&B** accommodation, can be found at the *Allargue Arms Hotel* (℡019756/51410; ❸), an old wayside inn overlooking Corgarff Castle and a cosy base for skiing, fishing or hiking trips.

The **Lecht Road**, crossing the area of bleak but wonderfully empty high country to the remote mountain village of Tomintoul (see p.571), passes the Lecht ski centre at 2090ft above sea level, but is frequently impassable in winter due to snow.

The coast

The **coast** of northeast Scotland from Aberdeen to Inverness has a rugged, sometimes bleak fringe with pleasant if undramatic farmland rolling inland. Still, if the weather is good, it's well worth spending a couple of days meandering through the various little fishing villages and along the miles of deserted, unspoilt beaches. It's not a part of the country that many visit, but it has its rewards for those who are prepared to explore and discover the many ruins, historic sites and intriguing small settlements which dot the area.

The largest coastal towns are **Peterhead** and **Fraserburgh**, both dominated by sizeable fishing fleets; while neither has much to offer, the latter's Museum of Scottish Lighthouses is one of the most attractive small museums in Scotland. More appealing to most visitors are the quieter spots along the Moray coast, including the charming villages of **Pennan**, **Gardenstown**, **Portsoy** and nearby **Cullen**. The other main attractions are **Duff House** in Banff, a branch of the National Gallery of Scotland; the working abbey at **Pluscarden** by Elgin; and the **Findhorn Foundation**, near Forres.

The main towns and larger villages are fairly well served by **buses**, while **trains** from Aberdeen and Inverness stop at Elgin, Forres and Nairn. Even so, it's preferable to have your own transport for reaching some of the far-flung places.

The coast road towards Peterhead

Fifteen miles north of Aberdeen, a turning (signposted to Collieston) leads off the main A92 coast road to **Forvie National Nature Reserve**. This area incorporates the Sands of Forvie, one of Britain's largest and least disturbed dune systems, and boasts a rich array of birdlife. There's a small but informative **visitor centre** (April–Sept daily 9am–5pm; call ☎01358/751330 for winter hours), from which a network of trails winds along the coast and through the dunes, with one leading to the site of a fifteenth-century village, buried by the shifting sands.

COLLIESTON itself is a pleasant hamlet with a harbour but little else; for somewhere to eat or stay it's worth making for **NEWBURGH**, essentially a satellite town of Aberdeen at the mouth of the Ythan River, itself a good place to spot wildfowl. You'll find the comfy *Udny Arms Hotel* on Main Street (☎01358/789444, ⓦwww.udny.co.uk; ❻), which has a decent if expensive **restaurant** serving local seafood and game.

Cruden Bay

Superb sandy beaches can also be found eight miles north of Forvie at **CRUDEN BAY**, from where a pleasant fifteen-minute walk leads to the huge pink-granite ruin of **Slains Castle**. The ruin itself is not especially interesting – it was over-modernized in the nineteenth century – though its stark clifftop beauty is striking and it claims notoriety as the place which inspired Bram Stoker to write *Dracula*. Stoker used to holiday here and another of his stories, *Mystery of the Sea*, is directly related to a local ghost story. The castle is surprisingly badly signposted: from the car park on the left at the end of Cruden Bay's Main Street, head for the sea, then along the cliffs; alternatively, pull into the Meikle Partans car park on A975 north of the village and follow the obvious path until you begin to see the ruins.

From a car park a little further up the A975, or a precarious three-mile walk north from Slains Castle along the cliffs, is the **Bullers of Buchan**, a splendid 245ft-deep sea chasm, where the ocean gushes in through a natural archway eroded by the sea. This is some of the finest cliff scenery in the country and attracts a huge number of (smelly) nesting seabirds.

Peterhead and around

PETERHEAD (Ⓦwww.peterhead.org.uk), the easternmost mainland town in Scotland, stands in sharp contrast to the picturesque fishing villages on this stretch of coast. As notable for its high-security prison and ugly power station as its busy harbour, it's an unashamedly functional place. Although in recent years the oil industry has created a surge in wealth and population, Peterhead's *raison d'être* is **fishing**, and it was for many years the busiest white-fish port in Europe. The boom is now over, however, and Peterhead has felt the consequences of the overfishing of the North Sea.

The oldest building in town is the 400-year-old **Ugie Salmon Fish House** on Golf Road at the mouth of the River Ugie, at the north end of town (Mon–Fri 9am–5pm, Sat 9am–noon; Ⓦwww.ugie-salmon.co.uk; free), where you can watch the traditional methods of oak-smoking salmon and trout in Scotland's oldest smokehouse; the finished product is for sale at reasonable prices. On the beach just off the main road, one of the town's newer buildings houses the **Peterhead Maritime Heritage**, a combined college and museum (June–Aug Mon–Sat 10.30am–5pm, Sun 11.30am–5pm; free) that tells the story of the town's fishing industry from the old herring fleet to the modern day. Listen out for the recordings of old fishermen and women, who still speak the distinctive Doric dialect.

Peterhead has no official tourist office, but you should be able to find somewhere **to stay**; in town there's the spick, span and welcoming *Invernettie Guest House* on South Road (carrickhouse@ukonline(☏01779/473530, Ⓦwww .invernettie.co.uk; ❸), while the old lighthouse cottages at remote Rattray Head (☏01364/532236, Ⓦwww.rattrayhead.net; ❸), halfway between Peterhead and Fraserburgh, offer B&B as well as a small tearoom (Easter–Sept daily noon–6pm) and a backpacker hostel. For **food**, the *Dolphin* serves good fish and chips from right next to the fish market in the harbour area, and there's a reasonable *Maritime Café* at Peterhead Maritime Heritage.

Fraserburgh and the north coast

Twenty miles north of Peterhead, **FRASERBURGH** (Ⓦwww.visitfraserburgh. com) is a large and fairly severe-looking place in the same vein as Peterhead. At the northern tip of the town, an eighteenth-century lighthouse protrudes from the top of sixteenth-century **Fraserburgh Castle**, where the highest wind speeds on mainland Britain were recorded in 1989 (they reached 140mph). The lighthouse was one of the first to be built in Scotland and is now part of the excellent **Museum of Scottish Lighthouses** (April–Oct Mon–Sat 10am– 5pm, Sun noon–5pm, plus July & Aug open till 6pm; Nov–March Mon–Sat 11am–4pm, Sun noon–4pm; £4.75), where you can see a collection of huge lenses and prisms gathered from decommissioned lighthouses, and a display on various members of the famous "Lighthouse" Stevenson family (including the father and grandfather of author Robert Louis Stevenson), who designed many of them. Highlight of the museum is the tour of Kinnaird Head light itself, preserved as it was when the last keeper left in 1991, with its century-old equipment still in perfect working order.

Next door, and also well worth a visit, is the **Fraserburgh Heritage Centre** (April–Oct Mon–Sat 11am–5pm, Sun 1–5pm; £2.50), a wide-ranging exhibition on the history of the town with small boats, audiovisual presentations and details of some experiments in wireless communication performed in town by Marconi in 1904.

Fraserburgh's **tourist office**, in Saltoun Square (April–Oct Mon–Sat 10am–1pm & 2–5pm; ☎01346/518315), gives out information about the surrounding area. The rest of the town centre isn't particularly inspiring; for a bite to eat, *Zanres* opposite the tourist office does decent fish and chips.

West of Fraserburgh

The coast road between Fraserburgh and Pennan, twelve miles west, is particularly attractive: inland there are villages with pretty churches and cottages, while countless paths lead off it to ruined castles, cliff-top walks and lonely beaches. **PENNAN** itself, a tiny fishing hamlet, lies just off the road, down a steep and hazardous hill. Consisting of little more than a single row of whitewashed stone cottages tucked between a cliff and the sea, the village leapt into the limelight when the British movie *Local Hero* was filmed here in 1982. You can stay at one of the identifiable landmarks from the film, the *Pennan Inn* (☎01346/561201, ✉thepennaninn@btinternet.com; ❹), which has recently been upgraded with particular attention paid to its restaurant, which specializes in local seafood and game.

Locals in tiny and equally appealing **CROVIE** (pronounced "crivie"), another village in the same style on the other side of Troup Head from Pennan, frequently have their doorsteps washed by the sea. Wedged in against the steep cliffs, it's so narrow that its residents have to park their cars at one end of the village and continue to their houses on foot. **GARDENSTOWN**, a short way west, is similar if a little larger and supports a hotel, the *Garden Arms* (☎01261/851260, ⓦwww.gardenarms.co.uk; ❷), as well as a couple of small art galleries and the small but excellent *Harbour Restaurant and Café* (☎01261/851690; booking recommended), which overlooks the collection of small local boats tied up to the quayside.

Macduff and Banff

Heading west along the coast from Pennan brings you, after ten miles, to **MACDUFF**, a famous spa town during the nineteenth century and now with a thriving and pleasant harbour. **Macduff Marine Aquarium**, 11 High Shore (daily 10am–5pm; £4.75; ⓦwww.marine-aquarium.com), has an intriguing display on local aquatic life, with a huge centrepiece aquarium tank open to the air. From the harbour, Puffin Cruises (☎01542/832560, ⓦwww.puffincruises.com) offer **boat trips** in a converted fishing trawler; they look for seabirds and dolphins, and offer an unusual angle on the coastline's fascinating little villages.

Macduff and its neighbour **BANFF** are separated by little more than the beautiful seven-arch bridge over the River Deveron. Banff's **tourist office** (April–June & Sept Mon–Sat 10am–1pm & 2–4pm; July & Aug Mon–Sat 10am–1pm & 2–5pm; ☎01261/812419) is housed in the old gatehouse of Duff House in St Mary Square.

Duff House

Banff has a mix of characterful old buildings and boarded-up shops, which give little clue to the extravagance of **Duff House** (generally April–Oct daily 11am–5pm; Nov–March Thurs–Sun 11am–4pm; ⓦwww.duffhouse.org.uk; HS; £5.50), the town's main attraction. Built to William Adam's design in 1730, this elegant four-floor Georgian Baroque house was originally intended for one of the northeast's richest men, William Braco, who became earl of Fife in 1759. It was clearly built to impress, and could have been even more splendid had Adam been allowed to build curving colonnades either side; Braco's refusal to pay for carved Corinthian columns to be shipped in from Queensferry caused such bitter argument that the laird never actually came to live here, and even went so far as to pull shut his coach curtains whenever he passed by.

The house has been painstakingly restored and reopened as an outpost of the **National Gallery of Scotland**'s extensive collection, and while the emphasis is on displaying period artwork rather than any broader selection of the Gallery's paintings, temporary exhibitions of work from the collections are mounted regularly. The downstairs rooms set the tone, principally the Rococo vestibule and the **dining room**, hung with ponderous eighteenth-century portraits, among which Allan Ramsay's *Elizabeth, Mrs Daniel Cunyngham* leaps out for its delightfully cool composition. Also on the other side of the ground floor, **Countess Agnes' Boudoir**, formerly Lord Macduff's dressing room, contains a riotous gilded Rococo mirror and El Greco's heartfelt *St Jerome in Penitence*, which dominates a wall of mainly religious art.

Ascending the **Great Staircase**, all eyes are drawn to the enormous copy of Raphael's *Transfiguration* by Inverness's Grigor Urquhart (1797–1846). Upstairs, the **North Drawing Room** contains the only piece of furniture original to the house, a 1760s mirror, but more obvious is the bewilderingly bold gold and cherry-red ceiling, a not entirely successful Victorian pastiche of Adam's style. In the **Great Drawing Room**, William's son Robert Adam's symmetrical classicism meets French opulence head on, and somehow it works. The best example is the 1764 furniture suite of two gilded sofas and two chairs originally designed by the younger Adam and built by Chippendale, combining the Classical reference of lion's-paw feet and the Rococo motif of florid gold shells. Beyond the house there are extensive **grounds** with an adventure playground, some pleasant parkland and riverside walks, and various odd buildings including a fishing "temple" and the Duff dynasty's mausoleum.

Practicalities

One option for **accommodation** is *The Knowes* (☎01261/832229, ⓦwww.knoweshotel.co.uk), a small hotel on the hill above Macduff with great outlooks over both towns. There are also numerous B&Bs in and around Macduff and Banff. The *Orchard* (☎01261/812146, ⓦwww.orchardbanff.co.uk; ❸) is superbly set on the edge of woodland in the grounds of Duff House, while the *St Helens Guest House* (☎01261/818241, ⓦwww.sthelensbanff.demon.co.uk; ❷) on Bellevue Road in Banff is another good option. **Camping** is best near the beach to the west of Banff, at the windy *Banff Links Caravan Park* (☎01261/812228; April–Oct).

For **food** it's best to head to Macduff, where *Milo's Restaurant* (☎01261/831222; closed Mon) overlooks the working harbour and has a great line-up of seafood dishes. Bar food with a view is available from *The Knowes Hotel*. More upmarket but still moderately priced is the French restaurant in the *County Hotel* in Banff (☎01261/815353).

Cullen and around

Twelve miles west of Banff is **CULLEN**, served by bus #305 from Aberdeen. Strikingly situated beneath a superb series of arched viaducts, which were built because the earl and countess of Seafield refused to allow the railway to pass through the grounds of Cullen House, the town is made up of two sections: Seatown, by the harbour, and the new town on the hillside. There's a lovely stretch of sheltered sand by Seatown, where the colourful houses – confusingly numbered according to the order in which they were built – huddle end-on to the sea.

You can pick up leaflets about local walks at the town's independent **tourist office** on the main square of the new town, but as it's run by volunteers the opening hours can be sporadic (generally June–Aug daily 11am–5pm). Grand *Seafield Hotel* (☎01542/840791, ⓦwww.theseafieldhotel.com; ❺) is a well-run nineteenth-century coaching **inn** which has an impressive if expensive dinner menu based around top-notch local produce. The local delicacy, **Cullen skink** – a soup made from milk (or cream), potato and smoked haddock – is available at the *Seafield* and elsewhere, including the bar of the *Royal Oak Hotel* at 43–45 Castle Terrace, and the *3 Kings* **pub** on North Castle Street, both tucked in under the towering viaducts of the now disused railway.

Six miles east is the quiet village of **PORTSOY**, renowned for its green marble once shipped to Versailles, and its annual traditional boat festival in early July. The *Shore Inn* by its atmospheric old stone harbour is a good spot for a beer or a meal on a sunny day.

Buckie and Spey Bay

West of Cullen, the scruffy working fishing town of **BUCKIE** marks one end of the **Speyside Way** long-distance footpath (see p.565). This follows the coast west for five miles to windy **Spey Bay**, at the mouth of the river of the same name and also reached by a small coastal road from Buckie. It's a remote spot bounded by sea and river and sky; interpretation is offered by a small but dedicated **wildlife centre** (April–Oct daily 10.30am–5pm; Nov–March Sat & Sun 10.30am–5pm; ⓦwww.wdcs.org/wildlifecentre; free), whose main mission is researching the Moray Firth dolphin population (for more on which, see p.604). The centre, run by the Whale and Dolphin Conservation Society, houses an exhibition and a café; alongside, the Tugnet **ice house**, a partially subterranean, thick-walled house with a turf roof used by fishermen in the days before electric refrigeration to store their ice and catches, makes for an atmospheric auditorium in which films of the underwater world are shown. If you want to head out onto the Firth itself to look for sea life, the centre will advise on accredited local operators. It is sometimes possible, however, to see dolphins feeding if you wander along the long pebbly spit by the mouth of the Spey; this is also a good spot to see otters and birds, including ospreys. Spey Bay makes for an attractively remote place to **stay**: the *Spey Bay Golf Links Hotel* (☎01343/820424, ⓦwww .speybay.com; ❺), is situated right on the shore, with its golf course stretching out to the west, while the simple *Beach House B&B* (☎01343/829220; ❷) has a living room with a huge picture window looking out to sea.

Elgin and around

The lively market town of **ELGIN**, just inland about fifteen miles west of Cullen, grew up in the thirteenth century around the River Lossie. Though quite a large town with lots of roundabouts and small factories, the centre has mostly kept its medieval street plan, and while the busy main street is choked with chain stores, it does open out onto an old cobbled marketplace with a tangle of wynds and pends on either side.

On North College Street, a few blocks from the tourist office and clearly signposted, is the lovely ruin of **Elgin Cathedral** (April–Sept daily 9.30am–6.30pm; Oct–March Sat–Wed 9.30am–4.30pm; HS; £3.30, joint ticket with Spynie Palace £3.80). Once considered Scotland's most beautiful cathedral, rivalling St Andrews in importance, it's little more than a shell today, though it does retain its original facade. Founded in 1224, the three-towered building was extensively rebuilt after a fire in 1270, and stood as the region's highest religious house until 1390 when the inimical Wolf of Badenoch (Alexander

△ Elgin Cathedral

Stewart, Earl of Buchan and illegitimate son of Robert II) burned the place down, along with the rest of the town, in retaliation for having been excommunicated by the bishop of Moray when he left his wife. The cathedral suffered further during the post-Reformation period, when all its valuables were stripped and the building was reduced to a common quarry for the locals. Unusual features include the Pictish cross slab in the middle of the ruins and the cracked gravestones with their *memento mori* of skulls and crossbones. Across the road from the cathedral, the three-acre **Biblical Garden** (May–Sept daily 10am–7pm; free) has been planted with all 110 plants mentioned in the Bible, interspersed with some rather stiff-looking statues depicting the parables.

At the very top of High Street is one of Britain's oldest museums, the **Elgin Museum** (April–Oct Mon–Fri 10am–5pm, Sat 11am–4pm; Nov–March open on request or if staff are in the building; ☏01343/543675; £2), which has been housed in this building since 1843. Following a major refurbishment, it has plenty of modern touches, with displays on local history and some weird anthropological artefacts including a shrunken head from Ecuador. In addition, you can see an excellent collection of fossils, some well-explained Pictish relics and a display on the important Birnie hoard of silver Roman dinarii from 197AD found nearby.

Elgin is on the edge of whisky country, and while the attractive local **distillery**, **Glen Moray** (Mon–Fri 9.30am–5pm, plus June to mid-Sept Sat 10am–4pm; £2; ⓦwww.glenmoray.com) isn't part of the official Malt Whisky Trail (see p.566), tours are still available – the distinctive thing here is that your guide is quite likely to be the stillman, mashman or one of the other workers from the distillery floor.

Practicalities

Elgin is well served by public transport, though the **train station** served by the Aberdeen–Inverness line is slightly detached from the city centre on the south side of town.

The **tourist office**, 17 High St (April–June & Sept Mon–Sat 10am–5pm, Sun 11am–3pm; July & Aug Mon–Sat 9am–6pm, Sun 11am–4pm; Oct–March Mon–Sat 10am–4pm; ℡01343/542666), will book local **accommodation** (£3). *The Lodge*, 20 Duff Ave (℡01343/549981, ⓦwww.thelodge-elgin.com; ❸), is a good-quality B&B in a house built for a former tea-plantation owner; while *The Pines*, East Road (℡01343/552495, ⓦwww.thepinesguesthouse.com; ❸) makes for a pleasant, dignified alternative. Five miles east of town, the *Old Church of Urquhart* (℡01343/843063, ⓦwww.oldkirk.co.uk; ❷) is the most appealing place to stay in the area, an unusual and comfortable B&B in an imaginatively converted church on Meft Road.

For **food**, there's inexpensive tapas from *Tapas del Mundo*, alongside *O'Flanagan's Irish Bar* on a small close off the High Street opposite Farmfoods, while you'll get a nice coffee or adventurous lunchtime sandwich from *Jolley's*, at 3 High St between the tourist office and the museum. For great **picnic** foods, head to the old-fashioned high-street store Gordon & McPhail, 58–60 South St, an Aladdin's cave of aromas, colours and delicacies, which sells one of the widest range of malt whiskies in the world.

Pluscarden Abbey

Set in an attractive, verdant valley seven miles southwest of Elgin, **Pluscarden Abbey** (daily 9am–5pm; free; ⓦwww.pluscardenabbey.org), looms impressively large in a peaceful clearing off an unmarked road. One of only two abbeys in Scotland with a permanent community of monks, it was founded in 1230 for a French order and, in 1390, became another of the properties burnt by the Wolf of Badenoch (see opposite); recovering from this, it became a priory of the Benedictine Abbey of Dunfermline in 1454 and continued as such until monastic life was suppressed in Scotland in 1560. The abbey's revival began in 1897 when the Catholic antiquarian, John, third Marquis of Bute, started to repair the building. In 1948 his son donated it to a small group of Benedictine monks from Gloucester, who established the present community. They are an active bunch, running stained-glass workshops, making honey and even recording Gregorian chants on CDs, all of which is detailed on their website. The abbey itself is airy and tranquil, with the monks' singing often eerily floating through from the connecting chapel. It is possible to **stay** here on retreat for a few days; see the website for details.

Lossiemouth, Spynie Palace and Duffus

Five miles north of Elgin across the flat land of the Laich of Moray, Elgin's nearest seaside town, **LOSSIEMOUTH** (generally known as Lossie), is a cheery golf-oriented seaside town blessed with lovely sandy beaches; the glorious duney spit of the East Beach is reached over a footbridge across the River Lossie from the town park. In the easternmost part of the older harbour's grid of stone streets, Pitgaveny Street has the tiny **Fisheries Museum** (April–Sept Mon–Sat 10.30am–5pm; £1.50), which includes some interesting scale models of fishing boats and a re-creation of the study of local-lad-made-good James Ramsay Macdonald (1866–1937), Britain's first Labour prime minister. The town's only blight is the frequent sky-tearing noise of military aircraft from the nearby RAF base.

Lossiemouth's development as a port came when the nearby waterways of **SPYNIE**, three miles inland, silted up and became useless to the traders of Elgin. Little remains of the settlement except hulking **Spynie Palace** (April–Sept daily 9.30am–6.30pm; Oct–March Sat & Sun 9.30am–4.30pm; HS; £2.50, joint ticket with Elgin Cathedral £3.80), home of the bishops of Moray from 1107 until 1686. The enormous rectangular David's Tower – visible for miles around – offers stunning views from the top over the Moray Firth and the Spynie Canal, the much-diminished sea loch.

Straight roads and water ditches crisscross the flat land west of Spynie. Past the sinister shapes of the planes and hangars of RAF Lossiemouth is the spread-eagled settlement of **DUFFUS**, five miles west of Lossie. Old Duffus is no more than a farm or two and a motte and bailey **castle** (free access), part of which leans at a rakish angle. New Duffus, two miles northwest, is best known as the gateway to **Gordonstoun School**, the spartan (but hugely expensive) public school favoured by royalty, although Prince Charles reportedly despised its fresh-air-and-cold-showers puritanism.

Burghead

Another of this coastline's tightly packed, stone-built fishing villages, the head-land at windswept **BURGHEAD** (served by hourly bus #331 from Elgin), was once the site of an important Iron Age fort and the ancient Pictish capital of Moray. In 1805–09 a fishing village was built on the promontory where the ancient fort had sat, in the course of which some unique Pictish stone carvings known as the **Burghead Bulls** were discovered. One is on display in the small **Burghead Visitor Centre** (Easter–Sept daily noon–4pm; entry by donation) built into the round white lookout tower at the tip of the promontory; others can be seen in Elgin Museum, the National Museum in Edinburgh and the British Museum in London. The tower offers great views of the Moray Firth, while inside are displays about Pictish times and the dramatic annual fire cere-mony known as the **Burning of the Clavie**, one of only a few that still take place in Scotland. A burning tar barrel is carried around the town on January 11 to mark the old calendar's new year, before being rolled into the sea, sparks and embers flying. Tucked away down King Street, a **well** (pick up the key from the porch of 69 King St), is the most remarkable surviving feature of Pictish times. Under a barrel roof, an impressive underground chamber fed by springs is believed to have been the water supply for the Iron Age strongholds.

Findhorn

A wide sweep of sandy beach stretches five miles around Burghead Bay to **FINDHORN**, a tidy village with some neat fishermen's cottages, a delight-ful harbour dotted with moored yachts, a small **Heritage Centre** (May & Sept Sat & Sun 2–5pm; June–Aug Wed–Mon 2–5pm; free) in the village's former salmon-net sheds and grass-roofed ice house, and a couple of good pubs: on a sunny day, a pint or some seafood on the terrace at the *Kimber-bey Inn* is hard to beat. For **B&B** here, try *Yellow Sands* (☎01309/691351, ⓦwww.yellowsands.com; ❸).

Like Lossiemouth, however, it's hard to escape the military presence in the area, with **RAF Kinloss**, one of the UK's most important front-line airfields, right on its doorstep. Findhorn is best known, however, for the controversial **Findhorn Foundation** (see box opposite), based beside the town's caravan park about a mile before you reach the village itself. Visitors are generally free to stroll around the community, but it's worth trying to take a more informed look at the different activities and projects by means of a **guided tour** (April–Sept Mon, Wed, Fri–Sun 2pm; £2); you can also guide yourself via a booklet (£3) available from the shop or visitor centre. During a tour you can stop off at the community's excellent **café** (daily 10am–5pm) beside the Universal Hall Arts

The Findhorn Foundation

In 1962, with little money and no employment, Eileen and Peter Caddy, their three children and friend Dorothy Maclean, settled on a caravan site at Findhorn. Dorothy believed she had a special relationship with what she called the "devas...the archetypal formative forces of light or energy that underlie all forms in nature – plants, trees, rivers", and from the uncompromising sandy soil they built a remarkable garden filled with plants and vegetables, far larger than had ever been seen in the area.

A few of those who came to see the phenomenon stayed to help out and tune into the spiritual aspect of the daily life of the nascent community. With its emphasis on inner discovery and development, but unattached to any particular doctrine or creed, the **Findhorn Foundation** has today blossomed into a permanent community of a couple of hundred people, with a well-developed series of courses and retreats on subjects ranging from astroshamanic healing to organic gardening, drawing another eight thousand or so visitors each year. The original caravan still stands, surrounded by a whole host of newer timber buildings and other caravans employing solar power, earth roofs and other green initiatives. The most intriguing of these are a group of round houses made from huge barrels reclaimed from a Speyside whisky distillery, while elsewhere you can see an ecological sewage treatment centre, a huge wind generator and various community businesses including a pottery and weaving studio.

The foundation is not without controversy: one community leader declared that "behind the benign and apparently religious front lies a hard core of New Agers experimenting with hallucinatory techniques marketed as spirituality." Findhorn is also accused of being overly well heeled: a glance into the shop or a tally of the smart cars parked outside the well-appointed eco-houses does give some substance to such ideas. However, there's little doubt that the community appeals to large numbers of people, and it is well known around the world. The reputation of the place is such that it attracts visitors both sympathetic and cynical – and both find something to feed their impressions.

Centre, an occasional venue for good touring folk or jazz bands, while the Phoenix Community Store is a richly stocked **delicatessen** with lots of organic produce and bread baked on site. The **Visitor Centre** (Mon–Fri 10am–4pm, also open Sat & Sun 1–4pm in summer; ☎01309/690311, ⊛www.findhorn .org) has information on staying within the community, either as part of an introductory "Experience Week", or simply overnighting – a number of the eco-houses offer B&B (❷). Despite the enormous growth of the community, it is still situated on Findhorn's caravan and **camping park** (☎01309/690203, ⊛www.findhornbayholidaypark.com; April–Oct) which has tent pitches and pitches, stationary caravans (❷) and some unusual eco-chalets. The foundation is located on the B9011 about five miles northeast of Forres and served by bus #336 linking Forres High Street with Findhorn and Elgin.

Forres

FORRES (⊛www.forresweb.net), four miles southwest of Findhorn, is one of Scotland's oldest agricultural towns, and of little note except for its pretty flower-filled parks and the twenty-foot **Sueno's Stone** on the eastern outskirts of town, one of the most remarkable Pictish stones in Scotland. Now housed in what looks like a huge glass telephone box as protection against further erosion, the stone was found buried in 1726 and mistakenly named after Swein Forkbeard, King of Denmark, though it more probably commemorates a battle between the people of Moray and the Norse settlers in Orkney. Carvings on the east face can be read as one of the earliest examples of war reportage, with the story told from the arrival of the leader at the top to the decapitated corpses of the vanquished at the bottom.

Forres is on the main Inverness–Aberdeen **train** line; the train station sits half a mile west of the tourist office near the north end of Market Street. **Bus** #10 between Aberdeen/Elgin and Inverness stops outside St Leonard's Church on High Street, a little way along from Forres' friendly **tourist office** at no. 116 (April–June & Sept–Oct Mon–Sat 10am–1pm & 2–5pm, July & Aug Mon–Sat 10am–6pm; ☎01309/672938). **Accommodation** includes the *Tormhor* B&B, 11 High St (☎01309/673837, Ⓦwww.tormhor.com; ❷), which has large, comfortable rooms in a Victorian house overlooking some colourful gardens, while three miles or so west of Forres at Dyke is the *Old Kirk* (☎01309/641414, Ⓦwww.oldkirk.co.uk; ❸), which has three rooms in a bright, modern conversion of a Victorian country church. The best places to **eat** are generally out of town: try *The Loft Bistro* (☎01343/850111, Ⓦwww.eastgrange .co.uk; closed Mon) at East Grange farm near Kinloss or the daytime café at *Logie Steading* (Ⓦwww.logie.co.uk), a conversion of an old farm outbuilding which also houses a secondhand bookshop, art gallery and other small shops, located six south of Forres.

A mile of so south of Forres on the A940, the **Dallas Dhu Historic Distillery** (April–Sept daily 9.30am–6.30pm; Oct–March Sat–Wed 9.30am–4.30pm; HS; £4) is an outpost of the Malt Whisky Trail (see p.566). Unlike most distilleries, this one isn't in production and there aren't guided tours: you're free to wander through the buildings at your own pace, making use of a free personal audio guide if you choose.

Brodie Castle

Four miles west of Forres and eight miles east of Nairn (see p.606), just off the A96, is **Brodie Castle** (April, July & Aug daily noon–4pm; May, June & Sept Sun–Thurs noon–4pm; NTS; £8). Dating from 1567, this is a classic Z-shaped Scottish tower house set in lovely grounds (open all year daily 9.30am–sunset; free) with drifts of daffodils in spring and an adventure playground. Inside, there are all the rooms you'd expect: a panelled dining room with fabulous plasterwork, several bedrooms complete with four-posters, and a massive Victorian kitchen and servants' quarters, all linked by winding passages. The collections of furniture, porcelain and especially paintings are outstanding, with works by Jacob Cuyp and Edwin Landseer, among others.

Travel details

Trains

Aberdeen to: Arbroath (every 30min; 1hr); Dundee (every 30min; 1hr 15min); Edinburgh (1–2 hourly; 2hr 35min); Elgin (Mon–Sat 10 daily, Sun 5 daily; 1hr 30min); Forres (Mon–Sat 10 daily, Sun 5 daily; 1hr 45min); Glasgow (hourly; 2hr 35min); Insch (Mon–Sat 10 daily, Sun 5 daily; 35min); Inverurie (Mon–Sat 10 daily, Sun 5 daily; 20min); London (5 daily direct; 7hr); Montrose (every 30min; 45min); Nairn (Mon–Sat 10 daily, Sun 5 daily; 2hr); Stonehaven (every 30min; 15min).

Dundee to: Aberdeen (every 30min; 1hr 15min); Arbroath (hourly; 20min); Edinburgh (1–2 hourly; 1hr 15min); Glasgow (hourly; 1hr 15min); Montrose (hourly; 15min).

Elgin to: Forres (hourly; 15min); Nairn (hourly; 25min).

Buses

Aberdeen to: Ballater (hourly; 1hr 45min); Banchory (every 30min; 55min); Banff (hourly; 1hr 55min); Braemar (hourly; 2hr 10min); Crathie for Balmoral (hourly; 1hr 55min); Cruden Bay (hourly;

50min); Cullen (hourly; 2hr 30min); Dundee (hourly; 2hr); Elgin (hourly; 2hr 35min); Forres (hourly; 2hr 35min); Fraserburgh (hourly; 1hr 20min); Inverurie (hourly; 45min); Macduff (hourly; 1hr 50min); Peterhead (every 30min; 1hr 15min); Stonehaven (every 30min; 25min).

Dundee to: Aberdeen (hourly; 2hr); Arbroath (hourly; 50min); Blairgowrie (hourly; 1hr); Forfar (hourly; 30min); Glamis (2 daily; 40min); Kirrie-muir (hourly; 1hr 10min); Meigle (hourly; 40min); Montrose (hourly; 1hr 10min).

Elgin to: Aberdeen (hourly; 2hr 35min); Burghead (Mon–Sat hourly; 30min); Duffus (Mon–Sat hourly; 15min); Forres (hourly; 25min); Inverurie (hourly; 1hr 45min); Lossiemouth (every 30min; 20min); Nairn (hourly; 40min); Pluscarden (1 daily schooldays only; 20min).

Forres to: Elgin (hourly; 25min); Findhorn (hourly; 20min).

Fraserburgh to: Banff (2 daily; 55min); Macduff (2 daily; 45min).

Montrose to: Brechin (hourly; 20min).

Ferries

Aberdeen to: Kirkwall, Orkney (Thurs, Sat & Sun plus Tues in summer; 6hr); Lerwick, Shetland (daily; 10–12hr overnight).

Flights

Aberdeen to: Belfast (Mon–Fri 1 daily; 1hr 15min); Birmingham (Mon–Fri 2 daily, Sat & Sun 1 daily; 1hr 30min); Dublin (1 daily; 1hr 5min); Glasgow (1 daily; 45min); Kirkwall, Orkney (2 daily; 55min); London Gatwick (4 daily; 1hr 30min); London Heathrow (5–7 daily; 1hr 30min); London Luton (2 daily; 1hr 30min); Manchester (Mon–Fri 6 daily, Sat & Sun 2 daily; 1hr 20min); Newcastle (Mon–Fri 4 daily, Sun 2 daily; 1hr); Sumburgh, Shetland (Mon–Fri 3 daily, Sat & Sun 2 daily; 1hr).

Dundee to: London City (Mon–Fri 4 daily, Sat 1 daily, Sun 3 daily; 1hr 25min).

The Cairngorms and Speyside

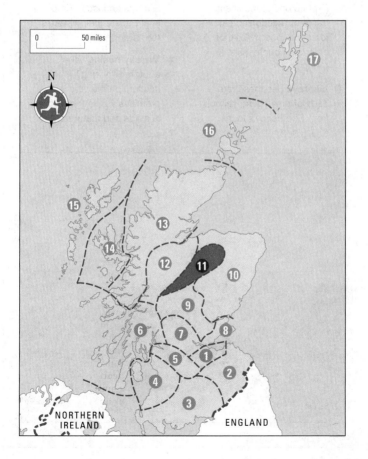

CHAPTER 11

Highlights

* **The Cairngorms** Scotland's grandest mountain massif, a place of rare plants, wild animals, inspiring vistas, and challenging outdoor activities. See p.557

* **Rothiemurchus Estate** Explore one of the finest tracts of Caledonian pine forest on foot, by bike or on cross-country skis. See p.559

* **Ospreys** See these rare birds of prey taking salmon from Strathspey's lochs. See p.562

* **Shinty** A wild mix between hockey and golf; watch a game at Kingussie or Newtonmore. See p.564

* **Speyside Way** Walking route taking in Glenfiddich, Glenlivet and Glen Grant, with the chance to drop in and taste their whiskies too. See p.565

* **Whisky nosing** Take a tutored "nosing" (tasting) on the very premises where the stuff is made and matured. See p.566

△ Walking in the Cairngorms

11

The Cairngorms and Speyside

Rising high in the heather-clad hills above remote Loch Laggan, forty miles due south of Inverness, the **River Spey**, Scotland's second longest river, drains northeast towards the Moray Firth through one of the Highlands' most spellbinding valleys. Famous for its ancient forests, salmon fishing and ospreys, the area around the upper section of the river, known as **Strathspey**, is dominated by the sculpted **Cairngorms**, Britain's most extensive mountain massif, unique in supporting subarctic tundra on its high plateau. Though the area has been admired and treasured for many years as one of Scotland's prime natural assets, the Cairngorms National Park was declared only in 2004, and even then with grumblings from conservationists about inadequate planning regulations and unnatural boundaries. Outdoor enthusiasts flock to the area to take advantage of the superb hiking, watersports and winter snows, aided by the fact that the area is easily accessible by road and rail from both the central belt and Inverness.

A string of villages along the river provides useful bases for setting out into the wilder country, principal among them **Aviemore**, a rather ugly straggle of housing and hotel developments which nevertheless has a lively, youthful feel to it. A little way north, **Grantown-on-Spey** is a more douce foil, with solid Victorian mansions but much less vitality, while smaller settlements such as **Boat of Garten** and **Kincraig** are quieter, well-kept villages popular with those who want to stay close to the natural surroundings.

Downriver, Strathspey gives way to the area known as **Speyside**, famous as the heart of Scotland's **malt whisky** industry. In addition to the Malt Whisky Trail which leads round a number of well-known distilleries in the vicinity of villages such as **Dufftown** and **Craigellachie**, the lesser-known **Speyside Way**, another of Scotland's long-distance footpaths, offers the chance to enjoy the scenery of the region, as well as its whiskies, on foot.

Strathspey

Of Strathspey's scattered settlements, **Aviemore** absorbs the largest number of visitors, particularly in midwinter when it metamorphoses into the UK's busiest ski

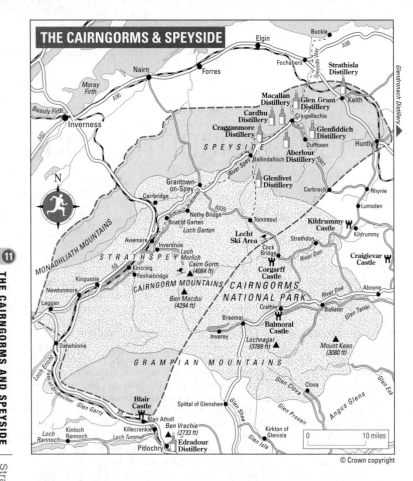

© Crown copyright

resort. The village itself isn't up to much, but it's a good first stop for information, to sort out somewhere to stay or to find out about nearby outdoor activities, which are likely to seem very enticing after a glimpse of the stunning mountain scenery provided by the 4000-foot summit plateau of the Cairngorms. The planned Georgian town of **Grantown-on-Spey** makes a good alternative base for summer visitors, but while it has more charm than Aviemore, there are fewer facilities. Further upriver, the sedate villages of **Newtonmore** and **Kingussie** are older-established holiday centres, popular more with anglers and grouse hunters than canoeists and climbers, or more recently those seeking to discover *Monarch of the Glen* country, made popular by the TV drama. Rather unusually for Scotland, the area boasts a wide choice of good-quality accommodation, particularly in the budget market, with various easygoing hostels run by and for outdoor enthusiasts.

Aviemore and around

The once-sleepy village of **AVIEMORE** was first developed as a ski and tourism resort in the mid-1960s and, over the years, it fell victim to profiteering

Cairngorms National Park

The **Cairngorms National Park** (ⓦ www.cairngorms.co.uk) covers some 1500 square miles and incorporates the **Cairngorms massif**, the largest mountainscape in the UK and the only sizeable plateau in the country over 2500ft. It's the biggest national park in Britain, and while Aviemore and the surrounding area are regarded as the main point of entry, particularly for those planning outdoor activities, it's also possible to access the eastern side of the park from both Deeside and Donside in Aberdeenshire (see p.537). Crossing the range is a significant challenge: by road the only connection is the A939 Tomintoul to Cock Bridge, frequently impassable in winter due to snow, while on foot the only way to avoid the high peaks is to follow the old cattle drovers' route called the **Lairig Ghru**, a very long day's walk between Inverdruie at the edge of Rothiemurchus and the Linn of Dee, near Inverey.

The name Cairngorm comes from the Gaelic *An Carm Gorm*, meaning "the blue hill" after the blueish-tinged stones found in the area, and within the park there are 52 summits over 2953ft, as well as a quarter of Scotland's native woodland, and a quarter of the UK's threatened wildlife species. The conservation of the landscape's unique flora and fauna is, of course, one of the principal reasons national park status was conferred. However, an important role for the park is to incorporate the communities living within it and integrate the array of outdoor activities enjoyed by visitors.

Vegetation in the area ranges from one of the largest tracts of ancient **Caledonian pine and birch forest** remaining in Scotland, at Rothiemurchus, to subarctic tundra on the high plateau, where **alpine flora** such as starry saxifrage and the star-shaped pink flowers of moss campion peek out of the pink granite in the few months of summer that the ground is free of snow. In the pine forests of the river valleys strikingly coloured **birds** such as crested tits, redwings and goldfinches can be observed, along with rarely seen **mammals** such as the red squirrel and pine marten. On the heather slopes above the forest, red and black grouse are often encountered, though their larger relative, the capercaillie, is a much rarer sight, having been reintroduced in 1837 after dying out in the seventeenth century. Birds of prey you're most likely to see are the **osprey**, best seen at the osprey observation centre (see p.562) at Loch Garten or fishing on the lochs around Aviemore, though golden eagles and peregrine falcons can occasionally be seen higher up. Venturing up to the plateau you'll have the chance of seeing the shy **ptarmigan**, another member of the grouse family, which nests on bare rock and has white plumage during winter, or even the dotterel and snow bunting, rare visitors from the Arctic, along with mountain (blue) hares, which also turn white in winter and are best seen in spring as they scurry across patches of brown hillside where the snow has melted.

developers with scant regard for the needs of the local community. Although a large-scale face-lift has removed some of the architectural eyesores of that era, the settlement remains dominated by a string of soulless shopping centres and sprawling housing estates surrounding a Victorian train station. That said, Aviemore is well equipped with services and facilities for visitors to the area and is the most convenient base for the Cairngorms, benefits which for most folk far outweigh its lack of aesthetic appeal.

The main attractions of Aviemore are its **outdoor pursuits**, though train enthusiasts are drawn to the restored **Strathspey Steam Railway**, which chugs the short distance between Aviemore and Broomhill, just beyond Boat of Garten village, five times daily through the summer (June–Sept; less regular service at other times; ☎01479/810725, ⓦwww.strathspeyrailway.co.uk for details). On a slightly more practical level, the most useful local **bus** route is the #31, which runs hourly from Aviemore to the Cairngorm mountain railway via Rothiemurchus and Loch Morlich.

Summary activities

In summer, the main activities around Aviemore are **walking** (see box on p.560) and **watersports**, and there are great opportunities for mountain biking, pony trekking and fly-fishing. Two centres offer sailing, windsurfing and canoeing: the Loch Morlich Watersports Centre (☎01479/861221, ⓦwww.lochmorlich .com), five miles or so east of Aviemore on the way to Cairn Gorm mountain, rents equipment and offers tuition in a lovely setting with a sandy beach, while six miles up-valley near Kincraig, the Loch Insh Watersports Centre (see p.563) offers the same facilities in equally beautiful surroundings. It also rents mountain bikes and boats for loch fishing, and gives ski instruction on a short dry slope. If you're looking for something that offers a bit more action, Full On Adventure (☎07885/835838, ⓦwww.fullonadventure.com) runs **white-water rafting** trips on the Findhorn river.

Riding and **pony trekking** are on offer up and down the valley: try Alvie Stables near Kincraig (☎01540/651409 or 07831/495397), or Strathspey Highland Ponies (☎01479/812345), who set out on hacks and treks from Rothiemurchus Visitor Centre at Inverdruie. **Fishing** is very much part of the local scene; you can fish for trout and salmon on the River Spey, and the Rothiemurchus Estate (ⓦwww.rothiemurchus.net) has a stocked trout-fishing loch at **Inverdruie**, where success is virtually guaranteed. Instruction and rod rental is available from the centre beside the loch. Fishing permits cost around £5–15 per day to fish a stocked loch and £25 on the Spey itself, and are sold at Speyside Sports (☎01479/810656) in Aviemore and at Loch Morlich Watersports Centre (see opposite), which also rents rods and tackle. The Aviemore tourist office has a helpful brochure on the complex series of permits required for the different lochs and waters in the Strathspey area.

The area is also great for **mountain biking**, with both Rothiemurchus and Glenmore estates more progressive in their attitude to catering for the sport with waymarked routes and maps than many. The Rothiemurchus Visitor Centre at Inverdruie has route maps, and you can also rent bikes here from Bothy Bikes (☎01479/810111, ⓦwww.bothybikes.co.uk), who have another shop in the Aviemore Shopping Centre beside the train station on Grampian Road. They hire out good-quality mountain bikes with front suspension, as well as offering advice and guided bike tours. To buy (and, in some instances, rent) other outdoor equipment, in particular **climbing** and **hill-walking** gear, try Cairngorm Mountain Sports in the centre of Aviemore (☎01479/810903).

Winter activities

Scottish **skiing** on a commercial level first really took off in Aviemore. By continental European and North American standards it's all on a tiny scale, but occasionally snow, sun and lack of crowds coincide and you can have a great day. February and March are usually the best times, but there's a chance of decent snow at any time between mid-November and April. Lots of places – not just in Aviemore itself – sell or rent equipment; for a rundown of ski schools and rental facilities in the area, check out the tourist office's *Ski Scotland* brochure or visit ⓦski.visitscotland.com.

The **Cairngorm Ski Area**, about eight miles southeast of Aviemore, above Loch Morlich in Glenmore Forest Park, is well served during winter by buses from Aviemore. You can rent skis, boards and other equipment from the Day Lodge at the foot of the ski area (☎01479/861261, ⓦwww .cairngormmountain.com, click 'winter'), which also has a shop, a bar and restaurant, as well as the base station for the **funicular railway**, the principal means of getting to the top of the ski slopes. Various types of ski pass are

△ Rothiemurchus Estate, Cairngorms

available from here – in person, by phone or online. The facilities include a ski school, cafés at three different levels and a separate terrain park for skiers and boarders. If there's lots of snow, the area around **Loch Morlich** and into the **Rothiemurchus Estate** provides enjoyable cross-country skiing through lovely woods, beside rushing burns and even over frozen lochs.

For a crash course in surviving Scottish winters, you could do worse than try a week at the National Outdoor Training Centre at *Glenmore Lodge* (see p.560) in the heart of the Glenmore Forest Park at the east end of Loch Morlich. This superbly equipped and organized centre offers winter and summer courses in hill walking, mountaineering, alpine ski-mountaineering, avalanche awareness and much besides, including an array of more recreational courses in kayaking, abseiling and the like. To add to the winter scene, there's a herd of reindeer at the **Cairngorm Reindeer Centre** by Loch Morlich (daily 10am–5pm; guided excursions to the main herd 11am, also 2.30pm May–Sept, £8; ☎01479/861228, ⓦwww.reindeer-company.demon.co.uk), while between Loch Morlich and Inverdruie the **Cairngorm Sleddog Adventure Centre** (☎07767/270526, ⓦwww.sled-dogs.co.uk), the UK's only sleddog centre, offers daily tours of the kennels and a small museum (2.30pm; £8), as well as three-hour trips on a wheeled or ski-based sled pulled by ten dogs (Oct–April only; £50 per person) and even a two-day course to learn how to take a team out yourself.

Practicalities

Aviemore's businesslike **tourist office** is in the heart of things at 7 The Parade, Grampian Rd (April–Oct Mon–Sat 9am–5pm, Sun 10am–4pm; Nov–March Mon–Fri 9am–5pm, Sat 10am–4pm). It offers an accommodation booking service and reams of leaflets on local attractions.

There's no shortage of **accommodation** locally. The *Corrour House Hotel* at Inverdruie, two miles southeast of Aviemore (☎01479/810220, ⓦwww .corrourhousehotel.co.uk; ❺), is secluded and upmarket, while the *Rowan Tree*

Walks around Aviemore

Ordnance Survey Explorer Maps nos. 402 & 403 or OS Outdoor Leisure Map no. 3.
Walking of all grades is a highlight of the Aviemore area, though before setting out you should heed the usual safety guidelines (see p.64). These are particularly important if you want to climb to the high tops, which include a number of Scotland's loftiest peaks. However, as well as the high mountain trails, there are some lovely and well-signposted **low-level walks** in the area. It takes an hour or so to complete the gentle circular walk around pretty **Loch an Eilean** (with its ruined castle) in the Rothiemurchus Estate, beginning at the end of the back road that turns east off the B970 two miles south of Aviemore. The helpful estate **visitor centres** at the lochside and by the roadside at Inverdruie provide more information on the many woodland trails that crisscross this area. A longer (2–3hr) walk through this estate, famous for its atmospheric native woodland of gnarled Caledonian pines and shimmering birch trees, starts at the near end of **Loch Morlich**. Cross the river by the bridge and follow the dirt road, turning off after about twenty minutes to follow the signs to Aviemore. The path goes through beautiful pine woods and past tumbling burns, and you can branch off to Coylumbridge and Loch an Eilean. Unless you're properly prepared for a 25-mile hike, don't take the track to the **Lairig Ghru**, a famous old cattle drovers' route through a dramatic cleft in the mountain range which eventually brings you out near Braemar on the far side of the Cairngorm range.

Another good shortish (half-day) walk leads along a well-surfaced forestry track from Glenmore Lodge up towards the **Ryvoan Pass**, taking in An Lochan Uaine, known as the "Green Loch" and living up to its name, with amazing colours that range from turquoise to slate grey depending on the weather. The track narrows once past the loch and leads east towards Deeside, so retrace your steps if you don't want a major trek. The **Glenmore Forest Park Visitor Centre** by the roadside at the turn-off to Glenmore Lodge is the starting point for the three-hour round-trip climb of Meall a' Bhuachaillie (2654ft), which offers excellent views and is usually accessible year-round. The centre has information on other trails in this section of the forest.

The **Speyside Way** (see box on p.565), the long-distance footpath which begins on the Moray Firth coast at Buckie and follows the course of the Spey through the heart of whisky country, now extends to Aviemore, with plans for further links down to Kingussie and Newtonmore. A pleasant day-trip involves walking the way from Aviemore to Boat of Garten, on to the RSPB osprey sanctuary at Loch Garten, and then returning on the Strathspey Steam Railway.

Country Hotel (℡01479/810207, ⌗www.rowantreehotel.com; ➎), by Loch Alvie, is a relaxed, comfortable alternative. In Aviemore, *Ravenscraig Guest House* (℡01479/810278, ⌗www.aviemoreonline.com; ➌), on the Grampian Road, has twelve rooms and is welcoming and family-friendly, or *Ardlogie Guest House* (℡01479/810747, ⌗www.ardlogie.co.uk; ➌) on Dalfaber Road is smaller and slightly cheaper. Aviemore's large SYHA **hostel** (℡0870/004 1104, ⌗www.syha.org.uk) is well placed within walking distance of the centre of the village; alternatively, the *Aviemore Bunkhouse* (℡01479/811181, ⌗www.aviemore-bunkhouse.com) is a large, modern place beside the Old Bridge Inn on Dalfaber Road, again within walking distance from the station. Towards the Cairngorms, there's another SYHA hostel at Loch Morlich (Christmas–Oct; ℡0870/004 1137), as well as excellent accommodation in twin rooms (with shared facilities) at *Glenmore Lodge* (℡01479/861256, ⌗www.glenmorelodge.org.uk; ➋) – full use of their superb facilities, which include a pool, weights room and indoor climbing wall is included. There's no shortage of **campsites** either: two of the best are *Rothiemurchus Caravan Park*, among the tall pine trees

at Coylumbridge on the way to Loch Morlich (☎01479/812800, ⓦwww
.rothiemurchus.net), and the Forestry Enterprise site beside the banks of Loch
Morlich (☎01479/861271).

All along Aviemore's main drag are bistros, hotels and takeaways serving fairly
predictable, run-of-the-mill **food**. One exception is the ⚞ *Mountain Café*
(☎01479/812473), above Cairngorm Mountain Sports, which serves an all-
day menu of wholesome snacks and freshly prepared meals, often using local
produce. Another good discovery is *The Einich* (☎01479/812334), tucked away
at the Rothiemurchus Visitor Centre at Inverdruie, which is open for lunch
every day and moderately priced evening meals Wednesday to Saturday. Alternatively, *The Old Bridge Inn* on the east side of the railway on Dalfaber Road,
dishes up decent pub grub and real ales in a mellow, cosy setting, while *Café
Mambo*, in Aviemore Shopping Centre on Grampian Road, matches its bright,
funky decor with a cheerful burger'n'chips-style menu.

Cairn Gorm mountain

From Aviemore, a road leads past Rothiemurchus and Loch Morlich and winds
its way up into the Cairngorms, reaching the Coire Cas car park at a height
of 2150ft. Here there's the base station for the ski area and the departure point
for the **Cairn Gorm Mountain Railway** (daily 10am–5.15pm; last train up
4.30pm; trains run every 15min; £8.50; ⓦwww.cairngormmountain.com), a
two-car funicular system that runs to the top of the ski area. A highly controversial, £15 million scheme which was bitterly opposed by conservationists
objecting to the man-made scar it creates in such a beautiful environment, the
railway whisks skiers in winter, and tourists at any time of year, along a mile and
a half of track to the top station at an altitude of 3600ft, not far from the summit
of Cairn Gorm mountain. The top station incorporates an exhibition/interpre-
tation area and a café/restaurant from which spectacular views can be had on
clear days, though you should note that there is no access beyond the confines
of the top station and its open-air viewing terrace unless you're embarking on
winter skiing; anyone wanting to walk on the subarctic Cairngorm plateau will
have to trudge up from the car park at the bottom. In winter the funicular starts
earlier in the day if skiing is possible.

At the base station there's a **ranger office** (daily: April–Oct 9am–5pm; Nov–
March 8.30am–4.30pm) where you can find out about various trails heading
out from the base station. If you're aiming to head to the summits, check here
for the latest weather report. The simplest of the walks is around a **Mountain
Garden Trail**, which features shrubs and trees native to the Cairngorms. The
Ptarmigan **restaurant** at the top station offers self-service meals through the
day and, in summer (July–Sept), more formal "sunset dining" on Friday and
Saturday evenings, as well as a ceilidh on Thursday evening (July & Aug only).
Pre-booking is required for both (☎01479/861336).

Carrbridge

Worth considering as an alternative to Aviemore – particularly as a skiing base
– **CARRBRIDGE** is a pleasant, quiet village about seven miles north. Look
out for the spindly Bridge of Carr at the northern end of the village, built in
1717 and still making a graceful stone arch over the River Dulnain. The main
attraction in the village is the **Landmark Forest Heritage Park** (daily: April
to mid-July 10am–6pm; mid-July to Aug 10am–7pm; Sept–March 10am–5pm;
£8.95 ⓦwww.landmark-centre.co.uk), which combines interactive exhibitions
with forest walks, nature trails, a maze and fun rides; it's more tastefully done than
some similar places and an excellent place for children to let off steam. For local

accommodation, both *Carrmoor Guest House*, Carr Road (☎01479/841244, ⓦwww.carrmoorguesthouse.co.uk; ❷), and the friendly *Cairn Hotel*, Main Road (☎01479/841212, ⓦwww.cairnhotel.co.uk; ❷), are central to the village, while *Feith Mhor Lodge* (☎01479/841621, ⓦwww.feithmhor.co.uk; ❸) is an attractive B&B just a mile southwest along Station Road with terrific views. The cosy, basic *Carrbridge Bunkhouse* (☎01479/841250, ⓦwww.carrbridge-bunkhouse .co.uk), a timber-lined cabin with its own sauna, is a good base for walkers half a mile or so north of the village on the Inverness road.

Loch Garten and around

The **Abernethy Forest RSPB Reserve** on the shore of **LOCH GARTEN**, seven miles northeast of Aviemore and eight miles south of Grantown-on-Spey, is famous as the nesting site of one of Britain's rarest birds. A little over fifty years ago, the **osprey**, known in North America as the fish hawk, had completely disappeared from the British Isles. Then, in 1954, a single pair of these exquisite white-and-brown raptors mysteriously reappeared and built a nest in a tree half a mile or so from the loch. Although efforts were made to keep the exact location secret, one year's eggs fell victim to a gang of thieves, and thereafter the area became the centre of an effective high-security operation. Now the birds are well established not only here but elsewhere, and there are believed to be up to 150 pairs nesting across the Highlands. The best time to visit is between April and August, when the ospreys return from West Africa to nest and the RSPB opens an **observation centre** (daily 10am–6pm; £3.50; ☎01479/821409), complete with powerful telescopes and CCTV monitoring of the nest. This is the place to come to get a glimpse of osprey chicks in their nest; you'll be luckier to see the birds perform their trademark swoop over water to pluck a fish out with their talons, though nearby Loch Garten, as well as Loch Morlich and Loch Insh, are good places to stake out in the hope of a sighting, while one of the best spots is the Rothiemurchus trout loch at Inverdruie. The reserve is also home to several other species of rare birds and animals, including the Scottish crossbill, capercaillie, whooper swan and red squirrel; once-weekly **guided walks** leave from the observation centre (Wed 9.30am), while during the spring lekking season (April to mid-May) when male capercaillie gather and joust with each other, the centre opens very early in the morning for "Caperwatch" (daily 5.30–8am; £3) so that you can see the activity both live and on CCTV.

Loch Garten is about a mile and a half west of **BOAT OF GARTEN** village: from the village, cross the Spey then take the Grantown road, and the reserve is signposted to the right. An attractive wee place, Boat of Garten has a number of good **accommodation** options: *Fraoch Lodge*, 15 Deshar Rd (☎01479/831331, ⓦwww.scotmountain.co.uk; ❶), is an excellent hostel with four twin rooms and a family room that sleeps four, and provides high-quality home-cooked meals along with good facilities such as a purpose-built drying room. It is enthusiastically run by experienced mountaineers, who also offer guided walking holidays and instruction in mountain skills. Alternatively, the *Old Ferryman's House* (☎01479/831370; ❷), just across the Spey, is a wonderfully homely, hospitable B&B, with no TVs, lots of books and delicious evening meals and breakfasts.

Kincraig

At **KINCRAIG**, six miles southwest of Aviemore on the B9152 towards Kingussie, there are a couple of unusual encounters with animals which offer a memorable diversion if you're not setting off on outdoor pursuits. While the style of the **Highland Wildlife Park** (daily: June–Aug 10am–7pm; April, May, Sept & Oct closes 6pm; Nov–March closes 4pm; last entry 2hr before closing; in snowy conditions call in advance; £8.50; T01540/651270, Wwww .highlandwildlifepark.org), with its various captive animals, may not appeal to everyone, it is accredited to the Royal Zoological Society of Scotland and offers a chance to see exotic foreigners such as wolves and bison, as well as many rarely seen natives, including pine martens, capercaillie, wildcat and eagles. Nearby, the engrossing **Working Sheepdogs** demonstrations at Leault Farm (May–Oct Sun–Fri noon & 4pm; Nov–April call T01540/651310 to arrange a visit; £4) afford the rare opportunity to see a champion shepherd herd a flock of sheep with up to eight dogs, using whistles and other commands. The fascinating hour-long display also includes a chance to see traditional hand-shearing, duck-herding and displays on how collie pups are trained. Meanwhile, the Loch Insh Watersports Centre (T01540/651272, Wwww.lochinsh.com) runs a **Wildlife Passenger Boat safari** around Loch Insh and into Inchmarsh RSPB reserve (four trips daily April–Oct; £8).

There are some good low-price **accommodation** options nearby. The Loch Insh Watersports Centre (see above) has basic but practical en-suite B&B and self-catering chalets (❷) as well as a decent waterfront café/restaurant (daily: Feb–Oct 10am–10pm; Nov–Jan 10am–6pm). At the remote *Glen Feshie Hostel* at Balachroick (T01540/651323), three miles from Loch Insh down beautiful Glen Feshie, the all-in price includes bed linen and as much porridge as you like for breakfast.

Grantown-on-Spey

Buses run from Aviemore and Inverness to the small town of **GRANTOWN-ON-SPEY** (Wwww.grantownonspey.com), about fifteen miles northeast of Aviemore, a relaxing alternative base for exploring the Strathspey area. Life is concentrated around the central square, with its attractive Georgian architecture, including a small **museum** and resource centre on Burnfield Avenue (March–Dec Mon–Sat 10am–4pm; £2; Wwww.grantownmuseum.co.uk), which tells the story of the town; it also offers **Internet access**. The **tourist office** is on the High Street (March–Oct Mon–Sat 9am–5pm, Sun 10am–4pm). Local **bike rental** is provided by Bike Hire Scotland (T07739/901396), which will deliver smart mountain bikes, along with maps, helmets and rucksacks, to your accommodation.

As with much of Speyside, there's a decent choice of **accommodation**. For B&B, *Parkburn Guest House* (T01479/873116, Wwww.parkburnguesthouse .co.uk; ❸) on the High Street is welcoming, while if you're after something more upmarket head for the large seventeenth-century *Garth Hotel*, at the north end of the square (T01479/872836, Wwww.garthhotel.com; ❺) or the smart *Auchendean Lodge Hotel* (T01479/851347, Wwww.auchendean.com; April–Oct; ❻), three miles southeast of Grantown near Dulnain Bridge, best known for its gourmet meals. In the budget range, there's a bunkhouse at *Ardenbeg Outdoor Centre* (T01479/872824, Wwww.ardenbeg.co.uk), on Grant Road, parallel to the High Street, which also serves as a base for courses in hill walking, climbing, canoeing and skiing, while a mile or two south of town at Nethy Bridge, between Grantown and Boat of Garten, is the tiny, eight-bed *Lazy Duck Hostel* (T01479/821642, Wwww.lazyduck.co.uk), a peaceful and comfortable retreat with great moorland walking on its doorstep.

To **eat out** in grand style, head for the *Auchendean Lodge Hotel* (see above) near Dulnain Bridge, where the highly rated meals sometimes include locally collected mushrooms. Within Grantown itself, the new ☘ *Glass House* restaurant on Grant Road (☎01479/872980) serves excellent, moderate to expensive contemporary Scottish food in a relaxed conservatory dining room. *Tyree House Hotel* on the square is the place to head for bar food or a **drink**.

Newtonmore and Kingussie

Twelve miles southwest of Aviemore, close neighbours **NEWTONMORE** and **KINGUSSIE** (pronounced "king-*yoos*-ee") are pleasant villages at the head of the Strathspey Valley separated by a couple of miles of farmland. However, on the **shinty** field their peaceful coexistence is forgotten and the two become bitter rivals; in recent years Kingussie has been the dominant force in the game, a fierce, home-grown relative of hockey (Ⓦwww.shinty.com). The chief attraction is the excellent **Highland Folk Museum** (☎01540/661307, Ⓦwww.highlandfolk.com), split between complementary sites in the two towns. The Kingussie section (April–Sept Mon–Sat 9.30am–5pm; Oct Mon–Fri 9.30am–4pm; rest of the year by appointment; guided tours on the hour; £2.50) contains an absorbing collection of artefacts typical of traditional Highland ways of life, as well as a farming museum, an old smokehouse, a mill, a Hebridean blackhouse and a traditional herb and flower garden; most days in summer there's a demonstration of various traditional crafts. The larger outdoor site at Newtonmore (April to end Aug daily 10.30am–5.30pm; Sept daily 11am–4.30pm; Oct Mon–Fri 11am–4.30pm; £5, or £6 for both sites), tries to create more of a living history museum, with an old vintage bus offering a jump-on/jump-off tour round reconstructions of a working croft, a water-powered sawmill, a church where recitals on traditional Highland instruments are given and a small village of blackhouses constructed using only authentic tools and materials.

Kingussie is also notable for the ruins of **Ruthven Barracks** (free access), standing east across the river on a hillock. The best-preserved garrison built to pacify the Highlands after the 1715 rebellion, it makes for great exploring by day and is impressively floodlit at night. Taken by the Jacobites in 1744, Ruthven was blown up in the wake of Culloden to prevent it from falling into enemy hands. It was also the place from where clan leader Lord George Murray dispatched his acrimonious letter to Bonnie Prince Charlie, holding him personally responsible for the string of blunders that had precipitated their defeat.

In Kingussie, the best place for local **tourist information** is the Highland Folk Museum (see above). The Wildcat Centre in Newtonmore (varied hours, though generally Mon–Fri 9.30am–12.30pm & 2.15–5.15pm, Sat 9.30am–12.30pm; Oct–March mornings only; ☎01540/673131) also offers local information and details of some well-organized walking trails in the area. Bike rental is available at Service Sports on the High Street in Kingussie (☎01540/661228). One of the most appealing places **to stay** on the whole of Speyside is the relaxed but stylish ☘ *The Cross* restaurant with rooms (☎01540/661166, Ⓦwww.thecross .co.uk; ❼) located in a converted tweed mill on the banks of the River Gynack. The best **B&B** accommodation is on the outskirts of the village: the *Auld Poor House* (☎01540/661558, Ⓦwww.yates128.freeserve.co.uk; ❷), on the road to Kincraig, is a comfortable place with a resident qualified masseuse, while *Ruthven Steadings* (☎01540/662328, Ⓦwww.ruthvensteadings.co.uk; ❷) has two spacious rooms and is just along the road from the striking ruined barracks. The best of a number of local **hostels** are in Newtonmore: the *Newtonmore Independent Hostel* (☎01540/673360, Ⓦwww.highlandhostel.co.uk) is a welcoming and well-equipped place, while the *Strathspey Mountain Hostel* (☎01540/673694, ⓦwww.newtonmore.com/strathspey), just up the road, is also of a high standard and welcomes families and groups.

The most ambitious **food** in the area is served at *The Cross* (see opposite; restaurant closed Sun & Mon), where the meals, though expensive, make imaginative use of local ingredients and there's a vast wine list. Cheaper food is available at several cafés and pubs in both towns – *Gilly's Kitchen* on the main street in Kingussie is open during the day for simple but good home-made soup, panini, and home baking, while the *Silverfjord Hotel* by the train station at Kingussie is a good spot for a bar snack or meal.

Speyside

Strictly speaking, the term **Speyside** refers to the entire region surrounding the Spey river, but to most people the name is synonymous with the **whisky triangle**, stretching from just north of Craigellachie, down towards Tomintoul in the south and east to Huntly. Indeed, there are more whisky distilleries and famous brands concentrated in this small area (including Glenfiddich and Glenlivet) than in any other part of the country. Running through the heart of the region is the River Spey, whose clean, clear, fast-running waters not only play such a vital part in the whisky industry, but are also home to thousands of salmon, making it one of Scotland's finest angling locations. Obviously fertile, the tranquil glens of the area have none of the ruggedness of other parts of the Highlands, and as such its charms are subtle rather than dramatic, with tourism blending into a local economy kept healthy by whisky and farming, rather than dominating it.

At the centre of Speyside is the quiet market town of **Dufftown**, full of solid, stone-built workers' houses and dotted with no fewer than nine whisky distilleries. Along with the well-kept nearby villages of **Craigellachie** and **Aberlour**, it makes the best base for a tour of whisky country, whether on the official Malt Whisky Trail or more independent explorations. Fewer visitors take the chance

The Speyside Way

The **Speyside Way**, with its beguiling blend of mountain, river, wildlife and whisky, is fast establishing itself as an appealing and less-taxing alternative to the popular West Highland and Southern Upland long-distance footpaths. Starting at **Buckie** on the Moray Firth coast (see p.545), it follows the fast-flowing River Spey from its mouth at Spey Bay south to **Aviemore** (see p.556), with branches linking it to **Dufftown**, Scotland's malt whisky capital, and **Tomintoul** on the remote edge of the Cairngorm mountains. Some 65 miles long without taking on the branch routes, the whole thing is a five- to seven-day expedition, but its proximity to main roads and small villages means that it is excellent for shorter walks or even bicycle trips, especially in the heart of **distillery** country between Craigellachie and Glenlivet: Glenfiddich, Glenlivet, Macallan and Cardhu distilleries, as well as the Speyside Cooperage, lie directly on or a short distance off the route. Other highlights include the chance to encounter an array of **wildlife**, from dolphins at Spey Bay to ospreys at Loch Garten, as well as the restored **railway** trips on offer at Dufftown and Aviemore. The path uses disused railway lines for much of its length, and there are simple campsites and good B&Bs at strategic points along the route. For more details contact the Speyside Way Visitor Centre at Aberlour (☎01340/881266, ⓦwww.speysideway.org).

Speyside is the heart of Scotland's **whisky** industry, with over fifty distilleries testimony to a unique combination of clear, clean water, benign climate and gentle upland terrain. Yet for all the advertising-influenced visions of timeless traditions and unspoilt glens, it's worth keeping in mind that in these parts whisky is a hard-edged, multimillion-pound business dominated by huge corporations, and to many working distilleries visitors are an afterthought, if not a downright nuisance. It sometimes comes as a surprise to visitors that a lot of distilleries are unglamorous industrial units, and by no means all are open to the public. Having said that, there are plenty located in attractive historic buildings which now go to some lengths to provide an engaging experience for visitors. Mostly this involves a tour around the essential stages in the whisky-making process, though for real enthusiasts a number of distilleries now offer pricier connoisseur tours with a tutored tasting (or **nosing**, as it's properly called) and in-depth studies of the distiller's art. Note that some tours have restrictions on children.

There are eight distilleries on the official **Malt Whisky Trail** (@www.maltwhiskytrail .com), a clearly signposted seventy-mile meander around the region. Unless you're seriously interested in whisky, it's best to just pick out a couple that appeal. All offer a guided tour (some are free, others charge but then give you a voucher which is redeemable against a bottle of whisky from the distillery shop), with a tasting to round it off; if you're driving you'll often be offered a miniature to take away with you. Most people travel the route by car, though you could cycle parts of it, or even walk using the Speyside Way (see box on p.565). The following are selected highlights:

Cardhu, on the B9102 at Knockando (Easter–June Mon–Fri 10am–5pm; July–Sept Mon–Sat 10am–5pm, Sun noon–4pm; Oct Mon–Fri 11am–4pm; Nov–Easter Mon–Fri tours at 11am, 1pm & 2pm; £4 including voucher). This distillery was established over a century ago when the founder's wife was nice enough to raise a red flag to warn local crofters if the authorities were on the lookout for their illegal stills. With attractive, pagoda-topped buildings in a nice location, it sells rich, full-bodied whisky with distinctive peaty flavours that comes in an attractive bulbous bottle.

Glen Grant, Rothes (April–Oct Mon–Sat 10am–4pm, Sun 12.30–4pm; free). A well-known, floral whisky aggressively marketed to the younger customer. A regular, well-informed tour, but the highlight here is the attractive Victorian gardens, a mix of well-tended lawns and mixed, mature trees which include a tumbling waterfall and a hidden whisky safe.

Glenfiddich, on the A941 just north of Dufftown (April to mid-Oct Mon–Sat 9.30am–4.30pm, Sun noon–4.30pm; rest of year Mon–Fri 9.30am–4.30pm; free). The biggest and slickest of all the Speyside distilleries, despite the fact that it's still owned by the same Grant family who founded it in 1887, this was the first distillery to offer regular tours to visitors. It's a light, sweet whisky packaged in triangular-shaped bottles – unusually, the bottling is still done on the premises and is part of the tours (which are offered in various languages). A Connoisseurs' Tour

to discover the more remote glens, such as **Glenlivet**, which push higher up towards the Cairngorm massif, nestled into which is Britain's highest village, **Tomintoul**, situated on the edge of both whisky country and a large expanse of wild uplands. Though not surrounded by distilleries, the market town of **Huntly** has an impressive ruined castle and serves as a useful point of entry if you're coming into the region from the Aberdeenshire side. While you'll also find distilleries in towns to the north such as Elgin and Forres, these are regarded as being on the periphery of the Speyside region, and we've included both towns in our account of the coastal route around Northeast Scotland (see chapter 10).

is available (£12), as well as an even more specialized tour of the linked Balvenie distillery (£20). Glenfiddich also has its own café-bar and an artists-in-residence programme each summer.

Glenlivet, on the B9008 to Tomintoul (April–Oct Mon–Sat 10am–4pm, Sun 12.30–4pm; free). A famous name in a lonely hillside setting. This was the first licensed distillery in the Highlands, following the 1823 Act of Parliament which aimed to reduce illicit distilling and smuggling. The Glenlivet twelve-year-old malt is a floral, fragrant, medium-bodied whisky. A stretch of the Speyside Way passes through the distillery grounds.

Strathisla, Keith (April–Oct Mon–Sat 10am–4pm, Sun 12.30–4pm; £5). A small, old-fashioned distillery claiming to be Scotland's oldest (1786); it's certainly one of the most attractive, with classic pagoda-shaped buildings and the River Isla rushing by. Inside there are some impressive and interesting bits of equipment such as an old-fashioned mashtun and brass-bound spirit safes. The malt itself has a rich, almost fruity taste and is pretty rare, but is used as the heart of the better known Chivas Regal blend. You can arrive here on board one of the restored trains of the Keith & Dufftown Railway (see p.568).

In addition, the **Speyside Cooperage** at Craigellachie (see p.569) is part of the official trail, and while there's no whisky made here, a visit offers a fascinating glimpse of a highly skilled and vital part of the industry.

There are also a number of other distilleries, not on the official trail, that you can visit:

Aberlour, on the outskirts of the village (April–Oct Mon–Sat 10.30am & 2pm, Sun 11.30am & 3pm; £7.50; booking essential ☎01340/881249). The twice-daily tours are also quite specialized, with a tutored nosing and the chance to buy and fill your own bottle of cask-strength single malt.

Cragganmore, at Ballindalloch (tours July–Sept Mon–Fri 2.30pm; booking essential ☎01479/874700; £4), also offers a personalized, exclusive tour by appointment which includes a tasting.

Glendronach, eight miles northeast of Huntly (Mon–Fri tours 10am & 2pm, shop 9am–4pm; free). An isolated distillery that makes much of its malt's place at the heart of the well-known *Teacher's* blend, as well as the fact that, uniquely, the stills are heated in the traditional method by coal fires.

Macallan, near Craigellachie (April–Oct Mon–Sat 9.30am–5pm, Nov–March Mon–Fri 11am–3pm; ☎01340/872280) can only take ten people on its tours, and therefore doesn't get the coaches pulling in. Three different tours leave from their small, modern visitor centre: the half-hour "Macallan experience" (free), a one-hour, in-depth "Spirit of Macallan" tour (£8), and the "Macallan Precious Whisky Tour" (£15) which includes a tutored nosing of four different Macallan whiskies. Bookings are essential for both the latter two tours, and all tours can be restricted during the "silent season" when whisky isn't distilled, which generally lasts from early July to mid-August.

Transport connections are poor through the area, with irregular buses connecting the main villages, and almost no service at all to remoter parts such as Glenlivet and Tomintoul. The only mainline railway stops in the area are at Keith, twelve miles northeast of Dufftown, and Huntly.

Dufftown

The cheery community of **DUFFTOWN**, founded in 1817 by James Duff, fourth Earl of Fife, proudly proclaims itself "Malt Whisky Capital of the World" for the reason that it produces more of the stuff than any other town in Britain.

△ Glenfiddich distillery, Dufftown

A more telling statistic, perhaps, is that as a result Dufftown also raises more capital for the exchequer per head of population than anywhere else in the country. There are nine distilleries around Dufftown (not all of them still working), as well as a cooperage and a coppersmith, and an extended stroll around the outskirts of the town gives a good idea of the density of whisky distilling going on, with glimpses of giant warehouses filled with barrels of the stuff and whiffs of fermenting barley or peat smoke lingering on the breeze.

There isn't a great deal to do in the town, but it's a useful starting point for orienting yourself towards the whisky trail. The small, volunteer-run **Whisky Museum** at 24 Fife St (Mon–Fri 1–4pm, Sat & Sun variable hours; free) has a slightly disorganized collection of illicit distilling equipment, books and old photographs. On the edge of town along the A941 is the town's largest working distillery, **Glenfiddich** (see box on p.566), as well as the old Dufftown train station, which has been restored by enthusiasts in recent years and is now the departure point for the **Keith & Dufftown Railway** (April–Sept 3 trips daily Sat & Sun, June–Aug also runs Fri; 40min; ☏01340/821181, ⓦwww.keith-dufftown .org.uk for journey times), which uses various restored diesel locomotives to chug through whisky country to Keith, home of the Strathisla distillery (see box on p.567). Beside the platform at Dufftown a permanent buffet car serves coffee, tea, soup and home-baked cakes. Behind Glenfiddich distillery, the ruin of the thirteenth-century **Balvenie Castle** (April–Sept daily 9.30am–6.30pm; HS; £2.50) sits on a mound overlooking vast piles of whisky barrels. The castle was a Stewart stronghold, which was abandoned after the 1745 uprising, when it was last used as a government garrison. There are more atmospheric remains to be seen if you're approaching Dufftown from the south along the A941; look out for the gaunt hill-top ruins of **Auchindoun Castle** about three miles before you reach town. Although you can't go inside, it's enjoyable to wander along the track from the main road to this three-storey keep encircled by Pictish earthworks.

Practicalities

Dufftown's four main streets converge on its main square, scene of a lively annual party on Hogmanay, when free drams are handed out to revellers. The official **tourist office** is located inside the handsome clocktower at the centre of the square (April–June, Sept & Oct Mon–Sat 10am–1pm & 2–5pm, Sun 11am–3pm; July & Aug Mon–Sat 10am–6pm, Sun 11am–3pm; ☎01340/820501), though an informal information and accommodation booking service has developed at The Whisky Shop (☎01340/821097) across the road. You'll certainly need to look no further than this for a vast array of whiskies and beers produced not just on Speyside but all over Scotland; nosings and other special events are organized regularly here, most notably the twice-yearly **Spirit of Speyside Whisky Festival** (ⓦwww.spiritofspeyside.com), which draws whisky experts and enthusiasts to the area late April and late September.

There's a handful of places to stay in Dufftown itself, although you may choose to look elsewhere on Speyside where you will feel a bit closer to the attractive countryside. The only **hostel** accommodation nearby is the small self-catering *Swan Bunkhouse* (☎01542/810334), located at Drummuir, three miles northeast of Dufftown; unfortunately there's no public transport this far. In town, *Morven*, on the main square (☎01340/820507, ⓦwww.dufftown .co.uk/morven.htm; ❶), offers simple, cheap **B&B**, while *Tannochbrae*, 22 Fife St (☎01340/820541, ⓦwww.tannochbrae.co.uk; ❸) is a pleasant, enthusiastically run place with a small restaurant, *Scott's*, on the ground floor. You can also rent **bikes** from here.

The smartest of Dufftown's **restaurants** are the expensive *La Faisanderie*, on the corner of The Square and Balvenie Street (☎01340/821273; closed Tues), which serves local produce such as trout and game in a French style and puts on a special whisky-tasting dinner on Fridays, and *Taste of Speyside*, 10 Balvenie St (☎01340/820860), just off The Square, which is moderately priced and manages to be even more Scottish in its presentation. Less pricey are *Scott's*, on Fife Street, or one of the two fish and chip shops in town. Whisky isn't in short supply in the local pubs and hotels, but for the largest collection in the area you have to head to the *Grouse Inn* at Cabrach, tucked away among the hills ten miles out along the A941 to Rhynie.

Craigellachie

Four miles north of Dufftown, the small settlement of **CRAIGELLACHIE** (pronounced "Craig-*ell*-ach-ee") sits above the confluence of the sparkling waters of the Fiddich and the Spey. From the village, you can look down on a beautiful iron bridge over the Spey built by Thomas Telford in 1815. The local distillery isn't open to the public, though Glen Grant with its attractive gardens is only a few miles up the road at Rothes, and, for an unusual alternative to a distillery tour, the **Speyside Cooperage** (Mon–Fri 9.30am–4pm; £3.10) is well worth a visit. After a short exhibition explaining the ancient and skilled art of cooperage, you're shown onto a balcony overlooking the large workshop where the oak casks for whisky are made and repaired by fast-working, highly skilled coopers.

For somewhere **to stay** in the village there's an extremely welcoming and tasteful B&B attached to the ⚜ *Green Hall Gallery* on Victoria Street (☎01340/871010, ⓦwww.aboutscotland.com/greenhall; ❸); just along the road, the grand *Craigellachie Hotel* (☎01340/881204, ⓦwww.craigellachie .com; ❼) is the epitome of sumptuous, "tartan-draped" Scottish hospitality, with classy cuisine and a bar lined with whisky bottles. In 2003 the hotel was the unlikely setting for peace talks about the disputed region of Nagorno-Karabakh in Central Asia. In Archiestown, a few miles west of Craigellachie, the pleasant, traditional *Archiestown Hotel* (☎01340/810218, ⓦwww.archiestownhotel.co.uk; ❻) caters for fishermen and outdoor types, and serves good evening **meals**. For more down-to-earth pub grub you're better off heading to the busy *Highlander Inn* (☎01340/881446, ⓦwww.whiskyinn.com; ❻) on Victoria Street in Craigellachie, which serves decent meals, has frequent folk **music sessions** in its bar, and five guestrooms. The tiny *Fiddichside Inn*, on the A95 just outside Craigellachie, is a wonderfully original and convivial **pub** with a garden by the river; quite unfazed by the demands of fashion, it has been in the hands of just two landladies (mother and daughter) for the last seventy years or so.

Aberlour

Two miles southwest from Craigellachie is **ABERLOUR**, officially "Charlestown of Aberlour". Founded in 1812 by Charles Grant, its long main street, neat, flower-filled central square and well-trimmed lawns running down to the Spey have all the markings of a planned village. Though you can visit the distillery here, it's another local produce, **shortbread**, which is exported in greater quantity around the world, mostly in tartan tins adorned with kilted warriors. A local baker, **Joseph Walker**, set up shop here at the turn of the twentieth century, quickly gaining a reputation for the product which seems to epitomize the Scottish sweet tooth. A small shop on the High Street, though not the original branch, has a suitably old-fashioned facade, and sells a range of shortbread, oatcakes and other bakery; if you're really keen, you can join the coach-loads who visit the factory shop on the outskirts of the village.

Aberlour is right on the Speyside Way (see box on p.565), and the **visitor centre** occupies half of the old train station, just back from the main square (May–Oct daily 10am–5pm; Nov–April open when ranger in office; ☎01340/881266, ⓦwww.speysideway.org). The centre has detailed information boards about natural history and other aspects of the way, a relief map of the entire route and films about the area; you can also buy maps of the route and pick up accommodation and transport information as well as the latest weather forecast. While the **campsite** here, *Aberlour Gardens Caravan Park* (☎01340/871586, ⓦwww .aberlourgardens.co.uk; March–Dec), is the best in the area, it's a walk of a mile and a half from either Aberlour or Craigellachie. Alternatively, there's simple and inexpensive **B&B** at *Knockside* (☎01340/881561, ⓦwww.speyside.moray .org/Aberlour/knockside.html; ❶), a mile southeast of the town with nice views. The best place to **eat and drink** is the *Mash Tun*, in the heart of Aberlour near the Spey, a pleasant, traditional pub which serves up good bar meals, real ales and all the local whiskies. To stock up for an encounter with the great outdoors, Walker's is the place for bakery, but you'll also find a range of lovely deli produce at the Spey Larder, right by the village square.

Glenlivet

Beyond Aberlour, the Spey and the main road both head generally southwest to Ballindalloch and, a dozen miles beyond that, Grantown-on-Spey, at the head of the Strathspey region (see p.563). South from Ballindalloch are the quieter, remote glens of the Avon (pronounced "*A'an*") and Livet rivers. The distillery at **GLENLIVET**, founded in 1824 by George Smith, is one of the most famous on Speyside, and certainly enjoys one of the more attractive settings. You can **stay** in George Smith's former house, right beside the distillery: 🏠

Minmore House (☎01807/590378, ⓦwww.minmorehousehotel.com; ❼), has a lovely country-house feel with antique furniture and a wood-panelled bar. The owner is a chef and the **meals**, available to non-residents if they book ahead, are superb.

Tomintoul

South of Glenlivet, deep into the foothills of the Cairngorms, **TOMINTOUL** (pronounced "*tom*-in-towel") is, at 1150ft, the highest village in the Scottish Highlands, and is the northern gateway to the **Lecht** ski area (see box below). Tomintoul owes its existence to the post-1745 landowners' panic when, as in other parts of the north, isolated inhabitants were forcibly moved to new, planned villages, where a firm eye could be kept on everybody. Its long, thin layout is reminiscent of a Wild West frontier town; Queen Victoria, passing through, wrote that it was "the most tumble-down, poor looking place I ever saw". A spur of the Speyside Way connects Ballindalloch through Glenlivet to Tomintoul, and there are plenty of other terrific walking opportunities in the area, as well as some great routes for mountain biking. Information and useful maps about the extensive Glenlivet Crown Estate (ⓦwww.crownestate.co.uk /glenlivet), its wildlife (including reindeer) and numerous paths and bike trails are available from the tourist office or the estate **ranger's office** at the far end of the long main street (open when staff present; ☎01807/580283). Land Rover and walking safaris are offered locally by Glenlivet Wildlife (☎01807/590241, ⓦwww.glenlivet-wildlife.co.uk), including trips out to see black grouse, birds of prey and roe deer.

In the central square, the **tourist office** (April–June, Sept & Oct Mon–Sat 9.30am–1pm & 2–5pm; July & Aug Mon–Sat 9am–6pm, Sun 1–5pm; ☎01807/580285) also acts as the local **museum** (same times; free), with mock-ups of an old farm kitchen and a smithie. It is possible to **camp** beside the Glenlivet Estate ranger's office, though there are no facilities. There's a recently renovated SYHA **hostel** situated in the old schoolhouse on Main Street (☎0870/004 1152; mid-March to Sept). Of the **B&Bs**, try *Findron Farmhouse*, a working farm half a mile south of town on the Braemar road (☎01807/580382, ⓦwww.findronfarmhouse.co.uk; ❶), while the *Glenavon* (☎01807/580218, ⓦwww.glenavon-hotel.co.uk; ❸) is the most convivial of the **hotels** gathered around the main square. For something to eat, head to the *Clockhouse* **restaurant** (☎01807/580378), also on the square. The Whisky Castle shop at 6 Main St not only stocks something like four hundred different types of whisky, but also operates as a coffee shop and rents out **bikes** (☎01807/580213).

Skiing and go-karting at the Lecht

The Lecht is the most remote of Scotland's ski areas, but it works hard to make itself appealing with a range of winter and summer activities. While its twenty runs include some gentle beginners' slopes there's little really challenging for experienced skiers other than a Snowboard Fun Park, with specially built jumps and ramps. Snow-making equipment helps extend the snow season beyond January and February, while there are also various summer activities, including quad bikes and "Deval karts", go-karts with balloon tyres imported from the Alps which you can use to speed down the slopes from the top of the chairlift. Day passes (summer and winter) start at around £20; ski and boot rental costs £14 a day from the ski school at the base station. For **information** on skiing and road conditions here, call the base station on ☎01975/651440 or check ⓦwww.lecht.co.uk or ⓦski.visitscotland.com.

Huntly and around

A small town set in attractive rolling farmland, the ancient burgh of **HUNTLY**, ten miles east of Dufftown and on the main train route from Aberdeen to Inverness, has little to offer other than its proximity to the Whisky Trail. It does boast, however, one of the smallest and prettiest, albeit rather skeletal, castles in the area. **Huntly Castle**, power centre of the Gordon family (April–Sept daily 9.30am–6.30pm; Oct–March Sun–Wed & Sat 9.30am–4.30pm, Thurs & Fri closed; HS; £3.30), sits in a peaceful clearing on the banks of the Deveron river, a ten-minute walk from the town centre down Castle Street and through an elegant arch. Built over a period of five centuries, it became the headquarters of the Counter-Reformation in Scotland in 1562. After the Battle of Corrichie, brought about by the wish of the fourth earl's third son to marry Mary, Queen of Scots, and which effectively ended the Gordons' 250-year rule, the castle was pillaged and its treasures sent to St Machar's Cathedral in Aberdeen. During the Civil War the earl of Huntly, who had supported Charles I and declared, "you can take my head off my shoulders, but not my heart from my sovereign", was shot against his castle's walls with his escort, after which the place was left to fall into ruin. Today you can still make out the twelfth-century **motte**, a grassy mound on the west side of the complex, while the main castle ruin, with its splendid **doorway** fronted by an elaborate coat of arms, dates from the mid-fifteenth century. In the basement, a narrow passage leads to the **prisons**, where medieval graffiti of tents, animals and people adorn the walls. Huntly was also the birthplace of the much-loved children's author George MacDonald, whose writing influenced Lewis Carroll, J.R.R. Tolkien and C.S. Lewis, among others. A plaque commemorates his birthplace on Duke Street, and you can get more information from the tourist office.

Seven miles south of Huntly and served by the occasional bus, the modest chateau-style **Leith Hall** (Easter weekend & May–Sept Fri–Tue noon–5pm; NTS; £8) is worth visiting, even when closed, for a wander around its 113-acre grounds (daily 9.30am to dusk; £3). Home to the Leith and Leith-Hay family since 1650, the vast estate of varied farm and woodlands includes ponds, eighteenth-century stables, a bird-observation hide and signposted countryside walks. Inside, you can see personal memorabilia of the successive Leith lairds, a number of whom were in the armed services overseas.

Huntly is on the fringe of whisky country, with the isolated **Glendronach Distillery** (see box on p.567) the nearest to town. Meanwhile, three miles northwest of Huntly, between the A920 to Dufftown and the A96 to Keith (signposted from both), the **North East Falconry Centre** (March–Oct daily 10.30am–5.30pm; ☎01466/760328, ⓦwww.huntly-falconry.co.uk; £4.95) is home to about fifty fabulous falcons, owls and eagles, with flying demonstrations four times a day.

Practicalities

Huntly's **tourist office** (April–June, Sept & Oct Mon–Sat 10am–1pm & 2–5pm; July & Aug Mon–Sat 10am–5.30pm, Sun 10am–4pm; ☎01466/792255) is on the main square, and can help organize places to stay locally. For luxurious **accommodation**, head for the former home of the duke of Gordon, the *Castle Hotel* (☎01466/792696, ⓦwww.castlehotel.uk.com; ❻), which stands at the end of a long driveway behind the castle ruins. At the other end of the scale there's the *Gordon Arms Hotel* (☎01466/792288, ⓦwww.gordonarms.demon .co.uk; ❷) in the main square, while you'll find decent, inexpensive B&B at *New Marnoch*, 48 King St (☎01466/792018; ❶). The *Auld Pit* on Duke Street is a reasonable **pub** with regular folk music, and serves pub meals, as does the

Gordon Arms, though your best bet for a decent **meal** is the *Castle Hotel*. **Bikes** can be rented from the Huntly Nordic & Outdoor Centre near the castle (℡01466/794428), where you can also brush up your cross-country skiing skills on all-weather tracks if there's no snow.

Travel details

11

THE CAIRNGORMS AND SPEYSIDE | Travel details

The Great Glen

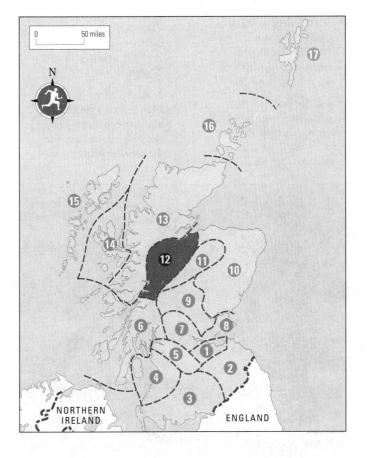

CHAPTER 12 # Highlights

✳ **Commando Memorial**
An exposed but dramatic
place to take in sweep-
ing views over Scotland's
highest ben (Nevis) and
its longest glen (the Great
Glen). See p.585

✳ **Glen Coe** Spectacular,
moody, poignant and full
of history – a glorious
place for hiking or simple
admiration. See p.586

✳ **Fishing on Loch Ness**
Chances of seeing the
famous monster Nessie
aren't high, but tales of
"the one that got away"

are bound to be unusual.
See p.593

✳ **Glen Affric** Some of Scotland's best hidden scenery,
with ancient Caledonian
forests and gushing rivers.
See p.594

✳ **Culloden battlefield** Tramp
the heather moor of Bonnie
Prince Charlie's last stand in
1746. See p.603

✳ **Dolphins of the Moray
Firth** Europe's most northerly school of bottle-nosed
dolphins can be seen from
the shore or on a boat trip.
See p.604

△ Dolphin-spotting around the Moray Firth

The Great Glen

T he **Great Glen**, a major geological faultline cutting diagonally across the Highlands from Fort William to Inverness, is the defining geographic feature of the north of Scotland. A huge rift valley was formed when the northwestern and southeastern sides of the fault slid in opposite directions for more than sixty miles, while the present landscape was shaped by glaciers that retreated only around 8000 BC. The glen is impressive more for its sheer scale than its beauty, but the imposing barrier of loch and mountain means that no one can travel into the northern Highlands without passing through it. With the two major service centres of the Highlands at either end it makes an obvious and rewarding route between the west and east coasts.

Of the Great Glen's four elongated lochs, the most famous is **Loch Ness**, home to the mythical monster; lochs **Oich**, **Lochy** and **Linnhe** (the last of these a sea loch) are less renowned though no less attractive. All four are linked by the Caledonian Canal. The southwestern end of the Great Glen is dominated by **Fort William**, the second-largest town in the Highland region, situated at the heart of the Lochaber area, a useful base with plenty of places to stay and eat and an excellent hub for accessing a host of outdoor activities. While the town itself is not one of the more charming places you'll encounter in Scotland, the surrounding countryside is a blend of rugged mountain terrain and tranquil sea loch. Dominating the scene to the south is **Ben Nevis**, Britain's highest peak, best approached from scenic Glen Nevis. The most famous glen of all, **Glen Coe**, lies on the main A82 road half an hour's drive south of Fort William, the two separated by the coastal inlet of **Loch Leven**. Nowadays the whole area is unashamedly given over to tourism, and Fort William is swamped by bus tours throughout the summer, but, as ever in the Highlands, within a thirty-minute drive you can be totally alone.

At the northeastern end of the Great Glen is the capital of the Highlands, **Inverness**, a pleasant, unhurried town with a couple of worthwhile sights, but used most often as a springboard to remoter areas further north. Inevitably, most transport links to the northern Highlands, including Ullapool, Thurso and the Orkney and Shetland islands, pass through Inverness.

The region has a turbulent and bloody **history**. Founded in 1655 and named in honour of William III, Fort William was successfully held by government troops during both of the Jacobite risings; the country to the southwest is inextricably associated with Bonnie Prince Charlie's flight after **Culloden**. Glen Coe is another historic site with a violent past, renowned as much for the infamous massacre of 1692 as for its magnificent scenery.

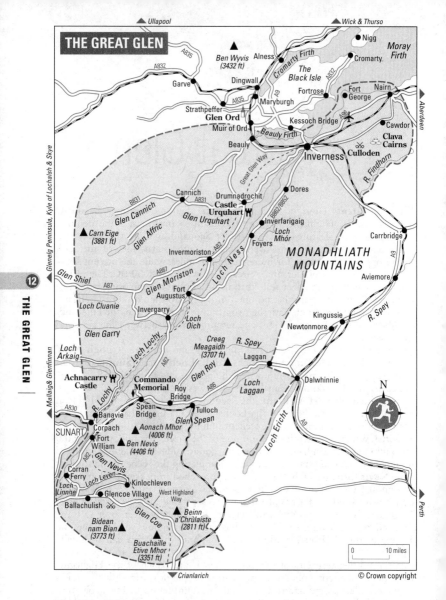

THE GREAT GLEN

Ullapool ▲   Wick & Thurso ▲

Nigg ●
Moray Firth

Ben Wyvis ▲
(3432 ft)   Alness ●   Cromarty Firth   Cromarty ●

Garve ●   Dingwall ●   The Black Isle   Fort George ●   Nairn ●

Strathpeffer ●   Maryburgh ●   Fortrose ●

Glen Ord

Muir of Ord ●   Kessoch Bridge ●   Cawdor ●

Beauly ●   Beauly Firth   **Clava Cairns**

Inverness ●   Culloden   R. Findhorn

Cannich ●   Drumnadrochit ●   Dores ●

Castle Urquhart ⚔   Great Glen Way

Glen Cannich   Glen Urquhart   Inverfarigaig ●   Carrbridge ●

Carn Eige ▲
(3881 ft)   Glen Affric   Loch Mhór   Foyers ●

Invermoriston ●   **MONADHLIATH MOUNTAINS**   Aviemore ●

Glen Shiel   Glen Moriston   Fort Augustus ●   Loch Ness

Loch Cluanie   Invergarry ●   'Loch Oich   Kingussie ●   R. Spey

Glen Garry   Loch Lochy   Newtonmore ●

Loch Arkaig   Creag Meagaidh ▲
(3707 ft)   R. Spey   Laggan ●

Achnacarry Castle ⚔   **Commando Memorial**   Roy Bridge   Glen Roy   Loch Laggan   Dalwhinnie ●

Banavie ●   Spean Bridge ●   Tulloch ●   Glen Spean

Corpach ●   **Aonach Mhor** ▲
(4006 ft)

SUNART   Fort William ●   **Ben Nevis** ▲
(4406 ft)   Loch Ericht

Corran Ferry ●   Glen Nevis   Loch Leven

Loch Linnhe   Kinlochleven ●   West Highland Way

Ballachulish ●   Glencoe Village ●   **Beinn a'Chrùlaiste** ▲
(2811 ft)

Bidean nam Bian ▲
(3773 ft)   Glen Coe

Buachaille Etive Mhor ▲
(3351 ft)

N

0   10 miles

Crianlarich ▼   © Crown copyright

Aberdeen ▶   Perth ▶

Glenelg Peninsula, Kyle of Lochalsh & Skye ◀   Mallaig & Glenfinnan ◀

⑫

THE GREAT GLEN

Transport

The main **A82** road runs the length of the Great Glen, although relatively high traffic levels mean that it's not a fast or particularly easy route to drive. The area is reasonably well served by **buses**, with several daily services between Inverness and Fort William, and a couple of extra buses covering the section between Fort William and Invergarry during school terms. However, the traditional and most rewarding way to travel through the Glen itself is by **boat**. A flotilla of kayaks, small yachts and pleasure vessels take advantage of the canal and its old wooden

The seventy-three-mile cleft of the Great Glen is the most obvious – and by far the flattest – way of traversing northern Scotland from coast to coast. The **Great Glen Way** long-distance footpath (ⓦwww.greatglenway.com) is a relatively undemanding five- to six-day hike that uses a combination of canal towpath and forest- and hill-tracks between Fort William and Inverness. Accommodation is readily available all the way along the route in campsites, hostels, bunkhouses and B&Bs, though in high season it's worth booking ahead and if you know you're going to arrive late somewhere it's worth checking that you can still get a meal where you're staying or somewhere nearby. The maps you'll need to do the whole thing are Ordnance Survey Landranger maps 41, 34 and 26. Alternatively, *The Great Glen Way and Cycle Route* published by Footprint (£4.50), concisely maps out the way. There are various guidebooks describing the route, including *The Great Glen Way* published by Rucksack Readers (£10.99). A **cycle path** also traverses the Glen, offering a tranquil alternative to the hazardous A82. The path, which shares some of its route with the footpath but also utilizes stretches of minor roads, is well signposted and can be managed in one long day or two easier days. Bikes can be rented at Fort William, Banavie at the Loch Linnhe end of the canal, Fort Augustus, Drumnadrochit and Inverness, from where you can tackle shorter sections. The Forestry Commission publishes *Cycling in the Forest, The Great Glen*, a handy booklet that highlights the various sections of the route (☎01320/366322 or 01397/702184, ⓦwww.forestry.gov.uk). The suggested **direction** for following both routes is from west to east – the direction of the prevailing southwesterly wind.

⑫

THE GREAT GLEN | Fort William

locks during the summer. Alternatively, an excellent **cycle path** traverses the Glen, as well as a long-distance footpath, the seventy-three-mile **Great Glen Way**, which takes five to six days to walk in full (see box above).

Fort William

With its stunning position on Loch Linnhe, tucked in below the snow-streaked bulk of Ben Nevis, **FORT WILLIAM** (known by the many walkers and climbers that come here as "Fort Bill"), should be a gem. Sadly, the same lack of taste that nearly saw the town renamed "Abernevis" in the 1950s is evident in the ribbon bungalow development and ill-advised dual carriageway – complete with grubby pedestrian underpass – which have wrecked the waterfront. The main street and the little squares off it are more appealing, though occupied by some decidedly tacky tourist gift shops. Ultimately, however, Fort William is an important regional centre, with facilities including a cinema, swimming pool and a large supermarket.

Arrival, information and accommodation

Just across the A82 dual carriageway, at the north end of the High Street, you'll find Fort William's **train station** (a stop on the scenic West Highland Railway direct from Glasgow; see p.582). Intercity **coaches** from Glasgow and Inverness stop outside the train station. The busy **tourist office** is on Cameron Square, just off High Street (April, May & Sept Mon–Sat 9am–5pm, Sun 10am–4pm; June–Aug Mon–Sat 9am–6pm, Sun 10am–4pm; Oct Mon–Fri 10am–5pm, Sat 10am–4pm, Sun 10am–2pm; Nov–March Mon–Fri 10am–5pm, Sat

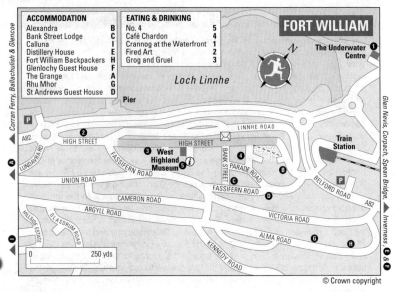

ACCOMMODATION
Alexandra	B
Bank Street Lodge	C
Calluna	I
Distillery House	E
Fort William Backpackers	H
Glenlochy Guest House	F
The Grange	A
Rhu Mhor	G
St Andrews Guest House	D

EATING & DRINKING
No. 4	5
Café Chardon	4
Crannog at the Waterfront	1
Fired Art	2
Grog and Gruel	3

FORT WILLIAM

Loch Linnhe

The Underwater Centre

Corran Ferry, Ballachulish & Glencoe

Glen Nevis, Corpach, Spean Bridge ▶ Inverness, E & F

Pier

A82

HIGH STREET

LINNHE ROAD

HIGH STREET

Train Station

LUNDAVRA RD

FASSIFERN ROAD

West Highland Museum

BANK STREET

PARADE ROAD

BELFORD ROAD

A82

UNION ROAD

FASSIFERN ROAD

CAMERON ROAD

ARGYLL ROAD

VICTORIA ROAD

HILLSIDE ESTATE

GLASDRUM ROAD

KENNEDY ROAD

ALMA ROAD

0   250 yds

© Crown copyright

10am–4pm; ☏01397/703781, Ⓦwww.visithighlands.com). You'll find a host of outdoor-activity specialists in town. High-spec **mountain bikes** are available for rent at Off Beat Bikes, 117 High St (☏01397/704008, Ⓦwww.offbeatbikes .co.uk); they know the best routes, issue free maps and also have a branch open at the Nevis Range gondola base station (June–Sept; ☏01397/705825) – a location which boasts forest rides and hosts an annual World Cup downhill mountain bike event in September. The Underwater Centre (☏01397/703786, Ⓦwww.theunderwatercentre.co.uk), at the water's edge beyond the train station and Morrison's supermarket, runs PADI courses and offers guided dives; and local **mountain guides** include Alan Kimber of *Calluna* (see opposite) and the **Snowgoose Mountain Centre** (☏01397/772467, Ⓦwww.highland -mountain-guides.co.uk), set beside the *Smiddy Bunkhouse and Blacksmith's Hostel* (see opposite), which offers instruction, rental and residential courses on activities such as hillwalking, mountaineering and canoeing.

Fort William's plentiful **accommodation** ranges from large luxury hotels to budget hostels and bunkhouses. Numerous B&Bs are also scattered across the town, many of them in the suburb of Corpach on the other side of Loch Linnhe, three miles along the Mallaig road (served by regular buses), where you'll also find a couple of good hostels.

In-town accommodation

Hotels and B&Bs
Alexandra Hotel The Parade ☏01397/702241, Ⓦwww.strathmorehotels.com. Established hotel in the town centre, with well-appointed rooms and a restaurant. ⑥
Distillery House North Rd ☏01397/700103, Ⓦwww.visit-fortwilliam.co.uk/distillery-house. Very comfortable, well-equipped upper-range

guesthouse situated ten minutes' walk north of the town centre near the Glen Nevis turn-off. ⑤
Glenlochy Guest House Nevis Bridge ☏01397/ 702909, Ⓦwww.glenlochy.co.uk. Opposite the *Distillery House*. Comfortable 12-bed B&B in peaceful surroundings. Non-smoking. ④
The Grange Grange Rd ☏01397/705516, Ⓦwww.thegrange-scotland.co.uk. Top-grade

accommodation in a striking old stone house, with four luxurious en-suite doubles and a spacious garden. Vegetarian breakfasts on request. Non-smoking. April–Oct. ⑥

Rhu Mhor Alma Rd ℡01397/702213, ⓦwww .rhumhor.co.uk. Congenial and characterful B&B, ten minutes' walk from the town centre, offering good breakfasts; vegetarians and vegans are catered for by arrangement. ②

St Andrews Guest House Fassifern Rd ℡01397/703038, ⓦwww.standrewsguesthouse .co.uk. Comfortable and extremely central B&B in an attractive converted granite choir school featuring various inscriptions and stained-glass windows. ②

Hostels and campsites

Bank Street Lodge Bank Street ℡01397/700070,
ⓦwww.bankstreetlodge.co.uk. A 43-bed centrally located lodge-cum-hostel that's handy for transport and the town centre.

Calluna Heathercroft, Connachie Rd ℡01397/700451, ⓦwww.fortwilliamholiday .co.uk; westcoast-mountainguides.co.uk. Well-run self-catering and hostel accommodation configured for individual, family and group stays. Free pick-up from town available. Owner is one of the area's top mountain guides, so there's plenty of outdoor advice available.

Fort William Backpackers Alma Rd ℡01397/700711, ⓦwww.scotlands-top-hostels .com. A busy 38-bed, rambling, archetypal backpacker hostel five minutes' walk up the hill from town, with great views and large communal areas.

Out-of-town accommodation

Hotels and B&Bs

Achintee Farm Guest House Glen Nevis ℡01397/702240, ⓦwww.achinteefarm.com. Friendly B&B with adjoining hostel located right by the *Ben Nevis Inn* (see below) at start of the Ben Nevis footpath. ④

Glenloy Lodge B&B Six miles north of town on B8004 north of Banavie at the start of the canal ℡01397/712700. A former hunting lodge with comfortable and secluded views to Ben Nevis and where pine martens occasionally visit. Excellent breakfast. ⑤

Inverlochy Castle Torlundy, two miles north of town on the A82 ℡01397/702177, ⓦwww .inverlochycastlehotel.co.uk. A grand country-house hotel set in wooded parkland with exceptional levels of service and outstanding, Michelin-star food – but all at a price. ⑨

Rhiw Goch Banavie ℡01397/772373, ⓦwww2 .prestel.co.uk/rhiwgoch. Comfortable and welcoming B&B overlooking Neptune's Staircase with great views to Ben Nevis. Good breakfasts. ③

Hostels and campsites

🏃 **Ben Nevis Bunkhouse** Achintee Farm, Glen Nevis ℡01397/702240, ⓦwww .achinteefarm.com. A more civilized option than the nearby SYHA place (see below), with hot showers and a self-catering kitchen adjoining to a smart B&B (see above). Located just over the river from the Ben Nevis Visitor Centre – reach it by following the Ben Nevis path across the river or by taking Achintee Rd along the north side of the River Nevis from Claggan.

Ben Nevis Inn Achintee, Glen Nevis ℡01397/701227. A basic and cosy 20-bed bunkhouse housed within the rustic and lively pub just north of the *Achintee Farm Guest House* (see above).

Farr Cottage Lodge Corpach, on the main A830 ℡01397/772315, ⓦwww.farrcottage.co.uk. Well-equipped, lively hostel with range of dorms and double/twin rooms ①. Offers a multitude of outdoor activities whilst evening entertainment includes whisky tastings.

Glen Nevis Caravan and Camping Park Glen Nevis, two miles up the Glen Nevis road ℡01397/702191, ⓦwww.glennevisholidays .co.uk. A range of cottages, lodges and holiday homes. Facilities include hot showers, a shop and restaurant, as well as disabled facilities.

Glen Nevis SYHA hostel Glen Nevis, two and a half miles up the Glen Nevis road opposite start of path to summit ℡0870/004 1120, ⓦwww .syha.org.uk. Though far from town, this friendly hostel is an excellent base for walkers. Very busy in summer.

Smiddy Bunkhouse & Blacksmith's Backpacker Lodge Corpach ℡01397/772467, ⓦwww.highland-mountain-guides.co.uk. A cosy 14-bed hostel and simpler 12-bed bunkhouse right next to Corpach train station at the entrance to the Caledonian Canal. Part of the Snowgoose Mountain Centre, offering year-round mountaineering, kayaking and other outdoor activities.

The Town

Fort William's downfall started in the nineteenth century, when the original fort, which gave the town its name, was demolished to make way for the train line. Today, the town is a sprawl of dual carriageways, and there's little to detain you except the splendid and idiosyncratic **West Highland Museum**, on Cameron Square, just off the High Street (June–Sept Mon–Sat 10am–5pm; July & Aug also Sun 2–5pm; Oct–May Mon–Sat 10am–4pm; £3). Its collections cover virtually every aspect of Highland life and the presentation is traditional, but very well done, making a refreshing change from state-of-the-art heritage centres. There's a secret portrait of Bonnie Prince Charlie, the long Spanish rifle used in the famous Appin Murder (see p.356) and even a 550kg slab of aluminium, the stuff that's processed locally into silver foil.

Excursions from town include the 84-mile round-trip to Mallaig (see p.623) on the West Highland Railway Line aboard the **Jacobite Steam Train** (end May to mid-Oct Mon–Fri; mid-July to end Aug also Sun; depart Fort William 10.20am, return 4pm; £26; ℡01463/239026, Ⓦwww.steamtrain.info). Heading along the shore of Loch Eil to the west coast via historic Glenfinnan (see p.620), the train passes through some of the region's most spectacular scenery, though these days it's as popular for its role as the locomotive used in the *Harry Potter* films. Several **cruises** also leave from the town pier every day, offering the chance to spot the marine life of Loch Linnhe, which includes seals and seabirds. Try Seal Island Cruises (March–Oct; 90min; £7.50; ℡01397/700714, Ⓦwww.oceanandoak.co.uk) or Seaventures, who offer exhilarating fast boat trips (March–Nov; 1–2hr, from £14; ℡01397/701687).

Eating and drinking

Fort William has a reasonable range of places to **eat** and **drink**. The pick of the bunch is the moderately priced *Crannog at the Waterfront* (℡01397/705589; Ⓦwww.oceanandoak.co.uk), located next to the Underwater Centre beyond the train station. Attentive staff offer the freshest of seafood, including oysters and langoustines, whilst you drink real ale or wine overlooking the loch. *No. 4* (℡01397/704222), adjacent to the tourist office, also offers moderately priced Scottish based dishes including seafood and game. On the High Street, the *Grog and Gruel* is the place to go for Scottish real ales, entertainment and some traditional pub grub. There are also a number of places out of town well worth seeking out for good food: for a smarter meal the *Old Pines* near Spean Bridge (see p.585; closed Mon) is worth seeking out, while *An Crann* (℡01397/773114; closed Sun), just outside Banavie (Highland Country bus #40) on the B8004, offers tasty Scottish dishes in a delightful, cosy setting. The most convivial atmosphere is in the ≽ *Ben Nevis Inn* (see p.581) up Glen Nevis, where you'll get some excellent, moderately priced food. Your best chance of a decent coffee in town is at *Fired Art*, a "paint-your-own-pottery" studio with its own café at 147 High St. A good place for **picnic food** as well as a snack is the *Café Chardon*, up a lane off High Street; they do excellent baguettes, croissants and pastries to eat in or take away.

Around Fort William

Any disappointment you harbour about the dispiriting flavour of Fort William town should be offset against the wealth of scenery and activities

△ Ben Nevis

in its immediate vicinity. Most obvious – on a clear day, at least – is **Ben Nevis**, the most popular, though hardly the most rewarding, of Scotland's high peaks, the path up which leaves from **Glen Nevis**, itself a starting point for excellent walks of various lengths and elevations. The mountain abutting Ben Nevis is **Aonach Mhor**, home of Scotland's most modern ski resort and in summer a honey-pot for downhill mountain-bike enthusiasts. Some of the best views of these peaks can be had from **Corpach**, a small village opposite Fort William which marks the start of the **Caledonian Canal** (see p.585).

The main road travelling up the Great Glen from Fort William towards Inverness is the A82, ten miles along which is the small settlement of **Spean Bridge**, a good waypoint for getting to various remote and attractive walking areas, notably glens **Spean** and **Roy**, found along the A86 trunk road, which links across the central highlands to the A9 and the Speyside region (see p.565).

Glen Nevis

A ten-minute drive south of Fort William, **GLEN NEVIS** is indisputably among the Highlands' most impressive glens: a classic U-shaped glacial valley hemmed in by steep bracken-covered slopes and swaths of blue-grey scree. Herds of shaggy Highland cattle graze the valley floor, where a sparkling river gushes through glades of trees. With the forbidding mass of Ben Nevis rising steeply to the north, it's not surprising this valley has been chosen as the location for scenes in several films, such as *Rob Roy* and *Braveheart*. Apart from its natural beauty, Glen Nevis is also the starting point for the ascent of Britain's highest peak, Ben Nevis, and you can rent **mountain equipment** and **mountain bikes** at the trailhead. The best map is *Harvey's Ben Nevis Walkers Map and Guide*, available from Fort William's tourist office and most local bookshops and outdoor stores. Highland Country **bus** #42 (every 1hr 20min) runs from the bus station in Fort William, beside the Morrison's supermarket

The Nevis Range

Seven miles northeast of Fort William by the A82, on the slopes of **Aonach Mhor**, one of the high mountains abutting Ben Nevis, the **Nevis Range** (℡01397/705825, ⓦwww.nevis-range.co.uk) is, in winter, Scotland's highest ski area. All year round, however, Highland Country bus #42 runs from Fort William five times a day (Mon–Sat; 3 on Sun) to the base station of the country's only **gondola** system (daily: 10am–5pm; July & Aug 9.30am–6pm; closed mid-Nov to mid-Dec for maintenance; £8 return). The one-and-a-half mile gondola trip (15min), rising 2000ft, gives an easy approach to some high-level walking as well as spectacular views from the terrace of the self-service restaurant at the top station. From the top of the gondola station, you can experience Britain's only World Cup standard **downhill mountain bike course** (mid-May to mid-Sept 11am–3pm; £10 includes gondola one-way), a hair-raising 3km route. It's not for the faint-hearted. There's also 25 miles of waymarked off-road bike routes, known as the Witch's Trails, on the mountainside and in the Leanachan Forest, ranging from gentle paths to cross-country scrambles. Off Beat Bikes (℡01397/704008, ⓦwww.offbeatbikes.co.uk) rents general mountain bikes as well as full-suspension bikes for the downhill course from their shops in Fort William and at the gondola base station (mid-May to mid-Sept).

and the train station, as far as the SYHA hostel, two and a half miles up the Glen Nevis road; some buses carry on another two and a half miles (late May to Oct only; 10min bus ride beyond the hostel) up the glen to the car park by the Lower Falls.

A great **low-level walk** (six miles round-trip) runs from the end of the road at the top of Glen Nevis. The good but very rocky path leads through a dramatic gorge with impressive falls and rapids, then opens out into a secret hanging valley, carpeted with wild flowers, with a high waterfall at the far end. It's a pretty place for a picnic and if you're really energetic you can walk the full twelve miles on over Rannoch Moor to **Corrour Station** (see p.486), where you can pick up one of three daily trains to take you back to Fort William.

Of all the walks in and around Glen Nevis, the **ascent of Ben Nevis** (4406ft), Britain's highest summit, inevitably attracts the most attention. Despite the fact that it's quite a slog up to the summit, and that it is by no means the most attractive mountain in Scotland, in high summer the trail is teeming with hikers, whatever the weather. However, this doesn't mean the mountain should be treated casually. It can snow round the summit any day of the year and more people perish here annually than on Everest, so take the necessary precautions (see p.64); in winter, of course, the mountain should be left to the experts. The most obvious **route** to the summit, a Victorian pony path up the whaleback south side of the mountain, built to service the observatory that once stood on the top, starts from the helpful Glen Nevis visitor centre (daily: Easter to mid-May & Oct 9am–5pm; mid-May to end Sept 9am–6pm) a mile and a half southeast of Fort William along the Glen Nevis road (bus #42 from An Aird in Fort William). Return via the main route or, if the weather is settled and you're confident enough, make a side trip from the wide saddle into the **Allt a'Mhuilinn glen** for spectacular views of the great cliffs on Ben Nevis's north face. Allow a full day for the climb (8hr).

Neptune's Staircase and Corpach

At the suburb of **BANAVIE**, three miles north of the centre of Fort William along the A830 to Mallaig, the Caledonian Canal climbs 64ft in less than half a mile via a punishing but picturesque series of eight locks known as **Neptune's Staircase**. There are stunning views from here of Ben Nevis and its neighbours, and it's a popular point from which to walk or cycle along the canal towpath. Bikes and Canadian canoes can be rented from *Rhiw Goch* B&B (see p.581) a half-mile up the B8004 in Banavie. If you do choose to cycle along the Caledonian Canal, look out for *The Eagle Inn* at Laggan Locks at the head of Loch Lochy, where fresh seafood and real ale are on offer aboard a cosy 1920s Dutch barge (℡077898/58567; Easter–Oct).

Back on the A830 and a mile west of Banavie is the suburb of **CORPACH**, the point where the canal enters from Loch Linnhe. The site of a mothballed paper mill, the main event here is the **Treasures of the Earth** exhibition (daily: July–Sept 9.30am–7pm; rest of the year 10am–5pm; closed Jan; £3.50) a useful rainy-day option for families, which has a dazzling array of rocks, crystals, gemstones and fossils.

Spean Bridge and Glen Spean

Ten miles northeast of Fort William, the village of **SPEAN BRIDGE** marks the junction of the A82 with the A86 from Dalwhinnie (see p.488) and Kingussie (see p.564). If you're here, it's well worth heading a mile out of the village on the A82 towards Inverness to the **Commando Memorial**, a group of bronze soldiers commemorating the men who trained in the area during World War II. The statue looks out on an awesome sweep of moor and mountain that takes in the wider Lochaber area and the Ben Nevis massif. A few hundred yards from the memorial, on the minor B8004 which heads towards Gairlochy, is the welcoming and upmarket *Old Pines Hotel and Restaurant* (℡01397/712324, ⓦwww.oldpines.co.uk; half-board ❽, B&B ❻).

At **ROY BRIDGE**, three miles east of Spean Bridge, a minor road turns off up **Glen Roy**. A couple of miles along the glen, you'll see the so-called "parallel roads": not roads at all, but ancient beaches at various levels along the valley sides which mark the shorelines of a loch confined here by a glacial dam in the last Ice Age. Back on the A86, two miles east of Roy Bridge, *Aite Cruinnichidh* (℡01397/712315, ⓦwww.highland-hostel.co.uk) is a comfortable **bunkhouse** in a beautiful setting, with good facilities (including a sauna) and local advice for walkers and cyclists. The nearby Roy Bridge Store is handy for provisions while Jimmy Couts (℡01397/712812, ⓦwww.fishing-scotland.co.uk), is the man to call for **fly-fishing** tuition and excursions.

Five miles further east, the railway line and road part company at **TULLOCH**, and trains swing south to pass Loch Treig and cross Rannoch Moor (see p.486). The station building at Tulloch is now a friendly **hostel**, *Station Lodge* (℡01397/732333, ⓦwww.stationlodge.co.uk), popular with climbers and walkers. The Caledonian sleeper train from London stops right at the door. Further east, the A86 runs alongside the artificial **Loch Laggan** with the picturesque Ardverikie Castle on its southern shore and the attractive walking area of **Creag Meagaidh National Nature Reserve** to the north. In Laggan itself, beyond the far end of the loch, there's the newly opened Laggan Wolftrax mountain-bike centre (℡01528/544786, ⓦwww.laggan.com/wolftrax.htm), boasting a café and nine miles of track to suit all abilities. Two miles east and after turning onto the A889, *The Pottery Bunkhouse* and coffee shop provides convenient, comfortable accommodation (℡01528/544231, ⓦwww.potterybunkhouse.co.uk).

Glen Coe and around

Despite its longstanding fame and popularity, **Glen Coe**, half an hour's drive south of Fort William on the main A82 road to Glasgow, can still fairly claim to be one of Scotland's most inspiring places. Arriving from the south across the desolate reaches of Rannoch Moor, you're likely to find the start of the glen, with **Buachaille Etive Mhor** to the south and **Beinn a'Chrùlaiste** to the north, is little short of forbidding. By the time you've reached the heart of the glen, with the three huge rock buttresses known as the **Three Sisters** on one side and the Anoach Eagach ridge on the other combining to close up the sky, you'll almost certainly feel compelled to stop simply to take it all in. Added

---

Walks around Glen Coe

Ordnance Survey Explorer Map no. 384.

Flanked by sheer-sided Munros, Glen Coe offers some of the Highlands' most challenging **hiking** routes, with long steep ascents over rough trails and notoriously unpredictable weather conditions that claim lives every year. The walks outlined below number among the glen's less ambitious routes, but still require a map. It's essential that you take the proper precautions (see p.64), and stick to the paths, both for your own safety and the sake of the soil, which has become badly eroded in places. For a broader selection of walks, get hold of the Ordnance Survey *Pathfinder Guide: Fort William and Glen Coe Walks*.

A good introduction to the splendours of Glen Coe is the half-day hike over the **Devil's Staircase**, which follows part of the old military road that once ran between Fort William and Stirling. The trail, part of the West Highland Way, starts at the village of **Kinlochleven** and is marked by thistle signs, which lead uphill to the 1804ft pass and down the other side into Glen Coe, where it affords stunning views of Loch Eilde and Buachaille Etive Mhor. The Devil's Staircase was named by four hundred soldiers who endured severe hardship to build it in the seventeenth century, but in fine, settled weather the trail is safe and a good option for families and less experienced hikers.

Set right in the heart of the glen, the half-day **Allt Coire Gabhail** hike starts at the car park opposite the distinctive Three Sisters massif on the main A82. From the road, drop down to the floor of the glen and cross the River Coe via the wooden bridge, where the path heads straight up the Allt Coire Gabhail for a couple of miles to a false summit directly ahead – actually the rim of the so-called "Lost Valley" which the Clan MacDonald used to flee to and hide their cattle in when attacked. Once in the valley, there are superb views of Bidean nan Bian, Gearr Aonach and Beinn Fhada, which improve as you continue on to its head, another twenty- to thirty-minute walk. Unless you're well equipped and experienced, turn around at this point, as the trail climbs to some of the glen's high ridges and peaks.

Undoubtedly one of the finest walks in the Glen Coe area not entailing the ascent of a Munro is the **Buachaille Etive Beag** circuit, which follows the textbook glacial valleys of Lairig Eilde and Lairig Gartain, ascending 1968ft in only nine miles of rough trail. Park near the waterfall at **The Study** – the gorge part of the A82 through Glen Coe – and walk up the road until you see a sign pointing south to "Loch Etiveside". The path angles up from here to the top of the pass, a rise of 787ft from the road. From here, follow the burn until you can pick up the trail heading up the eastern side of Stob Dubh (the "black peak"), which leads to the col of the Lairig Gartain, and onwards to the top of the pass. Drop down the other side to the main road, where the roughly parallel route of the old military road offers a gentler and safer return to the Study with superb views of the Three Sisters – finer than those ever seen by drivers.

to the heady mix is the infamous **massacre of Glen Coe** in 1692, nadir of the long-standing enmity between the clans MacDonald and Campbell. At its western end, Glen Coe meets Loch Leven: the main road goes west and over the bridge at **Ballachulish** en route to Fort William, while at the eastern end of the loch is the slowly reviving settlement of **Kinlochleven**, best known now as the site of the world's largest indoor ice-climbing centre and as a waypoint on the **West Highland Way** long-distance footpath (see box on p.589).

Glen Coe

Breathtakingly beautiful **Glen Coe** (literally "Valley of Weeping"), sixteen miles south of Fort William on the A82, is justifiably the best known of the Highland glens: a spectacular mountain valley between velvety-green conical peaks, their tops often wreathed in cloud, their flanks streaked by cascades of rock and scree. In 1692 it was the site of a notorious massacre, in which the MacDonalds were victims of a longstanding government desire to suppress the clans. Fed up with what they regarded as unacceptable lawlessness, and a groundswell of Jacobitism and Catholicism, the government offered a general pardon to all those who signed an oath of allegiance to William III by January 1, 1692. When clan chief **Alastair MacDonald** missed the deadline, a plot was hatched to make an example of "that damnable sept", and **Campbell of Glenlyon** was ordered to billet his soldiers in the homes of the MacDonalds, who for ten days entertained them with traditional Highland hospitality. In the early morning of February 13, the soldiers turned on their hosts, slaying between 38 and 45 and causing more than three hundred to flee in a blizzard.

Beyond the small village of **GLENCOE** at the western end of the glen, the glen itself (a property of the National Trust for Scotland since the 1930s) is virtually uninhabited, and provides outstanding climbing and walking. The NTS **visitor centre** (March daily 10am–4pm; April–Aug daily 9.30am–5.30pm; Sept & Oct daily 10am–5pm; Nov–Feb Fri–Mon 10am–4pm; NTS; £5), one mile south of the village is an interesting eco-friendly building where you'll find a good exhibition with a balanced account of the massacre alongside some entertaining material on rock- and hill-climbing down the years. There's also a cabin area providing information on the local weather and wildlife and after sampling the cakes in the café, there's often the chance to join informative ranger-led **guided walks** (Easter & June–Sept) which leave from the centre. Meanwhile, in Glencoe village, you can pay a visit to the delightful heather-roofed Glencoe Folk Museum (May–Sept 10am–5.30pm, closed Sun; £2). Artefacts within the refurbished 1720 croft include a chair that reputedly once belonged to Bonnie Prince Charlie.

At the eastern end of Glen Coe beyond the demanding Buachaille Etive Mhor, the landscape opens out onto the vast Rannoch Moor. From the **Glen Coe Mountain Resort** (☎01855/851226, ⒲www.glencoemountain.com; daily year-round, except Nov) a chairlift (£6) climbs 2400ft to Meall a Bhuiridh, giving spectacular views over Rannoch Moor and to Ben Nevis. At the base station, there's a simple but pleasant café.

Practicalities

To get to the heart of Glen Coe from Fort William by **public transport** the best option is to hop on the Glasgow-bound Scottish Citylink coach service (4 daily). The Highland County bus #44 from Fort William also stops at least five times a day at Glencoe village en route to Kinlochleven.

There's a good selection of **accommodation** in Glen Coe and the surrounding area. Basic options include an SYHA **hostel** (☎0870/004 1122, ⒲www.syha.org.uk) on a back road halfway between Glencoe village and the *Clachaig*

Inn (see below); the year-round *Red Squirrel* **campsite** (☎01855/811256) nearby; and a grassier NTS campsite (☎01855/811397; April–Oct) on the main road. Glencoe village has a few comfortable **B&Bs**, such as the secluded and friendly *Scorry Breac* (☎01855/811354, ⓦwww.scorrybreac.co.uk; ❷), while the best-known **hotel** in the area is the lively ᛤ *Clachaig Inn* (☎01855/811252, ⓦwww.clachaig.com; ❺), a great place to swap stories with fellow climbers and to reward your exertions with cask-conditioned ales and heaped platefuls of food; it's three miles south of Glencoe village on the minor road off the A82. Just over ten miles south of here through the glen and before heading into the empty wilds of Rannoch Moor, it's worth stopping for a pint at the atmospheric *Climber's Bar* within the historic though slightly run-down *Kingshouse Hotel* (☎01855/851259; ⓦwww.kingy.com; ❹). Further south still, at Bridge of Orchy station is the cosy *West Highland Way Sleeper Hostel* (☎01838/400548, ⓦwww .westhighlandwaysleeper.co.uk). Outdoor activity operators in Glencoe include **walking** and climbing specialists Glencoe Guides and Gear (☎01855/811402, ⓦwww.ice-factor.co.uk), while Vertical Descents (☎01855/821593, ⓦwww .verticaldescents.com) offers a type of white-water kayaking called "fun-yakking" (£35 for a half-day) and adrenalin-pumping canyoning trips (from £35) that can include scaling 100ft waterfalls.

Ballachulish and Onich

One mile west of Glencoe village, **BALLACHULISH** was, from 1693 to 1955, a major centre for the quarrying of roofing slates, shipping out 26 million of them at the height of production in the mid-nineteenth century. There's a short, well-maintained footpath leading from directly opposite Ballachulish tourist office into the now disused slate quarry – a few information boards tell the history of the quarry, which, like many former industrial sites, has an eerie stillness to it. Ballachulish has two parts – the main village on the south of the loch and North Ballachulish on the other side of the road bridge, which spans the mouth of Loch Leven. Beyond North Ballachulish on the road to Fort William is the roadside settlement of **ONICH**, a mile or so on from which is **CORRAN**, where a car ferry crosses the narrowest point of Loch Linnhe, providing access to the Morvern and Ardnamurchan peninsulas (see p.616).

Ballachulish's **tourist office** is on Albert Road, sharing space with a coffee and gift shop (daily 9am–5pm, May to end Aug until 6pm; ☎01855/811866). From here you can organize somewhere to stay locally using a freephone line. For a cheap bed, head to the welcoming *Inchree Hostel* (☎01855/821287, ⓦwww.inchreecentre.co.uk) at Onich, where accommodation is available in a bunkhouse or chalets and there's a decent real-ale **pub** and bistro called *The Four Seasons*. In Ballachulish village, *Fern Villa* (☎01855/811393, ⓦwww .fernvilla.com; ❷) is a friendly **B&B**, while *Cuildorag House* (☎01855/821529, ⓦwww.cuildoraghouse.com; ❷) in Onich is a particularly pleasant vegetarian and vegan B&B, renowned for its great breakfasts. **Hotels** include the *Ballachul-ish* (☎01855/821582, ⓦwww.freedomglen.co.uk; ❽), just below the southern end of the bridge, a grand but welcoming old place where residents have use of the pool and leisure centre at the nearby *Isles of Glencoe Hotel*: in the grounds you'll find Lochaber Watersports (☎01855/821391, ⓦwww.lochaberwaters ports.co.uk), where you can rent a small sailing dinghy, rowing boat or canoe.

Kinlochleven

At the easternmost end of Loch Leven, at the foot of the spectacular moun-tains known as the Mamores, the settlement of **KINLOCHLEVEN** is steadily reviving its fortunes after many years as a tourism backwater best known as the site of a huge, unsightly aluminium smelter built in 1904. The tale of the area's industrial past is told in **The Aluminium Story** (Mon–Fri 10am–1pm & 2–5pm, Oct–March closed Fri afternoon; free), a small series of displays in the same building as the town library and tourist information. The disused smelter is now the home of an innovative new indoor mountaineering centre called **The Ice Factor** (℡01855/831100, Ⓦwww.ice-factor.co.uk). Built at a cost of over £2.5 million, this impressive facility includes the world's largest artificial ice-climbing wall (13.5m) as well as a range of more traditional climbing walls and other facilities such as equipment hire, steam room, sauna and an inexpensive café. Alongside, another part of the aluminium smelter has been transformed into the **Atlas Brewery**, which you can tour on summer evenings (Easter–Sept Mon–Sat tour starts at 5.30pm; ℡01855/831111). As well as being close to Glen Coe, Kinlochleven stands at the foot of the Mamore hills, popular with Munro-baggers; it's also a convenient overnight stop on the **West Highland Way**, with Fort William a day's walk away.

For hikers looking to spend the night in Kinlochleven, the *Blackwater* **hostel** (℡01855/831253, Ⓦwww.blackwaterhostel.co.uk) beside the river, is decidedly upmarket, with TVs and en-suite facilities in dorms with two, three, four or eight beds, and a communal kitchen/dining area but no separate lounge. For £5 per person you can also **camp** here. Fine hospitality is to be found at the Edwardian-built *Edencoille Guest House* (℡01855/831358; ❷), while there are two good **hotels** in Kinlochleven: *MacDonald Hotel* (℡01855/831539, Ⓦwww.macdonaldhotel.co.uk; ❺), whose *Bothy Bar* is popular with walkers, and the *Tailrace Inn* on Riverside Road (℡01855/831777, Ⓦwww.tailraceinn.co.uk; ❹), offering reasonable rooms and food, along with regular entertainment.

Loch Ness and around

Twenty-three miles long, unfathomably deep, cold and often moody, **Loch Ness** is bounded by rugged heather-clad mountains rising steeply from a wooded shoreline and attractive glens opening up on either side. Its fame, however, is based overwhelmingly on its legendary inhabitant Nessie, the "Loch Ness monster", whose fame ensures a steady flow of hopeful visitors to the settlements dotted along the loch, in particular **Drumnadrochit**. Nearby, the impressive ruins of **Castle Urquhart** – a favourite monster-spotting location – perch atop a rock on the lochside and attract a deluge of bus parties during the summer. Almost as busy in high season is the village of **Fort Augustus**, at the more scenic southwest tip of Loch Ness, where you can watch queues of boats tackling one of the Caledonian Canal's longest flight of locks.

Away from the lochside, and seeing a fraction of Loch Ness's visitor numbers, the remote glens of **Urquhart** and **Affric** make an appealing contrast, with Affric in particular boasting narrow, winding roads, gushing streams and hillsides dotted with ancient Caledonian pine forests. More commonly encountered in these parts is the often bleak high country of **Glen Moriston**, a little to the southwest of Glen Affric, which holds the main road between Inverness and Skye.

Although most visitors use the tree-lined A82 road, which runs along the western shore of Loch Ness, the sinuous single-track B862/B852 (originally a military road built to link Fort Augustus and Fort George) that skirts the eastern shore is quieter and affords far more spectacular views. However, buses

Nessie

The world-famous **Loch Ness monster**, affectionately known as **Nessie** (and by serious aficionados as *Nessiteras rhombopteryx*), has been a local celebrity for some time. The first mention of a mystery creature crops up in St Adamnan's seventh-century biography of **St Columba**, who allegedly calmed an aquatic animal which had attacked one of his monks. Present-day interest, however, is probably greater outside Scotland than within the country, and dates from the building of the road along the loch's western shore in the early 1930s. In 1934 the *Daily Mail* published London surgeon R.K. Wilson's sensational photograph of the head and neck of the monster peering up out of the loch, and the hype has hardly diminished since. Recent encounters range from glimpses of ripples by anglers to the famous occasion in 1961 when thirty hotel guests saw a pair of humps break the water's surface and cruise for about half a mile before submerging.

Photographic evidence is showcased in the two "Monster Exhibitions" at Drum-nadrochit, but the most impressive of these exhibits – including the renowned black-and-white movie footage of Nessie's humps moving across the water, and Wilson's original head and shoulders shot – have now been exposed as fakes. Indeed, in few other places on earth has watching a rather lifeless and often grey expanse of water seemed so compelling, or have floating logs, otters and boat wakes been photographed so often and with such excitement. Yet while even hi-tech sonar sur-veys carried out over the past two decades have failed to come up with conclusive evidence, it's hard to dismiss Nessie as pure myth. After all, no one yet knows where the unknown layers of silt and mud at the bottom of the loch begin and end: best estimates say the loch is over 750 feet deep, deeper than much of the North Sea, while others point to the possibilities of underwater caves and undiscovered chan-nels connected to the sea. What scientists have found in the cold, murky depths, including pure white eels and rare arctic char, offers fertile grounds for speculation, with different theories declaring Nessie to be a remnant from the dinosaur age, a giant newt or a huge visiting Baltic sturgeon. With the possibility of a definitive answer sending shivers through the local tourist industry, monster-hunters are these days recruited over the web: ⓦwww.lochness.co.uk offers round-the-clock **web-cams** for views across the loch, while ⓦwww.lochnessinvestigation.org is packed with research information.

from Inverness along this road only run as far south as **Foyers**, so you'll need your own transport to complete the whole loop around the loch, a journey which includes a most impressive stretch between Fort Augustus and the high, hidden **Loch Mhor**, overlooked by the imposing Monadhliath range to the south.

Fort Augustus

FORT AUGUSTUS, a tiny, busy village at the scenic southwestern tip of Loch Ness, was named after George II's son, the chubby lad who later became the "Butcher" duke of Cumberland of Culloden fame; it was built as a barracks after the 1715 Jacobite rebellion. Today, it's dominated by comings and goings along the Caledonian Canal, which leaves Loch Ness here, and by its large former **Benedictine Abbey**, a campus of grey Victorian buildings founded on the site of the original fort in 1876 that was home until relatively recently to a small but active community of monks, but now has been converted into luxury flats. Traditional Highland culture is the subject of the lively and informative exhibition at the **Clansmen Centre** (Easter to mid-Oct daily 10am–6pm; £3.50), on the banks of the canal. Guides sporting sporrans and rough woollen plaids talk you through the daily life of the region's seventeenth-century inhabitants inside a mock-up of a turf-roofed stone croft, followed by demonstrations of weaponry in the back garden. Rather more sedate is the small **Caledonian Canal Heritage Centre** (daily July–Sept 10am–5pm; free), in Ardchattan House on the northern bank of the canal, where you can view old photographs and records about the history of the canal and watch a black-and-white film of the days when paddle boats and large barges passed through the locks every day. The new *Loch Ness Express* (Easter–Oct; 80min one way/2hr 30min return; £13 one-way, £25 return; ☎0800/3286426, ⓦwww.lochnessexpress.com) makes speedy daily trips up the length of Loch Ness and will carry bikes for free, while *Cruise Loch Ness* (March–Nov; 1hr; £8; ☎01320/366277, ⓦwww.cruiselochness.com) provide shorter trips.

Fort Augustus's helpful **tourist office** (daily: April–May 10am–5pm; June & Sept 9am–5pm; July & Aug 9am–6pm; Oct 10am–4.30pm; ☎01320/366779) hands out useful free walking leaflets and stocks maps of the Great Glen Way. They'll also advise on fishing permits for the loch or nearby river. There's **hostel** accommodation at *Morag's Lodge* (☎01320/366289) above the petrol station on the Loch Ness side of town, where the atmosphere livens up with the daily arrival of backpackers' minibus tours, and at the well-equipped, thirty-bed *Stravaigers Lodge* (☎01320/366257) on Glendoe Road. The *Old Pier* (☎01320/366418, ⓔjenny@oldpierhouse.com; ❹) is a particularly appealing **B&B** right on the loch at the north side of the village providing two roaring log fires in the evening and the option of renting two-person Canadian canoes (£10 per day) or even going horse riding (min £50 for two people) in the mountains. Of the **hotels**, try either the small, friendly *Caledonian* (☎01320/366256, ⓦwww.thecaledonianhotel.com; ❹) or the lovely *Lovat Arms Hotel* (☎01320/366366; ❺, opposite, built on the site of the 1718 Kilwhimen Barracks.

Either of the above hotels provides reasonable **food**, but for a lively atmosphere in a local pub, the *Lock Inn* has regular music and draws a mixed clientele of locals, yachties and backpackers, as does *Poachers* on the main road. The *Bothy Bite* beside the canal serves Scottish specialities, including a good range of moderately priced fish. There are some good **cycling** routes locally, notably along the Great Glen cycle route. The best place to rent bikes or watersports equipment, including boats and canoes, is at South Laggan, eight miles or so southwest at the head of Loch Lochy, from Monster Activities (☎01809/501340, ⓦwww.monsteractivities.com).

The east side of Loch Ness

The tranquil and scenic **east side** of Loch Ness is skirted by General Wade's old military highway, now the B862/B852. From Fort Augustus, the narrow single-track road swings up, away from the lochside through the near-deserted **Stratherrick** valley, dotted with tiny lochans. It's worth stopping for good-value, home-made food or a pint at the friendly 🏕 *Whitebridge Hotel* (☎01456/486226; ❹). Fifty metres further north is the beautifully preserved stone White Bridge built in 1732. From here, the road drops down to rejoin the shores of Loch Ness at **FOYERS**, where there are numerous marked forest trails and an impressive waterfall. Heading north through the village, turn right at the post office and *Waterfall Café* for the friendly *Foyers House* (☎01456/486405, ⓦwww.foyershouse-lochness.com; ❸). This secluded B&B with fabulous views of the loch from its terrace also has a **restaurant** serving up game pie, venison, local salmon and vegetarian options.

Past **Inverfarigaig** – where a road up a beautiful, steep-sided river valley leads east over to Loch Mhor – is the sleepy village of **DORES**, nestled at the northeastern end of Loch Ness, its whitewashed *Dores Inn* providing a pleasant pitstop. Only nine miles southwest of Inverness, the old **pub** is popular with Invernessians, who trickle out here on summer evenings for a stroll along the grey-pebble beach and some monster-spotting. Note that a local **bus** from Inverness runs down the east side of the loch to Foyers (3 daily Mon–Fri).

Invermoriston and west

On the other shore, heading north from Fort Augustus along the main A82, which follows the loch's northwestern side, **INVERMORISTON** is a tiny, attractive village just above the loch, from where you can follow well-marked woodland trails past a series of grand waterfalls.

The A887 leads west from Invermoriston to the west coast (via the A87) on the main commercial route to the Skye Bridge. Rugged and somewhat awesome, the stretch through **Glen Moriston**, beside **Loch Cluanie**, has serious peaks at either side and little sign of human habitation. At the western end of the loch, you'll find the isolated *Cluanie Inn* (☎01320/340238, ⓦwww .cluanie.co.uk; ❹), a popular place with outdoor types serving good food in its real-fire pub and offering some more expensive rooms (❼) with a sauna and jacuzzi. West from here, the road drops gradually down **Glen Shiel** into the superb mountainscape of Kintail (see p.626).

Drumnadrochit and around

Situated above a verdant, sheltered bay of Loch Ness fifteen miles southwest of Inverness, **DRUMNADROCHIT** is the southern gateway to remote Glen Affric and the epicentre of Nessie-hype, complete with a rash of tacky souvenir shops and two rival monster exhibitions whose head-to-head scramble for punters occasionally erupts into acrimonious exchanges, detailed with relish by the local press. Of the pair, the **Loch Ness 2000 Exhibition** (daily: Easter–May

△ Castle Urquhart overlooking Loch Ness

9.30am–5pm; June & Sept 9am–6pm; July & Aug 9am–8pm; Oct–Easter 10am–3.30pm; £5.95), though more expensive, is the better bet, offering an in-depth rundown of eyewitness accounts and information on various research projects that have attempted to shed further light on the mysteries of the loch. The **Original Loch Ness Monster Visitor Centre and Lodge Hotel** (daily: July & Aug 9am–9pm; rest of year 9am–5pm; Dec–March closes 4pm; £5) has a less impressive exhibition, though it's a worthwhile stop if only for the delicious array of home baking offered within the adjacent comfortable hotel (⑤) and to go in search of the resident ghost within the tartanized interior.

Cruises on the loch aboard *Deep Scan Cruises* run from the Loch Ness 2000 Exhibition (Easter to mid-Oct; 1hr; £10; ℡01456/450218), while the *Nessie Hunter* (hourly: Easter–Sept 9am–6pm; Oct–Dec 10am–3pm; 50min; £10; ℡01456/450395) can be booked at the Original Loch Ness Visitor Centre. A more relaxing alternative is to head out **fishing** with a local gillie – the boat costs around £20 each (flexible) based on a group of four for two hours; contact Bruce (Easter–Sept; ℡01456/450279). If you want to turn your back on all the hype and enjoy the surrounding scenery, you could opt for the well-run **pony trekking** available at the Highland Riding Centre (℡01456/450220), at Borlum Farm (ⓦwww.borlum.com), just two minutes north of Urquhart Castle.

Most photographs allegedly showing the monster have been taken a couple of miles east of Drumnadrochit, around the thirteenth-century ruined lochside **Castle Urquhart** (daily: April–Sept 9.30am–6.30pm; Oct–March 9.30am–4.30pm; HS; £6). Built as a strategic base to guard the Great Glen, the castle was taken by Edward I of England and later held by Robert the Bruce against Edward III, only to be blown up in 1692 to prevent it from falling to the Jacobites. Today it's one of Scotland's classic picture-postcard ruins, crawling with tourists by day but particularly splendid floodlit at night when all the crowds have gone. There's a footpath alongside the A82 road between Drumnadrochit and the castle, though the constant stream of cars, caravans and tour buses doesn't make it a particularly pleasant stroll.

Practicalities

Drumnadrochit's **tourist office** (April–June & Oct Mon–Sat 9am–5pm; July & Aug Mon–Sat 9am–6pm, Sun 10am–4pm; Sept Mon–Sat 9am–5pm, Sun 10am–4pm; Nov–March Mon–Fri 10am–1.30pm; ℡01456/459076) shares space with a Highland Council service point in the middle of the main car park in the village. There's a good range of **accommodation** around Drumnadrochit and in the adjoining village of Lewiston. A very welcoming **B&B** is *Gillyflowers* (℡01456/450641, ⓦwww.cali.co.uk/freeway/gillyflowers; ②), a renovated 1780s farmhouse on a country lane in Lewiston. **Hotels** include the friendly and secluded *Benleva* (℡01456/450080, ⓦwww.benleva.co.uk; ④), also in Lewiston, where real ale and delicious game and seafood are served by enthusiastic new owners. Two miles west of Drumnadrochit along the Cannich road is a particularly relaxed country-house hotel, *Polmaily House* (℡01456/450343, ⓦwww.polmaily.co.uk; ⑦). In addition to offering fine food and comfortable rooms, it's family-friendly with acres of space including a swimming pool. For **hostel** beds, head to the immaculate and friendly *Loch Ness Backpackers Lodge* (℡01456/450807, ⓦwww.lochness-backpackers.com), at Coiltie Farmhouse in Lewiston; follow the signs to the left when coming from Drumnadrochit. As well as dorm beds, it has one double and two family rooms (①) and facilities include bike rental and pony trekking, and even a special Sunday bus into Glen Affric can be arranged.

Most of the hotels in the area – the *Benleva* in particular – serve good bar **food**; in Drumnadrochit the *Glen Café* on the village green has a short and simple menu with basic grills, while the slightly more upmarket *Fiddlers' Café Bar* next door offers local steaks, salmon and hearty lunches.

Glen Affric

Due west of Drumnadrochit is a vast area of high peaks, remote glens and few roads. The reason most folk head this way is to explore the native forests and grand mountains of **Glen Affric**, generally held to be one of Scotland's most beautiful landscapes and heaven for walkers, climbers and mountain-bikers. If you're driving, note that the nearest petrol stations are in Drumnadrochit and in Beauly to the north. On weekdays there's a **bus** three times a day from Inverness to Cannich, but to get right into the heart of Glen Affric you'll need a car or a bike. If you're exploring the area, it's worth getting your hands on the excellent Glen Affric and Strathglass tourist map (Ⓦ www.glenaffric.info), which is usually available from local businesses and tourist offices.

The approach to the glen is through the small settlement of **CANNICH**, fourteen miles west of Drumnadrochit on the A831. Cannich is a quiet and uninspiring village, but it has an excellent campsite (Ⓣ 01456/415364) where mountain-bikes can be rented and there's the friendly *Glen Affric Backpackers Hostel* (Ⓣ 01456/415263, Ⓦ www.glenaffric.org) which offers inexpensive twin or four-bed rooms. Check the SYHA website (Ⓦ www.syha.org.uk) for updates on the status of the small youth hostel next door, which is due to be renovated in 2006. For food, try the modest *Slaters Arms* or buy supplies from the village Spar shop.

Hemmed in by a string of Munros, Glen Affric is great for picnics and pottering, particularly on a calm and sunny day, when the still water of the loch reflects the islands and surrounding hills. From the car park at the head of the single-track road along the glen, ten miles southwest of Cannich, there's a selection of **walks**: the trip around **Loch Affric** will take you a good five hours but captures the glen, its wildlife and Caledonian pine and birch woods in all their remote splendour. For details of **volunteer work** weeks based in Glen Affric helping with the restoration of the woodland, get in touch with Trees for Life (Ⓦ www.treesforlife .org.uk). You could also do some serious **hiking**. Munro-baggers are normally much in evidence, and it is possible to tramp 25 miles all the way through Glen Affric to Shiel Bridge, on the west coast near Kyle of Lochalsh, making use of the remote but recently revamped *Allt Beithe* SYHA hostel (Ⓣ 0870/155 3255, Ⓦ www.syha.org.uk; April–Oct) near the head of Glen Affric, which makes a convenient if rudimentary stopover halfway.

Inverness and around

Inverness, over a hundred miles from any other principal Scottish settlement and with a population of around 80,000, is the only "city" in the Highlands – an official status conferred in 2000 by the government. A good base for day-trips and a jumping-off point for many of the more remote parts of the region, it is not a compelling place to stay for long and inevitably you are drawn to the attractions of sea and mountains beyond. The approach to the city on the A9 over the barren Monadhliath Mountains from Perth and Aviemore provides a spectacular introduction to the district, with the **Great Glen** to the left, stretching southwestwards towards Fort William and, beyond, the massed peaks of Glen Affric. To the north is the huge, rounded form of Ben Wyvis, whilst to the east lies the **Moray Firth**, which has a lovely coastline boasting some of the region's best castles and historic sites. The gentle, undulating green landscape is well tended and tranquil, a fertile contrast to the windswept moorland and mountains that almost surround it.

A string of worthwhile sights punctuates the approaches to Inverness along the main route from Aberdeen. The low-key holiday resort of **Nairn**, with its long white-sand beaches and championship golf course, stands within striking distance of several monuments, including the whimsical **Cawdor Castle**, featured in Shakespeare's *Macbeth*, and **Fort George**, one of several impressive Hanoverian bastions erected in the wake of the Jacobite rebellion. The infamous battle and ensuing massacre that ended Bonnie Prince Charlie's uprising took place on the outskirts of Inverness at **Culloden**, where a visitor centre and memorial stones beside a heather-clad moor recall the gruesome events of 1746.

Inverness

Straddling a nexus of major road and rail routes, **INVERNESS** is the busy and prosperous hub of the Highlands, and an inevitable port of call if you're exploring the region by public transport. **Buses** and **trains** leave for communities right across the far north of Scotland, and it isn't uncommon for people from as far afield as Thurso, Durness and Kyle of Lochalsh to travel down for a day's shopping here – Britain's most northerly chain-store centre. Though boasting few conventional sights, the city's setting on the banks of the River Ness is appealing. Crowned by a pink crenellated **castle** and lavishly decorated with flowers, the compact centre still has some hints of its medieval street layout, although pedestrianization and some unsightly concrete blocks do a fairly efficient job of masking it. Within walking distance of the centre are peaceful spots along by the Ness, leafy parks and friendly B&Bs located in prosperous-looking stone houses.

The sheltered **harbour** and proximity to the open sea made Inverness an important entrepôt and shipbuilding centre during medieval times. David I, who first imposed a feudal system on Scotland, erected a castle on the banks of the Ness to oversee maritime trade in the early twelfth century, promoting it to royal burgh status soon after. Bolstered by receipts from the lucrative export of leather, salmon and timber, the town grew to become the kingdom's most prosperous northern outpost, and an obvious target for the marauding Highlanders who plagued this remote border area. A second wave of growth occurred during the eighteenth century as the Highland cattle trade flourished. The arrival of the **Caledonian Canal** and **rail** links with the east and south brought further prosperity, heralding a tourist boom that reached a fashionable zenith in the Victorian era, fostered by the Royal Family's enthusiasm for all things Scottish. Over the last thirty years, the town has become one of the fastest expanding in Britain, with its population virtually doubling due to the growing tourist industry and improved communications.

Arrival, information and accommodation

Inverness **airport** (℡01667/464000) is at Dalcross, seven miles east of the city; from here, bus #11 (Mon–Sat every 40min, reduced service Sun; journey time 20min; £3) goes into town, while a taxi costs around £12. The **bus station** (℡01463/233371) and **train station** (℡0845/748 4950) both lie just off Academy Street to the northeast of the centre. The **tourist office** (March to end May Mon–Sat 9am–5pm; end May to end Aug Mon–Sat 9am–6pm, Sun 10am–4pm; Sept to end Oct 9am–5pm, Sun 10am–4pm; ℡0845/2255121) is in an unsightly 1960s block on Castle Wynd, just five minutes' walk from the

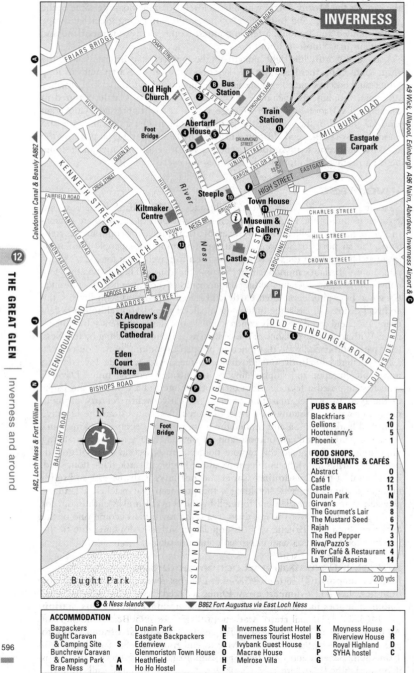

INVERNESS

A9 Wick, Ullapool & Edinburgh

A9 Wick, Ullapool, Edinburgh A96 Nairn, Aberdeen, Inverness Airport & **G**

FRIARS BRIDGE

CHAPEL STREET

LONGMAN ROAD

Library

Old High Church

B Bus Station

STROTHER'S LANE

Train Station

MILLBURN ROAD

Foot Bridge

Abertarff House

DRUMMOND STREET

Eastgate Carpark

UNION STREET

BARON TAYLOR'S ST

HIGH STREET

EASTGATE

E **9**

Steeple

Town House

CHARLES STREET

Kiltmaker Centre

i Museum & Art Gallery

HILL STREET

CROWN STREET

Castle

ARDCONNEL STREET

ARGYLE STREET

H

ADROSS PLACE

ARDROSS STREET

OLD EDINBURGH ROAD

St Andrew's Episcopal Cathedral

Eden Court Theatre

BISHOPS ROAD

N

Foot Bridge

Bught Park

PUBS & BARS

Blackfriars	2
Gellions	10
Hootenanny's	5
Phoenix	1

**FOOD SHOPS,
RESTAURANTS & CAFÉS**

Abstract	0
Café 1	12
Castle	11
Dunain Park	N
Girvan's	9
The Gourmet's Lair	8
The Mustard Seed	6
Rajah	7
The Red Pepper	3
Riva/Pazzo's	13
River Café & Restaurant	4
La Tortilla Asesina	14

0   200 yds

S & Ness Islands ▼   ▼ B862 Fort Augustus via East Loch Ness

ACCOMMODATION

Bazpackers	**I**	Dunain Park	**N**	Inverness Student Hotel	**K**	Moyness House	**J**
Bught Caravan & Camping Site	**S**	Eastgate Backpackers	**E**	Inverness Tourist Hostel	**B**	Riverview House	**D**
Bunchrew Caravan & Camping Park	**A**	Edenview	**Q**	Ivybank Guest House	**L**	Royal Highland	**P**
Brae Ness	**M**	Glenmoriston Town House	**O**	Macrae House	**G**	SYHA hostel	**C**
		Heathfield	**H**	Melrose Villa	**F**		
		Ho Ho Hostel	**F**				

© Crown copyright

Inverness is the departure point for a range of day **tours** and **cruises** to nearby attractions, including Loch Ness and the Moray Firth.

City Sightseeing runs an open-topped double-decker **city tour** of **Inverness** (May–Sept daily every 45min; £5.50), which you can hop on and off all day. You can buy tickets on board, at the tourist office or at their office in the train station (May–Sept daily 9am–6pm). An entertaining if slightly bizarre **Terror Tour** takes groups on foot around Inverness town centre (daily 7pm from the tourist office; £7), with grisly tales told along the way of ghosts, torture and witches. It ends with a free pint in a haunted pub. Telliesperie (℡01463 233729) also conducts storywalks, leaving daily from *Hootenanny's* on Church Street (1hr; £5) while the Inverness Historic Trail (July & Aug Mon–Sat 11am & 2pm; £3) leaves from the tourist office and provides a great insight into local history.

There are various tours of Loch Ness and Glen Affric leaving from the tourist office lasting from one hour to a whole day. Loch Ness cruises typically incorporate a visit to a monster exhibition at **Drumnadrochit** and **Urquhart Castle** – try Jacobite Cruises (℡01463/233999, ⒲www.jacobite.co.uk). Its courtesy bus runs from the tourist office to their dock at Tomnahurich Canal Bridge on Glenurquhart Road, a mile and a half south of Inverness town centre. **Discover Loch Ness** tours (℡01456/450168 or 0800/731 5565, ⒲www.discoverlochness.com) combines an insightful introduction to the monster-hype with visits to places of geological or historical interest. The new **Loch Ness Express** (℡0800/3286426; see p.591) also provides a daily return ferry service from Dochgarroch at the eastern end of Loch right down to Fort Augustus. A free shuttle bus runs to Dochgarroch from Inverness tourist office; the two-and-a-half-hour boat trip costs £13 one-way or £25 return.

Inverness is about the one place where transport connections allow you to embark on a major **grand tour** of the Highlands. It is possible, cabin fever notwithstanding, to catch the early train to Kyle of Lochalsh, a bus onto Skye and across the island to catch the ferry to Mallaig, which meets the train to Fort William, from where you can take a bus back to Inverness, all in less than twelve hours. Handy for exploring the northwest, Dearman Coaches (April–Sept Mon–Sat; £21, six-day rover ticket £36) have a daily service (bikes accepted) to **Ullapool**, **Lochinver**, **Durness**, **Smoo Cave** and back which stops at several hostels en route.

Enjoyable trips to **John O'Groats** and back in a day, with the chance to see puffins and visit prehistoric sites, are run by Puffin Express (℡01463/717181, ⒲www.puffinexpress.co.uk); they also put together a package which includes an overnight stop on **Orkney**. You can get to the islands and back with a gruelling full-day whistle-stop tour on the Orkney Bus, which leaves Inverness bus station every day during the summer (£46; advance bookings may be made at the tourist office or on ℡01955/611353, ⒲www.jogferry.co.uk).

See box on p.604 for details of **dolphin**-spotting cruises on the Moray Firth.

train station. It stocks a wide range of literature, including free maps of the city and environs, and the staff can book local accommodation for a £3 fee. There's also a Cal Mac ferry booking office.

Inverness is one of the few places in the Highlands where you're unlikely to have problems finding **accommodation**, although in July and August you'll have to book ahead. Inverness boasts several good **hotels**, and nearly every street in the older residential areas of town has a sprinkling of **B&Bs**. Good places to look include both banks of the river south of the Ness Bridge, and Kenneth Street and its offshoots on the west side of the river. There are several **hostels** in town, all reasonably central, and a couple of large **campsites**, one near the Ness Islands and the other further out to the west.

Hotels

Brae Ness 17 Ness Bank ☎01463/712266, Ⓦwww.braenesshotel.co.uk. A homely Georgian hotel with only ten rooms (all non-smoking) overlooking the river and St Andrews Cathedral. May–Sept. ❺

Dunain Park off the A82 Fort William road ☎01463/230512, Ⓦwww.dunainparkhotel .co.uk. Luxurious country-house hotel, three miles west of centre of town. Excellent food (dinner is around £25 per person) and charming, opulent rooms. ❼

Glenmoriston Town House Hotel 20 Ness Bank ☎01463/223777, Ⓦwww .glenmoriston.com. Classy and stylishly modern hotel harbouring a high-quality French restaurant, *Abstract*. ❼

Royal Highland 18 Academy St ☎01463/231926, Ⓦwww.royalhighlandhotel.co.uk. The old station hotel, dripping with the grandeur of the golden days of Highland travel. The restaurant, *Ash*, provides good food and cocktails. ❼

B&Bs

Edenview 26 Ness Bank ☎01463/234397, Ⓔedenview@clara.co.uk. Very pleasant B&B in a riverside location as good as that of the more expensive hotels, five minutes' walk from the centre. Non-smoking. March–Oct. ❸

Heathfield 2 Kenneth St ☎01463/230547. A very comfortable and friendly place at the quiet end of a street packed with B&Bs. All rooms centrally heated and some are en suite. Non-smoking. No credit cards. ❷

Ivybank Guest House 28 Old Edinburgh Rd ☎01463/232796, Ⓦwww.ivybankguesthouse .com. A grand Georgian home just up the hill from the castle, with open fires and a lovely wooden interior. ❷

Macrae House 24 Ness Bank ☎01463/243658, Ⓦwww.macraehouse.co.uk. Right on the river, friendly, and with large, comfortable rooms. Non-smoking. ❷

Melrose Villa 35 Kenneth St ☎01463/233745, Ⓦwww.melrosevilla.com. Very family-friendly, with excellent breakfasts. Three singles as well as doubles and twins, with most rooms en suite. ❸

Moyness House 6 Bruce Gardens ☎01463/233836, Ⓦwww.moyness.co.uk. Warm, welcoming, upmarket B&B on west side of Inverness, with original Victorian features and a nice walled garden. ❺

Riverview House 2 Moray Park, Island Bank Rd ☎01463/235557. A welcoming B&B in a characterful old house a little further down the river than some pricier guesthouses, but still an easy stroll from the centre. ❸

Hostels

Bazpackers top of Castle St ☎01463/717663. The most cosy and relaxed of the city's hostels, with thirty beds including two double rooms and a twin (❶); some dorms are mixed. Has good views and a garden, which is used for barbecues, as well as the usual cooking facilities. Non-smoking.

Eastgate Backpackers Hostel 38 Eastgate ☎01463/718756, Ⓦwww.eastgatebackpackers .com. Well-maintained former hotel with single, twin and double room (❶) accommodation. Bike rental, Internet access and dorms and two twin rooms. Left luggage storage and no curfew.

Ho Ho Hostel 23a High St ☎01463/221225, Ⓦwww.hohohostel.force9.co.uk. Formerly the grand Highland Club, a town base for lairds. Now a large, rather worn but central hostel with big rooms which tends to attract a partying crowd. They also have rather grubby, but cheap twins and doubles (❷) available at a nearby location, called *The Long Lie-in*.

Inverness Student Hotel 8 Culduthel Rd ☎01463/236556, Ⓦwww.scotlands-top-hostels .com. A busy 50-bed hostel with the usual facilities and fine views over the river. Part of the MacBackpackers group, so expect minibus tours to pull in most days.

Inverness Tourist Hostel 24 Rose St ☎01463/241962. A central, clean, well-equipped 60-bed hostel offering top-notch amenities including wide-screen TVs and Internet access.

SYHA hostel Victoria Drive, off Millburn Rd, about three-quarters of a mile east of the centre ☎0870/004 1127, Ⓦwww.syha.org.uk. One of SYHA's flagship hostels, fully equipped with large kitchens and communal areas, eco-friendly facilities and ten four-bed family rooms among the 166-bed total, but hardly central.

Campsites

Bught Caravan and Camping Site Bught Park ☎01463/236920. Inverness's main campsite, south of the centre, on the west bank of the river near the sports centre. Good facilities, but it can get very crowded at the height of the season. Easter to mid-Sept.

Bunchrew Caravan and Camping Park Bunchrew, three miles west of Inverness on the A862 ☎01463/237802, Ⓦwww.bunchrew -caravanpark.co.uk. Well-equipped site with lots of space for tents on the shores of the Beauly Firth, with hot water, showers, laundry and a shop. Very popular with families. March–Nov.

To much of the world, **tartan** is synonymous with Scotland. It's the natural choice of packaging for Scottish exports from shortbread to Sean Connery, and when the Scottish football team travels abroad to play a fixture, the high-spirited "Tartan Army" of fans is never far behind. Not surprisingly, tartan is big business for the tourist industry, yet the truth is that romantic fiction and commercial interest have enclosed this ancient Highland art form within an almost insurmountable wall of myth.

The original form of tartan, the kind that long ago was called **Helande**, was a fine, hard and almost showerproof cloth spun in Highland villages from the wool of the native sheep, dyed with preparations of local plants and with patterns woven by artist-weavers. It was worn as a huge single piece of cloth, or **plaid**, which was belted around the waist and draped over the upper body, rather like a knee-length toga. The natural colours of old tartans were clear but soft, and the broken pattern gave superb camouflage, unlike modern versions, where garish, clashing colours are often used to create impact.

The myth-makers were about four centuries ahead of themselves in dressing up the warriors of the film *Braveheart* in plaid: in fact tartan did not become popular in the Lowlands until the beginning of the eighteenth century, when it was adopted as the anti-Union badge of the **Jacobites**. After Culloden, a ban on the wearing of tartan in the Highlands lasted some 25 years; in that time it became a fondly held emblem for emigrant Highlanders in the colonies and was incorporated into the uniforms of the new Highland regiments in the British Army. Then Sir Walter Scott set to work glamorizing the clans, dressing George IV in a kilt (and, just as controversially, flesh-coloured tights) for his visit to Edinburgh in 1822. By the time Queen Victoria set the royal seal of approval on both the Highlands and tartan with her extended annual holidays at Balmoral, the concept of tartan as formal dress rather than rough Highland wear was assured.

Hand in hand with the gentrification of the kilt came "rules" about the correct form of attire and the idea that every clan had its own distinguishing tartan. To have the right to wear tartan, one had to belong, albeit remotely, to a clan, and so the way was paved for the "what's-my-tartan?" lists that appear in tartan picture books and souvenir shops. Great feats of genealogical gymnastics were performed in the concoction of these lists; where these left gaps, a more recent marketing phenomenon of themed tartans developed, with new patterns for different districts, companies and even football teams being produced.

Scotsmen today will commonly wear the **kilt** for weddings and other formal occasions; properly made kilts, however – comprising some four yards of 100 percent wool – are likely to set you back £300 or more, with the rest of the regalia at least doubling that figure. If the contents of your sporran don't stretch that far, most places selling kilts will rent outfits on a daily basis. The best place to find better-quality material is a recognized Highland outfitter rather than a souvenir shop: in Inverness, try the Scottish Kiltmaker Centre at the Highland House of Fraser shop (see p.600).

The Town

The logical place to begin a tour of Inverness is the central **Town House** on the High Street. Built in 1878, this Gothic pile hosted Prime Minister Lloyd George's emergency meeting to discuss the Irish crisis in September 1921, and now accommodates council offices. There's nothing of note inside, but look out for the old **Mercat Cross** next to the main entrance. The cross stands opposite a small square formerly used by merchants and traders and above the ancient *clach-na-cudainn*, or "**stone of tubs**" – so called because washerwomen used to rest their buckets on it on their way back from the river.

Looming above the Town House and dominating the horizon is **Inverness Castle**, a predominantly nineteenth-century red sandstone edifice perched picturesquely above the river. The original castle formed the core of the ancient town, which had rapidly developed as a port trading with Europe after its conversion to Christianity by St Columba in the sixth century. Robert the Bruce wrested the castle back from the English during the Wars of Independence, destroying much of the structure in the process, and while held by the Jacobites in both the 1715 and the 1745 rebellions, it was blown up by them to prevent it falling into government hands. Today's edifice houses the Sheriff Court and, in the summer and autumn months, the **Castle Garrison Encounter** (March–Oct Mon–Sat 10am–5pm; £6), an entertaining and noisy interactive exhibition in which the visitor plays the role of a new recruit in the eighteenth-century Hanoverian army. Around 7pm during the summer, a lone piper clad in full Highland garb performs for tourists on the castle esplanade.

Below the castle, the **Inverness Museum and Art Gallery** on Castle Wynd (Mon–Sat 9am–5pm; free; Ⓦ www.invernessmuseum.com) gives a good general overview of the development of the Highlands. Informative sections on geology, geography and history occupy the ground floor, while upstairs you'll find a muddled selection of silver, taxidermy, weapons and bagpipes, alongside an art gallery that occasionally attracts worthwhile touring exhibitions.

Leading north from the Town House, medieval **Church Street** is home to the town's oldest surviving buildings. On the corner with Bridge Street stands the **Steeple** (1791), whose spire had to be straightened after an earth tremor in 1816. Farther down Church Street is **Abertarff House**, reputedly the oldest complete building in Inverness and distinguished by its stepped gables and circular stair tower. It was erected in 1593 and is now owned by the National Trust for Scotland. The **Old High Church**, founded in 1171 and rebuilt on several occasions since, stands just along the street, hemmed in by a walled graveyard. Those Jacobites who survived the massacre of Culloden were brought here and incarcerated prior to their execution in the cemetery. If you look carefully you may see the bullet holes left on gravestones by the firing squads.

Along the River Ness

Just across Ness Bridge from Bridge Street is the **Kiltmaker Centre** in the Highland House of Fraser shop (June–Sept Mon–Sat 9am–9pm, Sun 10am–5pm; rest of year Mon–Sat 9am–5.30pm; £2). Entered through the factory shop, an imaginative small visitor centre, complete with the outfits worn by actors for the *Braveheart* and *Rob Roy* blockbuster films, sets out everything you ever wanted to know about tartan. There's an interesting seven-minute audio-visual film and on weekdays you can watch various tartan products being made in the workshop. The finished products are, of course, on sale in the showroom downstairs, along with all manner of Highland knitwear, woven woollies and Harris tweed.

Rising from the west bank directly opposite the castle, **St Andrews Episcopal Cathedral** was intended by its architects to be one of the grandest buildings in Scotland. However, funds ran out before the giant twin spires of the original design could be completed. The interior is pretty ordinary, too, though it does claim an unusual octagonal chapterhouse. Alongside the cathedral is **Eden Court Theatre** (Ⓦ www.eden-court.co.uk), closed in 2006 while it undergoes a multi-milllion pound refurbishment to make it the largest multi-arts centre in Scotland; it is due to reopen in spring 2007.

From here, you can wander a mile or so upriver to the peaceful **Ness Islands**, an attractive, informal public park reached and linked by footbridges. Laid out with mature trees and shrubs, the islands are the favourite haunt of local anglers.

The great **outdoors**

For outdoor
enthusiasts Scotland
is a vast adventure playground,
a wonderfully rugged and diverse
landscape where you can take a bracing
walk through an ancient oak forest or practise
ice-climbing for the Himalayas a thousand feet up
a mountainside. Hill walkers take to picking off Munros (a list of hills
over 3000ft in height), mountain bikers get muddy and if you're into
watersports, there's white water, waves and wind a plenty, as well as a stunning
coastline to explore by sea kayak or yacht. And while it's always tempting to
postpone your outdoor foray on account of the unreliable weather,
it's worth keeping in mind that the poorer the
conditions, the cosier the pub at the end of
the day.

Enjoying the view in the Highlands

To the hills

Of course, walking in Scotland needn't necessarily mean uphill, though it is hard to go far without encountering a slope, and anyway, a bit of elevation does wonders for the view. From the smooth, grassy hills and moors of the Southern Uplands to the wild and rugged country of the northwest Highlands, Scotland as a whole is remarkably well suited to **hill walking**: access is generally free, though there may be restricted access during lambing (dogs are particularly unwelcome in April and May) and deerstalking seasons (July 1 to October 20); there are a range of good paths or forest tracks; and, despite the popularity of walking, the hills aren't nearly as busy as, say, the Lake District in northern England.

On your bike

Cycling in the Cairngorms

Scotland is widely regarded as one of the world's top five **mountain bike** destinations, with over a thousand miles of remote terrain to challenge even the most accomplished cyclist. A growing number of dedicated mountain-bike centres such as those in Laggan, Glentress in the Borders or on the Black Isle, provide waymarked trails designed for every level of rider, with experiences on offer ranging from white-knuckle **black** runs to leisurely rides through

The crazy stuff

Scotland's long-standing image as a place to play a testing but well-mannered round of golf, or to pull on your waders and tweed cap to spend a relaxing day fishing, is fast being overtaken by the lycra and neon blur of adrenaline-junkies revelling in the wild conditions the country has to offer. Near Fort William there's a purpose built downhill **mountain bike track** which descends 1800ft in little over two miles – it's used for world championships and is definitely not one for Sunday riders. Out in Tiree there's also first-class sporting action in the annual **windsurfing Wave Classic**, while each year sailors and fell-runners team up for the exhausting **Scottish Islands Peak Race** to the top of the highest summits on the islands of Mull, Jura and Arran. In winter, there's downhill and cross-country **skiing** action in places such as Cairngorm National Park, Glen Shee and Ben Nevis, while Glencoe is popular with **ice-** and **rock-climbers** training for international high-altitude expeditions; in recent years some of the world's finest indoor facilities for both sports have been built at Kinlochleven near Fort William and at Ratho near Edinburgh. Thrill-seekers in Scotland aren't put off by the weather – it merely sets the agenda. A day of gentle zephyrs is perfect for a spot of **paragliding** in Ayrshire; a good dump of rain, on the other hand, will see **rafters** and **canoeists** heading for frothing white rivers such as the Tay, Orchy and Etive, while a brisk day has **kite-surfers** and blo-karters scurrying for stretches of sand such as the West Sands at St Andrews or some of the gloriously empty flat strands of the Outer Hebrides.

National Parks and well-managed Forestry Commission areas. A number of long-distance routes, including **The Great Glen Cycle Way** (see, p.579), have been established in Scotland using a combination of specially built cycle paths and quieter back roads. The rural roads are infinitely more enjoyable, particularly in the gentler landscapes of the south and east of the country, where generally amiable gradients and a decent density of pubs and B&Bs make the area perfect for cycle touring.

Worth a surf

One thing Scotland isn't short of is water, so it's no surprise that **watersports** of all types are popular both on inland lochs and around the coast. The waters of the Outer Hebrides in particular are regarded as world class for **sea-kayaking**, their innumerable skerries, sea-caves and remote white-sand beaches perfect for exploring by canoe; yacht racing and **sailing** are excellent on the protected Firth of Clyde; while **cruising** is the main focus on the west coast, commonly starting from a number of marinas in the area between Crinan and Oban. And though the climate can't quite match Bondi or Malibu, serious **surfers** will tell you that it's not the sun that counts, but the waves – and Scotland has a selection of excellent world-class quality breaks, including one of the finest in Europe near Thurso (see p.652). In addition, the

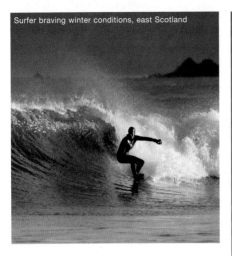
Surfer braving winter conditions, east Scotland

The best Scottish surf breaks

*Brimm's Ness Five miles west of Thurso; p.652. A selection of reef breaks that pick up the smallest of swells.
Fraserburgh 39 miles north of Aberdeen; p.542. A number of beach and reef breaks – beginners should stick to the beach.
Machrihanish Bay Mull of Kintyre; p.387. Four miles of beach breaks on one of Scotland's loneliest peninsulas.
Pease Bay Near Dunbar, 26 miles east of Edinburgh; p.164. A popular break suited to all abilities; can get very crowded.
*Thurso East Just below the castle; p.652. One of the best right-hand reef breaks in Europe.
*Torrisdale Bay Bettyhill, on the north coast of the Highlands; p.650. An excellent right-hand river-mouth break.
*Valtos On the Uig peninsula, Lewis; p.707. A break on one of the Outer Hebrides' most exquisite shell-sand beaches.
*Experienced surfers only

beaches of the **Moray Firth** offer a good North Sea swell, while the west coasts of islands **Coll**, **Tiree** and **Islay** get great swells from the Atlantic and have good beaches, as does the spectacular Sandwood Bay, one of Britain's most isolated beaches. Other remote spots include the Outer Hebrides and the Mull of Kintyre. Just pack some cocoa with the surf wax.

Long-distance footpaths

Now 25 years old, the doyen of Scotland's official long-distance footpaths is the 95-mile **West Highland Way** (see p.426), which involves a five-day trek along well-marked paths between north Glasgow and Fort William, via Loch Lomond and Rannoch Moor. Its popularity has spawned a series of other official routes, including the 73-mile **Great Glen Way** (see p.579) from Fort William to Inverness, the 84-mile **Speyside Way** (see p.565) through whisky country to the Cairngorms, and the daunting 212-mile **Southern Upland Way**, which travels coast to coast across Dumfries & Galloway and the Border region. These, and many other regional footpaths, such as Perthshire's **Cateran Trail** and Argyll's **Cowal Way**, often follow routes used for centuries as drove roads, along which clansmen would lead their cattle from the Highlands to markets in the Lowlands. Older still is the Borders' **St Cuthbert's Way** (see p.192), which follows an ancient pilgrimage route.

Hill climber on Liathach, Torridon

Further upstream still, the river runs close to the **Caledonian Canal**, designed by Thomas Telford in the early nineteenth century as a link between the east and west coasts, joining lochs Ness, Oich, Lochy and Linnhe. Today its main use is recreational, and there are cruises through part of it to Loch Ness (see box on p.597), while the towpath provides relaxing walks with good views.

Eating and drinking

Inverness has lots of eating places, including a few excellent-quality gourmet options, while for the budget-conscious there's no shortage of **pubs**, **cafés** and **restaurants** around the town centre. **Takeaways** cluster on Young Street, just across the river, and at the ends of Eastgate and Academy Street. The best place for **picnic food** is The Gourmet's Lair, a well-stocked deli at 8 Union St.

The liveliest **nightlife** revolves around the pubs and on, on Friday and Saturday nights, at *Bakoo* on High Street, the city's main nightclub. The far end of Academy Street has a cluster of good **pubs**; the public bar of the *Phoenix* is the most original town-centre place, though *Blackfriars* across the street has a better atmosphere with entertainment five nights a week, including ceilidhs popular with Australian backpackers searching for their roots. *Hootenanny's*, on Church Street, is a popular and lively pub, hosting lots of live gigs and ceilidhs. Over on Bridge Street, the *Gellions* is a legendary local watering hole with several other congenial places close by.

Cafés and restaurants

Abstract 20 Ness Bank ☎01463/223777, ⓦwww.abstractrestaurant.com. Best known for its appearance on the TV show *Ramsay's Kitchen Nightmares*, this award-winning French restaurant within *Glenmoriston Town House Hotel* (see p.598) positively oozes with style and chic. Closed Mon. Expensive.

Café 1 75 Castle St ☎01463/226200. Impressive contemporary Scottish cooking using good local ingredients in a bistro-style setting. Closed Sun. Moderate to expensive.

Castle Restaurant 41 Castle St. Classic, 40-year-old family-run café that does a roaring trade in down-to-earth Scottish food – meat pies, chicken and fish, dished up with piles of chips. Open at 8am for breakfast; closed Sun. Inexpensive.

Dunain Park Restaurant Dunain Park ☎01463/230512, ⓦwww.dunainparkhotel.co.uk. Scots-French restaurant in a country-house hotel (see p.598) set in lovely gardens just southwest of town; a good choice for a leisurely dinner. Expensive.

Girvan's 2–4 Stephen's Brae ☎01463/711900. Offers an uncomplicated but decent fare including Scottish meat and fish dishes. Doubles as a daytime patisserie.

La Tortilla Asesina 99 Castle St ☎01463/709809. Simple but lively tapas restaurant, serving all the

old favourites as well as some "tartan tapas" majoring on local ingredients. Moderate.

The Mustard Seed 16 Fraser St ☎01463/220220. The most stylish place in town for an informal meal – an airy converted church with stone walls, smart table settings and an upbeat approach, serving Scottish and European-influenced cuisine and a range of light, bistro-style dishes. Mouthwatering daily specials. Despite the wow factor, it's reasonably priced. Moderate.

Rajah Post Office Ave ☎01463/237190. An excellent Indian restaurant, tucked away in a back-street basement. Moderate.

The Red Pepper 74 Church St. Linked to the *Mustard Seed*, this is the city's hip coffee-bar hangout with lots of freshly made sandwiches. Takeaway available. Inexpensive.

Riva 4–6 Ness Walk ☎01463/237377. Reasonably authentic modern Italian bistro/café beside the river with antipasta, decent mains and good coffee and cakes. Next door is *Pazzo's Pizzeria* with standard moderately priced Italian fare. Moderate to expensive.

River Café and Restaurant 10 Bank St ☎01463/714884. Healthy wholefood lunches, great high tea with freshly baked cakes and tasty evening meals. Inexpensive to moderate.

Listings

Airport ☎01667/464000.
Bike rental Highland Cycles, 16a Telford St ☎01463/234789 (8.30am–5.30pm).

Bookshops Leakey's is located in a former church on Church St and filled with almost 100,000 second-hand books and a cosy café. Great spot

to browse with a warming wood stove in winter (Mon–Sat 10am–4.30pm). There's also Waterstones at 50–52 High St.

Car rental Budget is on Railway Terrace, behind the train station ☎01463/713333; Europcar has an office on Telfer St ☎01463/235337; Focus Vehicle Rental is at Shore St ☎01463/709517; Aberdeen 4x4 Self-Drive is at 15b Harbour Rd ☎01463/871083; and Sharps Reliable Wrecks is based at Inverness train station, Academy St ☎01463/236684 as well as the airport.

Cinemas With the Eden Court Theatre undergoing refurbishment, head for the seven-screen Warner Village complex (☎0870/240 6020), on the A96 Nairn road about two miles from the town centre.

Dentist Contact the Scotland-wide National Health Service Line (☎0800/224488) for local and emergency dentists or The Dental Clinic within Optical Express on High St (☎01463/248871).

Exchange American Express agents Alba Travel are at 43 Church St (Mon–Sat 9am–5pm; ☎01463/239188). The tourist office's *bureau de change* changes cash and currency for a small commission.

Hospital Raigmore Hospital (☎01463/704000) on the southeastern outskirts of town close to the A9.

Internet Highland libraries provide 30min free Internet access. There are also terminals in the tourist office and at Mailbox Etc outside the railway station.

Laundry Young Street Laundrette, 17 Young St (☎01463/242507).

Left luggage Train station lockers cost from £3 to £5 for 24hr (can only deposit 8am–6.30pm); the left-luggage room in the bus station costs £1 per item (Mon–Sat 8.30am–6pm, Sun 10am–6pm).

Library Inverness library (☎01463/236463), housed in the Neoclassical building on the northeast side of the bus station, has an excellent genealogical research unit (Mon–Fri 10am–1pm & 2–5pm; ext 9). Consultations with the resident genealogist cost £12 per hour, but are free if shorter than ten minutes. An appointment is advisable.

Outdoor supplies Blacks, 3–9 Academy St (☎01463/248617); Graham Tiso, 41 High St (☎01463/716617).

Pharmacy Boots, 1–11 Eastgate Shopping Centre (Mon–Wed & Fri 8.45am–6pm, Thurs 8.45am–7pm, Sat 8.30am–6pm, Sun 11am–5pm; ☎01463/225167).

Post office 14–16 Queensgate (Mon–Sat 9am–5.30pm; ☎0845/722 3344); also noon–5pm at Tesco's.

Public toilets Just behind tourist information on Castle St.

Radio The local radio station is Moray Firth Radio on 97.4FM and 1107AM.

Sports centre Inverness sports centre & Aquadome leisure pool (Mon–Fri 10am–8pm, Sat & Sun 9am–5pm; ☎01463/667502), a mile or so south of the town centre off the A82, has a large pool with flumes and waves, also gym, health suite and climbing wall.

Taxis Inverness Taxis ☎01463/220222; Tartan Taxis ☎01463/233033.

East of Inverness

East of Inverness lies the fertile, sheltered coastal strip of the **Moray Firth** and its hinterland, the pastoral countryside contrasting with the scenic splendours you'll encounter once you head further north into the Highlands. Primary target is **Culloden**, the most poignant battlefield site in Scotland, where Bonnie Prince Charlie's Jacobites were routed in 1746. Further east are **Cawdor Castle** and **Fort George**, two of the best-preserved fortified structures in the Highlands. **Nairn**, the main town of the district, has a pretty harbour as well as appealing walks and cycle routes.

The overloaded A96 traverses this stretch and the region is well served by public transport, with all the historic sites and castles accessible on day-trips from Inverness, or en route to Aberdeen. Highland Country **buses** run from either Queensgate or the main post office to Fort George (#11), Cawdor Castle (#13) and Culloden (#7). You can also purchase a £6 day-rover ticket for these journeys.

Culloden

The windswept moorland of **CULLODEN** (site open all year; free), five miles east of Inverness, witnessed the last-ever battle on British soil when, on April 16, 1746, the Jacobite cause was finally subdued – a turning point in the history of the Scottish nation.

The second Jacobite rebellion had begun on August 19, 1745, with the raising of the Stuarts' standard at **Glenfinnan** on the west coast (see p.620). Shortly after, Edinburgh fell into Jacobite hands, and Bonnie Prince Charlie began his march on London. The English had appointed the ambitious young duke of Cumberland to command their forces, and his pursuit, together with bad weather and lack of funds, eventually forced the Jacobites to retreat north. They ended up at Culloden, where, ill-fed and exhausted after a pointless night march, they were hopelessly outnumbered by the English. The open, flat ground of Culloden Moor was totally unsuitable for the Highlanders' style of courageous but undisciplined fighting, which needed steep hills and lots of cover to provide the element of surprise, and they were routed. After the battle, in which 1500 Highlanders were slaughtered (many of them as they lay wounded on the battlefield), Bonnie Prince Charlie fled west to the hills and islands, where loyal Highlanders sheltered and protected him. He eventually escaped to France, leaving his erstwhile supporters to their fate – and, in effect, ushering in the end of the clan system. The clans were disarmed, the wearing of tartan and playing of bagpipes forbidden, and the chiefs became landlords greedy for higher and higher rents. The battle also unleashed an orgy of violent reprisals on Scotland, as unruly English troops raped and pillaged their way across the region; within a century, the Highland way of life had changed out of all recognition.

The battle site

Today you can walk freely around the battle site; flags show the positions of the two armies, and **clan graves** are marked by simple headstones. The **Field of the English**, for many years unmarked, is a mass grave for the fifty or so English soldiers who died. Half a mile east of the battlefield, just beyond the crossroads on the main road, is the **Cumberland Stone**, thought for many years to have been the point from where the duke watched the battle. It is more likely, however, that he was much further forward and simply used the stone for shelter. Thirty Jacobites were burnt alive outside the old **Leanach cottage** next to the visitor centre; inside, it has been restored to its eighteenth-century appearance.

The dolphins of the Moray Firth

The **Moray Firth**, a great wedge-shaped bay forming the eastern coastline of the Highlands, is one of only three areas of UK waters that supports a resident population of **dolphins**. Over a hundred of these beautiful, intelligent marine mammals live in the estuary, the most northerly breeding ground for this particular species – the bottle-nosed dolphin (*Tursiops truncatus*) – in Europe, and you stand a good chance of spotting a few, either from the shore or a boat.

One of the best places in Scotland, if not in Europe, to look for them is **Chanonry Point**, on the Black Isle (see p.567) – a spit of sand protruding into a narrow, deep channel, where converging currents bring fish close to the surface, and thus the dolphins close to shore; a rising tide is the most likely time to see them. **Kessock Bridge**, one mile north of Inverness, is another prime dolphin-spotting location. You can go all the way down to the beach at the small village of North Kessock, underneath the road bridge, where there's a decent place to have a drink at the pub in the *North Kessock Hotel*, or you can stop above the village in a car park just off the A9 at the Dolphin Visitor Centre and listening post (June–Oct 9.30am–4.30pm; free), set up by a team of zoologists from Aberdeen University studying the dolphins, where hydrophones allow you to eavesdrop on the clicks and whistles of underwater conversations.

In addition, several companies run dolphin-spotting **boat trips** around the Moray Firth. However, researchers claim that the increased traffic is causing the dolphins unnecessary stress, particularly during the all-important breeding period when passing vessels are thought to force calves underwater for uncomfortably long periods. They have therefore devised a code of conduct for boat operators, based on the experiences of other countries where dolphin-watching has become disruptive. So if you decide to go on a cruise to see the dolphins, which also sometimes hold out the chance of spotting minke whales, porpoises, seals and otters, make sure the operator is a member of the Dolphin Space Programme's Accreditation Scheme (see ⓦwww.morayfirth -partnership.org and ⓦwww.wdcs.org). Operators currently accredited include Phoenix, based in Nairn (☎01667/456078); Moray Firth Cruises, Inverness (☎01463/717900); and the WDCS Wildlife Centre, Spey Bay (☎01343/820339; see p.545). In addition, Dolphin Trips Avoch (☎01381/622383, ⓦwww.dolphintripsavoch.co.uk) and the highly regarded Ecoventures, Cromarty (☎01381/600323, ⓦwww.ecoventures.co.uk) are based on the Black Isle, on the northern side of the firth. Trips cost from £10 for one hour. To reach the dolphin sites, hop on the Magic Mini bus (Mon–Sat; £5.10 return) at Inverness (Union Street) to Rosemarkie car park or take the Highland Country Bus (#26; Mon–Fri hourly, irregular Sat) from Inverness bus station to Avoch, Rosemarkie and Cromarty. Bus #12 runs hourly from Inverness Union Street to North Kessock.

The **visitor centre** (daily: Feb & March 11am–4pm; April & May 9am–5.30pm; June, July & Aug 9am–6pm; Sept & Oct 9am–5.30pm; Nov & Dec 11am–4pm; closed Jan; NTS; £5) provides background information through detailed displays and a film show, as well as a short play set on the day of the battle presented by local actors (June–Sept only; included in admission fee), or you can take the evocative hour-long guided **walking tour** (June–Sept 4 daily 10.30am–3pm; £4). In April, on the Saturday closest to the date of the battle, there's a small commemorative service. The visitor centre has a reference library, and will check for you if you think you have an ancestor who died here. A new visitor centre is being built which is due to be completed by 2007.

The Clava Cairns

If you're visiting Culloden with your own transport, a short detour is worthwhile to the **Clava Cairns**, an impressive collection of prehistoric burial chambers clustered around the south bank of the River Nairn, a mile southeast of the battlefield. Erected some time before 2000 BC, the cairns, which are encircled by standing stones in a spinney of mature beech trees, are of two different kinds: one large and one very small **ring-cairn**, and two **passage graves**, which have a narrow passageway from edge to centre. Though cremated remains have been found in both types of structure, and unburnt remains in the passage graves, little is known about the nomadic herdsmen who are thought to have built them.

Cawdor Castle

The pretty, if slightly self-satisfied, village of **CAWDOR**, eight miles east of Culloden, is the site of **Cawdor Castle** (May to mid-Oct daily 10am–5.30pm; £7, gardens only £3.70), a setting intimately linked to Shakespeare's *Macbeth*: the fulfilment of the witches' prediction that Macbeth was to become thane of Cawdor sets off his tragic desire to be king. Though visitors arrive here in their droves each summer because of the site's literary associations, the castle, which dates from the early fourteenth century, could not possibly have witnessed the grisly historical events on which the Bard's drama was based. However, the immaculately restored monument – a fairy-tale affair of towers, turrets, hidden passageways, dungeons, gargoyles and crenellations whimsically shooting off from the original keep – is still well worth a visit.

Six centuries on, the Campbells of Cawdor still spend their winters here, and the castle feels like a family home, albeit one with tapestries, pictures and opulent furniture (all catalogued with mischievous humour). As you explore, look out for the **Thorn Tree Room**, a vaulted chamber complete with the remains of an ancient holly tree that has been carbon-dated to 1372 – an ancient pagan fertility symbol believed to ward off fairies and evil spirits. The **grounds** of the castle are impressive, with an attractive walled garden, a topiarian maze, a small golf course, a putting green and nature trails. It's also worth visiting the village for a drink or meal at the traditional *Cawdor Tavern*, an old inn serving beautifully prepared, though pricey, dinners. To get here, use Highland Country **buses** #7 or #12 from Inverness.

Fort George

Eight miles of undulating coastal farmland separate Cawdor Castle from **Fort George** (daily: April–Sept 9.30am–6.30pm; Oct–March 9.30am–4.30pm; HS; £6), an old Hanoverian bastion with walls a mile long, considered by military architectural historians to be one of the finest fortifications in Europe. Crowning a sandy spit that juts into the middle of the Moray Firth, it was built between 1747 and 1769 as a base for George II's army, in case the Highlanders should attempt to rekindle the Jacobite flame. By the time of its completion, however, the uprising had been firmly quashed and the fort has been used ever since as a barracks; note the armed sentries at the main entrance and the periodic crack of live gunfire from the nearby firing ranges.

Apart from the sweeping panoramic views across the Firth from its ramparts, the main incentive to visit Fort George is the **Regimental Museum** of the Queen's Own Highlanders. Displayed in polished glass cases is a predictable array of regimental silver, coins, moth-eaten uniforms and medals, along with some macabre war trophies, ranging from blood-stained nineteenth-century Sudanese battle robes to Iraqi gas masks gleaned in the First Gulf War. The **chapel** is also worth a look – squat and solid outside, and all light and grace within.

Walking on the northern, grass-covered casemates, which look out into the estuary, you may be lucky enough to see the school of bottle-nosed **dolphins** (see box opposite) swimming in with the tide. This is also a good spot for bird-watching: a colony of kittiwakes occupies the fort's slate rooftops. Highland Country **bus** #11 from Queensgate in Inverness serves the fort.

Nairn

One of the driest and sunniest places in the whole of Scotland, **NAIRN**, sixteen miles east of Inverness, began its days as a peaceful community of fishermen and farmers. The former spoke Gaelic, the latter English, allowing James VI to boast that a town in his kingdom was so large that people at one end of the main street could not understand those at the other end. Nairn became popular in Victorian times, when the train line offered a convenient link to its revitalizing sea air and mild climate, and today its 11,000 strong population still relies on tourism, with all the ingredients for a traditional seaside holiday – a sandy beach, ice-cream shops and fish-and-chip stalls. It boasts two championship golf courses, and Thomas Telford's **harbour** is filled with leisure craft rather than fishing boats. The **Nairn Museum** (May–Sept Mon–Sat 10am–4.30pm; £2.50) at Viewfield House, King Street, provides a general insight into the history and prehistory of the area and also hosts the **Fishertown Museum**, with interesting exhibits illustrating the parsimonious and puritanical life of the fishing families.

Nairn no longer has a tourist office: for **accommodation**, *Bracadale House* on Albert Street (☎01667/452547, ⓦwww.bracadalehouse.com; March–Oct; ❸) is grand but affordable and has a Gaelic-speaking owner. *Greenlawns*, 13 Seafield St (☎01667/452738, ⓦwww.greenlawns.uk.com; ❷), is a spacious and friendly B&B with seven en-suite bedrooms. The *Swallow Golf View Hotel* (☎01667/452301, ⓦwww.swallowhotels.com; ❾) overlooks the sea (and, unsurprisingly, the golf course) and serves meals in its restaurant and conservatory. For a reasonably priced **meal** try the Italian restaurant at the *Aurora Hotel*, 2 Academy St (☎01667/453551, ⓦwww.aurorahotelnairn.com), while *The Classroom* is Nairn's fashionable coffee shop serving tasty light bites, lunches and dinners (11am–11pm). Also on High Street is *Ashers Tea-Room*, ideal for those seeking a decent cuppa. **Bike rental** is available from *Bike and Buggy* (☎01667/455416) at 2 Leopold St.

West of Inverness

West of Inverness, the Moray Firth becomes the **Beauly Firth**, a sheltered sea loch bounded by the Black Isle in the north and the wooded hills of the Aird to the south. At the head of the firth is the medieval village of **Beauly**, seat of the colourful Lovat clan, with the small settlement of **Muir of Ord**, known for its whisky, close by. Most northbound traffic uses Kessock Bridge to cross the Moray Firth from Inverness, so this whole area is quieter, and the A862, which skirts the shoreline and the mud flats, offers a more scenic alternative to the faster A9.

Beauly

The sleepy stone-built village of **BEAULY** lies ten miles west of Inverness, at the point where the Beauly River – one of Scotland's most renowned salmon-fishing streams – flows into the Firth. It's ranged around a single main street that widens into a spacious marketplace, at the north end of which stand the skeletal red sandstone remains of **Beauly Priory** (daily 10am–6pm; free). Founded in 1230 by the Bisset family for the Valliscaulian order, and later becoming Cistercian, it was destroyed during the Reformation and is now in ruins. Beside this, the **Beauly Centre** (daily 10am–6pm; £2) is set up in the manner of an old-time village store, with displays on weaving and the Fraser clan; you can also get local tourist information here and visit the bookshop. The locals will tell you the name Beauly was bestowed on the village by Mary, Queen of Scots, who, when staying at the priory in the summer of 1564, allegedly cried, *"Ah, quel beau lieu!"* ("What a beautiful place!"). In fact, the description "beau lieu" was bestowed by the Lovat family, who came to the region from France with the Normans in the eleventh century.

Beauly has a surprising number of **places to stay**. The most comfortable is the modern *Priory Hotel* (☎01463/782309, ⓦwww.priory-hotel.com; ⓺) within the picturesque village square. The *Lovat Arms Hotel* (☎01463/782313, ⓔlovat.arms@cali.co.uk; ⓸), at the opposite end of the main street, is more traditional and has a decent restaurant. If you're looking for something cheaper, try the *Heathmount Guest House* (☎01463/782411; ⓶), one of several pleasant **B&Bs** in a row of large Victorian houses just south of the *Lovat Arms* on the main road.

Around Beauly

Muir of Ord, a sprawling village four miles north of Beauly, is notable only for the **Glen Ord Distillery** (March–June Mon–Fri 10am–5pm; July–Sept also Sat 10am–5pm & Sun noon–4pm; Oct Mon–Fri 11am–4pm; Nov–Feb Mon–Fri 11.30am–3pm; £4 including discount voucher) on its northern outskirts. Here, as at other distilleries, the mysteries of whisky production are explained with a tour that winds up in the cellars, where you get to sample the 12-year-old Glen Ord single malt. No buses stop outside the distillery, but it's a ten-minute walk from Muir of Ord, which you can reach on the Stagecoach Inverness **bus** #19 from Union Street in Inverness, which travels via Beauly (Mon–Sat hourly); more helpfully, the **train** from Inverness stops at Muir of Ord station (Mon–Sat 6 daily; Sun 2 daily; 20min).

As a change from distilleries, you can visit a **winery** at **Moniack Castle** (Jan–March Mon–Fri 11am–4pm; April–Dec Mon–Sat 10am–5pm; £2), four miles east of Beauly, just off the A862, where you can taste and buy over thirty different home-made products, including silver-birch or meadowsweet wine, sloe-berry liqueur, juniper chutney and rosehip jam.

Travel details

Trains

Fort William to: Crianlarich (Mon–Sat 4 daily, 3 on Sun; 1hr 50min); Glasgow (Mon–Sat 3 daily, 2 on Sun; 3hr 45min); London (Sun–Fri 1 nightly; 12hr); Mallaig (Mon–Sat 3 daily, 2 on Sun; 1hr 25min). **Inverness** to: Aberdeen (Mon–Sat 10 daily; 5 on Sun; 2hr 15min); Aviemore (Mon–Sat 9 daily, 5 on Sun; 40min); Edinburgh (Mon–Sat 6 daily, 3 on Sun; 3hr 30min); Kyle of Lochalsh (Mon–Sat 2–3 daily, 1 on Sun; 2hr 30min); London (Mon–Fri & Sun 1 nightly; 11hr); Thurso (Mon–Sat 2 daily, 1 on Sun; 3hr 25min); Wick (Mon–Sat 2 daily, 1 on Sun; 3hr 45min).

Buses

Fort William to: Drumnadrochit (6 daily; 1hr 30min); Edinburgh (1 direct daily; 4hr); Fort Augustus (6 daily; 1hr); Glasgow (4 daily; 3hr); Inverness (6 daily; 2hr); Mallaig (1 daily; 2hr); Oban (Mon–Sat 4 daily; 1hr 30min); Portree, Skye (1 daily; 3hr). **Inverness** to: Aberdeen (hourly; 3hr 40min); Aviemore (10 daily; 45min); Drumnadrochit (8 daily; 25min); Fort Augustus (6 daily; 1hr); Fort William (6 daily; 2hr); Glasgow (6 daily direct; 3hr 35min–4hr 25min); Kyle of Lochalsh (3 daily; 2hr); Nairn (Mon–Sat 4 daily; 50min); Perth (10 daily; 2hr 35min); Portree (3 daily; 3hr); Thurso (Mon–Sat 5 daily, Sun

1 daily; 3hr 30min); Ullapool (2 Mon, Tues, Thurs & Sat; 3 Wed & Fri; 2hr 25min); Wick (Mon–Sat 4 daily, Sun 1 daily; 3hr).

Inverness to: Edinburgh (Mon–Fri 4 daily, Sat & Sun 1 daily; 45min); Glasgow (Mon–Fri 1 daily; 50min); Kirkwall (Mon–Fri 2 daily, 1 Sun; 45min); London (Gatwick 3 daily; Luton Mon–Fri 1 daily; 1hr 30min); Shetland (Mon–Fri 2 daily; 1hr 40min); Stornoway (Mon–Fri 4 daily; 40min).

The north and
northwest Highlands

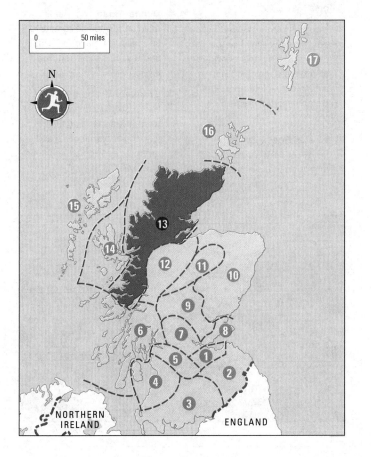

CHAPTER 13

Highlights

* **Loch Shiel** This romantic, unspoilt loch is where Bonnie Prince Charlie first raised an army. See p.620

* **West Highland Railway** From Glasgow to Mallaig via Fort William; the further north you travel, the more spectacular it gets. See p.621

* **Knoydart** Only reached by boat or a two-day hike over the mountains, this peninsula also boasts mainland Britain's most isolated pub, the welcoming *Old Forge*. See p.624

* **Wester Ross** Scotland's finest scenery – a heady mix of dramatic mountains, rugged sea lochs, sweeping bays and scattered islands. See p.630

* **Ceilidh Place, Ullapool** The best venue for modern Highland culture, with evenings of music, song and dance. See p.640

* **Dunnet Head** The true tip of mainland Britain, a remote spot with dramatic red cliffs and a wide sandy bay. See p.653

* **Cromarty** Set on the fertile Black Isle, this charming small town has some beautiful vernacular architecture and dramatic east-coast scenery. See p.657

△ West Highland Railway, Glenfinnan viaduct

The north and northwest Highlands

T he **north and northwest Highlands** – the area beyond the Great Glen – holds some of Scotland's most spectacular scenery: a classic combination of bare mountains, remote glens, dark lochs and tumbling rivers, surrounded on three sides by a magnificently rugged coastline. The inspiring landscape and the tranquillity and space which it offers are without doubt the main attractions of the region. You may be surprised at just how remote much of it still is: the vast peat bogs in the north, for example, are among the most extensive and unspoilt wilderness areas in Europe, while a handful of the west coast's isolated crofting villages can still be reached only by boat.

Exposed to slightly different weather conditions and, to some extent, different historical and cultural influences, each of the three coastlines has its own distinct character. The beautiful **west coast** with its indented shoreline and dramatic mountains in places like **Torridon** and **Assynt**, is a place whose charm and poetic scenery just about hold their own against the intrusions of the touring hordes in summer. West of Fort William lies the remote and tranquil **Ardnamurchan peninsula** and the "Road to the Isles" to the fishing port of **Mallaig**, railhead of the famous West Highland Railway. From Mallaig ferries cross to Skye, and there's also a service to **Knoydart**, a magical peninsula with no road access that's home to the remotest pub in Britain. The more direct route to Skye is across the famous Skye Bridge at **Kyle of Lochalsh**, not far from which are charming coastal villages such as **Glenelg** and **Plockton**. Between Kyle of Lochalsh and **Ullapool**, the main settlement in the northwest, lies **Wester Ross**, with quintessentially west-coast scenes of sparkling sea lochs, rocky headlands and sandy beaches set against some of Scotland's most dramatic mountains, with Skye and the Western Isles on the horizon.

The little-visited **north coast** stretching from stormy **Cape Wrath**, at the very northwest tip of the mainland, east to **John O'Groats** is yet more rugged than the west, with sheer cliffs and sand-filled bays bearing the brunt of frequently fierce Atlantic storms. The main settlement on this coast is **Thurso**, jumping-off point for the main ferry service to Orkney.

On the fertile **east coast** of the Highland region, stretching north from Inverness to the old herring port of **Wick**, green fields and woodland run down to the sweeping sandy beaches of the **Black Isle** and the **Cromarty**

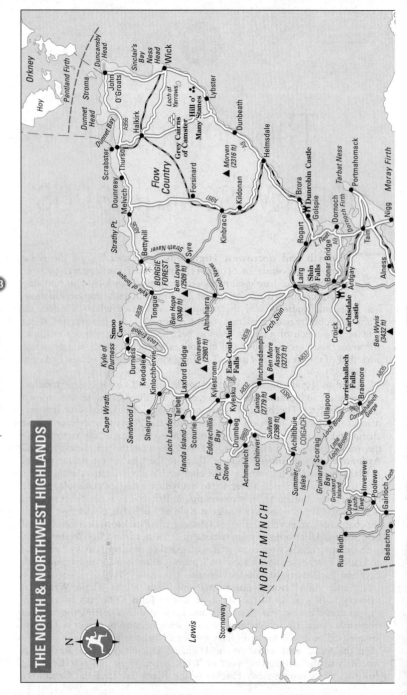

THE NORTH & NORTHWEST HIGHLANDS

N

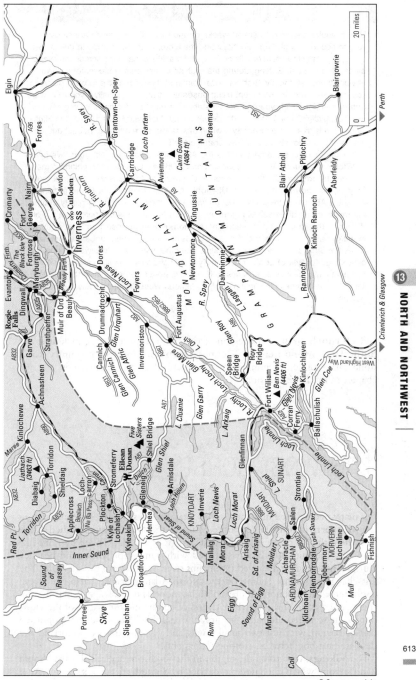

© Crown copyright

Unless you're prepared to spend weeks on the road, the Highlands are simply too vast to see in a single trip. Most visitors, therefore, base themselves in one or two areas, exploring the coast or hills on foot, and making longer hops across the interior by car, bus or train. Getting around the Highlands, particularly the remoter parts, is obviously easiest if you've got your own transport, but with a little forward planning you can see a surprising amount using **buses** and **trains**, especially if you fill in with **postbuses** (for which you can get timetables at most post offices, or see ⓦ www. postbus.royalmail.com). It is worth remembering, however, that much of the Highlands comes to a halt on **Sundays**, when bus services are sporadic at best and you may well find most shops and restaurants closed.

The key road on the **east coast** is the A9, which hugs the coast from Inverness to **Wick** and **Thurso**, with its connections to Orkney. One of the Highlands' main rail lines follows broadly the same route. Connections to the **west coast** are more fragmented: the quickest way to **Ullapool**, the largest settlement in the region, is along the A835 from Inverness, though with independent transport or plenty of time the much longer approach along the coast from the south is far more scenic. Fort William is the jumping-off point for the **Ardnamurchan** peninsula and the A830 to **Mallaig** – also known as the "Road to the Isles" – from where there are ferries to Skye, the Small Isles and the Outer Isles. The other main route to Skye is along the central A87 to **Kyle of Lochalsh**. Both Kyle of Lochalsh and Mallaig are also served by spectacular train lines: services to Kyle leave from Inverness, while the Fort William to Mallaig route is the final part of the famous **West Highland Railway** line (see box on p.621).

and **Dornoch firths**. This region is rich with historical sites, including the **Sutherland Monument** by Golspie, **Dornoch**'s fourteenth-century sandstone cathedral, and a number of places linked to the **Clearances**, a tragic chapter in the Highland story.

The west coast

For many people, the Highlands' starkly beautiful **west coast** – stretching from the **Morvern peninsula** (opposite Mull) in the south to wind-lashed **Cape Wrath** in the far north – is the finest part of Scotland. Serrated by fjord-like sea lochs, the long coastline is scattered with windswept white-sand beaches, cliff-girt headlands and rugged mountains sweeping up from the shoreline. The fast-changing weather rolling off the North Atlantic can be harsh, but it can also often create memorable plays of light, mood and landscape. When the sun shines, the sparkle of the sea, the richness of colour and the clarity of the views out to the scattered Hebrides are simply irresistible. This is the least populated part of Britain, with just two small towns, and yawning tracts of moorland and desolate peat bog between crofting settlements.

The **Vikings**, who ruled the region in the ninth century, called it the "South Land", from which the modern district of Sutherland takes its name. After

Culloden, the Clearances emptied most of the inland glens of the far north, however, and left the population clinging to the coastline, where a herring-fishing industry developed. Today, tourism, crofting, fishing and salmon farming are the mainstay of the local economy, supplemented by EU construction grants and subsidies to farm the sheep you'll encounter everywhere.

For visitors, **cycling** and **walking** are the obvious ways to make the most of the superb scenery, and countless lochans and crystal-clear rivers offer superlative trout and salmon **fishing**. The shattered cliffs of the far northwest are an ornithologist's dream, harbouring some of Europe's largest and most diverse **seabird colonies**, while the area's craggy mountaintops are the haunt of the elusive golden eagle.

The most visited part of the west coast is the stretch between Kyle of Lochalsh and Ullapool. Lying within easy reach of Inverness, this sector boasts the region's more obvious highlights: the awesome mountainscape of **Torridon**, **Gairloch**'s sandy beaches, the famous botanic gardens at **Inverewe** and **Ullapool** itself, a picturesque and bustling fishing town from where ferries leave for the Outer Hebrides. However, press on further north, or south, and you'll get a truer sense of the isolation that makes the west coast so special. Traversed by few roads, the remote northwest corner of Scotland is wild and bleak, receiving the full force of the North Atlantic's frequently ferocious weather. The scattered settlements of the far southwest, meanwhile, tend to be more sheltered, but they are separated by some of the most extensive wilderness areas in Britain – lonely peninsulas with evocative Gaelic names like **Ardnamurchan**, **Knoydart** and **Glenelg**.

Practicalities

Tempered by the Gulf Stream, the west coast's **weather** ranges from stupendous to diabolical. Never count on a sunny morning meaning a fine day; it can rain here at any time, and go on raining for days. Beware, too, of the dreaded **midge**, which drives even the hardiest of locals to distraction on warm summer evenings.

Without your own vehicle, **transport** can be a problem. There's a reasonable **train** service from Inverness to Kyle of Lochalsh and from Fort William to Mallaig, and a useful **summer bus** service connects Inverness to Ullapool, Lochinver, Scourie and Durness. However, services peter out as you venture further afield, where you'll have to rely on **postbuses**, which go just about everywhere, albeit slowly and at odd times of day. **Driving** is a much simpler option: the roads aren't busy, though they are frequently single-track and scattered with sheep. On such routes, you should refuel whenever you can since pumps are few and far between, and make sure your vehicle is in good condition; in a crisis, even if you manage to reach the nearest garage, spares may well have to be sent over from Inverness.

Morvern to Knoydart: the "Rough Bounds"

The remote and sparsely populated southwest corner of the Highlands, from the empty district of **Morvern** to the isolated peninsula of **Knoydart**, is a dramatic, lonely region of mountain and moorland fringed by a rocky, indented coast studded by stunning white beaches which enjoy wonderful views to Mull,

Skye and other islands. Its Gaelic name, *Garbh-chiochan*, translates as the "**Rough Bounds**", implying a region geographically and spiritually apart. Even if you have got a car, you should spend some time here exploring on foot; there are so few roads that some determined hiking is almost inevitable.

The southwest Highlands' main road is the A830, often described as "the Road to the Isles", which winds in tandem with the rail line through the glens from Fort William to the road- and railhead at **Mallaig**, a busy fishing port with ferry connections to Skye. Along the way, the road passes **Glenfinnan**, the much-photographed spot at the head of stunning **Loch Shiel** where Bonnie Prince Charlie gathered the clans to start the doomed Jacobite uprising of 1745. There are regular buses and trains along the main road; elsewhere in the region you'll usually have to rely on daily post- or schoolbuses. If you have your own transport, the five-minute ferry crossing at **Corran Ferry** (every 15min daily summer 7am–9pm; winter 7am–8pm; car and passengers £5.20; foot passengers and bicycles go free), a nine-mile drive south of Fort William down Loch Linnhe, provides a more direct point of entry for Morvern and the rugged **Ardnamurchan** peninsula.

Morvern

Bounded on three sides by sea lochs and in the north by desolate Glen Tarbet, the large, mountainous **Morvern** peninsula lies at the southwest corner of the Rough Bounds region. Its population is small and widely scattered, and much of the landscape can seem unremittingly bleak and empty – until, that is, you reach the coast which reveals some lovely views over to Mull. Most visitors only travel through here to get to **LOCHALINE** (pronounced "loch-*aa*lin"), a remote community on the **Sound of Mull**, from where a small car ferry chugs to **Fishnish** – the shortest crossing from the mainland (and a cheaper option than the main Oban–Craignure crossing if you're taking a car onto Mull). Lochaline village, little more than a scattering of houses around a small pier, has a diving centre specializing in underwater archeology (℡01967/421627; ⓦwww.lochalinedivecentre.co.uk) and is a popular anchorage for yachts cruising the west coast, but holds little else to detain you. For **accommodation**, the dive centre has a bunkhouse with simple twin rooms (❶), or try the straightforward *Lochaline Hotel* (℡01967/421657; ❶), which has five rooms and serves meals. The best reason to stop here, however, is to **eat** at the superb ⅄ *White House Restaurant* (℡01967/421777; ⓦwww.thewhitehouserestaurant.co.uk; Easter–Oct closed Mon; Oct–Dec Fri & Sat only; Jan–Easter closed), which specializes in delicious, freshly prepared dishes using local meat and seafood. It's a relaxed, friendly place, and not too expensive, particularly if you're in for lunch or coffee and home-baked scones. As you'd expect, **transport** links here (other than the Fishnish ferry) are extremely limited, with a bus running to and from Fort William on a Tuesday, Thursday and Friday only, plus a Saturday service in summer (check times with Shiel Buses ℡01967/431272). By request, the bus goes as far as the road end at **DRIMMIN** at the northwest corner of Morvern, from where it's possible to organize boat crossings over to Tobermory on Mull or Ardnamurchan through Ardnamurchan Charters (℡01972/500208).

Sunart and Ardgour

North of Morvern, the predominantly roadless regions of **Sunart** and **Ardgour** make up the country between Loch Shiel, Loch Sunart and Loch Linnhe: the heart of Jacobite support in the mid-eighteenth century and a Catholic stronghold to this day. The area's only real village is sleepy **STRONTIAN**, grouped around a green on an inlet of Loch Sunart. In 1722, lead mines here yielded the first-ever traces of the element **strontium**, which was named after the village. If you're interested, you can pick up a leaflet at the tourist office which explains the history of the mines and details some local routes to see what remains of the workings.

You can get to Strontian on the one **bus** a day (Mon–Sat) which links Fort William with Kilchoan (check times with Shiel Buses ☎01967/431272). Strontian's **tourist office** (Easter–May Mon–Sat 10am–5pm; June–Sept Mon–Sat 10am–5/5.30pm, Sun 10am–4pm; Oct Mon–Sat 10am–4pm; ☎01967/402382) is by the roadside as you pass through the village. Strontian has a couple of good **hotels**, the *Strontian Hotel* (☎01967/402029, ⓦwww.strontianhotel.supanet. com; ❸), on the main road looking over the water, and luxurious *Kilcamb Lodge* (☎01967/402257, ⓦwww.kilcamblodge.co.uk; ❼), a restored country house set in its own grounds on the lochside, whose **restaurant** serves excellent, if pricey, food. B&B is available at *Heatherbank* (☎01967/402201; ⓦwww .heatherbankbb.co.uk; ❷) and *Craigrowan Croft* (☎01967/402253; ⓦwww .craigrowancroft.co.uk; ❷), both a little way up the Ariundle turn-off. Six miles west of Strontian, only two miles before Salen, *Resipole Farm* (☎01967/431235, ⓦwww.resipole.co.uk; April–Oct) has a great set-up, with a **camping** and caravan park, self-catering accommodation and the *Farm Bar*, serving snacks and unexpectedly good evening meals.

The Ardnamurchan peninsula

The tortuous single-track B8007 road winds west from Salen to the wild **Ardnamurchan peninsula**, the most westerly point on the British mainland. The unspoilt landscape is relatively gentle and wooded at the eastern end, with much of the coastline of long Loch Sunart fringed by ancient oakwoods, which are protected as among the last remnants of the extensive temperate rainforests once common along the Atlantic coast of Europe (ⓦwww.sunartoakwoods.org .uk). The further west you travel, however, the trees disappear and are replaced by a wild, salt-sprayed moorland. The peninsula, which lost most of its inhabitants during the infamous Clearances (see p.804), has only a handful of tiny crofting settlements clinging to its jagged coastline and is sparsely populated – all the more so when you realize that many of the houses are seldom-used holiday cottages. Ardnamurchan, however, can be an inspiring place for its pristine, empty beaches, wonderful vistas of sea and island and the sense of nature all around. With its variety of undisturbed habitats the peninsula harbours a huge variety of birds, animals and wildflowers such as thrift and wild iris, making **walking** an obvious attraction. A variety of routes, from hill climbs to coastal scrambles, are detailed in a comprehensive guide to the peninsula produced annually by the local community (available from tourist offices and most shops on the peninsula, priced around £4), while **guided walks** are also available at most of the nature reserves dotted along the Loch Sunart shoreline; these are run under the auspices of the Highland Council Ranger Service (☎01967/402232). If you want to do some of your own wildlife spotting, it's worth stopping off at the turf-roofed Garbh Eilean hide (free access), not far from the road between Strontian and Salen, from where you can see seals, seabirds and the occasional otter or eagle.

Salen to Glenborrodale

The coastal hamlet of **SALEN** marks the turn-off for Ardnamurchan Point: from here it's a further 25 miles of scenic but slow driving along the single-track road which follows the northern shore of Loch Sunart. Salen is a sheltered anchorage, and yachties often row ashore for a drink at the *Salen Hotel* (℡01967/4311661, ⓦwww.salenhotel.co.uk; ❸), which has some neat rooms and serves good bar meals featuring fresh local seafood. There's not much more until you get to the engaging **Glenmore Natural History Centre** (April–Oct Mon–Sat 10.30am–5.30pm, Sun noon–5.30pm; ⓦwww .ardnamurchannaturalhistorycentre.co.uk; £2.50), which provides an inspiring introduction to the diverse flora, fauna and geology of Ardnamurchan just west of the hamlet of **GLENBORRODALE**. Originally set up by local photographer Michael MacGregor (whose stunning work enlivens postcard stands along the west coast), the centre is housed in a sensitively designed timber building called "The Living Building", complete with turf roof and wildlife ponds. CCTV cameras relay live pictures of the surrounding wildlife, catching the comings and goings of a pine marten's nest, underwater pools in the nearby river and a nearby heronry. The small **café** here serves sandwiches and good home-baked cakes, with evening meals served some evenings in summer (℡01972/500209). For coastal wildlife and whale-spotting **excursions** – or trips to Tobermory on Mull, the Treshnish Isles or Fingal's Cave – contact Ardnamurchan Charters at Glenborrodale (℡01972/500208, ⓦwww .west-scotland-marine.com).

Kilchoan and Ardnamurchan Point

KILCHOAN, nine miles west of the Glenmore Centre, is Ardnamurchan's main village – a straggling but appealing crofting township overlooking the Sound of Mull. A **car ferry** runs from here to Tobermory (Mon–Sat 8am–6.45pm 7 daily, plus June–Aug Sun 10.15am–4.45pm, 5 daily; 35min). The community centre in the village houses a **tourist office** (Easter–Oct daily 9am–5pm; ℡01972/510222, ⓦwww.ardnamurchan.com), which will help with and book accommodation, though year-round the community centre (and its simple tearoom) are open and will act as an informal source of local advice and assistance. For **boat trips** out of Kilchoan – either wildlife-spotting or fishing – contact Nick Peake (℡01972/510212, ⓔactivoutdoors.achnaha .scotland@virgin.net), who also leads guided walks to look for land-based wildlife such as eagles, pine martens and badgers. The only direct **bus** to Kilchoan leaves from Fort William at 1.25pm (Mon–Sat), travelling via the Corran Ferry and arriving two and a half hours later.

The road continues beyond Kilchoan to the rocky, windy **Ardnamurchan Point** and its famous **lighthouse**. The lighthouse buildings house a small café and an absorbing **exhibition** (daily April–Oct 10am–5pm; £5; ℡01972/510210), with well-assembled displays about lighthouses in general, their construction and the people who lived in them. Best of all is the chance to climb up the inside of the Egyptian-style lighthouse tower; at the top, a guide is on hand to tell some of the tall tales relating to the lighthouse and show you around the lighting mechanism. Whales are sometimes seen surfacing in the waters off the point – indeed, the Hebridean Whale and Dolphin Trust, based in Tobermory, often sends volunteers over to the lighthouse to sit by the massive old fog horn and peer out through binoculars counting sightings.

Also worth exploring around the peninsula are the myriad coves, beaches and headlands along the long coastline. The finest of the sandy beaches is about three miles north of the lighthouse at **Sanna Bay**, a shell-strewn strand and series of dunes which offers truly unforgettable vistas of the Small Isles to the north, circled by gulls, terns and guillemots.

Practicalities

Accommodation isn't plentiful in Kilchoan, and in summer you're well advised to book far ahead. You can normally camp in the gardens of the *Kilchoan House Hotel*, and there's also a simple campsite with lovely coastal views by the Ardnamurchan Study Centre (☏07787 812084, Ⓦwww .ardnamurchanstudycentre.co.uk), about half a mile past the Ferry Stores. For B&B, try *Doirlinn House* (☏01972/510209, Ⓔdorlinnhouse@yahoo .co.uk; ❷; March–Oct), or *Tigh a' Ghobhainn* (☏01972/510771, Ⓔmairihunter .kilchoan@virgin.net; ❷; March–Oct), both with lovely views over the Sound of Mull. Along the road between Salen and Kilchoan, at Glenborrodale, there's an exquisite upmarket guesthouse, *Feorag House* (☏01972/500248, Ⓦwww.feorag.co.uk; ❽ for dinner, B&B), which has three tasteful, modest rooms in a beautifully secluded modern house.

Most of the local hotels offer **food** to non-residents, among them *Kilchoan House Hotel* (☏01972/510200, Ⓦwww.kilchoanhousehotel.co.uk; ❹) and plain *Sonachan Hotel* (☏01972/510211, Ⓦwww.sonachan.com; ❶), which despite being hailed as the most westerly hotel on the British mainland is tucked inland away from the coast, halfway between Kilchoan and Ardnamurchan Point. The Ferry Stores in Kilchoan, the only **shop** west of Salen, makes an impressive effort to carry fresh food and local produce when it's available.

Acharacle and around

At the eastern end of Ardnamurchan, just north of Salen where the A861 heads north towards the district of Moidart, the main settlement is **ACHARACLE**, an ancient crofting village set back a few hundred yards from the seaward end of freshwater **Loch Shiel**. Surrounded by gentle hills, it's an attractive place, and being a couple of miles from the sea gives it a different feel to many of the area's other settlements. The pleasant *Loch Shiel House Hotel* (☏01967/431224, Ⓦwww.lochshielhotel.com; ❻) is a comfortable, friendly place to stay, stop for a drink or eat, while *Ardsheleach Lodge* (☏01967/431399, Ⓦwww.ardshealach-lodge.co.uk; ❻) is a restaurant with four rooms, serving lunches, afternoon teas and dinner in an attractive house in its own grounds with a great outlook over the loch and hills beyond.

You can get to Acharacle by **boat** from Glenfinnan at the head of Loch Shiel (Wed only; Easter to mid-Oct) with Loch Shiel Cruises (☏01687/470322, Ⓦwww.highlandcruises.co.uk), or on infrequent **buses** from Mallaig or Fort William. There are plenty of untaxing and attractive **walks** in the local area; Out of Doors, a shop just behind the hotel, stocks a book detailing these. Near this is the Bakehouse with good picnic fodder, which you can supplement with something from the tiny Moidart Smoke House, at Dalnabreac a couple of miles to the west of Acharacle. For evening **entertainment** your best bet is the *Clanranald Hotel* at Mingarry, again just west of Archaracle, which is run by a well-known local accordionist and band leader, Fergie Macdonald.

Castle Tioram

A mile north of Acharacle, a side road running north off the A861 winds for three miles or so past a secluded estuary lined with rhododendron thickets and fishing platforms to **Loch Moidart**, a calm and sheltered sea loch. Perched atop a rocky promontory protruding out into the loch is **Castle Tioram** (pronounced "cheerum"), one of Scotland's most atmospheric historic monuments. Reached via a sandy causeway that's only just above the high tide, the thirteenth-century fortress, whose Gaelic name means "dry land", was the seat of the MacDonalds of Clanranald until it was destroyed by their chief in 1715 to prevent it from falling into Hanoverian hands while he was away fighting for the Jacobites. Today, a certain amount of controversy surrounds the upkeep of the place: while the setting and approach are undoubtedly stunning, large notices and fences keep you from getting too close to the castle due to the danger of falling masonry.

The Road to the Isles

The "**Road to the Isles**" (ⓦ www.road-to-the-isles.org.uk) from Fort William to Mallaig, followed by the West Highland Railway and the narrow, winding A830, traverses the mountains and glens of the Rough Bounds before breaking out near **Arisaig** onto a spectacularly scenic coast of sheltered inlets, stunning white beaches and wonderful views to the islands of Rùm, Eigg, Muck and Skye. This is country commonly associated with **Bonnie Prince Charlie**, whose adventures of 1745–46 began and ended on this stretch of coast, with his first, defiant gathering of the clans at **Glenfinnan**.

Glenfinnan

GLENFINNAN, nineteen miles west of Fort William at the head of lovely Loch Shiel, was where Bonnie Prince Charlie raised his standard to signal the start of the Jacobite uprising of 1745. Surrounded by no more than two hundred loyal clansmen, the young rebel prince waited here to see if the Cameron of Loch Shiel would join his army. The drone of this powerful chief's pipers drifting up the glen was eagerly awaited, for without him the Stuarts' attempt to claim the English throne would have been sheer folly. Despite strong misgivings, Cameron did decide to support the uprising, and arrived at Glenfinnan on a sunny August 19 with eight hundred mèn, thereby encouraging other wavering clan leaders to follow suit. Assured of adequate backing, the prince raised his red-and-white silk colour, proclaimed his father as King James III of England and set off on the long march to London – from which only a handful of the soldiers gathered at

△ Glenfinnan monument, Loch Shiel

Scotland's most famous railway line, and a train journey counted by many as among the world's most scenic, is the brilliantly engineered **West Highland Railway**, running from Glasgow to Mallaig via Fort William. The line is in two sections: the southern part travels from **Glasgow** Queen Street station along the Clyde estuary and up Loch Long before switching to the banks of Loch Lomond on its way to **Crianlarich**, where the train divides, with one section heading for Oban. After climbing around Beinn Odhar on a unique horseshoe-shaped loop of viaducts, the line traverses desolate **Rannoch Moor**, where the track had to be laid on a mattress of tree roots, brushwood and thousands of tons of earth and ashes. By this point the line has diverged from the road, and travels through country which can otherwise be reached only by long-distance footpaths. The train then swings into Glen Roy, passing through the dramatic **Monessie Gorge** and entering **Fort William** from the northeast.

The second leg of the journey, from Fort William to Mallaig, is arguably even more spectacular, and from June to mid-October one of the scheduled services is pulled by the **Jacobite Steam Train** (Mon–Fri, also Sun late July & Aug; departs Fort William 10.20am, departs Mallaig 2.10pm; day-return £26; book on ☎01463/239026; ⊛ www .steamtrain.info). Shortly after leaving Fort William the railway crosses the Caledonian Canal beside Neptune's Staircase by way of a swing bridge at **Benavie**, before travelling along the shores of Locheil and crossing the magnificent 21-arch viaduct at **Glenfinnan**, where the steam train, in its "Hogwarts Express" livery, was filmed for the *Harry Potter* movies. At Glenfinnan station there's a small **museum** dedicated to the history of the West Highland line, as well as two old railway carriages which have been converted into a restaurant and a bunkhouse (see below). Not long afterwards the line reaches the coast, where there are unforgettable views of the Small Isles and Skye as it runs past the famous silver sands of **Morar** and up to **Mallaig**, where there are connections to the ferry which crosses to Armadale on Skye.

If you're planning on travelling the West Highland line, and in particular linking it to other train journeys (such as the similarly attractive route between Inverness and Kyle of Lochalsh), it's worth considering one of First ScotRail's multiday **rover tickets**, details of which are given on p.39.

Glenfinnan would return. The spot is marked by a column (now a little lopsided, Pisa-like), crowned with a clansman in full battle dress, erected as a tribute by Alexander Macdonald of Glenaladale in 1815.

Glenfinnan is a poignant place, a beautiful stage for the opening scene in a brutal drama which was to change the Highlands for ever. The **visitor centre** and café (daily: April, May, Sept & Oct 10am–5pm; June–Aug 9.30am–5.30pm; Nov Sat & Sun 10am–4pm; NTS; £3), opposite the monument, gives an account of the '45 uprising through to the rout at **Culloden** eight months later (see p.603). A **boat trip** on the loch with Loch Shiel Cruises (☎01687/470322, ⊛www.highlandcruises.co.uk), which offers a chance to view some very remote scenery and occasionally a golden eagle, is highly recommended.

Glenfinnan is one of the most spectacular parts of the **West Highland Railway** line (see box above), not only for the glimpse it offers of the monument and graceful Loch Shiel, but also the mighty 21-arched Loch nan Uamh **viaduct** built in 1901 and one of the first-ever large constructions made out of concrete. You can learn more of the history of this section of the railway at the **Glenfinnan Station Museum** (June–Sept daily 9.30am–4.30pm; 50p), set in the old booking office of the station. Right beside the station, two old railway carriages have been pressed into use as a highly original **restaurant** and **bunkhouse**; the *Dining Car* (June–Sept daily 10am–5pm; ☎01397/722300) is open for light lunches, home baking and evening meals if you phone ahead to make arrangements, while the *Sleeping Car* (☎01397/722295; year-round), a converted 1958 camping coach, sleeps ten in bunk beds. The best of the more conventional accommodation options locally is the *Lochailort Inn* (☎01687/470208, ⓦwww.lochailortinn.co.uk; ➒), about ten miles on from Glenfinnan towards Arisaig (and also on the train line, although you have to request to stop here).

Arisaig

West of Glenfinnan, the A830 runs alongside captivating Loch Eilt in the district of **Morar**, through Lochailort – where it meets the road from Acharacle – and on to a coast marked by acres of white sands, turquoise seas and rocky islets draped with orange seaweed. **ARISAIG**, scattered round a sandy bay at the west end of the Morar peninsula, makes a good base for exploring this area. A recently constructed **bypass** now whizzes cars (and, more importantly, fish lorries) on their way to Mallaig, but you shouldn't miss out on the slower coast road, which enjoys all the best of the scenery.

The only specific attraction in Arisaig village is the **Land, Sea and Islands Centre** (Easter to mid-Oct Mon–Sat 10am–4pm, Sun noon–4pm, winter closes 3pm; £2), a small, volunteer-run community project relating the social and natural history of the area. The displays include some intriguing detail on local events, including secret operations during World War II and the filming of various movies in the area, along with background on local characters such as the person who inspired Robert Louis Stevenson's pirate Long John Silver. If the weather's fine you could spend hours wandering along the beaches and quiet backroads, and there's a small seal colony at nearby **Rhumach**, reached via the single-track lane leading west out of Arisaig village along the headland. A **boat** also leaves from here daily during the summer for the Small Isles (see p.639), operated by Arisaig Marine (☎01687/450224, ⓦwww.arisaig.co.uk). **Accommodation** in the village is plentiful: *Kinloid Farm House* (☎01687/450366; ⓦwww.kinloid-arisaig.co.uk ➌; March–Oct) is one of several pleasant B&Bs with sea views, while the more upmarket *Old Library Lodge* (☎01687/450651, ⓦwww.oldlibrary.co.uk; ➎; April–Oct) has a handful of well-appointed rooms, though only two overlook the seafront. For **food**, the restaurant at the *Old Library* is quite upmarket, while there's bar food available at the *Arisaig Hotel*, just along the road.

Morar

Stretching for eight miles or so north of Arisaig is a string of stunning white-sand **beaches** backed by flowery machair, with barren granite hills and moorland rising up behind and wonderful seaward views of Eigg and Rùm. The next settlement of any significance is **MORAR**, where the famous beach scenes from *Local Hero* were shot. Since then, however, a bypass has been built around the village, and the white sands are no longer an unspoilt idyll. Of the string of **campsites** along the coast road try *Camusdarach* (☎01687/450221, ⓦwww.road-to-the-isles.org.uk/camusdarach), which isn't quite on the beach but is quieter and less officious than others nearby. **B&B** is also available in the converted billiard room of their attractive main house (➊). Alternatively, you can find B&B at the home of adventurer Tom McClean, *Invermorar House* (☎01687/462274; ⓦwww.road-to-the-isles.org.uk/invermorar.html; ➋; July & Aug only). He runs an adventure school on the north side of nearby **Loch Morar** – rumoured to be the home of a monster called Morag, a lesser-known rival to Nessie – which runs east of Morar village into the heart of a huge wilderness area.

Mallaig

A cluttered, noisy port whose pebble-dashed houses struggle for space with great lumps of granite tumbling down to the sea, **MALLAIG**, 47 miles west of Fort William along the A830 (regular buses and trains run this route), is not pretty. Before the railline reached here in 1901, it consisted of only a few cottages, but now it's a busy, bustling place and, as the main ferry stop for Skye, the Small Isles and Knoydart, is always full of visitors. The continuing source of the village's wealth is its **fishing** industry: on the quayside, piles of nets, tackle and ice crates lie scattered around a modern market. When the fleet is in, trawlers encircled by flocks of raucous gulls choke the harbour, and the pubs, among the liveliest on the west coast, host bouts of serious drinking.

Apart from the daily bustle of Mallaig's harbour, the main attraction in town is **Mallaig Marine World**, north of the train station near the harbour (March–Oct daily 9.30am–5.30pm; Nov–Feb Mon–Sat 11am–5.30pm; £3), where tanks of local sea creatures and informative exhibits about the port provide an unpretentious introduction to the local waters. Alongside the train station, the **Mallaig Heritage Centre** (April, May & Oct Mon–Sat 11am–4pm; June–Sept Mon–Sat 9.30am–4.30pm, Sun 1.30–4.30pm; phone for winter hours; ☎01687/462085; £1.80), displaying old photographs of the town and its environs, is worth a browse. The walking trail to **Mallaigmore**, a small cove with a white-sand beach and isolated croft, begins at the top of the harbour on East Bay; follow the road north past the tourist office and turn off right when you see the signpost between two houses. The round trip takes about an hour.

Practicalities

Mallaig is a compact place, concentrated around the harbour, where you'll find the **tourist office** (April–Oct Mon–Sat 10am–5pm; Nov–March Mon, Tues & Fri 11am–3pm), which will book accommodation for you, and the **bus** and **train stations**. The CalMac ticket office (☎01687/462403), serving passengers for Skye and the Small Isles, is also nearby, and you can arrange transport to Knoydart by calling Bruce Watt Cruises (☎01687/462320, ⓦwww .knoydart-ferry.co.uk), which sails to Inverie, on the Knoydart peninsula, every morning and afternoon (mid-May to mid-Sept Mon–Fri; otherwise Mon, Wed & Fri); the loch is sheltered, so crossings are rarely cancelled.

There are plenty of **places to stay**. The *West Highland Hotel* (☎01687/462210, ⓦwww.westhighlandhotel.co.uk; ❺) is a typically bland but comfortable Scottish Highland hotel; some rooms have excellent sea views. For **B&B**, head around the harbour to East Bay, where you'll find the cheery *Western Isles Guest House* (☎01687/462320, ⓦwww.road-to-the-isles.org.uk/western-isles. html; ❸). *Sheena's Backpackers' Lodge* (☎01687/462764), a refreshingly laid-back independent **hostel** overlooking the harbour, has mixed dorms, self-catering facilities and a sitting room. For **eating**, the *Fishmarket Restaurant* facing the backpacker lodge features lots of fresh seafood including crab and langoustines, often incorporating various exotic flavours. During the day, the *Tea Garden* at *Sheena's Lodge* is a great place to watch the world go by while you tuck into a bowl of cullen skink (soup made from smoked haddock), a pint of prawns or home-made scones. Also worth seeking out are the freshest of fish and chips – or a portion of scallops and chips if you're feeling decadent – served at the

Cornerstone, just across the road from the tourist office. To buy fresh or smoked fish, head to Andy Race's fish shop at the harbour.

The Knoydart peninsula

Many people regard the **Knoydart peninsula** as mainland Britain's most dramatic and unspoilt wilderness area. Flanked by **Loch Nevis** ("Loch of Heaven") in the south and the fjord-like inlet of **Loch Hourn** ("Loch of Hell") to the north, Knoydart's knobbly green peaks – three of them Munros – sweep straight out of the sea, shrouded for much of the time in a pall of grey mist. To get to the heart of the peninsula, you must catch a **boat** from Mallaig or Glenelg, or else **hike** for a couple of days across rugged moorland and mountains and sleep rough in old stone bothies (most of which are marked on Ordnance Survey maps). Unsurprisingly, the peninsula tends to attract walkers, lured by the network of well-maintained trails that wind east into the wild interior, where Bonnie Prince Charlie is rumoured to have hidden out after Culloden.

At the end of the eighteenth century, around a thousand people eked out a living from this inhospitable terrain through crofting and fishing. Evictions in 1853 began a dramatic decrease in the population, which continued to dwindle through the twentieth century as a succession of landowners ran the estate as a hunting and shooting playground, prompting a famous land raid in 1948 by a group of crofters known as the "Seven Men of Knoydart", who staked out and claimed ownership of portions of the estate. Although their bid failed, the memory of their cause was invoked when the crofters of Knoydart finally achieved control over the land they lived on in a community buy-out in 1998. These days the peninsula supports around seventy people, most of whom live in the hamlet of **INVERIE**. Nestled beside a sheltered bay on the south side of the peninsula, it has a pint-sized post office, a shop and mainland Britain's most remote pub, the *Old Forge*.

Practicalities

Bruce Watt Cruises' **boat** chugs into Inverie from Mallaig (see p.623). To arrange for a boat crossing from Arnisdale on the Glenelg peninsula to the north coast of Knoydart or Kinloch Hourn, contact Murray Morrison (see p.629).

There are two main **hiking routes** into Knoydart: the trailhead for the first is **KINLOCH HOURN**, a crofting hamlet at the far east end of Loch Hourn which you can get to by road (turn south off the A87 six miles west of Invergarry). From Kinloch Hourn, a well-marked path winds around the coast to Barrisdale and on to Inverie (see Ⓦwww.barisdale.com for more). The second path into Knoydart starts at the west side of **Loch Arkaig**, approaching the peninsula via Glen Dessary. These are both long hard slogs over rough, desolate country, so take wet-weather gear, a decent map, plenty of food, warm clothes and a good sleeping bag, and leave your name and expected time of arrival with someone when you set off.

Most of Knoydart's **accommodation** is concentrated in and around Inverie. *Torrie Shieling* (Ⓣ01687/462669, Ⓔtorrie@knoydart.org; £16 per person), an upmarket independent **hostel** located three-quarters of a mile east of the village on the side of the mountain, is popular with hikers and families, offering top-notch self-catering facilities, comfortable wooden beds in four-person rooms and the cosiness of open fires in the convivial living room. They also have a Land Rover and boat for ferrying guests around the peninsula, and to neighbouring lochs and islands. The Knoydart Foundation (Ⓦwww.knoydart-foundation.com) also runs a bunkhouse, with simple but adequate facilities, in some old steadings not far from *Torrie Shieling*. To book this call the foundation office (℡01687/462242). In Inverie itself there's just one guesthouse, the *Pier House* (℡01687/462347, ⓦwww.thepierhouseknoy dart.co.uk; ❻ for dinner, B&B), a great place to stay: they have their own **restaurant** serving à la carte evening meals, including some good veggie options. Dinner is available to non-residents (three courses from around £15). If you want total isolation and all the creature comforts book into the beautiful *Doune Stone Lodges* (℡01687/462667, ⓦwww.doune-knoydart.co.uk; full board ❼; min 3 nights), on the remote north side of the peninsula. Rebuilt from ruined crofts, this place has pine-fitted en-suite double rooms right on the shore; alongside the Doune dining room serves hearty meals. It's not easy to get to Doune by land, you'll have to get them to pick you up by boat from Mallaig. The ♉ *Old Forge* is one of Scotland's finer pubs, with a convivial atmosphere where visitors and locals mix, generous bar meals often featuring recently caught seafood, real ales, an open fire and a good chance of live music of an evening. You can rent **mountain bikes** from *Pier House*; they've established various mountain-bike trails in the area, and offer mountain walks for groups of four or more.

Kyle of Lochalsh and around

As the main gateway to Skye, **Kyle of Lochalsh** used to be an important transit point for tourists, locals and services. However, with the building of the Skye Bridge in 1995, Kyle was left as merely the terminus for the train route from Inverness, with little else to offer. Of much more interest to most visitors is nearby **Eilean Donan Castle**, one of Scotland's most famous and popular sights, perched at the end of a stone causeway on the shores of **Loch Duich**. It's not hard, however, to step off the tourist trail, with the **Glenelg** peninsula on the south side of Loch Duich testimony to how quickly the west coast can seem remote and undiscovered. A few miles north of Kyle of Lochalsh, the delightful village of **Plockton** is a refreshing alternative to its utilitarian neighbour, with cottages grouped around a yacht-filled bay and Highland cattle wandering the streets. Plockton lies on the southern shore of **Loch Carron**, a long inlet which, together with **Strathcarron** at the head of the loch, acts as a dividing line between the Kyle of Lochalsh district and the scenic splendours of Wester Ross to the north.

Kyle of Lochalsh

KYLE OF LOCHALSH is not particularly attractive and is ideally somewhere to pass through rather than linger in. With the building of the **Skye bridge**, traffic has little reason to stop before rumbling over the channel a mile to the west, leaving Kyle's shopkeepers bereft of the passing trade they used to enjoy. Just about the only reason to pause in Kyle is to take a ride on the *Atlantis* (℡01471/822716 or 0800/9804846, ⓦwww.seaprobe.freeserve.co.uk), the UK's only semi-submersible glass-bottomed **boat**, aboard which you can visit the protected seal and bird colonies on Seal Island or see the World War II wreck of *HMS Port Napier* (Easter–Oct; £6.50).

Buses run to Kyle of Lochalsh from Glasgow via Fort William and Invergarry (3 daily; 5hr 10min–6hr) and from Inverness via Invermoriston (3 daily; 2hr–2hr 30min). Book in advance for all of them (℡0870/550 5050, ⓦwww .citylink.co.uk). All continue at least as far as Portree on Skye. Buses also shuttle across the bridge to Kyleakin on Skye every thirty minutes or so. **Trains** run to Kyle of Lochalsh from Inverness (Mon–Sat 3 daily, 1 on Sun; 2hr 30min); curving north through Achnasheen and Glen Carron, the train line is a rail enthusiast's dream, even if scenically it doesn't quite match the West Highland line to Mallaig.

Kyle's **tourist office** (April–June, Sept & Oct Mon–Sat 9.30am–5pm; July & Aug Mon–Sat 9.30am–6pm, Sun 10am–4pm), on top of the small hill near the old ferry jetty, can book **accommodation** – a useful service as there are surprisingly few options. The best hotel is probably the welcoming *Kyle Hotel* in Main Street, with a menu including fresh seafood and game (℡01599/534204, Ⓦwww.kylehotel.co.uk; ❺). One of the most pleasant **B&Bs** in the area is the *Old Schoolhouse* at Erbusaig, built in the 1820s and located two miles north of Kyle towards Plockton (℡01599/534369, Ⓦwww.oldschoolhouse87.co.uk; ❹). There's a simple, bunkhouse in town, *Cúchulainn's* (℡01599/534492), above a pub across the main street from the tourist office. To **eat**, sample the steak and home-made puddings at the *Waverley Restaurant* (5.30–9.30pm, closed Thurs; ℡01599/534337) or for a snack visit *Sheila's Café* opposite the tourist office.

Loch Duich

Skirted on its northern shore by the A87, **Loch Duich**, the boot-shaped inlet just to the south of Kyle of Lochalsh, features prominently on the tourist trail, with buses from all over Europe thundering down the sixteen miles from **SHIEL BRIDGE** to Kyle of Lochalsh on their way to Skye. The main road, which connects to the Great Glen at Invermoriston (see p.592) and Invergarry, makes for a dramatic approach to the loch out of Glen Shiel, where, to the north, the much-photographed mountains known as the **Five Sisters of Kintail** surge impressively up to heights of 3000ft. With steep-sided hills hemming in both sides of the loch, it's sometimes hard to remember that this is, in fact, the sea. There's comfortable **accommodation** to be had in Shiel Bridge itself at the *Kintail Lodge Hotel* (℡01599/511275, Ⓦwww .kintaillodgehotel.co.uk; ❻); the hotel also offers **hostel** accommodation, dorm-style in the appropriately named *Wee Bunkhouse* and in twins and singles in the *Trekkers' Lodge*. At **RATAGAN**, a mile or so up the southern shore from Shiel Bridge, there's also an excellent SYHA **hostel** (℡0870/004 1147, Ⓦwww.syha.org.uk; March–Oct), popular with walkers newly arrived off the Glen Affric trek from Cannich (see p.594).

Eilean Donan Castle

After Edinburgh's hilltop fortress, **Eilean Donan Castle** (March & Nov 10am–4pm; April–Oct daily 10am–5.30pm; £4.75), ten miles north of Shiel Bridge on the A87, has to be Scotland's most photographed monument. Presiding over the once strategically important confluence of lochs Alsh, Long and Duich, the forbidding crenellated tower rises from the water's edge, joined to the shore by a narrow stone bridge and with sheer mountains as a backdrop. The original castle was established in 1230 by Alexander II to protect the area from the Vikings. Later, during a Jacobite uprising in 1719, it was occupied by troops dispatched by the king of Spain to help the "**Old Pretender**", James Stuart. However, when King George heard of their whereabouts, he sent frigates to take the Spaniards out, and the castle was blown up with their stocks of gunpowder. Thereafter, it lay in ruins until John Macrae-Gilstrap had it rebuilt between 1912 and 1932. Eilean Donan has since featured in several major **films**, including *Highlander*, *Entrapment* and the James Bond adventure *The World is*

Ordnance Survey Explorer Map no. 414.

The mountains of **Glen Shiel**, sweeping southeast from Loch Duich, offer some of the best hiking routes in Scotland. Rising dramatically from sea level to over 3000ft in less than a couple of miles, they are also exposed to the worst of the west coast's notoriously fickle weather. Don't underestimate either of these two routes. Tracing the paths on a map, they can appear short and easy to follow; nonetheless, unwary walkers die here every year, often because they failed to allow enough time to get off the mountain by nightfall, or because of a sudden change in the weather. Only attempt these routes if you're confident in your walking experience, and have a map, a compass and a detailed trekking guide – the SMC's *Hill Walks in Northwest Scotland* is recommended. Also make sure to follow the usual safety precautions outlined on p.64.

Taking in a bumper crop of Munros, the **Five Sisters traverse** is deservedly the most popular trek in the area. Allow a full day to complete the whole route, which begins at the first fire break on the left-hand side as you head southeast down the glen on the A87. Strike straight up from here and follow the ridge north along to Scurr na Moraich (2874ft), dropping down the other side to Morvich on the valley floor.

The distinctive chain of mountains across the glen from the Five Sisters is the **Kintail Ridge**, crossed by another famous hiking route that begins at the *Cluanie Inn* (see p.592) on the A87. From here, follow the well-worn path south around the base of the mountain until it meets up with a stalkers' trail, which winds steeply up Creag a' Mhaim (3108ft) and then west along the ridgeway, with breathtaking views south across Knoydart and the Hebridean Sea.

Not Enough. Three floors, including the banqueting hall, the bedrooms and the troops' quarters are open to the public, with various Jacobite and clan relics also on display, though like many of the region's most popular castles, the large numbers of people passing through make it hard to appreciate the real charm of the place.

There are several places to **stay** less than a mile away from the castle in the hamlet of **DORNIE**. The *Dornie Hotel*, Francis Street (℡01599/555205; ⑥), provides comfortable unpretentious rooms, while the *Loch Duich Hotel* (℡01599/555213; ⑨) has splendid doubles overlooking the loch; ask for the four-poster bed. Its small **restaurant** serves tasty bar snacks and evening meals. On Sunday nights they have a popular **folk music** session in the bar. Along from the *Dornie Hotel*, an eclectic bar meal menu is offered at the *Clachan Pub*.

The Glenelg peninsula

South of Loch Duich, the **Glenelg peninsula**, jutting out into the Sound of Sleat, is the isolated and little-known crofting area featured in Gavin Maxwell's otter novel *Ring of Bright Water*. Maxwell disguised the identity of this pristine stretch of coast by calling it "Camusfearnà", and it has remained a tranquil backwater in spite of the traffic that trickles through during the summer for the Kylerhea ferry to Skye (see p.677 for details of the wildlife sanctuary at Eilean Ban, once Maxwell's home).

The landward approach to the peninsula is from the east by turning off the fast A87 at Shiel Bridge on Loch Duich, from where a narrow single-track road climbs a tortuous series of switchbacks to the Mam Ratagan Pass (1115ft), affording spectacular views over the awesome **Five Sisters** massif. There's a terrific picnic stop half-way up the road. Following the route of an old drovers' trail, the road, covered weekdays from Kyle of Lochalsh by both the postbus and Skyeways bus service, drops down the other side through Glen More, with the magnificent Kintail Ridge visible to the southeast, towards the peninsula's main settlement, **GLENELG**, on the Sound of Sleat. One mile east of the village is Glenelg Candles and Coffee Shop (March–Oct daily) where within the delightful walled-garden of a Georgian manse, you'll receive a warm welcome and organic coffee from candle-maker Donna Stiven.

Glenelg itself is comprised of a row of picturesque whitewashed houses, surrounded by trees. The *Glenelg Inn* (☎01599/522273, ⓦwww.glenelg-inn .com; ❺) is a wonderful spot, boasting seven luxurious (en-suite) **rooms** overlooking the bay, moderately priced fresh food that's served all day and where, aside from its handy bank machine, there's also a good chance of finding live music from any local musicians who happen to be in the **pub**.

The six-car **Glenelg–Kylerhea ferry** shuttles across the Sound of Sleat and one of the fastest tidal races in the UK from a jetty northwest of the village. At the time of writing, the ferry is for sale but expected to continue running. Call the tourist office in Kyle of Lochalsh for information (☎01599/534390). In former times, this choppy channel where minke whale and dolphins may be spotted used to be an important drovers' crossing: 8000 cattle each year were herded head to tail across from Skye to the mainland.

One and a half miles south of Glenelg village, a left turn up Glen Beag leads to the **Glenelg Brochs**, some of the best-preserved Iron Age monuments in the country. Standing in a sheltered stream valley, the circular towers – Dun Telve and Dun Troddan – are thought to have been erected around 2000 years ago to protect the surrounding settlements from raiders. About a third of each main structure remains, with the curving dry-stone walls and internal passages still impressively intact.

Arnisdale

A narrow backroad snakes its way southwest beyond Glenelg village through a scattering of old crofting hamlets and timber forests. The views across the Sound of Sleat to Knoydart grow more spectacular at each bend, reaching a high point at a windy pass that takes in a vast sweep of sea, loch and islands. Below the road at **Sandaig** is where Gavin Maxwell and his otters lived in the 1950s: the site of his house is now marked by a cairn.

Swinging east, the road winds down to the waterside again, following the north shore of Loch Hourn as far as **ARNISDALE**, departure point for the boat to Knoydart (see p.624). Arnisdale is made up of the two hamlets of **Camusbane** and **Corran**, the former consisting of a single row of old cottages ranged behind a long pebble beach, with a massive scree slope behind, while the latter, a mile along the road, is a minuscule whitewashed fishing hamlet at the water's edge. Aside from the arrival of electricity and a red telephone box, the only major addition to this gorgeous hamlet in the last hundred years has been Mrs Nash's **B&B** and tea hut (☎01599/522336; ❶), where you can enjoy hot drinks and home-baked cake in a "shell garden", with breathtaking views on all sides.

From Monday to Saturday, you can get to Arnisdale on the 10am **postbus** from Kyle of Lochalsh (4hr 50min), returning on the 7.10am postbus from Arnisdale, or you can use the Skyeways bus service (☎01599/555477, ⓦwww .skyeways.co.uk; Mon–Fri 60min; £5.90 return) that operates a service between Kyle, Ratagan hostel and Glenelg post office. On request, the bus will go on to Arnisdale and Corran; similarly, the return bus from Glenelg can make arrangements to meet the Inverness or Glasgow buses at Kyle.

Murray Morrison's year-round **passenger ferry** from Arnisdale across Loch Hourn to Barrisdale (and to Kinlochhourn) provides an excellent means for walkers and cyclists to explore the most inaccessible parts of the Knoydart Peninsula (℡01599/522774, ⓦwww.arnisdaleferryservice.com; £10 single).

Plockton

A fifteen-minute train ride north of Kyle at the seaward end of islet-studded Loch Carron lies the unbelievably picturesque village of **PLOCKTON**: a chocolate-box row of neatly painted cottages ranged around the curve of a tiny harbour and backed by a craggy landscape of heather and pine. Originally known as Am Ploc, the settlement was a crofting hamlet until the end of the eighteenth century, when a local laird transformed it into a prosperous fishery, renaming it "Plocktown". Its fifteen minutes of fame came in the mid-1990s, when the BBC chose the village as the setting for the TV drama *Hamish Macbeth*. Though the resulting spin-off has since quietened, in high season it's packed full of tourists, yachties and second-home owners. The unique brilliance of Plockton's light has also made it something of an artists' hangout, and during the summer the waterfront, with its row of shaggy palm trees, even shaggier Highland cattle, flower gardens and pleasure boats, is invariably dotted with painters dabbing at their easels.

The friendly, cosy *Haven Hotel*, on Innes Street (℡01599/544223; ⑦), has king-size beds and is renowned for its excellent food, whilst the family-run *Plockton Inn*, also on Innes Street (℡01599/544222, ⓦwww.plocktoninn.co.uk; ⑤) is an equally friendly and informal alternative. The *Plockton Hotel*, Harbour Street (℡01599/544274, ⓦwww.plocktonhotel.co.uk; ⑥), overlooking the harbour with some rooms in a nearby cottage also serves excellent seafood. Of the fifteen or so **B&Bs**, *The Shieling* (℡01599/544282; ②) has a great location on a tiny headland at the top of the harbour, and the nearby *Heron's Flight* (℡01599/544220; March-Nov ③) enjoys uninterrupted views across the loch from its two upstairs bedrooms. At the cosy main-street retreat *An Caladh*, "the resting place on the shore" (℡01599/544356; ②), guests have the free use of two wooden sailing dinghies and can even watch the owner sail in with the morning catch of prawns. On the outskirts of Plockton, there's the attractive *Station Bunkhouse* (℡01599/544235) built in the shape of a signal box next to the railway station and featuring four- and six-person dorms and a cosy open-plan kitchen and living area.

There's a wealth of good places to **eat**: *The Haven,* the *Plockton Inn* and the *Plockton Hotel* all have excellent seafood **restaurants**, while *Off the Rails Restaurant and Tearoom* (ⓦwww.off-the-rails.co.uk), in the train station, serves evening fare that includes local shellfish and game. *The Buttery*, part of Plockton Stores on the seafront, is also open all day for snacks and inexpensive meals. Beside Plockton Stores, Calum's Seal Trips (℡01599/544306 or 07761/263828; Easter–Oct daily; £6) provides an interesting one-hour excursion. He also hires out rowing boats and canoes. **Bike rental** is available from Plockton Craft Shop (℡01599/544255) on the seafront.

Strathcarron and Kishorn

The sea lochs immediately north of Plockton are the dual inlets of **Loch Kishorn**, so deep it was once used as an oil-rig construction site, and **Loch Carron**, which cuts inland to **STRATHCARRON**, a useful linking point between the Kyle of Lochalsh and the Torridon area to the north. Strathcarron has a station on the Kyle–Inverness line and provides a postbus connection to Sheildaig and Torridon (Mon–Sat 10am). Duncan MacLennan's bus also provides a regular service to Torridon (12.30pm). Right by the station, housed in the old station building is the Strathcarron **tourist information, shop and post office** (Mon–Wed & Fri 9am–12.30pm & 1.30–5.30pm, Thurs 9am–1pm, Sat 9am–12.30pm; ☎01520/722218). Next door, the *Strathcarron Hotel* (☎01520/722227; ❸) serves bar meals and several real ales. A mile back, along the road to Kyle, the *Carron Pottery, Crafts and Restaurant* (☎01520/722488) serves up excellent food and offers some fine crafts.

From nearby **LOCHCARRON**, a pretty little village of whitewashed cottages stretched out along the northern shore of the loch, a single-track road leads over the hillside to **KISHORN**, at the head of the loch of the same name. The wooden chalet of the *Kishorn Seafood Bar* (☎01520/733240) is worth a stop for indulging in **fresh local shellfish** or coffee, home baking and bacon rolls.

Wester Ross

13

Wester Ross, the western seaboard of the old county of Ross-shire, is widely regarded as the most glamorous stretch of this coast. Here all the classic elements of Scotland's **coastal scenery** – dramatic mountains, sandy beaches, whitewashed crofting cottages and shimmering island views – come together in spectacular fashion. Though popular with generations of adventurous Scottish holiday-makers, only one or two places feel blighted by tourist numbers, with places such as **Applecross** and the peninsulas north and south of **Gairloch** maintaining an endearing simplicity and sense of isolation. There is some tough but wonderful **hiking** to be had in the mountains around **Torridon** and **Coigach**, while **boat trips** out among the islands and the prolific sea- and birdlife of the coast are another draw. The main settlement is the attractive fishing town of **Ullapool**, port for ferry services to Stornoway in the Western Isles, but a pleasant enough place to use as a base, not least for its active social and cultural scene.

The Applecross peninsula

The most dramatic approach to the **Applecross peninsula** (the English-sounding name is a corruption of the Gaelic *Apor Crosan*, meaning "estuary") is from the south, up a classic glacial U-shaped valley and over the infamous **Bealach na Bà** (literally "Pass of the Cattle"). Crossing the forbidding hills behind Kishorn and rising to 2053ft, with a gradient and switchback bends worthy of the Alps, this route – a popular cycling piste – is hair-raising in places, but the panoramic views across the Minch to Raasay and Skye more than compensate. The other way in is from the north: a beautiful coast road that meanders slowly from Shieldaig on Loch Torridon, with tantalizing glimpses of the Skye Cuillin to the south. This is the route the 11.30am postbus takes from Shieldaig on Loch Torridon; to reach Shieldaig, you need to catch the 10am postie from Strathcarron train station. No buses run over the Bealach na Bà.

The sheltered, fertile coast around **APPLECROSS** village (ⓦwww .applecross.info), where the Irish missionary monk Maelrhuba founded a monastery in 673 AD, comes as a surprise after the bleakness of the moorland approach. Maybe it's the journey, but Applecross feels like an idyllic place: you can wander along lanes banked with wild iris and orchids, and explore beaches and rock pools on the shore. There's a small **Heritage Centre** (April–Oct

Mon–Sat noon–4pm; Ⓦwww.applecrossheritage.org.uk) overlooking Clachan church and graveyard, and a number of short **waymarked trails** along the shore – great for walking off a pub lunch. If you're interested in something more exerting, contact the local experts Applecross Mountain & Sea (Ⓣ01520/744394, Ⓦwww.applecross.uk.com), which organizes mountain expeditions and sea kayaking around the coast.

The old, tastefully refurbished and family-run 🍴*Applecross Inn* (Ⓣ01520/744262, Ⓦwww.applecross.net; ❹), right beside the sea, is the focal point of the community, with **rooms** upstairs, and a lively bar that serves delicious, freshly prepared local seafood and produce (noon–9pm). Busy during the annual Fish Festival (June), the inn is the first stop for most folk coming here, but there are several excellent B&Bs on the peninsula. *Tigh na Mara* (Ⓣ01520/744277; ❸) at Lonbain provides views of Raasay whilst, nearer Shieldaig, *Tigh a' Chracaich* (Ⓣ01520/755367; ❸) is a great alternative. **Camping** is provided as you come into the village from the pass at the *Applecross Campsite* (Ⓣ01520/744268),, within which is the *Flower Tunnel* café-bar (daily 11am–9.30pm).

Loch Torridon

Loch Torridon marks the northern boundary of the Applecross peninsula, its awe-inspiring setting backed by the appealingly rugged mountains of **Liathach** and **Beinn Eighe**, tipped by streaks of white quartzite. The greater part of this area is composed of the reddish 750-million-year-old Torridonian sandstone, and some 15,000 acres of the massif are under the protection of the National Trust for Scotland. The trust looks after **Shieldaig Island**, where a heronry has been established among the tall Scots pines. The island lies in a sheltered bay off the prim but pretty village of **SHIELDAIG** ("herring bay") on the southern shore of Loch Torridon, where at the beginning of August the popular Shieldaig Fete is annually held. There's an attractive small **hotel** and friendly snug bar by the shore in the village, 🍴 *Tigh-an-Eilean* (Ⓣ01520/755251; March–Oct; ❼), the close-by *Rivendell* B&B (Ⓣ01520/755250; ❷) and

△ Loch Torridon

Ordnance Survey Explorer Map no. 433.

With the support of Scottish Natural Heritage (SNH), large tracts of Torridon's Beinn Eighe National Nature Reserve are being replanted with native trees including birch, Scots pine and rowan. There can be difficult conditions on virtually all hiking routes around Torridon, and the weather can change very rapidly. If you're relatively inexperienced but want to do the magnificent ridge walk along the **Liathach** (pronounced "lee-ach") massif, or the strenuous traverse of **Beinn Eighe** (pronounced "ben ay"), you can join a National Trust Ranger Service guided hike (July & Aug; Torridon Countryside Centre; ☎01445/791221).

For those confident to go it alone, one of many possible routes takes you behind Liathach and down the pass, **Coire Dubh**, to the main road in Glen Torridon. This is a great, straightforward walk if you're properly equipped (see p.64), covering thirteen miles and taking in superb landscapes. Allow yourself the whole day. Start at the stone bridge on the Diabaig road along the north side of Loch Torridon. Follow the Abhainn Coire Mhic Nobuil burn up to the fork at the wooden bridge and take the track east to the pass (a rather indistinct watershed) between Liathach and Beinn Eighe. The path becomes a little lost in the boggy area studded with lochans at the top of the pass, but the route is clear and, once over the watershed, the path is easy to follow. At this point you can, weather permitting, make the rewarding diversion up to the **Coire Mhic Fhearchair**, widely regarded as the most spectacular corrie in Scotland; otherwise continue down the Coire Dubh stream, ford the burn and follow its west bank down to the Torridon road, from where it's about four miles back to Loch Torridon.

A rewarding walk even in rough weather is the seven-mile hike up the coast from **Lower Diabaig**, ten miles northwest of Torridon village, to **Redpoint**. On a clear day, the views across to Raasay and Applecross from this gentle undulating path are superlative, but you'll have to return along the same trail, or else make your way back via Loch Maree on the A832. If you're staying in Shieldaig, the track that winds up the peninsula running north from the village makes a pleasant ninety-minute round walk.

a simple **campsite** affording terrific loch views a little way up the hill. Out of the village at Doireaonor, on the southwest side of Loch Shieldaig, west of Shieldaig across the inlet, *Tigh Fada* (☎01520/755248) offers self-catering accommodation in a delightful log cabin.

Loch Torridon prides itself on its **seafood**, either caught or farmed locally. *Tigh an Eilean* at Shieldaig serves impressive meals, while the very friendly *Loch Torridon Smoke House* (☎01520/755230), on the bypass behind Shieldaig, dishes up tea and home baking and a mouthwatering range of seafoods including hot smoked salmon.

At **TORRIDON** village, at the east end of the loch, the main road heads inland through Glen Torridon, while the minor road runs through the village along the northern shore of the loch. At the road junction, past the Torridon Mountain Rescue post, the National Trust for Scotland runs a **Countryside Centre** (Easter to end Sept Mon–Sat 10am–6pm; £3), where you can call in and learn a bit more about the local geology, flora and fauna. Nearby is a small but informative NTS Deer Museum (same hours as Countryside Centre). Oyster-catchers and otters may be spotted from the wildlife hide on the shore. The road, which continues beyond Torridon, is scenic and dramatic, winding first along the shore, then climbing and twisting past lochans, cliffs and gorges, past tiny **INVERALLIGIN** (good for free-range eggs and camping) and terminating at the green wooded slopes around **LOWER DIABAIG**. On the south side of the loch stands one of the area's grandest **hotels**, the smart, rambling Victorian *Loch Torridon Hotel* (℡01445/791242, ⓦwww.lochtorridonhotel.com; ❽), set amid well-tended lochside grounds. The hotel also runs the adjacent *Ben Damph Lodge* (March–Oct; ❺), a cyclist- and walker-friendly modern conversion of an old farmstead with neat twins and doubles and a bistro-bar. Torridon Activities, run from the hotel, offers residents and non-residents alike pursuits including hill walking, mountain-biking and sea kayaking. Close to the Countryside Centre is a rather unsightly SYHA **hostel** (℡0870/004 1154, ⓦwww .syha.org.uk; March–Oct) and a council-run **campsite**. Donnie and Morag MacDonald operate the well-stocked Torridon Stores (℡01445/791400) in Torridon village. The area's only shop, it sells everything from camping gas and midgy nets to fruit and veg and secondhand books.

Note that the chief transport connection with the Torridon region is **Achnasheen**, 18 miles northeast of Strathcarron at the head of Glen Carron. Another stop on the Kyle train line, Achnasheen marks a fork in the road from Inverness: one branch, the A890, follows the railway towards Strathcarron and Kyle; the other, the A832, snakes through the mountains to Kinlochewe, beside the Torridon hills. There are postbus links from the railway through to Torridon.

Loch Maree

About eight miles north of Loch Torridon, **Loch Maree**, dotted with Caledonian pine-covered islands, is one of the west's scenic highlights, best viewed from the A832 road that drops down to its southeastern tip through Glen Docherty. At the southeastern end of the loch, the A896 from Torridon meets the A832 from Achnasheen at the small settlement of **KINLOCHEWE** (ⓦwww.torridon-mountains.com), a good base if you're heading into the hills. There is a plain **bunkhouse** as well as good meals at the *Kinlochewe Hotel* (℡01445/760253, ⓦwww.kinlochewehotel.co.uk; ❹), but for a little extra head a mile southwest along the road towards Torridon to *Cromasaig* B&B (℡01455/760234, ⓦwww.cromasaig.com; ❷), a great place for hill-walkers set in the forest right at the foot of the track up Beinn Eighe. The *Cromasaig* folk also run the Moru outdoor shop at the old petrol station opposite the hotel and will furnish you with maps and guidebooks, as well as equipment and the weather forecast. The friendly Kinlochewe Store opposite the hotel contains the post office (which opens Mon–Sat 9–11am) and the *Teapot Café*, whilst 400yd up the road towards Gairloch is the petrol station and *Tipsy Laird* tearoom.

The A832 skirts the southern shore of Loch Maree, passing the **Beinn Eighe Nature Reserve**, the UK's oldest wildlife sanctuary. Parts of the Beinn Eighe reserve are forested with Caledonian pinewood, which once covered the whole of the country, and it is home to wildlife that includes pine martens, wildcats, buzzards and golden eagles. A mile north of Kinlochewe, the well-run **Beinn Eighe Visitor Centre** (Easter & May–Oct daily 10am–5pm) on the A832, uses excellent audiovisual presentations and child-friendly displays to inform visitors about the area's rare species. Outside, the "talking trails" are an imaginative innovation and provide an easy walk through the vicinity. Several interesting **walks** start from the car park, a mile north of the visitor centre.

Loch Maree is surrounded by some of Scotland's finest **deerstalking** country: the remote, privately owned Letterewe Lodge on the north shore, accessible only by helicopter or boat, lies at the heart of a famous deer forest. In 1877,

Queen Victoria stayed for a few days at the wonderfully sited *Loch Maree Hotel*; it offers dinner and B&B to guests (℡01445/760288; ❼), when not rented out as an exclusive self-catering lodge. An even better place **to stay** nearby is *The Old Mill* (℡01445/760271; ❽), a beautiful Highland lodge where rates include an absolutely fabulous dinner, bed and breakfast.

Gairloch and around

GAIRLOCH spreads itself around the northeastern corner of the wide sheltered bay of Loch Gairloch, with its sometimes sandy, sometimes rocky shores. During the summer, Gairloch thrives as a low-key holiday resort with several tempting sandy beaches and some excellent coastal walks within easy reach. The township is divided into several, pretty distinct areas spread over nearly two miles of shoreline: to the south, in **Flowerdale Bay**, are the old pier and harbour; past the bank, at the turn-off to Melvaig is **Achtercairn**, the centre of Gairloch, and along the north side of the bay, on the road to Melvaig, is **Strath**. The main supermarket and **tourist office** (June–Sept daily 9am–5.30pm; Oct Mon–Sat 9am–5.30pm; Nov–May Mon–Sat 10am–4pm) are in Achtercairn, right by the **Gairloch Heritage Museum** (March–Sept daily 10am–5pm; Oct Mon–Sat 10am–1pm); £3) has eclectic, appealing displays covering geology, archeology, fishing and farming that range from a mock-up of a croft house to an early knitting machine. Probably the most interesting section is the archive made by elderly locals – an array of photographs, maps, genealogies, lists of place names and taped recollections, mostly in Gaelic.

Gairloch has a good choice of **accommodation**, but you might prefer to stay out along the road north to Melvaig or south to Redpoint (see p.632). In Achtercairn, opposite the post office, a room-only option can be found at the *Mountain Lodge* (℡01445/712316; March–Dec; ❷). Next door, you can indulge in good coffee and fresh, though pricey, scones at the laid-back *Mountain Café*, which also features good views over the bay. There are also some very good **B&Bs**: in Strath, try Gaelic-speaking Miss Mackenzie's *Duisary* (℡01445/712252, ⓦwww.duisary.freeserve.co.uk; April–Oct; ❷); near the pier, head for *Heatherdale* (℡01445/712388, ⒺBrochod1@aol.com; March to end Oct; ❸); and further south still, just before the turn-off to Badachro, there's the atmospheric and tastefully furnished *Kerrysdale House* (℡01445/712292, ⓦwww.kerrysdalehouse.co.uk; ❷) set back in its own lovely gardens.

For **food**, head for the harbour where the *Old Inn* (ⓦwww.theoldinn.co.uk) offers seafood on its bar menu and a very good range of Scottish real ales. There's also the *Harbour Lights Café* for those in search of reasonably priced snacks and evening meals. Nearby, the *Creel Restaurant* offers delicious fare whilst the *Steading Restaurant*, tucked beside the Gairloch Museum, is another popular eatery. For **snacks**, try the *Mountain Lodge* or the bistro-style *Café Blueprint* across the road where you'll also find the chip shop.

One leisurely way to explore the coast is on a wildlife-spotting **cruise**. There several operators, but try Gairloch Marine Life Centre & Cruises (Easter–Oct; ℡01445/712636); pier-based, they run informative and enjoyable boat trips across the bay in search of dolphins, seals and even the odd whale. They also deploy a mini-sub that sends underwater pictures back to the boat whilst a hydrophone picks up audio from the sea life. You can **rent a boat** for the day through the Gairloch Chandlery (℡01445/712458, at the pier, or go **pony trekking** with Gairloch Trekking Centre (℡01445/712652; closed Thurs). There's also the scenic and testing nine-hole Gairloch golf course (℡01445/712407; £20). From the car park on the north side of the Flowerdale river, a sheltered glen enables walkers to enjoy a scenic woodland walk. Ask at the tourist office for directions.

Rubha Reidh and around

The area's real attraction, however, is its beautiful **coastline**. To get to one of the most impressive stretches, head around the north side of the bay and follow the single-track B8021 to **BIG SAND**, which has a cleaner and quieter **beach** than the one in Gairloch. An excellent **campsite** sits above the beach (℡01445/712152). Just before Big Sand, there's an SYHA **hostel** at Carn Dearg (℡0870/004 1110, ⓦwww.syha.org.uk; April–Sept), spectacularly set on the edge of a cliff with views to Skye. The B8021, and the postbus from Gairloch, terminate at the tiny crofting hamlet of Melvaig where a white-stone former Free Church provides a rustic setting for fabulous freshly prepared food at the *Mustn't Grumble* restaurant (℡01445/771212, ⓦwww.mustnt-grumble.com). The proprietor even runs a stretch limo and minibus service from Gairloch.

From Melvaig, it's another three miles out to **Rubha Reidh** (pronounced "roo-a-ray"). You can stay at the headland's still operational Stevenson-designed *Rua Reidh Lighthouse* (℡01445/771263, ⓦwww.ruareidh.co.uk; ❶), which looks straight out to the Outer Hebrides. Comfortable accommodation options include a bunkhouse, double and family rooms (meals extra; book ahead in high season). Fran, the cheerful owner, serves slap-up **afternoon teas** and home-made cakes (Tues & Thurs 11am–5pm); pre-booked evening meals are available and guided walking and climbing courses are offered.

Badachro and Redpoint

Three miles south of Gairloch, a narrow single-track lane (built with the Destitution Funds raised during the nineteenth-century potato famine) winds west from the main A832, past wooded coves and inlets on its way south of the loch to **BADACHRO**, a sleepy former fishing village in a very attractive setting with a wonderful pub, the ⚓ *Badachro Inn* (ⓦwww.badachroinn.com), right by the water's edge, where you can sit in the beer garden watching the boats come and go and tuck into deliciously fresh seafood with a real ale. Some 300m away, seek out the secluded *Shieldaig Lodge Hotel* (℡01445/741250, ⓦwww.shieldaiglodge.com; ❸) for comfortable accommodation in a former Victorian shooting lodge. Accessed via a floating bridge and a short drive away, *Dry Island* provides visitors to Badachro with a great B&B or self-catering option (℡01445/741263, ⓦwww.dryisland.co.uk; ❹). The owner will even run trips on his traditional fishing boat on which visitors can help haul in the creels.

Beyond Badachro, the road winds for five more miles along the shore to **REDPOINT**, a straggling hamlet with beautiful beaches of peach-coloured sand and great views to Raasay, Skye and the Western Isles. It also marks the trailhead for the wonderful coast walk to Lower Diabaig (see box on p.632). Even if you don't fancy a full-blown hike, following the path a mile or so brings you to the exquisite **beach** hidden on the south side of the headland, which you'll often have all to yourself.

Poolewe and around

It's a fifteen-minute hop by bus over the headland from Gairloch to the trim little village of **POOLEWE** which sits by a small bay at the sheltered southern end of Loch Ewe, where the (very short) River Ewe rushes down from Loch Maree. One of the area's best **walks** begins near here, signposted from the layby-cum-viewpoint on the main A832, a mile south of the village. It takes a couple of hours to follow the easy trail across open craggy moorland to the shores of **Loch Maree** (see p.633), and thence to the car park at Slattadale, seven miles southeast of Gairloch. If you reach Slattadale just before 7pm on a Tuesday, Thursday or Friday, you should be able to pick up the Wester bus from Inverness back to Poolewe or Aultbea.

For **accommodation** Poolewe has a popular and well-equipped **campsite** (℡01445/781249; May–Oct), whilst the family-run and refurbished *Poolewe Hotel* (℡01445/781241, Ⓦwww.poolewehotel.co.uk; ❺), on the Cove road, serves tasty dinners that include award-winning black pudding and fresh seafood. For a taste of luxury, relax at the award-winning *Pool House Hotel* (℡01445/781272, Ⓦwww.poolhousehotel.com; ❽) which once belonged to Osgood MacKenzie (see below). At Aultbea, *Cartmel* (℡01445/731375, Ⓦwww.cartmelguesthouse.com; ❸) is a very professional place with charming hosts. Four miles north of Poolewe at Inverasdale, *Bruach Ard* offers comfortable B&B lodging (℡01445/781765). In Poolewe itself, *The Bridge Cottage Coffee Shop and Gallery*, just up the Cove road from the village crossroads, is a cosy snack stop.

Inverewe Gardens

Half a mile across the bay from Poolewe on the A832, **Inverewe Gardens** (daily: April–Oct 9.30am–9pm or dusk; Nov–March 9.30am–4pm; NTS; £8), a verdant oasis of foliage and riotously colourful flower collections, forms a vivid contrast to the wild, heathery crags of the adjoining coast. The gardens were the brainchild of **Osgood MacKenzie**, who inherited the surrounding 12,000-acre estate from his stepfather, the laird of Gairloch, in 1862. Taking advantage of the area's famously temperate climate (a consequence of the Gulf Stream, which draws a warm sea current from Mexico to within a stone's throw of these shores), Mackenzie collected plants from all over the world for his walled garden, which still forms the nucleus of the complex. Protected from Loch Ewe's corrosive salt breezes by a dense brake of Scots pine, rowan, oak, beech and birch trees, the fragile plants flourished on rich soil brought here as ballast on Irish ships to overlay the previously infertile beach gravel and sea grass. By the time MacKenzie died in 1922, his garden sprawled over the whole peninsula, surrounded by a hundred acres of woodland. Today the National Trust for Scotland strives to develop the place along the lines envisaged by its founder.

Thousands of visitors pour through here annually, but the place rarely feels overcrowded. Interconnected by a labyrinthine network of twisting paths and walkways, a few accessible by wheelchair, more than a dozen gardens feature exotic plant collections from as far afield as Chile, China, Tasmania and the Himalayas. Strolling around the lotus ponds, palm trees and borders ablaze with exotic blooms, it's amazing to think you're at the same latitude as Hudson Bay. Mid-May to mid-June is the best time to see the rhododendrons and azaleas, while the herbaceous garden reaches its peak in July and August, as does the wonderful Victorian vegetable and flower garden beside the sea. Look out, too, for the grand old eucalyptus in the Peace Plot, which is the largest in the northern hemisphere, and the nearby Ghost Tree (*Davidia involucrata*), representing the earliest evolutionary stages of flowering trees. You'll need at least a couple of hours, particularly if you explore the Pinewood Trail and still leave time for the **visitor centre** (April–Sept daily 9.30am–5pm), which houses an informative display on the history of the garden and is the starting point for **guided walks** (May–Sept). The **restaurant** serves good food.

Gruinard Bay and Little Loch Broom

At **LAIDE**, ten miles north of Poolewe, the road skirts the shores of **Gruinard Bay**, offering fabulous views and, at the inner end of the bay, some excellent sandy beaches. During World War II, **Gruinard Island**, in the bay, was used as a testing ground for biological warfare, and for years was ringed by huge signs warning the public not to land. The **anthrax** spores released during the testing can live in the soil for up to a thousand years, but in 1987, after much protest, the Ministry of Defence had the island decontaminated and it was finally declared "safe" in 1990. As befits the stunning scenery, there are some lovely **accommodation** choices all along this stretch, including a reasonable campsite (℡01445/731225) and the welcoming *Old Smiddy Guest House* (℡01445/731696, Ⓦwww.oldsmiddyguesthouse.co.uk; ❸) on the main road in Laide and not to be confused with the well-run self-catering *Old Smiddy Cottages* run by Kate Macdonald (℡01445/731425). Another option is the remote but hospitable *Sheiling* B&B at Achgarve (℡01445/731487; ❸). To reach it, turn left at Laide post office and travel 1.5 miles down the road towards Mellon Udrigle. **Transport** is very patchy in these parts. On a Thursday only, a bus departs Gairloch (9am) and passes through Poolewe, Laide (post office; 9.40am) and Dundonnell en route to Ullapool.

To the east of Gruinard Bay lies **Little Loch Broom**, a narrow sea loch surrounded by a salt marsh that is covered with flowers in early summer. To the south, the loch is overlooked by the mass of **An Teallach** (3478ft); to the north, it is divided from Loch Broom by the rugged **Scoraig peninsula**, one of the remotest places on the British mainland, accessible only by boat or on foot. Formerly dotted with crofting townships, it is now deserted apart from tiny **SCORAIG** village, where a mostly self-sufficient community has established itself, complete with windmills, organic vegetable gardens and a thriving primary school. Understandably, Scoraig's inhabitants would rather not be regarded as tourist curiosities, so you should only venture out here if you're sympathetic to such a community. To reach Scoraig, you have two main options: you can drive to **BADRALLACH**, on the north side of Little Loch Broom, and walk from there, or try to plan a trip for when the postboat crosses the loch (℡01854/633333; Mon, Wed & Fri 11am). The boat is weather-dependent, so you should always call and check if it's running.

Accommodation in the area is limited, but there's the small *Northern Lights* **campsite** at Badcaul before which you will find the *Sail Mhor Croft* (℡01854/633224, Ⓦwww.sailmhor.co.uk), a small independent **hostel** in Camusnagaul in a lovely location on the lochside. Alternatively, heading two miles north you could stay at the head of Little Loch Broom, at the *Dundonnell* (℡01854/633204, Ⓦwww.dundonnellhotel.com; ❼), a smart, comfortable **hotel** which serves bar meals. Dundonnell is also where you'll find the nearest petrol station for miles around, the home of the An Teallach micro-brewery and the mountain rescue post. Heading north past the hotel, turn left and seven miles up the single-track road you'll find the very remote *Badrallach* campsite and bothy (℡01854/633281, Ⓦwww.badrallach.com; ❶). Take plenty of food if visiting this remote area.

Falls of Measach

The road heads inland before joining the A835, the main Inverness–Ullapool road, at **Braemore Junction**, above the head of Loch Broom. Just nearby, and easily accessible from a layby on the A835, are the spectacular 164ft **Falls of Measach**, which plunge through the mile-long Corrieshalloch Gorge, formed by glacial melt-waters. You can overlook the cascades from a precarious observation platform, or from the impressive, wobbly Victorian suspension bridge that spans the chasm, whose 197ft vertical sides are draped in a rich array of plantlife, with thickets of wych elm, goat willow and bird cherry miraculously thriving on the cliffs. The A835 from the head of Loch Broom to Ullapool is one of the so-called **Destitution Roads**, built to give employment to local people during the nineteenth-century potato famines.

Ullapool

ULLAPOOL (Ⓦ www.ullapool.co.uk), the northwest's principal centre of population, was founded at the height of the herring boom in 1788 by the British Fisheries Society, on a sheltered arm of land jutting into Loch Broom. The grid-plan town is still an important fishing centre, though the **ferry** link to Stornoway on Lewis (see p.700) means that in high season its personality is practically swamped by visitors. Note that visitors can now make a day-long return ferry/bus visit to Lewis with Caledonian MacBrayne (Ⓣ0870/565 0000; £26.25). Though busy, Ullapool remains a hugely appealing place and a good base for exploring the northwest Highlands. Regular **buses** run from here to Inverness and Durness, while there's an early-morning run through to the remote train station at Lairg. Accommodation is plentiful and Ullapool is an

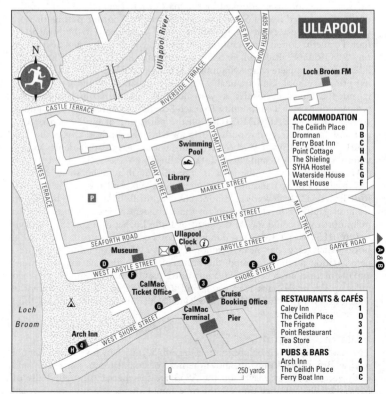

© Crown copyright

obvious hideaway if the weather is bad, with cosy pubs, a swimming pool and a lively **arts centre**, the *Ceilidh Place*.

Arrival, information and accommodation

Forming the backbone of its grid plan, Ullapool's two main arteries are the lochside **Shore Street** and, parallel to it, **Argyle Street**, further inland. **Buses** stop at the pier, in the town centre near the ferry dock, from where it's easy to get your bearings. The well-run **tourist office** (April, May & Sept Mon–Sat 9.30am–5pm; June–Aug Mon–Sat 9am–5pm, Sun 10am–4pm; Oct Mon–Fri 10am–5pm; Nov & Dec Mon–Fri 2–5.30pm), on Argyle Street, offers an accommodation booking service.

Ullapool has all kinds of **accommodation**, including a couple of welcoming hostels and some decent guesthouses and B&Bs, though it's worth booking ahead to get any of the places listed below.

Hotels, guesthouses and B&Bs

The Ceilidh Place West Argyle St ☎01854/612103, ⌨www.theceilidhplace .com. Tasteful and popular hotel, with the west coast's best bookshop, a relaxing first-floor lounge, a great bar/restaurant, sea views and a laid-back atmosphere. Also has a good-value bunkhouse for £15 per person. ❻

Dromnan Garve Rd ☎01854/612333, ⌨www .dromnan.co.uk. Excellent B&B run by very friendly hosts, who serve up a hearty breakfast. ❸

Ferry Boat Inn Shore St ☎01854/612366, ⌨www.ferryboat-inn.com. Traditional inn right on the waterfront with a friendly atmosphere and reasonable food. ❺

Point Cottage 22 West Shore St ☎01854/612494, ⌨www.pointcottage.co.uk. Rustic, very well-equipped and friendly B&B at the quieter end of the seafront. Guests can borrow OS maps that have been already marked up with walking routes. ❸

The Shieling Garve Rd ☎01854/612947. Another very friendly, comfortable guesthouse overlooking the loch, with immaculate, spacious rooms (nos 4 and 5 have the best views), superb breakfasts (try their home-made venison and leek sausages) and a sauna. ❸

Waterside House 6 West Shore St ☎01854/612140, ⌨www.waterside.uk.net. Three tastefully furnished en-suite rooms in a very pleasant, seafront B&B. ❸

Hostels and campsite

Broomfield Holiday Park West Shore St ☎01854/612020. Modest, good-value campsite, five minutes' walk from town. Exposed to the wind off Loch Broom but offers great views and warm showers.

SYHA hostel Shore St ☎0870/004 1156, ⌨www .syha.org.uk. Busy hostel on the front, with Internet access, laundry and lots of good information about local walks. March–Oct.

West House West Argyle St ☎01854/613126, ⌨www.scotpackers-hostels.co.uk. Lively, welcoming hostel with four- to six-bed dorms; some en suite. Internet access (£1). Bike rental available (£10 per day).

The Town

Day or night, most of the action in Ullapool centres on the **harbour**, which has an authentic and salty air, especially when the boats are in. By day, attention focuses on the comings and goings of the ferry, fishing boats and smaller craft, while in the evening, yachts swing on the current, the shops stay open late, and customers from the *Ferry Boat Inn* line the sea wall. During summer, booths advertise trips to the **Summer Isles** – a cluster of uninhabited islets two to three miles offshore – to view seabird colonies, dolphins and porpoises, but if you're lucky you'll spot marine life from the waterfront. Otters occasionally nose around the rocks near the *Ferry Boat Inn*, and seals swim past begging scraps from the boats moored in the middle of the loch.

The only conventional attraction in town is the award-winning **museum**, in the old parish church on West Argyle Street (April–Oct Mon–Sat 10am–5pm;

△ Ullapool

Nov–March Sat 10am–4pm; £4), where photographs, audiovisual and touch-screen displays provide an insight into life in a Highland community, including crofting, fishing, local religion and emigration. During the Clearances, Ullapool was one of the ports through which evicted crofters left to start new lives abroad.

Eating, drinking and entertainment

The two best **pubs** in Ullapool are the *Arch Inn*, home of the Ullapool football team, and the *Ferry Boat Inn* (known as the "FBI"), where you can enjoy a pint of real ale at the lochside – midges permitting. **Live Scottish folk music** is a special feature at *The Ceilidh Place* or on Thursday nights at the *FBI*. The atmospheric *Ceilidh Place* also runs a monthly art exhibition as part of its regular entertainment. All three pubs serve bar meals – the *FBI* is possibly the pick of the bunch.

There are several great places to eat in the town. Those in search of delicious fine dining should seek out the *Point Restaurant* (March–Oct Tues–Sat) above the *Arch Inn* on the shore, where the emphasis is on fresh, home-made dishes with local hot-smoked salmon and haggis among the treats. The *Caley Inn* on Quay Street combines Scottish fusion cuisine with the chance to sample several real ales whilst the nearby *Ceilidh Place* is another popular destination where modestly priced lunches, snacks and dinners are served in a pleasant bistro area. *The Frigate*, an airy café on the seafront serves good coffee but many a local seeks out the well-run *Tea Store*, on Argyll Street opposite the tourist information, for a tasty, inexpensive sandwich and refreshing cuppa.

Assynt

If you've come as far as Ullapool it really is worth continuing further north into the ever-more dramatic, remote and highly distinctive hills of **Assynt** (Ⓦwww.assynt.co.uk), which marks the transition from Wester Ross into Sutherland.

One of the least populated areas in Europe, this is a landscape not of mountain ranges but of extraordinary peaks rising individually from the moorland. It's an area of peaceful, slow backroads, which, after twisting through idyllic crofts, invariably end up at a deserted beach or windswept headland with superb clear-day views west to the Outer Hebrides. **Lochinver**, midway along the west coast, is the main settlement, though you're unlikely to want to stay there. Head, instead, for one of the crofting villages along the coast, like those around **Achiltibuie**, or – if you're keen to climb the mountains – head for **Inchnadamph**, which sits below the region's two Munros.

Coigach

Coigach (ⓦ www.coigach.com) is the peninsula immediately to the north of Loch Broom, accessible via a slow, winding, single-track road that leaves the A835 ten miles north of Ullapool, squeezing between the northern shore of Loch Lurgainn and the lower slopes of **Cul Beag** (2523ft) and craggy, Stac Pollaidh (2012ft). To the southeast, the awesome bulk of **Ben More Coigach** (2439ft) presides over the district, which contains some spectacular coastal scenery including a string of sandy beaches and the Summer Isles, scattered just offshore. Coigach's main settlement is **ACHILTIBUIE**, an old crofting village scattered across the hillside above a series of white-sand coves and rocks tapering into the Atlantic, from where a fleet of small fishing boats carries sheep and tourists to the enticing pastures of the **Summer Isles**, which lie a little way offshore. For **boat** trips round the isles, including some time ashore on the largest, Tanera Mor, Ian Macleod's boat *Hectoria* (☎01854/622200) usually runs twice a day from the pier (Easter–Oct).

The village attracts gardening enthusiasts, thanks to the unlikely presence of the **Hydroponicum** (April–Sept daily 10am–6pm; Oct Mon–Fri 11.30am–3.30pm; ⓦ www.thehydroponicum.com; £4.95; tours on the hour), a cross between a giant greenhouse and a futuristic scientific research station, and, it has to be said, something of an eyesore. Dubbed "The Garden of the Future", all kinds of flowers, fruits and vegetables are grown without using soil in conditions that concentrate the sun's heat while protecting the plants from winter (and summer) chill. Bumper crops of strawberries, salad leaves, figs and even bananas result – guided tours explain how it's all done and show you round the different "climate zones". You can taste whatever's being harvested in the subtropical setting of the functional *Lilypond Café*, which serves snacks and meals, including weekend evenings (7–9pm).

If in need of fuel or provisions, visit the well-stocked Achiltibuie Store, while for **accommodation**, the wonderfully understated *Summer Isles Hotel* (☎01854/622282, ⓔinfo@summerisleshotel.co.uk; ❼; Easter–Oct), just up the road from the Hydroponicum, enjoys a perfect setting with views over the islands. The hotel buys in Hydroponicum fruit and vegetables and has its own chicken run. An excellent set dinner in the **restaurant** costs about £40, although superb bar snacks and lunches feature crab, langoustines and smoked mackerel starting from £4. Note that children under 14 are not allowed in the bar area. Of Achiltibuie's several **B&Bs**, *Dornie House* (☎01854/622271, ⓔdorniehousebandb@aol.com; ❶; Easter–Nov), halfway to Altandhu, is welcoming and provides huge breakfasts.

Also worth a visit is the **Achiltibuie Smokehouse** (☎01854/622353; April–Sept Mon–Sat 9.30am–5pm; free), five miles northwest of the Hydroponicum at **ALTANDHU**, where you can see meat, fish and game being cured in the traditional way and can buy some afterwards. Next to this, the *Fuaran* bar serves lunches, snacks and evening meals, including fresh hand-dived scallops, and like everywhere else along this stretch, enjoys terrific views over to the Summer Isles.

There's also a beautifully situated twenty-bed SYHA **hostel** (℡0870/004 1101, ⓦwww.syha.org.uk; May–Sept), three miles southeast of Achiltibuie down the coast at **ACHININVER**, which is handy for accessing Coigach's mountain hikes. If you're reasonably experienced and can use a map and compass, you can walk to the hostel from Ullapool. The rock path, which winds along one of the region's most beautiful and unspoilt stretches of coastline, is over ten miles long, easy to follow in good weather, but very boggy and slippery when wet. Sound footwear, fluid, waterproofs and a map are essential.

Lochinver and around

The potholed and narrow road north from Achiltibuie through Inverkirkaig is unremittingly spectacular, threading its way through a tumultuous landscape of secret valleys, moorland and bare rock, past the startling shapes of Cul Beag (2523ft), Cul Mor (2785ft) and the distinctive sugar-loaf **Suilven** (2398ft). You pass thick-walled, idyllic crofts and the start of several community woodland walking trails established by Little Assynt Estate, and then a sheltered bay heralds your arrival at **LOCHINVER**, sixteen miles due north of Ullapool (although more than thirty by road). One of the busiest fishing harbours in Scotland, it's a workaday place from where large trucks head off for the continent. Like Gairloch, Lochinver is divided into quite distinct areas, with the harbour to the south, the centre of the village at the road junction half a mile or so to the north and Baddidarrach further west along the northern shore of Loch Inver. Halfway between the two is the **tourist office** (April to end Oct Mon–Sat 10am–5pm, June–Sept also Sun 10am–4pm), within the excellent **Assynt Visitor Centre**, which gives an interesting rundown on the area's geology, wildlife and history and has a CCTV link to a nearby heronry; a countryside ranger is available for advice, and there are a whole series of guided walks and activities put on from May to September. The area is popular with **fishing** enthusiasts. You can get information on permits at the tourist office or post office and at The Cottage, Culag Square (℡01571/844076), where boats are also rented.

Lochinver has a wide choice of good **B&Bs**: on the north side of the loch, *Ardglas House* (℡01571/844257, Ⓔguide@ardglas.co.uk; ❶) has superb views, whilst next-door *Davar* (℡01571/844501, Ⓔjean@davar36.fsnet.co.uk; ❷; March–Oct) is very welcoming. More central, close to the tourist office, comfortable *Polcraig* (℡01571/844429, Ⓔcathelmac@aol.com; ❷) serves up fabulous breakfasts and can arrange fishing. Combining fine dining with a relaxed, upmarket stay is the beautifully appointed *Albannach Hotel* at Baddidarrach (℡01571/844407, Ⓦwww.thealbannach.co.uk; ❾; March–Nov; no children under 12). An attractive nineteenth-century building set in a walled garden, its five-course menu includes fresh game and seafood. Lochinver's most popular **food** halt is the *Larder Riverside Bistro* on the main street: it is perhaps best known for excellent, though pricey, home-made pies such as wild boar, port and prune. Decent bar meals are available at the *Caberfeidh* next door, which is also the most convivial place to head for a drink, while the *Seamen's Mission*, down at the harbour, is a good option for the budget-conscious traveller. The local football team meet at the *Wayfarers Pub* at the pier.

Inverkirkaig Falls

Approaching Lochinver from the south, the road bends sharply through a wooded valley where a signpost for **Inverkirkaig Falls** marks the start of a long but gentle **walk** to the base of **Suilven** – the most distinctive mountain in Scotland, its huge sandstone dome rising above the heather boglands of Assynt. Serious hikers use the path to approach the mighty peak, but you can follow it for an easy three-to-four-hour ramble, taking in a waterfall and a tour of a secluded loch. Just by the start of the trail but tucked away among the dark pine trees, **Achins Bookshop** must rate as the Highland's best-hidden nook. You can browse the shelves of heavyweight classics and local-interest titles, then shuffle into the adjoining **coffee shop** for a bowl of soup or some home baking.

North of Lochinver

Heading **north** from Lochinver, there are two possible routes: the fast A837, which runs eastwards along the shore of Loch Assynt (see below) to join the northbound A894, or the narrow, more scenic B869 **coast road** that locals dub "The Breakdown Zone", because its ups and downs claim so many victims during summer. Hugging the indented shoreline, this route offers superb views of the Summer Isles, as well as a number of rewarding side-trips to beaches and dramatic cliffs. Post- and schoolbuses from Lochinver cover the route as far as Ardvar or Drumbeg (Mon–Sat).

The first village worthy of a detour is **ACHMELVICH**, three miles north-west of Lochinver, where a tiny bay cradles a stunning white-sand beach lapped by startlingly turquoise water. There's a **campsite** and a basic 36-bed SYHA **hostel** (⊕0870/004 1102, ⓦwww.syha.org.uk; April–Sept) just behind the largest beach. However, for total peace and quiet, head to other, equally seductive beaches beyond the headlands. Back to the B869, the giant peak of Suilven dominates the skyline. Further west, the crofting hamlet of Clachtoll is dominated by another beautiful bay with a campsite, and nearby which you'll find the former Clachtoll Salmon Station, now preserved by the Assynt Historical Society.

The side road that branches north off the B869 between **STOER** and **CLASHNESSIE**, ends abruptly by the automatic lighthouse at **Raffin**, Stevenson-built in 1870. You can continue for two miles along a boggy, slightly tricky track to the Point of Stoer, named after the colossal rock pillar that stands offshore known as "**The Old Man of Stoer**", surrounded by sheer cliffs and splashed with guano from the seabird colonies that nest on its two hundred-foot sides. Some five miles east of Clashnessie you could treat yourself to a **room** and delicious food at the *Drumbeg Hotel* (⊕01571/833236, ⓦwww.drumbeghotel.com; ❸).

Loch Assynt, Inchnadamph and around

The area east of Lochinver, traversed by the A837, centred on **Loch Assynt** and bounded by the gnarled peaks of the Ben More Assynt massif, is a wilderness of mountains, moorland, mist and scree. Dotted with lochs and lochans, it's also an angler's paradise, home to the only non-migratory fish in northern Scotland, the brown trout, and numerous other sought-after species, including the Atlantic salmon, sea trout, arctic char and a massive prize strain of cannibal ferox.

At **INCHNADAMPH** at the southeastern tip of Loch Assynt, the *Inchnadamph Hotel* (⊕01571/822202, ⓦwww.inchnadamphhotel.co.uk; ❺), is a seventeenth-century coaching inn which makes for a wonderful Highland retreat; inside, the walls are covered with the stuffed catches of past guests. The hotel offers fine old-fashioned cooking, usually with good vegetarian options, in its moderately priced restaurant and bar. It's popular with anglers, who get free fishing rights to Loch Assynt, as well as several hill lochs backing onto Ben More, haunts of the infamous ferox trout. Just along the road, the Assynt Field

Centre or *Inchnadamph Lodge* (☏01571/822218, ⓦwww.inch-lodge.co.uk; ❶) has basic, comfortable bunk rooms and spacious B&B accommodation. The lodge also serves as a study resource centre for groups interested in the area's fascinating geology, fauna and flora.

The displays within the grass-roofed, unstaffed **Knockan Crag** (Creag a' Chnocain; ⓦwww.knockan-crag.co.uk) visitor centre, nine miles south of Loch Assynt on the A835 to Ullapool and part of the Inverpolly National Nature Reserve, outline why this is one of the most important geological sites in the world. In 1859, the theory of thrust faults was developed by eminent geologist James Nicol, and two interpretive **trails** (one 15min, the other 1hr) show you how to detect the movement of rock plates in the nearby cliffs. A few miles further on in the village of Knockan itself, the *Birchbank Lodge* (☏01854/666215; ❸) is an excellent base if you're planning to fish in an area renowned for its wild brown trout lochs. The proprietors can advise both fishing enthusiasts and hill-walking guests.

Kylesku and around

KYLESKU, 33 miles north of Ullapool on the main A894 road, is the point where a curvaceous road bridge sweeps over the mouth of lochs Glencoul and Glendhu. Kylesku is a small, peaceful backwater where during World War II the deep lochs provided a secret training base for the brave crews of the x-craft mini-submarines. A small, poignant memorial to the crews stands in the car park at the northern end of the Kylesku road bridge.

The congenial *Kylesku Hotel* (☏01971/502231; ❺; March–Oct) by the water's edge above the old ferry slipway, has a welcoming bar popular with locals, and serves **fresh seafood** including lobster,s langoustines, mussels and local salmon. Alternatively, *Newton Lodge* (☏01971/502070, ⓔinfo@newtonlodge .co.uk; ❺; May–Sept) is a modern, friendly and comfortable small **hotel** a mile or so up the road towards Ullapool, with superb views over the loch and a small seal colony. Self-catering accommodation is available at *Kylesku Lodges* (☏01971/502003, ⓦwww.kyleskulodges.co.uk), where three-bedroom lodges offer great views to Quinaig (coo-in-yag) mountain and out to sea.

Statesman Cruises runs entertaining **boat trips** (March–Oct twice daily except Sat; round trip 2hr; £12.50; ☏01571/844446 or 01971/502345) from the jetty below the *Kylesku Hotel* to the 650ft **Eas-Coul-Aulin**, Britain's highest waterfall, located at the head of Loch Glencoul; otters, seals, porpoises and minke whales can occasionally be spotted along the way; you can also get dropped off in the morning and/or picked up in the afternoon if you arrange it beforehand. The boat also makes regular trips out to **Kerracher Gardens** (mid-May to mid-Sept Tues, Thurs & Sun; boat departs 1pm; £12.50) which are only accessible from the sea; this remarkable west-coast garden harnesses the Gulf Stream weather to create a riot of colour and exotic vegetation in the rugged Highland scenery.

The far northwest coast

The Sutherland coastline north of Kylesku is a bridge too far for some, yet for others the stark, elemental beauty of the Highlands is to be found on the **far northwest coast** as nowhere else. Here, the peaks become more widely spaced and settlements smaller and fewer, linked by twisting single-track roads and shoreside footpaths that make excellent hiking trails. From the Kylesku bridge to the beautiful strip of sand at **Sandwood Bay**, a day's hike from Cape Wrath, the area retains an exhilarating essence of wildness. One of the few conventional tourist attractions is the simple ferry that takes folk to see the puffins of the island wildlife reserve of **Handa**. Places to stay and eat can be thin on the ground, particularly out of season, but the lack of infrastructure is testimony to the isolation which this corner of Scotland delivers in such sweeping style.

Scourie and around

Ten miles north of Kylesku, the widely scattered crofting community of **SCOURIE**, on a bluff above the main road, surrounds a beautiful sandy beach whose safe bathing has made it a popular holiday destination for families; there's plenty to do for walkers and trout anglers, too. The mobile bank visits the area on Tuesday and Thursday afternoons. Scourie itself has some good **accommodation**, including the charming *Scourie Lodge* (℡01971/502248; ❺; March–Oct), an old shooting retreat surrounded by trees on the north side of the sandy bay, with a lovely garden and its own hens and ducks; the welcoming owners do great evening meals. There's a decent **campsite** by the bay, the *Scourie Caravan and Camping Park* (℡01971/502060), with the simple *Anchorage* café bar and adjoining hotel and a small supermarket. There's also a petrol station.

Tarbet and Handa Island

Visible just offshore to the north of Scourie is **Handa Island**, a huge chunk of red Torridon sandstone surrounded by sheer cliffs, carpeted with machair and purple-tinged moorland, and teeming with seabirds. A **wildlife reserve** administered by the Scottish Wildlife Trust (ⓦwww.swt.org.uk), Handa Island supports one of the largest seabird colonies in northwest Europe. It's a real treat for ornithologists, with razorbills and guillemots breeding on its guano-splashed cliffs during summer. From late May to mid-July, large numbers of puffins waddle comically over the turf-covered clifftops where they dig their burrows. Until the mid-nineteenth century, Handa supported a thriving, if somewhat eccentric, community of crofters, who survived on a diet of fish, potatoes and seabirds. The islanders, whose ruined cottages still cling to the slopes by the jetty, devised their own system of government, with a "queen" (Handa's oldest widow) and "parliament" (a council of men who met each morning to discuss the day's business). Uprooted by the 1846 potato famine, most of the villagers eventually emigrated to Canada's Cape Breton.

Weather permitting, **boats** (℡01971/502347) leave for Handa throughout the day (Easter to Sept Mon–Sat; £8) from the tiny cove of **TARBET**, three miles northwest of the main road and accessible by postbus from Scourie, where there's a small car park and jetty. You're encouraged to make a donation towards Handa's upkeep. You'll need about three hours to follow the **footpath** around the island – an easy and enjoyable walk taking in the north shore's Great Stack rock pillar and some fine views across the Minch: a detailed route guide is featured in the SWT's free leaflet, available from the warden's office when you arrive. Camping is not allowed on the island, but the SWT is currently revamping what is a popular **bothy** for bird-watchers (reservations essential on ℡01463/714746). In Tarbet, the *Croft House* (℡01971/502098; ❶) is a comfortable little **B&B** overlooking the bay. For **food**, Tarbet's unexpected *Seafood Restaurant* (Mon–Sat noon–8pm) serves delicious, moderately priced fish and vegetarian dishes, and a good selection of home-made cakes and desserts, in its conservatory just above the jetty.

Loch Laxford to Sandwood Bay

North of Scourie, the road sweeps inland through the starkest part of the High-lands; rocks piled on rocks, bog and water create an almost alien landscape, and the astonishingly bare, stony coastline looks increasingly inhospitable. Near the road junction at **RHICHONICH** and under the shadow of **Foinaven** (2980ft), a comfortable stay can be enjoyed at the *Rhichonich Hotel* (℡01971/521224, **⑤**). The hotel has the fishing rights to the local estate and can organize deer-stalk-ing, walking and bird-watching. A mile up the road, the B801 side road branches off to **KINLOCHBERVIE**, which for all the world seems to be a typical, strag-gling West Highland crofting community with a hotel (℡01971/521275; **⑥**) – until you turn a corner and encounter an incongruously huge fish market and modern concrete harbour. Trucks from all over Europe pick up cod and shellfish from here. There's a mobile bank and petrol pump and if you're in need of sustenance, try the **fish and chips** at the *Fishermen's Mission* (closed Sat & Sun); otherwise press on towards Oldshoremore.

A single-track road continues northwest of Kinlochbervie through isolated **OLDSHOREMORE**, a working crofters' village scattered above a stunning white-sand beach, to **BLAIRMORE**, where the enlarged car park is testament to the growing number of visitors making the four-mile walk across peaty moorland to **Sandwood Bay**. After an unremarkable walk-in, the shell-white sandy **beach** at the end of the rough track is a breathtaking sight and one of the most beautiful in Scotland. Flanked by rolling dunes and lashed by fierce gales for much of the year, the dramatic leaning rock stack to the south is said to be haunted by a bearded mariner – one of many sailors to have perished on this notoriously dangerous stretch of coast since the Vikings first navigated it over a millennium ago. Around the turn of the twentieth century, the beach, whose treacherous undercurrents make it unsuitable for swimming, also witnessed Britain's most recent recorded sighting of a **mermaid**. Turning back and past Blairmore at **SHEIGRA**, where the road ends, you can camp behind the beach, whilst provisions can be bought in the small store at Oldshoremore.

△ Sandwood Bay

It's possible to trek overland from Sandwood Bay north to Cape Wrath, the most northwesterly point in mainland Britain, a full day's walk away. If you're planning to meet the Cape Wrath minibus (see p.649) to Durness, contact them first since it won't run if the weather turns bad, leaving you stranded.

The north coast

Though a constant stream of sponsored walkers, caravans and tour groups makes it to the dull town of **John O'Groats**, surprisingly few visitors travel the whole length of the Highlands' wild **north coast**. Those that do, however, rarely return disappointed. Pounded by one of the world's most ferocious seaways, Scotland's rugged northern shore is backed by barren mountains in the west, and in the east by lochs and open rolling grasslands. Between its far ends, mile upon mile of crumbling cliffs and sheer rocky headlands shelter bays whose perfect white beaches are nearly always deserted, even in the height of summer – though, somewhat incongruously, they're also home to Scotland's best surfing waves (see p.67).

Though only a wee place, **Durness** is a good jumping-off point for nearby Balnakiel beach, one of the area's most beautiful sandy strands, and for rugged **Cape Wrath**, the windswept promontory at Scotland's northwest tip, which has retained an end-of-the-world mystique lost long ago by John O'Groats. Continuing east, **Loch Eriboll** is probably the most spectacular of the north-coast sea lochs, and **Tongue**, the most picturesque of the small crofting villages. **Thurso**, the largest town on the north coast, is really only visited by those en route to Orkney. More enticing are the huge seabird colonies clustered in clefts and on remote stacks at **Dunnet Head** and **Duncansby Head**, to the east of Thurso.

Public transport around this stretch of coast can be a slow and frustrating business: Thurso, the area's main town and springboard for Orkney, is well connected by **bus** and **train** with Inverness, but further west, after the main A836 peters out into a single-track road, you have to rely on **postbus** connections.

Durness and around

Scattered around a string of sheltered sandy coves and grassy clifftops, **DURNESS** (ⓦ www.durness.org), the most northwesterly village on the British mainland, straddles the turning point on the main A838 road as it swings east from the inland peat bogs of the interior to the north coast's fertile strip of limestone machair. First settled by the Picts around 400 BC, the area has been farmed ever since, its crofters being among the few not cleared off estate land during the nineteenth century. Today, Durness is the centre for several crofting communities and an unexpectedly pleasant base for a couple of days, with some good walks.

Durness village itself sits above its own sandy bay, Sango Sands, while half a mile to the east is **SMOO**, which used to be an RAF station. In between Durness and Smoo is the millennial village hall, which features a windblown and rather forlorn community garden that harbours a memorial commemorating the Beatle

John Lennon, who used to come to Durness on family holidays as a kid (and even revisited the place in the 1960s with Yoko). It's worth pausing at Smoo to see the two hundred foot-long **Smoo Cave**, a gaping hole in a sheer limestone cliff formed partly by the action of the sea and partly by the small burn that flows through it. Tucked away at the end of a narrow sheer-sided sea cove, the main chamber is accessible via steps from the car park by the A838. The much-hyped rock formations are less memorable than the short rubber-dinghy trip you have to make in the other two caverns, where the whole experience is enlivened after wet weather by a waterfall that crashes through the middle of the cavern. **Boat trips** (May–Sept) are run on request and weather permitting by Colin Coventry (☎01971/511704).

A narrow road winds a mile or so northwest of Durness to **BALNAKIEL**, passing **Balnakiel Craft Village** en route. Disabuse yourself of any notion of quaint cottages, as the craft village is housed in a grim 1940s military base, transformed in the 1960s into a sort of industrial estate for arts and crafts, thanks to the carrot of cheap rents for studio and living quarters. It's come a long way since those idealistic days. A dozen or so workshops continue to function, including a woodwind-instrument maker, a picture framer, painters, potters and leather-workers. There's also the friendly *Loch Croispol* bookshop which runs an excellent daytime café (daily 10am–5pm, but restricted winter opening) and serves Sunday lunch (☎01971/511777, Ⓦwww.scottish-books.org).

In tiny Balnakiel itself, a seventeenth-century **ruined chapel** overlooks the remote hamlet, but a church has stood here for at least 1200 years. A skull-and-crossbones stone set in the south wall marks the grave of Donald MacMurchow, a seventeenth-century highwayman and contract killer who murdered eighteen people for his clan chief (allegedly by throwing them from the top of the Smoo Cave). The "half-in, half-out" position of his grave was apparently a compromise between his grateful employer and the local clergy, who initially refused to allow such an evil man to be buried on church ground.

Balnakiel is also known for **golf course**, whose ninth and final hole involves a well-judged drive over the Atlantic; you can rent equipment from the club-house. The white-sand beach on the east side of **Balnakiel Bay** is a stunning sight in any weather, but most spectacular on sunny days when the water turns to brilliant turquoise. For the best views, walk along the path that winds north through the dunes (pockmarked from occasional naval bombing exercises) behind it; this eventually leads to **Faraid Head** – from the Gaelic *Fear Ard* (High Fellow) – where there's a very small colony of nesting puffins (ask the tourist office for directions). The fine views east to the mouth of Loch Eriboll and west to Cape Wrath make this round walk (3–4hr) the best in the Durness area.

Practicalities

Public transport is sparse; the key service is the Dearman Coaches link (May–Sept Mon–Sat 1 daily) from Inverness via Ullapool and Lochinver. The bus has a cycle carrier. Postbuses provide a more complicated year-round alternative and meet trains at Lairg; check schedules at the post office or tourist office. The helpful Durness **tourist office** (March–Oct Mon–Sat 10am–5pm; July & Aug also Sun 10am–4pm; Nov–Feb, Mon–Fri, 10am–1.30pm) has a small **visitor centre** that features excellent interpretive panels detailing the area's history, geology, flora and fauna, with insights into the daily life of the community.

In terms of **accommodation**, ☀ *Mackays Room and Restaurant*, at the western edge of the village stands out for its welcome, tasteful Highland decor and an emphasis on freshly prepared cooking with the personal touch

(☎01971/511202, ⓦwww.visitmackays.com; ❺). The proprietor also runs the clean and popular *Lazy Crofter Bunkhouse* (☎01971/511202, ⓦwww .durnesshostel.com) next door. The village has a basic SYHA **hostel** (☎0870/004 1113, ⓦwww.syha.org.uk; March–Oct), beside the Smoo Cave car park half a mile east of the village. Of the **B&Bs**, *Puffin Cottage* (☎01971/511208, ⓦwww.puffincottage.com; April–Sept; ❶) is very pleasant. There's a **campsite** (☎01971/511222), on an exposed spot near the tourist office, with views over Sango Sands; close by is the local village **pub.** In addition to Mackays and the restaurant at Loch Eriboll's *Port-Na-Con* guesthouse (see below), the *Seafood Platter* on the outskirts of the village towards Tongue is great value, serving the freshest of seafood and succulent steaks in a small, cosy restaurant. Opposite the tourist office is Wax and Wines, a delightful shop with candles and a host of **local wines** and spirits from flowers, fruit and herbs.

Cape Wrath

An excellent day-trip from Durness begins two miles southwest of Durness at **KEOLDALE**, where (tides and MOD permitting) a foot-passenger **ferry** (daily: May & Sept 11am & 1.30pm; June–Aug 9.30am, 11am & 1.30pm; ☎01971/511376 for ferry; £7 return) crosses the spectacular Kyle of Durness estuary to link up with a **minibus** (☎01971/511343; May–Sept) that runs the eleven miles out to **Cape Wrath**, the British mainland's most northwesterly point. Note that Garvie Island (An Garbh-eilean) is an air bombing range, and the military regularly close the road to Cape Wrath, so check with Durness tourist office or the MOD advisory line (☎0800/833300). The headland takes its name not from the stormy seas that crash against it for most of the year, but from the Norse word *hvarf*, meaning "turning place" – a throwback to the days when Viking warships used it as a navigation point during raids on the Scottish coast. These days, a Stevenson lighthouse warns ships away from the treacherous rocks; looking east to Orkney and west to the Outer Hebrides, it stands above the famous **Clo Mor cliffs**, the highest sea cliffs in Britain and a prime breeding site for seabirds. You can walk from here to remote Sandwood Bay (see p.646), visible to the south, although the route, which cuts inland across lochan-dotted moorland, is hard to follow in places. Hikers generally continue south from Sandwood to the trail end at Blairmore; if you hitch or walk the six miles from here to Kinlochbervie you can, with careful planning, catch a bus back to Durness.

Loch Eriboll

The road east of Durness passes several spectacular sandy bays en route to deep and sheltered **Loch Eriboll**, the north coast's most spectacular sea loch, ringed by ghost-like limestone mountains. Servicemen stationed here during World War II to protect passing Russian convoys nicknamed it "Loch 'Orrible", but if you're looking for somewhere wild and unspoilt, you'll find this a perfect spot. Porpoises and otters are a common sight along the rocky shore, and minke whales occasionally swim in from the open sea.

Overlooking its own landing stage at the water's edge, *Port-Na-Con* (☎01971/511367; Feb–Oct, otherwise by arrangement; ❷), seven miles from Durness on the west side of the loch, is a wonderful **B&B**. Top-notch food is served in its small **restaurant** (open all year), with a choice of vegetarian haggis, local kippers, fruit compote and home-made croissants for breakfast, and adventurous three-course evening meals for around £14; the menu always includes a gourmet vegetarian dish. Non-residents are welcome, although you'll need to book.

Tongue to Thurso

There's great drama in the landscape between Tongue and Thurso, as the A836 – still single-track for much of the way – wends its way over bleak and often totally uninhabited rocky moorland, intercut with sandy sea lochs. Tiny little **Tongue** is pleasant enough, as is the equally small settlement of **Bettyhill**, to the east, but the real reason to venture this far is to explore the countryside: **Ben Hope** (3040ft), the most northerly Munro, and the fascinating blanket bog of the **Flow Country** even further inland.

Tongue and around

The road takes a wonderfully slow and circuitous route around Loch Eriboll and east over the top of A' Mhoine moor to the pretty crofting township of **TONGUE**. Dominated by the ruins of **Castle Varrich** (Caisteal Bharraich), a medieval stronghold of the Mackays (three-mile return walk), the village is strewn above the east shore of the **Kyle of Tongue**, which you can cross either via a new causeway, or by following the longer and more scenic single-track road around its southern side. When the tide recedes, this shallow estuary becomes a mass of golden sand flats, superb on sunny days, with the sharp profiles of **Ben Hope** (3040ft) and **Ben Loyal** (2509ft) looming like twin sentinels to the south, and the Rabbit Islands a short way out to sea. Tongue's relatively temperate maritime climate even allows it to claim Britain's most northerly palm tree.

The best **accommodation** in Tongue is the *Tongue Hotel* (☎01847/611206, ⒲www.tonguehotel.co.uk; April–Oct; ❻), the plush former hunting lodge of the Duke of Sutherland, which serves delicious food and has a cosy downstairs bar. Close by is the modern *Ben Loyal Hotel* and the modest *Tigh-Nan-Ubhal* guesthouse (☎01847/611281; ❸). A half-mile south of the post office, a comfortable stay can be had at the *Rhian* guesthouse (☎01847/611257, ⒲www.rhiancottage .co.uk; ❸). The SYHA **hostel** (⒲www.syha.org.uk), right beside the causeway a mile north of the village centre on the Kyle's east shore is currently closed but expected to reopen in 2006.

Over on the western side of the Kyle, five miles away at **TALMINE**, a converted nineteenth-century church with great views out towards the Orkney Islands is the home of the popular *Cloisters* B&B (☎01847/601286, ⒲www .cloistertal.demon.co.uk; ❷). There is also a very basic **campsite** opposite the sandy beach.

Three miles east of Tongue sits the delightful and friendly *Strathtongue Old Manse* B&B (☎01847/611252, ⒲www.strathtongue.co.uk; ❸).

Bettyhill and around

Twelve miles east of Tongue, **BETTYHILL** is a major crofting village, set among rocky green hills. In Gaelic, it was known as *Am Blàran Odhar* (Little Dun-coloured Field), but the origins of the English name are unknown; however, it was definitely not named after Elizabeth, Countess of Sutherland, who presided over the Strathnaver Clearances. The story of those terrible times is told by local schoolchildren at the delightful and loyally maintained **Strathnaver Museum** (April–Oct, Mon–Sat 10am–1pm & 2–5pm; £1.90), housed in the old Farr church, set apart from the main village. Inside, you can see some Pictish stones and a 3800-year-old early Bronze Age beaker. In the churchyard that lies to the west of the church, stands the mysterious **Farr Stone**, a six-foot-high Pictish cross decorated with intricate interlacing and dating from around 800. The 24-mile Strathnaver Trail, running south from Bettyhill along the B873 to Altnaharra, highlights numerous historical sites from the Neolithic, Bronze and Iron Age periods.

A short stroll north of the church is the splendid sheltered **Farr beach**, which forms an unbroken arc of pure white sand between the Naver and Borgie rivers. Even more visually impressive is the River Naver's narrow tidal estuary, to the west of Bettyhill, and **Torrisdale beach** (popular with surfers; access off the road to Borgie five miles west of Bettyhill), which ends in a smooth white spit that forms part of the **Invernaver Nature Reserve**. During summer, arctic terns nest here on the riverbanks, which are dotted with clumps of rare Scottish primroses, and you stand a good chance of spotting an otter or two.

At the eastern end of Bettyhill, in the museum car park, the small **tourist office** (April–May & Sept–Oct Mon–Sat 10.30am–5pm; June, July & Aug daily 10.30am–5pm plus 8pm Fri & Sat) also runs *Elizabeth's Café*, a decent eating option. Nearby, the *Farr Bay Inn*, known locally as the "FBI" also serves good meals. The *Bettyhill Hotel* (℡01641/521352; ❷) provides good-value accommodation and bar meals whilst 100yd further east, *Dunveaden Guest House* (℡01641/521273; ❷) can organize fishing for guests. Bettyhill's large campsite affords excellent views over the bay. The most bizarre sight is a road sign proclaiming the village store to be "open 8 days per week". Sheltered in woods four or five miles west of Bettyhill, the *Borgie Lodge Hotel* (℡01641/521332, ⓦ www.borgielodgehotel.co.uk; ❻; Feb–Nov) is an upmarket base that's popular for salmon- and sea-fishing and boasts an excellent restaurant.

Melvich and Dounreay

As you move east from Bettyhill, the north coast changes dramatically as the hills on the horizon recede to be replaced by fields fringed with flagstone walls. At the hamlet of **MELVICH**, twelve miles east of Bettyhill, the A897 cuts south through Strath Halladale, the Flow Country (see p.652) and the Strath of Kildonan to Helmsdale on the east coast (see p.667). Melvich has some good **accommodation**, notably the wonderfully hospitable *Sheiling Guesthouse* (℡01641/531256, ⓦ www.thesheiling.co.uk; May–Sept; ❹) by the main road, whose impressive breakfasts feature locally smoked haddock and fresh herring. Good bar meals are on offer at the *Halladale Inn*, half-a-mile further east whilst the slightly run-down *Melvich Hotel* brews "Fast Reactor" ale on its premises. The *Strathy Inn* in Strathy is another good food stop on this stretch.

Five miles further east of Melvich, golfers can enjoy a round at Reay before continuing on the A836 past **Dounreay Nuclear Power Station** (ⓦ www .ukaea.org.uk/dounreay), a surreal collection of chimney stacks and box-like buildings, plus the famous golf-ball-shaped DFR (Dounreay Fast Reactor). Established back in 1955, Dounreay pioneered the development of fast reactor technology and was the first reactor in the world to provide mains electricity. The reactors themselves have long since closed, though Dounreay remains by the far the biggest employer on the north coast, with decommissioning estimated to take another 30 years at a cost of £2.7 billion. In recent years, an oyster-catcher has created its nest (May–June) outside the tiny teabar beside the helpful **visitor centre** (Easter to end Oct daily 10am–4pm; free). The centre details the processes (and, unsurprisingly, the benefits) of nuclear power, and seeks to offer explanations for a range of issues such as the area's "leukaemia cluster" (allegedly not connected with radiation), and the radioactive particles that continue to be found on the nearby beaches. A more green activity can be enjoyed walking along the short Achvarasdal woodland trail, half a mile south of Reay.

The Flow Country

From Melvich, you can head forty miles or so south towards Helmsdale on the A897, through the **Flow Country**, whose name comes from *flói*, an Old Norse word meaning "marshy ground". This huge expanse of "blanket bog" is a valuable "carbon sink" and home to a wide variety of wildlife. At the train station at **FORSINARD**, fourteen miles south of Melvich and easily accessible from Thurso, Wick and the south by train, there is an RSPB **visitor centre** (April–Oct daily 9am–6pm; ☎01641/571225), with CCTV coverage of hen harriers nesting, and also a **Peatland Centre**, which explains the wonders of peat. To get to grips with the whole concept of blanket bog, take a leaflet and follow the short **Dubh Lochan Trail** that's been laid out over the flagstones, through peat banks to some nearby black lochans. En route, you get to see bog asphodel, bogbean, sphagnum moss and the insect-trapping sundew and butterwort; you've also got a good chance of seeing greenshanks, golden plovers and hen harriers. There are also regular guided walks through the area from the visitor centre. The *Forsinard Hotel* (closed Feb), opposite the station, is popular with anglers and does standard **bar food**, but Sue Grimshaw's **B&B** (☎01641/571262; ❷), described by one guest as "heaven on earth", offers guests a comfortable stay and three-course evening meals made with local produce.

Thurso

Approached from the isolation of the west, **THURSO** feels like a metropolis. In reality, it's a relatively small service centre visited mostly by people passing through to the adjoining port of **Scrabster** to catch the ferry to Orkney or by increasing numbers of surfers attracted to the waves on the north coast. The birthplace in 1854 of William Smith, founder of the international Boys' Brigade, the town's name derives from the Norse word *Thorsa*, literally "River of the God Thor", and in Viking times this was a major gateway to the mainland. Later, ships set sail from here for the Baltic and Scandinavian ports loaded with meal, beef, hides and fish. Much of the town, however, dates from the 1790s, when Sir John Sinclair built a large new extension to the old fishing port. The nearby Dounreay Nuclear Power Station ensured continuing prosperity after World War II, tripling the population when workers from the plant (dubbed "atomics" by the locals) settled in Thurso.

Thurso's grid-plan streets boast some rather handsome Victorian architecture in the local, greyish sandstone, though there's nothing really specific to detain you. **Traill Street** is the main drag, turning into the pedestrianized Rotterdam Street and High Street precinct at its northern end. On the High Street, by the side of the old Victorian town hall, is **Thurso Heritage Museum** (June–Sept Mon–Sat 10am–1pm, 2–5pm; £1) whose most intriguing exhibits are the Ulbster Stone in the entrance, which features elephants, fish and other beasts, and the Skinnet Stone, intricately carved with enigmatic symbols and a runic cross. If you continue north up the High Street, you'll reach **Old St Peter's Church**, a substantial ruin with origins in the thirteenth century, and the old part of town, near the harbour.

Practicalities

Trains from Inverness (all of which go via Wick) arrive at Thurso **train station**, adjacent to the **bus station**, both a ten-minute walk down Princes Street and Sir George's Street to the helpful riverside **tourist office** (April–May & Oct Mon–Sat 10am–5pm; June–Sept Mon–Sat 10am–5pm, Sun 10am–4pm; closed Nov–Easter). The **Scrabster ferry terminal** is a mile or so northwest of town, with regular buses from the train station in the morning, and from Olrig Street in the afternoon. For more on **ferries to Orkney** from Scrabster, Gills Bay and John O' Groats, see p.670. Note that ferry tickets cannot be booked at the tourist office.

Thurso is well stocked with **accommodation**, including several **hostels**, the best of which is *Sandra's*, 24/26 Princes St (℡01847/894575, Ⓦwww .sandras-backpackers.ukf.net), a refurbished, clean and well-run place owned by the popular chippie downstairs. They also offer **bike rental** (£14) and **Internet** access. Aside from the upmarket *Forss Country House Hotel* (℡01847/861201; ❻), three miles west of Thurso on the A836, the *Royal Hotel* (℡01847/893191, Ⓦwww.british-trust-hotels.com; ❺) on Traill Street is among several comfortable and central hotels. Of the **B&Bs**, *Murray House*, 1 Campbell St (℡01847/895759, Ⓦwww.murrayhousebb.com; ❷), is central, comfortable and friendly; there's also *Tigh na Abhainn*, an old house by the river (℡01847/893443; ❷), or the long-established *Orcadia*, 27 Olrig St (℡01847/894395; ❶). The nearest **campsite** (℡01847/805503) sits out towards Scrabster alongside the main road, though there's a much nicer one at Dunnet Bay, a few miles east (see below).

By far the best place **to eat** in Thurso is the popular *Le Bistro*, 2 Traill St (℡01847/893737; Tues–Sat), where the reasonably priced menu includes traditional fare such as cullen skink soup. For fresh seafood, head for Scrabster and *The Captain's Galley* but if you're cooking your own supper there's a decent fishmonger and a bakery in Thurso's Rotterdam Street. Across from *Le Bistro*, the younger crowd may prefer a coffee at *Café Cardosi* or a pint in the *Central*, on Traill Street and there's always *Skinnandi's Nightclub* on Sir George's Street (Thurs–Sun). Thurso also has its very own entertainment complex, the *All St@r Factory*, down the Ormlie Road beyond the train station, with a two-screen **cinema**, a ten-pin bowling alley and a popular "night spot".

If you're coming to **surf**, Andy Bain of Thurso Surf offers surf lessons and advice (℡01847/831866, Ⓦwww.thursosurf.com; April–Sept) or you can try Tempest Surf (℡01847/892500) on Riverside Road.

Dunnet Head and the Castle of Mey

Thurso doesn't have much of a beach, so if you want to sink your toes into sand, head five miles east along the A836 to **Dunnet Bay**, a vast golden beach backed by huge dunes. The bay is popular with surfers, and even in the winter you can usually spot intrepid figures far out in the Pentland Firth's breakers. At the northeast end of the bay, there's a **Ranger Centre** (April–Sept Tues–Fri & Sun 2–5pm) beside the excellent campsite, where you can pick up information on good local history and nature walks, including a short self-guided trail into nearby **Dunnet Forest**, a failed plantation which has been left to go – literally – to seed, allowing a rich range of plant and animal life to thrive. To the north of the bay is the small village of **Dunnet**, where it's worth stopping in at **Mary-Ann's Cottage** (June–Sept Tues–Sun 2–4.30pm; £2), a farming croft vacated in 1990 by 93-year-old Mary-Ann Calder, whose grandfather had built the cottage, and maintained just as she left it, full of reminders of the three generations who lived and worked there over the last 150 years.

Despite the publicity that John O'Groats customarily receives, mainland Britain's most northerly point is in fact **Dunnet Head**, north of Dunnet along the B855, which runs for four miles over bleak heather and bog to the tip of the headland, crowned with a Stevenson lighthouse. At 345ft above sea level, stones hurled up from the sea have been known to break its windows. In early summer, puffins may be spotted on the impressive red cliffs whilst seals bathe off rocks below the weirdly eroded rock stacks. On a clear day you can see the whole northern coastline from Cape Wrath to Duncansby Head, and across the treacherous **Pentland Firth** to Orkney. In Brough, en route to the lighthouse, there's a small tearoom in the *Dunnet Head Educational Trust* (Easter–Sept 11am–5pm, closed Wed; ☎01847/851991, ⓦwww.dunnethead.com). Aside from information on the areas archeology, wildlife and transport links, behind the cottage a path leads to a seal-viewing area. Next door is *Windhaven Cottage* **B&B** (☎01847/851774; Easter–Sept; ❷).

Roughly fifteen miles east of Thurso, just off the A836, lies the late Queen Mother's former Scottish home and the most northerly castle on the UK mainland: the **Castle of Mey** (May to end July & mid-Aug to end Sept; Sat–Thurs 10.30am–4pm; ⓦwww.castleofmey.org.uk; £7). It's a modest little place, hidden behind high flagstone walls, with great views north to Orkney and a herd of the Queen Mum's beloved Aberdeen Angus grazing out front. The original castle was a sixteenth-century Z-plan affair, owned by the earls of Caithness until 1889, and bought in a state of disrepair the year her husband, George VI died. The Queen Mum used to spend every August here, and unusually for a royal palace, it's remarkably unstuffy inside, the walls hung with works by local amateur artists (and watercolours by Prince Charles), the sideboards cluttered with tacky joke ornaments and the video library well stocked with copies of *Fawlty Towers* and *Dad's Army*.

John O'Groats and around

Romantics expecting to find a magical meeting of land and water at **JOHN O'GROATS** (ⓦwww.visitjohnogroats.com) are invariably disappointed – sadly it remains an uninspiring tourist trap. The views north to Orkney are fine enough, but the village offers little more than a string of souvenir and craft shops and several refreshment stops thronged with coach parties. The village gets its name from the Dutchman, Jan de Groot, who obtained the ferry contract for the hazardous crossing to Orkney in 1496. The eight-sided house he built for his eight quarrelling sons (so that each one could enter by his own door) is echoed in the octagonal tower of the much-photographed but neglected *John O'Groats Hotel*. Aside from regular **buses** to Wick and Thurso, there are frequent if irregular links with Land's End (the far southwest tip of England), maintained by a succession of walkers, cyclists, vintage-car drivers and pushers of baths.

The **tourist office** (daily: May & Oct 10am–5pm; June 9.30am–6pm; July–Aug 9am–7pm; Sept 9am–6pm) is by the car park. One of the best **B&Bs** in the area is *Bencorragh House* (☎01955/611449, ⓦwww.bencorraghhouse.com; March–Oct; ❷), which has very pleasant farmhouse accommodation and spectacular views at Upper Gills near Canisbay, three miles southwest of John O'Groats. The small SYHA **hostel** (☎0870/004 1129, ⓦwww.syha.org.uk; April–Sept) is in Canisbay itself. Of the two local **campsites**, *Stroma View* (☎01955/611313; March–Sept), one mile along the Thurso road, is less exposed than the windswept but well-equipped John O'Groats campsite (☎01955/611323). There are several **boat trips** to be had: John O'Groats Ferries (☎01955/611353, ⓦwww .jogferry.co.uk) offers a leisurely afternoon cruise, which will take you round the seabird colonies and stacks of Duncansby Head or the seal colonies of Stroma (mid-June to Aug daily 2.30pm ; 1hr 30min; £14); North Coast Marine Adventures (Easter to Oct daily; ☎01955/611797, ⓦwww.northcoast-marine-adventures.co.uk) offers rather more high-adrenalin 30-minute trips in a rigid-inflatable (£13) and a one-hour wildlife scenic tour (£16).

If you're disappointed by John O'Groats, press on a couple of miles further east to **Duncansby Head**, which, with its lighthouse, dramatic cliffs and well-worn coastal path, has a lot more to offer. The birdlife here is prolific, and south of the headland lie some spectacular 200ft cliffs, cut by sheer-sided clefts known locally as *geos*, and several impressive sea stacks, including a very photogenic triangular one.

The east coast

The **east coast** of the Highlands, between Inverness and Wick, is nowhere near as spectacular as the west, with gently undulating moors, grassland and low cliffs where you might otherwise expect to find sea lochs and mountains. Washed by the cold waters of the North Sea, it's markedly cooler, too, although less prone to spells of permadrizzle and midges.

While many visitors speed up the main A9 road through this region in a head-long rush to the Orkneys' prehistoric sites, those who choose to dally will find a wealth of brochs, cairns and standing stones, many in remarkable condition. The area around the Black Isle and the Tain was a Pictish heartland, and has yielded many important finds. Further north, from around the ninth century AD onwards, the **Norse** influence was more keenly felt than in any other part of mainland Britain, and dozens of Scandinavian-sounding names recall the era when this was a Viking kingdom.

Culturally and scenically, much of the east coast is more lowland than highland, and Caithness in particular evolved more or less separately from the Highlands, avoiding the bloody tribal feuds that wrought such havoc further south and west. Later, however, the nineteenth-century **Clearances** hit the region hard, as countless ruined cottages and empty glens show. To make way for sheep, hundreds of thousands of crofters were evicted and forced to emigrate to New Zealand, Canada and Australia, or else take up fishing in one of the numerous herring ports established on the coast. The fishing heritage is a recurring theme along this coast, though there are only a handful of working boats scattered around the harbours today, and while oil boom has brought a transient prosperity to one or two places over the past few decades, the area remains one of the country's poorest, reliant on relatively thin pickings from sheep farming, fishing and tourism.

The one stretch of the east coast that's always been relatively rich is the **Black Isle** just over the Kessock Bridge heading north out of Inverness, whose main village, **Cromarty**, is the region's undisputed highlight, with a crop of elegant mansions and appealing fishermen's cottages clustered near the entrance to the Cromarty Firth. In late medieval times, pilgrims, including James IV of Scotland, poured through here en route to the red sandstone town of **Tain** to worship at the shrine of St Duthus, where the former sacred enclave has now been converted into one of the many "heritage centres" that punctuate the route north. Beyond **Dornoch**, a renowned golfing resort recently famous as the site of Madonna's wedding, the ersatz-Loire château **Dunrobin Castle** is the main tourist attraction, a monument as much to the iniquities of the Clearances as to the eccentricity of Victorian taste. The award-winning **Timespan Heritage Centre**, further north at Helmsdale recounts the human cost of the landlords' greed, while the area around the port of **Lybster** is littered with the remains of more ancient civilizations. **Wick**, the largest town on this section of coast, has an interesting past inevitably entwined with the fishing industry, whose story is told in another good heritage centre, but is otherwise uninspiring. The relatively flat landscapes of this northeast corner – windswept peat bog and farmland dotted with lochans and grey-and-white crofts – are a surprising contrast to the more rugged country south and west of here.

The Black Isle and around

Sandwiched between the Cromarty Firth to the north and, to the south, the Moray and Beauly firths which separate it from Inverness, the **Black Isle** is not an island at all, but a fertile peninsula whose rolling hills, prosperous farms and stands of deciduous woodland make it more reminiscent of Dorset or Sussex than the Highlands. It probably gained its name because of its mild climate: there's rarely frost, which leaves the fields "black" all winter; another explanation is that the name derives from the Gaelic word for black, *dubh* – a possible corruption of St Duthus (see p.660).

The Black Isle is littered with dozens of **prehistoric sites**, but the main incentive to make the detour east from the A9 is to visit the picturesque eighteenth-century town of **Cromarty**, huddled at the northeast tip of the peninsula. A string of villages along the south coast is also worth stopping off in en route, and one of them, Rosemarkie, has an outstanding small **museum** devoted to Pictish culture. Nearby Chanonry Point is among the best **dolphin-spotting** sites in Europe.

The southern Black Isle

Just across the Kessock Bridge from Inverness is a roadside lay-by which hosts a **tourist office** (Easter–Oct Mon–Sat 10am–5pm, Sun 10am–4pm; July & Aug Mon–Sat until 6pm; ☎01463/731505), as well as a small **dolphin and seal centre** (June–Sept daily 9.30am–4.30pm; free), which offers the chance to observe (and listen to) these popular creatures.

The most rewarding approach to Cromarty is along the south side of the Black Isle on the A832, which passes a **clootie well** just north of Munlochy, where a colourful, if somewhat motley, collection of rags has been hung on overhanging branches to bring luck and health. Ailing children used to be left here alone overnight in hopes of a miracle cure. Just south of Munlochy, kids not yet abandoned by their parents will enjoy the Black Isle Wildlife and Country Park (April–Oct daily 10am–6pm; £4), while the simple farm steading premises of the nearby **Black Isle Brewery** produces tasty organic ales and lager (tours Mon–Sat 10am–6pm, April–Oct also Sun 11.30am–5.30pm; free).

Fortrose and Rosemarkie

FORTROSE, six miles east of Munlochy, is a quietly elegant village dominated by the beautiful ruins of an early thirteenth-century **cathedral** (daily 9am–8pm; free access). Founded by King David I, it now languishes on a lovely green bordered by red sandstone and colourwashed houses, where a horde of gold coins dating from the time of Robert III was unearthed in 1880. There's

⑬

A memorial plaque in Fortrose remembers the seventeenth-century visionary **Cùin-neach Odhar** (Kenneth MacKenzie), known as the Brahan Seer, who was born at Uig on Skye and lived and worked on the estate of the count and countess of Sea-forth. Legend has it that he derived his powers of second sight from a small white divination stone passed on to him, through his mother, from a Viking princess. With the pebble pressed against his eye, Cùinneach foretold everything from outbreaks of measles in the village to the building of the Caledonian Canal, the Clearances and World War II. His visions brought him widespread fame, but also resulted in his untimely death. In 1660, Countess Seaforth, wife of the local laird, summoned the seer after her husband was late home from a trip to France. Reluctantly – when pressurized – he told the Countess that he had seen the earl "on his knees before a fair lady, his arm round her waist and her hand pressed to his lips". At this, she flew into a rage, accused him of sullying the family name and ordered him to be thrown head first into a barrel of boiling tar. However, just before the gruesome execution, which took place near Brahan Castle on Chanonry Point, Cùinneach made his last prediction: when a deaf and dumb earl inherited the estate, the Seaforth line would end. His prediction finally came true in 1815 when the last earl died.

also a memorial to the Seaforth family, whose demise the Brahan Seer famously predicted (see box above).

There's a memorial plaque to the seer at nearby **Chanonry Point**, reached by a backroad from the north end of Fortrose; the thirteenth hole of the golf course here marks the spot where he met his death. Jutting into a narrow channel in the Moray Firth (deepened to allow warships into the estuary during World War II), the point, fringed on one side by a beach of golden sand and shingle, is an excellent place to look for **dolphins** (see box on p.604). Come here when the tide is rising and you stand the best chance of spotting a couple leaping through the surf in search of fish brought to the surface by converging currents.

ROSEMARKIE, a lovely one-street village a mile north of Fortrose at the opposite (northwest) end of the beach, is thought to have been evangelized by St Boniface in the early eighth century. The cosy **Groam House Museum** (May–Sept Mon–Sat 10am–5pm, Sun 2–4.30pm; Oct–April Sat & Sun 2–4pm; free), at the bottom of the village, displays a bumper crop of intricately carved Pictish standing stones (among them the famous Rosemarkie Cross Slab), and shows an informative video highlighting Pictish sites in the region. A lovely mile-and-a-half **woodland walk**, along the banks of a sparkling burn to Fairy Glen, begins at the car park just beyond the village on the road to Cromarty. Good **bar food** in this area is available at the *Plough Inn*, just down the main street from the museum in Rosemarkie, or at *The Anderson* (☎01381/620236, ⓦwww.theanderson.co.uk), a pleasantly individual hotel just around the corner from the cathedral in Fortrose.

Cromarty

An ancient legend recalls that the twin headlands flanking the entrance to the **Cromarty Firth**, known as The Sutors (from the Gaelic word for shoemaker), were once a pair of giant cobblers who used to protect the Black Isle from pirates. Nowadays, however, the only giants in the area are Nigg and Invergordon's colossal oil rigs, marooned in the estuary like metal monsters marching out to sea. Built and serviced here for the Forties oil field in the North Sea, they form a surreal counterpoint to the web of tiny streets and chocolate-box workers' cottages of **CROMARTY**, the Black Isle's main settlement. The town, an ancient ferry crossing-point on the pilgrimage trail to St Duthus's shrine in Tain, lost much of its trade during the nineteenth century to places served by the railway; a branch line to the town was begun but never completed. Although a royal burgh since the fourth century, Cromarty didn't became a prominent port until 1772 when the entrepreneurial local landlord, George Ross, founded a hemp mill here, fuelling a period of prosperity during which Cromarty acquired some of Scotland's finest Georgian houses; these, together with the terraced fishers' cottages of the nineteenth-century herring boom, have left the town with a wonderfully well-preserved concentration of Scottish domestic architecture.

To get a sense of Cromarty's past, wander through the town's pretty streets to the **museum** housed in the old **Courthouse** on Church Street (daily: April–Oct 10am–5pm; Nov–Dec noon–4pm; £3.50), which tells the history of the town using audiovisuals and animated figures, including one of Sir Thomas Urquhart, an eccentric local laird who traced his ancestry back to Adam and Eve, and reportedly died laughing on hearing of the restoration of Charles II. You are also issued with an audio handset and a map for a walking tour around the town. **Hugh Miller**, a nineteenth-century stonemason turned author, geologist, folklorist and Free Church campaigner, was born in Cromarty, and his **birthplace** (Easter–Sept daily noon–5pm; Oct Sun–Wed noon–5pm; NTS; £5), a modest thatched cottage on Church Street, has been restored to give an idea of what Cromarty must have been like in his day.

Dolphin- and other wildlife-spotting trips are offered locally by *Ecoventures* (℡01381/600323, ⍈www.ecoventures.co.uk), who blast out through the Sutors to the Moray Firth in a powerful RIB. The tiny two-car **Nigg–Cromarty ferry** (June–Oct daily 8am–6.15pm), Scotland's smallest, also doubles up as a cruiser on Wednesday evenings in summer; you can catch it from the jetty near the lighthouse.

Practicalities

Nine **buses** a day run to Cromarty from Inverness (55min), returning from the car park at the bottom of Forsyth Place. During summer, **accommodation** is in short supply. Most upmarket is the traditional *Royal Hotel* (℡01381/600217, ⍈www.royalcromartyhotel.co.uk; ❹), down at the harbour, which has rather small but richly furnished rooms overlooking the Firth. For **B&B**, try one of the attractive old houses on Church Street, such as Mrs Robinson's at no. 7 (℡01381/600488; ❶), where you can also **rent bikes**. A little way out of the town in the direction of Dingwall, *Newfield B&B* (℡01381/610325, ⍈www .newfield-bb.co.uk; ❷) is also a pleasant option.

For something **to eat**, there are few more down-to-earth but satisfying restaurants in the Highlands than ⅛ *Sutor Creek* at 21 Bank St (℡01381/600855, ⍈www.sutorcreek.co.uk; closed Mon–Wed in winter). A small but friendly place run as a local cooperative, it serves delicious fresh pizza cooked in a wood-fired oven, though the imaginative toppings (and the daily blackboard specials) are local and seasonal rather than conventionally Italian.

Dingwall and the Cromarty Firth

Most traffic nowadays takes the upgraded A9 north from Inverness, bypassing the small market town of **DINGWALL** (from the Norse *thing*, "parliament", and *vollr*, "field"), a royal burgh since 1226 and former port that was left high and dry when the river receded during the nineteenth century. Today, it has succumbed to the curse of British provincial towns and acquired an ugly business park and characterless pedestrian shopping street. Dingwall's only real claim to fame is that it was the birthplace of Macbeth, whose family occupied the now ruined castle on Castle Street. You're unlikely to want to hang around here for long – for somewhere pleasant to stay move onto Strathpeffer or push on north.

Northeast of Dingwall, the **Cromarty Firth** has always been recognized as a perfect natural harbour. During World War I it was a major **naval base**, and today its sheltered waters are used as a centre for repairing North Sea oil rigs. The A862 road from Dingwall rejoins the A9 just after the main road crosses the firth on a long causeway; a few miles further along, look out for the extraordinary edifice on the hill behind **EVANTON**. This is the **Fyrish Monument**, built by a certain Sir Hector Munro, partly to give employment to the area and partly to commemorate his own capture of the Indian town of Seringapatam in 1781 – hence the design, resembling an Indian gateway. If you want to get a close-up look, it's a tough two-hour walk through pine woods to the top. An easier, but no less dramatic walk from the village, is to follow the Allt Graad river to the mile-long **Black Rock** gorge, an unexpected chasm which is a giddy 100ft deep in places but only 12–15ft wide. The best approach to the gorge is a half-hour walk along a track which leaves from *Black Rock Caravan Park*, set in a peaceful grassy glen, where there's also a simple but neat bunkhouse (℡01349/830917, ⊛www.blackrockscotland.co.uk).

Strathpeffer

STRATHPEFFER, a mannered and leafy Victorian spa town surrounded by wooded hills four miles west of Dingwall, is pleasant enough but does suffer from a high density of coach parties. During its heyday, this was a renowned European **health resort** reached by the tongue-twisting Strathpeffer Spa Express train from Aviemore. A recent face-lift has seen the town's attractive grand pavilion transformed into a performing arts centre, the Strathpeffer Pavilion (⊛www.strathpefferpavilion.org), and the nearby **Pump Room** (March–Oct Mon–Sat 10am–6pm, Sun 2–5pm; £2) converted into a visitor centre, where displays and videos tell the history of the resort and you can sample water from five different local wells which were supposed to treat all manner of ailments – most of today's visitors, however, find the sulphurous-smelling liquid more masochistic than medicinal.

Also making the most of the Victorian theme is the **Highland Museum of Childhood** (April–Oct Mon–Sat 10am–5pm, Sun 2–5pm; £2), located at the restored Victorian train station half a mile east of the main square. The museum looks at growing up in the Highlands, from home- and school-life to folklore and festivals, with some well-displayed photographs, display cabinets with toys and games and a colourful series of commissioned murals. In other parts of the station are a pleasant café and craft workshops.

Strathpeffer is within striking distance of the bleak **Ben Wyvis**, and so is also a popular base for walkers. One of the best hikes in the area is up the hill of Cnoc Mor, where the vitrified Iron Age hill fort of **Knock Farrel** affords superb panoramic views to the Cromarty Firth and the surrounding mountains.

Buses run regularly between Dingwall and Strathpeffer (11 daily Mon–Sat), dropping passengers in the square. **Tourist information** is available in the front section of Pump Room (see above for opening hours). The large **hotels** in the village are very popular with bus tours, so try one of the smaller places such as *Brunstane Lodge* (℡01997/421261, ⊛www.brunstanelodge.com; ❺); there's also **B&B** at the upmarket *Craigvar* (℡01997/421622, Ⓦwww.craigvar.com; ❹), which overlooks the square, or the hospitable and spacious *Dunraven Lodge* on Golf Course Road (℡01997/421210, wwww.dunravenlodge.co.uk; ❸). For **food**, cheap bar meals can be had at the *Strathpeffer Hotel*, while the *Richmond Hotel* offers similar fare. Anyone with a sweet tooth might enjoy paying a visit to *Mya* on Main Street, just across from the Pump Room, an attractive café (closed Sun & Mon) and artisan chocolate factory with a viewing window through to the production area where you can sometimes see the Belgian proprietor at work. There's also an excellent **bike** shop right on the Square, called *Square Wheels* (℡01997/421000, Ⓦwww.squarewheels.biz; closed Tues) which rents out bikes and offers good advice on some enjoyable local routes.

The Dornoch Firth and around

North of the Cromarty Firth, the hammer-shaped **Fearn peninsula** can still be approached from the south by the ancient ferry crossing from Cromarty to Nigg, though to the north the link is a more recent causeway over the **Dornoch Firth**, the inlet which marks the northern boundary of the peninsula. On the southern edge of the Dornoch Firth the A9 bypasses the quiet town of **Tain**, probably best known as the home of Glenmorangie whisky. Inland, at the head of the firth, there's not much to the village of **Bonar Bridge**, but fans of unusual hostels travel from far and wide to spend a night with the ghosts at the duchess of Sutherland's imposing former home, **Carbisdale Castle**. Further inland, the rather lonely village of **Lairg** is a connection point between west and east coasts, with roads spearing through the glens from northwest Sutherland and the railway making a laboured detour in from the east coast. Back on the coast, on the north side of the Dornoch Firth, the neat town of **Dornoch** itself, long known for its impressive cathedral and well-manicured golf courses, found renewed fame in 2000 as the venue for an outbreak of Madonna-mania, when it hosted the pop star's wedding to Guy Ritchie.

Tain

The peninsula's largest settlement is **TAIN**, an attractive if old-fashioned small town of grand whisky-coloured sandstone buildings that was the birthplace of **St Duthus**, an eleventh-century missionary who inspired great devotion in the Middle Ages. His miracle-working relics were enshrined in a sanctuary here in the eleventh century, and in 1360 St Duthus Collegiate Church was built, visited annually by James IV, who usually arrived here fresh from the arms of his mistress, Janet Kennedy, whom he had conveniently installed in nearby Moray. A good place to get to grips with the peninsula's past is the **Tain Through Time** exhibition (April–Oct Mon–Sat 10am–5pm, July & Aug till 6pm; £3.50), which makes creative use of three old buildings around the church and grave-yard, leading you round using an audioguide. The ticket price also includes a walking tour of the town and neighbouring **museum** on Castle Brae (just off the High St), housing an interesting display of the much-sought-after work of the Tain silversmiths, along with mediocre archeological finds and clan memo-rabilia. There's not a great deal more to see in the centre of Tain, but check out the High Street's castellated eighteenth-century **Tolbooth**, with its stone turrets and old curfew bell. Tain's other main attraction is the **Glenmorangie whisky distillery** where the highly rated malt is produced (℡01862/892477; shop Mon–Fri 9am–5pm, April–Oct also Sat 10am–4pm, June–Aug also Sun noon–4pm; tours Mon–Fri 10.30am–3.30pm, Sat 10.30am–2.30pm, Sun 12.30–2.30pm; £2.50 including discount voucher); it lies beside the A9 on the north side of town. Booking is recommended for the tours.

For **accommodation**, the *Carnegie Lodge Hotel* (℡01862/894039, Ⓦwww .carnegiehotel.co.uk; ❹) on Viewfield Road, tucked away behind a housing estate on the west side of the A9 from the main part of Tain, looks and feels a bit like a golf clubhouse but offers decent and reasonably priced rooms. The more modest *Golf View House* (℡01862/892856, Ⓦwww.golf-view.co.uk; Feb–Nov; ❸), three minutes' drive south of the town centre on Knockbreck Road, offers comfortable B&B, as does *Carringtons*, Morangie Road (℡01862/892635, wwww.stelogic.com/carringtons; ❷). The best option for **food** in Tain is the bistro at the *Carnegie Lodge Hotel*, while the *Royal Hotel* (℡01862/892013; ❺), a lovely sandstone building at the western end of the main street, does reasonable bar food. There's a decent deli in town, *Food Frenzi* on Market Street, for lunchtime sandwiches or picnic fare.

Portmahomack

Unless you're making use of the Cromarty–Nigg ferry, not many people visit the Fearn peninsula to the east of Tain. It has a couple of delightful discoveries, however, including the green, windswept village of **PORTMAHOMACK**, which huddles around a curving sandy beach. On the edge of the village the **Tarbat Discovery Centre** (April & Oct daily 2–5pm; May–Sept daily 10am–5pm; Nov Fri & Sat 2–4pm; £3.50) deals with the archeology of the Picts in the area, and has many original and replica examples of sculpture. From Portmahomack, narrow roads run through fertile farmland to the gorse-covered point at **Tarbat Ness**, where there's a lighthouse – one of the highest in Britain. A good seven-mile **walk** starts here (2–3hr round trip): head south from Tarbat Ness for three miles, following the narrow passage between the foot of the cliffs and the foreshore, until you get to the hamlet of Rockfield. A path leads past a row of fishermen's cottages from here to Portmahomack, then joins the tarmac road running northeast back to the lighthouse. Further south on the peninsula there are impressive Pictish **standing stones** at Hilton and at Shandwick, while near Fearn village is the unexpectedly well-groomed factory shop for *Anta* (April–Dec Mon–Sat 9.30am–5.30pm, Sun 11am–5pm; Ⓦwww.anta.co.uk; free), which sells attractive modern tweed and tartan fabrics, as well as pottery. There's a nice wee **café** inside.

In Portmahomack, the *Oystercatcher* on Main Street (℡01862/871560, Ⓦwww .the-oystercatcher.co.uk; closed Mon & Tues) is one of the **restaurant** highlights of this stretch of the east coast, serving a big selection of sumptuous seafood dishes. For **accommodation**, the *Oystercatcher* has a small double (❷) and a larger en-suite double (❺) above the restaurant, or try the *Caledonian Hotel* (℡01862/871345, Ⓦwww.caleyhotel.co.uk; ❹) further along Main Street with views out over the Dornoch Firth.

Bonar Bridge and around

Before the causeway was built across the Dornoch Firth, traffic heading along the coast used to skirt west around the estuary, crossing the Kyle of Sutherland at the village of **BONAR BRIDGE**. In the fourteenth and fifteenth centuries, the village harboured a large iron foundry. Ore was brought across the peat moors of the central Highlands from the west coast on sledges, and fuel for smelting came from the oak forest draped over the northern shores of the nearby kyle. However, James IV, passing through here on his way to Tain, was shocked to find the forest virtually clear-felled and ordered that oak saplings be planted in the gaps. Although now hemmed in by spruce plantations, the beautiful ancient woodland east of Bonar Bridge dates from this era.

Bonar Bridge has struggled since it was bypassed: there's little of note here other than the **bridge** itself, which has had three incarnations up to the present steel construction of 1973, all recalled on a stone plinth on the north side.

Carbisdale Castle

Towering high above the River Shin, three miles northwest of Bonar Bridge, the daunting neo-Gothic profile of **Carbisdale Castle** overlooks the Kyle of Sutherland, as well as the battlefield where the gallant marquis of Montrose was defeated in 1650, finally forcing Charles II to accede to the Scots' demand for Presbyterianism. The castle was erected between 1906 and 1917 for the dowager duchess of Sutherland, following a protracted family feud, during which the duchess was found in contempt of court for destroying important documents pertinent to a legal case, and locked up in London's Holloway prison for six weeks. However, by way of compensation, a castle was built for the duchess worthy of her rank. Designed in three distinct styles (to give the impression it was added to over a long period of time), Carbisdale was eventually acquired by a Norwegian shipping magnate in 1933, and finally gifted, along with its entire contents and estate, to the Scottish Youth Hostels Association, which has turned it into what must be one of the most opulent **hostels** in the world, full of white Italian marble sculptures, huge gilt-framed portraits, sweeping staircases and magnificent drawing rooms alongside standard facilities such as self-catering kitchens, games rooms, TV rooms and thirty dorms, including some recently upgraded four-bed family rooms (☎0870/004 1109, ⓦwww.carbisdale.org; March–Oct), often booked out by groups. The best way to get here by public transport is to take a **train** to nearby Culrain station, which lies within easy walking distance of the castle. **Buses** from Inverness (3 daily; 1hr 30min) and Tain (4 daily; 25min) only stop at **Ardgay**, three miles south.

Croick Church

A mile or so southwest of Bonar Bridge, the scattered village of **ARDGAY** stands at the mouth of Strath Carron, a wooded river valley winding west into the heart of the Highlands. It's worth heading ten miles up the strath to **Croick Church**, which harbours one of Scotland's most poignant and emotive reminders of the Clearances. Huddled behind a brake of wind-bent trees, the graveyard surrounding the tiny grey chapel sheltered eighteen families (92 individuals) evicted from nearby Glen Calvie during the spring of 1845 to make way for flocks of Cheviot sheep, introduced by the duke of Sutherland as a money earner. An evocative written record of the event is preserved on the diamond-shaped panes of the chapel windows, where the villagers scratched **graffiti memorials** still legible today: "Glen Calvie people was in the church-yard May 24th 1845", "Glen Calvie people the wicked generation", and "This place needs cleaning".

Lairg and around

North of Bonar Bridge, the A836 parallels the River Shin for eleven miles to **LAIRG** (ⓦwww.lairghighlands.org.uk), a bleak and scattered settlement at the eastern end of lonely **Loch Shin**. On fine days, the vast wastes of heather and deergrass surrounding the village can be beautiful, but in the rain it can be a deeply depressing landscape. Lairg is predominantly a transport hub and the railhead for a huge area to the northwest; there's nothing much to see in town. The Ferrycroft Countryside Centre and **tourist office**, on the west side of the river (daily: April–Oct 10am–4pm; June–Aug 10am–5pm; ☎01549/402160), is friendly and helpful, and has a good free display on the woodlands and history of the area; it's also the starting point for forest walks and an archeological trail. There's a simple café with Internet access at the centre. Four miles south of Lairg, on the opposite side of the river – along the A836, then the B864 – the **Falls of Shin** is one of the best places in Scotland to see **salmon** leaping on their upstream migration; there's a viewing platform, and an overpriced café/shop by the car park catering to bus parties. Oddly enough, you'll find a few lines in the shop which have come direct from Harrods – the reason being that the owner of the London store, Mohammed al-Fayed, owns a grand Highland estate nearby. More prosaically, Lairg hosts an annual lamb sale every August, the biggest one-day livestock market in Europe, when sheep from all over the north of Scotland are bought and sold.

Lairg's train station is a mile south of town on the road to Bonar Bridge; buses stop right on the lochside. Should you want to **stay**, *Ambleside* B&B (☎01549/402130; ❶) offers good views, as does the grander *Park House* (☎01549/402208, ⓦwww.fishinscotland.net/parkhouse; ❸) on Station Road, overlooking Loch Shin, which is a welcoming spot if you're planning on doing some walking, fishing or cycling in the area. In Lairg, the best bet for **food** is the bar menu at the *Nip Inn*, next to the post office, though *Park House* serves meals to residents.

Dornoch

DORNOCH, a genteel and appealing town eight miles north of Tain, lies on a flattish headland overlooking the **Dornoch Firth**. Surrounded by sand dunes and blessed with an exceptionally sunny climate by Scottish standards, it's something of a middle-class holiday resort, with solid Edwardian hotels, trees and flowers in profusion, and miles of sandy beaches giving good views across the estuary to the Fearn peninsula. The town is also renowned for its championship **golf course**, Scotland's most northerly first-class course. Dornoch was the scene for Scotland's most prestigious rock'n'roll wedding of recent times, when Madonna married Guy Ritchie at nearby **Skibo Castle** and had her son baptized in Dornoch cathedral. *Skibo*, an exclusive, private hotel used as a hideaway of the world's rich and powerful, is just to the west of Dornoch. Only members of the hugely expensive Carnegie Club (ⓦwww.carnegieclub.co.uk) or their guests, however, will get anywhere near the place.

Dating from the twelfth century, Dornoch became a royal burgh in 1628. Among its oldest buildings, which are all grouped round the spacious square, the exquisite **cathedral** was founded in 1224 and built of local sandstone. The original building was horribly damaged by marauding Mackays in 1570, and much of what you see today was restored by the countess of Sutherland in 1835, though her worst Victorian excesses were removed in the twentieth century, when the interior stonework was returned to its original state. The vaulted roof is particularly appealing; the stained-glass windows in the north wall were later additions, endowed by the expat Andrew Carnegie. Opposite, the fortified sixteenth-century **Bishop's Palace**, a fine example of vernacular architecture with stepped gables and towers, has been refurbished as a hotel (see p.664). Next door, the castellated **Old Town Jail** is home to a series of upmarket craft shops under the banner Jail Dornoch, while tucked in behind the *Castle Hotel* is the local **Historylinks Museum** (April & May Mon–Fri 10am–4pm; June–Sept daily 10am–4pm; £2), which tells the story of Dornoch, from local saints to the Madonna herself.

Practicalities

Local **tourist information** can be found beside the *Coffee Shop* in the cluster of buildings near the Cathedral (April–Sept daily 9.30am–5.30pm; Oct–March Mon–Sat 10am–5pm, Sun 11am–5pm), where there's also bike rental available. There's no shortage of **accommodation**: *Tordarroch B&B* (☎01862/810855; March–Oct; ❷), has a great location opposite the cathedral, as does the *Trevose* (☎01862/810269; March–Sept; ❷), which is swathed in roses. The character-ful *Dornoch Castle Hotel* (☎01862/810216, ⓦwww.dornochcastlehotel.com; ❺), in the Bishop's Palace on the Square, has a cosy old-style bar and relax-ing tea garden. The *Caravan Park* (☎01862/810423, ⓦwww.dornochcaravans .co.uk; April–Oct) is attractively set between the manicured golf course and the uncombed vegetation of the sand dunes which fringe the beach; it also offers **camping** although the site does get busy with caravans in July and August.

Expensive gourmet meals are available at the *2 Quail* **restaurant** (☎01862/811811; May–Sept Tues–Sat; Oct–April Thurs–Sat) on Castle Street, which also has tasteful rooms (❺); otherwise, try *Luigi's* on Castle Street, which is open during the day and in summer stays open into weekend evenings serv-ing familiar but decent Italian-style snacks and meals.

North to Wick

North of Dornoch, the A9 hugs the coastline for most of the sixty or so miles to **Wick**, the principal settlement in the far north of the mainland. Perhaps the most important landmark in the whole stretch is the **Sutherland Monument** near Golspie, erected in memory of the first duke of Sutherland, the landowner who oversaw the eviction of thousands of his tenants in a process known as the Clearances. The bitter memory of those times resonates through most of the small towns and villages on this stretch, including **Brora**, the gold-prospect-ing village of **Helmsdale**, **Dunbeath** and **Lybster**. With sites dotted around recalling Iron Age settlers and Viking rule, many of these settlements also hark back to the days of a thriving fishing trade, none more so than the main town of Wick, once the busiest herring port in Europe.

Golspie and around

Ten miles north of Dornoch on the A9 lies the straggling red sandstone town of **GOLSPIE**, whose status as an administrative centre does little to relieve its dullness. It does, however, boast an eighteen-hole golf course and a sandy beach, while half a mile further up the coast, the **Big Burn** has several rapids and waterfalls that can be seen from an attractive **woodland trail** beginning at the *Sutherland Arms Hotel*.

Dunrobin Castle

The main reason to stop in Golspie is to look around **Dunrobin Castle** (April–May & early Oct Mon–Sat 10.30am–4.30pm, Sun noon–4.30pm; June–Sept daily 10.30am–5.30pm; £6.70), overlooking the sea a mile north of town. Approached via a long tree-lined drive, this fairy-tale confection of turrets and pointed roofs – modelled by the architect Sir Charles Barry (designer of London's Houses of Parliament) on a Loire château – is the seat of the infamous

△Dunrobin Castle

Sutherland family, at one time Europe's biggest landowners, with a staggering 1.3 million acres, and the principal driving force behind the Clearances in this area. The castle is on a correspondingly vast scale, boasting 189 furnished rooms, of which the tour takes in only seventeen. Staring up at the pile from the midst of its elaborate **formal gardens**, it's worth remembering that such extravagance was paid for by uprooting literally thousands of crofters from the surrounding glens.

The castle's opulent **interior** is crammed full of fine furniture, paintings (including works by Landseer, Allan Ramsay and Sir Joshua Reynolds), tapestries and *objets d'art*. The attractive gardens are pleasant to wander around, and it's worth diverting through them to get to Dunrobin's unusual **museum**, housed in an eighteenth-century building at the edge of the garden. Inside, hundreds of disembodied animals' heads and horns peer down from the walls, alongside other more macabre appendages, from elephants' toes to rhinos' tails. Bagged mainly by the fifth duke and duchess of Sutherland, the trophies vie for space with other fascinating family memorabilia, including John O'Groat's bones, Chinese opium pipes and such curiosities as a "picnic gong from the South Pacific". Nearby, one corner of the gardens is home to various trained birds of prey; you can see them on their perches at any time or hang around for one of the flying falconry displays which take place three times daily.

Conveniently, the castle has its own **train** station on the main Inverness–Wick line; this is no surprise, really, as the duke built the railway.

The Sutherland Monument

Approaching Golspie, you can't miss the hundred-foot **monument** to the first duke of Sutherland, which peers proprietorially down from the summit of the 1293ft **Beinn a'Bhragaidh** (Ben Bhraggie). An inscription cut into its base recalls that the statue was erected in 1834 by "a mourning and grateful tenantry [to] a judicious, kind and liberal landlord [who would] open his hands to the distress of the widow, the sick and the traveller". Unsurprisingly, there's no reference to the fact that the duke, widely regarded as Scotland's own Josef Stalin, forcibly evicted 15,000 crofters from his million-acre estate – a fact which, in the words of one local historian, makes the monument "a grotesque representation of the many forces that destroyed the Highlands". The campaign to have the statue smashed and scattered over the hillside has largely died down; the general attitude now seems to be that the statue now stands as a useful reminder of the duke's infamy as much as his achievements.

It's worth the stiff **climb** to the top of the hill (round trip 1hr 30min) for the wonderful views south along the coast past Dornoch to the Moray Firth and west towards Lairg and Loch Shin. The path is steep and strenuous in places, however, and there's no view until you're out of the trees, about twenty minutes from the top. Head up Fountain Road about half-way along Golspie's main street; after crossing the railway line and passing through Rhives farm steading, follow the Beinn a'Bhragaidh footpath (BBFP) signs along the path into the woods.

Loch Fleet and Rogart

Just to the south of Golspie, the A9 fringes a tidal estuary on a causeway that was constructed in 1816 by Thomas Telford. The inlet, **Loch Fleet**, is part of a large nature reserve (open access) harbouring some delicate coastal and woodland vegetation, including Britain's greatest concentration of one-flowered wintergreen, also known as St Olaf's candlestick, as well as a range of birdlife including greylag geese and arctic terns, and sealife such as seals and otters. You can walk in the reserve by following the minor road south out of Golspie for three miles; from Balblair Bay a path leads into pine-forested Balblair Wood, while from Littleferry there are walks along the coastal heathland to the Moray Firth beaches.

Four miles northwest of Loch Fleet on the A839 to Lairg is one of Scotland's most unusual and imaginative **hostels**, *Sleeperzzz.com* (☎01408/641343, ⓦwww.sleeperzzz.com), where you can stay in one of two first-class railway carriages parked in a siding beside the station on the Inverness–Thurso line in the tiny settlement of **ROGART**. Each of the comfortable compartments has a bunk-bed on one side and the original seats on the other, while the two end compartments are used as a kitchen and common room. The owners have free **mountain bikes** available to let you explore the local countryside, and the place stands 100yd from a convivial local **pub**, the *Pittentrail Inn*, which serves warming evening meals. A small reduction is even offered to those arriving by train or bicycle.

Brora

BRORA, on the coast six miles north of Golspie, once boasted the only bridge in the region – hence the name, which means "River of the Bridge" in Norse. Until the 1960s, it was the only coal-mining village in the Highlands, having played host to the industry for four hundred years. These days, however, the small grey town holds little of interest, although as with all these towns the old harbour has a intriguing if rather woebegone feel to it. Three miles south of the town is the remarkably well-preserved Iron Age broch of **Carn Liath**, with great twelve-foot-thick walls and a number of obvious features intact, such as a staircase and entrance passage. The car park for the site is on the inland side of the A9, just before the broch if you're travelling north. A more interesting way to reach it is by walking along the coastal path which links Golspie and Brora. A mile or so north of town, the **Clynelish Distillery** (April–Sept Mon–Fri 10am–5pm; Oct 11am–4pm; Nov–March by appointment; ☎01408/623000; £2), will give you a guided tour and a sample dram.

There are a couple of good **B&Bs** in the area. The *Selkie* (☎01408/621717, Ⓦwww.selkiebroa.co.uk; April–Oct; ❷), on Harbour Road, is superbly located where the river meets the sea – otters and seals are frequent sights from the garden. *Clynelish Farm* (☎01408/621265, Ⓦwww.scotland2000.com/clynelish; March–Oct; ❷) – turn left after the petrol station – is a working Victorian stone farmhouse with en-suite rooms, built to provide employment for dispossessed crofters after the Clearances. The rooms here are spacious, with views over the fields to the Moray Firth, and evening meals are available by arrangement. The best place to **eat** in Brora is *The Quiet Piggy* (☎01408/622011, Ⓦwww .thequietpiggy.com) on Station Square, which serves light, contemporary lunches and grander, expensive evening meals based around beef, fish and game.

Helmsdale and around

Eleven scenic miles north along the A9 from Golspie, **HELMSDALE** is an old herring port, founded in the nineteenth century to house the evicted inhabitants of Strath Kildonan, which lies behind it. Today, the main draw in the sleepy grey village is the attractively designed **Timespan Heritage Centre** beside the river (April–Oct Mon–Sat 10am–5pm, Sun noon–5pm; £4). It's an ambitious venture for a place of this size, telling the local story of Viking raids, witch-burning, Clearances, fishing and gold-prospecting through high-tech displays, sound effects and an audiovisual programme. The centre also has an art gallery and a plain café.

There's no official tourism office in town, but you'll pick up local information at Strath Ullie Crafts on the harbour. At the end of Dunrobin Street is the *Bridge Hotel* (☎01431/821100, Ⓦwww.bridgehotel.net; ❺), a pleasantly grand and comfortable **hotel** with big open fireplaces and mounted antlers lining the walls. There are several good-value **B&Bs**, including *Broomhill House* on Navidale Road (☎01431/821259, Ⓦwww.blancebroomhill.com; ❷), which has bedrooms in a turret added to the former croft by a miner who struck it lucky in the Kildonan gold rush (see below). Alternatively, try *Bayview* (☎01431/821679, Ⓦwww.bayview-helmsdale.org.uk; ❶), just south of Helmsdale at Portgower. There's also a small SYHA **youth hostel** (☎0870/004 1124, Ⓦwww.syha.org.uk; April–Sept), beside the A9 as it climbs north up from the harbour.

If you're looking for somewhere to **eat** in Helmsdale, your eye may well be drawn to the bizarre *Mirage* restaurant (Ⓦwww.lamirage.org) on Dunrobin Street. The former proprietor of the *Mirage* became something of a local celebrity, modelling herself on the romantic novelist Barbara Cartland. The fittings and furnishings are suitably garish, complemented by framed photographs of visiting personalities covering the walls. There's a long menu, which includes large helpings of fish and chips. Immediately opposite, the *Wayfarer* offers a more conservative approach to bistro dining.

Baile an Or

From Helmsdale the single-track A897 runs up Strath Kildonan and across the Flow Country (see p.652) to the north coast, at first following the River Helmsdale, a strictly controlled and exclusive salmon river frequented by the Royal Family. Some eight miles up the Strath at **BAILE AN OR** (Gaelic for "goldfield"), gold was discovered in the bed of the Kildonan Burn in 1869; a **gold rush** ensued, hardly on the scale of the Yukon, but quite bizarre in the Scottish Highlands. A tiny amount of gold is still found by some hardy prospectors every year: should you fancy **gold-panning** yourself, you can rent the relevant equipment for £2.50 from Strath Ullie Crafts, which also sells a booklet with a few basic tips.

Dunbeath and around

Just north of Helmsdale, the A9 begins its long haul up the **Ord of Caithness**. This steep hill used to form a pretty impregnable obstacle, and the desolate road still gets blocked during winter snowstorms. Once over the pass, the landscape changes dramatically as heather-clad moors give way to miles of treeless green grazing lands, peppered with derelict crofts and latticed by long dry-stone walls. As you come over the pass, look out for signs to the ruined village of **Badbea**, reached via a ten-minute walk from the car park at the side of the A9. Built by tenants cleared from nearby Ousdale, the settlement now lies deserted, although its ruined hovels show what hardship the crofters had to endure: the cottages stood so near the windy cliff edge that children had to be tethered to prevent them from being blown into the sea.

DUNBEATH, hidden at the mouth of a small strath twelve miles north of Ord of Caithness, was another village founded to provide work in the wake of the Clearances. The local landlord built a harbour here in 1800, at the start of the herring boom, and the settlement briefly flourished. Today it's a sleepy place, with lobster pots stacked at the quayside and views of windswept Dunbeath Castle (no public access) on the opposite side of the bay. The novelist Neil Gunn was born here, in one of the terraced houses under the flyover that now swoops above the village; you can find out more about him at the **Dunbeath Heritage Centre** (April–Oct daily 10am–5pm; Nov–March Mon–Fri 11am–3pm; £2), signposted from the road. The staff can advise you on several good walks along the *Highland River* of Gunn's novel; his other famous book, *The Silver Darlings*, was also set on this coastline. The best of the handful of modest **B&Bs** here is *Tormore Farm* (☎01593/731240; May–Oct; ❶), a large farmhouse with four comfortable rooms, half a mile north of the harbour on the A9.

Just north of Dunbeath is the simple but moving **Laidhay Croft Museum** (Easter to Oct daily 10am–6pm; £2), which offers a useful perspective on the sometimes over-romanticized life of the Highlander before the Clearances. A little further up the coast, the **Clan Gunn Heritage Centre and Museum** (June–Sept Mon–Sat 11am–1pm & 2–4pm; £2) is mainly a place for members of the Clan Gunn and its septs, although it also doles out a bit more local history and a few titbits for those on the trail of Neil Gunn.

Lybster and around

The final stretch of road before Wick gives great views out to sea to the oil rigs perched on the horizon. The spectacular series of green-topped cliffs and churning bays are gorgeous in the sun and impressively bleak in bad weather. The planned village of **LYBSTER** (pronounced "libe-ster"), established at the height of the nineteenth-century herring boom, once had two hundred-odd boats working out of its harbour: now there are just one or two. The **Water Lines** heritage centre by the harbour (May–Sept daily 11am–5pm; £2.50) is an attractive modern display about the "silver darlings" and the fishermen that pursued them; there's a snug café downstairs. There's not much else to see here apart from the harbour area; the upper town is a grim collection of grey pebble-dashed bungalows centred on a broad main street.

The **Grey Cairns of Camster**, seven miles due north and one of the most memorable sights on the northeast coast, are a different story. Surrounded by bleak moorland, these two enormous reconstructed prehistoric burial chambers, originally built four or five thousand years ago, were immaculately designed, with corbelled dry-stone roofs in their hidden chambers, which you can crawl into through narrow passageways. More extraordinary ancient remains lie at **East Clyth**, two miles north of Lybster on the A99, where a path leads to the "**Hill o'Many Stanes**". Some two hundred boulders stand in the ground here, forming 22 parallel rows that run north to south; no one has yet worked out what they were used for, although archeological studies have shown there were once six hundred stones in place.

Another relatively unknown historic site in the area is the **Whaligoe staircase**, ten miles north of Lybster on the A99 at the north end of the village of Ulbster. The stairway, which has 365 steps constructed out of the distinctive local slab stone, leads steeply down from the side of the house beside the car park to a natural harbour surrounded by cliffs.

Wick

Originally a Viking settlement named *Vik* (meaning "bay"), **WICK** has been a royal burgh since 1589. It's actually two towns: Wick proper, and **Pultney-town**, immediately south across the river, a messy, rather run-down community planned by Thomas Telford in 1806 for the British Fisheries Society to encourage evicted crofters to take up fishing. Wick's heyday was in the mid-nineteenth century, when it was the busiest herring port in Europe, with a fleet of over 1100 boats, exporting tons of fish to Russia, Scandinavia and the West Indian slave plantations. Robert Louis Stevenson described it as "the meanest of man's towns, situated on the baldest of God's bays", and something of that down-at-heel atmosphere is apparent today. It's not somewhere you're likely to linger; if you're here for a few hours, the area around the harbour in Pultneytown, lined with rows of fishermen's cottages, is most worth a wander, with the acres of largely derelict net-mending sheds, stores and cooperages around the harbour giving some idea of the former scale of the fishing trade.

The town's story is told in the loyally maintained, but far from slick **Wick Heritage Centre** in Bank Row, Pultneytown (Easter–Oct Mon–Sat 10am–5pm; £2), which contains a fascinating array of artefacts from the old fishing days which verges on a jumble, including fully-rigged boats, original boat models, the old Noss Head lighthouse light and a great photographic collection dating from the 1880s. The other visitor attraction nearby is the fairly simple **Pulteney Distillery** (Mon–Fri 10am–1pm & 2pm–4pm; tours at 11am & 2pm or by arrangement ☎01955/602371; £3.50 includes discount voucher) on Huddart Street, a few blocks back from the sea. Much is made here of the maritime character of both the distillery and the whisky – the coopers who made barrels for the distillery, for example, also made them for storing cured herrings bound for Russia and Germany.

The **train** station and **bus** stops are next to each other immediately south and west of the bridge which crosses the Wick River in the centre of town. Frequent local buses run to Thurso and up the coast to John O'Groats. Wick also has an **airport** (☎01955/602215), a couple of miles north of the town, with direct flights from Edinburgh and Aberdeen.

There's no tourist office. The best of the **hotels** is *Mackay's*, on the south side of the river in the town centre (☎01955/602323, ⓦwww.mackayshotel.co.uk; ❺), while reasonable **B&B** options include *Quayside*, 25 Harbour Quay (☎01955/603229, ⓦwww.quaysidewick.co.uk; ❷), and *The Clachan*, 13 Randolph Place on South Road (☎01955/605384, wwww.theclachan.co.uk; ❷). Five miles towards Thurso is lovely *Bilbster House* (☎01955/621212,

ⓦ www.accommodationbilbster.com; April–Oct, in winter by arrangement; ❷).

Good **eating** options don't abound, though the moderately priced *Bord de l'Eau* (☎01955/604400; closed Mon) on Market Street, which runs along the north side of the river, offers a reasonable menu of classic French standards. Among the local **pubs**, try the *Alexander Bain* (named after the inventor of the fax machine, who lived locally) in Market Place, or the bar in *Mackay's Hotel*.

Travel details

Trains

Inverness to: Dingwall (Mon–Sat 7–8 daily, 2–4 on Sun; 25min); Helmsdale (Mon–Sat 3 daily, 1 on Sun; 2hr 20min); Kyle of Lochalsh (Mon–Sat 3–4 daily, 1–2 on Sun; 2hr 40min); Lairg (Mon–Sat 3–4 daily, 1–2 on Sun; 1hr 40min); Plockton (Mon–Sat 3–4 daily, 1–2 on Sun; 2hr 15min); Thurso (Mon–Sat 3 daily, 1 on Sun; 3hr 25min); Wick (Mon–Sat 3 daily, 1 on Sun; 3hr 45min).

Fort William to: Arisaig (Mon–Sat 4 daily, 1 on Sun; 1hr 10min); Glenfinnan (Mon–Sat 4 daily, 1 on Sun; 35min); Mallaig (Mon–Sat 4 daily, 1 on Sun; 1hr 25min).

Kyle of Lochalsh to: Dingwall (Mon–Sat 3–4 daily, 1–2 on Sun; 2hr); Inverness (Mon–Sat 3–4 daily, 1–2 on Sun; 2hr 40min); Plockton (Mon–Sat 3–4 daily, 1–2 on Sun; 15min).

Thurso to: Dingwall (Mon–Sat 3 daily, 1–2 on Sun; 3hr); Inverness (Mon–Sat 3 daily, 1–2 on Sun; 3hr 20min); Lairg (Mon–Sat 3 daily, 1–2 on Sun; 1hr 50min); Wick (Mon–Sat 3 daily, 1–2 on Sun; 35min).

Wick to: Dingwall (Mon–Sat 3 daily, 1–2 on Sun; 3hr 30min); Inverness (Mon–Sat 3 daily, 1–2 on Sun; 4hr); Lairg (Mon–Sat 3 daily, 1–2 on Sun; 2hr 20min).

Buses

Fort William to: Acharacle (Mon–Sat 2–3 daily; 1hr 30min); Inverness (6 daily; 2hr 15min); Kilchoan (1 daily; 3hr 35); Mallaig (Mon–Fri 1 daily; 1hr 30min).

Gairloch to: Inverness (Mon–Sat 1 daily; 2hr 45min); Redpoint (Mon–Fri 1–2 daily during school term only; 1hr 35min).

Inverness to: Durness (Mon–Sat 1 daily, May–Sept only; 5hr); Thurso (Mon–Sat 5 daily, 4 on Sun; 3hr 35min); Wick (Mon–Sat 5 daily, 4 on Sun; 2hr 55min).

Kyle of Lochalsh to: Fort William (3 daily; 1hr 50min); Glasgow (3 daily; 5hr); Inverness (2 daily; 2hr).

Lochinver to: Inverness (Easter–Sept 1 daily; 3hr 10min); Ullapool (Mon–Sat 2 daily; 1hr).

Thurso to: Inverness (4–5 daily; 3hr 30min); John O' Groats (Mon–Fri 5 daily, 2 on Sat; 1hr); Wick (Mon–Fri hourly, Sat & Sun 6 daily; 35min).

Ullapool to: Durness (Mon–Sat 1 daily, Easter–Sept only; 3hr); Inverness (Mon–Sat 2–3 daily; 1hr 30min).

Wick to: John O' Groats (4 daily Mon–Sat; 50min).

Ferries

To Lewis: Ullapool–Stornoway (Mon–Sat 2 daily; 2hr 45min).

To Mull: Kilchoan–Tobermory (Mon–Sat 7 daily; June–Aug also Sun 5 daily; 35min); Lochaline–Fishnish (Mon–Sat every 50min, Sun hourly; 15min).

To Orkney: Gill's Bay–St Margaret's Hope (3 daily; 1hr); John O'Groats–Burwick (passengers only; 2–4 daily; 40min); Scrabster–Stromness (2–3 daily; 2hr).

To Skye: Glenelg–Kylerhea (daily frequently; 15min); Mallaig–Armadale (Mon–Sat 8–9 daily; mid-May to mid-Sept also Sun; 30min).

To the Small Isles: Mallaig to Eigg, Rùm, Muck and Canna, see p.692.

Flights

Wick to: Edinburgh (Mon–Sat 1 daily; 1hr 10min); Inverness (Mon–Fri 2 daily; 35min); Kirkwall (Mon–Sat 1 daily; 25min).

Skye and the Small Isles

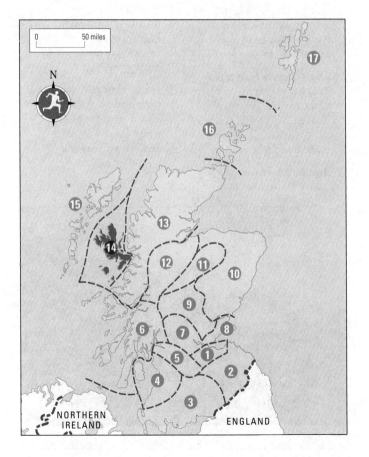

CHAPTER 14

Highlights

* **Isle of Raasay** Just off the coast of Skye, Raasay is well off the beaten track, yet offers a wide variety of outdoor pursuits from windsurfing to hill walking. **See p.678**

* **Skye Cuillin** The jagged peaks of the Skye Cuillin are the real reason why Skye is still a great place to go. **See p.679**

* **Loch Coruisk boat trip** Take the boat from Elgol to the remote, glacial Loch Coruisk in the midst of the Skye Cuillin, and walk back. **See p.679**

* **Trotternish** After the Skye Cuillin, the Trotternish peninsula is the most distinctive landscape on Skye, with its basalt intrusions and massive landslides. **See p.685**

* **Kinloch Castle, Isle of Rùm** Visit this outrageous Edwardian pile, or better still, stay in the hostel housed in the servants' quarters or in one of the castle's four-posters. **See p.688**

* **Isle of Eigg** Without doubt the friendliest of the Small Isles, with sandy beaches, a nice easy hill to climb and lots of peace and quiet. **See p.690**

△ Take to the hills of Skye Cuillin

Skye and the Small Isles

ome say the **Isle of Skye** (An t-Eilean Sgiathanach) was named after the Old Norse word for cloud (*skuy*), earning itself the Gaelic moniker Eilean a Cheo ("Island of Mist"). Yet, despite the unpredictability of the weather, tourism has been an important part of the island's economy for more than a hundred years, since the train line pushed through to Kyle of Lochalsh in the western Highlands in 1897. From here, it was the briefest of boat trips across to Skye, and the Edwardian bourgeoisie was soon swarming over to walk its mountains, whose beauty had been proclaimed by an earlier generation of Victorian climbers. Since the opening of the Skye Bridge, the island has been busier than ever, and at the height of the summer, the road system often begins to bottleneck with coach tours, minibuses and caravans. Yet Skye is a deceptively large island, and you'll get the most out of it – and escape the worst of the crowds – if you take the time to explore its more remote parts.

The Clearances saw an estimated 30,000 indigenous *Sgiathanachs* (pronounced "ski-anaks"), emigrate in the mid-nineteenth century, leaving a population today of around 9000. Nevertheless, Skye remains the most important centre for **Gaelic culture** and language outside of the Western Isles. Over a third of the population is fluent in Gaelic, the Gaelic college on Sleat is the most important in Scotland, and the Free Church maintains a strong presence. Yet tourism is by far the island's biggest earner and has attracted several thousand "white settlers" over the last couple of decades. As an English-speaking visitor, it's as well to be aware of the tensions that exist between these two communities within this idyllic island, even if you never experience them firsthand. For a taste of the resurgence of Gaelic culture, try and get here in time for the Skye and Lochalsh Festival, *Feis an Eilein* (W www.feisaneilein.com), which takes place over two weeks in July. A good way of finding out what's going on in the region is to read the weekly *West Highland Free Press* (W www.whfp.com), a refreshingly vociferous campaigning newspaper published in Broadford.

One way to avoid the crowds on Skye is to head off to the so-called **Small Isles** – the improbably named **Rùm**, **Eigg**, **Muck** and **Canna** – to the south. Each with a population of far less than a hundred, they are easily accessible by ferry from Mallaig and Arisaig, though with limited accommodation available, it's as well to do a bit of forward planning.

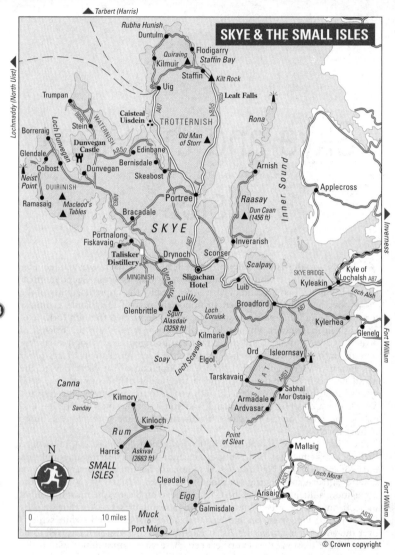

The map shows **SKYE & THE SMALL ISLES**, with locations including Tarbert (Harris), Lochmaddy (North Uist), Rubha Hunish, Duntulm, Quiraing, Flodigarry, Staffin Bay, Kilmuir, Staffin, Kilt Rock, Uig, Lealt Falls, Trumpan, Caisteal Uisdein, TROTTERNISH, Rona, Borreraig, Stein, WATERNISH, Old Man of Storr, Arnish, Applecross, Glendale, Dunvegan Castle, Edinbane, Bernisdale, Skeabost, Neist Point, Colbost, Dunvegan, DUIRINISH, Portree, Raasay, Dun Caan (1456 ft), Inner Sound, Ramasaig, Macleod's Tables, Bracadale, SKYE, Portnalong, Fiskavaig, Inverarish, Talisker Distillery, Drynoch, Sconser, Scalpay, MINGINISH, Glen Brittle, Sligachan Hotel, Luib, SKYE BRIDGE, Kyle of Lochalsh, Kyleakin, Loch Alsh, Broadford, Glenbrittle, Sgurr Alasdair (3258 ft), Cuillin, Loch Coruisk, Kylerhea, Kilmarie, Glenelg, Soay, Loch Scavaig, Elgol, Ord, Isleornsay, SLEAT, Tarskavaig, Sabhal Mor Ostaig, Canna, Kilmory, Armadale, Ardvasar, Sanday, Kinloch, Rum, Point of Sleat, Mallaig, Harris, Askival (2663 ft), SMALL ISLES, Cleadale, Loch Morat, Eigg, Arisaig, Muck, Galmisdale, Port Mór, with directions to Inverness, Fort William. Scale: 0 — 10 miles.

© Crown copyright

Skye

Jutting out from the mainland like a giant butterfly, the bare and bony promontories of **Skye** (ⓦwww.skye.co.uk) fringe a deeply indented coastline. The
island's most popular destination is the **Cuillin** ridge, whose jagged peaks
dominate the island during clear weather; to explore them at close quarters
you'll need to be a fairly experienced and determined walker. More accessible and equally dramatic in their own way are the rock formations of the
Trotternish peninsula, in the north, from which there are inspirational views

across to the Western Isles. If you want to escape the summer crush, shuffle off to **Glendale** and the cliffs of Neist Point or head for the **Isle of Raasay**, off Skye's east coast. Of the two main settlements, **Portree** is the only one with any charm, and a useful base for exploring the Trotternish; however, neither Portree nor Broadford, further south, is practical as a jumping-off point for the Cuillin, for which you need to head for Glenbrittle or Sligachan.

Most visitors still reach Skye via Kyle of Lochalsh, which is linked to Inverness by train, and to Kyleakin, on the eastern tip of the island, by the controversial **Skye Bridge**. This southeast corner of Skye is relatively dull, and the more scenic approach is by **ferry** from Mallaig, further south on the Morar peninsula (see p.623). Linked by train with Glasgow, the Mallaig boat takes thirty minutes to cross to **Armadale**, on the gentle southern slopes of the **Sleat peninsula**. A third option is the privately operated **car ferry** which leaves the mainland at Glenelg, south of Kyle of Lochalsh, to arrive at **Kylerhea**, from where the road heads inland towards **Portree**. If you're carrying on to the Western Isles, it's 57 miles from Armadale and 49 miles from Kyleakin to **Uig**, at the opposite end of Skye, where ferries leave for Tarbert on Harris and Lochmaddy on North Uist.

Skye has several substantial **campsites**, and numerous **hostels** or bunkhouses (all of which recommend advance bookings, particularly in July and August), plenty of B&Bs and a string of pricey, but excellent **hotels**. Most visitors arrive by car, as the **bus** services, while adequate between the villages, peter out in the more remote areas, and virtually close down on Sundays.

Sleat

Ferry services (Mon–Sat 8–9 daily; mid-May to mid-Sept also Sun; 30min) from Mallaig connect with the **Sleat** (pronounced "Slate") **peninsula**, Skye's southern tip, an uncharacteristically fertile area that has earned it the sobriquet "The Garden of Skye". The CalMac ferry terminal is at **ARMADALE** (Armadal), an elongated hamlet stretching along the wooded shoreline. If you've time to kill waiting for the ferry, take a look at the huge variety of Scottish and Irish knitwear on offer at Ragamuffin by the pier, or if you need a bite **to eat**, pop into the *Pasta Shed* next door, which does a great seafood pizza (eat-in or takeaway).

If you're leaving Skye on the early-morning ferry or you arrive late and need to stay near Armadale, your best bet is one of the **hostels** on the peninsula: Armadale SYHA hostel (☎0870/004 1103, ⓦwww.syha.org.uk; April–Sept) is a convenient ten-minute walk up the A851 towards Broadford and has a good position overlooking the bay; the *Flora MacDonald Hostel* (☎0783/447 6378, ⓦwww .isle-of-skye-tour-guide.co.uk), two miles further up the same road, beyond Sabhal Mòr Ostaig, is a converted barn with bunkbeds, family rooms and even B&B (❸); they will fetch you from the ferry. There are also two luxury options: a mile southwest towards neighbouring Ardvasar, the traditional, whitewashed *Ardvasar Hotel* (☎01471/844223, ⓦwww.ardvasarhotel.com; ❻) has a good restaurant specializing in local seafood, while six miles up the A851 overlooking Knock Bay, the *Toravaig House Hotel* (☎01471/833231, ⓦwww.skyehotel.co.uk; ❼) has immaculate, stylish, en-suite rooms and a smart, pricey restaurant. **Bike rental** is available from the SYHA hostel or the local petrol station (☎01471/844249), close to the pier; **boat trips** operate from Armadale with Sea.fari Adventures (☎01471/833316, ⓦwww.seafari.co.uk), who also have a shop on the pier; alternatively, you can go **horse riding** on Clydesdale and Shire horses with West Highland Heavy Horses (☎07769/588565, ⓦwww.westhighlandheavyhorses.com).

A little further along the A851, past the youth hostel, you'll find one of the best tourist attractions on the island, the **Armadale Castle Gardens** (April–Oct daily 9.30am–5.30pm; £4.80; ⓦwww.clandonald.com). Within the handsome forty-acre gardens lies the shell of the MacDonalds' neo-Gothic castle, a café and a library for those who want to chase up their ancestral Donald connections. The gardens' slick, purpose-built **Clan Donald Museum** has a good section on the Jacobite period and its aftermath, featuring a few Bonnie Prince Charlie keepsakes and a couple of cannonballs fired at the castle by HMS *Dartmouth*, sent by William and Mary to shell the castle, which "sent them scampering to the hills" (those who surrendered were hanged). There're also one or two top-notch works of art: a splendid portrait of a young, theatrical Glengarry (on whom Walter Scott modelled the hero of the Waverley novels) by Angelika Kauffman, and a portrait of his more conventional brother, MacDonell, by Raeburn.

Continuing northeast, it's another six miles to **ISLEORNSAY** (Eilean Iarmain), a secluded little village of whitewashed cottages that was once Skye's main fishing port. With the mountains of the mainland on the horizon, the views out across the bay are wonderful, overlooking a necklace of seaweed-encrusted rocks and the tidal **Isle of Ornsay**, which sports a trim lighthouse built by Robert Louis Stevenson's father. You can **stay** at one of Sir Iain Noble's enterprises, the mid-nineteenth-century *Isleornsay Hotel* – also known by its Gaelic name *Hotel Eilean Iarmain* – a pricey place with excellent service, whose **restaurant** serves great seafood (☎01471/833332, ⓦwww .eilean-iarmain.com; ❼), though you could just have a good bar meal by an open fire. There are various enterprises based in Isleornsay, among which is Sir Iain's Gaelic whisky company, Pràban na Linne, that markets a number of unpronounceable Gaelic-named blended and single malt whiskies; the company offers tastings at its head office (phone ☎01471/833496 for opening hours). Another couple of miles brings you to the turning for *Kinloch Lodge Hotel* (☎01471/833333, ⓦwww.claire-macdonald.com; B&B and dinner ❾), an old hunting lodge owned by Lord Macdonald of Macdonald, with excellent food guaranteed by wife Claire whose cookery books are internationally famous. If you need to work off the calories, you can go **sea kayaking** with *Skyak Adventures* (☎01471/833428, ⓦwww .skyakadventures.com), based at the bay to the south of Isleornsay.

Kyleakin and Kylerhea

The aforementioned Sir Iain Noble was also one of the leading advocates of (and investors in) the (now toll-free) **Skye Bridge**, which links the tidy hamlet of **KYLEAKIN** (Caol Acain – pronounced "kal*a*kin", with the stress on the second syllable) with the Kyle of Lochalsh (see p.625), just half a mile away on the mainland. Built in 1995 for a cool £30 million, the Skye Bridge was the most expensive toll bridge in Europe, and no cheaper than the ferry it replaced. Protests and non-payment eventually persuaded the Scottish Executive to buy out the firm (for £27 million) in 2004 and abolish the tolls. Strictly speaking there are two bridges which rest on an island in the middle, **Eilean Bàn**, whose lighthouse cottages were once the home of author and naturalist Gavin Maxwell. The house has been turned into a museum, but must be visited on a guided tour; numbers are limited and tours must be booked in advance through the **Bright Water Visitor Centre** in Kyleakin (April–Oct Mon–Fri 10am–5pm; free; ☎01599/530040, ⓦwww.eileanban.org). The centre itself is well worth a visit, as it's full of hands-on things for kids of all ages.

The other sight in Kyleakin are the scant remains of **Castle Moil**, a four-teenth-century keep poking out into the straits on top of a diminutive rocky knoll, which looks romantic when floodlit. One of its earliest inhabitants, an entrepreneurial Norwegian princess married to a MacDonald chief, hung a chain across the water and exacted a toll from every passing boat. With its ferry now defunct, Kyleakin has reinvented itself as something of a backpackers' hangout – to the consternation of some villagers (in summer, the population more than doubles). If you're looking for a party atmosphere, then head for *Saucy Mary's* (℡01599/534845, ⓦwww.saucymarys.com), a **pub and hostel** where there's often live music until the early hours; alternatively, snuggle down at the cosy *Dun Caan Hostel* (℡01599/534087, ⓦwww.skyerover.co.uk), or nearby *Skye Backpackers* (℡01599/534510, ⓦwww.scotlands-top-hostels.com), part of the MacBackpackers' circuit of hostels; there's also an SYHA hostel (℡0870/004 1134) in an ugly, modern building a couple of hundred yards from the old pier. **Bike rental** is available from *Dun Caan* and Skye Bikes (℡01599/534795) on the pier.

You can still go "over the sea to Skye" by taking the small **car ferry** (Easter to mid-May Mon–Sat 9am–5.45pm; mid-May to Aug Mon–Sat 9am–7.45pm, Sun 10am–5.45pm; Sept Mon–Sat 9am–5.45pm, Sun 10am–5.45pm; ℡01599/511302, ⓦwww.skyeferry.co.uk) which sets off every quarter- or half-hour from Glenelg and takes just five minutes to reach **KYLERHEA** (pronounced "kile-ray"), a peaceful little place some four miles down the coast from Kyleakin. From here you can walk half an hour up the coast to the Forestry Commission **Otter Hide**, where, if you're lucky, you may be able to spot one of these elusive creatures.

Broadford

Heading west out of Kyleakin or Kylerhea brings you eventually to the island's second-largest village, charmless **BROADFORD** (An t-Ath Leathann), whose mile-long main street curves round a wide bay. Despite its rather unlovely appearance, Broadford makes a useful base for exploring the southern half of Skye, and has one of Skye's best wet-weather retreats, the unusual **Skye Serpentarium** (Easter–Oct Mon–Sat 10am–5pm; July & Aug daily; £2.50; ⓦwww.skyeserpentarium.org.uk), housed in an old mill by the main road heading east out of town. There are over fifty animals on display, all of them abandoned or rescued, ranging from tiny tree frogs to large iguanas and there's usually a snake you can handle. Another popular activity in Broadford is to take a **boat trip** either on *Family's Pride II* (℡0800/783 2175, ⓦwww .glassbottomboat.co.uk; April–Oct), a glass-bottomed boat, or in a Rigid Inflatable Boat (RIB), both of which set off from Broadford pier.

Broadford's **tourist office** (Easter–Oct Mon–Fri 9.30am–5pm; June–Aug Mon–Fri 9.30am–5pm, Sat & Sun 9.30am–4pm; ℡01471/822713) is by the 24-hour garage on the main road, where there's a laundry, small shop and bureau de change. At the west end of the village there's a bank, a bakery, a tearoom and a post office. The SYHA **hostel** is on the west shore of Broad-ford Bay (℡0870/004 1106, ⓦwww.syha.org.uk; March–Oct). Two **B&Bs** which stand out are the delightful old croft-house *Lime Stone Cottage*, 4 Lime Park (℡01471/822142, ⓦwww.limestonecottage.co.uk; ❸), near the Serpen-tarium, and the modern, comfortable *Ptarmigan* (℡01471/822744, ⓦwww .ptarmigan-cottage.com; ❸), on the main road, with views over the bay. If you want a bite **to eat**, try the justifiably popular *Creelers Seafood Restaurant* (℡01471/822281, ⓦwww.skye-seafood-restaurant.co.uk) at the south end of the bay, which also does takeaway round the back. For top-notch French seafood, head for the award-winning *Rendezvous* (booking advisable, on ☏01471/822001) on the main road at Breakish, a mile or so east of Broadford. **Bike rental** is available from the SYHA hostel or from *Fairwinds* B&B, (☏01471/822270), just past the *Broadford Hotel*.

Isle of Raasay

Despite lying less than a mile offshore, the long, hilly island of **Raasay**, sees surprisingly few visitors. For much of its history, Raasay was the property of a branch of the staunchly Jacobite MacLeods of Lewis, and the island sent a hundred men and 26 pipers to the Battle of Culloden, as a consequence of which it was practically destroyed by government troops in the aftermath of the 1745 uprising. Bonnie Prince Charlie spent a miserable night in a "mean low hut" on Raasay during his flight and swore to replace the burnt turf cottages with proper stone houses (he never did). When the MacLeods were finally forced to sell up in 1843, the Clearances started in earnest, a period of the island's history immortalized in verse by Raasay poet, Sorley MacLean (Somhairle MacGill Eathain). In 1921, seven ex-servicemen and their families from the neighbouring isle of **Rona**, to the north, illegally squatted crofts on Raasay, and were imprisoned, causing a public outcry. As a result, both islands were bought by the government the following year and remain in state hands. Raasay's population now stands at around two hundred, many of them members of the Free Presbyterian Church. Strict observance of the Sabbath – no work or play on Sundays – is the most obvious manifestation for visitors, who should respect the islanders' feelings.

The ferry docks at the southern tip of the island, an easy fifteen-minute walk from **INVERARISH**, a tiny village set within thick woods on the island's southwest coast, where there are several walks you can follow. The grand Georgian mansion of **Raasay House** (now an outdoor centre) was built by the MacLeods in the late 1740s, to be all but ruined by government troops a few years later. The interior of Raasay is starkly barren, a rugged and rocky terrain of sandstone in the south and gneiss in the north, with the most obvious feature being the curiously truncated basalt cap on top of **Dun Caan** (1456ft), where Boswell "danced a Highland dance" on his visit to the island with Dr Johnson in 1773 – you may feel like doing the same if you're rewarded with a clear view over to the Cuillin and the Outer Hebrides. The trail to the top of the peak is fairly easy to follow, a splendid five-mile trek up through the forest and along the burn behind Inverarish. The quickest return is made down the northwest slope of Dun Caan, but – by going a couple of miles further – you can get back to the ferry along the path by the southeast shore, passing the abandoned crofters' village of Hallaig, whose steep incline led mothers to tether their children to stakes to prevent them rolling onto the shore.

The CalMac **car ferry** departs for Raasay from Sconser (Mon–Sat 9–11 daily, Sun 2 daily; 15min). Many visitors go for the day, since there's plenty to do within walking distance of the pier – if you do take a car, be warned, there's no petrol on the island. Comfortable **accommodation** in pleasantly casual rooms is available at the *Raasay Outdoor Centre* (☏01478/660266, ⓦ www.raasay-house .co.uk; ❶), where Boswell and Johnson stayed; there is also a café, open to all, with live music in the evenings. You can also **camp** in the grounds or stay in the bunkhouse, and they'll happily collect you from the ferry terminal. In addition, you can join in the centre's activity programme (£12–65): anything from sailing, windsurfing and canoeing, to climbing and hill walking to suit all

ages. Close by is the welcoming *Isle of Raasay Hotel* (℡01478/660222, Ⓦwww
.isleofraasayhotel.co.uk; ❹), which serves traditional Scottish food and where
the view of the Cuillin surpasses any other. A rough track cuts up the steep hillside from the village to Raasay's isolated but beautifully placed SYHA **hostel**
(℡0870/004 1146; Ⓦwww.syha.org.uk; May–Sept).

The Cuillin and the Red Hills

For many people, the **Cuillin**, whose sharp snow-capped peaks rise mirage-like
from the flatness of the surrounding terrain, are the *raison d'être* for a visit to
Skye. When the clouds finally disperse, they are the dominating feature of the
island, visible from every other peninsula. There are basically three approaches
to the Cuillin: from the south, by foot or by boat from Elgol; from the *Sligachan
Hotel* to the north; or from Glen Brittle to the west of the mountains. Glen
Sligachan is one of the most popular routes, dividing as it does the granite of
the round-topped **Red Hills** (sometimes known as the Red Cuillin) to the
east from the dark, coarse-grained jagged-edged gabbro of the real Cuillin (also
known as the Black Cuillin) to the west. With some twenty Munros between
them, these are mountains to be taken seriously, and many routes through the
Cuillin are for experienced climbers only (for more on safety, see p.64).

Elgol, Loch Coruisk and Glen Sligachan

The road to **ELGOL** (Ealaghol), fourteen miles southwest of Broadford at the
tip of the Strathaird peninsula, is one of the most dramatic on the island, leading
right into the heart of the Red Hills and then down a precipitous slope, with
a stunning view from the top down to Elgol pier. The chief reason for visiting
Elgol is, weather permitting, to take a boat across Loch Scavaig (March–Sept 2
daily; £20–30 return), past a seal colony, near the entrance of **Loch
Coruisk** (from *coire uish*, "cauldron of water"). An isolated, glacial loch, this
needle-like shaft of water, nearly two miles long but only a couple of hundred
yards wide, lies in the shadow of the highest peaks of the Black Cuillin, a
wonderfully overpowering landscape.

The journey by sea takes 45 minutes and passengers are dropped to spend
about one and a half (or six and a half) hours ashore. It's essential to book ahead
either online or over the phone between 7.30am to 10am (℡0800/731 3089,
Ⓦwww.bellajane.co.uk); RIB trips are also offered to the Small Isles. **Walkers**
can use the boat on a one-way trip (£15) simply to get to Loch Coruisk, from
where there are numerous possibilities for hiking amidst the Red Hills, the most
popular (and gentle) of which is the eight-mile trek north over the pass into
Glen Sligachan. Alternatively, you could walk round the coast to the sandy
bay of **Camasunary**, over two miles to the east – a difficult walk that involves
a tricky river crossing and negotiating "The Bad Step", an overhanging rock
with a thirty-foot drop to the sea – and either head north to Glen Sligachan,
continue south three miles along the coast to Elgol or continue east to the Am
Mam shoulder, for a stunning view of mountains and the islands of Soay, Rùm
and Canna. From Am Mam, the path leads down to the Elgol road, joining it
at Kilmarie.

The only public transport is the **postbus** from Broadford (Mon–Fri 2 daily,
Sat 1 daily), which delivers the post en route and takes over two hours to
reach Elgol in the morning. If you want a bite to eat, there's a coffee shop, or
the excellent seafood **restaurant** in *Coruisk House* (℡01471/866330, Ⓦwww
.seafood-skye.co.uk; April–Oct; ❺), which also offers **B&B** in its bright and
cheerful rooms. If you don't want to stay in Elgol, head for *Rowan Cottage*

(T01471/866287, Wwww.rowancottage-skye.co.uk; March–Oct; **4**) a lovely B&B a mile or so east in Glasnakille.

By far the most popular place to stay, though, is the **campsite** (April–Oct) by the *Sligachan Hotel* (T01478/650204, Wwww.sligachan.co.uk; **5**) on the A87, at the northern end of Glen Sligachan; the hotel also has a **bunkhouse**. Its huge *Seamus Bar* serves food for weary walkers until 11pm, and quenches their thirst with its own real ales, and often has live bands; there's also a more formal restaurant with splendid food.

Glen Brittle

Six miles along the A863 to Dunvegan from the *Sligachan Hotel*, a turning signed "Carbost and Portnalong" quickly leads to the entrance to stony **Glen Brittle**, edging the most spectacular peaks of the Cuillin; at the end of the glen, idyllically situated by the sea, is the village of **GLENBRITTLE**. Climbers and serious walkers tend to congregate at the SYHA **hostel** (T0870/004 1121, Wwww.syha.org.uk; April–Sept) or the beautifully situated **campsite** (T01478/640404; April–Oct), a mile or so further south behind the wide sandy beach at the foot of the glen. From mid-May to September, two buses a day (Mon–Sat only) from Portree make it to Glenbrittle; both the hostel and the campsite have grocery stores, the only ones for miles.

From the valley, a score of difficult and strenuous trails lead east into the **Black Cuillin**, a rough semicircle of peaks rising to about 3000ft, which surround Loch Coruisk. One of the easiest walks is the five-mile round-trip (3hr) from the campsite up **Coire Lagan**, to a crystal-cold lochan squeezed in among the sternest of rockfaces. Above the lochan is Skye's highest peak, **Sgurr Alasdair** (3258ft), one of the more difficult Munros, while Sgurr na Banachdich (3166ft) to the northwest is considered the most easily accessible Munro in the Cuillin (for the usual walking safety precautions, see p.64). The Mountain Rescue Service has produced a book of walks for those who are not climbers, available locally.

Dunvegan, Duirinish and Waternish

After the Portnalong and Glen Brittle turning, the A863 slips across bare rounded hills to skirt the bony sea cliffs and stacks of the west coast twenty miles or so north to **DUNVEGAN** (Dùn Bheagain). It's an unimpressive place, strung out along the east shore of the sea loch of the same name, though it does make quite a good base for exploring two interesting peninsulas: Duirinish and Waternish.

The main tourist trap in the village is **Dunvegan Castle** (daily: mid-March to Oct 10am–5pm; Nov to mid-March 11am–4pm; £7, gardens only £5; Wwww .dunvegancastle.com), which sprawls on top of a rocky outcrop, sandwiched between the sea and several acres of beautifully maintained gardens. It's been the seat of the Clan MacLeod since the thirteenth century, but the present greying, rectangular fortress, with its uniform battlements and dummy pepper pots, dates from the 1840s. Inside, you don't get a lot of castle for your money and the contents are far from stunning, but there are three famous items, the most intriguing of which is the battered remnants of the **Fairy Flag** which was allegedly carried back to Skye by Norwegian king, Harald Hardrada's Gaelic boatmen after the Battle of Stamford Bridge in 1066. The other two items are **Rory Mor's Horn**, a drinking vessel made from the horn of a mad bull which each new chief still has to drain at one draught "without setting down or falling down", and the **Dunvegan Cup**, made of bog oak covered in medieval silver filigree believed to have been given to Rory Mor by the O'Neils of Ulster in return for his help against England. Among the Jacobite mementoes are a lock of hair from the head of Bonnie Prince Charlie (whom the MacLeods, in fact, fought against) and Flora MacDonald's corsets. Elsewhere there's a "virtual" consumptive in the dungeon and an interesting display on the remote archipelago of St Kilda (see p.716), long the fiefdom of the MacLeods.

Duirinish and Glendale

The hammerhead **Duirinish peninsula** lies to the west of Dunvegan, much of it inaccessible to all except walkers prepared to scale or skirt the area's twin flat-topped basalt peaks: Healabhal Bheag (1600ft) and Healabhal Mhor (1538ft). The mountains are better known as **MacLeod's Tables**, for legend has it that the MacLeod chief held an open-air royal feast on the lower of the two for James V.

The main areas of habitation lie to the north, along the western shores of Loch Dunvegan, and in the broad green sweep of **Glen Dale** (Ⓦwww .glendale-skye.org.uk), attractively dotted with white farmhouses and dubbed "Little England" by the locals, due to its high percentage of "white settlers", English incomers searching for a better life. Glen Dale's current predicament is doubly ironic given its history, for it was here in 1882 that local crofters, following the example of their brethren in The Braes, staged a rent strike against their landlords, the MacLeods. Five locals – who became known as the "Glen Dale Martyrs" – were given two-month prison sentences, and eventually, in 1904, the crofters became the first owner-occupiers in the Highlands. All this, and a great deal more about nineteenth-century crofting, is told through fascinating contemporary news cuttings at **Colbost Folk Museum** (Easter–Oct daily 10am–6pm; £1.50), situated in a restored blackhouse, four miles up the road from Dunvegan. A guide is usually on hand to answer questions, the peat fire smokes all day, and there's a restored illegal whisky still round the back.

If you've got kids, you might like to pay a visit to the **Toy Museum** (Mon–Sat 10am–6pm; £2.50; Ⓦwww.toy-museum.co.uk), in **GLENDALE** itself, which has everything from early Meccano sets to fully equipped mini-crofters' kitchen, plus innumerable Sasha dolls and Marie and Donny Osmond string puppets. Beyond the village of Glendale itself, blustery but easy footpaths lead to the dramatically sited lighthouse on **Neist Point**, Skye's most westerly spot, which features some fearsome sea cliffs, and wonderful views across the sea to the Western Isles. Despite the fact that the present owner has put up "Keep Out!" notices, the locals continue to exert their right to roam right up to the lighthouse.

Waternish

Waternish is a thin and little-visited peninsula to the north of Dunvegan, whose prettiest village is **STEIN**, on the west coast looking out over Loch Bay and to the Western Isles. As you descend through the settlement, you eventually reach a row of whitewashed cottages built in 1787 by the British Fisheries Society. The place never really took off and by 1837 had been more or less abandoned. Today, however, it's coming back to life, particularly the pub, the sixteenth-century *Stein Inn*, which is well worth a visit.

At the end of the road is **Trumpan Church**, an evocative medieval ruin on a clifftop looking out to the Western Isles. This peaceful site was the scene of one of the bloodiest episodes in Skye history, when, in a revenge attack in 1578, the MacDonalds of Uist set fire to the church, while numerous MacLeods were attending a service inside. Everyone perished except one young girl who escaped by squeezing through a window, severing one of her breasts in the process. She raised the alarm, and the rest of the MacLeods quickly rallied and, bearing their famous Fairy Flag (see p.680), attacked the MacDonalds as they were launching their galleys. Every MacDonald was slaughtered and their bodies were thrown in a nearby dyke. In the churchyard, along with two medieval gravestones, you can also see the **Trial Stone**, a four-foot-high pillar with a hole drilled in it. Anyone accused of a crime was blindfolded and had to attempt to put their finger in it: success meant innocence; failure, death. Back on the A850, heading for Portree, a couple of miles before the junction with the A87, in Bernisdale, there are daily **sheepdog demonstrations** by a past finalist from the BBC's *One Man and his Dog* series; they're very popular, so booking is essential (℡01470/532331).

Practicalities

Dunvegan is by no means the most picturesque place on Skye, but it's a useful alternative base to Portree. It has a **tourist office** (Easter to mid-Oct Mon–Sat 9am–5.30pm; mid-Oct to Easter Mon–Fri 10am–1.30pm; ℡01470/521581) and boasts several good **hotels** and **B&Bs** dotted along the main road, such as the converted traditional croft *Roskhill House* (℡01470/521317, ⓦwww .roskhillhouse.co.uk; March–Nov; ❹) or the beautifully situated *Silverdale Guesthouse* (℡01470/521251, ⓦwww.silverdaleskye.com; ❸), just before you get to Colbost. There are a couple of excellent lochside **campsites**: one at Loch Greshornish, a mile north of Edinbane on the A850 (℡01470/582230, ⓦwww.skyecamp.com; April–Sept; bike and canoe rental available), and another on Loch Dunvegan (℡01470/521 531, ⓦwww.kinloch-campsite.co.uk; April–Nov), on the road to Colbost.

The culinary Mecca in the area is the expensive *Three Chimneys* **restaurant** (℡01470/511258, ⓦwww.threechimneys.co.uk; closed Sun lunch), located beside Colbost Folk Museum, which serves sublime three-course meals at £45 a head; the restaurant also has six fabulous rooms at the restaurant's adjacent *House Over-By* (❾), which cost £240 bed and breakfast. A good place to stay, with welcoming fires and good **pub food** is the sixteenth-century ⚓ *Stein Inn* (℡01470/592362, ⓦwww.steininn.co.uk; ❸), in Stein – next door is the much pricier *Lochbay Seafood Restaurant* (℡01470/592235; Easter–Oct closed Sat & Sun; Aug closed Sun), where you'll need to book ahead. Without doubt, the best place to eat in Dunvegan is *The Old School* (℡01470/521421) whose excellent food belies its appearance from outside. Otherwise, all the hotels do dinner and, on a more modest scale, there is a snug **café** attached to *Dunvegan Bakery* (confusingly the sign simply says "fish and chips").

Portree

Although referred to by the locals as "the village", **PORTREE**, with a population of around two thousand, is the only real town on Skye. It's also one of the most attractive fishing ports in northwest Scotland, its deep, cliff-edged harbour filled with fishing boats and circled by multicoloured restaurants and guesthouses. Originally known as *Kiltragleann* ("the church at the foot of the glen"), it takes its current name – some say – from *Portrigh* (Port of the King), after the state visit James V made in 1540 to assert his authority over the chieftains of Skye.

Information and accommodation

Hours vary enormously at Portree's **tourist office**, just off Bridge Street, so the ones here are just a guideline (April–Oct Mon–Sat 9am–8pm, Sun 10am–4pm;

Nov–March Mon–Sat 9am–5.30pm; ☎01478/612137). The office will, for a small fee, book **accommodation** for you – especially useful if you haven't booked ahead, and you can go online here. Accommodation prices tend to be higher in Portree than elsewhere on the island, especially in the town itself, though B&Bs on the outskirts are usually cheaper. The only **hostel** in Portree is the clean and smart *Portree Independent Hostel* (☎01478/613737, ⓦwww .portreehostel.f9.co.uk) housed in the Old Post Office on the Green. Torvaig **campsite** (☎01478/612209; April–Oct) is clean, well kept, with a friendly owner, and lies a mile and a half north of town off the A855 Staffin road.

Balloch Viewfield Rd ☎01478/612093, ⓦwww.balloch-skye.co.uk. Perfectly ordinary, reliable B&B (once visited by the Queen) just off the main road into Portree from the south. Open Easter–Oct. ❷

Bosville Bosville Terrace ☎01478/612846, ⓦwww.bosvillehotel.co.uk. Commands a good view of the harbour, and has a gourmet seafood restaurant. ❼

Cuillin Hills ten minutes' walk out of town along the northern shore of the bay ☎01478/612003, ⓦwww.cuillinhills-hotel-skye.co.uk. Very comfortable hotel, with a splendid view over the harbour and reasonably priced bar snacks. ❽

Medina Coolin Hills Gardens ☎01478/612821, ⓦwww.medinaskye.co.uk. Well-run B&B, with tasty breakfasts, in a quiet spot near the *Cuillin Hills Hotel*. ❸

Portree House Home Farm Rd ☎01478/611711, ⓦwww.portreehouse.co.uk. Built in 1810s by the MacDonalds, and set in lovely mature gardens, this hotel is just a few minutes' walk from the town centre. ❺

Skeabost House Skeabost, five miles northwest from Portree ☎01470/532202, ⓦwww.skeabost countryhouse.com. Late Victorian pile which offers the life of a country gent in the main building, with an original billiard room and, outdoors, fishing, golf and extensive gardens. Open March–Oct. ❽

🏃 **Viewfield House** ☎01478/612217, ⓦwww.viewfieldhouse.com. For real atmosphere and elegance, it's hard to beat this hotel on the southern outskirts of town, which has been in the hands of the MacDonalds for over two hundred years, and has a wonderful Victorian air, stuffed polecats and antiques. Open mid-April to mid-Oct. ❻

The Town

The **harbour** is well worth a stroll, with its attractive pier built by Thomas Telford in the early nineteenth century. Fishing boats still land a modest catch, some of which is sold through Anchor Seafoods (Tues–Fri only) at the end of the pier. The harbour is overlooked by **The Lump**, a steep and stumpy peninsula with a flagpole on it that was once the site of public hangings on the island, attracting crowds of up to 5000; it also sports a folly built by the celebrated Dr Ban, a visionary who wanted to make Portree into a second Oban. Up above the harbour is the spick-and-span town centre, spreading out from **Somerled Square**, built in the late eighteenth century as the island's administrative and commercial centre, and now housing the bus station and car park. The **Royal Hotel** on Bank Street occupies the site of *McNab's Inn* where Bonnie Prince Charlie took leave of Flora MacDonald (see box on p.686), and where, 27 years later, Boswell and Johnson had "a very good dinner, porter, port and punch".

A mile or so out of town on the Sligachan road is the **Aros Centre** (daily 9am–6pm; open later in summer; ⓦwww.aros.co.uk), one of Skye's most successful tourist attractions despite the fact that it's little more than one enormous souvenir shop. If it's wet, you can grab a live RSPB webcam centred on sea eagles' nests and an audiovisual roam around the island (£4). The best bit about Aros is that it hosts gigs (see p.684) and contains a **cinema**, a modern exhibition space, a licensed bar and a popular café, and there's a special play area for small kids. If it's fine, there are easy waymarked forest walks from the car park.

For a view of the contemporary visual art scene, it's well worth seeking out **An Tuireann**, an arts centre housed in a converted fever hospital on the Struan road (Mon–Sat 10am–5pm; free; ⓦ www.antuireann.org.uk), which puts on exhibitions, stages concerts and has an excellent small licensed café (Tues–Sat only) where even the counter is a work of art, with an imaginative range of food on offer.

Eating, drinking and nightlife

Eating out can be pretty pricey in Portree, with the likes of the *Bosville Hotel's* outstanding *Chandlery* restaurant (eves only) offering set menus from £28 a head, although the *Bosville Bistro* is much cheaper. Other options include *Harbour View* (Ⓣ01478/612069, ⓦ www.harbourviewskye.co.uk; closed Wed), a seafood restaurant, also on Bosville Terrace, with candlelit ambience and very fresh fish on the menu. The popular *Lower Deck Seafood Restaurant* (Ⓣ01478/613611) on the harbour has a wood-panelled warmth to it, and is reasonably priced at lunchtime (less so in the evenings, when booking is essential); for good **fish and chips**, pop next door to their excellent chippy. If you're after somewhere a bit more relaxed, look no further than *Café Arriba*, at the top of road down to the harbour, which offers an array of reasonably priced Mediterranean dishes. For a simple cuppa and a cake, there's the *Granary* bakery's **teashop** on Somerled Square. The *Café*, an ice-cream parlour on Wentworth Street, serves a selection of cakes, toasties and paninis. As for **pubs**, the bar of the *Pier Hotel* on the quayside is the fishermen's drinking hole, and the *Tongadale* on Wentworth Street is a lively, convivial place. Currently the most popular evening venue by far, though, is the *Isles Inn* on Somerled Square, which has excellent bar meals as well as live music.

The aforementioned Aros Centre has a **theatre**, which shows films and hosts Gaelic **concerts** (for more details phone Ⓣ01471/613649);

concerts and events also go on at An Tuireann (see p.683), and it's worth checking out what's on at the Portree Community Centre (Ⓣ01478/613736), which hosts ceilidhs and so forth. For **bike rental**, go to Island Cycles (closed Sun; Ⓣ01478/613121) below The Green; for **horse riding**, head for the Portree Riding Stables off the B885 to Struan, signposted "Peiness" (Ⓣ 01478/613124, ⓦ www.portreeriding.co.uk). Day or half-day **boat trips** leave the pier for daily excursions to Raasay and Rona (Ⓣ01478/613718); **diving** can be organized through Dive-and-Sea the Hebrides in Lochbay, towards Dunvegan (Ⓣ01470/592219, ⓦ www.dive-and-sea-the-hebrides.co.uk). Look out, too, for occasional **bird of prey displays** organized by the local Isle of Skye Falconry (Ⓣ01470/532489, ⓦ www.isleof skye-falconry.co.uk), which also runs courses.

△ Fish suppers at Portree

Trotternish

Protruding twenty miles north from Portree, the **Trotternish peninsula** boasts some of the island's most bizarre scenery, particularly on the east coast, where volcanic basalt has pressed down on the softer sandstone and limestone underneath, causing massive landslides. These, in turn, have created sheer cliffs, peppered with outcrops of hard, wizened basalt, which run the full length of the peninsula. These pinnacles and pillars are at their most eccentric in the **Quiraing**, above Staffin Bay, on the east coast. Trotternish is best explored with your own transport, but an occasional bus service (Mon–Sat 2–4 daily) along the road encircling the peninsula gives access to almost all the coast.

The east coast

The first geological eccentricity on the Trotternish peninsula, six miles north of Portree along the A855, is the **Old Man of Storr**, a distinctive column of rock, shaped like a willow leaf, which, along with its neighbours, is part of a massive landslip. Huge blocks of stone still occasionally break off the cliff face of the Storr (2358ft) above and slide downhill. At 165ft, the Old Man is a real challenge for climbers; less difficult is the half-hour trek up the new footpath to the foot of the column from the woods beside the car park.

Further north, **Staffin Bay** is spread out before you, dotted with white-washed and "spotty" houses; **STAFFIN** itself is a lively, largely Gaelic-speaking community where crofts have been handed down the generations. A single-track road cuts across the peninsula from the north end of the bay, allowing access to the **Quiraing**, a spectacular forest of mighty pinnacles and savage rock formations. There are two car parks: from the first, beside a cemetery, it's a steep half-hour climb to the rocks; from the second, on the saddle it's a longer but more gentle traverse. Once you're in the midst of the rocks, you should be able to make out the Prison to your right, and the 120-foot Needle, to your left; the Table, a great sunken platform where locals used to play shinty, lies above and beyond the Needle, another fifteen-minute scramble up the rocks; legend also maintains that a local warrior named Fraing hid his cattle there from the invading Norsemen.

Most **accommodation** choices on the east coast enjoy fantastic views out over the sea. Just beyond the Lealt Falls there's the very welcoming and comfortable *Glenview Inn* (☎01470/562248, ⓦwww.glenview-skye.co.uk; ❹), with an excellent restaurant, and a **campsite** (☎01470/562213; April–Sept) south of Staffin Bay. In fine weather, you can enjoy good bar snacks on the castellated terrace of the stylish *Flodigarry Country House Hotel* (☎01470/552203, ⓦwww.flodigarry.co.uk; ❻), three miles up the coast from Staffin. Behind the hotel (and now part of it) is the cottage where local heroine Flora MacDonald lived, and had six of her seven children, from 1751 to 1759. If the hotel's rooms are beyond your means, you can **camp** or stay at the neat and attractive *Dun Flodigarry* **hostel** (☎01470/552212), a couple of minutes' walk away.

Duntulm and Kilmuir

Beyond Flodigarry, at the tip of the Trotternish peninsula, by the road to Shulista, a public footpath leads past the ruins of a cleared hamlet to the spectacular sea stacks of **Rubha Hunish**, the most northerly point on Skye. A couple of miles further along the A855 lies **DUNTULM** (Duntuilm), whose heyday as a major MacDonald power base is recalled by the shattered remains of a headland fortress abandoned by the clan in 1732 after a clumsy nurse dropped the baby son and heir from a window onto the rocks below; on these same

Bonnie Prince Charlie

Prince Charles Edward Stewart – better known as **Bonnie Prince Charlie** or "The Young Pretender" – was born in Rome in 1720, where his father, "The Old Pretender", claimant to the British throne, was living in exile. At the age of 25, having little military experience, no knowledge of Gaelic, an imperfect grasp of English and a strong attachment to the Catholic faith, the prince set out for Scotland on a French ship, disguised as a seminarist from the Scots College in Paris. He arrived on the Outer Hebridean island of Eriskay (see p.719) on July 23, 1745, and was immediately implored to return to France by the clan chiefs, who were singularly unimpressed by his lack of army. Charles was unmoved and went on to raise the royal standard at Glenfinnan (see p.620), gather together a Highland army, win the Battle of Preston-pans, march on London and reach Derby before finally (and foolishly) agreeing to retreat. Back in Scotland, he won one last victory, at Falkirk, before the final disaster at Culloden in April 1746.

The prince spent the following five months in hiding, with a price of £30,000 on his head, and literally thousands of government troops searching for him. He certainly endured his fair share of cold and hunger whilst on the run, but the real price was paid by the Highlanders themselves, who risked their lives (and often paid for it with them) by aiding and abetting the prince. The most famous of these was, of course, 23-year-old **Flora MacDonald**, whom Charles met on South Uist in June 1746. Flora was persuaded – either by his beauty or her relatives, depending on which account you believe – to convey Charles "over the sea to Skye", disguised as an Irish servant girl by the name of Betty Burke. She was arrested just seven days after parting with the prince in Portree, and held in the Tower of London until July 1747. She went on to marry a local man, had seven children, and in 1774 emigrated to America, where her husband was taken prisoner during the American War of Independence. Flora returned to Scotland and was reunited with her husband on his release; they resettled in Skye and she died at the age of 68.

Charles eventually boarded a ship back to France in September 1746, but, despite his promises – "for all that has happened, Madam, I hope we shall meet in St James's yet" – never returned to Scotland, nor did he ever see Flora again. After mistreating a string of mistresses, he eventually got married at the age of 52 to the 19-year-old Princess of Stolberg, in an effort to produce a Stewart heir. They had no children, and she eventually fled from his violent drunkenness; in 1788, a none-too-"bonnie" Prince Charles died in the arms of his illegitimate daughter in Rome. Bonnie Prince Charlie became a legend in his own lifetime, but it was the Victorians who really milked the myth for all its sentimentality, conveniently overlooking the fact that the real conse-quence of 1745 was the virtual annihilation of the Highland way of life.

rocks, it is said, can be seen the keel marks of Viking longships. The imposing *Duntulm Castle Hotel* (March–Nov) is close by, and provides good pub food as well as wonderful views across the Minch to the Western Isles.

Heading down the west shore of the Trotternish, it's two miles to the **Skye Museum of Island Life** (Easter–Oct Mon–Sat 9.30am–5.30pm; £1.75), an impressive cluster of thatched blackhouses on an exposed hill overlooking Harris. The museum, run by locals, gives a fascinating insight into a way of life that was commonplace on Skye a hundred years ago. The blackhouse, now home to the ticket office, is much as it was when it was last inhab-ited in 1957, while the two houses to the east contain interesting snippets of local history. Behind the museum in the cemetery up the hill are the graves of **Flora MacDonald** and her husband. Thousands turned out for her funeral in 1790, creating a funeral procession a mile long – indeed, so widespread was her fame that the original family mausoleum fell victim to souvenir hunters and had to be replaced. The Celtic cross headstone is inscribed with a simple tribute by Dr Johnson, who visited her in 1773: "Her name will be mentioned in history, if courage and fidelity be virtues, mentioned with honour."

The land around **KILMUIR**, a mile or so to the south, used to be called the "Granary of Skye", since every inch was cultivated: even St Columba's Loch, where there are still indistinct remains of beehive cells and a chapel, was drained and the land eagerly reclaimed by crofters. **Accommodation** is available in the attractive *Kilmuir House*, previously the old manse (T01470/542262, W www.kilmuir-skye.co.uk; ❷). If you're looking for action, contact *Whitewave* (T01470/542414, W www.white-wave.co.uk), in Linicro; they organize everything from **windsurfing** and **sea kayaking** to **hill walking** and **archery**.

Uig

A further four miles south of Kilmuir is the ferry port of **UIG** (Uige), which curves its way round a dramatic, horseshoe-shaped bay, and is the arrival point for CalMac ferries from Tarbert (Harris) and Lochmaddy (North Uist); if you've time to spare while waiting for a ferry, pop into Uig Pottery (W www.uigpottery.co.uk), next to the pier car park. Most folk come to Uig to take the ferry to the Western Isles, but if you need to stay near the ferry terminal, there are a couple of decent inexpensive **B&Bs**: *Orasay*, 14 Idrigill (T01470/542316, W www.orasay.freeserve.co.uk; ❶), a minute's walk from the pier, and *Braigh-uige* (T01470/542228, W www.uig-skye.co.uk; March–Oct; ❶), on the other side of the bay near the church. The **campsite**, on a sloping field very close to the pier (T01470/542714, W www.uig-camping-skye.co.uk), is open all year and also offers **bike rental**. By contrast, the SYHA **hostel** (T0870/004 1155; April–Oct) is a fifteen-minute walk away, high up on the south side of the village, with exhilarating views over the bay. The *Pub at the Pier* offers basic **meals**, and serves beers from the Outer Hebrides and the nearby **brewery** (Mon–Fri tours by appointment; T01470/542477, W www.skyebrewery.co.uk).

The Small Isles

The history of the **Small Isles**, which lie to the south of Skye, is typical of the Hebrides: early Christianization, followed by a period of Norwegian rule that ended in 1266 when the islands fell into Scottish hands. Their support for the Jacobite cause resulted in hard times after the failed rebellion of 1745, but the biggest problems came with the introduction of the **potato** in the mid-eighteenth century. The consequences were as dramatic as they were unforeseen: the success of the crop and its nutritional value – when grown in conjunction with traditional cereals – eliminated famine at a stroke, prompting a population explosion. In 1750, there were a thousand islanders, but by 1800 their numbers had almost doubled.

At first, the problem of overcrowding was camouflaged by the **kelp** boom, in which the islanders were employed, and the islands' owners made a fortune, gathering and burning local seaweed to sell for use in the manufacture of gunpowder, soap and glass. But the economic bubble burst with the end of the Napoleonic Wars and, to maintain their profit margins, the owners resorted to drastic action. The first to sell up was Alexander MacLean, who sold Rùm as grazing land for **sheep**, got quotations for shipping its people to Nova Scotia and gave them a year's notice to quit. He also cleared Muck to graze cattle, as did the MacNeills on Canna. Only on Eigg was some compassion shown: the new owner, a certain Hugh MacPherson, who bought the island from the Clanranalds in 1827, actually gave some of his tenants extended leases.

Since the Clearances, each of the islands has been bought and sold several times, though only **Muck** is now privately owned by the benevolent laird, Lawrence MacEwen. **Eigg** hit the headlines in 1997, when the islanders finally managed to buy the island themselves and put an end to more than 150 years of property speculation. The other islands were bequeathed to national agencies: **Rùm**, by far the largest and most-visited of the group, possessing a cluster of formidable volcanic peaks and the architecturally remarkable Kinloch Castle, passed to the Nature Conservancy Council (now Scottish Natural Heritage) in 1957; and **Canna**, in many ways the prettiest of the isles with its high basalt cliffs, has been in the hands of the National Trust for Scotland since 1981.

Accommodation on the Small Isles is limited and requires **forward planning** at all times of year; formal public transport is nonexistent, but the locals will usually oblige if you have heavy baggage to shift.

Rùm

Like Skye, **Rùm** is dominated by its Cuillin, which, though reaching a height of only 2663ft at the summit of Askival, rises with comparable drama straight up from the sea in the south of the island. The majority of the island's twenty or so inhabitants now live in **KINLOCH**, on the sheltered east coast, and most are employed by Scottish Natural Heritage (SNH), which runs the island as a National Nature Reserve. SNH have been reintroducing native woodland to the island, and overseeing a long-term study of the vast red-deer population. However, the organization's most notable achievement to date is the reintroduction of **white-tailed (sea) eagles**, whose wingspan is even greater than that of the golden eagle. These magnificent birds of prey were last known to have bred on the Isle of Skye in 1916. After a caesura of some seventy years, the eagles returned, and have since mostly abandoned Rùm in favour of neighbouring islands. You can learn more about the history of the island, and its flora and fauna, in the small **museum** near the old pier.

Rùm's chief formal attraction is **Kinloch Castle** (guided tours most days around 2pm; £5), a squat red sandstone edifice fronted by colonnades and topped by crenellations and turrets, that dominates the village of Kinloch. Completed at enormous expense in 1900 – the red sandstone was shipped in from Dumfriesshire and the soil for the gardens from Ayrshire – and now in need of some serious restoration, its interior is a perfectly preserved example of Edwardian decadence, "a living memorial of the stalking, the fishing and the sailing, the tenantry and plenty of the days before 1914". From the galleried hall, with its tiger rugs, stags' heads and giant Japanese incense burners, to the "Extra Low Fast Cushion" of the Soho snooker table in the Billiard Room, the interior is packed with knick-knacks and technical gizmos accumulated by **Sir George Bullough** (1870–1939), the spendthrift son of self-made millionaire, Sir John Bullough, who bought the island as a sporting estate in 1888. As such, it was only really used for a few weeks each autumn, during the "season", yet employed an island workforce of one hundred all year round. Bullough's guests were woken at eight each morning by a piper; later on, an orchestrion, an electrically driven barrel organ (originally destined for Balmoral), crammed in under the stairs, would grind out an eccentric mixture of pre-dinner tunes: *The Ride of the Valkyries* and *Ma Blushin' Rosie* among others (a demo is included in the tour). The ballroom has a sprung floor, the library features a gruesome photographic collection from the Bulloughs' world tours, but the *pièce de résistance* has to be Bullough's **Edwardian bathrooms**, whose baths have hooded walnut shower cabinets, fitted with two taps and four dials, which allow bathers to fire high-pressure water at their bodies from every angle.

For those with limited time or energy, there are two gentle waymarked **trails**, both of which start from Kinloch, and take around two hours to complete. For longer walks, you must fill in route cards and pop them into the *White House* (Mon–Fri 9am–12.30pm), where the reserve manager can give useful advice; they also occasionally offer **guided walks** around the island including a night-time hike to see the shearwaters on the slopes of Hallival.

The island's best beach is at **KILMORY**, to the north (5hr return), where students get eaten alive by midges while studying red deer. When the island's human head count peaked at 450 in 1791, the hamlet of **HARRIS** on the southwest coast (6hr return) housed a large crofting community – all that remains now are several ruined blackhouses and the extravagant **Bullough Mausoleum**, built by Sir George to house the remains of his father in the style of a Greek Doric temple, overlooking the sea. This is, in fact, the second one to be constructed here: the first was lined with Italian marble mosaics, but when a friend remarked that it looked like a public lavatory Bullough had it dynamited and the current Neoclassical one erected.

Practicalities

Until Rùm passed into the hands of the SNH, it was known as the "Forbidden Isle" because of its exclusive use as a sporting estate for the rich; nowadays, visitors are made very welcome by the SNH staff. Day-trips are possible more or less daily in the summer, either via CalMac or the Sheerwater (see box, opposite). If you plan to stay the night, you do need to book in advance, as **accommodation** is fairly limited. Kinloch Castle was a luxury hotel until the early 1990s, and still lets a few of its four-poster rooms (⑤), but it's basically run as an independent **hostel** (☎01687/462037), with dormitories in the old servants' quarters. B&B is sometimes available on the island – ask at the hostel for the latest. There are also two simple mountain **bothies** (three nights maximum stay), in Dibidil, on the southeast coast, and Guirdil, on the northwest coast, and basic **camping** (toilets and a standpipe) on the foreshore near the old pier. You need to book ahead for both by contacting the reserve manager at the *White House* (☎01687/462026).

Wherever you're staying, you can either do self-catering – hostellers can use the hostel kitchen – or eat in the hostel's licensed **bistro**, which serves full breakfasts, offers packed lunches and charges just over £10 a head for a tasty three-course evening meal (advance booking essential). There is also a small shop/off-licence/post office on the north side of the bay. Bear in mind that Rùm is the wettest of the Small Isles, and is known for having some of the worst **midges** (see p.63) in Scotland – come prepared for both. Finally, note that overnight visitors cannot bring dogs, but day-trippers can.

Eigg

Eigg (ⓦwww.isleofeigg.org) is without doubt the most easily distinguishable of the Small Isles from a distance, since the island – which measures just five miles by three – is mostly made up of a basalt plateau 1000ft above sea level, and a great stump of columnar pitchstone lava, known as An Sgurr, rising out of the plateau another 290ft. It's also by far the most vibrant, populous and welcoming of the Small Isles, with a real strong sense of community. This was given an enormous boost by the 1997 buyout by the seventy-odd islanders (along with the local council and the Scottish Wildlife Trust), which ended Eigg's unhappy history of private ownership, most notoriously with the Olympic bobsleigher and gelatine heir Keith Schellenberg. The anniversary of the buyout is celebrated every year with an all-night ceilidh on the weekend nearest 12 June.

Ferries arrive at the new causeway, which juts out into **Galmisdale Bay**, at the southeast corner of the island where **An Laimhrig** (The Anchorage), the island's community centre, stands, housing a shop, post office, licensed tearoom and information centre. Davie's minibus meets incoming ferries, and will take you to wherever you need to go on the island (ⓣ01687/482494; £2). If time is limited, you could simply head through the woods for the nearby **Lodge**, the former laird's house and gardens, which the islanders plan to renovate in the future. With the island's great landmark, **An Sgurr** (1292ft), watching over

you wherever you go, many folk feel duty-bound to climb it, and enjoy the wonderful views over to Muck and Rùm. The easiest approach is to take the path that skirts the summit to the north, and ascend from the saddle to the west (3–4hr return).

Many visitors head off to **CLEADALE**, the main crofting settlement in the north of the island, where the beach, known as Camas Sgiotaig, or the **Singing Sands**, is comprised of quartz, which squeaks underfoot when dry (hence the name). The steep climb up to the ridge of **Ben Bhuidhe**, to the east, is hard going, but worth it for the views across to Rùm and Skye. A large colony of **Manx shearwaters** nests in burrows

△ An Sgurr, Eigg

around the base of Ben Bhuidhe; to view the birds, you need to be there just after dusk.

If you're just here for the day, make sure you pop into the **tearoom**, which has a lovely terrace looking out to sea. The nicest place **to stay** on Eigg is ⚓ *Kildonan House* (☎01687/482446; full board ❹), an eighteenth-century, wood-panelled house beautifully situated on the north side of Galmisdale Bay, with good home cooking. There are several **self-catering** options, which you can get off the island's website, plus *Glebe Barn* (☎01687/482417), a very comfortable **bunkhouse** where you must book ahead. Wild **camping** is also possible at Galmisdale Bay and in Cleadale with Sue Hollands (☎01687/482480, Ⓔsuehollands@talk21.com), who also rents out a bothy. **Bike rental** is available from Eigg Bikes (☎01687/482432), by the pier. You'll probably notice, as you walk around the island, that Eigg has no mains **electricity**; some houses have water-generated electricity, but others still run off noisy diesel generators.

Muck

Smallest and most southerly of the Small Isles, **Muck** (Ⓦwww.islemuck.com) is low-lying, mostly treeless and extremely fertile, and as such shares more characteristics with the likes of Coll and Tiree than its nearest neighbours. Its name derives from *muc*, the Gaelic for "pig" – or, as some would have it, *muc mara*, "sea pig" or porpoise, which abound in the surrounding waters – and has long caused much embarrassment to generations of lairds who preferred to call it the "Isle of Monk", because it had briefly belonged to the medieval church.

PORT MÓR, the village on the southeast corner of the island, is where visitors arrive and where most of the thirty or so residents live. A road, just over a mile in length, connects Port Mór with the island's main farm, **GALLANACH**, which overlooks the rocky seal-strewn skerries on the north side of the island. The nicest sandy beach is Camas na Cairidh, to the east of Gallanach. Despite its being only 452ft above sea level, it really is worth climbing **Beinn Airein** (2hr return), in the southwest corner of the island, for the 360-degree panoramic view of the surrounding islands.

You can **stay** with one of the MacEwen family, who have owned the island since 1896, at *Port Mór House* (☎01687/462365; full board ❹); the rooms are pine-clad and enjoy great views, and the food is delicious. Alternatively, you can stay at the island's **bunkhouse** (☎01687/462362), a characterful, wood-panelled bothy heated by a Rayburn stove – it's a seven-bed hostel, with three rooms, but can be booked exclusively as a self-catering unit. You can also hire the island **yurt** or the **tipi** (☎01687/462362, Ⓔjenny@isleofmuck.fsnet.co.uk), or **camp rough** on the island for free; ask at the craft shop for where to camp, and bring supplies with you, as there is no shop. For more **self-catering** options visit the island website.

The craft shop in Port Mór springs into life when day-trippers arrive, and doubles as a licensed **restaurant**. Willow basketmaking courses (☎01687/462362, Ⓔjenny@isleofmuck.fsnet.co.uk) are an island speciality.

Canna

Measuring a mere five miles by one, and with just a handful of full-time residents, **Canna** is run as a single farm and bird sanctuary by the NTS (National Trust for Scotland). The island enjoys the best harbour in the Small Isles, a horn-shaped haven at its southeastern corner protected by the tidal island of Sanday, now linked to Canna by a wooden footbridge. For visitors, the chief pastime is walking: from the dock it's about a mile across a grassy basalt plateau to the bony sea cliffs of the north shore, which rise to a peak around Compass Hill (458ft) – so called because its high metal content distorts compasses – in the northeastern corner of the island, from where you get great views across to Rùm and Skye. The cliffs of the buffeted western half of the island are a breeding ground for both Manx shearwaters and puffins, though both have suffered from the island's rat infestation. Some seven miles offshore, stands the **Heiskeir of Canna**, a curious mass of stone columns sticking up thirty feet above the water.

Accommodation is extremely limited. With permission from the NTS, you may **camp rough** on Canna, though you need to bring your own supplies, as there's no real shop to speak of. The NTS runs **self-catering** cottages, *Tighard*, a Victorian house half a mile from the jetty, which sleeps a maximum of ten people, and *Kate's Cottage*, a much simpler (and cheaper) bothy, which sleeps six, plus a hostel for groups in the distinctive St Edward's Church on Sanday. All the above should be booked through the NTS holidays department (☎0131/243 9300, ⓦwww.nts.org.uk). The NTS rep on Canna is Wendy MacKinnon, who can help answer most queries (☎01687/462465, ⓦwww.harbourview-canna .co.uk) and runs the *Harbour View* licensed **tearoom**, which serves lunch and dinner (March–Oct; advance booking essential).

Travel details

Trains

Aberdeen to: Kyle of Lochalsh (Mon–Sat 3 daily, 1 on Sun; 5hr).
Fort William to: Mallaig (4–5 daily; 1hr 25min).
Glasgow (Queen St) to: Mallaig (Mon–Sat 4 daily, 2 on Sun; 5hr 20min).
Inverness to: Kyle of Lochalsh (Mon–Sat 3–4 daily, 1–2 on Sun; 2hr 30min).

Buses

From the mainland

Glasgow to: Broadford (3–4 daily; 5hr 25min); Portree (3–4 daily; 6hr–6hr 30min); Uig (Mon–Sat 3–4 daily; 7hr 40min).
Inverness to: Broadford (2 daily; 2hr 50min); Portree (2 daily; 3hr 15min).
Kyle of Lochalsh to: Kyleakin (every 30min; 10min).

On Skye

Armadale to: Broadford (Mon–Sat 3–10 daily; 45min); Portree (Mon–Sat 3–10 daily; 1hr 20min); Sligachan (Mon–Sat 3–10 daily; 1hr 10min).
Broadford to: Portree (Mon–Sat 5–10 daily; 40min).
Dunvegan to: Glendale (Mon–Sat 1–2 daily; 30min).
Kyleakin to: Broadford (Mon–Sat 4–10 daily, 3–5 on Sun; 15min); Portree (Mon–Sat 4 daily, 3–5 on Sun; 1hr); Sligachan (Mon–Sat 7–8 daily, 5 on Sun; 45min); Uig (Mon–Sat 2 daily; 1hr 20min).
Portree to: Carbost (Mon–Fri 4–5 daily, 1 on Sat; 35min); Duntulm (Mon–Sat 2–4 daily; 1hr); Dunvegan (Mon–Sat 2–4 daily; 50min); Glenbrittle (April–Sept Mon–Sat 2 daily; 1hr); Staffin (Mon–Sat 2–4 daily; 40min); Uig (Mon–Sat 4–5 daily; 30min).

CalMac ferries

Summer timetable only.
To Canna: Eigg–Canna (Mon & Sat; 2hr 15min); Mallaig–Canna (Mon, Wed, Fri & Sat; 2hr 40min–3hr 50min); Muck–Canna (Sat; 1hr 35min); Rùm–Canna (Mon, Wed, Fri & Sat; 55min).
To Eigg: Canna–Eigg (Mon & Sat; 2hr 15min); Mallaig–Eigg (Mon, Tues & Thurs–Sat; 1hr 15min–2hr 25min); Muck–Eigg (Tues & Thurs–Sat; 30min); Rùm–Eigg (Mon & Sat; 1hr–3hr 30min).
To Muck: Canna–Muck (Sat; 1hr 35min); Eigg–Muck (Tues, Thurs & Sat; 30min); Mallaig–Muck (Tues, Thurs, Fri & Sat; 1hr 40min–4hr 20min); Rùm–Muck (Sat; 2hr 45min).
To Raasay: Sconser–Raasay (Mon–Sat 9–11 daily, Sun 2 daily; 15min).
To Rùm: Canna–Rùm (Mon, Wed, Fri & Sat; 55min); Eigg–Rùm (Mon & Sat; 1hr–3hr 30min); Mallaig–Rùm (Mon, Wed, Fri & Sat; 1hr 20min–2hr 30min); Muck–Rùm (Sat; 55min).
To Skye: Glenelg–Kylerhea (daily frequently; 15min); Mallaig–Armadale (Mon–Sat 8–9 daily; mid-May to mid-Sept also Sun; 30min).

The Western Isles

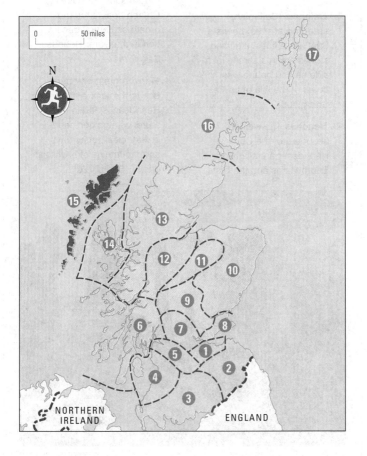

CHAPTER 15

Highlights

✻ **Gearrannan (Garenin), Lewis** A crofting village of painstakingly restored thatched blackhouses: you can stay in the hostel, or simply have a guided tour round the site. **See p.704**

✻ **Calanais (Callanish) standing stones, Lewis** Scotland's finest standing stones are in a serene loch-side setting on the west coast of the Isle of Lewis. **See p.705**

✻ **Beaches** The western seaboard of the Outer Hebrides, particularly on South Harris and the Uists, is strewn with stunning, deserted golden-sand beaches backed by flower-strewn machair. **See p.710**

✻ **Roghadal (Rodel) Church, Harris** Roghadal's pre-Reformation St Clement's Church boasts the most ornate sculptural decoration in the Outer Hebrides. **See p.712**

✻ **Barra** A great introduction to the Western Isles: a Hebridean island in miniature, with golden sands, crystal-clear rocky bays and mountains of Lewissian gneiss. **See p.720**

△ Calanais standing stones, Lewis

15

The Western Isles

Beyond Skye, across the unpredictable waters of the Minch, lie the wild and windy Outer Hebrides or Outer Isles, also known as the **Western Isles** (Ⓦwww.visithebrides.com), a 130-mile-long archipelago stretching from Lewis and Harris in the north to the Uists and Barra in the south. An elemental beauty pervades each of the more than two hundred islands that make up the Long Isle, as it's sometimes known, though only a handful are inhabited by a total population of just under 27,000 people. This is truly a land on the edge, where the turbulent seas of the Atlantic smash up against a geologically complex terrain whose rough rocks and mighty sea cliffs are interrupted by a thousand sheltered bays and, in the far west, a long line of sweeping sandy beaches. The islands' interiors are equally dramatic, a series of formidable mountain ranges soaring high above great chunks of flat, boggy peat moor, a barren wilderness enclosing a host of tiny lakes, or lochans.

However, the most significant difference between the Western Isles and the rest of the Hebrides is that here tourism is much less important to the islands' fragile economy, which is still mainly concentrated around crofting, fishing and weaving, and the percentage of "white settlers" is fairly low. In fact, the Outer Hebrides remain the heartland of **Gaelic** culture, with the language spoken by the vast majority of islanders, though its everyday usage remains under constant threat from the national dominance of English. Its survival is, in no small part, due to the efforts of the Western Islands Council and the Scottish Executive, and down to the influence of the Church in the region: the Free Church and its various Presbyterian offshoots, in Lewis, Harris and North Uist and the Roman Catholic church in South Uist and Barra.

The interior of the northernmost island, **Lewis**, is mostly peat moor, a barren and marshy tract that gives way abruptly to the bare peaks of **North Harris**. Linked only by a narrow isthmus, **South Harris**, presents some of the finest scenery in Scotland, with wide beaches of golden sand trimming the Atlantic in full view of the mountains and a rough boulder-strewn interior lying to the east. Across the Sound of Harris, to the south, a string of tiny, flatter isles – **North Uist**, **Benbecula**, **South Uist** – linked by causeways, offer breezy beaches, whose fine sands front a narrow band of boggy farmland, which, in turn, is mostly bordered by a lower range of hills to the east. Finally, tiny **Barra** contains all these landscapes in one small Hebridean package.

In direct contrast to their wonderful landscapes, villages in the Western Isles are rarely very picturesque in themselves, and are usually made up of scattered, relatively modern crofthouses dotted about the elementary road system. **Stornoway**, the only real town in the Outer Hebrides, is eminently

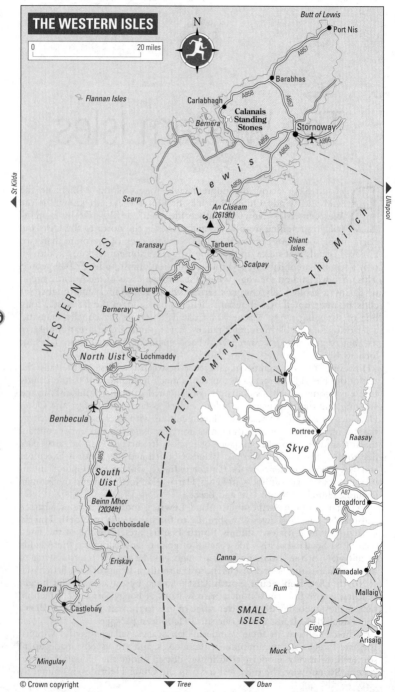

THE WESTERN ISLES

N

0 ——————— 20 miles

Butt of Lewis

Port Nis

A857

Barabhas

Flannan Isles

Carlabhagh   A858   A857

Calanais Standing Stones

Bernera   Stornoway

A858   A859   A866

L e w i s

A859

St Kilda

Scarp   An Cliseam
                            (2619ft)   *Shiant Isles*

Taransay   Tarbert   T h e   M i n c h

H a r r i s   *Scalpay*

W E S T E R N   I S L E S

Leverburgh   A859

Berneray

North Uist   Lochmaddy

A865   Uig

Benbecula

T h e   L i t t l e   M i n c h

A865   Portree   *Raasay*

South Uist   Skye

Beinn Mhor
(2034ft)

Lochboisdale   A87

Broadford

Eriskay

Canna   Armadale

Barra   *Rum*   Mallaig

Castlebay

SMALL ISLES

Eigg

Mingulay   *Muck*   Arisaig

▼ *Tiree*   ▼ *Oban*

Uig

Ullapool

Except in Stornoway, and Balivanich on Benbecula, **road signs** are now almost exclusively in **Gaelic**, a difficult language to the English-speaker's eye, with complex pronunciation (see p.855), though as a (very) general rule, the English names often provide a rough pronunciation guide. Particularly if you're driving, it's a good idea to buy the bilingual Western Isles **map**, produced by the local tourist board, Bord Turasachd nan Eilean, and available at most tourist offices. To reflect the signposting, we've put the Gaelic first in the text, with the English equivalent in brackets. Thereafter we've stuck to the Gaelic names, to try to familiarize readers with their (albeit variable) spellings – the only exceptions are in the names of islands and ferry terminals, where we've stuck to the English names (with the Gaelic in brackets) partly to reflect the ferry company CalMac's own policy.

unappealing. Many visitors, walkers and nature watchers forsake the main settlements altogether and retreat to secluded cottages, simple hostels and B&Bs.

Visiting the Western Isles

Several airlines operate fast and frequent daily **flights** from Glasgow, Edinburgh and Inverness to Stornoway on Lewis, and from Glasgow to Barra and Benbecula (Mon–Sat only). But be warned: the weather conditions on the islands are notoriously changeable, making flights prone to cancellation, delay and stomach-churning bumpiness. On Barra, the other complication is that you land on the beach, so the timetable is adjusted with the tides. CalMac **car ferries** run from Ullapool in the Highlands to Stornoway (Mon–Sat only); from Uig, on Skye, to Tarbert (Mon–Sat) and Lochmaddy (daily); and from Oban to South Uist and Barra (daily), via Tiree (Thurs only). There's also an **inter-island ferry** from Leverburgh, on Harris, to Berneray (Mon–Sat only), and thence to the Uists, and daily between Eriskay, at the foot of the Uists, and Barra (for more on ferry services, see "Travel details" on p.722).

Although travelling around the islands is time-consuming, for many people this is part of their charm. A series of inter-island causeways makes it possible to drive from one end of the Western Isles to the other with just two interruptions – the CalMac **ferry** trips from Harris to Berneray, and from Eriskay to Barra. The islands boast a low-key but efficient **bus** service, though there are no buses on Sundays. Note, however, local companies often offer very reasonable **car rental** rates though you're not permitted to take their vehicles off the Western Isles. Limited **bike rental** is also available, but bear in mind the wind makes cycling something of a challenge even for the fit and healthy. There are an increasing number of **boat trips** offered by companies such as the excellent Island Cruising (℡01851/672381, www.island-cruising.com), based in Uig, who will take folk out in their former marine research vessel on day-trips to the Shiants or Flannan Isles or, on longer trips out to Sula Sgeir and even **St Kilda** (see box on p.716); Kilda Cruises (℡01859/502060, www.kildacruises.co.uk) has a motor cruiser that leaves from Leverburgh for day-trips to similar destinations and takes just under three hours to reach St Kilda; Sea Trek (℡01851/672464, seatrek.co.uk), also based in Uig, offers RIB day-trips to St Kilda.

The islands' **hostels** are geared up for the outdoor life, occupying remote locations on or near the coast. Several of them are run by the Gatliff Hebridean Hostels Trust or GHHT (www.gatliff.org.uk), which has renovated several crofters' cottages. None of these has phones, so you can't book in advance – in the height of summer it's best to get there early to be sure of a bed, though it's also possible to camp at the hostels; each hostel has hot water and a simple kitchen. If you're after a little more comfort, then the islands have a generous sprinkling of reasonably priced **B&Bs** and **guesthouses** – many of which are a lot better value than the hotels, allow you to meet local folk and can be easily booked over the phone, or through the tourist offices for a small fee – again, in the height of summer it's best to book in advance.

The influence of the Atlantic Gulf Stream ensures a mild but moist climate, though you can expect the **strong Atlantic winds** to blow in rain on two out of every three days even in summer. Weather fronts, however, come and go at such dramatic speed in these parts that there's little chance of mist or fog settling and few problems with midges. Lastly, for a lively view on local life, read the **local papers**, in particular the weekly *West Highland Free Press* (Ⓦwww.whfp .com), published in Broadford on Skye (see p.677).

Lewis (Leodhas)

Shaped rather like the top of an ice-cream cone, **Lewis** is the largest and by far the most populous of the Western Isles and the northernmost island in the Hebridean archipelago. Most of the island's 20,000 inhabitants – over two-thirds of the Western Isles' total population – now live in the crofting and fishing villages strung out along the northwest coast, between **Calanais** and **Port Nis**, in one of the most densely populated rural areas in the country. On this coast you'll also find the islands' best-preserved **prehistoric remains** – Dùn Charlab-haigh broch and the Calanais standing stones – as well as a smattering of ancient crofters' houses in various stages of abandonment. The landscape is mostly flat peat bog – hence the island's name, derived from the Gaelic *leogach* (marshy) – but the shoreline is more dramatic especially around Rubha Robhanais (Butt of Lewis), a group of rough rocks on the island's northernmost tip, near Port Nis. To the south, where Lewis is physically joined with Harris, the land rises to just over 1800ft, providing an exhilarating backdrop for the excellent beaches that pepper the isolated coastline of **Uig**, to the west of Calanais. **Stornoway**, on the east coast, is the only real town in the Western Isles, but it's really only useful for stocking up on provisions and/or catching the bus: there are regular services to all parts of the island, and most usefully to Port Nis and Tarbert, and along the 45-mile round trip from Stornoway to Calanais, Carlabhagh, Arnol and back.

Some history

After Viking rule ended in 1266, Lewis became a virtually independent state, ruled over by the **MacLeod clan** for several centuries. King James VI, however, had other ideas: he declared the folk of Lewis to be "void of religion", and attempted to establish a colony, as in Ulster, by sending Fife Adventurers to attack Lewis. They were met with armed resistance by the MacLeods; so, in retaliation, James VI granted the lands to their archrivals, the MacKenzies of Kintail. The MacKenzie chiefs – the earls of Seaforth – chose to remain absentee landlords until 1844, when they sold Lewis to **Sir James Matheson**, who'd made a fortune from pushing opium to the Chinese. Matheson invested heavily in the island's infrastructure, though, as his critics point out, he made sure he recouped his money through tax or rent.

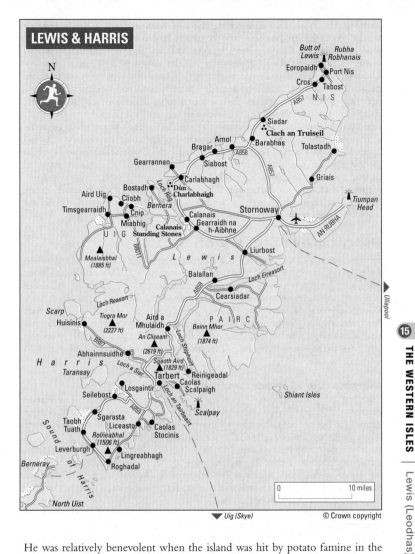

N

Butt of Lewis Rubha Robhanais
Eoropaidh Port Nis
Cros Tabost
A857
N I S
Siadar
Clach an Truiseil
Arnol Barabhas Tolastadh
Bragar A858
Gearrannan Siabost Griais
Carlabhagh A857
Bostadh **Dùn Charlabhaigh**
Aird Uig Cliobh Bernera Tiumpan Head
Timsgearraidh Cnip Calanais Stornoway
Miabhig Gearraidh na h-Aibhne
Calanais Standing Stones
U I G AN RUBHA
Mealaisbhal (1885 ft) L e w i s Liurbost
Balallan Loch Eireasort
Cearsiadar
Loch Reasort A859
Scarp Tiogra Mor (2227 ft) P A I R C
Huisinis Aird a Mhulaidh Beinn Mhor (1874 ft)
An Cliseam (2619 ft) Loch Shiphoirt
Abhainnsuidhe Sgaoth Aird (1829 ft)
H a r r i s Loch a Siar Tarbert Reinigeadal
Taransay Caolas Scalpaigh Shant Isles
Seilebost Losgaintir Scalpay
Sgarasta Caolas Stocinis
Taobh Tuath Liceasto
Roineabhal (1506 ft)
Leverburgh Lingreabhagh
Berneray Roghadal
North Uist

0 ——— 10 miles

© Crown copyright

Uig (Skye)

Ullapool

15

THE WESTERN ISLES | Lewis (Leodhas)

He was relatively benevolent when the island was hit by potato famine in the mid-1840s, but ultimately opted for solving the problem through eviction and emigration. His chief factor, Donald Munro, was utterly ruthless, and was only removed after the celebrated Bernera Riot of 1874 (see p.706). The 1886 Crofters' Act greatly curtailed the power of the Mathesons; it did not, however, right any of the wrongs of the past. Protests, such as the Pairc Deer Raid of 1887, in which starving crofters killed 200 deer from one of the sporting estates, and the Aignish land raids of the following year, continued against the Clearances of earlier that century.

When **Lord Leverhulme**, founder of the soap empire Unilever, acquired the island (along with Harris) in 1918, he was determined to drag Lewis out of its cycle of poverty by establishing an integrated fishing industry. To this end he founded MacFisheries, a nationwide chain of retail outlets for the fish which would be caught and processed on the islands: he built a cannery, an ice factory, roads, bridges and a light railway; he bought boats, and planned to use spotter planes to locate the shoals of herring. But the dream never came to fruition. Unfortunately, Leverhulme was implacably opposed to the island's centuries-old tradition of crofting, which he regarded as inefficient and "an entirely impossible way of life". He became involved in a long, drawn-out dispute over the distribution of land to returning ex-servicemen, the "land fit for heroes" promised by the Board of Agriculture. In the end, however, it was actually financial difficulties which prompted Leverhulme to pull out of Lewis in 1923, and concentrate on Harris. He generously gifted Lews Castle and Stornoway to its inhabitants and offered free crofts to those islanders who had not been involved in land raids. In the event, few crofters took up the offer – all they wanted was security of tenure, not ownership. Whatever the merits of Leverhulme's plans, his departure left a huge gap in the non-crofting economy, and between the wars thousands more emigrated.

Stornoway (Steornabhagh)

In these parts, **STORNOWAY** is a buzzing metropolis, with over 6000 inhabitants, a one-way system, pedestrian precinct with CCTV and all the trappings of a large town. It's a centre for employment, a social hub for the island and, perhaps most importantly of all, home to the Western Isles Council or **Comhairle nan Eilean Siar** (ⓦwww.cne-siar.gov.uk), set up in 1974, which has done so much to promote Gaelic language and culture and to try to stem the tide of anglicization. For the visitor, however, the town is unlikely to win any great praise – aesthetics are not its strong point, and the urban pleasures on offer are limited.

Information and accommodation

The best thing about Stornoway is the convenience of its services. The island's **airport** (ⓣ01851/707400, ⓦwww.hial.co.uk) is four miles east of the town centre: the hourly bus takes fifteen minutes, or else it's a £5 taxi ride into town. The swanky octagonal CalMac **ferry terminal** (ⓣ01851/702361) is on South Beach, close to the **bus station** (ⓣ01851/704327). You can get bus timetables, a map of the town, a parking disc and other useful information from the **tourist office**, near North Beach at 26 Cromwell St (April to mid-Oct Mon–Sat 9am–6pm, open 8–9pm to meet the evening ferry; mid-Oct to March Mon–Fri 9am–5pm; ⓣ01851/703088).

Of the **hotels**, the *Royal Hotel* on Cromwell Street (ⓣ01851/702109, ⓦwww.calahotels.com; ❺) is your best bet. Better value by far, however, is the *Park Guest House* (ⓣ01851/702485; ❹) on James Street, where the public areas have bags of lugubrious late Victorian character (the bedrooms significantly less), or the *Hebridean Guest House*, 61 Bayhead St (ⓣ01851/702268, ⓦwww.hebrideanguesthouse.co.uk; ❹), whose rooms are newly furnished in pine. Of the **B&Bs**, try *Fernlea*, a listed Victorian house, along leafy Matheson Road, at no. 9 (ⓣ01851/702125, ⓔmaureenmacmillan@amserve.com; ❸), or *Hal O The Wynd*, 2 Newton St (ⓣ01851/706073; ❸), conveniently situated right opposite the ferry terminal.

Fair Haven, 28 Francis St (ⓣ01851/705862, ⓦwww.hebrideansurf.co.uk; ❶), is primarily a hostel for surfers, but welcomes all; accommodation consists of bunk, family and single rooms and there's a good **restaurant** too. If you're **camping**, head out of Stornoway, unless you need to stay near town, in which case *Laxdale Holiday Park* (☎01851/703234, ⓦwww.laxdaleholidaypark.com) lies a mile or so along the road to Barabhas, on Laxdale Lane; the campsite has holiday caravans (short breaks available), a self-catering bungalow and a purpose-built **bunkhouse**, as well as a nice sheltered spot for tents.

The Town

For centuries, life in Stornoway has focused on its **harbour**, whose quayside was filled with barrels of pickled herring, and whose deep and sheltered waters were thronged with coastal steamers and fishing boats in their nineteenth-century heyday, when more than a thousand boats were based at the port. Today, most of the catch is landed on the mainland, and, despite the daily comings and goings of the CalMac ferry from Ullapool, the harbour is a shadow of its former commercial self. The nicest section is Cromwell Street Quay, by the tourist office, where the remaining fishing fleet ties up for the night.

Stornoway's commercial centre, to the east, is little more than a string of unprepossessing shops and bars. The one exception is the old **Town Hall** on South Beach, a splendid Scots Baronial building, its rooftop peppered with conical towers, above which a central clocktower rises. One block east along South Beach, and looking rather like a modern church, you'll find **An Lanntair** (Mon–Sat 10am–10pm; free; ⓦwww.lanntair.com) – Gaelic for "lantern" – Stornoway's long-awaited new arts centre, which houses a 250-seat auditorium and cinema, and gallery space for temporary exhibitions, plus a very pleasant café-bar.

Continuing up the pedestrian precinct into Francis Street, you'll eventually reach the **Museum nan Eilean** (April–Sept Mon–Sat 10am–5.30pm; Oct–March Tues–Fri 10am–5pm, Sat 10am–1pm; free; ⓦwww.cne-siar.gov.uk), housed in the old Victorian Nicolson Institute school. The ground-floor gallery explores the island's history until the MacKenzie takeover, and is full of artefacts found during peat-cutting, including a large Viking dish made from alderwood. The first-floor gallery includes lots of information about the herring and weaving industries and houses an old loom shed with one of the semi-automatic looms introduced by Lord Leverhulme in the 1920s.

Anyone remotely interested in Harris tweed should head for the **Lewis Loom Centre** (Mon–Sat 9–6pm; £1; ⓦwww.lewisloomcentre.co.uk), run by an eccentric and engaging man and located at the far end of Cromwell Street, in the Old Grainstore off Bayhead. There's an exhibition on the cloth, a shop, and three looms, one of which is a Hattersley, which you may catch going through its paces.

To the northwest of the town centre, across the bay, stands **Lews Castle** (ⓦwww.lews-castle.com), a castellated pomposity built by Sir James Matheson in 1863 after resettling the crofters who used to live here. As the former laird's pad, the castle is seen as a symbol of old oppression by many and it's currently in a state of some disrepair awaiting renovation. For the moment, however, the chief attraction is its mature wooded grounds (ⓦwww.lewiscastlegrounds.org.uk), a unique sight on the Western Isles, for which Matheson had to import thousands of tons of soil from the mainland. Hidden in amongst the trees is the **Woodland Centre** (Mon–Sat 10am–5pm; free), which has a straightforward exhibition on the history of the castle and the island upstairs, with a live CCTV link to a nearby nest box, and a decent **café** serving soup, salads and cakes downstairs.

Eating, drinking and nightlife

Food options have improved in Stornoway over the last couple of years. The best place is the ☀ *Thai Café*, 27 Church St, which serves inexpensive but authentic Thai food – as a consequence it's very popular, so book ahead (☎01851/701811; closed Sun). *HS-1*, in the *Royal Hotel*, is a stylish, modern place, offering everything from simple fare like baked potatoes to stir-fries and curry. *Sunsets*, the smart, modern restaurant below the *Fair Haven* surfers' hostel, serves good local food, as does the even more formal *Digby Chick* (☎01851/700026), on the corner of Bank Street and Point Street – both are expensive, but *Digby Chick* offers more reasonably priced lunch and early evening menus. The *Stornoway Balti House*, near the bus station on South Beach, is a good option on any night, but particularly on Sunday evenings, when most places are closed. Look out, too, for **Stornoway black puddings** (and the white and fruit ones), which are served throughout the Western Isles for breakfast. The best ones, renowned throughout Scotland, are made to a secret family recipe by Stornoway butcher Charles MacLeod, based at Ropework Park (ⓦwww.charlesmacleod.co.uk), near the Co-op.

As for **pubs**, *MacNeills* on Cromwell St is the liveliest central pub, with a mixed clientele of keen drinkers. *The Criterion*, a tiny wee pub on Point Street, is another option. There's sometimes **live music** at the Royal British Legion, opposite the ferry terminal, or the *Whalers Rest*, on Francis Street, and a regular programme of **gigs and films** at An Lanntair. Stornoway is also the focus of the annual **Hebridean Celtic Festival** (ⓦwww.hebceltfest.com), in mid-July, a jamboree of music with a festival tent in Lews Castle grounds, and other events in Stornoway and elsewhere on Lewis and Harris. Needless to say, nearly all pubs are closed on Sundays, though some hotel bars will serve food and drink to non-residents.

The road to Nis (Ness)

Northwest of Stornoway, the A857 crosses the vast, barren **peat bog** of the Lewis interior, an empty, undulating wilderness riddled with stretchmarks formed by peat cuttings and pockmarked with freshwater lochans. The whole area was once covered by forests, but these disappeared long ago, leaving a smothering deposit of peat that is, on average, six feet thick, and is still being formed in certain places. For the people of Lewis the peat continues to serve as a valuable energy resource; its pungent smoke is one of the most characteristic smells of the Western Isles.

Twelve miles across the peat bog the road approaches the west coast of Lewis and divides, heading southwest towards Calanais (see p.705), or northeast through **BARABHAS** (Barvas), and a whole string of bleak and fervently Presbyterian crofting and weaving villages. These scattered settlements have none of the photogenic qualities of Skye's whitewashed villages: the churches are plain and unadorned; the crofters' houses relatively modern and smothered in grey pebbledash rendering or harling; the stone cottages and enclosures of their forebears often lie half-abandoned in the front garden; a rusting assortment of discarded cars and vans store peat bags and the like.

Eventually, you reach the various densely populated settlements that make up the parish of **NIS** (Ness), at the northern tip of Lewis. Nis has the highest percentage of Gaelic speakers in the country, at over ninety percent, but the locals are perhaps best known for their annual culling of young gannets on **Sula Sgeir**, a tiny island forty miles north. For an insight into the social history of the area, take a look inside Ness Heritage Centre or **Comunn Eachdraidh**

Lewis wind farm

Tourists tend to cross the barren, almost intimidating, landscape of the Lewis **peat bog** at some speed – even the locals spend little time on the moor except to gather peat. Yet these natural wetlands have been identified as important "carbon sinks", which soak up greenhouse gases, and as a vital breeding ground for species such as red- and black-throated diver, golden plover, dunlin and greenshank. In a tricky little clash of ecological interests, however, plans are afoot to build the world's largest onshore **wind farm** (ⓦ www.lewiswind.com), with over two hundred wind turbines, each standing 400ft high, harnessing a renewable resource which Lewis has in vast quantities. Understandably, many locals are in favour of the project, which should create three hundred jobs, provide electricity for over a million people and pump millions into the local economy. An equal number, however, are concerned about the inevitable visual and environmental impact: over 100 miles of roads will need to be built, along with 40 miles of overhead cables, over 200 pylons, 9 electrical substations and at least 5 quarries. The council received around 5000 objections to the proposal, including ones from the RSPB, the Scottish Wildlife Trust and the John Muir Trust, but unanimously passed the planning application. Ultimately, it will be down to the Scottish ministers who will make a decision in 2006, and, after that, the European Commission.

Nis (Mon–Fri 10am–5pm; June–Sept also Sat; free; ⓦ www.c-e-n.org), on the left as you pass through **TABOST** (Habost). The road terminates at the fishing village of **PORT NIS** (Port of Ness), with a tiny harbour and lovely golden beach.

Shortly before you reach Port Nis, a minor road heads two miles northwest to the hamlet of **EOROPAIDH** (Europie) – pronounced "Yor-erpee". Here, by the road junction that leads to the Butt of Lewis, the simple stone structure of **Teampull Mholuaidh** (St Moluag's Church) stands amidst the runrig fields, which now act as sheep runs. Thought to date from the twelfth century, when the islands were still under Norse rule, but restored in 1912, the church features a strange south chapel with only a squint window connecting it to the nave.

From Eoropaidh, a narrow road twists to the bleak and blustery northern tip of the island, **Rubha Robhanais** – well known to devotees of the BBC shipping forecast as the **Butt of Lewis** – where a lighthouse sticks up above a series of sheer cliffs and stacks, alive with kittiwakes, fulmars and cormorants, with skuas and gannets feeding offshore; its a great place for marine mammal-spotting.

Practicalities

There are between four and six buses a day from Stornoway to Port Nis, Sundays excepted, and one or two **accommodation** possibilities. The best place to stay is *Galson Farm Guest House* (ⓣ 01851/850492, ⓦ www.galsonfarm .freeserve.co.uk; ❹), an eighteenth-century farmhouse in Gabhsann Bho Dheas (South Galson), halfway between Barabhas and Port Nis, with a **bunkhouse** close by (phone number as above). There are also a couple of very comfortable and welcoming **B&Bs**: *Tòm Gorm* (ⓣ 01851/810661; ❷), a modern house in Nis, and *Heatherview* (ⓣ 01851/850781; ❸), a much older crofthouse in Gabhsann bho Thuath (North Galson). The *Cross Inn* in Cros is about the only **pub** in the area, but look out for **live music** or other events going on at Taigh Dhonnchaidh (ⓦ www.taighdhonnchaidh.com), a new arts and music centre in Tabost.

Arnol and Siabost (Shawbost)

Heading southwest from the crossroads near Barabhas brings you to several villages that meander down towards the sea. In **ARNOL**, the remains of numerous blackhouses lie abandoned by the roadside; at the north end of the village, no. 42 has been preserved as the **Arnol Blackhouse** (Mon–Sat: April–Sept 9.30am–6.30pm; Oct–March 9.30am–4.30pm; HS; £4) to show exactly how a true blackhouse, or *taigh dubh,* would have been. The dark interior is lit and heated by a small peat fire, which is kept alight in the central hearth of bare earth, and is usually fairly smoky as there's no chimney; instead, smoke drifts through the thatch, helping to kill any creepy-crawlies, keep out the midges and turn the heathery sods and oat-straw thatch itself into next year's fertilizer. The animals slept in the byre, separated from the living quarters only by a low partition, while potatoes and grain were stored in the adjacent barn. The old woman who lived here moved out only very reluctantly in 1964, and even then only after the council had agreed to build a house with a byre for her animals (the building now houses the ticket office). Across the road is a ruined blackhouse, abandoned in 1920 when the family moved into the white house, or *taigh geal,* next door.

Returning to the main road, it's about a mile or so to **BRAGAR**, where it's difficult to miss the stark arch formed by the jawbone of a blue whale, washed up on the nearby coast in 1920. The spear sticking through the bone is the harpoon, which only went off when the local blacksmith was trying to remove it, badly injuring him. Another two miles on at **SIABOST** (Shawbost), you'll find the **Shawbost Museum** (April–Sept Mon–Sat 9am–6pm; free) in the new community centre, Ionad na Seann Sgoil, to the north of the school. The exhibits – most of them donated by locals – include a rare Lewis brick from the short-lived factory set up by Lord Leverhulme, an old hand-driven loom and a reconstructed living room with a traditional box bed. There's a great **B&B** in Siabost Bho Deas (South Shawbost) at *Airigh* (☎01851/710478, ⓦwww .airighbandb.co.uk; ❷), and behind the church is the *Eilean Fraoich* **campsite** (☎01851/710504; April–Oct). You can grab a bite to **eat** at the *Shawbost Inn.*

Carlabhagh (Carloway) and Gearrannan (Garenin)

The landscape becomes less monotonous as you approach the parish of **CARLABHAGH** (Carloway), with its crofthouses, boulders and hillocks rising out of the peat moor. A mile-long road leads off north to the beautifully remote coastal settlement of **GEARRANNAN** (Garenin), where nine thatched crofters' houses – the last of which was abandoned in 1974 – have been restored and give a great impression of what a **Baile Tughaidh**, or blackhouse village (Mon–Sat 9.30am–5.30pm; £2.50) must have been like. The first house you come to houses the ticket office and **café**, serving cheap and cheerful fare during the day and classic Scottish three-course meals for £25 a head in the evening (Wed–Sat only; phone ahead ☎01851/643416). The second house has been restored to its condition at the time of abandonment, so there's electric light, but no running water, lino flooring, but a peat fire and box beds – and a weaving machine in the byre. The third house has interpretive panels and a touch-screen computer telling the history of the village and the folk who lived there. Next door, there are public toilets and opposite is the GHHT **hostel** (ⓦwww.gatliff.org.uk); several others have been converted into **self-catering** houses (ⓦwww.gearrannan.com).

△ Gearrannan, Lewis

Just beyond Carlabhagh, about 400yd from the road, **Dùn Charlabhaigh Broch** perches on top of a conspicuous rocky outcrop overlooking the sea. Scotland's Atlantic coast is strewn with the remains of over five hundred brochs, or fortified towers, but this is one of the best preserved, its dry-stone circular walls reaching a height of more than 30ft on one side. The broch consists of two concentric walls, the inner one perpendicular, the outer one slanting inwards, the two originally fastened together by roughly hewn flagstones, which also served as lookout galleries reached via a narrow stairwell. The only entrance to the roofless inner yard is through a low doorway set beside a crude and cramped guard cell. As at Calanais (see below), there have been all sorts of theories about the purpose of the brochs, which date from between 100 BC and 100 AD; the most likely explanation is that they were built to provide protection from Roman slave-traders.

Dùn Charlabhaigh now has its very own **Doune Broch Centre** (June–Sept Mon–Sat 10am–6pm; free), situated at a discreet distance, stone-built and sporting a turf roof. It's a good wet-weather retreat, and fun for kids, who can walk through the hay-strewn mock-up of the broch as it might have been. A mile or so beyond the broch, beside a lochan, is the *Doune Braes Hotel* (℡01851/643252, ⓦwww.doune-braes.co.uk; ❺), a friendly, unpretentious former schoolhouse, whose bar serves up tasty seafood dishes.

Calanais (Callanish)

Five miles south of Carlabhagh lies the village of **CALANAIS** (Callanish), site of the islands' most dramatic prehistoric ruins, the **Calanais standing stones**, whose monoliths – nearly fifty of them – occupy a serene lochside setting. There's been years of heated debate about the origin and function of the stones – slabs of gnarled and finely grained gneiss up to 15ft high – though almost everyone agrees that they were lugged here by Neolithic peoples between 3000 and 1500 BC. It's also obvious that the planning and construction of the site – as well as several other lesser circles nearby – were spread over many generations. Such an endeavour could, it's been argued, only be prompted by the desire to predict the seasonal cycle upon which these early farmers were entirely dependent, and indeed many of the stones are aligned with the positions of the sun and the stars. This rational explanation, based on clear evidence that this part of Lewis was once a fertile farming area, dismisses as coincidence the ground plan of the site, which resembles a colossal Celtic cross, and explains away the central burial chamber as a later addition of no special significance. These two features have, however, fuelled all sorts of theories ranging from alien intervention to human sacrifice.

A blackhouse adjacent to the main stone circle has been refurbished as a **tearoom** – it has limited snacks but bags more atmosphere than the **Calanais Visitor Centre** (Mon–Sat: April–Sept 10am–6pm; Oct–March 10am–4pm; museum £1.75) on the other side of the stones (and thankfully out of view), to which all the signs direct you from the road. The centre runs a decent restaurant and a small museum on the site, but with so much information on the panels beside the stones there's little reason to visit it. You're politely asked not to walk between the stones, only along the path that surrounds them, though everyone ignores this. If you want to commune with standing stones in solitude, head for the smaller circles in more natural surroundings a mile or two southeast of Calanais, around Gearraidh na h-Aibhne (Garynahine).

There are several good **places to stay** in Calanais: try the modern *Eshcol Guest House* (☎01851/621357, ⊛www.eshcol.com; ❹), no beauty from the outside, but very well run and comfortable within, or the newly built *Leumadair Guest House* (☎01851/612 706, ⊛www.leumadair.co.uk; ❹). If it's just **food** you want, you should head to *Tigh Mealros* (☎01851/621333; closed Sun), in Gearraidh na h-Aibhne, which serves good, inexpensive lunches and evening meals, featuring local seafood.

Bernera (Bearnaraigh)

From Gearraidh na h-Aibhne, the main road leads back to Stornoway, while the B8011 heads off west to Uig (see opposite), and, a few miles on, the B8059 sets off north to the island of Great Bernera, usually referred to simply as **Bernera**. Joined to the mainland since 1953 via a narrow bridge that spans a small sea channel, Bernera is a rocky island, dotted with lochans, fringed by a few small lobster-fishing settlements and currently owned by Comte Robin de la Lanne Mirrlees, the Queen's former herald.

Bernera has an important place in Lewis history due to the **Bernera Riot** of 1874, when local crofters successfully defied the eviction orders delivered to them by the landlord, Sir James Matheson. At the central settlement of **BREACLEIT** (Breaclete), you'll find the **Bernera Museum** (June–Sept Mon–Sat 11am–6pm; £1.50), with a small exhibition on lobster fishing, a St Kilda mailboat and a mysterious 5000-year-old Neolithic stone tennis ball, but it's hardly worth the entrance fee, unless you're tracing your ancestry.

Much more interesting is the replica **Iron Age House** (times vary so contact the tourist office) that has been built above a precious little bay of golden sand beyond the cemetery at **BOSTADH** (Bosta), three miles north of Breacleit – follow the signs "to the shore". In 1992, gale-force winds revealed an entire late Iron Age or Pictish settlement hidden under the sand; due to its exposed position, the site has been refilled with sand, and a full-scale mock-up built instead, based on the "jelly baby" houses – after the shape – that were excavated. Inside, the house is incredibly spacious, and very dark, illuminated only by a central hearth and a few chinks of sunlight.

If you want to stay, there are a couple of simple **B&Bs** on the island: *Kelvindale* (T01851/612347; April–Oct; ❷) in Tobson, a couple of miles northwest of Breacleit, and *Garymilis* (T01851/612341, Egarymilis@talk21.com; Feb–Nov; ❷), in Circebost (Kirkibost), on the southeastern corner of the island.

Uig

It's a long drive along the partially upgraded B8011 to the remote parish of **UIG**, one of the areas of Lewis that suffered really badly from the Clearances. The landscape here is hillier, and more dramatic than elsewhere, a combination of myriad islets, wild cliff scenery and patches of pristine golden sand.

The main road takes you through the narrow canyon of Glèann Bhaltois (Glen Valtos) to **TIMSGEARRAIDH** (Timsgarry), which overlooks **Uig Sands** (Tràigh Uuige), the largest and most prized of all the golden strands on Lewis, where the sea goes out for miles at low tide; the best access point is from the car park near the cemetery in Eadar Dha Fhadhail. It was here in 1831 that a local cow rubbed itself against a sandbank and stumbled across the **Lewis Chessmen**, 78 twelfth-century Viking chesspieces carved from walrus ivory that now reside in Edinburgh's Museum of Scotland and the British Museum in London. You can see replicas of the chessmen in the **Uig Heritage Centre** (Mon–Sat noon–5pm; £1), housed in Uig School in Timsgearraidh. As well as putting on some excellent temporary exhibitions, the museum has bits and bobs from blackhouses and is staffed by locals, who are happy to answer any queries you have; there's also a welcome **tearoom** in the adjacent nursery during the holidays.

The most intriguing **place to stay** is *Baile na Cille* (T01851/672242, Wwww.bailenacille.com; Easter–Oct; ❹), in an idyllic setting overlooking the Uig Sands in Timsgearraidh. It's a chaotic kind of place, run by an eccentric couple, who are very welcoming to families – the Blairs have stayed here – and dish up wonderful, though expensive, set-menu dinners for £30 a head. The best B&B in the area is *Suainaval* (T01851/672386, Wwww.suainaval.com; ❷), in Cradhlastadh (Crowlista), run by a truly welcoming couple, and boasting superb views over Uig bay from the north.

An entirely different (but equally unusual) experience is to stay at the old RAF station in **AIRD UIG**, three miles north of Timsgearraidh. The concrete buildings themselves are something of an eyesore, but the position, overlooking a rocky inlet beside Gallan Head, is superb. An enterprising Irish-Breton couple offer **B&B** (T01851/672474, Wwww.bonaventurelewis.co.uk; ❷) and run the popular ✴ *Bonaventure* **restaurant** (booking advisable), which serves up outstanding French/Scottish three-course meals at around £25 a head. Alternatively, you can stay over in another part of the old barracks with the Western Isles Kite Company (WiKc), who run kite-surfing courses and also offer B&B (T01851/672707, Wwww.powerkitesales.co.uk; ❷).

Nearby, Sea Trek (T01851/672464, Wseatrek.co.uk), run by Murray MacLeod from Miabhaig jetty, offers **boat trips** in a RIB to Pabbay (Pabaigh Mòr) and other uninhabited islands in Loch Ròg (Loch Roag); they also do day-trips to the Flannan Isles, Mingulay and St Kilda, for which you must book in advance. For longer trips lasting four to six days, to St Kilda and other outlying islands, contact Island Cruising (T01851/672381, Wwww.island-cruising.com), which also sails from Loch Roag.

Harris (Na Hearadh)

Harris, whose name derives from the old Norse for "high land", is much hillier, more dramatic and much more immediately appealing, its boulder-strewn slopes descending to aquamarine bays of dazzling, white sand. The shift from Lewis to Harris is almost imperceptible, as the two are, in fact, one island, the "division" between them embedded in a historical split in the MacLeod clan, lost in the mists of time. The border was also, somewhat crazily, a county boundary until 1975, with Harris lying in Invernessshire, and Lewis belonging to Ross and Cromarty. Nowadays, the dividing line is rarely marked even on maps; for the record, it comprises Loch Reasort in the west, Loch Shìphoirt (Loch Seaforth) in the east, and the six miles in between (see map on p.699). Harris itself is more clearly divided by a minuscule isthmus, into the wild, inhospitable mountains of **North Harris** and the gentler landscape and sandy shores of **South Harris**.

Along with Lewis, Harris was purchased in 1918 by **Lord Leverhulme**, and after 1923, when he pulled out of Lewis, all his efforts were concentrated here. In contrast to Lewis, though, Leverhulme and his ambitious projects were broadly welcomed by the people of Harris. His most grandiose plans were drawn up for Leverburgh (see p.711), but he also purchased an old Norwegian whaling station in Bun Abhain Eadara in 1922, built a spinning mill at Geocrab

Harris tweed

Far from being a picturesque cottage industry, as it's sometimes presented, the production of **Harris tweed** is vital to the local economy, with a well-organized and unionized workforce. Traditionally the tweed was made by women, from the wool of their own sheep, to provide clothing for their families, using a 2500-year-old process. Each woman was responsible for plucking the wool by hand, washing and scouring it, dyeing it with lichen, heather flowers or ragwort, carding (smoothing and straightening the wool, often adding butter to grease it), spinning and weaving. Finally the cloth was dipped in stale urine and "waulked" by a group of women, who beat the cloth on a table to soften and shrink it whilst singing Gaelic waulking songs. Harris tweed was originally made all over the islands, and was known simply as *clò mór* (big cloth).

In the mid-nineteenth century, the countess of Dunmore, who owned a large part of Harris, started to sell surplus cloth to her aristocratic friends; she then sent two sisters from Srannda (Strond) to Paisley to learn the trade. On their return, they formed the genesis of the modern industry, which continues to serve as a vital source of employment, though demand (and therefore employment levels) can fluctuate wildly as fashions change. To earn the official Harris Tweed Association trademark of the Orb and the Maltese Cross – taken from the countess of Dunmore's coat of arms – the fabric has to be hand-woven on the Outer Hebrides from 100 percent pure new Scottish wool, while the other parts of the manufacturing process must take place only in the local mills.

The main centre of production is now Lewis, where the wool is dyed, carded and spun; you can see all these processes by visiting the **Lewis Loom Centre** in Stornoway (see p.701). In the last few decades, there has been a revival of traditional tweed-making techniques, with several small producers following old methods. One such producer is Soay Studio at the western end of Tarbert (May–Sept Tues–Thurs 9am–12.30pm & 1.30–4pm; ☏01859/502361), which uses indigenous plants and bushes to dye the cloth: yellow comes from rocket and broom; green from heather; grey and black from iris and oak; and, most popular of all, reddish brown from crotal, a flat grey lichen scraped off rocks.

and began the construction of four roads. Financial difficulties, a slump in the tweed industry and the lack of market for whale products meant that none of the schemes was a wholehearted success, and when he died in 1925 the plug was pulled on all of them by his executors.

Since the Leverhulme era, unemployment has been a constant problem in Harris. Crofting continues on a small scale, supplemented by the Harris tweed industry, though the main focus of this has, in fact, shifted to Lewis. The fishing industry continues to thrive on **Scalpay**, while the rest of the population gets by on whatever employment is available: roadworks, crafts, hunting and fishing and, of course, tourism. There's a regular **bus** connection between Stornoway and **Tarbert**, and an occasional service which circumnavigates South Harris (see also "Travel details" on p.722).

Tarbert (An Tairbeart)

The largest place on Harris is the ferry port of **TARBERT**, sheltered in a green valley on the narrow isthmus that marks the border between North and South Harris. The port's mountainous backdrop is impressive, and the town is attractively laid out on steep terraces sloping up from the dock. It boasts Harris's only **tourist office** (April–Oct Mon–Fri 9am–5pm, Sat 9am–1pm & 2–5pm, also open to greet the evening ferry; winter hours variable; ℡01859/502011), close to the ferry terminal. The office can arrange modest, inexpensive B&B **accommodation** and has a full set of bus timetables, but its real value is as a source of information on local walks.

If you wish to base yourself in Tarbert there's an excellent **hostel** called the *Rockview Bunkhouse* (℡01859/502626), on Main Street, which has laundry facilities and also offers **bike rental**. If you're looking for **accommodation** close to the ferry terminal, there's a very good **B&B**, *Tigh na Mara* (℡01859/502270, ⓦwww.tigh-na-mara.co.uk; ❷), or the long-established, but recently refurbished *Harris Hotel* (℡01859/502154, ⓦwww.harrishotel.com; ❺), five minutes' walk away. Another option is *Ardhasaig House* ℡01859/502066, ⓦwww.ardhasaig .co.uk; ❻), a small hotel up the Stornoway road, looking out over North Harris – it's newly modernized inside and TV-free. The lounge and bar of the *Harris Hotel* act as the local social centre, but the best **fish and chips** are actually dispensed by ✄ *Ad's Take-Away* (April–Oct; closed Sun), next to the hostel. Otherwise, you're best off heading for the very pleasant *First Fruits* **tearoom** (April–Sept; closed Sun), behind the tourist office, housed in an old stone-built cottage and serving real coffee, home-made cakes, toasties and so forth, plus evening meals (Tues–Fri).

North Harris (Ceann a Tuath na Hearadh)

Mountainous **North Harris** was run like a minor feudal fiefdom until 2003 when the locals were given the right to buy the 22,000-acre estate for a knock-down £2 million. If you're coming from Stornoway on the A859, it's a spectacular introduction to Harris, its bulging, pyramidal mountains of gneiss looming over the dramatic, fjord-like **Loch Shìphoirt** (Loch Seaforth). From **AIRD A' MHULAIDH** (Ardvourlie), you weave your way over a boulder-strewn saddle between mighty **Sgaoth Aird** (1829ft) and An Cliseam or the **Clisham** (2619ft), the highest peak in the Western Isles. This bitter terrain, littered with debris left behind by retreating glaciers, offers but the barest of vegetation, with an occasional cluster of crofters' houses sitting in the shadow of a host of pointed peaks, anywhere between 1000ft and 2500ft high.

Other than self-catering cottages, the only place to stay in this area is the GHHT **hostel** (Ⓦwww.gatliff.org.uk) in the lonely coastal hamlet of **REINIGEADAL** (Rhenigdale), until the 1990s only accessible by foot or boat. Nowadays, there's a road, and even a bus service, though this must be booked in advance (Ⓣ01859/502221). To reach the hostel on foot, walk east along the wonderfully undulating road to Caolas Scalpaigh (Kyles Scalpay). After a couple of miles, watch for the sign marking the start of the path which threads its way for three miles over the rocky landscape to Reinigeadal; you'll need to be properly equipped (see p.64) and should allow three hours for the one-way trip.

The road to Huisinis (Hushinish)

The most attractive road on North Harris is the winding, single-track B887, which clings to the northern shores of Loch a Siar (West Loch Tarbert), and gives easy access to the awesome mountain range of the (treeless) Forest of Harris to the north. Immediately as you turn down the B887, you pass through **BUN ABHÀINN EADARRA** (Bunavoneadar), where some Norwegians established a short-lived whaling station – the slipways and distinctive red-brick chimney can still be seen. Seven miles further on, the road takes you through the gates of **Amhuinnsuidhe Castle** (pronounced "Avan-soo-ee"), built in Scottish Baronial style in 1868 by the earl of Dunmore, and right past the front door, much to the annoyance of the castle's succession of owners. As it is, you have time to admire the lovely salmon-leap waterfalls and pristine castle grounds.

It's another five miles to the end of the road at the small crofting community of **HUISINIS** (Hushinish), where you are rewarded with a south-facing beach of shell sand that looks across to South Harris. A slipway to the north of the bay serves the nearby island of **Scarp**, a hulking mass of rock rising to over 1000ft, once home to more than two hundred people and abandoned as recently as 1971 (it's now a private holiday hideaway). The most bizarre moment in its history – and the subject of the film *The Rocket Post* – was undoubtedly in 1934, when the German scientist Gerhardt Zucher conducted an experiment at sending mail by rocket. Zucher made two attempts at launching his rocket from Scarp, but the letter-laden missile exploded before it even got off the ground, and the idea was shelved.

South Harris (Ceann a Deas na Hearadh)

The mountains of **South Harris** are less dramatic than in the north, but the scenery is equally breathtaking. There's a choice of routes from Tarbert to the ferry port of **Leverburgh**, which connects with North Uist: the east coast, known as Na Baigh (The Bays), is rugged and seemingly inhospitable, while the **west coast** is endowed with some of the finest stretches of golden sand in the whole of the archipelago, buffeted by the Atlantic winds. Paradoxically, most people on South Harris live along the harsh eastern coastline of **Bays** rather than the more fertile west side. But not by choice – they were evicted from their original crofts to make way for sheep-grazing.

The west coast

The main road from Tarbert into South Harris snakes its way south and west for ten miles across the boulder-strewn interior to reach the coast. Once there, you get a view of the most stunning **beach**, the vast golden strand of **Tràigh Losgaintir**. The road continues to ride above a chain of sweeping sands, backed by rich **machair**, that stretches for nine miles along the Atlantic coast. In good weather, the scenery is particularly impressive, foaming breakers rolling along the golden sands set against the rounded peaks of the mountains to the north and the islet-studded turquoise sea to the west – and even on the dullest day the sand manages to glow beneath the waves. A short distance out to sea is the large island of **Taransay** (Tarasaigh), which once held a population of nearly a hundred, but was abandoned as recently as 1974. In 2000 it was the scene of the BBC series *Castaway*, in which thirty-odd contestants were filmed living on the island for the best part of a year. Day-trips are possible to the island from Horgabost beach (Mon–Fri; £15); the island also has self-catering cottages (℡01859/502441, ⊛www.visit-taransay .com; April–Oct). *Beul-na-Mara* (℡01859/550205, ⊛www.beulnamara .co.uk; ➌) is a very good modern **B&B** in Seiilebost, overlooking the sands of Tràigh Losgaintir, but the most luxurious **guesthouse** in the area is five miles further south in **SGARASTA** (Scarista), where one of the first of the Hebridean Clearances took place in 1828, when thirty families were evicted and their homes burnt. Here, the beautifully furnished rooms of the Georgian former manse of *Scarista House* (℡01859/550238, ⊛www.scaristahouse .com; ➑) overlook yet more golden sands; the restaurant's meat and seafood are among the freshest and finest on the Western Isles, and among the most expensive, at nearly £40 a head.

There's a particularly magnificent stretch of machair by the golden sands close to the village of **TAOBH TUATH** (Northton), a lovely spot overlooked by the round-topped hill of Chaipabhal at the southwesternmost tip of the island. In the village is the tiny **MacGillivray Centre** (open all year at any time), though there's only limited information on the naturalist, William MacGillivray (1796–1852), after whom it's named, and a little on crofting and machair. There's more information on geology, flora and fauna to be found in **Seallam!** (Mon–Sat 10am–5pm; £2.50; ⊛www.seallam.com), on the main road, primarily a centre for eager ancestor hunters, but also providing interest for kids, literally at their level.

Leverburgh (An t-Ob)

From Taobh Tuath the road veers to the southeast to trim the island's south shore, eventually reaching the sprawling settlement of **LEVERBURGH** (An t-Ob), where a series of brown clapperboard houses strikes an odd Scandinavian note. Named after Lord Leverhulme, who planned to turn the place into the largest fishing port on the west coast of Scotland, it's a place that has languished for quite some time, but has picked up a fair amount since the establishment of the CalMac **car ferry** service to Berneray and the Uists. The hour-long journey across the skerry-strewn Sound of Harris is one of Scotland's most tortuous ferry routes, with the ship taking part in a virtual slalom race to avoid numerous hidden rocks – it's also a great crossing from which to spot seabirds and sea mammals.

There's a good choice of **accommodation** in Leverburgh: try *Caberfeidh House* (℡01859/520276; ➋), a lovely stone-built Victorian building by the turn-off to the ferry, *Sorrel Cottage* (℡01859/520319, ⊛www.sorrelcottage .co.uk; ➋), which specializes in vegetarian and seafood cooking and offers **bike rental**. A cheaper alternative is the quirky, timber-clad ⚓ *Am Bothan* (℡01859/520251, ⊛www.ambothan.com), a luxurious **bunkhouse** that's very welcoming, has great facilities and is only a few minutes' walk from the ferry. On the north side of the bay is the *An Clachan* co-op store which houses a small **information office**. For some local langoustines, home-made cakes and the usual comfort **food**, head for *The Anchorage*, over by the ferry slipway, and look out for the occasional live music night.

Roghadal (Rodel)

A mile or so from Rubha Reanais (Renish Point), the southern tip of Harris, is the old port of **ROGHADAL** (Rodel), with a smattering of ancient stone houses situated among the hillocks surrounding the dilapidated harbour where the ferry from Skye used to arrive. On top of one of these grassy humps, with sheep grazing in the graveyard, is **St Clement's Church** (Tur Chliamainn), burial place of the MacLeods of Harris and Dunvegan in Skye. Dating from the 1520s – in other words pre-Reformation, hence the big castellated tower (which you can climb) – the church was saved from ruination in the eighteenth century, and fully restored in 1873 by the countess of Dunmore. The bare interior is distinguished by its wall tombs, notably that of the founder, Alasdair Crotach (also known as Alexander MacLeod), whose heavily weathered effigy lies beneath an intriguing backdrop and canopy of sculpted reliefs depicting vernacular and religious scenes – elemental representations of, among others, a stag hunt, the Holy Trinity, St Michael and the devil and an angel weighing the souls of the dead. Look out, too, for the sheila-na-gig halfway up the south side of the church tower; unusually, she has a brother displaying his genitalia, below a carving of St Clement on the west face. Beyond the church, tucked away by a quiet harbour, the harling-smothered *Rodel* **hotel** (℡01859/520210, 🌐www.rodelhotel.co.uk; ❻) has been totally refurbished inside and serves decent bar **meals**.

North Uist (Uibhist a Tuath)

Compared to the mountainous scenery of Harris, **North Uist** – seventeen miles long and thirteen miles wide – is much flatter and for some comes as something of an anticlimax. Over half the surface area is covered by water, creating a distinctive peaty-brown lochan-studded "drowned landscape". Most visitors come here for the trout and salmon fishing and the deerstalking, both of which (along with poaching) are critical to the survival of the island's economy. Others come for the smattering of prehistoric sites, the birds, or the sheer peace of this windy isle and the solitude of North Uist's vast sandy beaches, which extend – almost without interruption – along the north and west coast.

There are two **car ferry** services to North Uist: the first is from Leverburgh on Harris to Berneray (Mon–Sat 3–4 daily, subject to tides; 1hr), from where there are regular **buses** to Lochmaddy, the principal village on the east coast; the second is from Uig on Skye (2 daily; 1hr 45min) and docks at Lochmaddy itself. Five or six daily buses leave for Lochboisdale in South Uist along the main road, and several buses travel some way round the coastal road. There is no public transport on Sundays.

Lochmaddy (Loch nam Madadh) and around

Despite being situated on the east coast, some distance away from any beach, the ferry port of **LOCHMADDY** – "Loch of the Dogs" – makes a good base for exploring the island. Occupying a narrow, bumpy promontory and overlooked by the brooding mountains of Lì a Tuath (North Lee) and Lì a Deas (South Lee) to the southeast, it's difficult to believe that this sleepy settlement was a large herring port as far back as the seventeenth century. Its most salient feature now is the sixteen incongruous brown weatherboarded houses, which arrived from Sweden in 1948.

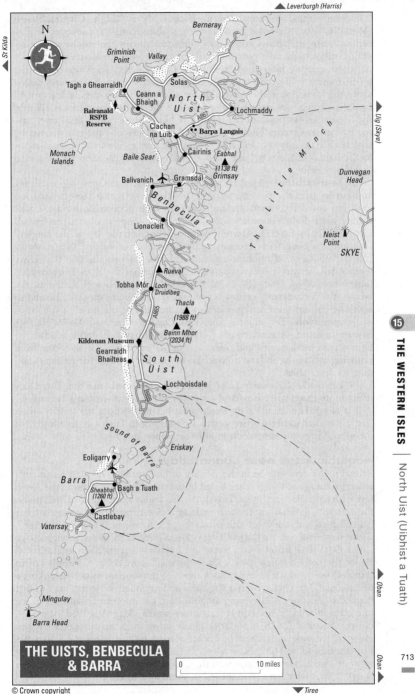

Leverburgh (Harris)

St Kilda

Uig (Skye)

Oban

Oban

Tiree

N

Berneray

Griminish
Point

Vallay

Tagh a Ghearraidh

A865

Solas

Ceann a
Bhaigh

*North
Uist*

Lochmaddy

**Balranald
RSPB
Reserve**

Clachan
na Luib

A865

Barpa Langais

*Monach
Islands*

Baile Sear

Cairinis

*Eabhal
(1138 ft)*
Grimsay

Balivanich

Gramsdal

Benbecula

The Little Minch

*Dunvegan
Head*

Lionacleit

*Neist
Point*

SKYE

Rueval

Tobha Mòr

*Loch
Druidibeg*

A865

*Thacla
(1988 ft)*

*Beinn Mhor
(2034 ft)*

Kildonan Museum

Gearraidh
Bhailteas

*South
Uist*

Lochboisdale

B888

Sound of Barra

Eriskay

Eoligarry

Barra

*Sheabhal
(1260 ft)*

Bagh a Tuath

Castlebay

Vatersay

Mingulay

Barra Head

**THE UISTS, BENBECULA
& BARRA**

0   10 miles

© Crown copyright

The only thing to keep you in Lochmaddy is **Taigh Chearsabhagh** (Mon–Sat 10am–5pm; Ⓦwww.taigh-chearsabhagh.org) a converted eighteenth-century merchant's house, now home to a vibrant community arts centre, with a simple airy café, post office, shop and excellent museum, which puts on some seriously innovative exhibitions. Taigh Chearsabhagh was one of the prime movers behind the commissioning of a series of seven sculptures dotted about the Uists. Ask at the arts centre for directions to the ones in and around Lochmaddy, the most interesting of which is the **Both nam Faileas** (Hut of the Shadow), 1km north of the town. The hut is an ingenious dry-stone, turf-roofed camera obscura built by sculptor Chris Drury that projects the nearby land, sea and skyscape onto its back wall – take time to allow your eyes to adjust to the light. On the way back keep a look out for otters, who love the tidal rapids hereabouts.

The **tourist office** (April to mid-Oct Mon–Sat 9am–5pm; also open for an hour to greet the evening ferry; Ⓣ01876/500321), near the quayside, has local bus and ferry timetables and can help with **accommodation**. Lochmaddy itself doesn't have the best options: the long-established *Lochmaddy Hotel* (Ⓣ01876/500331, Ⓦwww.lochmaddyhotel.co.uk; ❺) is the anglers' HQ, and has been fairly recently refurbished; the Georgian *Old Courthouse* (Ⓣ01876/500358, Ⓔmjohnson@oldcourthouse.fsnet.co.uk; ❸), the Uists' former jail, retains more character. A little further north is Lochmaddy's newest hotel, *Tigh Dearg* (Ⓣ01876/500700, Ⓦwww.tighdearghotel.co.uk; ❼), whose stylish modernity comes as something of a culture shock compared to anything else on the Uists; guests also get free use of the hotel's gym, sauna and steam room. Beyond lies the *Uist Outdoor Centre* (Ⓣ01876/500480, Ⓦwww.uistoutdoorcentre.co.uk), which has **hostel** accommodation in four-person bunk rooms and offers a wide range of outdoor activities, from canoeing round the indented coastline to "rubber tubing" for residents and non-residents alike.

The bar in the *Lochmaddy Hotel* is the lively local **pub**, but the *Tigh Dearg* offers more imaginative bar **food** (as well as formal four-course à la carte for £25 a head). The island's only **bank** is further inland from the tourist office. There is a small **general store**, petrol, a post office in Taigh Chearsabhagh, but the nearest large supermarket is in Solas (see opposite).

Neolithic sites near Lochmaddy

Several prehistoric sites lie in the vicinity of Lochmaddy. The most remarkable is **Barpa Langais**, a huge, chambered burial cairn a short walk from the A867, seven barren miles southwest. The stones are visible from the road and, unless the weather's good, it's not worth making a closer inspection as the chamber has collapsed and is now too dangerous to enter. A mile further down the A867, a side road leads off to *Langass Lodge* (Ⓣ01876/580285, Ⓦwww.langasslodge.co.uk; ❻), a small **hotel** whose restaurant and bar serves excellent local seafood. Beside the hotel, a rough track leads to the small stone circle of **Pobull Fhinn** (Finn's People), which enjoys a much more picturesque location overlooking a narrow loch. The circle covers a large area and, although the stones are not that huge, they occupy an intriguing amphitheatre cut into the hillside. For those interested in wildlife, the RSPB runs **otter walks** (May–Aug Wed 10am; £4; booking essential Ⓣ01876/560284) which set off from the car park at *Langass Lodge*. Three miles northwest of Lochmaddy along the A865 you'll find **Na Fir Bhreige** (The Three False Men), three standing stones which, depending on your legend, mark the graves of three spies buried alive or three men who deserted their wives and were turned to stone by a witch.

Berneray (Bhearnaraigh)

The ferry connection with Harris now leaves from the very southeastern point of **Berneray**, a low-lying island immediately to the north of North Uist and connected to the latter via a causeway. Two miles by three, with a population of just over a hundred, the island has a superb three-mile-long sandy beach on the west and north coast, backed by rabbit-free dunes and machair. Prince Charles, lover of Gaelic culture, was a frequent visitor at one time, and was memorably filmed helping local crofter "Splash" MacKillop pick potatoes. The other great draw is the wonderful GHHT **hostel** (ⓦ www.gatliff.org.uk), which occupies a pair of thatched blackhouses in a lovely spot by a beach, beyond Loch a Bhàigh and the main village. Alternatively you can follow in the prince's footsteps and stay (and help out) at "Splash" MacKillop's *Burnside Croft* **B&B** (ⓉT01876/540235, ⓦ www.burnsidecroft.fsnet.co.uk; Feb–Nov; ❷), in Borgh (Borve), overlooking the machair and dunes, and enjoy "story-telling evenings"; bike rental is also available. There's a **tearoom** called *The Lobster Pot* in the shop on the main road, near the junction, and a **bus** connection with Lochmaddy.

The coastal road via Solas (Sollas)

The A865, which skirts the northern and western shoreline of North Uist for more than thirty miles, takes you through the most scenic sections of the island. Once you've left the boggy east coast and passed the turning to Berneray and the Harris Ferry, the road reaches the parish of **SOLAS** (Sollas), which stands at the centre of a couple of superb tidal strands – sea green at high tide, golden sand at low tide – backed by large tracts of machair that are blanketed with wild flowers in summer. For a comfortable, friendly **B&B** with great views across Valley Strand, head for *Struan House* (ⓉT01876/560282; April–Sept; ❶), also known as *Struan Ruadh*.

Roughly three miles south of Scolpaig Tower, through the sand dunes, is the **Balranald RSPB Reserve**, best known for its corncrakes, once common throughout the British countryside but now among the country's rarest birds. Unfortunately, the birds are very good at hiding in long grass, so you're unlikely to see one; however, the males' loud "craking" is relatively easy to hear from May to July throughout the Uists and Barra: there are usually one or two making a loud noise right outside the RSPB **visitor centre**, from which you can pick up a leaflet outlining a two-hour walk along the headland, marked by posts. A wonderful carpet of flowers covers the machair in summer, and there are usually corn buntings and arctic terns inland, and gannets, Manx shearwaters and skuas out to sea. On a clear day you can see the unmistakable shape of St Kilda, seeming miraculously near.

Clachan

At **CLACHAN NA LUIB**, by the crossroads with the A867 from Lochmaddy, there's a post office and general store. Offshore, to the southwest, lie two flat, tidal, dune and machair islands, the larger of which is **Baleshare** (Baile Sear), with its fantastic three-mile-long beach, connected by causeway to North Uist. In Gaelic the island's name means "east village", its twin "west village" having disappeared under the sea during a freak storm in the fifteenth or sixteenth century. There are several decent **accommodation** options in the Clachan area: *Temple View Hotel* (ⓉT01876/580676, ⓦ www.templeviewhotel.co.uk; ❻) is a friendly family-run, small hotel overlooking the medieval ruined church

Britain's westernmost island chain is the NTS-owned **St Kilda** archipelago (ⓦwww .kilda.org.uk), roughly a hundred miles west southwest of the Butt of Lewis and over forty miles from its nearest landfall, Griminish Point on North Uist. Dominated by the highest cliffs and sea stacks in Britain, Hirta, St Kilda's main island, was occupied on and off for some two thousand years, with the last 36 Gaelic-speaking inhabitants evacuated at their own request in 1930. Immediately after evacuation, the island was bought by the marquess of Bute, who was keen to protect the island's population of somewhere between one and two million puffins, gannets, petrels and other seabirds. In 1957, having agreed to allow the army to build a missile-tracking radar station here linked to South Uist, the marquess bequeathed the island to the NTS (ⓣ01463/232034, ⓦwww.nts.org.uk). Despite its inaccessibility, several thousand visitors make it out to St Kilda each year; the resident NTS ranger usually gives a little talk, you get to see the museum, send a postcard and enjoy a drink at the army's pub, the *Puff Inn*. If you have your own yacht, you must have permission in order to land; several boat companies also offer **day-trips** to St Kilda for around £125 per person (see p.697). Between mid-May and mid-August, the NTS organizes volunteer **work parties**, which either restore and maintain the old buildings or take part in archeological digs. Volunteers are expected to work 24–36 hours a week for two weeks, for which they must pay around £500 per person, though, with only twelve people on each party and more applications than there are places, there's no guarantee you'll get on one. Volunteers meet at Oban, and should be prepared for a rough, fifteen-hour overnight crossing. For the armchair traveller, the best general book on St Kilda is Tom Steel's *The Life and Death of St Kilda*.

of **Teampull na Trionaid**; the nearby *Carinish Inn* (ⓣ01876/580673, ⓦwww .macinnesbros.co.uk; ⓹) is the local pub, offers a wide range of bar meals, and occasionally has live music. In an isolated position, overlooking Baleshare, is *Taigh mo Sheanair* (ⓣ01876/580246, ⓔcarnach@amserve.net), a very welcoming, family-run **hostel**, with bunk beds, en-suite rooms and a peat fire – you can also **camp**. The hostel is clearly signposted from the main road, from which it's a good fifteen-minute walk.

Benbecula (Beinn na Faoghla)

Blink and you could miss the pancake-flat island of **Benbecula** (put the stress on the second syllable), sandwiched between Protestant North Uist and Catholic South Uist (see map on p.713). Most visitors simply trundle along the main road that cuts across the middle of the island in less than five miles – not such a bad idea, since the island is scarred from the postwar presence of the Royal Artillery who until recently used to make up half the local population. Economically, of course, the area benefited enormously from the military presence, though the impact on the environment and the local Gaelic culture (with so many English speakers around) has been less positive.

The legacy of Benbecula's military past is only too evident in the depressing, barracks-like housing developments of **BALIVANICH** (Baile a Mhanaich), the grim, grey capital of Benbecula in the northwest. The only reason to come here at all is if you happen to be flying into or out of **Benbecula airport** (direct flights to Glasgow, Barra and Stornoway), need to take money out of the Bank of Scotland ATM (the only one on Benbecula and South Uist) or want to do some laundry (the laundrette is behind the bank). There's no tourist office and no real need **to stay** here, but if you've time to kill, you could head down to MacGillivray's, a long-established, old-fashioned shop selling everything from local tweeds to books, within easy walking distance of the airport, on the road to North Uist. If you need a bite to eat, you can stop by the *Stepping Stone* (closed Mon eve), a purpose-built **café/restaurant** divided into the *Food Base* café which serves up cheap filled rolls, hot meals and chips with everything, and the underwhelming £20-a-head *Sinteag* restaurant (evenings only), up the steps. **Car rental** is available at the airport from Ask Car Hire (☎01870/602818).

The chief **campsite** on the Uists is *Shell Bay* (☎01870/602447; April–Oct), in the south of the island at **LIONACLEIT** (Liniclate). Adjacent is the modern **Sgoil Lionacleit**, the only secondary school (and public swimming pool) on the Uists and Benbecula, and home to a small **Museum nan Eilean** (Mon–Sat only; phone for times; ☎01870/602864), which puts on temporary exhibitions on the history of the islands, as well as occasional live music and other events. Close to the school, **accommodation** is available at the comfortable *Lionacleit Guest House* (☎01870/602176, ⓦwww .lionacleit-guesthouse.com; ❹), and, just across the water in South Uist, the *Orasay Inn* (see p.718).

South Uist (Uibhist a Deas)

To the south of Benbecula, the island of **South Uist** (see map on p.713) is the largest and most varied of the southern chain of islands. The west coast boasts some of the region's finest machair and beaches – a necklace of gold and grey sand strung twenty miles from one end to the other – while the east coast features a ridge of high mountains rising to 2034ft at the summit of Beinn Mhor. Whatever you do, don't make the mistake of simply driving down the

△ South Uist beach

main A865 road, which runs down the centre of the island like a backbone. To reach the beaches (or even see them), you have to get off the main road and pass through the old crofters' villages that straggle along the west coast; to climb the mountains in the east, you need a detailed 1:25,000 Explorer map, in order to negotiate the island's maze of lochans. The only blot on South Uist's landscape is the old Royal Artillery missile range, which dominates the northwest corner of the island.

Tobha Mòr (Howmore) and around

One of the best places to gain access to the sandy shoreline is at **TOBHA MÒR** (Howmore), a pretty little crofting settlement with a fair number of restored houses, many still thatched, including one distinctively roofed in brown heather. A GHHT **hostel** (ⓦwww.gatliff.org.uk) occupies one such house near the village church, from where it's an easy walk across the flower-infested machair to the gorgeous beach. Close by the hostel are the shattered, lichen-encrusted remains of no fewer than four medieval churches and chapels, and a burial ground now harbouring just a few scattered graves.

Five miles south of Tobha Mòr, on the main road, the Kildonan Museum, or **Taigh-tasgaidh Chill Donnain** (April & May Mon–Sat 11am–4pm; June–Sept Mon–Sat 10am–5pm, Sun 2–5pm; £1.50), includes mock-ups of Hebridean kitchens through the ages, two lovely box beds and an impressive selection of old photos, accompanied by a firmly unsentimental yet poetic written text on crofting life in the last two centuries. Among the more unusual exhibits is a pair of ornamental shoes made of deer hooves. Pride of place goes to the sixteenth-century **Clanranald Stone**, carved with the arms of the clan who ruled over South Uist from 1370 to 1839, which used to lie in the church at Tobha Mòr. The museum also runs a café serving sandwiches and home-made cakes, and has a choice of historical videos for those really wet and windy days. A little to the south of the museum, the road passes a cairn that sits amongst the foundations of **Flora MacDonald**'s childhood home (see box on p.686); she was born nearby, but the house no longer stands.

Apart from the aforementioned hostel, there's the *Orasay Inn* (ⓣ01870 /610298, ⓔorasayinn@btinternet.com; ❹), a **hotel** in a peaceful spot off the road to Loch a Charnain (Lochcarnan), in the northeastern corner of the island. If you get a room looking east out towards the Minch, you can enjoy a bit of bird-watching from your balcony; the bar meals are also good value and the breakfasts are great. If you're amassing a picnic, try some "flaky smoked salmon", available throughout the Western Isles, as well as straight from its source, *Salar* (closed Sat & Sun), along the road to Loch a Charnain, beyond the *Orasay Inn* turn-off. Further south, you can stay at two inexpensive **B&Bs**: the modern farmhouse *Tigh-an-Droma* (ⓣ01870/620292, ⓔtighandroma@aol.com; ❶), overlooking Loch Druidibeg, or in the *Old Croft House* (ⓣ01870/620292, ⓔmmack6k@aol.com; ❷) in Cill Donnain (Kildonan). **Bike rental** (and repair) is available from Rothan Cycles (ⓣ01870/620283), on the main road in Tobha Mòr (Howmore).

Lochboisdale (Loch Baghasdail) and around

Although it is South Uist's chief settlement and ferry port, **LOCHBOIS-DALE**, occupying a narrow, bumpy promontory on the east coast, has less to offer than Lochmaddy. If you're arriving here late at night on the boat from Oban (or from Barra or Tiree), you should try to book accommodation in advance; otherwise, head for the **tourist office** (Easter to mid-Oct Mon–Sat 9am–5pm; open for an hour to meet the ferry; ☎01878/700286); next door is a useful coin-operated shower and toilet block (daily 9am–6pm). The town's only **hotel**, the *Lochboisdale* (☎01878/700332, Ⓦwww.lochboisdale.com; ❹) has been refusbished, and does decent bar meals, including succulent local cockles. There are also several small, perfectly friendly **B&Bs** within comfortable walking distance of the dock, one of the best (and nearest) being *Brae Lea House* (☎01878/700497, Ⓔbraelea@supanet.com; ❸). There's a bank, but the shops in Lochboisdale are pretty limited; the nearest supermarket is three miles west in Dalabrog (Daliburgh). Another place you could hole up in is the *Polochar Inn* (☎01878/700215, Ⓦwww.macinnesbros.co.uk; ❺), eight miles from Lochboisdale, right on the south coast overlooking the Sound of Barra, and with its own sandy beach close by.

Eriskay (Eiriosgaigh)

Famous for its patterned jerseys and a peculiar breed of pony, originally used for carrying peat and seaweed, the barren, hilly island of **Eriskay** is connected to the south of South Uist by a causeway, built in 2001. The island, which measures just over two miles by one, and shelters a small fishing community of about 150, makes a great day-trip from South Uist. The walk up to the island's highest point, **Ben Scrien** (607ft), is well worth the effort on a clear day, as you can see the whole island, plus Barra, South Uist and across the sea to Skye, Rùm, Coll and Tiree (2hr return from the village). On the way up or down, look out for the diminutive Eriskay ponies, who roam free on the hills but tend to graze around Loch Crakavaig, the island's freshwater source. Apart from one self-catering option (☎01878/720274), the only way to stay here is to **camp rough** (with permission). CalMac now runs a **car ferry to Barra** (4–5 daily; 40min) from a new harbour on the southwest coast of Eriskay.

For a small island, Eriskay has had more than its fair share of historical headlines. The island's main beach on the west coast, Coilleag a Phrionnsa (Prince's Cockle Strand), was where **Bonnie Prince Charlie** landed on Scottish soil on July 23, 1745 – the sea bindweed that grows there to this day is said to have sprung from the seeds Charles brought with him from France. The prince, as yet unaccustomed to hardship, spent his first night in a local blackhouse and ate a couple of flounders, though he apparently couldn't take the peat smoke and chose to sleep sitting up rather than endure the damp bed.

Eriskay's other claim to fame came in 1941 when the 8000-ton **SS Politician** or "*Polly*" as it's fondly known, sank on its way from Liverpool to Jamaica, along with its cargo of bicycle parts, £3 million in Jamaican currency and 264,000 bottles of whisky, inspiring Compton MacKenzie's book, and the Ealing comedy (filmed on Barra in 1948), *Whisky Galore!* (released as *Tight Little Island* in the US). The real story was somewhat less romantic, especially for the 36 islanders who were charged with illegal possession by the Customs and Excise officers, nineteen of whom were found guilty and imprisoned in Inverness. The ship's stern can still be seen at low tide northwest of Calvay Island in the Sound of Eriskay, and one of the original bottles (and lots of other related memorabilia) is on show in *Am Politician*, the island's purpose-built pub near the two cemeteries on the west coast where you can get something to eat when the bar's open (times vary).

Barra (Barraigh)

Just four miles wide and eight miles long, **Barra** (Ⓦwww.isleofbarra.com – see map on p.713) has a well-deserved reputation for being the Western Isles in miniature. It has sandy beaches, backed by machair, mountains of Lewissian gneiss, prehistoric ruins, Gaelic culture and a laid-back, welcoming Catholic population of just over 1300. Like some miniature feudal island state, it was ruled over for centuries, with relative benevolence, by the MacNeils. Unfortunately, however, the family sold the island in 1838 to Colonel Gordon of Cluny, who had also bought Benbecula, South Uist and Eriskay. The colonel deemed the starving crofters "redundant", and offered to turn Barra into a state penal colony. The government declined, so the colonel called in the police and proceeded with some of the most cruel forced Clearances in the Hebrides. In 1937, the 45th chief of the MacNeil clan bought back most of the island, and the island returned with relief to its more familiar, feudal roots.

Castlebay (Bàgh a Chaisteil)

The only settlement of any size is **CASTLEBAY** (Bàgh a Chaisteil), which curves around the barren rocky hills of a wide bay on the south side of the island. It's difficult to imagine it now, but Castlebay was a herring port of some significance back in the nineteenth century, with up to four hundred boats in the harbour and curing and packing factories ashore. Barra's religious allegiance is immediately announced by the large Catholic church, Our Lady, Star of the Sea, which overlooks the bay; to underline the point, there's a Madonna and Child on the slopes of **Sheabhal** (1260ft), the largest peak on Barra, and a fairly easy hike from the bay.

As its name suggests, Castlebay has a castle in its bay, the picturesque medieval islet-fortress of Caisteal Chiosmuil, or **Kisimul Castle** (April–Sept daily 9.30am–6.30pm; HS; £3.30), ancestral home of the MacNeil clan. The castle burnt down in the eighteenth century, but when the 45th MacNeil chief – conveniently enough, a wealthy American and trained architect – bought the island back in 1937, he set about restoring the castle. There's nothing much to see inside, but the whole experience is fun – head down to the slipway at the bottom of Main Street, where the HS ferryman will take you over (weather permitting; ☎01871/810313).

To learn more about the history of the island, and about the postal system of the Western Isles, it's worth paying a visit to the Barra Heritage Centre, known as **Dualchas** (March, April & Sept Mon, Wed & Fri 11am–4pm; May–Aug Mon–Sat 11am–4pm; Ⓦwww.barraheritage.com; £2), on the road that leads west out of town; the museum also has a handy **café** serving soup, toasties and cakes.

North to Cockle Strand and Eòlaigearraidh

If you head north from Castlebay, you have a choice of taking the west or the east coast road. The west coast road takes you past the island's finest sandy beaches, particularly those at **Halaman Bay** and near the village of Allathasdal (Allasdale). The east coast road winds its way in and out of various rocky bays, one of which, **Bàgh a Tuath** (Northbay) shelters a small fishing fleet and a little island sporting a statue of St Barr, better known as Finbarr, the island's Irish patron saint.

At the north end of the island, Barra is squeezed between two sandy bays: the dune-backed west side takes the full force of the Atlantic breakers, while the east side boasts the crunchy shell sands of Tràigh Mhòr, better known as **Cockle**

Strand. The beach is also used as the island's **airport**, with planes landing and taking off according to the tides, since at high tide the beach (and therefore the runway) is covered in water. As its name suggests, the strand is also famous for its cockles and cockleshells, the latter being used to make harling (the rendering used on most Scottish houses). The popular airport **café**, *Cafaidh Fosgailte* (closed Sun), serves home-made soup, sandwiches and cakes.

To the north of the airport is the scattered settlement of **EÒLAIGEARRAIDH** (Eoligarry), which boasts several sheltered sandy bays. Here, too, is **Cille-Bharra** (St Barr's Church), burial ground of the MacNeils (and the author Compton MacKenzie). The ground lies beside the ruins of a medieval church and two chapels, one of which has been re-roofed to provide shelter for several carved medieval gravestones and a replica of an eleventh-century rune-inscribed cross, the original of which is in the National Museum of Scotland in Edinburgh.

Barra practicalities

There are two **ferry terminals** on Barra: from Eriskay, you arrive at an uninhabited spot on the northeast of the island; from Oban, Lochboisdale or Tiree, you arrive at the main terminal in Castlebay itself. Barra Car Hire (℡01871/810243) will deliver **cars** to either terminal or the airport, and Barra Cycle Hire (℡01871/810438) will do the same with **bikes**. There's also a fairly decent **bus/postbus** service, which does the rounds of the island (Mon–Sat). Barra's **tourist office** (April–Oct Mon–Sat 9am–1pm & 2–5pm; also open to greet the ferry; ℡01871/810336) is situated on Main Street in Castlebay just round from the pier, and can help book accommodation, though it's as well to book in advance for B&Bs and hotels. Guided **sea kayaking** is available from the *Dunard Hostel* (ⓦwww.clearwaterpaddling.com), and those interested in a **boat trip** to any of the islands around Barra, including **Mingulay**, should phone Donald (℡01871/890384, ⓦwww.barrafishingcharters.com) or enquire at the tourist office.

For **accommodation** in Castlebay itself, the *Castlebay Hotel* (℡01871/810223, ⓦwww.castlebay-hotel.co.uk; ❺) is the more welcoming of the town's two hotels, followed by *Tigh-na-Mara* (℡01871/810304, ⓔtighnamara@aol.com; ❷), a Victorian guesthouse a couple of minutes' walk from the pier, overlooking the sea. Although architecturally something of a 1970s monstrosity, the *Isle of Barra Hotel* (℡01871/810383, ⓦwww.isleof barra.com/iob.html; Easter–early Oct; ❺) enjoys a classic location overlooking Halaman Bay. However, the best option outside Castlebay is *Northbay House* (℡01871/890255, ⓦwww.barraholidays.co.uk; April–Oct; ❸), a very nicely converted old school in Buaile nam Bodach (Balnabodach), or the *Old Croft House* (℡01871/890799, ⓔbernieandpaddy@tiscali.co.uk; ❷), half a mile further north in Bruairnis (Bruernish). Lastly, there's *Dunard Hostel* (℡01871/810443, ⓦwww.dunardhostel.co.uk), a relaxed, family-run place just 200yd west of the ferry terminal in Castlebay.

On Main Street, the *Kisimul* **café** (closed Sun) serves breakfast all day, and specializes in cheap-and-cheerful Scottish fry-ups. For more fancy fare, head to the *Castlebay Hotel*'s cosy **bar**, which regularly has cockles, crabs and scallops on its menu, and good views out over the bay. The only two watering holes in the north of the island are the airport terminal café (see above) and the *Heathbank Hotel*, a pub in Bagh a Tuath (Northbay). **Films** are occasionally shown on Saturday evenings at the local school – look out for the posters – where there is also a swimming pool (Tues–Sun), library and sports centre, all of which are open to the general public.

Travel details

Buses

Lewis & Harris

For more details, see ⓦ www.cne-siar.gov.uk/travel
Stornoway to: Arnol (Mon–Sat 4–6 daily; 35min); Barabhas (Mon–Sat 8–12 daily; 25min); Calanais (Mon–Sat 4–6 daily; 40min); Carlabhagh (Mon–Sat 4–6 daily; 1hr); Great Bernera (Mon–Sat 4 daily; 1hr); Leverburgh (Mon–Sat 4–5 daily; 1hr 55min); Port Nis (Mon–Sat 4–6 daily; 1hr); Siabost (Mon–Sat 4–6 daily; 45min); Tarbert (Mon–Sat 4–5 daily; 1hr 5min); Uig (Mon–Sat 3–4 daily; 1hr–1hr 30min).
Tarbert to: Huisinis (schooldays Mon–Fri 2–3 daily; school holidays Tues & Fri 3 daily; 45min); Leverburgh (Mon–Sat 9–11 daily; 45min–1hr); Rhenigadale (Mon–Sat 2 daily; 30min).

Uists & Benbecula

Berneray to: Lochmaddy (Mon–Sat 6–7 daily; 20–50min).
Lochboisdale to: Eriskay (Mon–Sat 6–7 daily; 35min).
Lochmaddy to: Balivanich (Mon–Sat 5–6 daily; 45min–2hr); Balranald (Mon–Sat 3 daily; 50min); Lochboisdale (Mon–Sat 5–6 daily; 2hr).

Barra

Castlebay to: airport/ferry for Eriskay (Mon–Sat 6–7 daily; 35–45min).

Ferries

Summer timetable only.
To Barra: Eriskay–Barra (5 daily; 40min); Lochboisdale–Castlebay (Mon & Tues; 1hr 30min); Oban–Castlebay (1 daily; 4hr 50min); Tiree–Castlebay (Thurs; 3hr).
To Harris: Berneray–Leverburgh (Mon–Sat 3–4 daily; 1hr); Uig–Tarbert (Mon–Sat 2 daily; 1hr 45min).
To Lewis: Ullapool–Stornoway (Mon–Sat 2–3 daily; 2hr 45min).
To North Uist: Leverburgh–Berneray (Mon–Sat 3–4 daily; 1hr); Uig–Lochmaddy (1–2 daily; 1hr 45min).
To South Uist: Castlebay–Lochboisdale (Mon, Tues & Fri–Sun; 1hr 40min); Oban–Lochboisdale (daily except Wed; 4hr 50min–6hr 40min).

Flights

Benbecula to: Barra (Mon–Fri 1 daily; 20min); Stornoway (Mon–Fri 2 daily; 30min).
Edinburgh to: Stornoway (Mon–Fri 3 daily, Sat & Sun 1–2 daily; 1hr).
Glasgow to: Barra (Mon–Sat 1 daily; 1hr 5min); Benbecula (Mon–Fri 2 daily, Sat 1 daily; 1hr); Stornoway (daily; 1hr 10min).
Inverness to: Stornoway (Mon–Fri 4 daily, Sat & Sun 1–2 daily; 35–40min).

Orkney

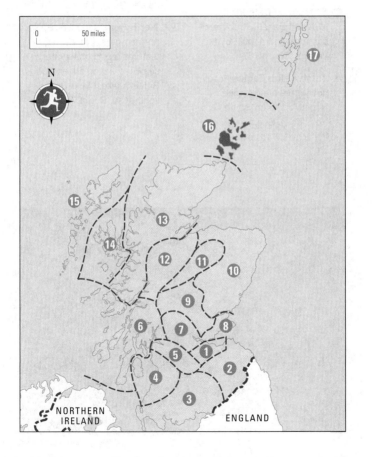

0   50 miles

N

17

16

15

13

14

12   11

10

9

6   7   8

5   1

4   2

3

NORTHERN
IRELAND   ENGLAND

CHAPTER 16

Highlights

* **Maes Howe** Orkney's, and Europe's, finest Neolithic chambered tomb. See p.732

* **Skara Brae** Mesmerizing Neolithic homes, crammed with domestic detail. See p.733

* **St Magnus Cathedral, Kirkwall** Beautiful red sandstone cathedral built by the Vikings. See p.737

* **Tomb of the Eagles** Fascinating, privately owned Neolithic site on South Ronaldsay. See p.742

* **Balfour Castle** Eat, sleep and live like a king in Orkney's most sumptuous castle hotel. See p.746

* **Westray** Thriving Orkney island with seabird colonies, sandy beaches and a ruined castle. See p.749

* **North Ronaldsay** Orkney's northernmost island features a bird observatory, seaweed-eating sheep and Britain's tallest land-based lighthouse. See p.755

△ St Magnus Cathedral, Kirkwall

16

Orkney

Just a short step from John O'Groats, **Orkney** is a unique and fiercely independent archipelago made up of seventy or so islands, with a population of less than 20,000. With the major exception of Hoy, which is high and rugged, the islands are mostly low-lying, gently sloping and richly fertile, and for centuries have provided a reasonably secure living for their inhabitants from farming and, to a much lesser extent, fishing. The locals tend to refer to themselves first as Orcadians, regarding Scotland as a separate entity, and proudly flying their own unofficial flag. For an Orcadian, the **Mainland** invariably means the largest island in Orkney rather than the rest of Scotland, and throughout their distinctive history they've been linked to lands much further afield, principally Scandinavia.

Orkney Mainland has two chief settlements: the old port of **Stromness**, an attractive old fishing town on the far southwestern shore, and the central capital of **Kirkwall**, which stands at the dividing point between East and West Mainland. The whole of Mainland is relatively heavily populated and farmed throughout, and is joined by causeways to a string of southern islands, the largest of which is **South Ronaldsay**. The island of **Hoy**, the second-largest in the archipelago, to the south of Mainland, presents a superbly dramatic landscape, with some of the highest sea cliffs in the country. Hoy, however, is atypical: Orkney's smaller, much quieter **northern islands** are low-lying, elemental but fertile outcrops of rock and sand, scattered across the ocean.

There is a peaceful continuity to Orcadian life reflected not only in the well-preserved treasury of Stone Age remains, but also in the rather conservative nature of society here today. For the visitor, the best time to come is in spring and summer when the days are long, the sandy beaches dazzling, the cliffs packed with seabirds and the meadows thick with wild flowers. In autumn and winter, the islands are often battered by gale-force winds and daylight is scarce, but the temperature stays remarkably mild thanks to the ameliorating effect of the Gulf Stream. Wind is, of course, a factor, throughout the year, though its almost constant presence does mean that midges are less of a problem, except on Hoy.

Some history

Small communities began to settle in the islands around 4000 BC, and the village at **Skara Brae** on the Mainland is one of the best-preserved Stone Age settlements in Europe. This and many of the other older archeological sites, including the **Stones of Stenness** and **Maes Howe**, are concentrated in West Mainland. Elsewhere the islands are scattered with chambered tombs and stone circles, a tribute to the well-developed religious and ceremonial practices taking place

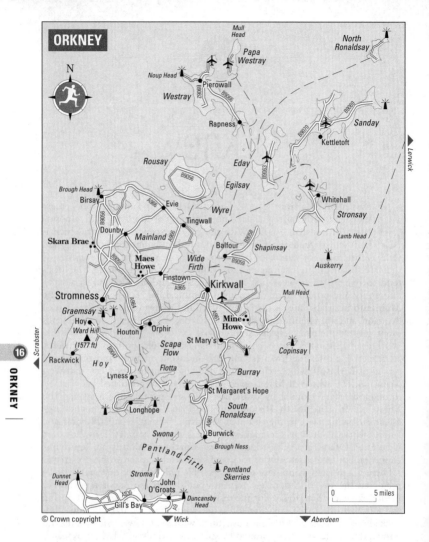

ORKNEY

N

Mull
Head

North
Ronaldsay

Papa
Westray

Noup Head

Pierowall

Westray

Rapness

Sanday

Kettletoft

Rousay

Eday

Egilsay

Brough Head

Birsay

Evie

Wyre

Tingwall

Whitehall

Stronsay

Dounby

Mainland

Lamb Head

Skara Brae

Balfour

Shapinsay

Maes
Howe

Wide
Firth

Auskerry

Finstown

Kirkwall

Stromness

Mull Head

Graemsay

Hoy

Mine
Howe

Ward Hill

Houton

Orphir

(1577 ft)

Scapa
Flow

St Mary's

Copinsay

Rackwick

Hoy

Flotta

Lyness

Burray

St Margaret's Hope

South
Ronaldsay

Longhope

Swona

Burwick

Brough Ness

Pentland Firth

Pentland
Skerries

Dunnet
Head

Stroma

John
O'Groats

Duncansby
Head

Gill's Bay

© Crown copyright

Wick

Aberdeen

0   5 miles

Scrabster

Lerwick

16

ORKNEY

here from around 2000 BC. More sophisticated **Iron Age** inhabitants built fortified villages incorporating stone towers known as brochs, protected by walls and
ramparts, the finest of which is the **Broch of Gurness** at Evie. Later, **Pictish**
culture spread to Orkney and the remains of several of their early Christian
settlements can still be seen, the best at the **Brough of Birsay**, where a group
of small houses is clustered around the remains of an early church. In the ninth
century or thereabouts, **Norse** settlers from Scandinavia arrived and the islands
became Norse earldoms, forming an outpost of a powerful, expansive culture
which was gradually forcing its way south. The last of the Norse earls was killed
in 1231, but they had a lasting impact on the islands, leaving behind not only
their language but also the great **St Magnus Cathedral** in Kirkwall, one of
Scotland's outstanding examples of medieval architecture.

After the end of Norse rule, the islands became the preserve of **Scottish earls**, who exploited and abused the islanders, although a steady increase in sea trade did offer some chance of escape. French and Spanish ships sheltered here in the sixteenth century, and the ships of the **Hudson's Bay Company** recruited hundreds of Orcadians to work in the Canadian fur trade. The islands were also an important staging post in the **whaling industry** and the herring boom, which drew great numbers of small Dutch, French and Scottish boats. More recently, the choice of **Scapa Flow**, Orkney's natural harbour, as the Royal Navy's main base brought plenty of money and activity during both world wars, and left the clifftops dotted with gun emplacements and the seabed scattered with wrecks – which these days make for wonderful diving opportunities.

After the war, things quietened down somewhat, although since the mid-1970s the large **oil terminal** on the island of Flotta, the establishment of the Orkney Islands Council (OIC), combined with EU development grants, have brought surprise windfalls, stemming the exodus of young people. Meanwhile, many disenchanted southerners have become "ferryloupers" (incomers), moving to Orkney in search of peace and the apparent simplicity of island life.

Arrival and island transport

Orkney is connected to the Scottish mainland by several **ferry** routes – and if you're coming by car, you should book your return journey in advance. Pentland Ferries (☎01856/831226, ⓦwww.pentlandferries.co.uk) operates the shortest car ferry crossing from **Gill's Bay**, on the north coast near John O'Groats (and linked by bus to Wick and Thurso) to **St Margaret's Hope** on South Ronaldsay (3–4 daily; 1hr). Services to **Stromness** from **Scrabster** (2–3 daily; 1hr 30min), which is connected to nearby Thurso by a shuttle bus, are run by Northlink Ferries (☎0845/600 0449, ⓦwww.northlinkferries .co.uk), which also operates ferries to **Kirkwall** from **Aberdeen** (4 weekly; 6hr) and from **Lerwick** in Shetland (3 weekly; 5hr 30min). John O'Groats Ferries (☎01955/611353, ⓦwww.jogferry.co.uk) runs a passenger ferry from **John O'Groats** to **Burwick** on South Ronaldsay (May & Sept 2 daily; June–Aug 4 daily; 40min), its departure timed to connect with the arrival of the Orkney Bus from Inverness; there's also a free taxi service from Thurso train station. The ferry is small and, except in fine weather, is recommended only for those with strong stomachs. Direct **flights** serve Kirkwall airport from Sumburgh in Shetland, Wick, Inverness and Aberdeen, and there are good connections from Edinburgh, Glasgow, Manchester, Birmingham and London. All can be booked through British Airways (☎0870/850 9850, ⓦwww.britishairways.com).

Bus services on the Orkney Mainland are infrequent, and skeletal on Sundays, making a Day Rover (£6) or Three-Day Rover (£15) of limited value (see ⓦwww.rapsons.co.uk for more details). On the smaller islands, a minibus usually meets the ferry and will take you to your destination. **Cycling** is not a bad option, though the wind can make it hard going; **renting a car** on Orkney will save you the steep ferry fares. If your time is limited, you may want to consider one of the informative bus or minibus **tours** on offer: Wildabout Orkney Tours (☎01856/851011, ⓦwww.orknet.co.uk/wildabout; March–Oct) has good-value tours of the chief sights on the Mainland and Hoy; other tours for specific islands are detailed in the text.

Getting to the other islands from the Mainland isn't difficult, though it is expensive: Orkney Ferries (☎01856/872044, ⓦwww.orkneyferries.co.uk) operates several **ferries** daily to Hoy, Shapinsay and Rousay, and between one and three a day, depending on route and season, to all the others except

North Ronaldsay, which has a weekly boat on Fridays. If you're taking a car on any of the ferries, it is essential to book your ticket well in advance. There are also a growing number of **boat trips** on offer: Explorer Fast Sea Charters (☎01856/741472, ⓦwww.explorercharters.co.uk) is based in Kirkwall and uses high-adrenalin RIBs to reach the outer isles, while Out West Charters (☎01856/850621, ⓦwww.outwestcharters.co.uk) uses a more sedate motorboat to take folk from Stromness to see the sea cliffs of Hoy.

There are also **flights** from Kirkwall to Eday, North Ronaldsay, Westray, Papa Westray, Sanday and Stronsay, operated by Loganair (☎01856/872494, ⓦwww .loganair.co.uk), using a tiny eight-seater plane. Loganair also offers **sightseeing flights** over Orkney, which are spectacular in fine weather (but cancelled in bad), as well as a discounted **Orkney Adventure** ticket, which allows you return tickets to three islands for around £70, and a special £12 offer on return flights to North Ronaldsay or Papa Westray if you stay over.

Stromness

STROMNESS has to be one of the most enchanting ports at which to arrive by boat, its picturesque waterfront a procession of tiny sandstone jetties and slate roofs nestling below the green hill of Brinkies Brae. As one of Orkney's main points of arrival, Stromness is a great introduction, and one that's well worth spending a day exploring, or using as a base in preference to Kirkwall. Its natural sheltered harbour (known as Hamnavoe) must have been used in Viking times, but the town itself only really took off in the eighteenth century when the Hudson's Bay Company made Stromness its main base from which to make the long journey across the North Atlantic, and crews from Stromness were also hired for herring and whaling expeditions – and, of course, pressganged into the Royal Navy. Today Stromness remains an important harbour town and fishing port, serving as Orkney's main ferry terminal, and is the focus of the popular four-day **Orkney Folk Festival** (ⓦwww.orkneyfolkfestival. com), held in May.

Information and accommodation

Arriving by ferry, you'll disembark at the modern ferry terminal, which also houses the **tourist office** (April–Oct Mon–Fri 8am–5pm, Sat 9am–4pm, Sun 10am–3pm; Nov–March Mon–Fri 9am–5pm; ☎01856/850716). **Accommodation** is actually quite thin on the ground in Stromness. As far as hotels go, the venerable Victorian *Stromness Hotel* (☎01856/850298, ⓦwww.stromnesshotel .com; ❻) – the town's first – is probably your best bet. For something with more character, head for the *Miller's House and Harbourside Guest House*, at 7 & 13 John St (☎01856/851969, ⓦwww.orkneyisles.co.uk/millershouse; ❷), in the town's oldest property (and a near neighbour). If you've your own transport, you might also consider *Thira* (☎01856/851181, ⓦwww.thiraorkney.co.uk; ❸), a modern house on the hill above town, boasting great views overlooking Hoy and good breakfasts.

The SYHA **hostel** in Stromness is undergoing much-needed refurbishment, with no date set for completion. An alternative is the laid-back family-run *Brown's Hostel*, 45–47 Victoria St (☎01856/850661, ⓦwww.brownshostel .co.uk), with bunk beds in very small, shared rooms and kitchen facilities. There's also a **campsite** (☎01856/873535; May to mid-Sept) in a superb setting a mile south of the ferry terminal at Point of Ness, with views out to

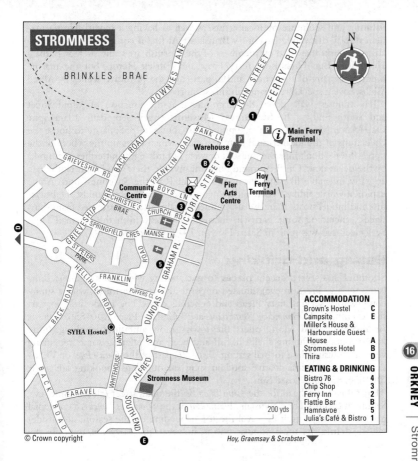

STROMNESS

BRINKLES BRAE

N

DOWNIES LANE

JOHN STREET

FERRY ROAD

A

1

BANK LN

P

i Main Ferry
Terminal

Warehouse

GRIEVESHIP RD

BACK ROAD

FRANKLIN ROAD

B

2

Hoy
Ferry
Terminal

Community
Centre

BOYS IN

C

Pier
Arts
Centre

CHRISTIE'S
BRAE

GRIEVESHIP TERR

SPRINGFIELD CRES

CHURCH RD

3

VICTORIA STREET

4

ST PETERS
PARK

MANSE LN

ROAD

GRAHAM PL

D

5

HELLIHOLE ROAD

FRANKLIN

PUFFERS CL

DUNDAS ST

SYHA Hostel

BACK ROAD

WHITEHOUSE LANE

ALFRED ST

Stromness Museum

FARAVEL

SOUTH END

BACK ROAD

0   200 yds

© Crown copyright   **E**   *Hoy, Graemsay & Scrabster* ▼

ACCOMMODATION	
Brown's Hostel	C
Campsite	E
Miller's House &	
Harbourside Guest	
House	A
Stromness Hotel	B
Thira	D

EATING & DRINKING	
Bistro 76	4
Chip Shop	3
Ferry Inn	2
Flattie Bar	B
Hamnavoe	5
Julia's Café & Bistro	1

16

ORKNEY | Stromness

Hoy; it's well equipped and even has its own lounge, but is extremely exposed,
especially if a southwesterly is blowing. **Bike rental** is available from Stromness
Cycle Hire, opposite the ferry terminal (☎01856/850750), and from Orkney
Cycle Hire, 54 Dundas St, near the museum (☎01856/850255).

The Town

Unlike Kirkwall, Orkney's capital, the old town of Stromness still hugs the
shoreline, its one and only street, a narrow winding affair, built long before
the advent of the motor car, still paved with great flagstones and fed by a tight
network of alleyways or closes. The central section, which begins at the *Stromness Hotel*, is known as **Victoria Street**, though in fact it takes on several other
names – Graham Place, Dundas Street, Alfred Street and South End – as it
threads its way southwards. On the east side of the street the houses are gable-
end-on to the waterfront, and originally each one would have had its own pier,
from which merchants would trade with passing ships.

You can visit the first of the old jetties, to the south of the modern harbour,
since it now houses the **Pier Arts Centre** (Tues–Sat 10.30am–12.30pm &
1.30–5pm; free). The art gallery hosts temporary exhibitions, often featuring

painting and sculpture by local artists, as well as having a remarkable permanent display of twentieth-century British art. At first it comes as a shock to see abstract works executed by members of the Cornish art scene such as Barbara Hepworth, Ben Nicholson, Terry Frost and Patrick Heron, but the marine themes of many of the works, and in particular the primitive scenes by Alfred Wallis, have a special resonance in this seaport.

Ten minutes' walk down the main street, at the junction of Alfred Street and South End, is the **Stromness Museum** (April–Sept daily 10am–5pm; Oct–March Mon–Sat 11am–3.30pm; £2.50), built in 1858, partly to house the collections of the local natural history society, which takes up the whole of the upper floor – don't miss the pull-out drawers of birds' eggs, butterflies and moths by the ticket desk. On the ground floor, meanwhile, there's a Halkett cloth boat, an early inflatable like the one used by John Rae, the Stromness-born Arctic explorer, whose fiddle, octant and shotgun are also on display. Amidst the beaver furs and model boats, there are also numerous salty artefacts gathered from shipwrecks, including some barnacle-encrusted crockery from the German High Seas Fleet that was sunk in Scapa Flow in 1919 (see box on p.741).

Eating and drinking

Stromness has several decent **places to eat**, starting with *Julia's Café and Bistro* (summer also Fri–Sun eve), situated opposite the ferry terminal, with a sunny conservatory, serving tasty meals and delicious cakes. The moderately expensive, evening-only *Hamnavoe Restaurant,* at 35 Graham Place (℡01856/850606; April–Sept; closed Mon), offers the town's most ambitious cooking, using local produce including shellfish, fish and beef, and offering some appetizing vegetarian dishes, in a formal setting. *Bistro 76*, part of the *Orca Hotel* on Victoria Street, serves imaginative food in snug surroundings (booking advisable; ℡01856/851803; closed Sun).

For **takeaways**, head for the *Chip Shop* on the main street (closed Thurs eve, Sat lunch & Sun). The downstairs *Flattie Bar* of the *Stromness Hotel* is a congenial place to warm yourself by a real fire (or, depending on the season, sit outside) with a **drink**; the most popular pub is, however, the *Ferry Inn*, opposite the hotel.

West Mainland

Stromness sits in the southwesternmost corner of the **West Mainland** – west of Kirkwall, that is – the great bulk of which is fertile, productive farmland, fenced off into a patchwork of fields used either to produce crops or for cattle-grazing. Fringed by spectacular coastline, particularly in the west, West Mainland is littered with some of the island's most impressive prehistoric sites, such as the village of **Skara Brae**, the standing **Stones of Stenness**, the chambered tomb of **Maes Howe** and the **Broch of Gurness**, as well as one of Orkney's best preserved medieval castles at **Birsay**. Despite the intensive farming, there are still some areas that are too barren to cultivate, and the high ground and wild coastline are protected by several interesting **wildlife reserves**.

Stenness

The parish of **Stenness**, northeast of Stromness along the main road to Kirkwall, slopes down from Ward Hill (881ft) to the lochs of Stenness and Harray,

△ Stones of Stenness

the first of which is tidal, the second of which is Orkney's most famous fresh-water trout loch. The two lochs are separated by a couple of promontories, now joined by a short causeway that may well have been a narrow isthmus around 3000 BC, when it stood at the heart of Orkney's most important Neolithic ceremonial complex, centred on the burial chamber of **Maes Howe**.

The most visible part of the complex between lochs Stenness and Harray is the **Stones of Stenness**, originally a circle of twelve rock slabs, now just four, the tallest of which is a real monster at over 16ft, though it's more remarkable for its incredible thinness. A broken table-top lies within the circle, which is surrounded by a much-diminished henge (a circular bank of earth and a ditch) with a couple of entrance causeways. Less than a mile to the northwest, past the awesome **Watch Stone** which stands beside the road at over 18ft in height, you reach another stone circle, the **Ring of Brodgar**, a much wider circle dramatically sited on raised ground. Here there were originally sixty stones, 27 of which now stand; of the henge, only the ditch survives.

Maes Howe

There are several quite large burial mounds visible to the south of the Ring of Brodgar, but these are entirely eclipsed by one of the most impressive Neolithic burial chambers in Europe, **Maes Howe** (April–Sept guided tours daily every 45min 9.45am–5.15pm; Oct–March Mon–Sat 9.45am–3.45pm, Sun 2–4.30pm; HS; £4; ☎01856/761606), which lies less than a mile northeast of the Stones of Stenness. Dating from around 3000 BC, its excellent state of preservation is partly due to the massive slabs of sandstone it was constructed from, the largest of which weighs over thirty tons. In the summer, to visit the tomb, you must first buy a **timed ticket** for a specific guided tour, either over the phone or direct from nearby **Tormiston Mill**, a converted nineteenth-century meal mill by the main road, which houses the **ticket office**, toilets and interpretive display on the ground floor, a shop and some of the original mill machinery on the middle floor, and a café, which calls itself a restaurant but isn't, on the top floor.

You enter the **central chamber** down a low, long passage, one wall of which is comprised of a single immense stone. Once inside, you can stand upright and admire the superb masonry of the lofty corbelled roof. Perhaps the most remarkable aspect of Maes Howe is that the tomb is aligned so that the rays of the winter solstice sun hit the top of the Barnhouse Stone, half a mile away, and reach right down the passage of Maes Howe to the ledge of one of the three cells built into the walls of the tomb. When Maes Howe was opened in 1861, it was found to be virtually empty, thanks to the work of generations of grave-robbers, who had left behind only a handful of human bones. The Vikings entered in the twelfth century, probably on their way to the Crusades, leaving large amounts of runic graffiti, some of which are cryptographic twig runes, cut into the walls of the main chamber and still clearly visible today. They include phrases such as "many a beautiful woman has stooped in here, however pompous she might be", and "these runes were carved by the man most skilled in runes in the entire western ocean", to the more prosaic "Thor and I bedded Helga".

Practicalities

Given the density of prehistoric sites around Stenness, and its central position on the Mainland, it's not a bad area in which to base yourself. For **accommodation** look no further than the carefully converted *Mill of Eyrland* (☎01856/850136, ⒲www.millofeyrland.co.uk; ❸), in a delightful setting by a millstream on the A964 to Orphir; it's filled with wonderful antiques and old mill machinery plus all mod cons, and serves enormous breakfasts. Alternatively, you could stay at *Holland House* (☎01856/771400, ⒲www.hollandhouseorkney .co.uk; ❸), a former manse halfway along the A986 to Dounby, that's tastefully furnished and serves up very good breakfasts (and dinners if required).

Skara Brae and around

Around seven miles north of Stromness, the parish of Sandwick contains the best known of Orkney's prehistoric monuments, the Neolithic village of **Skara Brae** (April–Sept daily 9.30am–6.30pm; Oct–March Mon–Sat 9.30am–4.30pm, Sun 2–4.30pm; HS; £6), beautifully situated beside the white curve of the Bay of Skaill. Here, the extensive remains of a small Neolithic fishing and farming village, dating back to 3000 BC, were discovered in 1850 after a fierce storm ripped off the dunes covering them. The village is amazingly well preserved, its houses huddled together and connected by narrow passages, which would originally have been covered over with turf. The houses themselves consist of a single, spacious living room, filled with domestic detail, including dressers, fireplaces, built-in cupboards, beds and boxes, all ingeniously constructed from slabs of stone.

Before you reach the site you must buy a ticket from the **visitor centre**, which houses an excellent **café/restaurant**, where you can also get takeaway sandwiches to order. If you want to, you can pay a visit to the small introductory **exhibition**, with a few replica finds, and some hands-on stuff for kids. You then proceed to a full-scale reproduction of House 7 (the best-preserved house), complete with a fake wood and skin roof. It's all a tad neat and tidy, with fetching uplighting – rather than dark, smoky and smelly – but it'll give you the general idea. Unfortunately, the sheer numbers now visiting Skara Brae mean that you can no longer explore the site itself properly, but only look down from the outer walls. Sadly, too, House 7 now sports a glass roof to protect it from the elements; however, House 1, which also contains a dresser, as yet does not. A short video, in the little building at the far end of the site, helps put the site in context.

In the summer months, your ticket to Skara Brae also covers entry to nearby **Skaill House**, an extensive range of buildings 300yd inland, home of the laird of Skaill. The original house was a simple two-storey block with a small courtyard, built for Bishop George Graham in the 1620s, but it has since been much extended. The last occupant of the house was Mrs Kathleen Scarth, who died in 1991; her bedroom has been left as it was, and is filled with old frocks, an ostrich feather fan and a "twist and slim exerciser".

With only infrequent bus connections, you really need your own transport to reach Sandwick parish. There's no main settlement as such, though there are a couple of **accommodation** options in the vicinity: try *Netherstove* (℡01856/841625, ⊛www.netherstove.com; May–Oct; ❷), a friendly modern farmhouse B&B a mile north of Skara Brae, or *Via House* (℡01856/841207, ⊛www.orkneyimages.com; ❷), a bohemian Orcadian farmhouse on the A967 just past the Loch of Stenness, which hosts regular evening **storytelling** sessions by the peat fire (Tues, Fri & Sun; advance booking essential).

Birsay and around

Occupying the northwest corner of the Mainland, the parish of **BIRSAY** (⊛www.birsay.org.uk) was the centre of Norse power in Orkney for several centuries before the earls moved to Kirkwall, some time after the construction of its cathedral. Today a tiny cluster of homes is gathered around the imposing sandstone ruins of the **Earl's Palace**, which was built in the second half of the sixteenth century by Robert Stewart, Earl of Orkney, using the forced labour of the islanders, who weren't even given food and drink for their work. By all accounts, it was a "sumptuous and stately dwelling", built in four wings around a central courtyard, its upper rooms decorated with painted ceilings and rich furnishings; surrounding the palace were flower and herb gardens, a bowling green and archery butts. The palace appears to have lasted barely a century before falling into rack and ruin; the crumbling walls and turrets retain much of their grandeur, although inside there is little remaining domestic detail. However, its vast scale makes the Earl's Palace in Kirkwall seem almost humble in comparison.

Just over half a mile northwest of the palace is the **Brough of Birsay**, a substantial Pictish settlement on a small tidal island that is only accessible during the two hours each side of low tide. Stromness and Kirkwall tourist offices have the tide times and Radio Orkney broadcasts them (93.7FM; Mon–Fri 7.30–8am). Once you reach the island, there's a small ticket office, where you must pay your **entrance fee** (mid-June to Sept daily; £2), and where you can see a few artefacts gathered from the site, including a game made from whalebone and an antler pin. The focus of the village was – and still is – the sandstone-built twelfth-century **St Peter's Church**, which is thought to have stood at the centre of a monastic complex of some sort – the foundations of a courtyard and outer buildings can be made out to the west. Close by is a large complex of Viking-era buildings, including several houses, a sauna and some sophisticated stone drains.

The best **accommodation** in Birsay is at *Linkshouse* (☎01856/721221, ⓦ www.ewaf.co.uk; ❷), a B&B in an old house with a bit of character close to Birsay village itself. The nearest watering hole is the **bar** of the *Barony Hotel*, overlooking the Loch of Boardhouse, to the southeast of Birsay village.

Kirbuster and Corrigall farm museums

Lying between the Loch of Boardhouse and the Loch of Hundland, the **Kirbuster Farm Museum** (March–Oct Mon–Sat 10.30am–1pm & 2–5pm, Sun 2–7pm; free) offers an interesting insight into life on an Orkney farmsteading in the mid-nineteenth century. Built in 1723, the farm is made up of a typical collection of flagstone buildings. Ducks, geese and sheep wander around the grassy open yard, which is entered through a whalebone archway. The most remarkable thing about Kirbuster, however, is that, despite being inhabited until as late as 1961, it has retained its firehoose, in which the smoke from the central peat fire is used to dry fish fillets, and eventually allowed simply to drift up towards a hole in the ceiling; the room even has the old neuk-beds, simple recesses in the stone walls, which would have originally been lined with wood. If you've enjoyed your time at Kirbuster – and kids almost certainly will – then it's definitely worth visiting **Corrigall Farm Museum** (same times), another eighteenth-century farmstead some five miles southeast of Kirbuster, beyond Dounby in the parish of Harray.

Evie and the Broch of Gurness

The village and parish of **EVIE**, on the north coast, look out across the turbulent waters of Eynhallow Sound towards the island of Rousay. Its chief draw is the **Broch of Gurness** (April–Sept daily 9.30am–6.30pm; HS; £3.30), the best-preserved broch on an archipelago replete with them, and one which is still surrounded by a remarkable complex of later buildings. As at Birsay, the sea has eaten away half the site, but the broch itself, dating from around 100 BC, still stands, its walls reaching a height of 12ft in places, its inner cells still intact. The compact group of homes clustered around the broch has also survived amazingly well, with much of their original and ingenious stone shelving and fireplaces still in place. The best view of the site is from the east, where you can clearly make out the "main street" leading towards the broch. The **visitor**

centre where you buy your ticket is also worth a quick once-over, especially for those with kids, who will enjoy using the quernstone corn grinder. The broch is clearly signposted from Evie, the road skirting the pristinely white **Sands of Evie**, a perfect picnic spot in fine weather.

One of the most secluded **accommodation** options on the Mainland is the artfully decorated ⚲ *Woodwick House* (☎01856/751330, ⓦwww.woodwick house.co.uk; ❹), southeast of the main village. The cheaper rooms have shared, slightly ancient bathrooms, but there are two residents' lounges, both with real fires and the wooded grounds are delightful (and feature a seventeenth-century doocot). At the other end of the scale, you can stay in the simple *Eviedale* **campsite**, run by Dale Farm (☎01856/751270, ⓦwww.creviedale.orknet .co.uk; April–Oct) and situated in a sheltered spot right by the junction of the road to Dounby. The local shop and post office are close by.

Kirkwall

Initial impressions of **KIRKWALL**, Orkney's capital, are not always favourable. It has nothing to match the picturesque harbour of Stromness, and its residential sprawl is far less appealing. However, it does have one great redeeming feature

△ Kirkwall harbour

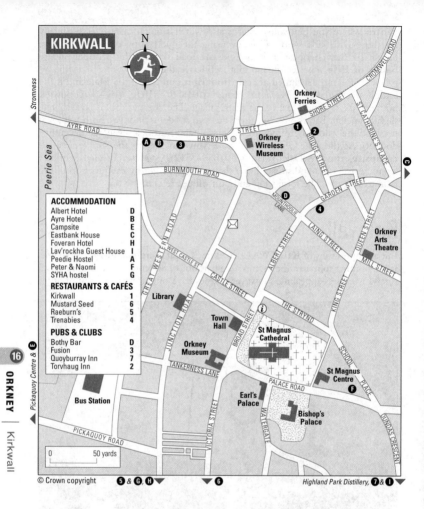

ACCOMMODATION

Albert Hotel	D
Ayre Hotel	B
Campsite	E
Eastbank House	C
Foveran Hotel	H
Lav'rockha Guest House	I
Peedie Hostel	A
Peter & Naomi	F
SYHA hostel	G

RESTAURANTS & CAFÉS

Kirkwall	1
Mustard Seed	6
Raeburn's	5
Trenabies	4

PUBS & CLUBS

Bothy Bar	D
Fusion	3
Quoyburray Inn	7
Torvhaug Inn	2

© Crown copyright

– its sandstone **cathedral**, without doubt the finest medieval building in the north of Scotland. In any case, if you're staying any length of time in Orkney you're more or less bound to find yourself in Kirkwall at some point, as the town is home to the islands' better-stocked shops, including the only large supermarket, and is the departure point for most of the ferries to Orkney's northern isles.

Part of the reason for Kirkwall's disappointing waterfront is that today's harbour is a largely modern invention; in the mid-nineteenth century, the shoreline ran along Junction Road, and before that it was flush with the west side of Broad Street. Nowadays, the town is very much divided into two main focal points: the old **harbour**, at the north end of the town, where visiting yachts moor and the small inter-island ferries come and go all year round, and the flagstoned **main street**, which changes its name four times – Bridge Street, Albert Street, Broad Street and Victoria Street – as it twists its way south from the harbour past the cathedral.

Arrival, information and accommodation

Northlink **ferries** from Shetland and Aberdeen (and all cruise ships) dock at the new Hatston terminal, a mile or so northwest of town; the buses waiting at Hatston will take you to Stromness, or into the centre of Kirkwall. Kirkwall **airport** is about three miles southeast of town on the A960; a bus (Mon–Sat 7–8 daily; 15min) will take you to Broad Street in the town centre, before terminating at the **bus station**, a few minutes' walk west of the centre. For **bike rental** head for Cycle Orkney, Tankerness Lane (℡01856/875777).

Kirkwall is an easy place in which to orientate yourself, with the prominent spire of St Magnus Cathedral clearly marking the town centre. The helpful **tourist office**, on Broad Street beside the cathedral graveyard (April–Sept daily 8.30am–8pm; Oct–March Mon–Sat 9.30am–5pm; ℡01856/872856), books accommodation, changes money and gives out a free plan of the town.

Accommodation

As for **accommodation**, Kirkwall has plenty of small rooms in ordinary B&Bs, and a host of blandly refurbished hotels, but nothing exceptional, so unless you're reliant on public transport, or have business in town, there's really no strong reason to base yourself here. Instead, head out into Orkney's wonderful countryside.

The SYHA **hostel** (℡0870/004 1133, Ⓦwww.syha.org.uk; April–Sept) is a good ten minutes' walk out of the centre on the road to Orphir, and is no beauty outside or in. A more central and more comfortable option is the small privately run *Peedie Hostel* (℡01856/875477), on the waterfront next door to the *Ayre Hotel*. There's also a **campsite** (℡01856/879900; mid-May to mid-Sept) behind the Pickaquoy Leisure Centre, five minutes' walk west of the bus station; the site is well equipped with laundry facilities, but it's hardly what you'd call picturesque.

Hotels and B&Bs

Albert Hotel Mounthoolie Lane ℡01856/876000, Ⓦwww.alberthotel.co.uk. Great central location, lively bar (with disco attached) and completely refurbished inside, this is a comfortable option. ❸

Ayre Hotel Ayre Rd ℡01856/873001, Ⓦwww.ayrehotel.co.uk. Despite harbourfront appearances – the hotel entrance is round the back – this is probably the smartest option in town, as well as being home to the local accordion and fiddle club (Wed). ❻

Eastbank House East Rd ℡01856/870179, Ⓦwww.eastbankhouse.co.uk. Former hospital, now converted into a simple four-storey guesthouse, with laundry facilities and a fully equipped kitchen for guests' use. ❸

Foveran Hotel Two miles southwest on the A964 to Orphir ℡01856/872389, Ⓦwww.foveranhotel.co.uk. Suitable should you have your own transport, this is a very friendly modern hotel, with comfortable rooms, a good restaurant and great views over Scapa Flow. ❻

Lav'rockha Guest House Inganess Rd ℡01856/876103, Ⓦwww.lavrockha.co.uk. Modern guesthouse near the Highland Park distillery southeast of the centre that's a cut above the rest. ❷

Peter & Naomi 13 Palace Rd ℡01856/872249. Probably Kirkwall's most central B&B, a modest Victorian villa right by the cathedral run by a friendly couple. ❸

The town and around

Standing at the very heart of Kirkwall, **St Magnus Cathedral** (Mon–Sat 9am–6pm, Sun 2–6pm) is the town's most compelling sight. This beautiful red sandstone building was begun in 1137 by the Orkney Earl Rognvald, who decided to make full use of a growing cult surrounding the figure of his uncle Magnus, killed on the orders of his cousin Haakon in 1117 (see p.748). When Magnus's body was buried in Birsay a heavenly light was said to have shone overhead, and his grave soon became a place of pilgrimage attributed with miraculous powers that drew pilgrims from far afield. When Rognvald finally took over the earldom he built the cathedral in his uncle's honour, moving the centre of religious and secular power from Birsay to Kirkwall.

Today much of the detail in the soft sandstone has worn away – the capitals around the main doors are reduced to artistically gnarled stumps – but it's still an immensely impressive building, its shape and style echoing the great cathedrals of Europe. Inside, the atmosphere is surprisingly intimate, the bulky sandstone columns drawing your eye up to the exposed brickwork arches, while around the walls is a series of mostly seventeenth-century tombstones, many carved with a skull and crossbones and other emblems of mortality, alongside chilling inscriptions calling on the reader to "remember death waits us all, the hour none knows". In the square pillars on either side of the high altar, the bones of Magnus and Rognvald are buried. In the southeastern corner of the cathedral lies the tomb of the Stromness-born Arctic explorer John Rae, who went off to try and find Sir John Franklin's expedition; he is depicted asleep, dressed in moleskins and furs, his rifle and Bible by his side. Beside Rae's tomb is Orkney's own poets' corner, with memorials to, among others, George Mackay Brown, Eric Linklater and Edwin Muir. Another poignant monument is the one to the dead of HMS *Royal Oak*, which was torpedoed in Scapa Flow in 1939 with the loss of 833 men.

To the south of the cathedral are the ruined remains of the **Bishop's Palace** (April–Sept daily 9.30am–6.30pm; Oct & Nov Mon–Sat 9.30am–4.30pm, Sun 2–4.30pm; HS; £2.50), residence of the bishop of Orkney since the twelfth century. It was here that the Norwegian King Haakon died in 1263 on his return from defeat at the Battle of Largs. Most of what you see now, however, dates from the time of Bishop Robert Reid, the founder of Edinburgh University, in the mid-sixteenth century. The walls still stand, as does the tall round tower in which the bishop had his private chambers; a narrow spiral staircase takes you to the top for a good view of the cathedral and across Kirkwall's rooftops. The ticket for the Bishop's Palace also covers entry to the neighbouring **Earl's Palace**, built by the infamous Earl Patrick Stewart around 1600 using forced labour, rather better preserved, and a lot more fun to explore. With its grand entrance, fancy oriel windows, dank dungeons, massive fireplaces and magnificent central hall, it has a confident solidity, and is reckoned to be one of the finest examples of Renaissance architecture in Scotland. The roof may be missing, but many domestic details remain, including a set of toilets and the stone shelves used by the clerk to do his filing. Earl Patrick enjoyed his palace for only a very short time before he was imprisoned and charged with treason. The earl might have been acquitted, but he foolishly ordered his son, Robert, to organize an insurrection; he held out four days in the palace against the Earl of Caithness, before being captured, sent to Edinburgh and hanged there; his father was beheaded at the same place five weeks later.

Opposite the cathedral stands the sixteenth-century Tankerness House, a former home for the clergy. It has been renovated countless times over the years, most recently in the 1960s in order to provide a home for the **Orkney Museum** (Mon–Sat 10.30am–5pm; May–Sept also Sun 2–5pm; free). A couple of rooms have been restored to how they would have been in 1820, when the building was a private home for the Baikie family. The rest house some of the islands' most treasured finds; among the more unusual of which are a witch's spell box, and a lovely whalebone plaque from a Viking boat grave discovered on Sanday. On a warm summer afternoon, the museum **gardens** (which can be entered either from the house itself or from a gate on Tankerness Lane) are thick with the buzz of bees and vibrantly coloured flora. In wet weather you can stay inside and watch a video of the traditional Orkney ball game, **The Ba'**, played at Christmas and New Year.

At the harbour end of Junction Road, at Kiln Corner, you can browse around the tiny **Orkney Wireless Museum** (April–Sept Mon–Sat 10am–4.30pm, Sun 2–4.30pm; £2; Ⓦwww.owm.org.uk), a single room packed to the roof with every variety of antique radio equipment you can imagine. The museum is particularly strong on technical flotsam from the two world wars, and there's even a working crystal set which you can listen to.

Highland Park

Further afield, a mile or so south of the town centre on the A961 to South Ronaldsay is the **Highland Park distillery** (April–Oct tours every 30min Mon–Fri 10am–5pm; July–Sept also Sat 10am–5pm & Sun noon–5pm; Nov–March Mon–Fri tours at 2pm; £3; Ⓣ01856/874619, Ⓦwww.highlandpark .co.uk), billed as "the most northerly legal distillery in Scotland". It's been in operation for more than two hundred years, although it was closed during World War II when the army used it as a food store and the huge vats served as communal baths. You can decide for yourself whether the taste still lingers by partaking of the customary dram after one of the regular guided tours of the beautiful old buildings, which include the distillery's very own peat-fired maltings.

Eating, drinking and entertainment

Given the quality of Orkney beef, and the quantity of shellfish caught in the vicinity, Kirkwall's **food** options are pretty disappointing. The best **café** in town is the venerable *Trenabies* on Albert Street, which does high teas, and more adventurous bistro fare in the evening; opposite is a great deli for **picnic** fodder. Another good café for lunch is the *Mustard Seed* (closed Wed & Sun), in the small Christian bookshop at 86 Victoria St, which serves home-made soups and imaginative, inexpensive main courses. Otherwise, there's nothing for it but to head for one of the town's hotels: the *Kirkwall*, on Harbour Street, is probably the best option, as it offers both **bar meals** and reasonable à la carte, though the bar meals at the *Albert* are OK, too. The best **fish and chips** is from *Raeburn's* at the corner of Union Street and Junction Road.

Kirkwall has its very own state-of-the-art **nightclub**, *Fusion* (Thurs–Sat; Ⓦwww.fusionclub.co.uk), which occasionally attracts top-name DJs and also stages live gigs. The liveliest **pub** is the *Torvhaug Inn* at the harbour end of Bridge Street; another good place to try is the *Bothy Bar* in the *Albert Hotel*, which sometimes has live music. The *Ayre Hotel* has regular Orkney Accordion & Fiddle Club nights on Wednesdays, and there's sometimes live music at the *Quoyburray Inn*, a couple of miles beyond the airport on the A960, and at other hotels in Kirkwall. Check the *Orcadian* listings for the latest (Ⓦwww.orcadian .co.uk).

Kirkwall's new **Pickaquoy Leisure Centre** (Ⓦwww.pickaquoy.com) – known locally as the "Picky" – is a short walk west of the town centre, up Pickaquoy Road past the supermarket. It now serves as one of the town's main large-scale venues, and also contains the New Phoenix **cinema** (Ⓣ01856/879900). There's a swimming pool on the other side of town, on Thomas Street.

Kirkwall's chief cultural bash is the week-long **St Magnus Festival** (Ⓦwww .stmagnusfestival.com), a superb arts festival based in Kirkwall and held in the middle of June. For many of the locals, though, the most important event is the agricultural **County Show** held in the middle of August in Kirkwall.

East Mainland and South Ronaldsay

Southeast from Kirkwall, the narrow spur of the **East Mainland** juts out into the North Sea and is joined, thanks to the remarkable Churchill Barriers, to several smaller islands, the largest of which are **Burray** and **South Ronaldsay**. As with the West Mainland, the land here is relatively densely populated and heavily farmed, but contains few of Orkney's more famous sights. Nevertheless, there are several interesting fishing villages, some good coastal walks to enjoy, an unusual new Iron Age site to explore at **Mine Howe** and, at the **Tomb of the Eagles**, one of the most enjoyable and memorable of Orkney's prehistoric sites.

East Mainland

The northern side of the **East Mainland** consists of three exposed peninsulas that jut out like giant claws. The most intriguing sight is the recently excavated Iron Age mound of **Mine Howe** (May Wed & Sun 11am–3pm; June to early Sept daily 11am–5pm; rest of Sept Wed & Sun 11am–2pm; £2.50), just off the A960 in the Tankerness peninsula, beyond the airport. Originally Mine Howe would have been a large mound surrounded by a deep ditch, but only a small section has been excavated. At the top of the mound a series of steps leads steeply down to a half-landing, and then plunges down even deeper to a small chamber some twenty feet below the surface. Visitors don a hard hat and grab a torch, before heading underground. The whole layout is unique and has left archeologists totally baffled, though, naturally, numerous theories as to its purpose abound, from execution by ritual drowning to a temple to the god of the underworld. Mine Howe's relationship to the nearby mound and broch of Longhowe remains a mystery too. A survey has revealed a ditch with a single entrance encompassing the site, beyond which are signs of a settlement, probably of Pictish origin.

The Churchill Barriers and Italian Chapel

To the south of the village of St Mary's is the first of four causeways known as the **Churchill Barriers**, built during World War II as anti-submarine barriers after the sinking of the battleship HMS *Royal Oak* on October 14, 1939. As you cross the barriers, you can still see the old blockships, which used to form the barrier, rusting away. More than two-thirds of the 1700-strong workforce who built the barriers were Italian POWs, whose legacy is the extraordinary **Italian Chapel** (daily dawn–dusk; free) on Lamb Holm. This, the so-called "miracle of Camp 60", must be one of the greatest adaptations ever, made from two Nissen huts, concrete, barbed wire and parts of a rusting blockship. It has a great false facade, and colourful *trompe l'oeil* decor, lovingly restored by the chapel's principal architect, Domenico Chiocchetti, who returned in 1960.

Burray

If you're travelling with children, you may like to stop off on the island of **Burray** in order to visit the **Orkney Fossil and Heritage Centre** (April–Sept daily 10am–6pm; £2.50), on the main road across the island. The UV room, where the rocks reveal their iridescent colours, is a particular favourite with kids. Upstairs, there's a lot of wartime memorabilia, books to read and a rocking horse to play on.

    BURRAY VILLAGE, on the south coast of the island, expanded in the nineteenth century during the boom years of the herring industry, but was

Apart from a few oil tankers, there's generally very little activity in the great natural harbour of **Scapa Flow**. Yet for the first half of the twentieth century, the Flow served as the main base of the Royal Navy, with over a hundred warships anchored here at any one time. The coastal defences required to make Scapa Flow safe to use as the country's chief naval headquarters were considerable and many are still visible all over Orkney, ranging from half-sunk blockships to the Churchill Barriers (see opposite) and the gun batteries that pepper the coastline. Unfortunately, these defences weren't sufficient to save **HMS Royal Oak** from being torpedoed by a German U-boat in October 1939, but they withstood several heavy German air raids during the course of 1940. Ironically, the worst disaster the Flow has ever witnessed was self-inflicted, when **HMS Vanguard** sank on July 9, 1917, after suffering an internal explosion, taking over a thousand of her crew with her and leaving only two survivors.

Scapa Flow's most celebrated moment in naval history, however, was when the entire **German High Seas Fleet** was interned here immediately after the end of World War I. A total of 74 ships, manned by several thousand German sailors, was anchored off the island of Cava awaiting the outcome of the Versailles Peace Conference. At around noon on Midsummer's Day, 1919, believing either that the majority of the German fleet was to be handed over, or that hostilities were about to resume, the commanding officer, Admiral von Reuter, ordered the fleet to be scuttled. By 5pm, every ship was beached or had sunk and nine German sailors had lost their lives, shot by outraged British servicemen. The British government were publicly indignant, but privately relieved since the scuttling avoided the diplomatic nightmare of dividing up the fleet between the Allies.

Between the wars, the largest **salvage operation** in history took place in Scapa Flow, with the firm of Cox & Danks alone raising twenty-six destroyers, one light cruiser, four battlecruisers and two battleships. Despite this, seven large German ships – three battleships and four light cruisers – remain on the seabed of Scapa Flow, along with four destroyers and a U-boat. Although the remaining vessels can only be salvaged on a piecemeal basis, their pre-atomic era steel is still extremely valuable as it is radiation-free and is in great demand in the space and nuclear industries. Scapa Flow is also considered one of the world's greatest dive sites. Scapa Scuba (℡01856/851218, @www.scapascuba.co.uk), based in Stromness, offers one-to-one **scuba-diving** tuition for beginners, lasting three hours, diving on one of the blockships sunk by the Churchill Barriers; they also offer wreck diving for those with more experience. If you don't want to get your feet wet, Roving Eye Enterprises (℡01856/811309, @www.rovingeye.co.uk) runs a boat fitted with an underwater camera, which does the diving for you, while you sit back and watch the video screen; their trip leaves from Houton Pier at 1.20pm, takes three hours, costs £25 and includes a visit to the Scapa Flow Visitor Centre in Lyness (see p.745).

16

ORKNEY | East Mainland and South Ronaldsay

badly affected by the sinking of the blockships during World War I. The two-storey warehouse, built in 1860 in order to cure and pack the herring, has since been converted into the *Sands Hotel* (℡01856/731298, @www.thesands hotel.co.uk; ❸), where you can find freshly caught local fish on the menu and six nicely refurbished **hotel** rooms. Alternatively, head for *Vestlaybanks* (℡01856/731305, @www.vestlaybanks.co.uk; ❷), a very comfortable **B&B** along the road to Littlequoy, which boasts great views over Scapa Flow.

South Ronaldsay

At the southern end of the series of four barriers is low-lying **South Ronaldsay**, the largest of the islands linked to the Mainland and, like the latter, rich farming country. It was traditionally the chief crossing-point to the Scottish mainland, as it's only six miles across the Pentland Firth from Caithness. Car **ferries** currently arrive at St Margaret's Hope, and there's a small passenger ferry between John O'Groats and Burwick, on the southernmost tip of the island (see p.757 for details).

St Margaret's Hope

The main settlement on South Ronaldsay is **ST MARGARET'S HOPE**, which local tradition says takes its name from Margaret, the Maid of Norway and daughter of the king of Norway, who is thought to have died here at the age of 8 in November 1290. As the granddaughter of Alexander III, Margaret had already been proclaimed queen of Scotland and was on her way to marry the English prince Edward (later Edward II), thereby unifying the two countries. Today, St Margaret's Hope – or "The Hope", as it's known locally – is a pleasing little gathering of stone-built houses overlooking a sheltered bay, and is by far the best base from which to explore the area. As is obvious from the architecture, and the piers, The Hope was once a thriving port. Nowadays, despite the presence of the Pentland Ferries terminal, it remains a very peaceful place.

The village smithy on Cromarty Square has been turned into a **Smiddy Museum** (June–Aug daily noon–4pm; May & Sept daily 2–4pm; Oct Sun 2–4pm; free), which is particularly fun for kids, who enjoy getting hands-on with the old tools, drills and giant bellows. There's also a small exhibition on the annual **Boys' Ploughing Match**, in which local boys compete with miniature hand-held ploughs. The competition, which is taken extremely seriously by all those involved, happens on the third Saturday in August, at the beautiful golden beach at the **Sands O' Wright** in Hoxa, a couple of miles west of The Hope. At the same time a **Festival of the Horse** takes place, with the local children dressing up in spectacular costumes and harnesses.

If you want **to stay** in St Margaret's Hope itself you should head for *The Creel* (℡01856/831311, Ⓦwww.thecreel.co.uk; ❻) on the harbourfront, with a view over the bay, and one of the best **restaurants** in Scotland and winner of all sorts of awards. At around £25 for two courses, it's expensive, but also friendly and relaxed. More modest bar meals are available from the *Murray Arms Hotel* (℡01856/831205, Ⓦwww.murrayarmshotel.com; ❹), on Back Road, which has rooms above the pub and a backpackers' **hostel** round the side.

Outside St Margaret's Hope, you're spoilt for choice with *Shoreside* (℡01856/831560, Ⓦwww.orkneyholiday.com; ❸), a **B&B** back down the road to Kirkwall, where you're guaranteed fresh fish and shellfish as the stuff comes from their own fishing boat, and *Roeberry House* (℡01856/831228; Ⓦwww.roeberry.co.uk; ❸), an imposing country house two miles west of the Hope along the B9043. Guests have their own flat, complete with lounge and kitchen, the Sands O' Right beach is nearby and the views are great. For a **hostel** with some character, head for *Wheems* (℡01856/831537; April–Oct), on the eastern side of South Ronaldsay, a mile and a half from the war memorial on the main road outside The Hope. Mattresses and clean linen are provided, and seasonal produce from the croft is on sale and **camping** is possible.

The Tomb of the Eagles

One of the most enjoyable archeological sights on Orkney is the Ibister chambered cairn at the southeastern corner of South Ronaldsay, known as the **Tomb of the Eagles** (daily: March 10am–noon; April–Oct 9.30am–6pm;

Nov–March by appointment; £5; ☎01856/831339, ⓦwww.tomboftheeagles
.co.uk). The cairn was discovered and excavated by local farmer, Ronald Simpson of Liddle, who still owns it, so a visit here makes a refreshing change from
the usual interpretive centre. First off, you get to look round the family's private
museum of prehistoric artefacts; this is the original hands-on museum, so visitors can actually touch and admire the painstaking craftsmanship of Neolithic
folk, and examine a skull. Next you get a brief guided tour of a nearby Bronze
Age **burnt mound**, which is basically a Neolithic rubbish dump, beside which
there was a large trough, where joints of meat were boiled by throwing in rocks
from the fire. Finally you get to walk out to the **chambered cairn**, by the
cliff's edge, where human remains were found alongside talons and carcasses
of sea eagles. To enter the cairn, you must lie on a trolley and pull yourself in
using an overhead rope – something that's guaranteed to put a smile on every
visitor's face.

Hoy

Hoy, Orkney's second-largest island, rises sharply out of the sea to the southwest of the Mainland. The least typical of the islands, but certainly the most
dramatic, its north and west sides are made up of great glacial valleys and
mountainous moorland rising to over 1500ft, dropping into the sea off the
red sandstone cliffs of St John's Head, and, to the south, forming the landmark
sea stack known as the **Old Man of Hoy**. The northern half of Hoy, though
a huge expanse, is virtually uninhabited, with just the cluster of houses at
Rackwick nestling dramatically in a bay between the cliffs. Meanwhile, most
of Hoy's four hundred or so residents live on the gentler, more fertile land in
the southeast, in and around the villages of **Lyness** and **Longhope**. This part
of the island is littered with buildings dating from the two world wars, when
Scapa Flow served as the main base for the Royal Navy.

Two **ferry services** run to Hoy: a passenger ferry from Stromness to
Moaness pier, by Hoy village (Mon–Fri 4–5 daily, Sat & Sun 2 daily; 25min;
☎01856/850624), which also serves the small island of Graemsay; and the
roll-on/roll-off car ferry from Houton on the Mainland to Lyness (Mon–Fri 6
daily, Sat & Sun 2–4 daily; 45min–1hr 25min; ☎01856/811397), which sometimes calls in at the oil terminal island of Flotta, and begins and ends its daily
schedule at Longhope. There's no bus service on Hoy, but those arriving on the
passenger ferry from Stromness should find a **minibus** waiting to take them to
Rackwick.

North Hoy

Walkers arriving by passenger ferry from Stromness at Moaness Pier, near the
tiny village of **HOY**, and heading for Rackwick (four miles southwest), can
either catch the minibus or take the well-marked footpath that goes past Sandy
Loch and along the large open valley beyond.

The minibus route to Rackwick is via the single-track road along another
valley to the south. En route, duckboards head across the heather to the
Dwarfie Stane, Orkney's most unusual chambered tomb, cut from a solid
block of sandstone and dating back to 3000 BC. The sheer effort that must
have been involved in carving out this tomb, with its two side-cells, is staggering, and as you crawl inside, the marks of the tools used by the Neolithic
builders on the ceiling are still visible. The tomb is also decorated with

copious Victorian graffiti, the most interesting of which is to be found on the northern exterior, where Major Mouncey, a former British spy in Persia and a confirmed eccentric who dressed in Persian garb, carved his name backwards in Latin, and also carved in Persian the words "I have sat two nights and so learnt patience."

RACKWICK is an old crofting and fishing village squeezed between towering sandstone cliffs on the west coast. In an area once quite extensively cultivated, these days only a few of Rackwick's houses are inhabited all year round, though the savage isolation of the place has provided inspiration to a number of artists and writers, including Orkney's George Mackay Brown, who wrote "when Rackwick weeps, its grief is long and forlorn and utterly desolate." A small farm building beside the hostel serves as a tiny **museum** (open anytime; free), with a few old photos and a brief rundown of Rackwick's rough history.

Despite its isolation, Rackwick has a steady stream of walkers and climbers passing through it en route to the **Old Man of Hoy**, a great sandstone column some 450ft high, perched on an old lava flow which protects it from the erosive power of the sea. The Old Man is a popular challenge for rock climbers, and a 1966 ascent, led by the mountaineer Chris Bonington, was the first televised climb in Britain. The well-trodden footpath from Rackwick is an easy three-mile walk (3hr round trip) – the great skuas will dive-bomb you only during the nesting season – and gives the reward of a great view of the stack. The surrounding cliffs provide ideal rocky ledges for the nests of thousands of seabirds, including guillemots, kittiwakes, razorbills, puffins and shags.

Continuing north along the clifftops, the path peters out before **St John's Head** which, at 1136ft, is one of the highest sea cliffs in the country and mostly too sheer even for nesting seabirds. Another, safer, option is to hike to the top of **Ward Hill** (1577ft), the highest mountain in Orkney, from which on a fine day you can see the whole archipelago laid out before you.

Practicalities

There are only a few places to stay in North Hoy. Luckily one of them is *The Glen* (℡01856/791262; ❷), in Rackwick, run by a friendly couple, whose family have lived on the island for centuries; they also offer dinner and will collect guests from Hoy. In addition, there are two council-run, SYHA-affiliated **hostels**, housed in converted schools; to book ahead, you must contact the education department at the Orkney Islands Council (℡01856/873535 ext 2415). The *North Hoy Hostel* (May to mid-Sept) in Hoy village is the larger of the two, but the *Rackwick Hostel* (mid-March to mid-Sept), with just eight beds, enjoys a better location. You can **camp** in Rackwick, either behind the hostel, down by the unusually attractive public toilets, or beside *Burnside Cottage* (℡01856/791316), the heather-thatched **bothy** in a beautiful setting right by the beach, which has no mattresses or kitchen facilities. **Bike rental** is available from Hoy's Moaness Pier (℡01856/791225). However, there's no shop in Rackwick, so take all your supplies with you; the post office shop in Hoy only sells chocolate, but the *Hoy Inn*, near the post office, serves very good **bar meals** in season. Be warned, too, that North Hoy is probably the worst place on Orkney for midges.

Lyness and Longhope

Along the sheltered eastern shore of Hoy, high moorland gives way to a gentler environment similar to that on the rest of Orkney. Hoy defines the western boundary of Scapa Flow, and **LYNESS** played a major role for the Royal Navy during both world wars. Many of the old wartime buildings have been cleared away over the last few decades, but the harbour and hills around Lyness are still scarred with the scattered remains of concrete structures which once served as hangars and storehouses during World War II, and are now used as barns and cowsheds. Among these are the remains of what was – incredibly – the biggest cinema in Europe, but perhaps the most unusual remaining building is the monochrome Art Deco facade of the old **Garrison Theatre**, on the main road south of Lyness, now a private home. Lyness also has a large **naval cemetery**, where many of the victims of the various disasters that have occurred in the Flow, such as the sinking of the *Royal Oak* now lie, alongside a handful of German graves.

The old oil pumphouse, which still stands opposite the Lyness ferry terminal, has been turned into the **Scapa Flow Visitor Centre & Museum** (April–Oct Mon–Sat 9am–4.30pm, Sun 10.30am–4pm; July–Sept Sun until 6.15pm; Nov–March Mon–Fri 9am–4.30pm; free), a fascinating insight into wartime Orkney. As well as the usual old photos, torpedoes, flags, guns and propellers, there's a paratrooper's folding bicycle, and a whole section devoted to the scuttling of the German High Seas Fleet and the sinking of the *Royal Oak*. The pumphouse itself retains much of its old equipment – you can even ask for a working demo of one of the oil-fired boilers – used to pump oil off tankers moored at Lyness into sixteen tanks, and from there into underground reservoirs cut into the neighbouring hillside. On request, an audiovisual show on the history of Scapa Flow is screened in the sole surviving tank, which has incredible acoustics. Even the **café** has an old NAAFI feel about it.

South Walls

To the east of Melsetter House, a causeway built during World War II connects Hoy with **South Walls** (pronounced "Waas"), a fertile tidal island which is more densely populated with farms and homes than Hoy. On the north side of South Walls is the main settlement of **LONGHOPE** (Ⓦwww.longhope .co.uk), an important safe anchorage during the Napoleonic Wars and World War I, but since then overshadowed by Lyness and Flotta. The **Longhope Lifeboat** capsized in strong gale-force winds in 1969 on its way to the aid of a Liberian freighter. The entire eight-man crew was killed, leaving seven widows and ten fatherless children; the crew of the freighter, by contrast, survived. There's a moving memorial to the men – six of whom came from just two families – in **Kirkhope Churchyard** on the road to Cantick Head Lighthouse. Just up the road before the causeway is the **Longhope Lifeboat Museum** (daily dawn–dusk; free) which houses the *Thomas McCunn*, a lifeboat in service from 1933 to 1962 and still launched for high days and holidays.

Evidence of Longhope's strategic importance during the Napoleonic Wars lies to the east of the village at the Point of Hackness, where the **Hackness Martello Tower** stands guard over the entrance to the bay, with a matching tower on the opposite promontory of Crockness. Built in 1815, these two circular sandstone Martello towers are the northernmost in Britain, and were built to protect merchant ships waiting for a Royal Navy escort from American and French privateers. You can visit Hackness Tower (if it's locked, a sign will tell you where to pick up the key) via a steep ladder connected to the upper floor, where nine men and one officer shared the circular room. Originally a portable ladder would have been used and retracted, making the place pretty much impregnable: the walls are up to 9ft high on the seaward side, and the tower even had its own water supply. Overlooking the bay at the nearby **Hackness**

Battery, positioned closer to the shore, yet more cannon were trained on the horizon.

Practicalities

South Hoy has a handful of good **accommodation** options, including *St John's Manse* (℡01856/791240; ❸), south of Lyness, overlooking Longhope; in Longhope itself is the welcoming *Stromabank Hotel*, a nicely converted old schoolhouse (℡01856/701494, ⓦwww.stromabank.co.uk; ❸), which also does good bar **food** (closed Thurs). **Self-catering** options include the Cantick Head lighthouse cottages (℡01856/701255; 4–6 people; £375–500 per week). There are two shops: one round the back of the *Hoy Hotel*, and one by the pier in Longhope.

Shapinsay

Just a few miles northeast of Kirkwall, **Shapinsay** is the most accessible of Orkney's northern isles. A gently undulating grid-plan patchwork of rich farmland, it's a bit like an island suburb of Kirkwall, which is clearly visible across the bay. Its chief attraction for visitors is **Balfour Castle** (May–Sept guided tours Sun 3pm; see below for details of the all-inclusive ticket), the imposing baronial pile designed by David Bryce and completed in 1848 by the Balfour family of Westray, who had made a small fortune in India the previous century. The Balfours died out in 1960 and the castle was bought by a Polish cavalry officer, Captain Tadeusz Zawadski, whose family now run the place as a hotel. The **guided tours** are great fun, and go down very well with children too, as they finish off with complimentary tea and home-made cakes in the servants' quarters. Before you enter the castle, you get to walk through the wooded grounds and view the vast kitchen gardens, which are surrounded by fifteen-foot-high walls, and once had coal-fired greenhouses to produce fruit and vegetables out of season. The interior of the castle is not that magnificent, though it has an attractively lived-in ambience and is pretty grand for Orkney; decorative otters crop up all over the place, as they feature prominently in the Balfour family crest.

Most folk visit Shapinsay on a day-trip, but if you're staying here for a few days you'd do well to explore one or two points of interest beyond the castle. If the weather's bad, you could head for the **Shapinsay Heritage Centre** (May–Sept Mon–Fri 11am–4.30pm, Sat & Sun 11am–6pm; free), above the old smithy, halfway along the village street. The east coast from the Bay of Linton to the Foot of Shapinsay has the most interesting cliffs and sea caves and is backed by the only open moorland on the island. On the far northeastern peninsula is Shapinsay's most striking ancient monument, the **Broch of Burroughston**, a well-preserved strongly fortified Iron Age broch with the substantial remains of living quarters within, a bar hole to make fast the door, and a guard-cell. The finest stretch of sandy beach is at the sweeping curve of **Sandgarth Bay** in the southeast.

Practicalities

Less than thirty minutes from Kirkwall by **ferry** (Mon–Fri 5 daily, Sat & Sun 4 daily), Shapinsay is an easy day-trip. If you want to visit the castle, you should phone ahead and book an **all-inclusive ticket** from Balfour Castle (£18), which includes a return ferry ticket. The ferry for the guided tour leaves at

2.15pm, but you can catch an earlier ferry if you want to have some time to explore the rest of the island. It's also possible **to stay** for dinner, bed and breakfast in lord-of-the-manor style at the ⚒ *Balfour Castle Hotel* (☎01856/711282, Ⓦwww.balfourcastle.co.uk; ❾); the rooms are vast and beautifully furnished, and you also get use of the library and the other public rooms. More modest **B&B** is available at *Girnigoe* (☎01856/711256, Ⓦwww.girnigoe.net; ❷), a very comfortable Orcadian croft close to the north shore of Veantro Bay that offers optional full board. Even if you're just coming for the day, it's worth popping into *The Smithy* (May–Sept; ☎01856/711722, Ⓦwww.shapinsaysmithy.com), the wonderfully cosy licensed **café** below the heritage centre, which serves delicious food (daily lunchtime plus Fri & Sat eve) and also offers **bike rental**.

Rousay, Egilsay and Wyre

Just over half a mile from the Mainland's northern shore, the hilly island of **Rousay** is one of the more accessible northern isles as well as being home to a number of intriguing prehistoric sites. The group of a dozen or so houses above the ferry terminal is the only settlement of any size, but a single road runs around the edge of the island, connecting a string of small farms which make use of the more cultivable coastal fringes. Many visitors come on a day-trip, as it's easy enough to reach the main points of archeological interest on the south coast by foot from the ferry terminal.

Rousay's diminutive neighbours, **Egilsay** and **Wyre**, contain a few medieval attractions of their own, which can either be visited on a day-trip from Rousay itself, or from the Mainland.

Trumland House to the Knowe of Yarso

Despite its long history of settlement, Rousay is today home to little more than two hundred people (many of them incomers), as this was one of the few parts of Orkney to suffer Highland-style Clearances, initially by George William Traill at Quandale in the northwest. His successor and nephew, Lieutenant General Traill-Burroughs, built a wall to force crofters onto a narrow coastal strip and eventually provoked so much distress and anger that a gunboat had to be sent to restore order. You can learn about the history and wildlife of the island from the well-laid-out display room of the **Rousay Heritage Centre** housed in the back of the ferry waiting room.

It was the aforementioned Burroughs who built **Trumland House**, the forbidding Jacobean-style pile designed by David Bryce in 1873, and hidden in the trees half a mile northwest of the ferry terminal. The house is currently undergoing much-needed restoration, as are the **gardens**, which can be visited (May–Sept Mon–Fri 10am–5pm; £2). The road west from Trumland House is bordered over the next couple of miles by a trio of intriguing prehistoric cairns, starting with **Taversoe Tuick**, discovered by workers during the building of a Victorian viewpoint. Dating back to 3500 BC, it's remarkable in that it exploits its sloping site by having two storeys, one entered from the upper side and one from the lower. A little further west is the **Blackhammar Cairn**, which is more promising inside than it looks from the outside. You enter through the roof via a ladder; the long interior is divided into "stalls" by large flagstones, rather like the more famous cairn at Midhowe (see p.748). Finally, there's the **Knowe of Yarso**, another stalled cairn dating from the same period that's a stiff climb up the hill from the road, but worth it, if only for the magnificent view.

The remains of 29 individuals were found inside, with the skulls neatly arranged around the walls; the bones of 36 deer were also buried here.

Midhowe Cairn and Broch

The southwestern side of Rousay is home to the most significant and impressive of the island's archeological remains, strung out along the shores of the tide races of Eynhallow Sound, which runs between the island and the Mainland. Approaching from the east, **Midhowe Cairn** comes as something of a surprise, both for its immense size – it's known as "the great ship of death" and measures nearly 100ft in length – and for the fact that it's now entirely surrounded by a stone-walled barn with a corrugated roof. Unfortunately, you can't actually explore the roofless communal burial chamber, dating back to 3500 BC, but only look down from the overhead walkway. The central corridor, 25yd long, is partitioned with slabs of rock, with twelve compartments on each side, where the remains of 25 people were discovered in a crouched position with their backs to the wall.

A couple of hundred yards beyond Midhowe Cairn is Rousay's finest archeological site, **Midhowe Broch**, whose compact layout suggests that it was originally built as a sort of fortified family house, surrounded by a complex series of ditches and ramparts. These are now partially obscured by later houses, many of which have shelving and stairs still intact. The broch itself looks as though it's about to slip into the sea: it was obviously shored up with flagstone buttresses back in the Iron Age, and has more recently been given extra sea defences by Historic Scotland. The interior of the broch, entered through an impressive doorway, is divided into two separate rooms, each with its own hearth, water tank and quernstone, all of which date from the final phase of occupation around the second century AD.

Egilsay and Wyre

Egilsay, the largest of the low-lying islands sheltering close to the eastern shore of Rousay, makes for an easy day-trip. The island is dominated by the ruins of **St Magnus Church**, with its distinctive round tower. Built around the twelfth century in a prominent position in the middle of the island, probably on the site of a much earlier version, the roofless church is the only surviving example of the traditional round-towered churches of Orkney and Shetland. It is possible that it was built as a shrine to Earl (later St) Magnus, who arranged to meet his cousin Haakon here in 1117, only to be treacherously killed on Haakon's orders by the latter's cook, Lifolf. A cenotaph marks the spot where the murder took place, about a quarter of a mile southeast of the church. Egilsay is almost entirely inhabited by incomers, and a large slice of the island's farmland is managed by the RSPB in a vain attempt to encourage corncrakes. If you're just here for the day, walk due east from the ferry terminal to the coast, where there's a beautiful sandy bay overlooking Eday.

The tiny, neighbouring island of **Wyre**, to the southwest, directly opposite Rousay's ferry terminal, is another possible day-trip, and is best known for **Cubbie Roo's Castle**, the "fine stone fort" and "really solid stronghold" mentioned in the *Orkneyinga Saga*, and built around 1150 by local farmer Kolbein Hruga. The castle gets another mention in *Haakon's Saga*, when those inside successfully withstood all attacks. The outer defences have survived well on three sides of the castle, which has a central keep, with walls to a height of around six feet, its central water tank still intact. Close by the castle stands **St Mary's Chapel**, a roofless twelfth-century church founded either by Kolbein or his son, Bjarni the Poet, who was bishop of Orkney. To learn more about Cubbie Roo or any other aspect of Wyre's history, pop into the **Wyre Heritage Centre**, near the chapel.

Practicalities

Rousay makes a good day-trip from the Mainland, with regular **car ferry** sailings from Tingwall (30min), linked to Kirkwall by buses. Most ferries also call in at Egilsay and Wyre, but some need to be booked the day before at the Tingwall ferry terminal (☎01856/751360). Alternatively, you can join one of the very informative **minibus tours** run by Rousay Traveller (June–Aug Tues–Fri; £16; ☎01856/821234), which connect with ferries and last between two and six hours, the longer ones allowing extended walks.

Accommodation on Rousay is limited. If you want to be near the ancient sites, your best bet is the **hostel** at *Trumland Farm* (☎01856/821252), a working organic farm half a mile or so west of the terminal. As well as a couple of dorms, you can also camp there, and they offer **bike rental**. The *Taversoe Inn*, further along the road, offers unpretentious accommodation (☎01856/821325, ⓔTaversoeHotel@aol.com; ❶) and does good bar meals. If you're up for exploring more of the island, head for *Ervadale* (☎01856/821351, ⓔervadale@aol.com; ❷), a traditional Orcadian crofthouse **B&B** in the north-eastern corner of the island, below Kierfea Hill. The *Pier* **pub**, right beside the terminal, serves bar meals at lunchtime and will make up fresh crab sandwiches if you phone in advance (☎01856/821359). Don't arrive expecting to be able to buy yourself many provisions, though, as Marion's Shop, the island's main general store, is in the northeastern corner of the island.

Westray

Although exposed to the full force of the Atlantic weather in the far northwest of Orkney, **Westray** (ⓦwww.westray-orkney.co.uk) shelters one of the most tightly knit, prosperous and independent island communities. It has a fairly stable population of six hundred or so, producing superb beef, scallops, shellfish and a large catch of white fish, with its own small fish-processing factory and an organic salmon farm. Old Orcadian families still dominate every aspect of life, giving the island a strong individual character. The landscape is very varied, with sea cliffs and a trio of hills in the west, and rich low-lying pastureland and sandy bays elsewhere. However, given that distances are fairly large – it's about twelve miles from the ferry terminal in the south to the cliffs of Noup Head in the far northwest – and that the boat from Kirkwall takes nearly an hour and a half, Westray is an island that repays a longer stay, especially as there's lots of good accommodation and the locals are extremely welcoming and genuinely interested in visitors.

The main village and harbour is **PIEROWALL** set around a wide bay in the north of the island, a good eight miles from the Rapness ferry terminal on the southernmost tip of the island. Pierowall is a place of some considerable size, relatively speaking, with a school, several shops, a bakery (Orkney's only one off the Mainland), and the excellent **Westray Heritage Centre** (May–Sept Mon & Sun 11.30am–5pm, Tues–Sat 2–5pm; July & Aug also Tues–Fri 10am–noon; £2). The latter is a very welcoming wet-weather retreat, with a mock-up of the sea cliffs of Noup Head (see p.750), a range of hands-on exhibits for kids and a good place for a cup of tea. The island's most impressive ruin, however, is the colossal sandstone hulk of **Noltland Castle**, which stands above the village half a mile west up the road to Noup Head. This Z-plan castle, pockmarked with over seventy gun loops, was begun around 1560 by Gilbert Balfour, a shady character from Fife, who was Master of the Household to Mary, Queen of Scots, and was implicated in the murder of her husband Lord Darnley in 1567. Balfour was eventually forced to flee to Sweden, where he was found guilty of plotting to murder the Swedish king and executed in 1576. To explore the castle, you must first pick up the key, which hangs outside the back door of the nearby farm.

The northwestern tip of Westray rises up sharply, culminating in the dramatic sea cliffs of **Noup Head**, which are particularly spectacular when a good westerly swell is up. During the summer months the guano-covered rock ledges are packed with over 100,000 nesting seabirds, primarily guillemots, razorbills, kittiwakes and fulmars, with puffins as well: a truly awesome sight, sound and smell.

The four-mile coastal walk along the top of Westray's red sandstone cliffs from Noup Head south to Inga Ness is thoroughly recommended, as is a quick ascent of **Fitty Hill** (557ft), Westray's highest point. Also in the south of the island is the tiny **Cross Kirk** which, although ruined, retains an original Romanesque arch, door and window. It's right by the sea, and on a fine day the nearby sandy beach is a lovely spot for a picnic, with views over to the north side of Rousay. The sea cliffs in the southeast of the island around **Stanger Head** are not quite as spectacular as at Noup Head, but it's here that you'll find **Castle o'Burrian**, a sea stack that was once an early Christian hermitage. It's now the best place on Westray at which to see **puffins** nesting; there's even a signpost to the puffins from the main road.

Practicalities

Westray is served by car **ferry** from Kirkwall (2–3 daily; 1hr 25min; ☎01856/872044), or you can **fly** on Loganair's tiny eight-seater plane from Kirkwall to Westray (Mon–Sat 2 daily; 12min). **Guided tours** of the island by minibus or bike can also be arranged with Westraak (☎01857/677777, ⓦwww.westraak.co.uk), who will meet you at the ferry. J&M Harcus of Pierowall (☎01857/677450) runs a **bus service** that will take you from Rapness to Pierowall, though you should phone ahead to check it's running. For **bike rental**, contact either of the hostels (see below).

Westray's finest **accommodation** is at the ⚼ *Cleaton House Hotel* (☎01857/677508, ⓦwww.cleatonhouse.co.uk; ⑤), a whitewashed Victorian manse about two miles southeast of Pierowall, with great views over to Papa Westray. *Cleaton House* is also the place to sample Westray's organic salmon, either in the **restaurant** or in the hotel's congenial **bar**, which serves real ale. Somewhat bizarrely, the hotel also has a **pétanque** pitch, which residents and non-residents alike are welcome to use. The *Pierowall Hotel* (☎01857/677472, ⓦwww.orknet.co.uk/pierowall; ③), in Pierowall itself, is less stylish and less expensive, but equally welcoming, with a popular bar and a well-justified reputation for excellent **fish and chips**, fresh off the boats (much of it fish you're unlikely to have heard of).

B&B is available at *No. 1 Broughton* (☎01857/677726, ⓦwww.no1broughton .co.uk; ③), a recently renovated mid-nineteenth-century house by the southern shore of Gill Bay, on the edge of Pierowall. Westray is positively spoilt for **hostels**: ⚼ *Bis Geos* (☎01857/677420, ⓦwww.bisgeos.co.uk), on the road to Noup Head, has unbeatable views along the cliffs and out to sea; inside, it's beautifully furnished, and there are also a couple of very good **self-catering**

cottages. ⚓ *The Barn* (☎01857/677214, ⓦwww.thebarnwestray.co.uk) is situated in an old farm at the southern edge of Pierowall; it's luxurious inside, is easier to get to, has a small **campsite** adjacent to it and a games room and genuinely friendly hosts.

Papa Westray

Across the short Papa Sound from Westray is the island of **Papa Westray**, known locally as "Papay" (ⓦwww.papawestray.co.uk). With a population hovering precariously around seventy, Papay has had to fight hard to keep itself viable over the last couple of decades, helped by a hefty influx of outsiders. With one of Orkney's best-preserved Neolithic settlements, and a large nesting seabird population, it's worthy of a stay in its own right or an easy day-trip from its neighbour.

Papay's visual focus is **Holland House**, occupying the high central point of the island and once seat of the local lairds, the Traill family, who ruled over Papay for three centuries. The main house, with its crow-stepped gables, is still in private hands, but the current owners are perfectly happy for visitors to explore the old buildings of the home farm, on the west side of the road, which include a kiln, a doocot and a horse-powered threshing mill. An old bothy for single male servants, decorated with red horse yokes, has even been restored and made into a small **museum** (open anytime; free), filled with bygone bits and bobs, from a wooden flea trap to a box bed. A road leads down from Holland House to the western shore, where Papay's prime prehistoric site, the **Knap of Howar**, stands overlooking Westray. Dating from around 3500 BC, this Neolithic farm building makes a fair claim to being the oldest-standing house in Europe. It's made up of two roofless buildings, linked by a little passageway; one has a hearth and copious stone shelves, and is thought to have been some kind of storehouse. Half a mile north along the coast from the Knap of Howar is **St Boniface Kirk**, a pre-Reformation church that has recently been restored. Inside, it's beautifully simple, with a bare flagstone floor, dry-stone walls, a little wooden gallery and just a couple of surviving box pews. The church is known to have seated at least 220, which meant they would have been squashed in, fourteen to a pew. In the surrounding graveyard there's a Viking **hogback grave**, decorated with carvings in imitation of the wooden shingles on the roof of a Viking longhouse.

The northern tip of the island around **North Hill** (157ft) is now an RSPB reserve. During the breeding season, you're asked to keep to the coastal fringe, where razorbills, guillemots, fulmars, kittiwakes and puffins nest, particularly around Fowl Craig on the east coast, where you can also view the rare Scottish primrose, which flowers in May and from July to late September. If you want to explore the interior of the reserve, which plays host to one of the largest arctic tern colonies in Europe as well as numerous arctic skuas, contact the warden (☎01857/644240), who conducts regular escorted walks.

Papay is an easy day-trip from Westray, with a regular **passenger ferry** service from Gill Pier in Pierowall (2–5 daily; 25min), which also takes bicycles. However, it's just as easy to stay on Papay and take a day-trip to Westray instead. On Tuesdays and Fridays, the **car ferry** from Kirkwall to Westray continues on to Papa Westray; at other times, a bus (which accepts a limited number of bicycles) from Rapness connects with the Pierowall passenger ferry. Papay is also connected to Westray by the **world's shortest scheduled flight** – two minutes in duration, or less with a following wind. You can also fly direct from Kirkwall to Papa Westray (Mon–Sat 2–3 daily, 1 on Sun) for a special return fare of £12 if you stay overnight.

Papay's Community Co-operative has a **minibus**, which will take you from the pier to wherever you want on the island, and can arrange a Papay Peedie Tour (mid-May to mid-Sept Tues, Thurs & Sat; £30; ☎01857/644321). It also runs a shop, a sixteen-bed SYHA-affiliated **hostel** (Ⓦwww.syha.org.uk) and the *Beltane House* **B&B** (☎01857/644267, Ⓔpapaybeltane2@hotmail.com; ❸), all housed within the old estate workers' cottages at Beltane, east of Holland House.

Eday

A long, thin island at the centre of Orkney's northern isles, **Eday** shares more characteristics with Rousay and Hoy than with its immediate neighbours, dominated as it is by a great block of heather-covered upland, with farmland confined to a narrow strip of coastal ground. However, Eday's hills have proved useful in their own way, providing huge quantities of peat which has been exported to the other peatless northern isles for fuel, and was even, for a time, exported to various whisky distillers. Eday's yellow sandstone has also been extensively quarried, and was used to build the St Magnus Cathedral in Kirkwall.

The island is sparsely inhabited and has no real village as such. The chief points of interest are all in the northern half of the island, along the signposted **Eday Heritage Walk**, which covers all the main sights and takes about three hours to complete. The walk initially follows the road heading northwest, past the bird hide overlooking **Mill Loch**, where several pairs of red-throated divers regularly breed. Clearly visible to the north of the road is the fifteen-foot **Stone of Setter**, Orkney's most distinctive standing stone, weathered into three thick, lichen-encrusted fingers. The stone clearly held centre stage in the Neolithic landscape, and is visible from the other nearby prehistoric sites. From here, passing the less spectacular Braeside and Huntersquoy chambered cairns en route, you can climb the hill to reach Eday's finest, the **Vinquoy Chambered Cairn**, which has a similar structure to that of Maes Howe. You can crawl into the tomb through the narrow entrance: a skylight inside lets light into the main, beehive chamber, now home to some lovely ferns, but not into the four side-cells. From the cairn, you can continue north to the viewpoint on the summit of **Vinquoy Hill** (248ft), and on to the very northernmost tip of the island, where lie the dramatic red sandstone sea cliffs of **Red Head**, where guillemots, razorbills, puffins and other seabirds nest in summer.

Visible on the east coast is **Carrick House**, the grandest home on Eday (Sun 2pm or by appointment; £2.50; ☎01857/622260). Built by the laird of Eday in 1633, it was extended in the original style by successive owners, but is best known for its associations with the pirate **John Gow** – on whom Sir Walter Scott's novel *The Pirate* is based – whose ship *The Revenge* ran aground on the Calf of Eday in 1725. He asked for help from the local laird, but was taken prisoner in Carrick House, before eventually being sent off to London where he was tortured and executed. Highlight of the house is the bloodstain on the floor of the living room, where John Gow was detained and stabbed whilst trying to escape.

Eday's **ferry** terminal is at Backaland pier in the south, not ideal for visiting the more interesting northern section of the island, although if you haven't got your own transport you should find it fairly easy to get a lift with someone off the ferry (1–2 daily; 1hr 15min–2hr). Alternatively, car rental and taxis can be organized through Mr A. Stewart by the pier (℡01857/622206); he also runs **minibus tours** (May–Aug Mon, Wed, Fri & Sun). It's also possible to do a day-trip on Loganair's Wednesday **flight** from Kirkwall to Eday (℡01856/872494 or 873457).

Eday has a handful of friendly **B&Bs** such as *Skaill Farm*, a traditional farm-house just south of the airport (℡01857/622271; ❸), all of whom offer full board – essential as Eday has no pub or restaurant. The other accommoda-tion options are renting one of the modern hacienda-style *Pirate Gow Chalets* (℡01856/879517, ⓦwww.pirategow.com; ❶), a series of self-catering units in Calfsound, which sleep up to three people, or staying at the SYHA-affiliated **hostel** (ⓦwww.syha.org.uk), situated in an exposed spot just north of the airport, though it's pretty bleak and basic. The hostel has no resident warden and is run by Eday Community Association (℡01857/622206; April–Sept), which can also advise on **camping**.

Stronsay

A low-lying, three-legged island to the southeast of Eday, **Stronsay** is strongly agricultural, its interior an almost uninterrupted patchwork of green pastures. The island features few real sights, but the coastline has enormous appeal: a beguiling combination of sandstone cliffs, home to several seabird colonies, interspersed with wide white sands and (in fine weather) clear turquoise bays. Stronsay has seen two economic booms in the last three hundred years. The first took place in the eighteenth century, and employed as many as three thousand people; it was built on collecting vast quantities of seaweed and exporting the **kelp** for use in the chemical industry, particularly in making iodine, soap and glass. In the following century, **fishing** on a grand scale came to dominate life here, as Whitehall harbour became one of the main Scottish centres for the curing of herring caught by French, Dutch and Scottish boats. By the 1840s, up to four hundred boats were working out of the port, attracting hundreds of women herring-gutters. By the 1930s, however, the herring stocks had been severely depleted and the industry began a long decline.

WHITEHALL, in the north of the island, is the only real village on Stronsay, made up of rows of stone-built fishermen's cottages set between two large piers. Wandering along the tranquil, rather forlorn harbourfront today, you'll find it hard to believe that the village once supported five thousand people in the fishing industry during the summer season, as well as a small army of coopers, coal merchants, butchers, bakers, several Italian ice-cream parlours and a cinema. It was said that, on a Sunday, you could walk across the decks of the boats all the way to **Papa Stronsay**, the tiny island that shelters Whitehall from the north, on which a new monastery for the Order of Transalpine Redemptorists has been built. The old fish market by Whitehall pier houses a small **museum**, with a few photos and artefacts from the herring days; ask at the adjacent café. If the weather's fine, you can choose which of the island's many arching, dazzlingly white beaches to relax on. The most dramatic section of coastline, featuring great layered slices of sandstone, lies in the southeast corner of the island. Signposts show the way to Orkney's biggest and most dramatic natural arch, the **Vat of Kirbuster**. Before you reach the arch there's a seaweedy, shal-low pool in a natural sandstone amphitheatre, where the water is warmed by the sun and kids and adults can safely wallow: close by is a rocky inlet for those who prefer colder, more adventurous swimming. You'll find progressively more nesting seabirds, including a few puffins, as you approach **Burgh Head**, further along down the coast.

Stronsay is served by a regular car **ferry** service from Kirkwall to White-hall (2 daily; 1hr 40min–2hr), and weekday Loganair **flights**, also from Kirkwall (Mon–Sat 2 daily; 25min). There's no bus service, but D.S. Peace (☎01857/616335) operates taxis and **rents cars**. Of the few **accommodation** options, a good choice is the *Stronsay Fish Mart* **hostel** (☎01857/616346) in the old fish market by the pier, with a well-equipped kitchen, washing machine and comfortable bunk-bedded rooms. The pub opposite is the refurbished *Stronsay Hotel* (☎01857/616213, ⓦwww.stronsay.co.uk/stronsayhotel; ❸), which once boasted the longest bar in the north of Scotland. Alternatively, head for the *Stronsay Bird Reserve* (☎01857/616363; ❷), a nicely positioned **B&B** in a lovely old crofthouse, run by bird enthusiasts who allow **camping** on the shores of Mill Bay. The *Stronsay Hotel* does good pub **food** – try the seafood taster – but otherwise, you'll need to bring your own supplies and make use of the island's two shops.

Sanday

Sanday (ⓦwww.sanday.co.uk), though the largest of the northern isles, is also the most insubstantial, a great low-lying, drifting dune strung out between several rocky points. The island's sweeping aquamarine bays and vast stretches of clean white sand are the finest in Orkney, and in dry, clear weather it's a superb place to spend a day or two. The sandy soil is, in fact, very fertile, and the island remains predominantly agricultural even today, holding its very own agricultural show each year at the beginning of August. The island has a long history as a shipping hazard, with many wrecks smashed against its shores, although the construction of the **Start Point Lighthouse** in 1802 on the island's exposed eastern tip reduced the risk for seafarers. Shipwrecks were, in fact, not an unwelcome sight on Sanday, as the island has no peat, and driftwood was the only source of fuel other than cow dung – it's even said that the locals used to pray for shipwrecks in church. The present Stevenson lighthouse, which dates from 1870, now sports very natty vertical black and white stripes. It actually stands on a tidal island, which is accessible only either side of low tide, so ask locally for the tide times before setting out (it takes an hour to walk there and back).

Sanday has particularly spectacular sand dunes to the south of the vast, shallow, tidal bay of **Cata Sand**. It's also rich in archeology, with hundreds of mostly unexcavated sites including cairns, brochs and burnt mounds. The most impressive is **Quoyness Chambered Cairn**, on the fertile farmland of Els Ness peninsula. The tomb, which dates from before 2000 BC, has been partially reconstructed, and rises to a height of around 13ft. The imposing, narrow entrance, flanked by high dry-stone walls, would originally have been roofed for the whole of the way into the thirteen-foot-long main chamber, where bones and skulls were discovered in the six small side-cells. Sanday also has a rather unusual attraction near the ferry terminal, the **Sanday Light Railway** (☎01857/600700, ⓦwww.sandaylightrailway.co.uk), a passenger-carrying seven-and-a-quarter-inch-gauge railway that winds its way round the farmhouse of Strangquoy in a lovely position looking over to Eday; phone to confirm when it's running.

Ferries to Sanday arrive at the Loth terminal at the southern tip of the island and are met by the **minibus** (book on ☎01857/600284), which will take you to most points. The airfield is in the centre of the island and there are regular Loganair **flights** to Kirkwall (Mon–Sat 1–2 daily; 10min). The fishing port of **Kettletoft** is where the ferry used to dock, and where you'll find the island's two **hotels**. Of the two, *The Belsair* (☎01857/600206, ✉laura@belsair.fsnet .co.uk; ❶) has the slightly more adventurous restaurant menu; the *Kettletoft* has a lively bar that's popular with the locals. Of the numerous **B&Bs**, try the *Marygarth Manse* (☎01857/600467; ❶), in Broughtown, who can also organize car and bike rental. If you're on a budget, head for nearby *Ayre's Rock* (☎01857/600410, ✉diane@ayresrock.fsnet.co.uk), a well-equipped **hostel** and **campsite** by the Bay of Brough with washing and laundry facilities, a chip shop (Sat only) and bike rental.

North Ronaldsay

North Ronaldsay – or "North Ron" as it's fondly known – is Orkney's most northerly island. Separated from Sanday by the treacherous waters of the North Ronaldsay Firth, it has a unique outpost atmosphere, brought about by its extreme isolation. Measuring just three miles by one and rising only 66ft above sea level, the island is almost overwhelmed by the enormity of the sky, the strength of wind and the ferocity of the sea – so much so that its very existence seems an act of tenacious defiance. With no natural harbours and precious little farmland, the islanders have been forced to make the most of what they have, and **seaweed** has played an important role in the local economy. During the eighteenth century, kelp was gathered here, burnt in pits and sent south for use in the chemicals industry.

The island's **sheep** are a unique, tough, goatlike breed, who feed mostly on seaweed, giving their flesh a dark tone and a rich, gamey taste, and making their thick wool highly prized. A high **dry-stone dyke**, completed in the mid-nineteenth century and running the thirteen miles around the edge of the island, keeps them off the farmland, except during lambing season, when the ewes are allowed onto the pastureland. North Ronaldsay sheep are also unusual in that they can't be rounded up by sheepdogs like ordinary sheep, but scatter far and wide at some considerable speed. Instead, once a year the islanders herd the sheep communally into a series of **dry-stone punds** near Dennis Head, for clipping and dipping, in what is one of the last acts of communal farming practised in Orkney.

The most frequent visitors to the island are ornithologists, who come in considerable numbers to catch a glimpse of the rare migrants who land here briefly on their spring and autumn migrations. As on Fair Isle (see p.775), there's a permanent **Bird Observatory**, which can give advice as to what birds have recently been sighted. **Holland House** – built by the Traill family who bought the island in 1727 – and the two lighthouses at Dennis Head, are the only features to interrupt the flat horizon. The attractive, stone-built **Old Beacon** was first lit in 1789, but the lantern was replaced by the huge bauble of masonry you now see as long ago as 1809. The **New Lighthouse** (May–Sept Sun 12.30–5.30pm; at other times by appointment; £3; ☎01857/633257), designed by Alan Stevenson in 1854 half a mile to the north, is the tallest land-based lighthouse in Britain, rising to a height of over 100ft. You can climb to the top of the lighthouse, don white gloves (to protect the brass) and admire the view

△ Old Beacon lighthouse, North Ronaldsay

– on a clear day you can see Fair Isle, and even Sumburgh and Fitful Head on Shetland.

The **ferry** from Kirkwall to North Ronaldsay runs only once a week (usually Fri; 2hr 40min–3hr), though day-trips are possible on occasional Sundays between late May and early September (phone ☎01856/872044 for details). Your best bet is to catch a Loganair **flight** from Kirkwall (2–3 daily; 15min): if you stay the night on the island, you're eligible for a £12 return fare. A **minibus** usually meets the ferries and planes (phone ☎01857/633244) and will take you off to the lighthouse. You can **stay** at the eco-friendly *Bird Observatory* (☎01857/633200, ⊛www.nrbo.f2s.com), which offers full board either in private guestrooms (❸) or in a **bunkhouse**; the observatory's *Obscafé* is a sort of pub/restaurant and serves decent meals. Full-board accommodation is also available at *Garso*, in the northeast (☎01857/633244, ⓔchristine@garso.fsnet .co.uk; ❸). The *Burrian Inn*, to the southeast of the war memorial, is the island's small **pub**, and does hot food. As part of an initiative to help regenerate the island, North Ron now stages its own annual **Rinansay Folk Festival**, over one weekend in June, with a return ferry fare included in the ticket price.

Travel details

Buses

On Orkney Mainland

Kirkwall to: Birsay (Mon–Fri 2 daily; 45min); Burwick (3–4 daily; 50min); Evie (Mon–Sat 4 daily; 30min); Houton (Mon–Fri 5 daily, 3 on Sat; 30min); St Margaret's Hope (Mon–Fri 4 daily, 2 on Sat; 40min); Skara Brae (June–Aug Mon–Fri 2 daily; 1hr 15min); Stromness (Mon–Fri hourly, 8 on Sat, 4 on Sun; 30min); Tingwall (Mon–Fri 4 daily, Sat & Sun 2–3 daily; 35min).

Stromness to: Skara Brae (3–4 daily; 20min); Tingwall (Wed & Fri 2 daily; 1hr).

Ferries

Summer timetable only.

To Orkney

Aberdeen to: Kirkwall (4 weekly; 6hr).
Gill's Bay to: St Margaret's Hope (3–4 daily; 1hr).
John O'Groats to: Burwick (passengers only; 2–4 daily; 40min).
Lerwick to: Kirkwall (3 weekly; 5hr 30min).
Scrabster to: Stromness (2–3 daily; 1hr 30min).

Inter-island ferries

To Eday: Kirkwall–Eday (1–2 daily; 1hr 15min–2hr).
To Egilsay: Tingwall–Egilsay (3–4 daily; 50min–1hr 45min).

To Flotta: Houton–Flotta (Mon–Fri 4 daily, Sat & Sun 2–3 daily; 45min–1hr).
To Hoy: Houton–Lyness (Mon–Fri 6 daily, Sat & Sun 2–4 daily; 45min–1hr 25min); Stromness–Hoy (passengers only; Mon–Fri 4–5 daily, Sat & Sun 2 daily; 25min).
To North Ronaldsay: Kirkwall–North Ronaldsay (1 weekly, usually Fri; 2hr 40min–3hr).
To Papa Westray: Kirkwall–Papa Westray (Tues & Fri; 2hr 15min); Pierowall (Westray)–Papa Westray (passengers only; 2–5 daily; 25min).
To Rousay: Tingwall–Rousay (5–6 daily; 30min).
To Sanday: Kirkwall–Sanday (2 daily; 1hr 25min).
To Shapinsay: Kirkwall–Shapinsay (Mon–Fri 5 daily, Sat & Sun 4 daily; 45min).
To Stronsay: Kirkwall–Whitehall (2 daily; 1hr 40min–2hr).
To Westray: Kirkwall–Westray (2–3 daily; 1hr 25min).
To Wyre: Rousay–Wyre (5–7 daily; 10–20min).

Inter-island flights

Kirkwall to: Eday (Wed; 8–26min); North Ronaldsay (2–3 daily; 15min); Papa Westray (Mon–Sat 2–3 daily, 1 on Sun; 12–19min); Sanday (Mon–Sat 1–2 daily; 10min); Stronsay (Mon–Sat 2 daily; 25min); Westray (Mon–Sat 2 daily; 12min).

Shetland

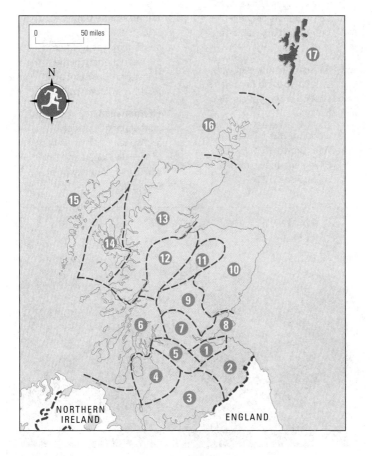

CHAPTER 17

Highlights

* **Traditional music** Catch some local music at the weekly Simmer 'n Sessions in Lerwick, or the annual Shetland Folk Festival. **See p.770**

* **Isle of Noss** Guaranteed seals, puffins and dive-bombing "bonxies". **See p.771**

* **Mousa** Remote islet with a 2000-year-old broch and nesting storm petrels. **See p.773**

* **Jarlshof** Site mingling Iron Age, Bronze Age, Pictish, Viking and medieval settlements. **See p.774**

* **Fair Isle** Magical little island half-way between Shetland and Orkney, with a lighthouse at each end and a world-famous bird observatory in the middle. **See p.775**

* **Lunna House** Superb B&B in an old laird's house that was used as the headquarters of the Norwegian Resistance in World War II. **See p.782**

* **Hermaness** More puffins, gannets and "bonxies", and spectacular views out to Muckle Flugga and Britain's most northerly point. **See p.789**

△ Mousa Broch

Shetland

Shetland is, in nearly all respects, a complete contrast with Orkney. Orkney lies within sight of the Scottish mainland, whereas Shetland lies beyond the horizon. Most maps plonk the islands in a box somewhere off Aberdeen, but in fact they're a lot closer to Bergen in Norway than Edinburgh, and to the Arctic Circle than Manchester. With little fertile ground, Shetlanders have traditionally been crofters rather than farmers, often looking to the sea for an uncertain living in fishing and whaling or the naval and merchant services. The 20,000 or so islanders tend to refer to themselves as Shetlanders first, and, with the unofficial Shetland flag widely displayed, they regard Scotland as a separate and quite distant entity. As in Orkney, "the mainland" is the one in their own archipelago, not the Scottish mainland.

Most folk come here for the unique wildlife and **landscape**, a product of the struggle between rock and the forces of water and ice that have, over millennia, tried to break it to pieces. Smoothed by the last glaciation, the surviving land has been exposed to the most violent weather experienced in the British Isles; it isn't for nothing that Shetlanders call the place "the Old Rock", and the coastline, a crust of cliffs with caves, blowholes and stacks, testifies to the continuing battle. Inland (a relative term, since you're never more than three miles from the sea), the terrain is a barren mix of moorland, often studded with peaty lochs.

The islands' capital, **Lerwick**, is a busy little port and the only town of any size, and the hub of all transport and communications. Many parts of Shetland can be reached from here on a day-trip. **South Mainland**, south of Lerwick, is a narrow finger of land that runs some 25 miles to **Sumburgh Head**; this area is particularly rich in archeological remains, including the Iron Age **Mousa Broch** and the ancient settlement of **Jarlshof**. A further 25 miles south of Sumburgh Head is the remote but thriving **Fair Isle**, synonymous with knitwear and exceptional birdlife. The **Westside** of Mainland is bleaker and more sparsely inhabited, as is **North Mainland**. A mile off the west coast, **Papa Stour** boasts some spectacular caves and stacks; much further out are the distinctive peaks and precipitous cliffs of the remote island of **Foula**. Shetland's three **North Isles** bring Britain to a dramatic, windswept end: **Yell** has the largest population of otters in Shetland; **Fetlar** is home to the rare red-necked phalarope; north of **Unst**, there's nothing until you reach the North Pole.

It's impossible to underestimate the influence of the **weather** in these parts. In winter, gales are routine and Shetlanders take even the occasional hurricane in their stride, marking a calm fine day as "a day atween weathers". Even in the summer months, more often than not, it will be windy and rainy; though,

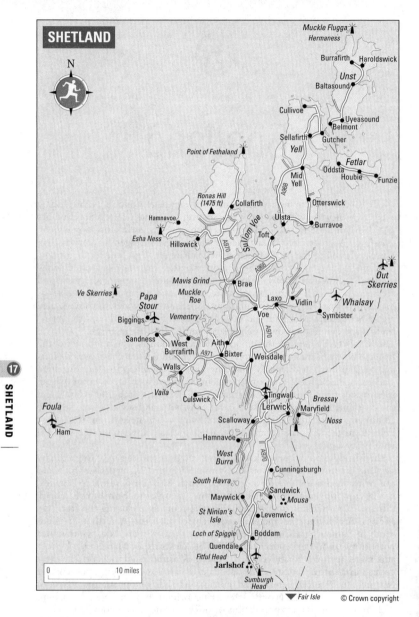

SHETLAND

N

Muckle Flugga
Hermaness
Burrafirth   Haroldswick
Unst
Baltasound
Cullivoe
Uyeasound
Sellafirth   Belmont
Yell   Gutcher
Point of Fethaland   Fetlar
Mid   Oddsta
Yell   Houbie   Funzie
Ronas Hill   Collafirth
(1475 ft)   Otterswick
Hamnavoe   Ulsta
Sullom Voe   Burravoe
Esha Ness   Toft
Hillswick
Out
Skerries
Mavis Grind   Brae
Ve Skerries   Muckle   Laxo   Vidlin   Whalsay
Papa   Roe
Stour   Voe   Symbister
Biggings   Vementry
Sandness   Aith
West   Weisdale
Burrafirth   Bixter
Walls
Vaila
Culswick   Tingwall   Bressay
Foula   Lerwick   Maryfield
Scalloway   Noss
Ham   Hamnavoe
West
Burra   Cunningsburgh
South Havra
Maywick   Sandwick
St Ninian's   Mousa
Isle   Levenwick
Loch of Spiggie   Boddam
Quendale
Fitful Head
Jarlshof
0   10 miles   Sumburgh
Head

▼ Fair Isle   © Crown copyright

as they say in the nearby Faroes, you can have all four seasons in one day. The
wind-chill factor is not to be taken lightly, and there is often a dampness or
drizzle in the air, even when it's not actually raining. Of course, there are some
good spells of dry, sunny weather (which often brings in sea mist) from May
to September, but it's the **simmer dim**, the twilight which lingers through the
small hours at this latitude, which makes Shetland summers so memorable. In

Shetland is famous for its diminutive **ponies**, but it is still something of a surprise to find so many of the wee beasts on the islands. Traditionally they were used exclusively as pack animals, although a ninth-century carving on Bressay shows a hooded priest riding a very small pony, and their tails were essential for making fishing nets. During the Industrial Revolution, Shetland ponies were exported to work in the mines in England, since they were the only animals small enough to cope with the low galleries. Shetlands then became the playthings of the English upper classes (the Queen Mother was patron of the Shetland Pony Stud Book Society) and they still enjoy the limelight at the Horse of the Year show.

June especially, the northern sky is an unfinished sunset of blue and burnished copper. Insomniac sheep and seabirds barely settle, and golfers, similarly afflicted, play midnight tournaments.

Some history

Since people first began to explore the North Atlantic, Shetland has been a stepping stone on routes between Britain, Ireland and Scandinavia, and people have lived here since **prehistoric times**, certainly from about 3500 BC. The **Norse settlers**, who began to arrive from about 800 AD, with substantial migration from around 900 AD, left the islands with a unique cultural character. Shetland started out as part of the Orkney earldom, but was ruled directly from Norway for nearly three hundred years after 1195. The Norse legacy is clearly evident today in place names and in the **dialect** (for more on which, see p.859); Shetland was never part of the Gaelic-speaking culture of Highland Scotland, and the later Scottish influence is essentially a Lowland one.

In 1469, Shetland followed Orkney in being **mortgaged to Scotland**, King Christian I of Norway being unable to raise the dowry for the marriage of his daughter, Margaret, to King James III. The Scottish king annexed Shetland in 1472 and the mortgage was never redeemed. Though Shetland retained links with other North Sea communities, religious and administrative practice gradually become Scottish, and **mainland lairds** set about grabbing what land and power they could. The economy soon fell increasingly into the hands of **merchant lairds**; they controlled the fish trade and the tenants who supplied it through a system of truck, or forced barter. It wasn't until the 1886 Crofters' Act and the simultaneous rise of **herring fishing** that ordinary Shetlanders gained some security. However, the boom and the prosperity it brought were short-lived and the economy soon slipped into depression.

During the two world wars, Shetland's role as gatekeeper between the North Sea and North Atlantic meant that the defence of the islands and control of the seas around them were critical: thousands of naval, army and air force personnel were drafted in and some notable relics, such as huge coastal guns, remain. **World War II** also cemented the old links with Norway, Shetland playing a remarkable role in supporting the Norwegian Resistance (see box on p.777). With a rebirth of the local economy in the 1960s, Shetland was able to claim, in the following decade, that the **oil industry** needed the islands more than they needed it. Careful negotiation, backed up by pioneering local legislation, produced a substantial income from oil, which the Shetland Islands Council (SIC) reinvested in the community, building roads, improving housing, keeping the price of ferry tickets down and pouring money into the outlying islands. With the oil boom days over, the islanders are having to think afresh how to carve out a living in the new millennium. **Tourism**, which has traditionally played only a minor role in the local economy, is beginning to develop. For the moment, however, comparatively few travellers make it out here, and those that do are as likely to be Faroese or Norwegian as British.

Arrival, transport and tours

NorthLink Orkney & Shetland Ferries (☎0845/600 0449, ⓦwww .northlinkferries.co.uk) operates a daily overnight **car ferry** from **Aberdeen** to Lerwick, either direct (12hr) or via Kirkwall (13hr). British Airways (☎0870/850 9850) runs **flights** nonstop to Shetland from Aberdeen, Inverness, Kirkwall and Wick, with connections into those airports from Edinburgh, Glasgow, Birmingham, Manchester and London; Highland Airways (☎0845/450 2245) also operates a daily Inverness to Shetland flight and Atlantic Airways run a summer-only service from London Stansted and the Faroes (☎01737/214255). Shetland's main airport is at **Sumburgh** (☎01950/461000), from where buses make short work of the 25-mile journey north to Lerwick. Standard airfares are high, but various cheaper tickets and special offers are sometimes available (see p.43). There are also British Airways **flights** linking Tingwall Airport, five miles west of Lerwick, to Fair Isle and less frequent Loganair flights to Whalsay, Out Skerries, Papa Stour and Foula. (Some Fair Isle flights leave from Sumburgh Airport.) Sample one-way fares include £25 Tingwall to Foula, and £28 Tingwall to Fair Isle; be sure to book well in advance, however, as the planes only take around eight passengers, and be prepared to be flexible, as flights are often cancelled due to the weather.

Public transport is pretty good in Shetland, with **buses** fanning out from Lerwick to just about every corner of Mainland, and even via ferries across to Yell and Unst. You can buy the full timetable (£1), which includes all ferries and flights, from Lerwick tourist office. Various **tours** are also available from specialists such as Shetland Wildlife (☎01950/422483, ⓦwww.shetlandwildlife .co.uk). Given the price of bringing a car on the ferry to Shetland, it might be worth considering using a local **car rental** firm once on the islands (see p.770). **Hitching** is viable and pretty safe, but **cycling** is hard going due to the almost constant wind.

The council-run **inter-island ferries** are excellent: journey times are mostly less than half an hour, and fares are much cheaper than those in Orkney or the

---

Onwards from Shetland

Thanks to the historical ties and the attraction of a short hop to continental Europe, **Norway** is a popular destination for Shetlanders and Orcadians. Norwegians often think of Shetland and Orkney as their western isles and, particularly in west Norway, old wartime bonds with Shetland are still strong. Norwegian yachts and sail-training vessels are frequent visitors to Lerwick and Kirkwall. Shetlanders can also go by ferry to the **Faroe Islands** – steep, angular shapes rising out of the North Atlantic – and on to **Iceland**.

From late May to early September the large, comfortable and fast Faroese car **ferry** Norröna, run by the Smyril Line (ⓦwww.smyril-line.com), makes weekly return trips from her home port in the Faroe Islands to Shetland, Norway, Iceland and Denmark. From Shetland, the voyages to **Bergen** in Norway or **Tórshavn** in the Faroe Islands both take around thirteen hours; to **Seydisfjördur** in Iceland, it takes thirty hours including a brief stop in the Faroes; on the way back there's a two-day stopover in Faroes while the ship makes a return trip to **Hanstholm** in Denmark.

Hebrides. Adults pay around £3 return on most routes, and a car plus driver can cross for around £10 return. It's also possible to take **boat trips** for pleasure, to explore the coastline and spot birds, seals, porpoises, dolphins and whales; operators include Shetland Wildlife (see opposite), Seabirds-and-Seals (☎01595/693434, ⓦwww.seabirds-and-seals.com) and Tom Jamieson from Sandwick for the Broch of Mousa (☎01950/431367, ⓦwww.mousaboattrips.co.uk).

Lerwick

For Shetlanders, there's only one place to stop, meet and do business, and that's "da toon", **LERWICK**. Very much the focus of Shetland's commercial life, Lerwick is home to about 6600 people, just less than a third of the islands' population. All year, its sheltered **harbour** at the heart of the town is busy with ferries, fishing boats, oil-rig supply vessels and a variety of more specialized craft including seismic survey and naval vessels from all round the North Sea. In summer, the quayside comes alive with local pleasure craft, visiting yachts, cruise liners, historic vessels such as the restored *Swan* and the occasional tall sailing

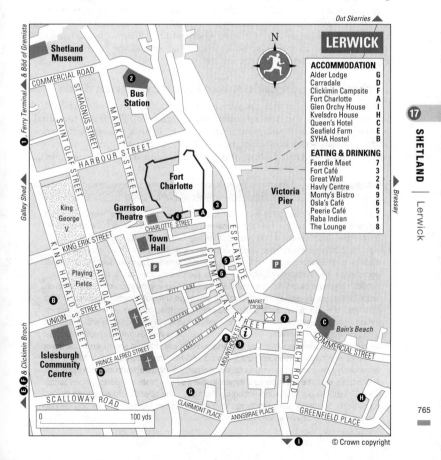

Out Skerries

LERWICK

ACCOMMODATION
Alder Lodge	G
Carradale	D
Clickimin Campsite	F
Fort Charlotte	A
Glen Orchy House	I
Kvelsdro House	H
Queen's Hotel	C
Seafield Farm	E
SYHA Hostel	B

EATING & DRINKING
Faerdie Maet	7
Fort Café	3
Great Wall	2
Havly Centre	4
Monty's Bistro	9
Osla's Café	6
Peerie Café	5
Raba Indian	1
The Lounge	8

17

SHETLAND | Lerwick

© Crown copyright

ship. Behind the old harbour is the compact town centre, made up of one long main street, Commercial Street; from here, narrow lanes, known as **closses**, rise westwards to the late Victorian new town.

Leir Vik ("muddy bay") began life as a temporary settlement, catering to the **Dutch** herring fleet in the seventeenth century, which brought in as many as twenty thousand men. It was burnt down in 1614 and 1625 by the jealous and disapproving folk of Scalloway, and again in 1702 by the French fleet. During the nineteenth century, with the presence of ever-larger Scottish, English and Scandinavian boats, it became a major **fishing** centre, and whalers called to pick up crews on their way to the northern hunting grounds. In 1839, the visiting Danish governor of the Faroes declared that "everything made me feel that I had come to the land of opulence". Business was conducted largely from buildings known as **lodberries** (from the Old Norse for "loading rock"), each typically having a store, a house and small yard on a private jetty. **Smuggling** was part of the daily routine, and secret tunnels – some of which still exist – connected the lodberries to illicit stores. During the late nineteenth century, the construction of the Esplanade along the shore isolated several lodberries from the sea, but further south beyond the *Queen's Hotel* are some that still show their original form. Lerwick expanded considerably at this time and the large houses and grand public buildings established then still dominate, notably the **Town Hall**, which remains the most prominent landmark. Another period of rapid growth began during the oil boom of the 1970s, with the farmland to the southwest disappearing under a suburban sprawl, the town's northern approaches becoming an industrial estate.

Arrival, information and accommodation

First impressions of Lerwick are very much dependent on the weather (and, if you arrive by boat, the crossing you've just experienced). The **ferry terminal** is situated in the unprepossessing north harbour, about a mile from the town centre: just walk south down Holmsgarth Road, east along North Road and on into Commercial Road. **Flying** into Sumburgh Airport, you can take one of

Böds

With only one official SYHA hostel in the whole of Shetland, it's worth knowing about the islands' unique network of **camping böds**, which are open from April to September. Traditionally, a böd was a small building beside the shore, where fishermen used to house their gear and occasionally sleep; the word was also applied to trading posts established by merchants of the Hanseatic League. Today, the tourist board uses the term pretty loosely: none of the places they run is strictly speaking a böd, ranging instead from stone-built cottages to weatherboarded sail lofts. In order to stay at a böd, you must **book in advance** through Shetland Amenity Trust (T 01595/694688, W www.camping-bods.com), as there are no live-in wardens. All the böds have some form of (primitive) heating system, cold water, toilets, a kitchen (though no stove or cooking utensils) and bunk beds (but as yet no mattresses), so a sleeping bag and bedding mat are pretty much essential. If you're on a camping trip, they're a great way to escape the wind and rain for a night or two; they're also remarkably good value, at around £5 per person per night. Except in June, July and August, it's even possible to pay for exclusive use of any of the böds; prices range from £35 to £90 per night depending on the size of the böd. **Camping rough** is also possible in Shetland, with the landowner's permission, but make sure you're fully equipped for the Shetland wind.

the regular buses to Lerwick; taxis (around £25) and car rental are also available. Buses stop on the Esplanade, very close to the old harbour and Market Cross, or at the Viking bus station on Commercial Road a little to the north of the town centre. Orientation within Lerwick is straightforward: the town is small and everything is within easy walking distance.

The **tourist office**, at the Market Cross on Commercial Street (May– Sept Mon–Sat 8am–6pm, Sun 10am–1pm; Oct–April Mon–Fri 9am–5pm; ☏01595/693434, ⊛www.visitshetland.com), is a good source of information, and will book accommodation for a small fee. At any time in the summer and over the Folk Festival weekend in April, accommodation can be in short supply, so it's a good idea to book in advance. Once you're here, pick up a copy of the annual *Shetland Visitor* magazine, and the weekly *Shetland Times*, to get an idea of what's going on.

Accommodation

Shetland's best **hotels** are not to be found in Lerwick, which has been spoilt in the past by the steady supply of visitors in the oil business. The town's **B&Bs** and **guesthouses** are usually better value for money, and will allow you to get closer to Shetland life.

The SYHA **hostel** (☏01595/692114, ⊜islesburgh@zetnet.co.uk; April–Sept) at Islesburgh House on King Harald Street, offers unusually comfortable surroundings and has family rooms, a café and laundry facilities. The *Clickimin* **campsite** (☏01595/741000, ⊜mail@srt.org.uk; May–Sept), enjoys the excellent facilities of the neighbouring Clickimin leisure centre, including good hot showers, but its sheltered suburban location, west of the town centre, is far from idyllic.

Hotels, guesthouses and B&Bs

Alder Lodge Guest House 6 Clairmont Place ☏01595/695705. Converted former Victorian bank that's probably the best middle-range accommodation available. ❸

Carradale Guest House 36 King Harald St ☏01595/692251, ⊛www.carradale.shetland .co.uk. Spacious, well-equipped guesthouse in a large, comfortable Victorian family home. ❷

Fort Charlotte Guest House 1 Charlotte St ☏01595/692140, ⊛www.fortcharlotte.co.uk. Small guesthouse with great central location, mostly en-suite rooms and a friendly proprietor. ❸

Glen Orchy House 20 Knab Rd ☏01595/692031, ⊛www.guesthouselerwick.com. A particularly comfortable, fully modernized former convent that's virtually a hotel, licensed and with good home-cooking. ❺

Kvelsdro House Hotel Greenfield Place ☏01595/692195, ⊛www.kgqhotels.co.uk. Lerwick's smartest and most luxurious establishment (pronounced "kelro"), with immaculate bedrooms and a good harbour view from the bar. It's hard to find, but locals will usually help out. ❻

Queen's Hotel Commercial St ☏01595/692826, ⊛www.kgqhotels.co.uk. A beautiful old building right on the waterfront with its feet in the sea and great views over Bressay Sound from many of its bedrooms, all of which are equipped with modern furnishings. ❻

Seafield Farm Off Sea Rd ☏01595/693853. A very friendly B&B in a huge modern farmhouse overlooking the sea, a mile or so southwest of the town centre and therefore best for those with their own transport. ❷

The Town

Lerwick's attractive, flagstone-clad **Commercial Street**, universally known to locals as "da street", is still very much the core of the town. Its narrow, winding form, set back one block from the Esplanade, provides shelter from the elements even on the worst days, and is where locals meet, shop, exchange news and gossip. The Street's northern end is marked by the towering walls of **Fort**

Charlotte (daily: June–Sept 9am–10pm; Oct–May 9am–4pm; free), which once stood directly above the beach. Begun for Charles II in 1665 during the wars with the Dutch, the fort was attacked and burnt down by the Dutch fleet in August 1673. In the 1780s it was repaired and given its name in honour of George III's queen. Since then, it's served as a prison and a Royal Navy training centre; it's now open to the public, except on rare occasions when it's used by the Territorial Army.

Although the narrow lanes or **closses** that connect the Street to Hillhead are now a desirable place to live, it's not so long ago that they were regarded as slumlike dens of iniquity, from which the better-off escaped to the Victorian new town laid out to the west on a grid plan. The steep stone-flagged lanes are now fun to explore, each one lined by tall houses with trees, fuchsias, flowering currants and honeysuckle pouring over the garden walls. If you look at the street signs, you can see that all the closses have two names: their former ones and their current titles, chosen in 1845 by the Police Commissioners – Reform, Fox and Pitt, reflecting the liberal political culture of the period, or derived from the writings of Sir Walter Scott.

Hillhead, up in the Victorian new town, is dominated by the splendid **Town Hall** (Mon–Thurs 9am–5pm, Fri 9am–4pm; free), a Scottish Baronial monument to civic pride, built by public subscription. Lerwick's chief tourist sight, however, is the **Shetland Museum** (Wed–Sat 10am–5pm; ⓦ www.shetland-museum.org.uk; free), which has recently moved to its new purpose-built waterfront premises at Hay's Dock, off Commercial Road. The museum was closed at the time of going to print, but will house the museum's wonderful collection of nauticalia. More unusual exhibits include Shetland's oldest

Up Helly-Aa

On the last Tuesday in January, whatever the weather, Lerwick's new town is the setting for the most spectacular part of the **Up Helly-Aa** (see the *Festivals* colour section), a huge fire festival, the largest of several held in Shetland from January to March. Around nine hundred torchbearing participants, all male and all in extraordinary costumes, march in procession behind a grand Viking longship. The annually appointed Guizer Jarl and his "squad" appear as Vikings and brandish shields and silver axes; each of the forty or so other squads is dressed for their part in the subsequent entertainment, perhaps as giant insects, space invaders or ballet dancers. Their circuitous route leads to the King George V Playing Field where, after due ceremony, all the torches are thrown into the longship, creating an enormous bonfire. A firework display follows, then the participants, known as "guizers", set off in their squads to do the rounds of more than a dozen "halls" (which usually include at least one hotel and the Town Hall) from around 8.30pm in the evening until 8am the next morning, performing some kind of act – usually a comedy routine – at each.

Up Helly-Aa itself is not that ancient, dating only from Victorian times, when it was introduced to replace the much older Christmas tradition of rolling burning tar barrels through the streets, which was banned in 1874. Seven years later a torchlight procession took place, which eventually developed into a full-blown Viking celebration, known as "Up Helly-Aa". Although this is essentially a community event with entry to halls by invitation only, visitors are welcome at the Town Hall, for which tickets are sold in early January; contact the tourist office well in advance. To catch some of the atmosphere of the event, check out the annual Up Helly-Aa exhibition in the **Galley Shed** on St Sunniva Street (mid-May to mid-Sept Tues 2–4pm & 7–9pm, Fri 7–9pm, Sat 2–4pm; £3), where you can see a full-size longship, costumes, shields and photographs.

telephone, fitted with a ceramic mouthpiece, and a carved head of Goliath by Adam Christie (1869–1950), a Shetlander who spent much of his life in Montrose Asylum.

Clickimin Broch and the Böd of Gremista

A mile or so southwest of the town centre on the road leading to Sumburgh, the much-restored **Clickimin Broch** stands on what was once a small island in Loch Clickimin. The settlement here began as a small farmstead around 700 BC and was later enclosed by a defensive wall. The main tower served as a castle and probably rose to around 40ft, as at Mousa (see p.773), though the remains are now not much more than 10ft high.

In earlier times the seasonal nature of the Shetland fishing industry led to the establishment of small stores, known as **böds** (see box on p.766), often incorporating sleeping accommodation, beside the beaches where fish were landed and dried. Just beyond Lerwick's main ferry terminal, a mile and a half north of the town centre, stands the **Böd of Gremista** (May to mid-Sept Wed–Sun 10am–1pm & 2–5pm; free; Ⓦ www.shetland-museum.org.uk), the birthplace of **Arthur Anderson** (1792–1868). The displays explore Anderson's life as beach boy (helping to cure and dry fish), naval seaman, businessman, philanthropist, Shetland's first native MP and founder of Shetland's first newspaper, the *Shetland Journal*.

Eating

Shetland produces a huge harvest of fresh fish from the surrounding seas, including shellfish and salmon, and from the land there's superb lamb and even local tomatoes, cucumbers and peppers, grown under glass. The most celebrated local delicacy is *reestit* mutton: steeped in brine, then air-dried, it's the base for a potato soup cooked and adored by the locals around New Year. Unfortunately, the **food** on offer in the majority of Lerwick's hotels and pubs doesn't do these ingredients justice.

Daytime cafés

Faerdie-Maet Commercial St (by the post office). Cosy café serving generously filled rolls to eat in or take away, as well as cakes, teas, real cappuccino and good ice cream. No smoking. Closed Sun.

Havly Centre 9 Charlotte St. Spacious Norwegian lunchtime café, with big comfy sofas and armchairs and a kids' corner; it offers home-made cakes, bread and pizzas. Closed Sun.

Osla's Café Commercial St. Situated opposite the *Grand Hotel*, the downstairs café-bar specializes in savoury and sweet pancakes; upstairs is the evening-only *La Piazza*, serving pizza and pasta. Closed Sun.

Peerie Café Esplanade. Funky designer shop/gallery/café in an old lodberry, with imaginative cakes, soup and sandwiches, and what is probably Britain's northernmost latte. Closed Sun.

Restaurants

Fort Café 2 Commercial St. Lerwick's best fish-and-chip shop, situated below Fort Charlotte: take

away or eat inside in the small café. Closed Sun lunch. Inexpensive.

Great Wall Viking Bus Station ☎01595/693988. A Chinese/Thai restaurant located above the bus station. Highly rated by the locals. Moderate.

Kvelsdro House Hotel Greenfield Place ☎01595/692195. The traditional bar meals or *table d'hôte*, served in the modern cocktail bar overlooking Bressay Sound, are above average in price and quality. Moderate to expensive.

🏃 **Monty's Bistro** 5 Mounthooly St ☎01595/696555. Unpretentious place serving inexpensive and delicious meals and snacks at lunchtimes, and accomplished contemporary cooking – the best in Lerwick – in the evening, with friendly service. Closed Sun & Mon. Moderate.

Raba Indian Restaurant 26 Commercial Rd ☎01595/695585. A consistently excellent curry house, with cheerful, efficient service and reasonable prices. Moderate.

Drinking, nightlife and entertainment

The friendliest **pub** in town is the upstairs bar in *The Lounge*, up Mount-hooly Street, where local musicians often do sessions. The Garrison Theatre (☎01595/692114, ⓦwww.islesburgh.org.uk), by the Town Hall, shows occasional **films** as well as putting on theatre productions, comedy acts and live gigs. The Islesburgh Community Centre has introduced regular **crafts and culture evenings** (late May to early Sept Mon & Wed 7–9.30pm), where you can buy local knitwear, chat to some locals and listen to traditional music.

In late April or early May, musicians from all over the world converge on Shetland for the excellent four-day **Shetland Folk Festival** (☎01595/694757, ⓦwww.shetlandfolkfestival.com), which embraces a wider range of musical styles than the title might suggest; there are concerts and dances in every corner of the islands. There are further musical gatherings in mid-June, when the newly founded three-day **Blues Festival** (ⓦwww.lerwick.plus.com/sbf/frameset. html) takes place, and in mid-October, there's an **Accordion and Fiddle Festival** (ⓦwww.shetlandaccordionandfiddle.com).

As well as the regular musical offerings at the Islesburgh (see above), there are **informal sessions**, known as Simmer 'n Sessions, held regularly over the summer in *The Lounge* and *Da Noost* (ⓦwww.shetland-music.com), two pubs on Commercial Street, as well as on visiting cruise ships and in various other venues on the islands. There are also full-on **gigs** featuring a surprising number of accomplished local groups: legendary local fiddler Aly Bain (see p.814) and the likes of Fiddlers Bid make occasional appearances. For details of **what's on**, listen in to *Good Evening Shetland* on BBC Radio Shetland, 92.7 FM (Mon–Fri 5.30pm), or buy the *Shetland Times* on Fridays (ⓦwww.shetlandtoday.co.uk). Some events are also advertised on Shetland's independent radio station SIBC, 96.2 FM. To pick up a CD or cassette of traditional Shetland music, head for High Level Music, up the steps by the chemists on the Market Cross.

Not surprisingly, another Shetland passion is **boating and yachting**, and regattas take place most summer weekends, in different venues throughout the islands. The sport of **yoal racing** has a big following, too, and teams from different districts compete passionately in large six-oared boats which used to serve as the backbone of Shetland's fishing industry. If you plan ahead, you could take a trip on the *Swan* (☎01595/697406, ⓦwww.theswan.shetland.co.uk), a restored wooden **sailing ship** built locally as a fishing smack in 1900, which undertakes various trips, from one to nine days' long, as far afield as Norway and the Faroes.

Listings

Airports Tingwall Airport ☎01595/840246; Sumburgh Airport ☎01950/460654.

Banks Clydesdale, Bank of Scotland and Royal Bank of Scotland are all on Commercial St; Lloyds TSB is the gleaming and locally controversial structure on the Esplanade.

Bike rental Grantfield Garage, Commercial Rd ☎01595/692709, ⓦwww.grantfieldgarage.co.uk.

Bookshops Shetland Times Bookshop, 71–79 Commercial St (☎01595/695531, ⓦwww .shetlandtoday.co.uk; closed Sun).

Bus information ☎01595/694100.

Car rental Bolts Car Hire, 26 North Rd

☎01595/693636, ⓦwww.boltscarhire.co.uk; John Leask & Sons, Esplanade ☎01595/693162, ⓦwww.leaskstravel.co.uk; Star Rent-a-Car, 22 Commercial Rd ☎01595/692075, ⓦwww .starrentacar.co.uk. All of these also have offices at Sumburgh Airport.

Consulates Denmark, Iceland and Sweden: Hay & Co., 66 Commercial Rd ☎01595/692533; Finland, France, Germany and Norway: Shearer Shipping Services, Garthspool ☎01595/692556.

Internet access At the tourist office or the SYIS opposite.

Laundry For self-service laundry head for
Manson's Dry Cleaners (closed Sat lunch & Sun),
behind the garage, west of the roundabout by the
Somerfield supermarket.
Medical care The Gilbert Bain Hospital
⊕01595/743000, and the Lerwick Health Centre
⊕01595/693201, are opposite each other on
Scalloway Rd.

Sports centre The large, modern Clickimin Leisure
Centre is in Lochside, on the west side of town by
Loch Clickimin (⊕01595/694555, ⊛www.srt
.org.uk), with a superb leisure pool, bowling, a café
and bar.

Bressay and Noss

Shielding Lerwick from the full force of the North Sea is the island of **Bressay**, dominated at its southern end by the conical Ward Hill (744ft) – "da Wart" – and accessible on an hourly car and passenger ferry from Lerwick (takes 5min). At the end of the nineteenth century, Bressay had a population of around eight hundred, due mostly to the prosperity brought by the Dutch herring fleet; now about four hundred people live here. If you've time to kill before the ferry, pop into the **Bressay Heritage Centre** (Tues, Wed, Fri & Sat 10am–4pm, Sun 11am–5.30pm; free; ⊛www.bressay-history-group.org), by the ferry terminal in **MARYFIELD**, where the local history group puts on temporary exhibitions. A short distance to the north lies **Gardie House**, built in 1724 and, in its Neoclassical detail, one of the finest of Shetland's laird houses, where the likes of Sir Walter Scott and minor royalty once stayed; it's now home to the lord lieutenant of Shetland.

In 1917, convoys of merchant ships would gather in Bressay Sound before travelling under naval escort across the Atlantic. Huge World War I gun batteries at Score Hill on Aith Ness in the north, and on Bard Head in the south, were constructed, and now provide a focus for a couple of interesting cliff and coastal walks. Another fine walk can be made to **Bressay Lighthouse**, three miles south of the ferry terminal at Kirkibuster Ness, built by the Stevensons in the 1850s. The lighthouse contains several self-catering cottages and will eventually house a camping **böd** (call Shetland Amenity Trust ⊕01595/694688 for the latest). **Accommodation** is available at *Maryfield House* near the ferry terminal (⊕01595/820207; ❹), the island's unremarkable hotel and pub.

Noss

The chief reason most visitors pass through Bressay is in order to visit the tiny but spectacular island of **Noss** – the name means "a point of rock" – just off Bressay's eastern shore. Sloping gently into the sea at its western end, and plunging vertically from over 500ft at its eastern end, Noss has the dramatic and distinctive outline of a half-sunk ocean liner. The island was inhabited until World War II but is now a nature reserve and sheep farm, partly managed by Scottish Natural Heritage, who operate an inflatable as a **ferry** from Bressay (May–Aug Tues, Wed & Fri–Sun; £3 return; phone ⊕0800/107 7818). The ferry departs from the landing stage below the car park overlooking Noss Sound, two miles from Maryfield – an easy stroll or short journey on bikes rented in Lerwick beforehand. A morning postcar takes over two hours to reach Noss Sound from Maryfield. If the weather is abnormally windy, check that the Noss ferry is running before setting off. A more convenient, but more expensive alternative is to join one of the **boat trips** that set out from Lerwick to see the rock arches and caves of Bressay and the cliffs and nesting seabirds on

17

SHETLAND | Bressay and Noss

△ Shetland ponies

Noss: try Seabirds and Seals (May–Aug 2 daily; £30; ☎01595/693434, ⓦwww
.seabirds-and-seals.com).

On the island, the old farmhouse, or Haa of Gungstie, contains a small **visitor
centre** (open whenever the ferry is operating), where the warden will give you
a quick briefing and a free map and guide. Nearby is a sandy beach, perfect for
a picnic in fine weather, while behind the Haa is a **Pony Pund**, a square stone
enclosure built for the breeding of Shetland ponies. As Noss is only one mile
wide, it's easy enough to do an entire circumference of the island in one day.
If you do, make sure you keep close to the coast, since otherwise you're likely
to be dive-bombed by the great skuas (locally known as "bonxies"). The most
memorable feature of Noss is its coastline of cliffs, rising to a peak at the massive
500-foot **Noup**, from which can be seen vast colonies of cliff-nesting gannets,
puffins, guillemots, shags, razorbills and fulmars: a truly wonderful sight and one
of the highlights of Shetland.

South Mainland

Shetland's **South Mainland** is a long, thin finger of land, only three or four
miles wide, but twenty-five miles long, ending in the cliffs of **Sumburgh Head**
and **Fitful Head**. It's a beautiful area with wild undulating landscapes, lots of
good green farmland, fabulous views out to sea and the mother of all brochs
on the island of **Mousa**, just off the east coast. The most concentrated points of
interest are at the southern end of the peninsula, with its seabird colonies, crofting museum, and, in particular, **Jarlshof**, Shetland's most impressive archeological treasure. The main road hugs the eastern side of the Clift Hills which form
the peninsula's backbone; on the west side, there's no road between Scalloway
and Maywick, except for a short spur from Easter to Wester Quarff.

Sandwick and Mousa

Halfway down the South Mainland, opposite the parish of **SANDWICK**, the island of **Mousa** boasts the most amazingly well-preserved broch in the whole of Scotland. Rising to more than 40ft, and looking rather like a Stone Age cooling tower, **Mousa Broch** has a remarkable presence, and features in both *Egil's Saga* and the *Orkneyinga Saga*, contemporary chronicles of Norse exploration and settlement. To get to the broch, simply head south from the jetty along the western coastline for about half a mile. The low entrance passage leads through two concentric walls to a central courtyard, divided into separate beehive chambers. Between the walls, a rough (very dark) staircase leads to the top parapet; a torch is provided for visitors.

To reach Mousa, take the small **passenger ferry** from Leebotton in the district of Sandwick (mid-April to mid-Sept 2 daily; takes 15min; £8 return; ☎01950/431367, ⓦwww.mousaboattrips.co.uk), though it's best to ring ahead to check the current schedule. From late May to late July, a large colony of around six thousand **storm petrels** breeds in and around the broch walls, fishing out at sea during the day and only returning to the nests after dark. The ferry also runs special late-night trips (Wed & Sat weather permitting), setting off in the "simmer dim" twilight around 11pm. Even if you've no interest in the storm petrels, which appear like bats as they flit about in the half-light, the chance to explore the broch at midnight is worth it alone.

St Ninian's Isle to Quendale

A little beyond Sandwick, on the main road south, it's possible to cross to **BIGTON**, on the west coast of the South Mainland. From the village, a signposted track heads down to a spectacular sandy causeway, or **tombolo**, leading to **St Ninian's Isle**. The tombolo – a concave strip of shell sand with Atlantic breakers crashing on either side, the best example of its kind in Britain – is usually exposed; you can walk over to the island, where there are the ruins of a church probably dating from the twelfth century and built on the site of an earlier, Pictish, one. The site was excavated in the 1950s and **treasure**, a hoard of 28 objects of Pictish silver, was found hidden in a larch box beneath a slab in the earlier building's floor; the larch probably came from the European mainland, as it didn't grow in Britain at that time. Replicas are in the Shetland Museum in Lerwick and the originals can be seen in the Museum of Scotland in Edinburgh.

Over on the east coast, a back road winds around to the **Croft House Museum** (May–Sept daily 10am–1pm & 2–5pm; free; ⓦwww.shetland -museum.org.uk) in Southvoe. Housed in a fairly well-to-do thatched croft built around 1870, the museum tries to re-create the feel of late-nineteenth-century crofting life, with a peat fire, traditional box beds and so forth. Adjacent to the living quarters is the byre for the cows and tatties, and the kiln for drying the grain. Crofting was mostly done by women in Shetland, while the men went out haaf fishing for the laird. Down by the nearby burn, there's also a restored thatched horizontal mill.

A few miles south of Loch Spiggie lies **QUENDALE**, overlooking a sandy south-facing bay. The village contains the beautifully restored full-size **Quendale Watermill** (mid-April to mid-Oct daily 10am–5pm; £2; ⓦwww .quendalemill.shetland.co.uk), built in the 1860s but not in operation since the early 1970s. You can explore the interior and watch a short video of the mill working, and there's a tearoom attached. Not far from Quendale, near the head of the rocky inlet of Cro Geo, on the other side of Garths Ness, lies a rusting ship's bow, all that remains of the **Braer oil tanker**, a Liberian-registered, American-owned ship that ran onto the rocks here at 11.13am on January 5, 1993, a wild Tuesday morning etched in the memory of every Shetlander. Although the *Braer* released twice the quantity of oil spilt even by the *Exxon Valdez* in Alaska, the damage was less serious than it might have been, due to the oil being churned and ultimately cleansed by huge waves built by hurricane-force winds which, unusually even for Shetland, blew for most of January.

Sumburgh

Shetland's southernmost parish is known as **Dunrossness** or "The Ness", a rolling agricultural landscape often compared with that of Orkney, dominated from the west by the great brooding mass of Fitful Head (929ft). The main road leads to **SUMBURGH**, whose **airport** is busy with helicopters and aircraft shuttling to and from the North Sea oilfields, as well as passenger services, and **GRUTNESS**, the minuscule ferry terminal for Fair Isle.

By the main road, just west of the airport, excavations are currently under way at **Old Scatness Broch & Iron Age Village** (May–Oct daily except Fri & Sat 10am–5.30pm; £2), where a vast Iron Age settlement is currently being excavated. First off, you get a guided tour of the site from a viewing platform, followed by a taste of life in a restored wheel-house in Norse and Pictish times, provided by costumed guides, and a weaving demonstration.

The Mainland comes to a dramatic end at **Sumburgh Head** (262ft), which rises sharply out of the land only to drop vertically into the sea about a mile or so southeast of Jarlshof. The Stevenson **lighthouse**, on the top of the cliff, is not open to the public, but the road up to the lighthouse is the perfect site for watching nesting kittiwakes, fulmars, shags, razorbills and guillemots, not to mention gannets diving for fish. This is also the easiest place in Shetland to get close to **puffins**: during the nesting season (May to early Aug), you simply need to look over the western wall, just before you enter the lighthouse complex, and watch them arriving at their burrows a few yards below with beakfuls of sand eels or giving flying lessons to their offspring.

Jarlshof

Of all the archeological sites in Shetland, **Jarlshof** (April–Sept daily 9.30am–6.30pm; HS; £3.30; Oct–March open access to grounds; free) is the largest and most impressive. What makes Jarlshof so amazing is the fact that you can walk right into a house built 1600 years ago, which is still intact to above head height. The site is big and confusing, scattered with the ruins of buildings dating from the Stone Age to the early seventeenth century. The name, which is misleading as it is not primarily a Viking site, was coined by Sir Walter Scott, who decided to use the ruins of the Old House in his novel *The Pirate*. However, it was only at the end of the nineteenth century that the Bronze Age, Iron Age and Viking settlements you see now were discovered, after a violent storm ripped off the top layer of turf.

The Bronze Age smithy and Iron Age dwellings nearest the entrance, dating from the second and first millennia BC, are nothing compared with the cells which cluster around the **broch**, close to the sea. Only half of the original broch survives, and its courtyard is now an Iron Age aisled roundhouse, with stone piers. However, it's difficult to distinguish the broch from the later Pictish **wheelhouses** which now surround it. Still, it's all great fun to explore, as, unlike at Skara Brae in Orkney, you're free to roam around the cells, checking out the in-built stone shelving, water tanks, beds and so on. Inland lies the maze of grass-topped foundations marking out the **Viking longhouses**, dating from the ninth century AD and covering a much larger area than the earlier structures. Towering over the whole complex are the ruins of the laird's house, built by Robert Stewart, Earl of Orkney and Lord of Shetland, in the late sixteenth century, and the **Old House of Sumburgh**, built by his son, Earl Patrick.

South Mainland practicalities

Accommodation in the South Mainland is provided by several comfortable modern B&Bs, such as *Setterbrae* (☎01950/440468, ⓦwww.setterbrae.co.uk; ❸), located a stone's throw from the *Spiggie Hotel* (☎01950/460563, ⓦwww .thespiggiehotel.co.uk; ❺), which has a lively bar serving real ales and a **restaurant** with great views over the Loch of Spiggie and out to Foula; both serve very reasonably priced and well-presented dishes. Over in Bigton, you can get soup and simple sandwiches at the *St Ninian's Isle Café* (closed Tues), whilst enjoying the views out to Foula. There's **hostel** accommodation at the modern *Cunningsburgh Village Club* (☎01950/477241; June–Aug), some ten miles south of Lerwick, and a **camping böd** in *Betty Mouat's Cottage* (☎01595/694688, ⓦwww.camping-bods.com; April–Sept), in Scatness, at the tip of the peninsula, close to the airport. At Levenwick, around eighteen miles south of Lerwick, a small, terraced **campsite** is run by the local community (☎01950/422207, ⓦwww.levenwick.shetland.co.uk; May–Sept), with hot showers, a tennis court and a superb view over the east coast.

Fair Isle

Fair Isle (ⓦwww.fairisle.org.uk) measures just three miles by one-and-a-half, marooned in the sea halfway between Shetland and Orkney and very different from both. The weather reflects its isolated position: you can almost guarantee that it'll be windy, though if you're lucky your visit might coincide with fine weather – what the islanders call "a given day". At one time Fair Isle's population was not far short of four hundred, but Clearances forced emigration from the middle of the nineteenth century. By the 1950s, the population had shrunk to just 44, a point at which evacuation and abandonment of the island were seriously considered. **George Waterston**, who'd bought the island and set up a bird observatory in 1948, passed it into the care of the NTS in 1954 and rejuvenation began. Today Fair Isle supports a vibrant community of around seventy people.

The north end of the island rises like a wall, while the Sheep Rock, a sculpted stack of rock and grass on the east side, is another dramatic feature. The croft land and the island's scattered houses are concentrated in the south, but the focus for many visitors is the **Bird Observatory**, built just above the sandy bay of North Haven where the ferry from Shetland Mainland arrives. It's one of the major European centres for ornithology, and its work in watching, trapping, recording and ringing birds goes on all year. Fair Isle is a landfall for a huge number and range of migrant birds during the spring and autumn passages. Migration routes converge here and more than 345 species, including many rarities, have been noted. As a result, Fair Isle is a haven for twitchers, who descend on the island in planes and boats whenever a major rarity is spotted; for more casual birders, however, there's also plenty of summer resident birdlife to enjoy. The high-pitched screeching that fills the sky above the airstrip comes from hundreds of arctic terns, and arctic skuas can also be seen here. Those in search of puffins should head for the cliffs around Furse, while to find gannets aim for the spectacular Stacks of Scroo.

Fair Isle is, of course, even better known for its **knitting** patterns, still produced with great skill by the local knitwear cooperative. There are samples on display at the island's **museum** (Mon 2–5pm, Wed 10am–noon, Fri 2–4.30pm; free; ☎01595/760244), situated next door to the Methodist Chapel. Particularly memorable are stories of shipwrecks; in 1868 the islanders undertook a heroic rescue of all 465 German emigrants aboard the *Lessing*. More famously, the *El Gran Grifon*, part of the retreating Spanish Armada, was lost here in 1588 and three hundred Spanish seamen were washed up on the island. Food was in such short supply that fifty died of starvation before help could be summoned from Shetland. The idea that the islanders borrowed all their patterns from the shipwrecked Spanish seamen is nowadays regarded as a patronizing myth.

Practicalities

For matters of administration and transport, Fair Isle is linked to Shetland. The passenger **ferry** connects Fair Isle with either Lerwick (on alternate Thurs; 4hr 30min) or Grutness in Sumburgh (Tues, Sat & alternate Thurs; 3hr); since the boat only takes a limited number of passengers, it's advisable to book in advance (☎01595/760222). The crossing can be very rough at times, so if you're at all susceptible to seasickness it might be worth considering catching a **flight** from Tingwall (Mon, Wed, Fri & Sat) or Sumburgh (Sat); a one-way ticket costs £28, and day-trips are possible (Mon, Wed & Fri).

Camping is not permitted, but there is full-board **accommodation** at the *Fair Isle Lodge & Bird Observatory* (☎01595/760258, ⓦwww.fairislebirdobs .co.uk; full board ⑤), in twins and singles or hostel-style dorms. To guests and visitors alike, the Bird Observatory offers tea, coffee and good home cooking for lunch and dinner; you might even be able to lend a hand with the observatory's research programme. A good **B&B** option – with full-board option – is *Upper Leogh* in the south of the island (☎01595/760248; ②), where you'll be well looked after. There is a shop/post office nearby (closed Thurs & Sun).

Central Mainland

The districts of Tingwall and Weisdale, plus the old capital of **Scalloway**, make up the **Central Mainland**, an area of minor interest in the grand scheme of things, but one that is very easy to reach from Lerwick. In fine weather, it's a captivating mix of farms, moors and lochs, and includes Shetland's only significant woodland; the scale of the scenery ranges from the intimate to the vast, with particularly spectacular views from high points above Whiteness and Weisdale. The area also holds strong historical associations, with the Norse parliament at **Law Ting Holm** and unhappy memories of Earl Patrick Stewart's harsh rule at Scalloway and of nineteenth-century Clearances at Weisdale.

Scalloway

Approaching **SCALLOWAY** from the shoulder of the steep hill to the east known as the **Scord**, there's a dramatic view over the town and the islands to the south and west. Once the capital of Shetland, Scalloway's importance waned through the eighteenth century as Lerwick, just six miles to the east,

The story of the **Shetland Bus**, the link between Shetland and Norway that helped to sustain the Norwegian Resistance through the years of Nazi occupation, is quite extraordinary. Constantly under threat of attack by enemy aircraft or naval action, small Norwegian fishing boats set out from Shetland to run arms and resistance workers into lonely fjords. The trip took at least 24 hours and on the return journey boats brought back Norwegians in danger of arrest by the Gestapo, or those who wanted to join Norwegian forces fighting with the Allies. For three years, through careful planning, the operation was remarkably successful: instructions to boats were passed in cryptic messages in BBC news broadcasts. Although local people knew what was going on, the secret was generally well kept. In total, 350 refugees were evacuated, and more than four hundred tons of arms, large amounts of explosives and sixty radio transmitters were landed in Norway.

Originally established at **Lunna** in the northeast of the Mainland, the service moved to **Scalloway** in 1942, partly because the village could offer good marine engineering facilities at Moore's Shipyard at the west end of Main Street, where a plaque records the morale-boosting visit of the Norwegian Crown Prince Olav. Many buildings in Scalloway were pressed into use to support the work: explosives and weapons were stored in the castle. **Kergord House** in Weisdale was used as a safe house and training centre for intelligence personnel and saboteurs. The hazards, tragedies and elations of the exercise are brilliantly described in David Howarth's book, *The Shetland Bus*; their legacy today is a heartfelt closeness between Shetland and Norway.

grew in trading success and status. Nowadays, Scalloway is fairly sleepy, though its prosperity, always closely linked to the fluctuations of the fishing industry, has recently been given a boost with investment in fish-processing factories, and in the impressive North Atlantic Fisheries College on the west side of the busy harbour.

In spite of modern developments nearby, Scalloway is dominated by the imposing shell of **Scalloway Castle**, a classic fortified tower house built with forced labour in 1600 by the infamous Earl Patrick Stewart, and thus seen as a powerful symbol of oppression. Stewart, who'd succeeded his father Robert to the earldom of Orkney and lordship of Shetland in 1592, held court in the castle and gained a reputation for enhancing his own power and wealth through the calculated use of harsh justice, frequently including confiscation of assets. He was eventually arrested and imprisoned in 1609, not for his ill-treatment of Shetlanders, but for his aggressive behaviour toward his fellow landowners; his son, Robert, attempted an insurrection and both were executed in Edinburgh in 1615. The castle itself is well preserved and fun to explore; if the door is locked, the key can be borrowed from the *Scalloway Hotel*.

On Main Street, the small **Scalloway Museum** (May–Sept Mon 9.30–11.30am & 2–4.30pm, Tues–Fri 10am–noon & 2–4.30pm, Sat 10am–12.30pm & 2–4.30pm; free), run by volunteers, holds a few local relics. It explains the importance of fishing and attempts to tell the story of the **Shetland Bus** (see box above), a memorial for which stands along the harbour at Mid Shore.

Scalloway has very little **accommodation** apart from the *Scalloway Hotel* (☎01595/880444; ❺), on the harbourfront, whose bar acts as the local pub. For **food**, head for *Da Haaf* (☎01595/880747; closed Sat & Sun), the unpretentious licensed restaurant in the North Atlantic Fisheries College, which serves a wide range of fresh fish, simply prepared, with broad harbour views to enjoy as well.

Tingwall and around

TINGWALL, the name for the loch-studded, fertile valley to the north of Scalloway, takes its name from the **Lawting** or Althing (from *thing*, the Old Norse for "parliament"), in existence from the eleventh to the sixteenth century, where local people and officials gathered to make or amend laws and discuss evidence. After the sixteenth century, judicial affairs were dealt with in Patrick Stewart's new castle at Scalloway. The Lawting was situated at **Law Ting Holm**, the small peninsula at the northern end of Loch Tingwall, that was once an island linked to the shore by a causeway.

Most of Shetland's inter-island flights leave from **Tingwall Airport** (☎01595/840246); taxis from Lerwick bus station cost just £1, but must be booked 24 hours in advance (☎01595/694617). If you're looking for somewhere to **stay** within easy striking distance of the airstrip, try the distinctive red *Herrislea House Hotel* (☎01595/840208; ❺), overlooking the airstrip by the main crossroads; its spacious **bar**, the idiosyncratically decorated *Starboard Tack*, doubles as Tingwall's social centre, serves good pub food and regularly features live **traditional music**. You can eat, or enjoy some draught Shetland ale whilst enjoying the view down Whiteness Voe, at the *Inn on the Hill*, on the A971.

The district of Weisdale, five miles or so northwest of Tingwall, is notable primarily for **Weisdale Mill** (Tues–Sat 10.30am–4.30pm, Sun noon–4.30pm; free), situated up the B9075 from the head of Weisdale Voe. Built for milling grain in 1855, this is now an attractively converted arts centre, housing the small, beautifully designed **Bonhoga Gallery**, in which touring and local exhibitions of painting, sculpture and other media are shown. Don't miss the small but fascinating **Shetland Textile Working Museum** (£1) in the basement, which puts on temporary exhibitions, and has pull-out drawers showing the knitted patterns unique to Shetland and Fair Isle. There's also a very pleasant café, serving soup, scones and snacks in the south-facing conservatory overlooking the stream.

The Westside

The western Mainland of Shetland – known as the **Westside** (Ⓦwww.walls.shetland.co.uk) – stretches west from Weisdale and Voe to Sandness. Although there are some important archeological remains and wildlife in the area, the area's greatest appeal lies in its outstanding **coastal scenery** and walks. At its heart, the Westside's rolling brown and purple moorland, dotted with patches of bright-green reseeded land, glistens with dozens of small, picturesque blue or silver lochs. On the west coast the rounded form of Sandness Hill (750ft) falls steeply away into the Atlantic. The coastal scenery, cut by several deep voes, is very varied; aside from dramatic cliffs, there are intimate coves and some fine beaches, as well as, just offshore, the stunning island of **Papa Stour**.

Around Bixter

The chief crossroads for the area is a few miles further on at **BIXTER**, a place of no particular consequence from where you can travel south to Skeld and Reawick, west to Walls, West Burrafirth and Sandness, or northwest along a scenic winding road towards Aith and eventually Voe (see p.782). Three miles southwest of Bixter lies the finest Neolithic structure in the Westside, dubbed the **Staneydale Temple** by the archeologist who excavated it because it resembled a temple on Malta. Whatever its true function, it was twice as large as the surrounding oval-shaped houses (now in ruins) and was certainly of great importance, perhaps as some kind of community centre. The horseshoe-shaped foundations measure more than 40ft by 20ft internally, with immensely thick walls, still around 4ft high, whose roof would have been supported by spruce posts (two postholes can still be clearly seen). To reach the temple, take the path marked out by black-and-white poles across the moorland for half a mile from the road.

Walls and Sandness

Once an important fishing port, **WALLS** (pronounced *waas*), appealingly set round its harbour, is now a quiet village which comes alive once a year in the middle of August for the Walls Agricultural Show, the biggest farming bash on the island. It has several good **accommodation** options: the nicely restored *Voe House* (℡01595/694688, Ⓦwww .camping-bods.com; April–Sept), the largest **camping böd** on Shetland, with its own peat fire, and the wonderfully welcoming *Skeoverick* (℡01595/809349; ❷), a lovely modern crofthouse B&B which lies a mile or so north of Walls. The only guesthouse in the area is 🍴 *Burrastow House* (℡01595/809307, Ⓦwww .users.zetnet.co.uk/burrastow-house-hotel; April–Oct; ❺), beautifully situated about three miles southwest of Walls; parts of the house date back to 1759, and have real character, others are more modern. With fresh Shetland ingredients and a French chef, the cooking is superb, though dinner is available to non-residents only at the weekend.

At the end of a long winding road across an undulating, uninhabited, boulder-strewn landscape, you eventually reach the fertile scattered crofting settlement of **SANDNESS** (pronounced *saaness*), which you can also reach by walking along the coast from Walls past the dramatic Deepdale and across Sandness Hill. It's an oasis of green meadows in the peat moorland, with a nice beach, too.

There's nowhere **to stay** in Sandness, but there is a croft B&B with great sea views, *Snarraness House* (℡01595/809375; ❶) in **WEST BURRAFIRTH**, the ferry terminal for Papa Stour, five miles or so north of Walls.

Papa Stour

A mile offshore from Sandness is the rocky island of **Papa Stour** (Ⓦwww .papastour.shetland.co.uk), created out of volcanic lava and ash, which has subsequently been eroded into some of the most impressive coastal scenery in Shetland. In good weather, it makes for a perfect day-trip, but in foul weather or a sea mist it can certainly appear pretty bleak. Its name, which means "big island of the priests", derives from its early Celtic Christian connections, and the island was home, in the eighteenth century, to people who were mistakenly believed to have been lepers (though in fact they were suffering from a hereditary skin disease caused by severe malnutrition). The land is very fertile, and once supported around three hundred inhabitants; but by the early 1970s the population crisis was such that the island advertised for incomers. All sorts turned up and Papa Stour was briefly dubbed "the hippie isle"; today the island struggles to sustain a community of twenty-five or so.

Papa Stour's main settlement, **BIGGINGS**, lies in the east near the pier, and it was here that excavation in the early 1980s revealed the remains of a thirteenth-century Norse house, which is thought to have belonged to Duke Haakon, heir to the Norwegian throne. There's an explanatory panel, but nothing much to see

– in any case, the chief reason to come to Papa Stour is to go **walking**; to reach the best of the coastal scenery, head for the far west of the island. From **Virda Field** (285ft), the highest point, in the far northwest, you can see the treacherous rocks of Ve Skerries, three miles or so northwest off the coast, where a lighthouse was erected as recently as 1979. The couple of miles of coastline from here southeast to Hamna Voe has some of the island's best stacks, blowholes and natural arches. Probably the most spectacular formation of all is the **Christie's Hole**, a gloup or partly roofed cleft, which extends far inland from the cliff line, and where shags nest on precipitous ledges. Other points of interest include a couple of defunct horizontal click-mills, below Dutch Loch, and the remains of a "meal road", so called because the workmen were paid in oatmeal or flour. In addition, several pairs of red-throated divers regularly breed on inland lochs such as Gorda Water.

The **ferry** runs from West Burrafirth on the Westside to the north side of Housa Voe on Papa Stour (Mon, Wed & Fri–Sun). Always book in advance, and reconfirm the day before departure (℡01595/810460); day-trips are only possible on Friday and Saturday. There's also a **flight** from Tingwall Airport every Tuesday, and again a day-trip is feasible; tickets cost around £17.50 one way. Papa Stour's airstrip is southwest of Biggings, by the school. There's currently no B&B on the island, but there is a small, clean, friendly **bunkhouse** (℡01595/873229, ✉fay@hurdiback.shetland.co.uk; April–Sept) at Hurdiback, near the pier and beside the island's only phone box; breakfast and dinner are available if you want. Ask around locally about the possibility of **boat rental**, if you want to look at the stacks from the sea. There's no shop, so day-trippers should bring their own picnic with them.

Foula

Southwest of Walls, at "the edge of the world", **Foula** is without a doubt the most isolated inhabited island in the British Isles, separated from the nearest point on Mainland Shetland by about fourteen miles of often turbulent ocean. Seen from the Mainland, its distinctive mountainous form changes subtly, depending upon the vantage point, but the outline is unforgettable. Its western **cliffs**, the second highest in Britain after those of St Kilda, rise at **The Kame** to some 1220ft above sea level; a clear day at The Kame offers a magnificent panorama stretching from Unst to Fair Isle. On a bad day, the exposure is complete and the cliffs generate turbulent blasts of wind known in Shetland as "flans", which rip through the hills with tremendous force.

Foula has been inhabited since prehistoric times, and the people here take pride in their separateness from Shetland, cherishing local traditions such as the observance of the **Julian calendar**, officially

△ Puffin, Shetland

dropped in Britain in 1752, where Old Yule is celebrated on January 6 and the New Year doesn't arrive until January 13. Foula was also the last place that **Norn**, the old Norse language of Orkney and Shetland, was spoken as a first language, in the eighteenth century. Foula's population, which peaked at around two hundred at the end of the nineteenth century, has fluctuated wildly over the years, dropping to three in 1720 following an epidemic of "muckle fever" or smallpox. Today, the community numbers around thirty.

Arriving on Foula, you can't help but be amazed by the sheer size of the island's immense, bare mountains, whose summits are often hidden in cloud, known on the Mainland as "Foula's hat". The gentler eastern slopes provide good crofting land and plentiful peat, and it is along this "green belt" that the island's population are scattered. The island, whose name is derived from the Old Norse for "bird island", also provides a home for a quarter of a million **birds**. Arctic terns wheel overhead at the airstrip, red-throated divers can usually be seen on the island's smaller lochs, while fulmars, guillemots, razorbills, puffins and gannets cling to the rock ledges. However, it is Foula's colony of **great skuas** or "bonxies" whom you can't fail to notice. From the edge of extinction a hundred years ago, the bonxies are now thriving, with an estimated three thousand pairs on Foula, making it the largest colony in Britain. During the nesting season, they attack anyone who comes near. Although their dive-bombing antics are primarily meant as a threat, they can make walking across the island's moorland interior fairly stressful: the best advice is to hold a stick above your head or stay on the road and the coast.

Practicalities

A day-trip to Foula by **ferry** isn't possible, as the summer passenger service from Mainland only runs on Tuesdays, Thursdays and Saturdays (2hr); it's essential to book and reconfirm (℡01595/753254). The boat arrives at Ham, in the middle of Foula's east coast, and has to be winched up onto the pier to protect it. However, there are regular **flights** from Tingwall (Mon–Wed & Fri; ℡01595/753226); tickets cost around £25 one way and day-trips are possible on Wednesdays (mid-Feb to mid-Oct) and Fridays. From May to September, Foula has its own resident part-time ranger, who usually greets new arrivals and offers local advice; it's also possible to arrange for guided walks (℡01595/753228). Foula's only **B&B** is *Leraback* (℡01595/753226, Ⓦwww.originart.com; ❸), near Ham, which does full board only, though they can also rent out a self-catering cottage on a daily basis; they will collect you from the airstrip or pier. There's no shop, so you'll need to take all your food and supplies with you. There's just one road, which runs along the eastern side of the island, and is used by Foula's remarkable fleet of clapped-out vehicles.

North Mainland

The **North Mainland**, stretching more than thirty miles north from the central belt around Lerwick, is wilder than much of Shetland, with almost relentlessly bleak moorland and some rugged and dramatic coastal scenery. It is all but split in two by the isthmus of Mavis Grind: to the south are the districts of Delting, home to Shetland's oil terminal (Sullom Voe) and town (Brae), Lunnasting (gateway to the islands of Whalsay and Out Skerries) and Nesting; to the north is the remote region of **Northmavine**, which boasts some of the most scenic cliffs in Shetland.

Voe and Lunnasting

If you're travelling north, you're bound to pass by **VOE**, as it sits at the main crossroads of the North Mainland. If you stay on the main road, it's easy to miss the picturesque old village, a tight huddle of homes and workshops down below the road around the pier (and signposted Lower Voe). Set at the head of a deep, sheltered, sea loch, Voe has a Scandinavian appearance, helped by the presence of the **Sail Loft**, now a large **camping böd** (℡01595/694688, ⓌWww .camping-bods.com; April–Sept); it has hot showers, a kitchen, and a solid-fuel heater in the smaller of the bedrooms. Across the road, the old butcher's is now the *Pierhead Restaurant & Bar*: the cosy wood-panelled **pub** has a real fire, occasional live music and offers a good bar menu, a longer version of which is on offer in the upstairs restaurant, featuring local mussels and the odd catch from the fishing boats.

LAXO, the ferry terminal for Whalsay (see p.784), lies two miles east of Voe. If you continue along the B9071 past the village, you'll pass **The Cabin** (open when the flag flies, which is mostly daily 10am–5pm; free; ℡01806/577243), a glorified garden shed packed to the rafters with wartime memorabilia collected over many years by the very welcoming proprietor, Andy Robertson. You can try on some of the uniforms and caps or pour over the many personal accounts of the war written by locals. Three miles or so further north past **VIDLIN**, the departure point for the Out Skerries (see p.785), is ⚓ **Lunna House** (℡01806/577311, Ⓦwww.lunnahouse.co.uk; ❷), with its distinctive red window surrounds, set above a sheltered harbour nine miles northeast of Voe. The house was originally built in 1660 by the Hunter family, but is best known as the initial headquarters from which the Shetland Bus resistance operation was conducted during World War II (see box, p.777). It's now a wonderful **place to stay**, with spacious bedrooms, lovely views and a top-class breakfast.

Down the hill lies the little whitewashed **Lunna Kirk**, built in 1753, with a beautiful tiny interior including a carved hexagonal pulpit. Among its more peculiar features is a "lepers' squint" on the outside wall, through which those believed to have the disease could participate in the service without risk of infecting the congregation; there was, however, no leprosy here, the outcasts in fact suffering from a hereditary, non-infectious skin condition brought on by malnutrition. In the graveyard, several unidentified Norwegian sailors, torpedoed by the Nazis, are buried.

Brae and Sullom Voe

BRAE, a sprawling settlement that still has the feel of a frontier town, was one of four expanded in some haste in the 1970s to accommodate the workforce for the huge **Sullom Voe Oil Terminal**, just to the northeast. Sullom Voe is the longest sea loch in Shetland and has always attracted the interest of outsiders in search of a deep-water harbour. During World War II it was home to the Norwegian Air Force and a base for RAF seaplanes. Although the oil terminal, built between 1975 and 1982, has passed its production peak, it is still the largest of its kind in Europe. Its size, however, isn't obvious from beyond the site boundary and few clues remain to the extraordinary scale of the construction effort, which for several years involved a workforce of six thousand accommodated in two large "construction villages" and two ships.

Brae may not, at first sight, appear to be somewhere to spend the night, but it does boast one of Shetland's finest **hotels**, *Busta House* (℡01806/522506, Ⓦwww.bustahouse.com; ❻), a lovely laird's house with stepped gables that has been tastefully enlarged over the last four hundred years and which sits across the bay of Busta Voe from the modern sprawl of Brae. Even if you're not staying the night here, it's worth coming for afternoon tea in the Long Room, for a stroll around the lovely wooded grounds or for a drink and an excellent bar meal in the hotel's pub-like bar. A cheaper alternative is the modern croft-house **B&B** of *Westayre* (T01806/522368, W www.westayre.shetland.co.uk; **2**), beyond Busta, overlooking a red sandy bay on the peaceful island of Muckle Roe, which is linked to the mainland by a bridge.

Northmavine

Northmavine, the northwest peninsula of North Mainland, is unquestionably one of the most picturesque areas of Shetland, with its often rugged scenery, magnificent coastline and wide open spaces. The peninsula begins a mile west of Brae at **Mavis Grind**, a narrow isthmus at which it's said you can throw a stone from the Atlantic to the North Sea, or at least to Sullom Voe.

HILLSWICK, the main settlement in the area, was once served by the steamboats of the North of Scotland, Orkney & Shetland Steam Navigation Company, and in the early 1900s the firm built the **St Magnus Hotel** to house their customers, importing it in the form of a timber kit from Norway. Despite various alterations over the years, it still stands overlooking St Magnus Bay, rather magnificently clad in black timber-framing and white weatherboarding. Nearer the shore is the much older Hillswick House and, attached to it, **Da Böd**, once the oldest pub in Shetland, said to have been founded by a German merchant in 1684, now an alternative veggie café and wildlife sanctuary called *The Booth* (T01806/503348; June–Sept; closed Mon).

The *St Magnus Hotel* is full to the rafters with contractors working at Sullom Voe, so if you want a decent **B&B** in the vicinity, look to *Almara* (T01806/503261, W www.almara.shetland.co.uk; **3**), a mile or two back down the road in Upper Urafirth, which will present you with good food, a family welcome and excellent views. The nicest sandiest **beach** to collapse on is on the west side of the Hillswick isthmus, overlooking Dore Holm, a short walk across the fields from the hotel.

Esha Ness

Just outside Hillswick, a side road leads west to the exposed headland of **Esha Ness** (pronounced "*A*ysha Ness"), celebrated for its splendid coastline views. Spectacular red granite **cliffs**, eaten away to form fantastic shapes by the elements, are spread out before you as the road climbs away from Hillswick: in the foreground are the stacks known as **The Drongs** off the Ness of Hillswick, while in the distance, the Westside and Papa Stour are visible.

A mile or so south off the main road is the **Tangwick Haa Museum** (May–Sept Mon–Fri 1–5pm, Sat & Sun 11am–7pm; free), housed in a seventeenth-century building, which, through photographs, old documents and fishing gear, tells the often moving story of this remote corner of Shetland and its role in the dangerous trade of deep-sea fishing and whaling. Kids and adults alike will also enjoy the shells, the Shetland wool and sand samples and the prize exhibit, the Gunnister Man, who was found preserved in peat in 1951. Over 250 years old now, he's down to his bones, for the most part, but his clothes are in good condition, as is his knitted purse, which contained three coins: two Dutch and one Swedish.

The northern branch of the road ends at the **Esha Ness Lighthouse**, a great place to view the red sandstone cliffs, stacks and blowholes of this stretch of coast. A useful information board at the lighthouse details some of the dramatic geological features here, and, if the weather's a bit rough, you should be treated to some spectacular crashing waves. One of the features to beware of at Esha Ness are the blowholes, some of which are hidden far inland. The best example is the **Holes of Scraada**, a partly roofed cleft where the sea suddenly appears 300yd inland from the cliff line. The incredible power of the sea can be seen in the various giant boulder fields above the cliffs: these **storm beaches** are formed by rocks torn from the cliffs in storms and deposited inland.

One of the few places to stay in Esha Ness is *Johnnie Notions* **camping böd** (℡01595/694688, Ⓦwww.camping-bods.com; April–Sept; no electricity), up a turning north off the main road, in the hamlet of **HAMNAVOE**. The house was originally the birthplace of **Johnnie "Notions" Williamson** (1740–1803), a man of many talents, including blacksmithing and weaving, whose fame rests on his work in protecting several thousand of the population against smallpox using a serum and a method of inoculation he'd invented himself, to the amazement of the medical profession. He used a scalpel to lift a flap of skin without drawing blood, then placed the serum he'd prepared underneath, dressing it with a cabbage leaf and a bandage.

Whalsay and Out Skerries

The island of **Whalsay**, known in Shetland as the "Bonnie Isle", is a friendly community of over a thousand, devoted almost entirely to fishing. The islands' crews operate a very successful pelagic fleet of immense super-trawlers which can fish far afield in all weathers and catch a wide range of species. The island is, in addition, extremely fertile, but crofting takes second place to fishing here; there are also plentiful supplies of peat, which can be seen in spring and summer, stacked neatly to dry out above huge peat banks, ready to be bagged for the winter.

Ferries from the Mainland arrive at the island's chief town, **SYMBISTER**, in the southwest, whose harbour is usually dominated by the presence of several of the island's sophisticated, multimillion-pound purse-netters, some over 180ft long. Across the busy harbour from the ferry berth stands the tiny grey granite **Pier House** (Mon–Sat 9am–1pm & 2–5pm, Sun 2–4pm; free), the key for which resides in the shop opposite. This picturesque little building, with a hoist built into one side, is thought to have been a Hanseatic merchants' store, and contains a good display on how the Germans traded salt, tobacco, spirits and cloth for Whalsay's salted, dried fish from medieval times until the eighteenth century; close by is the Harbour View house that is thought to have been a Hanseatic storehouse or booth.

About half a mile east of Symbister at the hamlet of **SODOM** – an anglicized version of Sudheim, meaning "South House" – is **Grieve House** (now a camping böd, see opposite), the modest former home of celebrated Scots poet, writer and republican **Hugh MacDiarmid** (1892–1978), born Christopher Grieve in the Borders town of Langholm. He stayed here from 1933 until 1942, writing about half of his output, including much of his best work: lonely, contemplative poems honouring fishing and fishermen, with whom he sometimes went out to sea.

Although the majority of folk live in or around Symbister, the rest of Whalsay – which measures roughly two miles by eight – is quite evenly and fairly densely populated. Of the prehistoric remains, the most notable are the two **Bronze Age houses** on the northeastern coast of the island, half a mile south of Skaw, known respectively as the "Benie Hoose" and "Yoxie Biggins". The latter is also known as the "Standing Stones of Yoxie", due to the use of megaliths to form large sections of the walls, many of which still stand.

Car ferries run regularly to Whalsay from Laxo on the Mainland (daily every 45min–1hr 15min; 30min); if you have a car, it's an idea to book ahead (℡01806/566259). In bad weather, especially southeasterly gales, the service operates from Vidlin instead. There are also request-only **flights** from Tingwall (Mon, Wed & Thurs; ℡01595/840246); day-trips are only possible on Thursdays. For **B&B** enquire at the post office; otherwise you can stay at the **camping böd** of *Grieve House* in Sodom (℡01595/694688, Ⓦwww .camping-bods.com; April–Sept; no electricity). The house has lovely views overlooking Linga Sound, but is hidden from the main road, so ask for directions at the shop on the brow of the hill along the road to the Loch of Huxter. A little further along the road is the *Oot Ower Lounge*, an agreeable **pub** overlooking the loch, and pretty much the only place to eat and drink on the island, though you must book ahead if you want a full meal (℡01806/566658). The island also has an eighteen-hole **golf course**, near the airstrip in Skaw, in the northeast, several shops and a **leisure centre** with an excellent swimming pool close to the school in Symbister.

Out Skerries

Lying four miles out to sea, off the northeast tip of Whalsay, the **Out Skerries** ("Oot Skerries" or plain "Skerries" as the locals call them), consist of three tiny low-lying rocky islands, Housay, Bruray and Grunay, the first two linked by a bridge, with a population of around eighty. That people live here at all is remarkable, and that it is one of Shetland's most dynamic communities is astonishing, its affluence based on fishing from a superb, small natural harbour sheltered by all three islands, and on salmon farming in a nearby inlet. There are good, if short, walks, with a few prehistoric remains, but the majority of visitors are divers exploring the wreck-strewn coastline, and ornithologists who come here when the wind is in the east, in the hope of catching a glimpse of rare migrants.

The Skerries' jetty and airstrip are both on the middle island of **Bruray**, which also boasts their highest point, Bruray Wart (173ft), an easy climb, and one which brings you up close to the islands' ingenious spiral channel collection system for rainwater, which can become scarce in summer. The easternmost island, **Grunay**, is now uninhabited, though you can clearly see the abandoned lighthouse keepers' cottages and the Stevenson-designed lighthouse on the outlying islet of Bound Skerry. The largest of the Skerries' trio, **Housay**, has the most indented and intriguing coastline, to which you should head if the weather's fine. En route, make sure you wander through the Battle Pund stone circle, a wide ring of boulders in the southeastern corner of the island.

Ferries to and from Skerries leave from Vidlin on the Mainland (Mon & Fri–Sun; 1hr 25min) and Lerwick (Tues & Thurs; 2hr 30min), but day-trips are only possible from Vidlin (Fri, Sat & Sun). Make sure you book your journey by 5pm the previous evening (℡01806/515226), or the ferry might not run. You can take your car over, but, with less than a mile of road to drive along, it's not worth it. There are also regular **flights** from Tingwall (Mon, Wed & Thurs), with day-trips possible on Thursdays. There is a shop, and a shower/toilet block by the pier, and **camping** is permitted, with permission. Alternatively, you can stay in *Rocklea* (℡01806/515228, Ⓦwww .rockleaok.co.uk; ❷), a friendly **B&B** on Bruray run by Mrs Johnson, who offers optional full board.

The North Isles

Many visitors never make it out to Shetland's trio of remote **North Isles**, which is a shame, as the ferry links are frequent and inexpensive, and the roads fast. Certainly, there is no dramatic shift in scenery: much of what awaits you is the familiar Shetland landscape of undulating peat moorland, dramatic coastal cliffs and silent glacial voes. However, with Lerwick that much further away, the spirit of independence and self-sufficiency in the North Isles is much more keenly felt. **Yell**, the largest of the three, is best known for its vast otter population, but is otherwise often overlooked. **Fetlar**, the smallest of the trio, is home to the rare red-necked phalarope, but **Unst** has probably the widest appeal, partly as the most northerly land mass in the British Isles, but also for its nesting seabird population.

Yell

Historically, **Yell** (Ⓦ www.yell-tourism.shetland.co.uk) hasn't had good write-ups. The writer Eric Linklater described it as "dull and dark", while the Scottish historian Buchanan claimed it was "so uncouth a place that no creature can live therein, except such as are born there". Certainly, if you keep to the fast main road, which links the island's two ferry terminals of Ulsta and Gutcher, you'll pass a lot of uninspiring peat moorland, but the landscape is relieved by several voes which cut deeply into it, providing superb natural harbours used as hiding places by German submarines during World War II. Yell's coastline, too, is gentler and greener than the interior and provides an ideal habitat for a large population of **otters**; locals will point out the best places to watch for them.

At **BURRAVOE**, in the southeastern corner of Yell, there's a lovely white-washed laird's house dating from 1672, with crow-stepped gables, that now houses the **Old Haa Museum** (late April to Sept Tues–Thurs & Sat 10am–4pm, Sun 2–5pm; free), which is stuffed with artefacts, and has lots of material on the history of the local herring and whaling industry; there's a very pleasant wood-panelled café on the ground floor, too. From May to August, you'll find thousands of **seabirds** (including puffins) nesting in the cliffs above Ladies Hole, less than a mile to the northeast of the village.

The island's largest village, **MID YELL**, has a couple of shops, a pub and a leisure centre with a good swimming pool. A mile or so to the northwest of the village, on an exposed hill above the main road, stands the spooky, abandoned **Windhouse**, dating in part from the early eighteenth century; skeletons were found under the floor and in its wood-panelled walls, and the house is now believed by many to be haunted (its ghost-free lodge is a camping böd; see below). In the north of Yell, the area around **CULLIVOE** has relatively gentle, but attractive, coastal scenery. The **Sands of Brekken** are made from crushed shells, and are beautifully sheltered in a cove a mile or two north of Cullivoe.

Ferries to Yell from Toft on the Mainland are frequent and inexpensive, and taking a car over is easy, too (1–2 hourly; 20min). One of the best **B&Bs** on Yell is *Hillhead* (Ⓣ 01957/722274, Ⓔ rita.leask@btopenworld.com; ❶), a comfortable modern house in Hamnavoe offering great home cooking; you can also stay with the very welcoming, storytelling Tullochs at *Gutcher Post Office* (Ⓣ 01957/744201, Ⓔ margaret.tulloch@btopenworld.com; ❷) by the Unst ferry terminal. A cheaper alternative is to stay in the **camping böd** at *Windhouse Lodge* (Ⓣ 01595/694688, Ⓦ www.camping-bods.com; April–Sept), the gatehouse on the main road near Mid Yell; it has a small wood- and peat-fired heater and hot showers. **Food** options on Yell are limited: the museum café in Burravoe (times as for museum) has soup, snacks and delicious home baking, while the functional *Hilltop Bar* in Mid Yell offers standard bar meals. Probably the best option is the funky, camp *Wind Dog Café* (Ⓦwww.winddogcafe.co.uk), opposite the post office at Gutcher, which offers evening meals (if you book ahead), provides Internet access, as well as hosting storytelling from the inimitable Tullochs and other events.

Fetlar

Fetlar is the most fertile of the North Isles, much of it grassy moorland and lush green meadows with masses of summer flowers. It's known as "the garden of Shetland", though that's pushing it a bit, as it's still, relatively speaking, an unforgiving, treeless landscape. Around nine hundred people once lived here and there might well be more than a hundred now were it not for the activities of **Sir Arthur Nicolson**, who in the first half of the nineteenth century cleared many of the people at forty days' notice to make room for sheep. Nicolson's architectural tastes were rather more eccentric than some other local tyrants; his rotting but still astonishing **Brough Lodge**, a rambling castellated composition complete with folly, built in stone and brick in the 1820s, can be seen a mile or so south of the ferry terminal. Today, Fetlar's population lives on the southern and eastern sides of the island. At the main settlement, **HOUBIE**, in the centre of the island on the south coast, there's the **Fetlar Interpretive Centre** (May–Sept Mon–Fri 1–5pm, Sat & Sun 2–5pm; £2; Ⓦwww.fetlar.com), a welcoming museum with information on Fetlar's outstanding birdlife and the archeological excavations that took place near Houbie.

Much of the northern half of the island around Fetlar's highest point, **Vord Hill** (522ft), is now an RSPB Reserve (mid-May to mid-July: phone for access ℡01957/733246). As well as harbouring important colonies of arctic skuas and whimbrels, Fetlar is perhaps best known for having harboured Britain's only breeding pair of **snowy owls**, which bred on Stackaberg, to the southwest of Vord Hill, from 1967 to 1975. Fetlar is also one of very few places in Britain where you'll see the graceful **red-necked phalarope** (late May–early Aug): the birds are unusual in that the female does the courting and then leaves the male in charge of incubation. The island boasts ninety percent of Britain's phalarope population, and a hide has been provided overlooking the marshes (or mires) to the east of the **Loch of Funzie** (pronounced "Finny"); the loch itself is also a good place at which to spot the phalaropes, and is a regular haunt of red-throated divers.

Ferries to Fetlar (5–6 daily; 25–40min) depart from both Gutcher on Yell and Belmont on Unst, though they are by no means as frequent as the ferries between the Mainland, Yell and Unst. The ferry docks at **Hamar's Ness**, three miles northwest of Houbie; the only public transport is an infrequent and small postcar (Mon, Wed & Fri 2 daily), so if you don't have a car you should try to negotiate a lift while on the ferry. If you do have a car, bear in mind that there's no petrol station on Fetlar, so fill up before you come across. **Accommodation** is in short supply, so book ahead either at *Gord* (℡01957/733227; ℮lynboxall@zetnet.co.uk; ❸), the comfortable modern house attached to the island shop in Houbie, which does dinner, bed and breakfast, or at the **camping böd** in Aithbank (℡01595/694688, Ⓦwww.camping-bods.com; April–Sept), a cosy wood-panelled cottage, a mile east of Houbie. The folk at *Gord* also run the *Garths* **campsite** (℡01957/733227; May–Sept), a simple field just to the west of Houbie, with toilets, showers and drying facilities. The post office, shop and **café** (closed Thurs & Sun) are all in one building in the middle of Houbie.

Unst

Much of **Unst** (Ⓦ www.unst.org) is rolling grassland – a blessed relief for some after the peaty moorland of Yell – but the coast is more dramatic: a fringe of cliffs relieved by some beautiful sandy beaches. As Britain's most northerly inhabited island, there is a surfeit of "most northerly" sights, which is fair enough, given that many visitors only come here in order to head straight for Hermaness, to see the seabirds and look out over Muckle Flugga and the northernmost tip of Britain, to the North Pole beyond. The island has been badly affected by the recent closure of the local RAF radar base at Saxa Vord, which used to employ a third of the island's population, which has now fallen to around six hundred.

On the south coast of the island, not far from the ferry terminal, is **UYEASOUND**, with Greenwell's Booth, an old Hanseatic merchants' warehouse by the pier, sadly now roofless. Further east lie the ruins of **Muness Castle**, a diminutive defensive structure, with matching bulging bastions and corbelled turrets at opposite corners. The castle was built in 1598 by the Scots incomer, Laurence Bruce, stepbrother and chief bullyboy of the infamous Earl Robert Stewart, and probably designed by Andrew Crawford, who shortly afterwards built Scalloway Castle for Robert's son Patrick. The inscription above the entrance asks visitors "not to hurt this vark aluayis", but the castle was sacked by Danish

△ Bobby's bus shelter, Unst

pirates in 1627 and never really re-roofed. To gain entry, you must get the keys and a torch from the nearby cottage.

Unst's main settlement is **BALTASOUND**, five miles north, whose herring industry used to boost the local population of around five hundred to as much as ten thousand during the fishing season. To learn more about the herring boom and other aspects of Unst's history, head for the excellent new **Unst Heritage Centre** (May–Sept daily 2–5pm; free), housed in the old school building by the main crossroads. As you leave Baltasound, heading north, be sure to take a look at **Bobby's bus shelter** (Ⓦ www.unstbusshelter.shetland .co.uk), an eccentric, fully furnished, award-winning Shetland bus shelter on the edge of the town.

From Baltasound, the main road crosses a giant boulder field of serpentine, a greyish-green, occasionally turquoise rock found widely on Unst, that weathers to a rusty orange. The **Keen of Hamar**, east of Baltasound, and clearly signposted from the main road, is one of the largest expanses of serpentine debris in Europe, and is home to an extraordinary array of plantlife. It's worth taking a walk on this barren, exposed, almost lunar landscape that's thought to resemble what most of northern Europe looked like at the end of the last Ice Age. With the help of one of the SNH leaflets (kept in a box by the stile), you can try and identify some of the area's numerous rare and minuscule plants, including Norwegian sandwort, frog orchid, moonwort and the mouse-eared Edmondston's chickweed, which flowers in June and July and is found nowhere else in the world.

Beyond the Keen of Hamar, the road drops down into **HAROLDSWICK**, where near the shore you'll find the **Unst Boat Haven** (May–Sept daily 2–5pm; free), displaying a beautifully presented collection of historic boats with many tools of the trade and information on fishing. The road that heads off northwest from Haroldswick leads eventually to the bleak headland of **Hermaness**, now a National Nature Reserve and home to more than 100,000 nesting seabirds. There's an excellent **visitor centre** in the former lighthouse keepers' shore station, where you can pick up a leaflet showing the marked routes across the heather, which allow you access into the reserve. Whatever you do, stick to the path so as to avoid annoying the vast numbers of nesting great skuas.

From Hermaness Hill, you can look down over the jagged rocks of the wonderfully named Vesta Skerry, Rumblings, Tipta Skerry and **Muckle Flugga**. There are few more dramatic settings for a lighthouse, and few sites could ever have presented as great a challenge to the builders, who erected it in 1858. Beyond the lighthouse is **Out Stack**, the most northerly bit of Britain, where Lady Franklin landed in 1849 in order to pray (in vain, as it turned out) for the safe return for her husband from his expedition to discover the Northwest Passage, undertaken four years previously. The views from here are inevitably marvellous, as is the birdlife; there's a huge gannetry on one of the stacks, and puffins burrow all along the clifftops. The walk down the west side of Unst towards Westing is one of the finest in Shetland: if the wind's blowing hard, the seascape is memorably dramatic.

Ferries shuttle regularly from Gutcher on Yell over to **BELMONT** on Unst (1–2 hourly; 10min); booking in advance is wise (Ⓣ01957/722259). By far the best and most unusual **accommodation** is historic *Buness House* (Ⓣ01957/711315, Ⓦ www.users.zetnet.co.uk/buness-house; ❻), a seventeenth-century haa in Baltasound still owned and run by the eccentric Edmondstons (of chickweed fame). Another very good bet is *Prestagaard* (Ⓣ01957/755234, Ⓦ www.prestegaard.shetland.co.uk; ❷), a modest Victorian B&B with just a couple of rooms in Uyeasound, where there's also the very handy *Gardiesfauld*

Hostel (☎01957/755240, ⓦwww.gardiesfauld.shetland.co.uk; April–Sept), a clean and modern place near the pier which allows **camping**, and offers **bike rental**. Make sure you book yourself in for dinner, bed and breakfast or self-cater, rather than resort to the bar food at the *Baltasound Hotel*. During the day, snacks and teas can be had at the **tearoom** in Nornova Knitwear just north of Muness Castle. The largest **shop** around is the NAAFI store within the old RAF base at Saxa Vord, which is now open to the public.

Travel details

Ferries to Shetland

Summer timetable only.
Aberdeen to: Lerwick (daily; 12hr).
Kirkwall (Orkney) to: Lerwick (3–4 weekly; 6hr).

Inter-island ferries

Summer timetable only.
To Bressay: Lerwick–Bressay (hourly; 7min).
To Fair Isle: Lerwick–Fair Isle (alternate Thurs; 4hr 30min); Grutness–Fair Isle (Tues, Sat & alternate Thurs; 3hr).
To Fetlar: Belmont (Unst) and Gutcher (Yell)–Hamar's Ness (5–6 daily; 25–40min).
To Foula: Scalloway–Foula (alternate Thurs; 3hr 30min); Walls–Foula (Tues, Sat & alternate Thurs; 2hr).
To Out Skerries: Lerwick–Skerries (Tues & Thurs; 2hr 30min); Vidlin–Skerries (1 on Mon, Fri–Sun 3 daily; 1hr 25min).
To Papa Stour: West Burrafirth–Papa Stour (Mon & Sun 1 daily, Wed, Fri & Sat 2 daily; 40min).
To Unst: Gutcher (Yell)–Belmont (1–2 hourly; 10min).
To Whalsay: Laxo–Symbister (every 45min; 30min).
To Yell: Toft–Ulsta (1–2 hourly; 20min).

Inter-island flights

Summer timetable only.
Sumburgh to: Fair Isle (Sat; 15min).

Tingwall to: Fair Isle (Mon, Wed & Fri 2 daily, 1 on Sat; 25min); Foula (Mon & Tues 1 daily, Wed & Fri 2 daily; 15min); Out Skerries, calling at Whalsay on request (Mon & Wed 1 daily, Thurs 2 daily; 20min); Papa Stour (Tues 2 daily; 10min).

Buses

Shetland Mainland

Lerwick to: Brae (Mon–Sat 4–6 daily, 1 on Sun in school term; 45min); Hamnavoe (Mon–Sat 2 daily; 30min); Hillswick (Mon–Sat 1 daily; 1hr 40min); Laxo (Mon–Sat 2 daily; 40min); Scalloway (Mon–Sat hourly; 15min); Sumburgh (Mon–Sat 5 daily, 3 on Sun; 45min); Toft (Mon–Sat 4–5 daily; 50min); Vidlin (Mon–Sat 2 daily; 45min); Voe (Mon–Sat 5–6 daily, 1 on Sun in school term; 30min); Walls (Mon–Sat 1–3 daily; 45min).

Unst

Baltasound to: Haroldswick (Mon–Sat 3–4 daily; 10min).
Belmont to: Baltasound (Mon–Sat 2–3 daily; 20min); Uyeasound (Mon–Sat 2–3 daily; 5min).

Yell

Mid Yell to: Gutcher (Mon–Sat 1–5 daily, Sun 1 daily in school term; 20min).
Ulsta to: Burravoe (Mon–Sat 1 daily; 15min); Gutcher (Mon–Sat 1–3 daily, 1 on Sun in school term; 30min).

SHETLAND | Travel details

Contexts

Contexts

History

S cotland's colourful and compelling **history** looms large. Peppered with tragic yet romantic heroes, the country's past has thrown up notable fighters, innovators and politicians. Often the nation's history has been defined either by fierce internecine conflict or epic struggles with its more populous and richer neighbour, England. Yet from earliest times the influences of Ireland, Scandinavia and continental Europe have been as important, particularly in aspects of Scotland's creative and cultural development. The result has been a sophistication and ambition few associate with the land of warring clans and burning castles.

Prehistoric Scotland

Scotland, like the rest of prehistoric Britain, was settled by successive waves of peoples arriving from the east. These first inhabitants were **hunter-gatherers**, whose heaps of animal bones and shells have been excavated, amongst other places, in the caves along the coast near East Wemyss in Fife. Around 4500 BC, **Neolithic farming peoples** from the European mainland began moving into Scotland. To provide themselves with land for their cereal crops and grazing for their livestock, they cleared large areas of upland forest, usually by fire, and in the process created the characteristic moorland landscapes of much of modern Scotland. These early farmers established permanent settlements, some of which, like the well-preserved village of **Skara Brae** on Orkney, were near the sea, enabling them to supplement their diet by fishing and develop their skills as boat-builders. The Neolithic settlements were not as isolated as was once imagined: geological evidence has, for instance, revealed that the stone used to make axe-heads found in the Hebrides was quarried in Northern Ireland.

Settlement spurred the development of more complex forms of religious belief. The Neolithic peoples built large chambered burial mounds or **cairns**, such as **Maes Howe** in Orkney. This reverence for human remains suggests a belief in some form of afterlife, a concept that the next wave of settlers, the **Beaker people**, certainly believed in. They placed pottery beakers filled with drink in the tombs of their dead to assist the passage of the deceased on their journey to, or their stay in, the next world. The Beaker people also built the mysterious **stone circles**, thirty of which have been discovered in Scotland. Such monuments were a massive commitment in terms of time and energy, with many of the stones carried from miles away, just as they were at Stonehenge in England, the most famous stone circle of all. One of the best-known Scottish circles is that of **Calanais** on the Isle of Lewis, where a dramatic series of monoliths (single standing stones) form avenues leading towards a circle made up of thirteen standing stones. The exact function of the circles is still unknown, but many of the stones are aligned with the position of the sun at certain points in its annual cycle, suggesting that the monuments are related to the changing of the seasons.

The Beaker people also brought the **Bronze Age** to Scotland. Bronze, an alloy of copper and tin, was stronger and more flexible than its predecessor, flint, which had long been used for axe-heads and knives. New materials led directly to the development of more effective weapons, and the sword and the shield made their first appearance around 1000 BC. Agricultural needs plus new weaponry added up to a state of endemic warfare as villagers raided their neighbours to steal livestock and grain. The Bronze Age peoples responded to the danger by developing a range of defences, among them the spectacular

hillforts, great earthwork defences, many of which are thought to have been occupied from around 1000 BC and remained in use throughout the Iron Age, sometimes far longer. Less spectacular but equally practical were the **crannogs**, smaller settlements built on artificial islands constructed of logs, earth, stones and brush, such as Cherry Island in Loch Ness.

Conflict in Scotland intensified in the first millennium BC as successive waves of **Celtic** settlers, arriving from the south, increased competition for land. Around 400 BC, the Celts brought the technology of **iron** with them and, as Winston Churchill put it, "Men armed with iron entered Britain and killed the men of bronze." These fractious times witnessed the construction of hundreds of **brochs** or fortified towers. Concentrated along the Atlantic coast and in the northern and western isles, the brochs were dry-stone fortifications (that is, built without mortar or cement) often over 40ft in height. Some historians claim they provided protection for small coastal settlements from the attentions of Roman slave traders. Much the best-preserved broch is on the Shetland island of **Mousa**; its double walls rise to about 40ft, only a little short of their original height. The Celts continued to migrate north almost up until Julius Caesar's first incursion into Britain in 55 BC.

At the end of the prehistoric period, immediately prior to the arrival of the Romans, Scotland was divided among a number of warring Iron Age tribes, who, apart from raiding, were preoccupied with wresting a living from the land, growing barley and oats, rearing sheep, hunting deer and fishing for salmon. The Romans were to write these people into history under the collective name Picti, or **Picts**, meaning painted people, after their body tattoos.

The Romans

The **Roman conquest** of Britain began in 43 AD, almost a century after Caesar's first invasion. By 80 AD the Roman governor, Agricola, felt secure enough in the south of Britain to begin an invasion of the north, building a string of forts across the Clyde–Forth line and defeating a large force of Scottish tribes at Mons Graupius. The long-term effect of his campaign, however, was slight. Work on a major fort – to be the base for 5000 soldiers – at Inchtuthill, on the Tay, was abandoned before it was finished, and the legions withdrew south. In 123 AD the emperor **Hadrian** decided to seal the frontier against the northern tribes and built **Hadrian's Wall**, which stretched from the Solway Firth to the Tyne and was the first formal division of the island of Britain. Twenty years later, the Romans again ventured north and built the **Antonine Wall** between the Clyde and the Forth. This was manned for about forty years, but thereafter the Romans, frustrated by the inhospitable terrain of the Highlands, largely gave up their attempt to subjugate the north, and instead adopted a policy of containment.

It was the Romans who produced the first **written** accounts of the peoples of Scotland. In the second century AD, the Greco–Egyptian geographer Ptolemy drew up the first-known map of Scotland, which identified seventeen tribal territories. Other descriptions were less scientific, compounding the mixture of fear and contempt with which the Romans regarded their Pictish neighbours. Dio Cassius, a Roman commentator writing in 197 AD, informed his readers:

They live in huts, go naked and unshod. They mostly have a democratic government, and are much addicted to robbery. They can bear hunger and cold and all manner of hardship; they will retire into their marshes and hold out for days with only their heads above water, and in the forest they will subsist on barks and roots.

The Dark Ages

In the years following the departure of the Romans, traditionally put at 450 AD, the population of Scotland changed considerably. By 500 the **Picts** occupied the northern isles, and the north and the east as far south as Fife. Today their settlements can be generally identified by place names with a "Pit" prefix, such as Pitlochry, and by the existence of carved symbol stones, like those found at Aberlemno in Angus. To the west, between Dumbarton and Carlisle, was a population of **Britons**. Many of the Briton leaders had Roman names, which suggests that they were a Romanized Celtic people, possibly a combination of tribes maintained by the Romans as a buffer between the Wall and the northern tribes, and peoples pushed west by the Anglo-Saxon invaders landing on the east coast. Both the Britons and the Picts spoke variations of P-Celtic, from which Welsh, Cornish and Breton developed.

On the west coast, to the north and west of the Britons, lived the **Scotti**, Irish-Celtic invaders who would eventually give their name to the whole country. The first Scotti arrived in the Western Isles from Ireland in the fourth century AD, and about a century later their great king, Fergus Mor, moved his base from Antrim to Dunadd, near Lochgilphead, where he founded the kingdom of Dalriada. The Scotti spoke Q-Celtic, the precursor of modern Gaelic. On the east coast, the Germanic **Angles** had sailed north along the coast to carve out an enclave around Dunbar in East Lothian. The final addition to the ethnic mix was also non-Celtic; from around 800 AD, **Norse** invaders began to arrive, settling mainly in the northern isles (see box below) and the northeast of the mainland.

The next few centuries saw almost constant warfare among the different groups. The main issue was land, but this was frequently complicated by the need of the warrior castes, who dominated all of these cultures, to exhibit martial prowess. Military conquests did play their part in bringing the peoples of Scotland together, but the most persuasive force was **Christianity**. Many of

C

The northern isles

With their sophisticated ships and navigational skills, the **Vikings**, who began their expansion in the eighth century, soon gained supremacy over the Pictish peoples in Shetland, Orkney, the extreme northeast corner of the mainland and the Western Isles. In 872, the king of Norway set up an earldom in **Orkney** from which **Shetland** was also governed: for the next six centuries the northern isles took a path distinct from the rest of what is now called Scotland, becoming a base for raiding and colonization in much of the rest of Britain and Ireland, and a link in the chain that connected Faroe, Iceland, Greenland and, more tenuously, North America. Norse culture flourished, and buildings such as St Magnus Cathedral in Kirkwall, Orkney, begun in 1137, give some idea of its energy. However, there were bouts of unrest, and finally Shetland was brought under direct rule from Norway at the end of the twelfth century.

When Norway united with Sweden under the Danish crown in the fourteenth century, Norse power began to wane and Scottish influence to increase. In 1469, a marriage was arranged between Margaret, daughter of the Danish king Christian I, and the future King James III of Scotland. Short of cash for her dowry, Christian mortgaged Orkney to Scotland in 1468, followed by Shetland in 1469; neither pledge was ever successfully redeemed. The laws, religion and administration of the northern isles became Scottish, though their Norse heritage is still very evident in place names, dialect and culture.

the Britons had been Christians since Roman times and it had been a Briton, St Ninian, who conducted the first missionary work among the Picts at the end of the fourth century. Attempts to convert the Picts were resumed in the sixth century by **St Columba**, who, as one of the Gaelic-speaking Scotti, demonstrated that Christianity could provide a bridge between the different tribes.

Christianity proved attractive to pagan kings because it seemed to offer them extra supernatural powers. As St Columba declared, when he inaugurated his cousin Aidan as king of Dalriada in 574, "Believe firmly, O Aidan, that none of your enemies will be able to resist you unless you first deal falsely against me and my successors." This combination of spiritual and political power, when taken with Columba's establishment of the island of **Iona** as a centre of Christian culture, opened the way for many peaceable contacts between the Picts and Scotti. Intermarriage became commonplace, and the Scotti king Kenneth MacAlpine, who united Dalriada and Pictland in 843, was the son of a Pictish princess (the Picts traced succession through the female line). Similarly, MacAlpine's creation of the united kingdom of **Alba**, later known as **Scotia**, was part of a process of integration rather than outright conquest. Kenneth and his successors gradually extended the frontiers of their kingdom by marriage and force of arms until, by 1034, almost all of what we now call Scotland was under their rule.

The Middle Ages

By the time of his death in 1034, **Malcolm II** was recognized as the king of Scotia. He was not, though, a national king in the sense that we understand the term, as under the Gaelic system kings were elected from the *derbfine*, a group made up of those whose great-grandfathers had been kings. The chosen successor, supposedly the fittest to rule, was known as the *tanist*. By the eleventh century, however, Scottish kings had become familiar with the principle of heredity, and were often tempted to bend the rules of tanistry. Thus, Malcolm secured the succession of his grandson **Duncan** by murdering a potential rival *tanist*. Duncan, in turn, was killed by **Macbeth** in 1040. Macbeth was not, therefore, the villain of Shakespeare's imagination, but simply an ambitious Scot of royal blood acting in a relatively conventional way.

C

CONTEXTS | History

Kings and queens of Scotland

Kenneth I 842–58	**Duncan I** 1034–40	**Margaret** 1286–90
Donald I 858–62	**Macbeth** 1040–57	**John Balliol** 1292–96
Constantine I 862–76	**Malcolm III** ("Canmore")	**Robert I** ("the Bruce")
Aed 876–78	1057–93	1306–29
Giric 878–89	**Donald III** 1093–94	**David II** 1329–71
Donald II 889–900	**Duncan II** 1094	**Robert II** 1371–90
Constantine II 900–43	**Donald III** 1094–97	**Robert III** 1390–1406
Malcolm I 943–54	**Edgar** 1097–1107	**James I** 1406–37
Indulf 954–62	**Alexander I** 1107–24	**James II** 1437–60
Duf 962–66	**David I** 1124–53	**James III** 1460–88
Culén 966–71	**Malcolm IV** 1153–65	**James IV** 1488–1513
Kenneth II 971–95	**William the Lion** 1165–	**James V** 1513–42
Constantine III 995–97	1214	**Mary** ("Queen of Scots")
Kenneth III 997–1005	**Alexander II** 1214–49	1542–67
Malcolm II 1005–34	**Alexander III** 1249–86	**James VI** 1567–1625

The victory over Macbeth in 1057 of **Malcolm III**, known as Canmore ("Bighead"), marked the beginning of a period of fundamental change in Scottish society. Having avenged his father Duncan, Malcolm III, who had spent the previous seventeen years at the English court, sought to apply to Scotland a range of ideas he had brought back with him. He and his heirs established a secure dynasty based on succession through the male line and introduced **feudalism** into Scotland, a system that was diametrically opposed to the Gaelic system, which rested on blood ties: the followers of a Gaelic king were his kindred, whereas the followers of a feudal king were vassals bought with land. The Canmores successfully feudalized much of southern and eastern Scotland by making grants to their Norman, Breton and Flemish followers but, beyond that, traditional clan-based forms of social relations persisted.

The Canmores, independent of the local nobility, who remained a military threat, also began to reform the **Church**. This development started with the efforts of **Margaret**, Malcolm III's English wife, who brought Scottish religious practices into line with those of the rest of Europe and was eventually canonized. **David I** continued the process by importing monks to found a series of monasteries, principally along the border at Kelso, Melrose, Jedburgh and Dryburgh. By 1200 the entire country was covered by a network of eleven bishoprics, although Church organization remained weak within the Highlands. Similarly, the dynasty founded a series of **royal burghs**, towns such as Edinburgh, Stirling and Berwick, and bestowed upon them charters recognizing them as centres of trade. The charters usually granted a measure of self-government, vested in the town corporation or guild, and the monarchy hoped this liberality would both encourage loyalty and increase the prosperity of the kingdom. Scotland's Gaelic-speaking clans had little influence within the burghs, and by 1550 Scots – a northern version of Anglo-Saxon – had become the main **language** throughout the Lowlands.

The policies of the Canmores laid the basis for a **cultural rift** in Scotland between the Highland and Lowland communities. Before that became an issue, however, the Scots had to face a major threat from the south. In 1286 Alexander III died, and a hotly disputed succession gave **Edward I**, King of England, an opportunity to subjugate Scotland. In 1291 Edward presided over a conference where the rival claimants to the Scottish throne presented their cases. Edward chose **John Balliol** in preference to **Robert the Bruce**, his main rival; he also obliged Balliol to pay him homage, thus turning Scotland into a vassal kingdom. Bruce refused to accept the decision, thereby continuing the conflict, and in 1295 Balliol renounced his allegiance to Edward and sided with France – the beginning of what is known as the "Auld Alliance". In the conflict that followed, the Bruce family sided with the English, Balliol was defeated and imprisoned, and Edward seized control of almost all of Scotland.

Edward had shown little mercy during his conquest of Scotland – he had, for example, had most of the population of Berwick massacred – and his cruelty seems to have provoked a truly national resistance. This focused on **William Wallace**, a man of relatively lowly origins who raised an army of peasants, lesser knights and townsmen that was fundamentally different to the armies raised by the nobility. Figures like Balliol, holding lands in England, France and Scotland, were part of an international aristocracy for whom warfare was merely the means by which they struggled for power. Wallace, by contrast, led proto-nationalist forces determined to expel the English from their country. Probably for that very reason Wallace never received the support of the nobility and, after a bitter ten-year campaign, he was betrayed and executed in London in 1305.

With Wallace out of the way, feudal intrigue resumed. In 1306 Robert the Bruce, the erstwhile ally of the English, defied Edward and had himself crowned king of Scotland. Edward died the following year, but the unrest dragged on until 1314, when Bruce decisively defeated a huge English army under Edward II at the battle of **Bannockburn**. At last Bruce was firmly in control of his kingdom, and in 1320 the Scots asserted their right to independence in a successful petition to the pope, now known as the **Declaration of Arbroath**.

In the years following Bruce's death in 1329, the Scottish monarchy gradually declined in influence. The last of the Bruce dynasty died in 1371, to be succeeded by the "Stewards", hence **Stewarts**, but thereafter a succession of Scottish rulers, culminating with James VI in 1567, came to the throne when still children. The power vacuum was filled by the nobility, whose key members exercised control as Scotland's regents while carving out territories where they ruled with the power, if not the title, of kings. At the close of the fifteenth century, the Douglas family alone controlled Galloway, Lothian, Stirlingshire, Clydesdale and Annandale. The more vigorous monarchs of the period, notably **James I**, did their best to curb the power of such dynasties, but their efforts were usually nullified at the next regency. **James IV**, the most talented of the early Stewarts, might have restored the authority of the Crown, but his invasion of England ended in a terrible defeat for the Scots – and his own death – at the battle of **Flodden Field**.

The reign of **Mary, Queen of Scots** typified the problems of the Scottish monarchy. Mary came to the throne when just one week old, and immediately caught the attention of the English king, Henry VIII, who sought, first by persuasion and then by military might, to secure her hand in marriage for his 5-year-old son, Edward. Beginning in 1544, the English launched a series of devastating attacks on Scotland, an episode Sir Walter Scott later called the "Rough Wooing", until, in the face of another English invasion in 1548, the Scots – or at least those not supporting Henry – turned to the "Auld Alliance". The French king proposed marriage between Mary and the Dauphin Francis, promising in return military assistance against the English. The 6-year-old queen sailed for France in 1548, leaving her loyal nobles and their French allies in control, and her husband succeeded to the French throne in 1559. When she returned thirteen years later, following the death of Francis, she had to pick her way through the rival ambitions of her nobility and deal with something entirely new – the religious Reformation.

The Reformation

The **Reformation** in Scotland was a complex social process, whose threads are often hard to unravel. Nevertheless, it is quite clear that, by the end of the sixteenth century, the established Church was held in general contempt. Many members of the higher clergy regarded their relationship with the Church purely in economic terms, and forty percent of known illegitimate births (ie those subsequently legitimized) were the product of the "celibate" clergy's liaisons.

Another spur to the Scottish Reformation was the identification of Protestantism with anti-French feeling. In 1554 Mary of Guise, the French mother of the absent Queen Mary, had become regent, and her habit of appointing Frenchmen to high office was seen as part of an attempt to subordinate Scotland's interests to those of France. There was considerable resentment, and in 1557 a group of nobles banded together to form the **Lords of the Congregation**, whose dual purpose was to oppose French influence and promote the reformed religion. With English military backing, the Protestant lords succeeded in deposing the

French regent in 1560, and, when the Scottish Parliament assembled shortly afterwards, it asserted the primacy of Protestantism by forbidding the Mass and abolishing the authority of the pope. The nobility proceeded to confiscate two-thirds of Church lands, a huge prize that did much to bolster their new beliefs.

Even without the economic incentives, Protestantism was a highly charged political doctrine. **Luther** had argued that each individual's conscience was capable of discerning God's will. This meant that a hierarchical priesthood, existing to interpret God's will, was unnecessary and that the people themselves might conclude their rulers were breaking God's laws, in which case the monarch should be opposed or even deposed. This point was made very clearly to Queen Mary by the Protestant

△ John Knox statue, Edinburgh

reformer **John Knox** at their first meeting in 1561. Subjects, he told her, were not bound to obey an ungodly monarch.

Knox, born in East Lothian, had returned to Scotland in 1559 from exile. He was a follower of the Genevan reformer Calvin, who combined Luther's views on individual conscience with a belief in predestination. Calvinism argued that an omnipotent God must know everything, including the destinies of every human being. Consequently, it was determined before birth who was to be part of the Elect, bound for heavenly glory, and who was not, a doctrine that placed enormous pressure on its adherents to demonstrate by their godly behaviour that they were of the Elect. This was the doctrine that Knox brought back to Scotland and laid out in his Articles of Confession of Faith, better known as the **Scot's Confession**, which was to form the basis of the reformed faith for over seventy years.

Mary ducked and weaved, trying to avoid an open breach with her Protestant subjects. The fires of popular displeasure were kept well stoked by Knox, however, who declared, "one Mass was more fearful than if ten thousand enemies were landed in any part of the realm." At the same time, Mary was engaged in a balancing act between the factions of the Scottish nobility. Her difficulties were exacerbated by her disastrous second marriage to **Lord Darnley**, a cruel and politically inept character, whose jealousy led to his involvement in the murder of Mary's favourite, David Rizzio, who was dragged from the queen's supper room at Holyrood and stabbed 56 times. The incident caused the Scottish Protestants more than a little unease, but they were entirely scandalized in 1567, when Darnley himself was murdered and Mary promptly married the **Earl of Bothwell**, widely believed to be the murderer. This was too much to bear, and the Scots rose in rebellion, driving Mary into exile in England at the age of just 25. The queen's illegitimate half-brother, the Earl of Moray, became regent, and her son, the infant James, was left behind to be raised a Protestant prince. Mary, meanwhile, became perceived as such a threat to the English throne that Queen Elizabeth I had her executed in 1587.

Knox could now concentrate on the organization of the reformed Church, or **Kirk**, which he envisaged as a body empowered to intervene in the daily lives of the people. **Andrew Melville**, another leading reformer, wished to push this theocratic vision further. He proposed the abolition of all traces of episcopacy – the rule of the bishops in the Church – and that the Kirk should adopt a **Presbyterian** structure, administered by a hierarchy of assemblies, part-elected and part-appointed. At the bottom of the chain, beneath the General Assembly, Synod and Presbytery, would be the Kirk session, responsible for church affairs, the performance of the minister and the morals of the parish. In 1592, the Melvillian party achieved a measure of success when presbyteries and synods were accepted as legal Church courts and the office of bishop was suspended.

James VI disliked Presbyterianism because its quasi-democratic structure – particularly the lack of royally appointed bishops – appeared to threaten his authority. He was, however, unable to resist the reformers until, strengthened by his installation as James I of England after Elizabeth's death in 1603, he restored the Scottish bishops in 1610. The argument about the nature of Kirk organization would lead to bloody conflict in the years after James's death.

The religious wars

Raised in Episcopalian England, **Charles I** had little understanding of Scottish reformism. He believed in the Divine Right of Kings, an authoritarian creed that claimed the monarch was God's representative on earth and, therefore, his authority had divine sanction, a concept entirely counter to Protestant thought. In 1637 Charles attempted to impose a new prayer book on the Kirk, laying down forms of worship in line with those favoured by the High Anglican Church. The reformers denounced these changes as "popery" and organized the **National Covenant**, a religious pledge that committed the signatories to "labour by all means lawful to recover the purity and liberty of the Gospel as it was established and professed".

Charles declared all the "**Covenanters**" to be rebels, a proclamation endorsed by his Scottish bishops. Consequently, when the king backed down from military action and called a General Assembly of the Kirk, the assembly promptly abolished the episcopacy. Charles pronounced the proceedings illegal, but lack of finance stopped him from mounting an effective military campaign – whereas the Covenanters, well financed by the Kirk, assembled a proficient army under Alexander Leslie. In desperation, Charles summoned the English Parliament, the first for eleven years, hoping it would pay for an army. But, like the calling of the General Assembly, the decision was a disaster and parliament was much keener to criticize his policies than to raise taxes. In response Charles declared war on parliament in 1642.

Until 1650, Scotland was ruled by the Covenanters, and the power of the Presbyterian Kirk grew considerably. Laws were passed establishing schools in every parish and, less usefully, banning trade with Catholic countries. The only effective opposition to the theocratic state came from the **Marquis of Montrose**, who had initially supported the Covenant but lined up with the king when war broke out. His army was drawn from the Highlands and Islands, where the Kirk's influence was weakest. Montrose was a gifted campaigner who won several notable victories against the Covenanters, but the reluctance of his troops to stay south of the Highland Line made it impossible for him to capitalize on his successes, and he was eventually captured and executed in 1650.

Largely confined to the peripheries of Scotland, Montrose's campaigns were a side show to the **Civil War** being waged further south. Here, the Covenanters and the English Parliamentarians faced the same royal enemy and in 1643 formed an alliance. Indeed, it was the Scots army that captured Charles at Newark in Nottinghamshire, in 1646. There was, however, friction between the allies. Many of the Parliamentarians, including Cromwell, were **Independents**, who favoured a looser form of doctrinal control within the state Church than did the Presbyterians, and were inclined towards religious toleration for the law-abiding sects outside the state Church. In addition, the Scots believed the English were tainted with **Erastianism** – a belief in placing the secular authority of parliament over the spiritual authority of the Church.

The Parliamentarians in turn suspected the Scots of hankering for the return of the monarchy, a suspicion confirmed when, at the invitation of the earl of Argyll, the future Charles II came back to Scotland in 1650. To regain his Scottish kingdom, Charles was obliged to renounce his father and sign the Covenant, two bitter pills taken to impress the population. In the event, the "Presbyterian restoration" was short-lived. Cromwell invaded, defeated the Scots at Dunbar and forced Charles into exile. Until the Restoration of 1660, Scotland was united with England and governed by seven commissioners.

Although the restoration of **Charles II** brought bishops back to the Kirk, they were integrated into an essentially Presbyterian structure of Kirk sessions and presbyteries, and the General Assembly, which had been abolished by Cromwell, was not re-established. Over three hundred clergymen, a third of the Scottish ministry, refused to accept the reinstatement of the bishops and were edged out of the Church, forced to hold open-air services, called **Conventicles**, which Charles did his best to suppress. Religious opposition inspired military resistance and the Lowlands witnessed scenes of brutal repression as the king's forces struggled to keep control in what was known as "The Killing Time". In the southwest, a particular stronghold of the Covenanters, the government imported Highlanders, the so-called "Highland Host", to root out the opposition, which they did with great barbarity.

Charles II was succeeded by his brother **James VII** (James II of England), whose ardent Catholicism caused a Protestant backlash in England. In 1689, he was forced into exile in France and the throne passed to **Mary**, his Protestant daughter, and her Dutch husband, **William of Orange**. In Scotland, William and Mary restored the full Presbyterian structure and abolished bishops, though they chose not to restore the political and legal functions of the Kirk, which remained subject to parliamentary control. This settlement ended Scotland's religious wars and completed its Reformation.

The Union

Although the question of Kirk organization was settled in 1690, the political issue of the relationship between the Crown and the Scottish Parliament was not. From 1689 to 1697, William was at war with France, a war partly financed by Scottish taxes and partly fought by Scottish soldiers. Yet many Scots, mindful of the Auld Alliance, disapproved of the war and others suffered financially from the disruption to trade with France. There were other economic irritants too, principally the legally sanctioned monopoly that English merchants had over trade with the English colonies. This monopoly inspired the **Darien Scheme**,

The Highlands

The country that was united with England in 1707 contained three distinct cultures: in south and east Scotland, they spoke **Scots**; the local dialect in Shetland, Orkney and much of the northeast, though Scots-based, contained elements of **Norn** (Old Norse), while the language of the rest of north and west Scotland, including the Western Isles, was **Gaelic**. These linguistic differences were paralleled by different forms of social organization and customs. The people of north and west Scotland were mostly **pastoralists**, moving their sheep and cattle to Highland pastures in the summer and returning to the glens in the winter. They lived in single-room dwellings, heated by a central peat fire and sometimes shared with livestock, and in hard times they would subsist on cakes made from the blood of their live cattle mixed with oatmeal. **Highlanders** supplemented their meagre income by raiding their clan neighbours and the prosperous Lowlands, whose inhabitants regarded their northern compatriots with a mixture of fear and contempt. In the early seventeenth century, Montgomerie, a Lowland poet, suggested that God had created the first Highlander out of horseshit. When God asked his creation what he would do, the reply was "I will doun to the Lowland, Lord, and thair steill a kow."

It would be a mistake, however, to infer from the primitive nature of Highland life that the institutions of this society had existed from time immemorial. This is especially true of the "**clan**", a term that only appears in its modern usage in the sixteenth century. In theory, the clan bound together blood relatives who shared a common ancestor, a concept clearly derived from the ancient Gaelic notion of kinship. But in practice many of the clans were of non-Gaelic origin – such as the Frasers, Sinclairs and Stewarts, all of Anglo-Norman descent – and it was the mythology of a common ancestor, rather than the actuality, that cemented the clans together. Furthermore, clans were often made up of people with a variety of surnames, and there are documented cases of individuals changing their names when they swapped allegiances.

At the upper end of Highland society was the **clan chief** (who might have been a minor figure, like MacDonald of Glen Coe, or a great lord, like the duke of Argyll, head of the Campbells), who provided protection for his followers: they would, in turn, fight for him when called upon to do so. Below the clan chief were the **chieftains of the septs**, or subunits of the clan, and then came the **tacksmen**, major tenants of the chief to whom they were frequently related. The tacksmen sublet their land to **tenants**, who were at the bottom of the social scale. The Highlanders wore a simple belted plaid wrapped around the body – rather than the kilt – and not until the late seventeenth century were certain **tartans** roughly associated with particular clans. The detailed codification of the tartan was produced by the Victorians, whose romantic vision of Highland life originated with George IV's visit to Scotland in 1822, when he appeared in an elaborate version of Highland dress, complete with flesh-coloured tights (for more on tartan, see box on p.599).

a plan to establish a Scottish colony in Panama. The colonists set off in 1698, but, thwarted by the opposition of both William and the English merchants, the scheme proved a miserable failure. The colony collapsed with the loss of £200,000 – an amount equal to half the value of the entire coinage in Scotland – and an angry Scottish Parliament threatened to refuse the king taxes as rioting broke out in the cities.

Meanwhile, in the north, the Highlanders blamed William for the massacre of the **MacDonalds of Glen Coe**. In 1691 William had offered pardons to those Highland chiefs who had opposed his accession, on condition that they took an oath of allegiance by New Year's Day 1692. Alasdair MacDonald of Glen Coe had turned up at the last minute, but his efforts to take the oath were frustrated by the king's officials, who were determined to see his clan, well known for their support of the Stewarts, destroyed. In February 1692, Captain Robert Campbell quartered his men in Glen Coe and, two weeks later, in the middle of the night, his troops acted on their secret orders and slaughtered as many MacDonalds as they could. Thirty-eight died, and the massacre caused a national scandal, especially among the clans, where "murder under trust" – killing those offering you shelter – was considered a particularly heinous crime.

The situation in Scotland was further complicated by the question of the succession. Mary died without leaving an heir and, on William's death in 1702, the crown passed to her sister **Anne**, who was also childless. In response, the English Parliament secured the Protestant succession by passing the Act of Settlement, which named the Electress Sophia of Hanover as the next in line to the throne. The Act did not, however, apply in Scotland, and the English feared that the Scots would invite James Edward Stewart back from France to be their king. Consequently, Parliament appointed commissioners charged with the consideration of "proper methods towards attaining a union with Scotland". The project seemed doomed to failure when the Scottish Parliament passed the **Act of Security** in 1703, stating that Scotland would not accept a Hanoverian monarch unless they had first received guarantees protecting their religion and their trade.

Nevertheless, despite the strength of anti-English feeling, the Scottish Parliament passed the **Act of Union** by 110 votes to 69 in January 1707. Some historians have explained the vote in terms of bribery and corruption. This certainly played a part (the duke of Hamilton, for example, switched sides at a key moment and was subsequently rewarded with an English dukedom), but there were other factors. Scottish politicians were divided between the Cavaliers – Jacobites (supporters of the Stewarts) and Episcopalians – and the Country party, whose Presbyterian members dreaded the return of the Stewarts more than they disliked the Hanoverians. There were commercial considerations too. In 1705 the English Parliament had passed the Alien Act, which threatened to impose severe penalties on cross-border trade, whereas the Union gave merchants of both countries free access to each other's markets. The Act of Union also guaranteed the Scottish legal system and the Presbyterian Kirk, and offered compensation to those who had lost money in the Darien Scheme.

Under the terms of the Act, both parliaments were to be replaced by a new British Parliament based in London, with the Scots apportioned 45 MPs and 16 peers. There were riots when the terms became known, but no sustained opposition.

The Jacobite risings

When James VII/II was deposed he had fled to France, where he planned the reconquest of his kingdom with the support of the French king. In 1702, James's successor, William, died, and the hopes of the Stewarts passed to his cousin James, the "Old Pretender" (Pretender in the sense of having pretensions to the throne; Old to distinguish him from his son Charles, the "Young Pretender"). James's followers became known as **Jacobites**, derived from Jacobus, the Latin equivalent of James. The British crown passed to Anne, however, and after her death and the accession of the Hanoverian George I, the first major **Jacobite uprising** occurred in 1715. Its timing appeared perfect. Scottish opinion was moving against the Union, which had failed to bring Scotland any tangible economic benefits. The English had also been accused of bad faith when, contrary to their pledges, they attempted to impose their legal practices on the Scots. Neither were Jacobite sentiments confined to Scotland. There were many in England who toasted the "king across the water" and showed no enthusiasm for the new German ruler. In September 1715 the fiercely Jacobite John Erskine, Earl of Mar, raised the Stewart standard at Braemar Castle. Just eight days later, he captured Perth, where he gathered an army of over 10,000 men, drawn mostly from the Episcopalians of northeast Scotland and from the Highlands. Mar's rebellion took the government by surprise. They had only 4000 soldiers in Scotland, under the command of the duke of Argyll, but Mar dithered until he lost the military advantage. There was an indecisive battle at Sheriffmuir in November, but by the time the Old Pretender arrived the following month 6000 veteran Dutch troops had reinforced Argyll. The rebellion disintegrated rapidly and James slunk back to exile in France in February 1716.

The **Jacobite uprising** of 1745, led by James's dashing son, Charles Edward Stewart (known as "**Bonnie Prince Charlie**"), had little chance of success. The Hanoverians had consolidated their hold on the English throne, Lowland society was uniformly loyalist, and even among the Highlanders Charles attracted only just over half of the 20,000 clansmen who could have marched with him. Nevertheless, after a decisive victory over government forces at Prestonpans, Charles made a spectacular advance into England, getting as far as Derby. London was in a state of panic: its shops were closed and the Bank of England, fearing a run on sterling, slowed withdrawals by paying out in sixpences. But Derby was as far south as Charles got. On December 6, threatened by superior forces, the Jacobites decided to retreat to Scotland. The duke of Cumberland was sent in pursuit and the two armies met on **Culloden Moor**, near Inverness, in April 1746. Outnumbered and outgunned, the Jacobites were swept from the field, losing over 1200 men compared to Cumberland's 300 or so. After the battle, many of the wounded Jacobites were slaughtered, an atrocity that earned Cumberland the nickname "Butcher". Jacobite hopes died at Culloden and the prince lived out the rest of his life in drunken exile.

In the aftermath of the uprising, the wearing of tartan, the bearing of arms and the playing of bagpipes were all banned. Rebel chiefs lost their land and the Highlands were placed under military occupation. Most significantly, the government prohibited the private armies of the chiefs, thereby effectively destroying the clan system.

The Highland Clearances

Once the clan chief was forbidden his own army, he had no need of the large tenantry that had previously been a vital military asset. Conversely, the second half of the eighteenth century saw the Highland population increase dramatically after the introduction of the easy-to-grow and nutritious **potato**. Between 1745 and 1811, the population of the Outer Hebrides, for example, rose from 13,000 to 24,500. The clan chiefs adopted different policies to deal with the new situation. Some encouraged emigration, and as many as 6000 Highlanders left for the Americas between 1800 and 1803 alone. Other landowners developed alternative forms of employment for their tenantry, mainly fishing and kelping. **Kelp** (brown seaweed) was gathered and burnt to produce soda ash, which was used in the manufacture of soap, glass and explosives. There was a rising market for soda ash until the 1810s, with the price increasing from £2 a ton in 1760 to £20 in 1808, making a fortune for some landowners and providing thousands of Highlanders with temporary employment. Other landowners developed **sheep runs** on the Highland pastures, introducing hardy breeds like the black-faced Linton and the Cheviot. But extensive sheep farming proved incompatible with a high peasant population, and many landowners decided to clear their estates of tenants, some of whom were forcibly moved to tiny plots of marginal land, where they were to farm as **crofters**.

The pace of these **Highland Clearances** accelerated after the end of the Napoleonic Wars in 1815, when the market price for kelp, fish and cattle declined, leaving sheep as the only profitable Highland product. The most notorious Clearances took place on the estates of the countess of Sutherland, who owned a million acres in northern Scotland. Between 1807 and 1821, around 15,000 people were thrown off her land, evictions carried out by Patrick Sellar, the estate factor, with considerable brutality. Those who failed to leave by the appointed time had their homes burnt in front of them, and one elderly woman, who failed to get out of her home after it was torched, subsequently died from her burns. The local sheriff charged Sellar with her death, but a jury of landowners acquitted him – and the sheriff was sacked. As the dispossessed Highlanders scratched a living from the acid soils of tiny crofts, they learnt through bitter experience the limitations of the clan. Famine followed, forcing large-scale emigration to America and Canada and leaving the huge uninhabited areas found in the region today.

By no means all landowners acted cruelly or insensitively, however, and many settlements around Scotland, from Inveraray on the west coast to Portsoy in the northeast, owe their existence to so-called "improving landlords", who invested in infrastructure such as fishing harbours, decent housing and communities of sustainable size. They created a legacy not only in the built environment but also brought economic prosperity to previously disadvantaged areas. Those left crofting, on the other hand, still eked out a precarious existence, often by taking seasonal employment away from home. In 1886, in response to the social unrest, Gladstone's Liberal government passed the **Crofters' Holdings Act**, which conceded three of the crofters' demands: security of tenure, fair rents to be decided independently and the right to pass on crofts by inheritance. But Gladstone did not attempt to increase the amount of land available for crofting and shortage of land remained a major problem until the **Land Settlement Act** of 1919 made provision for the creation of new crofts. Nevertheless, the population of the Highlands has continued to decline since then, with many of the region's young people finding city life more appealing.

Industrialization

Glasgow was the powerhouse of Scotland's **Industrial Revolution**. The passage from Glasgow to the Americas was much shorter than that from rival English ports and a lucrative transatlantic trade in tobacco had developed as early as the seventeenth century. This in turn stimulated Scottish manufacturing, since, under the terms of the Navigation Acts, Americans were not allowed to trade manufactured goods. Scottish-produced linen, paper and wrought iron were exchanged for Virginia tobacco and, when the American War of Independence disrupted the trade in the 1770s and 1780s, the Scots successfully turned to trade with the West Indies and, most important of all, to the production of cotton textiles.

Glasgow's west-coast location gave it ready access to the sources of raw cotton in the Americas, while the rapid growth of the British Empire provided an expanding market for its finished cloth. Initially, the city's **cotton industry**, like the earlier linen industry, was organized domestically, with spinners and weavers working in their homes, but increased demand required mass production and factories. In 1787, Scotland had only nineteen mills; by 1840 there were nearly two hundred.

The growth of the textile industry spurred the development of other industries. In the mid-eighteenth century, the **Carron Ironworks** was founded near Falkirk, specializing in the production of military munitions. Here, the capital and expertise were English, but the location was determined by Scottish coal reserves. By 1800 it was the largest ironworks in Europe. The basis of Scotland's **shipbuilding** industry was laid as early as 1802, when the steam vessel *Charlotte Dundas* was launched on the Forth–Clyde canal. Within thirty years, 95 steam vessels had been built in Scotland, most of them on Clydeside. The growth of the iron and shipbuilding industries, plus the extensive use of steam power, created a massive demand for coal, and pit shafts were sunk across the coalfields of southern Scotland.

Industrialization led to a concentration of Scotland's **population** in the central Lowlands. In 1840 one-third of the country's industrial workers lived in Lanarkshire alone, and Glasgow's population grew from 17,000 in the 1740s to over 200,000 a century later. Such sudden growth created urban overcrowding on a massive scale and, as late as 1861, 64 percent of the entire Scottish population lived in one- or two-room houses. For most Clydesiders, "house" meant a couple of small rooms in a grim tenement building, where many of the poorest families were displaced Highlanders and Irish immigrants, with the Irish arriving in Glasgow at the rate of a thousand a week during the potato famine of the 1840s.

By the late nineteenth century a measure of prosperity had emerged from industrialization, and the well-paid Clydeside engineers went to their forges wearing bowler hats and starched collars. They were confident of the future, but their optimism was misplaced. Scotland's industries were very much geared to the export market, and after **World War I** they found conditions much changed. During the war years, when exports had been curtailed by a combination of U-boat activity and war production, new industries had developed in India and Japan, and the eastern market for Scottish goods never recovered. The postwar world also witnessed a contraction of world trade, which hit the shipbuilding industry very hard and, in turn, damaged the steel and coal industries. By 1931, for instance, pig-iron production was at less than 25 percent of its 1920 output.

These difficulties were compounded by the financial collapse of the early 1930s, and by 1932 28 percent of the Scottish workforce was unemployed. Some 400,000 Scots emigrated between 1921 and 1931, and those who stayed endured some of the worst social conditions in the British Isles. By the late 1930s, Scotland had the highest infant mortality rate in Europe, while some thirty percent of homes had no toilet or bath. There was a partial economic recovery in the mid-1930s, but high unemployment remained until the start of **World War II**.

The Labour movement

In the late eighteenth century, conditions for the labouring population varied enormously. At one extreme, the handloom weavers, working from home, were well paid and much in demand, whereas the coal miners remained serfs, bought and sold with the pits they worked in, until 1799. During this period, the working class gave some support to the **radical movement**, a loosely connected groups of reformers, led by the lower middle class, who took their inspiration from the French Revolution. One of these groups, the "Friends of the People", campaigned for the extension of the right to vote, and such apparently innocuous activities earned one member, Thomas Muir, a sentence of fourteen years' transportation to Australia.

In 1820 the radicals called for a national strike and an insurrection to "show the world that we are determined to be free". At least sixty thousand workers downed tools for a week, and one group set off for the Carron Ironworks to seize arms. The government was, however, well prepared. It slammed radical leaders into prison and a heavy military presence kept control of the streets. The strike fizzled out and three leading radicals, all weavers, were later executed.

The 1832 **Scottish Reform Act** extended the franchise to include a large proportion of the middle class, and thereafter political radicalism assumed a more distinctive working-class character, though its ideals still harked back to the American and French revolutions. In the 1840s the **Chartists** led the campaign for working-class political rights by sending massive petitions to Parliament and organizing huge demonstrations. When Parliament rejected the petitions, the more determined Chartists – the "physical-force men" – urged insurrection. This call to arms was not taken up by the Scottish working class, however, and support for the Chartists fell away. The insurrectionary phase of Scottish labour was over.

During the next thirty years, as Scotland's economy prospered, skilled workers organized themselves into **craft unions**, such as the Amalgamated Society of Engineers, dedicated to negotiating improvements for their members within the status quo. Politically, the trade unions gave their allegiance to the Liberal Party, but the first major crack in the Liberal–trade union alliance came in 1888, when **Keir Hardie** left the Liberals to form the Scottish Socialist Party, which was later merged with the Independent Labour Party, founded in Bradford in 1893. Scottish socialism as represented by the ILP was ethical rather than Marxist in orientation, owing a great deal to the Kirk background of many of its members. But electoral progress was slow, partly because the Roman Catholic priesthood consistently preached against socialism.

In the early years of the twentieth century, two small Marxist groups established themselves on Clydeside: the **Socialist Labour Party**, which concentrated on workplace militancy, and the party-political **British Socialist Party**, whose most famous member was the Marxist lecturer John MacLean. During World War I, the local organizers of the SLP gained considerable influence by playing on the fears of the skilled workers, who felt their status was being undermined by the employment of unskilled workers. After the war, the influence of the shop stewards culminated in a massive campaign for the forty-hour working week. The strikes and demonstrations of the campaign, including one of a hundred thousand people in St George's Square, Glasgow, panicked the government into sending in the troops. But this was no Bolshevik Revolution; as Manny Shinwell, the seamen's leader and future Labour Party politician, observed, "[The troops] had nothing much to do but chat to the local people and drink their cups of tea." The rank and file may have had little interest in revolution, but many of the activists did go on to become leaders within the newly formed Communist Party of Great Britain.

The ILP, by then an affiliated part of the socialist **Labour Party**, made its electoral breakthrough in 1922, when it sent 29 Scottish MPs to Westminster. They set out with high hopes of social progress and reform, aspirations that were dashed, like trade union militancy, by the 1930s Depression. At the 1945 general election, Labour won forty seats in Scotland and, in more recent times, the party has dominated Scottish politics with its gradual eclipse of the Scottish

Conservatives. In 1955 the Conservatives held 36 Scottish seats; by 1995 they had just ten, and by 1997 none at all.

The ILP MPs of the 1920s combined their socialism with a brand of Scottish nationalism. In 1924, for instance, the MP James Maxton had declared his intentions to "make English-ridden, capitalist-ridden Scotland into the Scottish socialist Commonwealth". The Labour Party maintained an official policy of self-government for Scotland, endorsing home rule in 1945 and 1947, but these endorsements were made with less and less enthusiasm. In 1958 Labour abandoned the commitment altogether and adopted a unionist vision of Scotland, much to the chagrin of many Scottish activists.

In 1971 **Upper Clyde Shipbuilders** stood on the brink of closure, its demise symbolizing the failure of traditional Labour politicians to revive Scotland's industrial base, which had resumed its decline after the end of World War II. In the event, UCS was partly saved by the work-in organized by two communist shop stewards, Jimmy Reid and Jimmy Airlie. After fourteen months, the work-in finally succeeded in winning government support to keep part of the shipyard open, and Scots saw the broadly based campaign waged on its behalf as a national issue – Scottish industries set against an indifferent London government. Many socialist Scots, like James Jack, General Secretary of the Scottish TUC, moved towards some form of nationalism. Twenty-one years later, the closure of the steelworks at **Ravenscraig** in Motherwell revived many of the same emotions.

Towards devolution

The **National Party of Scotland** was formed in 1928, its membership mostly drawn from the non-industrial parts of the country. Very much a mixture of practical politicians and left-leaning eccentrics, such as the poet Hugh MacDiarmid, in 1934 it merged with the right-wing Scottish Party to create the **Scottish National Party**. The SNP achieved its electoral breakthrough in 1967 when Winnie Ewing won Hamilton from Labour in a by-election. The following year the SNP won 34 percent of the vote in local government elections,

and both the Labour and Conservative parties, wishing to head off the Nationalists, began to work on schemes to give Scotland a measure of self-government, the term **devolution** becoming common currency in Scottish politics.

The situation took a dynamic turn in 1974, when Labour were returned to power with a wafer-thin majority. The SNP held seven seats, which gave them considerable political leverage, and devolution was firmly on the agenda. The SNP had also run an excellent election campaign, concentrating on North Sea oil, which was now being piped ashore in significant quantities. Their two most popular slogans, "England expects... Scotland's oil" and "Rich Scots or Poor Britons?", seemed to have caught the mood of Scotland.

In 1979 the Labour government, struggling to hold onto office after its "winter

△ Scottish Devolution Referendum poster

of discontent" of strikes had decimated public services, put its devolution proposals before the Scottish people in a **referendum**. The "yes" vote gained 33 percent, the "no" vote 31 percent – but the required forty percent threshold had not been reached. Not for the first time, Scottish opinion had shifted away from home rule; the reluctance to embrace it was based on uncertainty about what might follow, a concern about too many layers of government and, in some areas, a fear that the resulting assembly might be dominated by the Clydeside conurbation. The incoming Conservative government of **Margaret Thatcher** set its face against any form of devolution. It argued that the majority of Scots had voted for parties committed to the Union – namely Labour, the Liberals and themselves – and that only a minority supported the separation advocated by the SNP. At the same time, the government asserted that any form of devolution would lead inevitably to the break-up of the United Kingdom and, therefore, that the devolution solutions put forward by other parties could not be what the Scottish people wanted, because the inescapable result would be separation.

As the Thatcher years rolled on, growing evidence from opinion polls and central and local government elections suggested that few Scottish voters accepted either this reasoning or the implication that Scots did not know what was good for them. The Conservatives' support in Scotland was further eroded by their introduction of the deeply unpopular Community Charge – universally nicknamed the **Poll Tax** – a form of local taxation that took little account of income. The fact that it had been imposed in Scotland a year earlier than in England and Wales was the source of further resentment.

Throughout the 1980s and early 1990s the case for devolution had been made consistently by both Labour and the Liberal Democrats. In 1989 they, together with a cross-section of Scottish organizations, including local government, churches and trade unions, cooperated in the establishment of the **Scottish Constitutional Convention**, a standing conference which developed detailed proposals for the introduction of a devolved Scottish legislature. Initially, the SNP saw the Convention as a diversion from their aim of an independent Scotland firmly attached to the European Union and did not join. Later, however, Nationalists began to argue that devolution might after all offer a stepping stone to independence.

In 1992, having largely rejected Conservative ideology and all but a few of the party's candidates, Scots found themselves still under a Tory government, this time with **John Major** at the helm. By the mid-1990s the momentum towards change was palpable, but without their hands directly on the levers of power, none of the main players could make it happen. Scotland's new political era began with the British general election of 1997, won by Tony Blair's **Labour Party**; the Conservatives were routed across the UK, losing every seat in Scotland. Under the stewardship of Scottish Secretary Donald Dewar, the new Labour government moved swiftly to publish its proposals for devolution and a **referendum** was organized for that September. The electorate responded with a clear endorsement: 75 percent of voters were in favour of establishing a separate Scottish Parliament.

The excitement generated in Scotland by the referendum helped imbue the subsequent establishment of the **parliament** with a palpable sense of destiny, something it had to cling to as many of the fears voiced in 1979 again resurfaced. By and large, however, the optimistic mood was carried through to Scotland's **general election** in 1999 – the first-ever, given that the last elected Scottish parliament in 1707 had not been under universal suffrage. The form of proportional representation adopted for the election made it unlikely that any one party would achieve an overall majority in the 129-seat assembly, and indeed the final result left Labour needing to enter into a coalition with the Liberal Democrats (or LibDems) to achieve a governing majority. The SNP won just under thirty percent of the vote, making them the second largest party. The leader of the Labour group, **Donald Dewar**, became Scotland's First Minister, while the new MSPs (Members of the Scottish Parliament) voted **Sir David Steel**, former leader of the British Liberal Party and one of the elder statesmen of Scottish politics, to be the Presiding Officer.

In a **ceremony** deliberately mixing pomp with down-to-earth, populist touches, the Queen came to the parliament's temporary home in the Church of Scotland Assembly Hall in Edinburgh to open the parliament officially on July 1, 1999. This marked the official transfer of power to the new assembly in matters of education, health, law and order, social work, local government, planning and the environment, economic development, agriculture and fisheries, sport and the arts (Westminster retains control over defence, foreign affairs, major economic and tax issues and social security). The new parliament has the power to initiate new legislation, and to pass bills without the endorsement of Westminster.

The delicate balancing act that the Labour–LibDem **coalition** faced in the first few years of the parliament was to prove that devolved government could still offer distinctive Scottish solutions without breaking from policies being pursued by the Labour government in Westminster. It made its mark with important decisions abolishing tuition fees for Scottish university students, repealing a law banning the promotion of homosexuality in school classrooms and granting state support for the elderly in care, all policies notably to the left of the Labour programme elsewhere in the UK. While the parliament has had to work hard to earn respect from a broadly cynical and demanding media, the general consensus is that the increased scrutiny under which Scottish affairs are now being conducted has brought a greater sense of realism and responsibility to the political scene.

A far greater blow to the credibility of the infant project came in 2000 with the untimely death of First Minister Donald Dewar, widely respected as the one politician of true stature in the parliament. The post of First Minister was taken up by **Henry McLeish**, another former Westminster MP, but within a year he had resigned over financial irregularities, to be replaced in 2001 by **Jack McConnell**, a Labour politician with no experience of the Westminster parliament.

McConnell led Labour to victory in Scotland's second post-devolution election in 2003, though again he had to rely on coalition with the LibDems to form a governing majority. The most notable development in this election was the rise of the **small parties**, with seventeen seats in the parliament going to Greens, the Scottish Socialists and various independent candidates. Most of these gains came through a clever marshalling of support in the second vote allowed under the proportional representation system, and were won at the expense of Labour and, more notably, the SNP, which has found its radical agenda for independence blunted by the more pragmatic demands of devolution.

Critics of the new dispensation are quick to point out the paucity of commanding political performers among MSPs, although it's much harder to find fault in their work rate, as thoroughly worked-over **legislation** on long-neglected issues such as land access, drink licensing and anti-social behaviour has been implemented. In addition, the Scottish Parliament has shown remarkable dynamism in tackling thorny issues, particularly when compared to the laborious procedures of Westminster, taking a lead in matters such as the outlawing of fox hunting with hounds and the banning of smoking in enclosed public places.

For many, however, the most notable progress made by the second parliament following devolution was the move it made down the Royal Mile to its brand-new home at **Holyrood**. The long-running saga of the building's construction, blighted from the start by political manoeuvering and serious mis-management, has dominated the Scottish political scene since the turn of the century. The middle years of the project were tainted by deaths within six months of each other, of both Donald Dewar and the building's Catalan architect, **Enric Miralles**, and while the final construction by and large represents their ambitious vision, neither emerged blameless from the official enquiry held into the severe time and budgetary overruns the project suffered. There's no doubt that the cost of the building, which grew from early estimates of around £40 million to a final bill more than ten times that amount, will continue to colour attitudes not just towards the building but also its occupants, for many years to come. Many people, however, praise the originality of the design, and its ability to provide a striking emblem of Scotland's new political age.

Prospects

Although Scots have had to readjust to finding the sometimes tawdry business of day-to-day politicking taking place in their own backyard rather than tucked away in London, a degree of idealism remains that the parliament will stimulate a vitality and originality in the way Scottish issues are tackled. Core to this is the realization that the parliament is here to stay and that it is the proper way for a nation as proud and singular as Scotland to conduct its affairs. Although almost entirely dictated from outwith the country, events such as the 2005 meeting of G8 world leaders at Gleneagles, with its accompanying **Make Poverty History** rally and Live8 pop concert in Edinburgh, served to shore up Scots' confidence that they can have a part to play in world affairs.

In recent years the Scottish **economy** has benefited from the general prosperity enjoyed in the UK as a whole. There have been hard times, however, particularly in central Scotland, where the decline of **heavy industry**, including deep coal-mining, steelmaking, shipbuilding and engineering, has been all but total, and **unemployment** has produced profound social problems in parts of Glasgow, Edinburgh and smaller towns. Hopes that employment in a broadening range of technology-based industries would underpin the new economy were shaken severely with the closure of factories run by giants such as Motorola and Hyundai; meanwhile another great hope, **tourism**, was still susceptible to downturns resulting from events such as the London terror attacks in 2005 and the foot and mouth disease epidemic of 2001. Financial services and insurance, on the other hand, have been a growth area in the central belt. In northeast Scotland, particularly around Aberdeen, the **oil industry** – although past its boom – continues to underpin an economy which might otherwise have struggled to cope with the uncertainties of agriculture and, especially, fishing.

Though there have been encouraging signs of recent progress, the **Highlands and Islands** remains an economically fragile area that needs special measures, distance from markets being an obvious and fundamental problem. The best options for the future are likely to lie in selective, high-quality development in fishing, fish farming and other food-based industries, activities which use the Internet and other advanced telecommunications technology, primary industries such as forestry and quarrying and, last but certainly not least, tourism. Increasingly, the local environment is seen as a major asset, and the establishment of a system of National Parks should go some way to creating a firm framework in which tourism can develop alongside local communities and the interests of the natural world. One of the keys to Highland development is the ownership and control of land. Some of the largest Highland estates continue to be owned and managed from afar, with little regard to local needs or priorities; the success of groups of crofters in buying estates in Assynt and Knoydart, as well as the purchase of the island of Eigg by its inhabitants, hints at a broadening of land ownership which many hope the land reforms brought in by the Scottish Parliament will do more to promote.

One aspect of Scottish life which has remained upbeat in the last decade or so is its **cultural life**. Writers such as Jim Kelman and A.L. Kennedy, pop groups Travis and Franz Ferdinand, classical composer James Macmillan and artists Andy Goldsworthy and Alison Watt have all given Scotland a substantial presence on the British arts scene. Also notable has been the revival of **Gaelic**, supported by large investments in broadcasting and publishing, and demonstrated by the popularity among young audiences – few of them Gaels – of folk/rock bands like Runrig and Capercaillie. But the transformation goes beyond that: old inhibitions about writing in Scots or in Shetland dialect have been laid to rest too, and much of the revival of cities such as Glasgow and Dundee is attributed to their focus on the arts. Indeed, contemporary culture is one of the healthiest aspects of Scotland today, and artists have often been able to articulate the richness of Scotland's post-devolution future with more ambition and colour than the country's frequently uninspiring politicians.

Music

S cottish indigenous **music** has begun the twenty-first century in remarkably fine health. Outstanding young musicians and bands abound, either faithfully re-creating the traditions of old or finding bold new ways to interpret and express them. After years of being stifled by the rigidly twee, cliché-ridden images of Scottishness as expressed by the likes of Andy Stewart and Jimmy Shand, the real spirit of Scots music enjoyed a significant rebirth towards the end of the twentieth century with a Celtic upsurge courtesy of bands like Silly Wizard, Tannahill Weavers and the Battlefield Band.

Scotland through the 1980s and 1990s saw an explosion of **roots** and **dance music** and, at the same time, a renewal and revisiting of traditions that had seemed perilously close to destruction. The influx of talent, energy and awareness in the national culture has been such that the scene is as vibrant now as it has been for years – from the thriving venues in Glasgow and the lively sessions in Edinburgh to the young musicians upholding their own tradition all over Shetland and the Orkneys. The revival has its own magazine *Living Tradition* and a selection of specialist record companies championing the music.

Things looked very different thirty years ago, when the stern disciplines and structures involved in effectively mastering Scottish **traditional music**, which allowed little scope for flair – particularly with bagpipe-playing – had seemed very outmoded alongside the poppier approach favoured south of the border. But taking their cue from the great Irish bands of the 1970s like Planxty and the Bothy Band, the young Scots musicians looked for new, more informal ways to express that tradition. Adopting non-traditional influences, they set about shaking the cobwebs off the old music. The virtuosos who've surfaced in their wake are themselves testament to the success of their musical revolution.

The Celtic folk band arrives

As in much of northern Europe, the story of Scotland's roots scene begins amid the **folk revival** of the 1960s, a time when folk song and traditional music engaged people who did not have strong family links with an ongoing tradition. For many in Scotland, traditional music had skipped a generation and they had to make a conscious effort to learn about it. At first, the main influences were largely American – skiffle music and artists like Pete Seeger – but soon people started to look to their own traditions, taking inspiration from the Gaelic songs of **Cathy-Ann McPhee**, then still current in rural outposts, or the old travelling singers like the **Stewarts of Blairgowrie**, **Isla Cameron**, **Lizzie Higgins** and, the greatest of them all, Lizzie's mother, **Jeannie Robertson**.

On the instrumental front, there were fewer obvious role models despite the continued presence of a great many people playing in **Scottish dance bands**, **pipe bands** and **Strathspey and Reel Societies** (fiddle orchestras). In the 1960s the action was coming out of Ireland and the recorded repertoire of bands like The Chieftains became the core of many a pub session in Scotland. Even in the early 1970s folk fiddle players were rare, although **Aly Bain** (see box on p.814) made a huge impression when he arrived from Shetland and, soon after, Shetland reels started to creep into the general folk repertoire.

The art of the traditional musician was largely considered a purely solo affair, but in the 1960s a new phenomena emerged to change these conceptions – the **Celtic folk band**. This soon created its own standard formula with a melody

Aly Bain has been a minor deity among Scottish musicians for well over three decades. A fiddle player of exquisite technique and individuality, he has been the driving force throughout that time of one of Scotland's all-time great bands, Boys of the Lough, while latterly teaming up with accordionist Phil Cunningham to act as roving ambassadors for Celtic music. In these guises, he has been instrumental in spreading the reach of Scottish music. First and foremost, though, Bain is a Shetlander, and his greatest legacy is the inspiration he has provided for a revival of Shetland's own characteristic tradition.

Aly was brought up in the capital of Shetland, Lerwick, and was inspired to play the fiddle by Bob **Duncan** – who endlessly played him records by the Strathspey king Scott Skinner – and later the old maestro, **Tom Anderson**. These two were the last of an apparently dying breed, and the youthful Aly was an odd sight dragging his fiddle along to join in with the old guys at the Shetland Fiddlers Society. Players like **Willie Hunter Jnr** and **Snr**, **Willie Pottinger** and **Alex Hughson** were legends locally, but they belonged to another age.

By the time the teenage Aly was persuaded to leave for the mainland, Shetland was changing by the minute, and the discovery of North Sea oil altered it beyond redemption, as the new industrial riches trampled its unique community spirit and sense of tradition. The old fiddlers gradually faded and died, and Shetland music, inflected with the eccentricity of the isolated environment and the influence of nearby Scandinavia, seemed destined to disappear too.

That it didn't was largely down to Aly. After a spell with Billy Connolly (then a folk artist) on the Scottish folk circuit, Aly found himself working with blues iconoclast Mike Whellans, and then the two of them tumbled into a link-up with two Irishmen, Robin Morton and Cathal McConnell, in a group they called **Boys of the Lough**. Aly's joyful artistry, unwavering integrity and unquenchable appetite and commitment to the music of his upbringing has kept Shetland music alive in a manner he could never have imagined. Even more importantly, it stung the imagination of the generation that followed.

These days, Aly spends as much time in Sweden as he does in Scotland, but Shetland music is buzzing again, with its own annual **festival** a treat of music-making and drinking. There are young musicians pouring out of the place, and a plethora of bands of all styles, including pop-oriented groups such as Rock, Salt & Nails and more recently Red Vans. The pick of the roots players, currently, is **Catriona MacDonald**, who was also taught by Tom Anderson in his last days. She is adept at classical music, and is fast becoming accomplished in Norwegian music; her mum went to school with Aly Bain – which in Shetland counts for an awful lot.

lead – usually fiddle or pipes – plus guitar, bouzouki and, more often than not, a singer, who became merely another element to the band rather than the focal point.

Instrumental in these developments was a Glasgow folk group, **The Clutha**, who in a folk scene dominated by singers and guitarists, boasted not one but two fiddlers, along with a concertina and four strong singers – including the superb **Gordeanna McCulloch**.

The Clutha were hugely influential and became even more successful when **Jimmy Anderson** introduced a set of chamber pipes into the line-up. Jimmy was not only a great piper but was also a pipe-maker and he "invented" a set of pipes to be played in the key of D which sounded much quieter than the Highland pipes. This was essential at that time, as virtually all the venues were acoustic, and sound systems were not up to the job of balancing out the sounds of pipes, fiddle and voices.

Key, too, to developments were the **Boys of the Lough**, a Scots-Irish group led by the Shetland fiddler **Aly Bain** (see box opposite) and **The Whistlebinkies**. Developing in the Glasgow folk scene alongside The Clutha, both these groups took a strong instrumental line, rather than The Clutha's song-based approach. These two bands were in many ways Scotland's equivalent of Ireland's The Chieftains and through their musical ability and recognition outside the folk clubs, played an important part in breaking down musical barriers.

The Whistlebinkies were notable for employing only traditional instruments, including fine clarsach (Celtic harp) from **Judith Peacock**. However, the most important, and definingly Scottish, element of all three of these bands was the presence of **bagpipes**. Clutha had piper **Jimmy Anderson**, the Whistlebinkies featured **Rab Wallace**, who had a firm background in the Scots piping scene, while The Boys also had an experienced piper in **Robin Morton**. They were pioneers for what was to become a revolution in the late 1970s with bands like Battlefield Band, Tannahill Weavers, Silly Wizard, Alba and Ossian.

Pibroch: Scots pipes

Bagpipes are synonymous with Scotland yet they are not a specifically Scots instrument. The pipes were once to be found right across Europe, and pockets remain, across the English border in Northumbria, all over Ireland, in Spain and Italy, and in Eastern Europe, where bagpipe festivals are still held in rural areas. In Scotland, bagpipes seem to have made their appearance around the fifteenth century, and over the next hundred years or so they took on several forms, including quieter varieties (small pipes), both bellows and mouth blown, which allowed a diversity of playing styles.

The Highland bagpipe form known as **pibroch** (*piobaireachd* in Gaelic) evolved around this time, created by clan pipers for military, gathering, lamenting and marching purposes. Legendary among the clan pipers of this era were the MacCrimmons (they of the famous *MacCrimmon's Lament*, composed during the Jacobite rebellion), although they were but one of several important piping clans, among which were the MacArthurs, MacKays and MacDonalds. In the seventeenth and eighteenth centuries, through the influence of the British army, reels and strathspeys joined the repertoire and a tradition of military pipe bands emerged. After World War II they were joined by civilian bands, alongside whom they developed a network of piping competitions.

The bagpipe tradition has continued uninterrupted, although for much of the last century under the domination of the military and the folklorist Piobaireachd Society. Recently, however, a number of Scottish musicians have revived the pipes in new and innovative forms. Following the lead of The Clutha, Boys of the Lough and Whistlebinkies, a new wave of young bands began to feature pipers, notably **Alba** with the then-teenage Alan McLeod, **Ossian** with Iain MacDonald and the **Battlefield Band** with Duncan McGillivray. Battlefield have subsequently used a selection of high-quality pipers, most recently the American Mike Katz. These players redefined the boundaries of pipe music using notes and finger movements outside the traditional range. They also showed the influence of Irish uillean pipe players (particularly Paddy Keenan of the **Bothy Band**) and Cape Breton style which many claim is the original, pre-military Scottish style.

In 1983 **Robin Morton** released *A Controversy of Pipers* on his Temple Records label, an album featuring six pipers from folk bands who were also top competitive players in the piping world. Up until this point, pipers in a folk band could be considered second-class by some in the piping establishment. This recording made a statement and soon the walls began to crumble.

Alongside all this came a revived interest in traditional piping, and in particular the strathspeys, slow airs and reels, which had tended to get submerged beneath the familiar military territory of marches and laments. The twentieth century's great bagpipe players, notably **John Burgess**, received a belated wider exposure. His legacy includes a masterful album and a renowned teaching career to ensure that the old piping tradition marches proudly into the twenty-first century.

Folk song and the club scene

While the folk bands were starting to catch up on the Irish and integrating bagpipes, **folk song** was also flourishing. The song tradition in Scotland is one of the strongest in Europe and in all areas of the country there are pockets of great singers and characters. In the 1960s the common ground was the folk club network and the various festivals dotted around the country.

The great modern pioneer of Scots folk song, and a man who perhaps rescued the whole British tradition, was the great singer and songwriter **Ewan MacColl**. Though born and raised in Salford in the north of England (about which he wrote one of his most famous songs, *Dirty Old Town*), he remained a fervently proud Scotsman all his life and saw folk song as a political tool of the working classes. He recorded the seminal *Scottish Popular Ballads* as early as 1956, and founded the first folk club in Britain. After MacColl, another of the building blocks of the 1960s folk revival was the Aberdeen group, **The Gaugers**. Song was the heart of this group – Tam Speirs, Arthur Watson and Peter Hall were all good singers – though they were also innovative in using instrumentation (fiddle, concertina and whistle) without a guitar or other rhythm instrument to tie the sound together.

Other significant Scots groups on the 1960s scene included the **Ian Campbell Folk Group**, Birmingham-based but largely Scots in character (and including future Fairport Daves, Swarbrick and Pegg, as well as Ian's sons, Ali

△ Ceilidh, Kirkwall

and Robin, who went on to form UB40). They flirted with commercialism and pop sensibilities – as virtually every folk group of the era was compelled to do – and were too often unfairly bracketed with England's derided Spinners as a result. So too were **The Corries**, although they laced their blandness with enterprise, inventing their own instrumentation and writing the new unofficial national anthem, *Flower of Scotland*.

Other more adventurous experiments grew out of the folk and acoustic club scene in mid-1960s Glasgow and Edinburgh. It was at Clive's Incredible Folk Club in Glasgow that **The Incredible String Band** made their debut, led by **Mike Heron** and **Robin Williamson**. They took an unfashionable glance back into their own past on the one hand, while plunging headlong into psychedelia and other uncharted areas on the other. Their success broke down significant barriers, both in and out of Scotland, and in their wake came a succession of Scottish folk-rock crossover musicians. Glasgow-born **Bert Jansch** launched folk super-group Pentangle with Jacqui McShee, John Renbourn and Danny Thompson, and the flute-playing **Ian Anderson** found rock success with Jethro Tull. Meanwhile, a more traditional Scottish sound was promoted by the likes of **Archie**, **Ray** and **Cilla Fisher**, who sang new and traditional ballads, individually and together.

The great figure, however, along with MacColl, was the singer and guitarist **Dick Gaughan**, whose passionate artistry towers like a colossus above three decades. He started out in the Edinburgh folk club scene with an impenetrable accent, a deep belief in the socialist commitment of traditional song and a guitar technique that had old masters of the art hanging on to the edge of their seats. For a couple of years in the early 1970s, he played with Aly Bain in the Boys of the Lough, knocking out fiery versions of trad Celtic material. Gaughan became frustrated, however, by the limitations of a primarily instrumental (and fiddle-dominated) group and subsequently joined the innovative band **Five Hand Reed** as lead singer and also playing electric guitar. Again playing Scots-Irish traditional material, they might have been the greatest folk-rock band of them all if they hadn't just missed the Fairport/Steeleye Span boat.

Leaving to pursue an independent career, Gaughan became a fixture on the folk circuit and made a series of albums exploring Scots and Irish traditional music and reinterpreting the material for guitar. His *Handful of Earth* (1981) was perhaps the single best solo folk album of the decade, a record of stunning intensity with enough contemporary relevance and historical belief to grip all generations of music fans. And though sparing in his output, and modest about his value in the genre, he's also become one of the best songwriters of his generation.

Crucial contributions to folk song came, too, from two giants of the Scottish folk scene who were probably more appreciated throughout Europe than at home – the late **Hamish Imlach** and **Alex Campbell** – and from song collectors and academics such as **Norman Buchan**, with his hugely influential songbook *101 Scottish Songs*, and **Peter Hall** with *The Scottish Folksinger*. **Robin Hall** and **Jimmie McGregor**, too, while like The Corries often derided for their high profile and their occasional lapses into opportunist populism, were a formidable presence for many years. There has also been a massive contribution from **Hamish Henderson** both as folklorist and researcher, an immense conduit of songs and tunes. That Henderson also penned some of the most telling songs in modern currency adds to his legend.

Gaelic rocking and fusions

Scottish music took an unexpected twist in 1978 with the low-key release of an album called *Play Gaelic*. It was made by a little-known ceilidh group called **Runrig**, who took their name from the old Scottish field system of agriculture, and worked primarily in the backwaters of the Highlands and Islands. The thing, though, that stopped people in their tracks was the fact

Ceilidhs, festivals and contacts

Scottish dances thrived for years under the auspices of the RSCDS, the Royal Scottish Country Dance Society. Their events tended to be fairly formal, with dancers who were largely skilled, but in the 1970s and 1980s more and more Scottish dances, or **ceilidhs** (pronounced "kay-lees"), adopted the English barn-dance practice of a "caller" to call out the moves. Nowadays there are two types of traditional dance events: ceilidh dances, usually with a caller and perhaps a more folky band, and **Scottish Country Dances**, usually with a more traditional Scottish dance band line-up and an expectation that the dancers will know the dance forms.

Scottish **music festivals** range from the Celtic Connections Festival (which takes place in Glasgow every January) where you can catch many of the top names in the Celtic music world in a comfortable concert setting, to lots of smaller festivals which offer a mix of concert, ceilidh and informal sessions. In recent years there has been an increase in the number of festivals where teaching takes a central role. Many of these are in the Highlands and Islands where the Feisean movement has introduced thousands of people to traditional music-making.

Scottish bands such as Capercaillie and Runrig feed the notion that folk music can be exciting, electric and diverse, without losing sight of its roots. However, the survival of traditional music depends on support from young players: they need to play it, listen to it and take it forward. In Scotland, change is coming from a grass-roots **Feisean Movement** (*feis* is Gaelic for festival). These festivals, held during summer months and school holidays, involve children receiving tuition in traditional music, drama, art, dance and Gaelic singing, with evening gigs in local venues. The teachers (and performers) are often leading musicians.

The idea began on the island of Barra, in the southern Hebrides, in 1981 and has spread to many parts of the Highlands and Islands. Its results have been remarkable. Beginners on the fiddle, clarsach, guitar, tin whistle or accordion have now begun to form bands and teach others. And the sheer numbers of young people coming through the Feis throughout the Highlands has resulted in more and more communities holding workshops and ceilidhs. In small communities there are great economic spin-offs for instrument-makers, music shops and teachers of traditional music.

Tuition projects have not been limited to the Highlands. In Edinburgh, Stan Reeves has made remarkable progress with the **Scots Music Group** within the Adult Learning Project (ALP), leading to several hundred people learning traditional instruments and an annual festival of fiddle music. In Glasgow, the **Glasgow Fiddle Workshop**, under the guidance of Ian Fraser, has made similar progress and is starting to widen its brief beyond fiddle tuition.

Contacts

ALP Scots Music Group ☎0131/347 9964, ⊛www.alpscotsmusic.org.

Feisean nan Gaidheal ☎01478/613355, ⊛www.feisean.org.

The Living Tradition ☎01563/571220, ⊛www.folkmusic.net. A traditional music magazine covering music from Britain and Ireland, with a focus, obviously, on Scotland. They also run a mail-order service for traditional recordings.

The Piping Centre ☎0141/353 0220, ⊛www.thepipingcentre.co.uk. The place to visit for anybody with an interest in piping. They have an exhibition, a teaching programme, concert space, café and even a hotel.

Royal Scottish Country Dance Society ☎0131/225 3854, ⊛www.rscds.org.

that they were writing original material in Gaelic. This was the first time any serious Scottish working band had achieved any sort of attention with Gaelic material, although Ossian were touching on it around a similar time, as were Nah-Oganaich.

Runrig marched on to unprecedented heights, appearing in front of rock audiences at concert halls around the world where only a part of the audience were Scots in exile. As their popularity grew the Gaelic content reduced, but they started a whole new ball rolling, chipping away at prejudices, adopting accordions and bagpipes, ever-sharper arrangements, electric instruments, full-blown rock styles, surviving the inevitable personnel changes and the continuous carping of critics accusing them of selling out with every new market conquered. They even made a concept album *Recovery*, which related the history of the Gael in one collection, provoking immense interest in the Gaelic language after years of it being regarded as moribund and defunct. They lost their main man **Donnie Munro** to politics during the 1990s but after an extended break made a solo comeback in 2000.

Capercaillie, too, rooted in the arrangements of **Manus Lunny** and the gorgeous singing of **Karen Matheson**, rose from Argyll pub sessions to flirt with mass commercial appeal, reworking Gaelic and traditional songs from the West Highlands and promoting Gaelic language and culture, primarily as a result of the songs learned by Matheson from her grandmother. They even got into the chart with one ancient Gaelic song, an ironic development considering the fact that Karen was actively discouraged from learning the language and her grandmother was made to feel ashamed of her Gaelic culture after moving to the Scottish mainland. Others have subsequently come to the fore, like **Margaret Bennett**, while the culture has remained defiantly intact courtesy of Scottish roots families in Cape Breton, Canada. **Mary Jane Lamond** is just one who's made the triumphant return journey back to Scotland with her repertoire of ancient Gaelic songs.

Of course, not everyone applauds. Critics point out that many singers using the language are not native Gaelic speakers and only learn the words phonetically, while further controversy has been caused by the "sampling" of archive recordings for use in backing tracks. For many people these songs are important and personal, and in the case of some of the religious singing, they felt very strongly that this use was in bad taste.

Nonetheless, the popularity of Gaelic roots bands undeniably paved the way for "purer" Scots musicians and singers: clarsach player **Alison Kinnaird**, for instance; singers **Savourna Stevenson**, **Christine Primrose**, **Flora McNeill**, **Cathy-Ann MacPhee**, **Heather Heywood** and **Jock Duncan**; and the **Wrigley sisters** from Orkney – who started out as teenagers playing traditional music with technical accomplishment and attitude, further demonstrating their vision in the fine band **Seelyhoo**.

And among the ranks of the roots or fusion bands, each with their own agendas and styles, have passed many – perhaps most – of Scotland's finest contemporary musicians. **Silly Wizard**, especially, featured a singer of cutting quality in **Andy M. Stewart** (and did he need that M.), while **Phil and Johnny Cunningham** went on to display pioneering zeal in their efforts on accordion and fiddle respectively to knit Scottish traditional material with other cultures. Phil Cunningham, in particular, has become an iconic figure in modern Scottish music, championing many up-and-coming musicians, composing modern symphonies for the accordion and even persuading ex-Fairground Attraction star **Eddi Reader** to turn her distinctive voice to a new interpretation of the songs of Robert Burns. The sudden death of Johnny Cunningham at the age of 46, shortly after completing an album with the Irish singer Susan McKeown in December 2003, robbed Scottish music of one of its very best and most influential instrumentalists. Apart from many years and numerous albums with Silly Wizard, he was also a key member of other leading bands – Relativity, Celtic Fiddle Festival and Nightnoise – and recorded with Bob Dylan, Bonnie Raitt and Hall & Oates as well as being an accomplished producer.

Mouth Music, too, were innovative: a Scots-origin (but recently Canadian) duo of **Martin Swan** and **Talitha MacKenzie**, who mixed Gaelic vocals (including the traditional "mouth music" techniques of sung rhythms) with African percussion and dance sounds. MacKenzie later went solo, radically transforming traditional Scottish songs, from which she clears the dust of folklore with wonderful multi-tracked vocals and the characteristic Mouth Music African rhythms. Swan's own subsequent work with various different incarnations of Mouth Music, often in partnership with Martin Furey, has wandered far from those 'Gaelic-Afro-pop' beginnings but has been constantly challenging and often groundbreaking, if failing to capture public imagination.

Another development was the fusion of traditional music and **jazz** by bands such as **The Easy Club** and the duo of piper **Hamish Moore** and jazz saxophonist **Dick Lee**. Moore has since come full circle, now taking his inspiration from a parallel Scottish culture which has developed in Cape Breton. Scottish interest in Cape Breton music has also led to the more or less lost tradition of Scottish step dancing being reintroduced.

Contemporary Celts

Young Celtic music artists have been leading from the front in the touchy subject of **fusion** and **electronica**. The **Easy Club** pioneered Celtic swing years ago, their example propagated by drummer/composer and Scottish National Jazz Orchestra member John Rae and his band **Celtic Feet**, while **Salsa Celtica** have made a considerable mark lacing their Celtic background with a genuinely deep love and understanding of Latin music. At the other end of the spectrum **Jennifer** and **Hazel Wrigley** and **Catriona MacDonald** have done some stirring conceptual work, even incorporating an almost classical mentality to the complex instrumental pieces they have created. MacDonald's increasing influence is also underlined by her leading role in the band of massed fiddle players, **Blazing Fiddles**, currently one of the Highlands' most active exponents of "the living tradition". The likes of **Deaf Shepherd**, **Mad Pudding** and **Tartan Amoebas** have also provided an explosive new edge to old notions of Celtic folk rock, while Cape Breton's **Natalie McMaster** has produced a succession of brilliant fiddle albums involving daring variants on a Scottish traditional theme.

Perhaps most intriguing – and controversial – are those bending the music to its limits by taking it into the realms of a modern club and dance scene involving an alien world of samples, sequencers, loops, computers and drum machines. Even Capercaillie – and one of their offshoots **Big Sky** – experimented in this area with mixed results, while the likes of **Simon Thoumire** and **Paul Mounsey** have been at the forefront of these technological forays. Multi-talented Mounsey lived in Brazil for a decade and has made it count with a series of alluring electronic experiments. The idea of marrying the common ingredients of Scottish and Latino music has also been explored to good effect by **Mac Umba**, one of several Scots bands who've made their mark abroad.

Shooglenifty, who captured the imagination of a new audience with a style they wryly described as "acid croft", and who played at the 2000 Sydney Olympics, are among those who've embraced technology with the most conviction. While most have treated it with kid gloves, Shooglenifty have gone in with the brashness of youth to utilize all the sounds and equipment around them to enhance the music without any caution or the sense of guilt of older musicians. **Peatbog Faeries**, too – featuring excellent piper Peter Morrison and fiddle player/throat singer Ben Ivitsky – have pushed back the boundaries in stirring futuristic fashion without compromising the tradition in any way. Yet the man who's been most responsible for shifting the goalposts is **Martyn Bennett**. A thrilling fiddle and bagpipe player originally from Newfoundland, he drove the music, inspiringly, right to the edge with his albums *Bothy Culture* and *Hardland*. He made his mark as a dreadlocked busker in Edinburgh but proved his credentials with an extraordinary adaptation of Sorley McLean's equally extraordinary poem *Hallaig*, featuring McLean's own reading of it recorded shortly before his death. He also recorded his own mother, the Gaelic singer Margaret Bennett, surrounding her voice with an innovative collection of natural soundscapes of the Isle of Skye on the enlightening album *Glen Lyon*. And if any further evidence were needed that the old and the new and apparently alien cultures can clash to resounding effect, then Bennett provided it on his brilliant final album *Grit*. Perhaps his greatest achievement, it married the voices of some of the great travelling singers he'd known in his youth, like Jeannie Robertson and Lizzie Higgins to his trademark techno beats and samples to brilliant effect. Sadly Bennett was by then too ill to play any instruments himself after a long valiant struggle with cancer and died at the age of 33 in 2005.

The new frontiers

As music generally has cross-fertilized, more Scots artists have crossed over from traditional roots into the mainstream without seemingly having any detrimental effect whatsoever on an ebullient traditional music scene. A browse round the music sessions frequently to be found in Edinburgh and Glasgow will tell you that.

Twin brothers Craig and Charlie Reid's incarnation as **The Proclaimers**, which shifted them from speccy geeks to unlikely pop stars (*Letter From America*, *I'm Gonna Be 500 Miles*) has now seen them acquire status as national treasures and part of Scottish heritage, guaranteed to send any festival home singing.

Almost equally unlikely is the rapid rise of ex-social worker **Karine Polwart**. She proved herself one of the most naturally gifted interpreters of traditional song in the band Malinky and showed glimpses of her songwriting talent in occasional duo MacAlias, before spending a year fronting Battlefield Band when Davy Steele was taken ill and subsequently died. Yet nobody was quite prepared for the outpouring of superb self-written songs when she finally launched her solo career with the *Faultlines* album, which was festooned in plaudits at the 2005 BBC Folk Awards and broke her into the mainstream.

If Polwart spearhead the new Scots charge on the mainstream, plenty of others have emerged at a grass-roots level. The young sisters who make up **Give Way** won the BBC Young Folk Award and have gone on to make three albums with their spirited take on traditional dance music, while the youthful **Julie Fowlis** from North Uist in the Outer Hebrides has even made Gaelic singing sound sexy and won much acclaim for her stirring album *Mar A Tha Mo Chridhe* (As My Heart Is).

Other new young artists determinedly making their mark include the wonderful young Black Isle fiddler **Lauren MacColl**, winner of the 2004 BBC Young Folk Award; and former Radio Scotland Young Traditional Musician of the Year and member of Unusual Suspects, **Emily Smith** from Dumfries, whose alluring voice and striking songs caused quite a stir on her album *A Different Life*.

Perhaps most startling of all of the new breed is **Alasdair Roberts**, a young singer discovered by Will Oldham and who initially started recording with a strange rock band Appendix Out. But with his hypnotic solo album *Farewell Sorrow*, remixed his own songs with traditional themes in fascinating manner and then followed it up in 2005 with a provocatively sparse series of murder ballads, *No Earthly Man*, which stripped the songs right back to their traditional roots in a way that divided opinion like no other.

Discography

In addition to the discs reviewed below, check out ✪www.musicscotland.com – a wonderful site with links to many label and artist pages.

General compilations

The Caledonian Companion (Greentrax, Scotland). A 1975 live recording of four of Scotland's most respected northeast musicians – Alex Green, Willie Fraser, Charlie Bremner and John Grant – featuring solo fiddle, mouth organ, whistle and diddling.

The Nineties Collection (Greentrax, Scotland). Sixteen artists, including four pipers and well-known names such as Aly Bain and Phil Cunningham play all-new tunes in a traditional style. Also available is a companion book containing over 200 tunes, published by Canongate Books, Scotland.

The Rough Guide to Scottish Music (World Music Network, UK). An entirely new compilation, this collection has a youthful feel, a reflection of the rude health of contemporary Celtic music, with tracks from the likes of Deaf Shepherd, Capercaillie and Cliar alongside the haunting vocals of Alison McMorland and the unusual bagpipe calypso of Robert Mathieson.

Traditional singers

Jock Duncan is an authentic bothy ballad singer from Pitlochry who gets to the heart of any song. He made his recording debut aged seventy, backed by musicians including his son, the piper Gordon Duncan, on *Ye Shine Whar Ye Stan'* (Springthyme, Scotland). Some of the traditional singing on this album is truly remarkable and the production from Battlefield Band founder Brian McNeill is impressive, too, creating an atmosphere that only falls a little short of the experience of a live performance.

Heather Heywood, from Ayrshire, is reckoned by many to be Scotland's foremost traditional singer of her generation. She performs largely core Scottish ballads and songs. *By Yon Castle Wa'* (Greentrax, Scotland) is a 1993 disc of epic ballads and contemporary songs, produced by Battlefield Band founder Brian McNeill. Heywood's forte is traditional song which she usually sings *a cappella.* McNeill makes the album accessible, without compromising the basic style, with the addition of accompaniment, including pipes – something which is difficult to do in live performance. This was a landmark recording in the traditional area.

Catherine-Ann MacPhee, from Barra, has a warm yet strong voice and her Gaelic has the soft pronunciation of the southern islands of the Outer Hebrides. *Canan Nan Gaidheal* (*The Language of the Gael*; Greentrax, Scotland) is a superb 1980s recording, re-released on CD, showing mature traditional singing from one of the best of the current generation of Gaelic singers.

Gordeanna McCulloch, the lead singer of seminal 1960s band, The Clutha, is another of the great voices of the Scottish folk revival. On *In Freenship's Name* (Greentrax, Scotland), her voice is a strong, sweet and flexible instrument, capable of a variety of tones. Here she is at home among some great Scots songs, all traditional bar one, and backed by some of Scotland's top musicians.

Eddi Reader is still best known as the flame-haired lead singer of Fairground Attraction, whose late-1980s number one *Perfect* remains a karaoke favourite. Reader's strong and distinctive voice took the Celtic Connections festival by storm in 2003 with her earthy interpretation of Burns's songs, captured on CD as *Eddi Reader Sings the Songs of Robert Burns* (Rough Trade, UK).

Jim Reid was, with Arbroath's Foundry Bar band, a well-known face at festivals and ceilidhs throughout Scotland for many years. One of the country's finest singers, whose *I Saw the Wild Geese Flee* (Springthyme, Scotland) is a selection of songs ranging from his own compositions to traditional ballads. Jim's version of *I Saw the Wild Geese Flee* alone makes this reissued album a classic.

Margaret Stewart and Allan MacDonald Lewis-born Stewart is a talented Gaelic singer; MacDonald is one of the famous piping family from Glenuig – his brother was the piper with Ossian and Battlefield Band. Their *Fhuair Mi Pog* (Greentrax, Scotland) is a fascinating CD of music and Gaelic song that works as terrific entertainment; lovely singing and great tunes, some of the best written by Allan himself.

Jane Turriff is a legendary song carrier. Born into the Aberdeenshire Stewart family in 1915, she grew up in a travelling family. *Singin is Ma Life* (Springthyme, Scotland) is a must for anyone interested in traditional song style. Content ranges from the "big" ballads such as *Dowie Dens of Yarrow* through to the classic C&W song *Empty Saddles*.

Sheena Wellington is a broadcaster and radio presenter, Fife Council's Traditional Arts development officer, and one of Scotland's leading traditional singers. *Strong Women* (Greentrax, Scotland) is a live recording showing off what Sheena does best: communicating traditional song to an audience.

Mick West, well known as a session singer, is now rated at home and abroad as one of the country's finest traditional singers. *Fine Flowers & Foolish Glances* (KRL, Scotland) is one of the most successful albums to use jazz musicians with a strong traditional singer. It may prove to be a classic.

Instrumentalists

Aly Bain, Shetland-born (see box on p.814), is one of the great movers in Scottish music's revival, through his band Boys of the

Lough and a panoply of solo and collaborative ventures. *Aly Bain and Friends* (Greentrax, Scotland) is one of the best-selling Scottish albums of modern times, compiled from a TV series Bain produced on traditional Scottish music. The "friends" include Boys of the Lough, Capercaillie, Hamish Moore and Dick Lee, and zydeco star Queen Ida and her Bonne Temps band. *The Silver Bow: The Fiddle Music of Shetland* (Topic, UK) is a collection of Shetland fiddle tunes notable for bringing together Bain with his old teacher, Tom Anderson. They played both individually and together on the album and the effect is never less than enthralling. On *The Pearl* (Whirlie, Scotland), Bain teams up with Phil Cunningham, Scotland's finest accordion-player, for some fabulous tunes from slow airs to Shetland reels, reflecting the incredible range of styles which this duo have mastered. Phil composed almost half of the tracks and he plays five of the six instruments featured.

John Burgess is arguably the twentieth century's greatest exponent of traditional bagpipes. On *King of the Highland Pipers* (Topic, UK), the maestro demonstrates his art to devastating effect through *piobaireachd*, strathspeys, hornpipes, reels and marches. Not for the faint-hearted!

Pete Clarke is a great fiddle-player whose skills with slow air playing also makes him in great demand as a song accompanist. *Fiddle Case* (Smiddymade, Scotland) comprises an hour of top-notch traditional music – not all Scottish fiddle though – with tunes from Europe and the US and even a couple of songs. There's a classical feel to some of the pieces which works well, with cello and flute parts.

Gordon Duncan, the son of bothy singer Jock, is one of Scotland's younger generation of pipers who is stretching the boundaries with some breathtaking solo piping. On *The Circular Breath* (Greentrax, Scotland), as well as performing on the great Highland bagpipe, Gordon plays the practice chanter and low whistle. He is joined by banjo-player Gerry O'Connor, Ian Carr on guitar, Ronald MacArthur on bass guitar, Jim Sutherland playing clay pots and Andy Cook on Ugandan harp.

Alasdair Fraser is a master fiddler, renowned for his slow airs and now for his leading of The Skyedance Band, whose members provided music for the film *Braveheart*. *Dawn Dance* (Culburnie, Scotland) is an album of completely self-penned tunes in the traditional style which bounces along, defying you to sit still while you listen. Fraser has a rare clarity of playing, without sacrificing the feel and enthusiasm essential to traditional music.

Willie Hunter and Violet Tulloch Hunter was one of the all-time greats of the Shetland fiddle and Tulloch is one of Shetland's leading piano accompanists. *The Willie Hunter Sessions* (Greentrax, Scotland) is a set of recordings made over several years including Scots and Shetland strathspeys, reels and slow airs. "Traditional chamber music" of the highest order.

William Jackson is one of Scotland's best-known traditional composers. He wrote some – and arranged most – of the music for folk band Ossian, and now works solo. *Inchcolm* (Linn Records, Scotland) brings Billy's harp-playing to centre stage. It is a collection of largely unrelated tracks with some orchestral interludes and forays into early and Eastern musics.

Mac-Talla is a Gaelic supergroup, which in 1994 made a small number of concert appearances and one spectacular recording – *Mairidh Gaol is Ceol* (Temple, Scotland), featuring glorious harmony and solo singing, accordion and harp – before settling back into their own individual paths having "made the statement". Mac-Talla's members included singers Arthur Cormack, Christine Primrose and Eilidh MacKenzie plus Alison Kinnaird on clarsach, and ex-Runrig musician Blair Douglas.

Iain McLachlan is a well-known and respected accordion-player who also plays fiddle and melodeon. From the writer of *The Dark Island*, *An Island Heritage* (Springthyme, Scotland) is real traditional music from the Western Isles played on accordion, fiddle, melodeon and pipes.

Hamish Moore is one of Scotland's finest contemporary pipers, playing Border pipes, Scottish small pipes and the great Highland bagpipe. Inspired by the Scottish culture he discovered in Cape Breton, on *Stepping on the Bridge* (Greentrax, Scotland) Moore plays Scottish pipes with Cape Breton accompanists to produce a lively glimpse of what piping may have been like before it became regimented.

Scott Skinner was a legendary Victorian-era fiddler, formidably kilted and moustachioed. *Music of Scott Skinner* (Topic, UK) is an essential roots album, featuring rare and authentic recordings by this elusive genius of the fiddle – and the weird strathspey style in particular – dating from 1908. Some of the quality is understandably distorted, though the collection is supplemented by modern interpretations by Bill Hardie.

"New Roots" groups

Battlefield Band has been perhaps the pre-eminent Scottish band of the last thirty years, despite numerous personnel changes. Some great musicians have come and gone – Brian McNeill has developed into one of Scotland's greatest modern songwriters – but Alan Reid remains a constant and the band even survived the death of its hugely popular singer Davy Steele and continues with one of the country's brightest young vocal talents Karine Polwart (also of Malinky and MacAlias). *Rain, Hail or Shine* (Temple, Scotland) features all the Battlefield Band trademarks in force – distinctive keyboard playing, well-chosen pipe tunes, guitar and bouzouki injecting excitement and tension, fine singing – and John McCusker's sharp fiddle-playing is a joy throughout.

Boys of the Lough have been a benchmark of taste for thirty years, with the virtuoso talents of Shetland fiddler Aly Bain and singer/flautist Cathal McConnell at the heart of the band. *The Boys of the Lough* (Shanachie, US) was the group's 1973 debut and remains one of their strongest sets, powered by contributions from Dick Gaughan and piper Robin Morton. *The Day Dawn* (Lough Records, Scotland) is characterized by quality, taste, superb singing and the relaxed easy style that comes from skilled musicians with years of experience. Along with the concertina and mandola of Dave Richardson, Aly on fiddle and Cathal on flute, whistle and vocals, this album features singer and uillean piper Christy O'Leary.

Capercaillie is a hugely influential and successful group that has taken Gaelic music to a worldwide audience in a modern contemporary style from a traditional base. They have in Karen Matteson one of the best singers around today. On *Beautiful Wasteland* (Survival Records, Scotland/Green Linnet, US), flute, whistle and uillean pipes pop up all over the place and a whole host of things are happening with fiddles, bouzoukis, keyboards and percussion.

Ceolbeg was not a full-time band but produced some of the finest albums of the genre, featuring some fabulous songs from their singer, Davy Steele. *An Unfair Dance* (Greentrax, Scotland) is an impressive collection of tunes played on a huge variety of instruments, with a great sense of light and shade.

Deaf Shepherd is a passionate contemporary band following in the footsteps of the Battlefield Band, rooted in the Scottish tradition and getting more skilled all the time. *Synergy* (Greentrax, Scotland) is a really varied album, including traditional and new material, and jumps from reels to jigs and back, involving vigorous fiddle-playing and powerful bouzouki. Poignant guitar, fiddle and whistle counter-melodies blend smoothly with the vocals.

The Easy Club, an admirably ambitious and sadly underrated group, took the baton from the more thoughtful Scots bands of the 1970s and ran with it at a pace, injecting traditional rhythms with a jazz sense. *Essential* (Eclectic, Scotland) is undoubtedly essential; MacColl's *First Time Ever I Saw Your Face* never sounded like this before.

Mouth Music – Talitha MacKenzie and Martin Swan – combined Gaelic nonsense songs (*puirt-a-beul*) with ambient dance, funk keyboards and African sampling. MacKenzie has gone on to a solo career but Mouth Music's first disc *Mouth Music* (Cooking Vinyl, UK) remains her finest hour, one of the best Celtic fusions committed to disc, featuring stunning rhythms, funk, Gaelic sea shanties and *puirt-a-beul*.

Ossian, a ground-breaking band formed in the 1970s, later reformed with a new line-up in 2004 featuring Iain MacInnes on pipes and Stuart Morrison on fiddle alongside founder members Billy Jackson on harp and Billy Ross on guitar and dulcimer. *The Carrying Stream* (Greentrax, Scotland) is a fine album, signalling the welcome return of Ossian's quintessentially Scottish sound. This is a collection of terrific tunes – first-rate jigs and reels, both traditional and contemporary, blended with songs in English, Scots and Gaelic.

Runrig, a band of Gaelic rock pioneers, was formed in North Uist in 1973 by brothers Rory (bass/vocals) and Calum MacDonald (drums/vocals), with singer Donnie Munro joining the following year. They worked their way up, over fifteen years, from ceilidhs to stadiums, going Top 10 in the UK charts in 1991. They are perhaps at their very best live, with memorable tunes and vocals and well-honed, subtle musicianship. *Alba* (Pinnacle, UK) is an excellent "best of" compilation from this most dynamic Gaelic band.

Seelyhoo, featuring the Wrigley sisters from Orkney, made their own statement with their own recordings. On *Leetera* (Greentrax, Scotland), they're joined by several other musicians in a band which came out of the Edinburgh session scene and exemplifies a fresh approach to traditional tunes and Gaelic song using fiddle, guitar, bass guitar, accordion, whistle, keyboard and percussion. Vibrant music from some of Scotland's young rising stars.

Shooglenifty is a brilliant, innovative band which has an impact well beyond the Scottish roots scene with its grafting of Scottish trad motifs and club-culture trance-dance. Live, they are unstoppable. *A Whisky Kiss* (Greentrax, Scotland) is the album that coined the term "acid croft", with elements of traditional music and house. A weird sound here, a strange tangent there, a sequence played in an odd way. There's nothing else like it.

Silly Wizard was a key roots band, featuring Andy M. Stewart (vocals, bouzouki, guitar), Phil (accordion, etc) and Johnny Cunningham (fiddle). Their albums are full of fresh, lively takes on the whole traditional repertoire and *Live Wizardry* (Green Linnet, US) features the band at its zenith in 1988, playing traditional and self-composed dance tunes and narrative ballads.

Andy M. Stewart, Phil Cunningham and Manus Lunny Two former members of Silly Wizard combine with an Irishman on *Fire In The Glen* (Shanachie, US), a formidable celebration of Scottish traditional music. Phil Cunningham's brilliance as an accordion-player is demonstrated on any number of albums, but it's especially impressive placed against the wonderful singing of Andy M. Stewart.

The Whistlebinkies – often dubbed the "Scottish Chieftains" – are one of the founding folk groups in Scotland and are still playing music with a difference. *A Wanton Fling* (Greentrax, Scotland) has all the freshness of early Binkies recordings, a combination of Lowland pipes, clarsach, flute, concertina and fiddle.

Wolfstone plays folk-rock from the Highlands – "stadium rock meets village-hall ceilidh" said one reviewer – full of passion and fire. *The Half Tail* (Green Linnet, Scotland) is a more subdued progressive sound than usual for Wolfstone, featuring amongst other tracks, a classic whaling song *Bonnie Ship the Diamond, The Last Leviathan* and catchy instrumental sets.

Folk singer-songwriters

Eric Bogle emigrated from Scotland to work in Australia as an accountant but when he returned home he was hailed for writing two of the great modern anti-war folk songs, *The Band Played Waltzing Matilda* and *Green Fields Of France* (or *No Man's Land* as he originally called it). Bogle's singing doesn't quite match his songwriting, but he has all-star support on *Something of Value* (Sonet, UK/Philo, US), which includes *Waltzing Matilda*.

Archie and Cilla Fisher The Fisher family – Archie, Ray and Cilla – were mainstays of the 1960s–70s Scottish folk club scene, reviving old ballads and creating new ones. *The Man With A Rhyme* (Folk Legacy, US) was Archie's finest hour, fourteen tracks from 1976 with the Fisher voice and guitar backed by concertina, banjo, dulcimers, cello, fiddle and flute. *Cilla and Artie* (Greentrax, Scotland), released in 1979 and featuring Cilla Fisher and Artie Trezise, still retains an ease and freshness; Cilla's imperious rendition of the late

Stan Rogers' *The Jeannie C* is in itself worth the acquisition.

Dick Gaughan is one of the most charismatic of Scottish performers – a singer/guitarist/songwriter who can make you laugh, cry and explode with anger with every twist and nuance of delivery. His later material is still up there with his classic albums of the 1980s, and in 2001 he forged a hugely successful working partnership with another great Scottish music legend Brian McNeill. *Handful of Earth* (Sonet, UK/Philo, US) is the Gaughan classic: a majestic album of traditional and modern songs, still formidable a decade on. When *Folk Roots* magazine asked its readers to nominate the album of the 1980s, it won by a street – and deservedly so.

Robin Laing is one of the best songwriters and performers to emerge out of the Scottish folk scene in the 1990s. *Walking In Time* (Greentrax, Scotland) includes four reworkings of traditional songs

– three by other writers and seven of Laing's own songs, accompanied by his own Spanish guitar. Producer Brian McNeill's multi-instrumental talents are also in evidence on most of the tracks.

Ewan MacColl was, simply, one of the all-time greats of British folk song. *In Black and White* (Cooking Vinyl, UK/Green Linnet, US) is a posthumous compilation, lovingly compiled by his family, showcasing MacColl's superb technique as a singer, his gift for choruses (*Dirty Old Town*), his colourful observation as a lyricist (*The Driver's Song*) and his raging sense of injustice (*Black And White*, written after the Sharpeville Massacre of 1963). A fitting epitaph.

Dougie MacLean, one-time member of Tannahill Weavers, has long carved out a successful solo career as an emotive singer-songwriter. *The Dougie MacLean Collection* (Putumayo, US) is a good selection from Dougie's extensive recorded output including perhaps his most famous song, the sentimental but moving confection of nostalgia and patriotism, *Caledonia*.

Adam McNaughtan has written many songs rich in Glasgow wit including one which has travelled the world, *Oor Hamlet*, a condensed version of Shakespeare's *Hamlet* to the tune of *The Mason's Apron*. He has a deep understanding of the tradition and is one of Scotland's national treasures. Adam's comic songs are masterpieces and on *Last Stand At Mount Florida* (Greentrax, Scotland) he is in excellent voice, accompanied by fellow Stramash members Finlay Allison, Bob Blair and John Eaglesham.

Brian McNeill is a man of amazing talents, the one-time fiddling founder of the Battlefield Band and a multi-instrumentalist and a songwriter of some substance. *No Gods* (Greentrax, Scotland) shows the broadening of McNeill's writing talent both in song and tunes. He is joined by ten backing musicians including masterful guitarist Tony MacManus.

by Pete Heywood and
Colin Irwin

(Taken from the *Rough Guide to World Music* and updated by Colin Irwin)

Scottish rock, pop and dance

Identifying certain **rock and pop** acts as specifically Scottish isn't always an easy – or helpful – task, given the amount of cross-pollination that goes on across the whole of the UK. As late as the 1970s, commercial success was very much dependent upon the London marketing scene – until, in the DIY spirit of punk, a small independent record label, **Postcard**, was set up in Glasgow to promote a hotbed of burgeoning rock talent. The label was to have a crucial and long-lasting effect on Scottish music. Starting out with virtually unknown acts such as Aztec Camera and Orange Juice, the subsequent nationwide popularity of these bands gave other Scottish labels and bands the confidence to challenge international markets. Proof that this independent spirit is still alive and well can be found in Glasgow's **Chemikal Underground** label, which signs both local and foreign acts.

The 1950s to the 1970s

The first popular music star from Scotland was London-based Glaswegian **Lonnie Donegan**, though like many who followed, he was generally regarded as British rather than Scottish. In the 1950s, he gave the world the hugely influential new style of **skiffle** (his version of country music and the blues) with the single *Rock Island Line* (1955); it sold three million copies within six months, influencing, among others, a Liverpool group named The Quarrymen, led by one John Lennon. The record was also a hit in the US, quite a feat for the time.

It wasn't until the mid-1960s that further serious Scottish talent would emerge, when singer-songwriter **Donovan** (born in Glasgow, raised mostly in Hertfordshire) caught the era's mood with *Catch The Wind* (1965); his Bob Dylan-like style led him to be labelled as a lightweight version of the real thing (it was released a year after *The Times They Are A-Changin'*). Despite commercial success, it became evident that while Donovan was a decent musical barometer, adapting passing styles from folk to flower power, he was always lagging behind the creative leaders. More original was the unorthodox Glaswegian **The Incredible String Band**, who merged multi-ethnic styles, blues and psychedelia, the result of which was their classic album *The Hangman's Beautiful Daughter* (1968). And in 1967, down in London, Edinburgh-born **Ian Anderson** began his career as the charismatic frontman for the legendary **Jethro Tull**.

At the close of the 1960s, Paisley boy **Gerry Rafferty** and his folky **Humblebums** (who also featured future comedian Billy Connolly), were having little impact. When the band split, Rafferty relocated to London and formed **Stealer's Wheel**, whose single *Stuck In The Middle With You* (1973) was made unforgettable by Quentin Tarantino's use of it in *Reservoir Dogs* in the 1990s. The group's success petered out, but in 1978 Rafferty's solo hit single *Baker Street* – all classic soft rock sheen – ensured his album *City to City* went platinum that year in the States.

In 1974 a bunch of Glaswegian expats in Australia formed the hard rock/heavy metal beast **AC/DC** that would produce the classic *Back In Black* (1980), while 1975 saw the **Average White Band** – formed in London although hailing from Glasgow and Dundee – with their classic *Pick Up The Pieces*, playing tightly arranged funk to an appreciative, loosened-up audience.

The 1970s also saw phenomenal success for teenybop bands. Between 1974 and 1976, Edinburgh's tartan-draped pin-ups, the **Bay City Rollers**, inspired besotted victims to scream loudly and buy enough records to give them nine Top 10 hits – despite there being a surfeit of cover versions and an admission that the band hadn't played on some tracks. Thankfully for non-fans, they went abroad to crack the US market, at which point home interest began to wane.

And then punk arrived. Of Scotland's very own clenched-fist malcontents, Glasgow's **Johnny and the Self Abusers** split up on the release of their first single. Slightly more staying power was provided by Dunfermline's **The Skids**, whose anthemic top-ten *Into The Valley* (1979) posited the group as musical warriors in full charge, an image that slotted in the punk ethos. In London itself, new wave group **The Tourists**, with vocals from Aberdeen's Annie Lennox, enjoyed a couple of hits before disbanding in 1980. Although short-lived, all three groups were nurturing some of the biggest rock stars of the 1980s – members of Simple Minds, Big Country and the Eurythmics respectively.

The 1980s

Arty post-punkers **Simple Minds** played grandiose synthesizer-driven rock, such as *Once Upon A Time* (1985), which typified both the best and worst of 1980s stadium; tellingly, their only US single to chart well was *Don't You (Forget About Me)* (1985), one of the decade's ultimate arena singalongs. **Big Country's** debut album *The Crossing* (1983) boasted soaring Celtic-sounding guitars, which proved popular both in the UK and the US; their second,

Steeltown (1984), was bleaker but notable for dealing with Scottish economic and industrial decline. The **Eurythmics** got off to a shaky start, but in 1983 their striking image was reaching a massive new audience thanks to the arrival of MTV, firstly with *Sweet Dreams (Are Made Of This)*. By 1990 they'd split, with **Annie Lennox** going on to enjoy solo success, though they continue to re-form periodically.

Meanwhile, Glasgow's independent record label Postcard was kick-starting a Scottish pop revolution. **Orange Juice**'s clean-sounding, soulful music reached its largest audience with *Rip It Up* (1982), and the group's singer-songwriter **Edwyn Collins** still maintains an intermittent career as both producer and solo artist (his *A Girl Like You* was a worldwide hit in 1995). Postcard also discovered the **Bluebells** (one of whom was Lonnie Donegan's son), whose *Young At Heart* first charted in 1980; and a fifteen-year-old **Roddy Frame**, whose group **Aztec Camera** later achieved success with the acoustic pop of the singles *Oblivious* (1982) and *Somewhere In My Heart* (1988); like Collins, Frame continues sporadically to produce solo material.

Complementing the poppy exuberance of these groups, rather more sedate American influences were evident in the underrated **Love And Money**, whose last album, *Dogs In The Traffic* (1991, turned out to be a blueprint, more or less, for the new solo career of founder member James Grant. **Wet Wet Wet**'s *Wishing I Was Lucky* (1987) was superb recession pop mixed with blue-eyed soul. Subsequent material was often over-produced, though the hits continued; in 1999 lead singer Marti Pellow left the band to go it alone. **Texas**' are now an international presence, but it took them a while to get there – after the success of *I Don't Want A Lover* (1989), things went quiet for nearly a decade until the global success of *White On Blonde* (1997) hauled them back into the limelight. Also from the 1980s, a more obvious presence was maintained by **Del Amitri**, whose easy-going trad-rock saw differing levels of success in the UK and the US until they were dropped by their label in 2002.

More original were Glasgow's **Blue Nile**, who have thus far produced just four mournful, shimmering albums in twenty years: *A Walk Across The Rooftops* (1984), *Hats* (1989), *Peace At Last* (1996) and *High* (2004). While the critics lavish praise on the songs – minimalist paeans to love – the public mostly ignore them. Following the success of *Sulk* (1982), a cult following was also to be the largest reward for Dundee's eclectic **Associates** and the solo work of frontman **Billy Mackenzie**. The **Silencers** too, whose second album *A Blues For Buddha* (1988) showcased a knack for cinematic tunes and hypnotic rhythms, managed to garner a small following – though mostly in France. Greater commercial success eventually went to Edinburgh man **Mike Scott**, who gathered together the **Waterboys** in London in 1982 and began the quest for what he termed "the Big Music," which resulted in anthemic singles like *The Whole of the Moon* (1985). Such loftiness was reduced in scope for the excellent *Fisherman's Blues* (1988), and his solo and group work continues to delight.

Throughout the mainstream-dominated mid-1980s, the alternative scene was brewing a heady concoction that would have far-reaching effects. Spearheading this movement was Manchester-based label **Creation**, formed by a Scot named Alan McGee, who was, in time, to talent-spot some of the UK's biggest acts, including Oasis. At the time, his most significant signing was **The Jesus and Mary Chain**, whose hedonistic image – sex, drugs and biker culture – found suitable expression in their benchmark debut *Psychocandy* (1984), where West Coast melodies were set to clanging feedback. Bubblegum pop and Velvet Underground influences would also surface in **The Pastels**, who appeared on *NME*'s seminal *C86* compilation, though they were never to scale the commercial heights of the Mary Chain. Similarly, Bathgate's **Goodbye Mr Mackenzie** featured Shirley Manson on vocals, whose success with Garbage in the 1990s would eclipse the work of her former band and their fine album *The Rattler* (1986). For a while, however, it seemed that the Glasgow suburb of Bellshill was to be alternative music's creative capital. From here came the closely related **Vaselines**, **BMX Bandits** and **Captain America** (who became **Eugenius**), who between them provided several rough gems that would resurface in the grunge years when Kurt Cobain paid them homage, plus band members for **Teenage Fanclub**, whose own *Bandwagonesque* (1991) is every bit as essential as Nirvana's *Nevermind*.

The 1990s to the present

Until the late 1980s, Scotland's most obvious contribution to dance music had been the hi-NRG disco of **Bronski Beat**, formed in London, whose album *Age of Consent* (1984), armed with the falsetto of Glaswegian **Jimmy Somerville**, addressed gay issues. But when the UK house scene increasingly went overground, achieving mainstream acceptance during the Ecstasy-fuelled dance-rock crossover period known as "Madchester", Scottish outfits were present and correct. As **The JAMMS**, Jimmy Cauty and Bill Drummond had already scored a major hit with *Doctorin' The Tardis* (1988), but as **The KLF**, their 1990 "Stadium House Trilogy" of singles brought the cash rolling in; they capitalized on their controversial image by later burning in public £1 million of that cash in what was either an act of art-terrorism or an expensive publicity stunt. The KLF were also a huge influence on ambient music when their classic *Chill Out* (1990) became the scene's very own *Dark Side Of The Moon*, and when Jimmy Cauty cofounded the influential **Orb**. Initially an indie guitar band, **The Shamen** got clubbers chanting "E's are good!" to the manic dancefloor hit *Ebeneezer Goode* (1992), while grand masters of being high as a kite, **Primal Scream** (formed by Bobby Gillespie, ex-drummer for the Jesus and Mary Chain) purveyed a Stonesy, dubbed-out bliss with the classic *Screamadelica* (1989).

Scotland's own dance scene has since flowered to become one of the liveliest in Europe. Independent labels such as **Soma** – who signed French dance act Daft Punk – **Bellboy Records** and **Hook Records** have all released top-quality dance tracks. DJs **Stuart MacMillan** and **Orde Meikle**, creators of Slam, perform globally, returning with world-class DJs to pack out Glasgow clubs. DJ **Howie B** helped break the boundaries of performance by mixing U2 live on their 1997 tour, while the camera-shy **Blue Boy** is a club favourite with his fusion of dance and funky soul, and the **Glasgow Underground** label ensures that deep house maintains a presence worthy of its influence. Treading the middle ground between dance and rock, Edinburgh-raised **Finlay Quaye** produced his laid-back and summery *Maverick A Strike* (1997), which threw reggae, rock and soul together, for which he received a Brit award in 1998. **The Beta Band**, meanwhile, were mixing various elements of dance, folk and psychedelia to create a hypnotic sound best exemplified by their *Best Of The Beta Band*; their strong critical acclaim wasn't matched by commercial success, though, and the group decided to quit in 2004. Fans of their esoteric style can catch up with activities of the perennially creative band members by checking out the two groups that they went on to found: **King Biscuit Time** and **The Aliens**.

The strong independent tradition carries on, with Glasgow still in the driving seat – a fact that has much to do with guitar group **The Delgados'** own record company, Chemikal Underground, as well as the Jeepster label. If there's a particular theme to the moment, "lo-fi" might just about encapsulate the folk-tinged wispiness of **Belle and Sebastian**, the minimalism of **Arab Strap** and the sonic experimentalism of **Mogwai**. The scene has also produced **Snow Patrol**, whose third album, *The Final Straw* (2004) belted out soaring choruses, pounding rhythms and aching laments to great commercial success. While their first two albums had hinted at singer-songwriter Gary Lightbody's ear for such a strong melody, his concurrent work with **The Reindeer Section** was perhaps a clearer statement of intent; a collective founded by Lightbody, made up from several members of pretty much every influential band on the Glasgow scene, they produced two albums, of which the second, *Son of Evil Reindeer*, in 2002, is a beguiling listen, trading in avant-garde experimentation for a touching, thoughtful simplicity. Also emerging as a creative force at the time was the more obviously Scottish **Mull Historical Society**, the work of Colin MacIntyre. His debut, *Loss* (2001), was a sparkling concoction that, while several steps removed from lo-fi with its clean production sound and jangling guitars, was still a kindred spirit to Snow Patrol's dedication to find the perfect pop tune.

Alan McGee also continues to maintain his Scottish connections with his label Poptones, to which he signed Glaswegians **The Cosmic Rough Riders**, a group every bit as inspired by the US West Coast bands of the 1960s as their name implies; their *Enjoy the Melodic Sunshine* (2000) is well worth investing in. Scottish acts aren't just watching from the commercial sidelines, however; **Travis** moved on from their early glam-rock style to produce the best-selling *The Man Who* (1999), brimming with tasteful angst, which they followed up in 2001 with *The Invisible Band* and in 2003 with *12 Memories*. In 2004 the big news was Glasgow's **Franz Ferdinand**, who won a Mercury award that year for their eponymous debut; their follow-up, *You Could Have It So Much Better* showcases the same garage-rock, post-punk style but takes things further, often in the conceptual direction of The Beatles. Against this rather male-dominated, often experimental background, it's refreshing to find singer-songwriter **KT Tunstall** can still uphold the virtues of her trade; her 2005 album *Eye To The Telescope*, a mature, melodic set that covers ballads and upbeat, jaunty numbers, went on to win a Mercury Music Prize nomination.

by Geoff Howard

Scotland's writers

Robert Burns

Scotland's national poet, **Robert Burns** *(1759–96) is celebrated not just for the lyrical genius in his prodigious output of poetry and song, but also for the fact that he was the ploughman-poet, a son of the soil who could give voice to Scottish nationalism and universal ideals of love and socialism. To a Mouse is one of his early poems, expressing both his intimacy with nature and a philosophical world view. Though written in Scots, its second-to-last stanza originates a phrase which is widely known in its anglicized form but which few attribute to Burns. We've added a boxed glossary explaining some unfamiliar Scots words. For a profile of Burns, see box on p.255.*

To a Mouse, On turning her up in her Nest, with the Plough, November 1785

Wee, sleeket, cowran, tim'rous beastie,
O, what a panic's in thy breastie!
Thou need na start awa sae hasty,
Wi' bickering brattle!
I wad be laith to rin an' chase thee,
Wi' murd'ring pattle!

I'm truly sorry Man's dominion
Has broken Nature's social union,
An' justifies that ill opinion,
Which makes thee startle,
At me, thy poor, earth-born companion,
An' fellow-mortal!

I doubt na, whyles, but thou may thieve;
What then? poor beastie, thou maun live!
A daimen-icker in a thrave
'S a sma' request.
I'll get a blessin wi' the lave,
An' never miss't!

They wee-bit housie, too, in ruin!
Its silly wa's the win's are strewin!
An' naething, now, to big a new ane,
O' foggage green!
An' bleak December's winds ensuin,
Baith snell an' keen!

Thou saw the fields laid bare an' wast,
An' weary Winter comin fast,
An' cozie here, beneath the blast,
Thou thought to dwell,
Till crash! the cruel coulter past
Out thro' thy cell.

That wee-bit heap o' leaves an' stibble
Has cost thee monie a weary nibble!
Now thou 's turn'd out, for a' thy trouble,
But house or hald,
To thole the Winter's sleety dribble
An' cranreuch cauld!

But Mousie, thou art no thy lane,
In proving foresight may be vain;
The best-laid schemes o' Mice an' Men
Gang aft agley,
An' lea'e us nought but grief an' pain,
For promis'd joy!

Still thou art blest, compar'd wi' me!
The present only toucheth thee:
But Och! I backward cast me e'e
On prospects drear!
An' forward, tho' I canna see,
I guess an' fear!

Glossary

Sleeket Glossy
Cowran Cowering
Na Not
Sae So
Wi' With
Brattle Clatter, hurry
Wad Would
Laith Loath, unwilling
Rin Run
Pattle Type of spade
Whyles Sometimes
Thieve Steal
Maun Must
Daimen-icker Occasional ear of corn
Thrave A measure of corn
Sma' Small
Lave Remainder
Silly Feeble

Wa's Walls
Win's Winds
Foggage Moss
Baith Both
Snell Bitter
Coulter Cutting blade
  of plough
Stibble Stubble
Monie Many
Hald Hold, dwelling
Cranreuch Hoar-frost
Cauld Cold
Lane Alone
Gang Go, depart
Aft Often
Agley Awry
Lea'e Leave
E'e Eye

Robert Louis Stevenson

*The son of a lighthouse engineer who grew up in Edinburgh's New Town, **Robert Louis Stevenson** (1850–94) is most famous worldwide for* Treasure Island *and* The Strange Case of Dr Jekyll and Mr Hyde. *An enduring favourite in Scotland is* Kidnapped, *in which the hero David Balfour crosses Scotland in a series of lively scrapes. Its sequel,* Catriona, *was written when Stevenson was living in Samoa, but as this extract from the opening chapter of the book shows, he was able to re-create vividly the feel and flavour of his home town. For more on Stevenson, see box on p.160.*

From Catriona

Here I was in this old, black city, which was for all the world like a rabbit-warren, not only by the number of its indwellers, but the complication of its passages and holes. It was, indeed, a place where no stranger had a chance to find a friend, let be another stranger. Suppose him even to hit on the right close, people dwelt so thronged in these tall houses, he might very well seek a day before he chanced on the right door. The ordinary course was to hire a lad they called a *caddie*, who was like a guide or pilot, led you where you had occasion, and (your errands being done) brought you again where you were lodging. But these caddies, being always employed in the same sort of services, and leaving it for obligation to be well informed of every house and person in the city, had grown to form a brother-hood of spies: and I knew from tales of Mr Campbell's how they communicated one with another, what a rage of curios-ity they conceived as to their employer's business, and how they were like eyes and fingers to the police. It would be a piece of little wisdom, the way I was

△ Robert Louis Stevenson

now placed, to take such a ferret to my tails. I had three visits to make, all immediately needful: to my kinsman Mr Balfour of Pilrig, to Stewart the Writer that was Appin's agent, and to William Grant Esquire of Prestongrange, Lord Advocate of Scotland. Mr Balfour was a non-committal visit; and besides (Pilrig being in the country) I made bold to find the way to it myself, with the help of my two legs and a Scots tongue. But the rest were in a different case. Not only was the visit to Appin's agent, in the midst of the cry about the Appin murder, dangerous in itself, but it was highly inconsistent with the other. I was like to have a bad enough time of it with my Lord Advocate Grant, the best of ways; but to go to him hot-foot from Appin's agent, was little likely to mend my own affairs, and might prove the mere ruin of friend Alan's. The whole thing, besides, gave me a look of running with the hare and hunting with the hounds that was little to my fancy. I determined, therefore, to be done at once with Mr Stewart and the whole Jacobitical side of my business, and to profit for that purpose by the guidance of the porter at my side. But it chanced I had scarce given him the address, when there came a sprinkle of rain – nothing to hurt, only for my new clothes – and we took shelter under a pend at the head of a close or alley.

Being strange to what I saw, I stepped a little farther in. The narrow paved way descended swiftly. Prodigious tall houses sprang upon each side and bulged out, one storey beyond another, as they rose. At the top only a ribbon of sky showed in. By what I could spy in the windows, and by the respectable persons that passed out and in, I saw the houses to be very well occupied; and the whole appearance of the place interested me like a tale.

I was still gazing, when there came a sudden brisk tramp of feet in time and a clash of steel behind me. Turning quickly, I was aware of a party of armed soldiers, and in their midst, a tall man in a great coat. He walked with a stoop that was like a piece of courtesy, genteel and insinuating: he waved his hands plausibly as he went, and his face was sly and handsome. I thought his eye took me in, but could not meet it. This procession went by to a door in the close, which a serving-man in a fine livery set open; and two of the soldier-lads carried the prisoner within, the rest lingering with their firelocks by the door.

There can nothing pass in the streets of a city without some following of idle folk and children. It was so now; but the more part melted away incontinent until but three were left. One was a girl; she was dressed like a lady, and had a screen of the Drummond colours on her head; but her comrades or (I should say) followers were ragged gillies, such as I have seen the matches of by the dozen in my Highland journey. They all spoke together earnestly in Gaelic, the sound of which was pleasant in my ears for the sake of Alan; and, though the rain was by again, and my porter plucked at me to be going, I even drew nearer where they were, to listen. The lady scolded sharply, the others making apologies and cringeing before her, so that I made sure she was come of a chief's house. All the while the three of them sought in their pockets, and by what I could make out, they had the matter of half a farthing among the party: which made me smile a little to see all Highland folk alike for fine obeisances and empty sporrans.

It chanced the girl turned suddenly about, so that I saw her face for the first time. There is no greater wonder than the way the face of a young woman fits in a man's mind, and stays there, and he could never tell you why; it just seems it was the thing he wanted. She had wonderful bright eyes like stars, and I daresay the eyes had a part in it; but what I remember the most clearly was the way her lips were a trifle open as she turned. And, whatever was the cause, I stood there staring like a fool. On her side, as she had not known there was anyone so near, she looked at me a little longer, and perhaps with more surprise, than was entirely civil.

Glossary

Close Narrow passageway leading to a block of flats

Pend A vaulted entranceway to a close or passageway

Gillies Most commonly attendants while hunting or fishing; used here simply to indicate lads or youths

Lewis Grassic Gibbon

Lewis Grassic Gibbon was the pen name of James Leslie Mitchell (1901–35), and though Mitchell achieved moderate success writing non-fiction in the early part of his career, recognition only really came when he adopted his pseudonym and re-created in fiction the language and life of the farming community known as the Mearns in north-east Scotland where he had grown up (see p.531). Sunset Song, the first of a trilogy known as A Scots Quair, is now widely regarded as the finest Scottish work of fiction in the twentieth century. In it, Gibbon introduces the spirited but tragic heroine Chris Guthrie, who after her mother's death and the departure of her brother Will overseas, is left to nurse her hard, unflinching father John through an illness at their farm Blawearie in the village of Kinraddie. This extract comes shortly after John Guthrie has died and Chris is left to battle with her own lack of emotion and uncertainty about the future. A glossary explains some of the distinctive northeast dialect used.

From Sunset Song

And the next forenoon the lawyer man came down from Stonehaven, it was Peter Semple, folk called him Simple Simon but swore that he was a swick. Father had trusted him, though, and faith! you'd be fell straight in your gait ere John Guthrie trusted you. Not that he'd listened to advice, father, he'd directed a will be made and the things to be set in that will; and when Mr Semple had said he was being fell sore on some of his family father had told him to mind his own business, and that was a clerk's. So Mr Semple drew up the will, it had been just after Will went off to the Argentine, and father had signed it; and now the Blawearie folk sat down in the parlour, with whisky and biscuits for Mr Semple, to hear it read. It was short and plain as you please, Chris watched the face of her uncle as the lawyer read and saw it go white in the gills, he'd expected something far different from that. And the will told that John Guthrie left all his possessions, in silver and belongings, to his daughter Christine, to be hers without let or condition, Mr Semple her guardian in such law matters as needed one, but Chris to control the goods and gear as she pleased. And folk were to say, soon as Kinraddie heard of the will, and faith! they seemed to have heard it all before it was well out of the envelope, that it was an unco will, old Guthrie had been fair spiteful to his sons, maybe Will would dispute his sister's tocher.

The money was over three hundred pounds in the bank, it was hard to believe that father could have saved all that. But he had; and Chris sat and stared at the lawyer, hearing him explain and explain this, that, and the next, in the way of lawyers: they presume you're a fool and double their fees. Three hundred pounds! And now she could do as she'd planned, she'd go up to the College again and pass her exams and go on to Aberdeen and get her degrees, come out as a teacher and finish with the filthy soss of a farm. She'd sell up the gear at Blawearie, the lease was dead, it had died with father, oh! she was free and free to do as she liked and dream as she liked at last!

And it was pity now that she'd all she wanted she felt no longer that fine thrill that had been with her while she made her secret plans. It was as though she'd lost it down in Kinraddie kirkyard; and she sat and stared so still and white at the lawyer man that he closed up his case with a snap. *So think it well over, Christine,* he said and she roused and said *Oh, I'll do that*; and off he went, Uncle Tam drew a long, deep breath, as though fair near choked he'd been *Not a word of his two poor, motherless boys!*

It seemed he'd expected Alec and Dod would be left their share, maybe that was why he'd been so eager to adopt them the year before. But Auntie cried *For shame, Tam, how are they motherless now that I've got them? And you'll come up and live with us when you've sold Blawearie's furnishings, Chris?* And her voice was kind but eyes were keen, Chris looked at her with her own eyes hard, *Ay, maybe* and got up and slipped from the room, *I'll go down and bring home the kye.*

And out she went, though it wasn't near kye-time yet, and wandered away over the fields; it was a cold and louring day, the sound of the sea came plain to her, as though heard in a shell, Kinraddie wilted under the greyness. In the ley field old Bob stood with his tail to the wind, his hair ruffled up by the wind, his head bent away from the smore of it. He heard her pass and give a bit neigh, but he didn't try to follow her, poor brute, he'd soon be over old for work. The wet fields squelched below her feet, oozing up their smell of red clay from under the sodden grasses, and up in the hills she saw the trail of the mist, great sailing shapes of it, going south on the wind into Forfar, past Laurencekirk they would sail, down the wide Howe with its sheltered glens and its late, drenched harvests, past Brechin smoking against its hill, with its ancient tower that the Pictish folk had reared, out of the Mearns, sailing and passing, sailing and passing, she minded Greek words of forgotten lessons, Παντα ρει, *Nothing endures.* And then a queer thought came to her there in the drookèd fields, that nothing endured at all, nothing but the land she passed across, tossed and turned and perpetually changed below the hands of the crofter folk since the oldest of them had set the Standing Stones by the loch of Blawearie and climbed there on their hold days and saw their terraced crops ride brave in the wind and sun. Sea and sky and the folk who wrote and fought and were learnéd, teaching and saying and praying, they lasted but as a breath, a mist of fog in the hills, but the land was forever, it moved and changed below you, but was forever, you were close to it and to you, not at a bleak remove it held you and hurted you. And she had thought to leave it all!

She walked weeping then, stricken and frightened because of that knowledge that had come on her, she could never leave it, this life of toiling days and the needs of beasts and the smoke of wood fires and the air that stung your throat so acrid, Autumn and Spring, she was bound and held as though they had prisoned her here. And her fine bit plannings! – they'd been just the dreamings of a child over toys it lacked, toys that would never content it when it heard the smore of a storm or the cry of sheep on the moors or smelt the pringling smell of a new-ploughed park under the drive of a coulter. She could no more teach a school than fly, night and day she'd want to be back, for all the fine clothes and gear she might get and hold, the books and the light and the learning.

The kye were in sight then, they stood in the lithe of the freestone dyke that ebbed and flowed over the shoulder of the long ley field, and they hugged to it close from the drive of the wind, not heeding her as she came among them, the smell of their bodies foul in her face – foul and known and enduring as the land itself. Oh, she hated and loved in a breath! Even their lover might hardly endure, but beside it the hate was no more than the whimpering and fear of a child that cowered from the wind in the lithe of its mother's skirts.

Glossary

Swick Sly cheat	**Smore** lit. smother; a wind thick with
Fell Cruel, exceedingly	fine rain
Unco Unusual, very	**Drookèd** Drenched
Tocher Inheritance	**Crofter** Smallholder farmers
Soss Mess	**Pringling** Prickling, tingling
Kye Cattle	**Coulter** Cutting blade of a plough
Louring Overcast, threatening	**Lithe** Shelter
Ley Fallow	

Alan Warner

*Born in Oban in 1964, **Alan Warner** was, along with the likes of Irvine Welsh, one of the writers to emerge from the Rebel Inc. group in the early 1990s, who portrayed the drug culture and street life of working-class urban Scotland with a vividness verging on glamour. Warner's first novel,* Morvern Callar, *tells the story of a headstrong and independent supermarket assistant in a Scottish west-coast town who takes off to the rave clubs of Ibiza. In this extract she is returning to her home in "the Port", a thinly disguised Oban.*

From Morvern Callar

We moved east to the Back Settlement then in west till we came in behind The Complex and down into the port through the long cutting by the signal box. With both hands I pulled down the cab window; the port looked same as ever round the bay. The cab swayed a little and a hiss came from the brake handle as

Coll nudged it over. As we ran along the platform edge I swung the seat round and bent down to pick up the bag. Woofit was up, circling and wagging his tail. The engine stopped moving and there was a dying honk of air as Coll snapped down the worn reddish-painted handle on the cab wall behind him. I opened the cab door and Woofit was out the train engine and sniffing around the passengers who were crowded up against the gate with Zipper checking tickets. I jumped down onto the platform.

Coll stood up in the cab doorway shouting Woofit away from the passengers. Coll sniffed and says, Mmm the only time these machines smell good is after youve been in them Morvern Callar.

I laughed and goes, I'd best be shooting, thanks for the hurl.

Aye no bother, no bother, you'd best away and find that man.

He'll be on the sesh.

No surprised. You take care you crazy thing.

You too, bye Woofit, I goes, kneeling and giving the dog a good clapping round the ears.

I crossed the square then looked up. There was still time to make it to the superstore.

Once across the carpark I moved through the sliding door and past the signing book. You saw The Seacow who was alone on tills turn and stare. I took the door up to the ladies' staffroom and Creeping Jesus's office. The staffroom was empty so I used the key on my locker then pushed aside the nylon uniform and the tights in a ball. I took out the schoolish shoes then rummaged through the shelf. I took a few things: make-up, a bottle paracetamol and vitamins, then put them in my bag.

I walked through, knocked on Creeping Jesus's door then stepped in.

Well, well, look whos arrived, our own suntanned supermodel, Creeping Jesus says.

There was a long bit of silentness.

Going to tell me why youre two weeks late for work then? Creeping Jesus says.

Thirteen days, I goes.

It's not just me suffers you know Morvern, the whole section suffers, working a man short.

I'm not a man.

Dont get smart.

Well, I'm not, I went then coughed.

Where've you been?

Thats none of your business just tell me where I stand, have I got a job? Cause if I dont then why should I be stood in your office like this?

What do you think Morvern?

Fine I goes.

It was the orangey plastic chair that always sat by the door I threw across his office at him. A back leg hit the front of the desk so the chair made a wobbling noise and shot off into the corner of the room. Creeping Jesus had got crouched down behind the desk, shouting about police.

Away crawl under the stone you came from, Creeping Jesus, I says. I wrenched the door open so bad-temperedly it crashed into the filing cabinets.

I walked out into the carpark, used the goldish lighter on a Silk Cut under one of the lights then crossed The Black Lynn that flows under the port.

In the night, rain was spotting down from the light's haloes. I walked into Haddows, asked for a half bottle voddy and counted out more of the money yon Tom and Susan subbed me. I walked quick up past Video Rental, St John's then the Phoenix. Cars were circling the port roads with elbows out windows. I dug my house keys from the bag.

On the mat were seven catalogues from model shops in the south and the letter with a queer postmark addressed to me. I picked them all up and dropped them on His desk. I put De Devil Dead by Lee Perry on the CD then I towelled my hair and twisted it up into a French roll. I put on the heater and immerser.

I'd forgot to get something for diluting the voddy and of course the fridge was bare so I opened this bottle of sweet wine and used that to dilute it. There was a can tinned potatoes so I opened it, drained the can then popped the potatoes in my mouth one after the other. While chewing I was just staring at the black window.

When that immerser had heated I gulped some more of the bogging-tasting drink then stripped in front of the fire, standing on one leg of the wet jeans to tug the other foot out.

After shaving my legs and having a good bath I used every clean towel on me and put SDI on the DC. In the scud with that religious music going I got down on the polished floorboards and tried hard with a wee prayer. I suddenly jumped up and paraded about all agitated. I took out De Devil Dead and put in From the Secret Laboratory by Lee Perry. I flicked forward to tracks 6 and 7. This time the praying went an awful lot better and when I'd finished I was shivering with perished coldness. I got dressed then put on the steerhide jacket from the wardrobe. I drank some more voddy then got the brolly and headed outside.

The wind tugged at the brolly and drops vibrated off of the edge as I hunched under.

I walked towards the phonebox, took the brolly down and got in. There was no answer at The Complex. I phoned V the D's out the Back Settlement.

Hello 206, she goes.

It's Morvern.

Morvern where are you? Your father's worried sick about you as if he doesn't have enough of his own problems.

I'm home.

We thought you'd been kidnapped or something.

Where is he then?

He's there in the port tonight. I've told him not to worry, I mean we'll get by, might have to put off the extension. Have you been to work?

Aye. Sacked.

Oh Morvern, she sighed and laughed. What are we going to do with the Callars? Surely you'll get a bit hotel work before the end of the season?

The pips started and I looked up at the ceiling.

Morvern . . .?

I put the phone down softly and listened to the rain on the roof of the box. I pushed out the door.

I used the shortcut up to the circular folly trying no to go skiteing in the runny mud. From the top of Jacob's Ladder I looked down on the port and the fishing boats tied up at the pier. I tried to look behind The Complex towards the mountains where the pass goes west to the village beyond the power station but there were only the moving clouds above orangey street light.

Going down Jacob's Ladder I tried to miss the puddles. Water was splattering over from the cliff above. No couples kissed on the benches of each platform.

I looked down on the dark street under the cliff and the dull lights of Red Hanna's local: The Politician Hotel.

I pushed open the door and shook water off the steerhide jacket's arms. All heads turned and followed me as I walked to the fridge where not only was Povie the butcher's extra meat kept but the Politician had placed the pool table cause it wouldnt fit anywhere else. I stuck my head in: five men were round the table, two were playing. A big hunk of meat was hung from one of the hooks and a man was holding it aside so the player could take a good shot. The other men were puffing into their hands.

Look it's one of the strippers, says a guy in a boilersuit.

Shh, thats yon engine driver's girl, another went as I turned round, stepped up to the bar and goes, Has Red Hanna been in the night?

A week past Friday, goes a voice behind me. I turned round.

An old greyhead was sat with tears coming from his eyes that he kept dabbing with a hanky. He was far from greeting though and it was a double he had in front him.

I'd Tod the Post, youre Morvern, Red Hanna's girl, you work in the super-store, eh?

Not any more I dont. Have you seen him then?

Not since he was in yon time, no like him to neglect us for so long.

Any inkling where he'll be?

Havent the foggiest. You'd be best parking yourself here and making an old fool happy; whats your pleasure?

Nah, I couldnt get you back.

Ah, sit yourself down. Red Hanna would skin me if he hears youve been in and no treated well. It's The Weekday Club the night, a'bhailaich, get the girl with the smashing suntan a drink.

A Southern Comfort and lemonade please, I goes.

A what says the barman.

Southern Comfort?

We dont have that here.

I looked at the bottles and says, A Sweetheart Stout please.

Extract from MORVERN CALLAR by Alan Warner, published by Jonathan Cape.
Used by permission of The Random House Group Limited.

Glossary

Hurl Lift	**Scud** Naked
Sesh lit. "session"; drinking bout	**Skiteing** Slipping
Bogging Foul	**A'bhailaich** (Gaelic) O boy, or My boy

Books

Out-of-print titles are indicated as o/p; these should be easy to track down in second-hand bookshops. Titles marked with 🏃 are particularly recommended.

Fiction

🏃 **Iain Banks** *The Bridge, Complicity, The Crow Road, Espedair Street, A Song of Stone, The Wasp Factory, DeadAir.* Just a few titles by this astonishingly prolific author, who also writes sci-fi as Iain M. Banks. His work can be funny, pacy, thought-provoking, imaginative and downright disgusting. It is never dull.

J.M. Barrie *Peter Pan.* Born and educated in Scotland, Barrie moved to London to work as a journalist. Aside from *Peter Pan*, his best-known work, he wrote a series of short stories and other works set in Kirriemuir where he was born.

Christopher Brookmyre *One Fine Day In the Middle of the Night, The Sacred Art of Stealing, A Big Boy Did It and Ran Away.* All very funny, racy novels that refuse to be categorized – you'll probably find them in the crime section, but they're as much politico-satirical.

George Mackay Brown *Beside the Ocean of Time.* A child's journey through the history of an Orkney island, and an adult's effort to make sense of the place's secrets in the late twentieth century. *Magnus* is his retelling of the death of St Magnus with parallels for modern times.

John Buchan *The Complete Richard Hannay.* This single volume includes *The 39 Steps, Greenmantle, Mr Standfast, The Three Hostages* and *The Island of Sheep.* Good gung-ho stories with a great feel for the Scottish landscape. Less well-known, but better, are Buchan's historical romances such as *Midwinter*, a Jacobite thriller, and *Witchwood*, a tale of religious strife in the seventeenth century.

Isla Dewar *Women Talking Dirty.* The outrageous, funny and poignant soul-bearing of two women in suburban Edinburgh who become friends over a bottle of vodka and post-match analysis. Her later novels, such as *Dancing in a Distant Place* and *Getting Out of the House* are gentler, but perceptive stories centring on a female character.

Anne Donovan *Hieroglyphics*, her first collection of short stories, and *Budda Da*, her first hilarious novel, were both nominated for major prizes, and rightly so.

Christine Marion Fraser *Kinvara.* Glasgow-born Fraser's family saga is centred on a lighthouse keeper on the west coast of Scotland. Her latest novels, *Children of Rhanna* and *Stranger on Rhanna*, trace the lives of four people who were brought up in a close-knit community on the island of Rhanna.

George MacDonald Fraser *The General Danced at Dawn, McAuslain Entire, The Sheikh and the Dustbin.* Touching and very funny collections of short stories detailing life in a Highland regiment after World War II by the author of the Flashman novels.

Janice Galloway *The Trick is to Keep Breathing.* The story of a woman's mind as she slowly spirals into depressive madness. Almost unwittingly readers are drawn into the vortex and suddenly find themselves empathizing with the heroine's confusion. A brilliantly written, intense book. Her much acclaimed novel *Foreign Parts* explores the friendship of two women.

🏃 **Lewis Grassic Gibbon** *A Scots Quair.* A landmark trilogy set in northeast Scotland during and after World

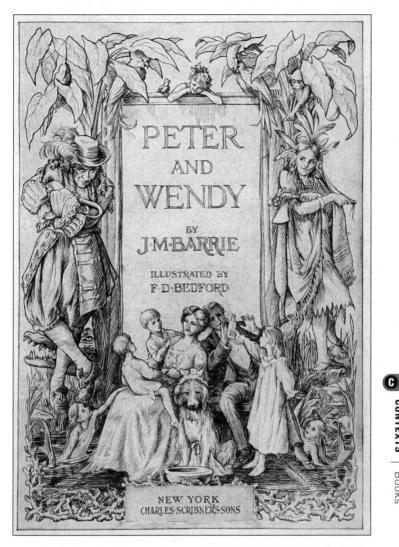

△ Illustration from the Peter Pan book by J.M Barrie

War I, the events seen through the eyes of Chris Guthrie, torn between her love for the land and her desire to escape a peasant culture. Strong, seminal work. (See p.836 for an extract from *Sunset Song*.)

Alasdair Gray *Lanark: A Life in Four Books*. A postmodern blend of social realism and labyrinthine fantasy. Gray's

extraordinary debut as a novelist, featuring his own allegorical illustrations, takes invention and comprehension to their limits.

Neil M. Gunn *The Silver Darlings*. Probably Gunn's most representative and best-known book, evocatively set on the northeast coast and telling the story of herring fishermen during the great years of the industry.

James Hogg *The Private Memoirs and Confessions of a Justified Sinner.* Complex, dark mid-nineteenth-century novel dealing with possession, myth and folklore, as it looks at the confession of an Edinburgh murderer from three different points of view.

Jackie Kay *Trumpet.* The protagonist is dead before the novel begins. He was a black Scottish jazz trumpeter, who left a wife in mourning and a son in deep shock, for the posthumous medical report revealed him to be a woman.

James Kelman *The Busconductor Hines.* The wildly funny story of a young Glasgow bus conductor with an intensely boring job and a limitless imagination. *How Late it Was, How Late* is Kelman's Booker Prize-winning and disturbing look at life as seen through the eyes of a foul-mouthed, blind Glaswegian drunk.

A.L. Kennedy *Looking for the Possible Dance.* Young Scottish writer dissects the difficulties of human relationships on a personal and wider social level. More recent novels *So I Am Glad, Original Bliss* and *Paradise* have the same deft touch, as does her collection of twelve short stories on the theme of longing, *Indelible Acts.*

Eric Linklater *The Dark of Summer.* Set on the Faroes, Shetland, Orkney (where the author was born) and in theatres of war, this novel exhibits the best of Linklater's compelling narrative style, although his comic *Private Angelo* is better known.

Alexander MacArthur and Kingsley Long *No Mean City.* Classic story of razor gangs in 1935 Glasgow.

Compton Mackenzie *Whisky Galore.* Comic novel based on a true story of the wartime wreck of a cargo of whisky on a Hebridean island. Full of predictable stereotypes but still funny.

Denise Mina *Garnethill, Exile* and *Resolution* form a tense and gritty trilogy set in the underside of Glasgow. Absorbing reading.

Naomi Mitchison *The Bull Calves* was written during World War II but set in 1747, with comment on the aftereffects of Jacobite rebellion wrapped in a historical setting. *Lobster on the Agenda,* written in 1952 closely mirrors contemporary life in Kyntyre where Mitchison lived, where the community is trying to look forward while hampered by the prejudices of the past.

Nancy Brysson Morrison *The Gowk Storm.* Published in 1933, this novel vividly portrays the lives of three sisters trapped in a claustrophobic and morally prejudiced society.

Neil Munro *Para Handy.* Engaging and witty stories relating the adventures of a Clyde puffer captain as he more or less legally steers his grubby ship up and down the west coast. Despite a fond – if slightly patronizing – view of the Gaelic mind, they are enormous fun.

Ian Rankin *The Hanging Garden, The Falls* and *Fleshmarket Close.* Superbly plotted dark stories featuring Rebus, the maverick police detective who haunts the bars of Edinburgh. Now a TV series and the subject of a guided tour in the city.

James Robertson *The Fanatic.* Stunning debut novel set in the present-day Edinburgh ghost tours; the current "ghost" becomes fascinated by the seventeenth-century character he portrays and, by delving into the history of the period, reveals secrets of the past and present. *Joseph Knight*, his latest novel, set in the aftermath of Culloden, tells of the search for a black slave brought back to Scotland from the Caribbean.

Dorothy L. Sayers *Five Red Herrings.* A complicated tale involving railway timetables set in Gatehouse of Fleet in Galloway, but solved, of course, by Lord Peter Wimsey.

Sir Walter Scott *The Waverley Novels.* The books that did much to create the romanticized version of Scottish life and history.

Iain Crichton Smith *Consider the Lilies*. Poetic lament about the Highland Clearances by Scotland's finest bilingual (English and Gaelic) writer.

Muriel Spark *The Prime of Miss Jean Brodie*. Wonderful evocation of middle-class Edinburgh life and aspirations, still apparent in that city today.

Robert Louis Stevenson *Dr Jekyll and Mr Hyde, The Master of Ballantrae, Weir of Hermiston*. Nineteenth-century tales of intrigue and adventure. For more on Stevenson, see p.834 & p.160.

Nigel Tranter *The Bruce Trilogy*. Massive tome about Robert the Bruce by a prolific and hugely popular author on Scottish themes. *The Flockmasters* deals with the Clearances and *Kettle*

of Fish with salmon poaching in the Tweed.

Alan Warner *Morvern Callar*. Bleakly humorous story of a supermarket shelf-packer from Oban who finds her boyfriend has committed suicide in her kitchen and tries to put it out of her mind with the aid of sex, drugs and booze until she finds an appalling solution. It'll grip you. (See p.838 for an extract.)

Irvine Welsh *Irvine Welsh Omnibus*. A compendium including *Trainspotting, The Acid House* and *Marabou Stork Nightmares*, all of which can also be found as separate titles. Welsh trawls through the horrors of drug addiction, sexual fantasy, urban decay and hopeless youth but, thankfully, his unflinching attention is not without humour. *Porno*, his latest, is a slightly less bleak sequel to *Trainspotting*.

Children's fiction

Eleanor Atkinson *Greyfriars Bobby*. Part of Edinburgh folklore, this tear-jerking true story of a faithful dog who nightly visited his master's grave, is suitable for 10-year-olds and over.

George Mackay Brown *Pictures in the Cave*. A collection of stories based on folk tales, told by a master poet. Suitable for 9-year-olds and over.

Rowena Farre *Seal Morning*. An absorbing account of a young girl growing up on a remote croft in the Highlands towards the beginning of the last century and the wild life she adopted. Eight-year-olds and upwards will love it and so will adults.

Kathleen Fidler *Desperate Journey*. Story of a family driven from Scotland in the Sutherland Clearances across the Atlantic to Canada. *The Droving Lad* is a thriller about a boy and his first experience of herding cattle from the Highlands to the Lowlands. Suitable for 9-year-olds and over.

Mairi Hedderwick *Katie Morag and the Two Grandmothers*. One of the many delightful stories of a little girl and the trouble she gets in on the west-coast island of Struay, beautifully illustrated by the author. Suitable for reading to under-5s.

Ted Hughes *Nessie the Mannerless Monster*. A verse story about the famous monster who goes to London to see the queen. Suitable for 5- to 8-year-olds.

Mollie Hunter *A Stranger Came Ashore*. Set in Shetland, this is a tragic and gripping historical tale. Suitable for 10-year-olds and over.

Jackie Kay *The Frog Who Dreamed She Was an Opera Singer*. Collection of poems, funny and appealing, for 8-year-olds upward. *Strawgirl* is the story of a mixed-race child growing up on a Highland farm in a white community, for 10-year-olds upwards.

Gavin Maxwell *Ring of Bright Water*. Heart-warming true story of the author's relationship with three otters. Suitable for 5-to-8-year-olds.

Aileen Paterson *Maisie Goes to Glasgow.* There are lots of adventures of this mischievous cat, mostly set in Scotland. Suitable for 5- to 8-year-olds.

Stephen Potts *Hunting Gumnor.* A haunting story set on a Scottish island, both an adventure and a fantasy, which affirms the values of island life and the creatures that live there. Suitable for ages 10 and upwards.

Robert Louis Stevenson *Kidnapped.* A thrilling historical adventure set in eighteenth-century Scotland. Every bit as exciting as the better-known *Treasure Island.*

Andrew Wolffe *Rory and his Christmas Surprise.* The latest edition to the delightfully illustrated books about Rory, a small boy, and his dog, Scruff McDuff, who live by the sea. Suitable for reading to young children.

Poetry

George Mackay Brown *Selected Poems 1954–1983.* Brown's work is as haunting, beautiful and gritty as the Orkney islands which inspire it. The most recent collection is the posthumous *Travellers,* featuring work either previously unpublished or appearing only in newspapers and periodicals.

Robert Burns *Selected Poems.* Scotland's most famous bard. Immensely popular all over the world, his best-known works are his earlier ones, including *Auld Lang Syne* and *My Love Is Like A Red, Red Rose.* (See p.833 for an example of his work.)

Cockburn and Marsack (eds) *Intimate Expanses: XXV Scottish Poems 1978–2002.* There's one for each year from a variety of poets.

Crawford and Imlah (eds) *The New Penguin Book of Scottish Verse.* A historical survey of Scottish verse and its many languages, from St Columba to Don Paterson.

Carol Anne Duffy *Selected Poems.* Some of her work reflects her childhood in Glasgow; all of it is personal and packed with striking images. *The World's Wife* is a playful reflection on the lives of Mrs Midas, Mrs Aesop, Frau Freud etc, while *Rapture* celebrates love in all its forms.

William Dunbar *The Poems of William Dunbar.* An important literary figure in his time, his poetry reveals the concerns and attitudes to life at the court of James IV.

Douglas Dunn *New Selected Poems 1964–99.* A writer of delicately wrought poetry, ranging from the intensely private to poems involved with Scottish issues. He also edited *The Faber Book of Twentieth-Century Scottish Poetry,* featuring all the big names (except for Dunn himself) and some lesser-known works.

Kathleen Jamie *The Queen of Sheba, The Donkey's Ears* and *Jizzen.* Although often set in Scotland, her work has a wider significance; its tone is strong, almost angry, and its themes both personal and universal. Her latest volume, *The Tree House,* is rooted in the natural world and its relationship to ours.

Jackie Kay *The Adoption Papers* and *Other Lovers.* Her poetry explores being black, Scottish and gay and deals with personal relationships in an accessibly intimate way. Latest collection of poetry, *Life Mask,* investigates some of the difficult moments in her own life, such as meeting her father in Nigeria for the first time.

Liz Lochhead *Bagpipe Muzak; True Confessions.* A strong straightforward style, coupled with shrewd observations, Lochhead speaks with immediacy on personal relationships. Some of her best work is in *Dreaming Frankenstein & Collected Poems.* Her latest major body of poetry, *The Colour of Black and White,* conveys her voice in a variety of styles.

Norman MacCaig *Selected Poems*. Justly celebrated for its keen observation of the natural world, MacCaig's work remains intellectually challenging without being arid. His poetry, rooted in the Highlands, uses detail to explore a universal landscape. *Norman MacCaig; A Celebration* is an anthology written for his 85th birthday, and includes work by more than ninety writers, including Ted Hughes and Seamus Heaney.

Hugh MacDiarmid *Selected Poems*. Immensely influential, not least for his nationalist views and his use of Scots, MacDiarmid's poetry is richly challenging. *A Drunk Man Looks at a Thistle* is acknowledged as a masterpiece of Scottish literature.

Sorley Maclean (Somhairle Macgill-Eain) *From Wood to Ridge: Collected Poems*. Written in Gaelic, his poems have been translated in bilingual editions all over the world; they deal with the sorrows of poverty, war and love.

William McGonagall *McGonagall: A Selection* (edited by Colin Walker). Verse so bad you have to read it – or perhaps not.

McMillan and Byrne (eds) *Modern Scottish Women Poets*. The work of over a hundred women writers of the twen-

tieth century, some of whom have sunk into undeserved oblivion.

John McQueen and Tom Scott (eds) *The Oxford Book of Scottish Verse*. Claims to be the most comprehensive anthology of Scottish poetry ever published.

Edwin Morgan *New Selected Poems*. A love of words and their sounds is evident in his poems, which are refreshingly varied and often experimental. He comments on the Scottish scene with shrewdness and humour.

Edwin Muir *Collected Poems*. Muir's childhood on Orkney at the turn of the century remained with him as a dream of paradise from which he was banished to Glasgow. His poems are passionately concerned with Scotland.

Don Paterson *God's Gift to Women* and *Nil Nil*. A writer whose work examines the working class, sex and drink with a wry sense of humour and an exciting, innovative voice. His latest work, *Landing Light* is more intimate.

Iain Crichton Smith *Collected Poems*. Born on the Isle of Lewis, Crichton Smith wrote with feeling and sometimes bitterness, in both Gaelic and English, of the life of the rural communities, the iniquities of the Free Church, the need to revive Gaelic culture and the glory of the Scottish landscape.

Folklore and legend

Margaret Bennett *Scottish Customs from the Cradle to the Grave*. Fascinating and sympathetic extensive oral history.

Alan J. Bruford and Donald Archie McDonald (eds) *Scottish Traditional Tales*. A huge collection of folk stories from all over Scotland, taken from tape archives.

Neil Philip (ed.) *The Penguin Book of Scottish Folk Tales*. A collection of over a hundred folk tales from all over Scotland.

Nigel Tranter *Tales and Traditions of Scottish Castles*. The myths and legends of some of Scotland's more famous castles.

History, politics and culture

Historic Scotland. A series of books covering many aspects of Scotland's history and prehistory, including the Picts, Vikings, Romans and Celts. All are

colourful, accessible and well presented. Available at many Historic Scotland properties as well as bookshops.

Scotland's Past in Action "Building Railways"; "Feeding Scotland"; "Fishing and Whaling". Some of the titles in an attractive series of small illustrated books, produced by the National Museums of Scotland.

Adamnan (trans. John Marsden) *The Illustrated Life of Columba*. The original story of the life of St Columba, annotated and accompanied by beautiful photos of the places associated with him, in particular the Hebridean island of Iona.

Ian Adams and Meredith Somerville *Cargoes of Despair and Hope*. Riveting mixture of contemporary documents and letters telling the story of Scottish emigration to North America from 1603 to 1803.

Neal Ascherson *Stone Voices*. Intelligent, thought-provoking ponderings on the nature of Scotland and the road to devolution from Scots-born *Observer* journalist, interspersed with personal anecdotes.

Bella Bathurst *The Lighthouse Stevensons*. Straightforward account of the fascinating lives and amazing achievements of Robert Louis Stevenson's family, who built many of the island lighthouses round Scotland.

Colin Bell *Scotland's Century – An Autobiography of the Nation*. Richly illustrated and readable account of the social history of Scotland, based on radio interviews with people from all walks of life.

Tom Devine *The Scottish Nation 1700–2000*. Best post-Union history, from the last Scottish Parliament to the new one.

G. Donaldson and R.S. Morpeth (eds) *A Dictionary of Scottish History*. A user-friendly volume listing dates, facts and potted biographies.

Ninian Dunnett *Out on the Edge*. A readable series of interviews with Scots, probing the national psyche.

George MacDonald Fraser *The Steel Bonnets*. Immensely enjoyable and erudite account of sixteenth-century cattle-rustling, feud, blackmail, murder and mayhem in the border country between England and Scotland.

John Guy *My Heart is My Own*. Somehow, although you know the story, Guy manages to make the tale of Mary, Queen of Scots a real page-turner as well as historically informative.

David Howarth *The Shetland Bus*. Wonderfully detailed story of the espionage and resistance operations carried out from Shetland by British and Norwegian servicemen, written by someone who was directly involved.

Michael Lynch *Scotland: A New History*. Probably the best available overview of Scottish history, taking the story up to 1992. He is also the editor of the more weighty *Oxford Companion to Scottish History*.

James MacKay *William Wallace*. An authoritative biography, and the best of a rash of books capitalizing on the success of the movie *Braveheart* – the book is more of a stickler for historical fact than the film.

Fitzroy Maclean *Bonnie Prince Charlie*. Very readable and more or less definitive biography of Scotland's most romanticized historical figure, written by the "real" James Bond.

John Prebble *Glencoe, Culloden, The Highland Clearances*. Emotive, subjective and accessible accounts of key events in Highland history.

John Purser *Scotland's Music*. Comprehensive overview of traditional and classical music in Scotland; thorough and scholarly but readable.

T.C. Smout *A History of the Scottish People 1560–1830* and *A Century of the Scottish People 1830–1950*. Widely acclaimed books, brimful of interest for those keen on social history. Smout combines enormous learning with a clear and entertaining style.

Martin Wallace *A Little Book of Celtic Saints*. A small but informative volume.

Art, architecture and historic sites

Exploring Scotland's Heritage. Detailed, beautifully illustrated series produced by the Stationery Office, with the emphasis on historic buildings and archeological sites. Recently updated titles cover Orkney, Shetland, the Highlands, Aberdeen and Northeast Scotland, Fife, Perthshire and Angus, and Argyll and the Western Isles.

Jude Burkhauser *Glasgow Girls: Women in Art and Design 1880–1920*. The lively contribution of women to the development of the Glaswegian Art Nouveau movement is recognized in this authoritative account.

Alan Crawford *Charles Rennie Mackintosh*. Part of the World of Art series, describing the major contribution of Scotland's premier architect and designer.

Kitty Cruft and Andrew Fraser (eds) *James Craig 1744–95*. Distinguished authors offer reassessments of Craig's achievement in designing Edinburgh's New Town.

Bill Hare *Contemporary Painting in Scotland*. Features the work of 48 contemporary artists including John Bellany, Bruce McLean and Elizabeth Blackadder, and gives special attention to the "New Painting" that emerged in the 1980s and developed into a distinctive Scottish style. Expensive and serious.

Philip Long & Elizabeth Cumming *The Scottish Colourists*

1900–30. A recognition of the importance of the work of this group of artists; lavishly illustrated.

Duncan MacMillan *Scottish Art 1460–1990*. Lavish overview of Scottish painting with good sections on landscape, portraiture and the Glasgow Boys. Also a detailed look at modern art in *Scottish Art in the 20th Century 1890–2001*.

Charles McKean, David Walker and Frank Walker *Central Glasgow*. An architectural romp through the city centre and West End, with plenty of photographs and informed comment; part of the Rutland Press series of illustrated guides to Scottish architecture. Whilst authoritative, they are not at all stuffy and are conveniently pocket-sized. In addition, the Rutland Press has produced studies of such notable figures as James Miller, Basil Spence and Peter Womersley.

Colin McWilliam (ed.) *The Buildings of Scotland*. There are volumes on various regions of Scotland, including Fife, Edinburgh and Lothian, and Argyll and Bute, all of which provide comprehensive and scholarly coverage of every building of importance. Though easy to follow, they would best suit visitors intending to spend more than a couple of weeks in Scotland.

Steven Parissien *Adam Style*. A well-illustrated account of the birth of the Neoclassical style named for the two Scottish Adam brothers, Robert and James.

Guides and picture books

Scottish Wild Flowers, Scottish Birds. Well-illustrated and informative small guides by Collins. Also in the guide series are *Clans and Tartans* and *Scottish Surnames* which are a first step on the road to genealogy.

Colin Baxter *Scotland from the Air, Portrait of Scotland*; with Jim Crumley:

Portrait of Edinburgh; with Jack McLean: *The City of Glasgow*. Best known for his ubiquitous postcards, Baxter's photographs succeed in capturing the grandeur of Scotland's moody landscapes and characterful cityscapes in many lavishly illustrated books.

Derek Cooper *Skye*. A gazetteer and guide and an indispensable mine of information; although written in 1970, it has been updated and revised.

🏃 **Hamish Haswell-Smith** *The Scottish Islands.* An exhaustive and impressive gazetteer with maps and absorbing information on all the Scottish islands. Filled with attractive sketches and paintings, the book is breathtaking in its thoroughness and lovingly gathered detail.

Ranald Macinnes *The Aberdeen Guide.* Series of city walks with detailed architectural and historical background.

Magnus Magnusson and Graham White (eds) *The Nature of Scotland – Landscape, Wildlife and People.* Glossy picture-based book on Scotland's natural heritage, from geology to farming and conservation. Good section on crofting.

Andrew Murray Scott *Discovering Dundee: The Story of a City.* A good popular history of the city and some of its famous citizens.

N.S. Newton *The Life and Times of Inverness.* Inverness has a long history on account of its crucial position at the head of the Great Glen.

Donald Omand *The Borders Book.* An entertaining history of the much disputed land between England and Scotland, from prehistory to its present passion for rugby.

Paul Ramsay *Lochs & Glens of Scotland.* Informative text and stunning photographs of the Highlands that make you want to book a holiday immediately.

Cecil Sinclair *Tracing your Scottish Ancestors.* Probably the best guide to ancestry research in the Scottish Record Office – definitely worth reading before visiting General Register House.

David Williams *The Glasgow Guide.* Thirteen walks round Glasgow, with the emphasis on historical points of interest: buildings, graveyards, museums and architecture.

Michael and Elspeth Wills *Walks in Edinburgh's Old Town.* A small guide which takes you into the nooks and crannies of Scotland's most historically intense city centre. Also *Walks in Edinburgh's New Town* to get you up to date.

Memoirs and travelogues

George Mackay Brown *Letters from Hamnavoe.* A selection of writings from a weekly column in *The Orcadian,* chronicling everyday life in Orkney during the early 1970s. Gentle and perceptive.

David Craig *On the Crofter's Trail.* Using anecdotes and interviews with descendants, Craig conveys the hardship and tragedy of the Highland Clearances without being mawkish.

🏃 **Elizabeth Grant of Rothiemurchus** *Memoirs of a Highland Lady.* Hugely readable recollections written with wit and perception at the turn of the eighteenth century, charting social changes in Edinburgh, London and particularly Speyside.

Peter Hill *Stargazing.* Engaging account of being a tyro lighthouse keeper

on three of Scotland's most famous lighthouses: Pladda, Ailsa Craig and Hyskeir.

Kathleen Jamie *Findings.* Jamie brings her poetic eye to bear on travels round her native Scotland.

🏃 **Samuel Johnson and James Boswell** *A Journey to the Western Isles of Scotland* and *The Journal of a Tour to the Hebrides.* Lively accounts of a famous journey around the islands taken by the great lexicographer Dr Samuel Johnson and his biographer and friend.

John Lister-Kaye *Song of the Rolling Earth.* The author tells what led him to become a passionate naturalist and turn a derelict Highland estate into a field study centre where he encourages others to live in harmony with the natural environment. An inspiring story.

Alasdair MacLean *Night Falls on Ardnamurchan.* First published in 1984 and recently reprinted, this is a classic story of the life and death of the Highland community in which the author grew up.

Iain Mitchell *Isles of the West, Isle of the North.* In the first book, Mitchell sails round the Inner Hebrides, talking to locals and incomers, siding with the former, caricaturing the latter, and, with a fair bit of justification, laying into the likes of the RSPB and SNH. *Isles of the North* gives Orkney and Shetland the same treatment, before heading off to Norway to find out how it can be done differently.

Edwin Muir *Scottish Journey.* A classic travelogue written in 1935 with sympathetic insight by the Orcadian writer on his return to Scotland from London.

June Skinner Sawyers *The Road North.* An entertaining collection of three hundred years of some of the best Scottish travel writing, divided into regions.

🏃 **Robert Louis Stevenson** *Edinburgh: Picturesque Notes.* Charming evocation of Stevenson's birthplace – its moods, curiosities and influences on his work. First published in 1879.

David Thomson *Nairn in Darkness and Light.* Beautifully written evocation of Nairn in the 1920s.

Betsy Whyte *The Yellow on the Broom.* A fascinating glimpse of childhood in a traveller family, both on the road and in council housing for part of the year to comply with school attendance. Also *Red Rowans and Wild Honey.*

Wildlife and outdoor pursuits

Bartholomew Walks Series. The series covers individual areas of Scotland, including Perthshire, Loch Lomond and the Trossachs, Oban, Mull and Lochaber, and Skye and Wester Ross. Each booklet has a range of walks of varying lengths with clear maps and descriptions.

Ordnance Survey Pathfinder Series. Top-quality maps, colour pictures and clear text. Titles include "Loch Lomond and the Trossachs", "Fort William and Glen Coe" and "Perthshire".

Scotland for Game, Sea and Coarse Fishing. General guide on what to fish, where and for how much, along with notes on records, regulations and convenient accommodation. Published in association with the Scottish Tourist Board.

Donald Bennet *The Munros.* Authoritative and attractively illustrated hill walkers' guides to the Scottish peaks. Scottish Mountaineering Trust also publishes guides to districts and specific climbs, as well as *The Corbetts* by Scott Johnstone et al.

🏃 **Hamish Brown** *Hamish's Mountain Walk / Climbing the*

Corbetts. The best of the travel narratives about walking in the Scottish Highlands. *The Fife Coastal Path* takes you from the Forth Bridge to St Andrews with maps, photos and info.

Anthony Burton *The Caledonian Canal.* A book for walkers, cyclists and boaters with maps and details of boat rental, accommodation and the like. The author has also covered *The Southern Upland Way* and *The West Highland Way.*

Andrew Dempster *Classic Mountain Scrambles in Scotland.* Guide to hill walks in Scotland that combine straightforward walking with some rock-climbing.

Derek Douglas *The Thistle: A Chronicle of Scottish Rugby.* History of the game for enthusiasts, from Victorian times to the present day, with some good photos.

David Hamilton *The Scottish Golf Guide.* An inexpensive paperback with descriptions of and useful information about 84 of Scotland's best courses from the remote to the Open Championship.

John Hancox *Collins Pocket Reference – Cycling in Scotland*. Spiral-bound edition with over fifty road routes of all grades up and down the country, each with a useful route map. For more off-road mountain bike routes, try *Scotland: The Central Valley* by Derek Purdy in the *Ride Your Bike* series, or *101 Bike Routes in Scotland* by Harry Henniker.

🏃 George Hendry *Midges in Scotland*. Everything you ever wanted to know about *Culicoides impunctatus* – a strangely satisfying read on warm, damp nights in the Highlands.

Philip Lusby & Jenny Wright *Scottish Wild Plants*. Beautifully produced book about the rarer plants of Scotland, their discovery and conservation, produced in conjunction with the Royal Botanic Gardens of Edinburgh.

Michael Madders and Julia Welstead *Where to Watch Birds in Scotland*. Region-by-region guide with maps, details on access and habitat, and notes on what to see when.

Jenny Parke *Ski & Snowboard: Scotland*. Informative book about where to find the best slopes, with loads of useful advice.

Ralph Storer *100 Best Routes on Scottish Mountains*. A compilation of the best day-walks in Scotland, including some of the classics overlooked by the Munroing guides.

Food and drink

Iain Banks *Raw Spirit*. A cross between a travel book and autobiography, with info on whisky thrown in for good measure.

Annette Hope *A Caledonian Feast*. Authoritative and entertaining history of Scottish food and social life from the ninth to the twentieth centuries. Lots of recipes.

Michael Jackson *Malt Whisky Companion*. An attractively put-together tome, considered by many to be the bible of malt whisky tasting.

Wallace Lockhart *The Scots and Their Fish*. Tells the history of fish and fishing in Scotland, and ends with a selection of traditional recipes.

Claire Macdonald. *Simply Seasonal*. Lady Claire Macdonald of Macdonald has become widely known in Scottish cookery circles. She promotes the use of native food and runs a successful hotel on Skye.

🏃 Nick Nairn *Wild Harvest, Wild Harvest 2, Island Harvest, New Scottish Cookery*. Glossy TV tie-ins by an engaging young, talented Scottish chef, who took up the challenge of gathering and eating from the wild and is now promoting imaginative ways to serve Scottish traditional fare.

Language

Language

Language

L
anguage is a thorny, complex and often highly political issue in Scotland. If you're not from Scotland yourself, you're most likely to be addressed in a variety of **English**, spoken in a Scottish accent. Even then, you're likely to hear phrases and words that are part of what is known as Lowland Scottish or **Scots**, which is now officially recognized as a distinct language in its own right. To a lesser extent, **Gaelic**, too, remains a living language, particularly in the *Gàidhealtachd* or Gaelic-speaking areas of the Western Isles, parts of Skye and a few scattered Hebridean islands. In Orkney and Shetland, the local dialect of Scots contains many words carried over from **Norn**, the Norse language spoken in the Northern Isles from the time of the Vikings until the eighteenth century.

Scots

Lowland Scottish or **Scots** is spoken by thirty percent of the Scottish population, according to the latest survey. It began life as a northern branch of Anglo-Saxon, and emerged as a distinct language in the Middle Ages. From the 1370s until the Union in 1707, it was the country's main literary and documentary language. Since the eighteenth century, however, it has been systematically repressed to give preference to English.

Robbie Burns is the most obvious literary exponent of the Scots language, but there was a revival in the last century led by poets such as Hugh MacDiarmid. (For examples of the works of both writers, see "Books".) Only very recently has Scots enjoyed something of a renaissance, getting itself on the Scottish school curriculum in 1996, and achieving official recognition as a distinct language in 1998. Despite these enormous political achievements, many people (rightly or wrongly) still regard Scots as a dialect of English.

HarperCollins in the UK publishes a handy, pocket-sized Scots dictionary as a guide to the mysteries of Scottish vocabulary and idiom.

Gaelic

Scottish **Gaelic** (*Gàidhlig*, pronounced "gallic") is one of only four Celtic languages to survive into the modern age (Welsh, Breton and Irish Gaelic are the other three). Manx, the old language of the Isle of Man, died out early last century, while Cornish was finished as a community language way back in the eighteenth century. Scottish Gaelic is most closely related to Irish Gaelic and Manx – hardly surprising since Gaelic was introduced to Scotland from Ireland around the third century BC. Some folk still argue that Scottish Gaelic is merely a dialect of its parent language, Irish Gaelic, and indeed the two languages remain more or less mutually intelligible. From the fifth to the twelfth centuries, Gaelic enjoyed an expansionist phase, gradually becoming the national language, thanks partly to the backing of the Celtic Church in Iona.

At the end of this period, Gaelic was spoken throughout virtually all of what is now Scotland, the main exceptions being Orkney and Shetland.

From that high point onwards Gaelic began a steady decline. Even before Union with England, power, religious ideology and wealth gradually passed into non-Gaelic hands. The royal court was transferred to Edinburgh and an Anglo-Norman legal system was put in place. The Celtic Church was Romanized by the introduction of foreign clergy, and, most important of all, English and Flemish merchants colonized the new trading towns of the east coast. In addition, the pro-English attitudes held by the Covenanters led to strong anti-Gaelic feeling within the Church of Scotland from its inception.

The two abortive Jacobite rebellions of 1715 and 1745 furthered the language's decline, as did the Clearances that took place in the Gaelic-speaking Highlands from the 1770s to the 1850s, which forced thousands to migrate to central Scotland's new industrial belt or emigrate to North America. Although efforts were made to halt the decline in the first half of the nineteenth century, the 1872 Education Act gave no official recognition to Gaelic, and children were severely punished if they were caught speaking the language in school.

The 2001 census put the number of Gaelic speakers at under 60,000 (just over one percent of the population), the majority of whom live in the *Gàidhealtachd*, though there is thought to be an extended Gaelic community of perhaps 250,000 who have some understanding of the language. Since the 1980s, great efforts have been made to try and save the language, including the introduction of bilingual primary and nursery schools, and a huge increase in the amount of broadcasting time given to Gaelic-language and Gaelic music programmes, and the establishment of highly successful Gaelic colleges such as Sabhal Mòr Ostaig (@www.smo.uhi.ac.uk).

Gaelic grammar and pronunciation

Gaelic is a highly complex tongue, with a fiendish, antiquated **grammar** and, with only eighteen letters, an intimidating system of spelling. **Pronunciation** is easier than it appears at first glance; one general rule to remember is that the **stress** always falls on the first syllable of a word. The general rule of syntax is that the verb starts the sentence whether it's a question or not, followed by the subject and then the object; adjectives generally follow the word they are describing.

Gaelic has both short and long vowels, the latter being denoted by an acute or grave accent.

Short and long vowels

a as in cat; before nn and ll, as in cow
à as in bar
e as in pet
é like rain
i as in sight
í like free
o as in pot
ò like enthral
ó like cow
u like scoot
ù like loo

Vowel combinations

Gaelic is littered with diphthongs, which, rather like in English, can be pronounced in several different ways depending on the individual word.

ai like cat, or pet; before dh or gh, like street
ao like the sound in the middle of colonel
ei like mate
ea like pet, or cat, and sometimes like mate; before ll or nn like cow
èa as in hear
eu like train, or fear

ia like fear

io like fear, or shorter than street

ua like wooer

Consonants

The consonants listed below are those that differ substantially from the English.

b at the beginning of a word as in big; in the middle or at the end of a word like the p in pair

bh at the beginning of a word like the v in van; elsewhere it is silent

c as in cat; after a vowel it has aspiration before it

ch always as in loch, never as in church

cn like the cr in crowd

d like the d in dog, but with the tongue pressed against the back of the upper teeth; at the beginning of a word or before e or i, like the j in jam; in the middle or at the end of a word like the t in cat; after i like the ch in church

dh before and after a, o or u is an aspirated g, rather like a gargle; before e or i like the y in yes; elsewhere silent

fh usually silent; sometimes like the h in house

g at the beginning of a word as in get; before e like the y in yes; in the middle or end of a word like the ck in sock; after i like the ch in loch

gh at the beginning of a word as in get; before or after a, o or u rather like a gargle; after i sometimes like the y in gay, but often silent

l after i and sometimes before e like the l in lot; elsewhere a peculiarly Gaelic sound produced by flattening the front of the tongue against the palate

mh like the v in van

p at the beginning of a word as in pet; elsewhere it has aspiration before it

rt pronounced as sht

s before e or i like the sh in ship; otherwise as in English

sh before a, o or u like the h in house; before e like the ch in loch

t before e or i like the ch in church; in the middle or at the end of a word it has aspiration before it; otherwise as in English

th at the beginning of a word, like the h in house; elsewhere, and in the word thu, silent

Gaelic phrases and vocabulary

The choice is limited when it comes to **teach–yourself Gaelic** courses, but the BBC *Can Seo* cassette and book are perfect for starting you off. Drier and more academic is *Teach Yourself Gaelic*, which is aimed at bringing beginners to working competence. *Everyday Gaelic* by Morag MacNeill is the best phrasebook around. You can also get learning materials online from ⓦwww .smo.uhi.ac.uk.

Basic words and greetings in Gaelic

tha	yes
chan eil	no
hallo	hello
ciamar a tha thu?	how are you?
tha gu math	fine
tapadh leat	thank you
fàilte	welcome
thig a-staigh	come in
latha math	good day
mar sin leat	goodbye
oidhche mhath	goodnight
slàinte	cheers

an-dé	yesterday
an-diugh	today
maireach	tomorrow
taigh-òsda	hotel
taigh	house
sgeul	story
òran	song
ceòl	music
leabhar	book
aran	bread
uisge	water
uisge beatha	whisky
post oifis	post office
Dun Eideann	Edinburgh
Glaschu	Glasgow

Ameireaga	America	drum, from druim	ridge
Eire	Ireland	dubh	black
Sasainn	England	dun or dum, from dùn	fort
Lunnain	London	eilean	island

Gaelic geographical and place-name terms

The purpose of this list is to help with place-name derivations from Gaelic and with more detailed map reading.

abhainn	river	ess, from eas	waterfall
ach or auch, from achadh	field	fin, from fionn	white
ail, aileach	rock	gair or gare, from geàrr	short
Alba	Scotland	garv, from garbh	rough
aonach	ridge	geodha	cove
ard, ardan or arden, from àird	a point of land or height	glen, from gleann	valley
aros	dwelling	gower or gour, from gabhar	goat
ault, from allt	stream	inch, from innis	meadow or island
bad	brake or clump of trees	inver, from inbhir	river mouth
bagh	bay	ken or kin, from ceann	head
bal or bally, from baile	town, village	knock, from cnoc	hill
balloch, from bealach	mountain pass	kyle, from caolas	narrow strait
ban	white, fair	lag	hollow
bàrr	summit	larach	site of an old ruin
beg, from beag	small	liath	grey
ben, from beinn	mountain	loch	lake
blair, from blàr	field or battlefield	meall	round hill
cairn, from càrn	pile of stones	mon, from monadh	hill
camas	bay, harbour	more, from mór	large, great
cnoc	hill	rannoch, from raineach	bracken
coll or colly, from coille	wood or forest	ross, from ros	promontory
corran	a spit or point jutting into the sea	rubha	promontory
		sgeir	sea rock
		sgurr	sharp point
corrie, from coire	round hollow in mountainside, whirlpool	sron	nose, prow or promontory
		strath, from srath	broad valley
		tarbet, from tairbeart	isthmus
craig, from creag	rock, crag	tigh	house
cruach	bold hill	tir or tyre, from tìr	land
		torr	hill, castle
		tràigh	shore
		uig	shelter
		uisge	water

Norn

Between the tenth and seventeenth centuries, the chief language of Orkney and Shetland was **Norn**, a Scandinavian tongue close to modern Faroese and Icelandic. After the end of Norse rule, and with the transformation of the Church, the law, commerce and education, Norn gradually lost out to Scots and English, eventually petering out completely in the eighteenth century. Today, Orkney and Shetland have their own dialects, and individual islands and communities within each group have local variations. The **dialects** have a Scots base, with some Old Norse words; however, they don't sound strongly Scottish, with the Orkney accent – which has been likened to the Welsh one – especially distinctive. Listed below are some of the words you're most likely to hear, including some common elements in place names.

Norn phrases and vocabulary

ayre	beach	muckle	large
bister	farm	noost	hollow place where a boat is drawn up
böd	fisherman's store		
bruck	rubbish	noup	steep headland
burra	heath rush	peerie /peedie	small
crö	sheepfold	plantiecrub (or plantiecrö)	small dry-stone enclosure for growing cabbages
eela	rod-fishing from small boats		
ferrylouper	incomer (Orkney)	quoy	enclosed, cultivated common land
fourareen	four-oared boat		
foy	party or festival	roost	tide race
geo	coastal inlet	scattald	common grazing land
haa	laird's house	scord	gap or pass in a ridge of hills
hap	hand-knitted shawl		
howe	mound	setter	farm
kame	ridge of hills	shaela	dark grey
kishie	basket	sixern	six-oared boat
mool	headland	soothmoother	incomer (Shetland)
moorit	brown	voe	sea inlet
mootie	tiny		

Glossary

Auld Old.

Aye Yes.

Bairn Baby.

Baronial see "Scottish Baronial" below.

Ben Hill or mountain.

Blackhouse Thick-walled traditional dwelling.

Bonnie Pretty.

Bothy Primitive cottage or hut; farmworker's or shepherd's mountain shelter.

Brae Slope or hill.

Brig Bridge.

Broch Circular prehistoric stone fort.

Burn Small stream or brook.

Byre Shelter for cattle; cottage.

Cairn Mound of stones.

CalMac Caledonian MacBrayne ferry company.

Carse Riverside area of flat alluvium.

Ceilidh (pronounced "kay-lee") Social gathering involving dancing, drinking, singing and storytelling.

Central belt The densely populated strip of central Scotland between the Forth and Clyde estuaries, incorporating the conurbations of Edinburgh, Glasgow and Stirling.

Clan Extended family.

Clearances Policy adopted by late eighteenth- and early nineteenth-century landowners to evict tenant crofters in order to create space for more profitable sheep-grazing. Families cleared from the Highlands were often put on emigrant ships to North America or the colonies.

Corbett A mountain between 2500ft and 3000ft high.

Corbie-stepped Architectural term; any set of steps on a gable.

Covenanters Supporter of the Presbyterian Church in the seventeenth century.

Crannog Celtic lake or bog dwelling.

Croft Small plot of farmland with house, common in the Highlands.

Crow-stepped Same as corbie-stepped.

Dolmen Grave chamber.

Dram Literally, one-sixteenth of a fluid ounce. Usually refers to any small measure of whisky.

Dun Fortified mound.

First-foot The first person to enter a household after midnight on Hogmanay (see below).

Firth A wide sea inlet or estuary.

Gillie Personal guide used on hunting or fishing trips.

Glen Deep, narrow mountain valley.

Harling Limestone and gravel mix used to cover buildings.

Hogmanay New Year's Eve.

Howe Valley.

Howff Meeting place; pub.

HS Historic Scotland, a government-funded heritage organization.

Jacobite Supporter of the Stewart claim to the throne, most famously Bonnie Prince Charlie.

Ken Knowledge; understanding.

Kilt Knee-length tartan skirt worn by Highland men.

Kirk Church.

Laird Landowner; aristocrat.

Law Rounded hill.

Links Grassy coastal land; coastal golf course.

Loch Lake.

Lochan Little loch.

Mac/Mc These prefixes in Scottish surnames derive from the Gaelic, meaning "son of". In Scots "Mac" is used for both sexes. In Gaelic "Nic" is used for women: Donnchadh Mac Aoidh is Duncan MacKay, Iseabail Nic Aoidh is Isabel MacKay.

Machair Sandy, grassy, lime-rich coastal land, generally used for grazing.

Manse Official home of a Presbyterian minister.

Mercat Cross lit. Market Cross. The decorative stone or wooden pillar which in medieval towns and cities indicated the central gathering point for the local market; often also the site of proclamations and occasionally other government business such as public executions. Not many remain in situ, though the spot where they sat is often remembered in place names or locals' street knowledge.

Munro A mountain over 3000ft high.

Munro-bagging The sport of trying to climb as many Munros as possible.

NTS The National Trust for Scotland, a heritage organization.

Peel Fortified tower, built to withstand Border raids.

Pend Archway or vaulted passage.

Presbyterian The form of Church government used in the official (Protestant) Church of Scotland, established by John Knox during the Reformation.

Runrig A common form of land tenure in which separate ridges are cultivated by different occupiers under joint agreement.

RSPB Royal Society for the Protection of Birds.

Sassenach Literally "Saxon"; used by Highlanders to refer to Lowlanders, though commonly used to describe the English.

Scottish Baronial Style of architecture favoured by the Scottish land-owning class featuring crow-stepped gables and round turrets.

Shinty Stick and ball game played in the Highlands, with similarities to hockey.

Smiddy Smithy.

SNH Scottish Natural Heritage, a government-funded conservation body.

SNP Scottish National Party.

Sporran Leather purse worn in front of, or at the side of, a kilt.

Tartan Check-patterned woollen cloth, particular patterns being associated with particular clans.

Thane A landowner of high rank; the chief of a clan.

Trews Tartan trousers.

Wee Small.

Wee Frees Followers of the Free Presbyterian or Free Church of Scotland.

Wynd Narrow lane.

Yett Gate or door.

Travel
store

TRAVEL

& MORE

Small print and

A Rough Guide to Rough Guides

Published in 1982, the first Rough Guide – to Greece – was a student scheme that became a publishing phenomenon. Mark Ellingham, a recent graduate in English from Bristol University, had been travelling in Greece the previous summer and couldn't find the right guidebook. With a small group of friends he wrote his own guide, combining a highly contemporary, journalistic style with a thoroughly practical approach to travellers' needs.

The immediate success of the book spawned a series that rapidly covered dozens of destinations. And, in addition to impecunious backpackers, Rough Guides soon acquired a much broader and older readership that relished the guides' wit and inquisitiveness as much as their enthusiastic, critical approach and value-for-money ethos.

These days, Rough Guides include recommendations from shoestring to luxury and cover more than 200 destinations around the globe, including almost every country in the Americas and Europe, more than half of Africa and most of Asia and Australasia. Our ever-growing team of authors and photographers is spread all over the world, particularly in Europe, the USA and Australia.

In the early 1990s, Rough Guides branched out of travel, with the publication of Rough Guides to World Music, Classical Music and the Internet. All three have become benchmark titles in their fields, spearheading the publication of a wide range of books under the Rough Guide name.

Including the travel series, Rough Guides now number more than 350 titles, covering: phrasebooks, waterproof maps, music guides from Opera to Heavy Metal, reference works as diverse as Conspiracy Theories and Shakespeare, and popular culture books from iPods to Poker. Rough Guides also produce a series of more than 120 World Music CDs in partnership with World Music Network.

Visit www.roughguides.com to see our latest publications.

Rough Guide travel images are available for commercial licensing at www.roughguidespictures.com

ROUGH
GUIDES

SMALL PRINT

Rough Guide credits

Text editors: Karoline Densley and Helena Smith
Layout: Ajay Verma
Cartography: Maxine Repath
Picture editor: Mark Thomas
Production: Aimee Hampson
Proofreader: Jennifer Speake
Cover design: Chloë Roberts
Photographer: Helena Smith
Editorial: London Kate Berens, Claire Saunders, Geoff Howard, Ruth Blackmore, Polly Thomas, Richard Lim, Clifton Wilkinson, Alison Murchie, Andy Turner, Keith Drew, Edward Aves, Nikki Birrell, Helen Marsden, Alice Park, Sarah Eno, David Paul, Lucy White, Joe Staines, Duncan Clark, Peter Buckley, Matthew Milton, Tracy Hopkins, Ruth Tidball; **New York** Andrew Rosenberg, Richard Koss, Steven Horak, AnneLise Sorensen, Amy Hegarty, Hunter Slaton, April Isaacs, Sean Mahoney
Design & Pictures: London Simon Bracken, Dan May, Diana Jarvis, Jj Luck, Harriet Mills; **Delhi** Umesh Aggarwal, Madhulita Mohapatra, Jessica Subramanian, Amit Verma, Ankur Guha, Pradeep Thapliyal

Production: Katherine Owers, Sophie Hewat;
Cartography: London Ed Wright, Katie Lloyd-Jones; **Delhi** Manish Chandra, Jai Prakash Mishra, Rajesh Chhibber, Ashutosh Bharti, Rajesh Mishra, Animesh Pathak, Jasbir Sandhu, Karobi Gogoi, Amod Singh
Online: New York Jennifer Gold, Suzanne Welles, Kristin Mingrone; **Delhi** Manik Chauhan, Narender Kumar, Manish Shekhar Jha, Lalit K. Sharma, Rakesh Kumar, Chhandita Chakravarty
Marketing & Publicity: London Richard Trillo, Niki Hanmer, David Wearn, Demelza Dallow, Louise Maher; **New York** Geoff Colquitt, Megan Kennedy, Katy Ball; **Delhi** Reem Khokhar
Custom publishing and foreign rights: Philippa Hopkins
Manager India: Punita Singh
Series editor: Mark Ellingham
Reference Director: Andrew Lockett
PA to Managing and Publishing Directors: Megan McIntyre
Publishing Director: Martin Dunford
Managing Director: Kevin Fitzgerald

Publishing information

This seventh edition published April 2006 by
Rough Guides Ltd,
80 Strand, London WC2R 0RL
345 Hudson St, 4th Floor,
New York, NY 10014, USA
14 Local Shopping Centre, Panchsheel Park,
New Delhi 110017, India
Distributed by the Penguin Group
Penguin Books Ltd,
80 Strand, London WC2R 0RL
Penguin Putnam, Inc.
375 Hudson Street, NY 10014, USA
Penguin Group (Australia)
250 Camberwell Road, Camberwell,
Victoria 3124, Australia
Penguin Books Canada Ltd,
10 Alcorn Avenue, Toronto, Ontario,
Canada M4V 1E4
Penguin Group (New Zealand)
Cnr Rosedale and Airborne Roads
Albany, Auckland, New Zealand
Cover design by Peter Dyer.

Typeset in Bembo and Helvetica to an original design by Henry Iles.
Printed in LegoPrint S.p.A in Italy
© Rob Humphreys, Donald Reid 2006

888pp includes index
A catalogue record for this book is available from the British Library
ISBN 13: 781-8-43536-666-6
ISBN 10: 1-84353-666-8

1 3 5 7 9 8 6 4 2

SMALL PRINT

Help us update

We've gone to a lot of effort to ensure that the seventh edition of **The Rough Guide to Scotland** is accurate and up to date. However, things change – places get "discovered", opening hours are notoriously fickle, restaurants and rooms raise prices or lower standards. If you feel we've got it wrong or left something out, we'd like to know, and if you can remember the address, the price, the time, the phone number, so much the better.

We'll credit all contributions, and send a copy of the next edition (or any other Rough Guide

if you prefer) for the best letters. Everyone who writes to us and isn't already a subscriber will receive a copy of our full-colour thrice-yearly newsletter. Please mark letters: **"Rough Guide Scotland Update"** and send to: Rough Guides, 80 Strand, London WC2R 0RL, or Rough Guides, 4th Floor, 345 Hudson St, New York, NY 10014. Or send an email to **mail@roughguides.com**

Have your questions answered and tell others about your trip at
www.roughguides.atinfopop.com

Acknowledgements

The authors would like to thank the National Trust for Scotland, Historic Scotland, VisitScotland (in various guises), Deborah Brown at CalMac and Karoline for trawling through Scotland twice.

Rob Humphreys would also like to thank Alasdair Enticknap for frontline dispatches, Val & Gordon for heading once more for the Borders and for sampling D&G, Val (again) for the Northern Isles, Kate, Stan & Josh for going to Skye out of season, and to Kate for lugging a rucksack around the Hebrides.

Donald Reid would also like to thank Rob, Karoline and Helena for staying the course

and all they add to the book, Colin Hutchison for paddling so enthusiastically and effectively through the choppy waters, Barry Shelby for his west-coast wisdom, Henry Hepburn for Doric duties, and Robin Lee and Isla Leavery-Yap for capital contributions. Around the country there has been an abundance of useful insight, generous hospitality, timely assistance and friendly faces. Thanks to all. Granny R and Granny and Grandpa K had extra duties this time, but their support and encouragement was as valuable as ever. Mo did more than her fair share of the carrying and Riona explored exhaustively, but they kept me together, for which particular love and thanks.

Readers' letters

Thanks to all those readers of the sixth edition who took the trouble to write in with their amendments and additions. Apologies for any misspellings or omissions.

Gaele Amiot-Cadey, Helen Bennell, Anders Berglund, Ian and John Besch, Katy Broadhead, Adam Butler, Mary Byrne, Michaela Carlowe, Matt and Carrie, Guy and Varry Cocker, Jim Craig, Olga Crawford, Carolyn Datta, Linda Davis, Mike Dean, James Dress, Norinda Fennema, Chris Fort, Paul Gaskell, Andrew Godley, Colin Good, Phillip Greenstein, Matthew Hall, Alastair Hamilton, Andy Hamnett, Aybike Hatemi, Andrea Hemingway, Catherine Henderson, Ian and Mayumi Hepburn, Les and Faye Hinzman, Annelies van 't Hof, R Holland, Jerry Holmes, David Hopkinson, David Hoult, Linda Howe, Marian Hoyle, Margaret Hughes, David & Catriona Jones, Jody Joseph, Cindy Kasfikis, JC Kershaw, John F. King, Sheelagh Knapp, Reto Kromer, Mike and Cassandra Lawton, Andrea, Jochem, Bastian and Nils Liebermann, Jeff Lyons, Frank Maas, Doug MacDougall, Mrs Barbara MacGregor, Karin Mackinnon, Brent Marshall, Ben Mccallum, Karen McCaughtrie, Jim Murchison, Steve Murray, Steven & Judith Niechcial, Tom Paton, Alex Pattison-Appleton, Trevor Pollard, Hugh Raven, Grace Rose-Miller, Sheila Rowell, Mary Ellen Ryan, Ed Schlenk, Jackie Scott, Millicent Scott, Karen See, Alberto Saz Serraro, Annette Spencer, Rachel and Kerry Sutton-Spence, Sue Taylor, Stuart Todd, Mrs R. Thomas, Liz Wadsworth, David White, Adrian Wood, Helen Woods.

SMALL PRINT

Photo credits

All photos © Rough Guides except the following:

Introduction

Eilean Donan Castle © David Norton/Alamy
Otter, Aviemore © Niall Benvie/Corbis
Man drinking malt whisky © Bo Zaunders/Corbis
Trotternish, Isle of Skye © Rob Humphreys
Mountain walking on the Cuillin Ridge © Donald Reid
Buachaille Etive © Steve Austin/Corbis

Things not to miss

01 Mousa Broch © Christa Kniiff/Alamy
06 The Burrell Collection, Glasgow © David Lyons/Alamy
07 Distillery, Islay © Simon Grosset/Alamy
08 Shetland Folk Festival © Doug Houghton
09 Minke whale © Visual & Weitten SL/Alamy
10 Dunnottar Castle © Doug Houghton
13 Eigg © Rob Humphreys
16 Kinloch Castle, Rùm © Michael Jenner
26 Skiing in the Cairngorms © Bridget Clyde/Alamy
27 Flying above Orkney © Rob Humphreys
33 Glen Coe © Doug Houghton
35 South Harris Beach © Rob Humphreys
36 Maes Howe, Orkney © Doug Houghton

Architecture colour insert

Glasgow School of Art © Mark Fiennes/Accaid/Alamy

Festivals colour insert

Edinburgh Festival © Gideon Mendel/Corbis
Competitor at the Highland Games © David Robertson/Alamy
Haggis © Gibson & Smith/ Getty Images
Up Helly-Aa, Lerwick, Shetland © Homer Sykes/Alamy

The great outdoors colour insert

Mountain-biking through the Great Glen © John James/Alamy
Walking in the Highlands © Posing Productions/Photonica/Getty Images
Mountain-biking, Scotland © Stockshot/Alamy
Kayaks, Elgol © South West images Scotland/Alamy
Surfer, East Scotland © Arch White/Alamy
Hill climber on Munrow Liathach, Torridon © Javier Corripio/Alamy

Black and whites

p.076 Edinburgh Castle from Princes Street Gardens © Mark Thomas
p.210 View over the River Dee to Kirkcudbright © South West Images Scotland
p.220 Midsteeple, Dumfries © Ron Humphreys
p.239 Book shop, Wigtown © David Pattison/Alamy
p.268 Brodick Castle, Arran © Stephen Crawford/Alamy
p.332 Restored water wheel, Lanark Mills © Martin Bond/Alamy
p.370 Cloisters at Iona Abbey © Jon Sparks/Alamy
p.376 Tiree Wave Classic: Triple Crown © TNT Magazine/Alamy
p.392 Whisky barrels, Islay © Rob Humphreys
p.446 St Andrews University © Doug Houghton
p.466 Loch Tay Crannog Centre © Doug Houghton
p.546 Ellgin Cathedral and River Lossie, Moray © Doug Houghton
p.554 Mountaineers traversing Cairngorm Plateau © Roger Antrobus/Alamy
p. 568 Glenfiddich distillery, Dufftown © Jiri Rezac/Alamy
p.576 Bottlenose dolphins, Moray Firth © Ronal Weir/Alamy
p.646 Sandwood Bay beach, Sutherland © Jesus Rodriguez/Alamy
p.690 An Sgurr, Eigg © Rob Humphreys
p.716 beach on South Uist © Jill Mead/Axiom
p.734 Kirkwall Habour © Rob Humphreys
p.756 Lighthouse on Dennis Head, North Ronaldsay © Simon Stirrup/Alamy
p.760 Mousa Broch, Shetland © Ronald Weir/Alamy
p.772 Shetland ponies © Rob Humphreys
p.780 Puffin on Noss, Shetland © Rob Humphreys
p.788 Bobby's bus shelter, Unst © Rob Humphreys
p.808 Scottish Devolution Referendum poster © Davis Gordon/Alamy
p.835 Scottish novelist and poet Robert Louis Stevenson © Hulton Archive/Getty Images
p.843 Book illustration from Peter Pan by J.M. Barrie © Blue Lantern Studio/Corbis

SMALL PRINT

Index

Map entries are in colour.

INDEX